Constant-Growth Dividend Discount Model

If the initial dividend is \$1 (paid in 1 year), and if the dividen[...] ...alue of the dividend stream is $P_0 = \dfrac{\text{DIV}_1}{r - g}$ (page 236)

CAPITAL BUDGETING

Break-Even Point

The sales revenue necessary for the firm to break even (in terms of accounting profits) is

$$\text{Break-even revenue} = \frac{\text{fixed costs including depreciation}}{\text{additional profit from each additional dollar of sales}} \quad \text{(page 341)}$$

Operating Leverage

The degree of operating leverage, DOL, is the sensitivity of profits to changes in sales:

$$\text{DOL} = \frac{\text{percentage change in profits}}{\text{percentage change in sales}} = 1 + \frac{\text{fixed costs}}{\text{profits}} \quad \text{(pages 346–47)}$$

RISK AND RETURN

Measures of Risk and Return

Mean or expected return = probability-weighted average of possible outcomes (page 369)

Variance = σ^2 = probability-weighted average of squared deviations around the expected return (page 371)

Standard deviation = $\sigma = \sqrt{\text{Variance}}$ (page 371)

Variance of a sample of observations = sum of the square deviations around the average return, divided by the number of observations minus 1 (page 372)

Standard deviation of a sample = $\sqrt{\text{sample variance}}$ (page 373)

$$\text{Beta of stock } j = \frac{\text{covariance between stock and market return}}{\text{variance of market return}}$$

$$= \frac{\text{cov}(r_j, r_m)}{\sigma_m^2} \quad \text{(page 397)}$$

Capital Asset Pricing Model

The expected rate of return on a risky security equals the rate of return on risk-free assets plus a risk premium that depends on the security beta and the market risk premium $(r_m - r_f)$:

$$\text{Security's expected return} = r = r_f + \beta \times (r_m - r_f) = r_f + \beta \times \text{MRP} \quad \text{(page 403)}$$

CAPITAL STRUCTURE

Weighted-Average Cost of Capital

$$\text{WACC} = \left[\frac{D}{V} \times (1 - T_c) r_{\text{debt}}\right] + \left[\frac{E}{V} \times r_{\text{equity}}\right]$$

where T_c is the corporate tax rate, D is debt, E is equity, and $V = D + E$ (page 427)

Return on Assets

Return on assets equals the weighted average of the returns of the firm's outstanding securities:

$$r_{\text{assets}} = r_{\text{debt}} \frac{D}{V} + r_{\text{equity}} \frac{E}{V} \quad \text{(pages 425 and 531)}$$

Value of Interest Tax Shields

If a firm maintains a fixed amount of debt in perpetuity, then the present value of the tax savings equals $T_c \times \text{Debt}$ (page 534)

Du Pont Formulas

Return on assets (ROA) = asset turnover × operating profit margin (page 110)

$$\text{Return on equity (ROE)} = \frac{\text{asset}}{\text{equity}} \times \text{asset turnover} \times \text{operating profit margin} \times \text{debt burden} \quad \text{(page 114)}$$

(continued on inside back cover)

Fifth Canadian Edition

Fundamentals of CORPORATE FINANCE

Richard A. Brealey
London Business School

Stewart C. Myers
Sloan School of Management
Massachusetts Institute of Technology

Alan J. Marcus
Wallace E. Carroll School of Management, Boston College

Elizabeth M. Maynes
Schulich School of Business, York University

Devashis Mitra
Faculty of Business Administration, University of New Brunswick

McGraw-Hill Ryerson
Connect. Learn. Succeed.

The McGraw-Hill Companies

McGraw-Hill Ryerson
Connect. Learn. Succeed.

FUNDAMENTALS OF CORPORATE FINANCE
FIFTH CANADIAN EDITION

ISBN-13: 978-0-07-040089-4
ISBN-10: 0-07-040089-X

2 3 4 5 6 7 8 9 CTPS 1 9 8 7 6 5 4 3

Printed and bound in China

Sr. Sponsoring Editor: *Kimberley Veevers*
Marketing Manager: *Jeremy Guimond*
Developmental Editor: *Daphne Scriabin*
Senior Editorial Associate: *Christine Lomas*
Photo/Permissions Editor: *Indu Arora*
Supervising Editor: *Graeme Powell*
Copy Editor: *Rodney Rawlings*
Production Coordinator: *Scott Morrison*
Cover and Interior Design: *Laserwords*
Cover Image: *JFunk/Shutterstock*
Page Layout: *Laserwords Private Limited*
Printer: *CTPS*

Library and Archives Canada Cataloguing in Publication

Fundamentals of corporate finance / Richard A. Brealey . . . [et al.]—5th ed.

Includes bibliographical references and index.
ISBN 978-0-07-040089-4

1. Corporations—Finance—Textbooks. I. Brealey, Richard A

HG4026.F85 2012 658.15 C2011-905920-7

Dedications

Richard A. Brealey, Stewart C. Myers, Alan J. Marcus:
To our Families

Elizabeth Maynes to David and Bruce
Devashis Mitra to Anusha and Koumari

About the Authors

RICHARD A. BREALEY

Professor of Finance at the London Business School. He is the former president of the European Finance Association and a former director of the American Finance Association. He is a fellow of the British Academy and has served as a special advisor to the Governor of the Bank of England and as director of a number of financial institutions. Professor Brealey is also the author (with Professor Myers and Franklin Allen) of this book's sister text, *Principles of Corporate Finance*.

STEWART C. MYERS

Gordon Y. Billard Professor of Finance at MIT's Sloan School of Management. He is past president of the American Finance Association and a research associate of the National Bureau of Economic Research. His research has focused on financing decisions, valuation methods, the cost of capital, and financial aspects of government regulation of business. Dr. Myers is a director of The Brattle Group, Inc., and is active as a financial consultant. He is also the author (with Professor Brealey and Franklin Allen) of this book's sister text, *Principles of Corporate Finance*.

ALAN J. MARCUS

Professor of Finance in the Wallace E. Carroll School of Management at Boston College. His main research interests are in derivatives and securities markets. He is co-author (with Zvi Bodie and Alex Kane) of the texts *Investments* and *Essentials of Investments.* Professor Marcus has served as a research fellow at the National Bureau of Economic Research. Professor Marcus also spent two years at Freddie Mac, where he helped to develop mortgage pricing and credit risk models. He currently serves on the Research Foundation Advisory Board of the CFA Institute.

ELIZABETH M. MAYNES

Director, BBA and iBBA Programs, and Associate Professor of Finance at the Schulich School of Business, York University, Toronto. Her main research interests are in corporate finance, including equity issuance and the role and value of voting rights of shareholders, and in experimental economics and finance, where theories are tested with human subjects. Some of the issues examined using the experimental methodology include peoples' decisions about whether to evade tax, whether to tender shares in a takeover bid, and how much to contribute toward a public good. Her research has been funded by the Social Sciences and Humanities Research Council of Canada and the Financial Research Foundation. Professor Maynes has extensive experience teaching introductory and corporate finance to undergraduate, MBA, and EMBA students, and to managers.

DEVASHIS MITRA

Professor of Finance and Entrepreneurship at the Faculty of Business Administration, University of New Brunswick, Fredericton. He has extensive experience teaching introductory and advanced courses to undergraduate and MBA students. His teaching interests are in corporate finance, entrepreneurial finance, and international finance. Professor Mitra has conducted research in areas such as dividend policy, working capital, international capital budgeting, financial markets, and venture capital. Professor Mitra's research projects have been funded by the Social Sciences and Humanities Research Council of Canada and the Shastri Indo-Canadian Institute. He served as Associate Dean (International) and as Associate Dean (Accreditation and Research) of his faculty and is a past Division Chair, Academic Reviewer, and Program Chair at conferences of the Administrative Sciences Association of Canada.

Contents in Brief

PREFACE XIII

PART ONE | **INTRODUCTION 1**

Chapter 1 Goals and Governance of the Firm 1
Chapter 2 Financial Markets and Institutions 32
Chapter 3 Accounting and Finance 58
Chapter 4 Measuring Corporate Performance 98

PART TWO | **VALUE 131**

Chapter 5 The Time Value of Money 131
Chapter 6 Valuing Bonds 182
Chapter 7 Valuing Stocks 219
Chapter 8 Net Present Value and Other Investment Criteria 262
Chapter 9 Using Discounted Cash Flow Analysis to Make Investment Decisions 299
Chapter 10 Project Analysis 333

PART THREE | **RISK 360**

Chapter 11 Introduction to Risk, Return, and the Opportunity Cost of Capital 360
Chapter 12 Risk, Return, and Capital Budgeting 392
Chapter 13 The Weighted-Average Cost of Capital and Company Valuation 420

PART FOUR | **FINANCING 451**

Chapter 14 Introduction to Corporate Financing and Governance 451
Chapter 15 Venture Capital, IPOs, and Seasoned Offerings 488

PART FIVE | **DEBT AND PAYOUT POLICY 523**

Chapter 16 Debt Policy 523
Chapter 17 Leasing 560
Chapter 18 Payout Policy 584

PART SIX | **FINANCIAL PLANNING 608**

Chapter 19 Long-Term Financial Planning 608
Chapter 20 Short-Term Financial Planning 635

PART SEVEN | **SHORT-TERM FINANCIAL DECISIONS 673**

Chapter 21 Cash and Inventory Management 673
Chapter 22 Credit Management and Collection 701

PART EIGHT | **SPECIAL TOPICS 722**

Chapter 23 Mergers, Acquisitions, and Corporate Control 722
Chapter 24 International Financial Management 754
Chapter 25 Options 784
Chapter 26 Risk Management 809

APPENDIX A: Present Value Tables 829
APPENDIX B: Answers to Selected End-of-Chapter Problems 837
Glossary 845
Index 850

Table of Contents

Preface xiii

PART ONE
INTRODUCTION 1

CHAPTER 1
Goals and Governance of the Firm 1

1.1 Investment and Financing Decisions 2
The Investment (Capital Budgeting) Decision 5
The Financing Decision 6

1.2 What is a Corporation? 8

1.3 Other Forms of Business Organization 10
Sole Proprietorships 10
Partnerships 11
Hybrid Forms of Business Organization 11

1.4 Who is the Financial Manager? 12

1.5 Goals of the Corporation 13
Shareholders Want Managers to Maximize Market Value 13
Ethics and Management Objectives 14
Do Managers Really Maximize Firm Value? 16

1.6 Careers in Finance 22

1.7 Topics Covered in this Book 24
Snippets of History 25

1.8 Summary 28

CHAPTER 2
Financial Markets and Institutions 32

2.1 The Importance of Financial Markets and Institutions 33

2.2 The Flow of Savings to Corporations 35
The Stock Market 37
Agency Problems and Corporate Governance 38
Other Financial Markets 38
Financial Intermediaries 39
Financial Institutions 43
Total Financing of Canadian Corporations 45

2.3 Functions of Financial Markets and Intermediaries 46
Transporting Cash Across Time 47
Risk Transfer and Diversification 47
Liquidity 48
The Payment Mechanism 48
Information Provided by Financial Markets 48

2.4 Value Maximization and the Cost of Capital 50
Value Maximization 50
The Opportunity Cost of Capital 51

2.5 The Crisis of 2007–2009 52

2.6 Summary 53

CHAPTER 3
Accounting and Finance 58

3.1 The Statement of Financial Position or Balance Sheet 59
Book Values and Market Values 66

3.2 The Income Statement and Statement of Comprehensive Income 68
Consolidated Statement of Changes in Equity 70
Profits versus Cash Flow 72

3.3 The Statement of Cash Flows 75

3.4 Cash Flow from Assets, Financing Flow, and Free Cash Flow 78

3.5 Accounting Practice and Accounting Malpractice 81

3.6 Taxes 83
Corporate Tax 83
Personal Tax 85

3.7 Summary 89

CHAPTER 4
Measuring Corporate Performance 98

4.1 Measuring Market Value and Market Value Added 99

4.2 Economic Value Added and Accounting Rates of Return 102
Accounting Rates of Return 105
Problems with EVA and Accounting Rates of Return 107

4.3 Measuring Efficiency 108

4.4 Analyzing the Return on Assets: The Du Pont System 109
The Du Pont System 110

4.5 Measuring Financial Leverage 111
EBITDA 113
Leverage and the Return on Equity 114

4.6 Measuring Liquidity 115

4.7 Calculating Sustainable Growth 116

4.8 Interpreting Financial Ratios 117

4.9 The Role of Financial Ratios—and a Final Note on Transparency 121
Transparency 122
4.10 Summary 123

PART TWO
VALUE 131

CHAPTER 5
The Time Value of Money 131

5.1 Future Values and Compound Interest 132
5.2 Present Values 136
Finding the Interest Rate 140
Finding the Investment Period 141
5.3 Multiple Cash Flows 142
Future Value of Multiple Cash Flows 142
Present Value of Multiple Cash Flows 145
5.4 Level Cash Flows: Perpetuities and Annuities 147
How to Value Perpetuities 147
How to Value Annuities 149
Annuities Due 153
Future Value of an Annuity 155
Cash Flows Growing at a Constant Rate—Variations on Perpetuities and Annuities 158
5.5 Inflation and the Time Value of Money 160
Real versus Nominal Cash Flows 160
Inflation and Interest Rates 162
Valuing Real Cash Payments 164
Real or Nominal? 165
5.6 Effective Annual Interest Rates 165
5.7 Summary 168

CHAPTER 6
Valuing Bonds 182

6.1 Bonds and the Bond Market 184
Bond Market Data 184
6.2 Interest Rates and Bond Prices 186
How Bond Prices Vary with Interest Rates 188
6.3 Current Yield and Yield to Maturity 190
6.4 Bond Rates of Return 192
Taxes and Rates of Return 196
Multiperiod Rates of Return 197
6.5 The Yield Curve 198
Nominal and Real Rates of Interest 199
The Determinants of the Yield Curve 201
Expectations Theory 201
Interest Rate Risk and the Liquidity Premium 202
6.6 Corporate Bonds and the Risk of Default 203
Variations in Corporate Bonds 206
6.7 Summary 209
Appendix 6A: A More Detailed Look at the Yield Curve 216
Appendix 6B: Duration: Measuring the Life of a Bond (available on Connect)

CHAPTER 7
Valuing Stocks 219

7.1 Stocks and Stock Markets 220
Reading Stock Market Listings 222
7.2 Market Values, Book Values, and Liquidation Values 225
7.3 Valuing Common Stocks 228
Valuation by Comparables 228
Price and Intrinsic Value 229
The Dividend Discount Model 231
7.4 Simplifying the Dividend Discount Model 234
The Dividend Discount Model with No Growth 234
The Constant-Growth Dividend Discount Model 235
Estimating Expected Rates of Return 237
Non-Constant Growth 238
7.5 Growth Stocks and Income Stocks 240
7.6 There are No Free Lunches on Bay Street 243
Method 1: Technical Analysis 244
Method 2: Fundamental Analysis 247
A Theory to Fit the Facts 248
7.7 Market Anomalies and Behavioural Finance 249
Market Anomalies 249
Behavioural Finance 250
7.8 Summary 251

CHAPTER 8
Net Present Value and Other Investment Criteria 262

8.1 Net Present Value 264
A Comment on Risk and Present Value 265
Valuing Long-Lived Projects 265
Using the NPV Rule to Choose Among Projects 269
8.2 Other Investment Criteria 269
Payback 270
Discounted Payback 271

Internal Rate of Return 272
A Closer Look at the Rate of Return Rule 274
Calculating the Rate of Return for Long-Lived Projects 274
A Word of Caution 277
Some Pitfalls of the IRR Rule 277

8.3 More Examples of Mutually Exclusive Projects 281
Investment Timing 282
Long-versus Short-Lived Equipment 283
Replacing an Old Machine 285

8.4 Capital Rationing 286
Soft Rationing 286
Hard Rationing 286
Pitfalls of the Profitability Index 288

8.5 A Last Look 288

8.6 Summary 289

CHAPTER 9
Using Discounted Cash Flow Analysis to Make Investment Decisions 299

9.1 Identifying Cash Flows 301
Discount Cash Flows, Not Profits 301
Discount Incremental Cash Flows 303
Include All Indirect Effects 303
Forget Sunk Costs 303
Include Opportunity Costs 304
Recognize the Investment in Working Capital 304
Remember Shutdown Cash Flows 305
Beware of Allocated Overhead Costs 305
Discount Nominal Cash Flows by the Nominal Cost of Capital 306
Separate Investment and Financing Decisions 307

9.2 Calculating Cash Flows 307
Capital Investment 308
Investment in Working Capital 308
Operating Cash Flow 309

9.3 Business Taxes in Canada and the Capital Budgeting Decision 311
Depreciation and Capital Cost Allowance 311
The Asset Class System 312
Sale of Assets 314
Termination of Asset Pool 314
Present Values of CCA Tax Shields 315

9.4 Example: Blooper Industries 317
Calculating Blooper's Project Cash Flows 318
Calculating the NPV of Blooper's Project 320
Further Notes and Wrinkles Arising from Blooper's Project 321

9.5 Summary 324

Appendix 9A: Deriving the CCA Tax Shield (available on Connect)

CHAPTER 10
Project Analysis 333

10.1 How Firms Organize the Investment Process 334
Stage 1: The Capital Budget 335
Stage 2: Project Authorizations 335
Problems and Some Solutions 336

10.2 Some "What If" Questions 337
Sensitivity Analysis 337
Scenario Analysis 340

10.3 Break-Even Analysis 341
Accounting Break-Even Analysis 341
NPV Break-Even Analysis 343
Operating Leverage 346

10.4 Real Options and the Value of Flexibility 348
The Option to Expand 348
A Second Real Option: The Option to Abandon 350
A Third Real Option: The Timing Option 351
A Fourth Real Option: Flexible Production Facilities 352

10.5 Summary 352

PART THREE
RISK 360

CHAPTER 11
Introduction to Risk, Return, and the Opportunity Cost of Capital 360

11.1 Rates of Return: A Review 361

11.2 Eighty-Five Years of Capital Market History 363
Market Indexes 363
The Historical Record 364
Using Historical Evidence to Estimate Today's Cost of Capital 367

11.3 Measuring Risk 369
Variance and Standard Deviation 369
A Note on Calculating Variance 372
Measuring the Variation in Stock Returns 372

11.4 Risk and Diversification 374
Diversification 374
Asset versus Portfolio Risk 375
Covariance and Correlation 378
Correlation and Portfolio Diversification 379
Market Risk versus Unique Risk 382

11.5 Thinking About Risk 383
Message 1: Some Risks Look Big and Dangerous but Really are Diversifiable 383

Message 2: Market Risks are Macro Risks 384
Message 3: Risk Can be Measured 385

11.6 Summary 385

CHAPTER 12
Risk, Return, and Capital Budgeting 392

12.1 Measuring Market Risk 393
Measuring Beta 394
Betas for Cameco and Royal Bank 397
Total Risk and Market Risk 398
Portfolio Betas 399

12.2 Risk and Return and Capital Asset Pricing Model, CAPM 400
Why the CAPM Makes Sense 403
The Security Market Line 404
How Well Does the CAPM Work? 405
Using the CAPM to Estimate Expected Returns 408

12.3 Capital Budgeting and Project Risk 408
Company Risk versus Project Risk 409
Determinants of Project Risk 410
Don't Add Fudge Factors to Discount Rates 411

12.4 Summary 412

CHAPTER 13
The Weighted-Average Cost of Capital and Company Valuation 420

13.1 Geothermal's Cost of Capital 421

13.2 The Weighted-Average Cost of Capital 423
Calculating Company Cost of Capital as a Weighted Average 424
Use Market Weights, Not Book Weights 426
Taxes and the Weighted-Average Cost of Capital 427
What If There are Three (or More) Sources of Financing? 428
Wrapping Up Geothermal 428
Checking Our Logic 429

13.3 Measuring Capital Structure 430

13.4 Calculating Required Rates of Return 432
The Expected Return on Bonds 432
The Expected Return on Common Stock 432
The Expected Return on Preferred Stock 434

13.5 Calculating the Weighted-Average Cost of Capital 434
Real Company WACC 435

13.6 Interpreting the Weighted-Average Cost of Capital 435
When You Can and Can't Use WACC 435
Some Common Mistakes 436
How Changing Capital Structure Affects WACC When the Corporate Tax Rate is Zero 436
How Changing Capital Structure Affects Debt and Equity when the Corporate Tax Rate is Zero 437
What Happens if Capital Structure Changes and the Corporate Tax Rate is Not Zero? 438
Revisiting the Project Cost of Capital 440

13.7 Valuing Entire Businesses 440
Calculating the Value of the Concatenator Business 442

13.8 Summary 443

PART FOUR
FINANCING 451

CHAPTER 14
Introduction to Corporate Financing and Governance 451

14.1 Creating Value with Financing Decisions 453

14.2 Common Stock 454
Book Value versus Market Value 455
Dividends 456
Ownership of the Corporation 456
Voting Procedures 456
Classes of Stock 457
Corporate Governance in Canada and Elsewhere 458

14.3 Preferred Stock 461

14.4 Corporate Debt 463
Debt Comes in Many Forms 463
Innovation in the Debt Market 468

14.5 Convertible Securities 472

14.6 Patterns of Corporate Financing 473
Do Firms Rely Too Heavily on Internal Funds? 474
External Sources of Capital 474

14.7 Summary 476

Appendix 14A: The Bond Refunding Decision 481

CHAPTER 15
Venture Capital, IPOs, and Seasoned Offerings 488

15.1 Venture Capital 490
Venture Capital Companies 491

15.2 The Initial Public Offering 492
Arranging a Public Issue 493

15.3 The Underwriters 497
Who are the Underwriters? 498

15.4 Listing on the Stock Market 500

15.5 Rights Issues and General Cash Offers by Public Companies 501
Rights Issues 501
General Cash Offers 503
Costs of the General Cash Offer 504
Market Reaction to Stock Issues 504

15.6 The Private Placement 505

15.7 Summary 506

Appendix 15A: The Financing of New and Small Enterprises 512

Other Sources of Small Business Financing 517

Appendix 15B: Hotch Pot's New Issue Prospectus 519

PART FIVE
DEBT AND PAYOUT POLICY 523

CHAPTER 16
Debt Policy 523

16.1 How Borrowing Affects Value in a Tax-Free Economy 525
MM's Argument 526
How Borrowing Affects Earnings per Share 526
How Borrowing Affects Risk and Return 529
Debt and the Cost of Equity 530

16.2 Capital Structure and Corporate Taxes 533
Debt and Taxes at River Cruises 533
How Interest Tax Shields Contribute to the Value of Shareholders' Equity 535
Corporate Taxes and the Weighted-Average Cost of Capital 535
The Implications of Corporate Taxes for Capital Structure 536

16.3 Costs of Financial Distress 537
Bankruptcy Costs 538
Evidence on Bankruptcy Costs 539
Direct versus Indirect Costs of Bankruptcy 540
Financial Distress without Bankruptcy 540
Costs of Distress Vary with Type of Asset 542

16.4 Explaining Financing Choices 544
The Trade-Off Theory 544
A Pecking-Order Theory 544
The Two Faces of Financial Slack 545

16.5 Bankruptcy Procedures 548
The Choice Between Liquidation and Reorganization 551

16.6 Summary 552

CHAPTER 17
Leasing 560

17.1 What is a Lease? 561
Leasing Industry 562

17.2 Why Lease? 563
Sensible Reasons for Leasing 563
Some Dubious Reasons for Leasing 564

17.3 Valuing Leases 567
Operating Leases 567
Financial Leases 568
Cash Flows of a Financial Lease 568
Who Really Owns the Leased Asset? 570
Leasing and the Canada Revenue Agency (CRA) 571
First Pass at Valuing a Financial Lease Contract 571
Financial Lease Evaluation 574
Using Formulas to Evaluate Financial Leases 574

17.4 When Do Financial Leases Pay? 576

17.5 Summary 577

CHAPTER 18
Payout Policy 584

18.1 How Dividends are Paid 585
Cash Dividends 585
Some Legal Limitations on Dividends 587
Stock Dividends, Stock Splits, and Reverse Splits 587
Dividend Reinvestment Plans and Share Purchase Plans 588

18.2 Share Repurchase 588
Why Repurchases are Like Dividends 589
Repurchases and Share Valuation 590

18.3 How Do Companies Decide on How Much to Pay Out? 591
The Role of Share Repurchase Decisions 592
The Information Content of Dividends and Repurchases 592

18.4 Why Payout Policy Should Not Matter 594
Payout Policy is Irrelevant in Efficient Financial Markets 595
The Assumptions Behind Dividend-Irrelevance 597

18.5 Why Dividends May Increase Firm Value 597
Market Imperfections 597

18.6 Why Dividends May Reduce Firm Value 598
Why Pay Any Dividends at All? 599
Dividends versus Capital Gains 599
Dividend Clientele Effects 600

18.7 Summary 600

PART SIX
FINANCIAL PLANNING 608

CHAPTER 19
Long-Term Financial Planning 608

19.1 What is Financial Planning? 609
Financial Planning Focuses on the Big Picture 610
Why Build Financial Plans? 610
19.2 Financial Planning Models 611
Components of a Financial Planning Model 612
Percentage-of-Sales Models 613
An Improved Model 615
19.3 Tips for Planners 620
Pitfalls in Model Design 620
The Assumption in Percentage-of-Sales Models 620
Forecasting Interest Expense 622
The Role of Financial Planning Models 623
19.4 External Financing and Growth 623
19.5 Summary 627

CHAPTER 20
Short-Term Financial Planning 635

20.1 Links Between Long-Term and Short-Term Financing 637
20.2 Working Capital 640
The Components of Working Capital 641
Net Working Capital, Operating Cycle, and the Cash Conversion Cycle 642
The Working Capital Trade-Off 645
20.3 Tracing Changes in Cash and Working Capital 647
20.4 Cash Budgeting 649
Forecast Sources of Cash 649
Forecast Uses of Cash 651
The Cash Balance 651
20.5 A Short-Term Financing Plan 653
Dynamic Mattress's Financing Plan 654
Evaluating the Plan 655
20.6 Sources of Short-Term Financing 655
Bank Loans 656
Secured Loans 657
Commercial Paper 658
Banker's Acceptance 660
20.7 The Cost of Bank Loans 660
Simple Interest 660
Discount Interest 661
Interest with Compensating Balances 661
20.8 Summary 662

PART SEVEN
SHORT-TERM FINANCIAL DECISIONS 673

CHAPTER 21
Cash and Inventory Management 673

21.1 Cash Collection, Disbursement, and Float 675
Float 675
Valuing Float 676
21.2 The Payment System and the Float 677
21.3 Managing Float 680
Speeding Up Cheque Collections 680
Controlling Cheque Disbursements 681
Electronic Funds Transfer 682
21.4 Managing Inventories and Cash Balances 684
Inventory Management Models 684
Just-in-Time Inventory Management 687
Managing Inventories of Cash 687
Uncertain Cash Flows 689
Cash Management in Large Domestic and International Corporations 691
21.5 Investing Idle Cash: The Money Market 692
21.6 Summary 695

CHAPTER 22
Credit Management and Collection 701

22.1 Terms of Sale 703
22.2 Credit Agreements 705
22.3 Credit Analysis 706
Financial Ratio Analysis 706
Numerical Credit Scoring 706
When to Stop Looking for Clues 708
22.4 The Credit Decision 708
Credit Decisions with Repeat Orders 710
Evaluating a Credit Policy Switch 712
Some General Principles 712
22.5 Collection Policy 713
22.6 Summary 714

PART EIGHT
SPECIAL TOPICS 722

CHAPTER 23
Mergers, Acquisitions, and Corporate Control 722

23.1 Sensible Motives for Mergers 724
Increased Revenues 727

Economies of Scale 727
Economies of Vertical Integration 727
Combining Complementary Resources 728
Merging to Reduce Taxes 728
Mergers as a Use for Surplus Funds 728

23.2 Dubious Reasons for Mergers 729
Diversification 729
The Bootstrap Game 729

23.3 The Mechanics of a Merger 730
The Form of Acquisition 730
Mergers, Antitrust Law, and Popular Opposition 732

23.4 Evaluating Mergers 733
Mergers Financed by Cash 733
Mergers Financed by Stock 735
Some Tax Issues 736
A Warning 736
Another Warning 736

23.5 The Market for Corporate Control 737
Ownership Structure and the Effectiveness of the Market for Corporate Control 737

23.6 Method 1: Proxy Contests 738

23.7 Method 2: Takeover Bids 739
Takeover Bid Tactics 740

23.8 Method 3: Leveraged Buyouts 741
Barbarians at the Gate? 743
Recent LBO Activity 744

23.9 Method 4: Divestitures, Spin-Offs, and Equity Carve-Outs 746

23.10 The Benefits and Costs of Mergers 747

23.11 Summary 748

CHAPTER 24
International Financial Management 754

24.1 Foreign Exchange Markets 755
Spot Exchange Rates 756
Forward Exchange Rates 758

24.2 Some Basic Relationships 760
Exchange Rates and Inflation 760
Inflation and Interest Rates 763
Interest Rates and Exchange Rates 764
The Forward Rate and the Expected Spot Rate 766
Some Implications 767

24.3 Hedging Exchange Rate Risk 768
Transaction Risk 768
Economic Risk 769

24.4 International Capital Budgeting 770
Net Present Value Analysis 770
The Cost of Capital for Foreign Investment 771
Political Risk 772
Avoiding Fudge Factors 776

24.5 Summary 776

CHAPTER 25
Options 784

25.1 Calls and Puts 785
Selling Calls and Puts 788
Payoff Diagrams are Not Profit Diagrams 789
Financial Alchemy with Options 790
Some More Option Magic 790

25.2 What Determines Option Values? 792
Upper and Lower Limits on Option Values 792
The Determinants of Option Value 793
Option-Valuation Models 795

25.3 Spotting the Option 797
Options on Real Assets 797
Options on Financial Assets 799

25.4 Summary 802

Appendix 25A: The Black-Scholes Option Valuation Model (available on Connect)

CHAPTER 26
Risk Management 809

26.1 Why Hedge? 810
The Evidence on Risk Management 812

26.2 Reducing Risk with Options 812

26.3 Futures Contracts 813
The Mechanics of Futures Trading 817
Commodity and Financial Futures 818

26.4 Forward Contracts 819

26.5 Swaps 819

26.6 Innovation in the Derivatives Market 822

26.7 Is "Derivative" a Four-Letter Word? 822

26.8 Summary 824

Appendix A: Present Value Tables 829

Appendix B: Answers to Selected End-of-Chapter Problems 837

Glossary 845

Index 850

Preface

This book is about corporate finance. It focuses on how companies invest in real assets and how they raise the money to pay for these investments. It also provides a broad introduction to the financial landscape, discussing, for example, the major players in financial markets, the role of financial institutions in the economy, and how securities are traded and valued by investors. The book offers a framework for systematically thinking about most of the important financial problems that both firms and individuals are likely to confront.

Financial management is important, interesting, and challenging. It is *important* because today's capital investment decisions may determine the businesses that the firm is in 10, 20, or more years ahead. Also, a firm's success or failure depends in large part on its ability to find the capital that it needs.

Finance is *interesting* for several reasons. Financial decisions often involve huge sums of money. Large investment projects or acquisitions may involve billions of dollars. Also, the financial community is international and fast-moving, with colourful heroes and a sprinkling of unpleasant villains.

Finance is *challenging*. Financial decisions are rarely cut and dried, and the financial markets in which companies operate are changing rapidly. Good managers can cope with routine problems, but only the best managers can respond to change. To handle new problems, you need more than rules of thumb; you need to understand why companies and financial markets behave as they do and when common practice may not be best practice. Once you have a consistent framework for making financial decisions, complex problems become more manageable.

This book provides that framework. It is not an encyclopedia of finance. It focuses instead on setting out the basic *principles* of financial management and applying them to the main decisions faced by the financial manager. It explains why the firm's owners would like the manager to increase firm value and shows how managers choose between investments that may pay off at different points of time or have different degrees of risk. It also describes the main features of financial markets and discusses why companies may prefer a particular source of finance.

Some texts shy away from modern finance, sticking instead with more traditional, procedural, or institutional approaches. These are supposed to be easier or more practical. We disagree emphatically. The concepts of modern finance, properly explained, make the subject simpler, not more difficult. They are also more practical. The tools of financial management are easier to grasp and use effectively when presented in a consistent conceptual framework. Modern finance provides that framework.

Modern financial management is not "rocket science." It is a set of ideas that can be made clear by words, graphs, and numerical examples. The ideas provide the "why" behind the tools that good financial managers use to make investment and financing decisions.

WHY USE OUR BOOK

We wrote this book to make financial management clear, useful, interesting, and fun for the beginning student. We set out to show that modern finance and good financial practice go together—even for the financial novice. The key to this is a thorough understanding of the principles and mechanics of the time value of money. This material underlies almost all of this text, and we spend a lengthy Chapter 5 providing extensive practice with this key concept.

The second component of our approach is the extensive use of numerical examples. Each chapter presents detailed numerical examples to help the reader become familiar and comfortable with the material. We have peppered the book with real-life illustrations of the chapters' topics. Some of these are excerpts from the financial press found in Finance in Action boxes; others are built into the text as examples. By connecting concepts with practice, we strive to give students a working ability to make financial decisions.

We have streamlined the treatment of most topics to avoid getting bogged down in unnecessary detail that can overwhelm a beginner. We don't assume users will have a lot of background knowledge.

We have written the book in a relaxed and informal writing style. We use mathematical notation only where necessary. Even when we present an equation, we usually write it in words before using symbols. This approach has two advantages: it is less intimidating and it focuses attention on the underlying concept rather than just the formula.

WAYS TO USE OUR BOOK

There are about as many effective ways to organize a course in corporate finance as there are teachers. For this reason, we have ensured that the text is modular, so that topics can be introduced in different sequences. Nonetheless, in this edition we have changed the sequencing of chapters to improve the logical flow of topics. For instance, the chapter on financial statement analysis has been moved ahead and is now Chapter 4 (Measuring Corporate Performance) as we recognize that many instructors will prefer to go directly to this topic after covering Chapter 3 (Accounting and Finance), as a gentler transition from a typical prerequisite accounting course. Also, recognizing that firms have the choice of making investment decisions by either taking on debt in order to purchase assets or by leasing those assets, the chapter on leasing has been moved forward as Chapter 17 and now follows the one on debt policy (Chapter 16). We have made sure that Part Six (Financial Planning) can easily follow Part One (Introduction). Similarly, we discuss working capital after the basic principles of valuation and financing, but we recognize that many instructors prefer to reverse that order. There should be no difficulty in using Part Seven (Short-Term Financial Decisions) out of order. When we discuss project valuation in Part Two (Value), we stress that the opportunity cost of capital depends on project risk. But we do not discuss how to measure risk or how return and risk are linked until Part Three (Risk). This ordering can easily be modified. For example, the chapters on risk and return can be introduced before, after, or midway through the material on project valuation.

CHANGES IN THE FIFTH CANADIAN EDITION

This fifth Canadian edition of *Fundamentals* includes many updates. We have enhanced the analytical tools used with the book: more spreadsheet boxes are integrated into the chapters; end-of-chapter problems include exercises that ask students to use a variety of Internet resources to solve financial problems and integrative mini cases. The location of some chapters in the book has been altered to improve the logical flow of topics. In addition, we have rewritten, rearranged, and added material to improve readability and update coverage across chapters. The following are some examples of the changes that we have made.

Chapter 1 (Goals and Governance of the Firm) has been largely rewritten to improve readability and interest. This chapter and Chapter 2 include the real-life case of Research In Motion and its founder Mike Lazaridis, illustrating how financial markets help infant firms grow into healthy adults. The section on business organizations has new material on private corporations and the pros and cons of being a public corporation. Examples of investment and financial decisions of well-known companies are used to illustrate the main activities of financial managers, the role of financial markets, and the goals of a corporation. Keeping in mind the currency of certain themes, the chapter includes new discussion on the global financial crisis, big government bailouts, credit default swaps, and the subprime mortgage crisis. New content on the ethical issues that confront managers includes a Finance in Action article on the value of ethical dealings to maintain reputation in the context of the recent global financial crisis.

Chapter 2 (Financial Markets and Institutions) opens with the history of Research In Motion. It includes new coverage of agency problems and corporate governance and a new Finance in Action article on prediction markets. Coverage of financial intermediaries has expanded coverage of exchange traded funds (EFTs) and hedge funds. A non-technical introduction to the idea of the opportunity cost of capital provides context for the later discussion of present value.

Chapter 3 (Accounting and Finance) includes a discussion of new Canadian accounting standards for public companies, which are the International Financial Reporting Standards (IFRS). The discussion of profits versus cash flow includes more examples of how accrual accounting impacts cash flow. The tax rates have also been updated.

Chapter 4 (Measuring Corporate Performance—*formerly titled* Financial Statement Analysis) was previously Chapter 17 of the text. In response to user comments, we have moved this chapter to Part One to accompany the previous chapter on accounting and finance. We also have extensively rewritten the chapter with a sharper focus on how financial data can be used to measure contributions to firm value.

Chapter 5 (The Time Value of Money) has been updated and rearranged to improve logical flow. The chapter includes new spreadsheet applications.

Chapter 6 (Valuing Bonds) has been updated. The discussion of the risk of default has been extended to include possible default of European governments' debt.

Chapter 7 (Valuing Stocks) starts with a review of stock markets and trading procedures and motivates stock valuation with an example of an investor considering whether to purchase a particular stock, RIM. We begin this discussion with valuation by comparables and the distinction between price and intrinsic value. Then the details of dividend discount model are discussed. The chapter ends with a discussion of market efficiency.

Chapter 8 (Net Present Value and Other Investment Criteria) has been streamlined and reorganized. The chapter includes a new discussion, "Modified Internal Rate of Return."

Chapter 9 (Using Discounted Cash Flow Analysis to Make Investment Decisions) has been updated and the discussion of project cash flow has been reworked to more carefully show how each of its components can be estimated. The chapter works through a realistic comprehensive example of capital budgeting analysis and includes updated information on capital cost allowance (CCA). An appendix showing how the CCA tax shield is derived is available to the reader on Connect.

Chapter 10 (Project Analysis). The updated chapter includes revised coverage of NPV breakeven analysis. New Finance in Action material includes an article on the uncertainty associated with development costs in the mining industry.

Chapter 11 (Introduction to Risk, Return, and the Opportunity Cost of Capital) starts with a historical survey of returns on bonds and stocks and goes on to distinguish between the unique risk and market risk of individual stocks.

Chapter 12 (Risk, Return, and Capital Budgeting) market data has been updated and shows how to measure market risk and discusses the relationship between risk and expected return.

Chapter 13 (The Weighted-Average Cost of Capital and Company Valuation) market data has been updated. A new discussion of the choice of the risk-free security, Treasury bill, or long-term government bond when implementing CAPM has been added.

Chapter 14 (Introduction to Corporate Financing and Governance) has been extensively updated, and includes new discussion on the recent subprime crisis in the United States and its impact on credit markets and economic activity in countries around the world, including Canada. Two new Finance in Action boxes discuss the fallout from the crisis and another examines the bounce back of corporate financing activity in Canada, in which debt markets have played an important role.

Chapter 15 (Venture Capital, IPOs, and Seasoned Offerings). The chapter has updated material on developments in the IPO market. An appendix to the chapter discussing the financing of new and small enterprises has been rewritten to reflect changes in the venture capital industry and other sources of small business financing in Canada.

Chapter 16 (Debt Policy) has been updated with Canadian examples and statistics in the discussions on costs of financial distress and explaining financing choices.

Chapter 17 (Leasing) has been moved forward and included with the other two chapters on financing decisions, namely debt policy and payout policy. The chapter has been updated to include two new Finance in Action boxes assessing the impact of accounting under IFRS on the retail and transportation industries.

Chapter 18 (Payout Policy) has been extensively updated and revised to reflect its broader focus on share repurchases along with dividend policy. A new Finance in Action box discusses George Weston's special dividend payout.

Chapter 19 (Long-Term Financial Planning—*formerly titled* Financial Planning). The concept of net operating working capital (= operating current assets – operating current liabilities) has been added. All interest-bearing liabilities, including operating lines of credit, are classified as sources of financing, not included in the operating current liabilities. The discussion of forecasting interest expense explains the implications of calculating the current year's interest expense on the basis of the assumption of when the new debt is acquired.

Chapter 20 (Short-Term Financial Planning) has been updated with new examples of short-term financing. A new Finance in Action has been added that deals with the importance of working capital management for coping with the financial crisis.

Chapter 21 (Cash and Inventory Management) has an updated table of payments methods in different countries around the world. The discussion of just-in-time inventory management has been extended to talk about the risk of not holding inventory. The Finance in Action article deals with the impact of environment disasters, such as Iceland's volcano ash and Japan's earthquake and tsunami, on the access to supplies. The discussion of the various types of short-term investments includes asset-backed commercial paper. A new Finance in Action article deals with the asset-backed commercial paper crisis and how it was resolved.

Chapter 22 (Credit Management and Collection) emphasizes that buying goods on credit is in effect a loan from the supplier. The equation for calculating the effective annual interest rate when using trade credit has been revised to show various ways to assess the impact of forgoing the cash discount.

Chapter 23 (Mergers, Acquisitions, and Corporate Control) has been fully reorganized, and now begins with an overview of why mergers and other forms of reorganization may make sense. Next are the mechanics of acquisitions and barriers to mergers, including antitrust law, political and public opposition, and merger evaluation. Then we progress to the market for corporate control and discuss various methods for achieving corporate control: proxy contests, takeovers, leveraged buyouts and then divestitures, equity spin-offs, and carve-outs. The chapter has many new examples and data.

Chapter 24 (International Financial Management) has new discussion on the global financial crisis including two Finance in Action articles on the effects of the crisis on Greece and on other Eurozone countries. Another new Finance in Action box discusses the implications of a strengthening Canadian dollar and the possibility of it being overvalued.

Chapter 25 (Options) has updated market and institutional information. A new subsection, Payoff Diagrams Are Not Profit Diagrams, provides new drawings of call and option payoffs with the costs of the call and option subtracted from the payoff. This shows the net payoff from the option. Also a new subsection on executive and employee stock options has been added. The discussion includes option backdating issues and an example of a company that had its shareholders approve a stock option exchange program for its employees.

Chapter 26 (Risk Management) includes updated discussion on different ways to manage risk. The chapter includes new writeup on derivative instruments such as credit default swaps in the context of the global financial crisis. Two new Finance in Action articles provide further context. The first examines the role of Goldman Sachs in their dealings with mortgage-related instruments and with AIG, the giant insurer. The second examines Goldman's role in the financial crisis through some of its speculative activities with derivative products.

PEDAGOGY WALK-THROUGH

To provide guidance and insights throughout the text, we include a number of proven pedagogical aids:

CHAPTER OPENING

Each chapter begins with numbered learning objectives (LOs) included to provide a quick introduction to the material students will learn and should understand fully before moving to the next chapter. This is followed by a narrative to set the tone for what follows.

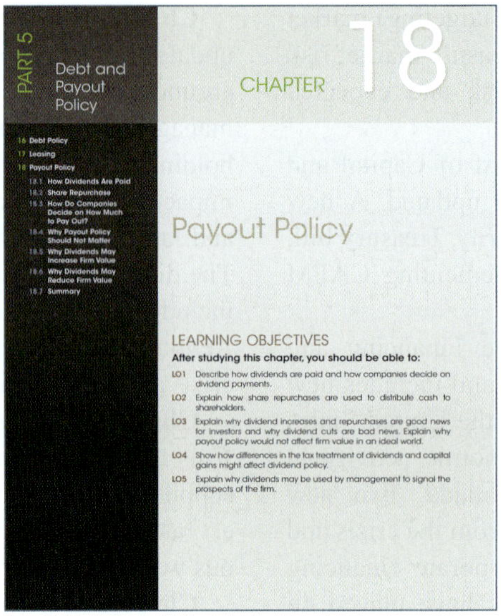

PART 5

Debt and Payout Policy

16 Debt Policy
17 Leasing
18 Payout Policy
18.1 How Dividends Are Paid
18.2 Share Repurchase
18.3 How Do Companies Decide on How Much to Pay Out?
18.4 Why Payout Policy Should Not Matter
18.5 Why Dividends May Increase Firm Value
18.6 Why Dividends May Reduce Firm Value
18.7 Summary

CHAPTER 18

Payout Policy

LEARNING OBJECTIVES

After studying this chapter, you should be able to:

LO1 Describe how dividends are paid and how companies decide on dividend payments.

LO2 Explain how share repurchases are used to distribute cash to shareholders.

LO3 Explain why dividend increases and repurchases are good news for investors and why dividend cuts are bad news. Explain why payout policy would not affect firm value in an ideal world.

LO4 Show how differences in the tax treatment of dividends and capital gains might affect dividend policy.

LO5 Explain why dividends may be used by management to signal the prospects of the firm.

This investor is obviously delighted with his extra cash, but can companies increase share value simply by increasing their dividend payout?

Everett Collection

In this chapter we explain how companies set their payout policy, and discuss the controversial question of how dividend policy affects value.

Shareholders invest in the company when they buy newly issued shares and when the company reinvests earnings on the shareholders' behalf. The shareholders do not usually demand a prompt cash return on their investment. Some long-established companies have never yet paid a cash dividend. Sooner or later, however, most corporations do pay out cash to their shareholders. They pay dividends, or they use cash to buy back previously issued shares.

How much should a company pay out in a given year? Should the payout come as dividends or share repurchases? The answers to these two questions are the corporation's *payout policy*.

We start the chapter with a discussion of how dividends are paid. We then show that in an ideal world, the value of a firm would be independent of its dividend policy. This demonstration is in the same spirit as the Modigliani and Miller debt-irrelevance proposition of Chapter 16.

That leads us to look at the real-world complications that might favour one dividend policy over another. These complications include transaction costs, taxes, and the signals that investors might read into the firm's payout announcement.

LO1 18.1 HOW DIVIDENDS ARE PAID

CASH DIVIDENDS

cash dividend Payment of cash by the firm to its shareholders.

On February 23, 2011, Maple Leaf Foods Inc. (MFI) announced a regular quarterly **cash dividend** of $.04 per share, making a total payment of $.16 for the year; soon after, its board of directors met and approved the decision. The term *regular* indicates that MFI expected to maintain the payment in the future. If it did not want to give that kind of assurance, it could have declared both a regular and an *extra dividend*. In July 2004, Microsoft did just that. The cash-rich software giant declared a whopping US$32 billion *special dividend*, because it could not find any other way to spend its sizeable cash flows. The company also declared a US$3.5 billion regular quarterly dividend and still had $20 billion cash on hand. Investors realize that extra dividends are less likely to be repeated.[1] The nearby Finance in Action box discusses the aftermath of a special dividend declared by another cash-rich company, George Weston.

Who receives the MFI dividend? That may seem an obvious question, but because shares trade constantly, the firm's records of who owns its shares can never be fully up to date. So MFI announced that it would send a dividend cheque to all shareholders recorded in its books on March 10, 2011. This is known as the *record date*.

[1] Companies also use the term "special dividend" for payments that are unlikely to be repeated.

NUMBERED EXAMPLES

Numbered and titled examples are extensively integrated into the chapters to provide detailed applications and illustrations of the text material.

FINANCE IN ACTION BOXES

Almost every chapter includes at least one Finance in Action box. These are excerpts, usually from the financial press, providing real-life illustrations of the chapter's topics such as in the growth of leveraged buyouts.

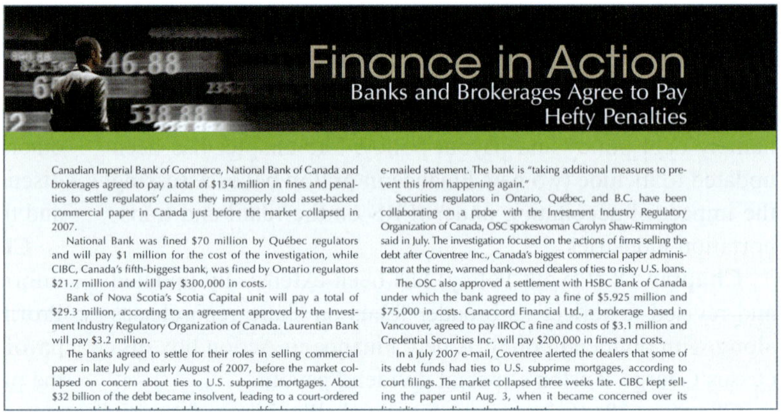

Finance in Action

Banks and Brokerages Agree to Pay Hefty Penalties

Canadian Imperial Bank of Commerce, National Bank of Canada and brokerages agreed to pay a total of $134 million in fines and penalties to settle regulators' claims they improperly sold asset-backed commercial paper in Canada just before the market collapsed in 2007.

National Bank was fined $70 million by Québec regulators and will pay $1 million for the cost of the investigation, while CIBC, Canada's fifth-biggest bank, was fined by Ontario regulators $21.7 million and will pay $300,000 in costs.

Bank of Nova Scotia's Scotia Capital unit will pay a total of $29.3 million, according to an agreement approved by the Investment Industry Regulatory Organization of Canada. Laurentian Bank will pay $3.2 million.

The banks agreed to settle for their roles in selling commercial paper in late July and early August of 2007, before the market collapsed on concern about ties to U.S. subprime mortgages. About $32 billion of the debt became insolvent, leading to a court-ordered

e-mailed statement. The bank is "taking additional measures to prevent this from happening again."

Securities regulators in Ontario, Québec, and B.C. have been collaborating on a probe with the Investment Industry Regulatory Organization of Canada, OSC spokeswoman Carolyn Shaw-Rimmington said in July. The investigation focused on the actions of firms selling the debt after Coventree Inc., Canada's biggest commercial paper administrator at the time, warned bank-owned dealers of ties to risky U.S. loans.

The OSC also approved a settlement with HSBC Bank of Canada under which the bank agreed to pay a fine of $5.925 million and $75,000 in costs. Canaccord Financial Ltd., a brokerage based in Vancouver, agreed to pay IIROC a fine and costs of $3.1 million and Credential Securities Inc. will pay $200,000 in fines and costs.

In a July 2007 e-mail, Coventree alerted the dealers that some of its debt funds had ties to U.S. subprime mortgages, according to court filings. The market collapsed three weeks late. CIBC kept selling the paper until Aug. 3, when it became concerned over its

INTERNATIONAL ICON

An international icon appears where the authors discuss global issues.

ETHICS ICON

An ethics icon appears where the authors discuss ethical issues or the implications of unethical practices.

KEY POINTS

These marginal boxes, identified with a key icon, summarize the importance of the adjoining material, at the same time helping students focus on the most critical content.

The value of a stock is the present value of the dividends it will pay over the investor's horizon plus the present value of the expected stock price at the end of that horizon.

CHECK POINT QUESTIONS

Numbered Check Point boxes with questions are provided in each chapter to enable students to check their understanding as they read. Both conceptual and calculation-type questions have been included in this edition. Answers are provided at the end of each chapter.

Check Point 3.6 Would the following activities increase or decrease the firm's cash balances?

a. Inventories are increased.
b. The firm reduces its trade payables.
c. The firm issues additional common stock.
d. The firm buys new equipment.

KEY FORMULAS

Key mathematical formulas, identified by a number, are called out in the text. A summary of these key formulas can be found by visiting Connect.

KEY TERMS

Key terms, when introduced, appear in colour and bold in the main text and are defined in the margin. A glossary made up of all these definitions is also available at the back of the book and on Connect.

CALCULATOR BOXES AND EXERCISES

In a continued effort to help students grasp the critical concept of time value of money, many pedagogical tools have been added throughout the text. Financial Calculator boxes provide examples of solving a variety of problems with directions for the three most popular financial calculators.

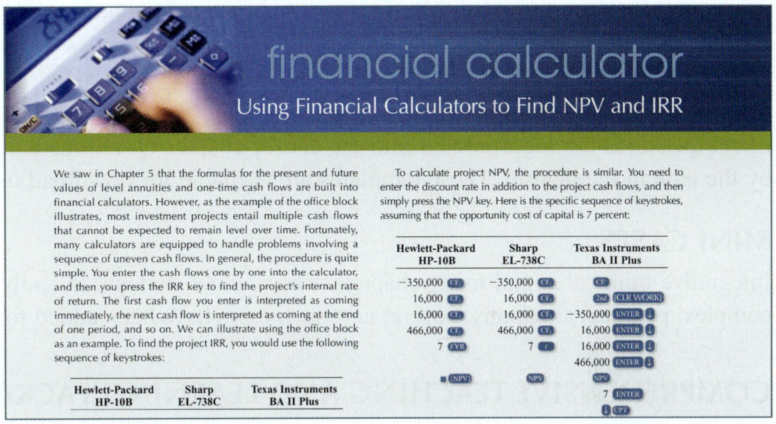

EXCEL SPREADSHEETS & EXHIBITS

Excel Spreadsheet boxes are integrated into many chapters and provide the student with detailed examples of how to use spreadsheets in applying financial concepts. They give students a valuable introduction to financial modelling. We show how spreadsheets can be used in time-value-of-money and security valuation problems, in capital budgeting, and in long- and short-term planning applications. Questions that apply to the spreadsheet are included. These spreadsheets are also available on Connect. Selected Exhibits are set as Excel Spreadsheets.

	A	B	C	D
1		Returns, Percent		Formulas Used in
2	Month	TSX	CAMECO	Column C
3	May 2010	−3.48	2.84	
4	June 2010	−3.71	−11.81	
5	July 2010	3.96	15.64	
6	August 2010	1.90	−0.61	
7	September 2010	4.09	10.18	
8	October 2010	2.71	10.31	
9	November 2010	2.37	17.78	
10	December 2010	4.09	18.64	
11				
12	Standard deviation (monthly)	3.25	9.58	=STDEV(C3:C10)
13	Standard deviation, annualized	11.25	33.19	=C10*SQRT(12)
14	Beta, using SLOPE		2.21	=SLOPE(C3:C10,B3:B10)
15	Correlation		0.748	=CORREL(B3:B10,C3:C10)

END-OF-CHAPTER MATERIAL

The end-of-chapter features offered to support the concepts presented are Summary, Related Web Links, Key Terms, Questions and Problems, Solutions to Check Points, and Mini Cases. To help students achieve the stated learning objectives, the LO numbers are included in the chapter Summaries and the Questions and Problems. The Questions and Problems incorporate Internet questions, questions with guided steps, integrative questions, qualitative/conceptual questions, and questions that require the use of Excel or an equivalent spreadsheet to solve. Questions are grouped according to level of difficulty; those whose answers are provided in Appendix B are identified by an asterisk on the question number.

Questions and Problems

connect Practise and learn online with *Connect*. Questions with online Excel templates or datasets are marked with .

*Answers in Appendix B

BASIC

1. **Financial Planning.** True or false? Explain. (LO1)
   a. Financial planning should attempt to minimize risk.
   b. The primary aim of financial planning is to obtain better forecasts of future cash flows and earnings.
   c. Financial planning is necessary because financing and investment decisions interact and should not be made independently.
   d. Firms' planning horizons rarely exceed three years

8. **Financial Targets.** Managers sometimes state a target growth rate for sales or earnings per share. Do you think that either one makes sense as a corporate goal? If not, why do you think that managers focus on them? (LO1)

INTERMEDIATE

*9. **Percentage-of-Sales Models.** Here are the abbreviated financial statements for Planners Peanuts:

CHALLENGE

27. **Capacity Use and External Financing.** Now suppose that the long-term assets of Growth Industries (from the previous problem) are operating at only 75 percent of capacity. What is required external financing over the next year? (LO4)

28. **Capacity Use and External Financing.** If Growth Industries from problem 26 is operating at only 75 percent

breach the bank's requirement that the company's debt ratio not exceed 60 percent?

b. Same scenario as (a), except that the interest rate on debt is 15 percent.
c. Same scenario as (a), except that Yummy Food keeps its debt ratio at 40 percent.
d. Same scenario as (a), except that cost of goods sold is 95 percent of sales each year.
e. Same scenario as (a), except each year's interest

INTERNET PROBLEMS

Many problems are provided that are meant to be solved using the wealth of material available on the Internet.

EXCEL QUESTIONS

Excel questions are incorporated into the end-of-chapter Questions and Problems, and are identified by the icon in the margin. These templates are available for download on Connect.

MINI CASES

Integrative mini cases end many chapters. These allow students to apply their knowledge to relatively complex, practical situations. Several new such cases have been added for this edition.

COMPREHENSIVE TEACHING AND LEARNING PACKAGE

CONNECT™

McGraw-Hill Connect™ is a web-based assignment and assessment platform that gives students the means to better connect with their coursework, with their instructors, and with the important concepts that they will need to know for success now and in the future. With Connect, instructors can deliver assignments, quizzes and tests easily online. Students can practice important skills at their own pace and on their own schedule. With Connect, students also get 24/7 online access to an eBook—an online edition of the text—to aid them in successfully completing their work, wherever and whenever they choose.

Key Features

Simple Assignment Management With Connect, creating assignments is easier than ever, so you can spend more time teaching and less time managing.

- Create and deliver assignments easily with new banks of homework questions and test bank material to assign online
- Streamline lesson planning, student progress reporting, and assignment grading to make classroom management more efficient than ever
- Go paperless with the eBook and online submission and grading of student assignments

Smart Grading When it comes to studying, time is precious. Connect helps students learn more efficiently by providing feedback and practice material when they need it, where they need it.

- Automatically score assignments, giving students immediate feedback on their work and side-by-side comparisons with correct answers
- Access and review each response; manually change grades or leave comments for students to review
- Reinforce classroom concepts with practice tests and instant quizzes

Instructor Library The Connect Instructor Library is your course creation hub. It provides all the critical resources you'll need to build your course, just how you want to teach it.

Instructor's Manual

This supplement was completed by our authors, and includes a descriptive preface containing alternative course formats and case teaching methods, a chapter overview and outline, key terms and concepts. Complete solutions to all end-of-chapter problems are included.

Computerized Test Bank

For the computerized test bank, Sepand Jazzi of Kwantlen Polytechnic University has adapted test questions that consist of true/false, multiple choice, and short answer questions. Questions are identified by level of difficulty and complete answers are provided for all questions and problems, along with reference to the relevant chapter Learning Objective(s).

Microsoft® PowerPoint® Slides

These visually stimulating slides have been fully updated, by Helen Prankie of Humber College, with colourful graphs, charts, and lists. The slides can be edited or manipulated to fit the needs of a particular course.

Image Gallery

The complete set of figures from the text can be downloaded from the image gallery on Connect and easily embedded into instructors' PowerPoint slides.

- Assign eBook readings and draw from a rich collection of textbook-specific assignments
- Access instructor resources, including ready-made PowerPoint presentations and media to use in your lectures
- View assignments and resources created for past sections
- Post your own resources for students to use

eBook Connect reinvents the textbook learning experience for the modern student. Every Connect subject area is seamlessly integrated with Connect eBooks, which are designed to keep students focused on the concepts key to their success.

- Provide students with a Connect eBook, allowing for anytime, anywhere access to the textbook
- Merge media, animation, and assessments with the text's narrative to engage students and improve learning and retention
- Pinpoint and connect key concepts in a snap using the powerful eBook search engine
- Manage notes, highlights, and bookmarks in one place for simple, comprehensive review

SUPERIOR SERVICE

Service takes on a whole new meaning with McGraw-Hill Ryerson and *Fundamentals of Corporate Finance*. More than just bringing you the textbook, we have consistently raised the bar in terms of innovation and educational research. These investments in learning and the education community have helped us to understand the needs of students and educators across the country, and allowed us to foster the growth of truly innovative, integrated learning.

INTEGRATED LEARNING

Your Integrated *i*Learning Sales Specialist is a McGraw-Hill Ryerson representative who has the experience, product knowledge, training, and support to help you assess and integrate any of our products, technology, and services into your course for optimal teaching and learning performance. Whether it's helping your students improve their grades, or putting your entire course online, your *i*Learning Sales Specialist is there to help you do it. Contact your *i*Learning Sales Specialist today to learn how to maximize all of McGraw-Hill Ryerson's resources!

COURSE MANAGEMENT

McGraw-Hill Ryerson offers a range of flexible integration solutions for Blackboard, WebCT, Desire2Learn, Moodle, and other leading learning management platforms. Please contact your local McGraw-Hill Ryerson *i*Learning Sales Specialist for details.

TEGRITY

Tegrity is a service that makes class time available all the time by automatically capturing every lecture in a searchable format for students to review when they study and complete assignments. With a simple one-click start-and-stop process, you capture all computer screens and corresponding audio. Students can replay any part of any class with easy-to-use browser-based viewing on a PC or Mac. Educators know that the more students can see, hear, and experience class resources, the better they learn.

ADDITIONAL TECHNOLOGY AND LEARNING SOLUTIONS

To see the latest technology and Learning Solutions offered by McGraw-Hill Ryerson and its partners, please visit us online. **www.mcgrawhill.ca/he/solutions**

ACKNOWLEDGMENTS

We take this opportunity to thank all of the individuals who helped us prepare this fifth edition. We want to express our appreciation to those instructors whose insightful comments and suggestions were invaluable to us during this revision.

Ben Amoako-Adu, Wilfrid Laurier University
Larry Bauer, Memorial University
David Birkett, University of Guelph
Keith Cheung, University of Windsor
Larbi Hammami, McGill University
Shahriar Hasan, Thompson Rivers University
Hui Huang, University of Waterloo
Andy Lin, Vancouver Island University
Ildebrando Lucas, Algonquin College
Usman Malik, Humber College
Andreas Marosi, University of Alberta
Diana Mok, University of Western Ontario
Martin Moy, Cape Breton University
Howard Nemiroff, Carleton University
Ian Rakita, Concordia University
Shahbaz Sheikh, University of Western Ontario
Francis Tapon, University of Guelph
Lachlan Whatley, Trinity Western University
Semih Yildrim, York University

We owe much to our colleagues at the University of New Brunswick and the Schulich School of Business, York University.

We extend much gratitude to professors Dr. Tom Beechy, Ingrid McLeod-Dick and Elizabeth Farrell, accounting experts at the Schulich School of Business, York University, who provided tremendous assistance regarding the treatment of IFRS in this text.

Thanks go to Professors Gopalan Srinivasan, Eben Otuteye and Muhammad Rashid, University of New Brunswick, for useful suggestions, and also to the Faculty of Business Administration, University of New Brunswick, for some research support on this project.

We would like to express our appreciation to Navid Kheradmand and Drew Cameron, University of New Brunswick, for adept research and computational assistance and to Danielle LeBlanc, University of New Brunswick for calculator work on some end-of-chapter problem solutions. Thanks to Andy Thi, David Jiang and Becky Zhou, Schulich undergraduate students, who did editing and calculator work. Thanks to David Birkett, University of Guelph, for the technical review of the text. In addition, we would like to thank our supplement authors William Lim, Helen Prankie and Sepand Jazzi. Their efforts will help students and instructors alike.

We are also grateful to the talented staff at McGraw-Hill Ryerson, especially Kimberley Veevers, Sponsoring Editor; Daphne Scriabin, Developmental Editor; and Graeme Powell, Supervising Editor. We want to thank copy editor Rodney Rawlings for his energetic attention to the details.

Finally, we cannot overstate our indebtedness to our spouses, Bruce Rhodes and Koumari Mitra, and to David Rhodes, Elizabeth's son, and Anusha Mitra, Devashis' daughter. They supported us and forgave us when we were very absorbed in the project.

PART I

Introduction

1 Goals and Governance of the Firm
- 1.1 Investment and Financing Decisions
- 1.2 What Is a Corporation?
- 1.3 Other Forms of Business Organization
- 1.4 Who Is the Financial Manager?
- 1.5 Goals of the Corporation
- 1.6 Careers in Finance
- 1.7 Topics Covered in This Book
- 1.8 Summary

2 Financial Markets and Institutions

3 Accounting and Finance

4 Measuring Corporate Performance

CHAPTER 1

Goals and Governance of the Firm

LEARNING OBJECTIVES

After studying this chapter, you should be able to:

LO1 Give examples of the investment and financing decisions that financial managers make.

LO2 Distinguish between real and financial assets.

LO3 Cite some of the advantages and disadvantages of organizing a business as a corporation.

LO4 Describe the responsibilities of the CFO, the treasurer, and the controller.

LO5 Explain why maximizing market value is the logical financial goal of the corporation.

LO6 Explain why value maximization is usually consistent with ethical behaviour.

LO7 Explain how corporations mitigate conflicts and encourage cooperative behaviour.

LO8 Give examples of career paths in finance.

A meeting of the corporation's directors.

Corporate finance boils down to the investment and financing decisions made by corporations. Financial managers in corporations work with other managers to identify investment opportunities, to analyze and value the opportunities, and to decide whether and how much to invest. Financial managers also have to raise the money to finance the corporation's investments. Therefore we start this chapter with examples of recent investment and financing decisions by major Canadian and foreign corporations. We also review what a corporation is and describe the special roles of a corporation's top financial managers, including the chief financial officer (CFO), treasurer, and controller. Later in the chapter we will review several possible career paths in finance.

Next we turn to the financial goals of the corporation. Should it maximize value, or is surviving and avoiding bankruptcy enough? Should it strive to be a good corporate citizen? If the firm maximizes value for its stockholders, can it also be a good corporate citizen? We also consider the conflicts of interest that arise in large corporations, and review the mechanisms that align the interests of the firm's managers with the interests of stockholders. Finally, we look ahead to the rest of this book and back to some entertaining snippets of financial history.

LO1, 2 1.1 INVESTMENT AND FINANCING DECISIONS

Mike Lazaridis is best known today as one of the founders of Research In Motion (RIM), the rapidly growing Canadian technology company known for its BlackBerry brand of handheld smart phones. But just over 25 years ago, Lazaridis had dropped out from University of Waterloo to operate Research In Motion with his childhood friend and business partner, Doug Fregin, in their small office in downtown Waterloo. In the early years, the duo secured minor contracts from large corporations such as General Motors, Kodak, and Ericsson that helped legitimize the business. For General Motors, the company created networked display terminals that could display messages to the assembly line on big LED screens. Kodak accepted RIM's bid to develop the first "DigiSync Film Barcode Reader," which revolutionized the way movies were edited in Hollywood. RIM even won an Oscar in technical achievement for the "DigiSync" innovation. Ericsson hired Lazaridis and Fregin to develop software for one of its new projects that would later be known as the "Viking Express." The software that RIM developed would prove to be the critical missing piece to the commercial wireless e-mail puzzle. Lazaridis and Fregin had experienced their first taste of the wireless e-mail dream that would come to define the entire company some years later.

Eight years in, the company was surviving, but it was still far from being the Research In Motion we know today. It had added 14 employees and was operating four different business lines providing yearly revenue of around $500,000. With a strong engineering and computer networking foundation in place, Lazaridis brought in Jim Balsillie in 1992 as co-CEO to navigate the company with sound business practices. With Balsillie came his personal investment of $250,000. From that point on, through a series of personal and business connections, the company was able to secure major technological research and development funding from myriad sources, including loan and assistance programs from federal and provincial governments and private organizations. This period also saw RIM's *initial public offering (IPO)*; it was the first time the firm allowed the general public to buy shares. The new shareholders became part owners of the company in proportion to the number of shares they purchased, and the company used the funds raised for its investment outlays. RIM was able to focus on its core business.

Following years of successes and failures developing software and less-popular mobile handhelds, Research In Motion eventually found its way in 1997. The RIM Inter@ctive Pager 950 Wireless Handheld would come to be known as the company's first BlackBerry. The 950 was a compact device that supported a 31-key PC-style keyboard and a 1,000-entry address book. Its key feature, however, was the ease and reliability of its portable e-mail functionality. The response time for receiving an e-mail was an amazing 20 seconds. The device would alert the user that an e-mail had been received without his or her having to click the "get mail" button other devices required. RIM was tasked by IBM to outfit its North American field workers with the devices. Other large companies such as Bellsouth signed on to buy hundreds of thousands of the product. Needless to say, this was RIM's first real taste of major commercial success.

In the 12 years since the first BlackBerry, Research In Motion has become one of Canada's biggest corporate success stories in recent history. According to *The Globe and Mail*, RIM is currently the fourth-most-profitable company in Canada, behind only three of the largest banks in the country. With annual sales of $15 billion, and a stock market value of over $30 billion, the company employs almost 14,000 full-time workers. There are currently 10 different BlackBerry models available, all of which have come a long way since the RIM 950. The newest BlackBerrys are equipped with wireless and 3G network Internet, e-mail and text messaging, a phone, GPS, a camera, an MP3 player, and countless other features.

In retrospect, Research In Motion's success was hardly a sure thing. Mike Lazaridis, Doug Fregin, and Jim Balsillie's ideas were inspired, but their implementation was complex and difficult. It took time and considerable effort to build a customer base. Beyond the challenges posed by its product innovation, the firm also needed to be *good at finance*. It had the good fortune to get a long head start from potential competitors, but a series of bad financial decisions would have sunk the company.

Research In Motion had to make good *investment decisions*. In the beginning, these decisions were constrained. Contracts had to be carefully vetted for their chances of working out favourably. Given the company's scarce resources, every new contract it decided to undertake might have led to the demise of the entire firm if it had failed. As the company grew, RIM's investment decisions became more complex. Should it incorporate a phone into the device? When should it expand into Europe and Asia? How many unique devices should it develop? Which companies should it acquire as it expanded its range of services and devices?

Research In Motion also had to make good *financing decisions*. For example, how should it raise the money it needed for investment? In the beginning, these choices were also constrained. Available sources of financing were limited to family money, and bank loans. As the company grew, its range of choices expanded. Every new software contract the company received attracted more and more attention from the Canadian Government who were attempting to establish Canada as a worldwide technology leader in the 1990s. According to Innovation Strategy Canada, federal and provincial governments lent or simply gave the company close to $50 million during its "make-or-break" period in the mid and late 1990s. Jim Balsillie had some major decisions to make when deciding how the company would finance its operations.

The initial public offering was one of those trying times. For example, how many shares should the company try to sell? At what price? As the company grew, it periodically raised more

TABLE 1.1 Examples of recent investment and financing decisions by major corporations. Unless otherwise stated, revenues, investment costs, and financing proceeds are in Canadian dollars.

Company (2009 revenues in $ millions)	Recent Investment (Capital Budgeting) Decision	Recent Financing Decision
Nokia ($59,972)—Finnish, world's leading mobile phone supplier	In 2007, agreed to buy Navteq Corp. for $8.1 billion to gain digital maps of 69 countries.	Will finance half the acquisition with its own cash, and use borrowed money for the rest.
Royal Bank of Canada (38,143)—Canada's largest bank	Acquired the fund manager Phillips Hagar and North for $1.4 billion in May 2008.	Offered Phillips Hagarand North shareholders 27 million common shares for the company.
EnCana Corporation ($11,335)—Canadian oil and gas producer	Purchased Deep Bossier natural gas assets and land interests in East Texas for US$2.55 billion in 2007.	Completed a public offering in the United States of senior unsecured notes in the aggregate principal amount of US$500 million in May 2009.
Research In Motion ($15,252; 20101)—Canadian, world-leading designer, manufacturer and marketer of mobile communication devices (BlackBerry)	Spent $148 million in March 2009 to acquire Certicom Corp. and Torch Mobile Inc., whose technologies will be incorporated into future RIM mobile devices.	In November 2009, the company established an $800 million common share repurchase program.
Shaw Communications ($3,148)—Canadian cable company	In February 2009, acquired the Campbell River cable system in British Columbia for $46.3 million and the Mountain Cable system in Ontario for $300 million just 8 months later.	Issued $600 million 6.5% senior notes in March 2009.
Diageo ($15,687)—British, world leading beverage company	Purchased the exclusive perpetual distribution rights to Ketel One Vodka products in June 2008 for $708 million.	In 2008, issued $1.5 billion 5-year and 1.27 billion 6-year bonds
Walmart ($416,337)—U.S., world's largest retailer	Spent $100 million in 2010 to purchase Vudu, an online movie service being built into an increasing amount of Blu-ray players.	Has set up a $15 billion share repurchase program in 2010.
McCain Foods (N/A)—Canadian, privately owned world-leading frozen french fry processor	Investing £10m ($20 million) to build three wind turbines at the United Kingdom's largest french fry factory	(No information provided, as this is a private corporation.)
TransCanada ($8,966)—Canadian oil and gas pipeline operator	Spent $3.9 billion in 2009 to extend two oil pipelines from Alberta to the U.S. Midwest	Issued 22 million preferred shares in September 2009, resulting in gross proceeds of $600 million.

funds by selling additional stock to the public, and it borrowed money from banks. At each point, it needed to decide on the proper form and terms of financing as well as the amounts to be raised.[1]

The particulars may differ, but all successful companies, such as Research In Motion, have to make good investment and financing decisions. Also, as with RIM, those decisions range from prosaic and obvious to difficult, complicated, and strategically crucial.

Table 1.1 lists nine corporations, of which six are Canadian. Three are foreign: Diageo's headquarters are in Britain, Nokia's in Finland, and Walmart's in the United States. We have chosen large corporations that you may be familiar with. Earlier you learned about RIM's

[1] The following sources were helpful in writing this section: Claire Gagné, "Douglas Fregin—The Other RIM Guy," *Canadian Business Online*, December 5, 2005, **www.canadianbusiness.com/after_hours/lifestyle_activities/article.jsp?content=20051205_72913_72913**; Barrie McKenna, Paul Waldie, and Simon Avery, "Patently Absurd: The Inside Story of RIM's Wireless War," *The Globe and Mail*, January 28, 2006, B4.

BlackBerry, but did you know that Nokia is the world's largest producer of mobile phones? You may have eaten McCain's frozen french fries and heard of Smirnoff and Johnny Walker, two of the world's leading beverages produced by Diageo.

What do these companies have to be "good at" in order to succeed in their businesses? The first answer is obvious: producing goods and services that meet their customers' needs. For example, Shaw Communications has to ensure that its cable system provides reliable television and Internet service to its 3.4 million Canadian customers. McCain's has to strive to produce frozen fries at least as good as those made by its competitors.

But each of these companies also has to be good at finance. This means that each has to make good investment decisions and good financing decisions. Superior investment and financing decisions might put these companies a step ahead of their competitors. A series of bad investment or financing decisions might cause severe damage.

Table 1.1 gives for each company an example of a recent investment and financing decision. *Making good investment and financing decisions is the chief task of the financial manager*. Let us consider each class of decisions in more detail.

THE INVESTMENT (CAPITAL BUDGETING) DECISION

capital budgeting decision or **investment decision** Decision about which real assets the firm should acquire.

The investment decision starts with the identification of investment opportunities, often referred to as *capital investment projects*. The financial manager has to help the firm identify promising projects and decide how much to invest in each project. The investment decision is also called the **capital budgeting decision**, because most firms prepare an annual budget listing authorized capital investments.

Some investments are in tangible assets, such as investment in TransCanada's new oil pipeline and EnCana's natural gas project. But you can see from Table 1.1 that the scope of the investment decision is much broader. It includes investment in intangible assets, including research and development (R&D) and acquisition of patents and trademarks. RIM recently spent over $1.2 billion on R&D and the purchase of patents. Major pharmaceutical companies invest billions every year in R&D for new drugs. Consumer product companies, such as Diageo and McCain, spend millions to advertise products. In this case the intangible asset is brand recognition and acceptance.

The world of business can be intensely competitive, and corporations survive and prosper only if they can keep launching new products or services. In some cases the costs and risks of doing so are amazingly large. Nokia has spent billions over the past four years to build itself into a consumer Web media company. It has purchased the biggest digital-map database, Navteq, and already owns Enpocket, the largest mobile advertising agency. It operates services for downloading music, games, and turn-by-turn navigation. It runs the consumer e-mail service for dozens of carriers worldwide and recently bought a Web photo and video sharing site called Twango. By offering these services, Nokia is in competition with the major Internet companies, Google and Yahoo, and the Apple iPhone. Google offers mobile phone services and has developed its own mobile device, Nexus One. More recently, Google has been involved with the Android smart phone operating system.

Not all capital investments succeed. The Iridium communications satellite system, which offered its users instant telephone connections worldwide, soaked up $5 billion in investment before it started operations in 1998. It needed 400,000 subscribers to break even, but attracted only a small fraction of that target. Iridium defaulted on its debt and filed for bankruptcy in 1999. The Iridium system was sold a year later for just $25 million.

The investment in Iridium, though it looks stupid in hindsight, may have been rational given what was known in the early 1990s when the go-ahead decision was made. It may have been a good decision thwarted by bad luck. There are no guarantees in finance. But you can tilt the odds in your favour if you learn the tools of investment analysis and apply them intelligently. We will cover these tools in detail later in this book.

Today's capital investments generate future returns. Often the returns come in the distant future. Nokia is committing billions to acquire mobile information services, because it believes future sales will generate cash returns. Those cash returns have to recover the $9 billion investment and provide at least an adequate profit on that investment. The longer Nokia has to wait for cash to flow back, the greater its required profit. Thus, the financial manager has to pay attention to the timing of project returns, not just their cumulative amount. In addition, these returns are rarely certain. A new project might be either a smashing success or a dismal failure like Iridium.

The financial manager needs a way of putting a value on the uncertain future cash inflows generated by capital investment projects. This value should account for the amounts, timing, and risk of the future cash flows. If a project's value is greater than its required investment, the project is attractive financially. An effective financial manager guides his or her firm to invest in projects that add more value than the investment required. In other words, the financial manager helps the firm to invest in projects that are worth more than they cost.

But do not think of financial managers making major investment decisions in solitary confinement. Financial managers may work as part of a team of engineers and managers from manufacturing, marketing, and other business functions. Often the final investment decision is made by senior non-financial management.

Also, do not think of the financial manager as making billion-dollar investments daily. Most investment decisions are smaller and simpler, such as the purchase of a truck, machine tool, or computer system. But the objective is still to add value, that is, to find and make investments that are worth more than they cost. Most firms make thousands of small investment decisions every year. The cumulative value added by the small decisions can be just as large as the value added by occasional big decisions such as those shown in Table 1.1.

THE FINANCING DECISION

financing decision Decision on how to raise the money to pay for investments in real assets.

capital structure A firm's mix of long-term financing.

The financial manager's second main responsibility is to raise the money that the firm needs for its investments and operations. This is the **financing decision**. When a company needs to raise money, it can invite investors to put up cash in exchange for a share of future profits, or it can promise to pay back the investors' cash plus a fixed rate of interest. In the first case, the investors receive shares of stock and become shareholders, part owners of the corporation. The investors in this case are referred to as *equity investors*, who contribute equity financing. In the second case, the investors are lenders, that is, *debt investors*, who one day have to be repaid. The choice between debt and equity financing is often called the **capital structure** decision. Here "capital" refers to the firm's sources of long-term financing. A firm that is seeking to raise long-term financing is said to be *raising capital*.

The financing choices available to large corporations seem almost endless. Suppose the firm decides to borrow. Should it issue debt to investors, or should it borrow from a bank? Should it borrow for 1 year or 20 years? If it borrows for 20 years, should it reserve the right to pay off the debt early if interest rates fall? Should it borrow in its domestic currency or a foreign currency? As Table 1.1 shows, EnCana raised $500 million in U.S. dollars, rather than Canadian dollars. This makes sense, because EnCana is paid in U.S. dollars for its exports of oil and gas to the United States. We will look at these and other choices in later chapters.

The decision to take out a 20-year loan or to issue new shares of stock obviously has long-term consequences. But the financial manager is also involved in many important short-term decisions. For example, he or she has to make sure that there is enough cash on hand to pay next week's bills and that any spare cash is put to work to earn interest. These are short-term financing decisions (how to raise cash to meet a short-term need) and short-term investment decisions (how to invest spare cash for brief periods).

The financial manager is involved in many other day-to-day activities that are essential to the smooth operation of the firm but not dramatic enough to show up in Table 1.1. For example, if the firm sells goods or services on credit, it has to make sure its customers pay their bills on time. Corporations that operate internationally must constantly transfer cash from one currency to another. Manufacturing companies must decide how much to invest in inventories of raw materials and finished goods.

Businesses are inherently risky, so the financial manager has to identify risks and make sure they are managed properly. For example, the manager will want to ensure that the firm's operations will not be severely damaged by a rise in oil prices or a fall in the dollar. In later chapters we will look at how managers assess risk and at some of the ways firms can be protected from nasty surprises.

Check Point 1.1

Are the following capital budgeting or financing decisions?

a. Ballard Power decides to spend $500 million to develop a new hydrogen fuel cell.
b. Bayer Inc. decides to raise 350 million euros (€350 million) through a bank loan.
c. Nova Corporation constructs a pipeline to transport natural gas to Chile's remote southern Magallanes region.
d. BCE Inc. completes a $1 billion public debt offering that replaces existing debt at a significantly lower cost.
e. Biochem Pharma buys a licence to produce and sell a new drug developed by a biotech firm.
f. Volkswagen issues new shares to help finance the acquisition of a 49.9 percent stake in Porsche, a luxury carmaker.

Financing and investment decisions (both long- and short-term) are interconnected. The amount of investment determines the amount of financing that has to be raised, and the investors who contribute financing today expect a return on that investment in the future. Thus, the investments that the firm makes today have to generate future returns for payout to investors.

Figure 1.1 traces how money flows from investors to the firm and back to investors. The flow starts when cash is raised from investors (arrow 1 in the figure). The cash is used to pay for the real assets (investment projects) needed for the firm's operations (arrow 2). Later, if the firm does well, the operations generate enough cash inflow to more than repay the initial investment (arrow 3). Finally, the cash is either reinvested (arrow 4a) or returned to the investors who furnished the money in the first place (arrow 4b). Of course, the choice between arrows 4a and 4b is constrained by the promises made when cash was raised at arrow 1. For example, if the firm borrows money from a bank at arrow 1, it has to repay this money plus interest at arrow 4b.

You can see examples in Table 1.1 of the flows represented by arrows 4a and 4b. RIM finances its R&D by reinvesting earnings (arrow 4a). Shaw Communications has decided to return cash to shareholders by buying back its stock and paying dividends (arrow 4b).

Notice in Figure 1.1 how the financial manager stands between the firm and outside investors. On the one hand, the financial manager helps manage the firm's operations, particularly by helping to make good investment decisions. On the other, the financial manager deals with investors—not just with shareholders but also with banks and other financial institutions and

FIGURE 1.1
Flow of cash between investors and the firm's operations. Key: (1) cash raised by selling financial assets to investors; (2) cash invested in the firm's operations; (3) cash generated by the firm's operations; (4a) cash reinvested; (4b) cash returned to investors.

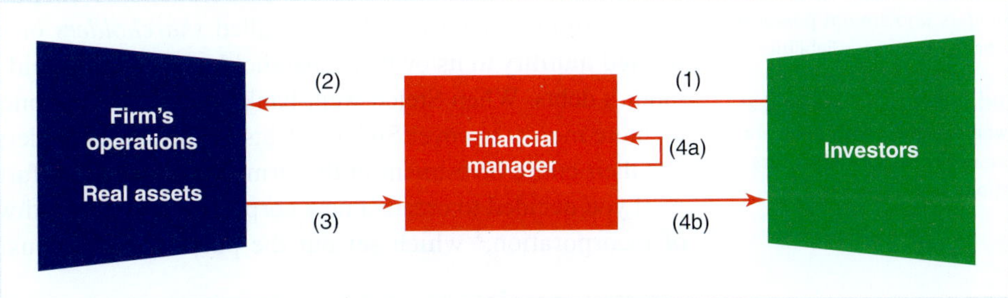

with financial markets, such as the Toronto Stock Exchange. We will say more about financial markets and institutions in the next chapter.

real assets Assets used to produce goods and services.

financial assets Claims to the income generated by real assets. Also called *securities*.

Figure 1.1 also distinguishes real from financial assets. **Real assets** are used to produce the firm's products and services. They include tangible assets such as machinery, factories, and offices and intangible assets such as technical knowledge, trademarks, and patents. The firm finances its investments in real assets by issuing **financial assets** to investors. A share of stock is a financial asset, which has value as a claim on the firm's real assets and the income that those assets will produce. A bank loan is a financial asset also. It gives the bank the right to get its money back plus interest. If the firm's operations can't generate enough income to pay what the bank is owed, the bank can force the firm into bankruptcy and stake a claim on its real assets.

Shares of stock and other financial assets that can be purchased and traded by investors are called *securities*.

Check Point 1.2

Which of the following are financial assets and which are real assets?

a. A patent
b. A share of stock issued by Royal Bank
c. A blast furnace in a steel-making factory
d. A mortgage loan taken out to help pay for a new home
e. After a successful advertising campaign, the belief by potential customers that your brand of potato chips is extra crispy
f. An IOU ("I owe you") from your brother-in-law

LO3 1.2 WHAT IS A CORPORATION?

public company Corporation whose shares are listed for trading on a stock exchange.

private company Corporation whose shares are privately owned.

More than 5,000 public companies exist in Canada, about 15,000 in the United Sates, and many more around the world. "Public" means that the company's shares are traded in a securities market such as the Toronto Stock Exchange. **Public companies** have a lot of flexibility when raising financing. They can offer shares for sale to any and all investors. In return, public companies are required to provide investors with detailed financial information in their annual reports and make timely disclosure of significant corporate events. Access to information is crucial for making decisions on whether to buy or sell the shares of a public company. Hundreds of thousands of **private companies** also exist, but their shares cannot be freely traded among investors and do not raise money in the stock market. Consequently, private companies are not required to provide much financial information, so little information is publicly available. You cannot purchase the shares of these private companies, except by negotiation with existing owners.

The nine major companies in Table 1.1 are a tiny subsample from the list of corporations operating around the world. Eight of the nine companies in Table 1.1 are public, and one, McCain Foods, is private. Members of the McCain family own all of its shares. As a private corporation, McCain Foods does not release detailed financial information but does report its annual revenue.

corporation Business owned by shareholders who are not personally liable for the business's liabilities.

limited liability Principle that the owners of the corporation are not personally responsible for its obligations.

Nearly all large businesses are corporations. A **corporation** is a permanent entity, legally distinct from its owners, who are called *shareholders* or *stockholders*.[2] A corporation confers **limited liability** to its owners: shareholders cannot be held personally responsible for the corporation's debts. When Stelco went bankrupt in 2004, no one demanded that the stockholders put up more money to cover Stelco's debts. All the stockholders ended up with worthless shares and lost their entire investment in the firm, but they had no further liability.

If you decided to create a new corporation, you would work with a lawyer to prepare articles of incorporation,[3] which set out the purpose of the business and how it is to be financed,

[2] "Shareholder" and "stockholder" mean exactly the same thing and are used interchangeably.

[3] They are also called *letters patent* or *memoranda of association* in some provinces.

managed, and governed. You may incorporate your firm federally, under the *Canadian Business Corporation Act*, or provincially, under the relevant provincial laws. For many purposes, the corporation is considered a resident of its jurisdiction. For example, it can borrow or lend money and it can sue or be sued. It pays its own taxes—but it cannot vote!

Corporations can, in principle, live forever, and in practice they can survive many human lifetimes. One of the oldest corporations is the Hudson's Bay Company, which was formed in 1670 to profit from the fur trade between northern Canada and England by sea, via Hudson's Bay. It still operates as one of Canada's leading retail chains. However, it is no longer a public company, because all its shares were purchased in a takeover in 2006 by Jerry Zucker, a wealthy American financier. Hudson's Bay is now a private company.[4]

EXAMPLE 1.1 BUSINESS ORGANIZATION

Suppose you own a commercial building and operate a restaurant in it. You have invested in the building itself, kitchen equipment, dining-room furnishings, a computer system to keep track of supplies and reservations, plus various other assets. If you do not incorporate, you own these assets personally, as the sole proprietor of the business. If you have borrowed money from a bank to start the business, you are personally responsible for this debt. If the business loses money and cannot pay the bank, the bank can demand that you raise cash by selling other assets—your car or house, for example—in order to repay the loan. But if you incorporate the restaurant business, and the corporation borrows from the bank, your other assets are shielded from the restaurant's debts. Of course, this also means that the bank will be more cautious in lending if your restaurant is incorporated, because the bank will have no access to your other assets.

Notice that if you incorporate your business, you exchange direct ownership of its real assets (the building, kitchen equipment, etc.) for indirect ownership via financial assets (the shares of the new corporation).

All corporations have a board of directors, a group elected by shareholders and given the responsibility for overseeing the activities of the corporation, including the appointment of top managers and the monitoring of their performance.

The legal separation of ownership and management is one distinctive feature of corporations. Separation gives corporations permanence. If managers are fired and replaced, the corporation survives. All of today's shareholders can sell out to new investors without necessarily affecting the conduct of the corporation's business. One advantage of being a public company is the convenience of the stock market for selling shares. Shareholders of private corporations can also sell their shares to new investors, but the process is more time-consuming and subject to legal restrictions.

Although all corporations have boards of directors, the extent of the actual separation of shareholders and management differs. In a private corporation, the shareholders are on the board of directors and often are also top managers. In public corporations, this is neither feasible nor desirable. Large, public corporations have thousands of shareholders. An individual may have 100 shares, receive 100 votes, and be entitled to a tiny fraction of the firm's income and value. A pension fund or insurance company may own millions of shares, receive millions of votes, and have a correspondingly large stake in that same firm's performance. Thus, shareholders of public corporations do not usually manage them. Some public corporations have a shareholder who owns more than 50 percent of the shares. In such closely held public corporations, this controlling

[4] After the death of Mr. Zucker in April 2008, the Zucker family decided to sell their Hudson's Bay shares. The shares were sold in July 2008 to NRDC Equity Partners, a private equity firm that acquires operating companies in the retail, leisure, lodging, and commercial real estate sectors. NRDC will merge Hudson's Bay with other stores it owns, including Lord & Taylor, a chain of American upscale department stores. The new combined private company will have annual sales of about $8 billion, 75,000 employees, and some 650 stores with over 5,000,000 square metres of retail space across all ten Canadian provinces and nine U.S. states, mainly in the Northeast.

shareholder may be very involved in the day-to-day management of the firm. Regardless of the ownership structure, in public companies, the board of directors plays a critical role as the shareholders' representative, and is supposed to ensure that management is acting in the shareholders' best interests.

Given these advantages, you may wonder why all businesses are not organized as public corporations. One reason is the cost, in both time and money, of managing the corporation's legal machinery. Public corporations must pay stock exchanges for listing their shares and also must abide by the rules of stock exchanges, accounting standards, and securities laws. These requirements include compliance with the relevant corporate governance policies, which are given to the board of directors so that they do a proper job of ensuring that the business is operating appropriately. Stocks listed on the Toronto Stock Exchange have to comply with Canadian corporate governance policies, created jointly by the provincial securities commissions.[5] These policies include rules for proper auditing, give guidelines for ensuring board independence, and require companies to disclose their governance policies. In contrast, U.S. public companies must comply with the *Sarbanes-Oxley Act*, a set of disclosure and corporate governance laws that dictate how the governance has to be set up. Some market watchers believe that the *Sarbanes-Oxley* rules are so strict that they are causing public companies to go private. These regulatory and financial costs are particularly burdensome for small businesses.

There is also an important tax drawback to corporations. Because the corporation is a separate legal entity, it is taxed separately. So corporations pay tax on their profits, and shareholders are taxed again when they receive dividends from the company or sell their shares at a profit.[6] By contrast, income generated by businesses that are not incorporated is taxed just once as personal income.

To summarize, the corporation is a distinct, permanent legal entity. Its advantages are limited liability and the ease with which ownership and management can be separated. These advantages are especially important for large firms. Public companies have the added advantage of the financial flexibility of publicly traded shares. A disadvantage of corporate organization is double taxation. For public corporations, the additional disadvantages are the expense of maintaining a stock listing, compliance with governance requirements, and sharing of information with the public.

LO3 1.3 OTHER FORMS OF BUSINESS ORGANIZATION

This book focuses on corporations, which tend to be larger firms with many shareholders. But there are other forms of organizations that range from small "mom and pop" proprietorship businesses to larger partnerships. Let us look at these in more detail.

SOLE PROPRIETORSHIPS

sole proprietor Sole owner of a business that has no partners and no shareholders. Personally liable for all the firm's obligations.

A **sole proprietorship** is a business owned and operated by one individual. As the sole proprietor, you bear all of the costs and keep all of the profits after the Canada Revenue Agency (CRA) has taken its cut. The advantages of a proprietorship are the ease with which it can be established and the lack of regulations governing it. This makes it well suited for a small company with an informal business structure. However, the sole proprietor is not protected by limited liability, but is responsible for all the business's debts and other liabilities. Suppose you start a sole proprietorship and the business borrows from the bank. If subsequently the business cannot repay the loan,

---

[5] *National Policy 58-201 Corporate Governance Guidelines* and *National Instrument 58-101 Disclosure of Corporate Governance Practices* set out the rules for companies listed on the Toronto Stock Exchange. They can be found at **www.tsx.com/en/listings/tsx_issuer_resources/corporate_governance.html**.

[6] To avoid taxing the same income twice, Canada's tax system, like that of several other countries, allows shareholders some credit for the taxes their company has already paid. Although this feature of Canadian tax law reduces the "double taxation" of dividend income, it does not usually eliminate it completely. We will discuss the dividend tax credit in more detail in Chapter 3.

the bank has a claim against your personal belongings. It might force you into personal bankruptcy if the business debts are big enough. Thus, as sole proprietor you have unlimited liability.

PARTNERSHIPS

partnership Business owned by two or more people who are personally responsible for all its liabilities.

Instead of being on your own, you may wish to pool money and expertise with friends or business associates. If so, a sole proprietorship is obviously inappropriate. Instead, you can form a **partnership**. Your partnership agreement will set out how management decisions are to be made and the proportion of the profits to which each partner is entitled. The partners then pay personal income tax on their share of these profits. Both sole proprietorships and partnerships are flow-through entities because the businesses do not pay income tax on operating profits and do not have to file a tax return, unlike corporations.

Partners, like sole proprietors, have the disadvantage of unlimited liability. If the business runs into financial difficulties, each partner has unlimited liability for all the business's debts, not just his or her share. The moral is clear and simple: "Know thy partner." Many professional businesses are organized as partnerships. They include accounting, legal, and management consulting firms. Several large Canadian investment dealers, such as BMO Nesbitt Burns, Scotia Capital, and CIBC World Markets, have their origins in partnerships, as do most large investment banks in the United States, such as Morgan Stanley, Salomon, Smith Barney, Merrill Lynch, and Goldman Sachs.[7] A number of large and growing Canadian companies, such as Saputo Inc. and the Jean Coutu Group, and international companies, such as Microsoft and Apple Computer, also started life as partnerships. But eventually these companies and their financing requirements grew too large for them to continue as partnerships and they became corporations.

HYBRID FORMS OF BUSINESS ORGANIZATION

Some business forms do not fit neatly into any one category, but are hybrids. For example, in a limited partnership, partners are classified as general or limited. General partners manage the business and have unlimited personal liability for the business's debts. Limited partners are liable only for the money they contribute to the business and cannot take part in the day-to-day management of the partnership.

Many provinces allow limited liability partnerships (LLPs) or, equivalently, limited liability companies (LLCs). These are partnerships in which all partners have limited liability. Both limited partnerships and limited liability partnerships are flow-through entities, with earnings taxed in the hands of the partners, avoiding the double taxation of corporate earnings. Another variation is the professional corporation (PC), which is commonly used by doctors, lawyers, and accountants.[8] In this case, the business has limited liability and is taxed as a corporation, but the professionals can still be sued personally, for example for malpractice.

Another hybrid business form is the income trust. An income trust is an investment fund, legally known as a mutual fund trust. Mutual fund trusts sell units to investors to raise money to purchase shares and debt of operating businesses. Mutual fund trusts are not operating companies but flow-through entities, in which the earnings on the investments are not taxed at the fund level, but rather are taxed in the hands of the unitholders. Unlike typical investment funds, which invest in many different companies, an income trust invests in only one company, making a unit similar to a share. Clever lawyers and financial experts were able to structure income trusts to dramatically reduce the taxes paid by the underlying business enterprise. One way this was accomplished was by having the income trust own both the debt and the equity of the underlying corporation. This allowed the corporation to be financed with a lot of debt, reducing its taxes. Income trusts became very popular, with some corporations converting to the trust structures and

[7] Canadian investment dealers assist investors in buying and selling securities for a fee. They also assist firms in issuing new securities. In the United States, the term "investment bank" is used instead of "investment dealer."

[8] For further discussion, see John Willes, *Contemporary Canadian Business Law*, 8th ed. (Whitby, ON: McGraw-Hill Ryerson, 2006).

other business going public as trusts. On October 31, 2006, the Canadian federal government, fearing significant loss of tax revenue, changed the rules for the taxation of income trusts, taking away their tax advantage, and the income trust boom came to a sudden end.[9]

Check Point 1.3

Which form of business organization might best suit the following?

a. A consulting firm with several senior consultants and support staff.

b. A house painting company owned and operated by a university student who hires some friends for occasional help.

c. A paper goods company with sales of $100 million and 2,000 employees.

LO4 1.4 WHO IS THE FINANCIAL MANAGER?

In this book we will use the term *financial manager* to refer to anyone responsible for a significant corporate investment or financing decision. But except in the smallest firms, no single person is responsible for all the decisions discussed in this book. Responsibility is dispersed throughout the firm. Top management is, of course, constantly involved in financial decisions. But the engineer who designs a new production facility is also involved: the design determines the kind of asset in which the firm will invest. Likewise, the marketing manager who undertakes a major advertising campaign is making an investment decision: the campaign is an investment in an intangible asset that will pay off in future sales and earnings.

treasurer Manager responsible for financing, cash management, and relationships with financial markets and institutions.

controller Officer responsible for budgeting, accounting, and auditing.

chief financial officer (CFO) Officer who oversees the treasurer and controller and sets overall financial strategy.

Nevertheless, there are managers who specialize in finance, and their functions are summarized in Figure 1.2. The **treasurer** is usually the person most directly responsible for looking after the firm's cash, raising new capital, and maintaining relationships with banks and other investors who hold the firm's securities.

For small firms, the treasurer is likely to be the only financial executive. Larger corporations usually also have a **controller**, who prepares the financial statements, manages the firm's internal accounting, and looks after its tax affairs. You can see that the treasurer and controller have different roles: the treasurer's main function is to obtain and manage the firm's capital, whereas the controller ensures that the money is used efficiently.

The largest firms usually appoint a **chief financial officer (CFO)** to oversee both the treasurer's and the controller's work. The CFO is deeply involved in financial policymaking and corporate planning. Often he or she will have general responsibilities beyond strictly financial issues.

FIGURE 1.2
The financial managers in large corporations.

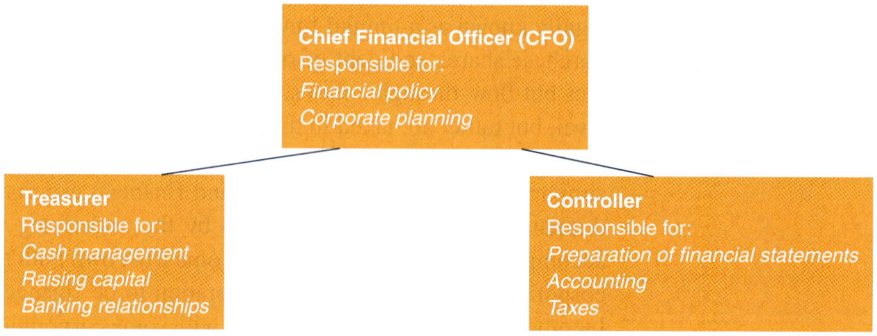

[9] To read more about the new rules for income trust taxation, see **en.wikipedia.org/wiki/Income_trust#The_Conservatives_propose_new_rules_for_income_trusts**.

Usually the treasurer, controller, or CFO is responsible for organizing and supervising the capital budgeting process. However, major capital investment projects are so closely tied to plans for product development, production, and marketing that managers from these other areas are inevitably drawn into planning and analyzing the projects. If the firm has staff members specializing in corporate planning, they are naturally involved in capital budgeting too.

Because of the importance of many financial issues, ultimate decisions often rest by law or by custom with the board of directors.[10] For example, only the board has the legal power to declare a dividend or to sanction a public issue of securities. Boards usually delegate decision-making authority for small- or medium-sized investment outlays, but the authority to approve large investments is almost never delegated.

Check Point 1.4

Sal and Sally went to business school together 10 years ago. They have just been hired by a midsized corporation that wants to bring in new financial managers. Sal studied finance, with an emphasis on financial markets and institutions. Sally majored in accounting and became a chartered accountant (CA) five years ago. Who is more suited to be treasurer? Controller? Briefly explain.

LO5, 6, 7 1.5 GOALS OF THE CORPORATION

SHAREHOLDERS WANT MANAGERS TO MAXIMIZE MARKET VALUE

For small firms, shareholders and management may be one and the same. But for large companies, separation of ownership and management is a practical necessity. For example, Royal Bank has over 1.2 billion shares outstanding, some owned by large institutional investors and others by thousands of individuals. There is no way that these shareholders can be actively involved in management; it would be like trying to run Toronto or Vancouver by town meetings. Authority has to be delegated.

How can shareholders decide how to delegate decision making when they all have different tastes, wealth, time horizons, and personal opportunities? Delegation can work only if the shareholders have a common objective. Fortunately there is a natural financial objective on which almost all shareholders can agree: to maximize the current value of their investment.

A smart and effective financial manager makes decisions that increase the current value of the company's shares and the wealth of its shareholders. That increased wealth can then be put to whatever purposes the shareholders want. They can give their money to charity or spend it in glitzy nightclubs; they can save it or spend it now. Whatever their personal tastes or objectives, they can all do more when their shares are worth more.

Sometimes you hear managers speak as if the corporation has other goals. For example, they may say that their job is to "maximize profits." That sounds reasonable. After all, don't shareholders want their company to be profitable? But taken literally, profit maximization is not a well-defined corporate objective. Here are three reasons:

1. "Maximizing profits" leaves open the question of "which year's profits?" The company may be able to increase current profits by cutting back on maintenance or staff training, but shareholders may not welcome this if profits are damaged in future years.
2. A company may be able to increase future profits by cutting this year's dividend and investing the freed-up cash in the firm. That is not in the shareholders' best interests if the company earns only a very low rate of return on the extra investment.
3. Different accountants may calculate profits in different ways. So a decision that improves profits using one set of accounting rules may reduce them using another.

---

[10] Often the firm's chief financial officer is also a member of its board of directors.

In a free economy a firm is unlikely to survive if it pursues goals that reduce the firm's value. Suppose, for example, that a firm's only goal is to increase its market share. It aggressively reduces prices to capture new customers, even when the price discounts cause continuing losses. What would happen to such a firm? As losses mount, it will find it more and more difficult to borrow money, and it may not even have sufficient profits to repay existing debts. Sooner or later, however, outside investors would see an opportunity for easy money. They could offer to buy the firm from its current shareholders and, once they have tossed out existing management, increase the firm's value by changing its policies. They would profit by the difference between the price paid for the firm and the higher value it would have under new management. Managers who pursue goals that destroy value often land in early retirement.

The natural financial objective of the corporation is to maximize current market value. Managers who consistently ignore this objective are likely to be replaced.

ETHICS AND MANAGEMENT OBJECTIVES

Crime Does Not Pay For a public company, maximizing current market value means maximizing today's stock price. (The firm's market value is the total amount that investors are willing to pay for all of its shares.) Does that objective justify pumping up stock price by fraud or deception? Of course not. But there will be occasional bad apples in the barrel, companies that attempt to increase market value in unethical ways.

The years since 2001 have revealed an unusual number of bad apples. For example, telecom giant WorldCom admitted that it failed to report US$3.8 billion of operating expenses. (The expenses were classified as investments, contrary to the rules of accounting.) Thus, WorldCom's income was overstated by US$3.8 billion. In the meantime, the company had run up US$41 billion of debt. When the company's true profitability was discovered, it went bankrupt within a month—the largest U.S. bankruptcy ever.

The second-largest bankruptcy was Enron, the energy trading and investment company. In late 2001 it announced over US$1.7 billion in losses that had previously been concealed in "special purpose entities" (SPEs). We need not delve into SPEs here, except to say that the company broke basic rules of accounting and that one of Enron's top financial executives allegedly used SPEs to pocket millions at the expense of Enron and its shareholders. The bad news came out all at once in October and November 2001, and Enron was bankrupt by year-end.

In 2003, Italian food giant Parmalat filed for bankruptcy protection after it was revealed that the company had manipulated its financial statements to conceal a deficit of 10 billion euros (about $16.4 billion). Canadian corporations were not immune from this problem either. Nortel Networks, once hailed as an icon of high technology, released revised financial statements in early 2005 that effectively reduced its 2003 profit from US$732 million to US$434 million. The former CEO, CFO, and controller, all of whom had received bonuses based on the faulty accounting of higher profits, were arrested by the RCMP in June 2008 and charged with fraudulently misstating the 2002 and 2003 financial results.

We suspect that WorldCom, Enron, and Parmalat's accounting misdeeds were in part a desperate attempt to stave off bankruptcy. In the end these misdeeds were the proximate cause of bankruptcy. Crime, fraud, and deceit do not pay. In April 2010, Goldman Sachs, Wall Street's venerable investment bank, was embroiled in charges of fraud from the U.S. Securities and Exchange Commission. The Finance in Action box here describes the nature of the charges. At the time of writing, in July 2010, Goldman agreed to pay US$550 million to settle the civil fraud charges.

The Ethics of Maximizing Value Let us shift the focus back to the great majority of financial managers, who are honest and conscientious. Some idealists say these managers should not be obliged to act in the selfish interests of their stockholders. Some realists argue that, regardless of what managers ought to do, they in fact look after themselves rather than their shareholders.

Finance in Action

The Charges Against Goldman Sachs

Goldman Sachs Group Inc was charged with fraud by the U.S. Securities and Exchange Commission over its marketing of a debt product tied to subprime mortgages that was designed to fail.

The lawsuit is the biggest crisis in years for Goldman, which emerged from the global financial crisis as Wall Street's most influential bank.

It is also a huge test for Chief Executive Lloyd Blankfein, who has faced a firestorm of criticism over the bank's pay and business practices. It comes as lawmakers in Washington debate sweeping reform of financial industry regulation.

The SEC alleged that Paulson & Co, a major hedge fund run by billionaire John Paulson, worked with Goldman in creating a collateralized debt obligation, and stood to benefit as its value fell, costing investors more than US$1-billion. That is roughly the amount that Paulson is estimated to have made by betting against the CDO.

Fabrice Tourre, a Goldman vice president who the SEC said was principally responsible for creating the product, was also charged with fraud. Paulson was not charged.

Goldman vowed to fight the SEC civil suit.

It is a regulatory and public relations nightmare for Mr. Blankfein, who has spent 18 months fending off complaints that Goldman is an unfair beneficiary of taxpayer bailouts of Wall Street. He became CEO less than a year before the product challenged by the SEC was created.

In afternoon trading, Goldman shares sank US$24.92, or 13.5%, to US$159.35 on the New York Stock Exchange, after earlier falling to US$155.57.

The news sent broader U.S. stock indexes down more than 1%, and major bank indexes down more than 3%.

In its lawsuit, the SEC alleged that Goldman structured and marketed a synthetic CDO, ABACUS, that hinged on the performance of subprime residential mortgage-backed securities. It alleged that Goldman did not tell investors "vital information" about ABACUS, including that Paulson & Co was involved in choosing which securities would be part of the portfolio. It also alleged that Paulson took a short position against the CDO in a bet that its value would fall. According to the SEC, the marketing materials for the CDO showed that a third party, ACA Management LLC, chose the securities underlying the CDO, without revealing Paulson's involvement.

Paulson & Co paid Goldman US$15-million to structure and market the ABACUS CDO, which closed on April 26, 2007, the SEC said. Little more than nine months later, 99 percent of the portfolio had been downgraded, the SEC said.

"In sum," the complaint said, "Goldman Sachs arranged a transaction at Paulson's request in which Paulson heavily influenced the selection of the portfolio to suit its economic interests, but failed to disclose to investors . . . Paulson's role in the portfolio selection process or its adverse economic interests."

Source: Adapted from J. Stempel and S. Eder, "Goldman Sachs Charged with Fraud," *National Post*, April 16, 2010, **www.nationalpost.com/m/story.html?id=2915173&s=Home**. © Thomson Reuters 2010.

Let us respond to the idealists first. Does maximizing value mean that managers must act as greedy mercenaries riding roughshod over the weak and helpless? No, in most instances there is little conflict between doing well (maximizing value) and doing good.

The first step in doing well is doing good by your customers. Here is how Adam Smith put the case in 1776:

> It is not from the benevolence of the butcher, the brewer, or the baker, that we expect our dinner, but from their regard to their own interest. We address ourselves, not to their humanity but to their self-love, and never talk to them of our own necessities but of their advantages.[11]

By striving to enrich themselves and their shareholders, businesspeople have to provide their customers with the products and services they truly desire.

Of course, ethical issues do arise in business as in other walks of life. When the stakes are high, competition is intense, and a deadline is looming, it's easy for financial managers to blunder, and not to inquire as deeply as they should about the legality or morality of their actions.

Written rules and laws can help only so much. In business, as in other day-to-day affairs, there are also unwritten rules of behaviour. These work because everyone knows that such rules are in the general interest. But they are reinforced because good managers know that their firm's reputation is one of its most important assets and therefore playing fair and keeping one's word are simply good business practices. Thus, huge financial deals are regularly completed on a handshake and each side knows that the other will not renege if things turn sour. For example, the motto of the London Stock Exchange is "My word is my bond."

Reputation is particularly important in finance. If you buy a well-known brand in a store, you can be fairly sure what you are getting. But in financial transactions the other party may have more

[11] Adam Smith, *An Inquiry into the Nature and Causes of the Wealth of Nations* (New York: Random House, 1937; first published 1776), 14.

information than you and it is less easy to be sure of the quality of what you are buying. The reaction of honest financial firms is to build long-term relationships with their customers and establish a name for fair dealing and financial integrity. Major banks and securities firms protect their reputations by emphasizing their long history and their responsible behaviour when seeking new customers. When something happens to undermine that reputation the costs can be enormous.

Of course, trust is sometimes misplaced. Charlatans and swindlers are often able to hide behind booming markets, for it is only "when the tide goes out that you learn who's been swimming naked." The tide went out in 2008 and a number of frauds were exposed. One notorious example was the Ponzi scheme run by the disgraced financier Bernard Madoff.[12] Individuals and institutions invested around $20 billion with Madoff and were told that their investments had grown to $65 billion. That figure turned out to be completely fictitious. (It's not clear what Madoff did with all this money, but much of it was apparently paid out to early investors in the scheme to create an impression of superior investment performance.) With hindsight, the investors should not have trusted Madoff or the financial advisors who steered money to him.

Madoff's Ponzi scheme was (we hope) a once-in-a-lifetime event. (Ponzi schemes pop up frequently, but none has approached the scope and duration of Madoff's.) It was astonishingly unethical, illegal, and bound to end in tears. More complex ethical issues were raised by the banking crisis of 2007–2009. Earlier we discussed the problems of Goldman Sachs. Some observers believed that Goldman's actions reflected all that is worst on Wall Street. Others see them as simply an example of an investment bank performing one of its main functions as an intermediary between willing buyers and sellers.

The Finance in Action box here reports on a difficult decision made by the management of the National Bank of Canada to protect the bank's reputation as a trustworthy investment company. Management chose to repay investors the full amount invested in their money market funds, even though the investments had lost value. This cost National Bank shareholders in the short run; but in management's opinion, had the money market funds not been fully repaid, shareholders would have lost more in the long run, because the firm would lose business from customers who now distrusted the company.

It is not always easy to know what is ethical behaviour, and there can be many grey areas. For example, should the firm be prepared to do business with a corrupt or repressive government? Should it employ child labour in countries where that is the norm? The next Finance in Action box presents several simple situations that call for an ethically based decision, along with survey responses on the proper course of action in each circumstance. Compare your decisions with those of the general public.

Check Point 1.5

Without knowing anything about the personal ethics of the owners, which of the two following companies would you trust more to keep its word in a business deal?

a. Harry's Hardware has been in business for 50 years. Harry's grandchildren, now almost adults, plan to take over and operate the business. Hardware stores require considerable investment in customer relations to become established.

b. Victor's Videos just opened for business. It rents a storefront in a strip mall and has financed its inventory with a bank loan. Victor has little of his own money invested in the business. Video shops usually command little customer loyalty.

DO MANAGERS REALLY MAXIMIZE FIRM VALUE?

Owner-managers of private corporations, sole proprietorships, and partnerships have no conflicts of interest in their management of the business. They work for themselves, reaping the rewards of good work and suffering the penalties of bad work. Their personal well-being is tied to the value of the firm.

[12] The quotation is from Warren Buffett's annual letter to the shareholders of Berkshire Hathaway, March 2008.

Finance in Action

The Cost of Protecting a Bank's Reputation

Investors looking for a safe place to hold surplus cash often invest in *money market funds*—mutual funds that invest in short-term government securities, known as *Treasury bills*, and in *commercial paper*, which is short-term securities sold by high-quality corporations and banks. Some money market funds also invest in *asset-backed commercial paper* (ABCP), short-term debt issued by finance companies. Finance companies purchase cash-flow-generating debts of other companies, such as credit card receivables, mortgages, and car loans. They then package the debts into pools, creating asset-backed commercial paper. The ABCP receive cash flows from the payment of credit card bills, mortgages and car loans.

Money market funds are structured so the units sell for a fixed price; this is traditionally set at $1, but many today are priced at $10. The price is never to fall below that level, and if there is a surplus of cash, investors receive more units to lower the unit price. The key to running a money market mutual fund is to never "break the buck," meaning never to let the unit price fall below $1 (or $10). That means never lose money.

In August 2007, the asset-backed commercial paper market went into crisis, as a result of severe financial trouble in the U.S. subprime mortgage market. With U.S. mortgage holders defaulting on their mortgage payments, cash was not being paid to holders of the asset-backed commercial paper. Although much of the Canadian ABCP had no direct connection to the troubled U.S. mortgages, investors became suspicious of all asset-backed securities, refusing to invest in new asset-backed commercial paper. The finance companies were unable to repay such securities that were maturing. In response to the crisis, Canadian financial institutions agreed to freeze all $33 billion of troubled Canadian asset-backed commercial paper, to prevent funds from going bankrupt.

Some money market funds were heavily invested in ACBP and on the verge of losing money, breaking the confidence of investors who had trusted money market funds as a safe investment. The National Bank of Canada, with about $2 billion of troubled financial paper in its money market funds, was the first Canadian bank to buy up the troubled ABCP.

It was not an easy decision to make. In a *Globe and Mail* article it was reported that the National Bank's chief executive officer, Louis Vachon, knew that buying up the ABCP would be expensive, severely cutting the bank's earnings, making shareholders angry.[1] On the other hand, if they did nothing, the money market investors would be furious because of their units would be worth less than $10. Such a loss would severely damage the reputation of the National Bank as a safe place to put money. It would also affect confidence in all investment products sold by the Bank. Mr. Vachon reported that he and the board of directors decided that maintaining the Bank's reputation was their top concern.

By the end of November, 2008 the cost of the buyback was revealed: a $365 million reduction the firm's earnings. The stock price was down almost 20 percent on the year. However, CEO Vachon was quoted as being satisfied that they did the right thing to protect their reputation.

[1] Boyd Erman, "Take the Hit, Avoid the Crisis," *The Globe and Mail*, December 1, 2007, B3.

In most large public companies the managers are not the owners and they might be tempted to act in ways that are not in the best interests of the owners. For example, they might buy luxurious corporate jets for their travel, or overindulge in expense-account dinners. They might shy away from attractive but risky projects because they are worried more about the safety of their jobs than the potential for superior profits. They might engage in empire building, adding unnecessary capacity or employees. Such problems can arise because the managers of the firm, who are hired as agents of the owners, may have their own axes to grind. Therefore these conflicts are called **agency problems**.

agency problems Conflict of interest between the firm's owners and managers.

These agency problems can sometimes lead to outrageous behaviour. For example, when Dennis Kozlowski, the CEO of Tyco, threw a $2 million 40th birthday bash for his wife, he charged half of the cost to the company. This of course was an extreme case of an agency conflict, as well as being illegal. In normal business dealings, agency problems commonly arise whenever managers think just a little less hard about spending money that is not their own.

Think of the company's net revenue as a pie that is divided among a number of claimants. These include the management and the work force as well as the lenders and shareholders who put up the money to establish and maintain the business. The government is a claimant, too, since it gets to tax the profits of the enterprise. It is common to hear these claimants called **stakeholders** in the firm. Each has a stake in the firm and their interests may not coincide.

stakeholder Anyone with a financial interest in the firm.

All these stakeholders are bound together in a complex web of contracts and understandings. For example, when banks lend money to the firm, they insist on a formal contract stating the rate of interest and repayment dates, perhaps putting restrictions on dividends or additional borrowing.

Similarly, large companies have carefully worked out personnel policies that establish employees' rights and responsibilities. But you can't devise written rules to cover every possible future event. So the written contracts are supplemented by understandings. For example, managers understand that in return for a fat salary they are expected to work hard and not spend the firm's money on unwarranted personal luxuries.

What enforces these understandings? Is it realistic to expect managers always to act on behalf of the shareholders? The shareholders can't spend their lives watching through binoculars to check that managers are not shirking or dissipating company funds on the latest executive jet. Companies do act on allegations of impropriety by senior managers. Recently, Chicago-based Hollinger International filed a $1.25 billion lawsuit against Conrad Black, its former chairman and CEO, and David Radler, former chief operating officer. The lawsuit alleged that Lord Black and others used Hollinger "as a cash cow to be milked of every possible drop of cash" and improperly took millions of dollars in management fees, non-competition payments, and bonuses. According to the lawsuit, the company paid $90,000 to refurbish a Rolls-Royce limousine and $4.7 million to $6.5 million a year for two corporate jets, which were often used for personal purposes by the senior executives.[13] In 2007, Black was found guilty on three counts of fraud and one count of obstruction of justice, sentenced to 6½ years in prison, fined $125,000, and ordered to repay US$6.1 million. Presently, Black is serving a reduced sentence after a successful Supreme Court appeal.

A closer look reveals several arrangements that help to ensure that the shareholders and managers are working toward common goals.

Compensation Plans Managers are spurred on by incentive schemes that provide big returns if shareholders gain but are valueless if they do not. For example, Larry Ellison, CEO of the business software giant Oracle Corporation, received total compensation for 2007 estimated at between $60 and $70 million. Only a small fraction ($1 million) of that amount was salary, however. A larger amount, a bit more than $6 million, was bonus and incentive pay, and the lion's share was in the form of stock and option grants. Those options will be worthless if Oracle's share price falls from its 2007 level but will be highly valuable if the price rises. Moreover, as founder of Oracle, Ellison holds over 1 billion shares in the firm. No one can say for certain how hard Ellison would have worked with a different compensation package. But one thing is clear: he has a huge personal stake in the success of the firm—and in increasing its market value.

Of course, if employee compensation plans are not designed properly, they can create incentives for errant behaviour by management. In 2004, Nortel Networks admitted that accounting mistakes would halve its reported profits for 2003 and would lead to a second restatement of the company's earnings since 2001. It was later revealed that the company's controversial "return to profitability" bonus plan, which allowed many employees to receive large payouts based on results of one fiscal quarter, may have given senior management an incentive to manipulate profits. Millions of dollars were paid out to executives under this bonus program, including over $2 million to its CEO. In April 2004, Nortel's board of directors sought to take corrective action by firing its CEO, CFO, and controller. In 2010, Tony Hayward, CEO of British Petroleum, was replaced following strong criticism of his handling of the oil spill in the Gulf of Mexico, now infamously known as the largest in U.S. history. He was, however, compensated handsomely with a pension of over a million dollars per year.

As discussed in the Finance in Action Box here, some criticize executive stock options for being too favourable for managers and for distorting management's incentives. Stock options have also drawn the attention of securities regulators because of the practice of backdating. *Backdating* occurs when the date on the options is not the actual date of the option grant but rather a date in the past when the stock price was lower. In March 2007 the co-chair of Research In Motion's board of directors, Jim Balsillie, resigned because of a backdating scandal. The Ontario Securities Commission and the U.S. Securities and Exchange Commission investigated

[13] See, for instance, Richard Blackwell, "Hollinger Paid Expenses: Lawsuit," *The Globe and Mail*, May 11, 2004.

Finance in Action

Things Are Not Always Fair in Love or Economics

What constitutes fair behaviour by companies? One survey asked a number of individuals to state whether they regarded a particular action as acceptable or unfair. Before we tell you how they responded, think how you would rate each of the following actions:

1a. A small photocopying shop has one employee who has worked in the shop for 6 months and earns $9 per hour. Business continues to be satisfactory, but a factory in the area has closed and unemployment has increased. Other small shops in the area have now hired reliable workers at $7 an hour to perform jobs similar to those done by the photocopying shop employee. The owner of the photocopying shop reduces the employee's wage to $7.

1b. Now suppose that the shop does not reduce the employee's wage but she leaves. The owner decides to pay a replacement $7 an hour.

2. A house painter employs two assistants and pays them $9 per hour. The painter decides to quit house painting and go into the business of providing landscape services, where the going wage is lower. He reduces the workers' wages to $7 per hour for the landscaping work.

3a. A small company employs several workers and has been paying them average wages. There is severe unemployment in the area and the company could easily replace its current employees with good workers at a lower wage. The company has been making money. The owners reduce the current workers' wages by 5 percent.

3b. Now suppose instead that the company has been losing money and the owners reduce wages by 5 percent.

4. A grocery store has several months' supply of peanut butter in stock on shelves in the storeroom. The owner hears that the wholesale price of peanut butter has increased and immediately raises the price on the current stock of peanut butter.

5. A hardware store has been selling snow shovels for $15. The morning after a large snowstorm, the store raises the price to $20.

6. A store has been sold out of popular Beanie Baby dolls for a month. A week before Christmas a single doll is discovered in a storeroom. The managers know that many customers would like to buy the doll. They announce over the store's public address system that the doll will be sold by auction to the customer who offers to pay the most.

Now compare your responses with the responses of a random sample of individuals:

	Percent Rating the Action As:	
Action	**Acceptable**	**Unfair**
1a	17	83
1b	73	27
2	63	37
3a	23	77
3b	68	32
4	21	79
5	18	82
6	26	74

Source: Adapted from D. Kahneman, J. L. Knetsch, and R. Thaler, "Fairness as a Constraint on Profit Seeking: Entitlements in the Market," *American Economic Review* 76 (September 1986): 728–741. Reprinted by permission of American Economic Association and the authors.

the allegations of backdating of RIM's stock options. Four senior executives of the company, including co-CEOs Jim Balsillie and Mike Lazaridis, were charged with illegally granting stock options to executives and employees over an eight-year period from 1998 to 2006. The executives agreed to pay fines of up to US$500,000 and to give back the value of backdated options of over US$800,000.

As we shall see next, corporate boards often do act to replace managers who are perceived not to have acted in the best interest of shareholders.

The Board of Directors Boards of directors have often been portrayed as passive supporters of top management. But response to the corporate scandals of 2001–2002 has tipped the balance toward greater independence. The *Sarbanes-Oxley Act* requires that corporations place more independent directors on the board, that is, more directors who are not managers or not affiliated with management. More than half of all directors are now independent. Boards also now meet in sessions without the CEO present. In addition, institutional shareholders, particularly pension funds and hedge funds, have become more active in monitoring firm performance and proposing changes to corporate governance.

Not surprisingly, more chief executives have been forced out in recent years, among them the CEOs of Hollinger International, Nortel Networks, Citigroup, Merrill Lynch, Boeing, Sun

Microsystems, and Pfizer. Boards in Europe, which traditionally have been more management-friendly, have also become more willing to replace underperforming managers. The list of European departures includes senior management from Deutsche Telekom, Airbus, UBS, and Volkswagen.

If shareholders believe that the corporation is underperforming and that the board of directors is not sufficiently aggressive in holding managers to task, they can try to replace the board in the next election. The dissident shareholders will attempt to convince other shareholders to vote for their slate of candidates to the board. If they succeed, a new board will be elected, and it can replace the current management team.

Conrad Black had to leave his position as CEO of Hollinger International following revelations of the payment of millions of dollars in so-called "non-compete" fees to related companies and executives allegedly made without the approval of the board of directors. A shareholder had requested the company's board take action on such fees.

Takeovers Poorly performing companies are also more likely to be taken over by another firm. After the takeover, the old management team may find itself out on the street. In recent years, the CEOs of Canadian Airlines and Chapters were replaced following such takeovers. Recently, when the share price of beleaguered Nortel Networks plummeted after the company had admitted to accounting mistakes and fired its CEO, investment bankers reportedly tried to put together a hostile takeover bid for the company. We discuss takeovers in Chapter 23.

Specialist Monitoring Finally, managers are subject to the scrutiny of specialists. Their actions are monitored by the security analysts who advise investors to buy, hold, or sell the company's shares. Managers are also reviewed by banks, which keep an eagle eye on the progress of firms receiving their loans.

Legal and Regulatory Requirements CEOs and financial managers have a legal duty to act responsibly and in the interests of investors. For example, the Ontario Securities Commission sets accounting and reporting standards for public companies that trade on the Toronto Stock Exchange in order to ensure consistency and transparency. The Ontario securities Commission also prohibits insider trading, that is, the purchase or sale of shares based on information not available to public investors. In 2002, in response to Enron, WorldCom, and other debacles of the late 1900s and early 2000s, Congress in the United States passed the *Sarbanes-Oxley Act*, known widely as SOX. In addition to its restrictions on board activities, SOX requires each CFO to sign off personally on the corporation's accounting procedures and results. Ontario recently introduced legislation to improve corporate governance and disclosure practices under an enactment which is popularly known as Bill C-198 or "Canada's *Sarbanes-Oxley*."[14]

We do not want to leave the impression that corporate life is a series of squabbles and endless micromanagement. It isn't, because practical corporate finance has evolved to reconcile personal and corporate interests—to keep everyone working together to increase the value of the whole pie, not merely the size of each person's slice.

The agency problem is mitigated in practice through several devices: compensation plans that tie the fortune of the manager to the fortunes of the firm; monitoring by lenders, stock market analysts, and investors; and ultimately, the threat that poor performance will result in the removal of the manager.

Check Point 1.6

Corporations are now required to publish the amount and form of compensation (for example, stock options versus salary versus performance bonuses) received by their top executives. Of what use would that information be to a potential investor in the firm?

[14] Actually the omnibus bill introduced by the Ontario government was titled *Keeping the Promise for a Strong Economy Act (Budget Measures), 2002.*

Finance in Action

Why Stock Options Should Be Banned

Options are inherently flawed because they distort the risks and rewards of owning stock. The deal works like this: Each year, a company issues an executive the right to buy stock at a future date for a set price. So, let's say you get an option to buy your company's stock for $10. You wait for a year or so until the option "vests," by then hopefully the stock has gone up to, say, $20. You exercise your option to buy at $10, turn around and sell the stock into the market at $20, pocket the difference and go yacht shopping. This simple transaction has unleashed tens of billions of dollars into CEO bank accounts in recent years.

Executives insist that options are a great incentive, ensuring corporate managers stay focused on the stock price, and thus the shareholders. Sounds great, except executives holding stock options have none of their own capital at risk. If the stock goes down, and your options are considered "underwater," you may miss out on a windfall, but since you paid nothing for them in the first place, you've lost nothing. Heads the insiders win, tails the shareholders lose.

For many executives, even those odds aren't good enough. When hundreds of tech companies saw their stock prices collapse in 2001, rendering their options worthless, many appeased their executives by "re-pricing" options—changing exercise prices and vesting periods to yield another hefty payday for insiders while ordinary investors licked their wounds. Others simply signed deals with banks, trading options for cash. This little trick was called monetizing, and although perfectly legal, it meant insiders had already hedged against the crash of their company's stock, and investors were none the wiser.

There's no shortage of staunch capitalists opposed to this kind of gerrymandering. Paul Volcker, the renowned former chairman of the US Federal Reserve, abhors options because they emphasize short-term stock movements at the expense of the long-term health of the company. Corporate sage Warren Buffett objects on the grounds that options provide a benefit to executives that isn't available to ordinary investors. Both are valid criticisms, but they miss the more fundamental problem exposed over the past few years: Options are ripe for fraud.

US regulators are currently investigating the widespread practice of "backdating"—retroactively manipulating the date of options grants to maximize the payout for executives at the expense of shareholders. Among the hundreds of companies under investigation is Canada's own tech titan Research In Motion. Already, dozens of executives have taken the fall for this, and the staggering costs are just now coming into focus. In October, Andrew McKelvey, chief executive of Monster Worldwide, stepped down over allegations surrounding tens of millions of dollars in options grants he collected. Last week, Monster said it had understated its options costs by US$339.6 million over six years.

Home Depot has said it too under-reported the cost of its options program—by about US$200 million over 25 years. But, they were quick to add, it was all an innocent mistake. One suspects that if Home Depot made some other $200-million mistake, like say, buying too many garden hoses, to the tune of $7 million a year for a quarter-century, heads would roll and quickly. But when it comes to options, everybody is expected to shrug and say, "Well, at least they didn't do it on purpose."

Enough. If you want to keep executives focused on the interests of shareholders, pay part of their annual salary and bonus in stock and require them to hold that stock until after they quit or retire. It's not elegant, but it's clear and it's fair. And executives, like children, sometimes need a firm hand to guide them.

Source: "Why Stock Options Should be Banned," by Steve Maich, Maclean's Magazine, January 1, 2007. Reprinted by permission of Maclean's Magazine.

We have covered several types of constraints and incentives designed to mitigate agency costs and ensure cooperative and ethical behaviour. All these mechanisms help ensure effective corporate governance. When scandals happen, we say that corporate governance has broken down. When corporations compete effectively and ethically and deliver value to shareholders, we are comforted that corporate governance is working properly.[15]

Check Point 1.7

What is an agency problem? Give two or three examples of decisions by managers that lead to agency costs.

[15] We will also be discussing issues pertaining to corporate governance in Chapters 2 and 13.

LO1 1.6 CAREERS IN FINANCE

In Canada, well over half a million people work in financial services, and many others work as financial managers in corporations. We can't tell you what each person does all day, but we can give you some idea of the variety of careers in finance. The Finance in Action box here summarizes the experience of a small sample of recent (fictitious) graduates.

We explained earlier that corporations face two principal financial decisions: the investment decision and the financing decision. Therefore, as a newly recruited financial analyst, you may help to analyze a major new investment project. Or you may instead help raise the money to pay for it, perhaps by negotiating a bank loan or by arranging to lease the plant and equipment. Other financial analysts work on short-term financial issues, such as collecting and investing the company's cash or checking whether customers are likely to pay their bills. Financial analysts are also involved in monitoring and controlling risk. For example, they might help arrange insurance for the firm's plant and equipment, or assist with the purchase and sale of options, futures, and other tools for managing risk.

Instead of working in the finance department of a corporation, you may join a financial institution. The largest employers are the banks. Banks collect deposits and re-lend the cash to corporations and individuals. If you join a bank, you may work in a branch, where individuals and small businesses come to deposit cash or to seek a loan. Alternatively, you may be employed by one of the corporate banking groups, located in a major financial centre, and help to analyze a \$500 million loan to a large corporation.

Banks do many things in addition to lending money, and they probably provide a greater variety of jobs than other financial institutions. For example, individuals and businesses use banks to make payments to each other. So if you work in the cash management department of a large bank, you may help companies electronically transfer huge sums of money in wages, taxes, and payments to suppliers. Banks also buy and sell foreign exchange, so you could find yourself working in front of one of those computer screens in a foreign exchange dealing room. Another bank job is in the derivatives group, which helps companies manage their risk by buying and selling options, futures, and so on. This is where the mathematicians and the computer buffs thrive.

Investment dealers are financial firms involved in helping firms issue securities (underwriting) and in the trading of securities (brokerage). Some large investment dealers, such as Scotia Capital and Genuity Capital Markets, engage in investment banking,[16] which includes helping companies sell their securities to investors and assisting firms in major reorganizations such as takeovers. When firms issue securities or try to take over another firm, a lot of money is at stake and the firms may need to move quickly. Thus, working in investment banking can be a high-pressure activity with long hours. It can also pay very well.

Investment dealers can also be involved in the trading of securities, such as stocks and bonds. They employ sales staff and dealers who make the trades. They also employ financial analysts to analyze the securities and help customers decide which ones to buy or sell. Thus, investment dealers are part of the business of "managing money," that is, deciding which companies' shares to invest in, or how to balance investment in shares with safer securities, such as the bonds (debt securities) issued by the Government of Canada. Investment dealers can provide investment advice to retail, corporate, and institutional clients. Caldwell Securities, for example, gives wealth management advice to retail clients, whereas Scotia Capital focuses on corporate and institutional clients.

The distinction between banks and investment dealers is blurry. All large Canadian banks own investment dealers. For example, RBC Dominion Securities (an investment dealer, focused on wealth management for individuals and businesses), RBC Capital Markets (an investment dealer

---

[16] In the United States, firms engaged in investment banking activities, such as Merrill Lynch and Goldman Sachs, are known as *investment banks*.

Finance in Action

Working in Finance

Susan Webb, Research Analyst, Mutual Fund Group

After majoring in biochemistry, I joined the research department of a large mutual fund group. Because of my background, I was assigned to work with the senior pharmaceuticals analyst. I start the day by reading the business sections of *The Globe and Mail* and *National Post* and reviewing the analyses that come in each day from stockbroking firms. Sometimes we need to revise our earnings forecasts and meet with the portfolio managers to discuss possible trades. The remainder of my day is spent mainly in analyzing companies and developing forecasts of revenues and earnings. I meet frequently with pharmaceutical analysts in stockbroking firms, and we regularly visit company management. In the evenings I study for the Chartered Financial Analyst (CFA) exam. Since I did not study finance at university, this is quite challenging. I hope eventually to move from a research role to become a portfolio manager.

Richard Gradley, Project Finance, Large Energy Company

After leaving university, I joined the finance department of a large engineering and construction company. I spent my first year helping to analyze capital investment proposals. I then moved to the project finance group, which is responsible for analyzing engineering infrastructure and construction projects around the world. Recently, I have been involved in a proposal to set up a company that would build and operate a large electricity plant in southeast Asia. We built a spreadsheet model of the project to ensure that it was viable. We had to check that the contracts with the builders, operators, suppliers, and so on were all in place before we could arrange bank financing for the project.

Albert Rodriguez, Emerging Markets Group, Major Toronto Bank

I joined the bank after majoring in finance. I spent the first six months in the bank's training program, rotating between departments. I was assigned to the Latin America team just before the 1998 Brazilian crisis when interest rates jumped to nearly 50 percent and the currency fell by 40 percent. There was a lot of activity, with everyone trying to figure out what was likely to happen next and how it would affect our business. My job is largely concerned with analyzing economies and assessing the prospects for bank business. There are plenty of opportunities to work abroad, and I hope to spend some time in one of our Latin American offices, such as Argentina or Brazil.

Emma Kuletsky, Branch Manager, Chartered Bank

My job is to help look after customers in a large branch. They seem to expect me to know about everything. I help them with financial planning and with their applications for loans. In a typical day, I may have to interview a new customer who wants to open an account with the bank and calm an old one who thinks she has been overcharged for a wire transfer. I like dealing with people, and one day I hope to be manager of a branch like this one.

focused on investment banking), and the Royal Bank of Canada (a chartered bank) are all owned by Royal Bank Financial Group. There are also independent investment dealers, both in the wealth management and the investment banking areas. All are members of the Investment Dealers Association, **www.ida.ca**.

The insurance industry is another large employer. Much of the insurance industry is involved in designing and selling insurance policies on people's lives and property, but businesses are also major customers. So if you work for an insurance company or a large insurance broker, you could find yourself arranging insurance on a Learjet 60 in Canada or a pipeline in Chile.

Life insurance companies are major lenders to corporations and to investors in commercial real estate. (Life insurance companies invest the insurance premiums received from policyholders into medium- and long-term loans; banks specialize in shorter-term loans). So you could end up negotiating a $50-million loan for the construction of a new shopping centre or investigating the creditworthiness of a family-owned manufacturing firm that has applied for a loan to expand production.

There are other financing firms to work for. Take mutual funds for example. A mutual fund collects money from individuals and invests in a portfolio of stocks or bonds. A financial analyst for a mutual fund analyzes the prospects for the securities and works with the investment manager to decide which ones should be bought and sold. Many other financial institutions also contain investment management departments. For example, you might work as a financial analyst in the investment department of an insurance company. (Insurance companies also invest in

TABLE 1.2
Representative salaries for jobs in finance.

Career	Annual Salary
Commercial Banking	
Junior loan officer	$60,000
Department manager	$100,000
Corporate Finance	
Financial analyst	$40–50,000
Tax manager	$90–130,000
Chief financial officer	$260–390,000
Investment Banking (bulge bracket)	
First-year analyst	$60–150,000
First-year associate	$150–250,000
Vice-president	$350K–1 million
Director/principal	$400K–1.5 million
Managing director/partner	$500K–20 million
Department head	$800K–70 million
Money Management	
Portfolio manager	$500,000
Bank trust department	$90–180,000

Note: "Bulge bracket" refers to a few of the largest investment banks.

Source: Careers-in-Business, LLC, **www.careers-in-business.com**. © 1997–2009. All rights reserved.

traded securities). Or you could be a financial analyst in the trust department of a bank that manages money for retirement funds, universities, and charitable bodies.

Many of the chartered banks, investment dealers, insurance companies, and stockbroking firms are headquartered in and around Toronto but have operations across Canada. Of course, large financial institutions have their headquarters in other cities as well. For instance, National Bank of Canada, Caisse de dépôt et placement du Québec, and Desjardins-Laurentian Financial Corporation are headquartered in Montréal, while Great-West Life Assurance and Investors Group are headquartered in Winnipeg. Many financial institutions have significant business interests outside Canada. Finance is a global business, so you may spend some time working in an overseas branch or travel occasionally to one of the major international financial centres, such as New York, London, Frankfurt, Hong Kong, or Singapore.

Finance professionals tend to be well paid. Starting salaries for new graduates are in the region of $50,000, rather more in a major Toronto investment dealer and somewhat less in a bank. But let us look ahead a little: Table 1.2 gives you an idea of the compensation that you can look forward to when you become a financial manager.

1.7 TOPICS COVERED IN THIS BOOK

This book covers investment decisions first, then financing decisions, and then a variety of planning issues that require understanding of both investments and financing. But first there are two further introductory chapters that should be helpful to readers making a first acquaintance with financial management. Chapter 2 is an overview of financial markets and institutions. Chapter 3 reviews the basic concepts of accounting, and Chapter 4 demonstrates the techniques of financial statement analysis.

In Parts Two and Three we look at different aspects of the investment decision. The first is the problem of how to value assets, and the second is the link between risk and value. Our discussion of these topics occupies Chapters 5 through 13.

Nine chapters devoted to the simple problem of finding real assets that are worth more than they cost may seem excessive, but that problem is not so simple in practice. We will require a theory of how long-lived, risky assets are valued, and that requirement will lead us to basic questions about capital markets. For example:

- How are corporate bonds and stocks valued in capital markets?
- What risks are borne by investors in corporate securities? How can these risks be measured?
- What compensation do investors demand for bearing risk?
- What rate of return can investors in common stocks reasonably expect to receive?
- Do stock prices accurately reflect the underlying value of the firm?

Intelligent capital budgeting and financing decisions require answers to these and other questions about how capital markets work.

Financing decisions occupy Parts Four and Five. The two chapters in Part Four describe the kinds of securities corporations use to raise money and explain how and when they are issued. These chapters also describe the sources of financing of new and small business ventures.

Part Five continues the analysis of the financing decision, covering dividend policy, the decision to lease, and debt policy. We will also describe what happens when firms find themselves in financial distress because of poor operating performance, excessive borrowing, or both.

Part Six covers financial planning. Decisions about investment, dividend policy, debt policy, and other financial issues cannot be reached independently. They have to add up to a sensible overall financial plan for the firm, one that increases the value of the shareholders' investment yet retains enough flexibility for the firm to avoid financial distress and pursue unexpected new opportunities.

Part Seven is devoted to decisions about the firm's short-term assets and liabilities. We discuss channels for short-term borrowing or investment, management of liquid assets (cash and marketable securities), and management of accounts receivable (money lent by the firm to its customers) and inventories.

Part Eight covers four important problems that require decisions about both investment and financing. First, we look at mergers and acquisitions. Then we consider international financial management; because, although all the financial problems of doing business at home are present overseas, the international financial manager faces the additional complications created by multiple currencies, different tax systems, and special regulations imposed by foreign institutions and governments. Finally, we look at risk management and the specialized securities, including futures and options, that managers can use to hedge or lay off risks.

SNIPPETS OF HISTORY

Now let's lighten up a little. In this book we will describe how financial decisions are made today. But financial markets also have an interesting history. Look at the Finance in Action box here, which lays out bits of this history, starting in prehistoric times, when the growth of bacteria anticipated the mathematics of compound interest, and continuing nearly to the present. We have keyed each of these episodes to the chapter of the book that discusses it.

Finance in Action

Finance Through the Ages

Date unknown ***Compound Growth.*** Bacteria start to propagate by subdividing. They thereby demonstrate the power of compound growth. *(Chapter 5)*

c. 1800 B.C. ***Interest Rates.*** In Babylonia, Hammurabi's Code established maximum interest rates on loans. Borrowers often mortgaged their property and sometimes their spouses, but in these cases the lender was obliged to return the spouse in good condition within three years. *(Chapter 4)*

c. 1000 B.C. ***Options.*** One of the earliest recorded options is described by Aristotle. The philosopher Thales knew by the stars that there would be a great olive harvest, so having a little money, he bought options for the use of olive presses. When the harvest came Thales was able to rent the presses at great profit. Today financial managers need to be able to evaluate options to buy or sell a wide variety of assets. *(Chapter 25)*

15th century ***International Banking.*** Modern international banking has its origins in the great Florentine banking houses. But the entire European network of the Medici empire employed only 57 people in eight offices. Today the RBC Financial Group has over 75,000 employees and an international network of 1,197 branches in over 50 countries. *(Chapter 24)*

1650 ***Futures.*** Futures markets allow companies to protect themselves against fluctuations in commodity prices. During the Tokugawa era in Japan, feudal lords collected rents in the form of rice but often they wished to trade their future rice deliveries. In Canada, the Winnipeg Commodity Exchange started operating in 1887 and established futures markets in wheat, oats, and flax seed in 1904. *(Chapter 26)*

17th century ***Joint Stock Corporations.*** Although for a long time investors have combined forces to be joint owners of an enterprise, the modern corporation with a large number of shareholders originates with the formation in England of the great trading firms such as the East India Company (est. 1599). Another early trading firm, Hudson's Bay (est. 1670), still survives and is one of Canada's largest companies. *(Chapter 15)*

17th century ***Money.*** Through the 17th century until well into the 19th, coins from many countries such as England, France, Portugal, and Spain circulated freely in the French and British colonies in North America. Colonies rated coins differently, sometimes deliberately overrating (overvaluing) or underrating (undervaluing) them relative to others, based on their weight in gold or silver, in order to encourage or discourage their use. In such circumstances, overrated coins drove underrated coins from circulation—an application of Gresham's Law, "Bad money drives out good." A chronic coin shortage encouraged the introduction of paper money. For instance, in 1685, card money was introduced in New France, which initially consisted of playing cards cut to different sizes according to denomination and signed by colonial officials. The first bank notes in Canada denominated in dollars were issued by the Montreal Bank in 1817. A distinctive Canadian currency came into being when the Province of Canada revised the *Currency Act* in 1857, requiring all provincial accounts to be kept in dollars. Silver and bronze coins bearing "Canada" were issued for the first time. Private bank notes were gradually phased out when the Bank of Canada started operations in 1935 and was given the sole right to issue bank notes.[17] *(Chapter 21)*

1720 ***New Issue Speculation.*** From time to time investors have been tempted by speculative new issues. During the South Sea Bubble in England, one company was launched to develop perpetual motion. Another enterprising individual announced a company "for carrying on an undertaking of great advantage but nobody to know what it is." Within five hours he had raised £2000; within six hours he was on his way out of the country. *(Chapter 15)*

1792 ***Formation of Stock Exchanges.*** In North America the New York Stock Exchange (NYSE) was founded in 1792 when a group of brokers met under a buttonwood tree and arranged to trade shares with one another at agreed rates of commission. Today the NYSE is the largest stock exchange in the world, trading on average about a billion shares a day. The Toronto Stock Exchange was established in 1852. Today the Toronto Stock Exchange (TSX) belongs to the TSX Group and is Canada's largest stock exchange. In January 2010, the TSE traded an average of 438.0 million shares valued at about $5.09 billion each day. *(Chapter 7)*

1929 ***Stock Market Crashes.*** Common stocks are risky investments. In September 1929, stock prices in the United States reached an all-time high, and the economist Irving Fisher forecast that they were at "a permanently high plateau." Some three years later stock prices were almost 90 percent lower, and it was to be a quarter of a century before the prices of September 1929 were seen again. Contrary to popular impression, no Wall Street broker jumped out the window. *(Chapter 11)*

1960s ***Eurodollar Market.*** In the 1950s, the Soviet Union transferred its dollar holdings from the United States to a Russian-owned bank in Paris. This bank was best known by its telex address, EUROBANK, and consequently dollars held outside the United States came to be known as eurodollars. In the 1960s, U.S. taxes and regulation made it much cheaper to borrow and lend dollars in Europe rather than in the United States and a huge market in eurodollars arose. *(Chapter 14)*

1972 ***Financial Futures.*** Financial futures allow companies to protect themselves against fluctuations in interest rates, exchange rates, and so on. It is said that they originated from a remark by the economist Milton Friedman that he was unable to profit from his view that sterling was overpriced. The Chicago Mercantile founded the first financial futures market. Today futures exchanges in the United States trade 200 million contracts a year of financial futures. In Canada, a market for futures contracts on treasury coupons and long-term government bonds was created in 1979. Canadian financial futures are traded on the Montreal Exchange. *(Chapter 26)*

1986 ***Capital Investment Decisions.*** The largest investment project undertaken by private companies was the construction of the

[17] Information for this excerpt was compiled from J. Powell, "A History of the Canadian Dollar," at the Bank of Canada site, **www.bankofcanada.ca/en/dollar_book/index.html**.

tunnel under the English Channel. It started in 1986 and was completed in 1994 at a total cost of US$15 billion. *(Chapters 8, 9)*

1988 ***Mergers.*** The 1980s saw a wave of takeovers culminating in the US$25 billion takeover of RJR Nabisco. Over a period of six weeks, three groups battled for control of the company. As one of the contestants put it, "We were charging through the rice paddies, not stopping for anything and taking no prisoners." The takeover was the largest in history and generated almost $1 billion in fees for the banks and advisors. *(Chapter 23)*

1993 ***Inflation.*** Financial managers need to recognize the effect of inflation on interest rates and on the profitability of a firm's investments. In the United States inflation has been relatively modest, but some countries have suffered from hyperinflation. In Hungary after World War II the government issued banknotes worth 1,000 trillion pengoes. In Yugoslavia in October 1993 prices rose by nearly 2,000 percent and a dollar bought 105 million dinars. *(Chapter 5)*

1780 and 1991 ***Inflation-Indexed Debt.*** In 1780, Massachusetts paid Revolutionary War soldiers with interest-bearing notes rather than its rapidly eroding currency. Interest and principal payments on the notes were tied to the rate of subsequent inflation. In 1991, the Canadian government issued inflation-indexed bonds. The U.S. Treasury followed Canada in 1997. *(Chapter 6)*

1993 ***Controlling Risk.*** When a company fails to keep close tabs on the risks being taken by its employees, it can get into serious trouble. This was the fate of Barings, a 220-year-old British bank that counted the Queen among its clients. In 1993 it discovered that Nick Leeson, a trader in its Singapore office, had hidden losses of US$1.3 billion (£869 million) from unauthorized bets on the Japanese equity market. The losses wiped out Barings and landed Leeson in jail with a six-year sentence. *(Chapter 26)*

1999 ***The Euro.*** Large corporations do business in many currencies. In 1999 a new currency came into existence when 11 European countries adopted the euro in place of their separate currencies. This was not the first time different countries had agreed on a common currency. In 1865, France, Belgium, Switzerland, and Italy came together in the Latin Monetary Union, and they were joined by Greece and Romania the following year. Members of the European Monetary Union (EMU) hope the euro will be a longer-lasting success than earlier experiments. *(Chapter 24)*

2002 ***Financial Scandals.*** A seemingly endless series of financial and accounting scandals climaxed in this year. Resulting bankruptcies included Enron (and its accounting firm, Arthur Andersen), WorldCom, and the Italian food company Parmalat. The U.S. Congress passed the *Sarbanes-Oxley Act* to increase the accountability of corporations and executives. *(Chapters 1, 14)*

2008 ***Global Financial Crisis.*** World stock markets began experiencing unprecedented turmoil by late summer 2008. The S&P/TSX Composite Index, the major stock market index of the Toronto Stock Exchange, plummeted about 30 percent. The S&P/500, a major U.S. stock market index, dropped about 37 percent over the same period. The Hang Seng Composite Index, the main stock market index for the Hong Kong Stock Exchange, dropped almost 50 percent, and the FTSE 100, the index of the top 100 firms listed on the London Stock Exchange, dropped about 35 percent. Much of the stock market turmoil was a consequence of the financial troubles of the world's banks and other financial institutions. Reacting to asset write-downs and operating losses of financial institutions, the stock prices of financial institutions fell. Since the financial sector plays a major role in supporting the activities of the rest of the economy, the crisis spread from the financial sector to the real economy. Banks in financial trouble were unable to make loans, creating financial problems for other companies. This "credit crunch" inflicted real damage to the world economy. *(Chapters 1, 14, 26)*

2008 ***Subprime Mortgage Crisis.*** One cause of the financial institutions' troubles has been named the "subprime mortgage crisis." Many put the blame on the mortgage lending practices of U.S. banks, who provided mortgages to people with above-average risk of being unable to keep up with their mortgage payments. The availability of cheap mortgages, due to low interest rates and the willingness to lend to these "subprime" borrowers, caused a significant increase in the demand for housing and also for mortgages. The United States and the rest of the world enjoyed economic growth fuelled by the U.S. housing boom. However, when the U.S. economy started to slow down in 2006 and 2007, some workers lost their jobs and began to miss their mortgage payments. The rising price of oil has been named by some as a significant cause of the slowdown. Although the bad mortgages originated in the U.S., financial institutions from around the world had investments in those mortgages; the defaults affected cash flows and caused losses for financial institutions around the world. In Canada, this led to a liquidity crisis for asset-backed commercial paper. *(Chapter 14)*

2008 ***Credit Default Swaps.*** These are financial instruments that provide a form of insurance to investors in debt securities (such as bonds or mortgages) in the event that these securities go into default. Unlike traditional insurance contracts, credit default swaps were completely unregulated and, by some estimates, the market for these instruments had proliferated to over US$45 trillion. The excessive supply of these instruments contributed significantly to the financial crisis. *(Chapters 14, 26)*

2008 ***Big Government Bailouts.*** Governments stepped in to provide financial support to foundering banks and insurance companies, hoping to reestablish confidence in the financial system. For instance, the U.S. federal government spent US$85 billion to bail out one of the world's biggest insurance companies, American International Group (AIG), which risked defaulting on its credit default swaps issues. Interest rates were cut, to stimulate lending; some banks were given loan guarantees; and others were taken over by their government. These large bailouts are now widely acknowledged to have prevented a severe global recession, led by the United States. *(Chapters 14, 26)*

2010 ***The Euro (an update).*** In early 2001, Greece became the 12th country to adopt the euro and join the euro zone. Slovenia joined in 2007 followed by Cyprus and Malta in 2008 and

(Continued)

Finance Through the Ages

FINANCE IN ACTION

Slovakia in 2009. By January 2009, euro notes and coins were in circulation in the 16 participating countries. More than 90 percent of cash payments in these countries are now carried out in euros. Consumers can still use the respective national currencies, although they are being phased out. The euro zone is going through challenging times as a number of weak links between the member countries have surfaced. Several governments are running deficits due to recession in the past two years and now have to borrow heavily to plug the gap. The countries include Greece, Portugal, Ireland, and perhaps even Spain and Italy (the third-biggest economy to use the common currency). The value of the euro has declined against other major world currencies. Financial markets have fallen sharply on fears of a Greek debt default and a possible domino effect through other European Union countries. Some have even questioned whether the euro currency zone can survive the crisis.[18] *(Chapter 24)*

[18] For more information about the euro, you can visit the Web site of the *Financial Times* at **specials.ft.com/euro**.

1.8 SUMMARY

1. **What are the two major decisions made by financial managers? LO1**

   Financial management can be broken down into (1) the investment, or capital budgeting, decision and (2) the financing decision. The firm has to decide (1) how much to invest and which real assets to invest in and (2) how to raise the necessary cash.

2. **What does "real asset" mean? What is a "financial asset"? LO2**

   Real assets include all assets used in the production or sale of the firms' products or services. Real assets can be tangible (plant and equipment, for example) or intangible (patents or trademarks, for example). Financial assets are securities (such as shares) sold by the firm to raise money, and represent claims on the firm's real assets and the cash generated by those assets.

3. **What are the advantages and disadvantages of the most common forms of business organization? Which forms are most suitable to different types of businesses? LO3**

   Businesses may be organized as sole proprietorships, partnerships, or corporations. A corporation is legally distinct from its owners. Therefore, the shareholders who own a corporation enjoy limited liability for its obligations. Ownership and management of corporations are usually separate, which means that the firm's operations need not be disrupted by changes in ownership. On the other hand, corporations are subject to double taxation. Large public companies are always corporations.

4. **Who are the major financial managers? LO4**

   Almost all managers are involved to some degree in investment decisions, but some managers specialize in finance, for example, the treasurer, controller, and CFO. The treasurer is most directly responsible for raising capital and maintaining relationships with banks and investors that hold the firm's securities. The controller is responsible for preparing financial statements and managing budgets. In large firms, a chief financial officer who oversees both the treasurer and the controller will also be involved in financial policymaking and corporate planning.

5. **Why does it make sense for corporations to maximize their market value? LO5**

   Value maximization is the natural financial goal of the firm. Maximizing value maximizes the wealth of the firm's owners, its shareholders. Shareholders can invest or consume that wealth as they wish.

6. **Is value maximization ethical? LO6**

   Modern finance does not condone attempts to pump up stock price by unethical means. But there need be no conflict between ethics and value maximization. The surest route to maximum value starts with products and services that satisfy customers. A good reputation with customers, employees, and other stakeholders is also important for the firms' long-term profitability and value.

7. **How do corporations ensure that managers' and stockholders' interests coincide?** LO7

Conflicts of interest between managers and stockholders can lead to agency problems. These problems are kept in check by compensation plans that link the well-being of employees to that of the firm; by monitoring of management by the board of directors, security holders, and creditors; and by the threat of takeover.

Related Web Links

canadabusiness.ca, ic.gc.ca/epic/site/cd-dgc.nsf/en/Home Information and help in setting up a firm as a corporation, partnership, or proprietorship

tsx.com/en/listings/sector_profiles/income_trusts/index.html Information on Canadian income trusts

careers-in-finance.com, workopolis.com, payscale.com Career information and salary data

corpgov.net/wordpress Discussion of U.S. corporate governance issues

ccgg.ca Governance guidelines for Canadian corporations

thecorporatelibrary.com Discussion of recent issues regarding the role of directors and management

rotman.utoronto.ca/CCBE Corporate governance ratings for Canadian public companies

otpp.com/wps/wcm/connect/otpp_en/Home/Corporate+Info/Plan+Governance Ontario Teachers' Pension Plan corporate governance policy

businessethics.ca, greenmoneyjournal.com, cbsr.ca Web sites focused on responsible corporate behaviour

Key Terms

agency problems	17	corporation	8	public company	8
capital budgeting decision (*or* investment decision)	5	financial assets	8	real assets	8
capital structure	6	financing decision	6	sole proprietor	10
chief financial officer (CFO)	12	limited liability	8	stakeholder	17
controller	12	partnership	11	treasurer	12
		private company	8		

Questions and Problems

Practise and learn online with *Connect*. Questions with online Excel templates or datasets are marked with .

*Answers in Appendix B

BASIC

*1. **Financial Decisions.** Fit each of the following terms into the most appropriate space: financing, real, stock, investment, executive airplanes, financial, capital budgeting, brand names. (LO1)

Companies usually buy ______ assets. These include both tangible assets such as ______ and intangible assets such as ______. In order to pay for these assets, they sell ______ assets such as ______. The decision regarding which assets to buy is usually termed the ______ or ______ decision. The decision regarding how to raise the money is usually termed the ______ decision.

2. **Value Maximization.** Give an example of an action that might increase profits but at the same time reduce stock price. (LO5)

3. **Corporations.** What is the advantage of separating ownership and management in large corporations? What is the difference between public and private corporations? (LO3)

4. **Corporate Organization.** What are the advantages and disadvantages of organizing a firm as a proprietorship, partnership, or corporation? In what sense are LLPs or professional corporations hybrid forms of business organization? (LO3)

5. **Corporate Organization.** What do we mean when we say that corporate income is subject to double taxation? (LO3)

6. **Financial Managers.** Which of the following statements more accurately describes the treasurer than the controller? (LO4)

   a. Likely to be the only financial executive in small firms
   b. Monitors capital expenditures to ensure that they are not misappropriated

c. Responsible for investing the firm's spare cash
d. Responsible for arranging any issue of common stock
e. Responsible for the company's tax affairs

7. **Internet.** Go to the Web page of TD Financial Group, **www.td.com**, and look at the activities of their various businesses. If you are an investment banker, which business would you work for? If you want to trade securities, where would you work? Where would you work as a retail investment advisor? (LO3)

INTERMEDIATE

8. **Real Versus Financial Assets.** Which of the following are real assets and which ones are financial? (LO2)
   *a. A share of stock
   b. A personal IOU
   c. A trademark
   *d. A truck
   e. Undeveloped land
   *f. The balance in the firm's chequing account
   *g. An experienced and hardworking sales force
   h. A bank loan agreement

9. **Basic Finance Concepts.** Explain the differences between each pair of concepts: (LO1)
   a. Real versus financial assets
   b. Investment versus financing decisions
   c. Capital budgeting versus capital structure decisions

10. **The Financial Manager.** Give two examples of capital budgeting decisions and financing decisions. (LO4)

11. **Goals of the Firm.** You may have heard big business criticized for focusing on short-term performance at the expense of long-term results. Explain why a firm that strives to maximize stock price should be less subject to an overemphasis on short-term results than one that maximizes profits. (LO5)

12. **Goals of the Firm.** We claim that the goal of the firm is to maximize stock price. Are the following actions necessarily consistent with that goal? (LO5)
   a. The firm adds a cost-of-living adjustment to the pensions of its retired employees.
   b. The firm reduces its dividend payment, choosing to reinvest more of earnings in the business.
   c. The firm buys a corporate jet for its executives.

13. **Goals of the Firm.** Explain why each of the following may not be appropriate corporate goals: (LO5)
   a. Increase market share
   b. Minimize costs
   c. Underprice any competitors
   d. Expand profits

*14. **Agency Issues.** Sometimes lawyers work on a contingency basis. They collect a percentage of their client's settlement instead of receiving a fixed fee. Why might clients prefer this arrangement? Would this sort of arrangement be more appropriate for clients who use lawyers regularly or infrequently? (LO7)

15. **Reputation.** As you drive down a deserted highway, you are overcome with a sudden desire for a hamburger. Fortunately, just ahead are two hamburger outlets; one is owned by a national brand, the other appears to be owned by "Joe." Which outlet has the greater incentive to serve you cat meat? Why? (LO6)

*16. **Agency Problems.** If agency problems can be mitigated by tying the manager's compensation to the fortunes of the firm, why don't firms compensate managers exclusively with shares in the firm? (LO7)

*17. **Agency Problems.** Many firms have devised defences that make it much more costly or difficult for other firms to take them over. How might such takeover defences affect the firm's agency problems? Are managers of firms with formidable takeover defences more or less likely to act in the firm's interests rather than their own? (LO7)

18. **Agency Issues.** One of the "Finance Through the Ages" episodes that we cite on pages 26–28 is the 1993 collapse of Barings Bank when one of its traders lost US$1.3 billion. Traders are compensated in large part according to their trading profits. How might this practice have contributed to an agency problem? (LO7)

19. **Agency Issues.** Discuss which of the following forms of compensation is most likely to align the interests of managers and shareholders: (LO7)
   a. A fixed salary
   b. A salary linked to company profits
   c. A salary paid partly in the form of the company's shares
   d. Stock options to buy shares at an attractive price

20. **Agency Issues.** When a company's stock is widely held, it may not pay an individual shareholder to spend time monitoring the manager's performance and trying to replace poor management. Explain why. Do you think that a bank that has made a large loan to the company is in a different position? (LO7)

21. **Ethics.** In some countries, such as Japan and Germany, corporations develop close long-term relationships with one bank and rely on that bank for a large part of their financing needs. In the United States or Canada, companies are more likely to shop around. Do you think this practice is more or less likely to encourage ethical behaviour on the part of the corporation? (LO6)

22. **Ethics.** Is there a conflict between "doing well" and "doing good"? In other words, are policies that increase the value of the firm (doing well) necessarily at odds with socially responsible policies (doing good)? When

there are conflicts, how might government regulations or laws tilt the firm toward doing good? For example, how do taxes or fees charged on pollutants affect the firm's decision to pollute? Can you cite other examples of "incentives" used by governments to align private with public ones? (LO6)

23. **Ethics.** The following report appeared in *Financial Times* (October 28, 1999, p. 1): "Coca-Cola is testing a vending machine that automatically raises the price of the world's favourite soft drink when the temperature increases. . . . [T]he new machine, believed to have been tested in Japan, may well create controversy by using hot weather to charge extra. One rival said the idea of charging more when temperatures rose was 'incredible.'" Discuss. (LO6)

24. **Internet.** Canada Business, **www.canadabusiness.ca**, is a Government of Canada Web site for businesses. Click on "Starting a Business," then on "Forms of Business Organization." Pick a province and review the differences between sole proprietorships, partnerships, and corporations. Then look at the "not for profit" organizations. How do they differ from for-profit organizations? (LO3)

25. **Internet.** To learn about careers in finance, go to **www.careers-in-finance.com**. This site describes jobs in commercial banking, corporate finance, financial planning, insurance, investment banking, money management, and real estate. For each area the site describes the types of jobs available, the skills and talents needed, salary ranges, and so on. Pick a field. Which jobs do you think would best suit you? Now compare the skills needed for these jobs. How do you match up? How will you match up when your education is completed? (LO4)

26. **Internet.** Go to Job Futures, **www.workingincanada.gc.ca**, a career and education Web site provided by the Government of Canada. Type in a job title that you find interesting and pick your province or territory. Explore some of the job's essential skills, main duties, and wages. (LO4)

Solutions to Check Points

1.1 a. The development of a fuel cell is a capital budgeting decision. The investment of $500 million will purchase a real asset, the fuel cell.
b. The bank loan is a financing decision. This is how Volkswagen will raise money for its investment.
c. Capital budgeting.
d. Financing.
e. Capital budgeting. Though intangible, the licence is a real asset that is expected to produce future sales and profits.
f. Financing.

1.2 a. A patent is a real asset. Real assets can be intangible assets.
b. Financial.
c. Real.
d. Financial.
e. Real.
f. Financial.

1.3 a. The consulting firm is most suited to a partnership or limited liability partnership. Each senior consultant might be a partner, with partial responsibility for managing the firm and its clients.
b. The university student would set up the business as a sole proprietorship. She is the only manager and has little need for partners to contribute capital.
c. The large firm would be set up as a corporation. It requires great amounts of capital, and with the budgetary, payroll, and management issues that arise with such a large number of employees, it probably needs a professional management team.

1.4 Sal would more likely be the treasurer and Sally the controller. The treasurer raises money from the credit and financial markets and requires background in financial institutions. The controller is more of an overseer who requires background in accounting.

1.5 Harry's has a far bigger stake in the reputation of the business than Victor's. The former has been in business for a long time. The owners have spent years establishing customer loyalty. In contrast, Victor's has just been established. The owner has little of his own money tied up in the firm, and so has little to lose if the business fails. In addition, the nature of the business results in little customer loyalty. Harry's is probably more reliable.

1.6 An investor would like top management to be compensated according to the fortunes of the firm. If management is willing to bet its own compensation on the success of the firm, that is good news; first, because it shows management has confidence in the firm, and second, because it gives managers greater incentives to work hard to make the firm succeed.

1.7 Agency problems arise when managers and shareholders have different objectives. Managers may empire build with excessive investment and growth. Managers may be unduly risk-averse, or they may try to take excessive salaries or perquisites.

PART 1 Introduction

1 Goals and Governance of the Firm
2 Financial Markets and Institutions
2.1 The Importance of Financial Markets and Institutions
2.2 The Flow of Savings to Corporations
2.3 Functions of Financial Markets and Intermediaries
2.4 Value Maximization and the Cost of Capital
2.5 The Crisis of 2007–2009
2.6 Summary
3 Accounting and Finance
4 Measuring Corporate Performance

CHAPTER 2

Financial Markets and Institutions

LEARNING OBJECTIVES

After studying this chapter, you should be able to:

LO1 Describe how financial markets and institutions channel savings to corporate investment.

LO2 Describe the basic structure of mutual funds, pension funds, banks, and insurance companies.

LO3 Enumerate the functions of financial markets and institutions.

LO4 Explain why the cost of capital for corporate investment is determined by investment opportunities in financial markets.

The Toronto Stock Exchange is an important Canadian financial market.

Courtesy of the Toronto Stock Exchange.

If a corporation needs to issue more shares of stock, its financial manager must understand how the stock market works. If the corporation wants to take out a bank loan, the financial manager must understand how banks and other financial institutions work. That much is obvious. But the capital investment decision also requires a broader understanding of financial markets. We have said that a successful investment is one that increases the market value of the firm. How do investors value the firm? What level of profitability do investors require from the firm's capital investments? To answer these questions, we will need to think clearly about the cost of the capital that the firm raises from outside investors.

Financial markets and institutions are the firm's financial environment. You don't have to understand everything about that environment to begin the study of financial management, but a general understanding provides useful context for the work ahead. For example, that context will help you to understand why you are calculating the yield to maturity of a bond in Chapter 6, the net present value of a capital investment in Chapter 8, or the weighted-average cost of capital for a company in Chapter 13.

This chapter does three things. First, it surveys financial markets and institutions. We will cover the stock and bond markets, mutual and pension funds, and banks and insurance companies. Second, we will set out the functions of financial markets and institutions: What do they do for corporations and for the economy? Third, it offers another look at why maximizing value is the natural financial objective of the corporation, and it defines the cost of capital for corporate investment.

LO1 2.1 THE IMPORTANCE OF FINANCIAL MARKETS AND INSTITUTIONS

We saw in the last chapter why a corporation's financing and investment decisions are important to its profitability and growth. Here we shift attention to the corporation's financial environment, particularly to the financial markets and institutions that supply financing for investment by corporations.

It's easy to take modern financial markets and institutions for granted and to miss their contribution to the growth of the firm and the productivity of the overall economy. All large, successful corporations can be traced back to one or a handful of entrepreneurs with nothing more than an idea for a new business. For example, both Hewlett-Packard and Apple Computer started up in California garages. Research In Motion's founder, Mike Lazaridis, dropped out of university in the spring of 1984, when General Motors of Canada Ltd. granted his then-nonexistent

TABLE 2.1 Examples of financing decisions by Research In Motion.

March 1984: Research In Motion founded	Mike Lazaridis and Doug Fregin start an electronics and computer science consulting business, financed by loans from friends and family. General Motors hires RIM to work on automation project.
1987:	RIM signs contract with Rogers Cantel Mobile Communications to work on wireless digital network systems.
1992:	Jim Balsillie joins RIM to handle corporate finance and business development and invests $250,000 of his own money in RIM shares.
1995:	Ontario Government invests $4.7 million through the Ontario Technology Fund.
October 1997: Initial public offering, listing shares on the Toronto Stock exchange	RIM raises $104 million, after fees and expenses, by selling shares to public investors for $7.25 per share.
1998: BlackBerry® Wireless handheld is introduced	Canadian federal government invests $5.7 million through technology partnerships Canada, and Intel makes $4.1 million equity investment.
1999: Lists shares for trading on Nasdaq stock exchange	RIM raises $250 million selling additional shares to the public.
2000:	RIM completes a 6,000,000-common-share public offering raising US$611 million. Nortel makes US$25 million equity investment.
October 2001: Acquisition of Plazmic Inc., to service users with Java-capable devices	Acquisition is financed with 387,000 shares of RIM.
January 2004: Public offering	RIM make public offering of 12,075,000 shares raising $1.2 billion.
May 2004:	RIM common stock is split 2-for-1.
March 2006: RIM signs a settlement agreement with NTP, Inc. worth US$612.5 million; company continues to face ongoing patent infringement lawsuits from various companies	RIM sells 2,837,000 of common stock and issues additional shares on conversion of restricted share units (RSUs). The transactions provide "sufficient liquidity" to defend the company against pending litigation.
August 2007: RIM healthy and profitable thanks to launches of BlackBerry® Pearl, BlackBerry® Curve, and BlackBerry® Mobile Voice System, with services in more than 200 countries	RIM common stock is split 3-for-1.
2010:	RIM begins a $775 million share repurchase program. The board of governors has authorized the repurchase and cancellation of $1.2 billion worth of common stock (nearly 3.6% of all common shares).
Since startup to March 2010:	RIM shareholders reinvest $7.6 billion of earnings. Thus RIM's 2010 balance sheet shows cumulative retained earnings of UD$7.6 billion.

company an industrial automation contract. But they could not have grown from those humble beginnings without access to well-functioning financial markets and institutions.

Table 2.1 gives examples of the sources of financing tapped by Research In Motion (RIM) from its startup in 1984 to early in 2008. The original financing of RIM came from friends and family. RIM was also able to get financing through contracts with its customers. Then as RIM grew, it was able to obtain several rounds of financing by selling its shares to other companies and from government-sponsored investment funds. (We discuss venture capital in Chapter 15.) In October 1997, it raised $104 million in an initial public offering (IPO) of its shares to public investors.

Finance in Action

Founder of Microcredit Movement Wins Nobel Peace Prize

Bangladesh's Muhammad Yunus and the bank he founded, Grameen Bank, which created a new category of banking by granting millions of small loans to poor people with no collateral—helping to establish the microcredit movement across the developing world—won the 2006 Nobel Peace Prize. On its Web site, the Norwegian Nobel Committee said it awarded the prize to Yunus and the bank "for their efforts to create economic and social benefit from below."

The Grameen Bank lends small amounts of money to people who would normally be refused loans by mainstream banks. Back in 1976, Yunus was struck by the plight of 22-year-old Sophia Khatoon, who was struggling to survive in a small Bangladeshi village called Jobra. She worked seven days a week making finely woven bamboo furniture. Because she had no working capital, she was forced to buy her materials on credit. Professor Yunus, then a professor of economics at a nearby university, calculated that she was paying 10 percent interest per day—more than 3,000 percent per year.

He lent her 50 taka (a few dollars) and within months she was able to make her business viable, increasing her income sevenfold and repaying the loan.

After this, Professor Yunus extended his lending to other very poor people, and then tried to interest the mainstream banks in doing the same. They weren't interested, so Professor Yunus became a full-time banker. As of July 2010, the Grameen Bank has extended loans totalling US$9.43 billion, and 94 percent of its borrowers are women. To date, its loan recovery rate has been 88.6 percent.[1]

According the 2009 State of the Microcredit Summit Campaign Report (**www.microcreditsummit.org**), there are now 3,552 microcredit institutions worldwide, reaching more than 154 million clients.

[1] Grameen Bank, **www.grameen-info.org**.

Source: Courtesy of Global Education, **www.globaleducation.edna.edu.au**.

Once RIM was a public company, it could raise financing from many sources. On three occasions, it sold more shares to the public in follow-on offers. RIM was also able to pay for acquisitions by issuing more shares. We have shown examples in Table 2.1.

RIM has never paid cash dividends to shareholders, but it has distributed cash to investors through stock repurchases starting in 2001. But RIM hit a rough patch in 2002 and 2003 and had negative operating earnings and laid off 10 percent of its workforce. However, investors still believed in the technology, and the company was able to raise new equity financing in 2004. Cumulative retained earnings were $7.6 billion by the end of February 2010.

RIM is well known for its product innovations, particularly the BlackBerry. RIM is not special because of its financing; its story in this regard is not very different from that of many other successful companies. But access to financing was vital to RIM's growth and profitability. Would we have the BlackBerry today had RIM been forced to operate in a country with a primitive financial system? Probably not.

A modern financial system offers financing in many different forms, depending on the company's age, its growth rate, and the nature of its business. For example, RIM relied on venture capital financing in its early years and only later floated its shares in public stock markets. Table 2.1 does not begin to cover the range of financing channels open to modern corporations. We will encounter many other channels later in the book, and new channels are opening up all the time. The nearby box describes one recent financial innovation, microcredit funds, that make small loans to businesspeople in the poorer parts of the world.

LO1, 2 2.2 THE FLOW OF SAVINGS TO CORPORATIONS

The money that corporations invest in real assets comes ultimately from savings by investors. But there can be many stops on the road between savings and corporate investment. The road can pass through financial markets, financial intermediaries, or both.

Let's start with the simplest case of a small, privately owned corporation, such as RIM in its earliest years. The red arrows in Figure 2.1 (which we repeat from Chapter 1) show the flow of

FIGURE 2.1
Flow of savings to corporate investment (red arrows) in a private corporation. Investors purchase shares with personal savings (1), which are invested (2). The business generates cash (3), which is reinvested (4a) or paid out to shareholders (4b). Reinvestment (4a) represents additional savings on behalf of shareholders.

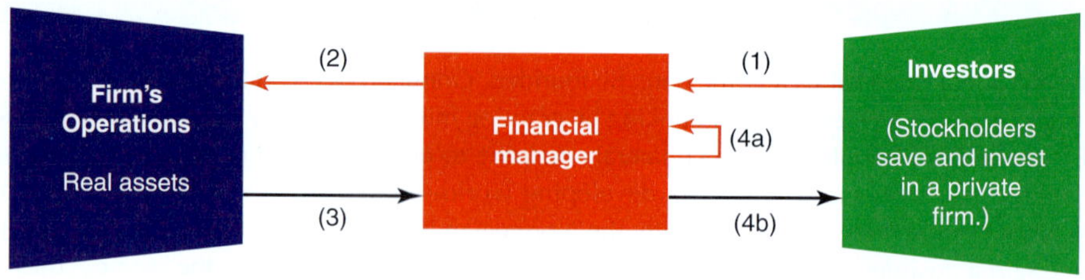

savings to investment in this simple case. There are two possible paths: the firm can sell new shares (arrow 1) or it can reinvest cash back into the firm's operations (arrow 4a). Reinvestment means additional savings by existing shareholders. The reinvested cash could have been paid out to those shareholders (arrow 4b) and spent by them on personal consumption. By not taking and spending the cash, shareholders have reinvested their savings in the corporation.

Cash retained and reinvested in the firm's operations is cash saved and invested on behalf of the firm's shareholders.

Of course, this small corporation has other financing choices. It might take out a bank loan, for example. The bank in turn may have raised money by attracting savings accounts. In this case investors' savings flow through the bank to the firm.

Now consider a large, public firm, such as RIM in 2010. What's different? Scale, for one thing: RIM's annual revenues in 2010 were US$14.9 billion and its balance sheet showed total assets of US$10.2 billion. Financing requirements are correspondingly large, and the linkages between investors and the corporation are much more diverse.

The flow of savings to large public corporations is shown in Figure 2.2. Notice two key differences from Figure 2.1. First, public corporations can draw savings from investors worldwide. Second, the savings flow through financial markets, financial intermediaries, or both. Suppose,

FIGURE 2.2
Flow of savings to a large public corporation (red arrows). Savings, which can come from investors worldwide, might flow through financial markets or financial intermediaries. Savings might also flow into financial intermediaries through financial markets or into financial markets through financial intermediaries.

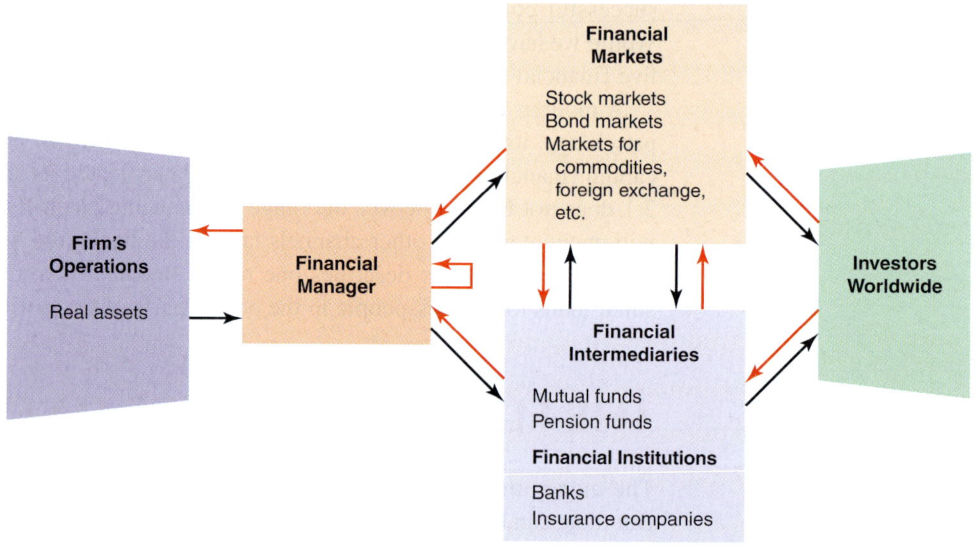

for example, that Bank of Montreal raises $300 million by a new issue of shares. An Italian investor buys 1,000 of the new shares for $60 per share. Now Bank of Montreal takes that $60,000, along with money raised by the rest of the issue, and provides a $300 million mortgage to RIM. The Italian investor's savings end up flowing through financial markets (the stock market), to a financial intermediary (Bank of Montreal), and finally to RIM.

Of course, our Italian friend's $60,000 doesn't literally arrive at RIM in an envelope marked "From L. DaVinci." Investments by the purchasers of Bank of Montreal's stock issue are pooled, not segregated. Sr. DaVinci would own a share of all of Bank of Montreal's assets, not just one loan to RIM. Nevertheless, investors' savings flow through the financial markets and the bank to finance RIM's capital investments.

THE STOCK MARKET

financial market Market in which securities are issued and traded.

A **financial market** is a market in which securities are issued and traded. A security is just a traded financial asset, such as a share of stock. For a corporation, the stock market is probably the most important financial market.

As corporations grow, their requirements for outside capital can expand dramatically. At some point the firm will decide to "go public" by issuing shares on an organized exchange such as the Toronto Stock Exchange (TSX) in Canada or the New York Stock Exchange (NYSE) in the United States; that first issue is called an *initial public offering* or *IPO*. The sale of the securities is usually managed by a group of investment dealers such as CIBC World Markets or RBC Dominion Securities. The buyers of the IPO are helping to finance the firm's investment in real assets. In return, the buyers become part-owners of the firm and share in its future success or failure. Most investors in the Internet IPOs of 1999 and 2000 are by now sorely disappointed, but many IPOs pay off handsomely. If only we had bought RIM shares on their IPO day in 1997 when they were sold for $7.25 per share. As of July 2010, one share would have been worth $319.98![1]

An IPO is not the only occasion on which newly issued stock is sold to the public. Established firms also issue new shares from time to time. RIM has made three public stock offerings since its initial IPO. Such offers are known as *seasoned equity offers* or *follow-on offers*.

primary market Market for the sale of new securities by corporations.

secondary market Market in which already issued securities are traded among investors.

A new issue of shares increases both the amount of cash held by the company and the number of shares held by the public. Such an issue is known as a primary issue and it is sold in the **primary market**. But in addition to helping companies raise new cash, financial markets also allow investors to trade stocks or bonds between themselves. For example, Voth might decide to raise some cash by selling her RIM stock at the same time that Schloo invests his spare cash in RIM. The result is simply a transfer of ownership from Voth to Schloo, which has no effect on the company itself. Such purchases and sales of existing securities are known as secondary transactions, and they take place in the **secondary market**.

Stock markets are also called *equity markets*, since shareholders are said to own the common equity of the firm. You will hear financial managers refer to the capital structure decision as "the choice between debt and equity financing."

The Toronto Stock Exchange is the main stock exchange for trading shares of large Canadian corporations. Trading in the shares of smaller and emerging Canadian companies is done through the TSX Venture Exchange (TSX-V) and the Canadian National Stock Exchange (CNSX), Canada's new stock exchange for emerging companies. All Canadian stock exchanges are fully electronic. The New York Stock Exchange lists the largest companies in the United States, and is one of the few stock markets in which stocks are physically bought and sold by traders on the trading floor. But even the NYSE has now introduced electronic trading, and in time all of its trading will be electronic. The other big U.S. stock market is the Nasdaq, a fully

---

[1] RIM's quoted closing stock price on July 9, 2010, was US$53.33. Taking into account the two stock splits, one share in 1997 is equivalent to six shares in 2010, making the original share worth US$319.98.

electronic market. Nasdaq is a dealer network, providing trading with a large choice of electronically linked dealers. Trading also occurs through electronic communication networks (ECNs) and alternative trading systems (ATS) that provide competitive alternatives to existing stock markets. Pure Trading, **www.puretrading.ca**, is the first Canadian ATS that offers trading of TSX-listed stocks.

Now may be a good point to stress that the financial manager plays on a global stage and needs to be familiar with markets around the world. For example, larger Canadian companies having sizable global operations, such as RIM or Canadian Imperial Bank of Commerce, tend to be cross-listed on the TSX as well as other large international exchanges such as the NYSE and Nasdaq. Conversely, foreign-based businesses list their shares for trading on the TSX.

We return to the trading and pricing of shares in Chapter 7.

AGENCY PROBLEMS AND CORPORATE GOVERNANCE

The flow of savings to public corporations, as in Figure 2.2, requires *separation of ownership and control*: the ultimate owners of a corporation are not its managers. That creates the *agency problems* we noted in the previous chapter. Agency problems exist because managers will consider their own interests as well as shareholders'. Corporations try to align managers' and shareholders' interests (by granting stock or options to top management, for example), but the alignment can never be perfect.

Separation of ownership and control is necessary because outside investors cannot know enough about the firm's problems and prospects to make good financial decisions. If investors did have that knowledge, they would not need managers. The investors could manage the firm on their own.

Financial markets and institutions are supposed to move financing to all firms that can invest at superior rates of return. Financing moves from investors to firms only if investors are protected. This creates the need for a system of *corporate governance*, so that financing can flow to the right firms at the right times. Good corporate governance protects investors and thus supports the development of financial markets and the financing required for economic growth. Governance includes standards for accounting and disclosure to investors, requirements for boards of directors, and legal sanctions for fraud or self-dealing by management. The Sarbanes-Oxley (SOX) Act of 2002 in the United States or the Ontario government's Bill C-198 were attempts to tighten corporate governance.

Although we discussed agency problems and governance in the previous chapter, these topics are worth revisiting. Think again of the financial history of RIM in Table 2.1 and at the start of Chapter 1. The company survived and grew because it had access to financing from outside investors. That financing was forthcoming because the investors trusted the company to invest wisely. In other words, the investors trusted the Canadian system of corporate governance, and they trusted the directors and managers of the firm to try to increase shareholder value.

OTHER FINANCIAL MARKETS

Debt securities are also traded in financial markets. For example, EnCana issued long-term bonds to investors. The bonds are securities representing EnCana's promise to make regular interest payments and to repay investors' money on a specified future date.

A few corporate debt securities are traded on the Toronto or New York stock exchanges, but many corporate debt securities are traded over the counter, not on Nasdaq but on a network of banks and securities dealers. Government debt is also traded over the counter. There are also a growing number of electronic markets where debt is traded, such as CanDeal, **www.candeal.ca**.

A bond is a more complex security than a share of stock. A share is just a proportional ownership claim on the firm, with no definite maturity. Bonds and other debt securities can vary in maturity, the degree of protection or collateral offered by the issuer, and the level and timing of interest payments. Some bonds make "floating" interest payments tied to the future level of interest rates. Some can be "called" (repurchased and retired) by the issuing company before the bonds' stated maturity date. Some bonds can be converted into other securities, usually the stock of the issuing company. You don't need to master these distinctions now; just be aware that the debt or **fixed-income market** is a complicated and challenging place. A corporation must not only decide between debt and equity finance but also consider the design of debt. We return to the trading and pricing of debt securities in Chapter 6.

fixed-income market Market for debt securities.

The markets for long-term debt and equity are called **capital markets**. A firm's capital is its long-term financing. Short-term securities are traded in the **money markets**. "Short term" means less than one year. For example, large, creditworthy corporations raise short-term financing by issues of commercial paper, which are debt issues with maturities of at most one year. Commercial paper is issued in the money market.

capital market Market for long-term financing.

money market Market for short-term financing (less than one year).

Check Point 2.1

Do you understand the following distinctions? Briefly explain in each case.

a. Primary versus secondary market
b. Initial public offer versus seasoned equity offer
c. Capital market versus money market
d. Stock market versus fixed-income market

The financial manager regularly encounters other financial markets. Here are three examples, with references to the chapters where they are discussed:

- *Foreign-exchange markets* (Chapter 24). Any corporation engaged in international trade must be able to transfer money from dollars to other currencies, or vice versa. Foreign exchange ("FOREX" or "FX") is traded over the counter through a network of the largest international banks.
- *Commodities markets* (Chapter 26). Dozens of commodities are traded on organized exchanges, such as the New York Mercantile Exchange or the Chicago Board of Trade in the United States or the Intercontinental Exchange. You can buy or sell corn, wheat, canola oil, cotton, fuel oil, natural gas, copper, silver, platinum, and so on.
- *Markets for options and other derivatives* (Chapters 25 and 26). Derivatives are securities whose payoffs depend on the prices of other securities or commodities. For example, you can buy an option to purchase Nortel Network shares at a fixed price on a fixed future date. The option's payoff depends on the price of Nortel shares on that date. Commodities can be traded by a different kind of derivative security called a futures contract.

Commodity and derivative markets are not sources of financing, but markets in which the financial manager can adjust the firm's exposure to various business risks. For example, an electricity-generating company might wish to "lock in" the future price of natural gas or fuel oil by trading in commodity markets, eliminating the risk of a sudden jump in the price of its raw materials.

Wherever there is uncertainty, investors may be interested in trading, either to speculate or to lay off their risks, and a market may arise to meet that trading demand. In recent years several new markets have been created that allow punters to bet on a single event. The nearby box discusses how prices in these markets can reveal people's predictions about the future.

FINANCIAL INTERMEDIARIES

A **financial intermediary** is an organization that raises money from investors and provides financing for individuals, companies, and other organizations. For corporations, intermediaries are important sources of financing. Intermediaries are a stop on the road between savings and real investment. We will look at five classes of intermediaries: mutual funds, exchange-traded funds, hedge funds, private equity funds, and pension funds.

financial intermediary An organization that raises money from investors and provides financing for individuals, corporations, or other organizations.

Finance in Action

Prediction Markets

Stock markets have long let traders bet on their favoured stocks. Now *prediction markets* allow them to bet on almost anything else. These markets reveal the collective guess of traders on issues as diverse as the next presidential election, the winner of the Academy Awards, the amount of snow that will fall on Central Park this winter, or the severity of the next influenza season.

Prediction markets are conducted on the Iowa Electronic Market at the University of Iowa (**www.biz.uiowa.edu/iem**) and on online exchanges such as **www.intrade.com** or **www.betfair.com**. Take the 2008 presidential primary races as an example. You could bet that Barack Obama would be the Democratic candidate by buying one of his contracts. Each Obama contract would pay $1 if he won the Democratic nomination and nothing if he lost. If you thought the probability of his victory in the primaries was 55 percent, you would be prepared to pay up to $.55 for his contract. Someone relatively pessimistic about his chances would be happy to *sell* you such a contract, for that sale would turn a profit if Obama eventually were to lose the nomination. With many participants buying and selling contracts, the market price of a contract reveals the aggregated wisdom of the crowd.

Take a look at the figure here, from the Iowa Electronic Market, which shows the prices of the three major Democratic contenders (Hillary Clinton, Barack Obama, and John Edwards) through the end of February 2008. Notice the dramatic increase in the Obama contract price after his January win in the Iowa caucuses, the equally dramatic decrease the next week when Clinton won the New Hampshire primary, and the substantial run-up in Obama's price in February as he went on to win a lengthy succession of state primaries and caucuses.

The predictive accuracy of these markets compares favourably to several major polls. This may not be surprising, since participants are putting their money where their mouths are when making their predictions. Businesses have also experimented with these markets. For example, Hewlett-Packard set up a market to predict its printer sales and plan accordingly. You can trade "weather contracts" on the Chicago Mercantile Exchange that pay off depending on average temperatures in a variety of cities. The CME has also experimented with economic prediction contracts that allow trading on macroeconomic variables such as gross domestic product or inflation rates.

Prediction markets allowed you to bet on three candidates for the Democratic nomination.

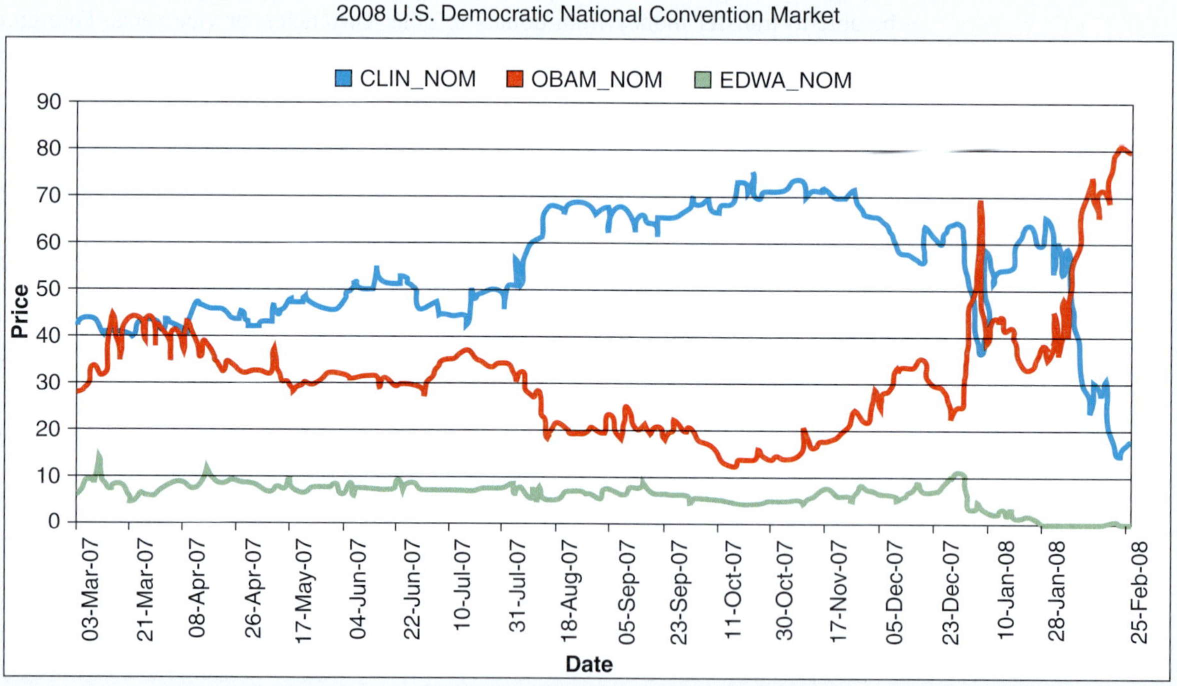

Source: Iowa Electronic Market, February 2008, **www.biz.uiowa.edu/iem**.

mutual fund A managed investment fund, pooling the savings of many investors and investing in a portfolio of securities.

Mutual funds and **exchange-traded funds (ETFs)**, raise money by selling units to investors. The investors' money is pooled and invested in a portfolio of securities. The AIM Canadian Premier Fund, for example, had about $649.4 million in total assets in May 2010. It held a portfolio of 83 stocks, 54 percent Canadian and 46 percent international. You could buy additional

exchange-traded fund (ETF) An investment fund, traded on a stock exchange, that pools the savings of many investors and invests in a portfolio of securities, selected to replicate an established securities index.

units in this mutual fund with an initial investment of as little as $500. By doing so, you would contribute $500 more to the portfolio and gain a tiny percentage of the portfolio's subsequent dividends and price appreciation.[2] You might also sell your units back to the fund if you decided to cash out of your investment.[3] By contrast, to invest in an ETF, units are purchased on a stock exchange. For example, the iShares DEX Universe Bond Index Fund ETF (XBB) trades on the Toronto Stock Exchange. The funds are invested in a portfolio of 326 federal, provincial, corporate, and municipal domestically issued Canadian bonds.

The advantages of a mutual fund or an ETF should be clear: unless you are very wealthy, you cannot buy and manage a 83-stock or a 326-bond portfolio on your own, at least not efficiently.

Mutual funds and exchange-traded funds offer investors low-cost diversification and professional management. For most investors, it's more efficient to buy a mutual fund or an ETF than to assemble a diversified portfolio of stocks and bonds.

Many mutual funds are actively managed. The fund managers try their best to "beat the market," that is, to generate superior performance by finding the stocks with better-than-average returns. Whether they can pick winners consistently is another question, which we will address in Chapter 6. By contrast, some mutual funds and all ETFs are passively managed index funds. The fund manager's job is to invest in securities to replicate the performance of an established market index. The iShares DEX Universe Bond Index Fund ETF matches the performance of the DEX Universe Bond Index, an index designed to measure the performance of the Canadian bond market.

In exchange for their services, the fund's managers take a management fee. There are also the expenses of running the fund. For AIM Canadian Premier, the management expense ratio (MER), which measures the total costs of operating the fund as a percentage of average total assets, is 2.43 percent. The MER differs across funds and fund managers. For instance, money market funds, which invest in short-term debt securities, tend to have low MERs. Passively managed funds, such as ETFs, have lower MERs. The MER for the iShares CDN Bond Index Fund is only 0.3 percent. In some cases mutual fund fees and expenses add up to over 3 percent per year. That's a big bite out of your investment return.

Mutual funds and ETFs are a stop on the road from savings to corporate investment. Suppose Canadian Premier purchases part of the new issue of shares by Bank of Montreal, which lends to RIM. Again we show the flow of savings to investment by red arrows:

Over 2,000 mutual funds and 60 ETFs operate in Canada. In fact there are more mutual funds than public companies listed on the Toronto Stock Exchange! Funds pursue a wide variety of investment strategies. Some funds specialize in safe stocks with generous dividend payouts. Some specialize in high-tech growth stocks. Some "balanced" funds offer mixtures of stocks and bonds. Some specialize in particular countries or regions. For example, the Fidelity Investments mutual fund group sponsors funds for Japan, China, Europe, Latin America, and so on.

hedge fund A private investment pool, open to wealthy or institutional investors, that is only lightly regulated and therefore can pursue more speculative policies than mutual funds.

You may have heard of another type of financial intermediary: **hedge funds**. Like mutual funds, these receive money from investors and then invest in a portfolio of securities. But they differ from mutual funds in at least two ways. First, because hedge funds usually follow complex, high-risk investment strategies, access is restricted to knowledgeable investors such as pension funds, endowment funds, and wealthy individuals. Don't try to send a cheque for $3,000 or

[2] Mutual funds and exchange-traded funds are not corporations, but investment companies. They pay no tax, providing that all income from dividends and price appreciation is passed on to the funds' unitholders. The unitholders pay personal tax on this income.

[3] AIM Canadian Premier, like most mutual funds, is an open-end fund. It stands ready to issue units to new investors in the fund and to buy back existing units when its unitholders decide to cash out. The purchase and sale prices depend on the fund's net asset value (NAV) on the day of purchase or redemption. Closed-end funds have a fixed number of units traded on an exchange. If you want to invest in a closed-end fund, you must buy units from another unitholder in the fund. ETFs are closed-end funds.

$5,000 to a hedge fund. The hedge fund is not in the "retail" investment business. Second, hedge funds try to attract the most talented managers by compensating them with potentially lucrative, performance-related fees.[4] In contrast, mutual funds usually pay a fixed percentage of assets under management.

Hedge funds follow many different investment strategies that may not generally be available to traditional mutual funds such as taking both long and short positions in stocks and using arbitrage, leverage, options, futures, bonds, and other financial instruments to capitalize on market conditions. For instance, some hedge funds try to make a profit by identifying overvalued stocks or markets and selling short. (We will not go into procedures for short selling here. Just remember that short sellers profit when prices *fall*.)[5] "Vulture funds" specialize in the securities of distressed corporations. Some hedge funds take bets on firms involved in merger negotiations, others look for mispricing of convertible bonds, and some take positions in currencies and interest rates. Hedge funds manage less money than mutual funds, but they sometimes take very big positions and have a large impact on the market. Some hedge funds are open only to "accredited investors," a category of investors deemed to be smart and rich enough to take on a lot of risk. Accredited investors include institutions and wealthy individuals. Some hedge funds are open to anyone, although they often have larger minimum contributions than mutual funds.

private equity fund Investment fund focused on investing in equity of privately owned businesses

A **private equity fund**, another type of financial intermediary, invests in the equity of private businesses, where the equity is not publicly traded on a stock market. Often, private equity funds provide financing and help nurture growing or troubled companies toward stable long-term growth. Some important categories of private equity investments include venture capital, angel investing, and leveraged buyouts.[6] We will discuss venture capital and angel investing in more detail in Chapter 15. Leveraged buyouts are discussed further in Chapter 23. Some large, established companies that have received private equity funding are Polaroid, Universal Studios, and BCE.

pension fund Investment plan set up by an employer to provide for employees' retirement.

A **pension fund** set up by a corporation or other organization on behalf of its employees is another way to pool and invest savings. There are several types of pension plan. Here is just one example. In a defined contribution plan,[7] a percentage of the employee's monthly paycheque is contributed to a pension fund. (The employer and employee might each contribute 5 percent, for example.) Contributions from all participating employees are pooled and invested in securities or mutual funds. (Usually the employees can choose from a menu of funds with different investment strategies.) Each employee's balance in the plan grows over the years as contributions continue and investment income accumulates. When retirement age arrives, the balance in the plan can be used to finance living expenses.

Pension funds are designed for long-term investment. They provide professional management and diversification. They also have an important tax advantage: Contributions are tax-deductible, and investment returns inside the plan are not taxed until cash is finally withdrawn.[8]

---

[4] Sometimes these fees can be very large indeed. For example, *Trader Monthly Magazine* estimated that the top-performing hedge fund manager in 2006 earned over $1.5 billion.

[5] A short seller borrows a security from another investor and sells it. Of course, the seller must sooner or later buy the security back and return it to its original owner. He or she earns a profit if the security can be bought back at a lower price than it was sold for.

[6] A recent study that interviewed CEOs in the United Kingdom found that the respondents felt that the boards of private equity firms were more effective in overseeing the affairs of private equity firms. See V. Acharya, C. Kehoe, and M. Reyner, "The Voice of Experience: Public Versus Private Equity," *McKinsey Quarterly: The Online Journal of Mckinsey & Co.*, December 2008, at **www.mckinseyquarterly.com/home.aspx**.

[7] In a *defined contribution plan*, each employee owns a portion of the pension fund and accumulates an investment balance to pay for retirement. The amount available for retirement depends on the accumulated contributions and on the rate of return earned on the invested contributions. In a *defined benefit plan*, the employer promises a certain level of retirement benefits (set by a formula) and the employer invests in the pension plan. The plan's accumulated investment value has to be large enough to cover the promised benefits. If not, the employer has to put in more money.

[8] Defined benefit pension plans share these same advantages, except that the employer invests rather than the employees. In a defined benefit plan, the advantage of tax deferral on investment income accrues to the employer. This deferral reduces the cost of funding the plan.

Pension plans are among the most important vehicles for savings. Some pension plans, such as Caisse de dépôt et placement du Québec or the Ontario Teachers' Plan are among the largest and most influential investors in the country. For instance, the Ontario Teachers' Plan held over \$96.4 billion in net assets, that is, assets minus liabilities, as at December 2009. A significant proportion of the plan's assets comprised equity and bond securities.

Check Point 2.2 Individual investors can buy bonds and stocks directly, or they can put their money in a mutual fund, ETF, or a defined-contribution pension fund. What are the advantages of the second strategy?

FINANCIAL INSTITUTIONS

financial institution A bank, insurance company, or similar financial intermediary.

Banks and insurance companies are **financial institutions**.[9] A financial institution is an intermediary that does more than just pool and invest savings. Institutions raise financing in special ways—for example, by accepting deposits or selling insurance policies—and they provide additional financial services. Unlike a mutual fund, they not only invest in securities but also loan money directly to individuals, businesses, or other organizations.

Banks lend money to corporations. (In the United States, they are generally not allowed to make equity investments in corporations, although banks in most other countries can do so.) Suppose that a grocery chain negotiates a short-term bank loan for \$2.5 million. The flow of savings is like this:

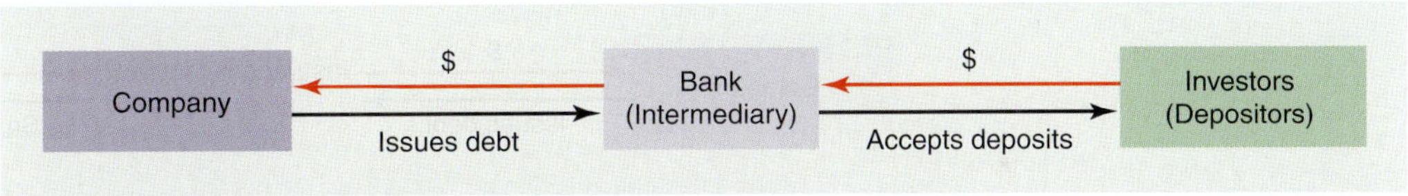

The bank provides a service. To cover the costs of this service, it charges borrowers a higher interest rate than it pays its depositors.

At present, Canadian residents are served by 76 banks that operate in different parts of the country and manage over \$2.9 trillion in assets. Of these, 22 are domestic banks, known as Schedule I banks, while the remaining 25 are foreign bank subsidiaries, or Schedule II banks, and 29 foreign bank branches, or Schedule III banks. The "Big Six" Schedule I banks account for about 88 percent of the country's bank industry assets and over 50 percent of the total domestic assets held by the financial sector.[10] Schedule II banks include Citibank Canada and HSBC Bank Canada. Branches of foreign banks operating in Canada, Schedule III banks, include Capital One Bank, and Deutsche Bank AG. Banks are, however, only one group of financial intermediaries operating in Canada. There are many others such as caisses populaires, credit unions, insurance companies, pension funds, and trust companies.

Like banks, trust companies, credit unions, and caisses populaires accept deposits and make loans. In addition, trust companies engage in fiduciary services such as managing assets, like registered retirement savings plans, for estates or pension plans. Credit unions and caisses populaires are typically run as cooperatives and are an important source of financing for residential

[9] We may be drawing too fine a distinction between financial intermediaries and institutions. A mutual fund might be considered a financial institution. But "financial institution" usually suggests a more complicated intermediary, such as a bank.

[10] In 2010, the largest banks, in order of assets, were Royal Bank of Canada, the Toronto Dominion Bank, Scotiabank, Bank of Montreal, CIBC, and National Bank of Canada. Shares in these banks are widely held by a large number of shareholders. For more information and statistics about Canada's banking industry, you can visit the Web site of the Canadian Bankers Association at **www.cba.ca**.

mortgages as well as small and medium enterprises. Caisses populaires are mainly located in Québec, with some operating in Manitoba, Ontario, and the Maritime provinces. Credit unions can be found across Canada but are particularly active in British Columbia and Saskatchewan. Some of Canada's caisses populaires and credit unions are very large. Québec-based Mouvement des caisses Desjardins is a conglomerate involved in a wide array of activities and ranks among the top eight financial institutions in the country, based on assets. Mouvement des caisses Desjardins includes a network of 450 caisses populaires and caisses d'économie (credit unions) in Québec and 20 in Ontario and their 914 service centres, including 871 in Québec and 43 in Ontario all assembled under the Fédération des caisses Desjardins du Québec.

Insurance companies include health, life, property, and casualty insurance companies. They are massive investors in corporate stocks and bonds and they often make long-term loans directly to corporations. In Canada, large pension funds and insurance companies, particularly life and health insurance firms, invest more in the long-term financing of businesses than do banks. They are massive investors in corporate stocks and bonds and occasionally make long-term loans directly to corporations.

A worldwide trend is the growth of financial institutions offering financial products that comply with the special loan-related requirements of practising Muslims. These Sharia-compliant products cannot explicitly charge or pay interest. As you will read in the nearby Finance in Action box, although only a few Canadian financial institutions are currently offering Sharia-compliant products, many more are expected to as the financial services sector responds to the growing demand.

Suppose a company needs a loan for nine years, not nine months. It might issue a bond directly to investors, or negotiate a nine-year loan with an insurance company:

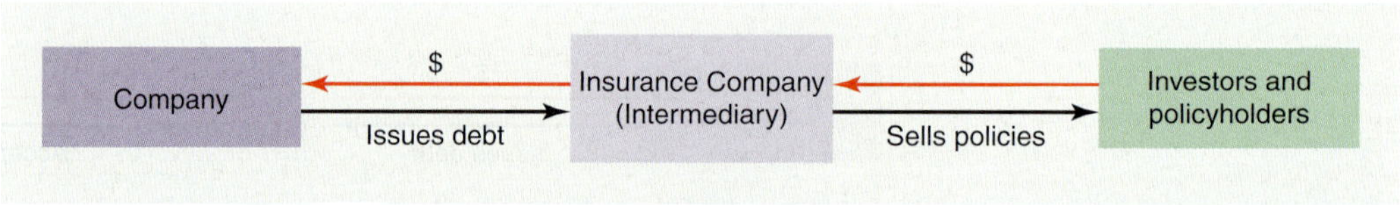

The money to make the loan comes mainly from the sale of insurance policies. Say you buy a fire insurance policy on your home. You pay cash to the insurance company and get a financial asset (the policy) in exchange. You receive no interest payments on this financial asset, but if a fire does strike, the company is obliged to cover the damages up to the policy limit. This is the return on your investment.

The company will issue not just one policy, but thousands. Normally the incidence of fires "averages out," leaving the company with a predictable obligation to its policyholders as a group. Of course, the insurance company has to charge enough for its policies to cover selling and administrative costs, pay policyholders' claims, and generate a profit for its shareholders.

Why is a financial intermediary different from a manufacturing corporation? First, it may raise money differently; for example, by taking deposits or selling insurance policies. Second, it invests that money in financial assets; for example, in stocks, bonds, or loans to businesses or individuals. The manufacturing company's main investments are in plant, equipment, and other real assets.

Check Point 2.3 What are the key differences between a mutual fund and a bank or an insurance company?

Finance in Action

The Fast-Growing Islamic Financial Sector

The Islamic financial sector has grown rapidly from its beginning in 1975, when the Islamic Development Bank and Dubai Islamic Bank were the first financial institutions to offer Sharia-compliant financial services. Now more than 600 financial institutions are providing such services. These institutions grew at more than four times the rate of Western (interest-related) financial services in 2009.

According to the November 2009 issue of *The Banker*, the Top 500 Islamic Financial Institutions grew 28.6 percent in 2009, ending the year with US$822 billion in Sharia-compliant assets.[1] This was the third consecutive comprehensive listing of Top 500 Islamic financial institutions, drawn from banks—both fully Islamic and those offering Islamic windows or selling Islamic products—investment banks and finance companies, and insurance companies. Of the 626 financial institutions reporting in 2009, 435 are operating under full Sharia-compliant principles and 191 are conventional institutions operating with Sharia-compliant windows.

Islamic banking refers to a system of banking or banking activity that is consistent with Islamic law or Sharia principles. Islamic law prohibits investing in businesses considered unlawful, or *haraam* (such as businesses that sell alcohol or pork, or businesses that produce media such as gossip columns or pornography, which are contrary to Islamic values). Trading in tangible assets or services is permitted, but simply making money from money is forbidden. Islamic law prohibits the collection and payment of interest, called *usury* in English or *riba* in some Islamic languages.

Sharia-compliant products are based on risk-sharing. Islamic mortgages are often structured as rent-to-own agreements. Both the client (the home buyer) and the Sharia-compliant financial institution are co-equity owners in the home. Instead of paying interest, the client pays rent and a principal payment each month to the bank. In the end, total monthly payments amount to roughly the same as under a conventional mortgage.

Many of the world's largest conventional financial institutions, including Citigroup and HSBC, provide Sharia-compliant financial products to cater to the large and increasingly affluent Muslim population. Muslims account for almost one-quarter of the world's population and Islam is widely considered to be the world's fastest-growing religion.

London, England, is a thriving centre for the sector—not only do domestic U.K. banks offer a range of Islam compliant products, but also London is the home to a multibillion-dollar market in Sharia-compliant bonds, known as the "Sukuk market."

Despite the growth of the Islamic finance sector around the world, growth is building slowly in North America. But experts say the largely untapped market in Canada includes close to a million Canadian Muslims, as well as non-Muslims interested in ethical investments, and oil-rich foreign investors from the Middle East.

Although a small number of grassroots Islamic financial institutions and organizations now offer retail products or services in Canada, no large Canadian financial institution currently distributes Sharia-compliant financial services or products in Canada. Co-operators Insurance was the first Canadian insurance provider to create Sharia-compliant insurance products, known as "Takaful insurance." In 2007, they had written 27 policies in partnership with Muslim housing cooperatives. UM Financial Inc. has offered a Sharia-based mortgage product, and plans to offer others.[2]

[1] *The Banker*, **www.thebanker.com**, is the global finance magazine of the *Financial Times*, Britain's top financial newspaper. The survey can be found at **www.mifc.com/index.php?ch=151&pg=735&ac=395&bb=657**.

[2] *The Co-operators Sustainability Report 2007*, **www.cooperators.ca/~/media/Cooperators%20Media/Section%20Media/AboutUs/Sustainability/sustainability-report-2007.ashx**, accessed August 3, 2011, and UM Financial, **www.umfinancial.com**.

Other Sources: "Islamic Banking," *Wikipedia*, **en.wikipedia.org/wiki/Islamic_banking**, accessed August 18, 2008; Tavia Grant, "A Hot New Banking Trend: Sharia-Compliant Finance," *The Globe and Mail*, May 7, 2007, B1.

TOTAL FINANCING OF CANADIAN CORPORATIONS

The pie chart in Figure 2.3 shows the investors in Canadian bonds. Notice the importance of non-residents and institutional investors such as banks, other financial institutions, insurance companies, pension plans, and, to a lesser extent, mutual funds. Individual investors, and non-financial businesses and governments hold smaller slices of the debt pie.

The pie chart in Figure 2.4 shows holdings of shares issued by Canadian corporations. Here, individual investors and non-financial businesses make a much stronger showing, almost 53 percent of the total. Insurance companies, pension funds, mutual funds, banks, and other financial institutions add up to about 36 percent of the total.

The aggregate amounts represented in these figures are enormous. There is $1.90 trillion of debt behind Figure 2.3 and $1.73 trillion of equity behind Figure 2.4—$1,729,014,000,000, to be exact. Chapter 15 reviews corporate financing patterns in more detail.

FIGURE 2.3
Holdings of Canadian bonds and debentures, 2009. Total amount is $1.90 trillion.

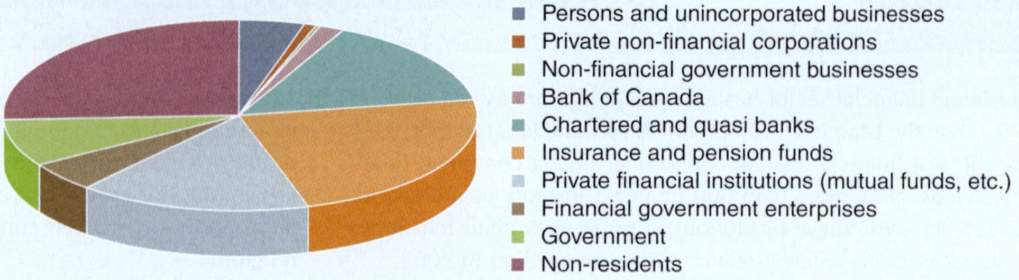

Sources: Statistics Canada, "Other Canadian Bonds," Table 378-0051: "National Balance Sheet Accounts, by Sectors, Annual (Dollars × 1,000,000)," **www.statscan.ca**; Statistics Canada, CANSIM database, Table 378-0081, **cansim2.statcan.ca**.

Notes:

- "Other Canadian Bonds" comprises mainly bonds and debentures issued by Canadian corporations.
- "National Balance Sheet": the bonds category has been pulled from each category.
- *Investment dealers* include investment dealers, issuers of asset-backed securities, and sales, finance, and consumer loan companies.
- *Insurance companies* include life, accident, and property and casualty insurance companies.
- *Banks* include chartered banks and near-banks, which comprise Québec saving banks, credit unions, and caisses populaires; trust companies; mortgage loan companies; and sales, finance, and consumer loan companies.
- *Non-financial business enterprises* include non-financial private corporations and non-financial government business enterprises.
- *Mutual funds etc.* includes mutual funds and segregated funds offered by life insurance companies.
- *Other financial institutions* includes investment dealers and issuers of asset-backed securities.

FIGURE 2.4
Holdings of Canadian corporate equities, 2009. Total amount is $1.73 trillion.

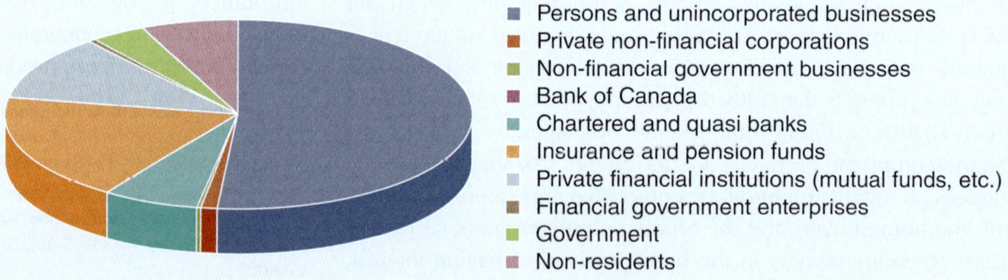

Sources: Statistics Canada, "Shares," Table 378-0051: "National Balance Sheet Accounts, by Sectors, Annual (Dollars × 1,000,000)," **www.statscan.ca**; Statistics Canada, CANSIM database, Table 378-0081, **cansim2.statcan.ca**.

Notes:

- "Shares" includes common and preferred shares in addition to some other items such as contributed surplus and mutual fund shares.
- *Investment dealers* include investment dealers, issuers of asset-backed securities, and sales, finance, and consumer loan companies.
- *Insurance companies* include life, accident, and property and casualty insurance companies.
- *Banks* include chartered banks and near-banks, which comprise Québec saving banks, credit unions, and caisses populaires; trust companies; mortgage loan companies; and sales, finance, and consumer loan companies.
- *Non-financial business enterprises* include non-financial private corporations and non-financial government business enterprises.
- *Mutual funds etc.* includes mutual funds and segregated funds offered by life insurance companies.
- *Other financial institutions* includes investment dealers and issuers of asset-backed securities.

LO3 2.3 FUNCTIONS OF FINANCIAL MARKETS AND INTERMEDIARIES

Financial markets and intermediaries provide financing for business. They channel savings to real investment. That much should be clear from the first section of this chapter. But there are other functions that may not be quite so obvious and we'll enumerate them.

TRANSPORTING CASH ACROSS TIME

Individuals need to transport expenditures in time. If you have money now that you wish to save for a rainy day, you can (for example) put the money in a savings account at a bank and withdraw it with interest later. If you don't have money today, say to buy a car, you can borrow money from the bank and pay off the loan later. Modern finance provides a kind of time machine. Lenders transport money forward in time, borrowers transport it back. Both are happier than if they were forced to spend income as it arrives. Of course, individuals are not alone in needing to raise cash from time to time. Firms with good investment opportunities, but a shortage of internally generated cash, raise cash by borrowing or selling new shares. Many governments run deficits and finance current outlays by issuing debt.

Young people saving for retirement may transport their current earnings 30 or 40 years into the future by means of a pension fund. They may even transport income to their heirs by purchase of a life insurance policy.

In principle, individuals or firms with cash surpluses could take out newspaper advertisements or surf the Internet looking for counterparties with cash shortages. But it is usually cheaper and more convenient to use financial markets and intermediaries. It is not just a matter of avoiding the cost of searching for the right counterparty. Follow-up is needed. For example, banks don't just loan money and walk away. They monitor the borrower to make sure that the loan is used for its intended purpose and that the borrower's credit stays solid.

RISK TRANSFER AND DIVERSIFICATION

Financial markets and intermediaries allow investors and businesses to reduce and reallocate risk. Insurance companies are an obvious example. When you buy homeowner's insurance, you greatly reduce the risk of loss from fire, theft, or accidents. But your policy is not a risky bet for the insurance company. It diversifies by issuing thousands of policies, and it expects losses to average out over the policies.[11] The insurance company allows you to pool risk with thousands of other homeowners.

Investors should diversify too. For example, you can buy units of a mutual fund or units of an exchange-traded fund that hold hundreds of stocks. In fact, you can buy index funds that invest in all the stocks in the popular market indexes.[12] Various mutual funds and ETFs hold the stocks of the Standard & Poor's Composite stock market index, the S&P 500, which tracks the performance of the largest U.S. stocks. Similarly, mutual funds and ETFs seek to approximate the performance of the S&P/TSX Composite Index. This index includes the largest and most liquid companies listed on the TSX. For example, the CIBC Canadian Index Fund (a mutual fund) and iShares S&P/TSX Capped Composite Index Fund (an ETF) both replicate the S&P/TSX Composite. The management expense ratio, MER, of the CIBC fund is 1.09 percent and the iShare fund MER is 0.25 percent. If you buy such index funds, you are insulated from the company-specific risks of the companies in the respective indexes. These risks are averaged out by diversification. Of course, you are still left with the risk that the level of the stock market as a whole will fall. In fact, we will see in Chapter 11 that investors are mostly concerned with market risk, not the specific risks of individual companies.

Financial markets provide other mechanisms for sharing risks. For example, a wheat farmer and a baking company are each exposed to fluctuations in the price of wheat. The farmer worries about low prices, the baker about high prices. They can both rest easier if the baker agrees with the farmer to buy wheat in the future at a fixed price. The farmer and baker would not negotiate the trade face to face, however. They would each trade in commodity markets, the farmer as a seller and the baker as a buyer.

---

[11] Unfortunately for insurance companies, the losses don't always average out. Hurricanes and earthquakes can damage thousands of homes at once. The potential losses are so great that property insurance companies buy reinsurance against such catastrophes.

[12] Index funds don't always own every stock in the index, but they own most of them—enough that the performance of the fund tracks the index almost perfectly.

LIQUIDITY

liquidity The ability to sell or exchange an asset for cash on short notice.

Markets and intermediaries also provide **liquidity**, that is, the ability to turn an investment back into cash when needed. Suppose you deposit $5,000 in a savings bank on February 1. During that month, the bank uses your deposit and other new deposits to make a six-month construction loan to a real estate developer. On March 1, you realize that you need your $5,000 back. The bank can give it to you. Because the bank has thousands of depositors, and other sources of financing if necessary, it can make illiquid loans financed by liquid deposits. If you lend out your money for six months directly to a real estate developer, you will have a hard time retrieving it one month later.

The shares of public companies are liquid because they are traded more or less continuously in the stock market. An Italian investor who puts $60,000 into Royal Bank of Canada shares can recover that money on short notice. (A $60,000 sell order is a drop in the bucket, compared with the normal trading volume of Royal Bank of Canada shares.) Mutual funds can redeem their shares for cash on short notice because the funds invest in traded securities, which can be sold as necessary.

Of course, liquidity is a matter of degree. Foreign-exchange markets for major currencies are exceptionally liquid. Royal Bank of Canada or Deutsche Bank could buy $200 million worth of yen or euros in the blink of an eye, with hardly any affect on foreign exchange rates. Government securities are also very liquid, and the shares of the largest companies on the major international stock exchanges only slightly less so.

Liquidity is most important when you're in a hurry. If you try to sell $500,000 worth of the shares of a small, thinly traded public company all at once, you will probably knock down the price to some extent. If you're patient and don't surprise other investors with a large, sudden sell order, you might be able to unload your shares on better terms. It's the same problem you will face in selling real estate. A house or condominium is not a liquid asset in a panic sale. If you're determined to sell in an afternoon, you won't get full value.

THE PAYMENT MECHANISM

Think how inconvenient life would be if you had to pay for every purchase in cash or if General Motors of Canada had to ship truckloads of hundred-dollar bills round the country to pay its suppliers. Chequing accounts, credit cards, and electronic transfers allow individuals and firms to send and receive payments quickly and safely over long distances. Banks are the obvious providers of payment services, but they are not alone. For example, if you buy shares in a money market mutual fund, your money is pooled with that of other investors and used to buy safe, short-term securities. You can then write cheques on this mutual fund investment, just as if you had a bank deposit.

INFORMATION PROVIDED BY FINANCIAL MARKETS

In well-functioning financial markets, you can see what securities and commodities are worth, and you can see—or at least estimate—the rates of return that investors can expect on their savings. The information provided by financial markets is often essential to a financial manager's job. Here are three examples of how this information can be used.

Commodity Prices Catalytic converters are used in the exhaust systems of cars and light trucks to reduce pollution. The catalysts include platinum, which is traded on the New York Mercantile Exchange, NYMEX.

In July a manufacturer of catalytic converters is planning production for the following January. How much per ounce should the company budget for purchases of platinum in that month? Easy: the company's CFO looks up the market price of platinum on the NYMEX—$1,532 per ounce (1 ounce = 28.35 grams) for delivery in January. (This was the closing price for platinum on July 9, 2010, for delivery in January, 2011.) The CFO can lock in that price if she wishes. The details of such a trade are covered in Chapter 26.

TABLE 2.2
Interest rates on 10-year Canadian corporate bonds, July 31, 2008. The interest rate is lowest for highest-quality issuers. The rate rises as credit quality rating declines.

Credit Rating	Interest Rate (%)
AA-rated	4.78
A-rated	5.16
BBB-rated	6.22

Source: "Fair Market Value Yield Curve" data, from Bloomberg, **www.bloomberg.com**.

Interest Rates The CFO of Catalytic Concepts has to raise $400 million in new financing. She considers an issue of 10-year bonds. What will the interest rate on the bonds be? To find out, the CFO looks up the average interest rates on existing Canadian bonds traded in financial markets, as reported by Bloomberg, a company that specializes in financial analysis.

The results are shown in Table 2.2.[13] Notice how the interest rate climbs as credit quality deteriorates: companies with AA-rated bonds ("double-A"), which are the second-safest after AAA ("triple-A") corporate bonds, can borrow for 10 years at a 4.78 percent interest rate. The interest rates for A- and BBB-rated bonds climb from 5.16 percent to 6.22 percent, respectively. Triple-B companies are still regarded as investment-grade, that is, good quality, but the next step down takes the investor into junk-bond territory. Although Canadian junk bonds exist, there are not enough bonds with BB, B, or CCC ratings for Bloomberg to be willing to report an average.

There will be more on bond ratings and interest rates in Chapter 6. But you can see how a financial manager can use information from fixed-income markets to forecast the interest rate on new debt financing. For example, if Catalytic Concepts can qualify as a BBB-rated company, and interest rates are as shown in Table 2.2, it should be able to raise new debt financing for approximately 6.2 percent.

Company and Stock Values How much was the Bank of Montreal's stock worth on July 12, 2010? How about Telus, BCE Inc., TransCanada, Loblaw, or Research In Motion? Table 2.3 shows the answers. We simply multiplied the number of shares outstanding by the price per share in the stock market. Investors valued the Bank of Montreal at about $33.5 billion, TransCanada at roughly $25.3 billion. To value the entire company, or the enterprise value, add the value of the company's debt to its stock value.

Stock prices and company values summarize investors' collective assessment of how well a company is doing, both its current performance and its future prospects. Thus an increase in stock price sends a positive signal from investors to managers.[14] That is why top management's compensation is linked to stock prices. A manager who owns shares in his company will be

TABLE 2.3
Calculating the total market values of the stock of Bank of Montreal and other companies. Stock prices are as of July 12, 2010, shares and market values in millions.

Company	Stock Price ×	Number of Shares =	Market Value
Bank of Montreal (BMO)	$60.17	557.79	$33,561.96
Telus Corp. (T.TO)	$41.15	316.29	$13,015.44
BCE Inc. (BCE)	$31.51	761.29	$23,714.04
TransCanada (TRP)	$36.60	692.07	$25,329.69
Loblaw (L)	$39.80	277.44	$11,042.01
Research In Motion (RIM)	$55.83	545.07	$30,431.10

Source: Globe Investors, **www.globeinvestor.com**, accessed July 12, 2010.

[13] Bloomberg does not report an interest rate for Canadian AAA-rated bonds, the bonds of the largest, safest companies, because there are too few AAA-rated Canadian companies to be able to create a reliable average.

[14] We can't claim that investors' assessments of value are always correct. Finance can be a dangerous business—dangerous for your wealth, that is. In hindsight we see horrible mistakes by investors, most recently the gross overvaluation of Internet and telecom companies. On average, however, it appears that financial markets collect and assess information quickly and accurately. We'll discuss this issue again in Chapter 7.

motivated to increase the company's market value. This reduces agency costs by aligning the interests of managers and stockholders.

This is one important advantage of going public. A private company can't use its stock price as a measure of performance. It can still compensate managers with shares, but the shares will not be valued in a financial market.

Check Point 2.4

Which of the functions described in this section require financial markets? Explain briefly.

LO4 2.4 VALUE MAXIMIZATION AND THE COST OF CAPITAL

In Chapter 1 we stated the financial objective of the firm: maximize the current market value of shareholders' investment. This simple, unqualified goal makes sense when the shareholders have access to well-functioning financial markets and institutions. Access allows them to share risks and transport savings across time. Access gives them the flexibility to manage their own savings and investment plans, leaving the corporation's financial managers with only one task, to increase market value.

A corporation's roster of shareholders will usually include both risk-averse and risk-tolerant investors. You might expect the risk-averse to say, "Sure, maximize value, but don't touch too many high-risk projects." Instead, they say, "Risky projects are OK, provided that expected profits are more than enough to offset the risks. If this firm ends up too risky for my taste, I'll adjust my investment portfolio to make it safer." For example, the risk-averse shareholder can shift more of his or her portfolio to safe assets, such as Canadian government bonds. The shareholder can also just say goodbye, selling off shares of the risky firm and buying shares in a safer one. If the risky investments increase market value, the departing shareholder is better off than he or she would be if the risky investments were turned down.

VALUE MAXIMIZATION

Fast-Track Wireless shares trade for \$20. The company invests \$3 per share in a high-risk, but potentially revolutionary, WhyFi technology. Investors note the risk of failure but are even more impressed with the technology's upside. They conclude that the possibility of very high future profits is worth \$6 per share. The net value added is \$6 − 3 = +\$3, and the share price increases from \$20 to \$23.

Caspar Milquetoast, a thoughtful but timid shareholder, notes the downside risks and decides that it's time for a change. He sells out to more risk-tolerant investors. But he sells at \$23 per share, not \$20. Thus he captures the value added by the WhyFi project without having to bear the project's risks. The risks are transferred to other investors. In a well-functioning stock market, there is always a pool of investors ready to bear downside risks if the upside potential is sufficiently attractive. We know that the upside potential was sufficient in this case, because Fast-Track stock attracted investors willing to pay \$23 per share.

The same principles apply to the timing of a corporation's cash flows, as the following Check Point illustrates.

Check Point 2.5

Rhonda and Reggie Hotspur are working hard to save for their children's university educations. They don't need more cash for current consumption but will face big tuition bills in 2020. Should they therefore avoid investing in stocks that pay generous current cash dividends? Explain briefly.

THE OPPORTUNITY COST OF CAPITAL

cost of capital Minimum acceptable rate of return on capital investment.

Financial managers look to financial markets to measure, or at least estimate, the cost of capital for the firm's investment projects. The **cost of capital** is the minimum acceptable rate of return for capital investments. Investment projects offering rates of return higher than the cost of capital add value to the firm. Projects offering rates of return less than the cost of capital actually subtract value and should not be undertaken.[15]

Let's think again about the value added by risky corporate investments, for example, Fast-Track's WhyFi project. That project increased Fast-Track's overall market value and the price of each of its shares. The project was worth more than it cost because it offered a superior rate of return, even after accounting for the risks of failure.

What does "superior rate of return" mean? It means an expected rate of return higher than the return investors might achieve from alternative investments at the same level of risk. For example, suppose that the WhyFi project is just as risky as the shares of other high-tech growth companies, and that the expected return on those companies' shares is 15 percent. If the WhyFi project offers a 20 percent expected return, the project adds value. If the project offered only 10 percent, investing in it would destroy value, because the project return would be less than the 15 percent return that shareholders could obtain by investing on their own.

When the financial manager invests at a superior rate of return, stockholders applaud and stock price increases. If the financial manager invests at an inferior rate, shareholders boo, stock price falls, and shareholders want their money back so that they can invest on their own.

You can see why the rates of return on investments outside the corporation set the minimum return for investment projects inside the corporation. In other words, the expected rates of return on investments in financial markets determine the cost of capital for corporate investments.

The cost of capital for corporate investment is set by the rates of return on investment opportunities in financial markets.

Figure 2.5 summarizes this trade-off. The firm can invest, or it can pay out cash to shareholders. Shareholders can invest for themselves in financial markets. Capital investments by the firm should therefore offer rates of return at least as high as those available in financial markets at the same level of risk. If they do not, the firm should not invest.

You can see why financial managers refer to the opportunity cost of capital. When the firm invests, shareholders lose the opportunity to invest in financial markets.

For safe investments, you can observe the opportunity cost of capital by looking up current interest rates on safe debt securities. For risky investments, the opportunity cost of capital has to be estimated. That is one of the harder tasks in financial management. We will return to this task in Chapter 8 and in several later chapters.

FIGURE 2.5
The firm can either keep and reinvest cash or return it to investors. (Arrows represent possible cash flows or transfers.) If cash is reinvested, the opportunity cost is the expected rate of return that shareholders could have obtained by investing in financial assets.

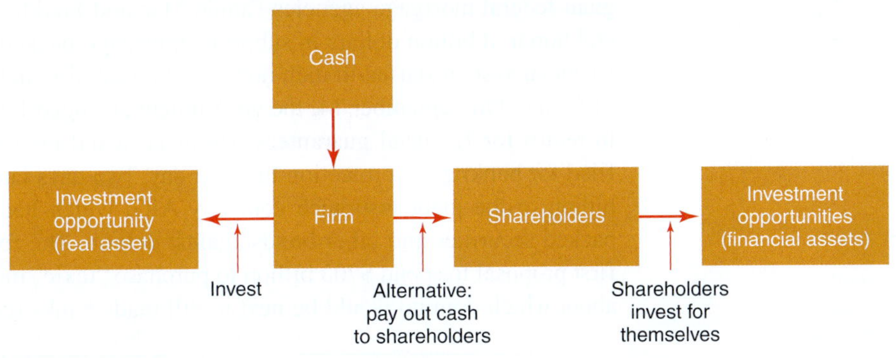

[15] Of course, there are exceptions when the company invests for other reasons. Think of an investment in pollution control equipment for a factory. The equipment may not generate significant cash returns, so the rate of return on investment may be negative. But firms still invest in pollution control, not to earn direct profits, but to meet legal and ethical obligations.

Notice that the opportunity cost of capital is generally not the interest rate that the firm pays on a loan from a bank or insurance company. If the company is making a risky investment, the opportunity cost is the expected return that investors can achieve in financial markets at the same level of risk. The expected return on risky securities will normally be well above the interest rate on corporate borrowing.

Check Point 2.6

Investing $100,000 in additional raw materials today—mostly in palladium—should allow Cryogenic Concepts to increase production and earn an additional $112,000 next year. This payoff would cover the investment today, plus a 12 percent return. Palladium is traded in commodity markets. The CFO has studied the history of returns on investments in palladium and believes that investors in that precious metal can reasonably expect a 15 percent return. Is Cryogenic's investment in palladium a good idea? Why or why not?

2.5 THE CRISIS OF 2007–2009

The financial crisis of 2007–2009 raised many questions, but it settled one question conclusively: Yes, *financial markets and institutions are important*. When financial markets and institutions ceased to operate properly, the world was pushed into a global recession.

The financial crisis had its roots in the easy-money policies that were pursued by the U.S. Federal Reserve and other central banks following the collapse of the Internet and telecom stock bubble in 2000. At the same time, large balance-of-payments surpluses in Asian economies were invested back into U.S. debt securities. This also helped to push down interest rates and contribute to the lax credit. Banks took advantage of this cheap money to expand the supply of *subprime mortgages* to low-income borrowers. Many banks tempted would-be homeowners with low initial payments, offset by significantly higher payments later.[16] (Some home buyers were betting on escalating housing prices so that they could resell or refinance before the higher payments kicked in.) One lender is even said to have advertised what it dubbed its "NINJA" loan—*NINJA* standing for "no income, no job, and no assets." Most subprime mortgages were then packaged together into *mortgage-backed securities* that could be resold. But, instead of selling these securities to investors who could best bear the risk, many banks kept large quantities of the loans on their own books or sold them to other banks.

The crisis peaked in September 2008, when the U.S. government was obliged to take over the giant federal mortgage agencies Fannie Mae and Freddie Mac, both of which had invested several hundred billion dollars in subprime mortgage-backed securities. Over the next few days the financial system started to melt down. Both Merrill Lynch and Lehman Brothers were in danger of failing. On September 14, the government arranged for Bank of America to take over Merrill in return for financial guarantees. However, it did nothing to rescue Lehman Brothers, which filed for bankruptcy protection the next day. Two days later the government reluctantly lent $85 billion to the giant insurance company AIG, which had insured huge volumes of mortgage-backed securities and other bonds against default. The following day, the Treasury unveiled its first proposal to spend $700 billion to purchase "toxic" mortgage-backed securities. Uncertainty about which domino would be next to fall made banks reluctant to lend to one another, and the

[16] With a so-called *option ARM loan*, the minimum mortgage payment was often not even sufficient to cover that month's interest on the loan. The unpaid interest was then added to the amount of the mortgage, so the homeowner was burdened by an ever-increasing mortgage that one day would need to be paid off. The widespread availability of mortgage finance fuelled a dramatic increase in house prices, which doubled in the five years ending June 2006. At that point prices started to slide, and homeowners began to default on their mortgages. A year later Bear Stearns, a large investment bank, announced huge losses on the mortgage investments that were held in two of its hedge funds. By the spring of 2008 Bear Stearns was on the verge of bankruptcy, and the U.S. Federal Reserve arranged for it to be acquired by JPMorgan Chase.

interest rate that they charged for such loans rose to 4.6 percent above the rate on U.S. Treasury debt. (Normally this spread above Treasuries is less than .5 percent.) This had an immediate knock-on effect on the supply of credit to industry, and the economy suffered one of its worst setbacks since the Great Depression. Unemployment rose rapidly, and business bankruptcies tripled.

Few developed economies escaped the crisis. As well as suffering from a collapse in their own housing markets, many foreign banks had made large investments in U.S. subprime mortgages. A roll call of all the banks that had to be bailed out by their governments would fill several pages, but here are just a few members of that unhappy band: the Royal Bank of Scotland in the United Kingdom, UBS in Switzerland, Allied Irish Bank in Ireland, Fortis in Belgium, ING in Holland, Hypo Group in Austria, and West Lb in Germany.

Who was responsible for the financial crisis? In part, the U.S. Federal Reserve, for its policy of easy money. The U.S. government also must take some of the blame for encouraging banks to expand credit for low-income housing. The rating agencies were at fault for providing triple-A ratings for many mortgage bonds that shortly afterward went into default. Last but not least, the bankers themselves were guilty of promoting and reselling the subprime mortgages. As we suggested in the last chapter, managers were probably aware that a strategy of originating massive amounts of subprime debt was likely to end badly. Perhaps they were trying to squeeze in one more fat bonus before the game ended. That is why we described the mess as largely an *agency* problem—a failure to incentivize managers to act in shareholders' interests. The banking crisis and subsequent recession left many governments with huge mountains of debt. By 2010 investors were becoming increasingly concerned about the position of Greece, where for many years government spending had been running well ahead of revenues. Greece's position was complicated by its membership in the single-currency euro club. Although much of the country's borrowing was in euros, the government had no control over its currency and could not simply print more euros to service its debt. Investors began to contemplate the possibility of a Greek government default and became increasingly reluctant to lend to the country. Greece is still afloat, thanks partly to a rescue package from the International Monetary Fund, the European Commission, and the European Central Bank. Attention has shifted to Ireland, where in the midst of a brutal recession, the government put up 34 billion euros to take over the Anglo Irish bank. We will discuss the crisis more in Chapters 14 and 24.

2.6 SUMMARY

1. **Where does the financing for corporations come from?** LO1

   The ultimate source of financing is individuals' savings. The savings flow through **financial markets** and **intermediaries**. The intermediaries include mutual funds, exchange-traded funds, pension funds, and financial institutions, such as banks and insurance companies.

2. **Why do non-financial corporations need financial markets and institutions?** LO1

   Corporations need access to financing in order to innovate and grow. The financial system offers different types of financing, depending on the corporation's age and the nature of its business. A high-tech startup will seek venture capital financing, for example. A mature firm will rely more on bond markets.

3. **What if a corporation finances investment by retaining and reinvesting cash generated from its operations?** LO1

In that case the corporation is saving on behalf of its shareholders. Although shareholders will receive smaller dividends now, reinvestment of their funds may help generate more wealth and provide higher future returns.

4. **What are the key advantages of mutual funds, exchange-traded funds, and pension funds?** LO2

   Mutual funds, **exchange-traded funds**, and **pension funds** allow investors to diversify in professionally managed portfolios. Pension funds offer an additional tax advantage, because the returns on pension investments are not taxed until withdrawn from the plan.

5. **What are the functions of financial markets?** LO3

   Financial markets help channel savings to corporate investment, and they help match up borrowers and lenders. They provide **liquidity** and diversification opportunities for investors. Trading in financial markets provides a wealth of useful information for the financial manager.

6. **Do financial institutions have different functions?** LO3

   Financial institutions carry out a number of similar functions but in different ways. They channel savings to corporate investment, and they serve as intermediaries between borrowers and lenders. Banks also provide liquidity for depositors and, of course, play a special role in the economy's payments systems. Insurance companies allow policyholders to pool risks.

7. **How does the financial manager identify the cost of the capital raised by a corporation?** LO4

   The **cost of capital** is the minimum acceptable rate of return on capital investment. It's an opportunity cost, that is, a rate of return that investors could earn in financial markets. For a safe capital investment, the opportunity cost is the interest rate on safe debt securities, such as high-grade corporate bonds. For riskier capital investments, the opportunity cost is the expected rate of return on risky securities, investments in the stock market, for example.

8. **What happens when financial markets and institutions no longer function well?** LO3

   The financial crisis of 2007–2009 provided a dramatic illustration. The huge expansion in subprime mortgage lending in the United States led to a collapse of the banking system. The government was forced into a costly bailout of banks and other financial institutions. As the credit markets seized up, the country suffered a deep recession.

Related Web Links

tsx.com The TSX Group, which includes the Toronto Stock Exchange and the TSX Venture Exchange

cnsx.ca The CNSX Stock Exchange

nyse.com The New York Stock Exchange

nasdaq.com.ca The Nasdaq stock market

world-stock-exchanges.net Links to exchanges around the world

globefund.com Information on Canadian mutual funds and ETFs, including performance data

cba.ca The Canadian Bankers' Association; contains information on Canada's banking industry

ific.ca The Investment Funds Institute of Canada; contains information on Canada's mutual fund industry

etf.stock-encyclopedia.com Information on exchange-traded funds around the world

insurance-canada.ca Provides consumers and industry professionals with information on insurance in Canada

standardandpoors.com Web site of Standard & Poor's, a leading international provider of independent credit ratings and indexes, risk evaluation, investment research, data, and valuations

otpp.com Web site of Ontario Teachers' Pension Plan, which invests and administers the pensions of Ontario teachers

cdp.ca Web site of Caisse de dépôt et placement du Québec, a leading institutional and pension fund manager

Key Terms

capital market	39	financial market	37	mutual fund	40
cost of capital	51	fixed-income market	39	pension fund	42
exchange-traded fund	41	hedge fund	41	primary market	37
financial institution	43	liquidity	48	private equity fund	42
financial intermediary	39	money market	39	secondary market	37

Questions and Problems

connect Practise and learn online with *Connect*. Questions with online Excel templates or datasets are marked with .

*Answers in Appendix B

BASIC

1. **Corporate Financing.** How can a small, private firm finance its capital investments? Give a couple of examples. (LO1)
2. **Corporate Financing.** Is it possible for an individual to save and invest in a corporation without lending money to it or purchasing additional shares? Explain. (LO1)

*3. **Financial Markets.** The stock and bond markets are not the only financial markets. Give two or three additional examples. (LO1)

*4. **Financial Intermediaries.** You are a beginning investor with only $5,000 in savings. How can you achieve a widely diversified portfolio at reasonable cost? (LO2)

5. **Financial Intermediaries.** What are the key advantages of a defined contribution pension plan as a vehicle for retirement savings? (LO2)
6. **Financial Intermediaries.** Is an insurance company also a financial intermediary? How does the insurance company channel savings to corporate investment? (LO2)
7. **Corporate Financing.** What are the largest institutional investors in bonds? In shares? (LO2)

*8. **Financial Markets.** You discover a six-ounce gold nugget. A friend offers to pay you $2,500 for it. How do you check whether this is a fair price? (LO3)

9. **Financial Markets.** What kinds of useful information can a financial manager obtain from financial markets? Give examples. (LO3)
10. **Cost of Capital.** Why do financial managers refer to the opportunity cost of capital? How would you find the opportunity cost of capital for a safe investment? (LO4)
11. **Value Maximization.** The objective of value maximization makes sense when shareholders have access to financial markets and institutions. Briefly explain why. (LO4)

INTERMEDIATE

12. True or false? (LO1)
    a. Financing for public corporations must flow through financial markets.
    b. Financing for private corporations must flow through financial intermediaries.
    c. The sale of policies is a source of financing for insurance companies.
    d. Almost all foreign-exchange trading occurs on the floors of the FOREX exchanges in New York and London.
    e. The opportunity cost of capital is the capital outlay required to undertake a real investment opportunity.
    f. The cost of capital is the interest rate paid on borrowing from a bank or other financial institution.
13. **Liquidity.** Securities traded in active financial markets are liquid assets. Explain why liquidity is important to individual investors and to mutual funds. (LO2)
14. **Liquidity.** Bank deposits are liquid; you can withdraw money on demand. How can the bank provide this liquidity and at the same time make illiquid loans to businesses? (LO2)
15. **Corporate Financing.** Financial markets and intermediaries channel savings from investors to corporate investments. The savings make this journey by many different routes. Give a specific example for each of the following routes: (LO1)
    a. Investor to financial intermediary, to financial markets, and to the corporation.
    b. Investor to financial markets, to a financial intermediary, and to the corporation.
    c. Investor to financial markets, to a financial intermediary, back to financial markets, and to the corporation.
16. **Mutual Funds.** Why are mutual funds and exchange-traded funds called financial intermediaries? Why does it make sense for an individual to invest her savings in a mutual fund or ETF rather than directly in individual stocks and bonds? (LO2)
17. **Value Maximization.** Fritz is risk-averse and content with a relatively low but safe return on his investments. Frieda is risk-tolerant and seeks a very high rate of return on her invested savings. Yet both shareholders will applaud a low-risk capital investment that offers a superior rate of return. Why? What is meant by "superior"? (LO4)
18. **Cost of Capital.** In a stroke of good luck, your company has uncovered an opportunity to invest for 10 years at a guaranteed 8 percent rate of return. What is the opportunity cost of capital? Assume interest rates as in Table 2.2. (LO4)

*19. **Cost of Capital.** Pollution Busters, Inc., is considering a purchase of 10 additional carbon sequesters for

$100,000 apiece. The sequesters last for only one year until saturated with carbon. Then the carbon is removed and sold. (LO4)

a. Suppose the government guarantees the price of carbon. At this price, the payoff after 1 year is guaranteed to be $115,000. How would you determine the opportunity cost of capital for this investment?

b. Suppose instead that the sequestered carbon has to be sold on the London Carbon Exchange. Carbon prices have been extremely volatile, but Pollution Busters' CFO learns that average rates of return from investment on that exchange have been about 20 percent. She thinks this is a reasonable forecast for the future. What is the opportunity cost of capital in this case? Is the purchase of an additional sequester a worthwhile capital investment if she expects that the price of extracted carbon will be $115,000?

20. **Financial Institutions.** We mentioned banks and insurance companies as two examples of financial institutions. What other types of financial institutions can you identify? (LO2)

21. **Internet.** Barclays Canada provides many of the exchange-traded funds listed on the TSX. Go to **www.ishares.ca** and explore three different ETFs. The list is found on the left side of the home page. For each ETF, find out the name of the market index that the ETF is replicating. Note the EFT's top five holdings, past returns, and fund fees. (LO2)

22. **Internet.** Go to **www.globefund.com**, find "Research a Fund" on the right. Next, click on "Fund Company" under "Look Up By" on the left. Select a fund company, then pick three funds operated by the fund company and get the fund profiles for each. Note the funds' investment objectives, top five holdings, risks, past returns, and fund fees. Note the name of the index chosen as the benchmark for measuring the funds' performances. (LO2)

23. **Internet.** We mentioned in Chapter 1 that large banks have their fingers in many pies. The Web sites of the very largest banks are equally massive. The Royal Bank of Canada (**www.royalbank.com**) and Scotiabank (**www.scotiabank.com**) are examples of two of Canada's largest banks with relatively straightforward Web sites. Use these sites to find what services banks provide to individuals, small businesses, and large corporations. (LO2, LO3, LO4)

CHALLENGE

24. **Internet.** Go to **www.globefund.com**, find "Fund Filter" under "Inside Funds" in the middle of the page. Select an asset class that interests you. For example, under the "Aggressive Growth" category, pick "Science and Technology," and click on "Get Results." Click on each of the tabs across the page and see what information is provided for the mutual funds. (LO3)

25. **Internet.** Using the Fund Filter from question 24, find a mutual fund offering a similar investment objective for each of the ETFs you found in question 21. Compare the top five holdings, risks, past returns, and fund fees. Note the name of the index chosen as the benchmark for measuring the mutual fund's performances. (LO3)

26. **Financial Markets.** In most years, new issues of stock are a tiny fraction of total stock market trading. In other words, secondary market volume is much greater than primary market volume. Does the fact that firms only occasionally sell new shares mean that the stock market is largely irrelevant to the financial manager? (LO2, LO3)

Solutions to Check Points

2.1 a. Corporations sell securities in the primary market. The securities are later traded in the secondary market.

b. The first public offering of shares by a corporation is its initial public offer. Any public offering of shares after that is a seasoned equity offer.

c. The capital market is for long-term financing, the money market for short-term financing.

d. The market for stocks versus the market for bonds and other debt securities.

2.2 Efficient diversification and professional management. Pension funds offer an additional advantage, because investment returns are not taxed until withdrawn from the fund.

2.3 Mutual funds are financial intermediaries that pool and invest money raised from investors in portfolios of securities. Banks and insurance companies are financial institutions that do more than just pool and invest savings. These financial institutions raise money in special ways, such as by accepting deposits or selling insurance policies. They not only invest in securities but also lend directly to businesses. They provide various other financial services as well.

2.4 Liquidity, risk reduction by investment in diversified portfolios of securities (through a mutual fund, for example), information provided by trading.

2.5 Rhonda and Reggie need not avoid high-dividend stocks. They can reinvest the dividends and keep reinvesting until it's time to pay the tuition bills. (They will have to pay taxes on the dividends, however, which could affect their investment strategy. We discuss dividends and taxes in Chapter 18.)

2.6 It is not a good investment if the opportunity cost of capital is 15 percent. The investment offers only a 12 percent return.

PART 1 Introduction

1 Goals and Governance of the Firm
2 Financial Markets and Institutions
3 Accounting and Finance
3.1 The Statement of Financial Position or Balance Sheet
3.2 The Income Statement and Statement of Comprehensive Income
3.3 The Statement of Cash Flows
3.4 Cash Flow from Assets, Financing Flow, and Free Cash Flow
3.5 Accounting Practice and Accounting Malpractice
3.6 Taxes
3.7 Summary
4 Measuring Corporate Performance

CHAPTER 3

Accounting and Finance

LEARNING OBJECTIVES

After studying this chapter, you should be able to:

LO1 Describe the information contained in the statement of financial position (balance sheet), the income statement and the statement of comprehensive income, the statement of changes in equity, and the statement of cash flows, using the various names given to standard items on various financial statements.

LO2 Distinguish between market and book values.

LO3 Explain why accounting income differs from cash flow.

LO4 Use the statement of cash flow to calculate cash flow from assets, financing flow, and free cash flow.

LO5 Outline the essential features of the taxation of corporate and personal income.

Accounting is not the same as finance, but if you don't understand the basics of accounting, you won't understand finance either.

© Tom Grill/Corbis.

In Chapter 1 we pointed out that a large corporation is a team effort. All the players—the shareholders, lenders, directors, management, and employees—have a stake in the company's success and all therefore need to monitor its progress. For this reason the company prepares regular financial accounts and arranges for an independent firm of auditors to certify that these accounts present a "true and fair view."

Until the mid-19th century most businesses were owner-managed and seldom required outside capital beyond personal loans to the proprietor. When businesses were small and there were few outside stakeholders in the firm, accounting could be less formal. But with the Industrial Revolution and the creation of large railroad and canal companies, shareholders and bankers demanded information that would help them gauge a firm's financial strength. That was when the accounting profession began to come of age.

Although this is not an accounting textbook, we will be referring to financial statements throughout this book. Financial statements are an important source of information about companies. In this chapter we introduce the major financial statements: the statement of financial position (balance sheet), the income statement and the statement of comprehensive income, the statement of changes in equity, and the statement of cash flows. We discuss the important differences between income and cash flow and between book values and market values. We also discuss the Canadian tax system.

LO1, 2 3.1 THE STATEMENT OF FINANCIAL POSITION OR BALANCE SHEET

Public companies must publish their financial statements on a regular basis, providing investors with access to information about the companies' financial situation. Companies listed for trading in the U.S. register with the SEC, the Securities and Exchange Commission, and file their statements each quarter (10Q) and annually (10K). United Kingdom companies register and file with the Companies House. Companies listed for trading on Canadian stock exchanges—the Toronto Stock Exchange and the TSX Venture Exchange—file quarterly and annual reports with the Canadian Securities Administrators (CSA), an organization created by Canada's provincial and based on AstraZeneca's December 31, 2010, consolidated statement of financial position, but we have changed the sequence of assets to be similar to that of a typical Canadian SFP or balance sheet.

You can see in Table 3.1 that AZN had US$11,068 million of *cash and cash equivalents*. *Cash* includes money on hand and money immediately accessible in bank accounts. *Cash equivalents* include short-term deposits, which normally mature in three months or less, providing the company with interest income and also high liquidity.[5] Next are *trade and other receivables*, called *accounts receivable* or *receivables* by some companies. Included are *trade receivables* of $6,247 million which is the value of AZN sales of goods and services for which AZN had not received payment from customers by December 31, 2010.[6] These customers are expected to soon pay these invoices/bills so trade receivables (unpaid bills) are an asset. *Other receivables* include receivables not arising from sales and also prepaid expenses, accounting for payments made by AZN for goods or services not yet provided by their suppliers. Prepaid expenses, such as insurance, are assets because suppliers have to deliver the goods or services at some future date. The next asset, *inventories*, includes (1) raw materials and ingredients that the firm bought from suppliers, $539m, (2) work in process, $665m, and (3) finished products waiting to be sold, $478m. *Other investments* of $1,482 million include other short-term investments such as longer-term bank deposits and equity securities being traded. *Derivatives financial instruments*, $9 million, are used to manage the company's foreign currency risk. The last item, *income taxes receivable*, amounting to $3,043 million, represents amount due from governments for income taxes that have been overpaid in the past. All these assets are classified as *current assets*, ones likely to be used up or turned into cash within a year.

The second group of assets are those that will not be turned into cash soon, hence the title *non-current assets*. The first non-current asset category is *property, plant, and equipment* (PP&E), which are tangible assets used in the revenue-producing activities of the company.[7] The book value of AZN's property, plant, and equipment is $6,957 million. The first step in accounting for PP&E is recording the initial cost of acquiring the assets. Then, under IFRS, the company must select one of two methods for measuring the asset value over time: cost method or revaluation method.[8]

The *cost method* results in the asset being carried at its original cost less accumulated depreciation booked to date, less any impairment losses accumulated to date. One of the big changes under IRFS is the option to use *the revaluation method* for valuing property, plant, and equipment. Using this method, every few years the company has to revalue the assets—that is, calculate their **fair value**, what they would be worth if sold to another user. In other words, its market value. The best measure of its fair value would be any existing actual market price for that asset. IFRS provides guidelines for determining the fair value when there is no actual quoted market value. Under the revaluation method, accumulated depreciation and impairment losses are still deducted. You must read the notes of the financial statement to find which method is used to calculate the book value of property, plant, and equipment. The company must use the same method for all assets of the same type.

fair value Estimated market value.

Depreciation is an expense that allocates the cost of the asset over its useful life. Under the cost method, the depreciation is based on the asset's original cost. Under the revaluation method, the depreciation is based on the asset's revalued amounts. To calculate depreciation, the expected number of years of the asset use and its residual value, the expected value when disposed, must be estimated. Residual value could be zero. A commonly used method for calculating depreciation

---

[5] In a company's annual report are "Notes to the Financial Statement" providing details about the various items on financial statements. Cash and cash equivalents note 13 reports that AZN has $1,750 million cash at bank and in hand, $9,318 million in short-term deposits, for a total of $11,068 million. Also, AZN had $87 million in bank overdrafts, indicating cash used that was borrowed through bank accounts. So taking into account that cash will soon be used to get rid of the overdraft gives cash and equivalents of $11,068 − $87 = $10,981 million.

[6] All IFRS users must report trade receivables and typically put it in a note. See note 12 of the AZN annual report.

[7] Sometimes tangible long-term assets, such as property, plant, and equipment, are called *fixed assets*.

[8] In U.S. GAAP and former Canadian GAAP, the historical cost method is similar to the IFRS cost method. The main difference is in how depreciation is calculated.

is the straight-line method. For example, a delivery van was purchased for $30,000, it was expected to be used for 10 years and its estimated residual value was zero. Then the annual depreciation is (acquisition cost − residual value)/estimated useful life in years = ($30,000 − $0)/10 = $3,000. After one year, the book value of the van would be acquisition cost − accumulated depreciation, $30,000 − $3,000 = $27,000. After two years, the book value of the van would be $24,000 (= $30,000 − $3,000 − $3,000), since the accumulated depreciation now totals $6,000. IFRS requires that each year the company review the residual value and the asset's useful life and use any revised numbers in calculating that year's depreciation. AstraZeneca uses this method. Reviews are made each year to estimate the remaining life and residual values of each productive asset, taking into account commercial and technological obsolescence as well as normal wear and tear.

Every year, the company must also assess whether the asset has been impaired. Impairment tests determine if the asset's value has deteriorated below its book value and should be written down. The method is to compare the book value of the asset to its recoverable amount,[9] which is an estimate of its fair value. Let's look at the example of the van used in earlier. At the end of year 2, the van has a book value of $24,000. If it is determined that the van only has a recoverable amount of $20,000, the van would be written down to $20,000 and an impairment loss of $4,000 would be expensed. However, if in a future year it is found that circumstances have changed and the van's value has increased, a portion of this impairment loss may be reversed.

Every year a company purchases any new property, plant, and equipment, making *capital expenditure*, the value of PP&E is initially increased by the purchase cost. Depreciation expense is calculated each year and added to prior's depreciation, and the result is called *accumulated depreciation*. Impairment losses and reversals are also accumulated. AZN uses the cost method and its book value of PP&E is the sum of all asset purchases minus the accumulated depreciation minus accumulated impairment losses and plus any loss reversals. This is also called *net PP&E*.

Check Point 3.1

Note 7 of AZN's annual report shows the purchase cost of all its property, plant, and equipment, $15,583 million, and the accumulated depreciation and impairment, $8,626 million, as of 2010.

a. How do these numbers relate to the 2010 net PP&E in Table 3.1?
b. If the 2011 PP&E capital expenditure was $800 million, and depreciation and impairment expense $1,020 million, what values would be in note 7, and what would the 2011 net PP&E be? Explain the change in net PP&E from 2010 to 2011.
c. If the 2011 net PP&E was $7,000 million, and 2011 depreciation and impairment expense $1,020, what must the PP&E capital expenditure (gross investment) in 2011 have been?

The property, plant, and equipment on AstraZeneca's SFP are all tangible assets, assets with physical presence. *Intangible assets* are long-lived assets that do not have physical substance. AZN's intangible assets, shown as $12,158 million, include patents and licences for drugs bought from other companies and new drugs under development. AZN makes frequent purchases of drug patents from other companies, so it has a large value for intangible assets. Since patents and licences do not last forever, the book value of the intangible assets decreases over their useful economic life. The expense for the use of intangible assets is called *amortization*, which is similar to the depreciation expense for the use of property, plant, and equipment. Intangible assets are also tested annually for impairment. The value of AstraZeneca's intangible assets is their net value, the original cost minus the accumulated amortization minus the accumulated impairment losses (plus reversals).

[9] The recoverable amount is the higher of the asset's value to the company as it is continued to be used, or its fair value on sale less selling costs.

Goodwill is not an identifiable asset. It is generated when a company buys another company. *Goodwill* is the difference between the purchase price of the acquired company and the estimated fair market value of the identifiable net assets acquired (tangible and intangible assets minus the liabilities). Factors that might generate goodwill could include a strong brand name, reputation for quality products, highly skilled workers, and *synergy*, the value created by combining two companies. Goodwill is not depreciated or amortized, because it has an unlimited life. The goodwill must be evaluated each year and is written down if the recoverable value is less than the current book value. In the past, AstraZeneca has purchased other drug companies, paying $9,871 million for goodwill.

The next non-current asset, $221 million of *other investments* are shares of other companies. In other companies, non-current investments might also include derivatives, long-term bank deposits, bonds of other companies, and foreign currency options. Under IFRS, depending on the nature of the investment and management's intent, the investments may be reported at fair value or (amortized) cost. If these assets are available for sale, companies report these financial assets at fair value, their estimated market value. These assets are not needed to operate AstraZeneca's business. They are investments made to use spare cash and are also called *non-operating assets*. If the assets are held for strategic purposes, where the company has 20 percent ownership, these investments would be reported at cost with adjustments for AZN's portion of profits and losses accumulated since the date of purchase. AZN also has long-term derivative assets (discussed earlier) amounting to $324 million.

The final entry on the asset side is *deferred tax assets*, worth $1,475 million. Deferred tax assets are expected future income tax. We will talk about this when we deal with the next financial statement, the company's comprehensive income statement.

As of December 31, 2010, the total assets of AstraZeneca, including all of its subsidiaries, were $25,131 million current assets plus $30,996 million non-current assets, for a total of $56,127 million.

Now look at the right side of AZN's statement of financial position, which shows the obligations of the company and where the money to buy the assets came from. The accountant starts by looking at the company's liabilities—that is, the money owed by the company. Listed first are those liabilities to be paid off within a year, *current liabilities*. Next are the *non-current liabilities*, obligations that come due in more than one year.

The first current liability, *interest-bearing loans and borrowings*, shows the amount of money the company must pay its lenders within the next year and is sometimes called *short-term debt*. Of the $125 million owed by AZN, $87 million is the bank overdraft and $38 million are short-term loans due within the year. The next entry, $8,861 million of *trade and other payables*, also known as *accounts payable*, is made up of trade payables of $2,257 million and other payables of $6,404 million.[10] *Trade payables* are AZN's unpaid bills/invoices for supplies and other services that have been used to produce products. *Other payables* are other items, such as salaries, payroll taxes, rebates, that have been used but haven't yet been paid for and are expected to be paid within the next year. Other payables due in more than one year, $373 million, are in the list of non-current liabilities.

A *provision* is an estimated liability for a probable cost that will arise due to a past action. AZN is undergoing a global restructuring program and has estimated the future costs arising from its commitment to the restructuring. Other provisions relate to environmental obligations, pending lawsuits, and management bonuses. Provisions of $1,095 million that are due within the next year are shown as current, and $843 million of provisions that are due after one year are listed as non-current. *Derivative financial instruments* are used to manage the company's exposure to currency rate changes. The final current liability is *income taxes payable* of $6,898 million, representing income taxes due within the next year.

---

[10] All IFRS users must report trade payables and typically put it in a note. See note 16 of the AZN annual report.

AstraZeneca's current assets total $25,131 million; its current liabilities amount to $16,787 million. Therefore the difference between the value of AZN's current assets and its current liabilities is $25,131 − $16,787 = $8,344 million. This figure is known as AZN's *net current assets* or *net working capital*. It roughly measures the company's potential reservoir of cash.

The first non-current liabilities are $9,097 million of *interest-bearing loans and borrowings*. Financial statement note 17 shows that AZN has issued seven bonds to borrow money in U.S. dollars, euros, and pounds sterling. The bonds have different maturity dates, ranging from 2012 to 2037. When each bond matures, AstraZeneca will have to pay back the money they borrowed. *Deferred tax liabilities* of $3,145 million represent future potential income tax obligations. The *retirement benefit obligations*, $2,472 million, is the estimated deficit in the company's employees' pension plan.[11]

Total non-current liabilities, $15,930 million, plus current liabilities equals $32,717 million and are the total financial obligations of AZN. The suppliers and lenders have first claim on the firm's assets. What is left over after the liabilities have been paid off belongs to the shareholders. This figure is known as the *shareholders' equity* or *total equity*. The book value of AZN's *total equity* is $23,410 million, which equals total assets minus total liabilities, $56,127 − $32,717 million.

Since AZN's accountants are required to prepare a consolidated statement, all of the assets and liabilities of AZN and its subsidiaries are included in the statement of financial position, as if AZN were the 100 percent owner of the equity of its subsidiaries. In the equity section of Table 3.1, the value of equity of subsidiaries not owned by AstraZeneca PLC, the parent company, is shown as the $197 million *non-controlling interest*. The book value of equity owned by the shareholders of AstraZeneca PLC, parent company, is the *total equity attributable to equity holders of the company* and equals total equity minus non-controlling interest, $23,410 million − $197 million = $23,213 million.

The equity of AZN PLC consists of the AZN shares sold to investors and the reinvestment of earnings. *Share capital* plus *share premium account*, $352 million + $2,672 million, shows the value of shares sold to investors. Share capital is the par value of its equity, $.25 per share times the number of outstanding shares. Shares are typically sold for more than their par value, so the share premium account captures the difference between the price the shares were sold for and the par value. Canadian companies do not generally have par value for their equity, so the typical entry for the issued equity is called *share capital*. The next line, *retained earnings and reserves*, is $20,189 million. The retained earnings are the earnings (or profits or net income) that AZN has not paid out as dividends and hence reinvested into the firm on shareholders' behalf. Reserves are part of the firm's earnings that cannot be paid out to shareholders due to legal restrictions and includes accumulated income arising from *other comprehensive income*. Because of the complexity of AZN's equity reserves, we have combined them with retained earnings. Such legal requirements are rare in Canada, so a typical Canadian company does not have equity reserves and reports separately *retained earnings* and *accumulated other comprehensive income (loss)* on its SFP.

In the next section we will look at the statement of comprehensive income, which shows profits from operations and also other comprehensive income. Then we will look at the statement of changes in equity, which shows the connection of profits to equity on the statement of financial position.

Figure 3.1 shows how the separate items in the SFP link together. There are two classes of assets: current assets, which will soon be used or turned into cash, and non-current assets, which may be either tangible or intangible. There are also two classes of liabilities—current liabilities, which are due for payment shortly, and non-current liabilities.

---

[11] A pension plan deficit results when the obligations of the pension payments is more than the pension assets available to fund the payments.

FIGURE 3.1
The main statement of financial position (balance sheet) items.

Assets		Liabilities and equity
Current assets: Cash and cash equivalents Receivables Inventories + Non-current assets: Tangible assets Intangible assets	=	Current liabilities: Short-term debt Payables + Non-current liabilities: Long-term debt Other payables + Shareholders' equity

The difference between the assets and the liabilities represents the amount of the shareholders' equity. This is the basic SFP identity. Shareholders are sometimes called *residual claimants* on the firm. We mean by this that shareholders' equity is what is left over when the liabilities of the firm are subtracted from its assets:

$$\text{Shareholders' equity} = \text{Total assets} - \text{Total liabilities}$$

Check Point 3.2

Suppose that AstraZeneca borrows $500 million by issuing new long-term bonds. It places $100 million of the proceeds in the bank and uses $400 million to buy new machinery. What items of the SFP would change? Would total equity change?

By the way, it is easy to obtain the financial statement of almost any publicly traded company. Most companies make their annual reports available on the Web. The site **www.sedar.com** allows you to access all Canadian public securities' filings, including annual reports. If the company trades on a U.S. stock exchange, you can also likely find key financial statements for it at Yahoo Finance, **finance.yahoo.com**. Also, various stock exchanges, including the Toronto Stock Exchange and the London England Stock Exchange, provide financial statements for listed companies. However, if you don't use the company's annual report, you won't get the notes for financial statements and won't know details about the company's accounting policies.

BOOK VALUES AND MARKET VALUES

Throughout this book we will sometimes make a distinction between the book values of the assets shown in the statement of financial position and the market value of the firm's assets.

As explained earlier in this chapter, the company has choices allowed under IFRS for reporting some of its asset values. We saw that property, plant, and equipment may be reported using the cost method or the revaluation method. If the revaluation method is used, then these assets will be reported close to their market value. We also saw that investments may be reported at fair value or cost, depending on the nature and management's intent for the investments. When cost is used, the book values are "backward-looking" measures of value, based on the past cost of the asset, not its current market price or value to the firm. You have to read the notes attached to the financial statements to know which assets are reported at fair value and which are at cost.

The market values of assets and liabilities might not equal their book values, depending on the accounting rules used. Some book values are based on historical or original values, but others are based on fair value, which is closer to market value. Market values measure current values of assets and liabilities.

The difference between the market values of assets and liabilities is the market value of the shareholders' equity claim. The stock price is simply the market value of shareholders' equity divided by the number of outstanding shares.

The difference between book value and market value is greater for some assets than for others. It is zero in the case of cash but potentially very large for property, plant, and equipment and intangible assets valued using the cost method. The purpose of depreciation is to allocate the original cost of the asset over its useful life, and the rules governing the depreciation of asset values do not reflect actual loss (or gain) of market value. As a result, the book value of assets recognized using the cost approach will not be equal to the asset's market value in many cases.

The same goes for the right-hand side of the SFP. Most IFRS users simply record the amount of money they have promised to pay. For short-term liabilities this figure is generally close to the market value of that promise. For example, if you owe the bank $1 million tomorrow, the accounts show a book liability of $1 million. As long as you are not bankrupt, that $1 million is also roughly the value to the bank of your promise. But now suppose that $1 million is not due to be repaid for several years. The accounts still show a liability of $1 million, but how much your debt is worth depends on what happens to interest rates in the market. If market interest rates rise after you have issued the debt, lenders might not be prepared to pay as much as $1 million for your debt; if interest rates fall, they might be prepared to pay more than $1 million.[12] Thus the market value of a long-term liability might be higher or lower than its book value.

The difference between book value and market value is likely to be greatest for shareholders' equity. The book value of equity measures the cash that the company received on the original issue of shares in the past plus the profits that the company has retained and reinvested in the business on their behalf. But this often bears little resemblance to the total market value that investors place on the shares. One of the reasons for the gap between book value of equity and its market value is the fact that all accounting standards including IFRS dictate which assets can be listed on the statement of financial position. For example, a company cannot include the value of its brand name as an asset, unless it was purchased originally from another company. Some missing assets can be captured on a statement of financial position as "goodwill" only when the company purchases another company. Goodwill, the difference between the purchase price and the fair value of all identifiable assets, reflects the value of assets that cannot be isolated and separately reported on the statement of financial position of the acquired company.

If the market price of the firm's shares falls through the floor, don't try telling the shareholders that the book value is satisfactory—they won't want to hear it. Shareholders are concerned with the market value of their shares; market value, not book value, is the price at which they can sell their shares. Managers who wish to keep their shareholders happy will focus on market values.

We will often find it useful to think about the firm in terms of a *market-value statement of financial position*. Like a conventional SFP, a market-value SFP lists the firm's assets, but it records each asset at its current market value rather than at historical cost less depreciation. Similarly, each liability is shown at its market value.

EXAMPLE 3.1 MARKET-VALUE VERSUS BOOK-VALUE SFP

Jupiter has developed a revolutionary auto production process that enables it to produce cars 20 percent more efficiently than any rival. It has invested $10 billion in building its new plant. To finance the investment, Jupiter borrowed $4 billion and raised the remaining funds by selling shares of stock in the firm. There are currently 100 million shares of stock outstanding. Investors are very excited about Jupiter's prospects. They believe that the flow of profits from the new plant justifies a stock price of $75.

(Continued)

[12] We will show you how changing interest rates affect the market value of debt in Chapter 5.

(Concluded)

If these are Jupiter's only assets, the book-value SFP immediately after it has made the investment is as follows:

Book-Value SFP for Jupiter Motors
($ billions)

Assets		**Liabilities and Shareholders' Equity**	
Auto plant	$10	Debt	$4
		Shareholders' equity	6

Investors are putting a market value on Jupiter's equity of $7.5 billion ($75 per share × 100 million shares). We assume that the debt outstanding is worth $4 billion.[13] Therefore, if you owned all Jupiter's shares and all its debt, the value of your investment would be 7.5 + 4 = $11.5 billion. In this case you would own the company lock, stock, and barrel and would be entitled to all its cash flows. Because you can buy the entire company for $11.5 billion, the total market value of Jupiter's assets must also be $11.5 billion. In other words, the market value of the assets must be equal to the market value of the liabilities plus the market value of the shareholders' equity.

We can now draw up the market-value SFP as follows:

Market Value SFP for Jupiter Motors
($ billions)

Assets		**Liabilities and Shareholders' Equity**	
Auto plant	$11.5	Debt	$ 4
		Shareholders' equity	7.5

Notice that the market value of Jupiter's plant is $1.5 billion more than the plant cost to build. The difference is due to the superior profits that investors expect the plant to earn. Thus in contrast to the company's SFP, the market-value SFP is forward-looking. It depends on the benefits that investors expect the assets to provide.

Is it surprising that market value exceeds book value? It shouldn't be. Firms find it attractive to raise money to invest in various projects because they believe the projects will be worth more than they cost. Otherwise why bother? You will usually find that shares of stock sell for more than the value shown in the company's SFP.

Check Point 3.3

a. What would Jupiter's price per share be if the auto plant had a market value of $14 billion?

b. How would you reassess the value of the auto plant if the value of outstanding stock were $8 billion?

LO1, 3 3.2 THE INCOME STATEMENT AND STATEMENT OF COMPREHENSIVE INCOME

If AstraZeneca's statement of financial position resembles a snapshot of the firm at a particular time, its **statement of comprehensive income (SCI)** is like a video. It shows how much accounting income the firm has generated during the past year. *Comprehensive income* is the sum of two

[13] Jupiter has borrowed $4 billion to finance its investment, but if the interest rate has changed in the meantime, the debt could be worth more or less than $4 billion.

statement of comprehensive income (SCI) Financial statement that shows profits and other comprehensive income of a firm over a period of time. Without an income statement, SCI starts with the profit section, which has the same content as the income statement.

income statement Financial statement that shows the revenues, expenses, and profit or net earnings or net income from operations of a firm over a period of time. The same as the profit section on the SCI.

parts: *profit*, called "net earnings" or "net income" by some firms, and *other comprehensive income (OCI)*. Profit is the accountants' measurement of what the firm earned from its operating activities. Negative profit is called a *loss*. The *profit section* is the biggest part of the statement of comprehensive income and shows the firm's revenues, operating expenses, finance income and expense, and the taxes arising from operating profit, and ends with profit (or net earnings or net income). The other comprehensive income is typically a relatively small amount and captures the change in value of certain assets and liabilities. Sometimes the profit section is reported on a separate statement, called the **income statement**, and then the statement of comprehensive income starts with profit (or net earnings or net income), lists the other comprehensive income, and ends with total comprehensive income, the sum of profit and other comprehensive income.

Look at AZN's statement of comprehensive income in Table 3.2, which starts with the profits section. During 2010 AstraZeneca sold its products for $33,269 million. Numbers in brackets on any financial statement tells you that the number is subtracted, which is a characteristic of costs. The costs of producing the products, *cost of sales*, were $6,389 million. Included in the cost of sales are the costs of raw materials, labour, and depreciation and amortization. *Gross profit*, revenue minus cost of sales, $33,269 − $6,389, was $26,880 million. The costs of distributing the products, *distribution costs*, were $335 million. *Selling, general, and administrative costs*, $10,445 million, include advertising, cost of legal activities, head office costs, and other operating costs. For a pharmaceutical company a crucial operating activity is research to find new drugs to solve health issues. AstraZeneca spent $5,318 million in 2010 on *research and development* of new drugs. These operating costs, the four numbers in brackets, added up to $22,487 million. The *other operating income and expense* of $712 million includes royalties from drug

TABLE 3.2

Consolidated Statement of Comprehensive Income for AstraZeneca, for the Year Ended December 31 (US$ millions)

	2010
Revenue	33,269
Cost of sales	(6,389)
Gross profit	26,880
Distribution costs	(335)
Research and development	(5,318)
Selling, general, administrative costs	(10,445)
Other operating income and expense	712
Operating profit	11,494
Finance income	516
Finance expense	(1,033)
Profit before tax	10,977
Taxation	(2,896)
Profit for the period	8,081
Other comprehensive income for the period, net of tax	25
Total comprehensive income for the period	8,106
Profit attributable to:	
Owners of the parent	8,053
Non-controlling interests	28
Total comprehensive income attributable to:	
Owners of the parent	8,058
Non-controlling interests	48

Source: Reprinted by permission of Astra Zeneca PLC.

licences sold by AstraZeneca, and some other operating expenses. Thus AstraZeneca's total *earnings before interest and taxes (EBIT)*, or *operating profit*, were

$$\begin{aligned}\textbf{EBIT} &= \textbf{revenues} - \textbf{operating costs} + \textbf{other operating income and expense} \\ &= \$33{,}269 - \$22{,}487 + \$712 \qquad (3.1) \\ &= \$11{,}494 \textbf{ million}\end{aligned}$$

The next entry, *finance income*, shows $516 million income on AZN's investment in financial assets. Most of this amount was interest income on its bank deposits and pension plan assets. However, some of the finance income is the gain in fair value of some of investment assets. This equals the increase in the market value of these financial assets since the last report date.

We saw on its SFP that AstraZeneca has partly financed its investment in assets by borrowing. AstraZeneca must pay interest on its bank overdrafts, bank loans, and bonds it has sold. The next entry, $1,033 million *finance expense*, includes the interest that AstraZeneca paid on its debt. Also included in this are losses from the reduction in fair value of some financial instruments and foreign exchange. Finally, a further slice of the profit went to governments as *taxation*. Taxes amounted to $2,896 million, so the *profit for the period* (or net earnings) was $8,081 million. This is the end of the profit section and if AZN had created an income statement, all the entries up to and including *profit for the period* would have been on its income statement. Remember, some companies use the term *net earnings* or *net income* when referring to what the company generated from its operations.

The next line on the statement of comprehensive income, *other comprehensive income for the period, net of tax* captures changes in value of certain assets and liabilities not included in the operating cost measures under IFRS. For example, a company that makes equity investments and records their fair value on the SFP can include gains or losses on the equity investment in the other comprehensive income, if these investments are not held for trading purposes. The other comprehensive income, net of tax was $25 million. Adding the profit to the after-tax other net comprehensive income gives the *total comprehensive income for the period*, $8,106 million.

The final section allocates the profit and the total comprehensive income between the *owners of the parent* (the shareholders of AstraZeneca PLC) and the *non-controlling interest*, representing the part of the equity of subsidiaries that is not owned by the parent, AstraZeneca PLC. Following the principles of consolidation, AstraZeneca's accountants included all of the revenues and expenses of all subsidiaries as if AstraZeneca PLC was the 100 percent owner. So the total comprehensive income that is attributable to the shareholders of AstraZeneca PLC is $8,053 million. What did AZN do with the profits from operations and other comprehensive income that belong to its shareholders?

CONSOLIDATED STATEMENT OF CHANGES IN EQUITY

statement of changes in equity Financial statement that explains the change from the previous period of each component of equity on the statement of financial position (balance sheet).

Under IFRS, transactions with the owners of the firm's equity (shareholders) are excluded from the statement of comprehensive income and instead are reported in a separate financial statement, the **statement of changes in equity**. It explains the change of each component of equity shown on the statement of financial position.

In Table 3.3 is the consolidated statement of changes in equity for AstraZeneca for 2010 year. The first line is the book value of each component of equity as of December 31, 2009. Next rows show the changes in each component and *net movement* is the sum of the changes during 2010. The final line is the balance as of the end of 2010, equals the value as of December 31, 2009 plus the net movement. If you look back to Table 3.1, you will see that each entry in the equity section corresponds to a bottom line of a column in Table 3.3.

The first two columns, *share capital* and *share premium*, start with the book values as of December 31, 2009, and then show the impact of the sale of new shares and repurchase of existing shares that occurred in 2010. The issue of new shares increased share capital $2 million and increased share premium $492 million. Shares repurchased decreased share capital $13 million,

TABLE 3.3

Consolidated Statement of Changes in Equity for AstraZeneca, for the Year Ended December 31 (US$ millions)

	Share Capital	Share Premium	Retained Earnings & Reserves	Total Parent's Equity	Non-controlling Interest	Total Equity
Balance, December 31, 2009	363	2,180	18,117	20,660	161	20,821
Total comprehensive income for 2010			8,058	8,058	48	8,106
Transactions with owners in 2010						
Dividends			(3,494)	(3,494)		(3,494)
Issue of ordinary shares	2	492		494		494
Repurchase of ordinary shares	(13)		(2,591)	(2,604)		(2,604)
Share-based payments			99	99		99
Transfer from non-controlling interests to payables					(11)	(11)
Dividend paid by subsidiary to non-controlling interest					(1)	(1)
Net movement	(11)	492	2,072	2,553	36	2,589
Balance, December 31, 2010	352	2,672	20,189	23,213	197	23,410

Source: Reprinted by permission of Astra Zeneca PLC.

so net movement (change) of share capital was \$2 million − \$13 million = −\$11 million, and the value of share capital as of December 31, 2010 was \$363 million − \$11 million = \$352 million. The \$492 million net movement of share premium in 2010 increased share premium to \$2,672 million.

The third column, *retained earnings & reserves*, was \$18,117 million at the end of 2009. The next line is the 2010 total comprehensive income of owners of AZN, \$8,058. Remember, total comprehensive income is the sum of profit for the period plus other comprehensive income. Next, the 2010 dividends paid to AZN's shareholders, \$3,494 million, are subtracted. Also, \$2,591 million is removed due to the price paid on the repurchase of shares. Share-based payments, \$99 million, reflects cash raised from stock options. So, the change in retained earnings and reserves equals comprehensive income minus dividends minus impact of share repurchases and any change due to share-based payments, \$2,072.

The next column, *total parent's equity*, is the equity of the parent company, which equals the sum of share capital, share premium, and retained earnings and reserves. The book value of AZN shareholders' equity as of December 2009 was \$20,660 million. Then add the 2010 owners' comprehensive income plus all of the changes in the other components of owner's equity, net movement of \$2,553 million, to get the total owner's equity of \$23,213 million as of the end of 2010. The next column, *non-controlling interest*, starts with its value as of December 31, 2009, \$161 million, and adds the comprehensive income of the non-controlling interest, \$48 million, and subtracts a transfer from non-controlling interest to payables, −\$11 million, and the dividends paid to the non-controlling interest, −\$1, generating a net movement of \$36 million. So the value of the non-controlling interest as of December 31, 2010, was \$197 million.

The last column adds all of the other columns to show the change in total equity. The total shareholders' equity as of December 31, 2010, equals the shareholders equity at the start of year, \$20,821 million, plus the net movement of \$2,589, resulting in total shareholders' equity of \$23,410 million at December 31, 2010. If you look back at the bottom line of the statement of financial position in Table 3.1, you will see the same total shareholder equity value at the end of December 2010.

Every column in the statement of changes in equity corresponds to an item in the equity section of the statement of financial position. If a firm has preferred shares, another type of equity, there will be a preferred equity column showing issues and repurchases of preferred shares. If a company reports *retained earnings* separately from *accumulated other comprehensive income* on its SFP, the change in retained earnings depends only on profit for the period (or net earnings or net income) and dividends paid to shareholders. The change in accumulated other comprehensive income depends on other comprehensive income for the period.

Check Point 3.4

On December 31, 2011, the SFP of Can Corp, a fake public Canadian company, had \$10 million of share capital, \$25 million of retained earnings, and \$1 million of accumulated other comprehensive income. The company had no subsidiaries. Can Corp 2012 net earnings were \$2.5 million and its other comprehensive income was \$0.1 million. In 2012, the company issued \$2 million of new equity and paid \$1 million in dividends. Create the 2012 statement of changes in equity for Can Corp.

PROFITS VERSUS CASH FLOW

It is important to distinguish between AstraZeneca's total comprehensive income, profits plus other comprehensive income, and the cash that the company generates, its *cash flow*. *Cash inflow* means cash received by the firm and *cash outflow* is cash paid out. Since other comprehensive income just captures changes in the book value of certain assets and liabilities, it is not a source of cash. Also, profits are not equal to the cash generated by operations. Here are two reasons why accounting profits or losses and cash flow are not the same:

1. *Depreciation, amortization, and impairment.* When accountants prepare the profit section of the SCI or an income statement, they do not simply add up the cash inflows and cash outflows. Instead the accountants start with the cash payments, outflows, but then divide these payments into two groups—current expenditures (such as wages) and capital expenditures (such as the purchase of new machinery). Current expenditures are deducted from current revenues. However, rather than deducting the cost of machinery in the year it is purchased, the accountants make an annual charge for depreciation. Thus the cost of machinery is spread over its estimated life.

   When calculating profits (or net earnings or net income), the accountants *do not* deduct the expenditure on new equipment that year, even though cash is paid out. However, the accountants *do* deduct depreciation on assets previously purchased, even though no cash is currently paid out.

   For example, suppose a \$100,000 investment is depreciated by \$10,000 a year. This depreciation is treated as an annual expense, although the cash actually went out the door when the asset was first purchased. For this reason, the deduction for depreciation is classified as a *non-cash* expense. Similarly, amortization of intangible assets also is incorporated into the costs of operating but are non-cash expenses. Impairment losses also represent non-cash expenses.

> To calculate the cash produced by the business, it is necessary to add back the depreciation and amortization charges and impairment losses (which are not cash payments) and subtract the expenditure on new capital equipment and new intangibles (which are cash payments).

2. *Cash versus accrual accounting.* Consider a manufacturer that spends \$60 to produce goods in period 1. In period 2 it sells these goods for \$100, but its customers do not pay their bills until period 3. So there is a \$60 cash *outflow* in period 1 to pay for the production of the goods and \$100 cash *inflow* in period 3 when the customers pay for their purchases. An income statement reporting a loss in period 1 (when cash flow was −\$60), zero profit in period 2 (when there was no cash flow), and extreme profit in period 3 (when cash flow was +\$100) would be misleading. Accounting rules for creating an income statement are used to provide a more reasonable measure of the firm's profitability.

Transactions are recognized in the books when incurred, which may not be at the same time as the cash flows. This is the concept of *accrual accounting*. Revenues are *recognized*, put on the income statement, in the period when the sale occurred, regardless of when the cash is actually received. The costs of producing the goods sold are also put on the income statement as expenses for the same period as the revenue recognition. This provides a reasonable measure of the firm's profits. This practice is known as *matching*. The accountant gathers all expenses that are associated with a sale and deducts them from the revenues to calculate profit, even though expenses may have occurred in an earlier period and sales haven't been paid. For our company, the income statement would be:

Period:	**1**	**2**	**3**
Revenues	0	100	0
Cost of goods sold	0	(60)	0
Profit	0	40	0

Of course, the accountant cannot ignore the actual timing of the cash expenditures and payments. To account for the fact that the firm spent money to produce the goods in period 1, the expenditure will be shown as a period 1 *investment* in inventories, which is an increase in inventories on the SFP. Subsequently in period 2, when the goods are sold, the inventories will decline. For our company, inventories increase $60 in period 1 to recognize the production of unsold goods and then decrease $60 in period 2, to recognize the sale of existing goods.

The cash flow due to the production of the goods can be calculated using information from the income statement and the SFP. Start with the cost of goods sold from the income statement, and then *subtract* the increase in inventories or *add* the decrease in inventories. In this example, we have assumed that all of the costs of producing the inventory was paid for in period 1. Thus the cash flow due to production is:

Period:	**1**	**2**
Cost of goods sold	0	(60)
(Increase) or decrease in inventories	(60)	60
= Cash inflow (outflow) due to production of goods	(60)	0

The accountant also does not ignore the fact that the firm has to wait until period 3 to collect its bills/invoices from its customers, even though sales are shown on the income statement in period 2. When the sale is made in period 2, the figure for trade receivables in the SFP is increased by $100 to because of the $100 unpaid bills of the company's customers. Later, when the customers pay those bills in period 3, accounts receivable are reduced by $100. This cash payment has no impact on the income statement and hence does not affect accounting profits in period 3.

To calculate the company's total cash flow from its sales, start with revenues, subtract cost of goods sold, subtract the increase (investment) in trade receivables and inventories, and add the decrease in trade receivables and inventories.

To calculate the cash that the company receives from sales using information from the income statement and the SFP, start with revenues from the income statement and then *subtract* the increase in receivables or *add* the decrease in receivables. Thus cash inflow (outflow) from sales is:

Period:	**1**	**2**	**3**
Revenues	0	100	0
(Increase) or decrease in receivables	0	(100)	100
= Cash inflow (outflow) from sales	0	0	100

To calculate the company's total cash flow, start with revenues, subtract cost of goods sold, subtract the increase (investment) in trade receivables and inventories, add the decrease in trade receivables and inventories, add the increase in trade payables, and subtract the decrease in trade payables.

Up to now, we've assumed that the manufacturer paid all the costs of producing the inventory in period 1. If suppliers let the manufacturer pay for purchases after the delivery of the supplies, the accountant will need to keep track of the manufacturer's unpaid bills. This is recorded as accounts payable, listed as a liability. Suppose $40 of the cost of producing the good is paid for, not in period 1, but in period 2. In period 1, accounts payable would increase $40, recognizing the unpaid bills. Then in period 2, when the manufacturer pays its outstanding bills, accounts payable would decrease $40, indicating the use of cash. The cash flows due to production would now be:

Period:	**1**	**2**
Cost of goods sold	0	(60)
(Increase) or decrease in inventories	(60)	60
Increase or (decrease) in payables	40	(40)
Cash inflow (outflow) due to production of goods	(20)	(40)

EXAMPLE 3.2

Suppose it costs a firm $100 to produce some goods in period 1. In period 1 it pays employees $40 for their work but pays suppliers for the $60 of raw materials in period 2. It sells those goods for $150 in period 2 but does not collect payment from its customers until period 3. On the period 2 income statement are $150 revenues, ($100) cost of goods sold, and $50 profit. This table shows the cash flow each period:

Period:	**1**	**2**	**3**
Revenues	0	150	0
Cost of goods sold	0	(100)	0
(Increase) or decrease in receivables	0	(150)	150
(Increase) or decrease in inventories	(100)	100	0
Increase or (decrease) in payables	60	(60)	0
= Net cash inflow (outflow)	(40)	(60)	150

Think about why this makes sense. In period 1, it costs $100 for the firm to produce the product but the firm only pays $40 to its employees. The unpaid bills are captured as a $60 increase in payables. The product is not sold then, so the cost of producing the product is not recognized on the income statement in this period. Instead, the cost of the goods is recognized as an investment in inventory. The period 1 net cash flow is minus $40. In period 2, the product is sold, but customers don't pay for the products. Instead, under accrual accounting, $150 is booked as a sale, with a corresponding investment in accounts receivable. At the same time, the $100 cost of goods sold is recognized in this period, and because the product is sold, the investment in inventories is reversed. But the firm pays its bills, causing its payables to decrease $60, using $60 of cash. Finally, in period 3, $150 cash is collected. Accounts receivable is reduced by the $150 cash inflow.

Check Point 3.5

It cost a firm $200 to produce goods in period 1. The firm must pay $130 of its production cost in period 1 and the rest of the costs will be paid in period 2. No goods are produced in any other period. In period 2 it sells half of these goods for $150 but does not collect payments until one period later. In period 3, it sells the other half of the goods for $150 and collects payment in period 4. Calculate the profits and cash flows for the firm in period 1 to 4. Create a table like that in Example 3.2.

LO1 3.3 THE STATEMENT OF CASH FLOWS

The firm requires *cash* when it buys new plant and machinery or when it pays interest to the bank and dividends to the shareholders. Therefore, the financial manager needs to keep track of the cash that is coming in and going out.

We have seen that the firm's cash flow can be quite different from its profit (net earnings or net income) for the period. These items are from the income statement or the profit section of the statement of comprehensive income, SCI. These differences can arise for at least two reasons:

1. The income statement or SCI does not recognize capital expenditures as expenses in the year that the capital goods are paid for. Instead, it spreads those expenses over time in the form of an annual depreciation or amortization expenses.
2. The income statement or SCI uses the accrual method of accounting, which means that revenues and expenses are recognized when sales are made rather than when the cash is received or paid out.

statement of cash flows Financial statement that shows the firm's cash receipts and cash payments over a period of time.

The **statement of cash flows** shows the firm's cash inflows and outflows from operations as well as from its investment and financing activities. Table 3.4 is the cash flow statement for AstraZeneca.

The statement of cash flows contains three sections. The first section shows the cash generated from AZN's operating activities, such as the production and sale of pharmaceutical products. Next is the cash that AZN has invested in plant and equipment, in the acquisition of new businesses, and in other financial securities. The final section reports cash flows from financing activities such as the issuance of new debt, loans, or shares and also debt repayments and share repurchases. The sum of cash inflows or outflows from each section gives the change in AZN's cash and cash equivalents. We will look at these sections in turn.

The first section, cash flows from operating activities, for any firm's statement of cash flow starts with a profit number from the profit section of the statement of comprehensive income (or income statement). Then adjustments are made to remove those parts of the profits that do not involve cash coming in or going out. This involves adding back non-cash expenses and subtracting non-cash income. The first line could be net earnings (net income), which is after taxes. Taxes on the income statement typically do not equal actual cash taxes paid. So if the first line is net income you will see an entry *deferred taxes*, which gets rid of non-cash taxes. The first line of AZN's cash flow from operations is *profit before tax*. By starting with profits before tax, no adjustment needs to be made for non-cash taxes. Depreciation, amortization, and impairment allowances are added back, because these are not cash flows even though they are treated as expenses in the income statement. If these numbers aren't shown separately on the SCI they would be included in various expenses.

In the SCI, Table 3.2, finance income was \$516 million and finance expense was −\$1,033 million. Finance income and expense, the sum of these two is \$516 − \$1,033 = −\$517 million. On the statement of cash flow, finance income and expense are added back to remove their impact on profits. This is done because both finance income and finance expense have non-cash based items, such as changes in the fair values of the financial instruments as well as accrued interest income and interest expense. Under IFRS, the actual cash flows for interest paid and interest received must be shown separately on the statement of cash flows. There are also choices as to where these amounts are shown. Interest paid may be reported as either an operating activity or a financing activity. Interest received may be classified as either an operating or an investing activity. AZN has chosen to report interest paid as an operating activity, and interest received as an investing activity. One final choice allowed under IFRS is to report dividends paid as either an operating activity or a financing activity. Dividends paid by AZN are included as a financing activity.

Additions to current assets, excluding cash and equivalents, need to be *subtracted* from profits in order to adjust for accrued amounts in the statement of comprehensive income. As we showed

TABLE 3.4

Consolidated Statement of Cash Flows for AstraZeneca, for the Year Ended December 31 (US$ millions)	2010
Cash flows from operating activities:	
Profit before tax	10,977
Finance income and expense	517
Depreciation, amortization, and impairment	2,741
	14,235
Decrease (increase) in trade and other receivables	10
Decrease (increase) in inventories	88
Increase (decrease) in trade and other payables and provisions	(16)
Other non-cash movements	(463)
Cash generated from operations	13,854
Interest paid	(641)
Tax paid	(2,533)
Net cash inflow from operating activities	10,680
Cash flows from investing activities:	
Acquisitions of business operations	(348)
Movement in short-term investments and fixed deposits	(239)
Purchase of property, plant, and equipment	(791)
Disposal of property, plant, and equipment	83
Purchase of intangible assets	(1,390)
Disposal of intangible assets	210
Purchase of non-current asset investments	(34)
Disposal of non-current assets investments	5
Interest received	174
Payments made by subsidiaries to non-controlling interests	(10)
Net cash inflow (outflow) from investing activities	(2,340)
Net cash inflow (outflow) before financing activities	8,340
Cash flows from financing activities:	
Proceeds from issue of share capital	494
Repurchase of shares	(2,604)
Issue of loans	
Repayment of loans	(1,741)
Dividends paid	(3,361)
Movement in short-term borrowings	(8)
Net cash inflow (outflow) from financing activities	(7,220)
Net increase (decrease) in cash and cash equivalents in the period	1,120
Cash and cash equivalents at beginning of the period	9,828
Effect of exchange rate fluctuations on cash held	33
Cash and cash equivalents at the end of the period	10,981

Source: Reprinted by permission of Astra Zeneca PLC.

in the previous section, revenues include unpaid bills. So the increase in accounts receivable is subtracted to get to actual cash from sales. Likewise, any decrease in current assets needs to be added, since they capture cash that did not get reported on the statement of comprehensive income. Conversely, any additions (reductions) to current liabilities need to be added (subtracted) because these produce (use) cash. Changes in those current assets and current liabilities that are directly related to the firm's operations are included in the cash flow from operating activities. In Table 3.4 the decrease of $10 million in trade and other receivables is *added* to profit, because this is due to receipts of cash from customers for sales made in a previous year. In addition, inventories decreased $88 million, but the cash generated by this reduction in inventories was not included in the cost of sales so must be recognized as a source of cash on this statement. On the other hand, AZN does not pay all its bills immediately. These delayed payments show up in trade and other payables and provisions. In 2010 AZN had fewer unpaid bills: trade and other payables and provisions decreased by $16 million, using $16 million of cash. Adding up all of these changes in current assets used in operations and current liabilities related to operations gives the change in net operating working capital, $10 + $88 − $16 = $82 million. Since this number from the statement of cash flow is positive, AZN received cash from the reduction of its net working capital. Another adjustment for non-cash based items are *other non-cash movements*. In this case cash is reduced by $463 million to offset some earnings that were not cash-based. Adding up all these adjustments to profits from operations gives the *cash generated from operations*, $13,854 million. From that is subtracted the actual cash *interest paid* and the cash *taxes paid*, revealing that the *net cash inflow from operating activities* was $10,680 million. Note, if the first line had been net income, rather than profit before tax, there would not be a subtraction of cash taxes paid because net income is after tax.

Next are the cash inflows and outflows related to investing activities. All the negative numbers are cash outflows for purchases of assets. AZN bought another business and spent $348 million cash, *acquisition of business operations*. They also spent $239 million on new short-term investments and fixed deposits, *movement in short-term investments and fixed deposits*. Although depreciation and amortization are expenses on the SCI that are the accountant's allocation to the current year of the original cost for capital equipment and intangible assets, they are not cash payments. However, cash does go out the door when the firm actually buys and pays for new capital equipment and new intangibles. AZN spent $791 million on the *purchase of property, plant, and equipment* and $1,390 million on the *purchase of intangible assets*. It also spent $34 million on *non-current-asset investments*. Also, $10 million of cash was paid by subsidiaries to non-controlling interest. Total cash used for investments was −$2,812 million. But $298 million cash was generated by the disposal of some property, plant, and equipment, intangible assets, and non-current-asset investments, and $174 million of interest income was received, generating a total cash inflow of $472 million from investing activities. The net cash used in investing activities was −$2,812 million + $472 million = −$2,340 million. The total net cash flow before dealing with financing activities is $8,340 million, with $10,680 million from operating activities minus the net $2,340 million spent on investment activities.

Finally, the third section of the cash flow statement shows the cash related to financing activities. Some activities were with shareholders: AZN raised $494 million by issuing new shares, and AZN spent $2,604 million to buy back shares and paid $3,361 million in dividends to shareholders. So the total cash flow to shareholders was $5,471 million (= −$494 + $2,604 + 3,361). Activities with lenders involved $1,741 loan repayment loans and $8 million reduction in short-term borrowings, which adds up to $1,749 million payment to lenders. The total net cash paid out to investors was $7,220 million (5,471 + 1,749).

To summarize, the cash flow statement tells us that AstraZeneca generated $10,680 million from operations, spent $2,340 million on net investment activities, and spent $7,220 million on net financing activities. AstraZeneca earned more cash than it spent. Therefore, its cash and cash equivalents balance increased by $1,120 million. To calculate this change in cash balance, we subtract the uses of cash from the sources of cash. Brackets indicate that the number is subtracted rather than added:

US$ Millions	
Cash inflow (outflow) from operating activities	$10,680
Cash inflow (outflow) from investing activities	(2,340)
Cash inflow (outflow) from financing activities	(7,220)
= Change in cash and cash equivalents	$ 1,120

The balance of cash and cash equivalents at the beginning of 2010 was $9,828 million. The net increase in cash and equivalents from the statement of cash flow was $1,120 million, plus another $33 million due to changes in currency exchange rates, which equals $1,153 million, increasing the cash and cash equivalents to $10,981 million as of the end of 2010. The last few lines of the statement of cash flow shows this change cash and cash equivalents. Typically, the bottom line of the statement of cash flows, the cash and cash equivalents at the end of the period, is equal to the cash and cash equivalents balance on the statement of financial position. However, AZN had $87 million bank overdraft, which isn't taken into account on the statement of cash flows. Add the cash from the overdraft to the bottom line of the statement cash flow, $87 million + $10,981 million, which equal $11,068 million, the SFP 2010 cash and cash equivalents.

Check Point 3.6

Would the following activities increase or decrease the firm's cash balances?

a. Inventories are increased.
b. The firm reduces its trade payables.
c. The firm issues additional common stock.
d. The firm buys new equipment.

LO4 3.4 CASH FLOW FROM ASSETS, FINANCING FLOW, AND FREE CASH FLOW

The statement of cash flows provides information about cash generated and used in the firm's activities. Cash flows can be expressed as an equation for the change in cash and cash equivalents. A term in brackets, such as "(outflow)," means that the number is negative and so it is subtracted:

$$\begin{aligned}\textbf{Change in cash and cash equivalents}\\ &= \textbf{Cash inflow (outflow) from operating activities}\\ &+ \textbf{Cash inflow (outflow) from investing activities}\\ &+ \textbf{Cash inflow (outflow) from financing activities}\end{aligned} \tag{3.2}$$

Using equation 3.2, we can calculate AstraZeneca's change in cash and cash equivalents:

$$\text{Change in cash and cash equivalents} = \$10{,}680 + (-\$2{,}340) + (-\$7{,}220) = \$1{,}120$$

Since the cash flows from investing activities and from financing activities were negative, both were cash outflows, they are subtracted from the positive cash inflow from the operating activities.

cash flow from assets
Cash flow generated by the firm's operations, after investment in working capital and operating assets.

Information in the statement of cash flows can be used to measure a company's **cash flow from assets**. *Cash flow from assets* is the cash generated from operating activities, taking into account its investments:

$$\textbf{Cash flow from assets} = \textbf{Cash inflow (outflow) from operating activities} + \textbf{Cash inflow (outflow) investing activities} \quad (3.3)$$

Using equation 3.3, we can calculate AstraZeneca's cash flow from assets in 2010:

$$\begin{aligned}\text{Cash flow from assets} &= \text{Cash inflow (outflow) from operating activities} \\ &\quad + \text{Cash inflow (outflow) investing activities} \\ &= \$10{,}680 \text{ million} + (-\$2{,}340 \text{ million}) = \$8{,}340 \text{ million}\end{aligned}$$

So AZN's use of its assets, by operating its business, generated $8,340 million cash flow from assets.

financing flow Cash flow to lenders and shareholders plus increase in cash balances; also equals cash flow from assets.

Information in the statement of cash flows can also be used to measure a company's **financing flow**. Financing flow is the change in the company's cash plus the cash paid to investors (or minus the cash received from investors):

$$\textbf{Financing flow} = \textbf{Change in cash and cash equivalents} - \textbf{Cash inflow (outflow) from financing activities} \quad (3.4)$$

Using equation 3.4, we can calculate AstraZeneca's financing flow in 2010:

$$\begin{aligned}\text{Financing flow} &= \text{Change in cash and cash equivalent} \\ &\quad - \text{Cash from (used in) financing activities} \\ &= \$1{,}120 \text{ million} - (-\$7{,}220 \text{ million}) \\ &= \$1{,}120 \text{ million} + \$7{,}220 \text{ million} \\ &= \$8{,}340 \text{ million}\end{aligned}$$

The financing flow equation shows that AZN put $1,120 million into its bank and also paid out $7,220 million to its investors. Did you notice that AZN's cash flow from assets equalled its financing flow? Look back at equation 3.2 and you will see that the first two terms in the equation, *cash inflow (outflow) from operating activities* + *cash inflow (outflow) from investing activities*, are the definition of *cash flows from assets*. So put *cash flow from assets* in equation 3.2 to create another expression for the statement of cash flow:

$$\textbf{Change in cash and cash equivalents} = \textbf{Cash flow from assets} + \textbf{Cash inflow (outflow) from financing activities} \quad (3.5)$$

Now rearrange equation 3.4 to show cash flow from assets:

$$\textbf{Cash flow from assets} = \textbf{Increase (decrease) in cash and cash equivalents} - \textbf{Cash inflow (outflow) from financing activities} \quad (3.6)$$

Look back at equation 3.4, the equation for financing flow, and you will see that it is same as equation 3.6. So, because of the statement of cash flow and the definitions of cash flow from assets and financing flow, it is true that *cash flow from assets* = *financing flow*. Looking at the details of the financing flow tells you what the company did with its cash flow from assets.

Of the $8,340 million cash flow generated by its assets in 2010, AZN put $1,120 million into the company's bank account and other short-term investments. Also, its financing activities resulted in a net cash outflow of $7,220 million to its lenders (or bondholders) and shareholders. In other words, AstraZeneca's negative net cash flow *from* financing activities means that the net cash flow *to* providers of financings was positive. The negative numbers in financing activities section in Table 3.4 are cash flow to investors and include the repayment of short-term borrowing, repayment of loans, repurchase of shares and dividends to shareholders. In the previous section we calculated the $1,749 million cash flow to lenders and $5,471 million to shareholders.

free cash flow Another term for cash flow from assets.

The financial flow equals the cash flow from assets. Another name for cash flow from assets and financial flow is **free cash flow**. It's *free* because it's the cash remaining after the firm has made its investment in new operating assets. It's free to be put into the bank as spare cash and/or paid out to company's investors.

You may have noticed that one category of payment to bondholders is not listed in the financial activities section of the statement of cash flows for AZN: interest payments. As discussed earlier, interest paid may be classified as either an operating or a financing activity. AZN has chosen to include this as an operating activity. However, to measure cash flow from assets, independently of how the firm chooses to finance itself, interest paid should be classified as a financing activity. To do this, add back the interest paid to cash flow from assets and also add interest paid as a financing flow.[14]

AstraZeneca spent $641 million on interest. Its cash flow from assets, adjusted to remove the interest expense is

$$\begin{aligned}\textbf{Cash flow from assets (adjusted)} &= \textbf{Cash flow from assets} + \textbf{Interest paid} \\ &= \$8{,}340 \textbf{ million} + \$641 \textbf{ million} = \$8{,}981 \textbf{ million}\end{aligned} \quad (3.7)$$

As you would expect, treating interest paid as a financing flow increases AstraZeneca's cash flow from assets. Likewise the cash flow to bondholders and shareholders now includes interest paid, increasing financing flows to $7,861 million = $7,220 + $641 million. You can make the same adjustment to the equation for the financing flow, equation 3.5, by adding interest paid as another financing flow.

Check Point 3.7

A firm's net earnings for the year were $7.3 million and its depreciation expense was $1.9 million. Working capital increased $2.6 million and $3.5 million was spent on new equipment. The company issued $1.5 million of new debt, raised no new equity, and paid $.6 million in interest and $2 million in dividends. What was cash flow from assets for the year, treating interest as a financing flow? What was the cash flow from financing activities with lenders and shareholders? Show that change in cash was a $2.6 million increase. What was financing flow for the year assuming that interest paid is included as a financing activity?

Why is it important to understand a company's cash flow from assets and financing flow? Financial managers care about the cash flow from assets and financing flow because it is their job to manage the company's inflows and outflows of cash. For a company with positive cash flow from assets, managers must decide how much of that cash to pay out to shareholders, either as dividends or through share repurchases, and whether to pay off their debt or stockpile the surplus cash in the bank. Cash flow from assets can also be negative. In this case, managers must decide whether to raise new financing by borrowing or issuing shares, or draw down cash reserves. Financing decisions and dividend policy decisions are at the very heart of financial management, and we will look at them in depth in later chapters.[15]

Investors are also interested in understanding a company's free cash flow. For example, if free cash flow is negative, can the firm survive? Negative free cash flow is quite common for new and growing firms, having greater investment expenditures than cash flow from operations. However, this is not sustainable in the long run. Investors will refuse to pour money into the business if they have no hope of receiving any return of cash flow. If the company's cash flow from assets is continuously negative, the financial managers may fail in their attempts

[14] To be really precise, we should be using the *after-tax* interest expense. In Section 3.6 you will learn that interest expense is tax-deductible for a corporation. Thus the actual *cash* spent on interest is the after-tax amount, interest expense × (1 − tax rate). This adjustment is necessary for some methods of business valuation.

[15] We will discuss financing and dividend policies in Chapters 16, 17, and 18.

to raise the needed financing to keep the company going and the company may fall into bankruptcy.

Free cash flow is also an important component used in the valuation of the company's assets. As we shall see in Chapter 5, the value of an asset depends on the cash flows you expect to receive. The value of a company's assets will depend on the cash flow those assets generate—its cash flow from assets. In Chapter 9 we will show you how to evaluate a firm's investment projects by measuring the project's cash flows. Those cash flows are the same as the firm's cash flow from assets. We will return to identifying and calculating cash flows in Chapter 9.

3.5 ACCOUNTING PRACTICE AND ACCOUNTING MALPRACTICE

Managers of public companies face constant scrutiny. Much of that scrutiny focuses on earnings. Security analysts forecast earnings per share, and investors wait to see whether the company can meet or beat the forecasts. A shortfall, even if it is only a cent or two, can be a big disappointment. Investors might judge that if you could not find that extra cent or two of earnings, the firm must be in a really bad way.

Managers complain about this pressure, but do they do anything about it? Unfortunately, the answer appears to be yes, according to Graham, Harvey and Rajgopal, who surveyed about 400 senior managers.[16] Most of the managers said that accounting earnings were the single most important number reported to investors. Most admitted to adjusting their firms' operations and investments to produce the earnings that investors were looking for. For example, 80 percent were prepared to decrease discretionary spending in R&D, advertising, or maintenance to meet earnings targets.

Of course, managers may not need to adjust the firm's operations if they can instead adjust their accounting methods. Canadian accounting rules are spelled out by the Accounting Standards Board (AcSB) and it requires that public companies use IFRS. Yet, inevitably, rules and principles leave room for discretion, and managers under pressure to perform are tempted to take advantage of this leeway to satisfy investors. In more extreme cases, managers may simply break the rules.

Here are some examples of grey areas that demand judgment calls, and may tempt those who wish to conceal unflattering information to misuse any leeway in accounting rules:

1. *Allowance for bad debts.* Most firms sell goods on credit and must make an allowance for the fact that some customers will not pay. But it can sometimes be tempting to take a rosy view of the proportion of bills that will go unpaid.
2. *Revenue recognition.* As we saw above, firms record a sale when it is made, not when the customer actually pays. But there are occasions when it can be hard to know when the sale occurs. An extreme (and potentially fraudulent) version of this problem is known as "channel stuffing." The firm "sells" large quantities of goods to customers but gives them the right to later refuse delivery or return the product. The revenue from the "sale" is booked immediately, but the likely returns are not recognized until they occur in a future accounting period. Channel stuffing hit the headlines in 1997 when the head of Sunbeam Corporation, "Chainsaw" Al Dunlap, allegedly moved millions of dollars of appliances to distributors and retailers to produce record earnings.

Investors worry that some companies may be particularly tempted to inflate their earnings in such ways. They refer to such companies as having "low-quality" earnings, and they place a correspondingly lower value on the firms' stock.

[16] J. R. Graham, C. R. Harvey, and S. Rajgopal, "The Economic Implications of Corporate Financial Reporting," *Journal of Accounting and Economics* 40 (2005): 3–73.

Firms that aggressively exploit any latitude in the accounting rules are liable to find that it is only a small step further to produce fraudulent accounts. The years between 2000 and 2004 were filled with a seemingly unending series of accounting scandals in the United States and, to a lesser extent, in Canada. Enron and its auditor Arthur Andersen came to symbolize the crisis in corporate accounting. Enron broke accounting rules to hide its debt and overstate earnings in 2001. It subsequently went bankrupt. Arthur Andersen was convicted of shredding documents that would have provided evidence concerning Enron's activities. A few months later WorldCom admitted to inflating its profits by booking nearly $4 billion of expenses as capital expenditures. Other firms such as Global Crossing and Qwest Communications were also found to have misstated profits significantly. At the end of 2004, mortgage giant Fannie Mae was found to have improperly accounted for transactions in derivative contracts, reducing its stated profits back to 2001 by US$9 billion. In 2004, Nortel Networks, one of Canada's largest companies, came under scrutiny for accounting problems that led to overstated profits. The Nortel board of directors fired the CEO, the CFO, and the controller and initiated an investigation to assess who was responsible for the accounting manipulations. Four Nortel executives were subsequently charged for financial fraud by the Securities and Exchange Commission in the United States. Subsequently, Nortel went bankrupt.

Accounting fraud is not just a North American problem. In 2003, Parmalat, an Italian multinational dairy producer, was dubbed "Europe's Enron" and went bankrupt after it was discovered the company had been falsifying its financial statements, including overstating its cash and sales. The French media and entertainment firm Vivendi Universal nearly ended up in bankruptcy after it was accused of accounting fraud. In each case, the stock of the company plummeted on the news of the frauds, and the negative effects spilled over to other companies as investors lost faith in many firms' financial statements.

In response to the numerous scandals, the U.S. Congress passed the *Sarbanes-Oxley Act* (SOX) in 2002. The act attempts to ensure that a firm's financial reports accurately represent its financial condition. The act created the Public Company Accounting Oversight Board to oversee the auditing of public companies. Under this act, CEOs and CFOs are now required to personally sign off on their firm's financial statements, and independent experts now have to serve on the audit committee of the board of directors.

But managers and investors worry that these reforms have gone too far. The costs of SOX and the burden of meeting detailed, inflexible regulations are pushing some corporations to return from public to private ownership. Some blame SOX and onerous regulation in the United States for the fact that an increasing number of foreign companies have chosen to list their shares in London rather than New York. In Canada, CEOs and CFOs are required to certify that the company is providing proper disclosure.

There is also a vigorous debate over "rules-based" versus "principles-based" approaches to accounting standards. The United States follows a rules-based approach, with hundreds of pages of rules governing virtually every circumstance that possibly can be anticipated. In contrast, the IFRS takes a principles-based approach to accounting. It sets out general approaches that financial statements should take to recognizing and measuring assets, and leaves more room for discretion and professional judgment as long as firms can defend the consistency of their approach within the spirit of the standards. While this seems to give firms considerably more leeway than the U.S.'s rules-based system, critics of the U.S. approach argue that, once firms find a loophole in GAAP, they are not legally bound to obey even the spirit of the rules. The International Accounting Standards Board (IASB) and the United States Financial Accounting Standards Board (FASB) have been engaged for years in attempts to coordinate their systems, and many in the United States have lobbied for the greater simplicity that principles-based accounting standards might offer. However, the nearby box shows how not all Canadian accountants are convinced that the switch to IFRS which allows for a lot more choices will improve accounting. Only time will tell what the impact of the change to IFRS will have on the quality of financial statements.

Finance in Action

Accounting for Trouble?

Canada is in the midst of a seismic shift in accounting standards—one that will tie the country more tightly to international commerce, but might also result in investors being taken for a ride.

Starting this year, Canadian public companies will issue financial statements using international financial reporting standards (IFRS) instead of the generally accepted accounting principles (GAAP) that have been in place for decades. Many countries have unique accounting standards that are difficult to reconcile. In part to remedy this, the European Union began to implement IFRS to harmonize reporting among member countries. Others have signed up in the past few years, including Australia and Chile. The Accounting Standards Board in Canada, which oversees financial reporting methods, decided in 2006 to replace Canadian GAAP with IFRS. (The U.S., meanwhile, is incorporating aspects of the international standards over the next few years, but wholesale adoption is still in debate.)

"In the end, we feel IFRS makes more sense for us," says Ron Salole, a director of the AcSB. The primary benefit of a common set of accounting principles is the increased comparability between companies around the world, which ultimately reduces the cost of capital. "If you want to operate in a global economy, then having unique standards will not find favour," he says.

Or so the argument goes. "This is a matter of tight rules versus [worthless] rules," argues Toronto based forensic accountant Al Rosen. IFRS is a major step back from Canadian GAAP, he says, and will permit unethical managers to hide, massage and choose numbers to make their companies look good. "This is a Ponzi scheme in progress," he says. Investors, who are supposed to benefit through increased comparability, could end up the victims of unfair accounting.

A key difference under IFRS is that managers have more choice in how they report certain information. Take revenue recognition. Canadian accounting standards had stringent criteria around when and how a company could record revenue on goods and services. Under IFRS, the guidelines are more vague, potentially permitting unscrupulous managers to pump up revenue or mask bad debt. A company issuing loans, such as mortgages, could record cash coming in on loans that are going unpaid.

Rosen is also fuming about related-party transactions. IFRS does away with fair market valuation of self-dealings—for instance, if a private company owned by a couple of executives sells an asset to the public company employing them—meaning investors have little to no assurance the goods and services are transacted at legitimate prices.

Along with his son Mark, Rosen claims to have identified a litany of such problems with IFRS, and the two have given numerous presentations to banks and institutional investors. "The level of knowledge in Canada of all the dirty tricks is near zero," says the elder Rosen.

Supporters of IFRS will agree there is more leeway in reporting in some areas, but trust auditors to exercise their professional judgment to prevent accounting shenanigans from occurring. "The missing element is whether we are going to have enough educated people with sufficient backbone to apply their judgment in the face of client pressure," says Barry Epstein, a financial reporting author and litigation consultant in Chicago. "The auditors are the frontline troops, so that's where the action will be."

Salole argues no standards, however stringent, will stop unethical executives from manipulating financial statements. The areas in which IFRS allow for greater choice reflect a more complex business world in which no two transactions are exactly alike. "Bringing in your professional judgment still doesn't mean you can cherry-pick accounting," he says. Managers will have to justify their accounting decisions in financial statements under IFRS, as well, giving investors more information to chew over. In some cases, these disclosures are more rigorous than what existed under Canadian GAAP.

In any event, there is no turning back, and Rosen is not looking forward to it. "This is just going to dwarf the fiasco of Nortel," he says. "There's no doubt in my mind." . . .

Source: Castaldo, Joe, "Accounting for Trouble?", Canadian Business, February 14, 2011, p. 15–16. Reprinted by permission of Canadian Business.

LO5 3.6 TAXES

Taxes often have a major effect on financial decisions. Therefore, we should explain how corporations and investors are taxed.

CORPORATE TAX

Canadian companies pay both federal and provincial tax on their taxable income. The 2011 general federal corporate tax rate is 16.5 percent. To assist small businesses, the federal tax rate is only 11 percent on the first $400,000 of the taxable income of Canadian-controlled private corporations. The appropriate provincial corporate tax rate is added to the federal rate to give the overall tax rate.[17] For example, a small business operating in New Brunswick pays 11 percent

[17] Not all corporate income is subject to provincial taxation, for instance income earned outside Canada. In this case, 10 percentage points are added to the federal rate, giving a basic federal rate of 26.5 percent.

TABLE 3.5
Federal and provincial corporate tax rates, 2011.

	General Rate (%)		Small Business Rate (%), Income Up to $400,000	
Federal		**16.5**		**11**
	Prov.	**Fed. + Prov.**	**Prov.**	**Fed. + Prov.**
British Columbia	10	26.5	2.5	13.5
Alberta	10	26.5	3	14
Saskatchewan	12	28.5	4.5	15.5
Manitoba	12	28.5	0	11
Ontario[1]	11.5	28.0	4.5	15.5
Québec	11.9	28.4	8	19
New Brunswick[2]	10	26.5	5	16
Nova Scotia	16	32.5	5	16
Prince Edward Island	16	32.5	1	12
Newfoundland and Labrador	14	30.5	4	15
Northwest Territories	11.5	28.0	4	15
Nunavut	12	28.5	4	15
Yukon	15	31.5	4	15
Average rate	**12.5**	**29.0**	**3.8**	**14.8**

[1] Prior to July 1, 2011, Ontario 2011 general rate was 12%.
[2] Prior to July 1, 2011, New Brunswick 2011 general rate was 11%.
Source: KPMG, "Canadian Corporate Tax Tables," **www.kpmg.com/ca/en/issuesandinsights/articlespublications/pages/taxrates.aspx**, accessed August 7, 2011.

federal tax plus 5 percent provincial tax, giving a 16 percent total tax rate.[18] Table 3.5 summarizes the main federal and provincial rates for 2011.[19] Visit Canada Revenue Agency's site, **www.cra-arc.gc.ca**, for information on current rates. Web sites of provincial governments carry up-to-date information on provincial tax rates.

When firms calculate taxable income, they are allowed to deduct expenses such as labour and material costs, marketing and selling costs, and administration expenditures. However, the costs of new equipment, new factories, and other non-current assets cannot be deducted all at once; instead, they are deducted over time, depreciating the cost of the assets. The allowable depreciation for tax purposes is determined by the *Income Tax Act* and is called the *capital cost allowance* (CCA).[20] The deductions allowed for CCA may be different from the depreciation recorded for accounting purposes, resulting in a taxable income that is different than accounting income. As a result, taxes paid to Canada Revenue Agency (CRA) may be very different from the tax expense reported in the income statement.[21]

The company is also allowed to deduct interest paid to debtholders when calculating its taxable income, but dividends paid to shareholders are not deductible. These dividends are therefore paid out of after-tax earnings. Table 3.6 provides an example of how interest payments reduce corporate taxes. Although both companies have earnings before interest and taxes of $100 and have a 29 percent tax rate, firm A pays only $17.4 in tax, leaving it with $100 − $17.4, or $82.6,

---

[18] The federal corporate is expected to drop to 15 percent in 2012.

[19] KPMG Web site has documents on tax rates for businesses and individuals, found at **www.kpmg.com/Ca/en/IssuesAndInsights/ArticlesPublications/Pages/taxrates.aspx**.

[20] We will tell you more about these allowances in Chapter 9.

[21] The capital cost allowance is a type of accelerated depreciation, allowing bigger deductions at the beginning of the life of an asset. This reduces taxable income and taxes relative to what they would be according to the IFRS depreciation used in the income statement. Deferred taxes, a liability account on the balance sheet, is an adjustment needed to reconcile the tax expense on the income statement with the actual taxes paid to CRA.

TABLE 3.6
Firms A and B both have earnings before interest and taxes (EBIT) of $100 million, but A pays out part of its profits as debt interest. This reduces the corporate tax paid by A.

	Firm A	Firm B
	($ millions)	
EBIT	$100	$100
Interest	(40)	0
Pretax income	60	100
Tax (29% of pretax income)	(17.4)	(29)
Net income	42.6	71

to pay to bondholders and shareholders. Firm B has only $100 − $29, or $71, to distribute to bondholders and shareholders.

The bad news about taxes is that every extra dollar of revenues increases taxable income by $1 and results in 29 cents of extra taxes. The good news is that every extra dollar of expense reduces taxable income by $1 and therefore reduces taxes by 29 cents. For example, if the firm borrows money, every dollar of interest it pays on the loan reduces taxes by 29 cents. Therefore, after-tax earnings is reduced by only 71 cents.

Check Point 3.8

Recalculate the figures in Table 3.6 assuming that firm A now has to make interest payments of $60 million. What happens to taxes paid? Does net income fall by the additional $20 million interest payment compared with the case considered in the table, where interest expense was only $40 million?

When firms make profits, they pay 29 percent of the profits to CRA. But the process doesn't work in reverse; if the firm makes an operating loss, CRA does not send it a cheque for 29 percent of the loss. However, the firm can carry the losses back, deduct them from taxable income in earlier years, and claim a refund of past taxes paid. Losses can also be carried forward and deducted from taxable income in the future. Currently, operating losses can be carried back a maximum of three years and carried forward for up to twenty years.

The United States, European countries, and most other countries in the world also charge corporate taxes based on corporate profits, allowing companies to deduct the costs of operations, including interest expense. However, the tax systems and tax rates differ in each country. To learn more about taxation in different countries, check out the site **www.worldwide-tax.com**. A company such as AstraZeneca, with subsidiaries operating in various countries, has to pay taxes in each of the countries, based on the profits earned by its subsidiary in that country. Since a subsidiary is a separate legal corporation, although at least 50 percent of its shares are owned by its parent, it is taxed separately from the parent. So AstraZeneca's Canadian subsidiary is treated like a Canadian corporation and pays Canadian corporate taxes on the basis of the earnings of the Canadian subsidiary.

PERSONAL TAX

Table 3.7 shows the 2011 Canadian federal and provincial personal tax rates for employment income, interest income, and unincorporated business income. Dividends and capital gains are taxed at special rates, and we discuss them later in the section.

marginal tax rate Additional taxes owed per dollar of additional income.

The tax rates presented in Table 3.7 are **marginal tax rates**, and they apply to various income tax brackets. The marginal tax rate is the tax the individual pays on each extra dollar of income. As a federal taxpayer, you would pay 15 cents for each extra dollar of income you earn when your income is below $41,544, but you would pay 22 cents of tax on each dollar of income in excess of $41,544 and up to $83,088. As outlined in the table, the federal personal tax system has four income brackets and marginal tax rates. This is a progressive tax system—the higher the income, the higher the tax rate. Almost all provincial and territorial systems are progressive. Alberta is the exception, where a flat tax rate of 10 percent is charged on all income.

TABLE 3.7
Federal and provincial personal income tax rates, 2011.

Tax Rates and Taxable Income Brackets, 2011					
	Rate, %	Income Bracket, $		Rate, %	Income Bracket, $
Federal	15	0–41,544	Nova Scotia	8.79	0–29,590
	22	41,545–83,088		14.95	29,591–59,180
	26	83,089–128,800		16.67	59,181–93,000
	29	128,801 and over		17.5	93,001–150,000
				21	150,001 and over
British Columbia	5.06	0–36,146	Prince Edward Island	9.8	0–31,984
	7.7	36,147–72,293		13.8	31,985–63,969
	10.5	72,294–83,001		16.7	63,970 and over
	12.29	83,002–100,787	Newfoundland and Labrador	7.7	0–31,904
	14.7	100,788 and over		12.5	31,905–63,807
Alberta	10	All income		13.3	63,808 and over
			Northwest Territories	5.9	0–37626
Saskatchewan	11	40,919		8.6	37,627–75,253
	13	40,920–116,911		12.2	75,254–122,345
	15	116,912 and over		14.05	122,346 and over
Manitoba	10.8	0–31,000	Nunavut	4	0–39,612
	12.75	31,001–67,000		7	39,613–79,224
	17.4	67,001 and over		9	79,225–128,800
Ontario	5.05	0–37,774		11.5	128,801 and over
	9.15	37,775–75,550	Yukon	7.04	0–41,544
	11.16	75,551 and over		9.68	41,545–83,088
Québec	16	0–39,060		11.44	83,089–128,800
	20	39,061–78,120		12.76	128,801 and over
	24	78,121 and over			
New Brunswick	9.1	0–37,150			
	12.1	37,151–74,300			
	12.4	74,301–120,796			
	14.3	120,797 and over			

Note: All surtaxes have been ignored.

Sources: 1) KPMG, Federal and Provincial Personal Income Tax Rates, Brackets and Surtaxes for 2011. Reprinted with permission of KPMG LLP (Canada).; 2) Canada Revenue Agency website: **www.cra-arc.gc.ca/tx/indvdls/fq/txrts-eng.html#provincial**, accessed on January 22, 2011.

For example, suppose you live in Saskatchewan and your taxable income is $50,000. Your federal tax is 15 percent of the first $41,544 and 22 percent on the remaining $8,456:

$$\text{Federal tax} = (.15 \times \$41{,}544) + (.22 \times \$8{,}456) = \$8{,}091.92$$

From Table 3.7 we see that the Saskatchewan provincial tax rate is 11 percent on the first $40,919 of taxable income and 13 percent on income in excess of $40,919 and up to $116,911. Your provincial tax is

$$\text{Provincial tax} = (.11 \times \$40{,}919) + (.13 \times \$9{,}081) = \$5{,}681.62$$

As you can see, taxpayers end up calculating their taxes twice: once for the federal government and once for their provincial government. No wonder computerized tax preparation software is popular!

average tax rate Total taxes owed divided by total income.

What is your tax rate? The **average tax rate** is simply the total tax bill divided by total income. In this example, total tax is \$8,091.92 + \$5,681.62, or \$13,773.54, giving an average tax rate of \$13,773.54/\$50,000 = .275, or 27.5 percent. At the margin, however, an extra dollar of income is taxed at 22 percent federally and 13 percent provincially, making a combined marginal tax rate of 22 percent plus 13 percent, or 35 percent. The marginal tax rate is usually the most important for making financial decisions, because different types of income are taxed at different marginal rates, as we will discuss next.

Financial managers need to know about personal tax rates because dividends and interest payments that companies make to individuals are both subject to tax. If these payments are heavily taxed, individuals will be more reluctant to buy the company's shares or bonds. Remember that every dollar of income the company earns is taxed at the corporate rate. If the company then pays a dividend out of this after-tax income, the shareholder also pays personal income tax on that dividend. Thus the income paid out as a dividend is taxed twice, once in the hands of the firm and once in the hands of the shareholder. Suppose instead that the company earns a dollar that is then paid out as interest. This dollar escapes corporate tax, but an individual who received the interest has to pay personal tax.

The personal tax rates in Table 3.7 apply to interest income but not to dividend income. In Canada, dividends paid by Canadian companies to individuals are taxed at a lower rate, giving credit for some of the corporate tax already paid.

The calculation of personal tax on dividends depends on whether the dividends are categorized as "eligible" or "non-eligible." Eligible dividends include dividends paid by public or other corporations which are Canadian residents and are not Canadian-controlled private companies (CCPCs). Companies that pay eligible dividends should be subject to the federal general corporate income tax rate, which at the time of writing is at 16.5 percent. Under some conditions, CCPCs can also pay eligible dividends.[22] The company paying the dividend declares whether it is an eligible or non-eligible dividend.

EXAMPLE 3.3 CALCULATING THE TAX ON DIVIDENDS

To see how we would calculate dividends on personal taxes, let us examine the following example:

Suppose you receive \$50 of eligible dividends, and your marginal federal tax rate is 26 percent and your Ontario provincial marginal tax rate is 11.16 percent. To calculate your federal tax, first "gross up" your dividends to 141 percent- of the actual dividends received, to get *grossed-up* or *taxable* dividends:

$$\begin{aligned}\text{Grossed-up dividends} &= \text{Gross-up factor} \times \text{dividends}\\ &= 1.41 \times \$50, \text{ or } \$70.5\end{aligned}$$

The gross federal tax on the grossed-up dividends is

$$\begin{aligned}\text{Gross federal tax} &= \text{federal tax rate} \times \text{grossed-up dividends}\\ &= .26 \times \$70.5, \text{ or } \$18.33\end{aligned}$$

However, you don't pay this amount! Subtract the federal dividend tax credit of 16.44 percent of the grossed-up dividend (or 23.17 percent of the actual dividend paid):

$$\begin{aligned}\text{Federal dividend tax credit} &= \text{federal dividend tax credit} \times \text{grossed-up dividends}\\ &= .1644 \times \$70.50, \text{ or } \$11.59\end{aligned}$$

Your net federal dividend tax is gross federal tax less the dividend tax credit:

$$\begin{aligned}\text{Federal dividend tax} &= \text{gross federal dividend tax} - \text{federal dividend tax credit}\\ &= \$18.33 - \$11.59 = \$6.74\end{aligned}$$

(Continued)

[22] These conditions include the following: The CCPC should be subject to the federal general corporate income tax rate and not the small business tax rate. Earnings of such CCPCs should not be in the form of investment income other than eligible dividends from public corporations.

(Concluded)

To calculate the provincial tax on the $50 dividend, repeat the steps using the appropriate provincial tax rate and provincial dividend tax credit. We note from Table 3.8 that the Ontario dividend tax credit is 6.4 percent of grossed-up dividends.

$$\begin{aligned}\text{Ontario dividend tax} &= \text{gross Ontario dividend tax} - \text{Ontario dividend tax credit}\\ &= .1116 \times \$70.50 - .064 \times \$70.50 = \$3.36\end{aligned}$$

Total dividend tax is $6.74 + $3.36, or $10.10.

In Example 3.3, the after-tax dividend income is the $50 dividend less the $10.10 in taxes, or $39.90. The effective tax rate on eligible dividend income equals the dividend tax divided by dividends received, $10.10/$50, or 20.2 percent. This is substantially less than the combined federal–provincial marginal tax rate on salary and interest income of 26 percent + 11.16 percent, or 37.16 percent. Of course, if the dividend is non-eligible, different gross up and tax rates would apply, as shown in Table 3.8. The effective tax rate on non-eligible dividends will be higher than the applicable rate on eligible dividends. We should keep in mind that companies that pay non-eligible dividends also tend to be taxed at the small business rate and, therefore, generally pay lower corporate taxes than companies that pay eligible dividends.

In addition to salary, interest, and dividend income, individuals can also earn capital gains income. A capital gain occurs when an asset is sold for more than its original purchase price. If you sell the asset for less than the original purchase price, you have a capital loss. Currently, 50 percent of capital gains are taxable; in other words, capital gains are taxed at one-half of the regular or full personal tax rate. Capital losses can be used to reduce your capital gains. If you don't have a capital gain in the current year to offset capital loss, you can carry the loss back up to three years or carry it forward indefinitely to reduce capital gains from another year. Capital gains and losses are *realized* only when you sell the asset. If you don't sell, you pay no tax.

TABLE 3.8

Dividend Tax Credit, 2011, on Grossed-Up Amount*		
	Eligible Dividend	Non-eligible Dividend
Federal	**16.44%**	**13.33%**
Alberta	10%	3.48%
British Columbia	10.31%	3.40%
Manitoba	11%	2.50%
New Brunswick	12%	5.30%
Newfoundland and Labrador	11%	5%
Northwest territories	10.78%	6%
Nova Scotia	8.29%	7.70%
Nunavut	5.82%	4%
Ontario	6.40%	4.50%
Prince Edward Island	10.50%	2.10%
Québec	11.90%	8%
Saskatchewan	11%	6%
Yukon	10.31%	4.45%

*The grossed-up amount is calculated for eligible dividends by multiplying the actual dividend by a gross-up factor of 1.41. For non-eligible dividends, the applicable gross-up factor is 1.25.

Source: TaxTips sites, **www.taxtips.ca/dtc/enhanceddtc/enhanceddtcrates.htm** and **www.taxtips.ca/dtc/smallbusdtc.htm**.

EXAMPLE 3.4 **DETERMINING CAPITAL GAINS TAX**

You bought shares in Bio-technics stock when it was selling for 10 cents a share. Its market price is now $1 a share. As long as you hold on to the stock, there is no tax to pay on your gain. But if you sell for $1, you realize a capital gain of 90 cents and have to pay tax. If your combined marginal federal and provincial tax rate is 40 percent, the capital gains tax rate is 20 percent, and the capital gains tax is .2 × $0.90, or $0.18. Your after-tax capital gain is $0.90 − $0.18, or $0.72 per share sold.

Check Point 3.9

Suppose in 2011 you lived in British Columbia and earned interest income of $1,000 and dividend income of $1,000, and realized a capital gain of $1,000. Calculate the tax, the after-tax income, and the tax rate for each of the different types of income assuming you are in the lowest tax bracket. Redo the calculations assuming you are in the highest tax bracket. Rank high and low income taxpayers' tax rates on the different types of income.

The tax rates in Table 3.7 apply to individuals. But financial institutions are major investors in shares and bonds. These institutions often have special rates of tax. For example, pension funds, which hold huge numbers of shares, are not taxed on either dividend income or capital gains.

The financial policies of companies affect the taxes paid by both the company and its investors, the bondholders and shareholders. By selecting financial policies that minimize investors' taxes, financial managers can increase the wealth of their investors. We will return to the important issue of investor taxation when we examine financing and dividend payout decisions of companies in Chapters 16 and 17.

3.7 SUMMARY

1. **What information is contained in the statement of financial position (balance sheet), income statement and statement of comprehensive income, statement of changes in equity, and statement of cash flows?** LO1

Investors and other stakeholders in the firm need regular financial information to help them monitor the firm's progress. Accountants summarize this information in a statement of financial position (balance sheet), income statement and statement of comprehensive income, statement of changes in equity and statement of cash flows.

The **statement of financial position (balance sheet)** provides a snapshot of the firm's assets, liabilities and equity at a specific date. The assets consist of current assets that can be rapidly turned into cash within the next year and non-current assets, which include tangible assets such as plant and machinery. The liabilities consist of current liabilities that are due for payment shortly and non-current liabilities such as long-term debts. The difference between the assets and the liabilities represents the amount of the shareholders' equity.

The **income statement** measures the profit (net earnings or net income) from the operating activities of the company during the year. It shows the difference between revenues and expenses. The **statement of comprehensive income** includes profits plus other comprehensive income.

The **statement of changes in equity** provides information to explain the change from the previous period of each component of equity on the statement of financial position.

The **statement of cash flows** measures the sources and uses of cash during the year. The change in the company's cash balance is the difference between the sources and uses.

2. **What is the difference between market and book value? LO2**

It is important to distinguish between the book values that are shown in the company accounts and the market values of the assets and liabilities. Some **book values** are historical measures based on the original cost of an asset. For example, if the firm uses the cost method for valuing property, plant, and equipment the assets in the SFP are shown at their historical cost less an allowance for depreciation (and any impairment losses). Similarly, the figure for shareholders' equity measures the cash that shareholders have contributed in the past and what the company has reinvested on their behalf. In contrast, **market value** is the current price of an asset, liability or equity.

3. **Why does accounting income differ from cash flow? LO3**

Profit or net income is not the same as cash flow. There are three reasons for this: (1) investment in fixed assets is not deducted immediately from income but is instead spread over the expected life of the equipment, (2) the accountant records revenues when a sale is made rather than when the customer actually pays the bill, and at the same time, deducts the production costs even though those costs may have been incurred earlier, and (3) other comprehensive income, a component of total comprehensive income, is not due to operating activities but captures changes in book value of certain asset and liabilities due to accounting methods.

4. **What is cash flow from assets, financing flow and free cash flow? LO4**

The three sections of statement of cash flow show a firm's cash flows from operating activities, cash flow from investment activities, and cash flows from financing activities. The sum of all of the different cash flows equals the change in cash and cash equivalents. **Cash flow from assets**, the net cash generated by the operation of the firm, equals the sum of cash flow from operating activities and investment activities. **Financing flow** equals cash flow from financing activities minus change in cash and cash equivalents. Cash flow from financing activities can be separated into cash flows to bondholders (lenders) and to shareholders. Cash flow from assets equals financing flow. Cash flow from assets is also called **free cash flow** because it is the cash flow available to pay out to lenders and shareholders.

5. **What are the essential features of the taxation of corporate and personal income? LO5**

For large companies the marginal rate of tax on income is around 29 percent and around 15 percent for small businesses. In calculating taxable income the company deducts operating costs, an allowance for depreciation and interest payments. It cannot deduct dividend payments to the shareholders.

Individuals are also taxed on their income, which includes dividends and interest on their investments. Dividends are taxed at lower rates than interest and employment income. Capital gains are taxed at one-half the personal tax rate, but only when the investment is sold and the gain realized.

Related Web Links

sedar.com Annual reports and other documents of Canadian public companies

AnnualReports.com Links to financial statements and other documents of U.S. listed public companies

annualreports.co.uk Link to financial statement of U.K. companies

kpmg.com/Ca/en/IssuesAndInsights/ArticlesPublications/Pages/taxrates.aspx KPG tax site

iasb.org Site of the International Accounting Standards Board

Key Terms

average tax rate 87
book value *or* carrying value 61
cash flow from assets 78
International Financial Reporting Standards (IFRS) 60
fair value 62
financing flow 79
free cash flow 80
income statement 69
marginal tax rate 85
statement of cash flows 75
statement of changes in equity 70
statement of comprehensive income 69
statement of financial position (SFP) *or* balance sheet 61
subsidiary 60

Questions and Problems

connect™ Practise and learn online with *Connect*. Questions with online Excel templates or datasets are marked with .

*Answers in Appendix B

Notes: Different names for the same concepts are used in questions and problems to help you get familiar with the various names. For example, *balance sheet* and *statement of financial position* stand for the same financial statement. *Profit*, *net earnings*, and *net income* are different names for what the firm earned from its operations (excluding other comprehensive income). *Cost of sales* and *cost of goods sold* both measure the cost of producing goods. *Owners' equity* and *shareholders' equity* are both terms for book value of the firm's equity.

BASIC

*1. **Statement of Financial Position (SFP).** Construct an SFP for Sophie's Sofas given the following data. What is shareholders' equity? (LO1)

Cash and cash equivalents = $10,000
Inventory of sofas = $200,000
Store and property, net = $100,000
Trade receivables = $22,000
Trade payables = $17,000
Long-term debt = $170,000

2. **Financial Statements.** Earlier in the chapter, we characterized the statement of financial position as providing a snapshot of the firm at one point in time and the statement of comprehensive income as providing a video. What did we mean by this? Is the statement of cash flows more like a snapshot or a video? (LO1)

3. **Profit Versus Cash Flow.** Explain why profit (net earnings) generally differs from a firm's cash inflows. (LO3)

4. **Net Working Capital.** QuickGrow is in an expanding market, and its sales are increasing by 25 percent annually. Would you expect its net working capital to be increasing or decreasing? Explain. (LO3)

5. **Tax Rates.** Using Table 3.7, calculate the combined federal and provincial marginal and average tax rates for both an Albertan and Newfoundlander with the following incomes: (LO5)

a. $20,000
*b. $60,000
c. $100,000
d. $3,000,000

6. **Tax Rates.** What would be the marginal and average tax rates for a Manitoban corporation with an income level of $100,000? (LO5)

*7. **Taxes.** John Flynn lives in Nova Scotia. In 2011 he earned $1,500 in interest income and $3,000 in dividend income, and realized a $2,000 capital gain. Calculate his after-tax income and tax rate for each type of income, assuming that his marginal federal tax rate was 26 percent, his marginal provincial tax rate was 16.67 percent, the dividend gross-up factor is 141 percent, the federal dividend tax credit is 16.44 percent of grossed-up dividends, and the provincial dividend tax credit is 8.29 percent of grossed-up dividends. (LO5)

8. **Cash Flows.** What impact will the following actions have on the firm's cash balance? (LO3)

a. The firm sells some goods from inventory.
b. The firm sells some machinery to a bank and leases it back for a period of 20 years.
c. The firm buys back 1 million shares from existing shareholders.

*9. **Statement of Changes in Equity.** On the Brandex Inc. SFP as the year-end 2012 the share capital was $1,100,000, retained earnings were $3,000,000, accumulated other comprehensive income was $400,000, and total equity was $4,500,000. Year-end 2013 SFP retained earnings were $3,300,000. In 2013 net earnings were $900,000 and other comprehensive income was $0. There were no stock repurchases or stock issues during the year. What were dividends paid by the firm in 2013? (LO1)

INTERMEDIATE

10. **Taxes.** You set up your tax preparation firm as an incorporated business in Nova Scotia. You took $70,000 from the firm as your salary. The firm's taxable income for the year (net of your salary) was $30,000. How much tax must be paid, including both your personal taxes and the firm's taxes? By how much will you reduce the total tax bill by reducing your salary to $50,000, thereby leaving the firm with taxable income of $50,000? Use the tax rates presented in Tables 3.5 and 3.7. (LO5)

11. **Market Versus Book Values.** The founder of Alchemy Products, Inc., discovered a way to turn lead into gold and patented this new technology. He then formed a corporation and invested $900,000 in setting up a production plant. As an IFRS user, the patent is on the SFP as an intangible asset, with $100,000 book value, the cost of registering the patent. Now he believes that he could sell his patent for $50 million. (LO2)
   *a. What are the book value and market value of the firm?
   *b. If there are 2 million shares of stock in the new corporation, what would be the price per share and the book value per share?
   c. Why are the price per share and book value per share so different?

*12. **Income Statement and Statement of Cash Flow.** Sheryl's Shingles had sales of $10,000 in 2011. The cost of sales was $6,500, general and administrative expenses were $1,000, and interest expenses were $500. Net working capital increased $200 and capital expenditures were $900. Total depreciation expense included in the costs was $1,000. The firm's tax rate is 35 percent.
   a. What are earnings before interest and taxes? (LO1)
   b. What is net earnings? (LO1)
   c. What is cash flow from operating activities if you start with net earnings? What if you start with profit before tax? (LO1)
   d. What is cash flow from assets? (LO4)

13. **Cash Flow.** Can cash flow from operating activities be positive if profit before tax is negative? Can operating cash flow be negative if profit before tax is positive? Give examples. (LO3)

14. **Cash Flows.** Ponzi Products produced 100 chain letter kits in the first quarter, Q1, resulting in a Q1 total cash outlay of $10 per unit. It will sell 50 of the kits next quarter, Q2, at a price of $11, and the other 50 kits in Q3 at a price of $12. It takes a full quarter for it to collect its bills from its customers. (Ignore possible sales in earlier or later quarters.) In your answers, state any assumptions you make.
   a. Prepare an income statement for Ponzi for Q1, Q2, Q3, and Q4. Ignore taxes. (LO1)
   b. What is Ponzi's net working capital in each quarter? (LO1)
   c. What are the cash flows for the company in each of the four quarters? (LO3)

15. **Profits Versus Cash Flow.** During the last year of operations, trade receivables increased by $10,000, trade payables increased by $5,000, and inventories decreased by $2,000. What is the total impact of these changes on the difference between profits and cash flow? (LO3)

16. **Income Statement.** A firm's income statement includes the following data. The firm's average tax rate was 20 percent. No depreciation is included in cost of goods sold or administrative expenses. (LO1)

Cost of goods sold	$8,000
Income taxes	2,000
Administrative expenses	3,000
Interest expense	1,000
Depreciation	1,000

   a. What was the firm's profit before tax and net income?
   b. What must have been the firm's revenues?
   c. What was EBIT?

17. **Profits Versus Cash Flow.** Butterfly Tractors had $14 million in sales last year. Cost of sales, including depreciation, was $8 million, depreciation expense was $2 million, interest payment on outstanding debt was $1 million, capital expenditures were $1 million, and the firm's tax rate was 35 percent. (LO3, LO4)
   a. What were the firm's net income, cash flows from operations, and cash flow from assets?
   b. What would happen to net income and cash flows if depreciation were increased by $1 million? How do you explain the differing impact of depreciation on income versus cash flow?
   c. Would you expect the change in income and cash flows from the change in depreciation to have a positive or negative impact on the firm's stock price?
   d. Now consider the impact on net income and cash flow if the firm's interest expense were $1 million higher. Why is this case different from part (b)?

18. **Cash Flow.** In April, Candy Canes, Inc., buys $50,000 of raw materials, sugar and peppermint, and pays for them in May. In May it uses all of the raw materials to produces candy. Total cost of the candy is $100,000 and all costs are paid in May. All candy is sold to distributors in May for $150,000, but it does not receive payment

until June. For each month, what the firm's sales, net income, and operating cash flow. (LO3)

19. **Financing Flow.** Interest expense for Rhodes Manufacturing was $500,000 in 2011. During 2011, $3.7 million in old debt was repaid and $2.0 million was raised through new borrowing. Dividends of $425,000 were paid and $1.75 million was raised through new share sales. (LO4)
    a. Calculate the cash flow to bondholders. Treat interest as a financing flow.
    b. Calculate the cash flow to shareholders.
    c. If cash and marketable securities increased $300,000 in 2011, what were the 2011 financing flow and cash flow from assets? Treat interest as a financing flow.

*20. **Financial Statements.** Here are incomplete 2011 and 2012 SFPs for Nobel Corp.

Nobel Corp. Statement of Financial Position, as of End of Year

Assets	2012	2011
Current assets	$ 420	$ 310
PP&E	1,420	1,200
Liabilities and Shareholders' Equity		
Trade payables	$ 240	$ 210
Long-term debt	920	830

a. What was shareholders' equity at the end of 2011 and 2012? (LO1)
b. If Nobel paid dividends of $100 in 2011, what must have been 2011 net income? Assume no shares were issued or repurchased and no other comprehensive income. (LO1)
c. If Nobel purchased $300 in equipment during the year, what must have been the depreciation expense on the income statement? No impairment charges were made. (LO1)
d. What was the change in net working capital between 2011 and 2012? (LO1)
e. If Nobel issued $200 of new long-term debt in 2012, how much debt must have been paid off during the year? (LO1)
f. What were the 2012 cash flow from operations and cash flow from assets? (LO4)
g. What were the 2012 cash flow to bondholders, cash flow to shareholders, and the financing flow? State all assumptions you make. (LO4)

21. **Financial Statements.** South Sea Baubles has the following incomplete balance sheet and income statement.

South Sea Baubles Balance Sheet, as of End of Year ($ millions)

Assets	2012	2011
Current assets	$ 140	$ 90
Net fixed assets	900	800
Liabilities and Shareholders' Equity		
Current liabilities	$ 60	$ 50
Long-term debt	750	600

Income Statement, 2012 ($ millions)

Revenue	$1,950
Cost of goods sold	(1,030)
Depreciation	350
Interest expense	240

a. What is shareholders' equity in 2011 and 2012? (LO1)
b. What is net working capital in 2011 and 2012? (LO1)
c. What is taxable income and taxes paid in 2012? Assume the firm pays taxes equal to 35 percent of taxable income. (LO4)
d. What is cash flow provided by operations during 2012? Pay attention to changes in net working capital. (LO3)
e. What must have been South Sea's gross investment in fixed assets (capital expenditure) during 2012? See Check Point 3.1. (LO1)
f. If South Sea reduced its outstanding accounts payable by $35 million during 2008, what must have happened to its other current liabilities? (LO1)
g. What are the 2012 cash flow from assets, and cash flow to bondholders and shareholders? State all assumptions you make. (LO4)

22. **Internet.** The schedule of tax rates for individuals changes periodically. Find the latest schedules on **www.cra-arc.gc.ca**, click on information for individuals and then on all rates. What is your marginal tax rate if you are single with a taxable income of $70,000? What is your average tax rate? (LO5)

CHALLENGE

Here are some data on Fincorp, Inc., that you should use for problems 23 to 32. Fincorp follows IFRS. The statement of financial position items correspond to values at year-end of 2011 and 2012, while the statement of comprehensive income items correspond to revenues or expenses during the year ending in either 2011 or 2012. All values are in thousands of dollars.

	2012	2011
Trade payables	$ 350	$ 300
Revenue	4,100	4,000
Depreciation	(320)	(300)
Short-term investments	550	430
Inventories	350	300
Long-term debt	2,400	3,000
Provisions	770	680
Administrative expenses	(550)	(500)
Federal and provincial taxes[a]	(420)	(400)
Trade receivables	450	400
Finance income	120	50
Finance expense[b]	(150)	(150)
Property, plant, and equipment[c]	5,800	5,000
Dividends paid	(410)	(410)
Cost of goods sold	(1,700)	(1,600)
Cash and cash equivalents	300	800

[a] Taxes are paid in their entirety in the year in which the tax obligation is incurred.
[b] Finance income is gain in value of short-term investments.
[c] Property, plant, and equipment are net of accumulated depreciation and impairment losses since the assets were installed.

23. **SFP.** Construct an SFP for Fincorp for 2011 and 2012. What is shareholders' equity? (LO1)

*24. **Working Capital.** What happened to net working capital during the year? What about non-cash net working capital? (LO1)

25. **Income Statement.** Construct an income statement for Fincorp for 2011 and 2012. What was the addition to retained earnings for 2012? How does that compare with the increase in shareholders' equity between the two years? (LO1)

*26. **Earnings per Share.** Suppose that Fincorp has 500,000 shares outstanding. What were earnings per share? (LO1)

27. **Taxes.** What was the firm's average tax bracket for each year? Do you have enough information to determine the marginal tax bracket? (LO4)

28. **SFP.** Examine the values for depreciation in 2012 and the balance for property, plant, and equipment in 2011 and 2012. What was Fincorp's gross investment in property, plant, and equipment during 2012? (LO1)

29. **Cash Flows.** Construct a statement of cash flows for Fincorp for 2012 using Table 3.4 as a guide. Treat interest as an operating expense and assume that interest paid is equal to finance expense for the year. (LO1)

30. **Operating Cash Flow.** Calculate Fincorp's operating cash flow starting with profit before taxes. Treat interest as a financing flow. (LO1)

31. **Free Cash Flows.** (LO4)
   a. Using the data for Fincorp, determine the cash flow from assets, cash flow to bondholders, cash flow to shareholders, and financing flows. Treat interest as a financing flow.
   b. Assuming that Fincorp's tax rate is 28 percent, calculate its after-tax interest expense. Why is it appropriate to convert the interest expense to its after-tax cost but not appropriate to adjust dividends?
   c. Using the after-tax interest expense, recalculate cash flow from assets and financing flow. Compare with your answers in problem (a). In what ways are the values different?

*32. **Book Versus Market Value.** Now suppose that the *market value* (in thousands of dollars) of Fincorp's fixed assets in 2012 is $6,000, and that the value of its long-term debt is only $2,400. In addition, the consensus among investors is that Fincorp's past investments in developing the skills of its employees are worth $2,900. This investment of course does not show up on the balance sheet. What will be the price per share of Fincorp stock? (LO2)

33. **Cash Flow from Assets and Financing Flow.** Using the financial statements for Small Time Products, calculate cash flow from assets and financing flow in 2012. Treat interest as a financing flow. (LO4)

2012 Income Statement

Revenue	$1,301
Cost of goods sold	1,031
Depreciation	140
Interest expense	38
Taxes	29
Net income	63

Small Time Products Statement of Financial Position for 2011 and 2012, as of Year-End

	2011	2012
Cash and cash equivalents	$ 41	42
Trade receivable	70	86
Inventory	12	14
Current assets	123	142
Net property and equipment	886	974
Total assets	1,009	1,116
Bank loan	40	40
Accounts payable	108	120
Current liabilities	148	160
Long-term debt	420	464
Capital stock	100	110
Retained earnings	341	382
Total liabilities and shareholders' equity	1,009	1,116

34. **Taxes.** Reconsider the data in problem 10. What are the total personal and corporate taxes if you pay yourself a salary of $50,000 and a dividend of $20,000? (LO4)

35. **Internet.** Go to **www.sedar.com**, the Web site where public Canadian companies must post their annual reports and other corporate documents. Click on "Search Database," then "Public Company." Select document type "Annual Report" then "Search" and you will get a list of recent annual reports. Pick one and read it. What do you learn about the nature of the business and of the company's successes and failures? What type of assets and liabilities are listed on the balance sheet? Using the cash flow statement, calculate the cash flow from assets and the financing flow. Treat interest as a financing flow. (LO1, LO4)

36. **Internet.** For a wider choice of financial statements, you might go to **www.annualreports.com**. Browse through this site to see the wide range of companies, listed in different international stock exchanges, included here. How many stock exchanges are covered by this site? Select a large non-financial company and find its latest financial statements. For this company, draw up a simplified statement of financial position, income statement, and statement of cash flows as in Tables 3.1, 3.2, and 3.4. Some companies' financial statements can be extremely complex; try to find a relatively straightforward business. Also, as far as possible, use the same headings as in these tables, and do not hesitate to group some items as "other current assets" or "other expenses," etc. Look first at your simplified balance sheet. How much was the company owed by its customers in the form of unpaid bills? What liabilities does the company need to meet within a year? What was the original cost of the company's fixed assets? Now look at the income statement. What were the company's earnings before interest and taxes (EBIT)? Finally, turn to the cash-flow statement. Did changes in working capital add to cash or use it up? (LO1)

Solutions to Check Points

3.1 a. PP&E book value, net PP&E, = cost − accumulated depreciation and impairment. So 2010 net PP&E = $15,583 million − $8,626 million = $6,957 million and this is the 2010 PP&E value on the SFP in Table 3.1.

b. The capital expenditure (capex) is the amount spent to purchase new PP&E. In the 2011 annual report, note 7 would be

2011 PP&E cost = 2010 cost + 2011 capex
= $15,583 million + $800 million
= $16,383 million

2011 accumulated depreciation and impairment
= 2010 value + 2011 depreciation and impairment expense
= $8,626 million + $1,000 million + $20 million
= $9,646 million

2011 net PP&E
= 2011 PP&E cost + 2011 accumulated depreciation and impairment
= $16,383 million − $9,646 million
= $6,737 million

Change in net PP&E
= 2011 net PP&E − 2010 net PP&E
= $6,737 million − $6,957 million = −$220

Notice that 2011 capital expenditure − 2011 depreciation and impairment expense = $800 − $1020 = −$220. So the change in the book value of PP&E equals capital expenditures minus the depreciation and impairment expense. This can be written as

Change in net PP&E
= Capital expenditure − Depreciation and impairment expense

c. Rearrange the above equation to solve for capital expenditures:

Capital expenditure
= Change in net PP&E + Depreciation and impairment expense
= ($7,000 million − $6,957 million) + $1,020 million
= $1,063 million

So, given the change in net PP&E from 2010 to 2011 and knowing the depreciation and impairment expense that have affected the book value, you can calculate the capital expenditure.

3.2 Cash and equivalents would increase by $100 million. Property and equipment would increase by $400 million. Long-term debt would increase by $500 million. Total equity would not increase: assets and liabilities have increased equally, leaving total equity unchanged.

3.3 a. If the auto plant were worth $14 billion, the equity in the firm would be worth $14 billion − $4 billion = $10 billion. With 100 million shares outstanding, each share would be worth $100.

b. If the outstanding stock were worth \$8 billion, we would infer that the market values the auto plant at \$8 billion + \$4 billion = \$12 billion.

3.4 Statement of changes in equity for Can Corp (value in millions of dollars):

	Share Capital	Retained Earnings	Accumulated Other Comprehensive Income	Total Equity
Balance, December 31, 2011	10	25	1	36
Net earnings for 2012		2.5		2.5
Other comprehensive Income for 2012			0.1	0.1
Transactions with owners in 2012				
Dividends		(1)		(1)
Issue of ordinary shares	2			2
Net movement	2	1.5	0.1	3.6
Balance, December 31, 2012	12	26.5	1.1	39.6

3.5 The profits for the firm are recognized in periods 2 and 3 when the sales take place. Because 50 percent of the goods are sold in periods 2 and 3, each period cost of goods sold is 50 percent of the total cost of producing the goods, (\$100). So in both of those periods, profits are sale − cost of goods sold, \$150 − \$100 = \$50. Cash flows are derived as follows:

Period:	1	2	3	4
Sales	0	150	150	0
(Increase) or decrease in receivables	0	(150)	0	150
Cost of goods sold	0	(100)	(100)	0
(Increase) or decrease in inventories	(200)	100	100	
Increase or (decrease) in payables	70	(70)	0	0
= Net cash inflow (outflow)	(130)	(70)	150	150

In period 1, \$130 of cash is used to produce, but the rest of the cost, \$200 − \$130 = \$70, isn't paid but is recognized as an increase in accounts payable. In period 2, half the units are sold for \$150 but no cash is collected, so the \$150 is treated as an increase in accounts receivable. Also, half of the \$200 cost of production is recognized as cost of goods sold, and the same amount is taken out of inventory. But \$70 is spent to pay for the firm's bills. In period 3, the firm sells another \$150 of product but collects \$150 from its previous sales. The uncollected sales in period 3 increases receivables by \$150 but the collected cash from the period 2 sales reduces receivables by \$150. So the total change in receivables is zero. Net cash flow is the \$150 collected in this period on the sale that occurred in period 2. In period 4, cash flow is again \$150, as the accounts receivable from the sale in period 3 are collected.

3.6 a. An increase in inventories uses cash, reducing the firm's net cash balance.

b. A reduction in accounts payable uses cash, because it captures the fact that the company paid its bills, reducing the firm's net cash balance.

c. An issue of common stock is a source of cash.

d. The purchase of new equipment is a use of cash, and it reduces the firm's net cash balance.

3.7 **Cash flow from assets** = Cash flow from operating activities + cash flow from investing activities.

Cash flow from operating activities = Net income + depreciation + interest expense − increase in working capital = 7.3 + 1.9 + 0.6—2.6 = \$7.2 million.

Cash flow from investing activities = −\$3.5 million.

So: **Cash flow from assets** = 7.2 − 3.5 = \$3.7 million.

Cash flow from financing activities = cash flow from lenders + cash flow from shareholders.

Cash flow from lenders = −interest paid + new debt = −0.6 + 1.5 = \$.9 million.

Cash flow from shareholders = −dividends paid + new equity = −2 + 0 = −\$2 million.

So: **Cash flow from financing activities** = 0.9 − \$2 = −\$1.1 million.

Change in cash = cash flow from assets + cash flow from financing activities = 3.7 − 1.1 = \$2.6 million.

Financing flow = change in cash − cash from financing activities = 2.6 − (− 1.1) = 2.6 + 1.1 = \$3.7 million.

3.8

	Firm A	Firm B
	(\$ millions)	
EBIT	100	100
Interest	60	0
Pretax income	40	100
Tax (29% of pre-tax income)	11.6	29
Net income	28.4	71

Taxes owed by firm A fall from \$17.4 million to \$11.6 million. The reduction in taxes, \$5.8, is 29 percent of the extra \$20 million of interest income (5.8/20 = .29 or 29%). Net income falls by \$14.2 million, from \$42.6 million to \$28.4 million. It does not fall by the full \$20 million of extra interest expense; it falls by interest expense less the reduction in taxes, or \$20 million − \$5.8 million = \$14.2 million.

3.9		Lowest Tax Bracket	Highest Tax Bracket
	Federal tax rate	15.0%	29%
	B.C. tax rate	5.06%	14.70%
	Combined tax rate	20.06%	43.70%
1.	Interest income	$1,000	$1,000
	Tax on interest income	.2006 × $1,000 = $200.60	.437 × $1,000 = $437
	After-tax interest income	$1,000 − $200.6 = $799.4	$1,000 − $437 = $563
	Interest income tax rate	$200.6/$1,000 = 20.06%	$437/$1,000 = 43.7%
2.A.	Dividend income (eligible)	$1,000	$1,000
	Grossed-up dividend	1.41 × $1,000 = $1,410	1.41 × $1,000 = $1,410
	Gross federal tax	.15 × $1,410 = $211.5	.29 × $1,410 = $408.90
	Less: Federal dividend tax credit	.1644 × $1,410 = $231.80	.1644 × $1,410 = $231.80
	Net federal dividend tax	$0 ($211.5 − $231.80 < 0)	$408.9 − $231.80 = $177.1
	Gross provincial tax	.0506 × $1,410 = $71.35	.147 × $1,410 = $207.27
	Less: Provincial dividend tax credit	.1031 × $1,410 = $145.37	.1031 × $1,410 = $145.37
	Net provincial dividend tax	$0 ($71.35 − $145 < 0)	$207.27 − $145.37 = $61.90
	Net tax on dividend income	$0	$177.1 + $61.90 = $239.00
	After-tax dividend income	$1,000	$1,000 − $239 = $761
	Dividend tax-rate	0%	$239/$1,000 = 23.9%
2.B.	Dividend income (non-eligible)	$1,000	$1,000
	Grossed-up dividend	1.25 × $1,000 = $1,250	1.25 × $1,000 = $1,250
	Gross federal tax	.15 × $1,250 = $187.5	.29 × $1,250 = $362.5
	Less: Federal dividend tax credit	.1333 × $1,250 = $166.63	.1333 × $1,250 = $166.63
	Net federal dividend tax	$187.5 − $166.63 = $20.88	$362.5 – $166.63 = $195.88
	Gross provincial tax	.0506 × $1,250 = $63.25	.147 × $1,250 = $183.75
	Less: Provincial dividend tax credit	.034 × $1,250 = $42.50	.034 × $1,250 = $42.50
	Net provincial dividend tax	$63.25 − $42.50 = $20.75	$183.75 − $42.50 = $141.25
	Net tax on dividend income	$20.88 + $20.75 = $41.63	$195.88 + $141.25 = $337.13
	After-tax dividend income	$1,000 − $41.63 = $899.7	$1,000 − $337.13 = $662.88
	Dividend tax-rate	$41.63/$1000 = 4.163%	$337.13/$1,000 = 33.71%
3.	Capital gains income	$1,000	$1,000
	Tax on capital gains	.2006 × .5 × $1,000 = $100.3	.437 × .5 × $1,000 = $218.5
	After-tax capital gains	$1,000 − $100.3 = $899.7	$1,000 − $218.5 = $781.5
	Capital gains tax rate	$100.3/$1000 = 10.03%	$218.5/$1000 = 21.85%

For the low-income investor, dividends are taxed least (0% if the dividends are eligible or 4.79% if the dividends are non-eligible), then capital gains (10.03%), and finally interest (20.06%). For the high-income investor, eligible dividends are taxed least (23.9%), followed by capital gains (21.85%), followed by non-eligible dividends (33.71%), and finally interest income (43.7%).

Notice that while non-eligible dividends are taxed at higher rates than eligible dividends, the companies paying non-eligible dividends are typically taxed at lower small business rates than those paying eligible dividends. The latter are taxed at general applicable corporate tax rates.

PART 1 Introduction

1 Goals and Governance of the Firm
2 Financial Markets and Institutions
3 Accounting and Finance
4 Measuring Corporate Performance
4.1 Measuring Market Value and Market Value Added
4.2 Economic Value Added and Accounting Rates of Return
4.3 Measuring Efficiency
4.4 Analyzing the Return on Assets: The Du Pont System
4.5 Measuring Financial Leverage
4.6 Measuring Liquidity
4.7 Calculating Sustainable Growth
4.8 Interpreting Financial Ratios
4.9 The Role of Financial Ratios—and a Final Note on Transparency
4.10 Summary

CHAPTER 4

Measuring Corporate Performance

LEARNING OBJECTIVES

After studying this chapter, you should be able to:

LO1 Calculate and interpret market value and market value added for a public corporation.

LO2 Calculate and interpret some key measures of firm performance, including economic value added (EVA), and rates of return on capital, assets, and equity.

LO3 Calculate and interpret measures of a firm's operating efficiency, leverage, and liquidity.

LO4 Show how profitability depends on the efficient use of assets and on profits as a fraction of sales.

LO5 Explain how a company's sustainable growth depends on both its payout policy and its return on equity.

LO6 Compare the company's financial standing with its main competitors and with its own position in earlier years.

When you need to judge how well management has performed, it is useful to start with some key financial ratios.

In Chapter 1 we introduced the basic objective of corporate finance: to maximize the current value of shareholders' investment in the firm. For public corporations, this value is set in the stock market. It equals market price per share multiplied by the number of shares outstanding. Of course, the fluctuations in market value partly reflect events that are outside the financial manager's control. Nevertheless, good financial managers always strive to add value by superior investment and financing decisions.

How can we judge whether managers are doing a good job at adding value or where there may be opportunity for improvement? We need measures of value added. We also need measures that help explain where the value added comes from. For example, value added depends on profitability, so we need measures of profitability. Profitability in turn depends on profit margins and on how efficiently the firm uses its assets. We will describe standard measures of profitability and efficiency in this chapter.

Value also depends on sound financing. Value is destroyed if the firm is financed recklessly and can't pay its debts. Value is also destroyed if the firm does not maintain adequate liquidity and therefore has difficulty finding the cash to pay its bills. Therefore, we will describe the measures that financial managers use to assess debt policy and liquidity.

These financial measures are financial ratios calculated from the firm's statement of comprehensive income and statement of financial position. Therefore, we will have to take care to remember the limitations of these accounting data.

You have probably heard stories of whizzes who can take a company's accounts apart in minutes, calculate some financial ratios, and divine the company's future. Such people are like abominable snowmen: often spoken of but never truly seen. Financial ratios are no substitute for a crystal ball. They are just a convenient way to analyze large quantities of financial data and to compare firms' performances. The ratios help you to ask the right questions, but they seldom answer them.

LO1 4.1 MEASURING MARKET VALUE AND MARKET VALUE ADDED

It is New Year's Day, 2011. Your New Year's resolutions have sparked an intense financial interest in AstraZeneca (AZN). Perhaps you are a mutual-fund manager trying to decide whether to allocate $25 million of new money to AstraZeneca stock. Perhaps you are an AZN shareholder pondering a sellout. You could be an investment banker seeking business from AstraZeneca or a bondholder concerned with AstraZeneca's credit standing. You could be the treasurer or CFO of AstraZeneca or of one of its competitors. You want to understand AstraZeneca's value and financial performance. How would you start?

AstraZeneca PLC common stock closed 2010 on the New York Stock Exchange (NYSE) at a price of US$46.19 per share. There were 1,438 million shares outstanding, so AstraZeneca's

market capitalization Total market value of equity, equal to share price times number of shares outstanding.

market capitalization or "market cap" was $46.19 × 1,438 = $66,421.22 million, just over $66 billion. This is a big number, of course, but AstraZeneca is a big company. AstraZeneca's shareholders have, over the years, invested billions in the company. Therefore, you decide to compare AstraZeneca's market capitalization to the book value of AstraZeneca's equity. The book value of equity is the sum of the funds invested by shareholders when they purchase shares plus earnings reinvested by the company on behalf of the shareholders. So the book value of equity measures shareholders' cumulative investment in the firm.

market value added Market capitalization minus book value of equity.

You turn to AstraZeneca's statement of comprehensive income and statement of financial position in Tables 4.1 and 4.2. Financial analysts typically recast (restate) financial statements into a format that makes them more convenient to use to calculate financial ratios.[1] At the end of 2010, the book value of AstraZeneca's equity, excluding non-controlling interest, was $23,213 million.[2] Therefore, AstraZeneca PLC **market value added**, the difference between the market

TABLE 4.1
Consolidated statement of comprehensive income for AstraZeneca PLC, for years ending December 31, 2009 and 2010 (US$ millions).

	2010	2009
Revenue	33,269	32,804
Cost of sales	(6,389)	(5,775)
Gross profit	26,880	27,029
Distribution costs	(335)	(298)
Research and development	(5,318)	(4,409)
Selling, general, administrative cost	(10,445)	(11,332)
Other operating income and expense	712	553
Operating profit	11,494	11,543
Finance income	516	462
Finance expense	(1,033)	(1,198)
Profit before tax	10,977	10,807
Taxation	(2,896)	(3,263)
Profit for the period	8,081	7,544
Other comprehensive income for the period, net of income tax	25	(54)
Total comprehensive income for the period	8,106	7,490
Profit attributable to:		
Owners of the company	8,053	7,521
Non-controlling interests	28	23
Total profit	8,081	7,544
Total comprehensive income attributable to:		
Owners of the company	8,058	7,467
Non-controlling interests	48	23
Total comprehensive income	8,106	7,490

Source: Reprinted by permission of Astra Zeneca PLC.

[1] We are pretending that you actually had these statements on January 1, 2011. They were not published until March. Also, these statements, taken from Chapter 3, have had minor restatement, separating trade receivables from other receivables and separating trade payables from other payables. We have not done a major recast, but what an analyst might do is dig through the financial statement notes to collect additional information. For example, prepaid expenses are included in current other receivables, and could be reported as a separate line in current assets. Read Chapter 21 of Beechy, Conrod, and Farrell, *Intermediate Accounting, Volume 2*, 5th ed. (Toronto: McGraw-Hill Ryerson, 2011), to learn more about recasting IFRS statements for purposes of financial statement analysis.

[2] The consolidated financial statements include the assets, liabilities, and equity of the parent company and its subsidiaries. When you see non-controlling or minority interests on a financial statement, it tells you that the parent does not own 100 percent of its subsidiaries. So the book value of a share of AstraZeneca PLC does not include the book value of non-controlling interest equity. That interest is the value of equity of subsidiaries not owned by the parent, AstraZeneca PLC. Likewise, the price of a share of AstraZeneca PLC reflects the market value of AstraZeneca PLC and the market value of its share of the subsidiaries. If a company owns 100 percent of its subsidiaries, there would no non-controlling interest.

TABLE 4.2 Consolidated statement of financial position for AstraZeneca PLC, as of December 31, 2009 and 2010 (US$ millions).

Assets	2010	2009	Liabilities	2010	2009
Current assets:			**Liabilities and equity:**		
Cash and cash equivalents	11,068	9,918	Interest-bearing loans and borrowings	125	1,926
Trade receivables	5,864	5,782	Trade payables	2,257	2,316
Other receivables	5,026	4,802	Income tax payable, provisions, other payables	14,397	13,308
Inventories	1,682	1,750	Derivative financial instruments	8	90
Other investments, including derivatives	1,491	1,508	**Total current liabilities**	16,787	17,640
Total current assets	25,131	23,760			
			Non-current liabilities:		
Non-current assets:			Interest-bearing loans and borrowings	9,097	9,137
Property, plant, and equipment	6957	7,307	Deferred tax liabilities, provisions, and other payables	4,361	3,968
Intangible assets	12,158	12,226	Retirement benefit obligations	2,472	3,354
Goodwill	9,871	9,889	**Total non-current liabilities**	15,930	16,459
Other investments, including derivatives	535	446	**Total liabilities**	32,717	34,099
Deferred tax assets	1475	1,292			
Total non-current assets	30,996	31,160	**Equity**		
Total assets	56,127	54,920	Share capital	352	363
			Share premium account	2,672	2,180
			Retained earnings and reserves	20,189	18,117
			Total equity attributable to equity holders of the company	23,213	20,660
			Non-controlling interest	197	161
			Total equity	23,410	20,821
			Total liabilities and equity	56,127	54,920

Source: Reprinted by permission of Astra Zeneca PLC.

value of the firm's shares and the amount of money that shareholders have invested in the firm, was $66,421.22 − $23,213 = $43,208.22 million. In other words, AstraZeneca shareholders contributed about $23 billion and ended up with shares worth about $66 billion. They have accumulated about $43 billion in market value added.

The consultancy firm EVA Dimensions calculates market value added for many firms. Table 4.3 shows a few Canadian firms and one U.K. firm, GlaxoSmithKline (GSK), which heads the group. It has created US$88.220 billion of wealth for its shareholders. Loblaw is at the bottom, with market value of only US$4.4 billion.

GlaxoSmithKline is a large firm. Its managers have lots of assets to work with. A small firm could not hope to create so much extra value. Therefore, financial managers and analysts also like to calculate how much value has been added for each dollar that shareholders have invested. To do this, they compute the ratio of market value to book value. For example, AstraZeneca's **market-to-book ratio** as the end of 2010 was[3]

market-to-book ratio Ratio of market value to book value of equity.

$$\text{Market-to-book} = \frac{\text{market value of equity}}{\text{book value equity}} = \frac{\$66{,}421.22}{\$23{,}213} = 2.86$$

[3] The market-to-book ratio can also be calculated by dividing stock price by book value per share.

TABLE 4.3 Stock market measures of company performance, December 31, 2010. Companies are ranked by market value added (US$ millions).

	Market Value Added	Market-to-Book Ratio		Market Value Added	Market-to-Book Ratio
GlaxoSmithKline PLC	88,220	7.45	Enbridge Inc.	14,175	2.89
Royal Bank of Canada	43,270	2.27	Husky Energy Inc.	8,054	1.52
Toronto Dominion Bank	25,619	1.66	George Weston Ltd.	5,518	2.03
Research In Motion LTD	25,560	3.86	Magna International Inc.	4,548	1.56
Imperial Oil Ltd.	23,145	3.06	Loblaw Companies Ltd.	4,402	1.64
Suncor Energy Inc.	22,965	1.62			

Source: We are grateful to EVA Dimension for providing these statistics.

In other words, investors have responded positively to AstraZeneca operating strategy, causing the stock price to be 2.86 times the value of the shareholders' investment in AstraZeneca.

Table 4.3 also shows market-to-book ratios. Although GSK's market-to-book ratio is the largest at 7.45, Loblaw, with the smallest market value added, does not have the smallest market-to-book ratio.

Check Point 4.1

Shares of Notung Cutlery Corp. closed 2010 at $75 per share. The company had 14.5 million shares outstanding. The book value of equity was $610 million. Compute Notung's market capitalization, market value added, and market-to-book ratio.

The market-value performance measures in Table 4.3 have three drawbacks. First, the market value of the company's shares reflects investors' expectations about future performance. Investors pay attention to current profits and investment, of course, but they also avidly forecast investment and growth. Second, market values fluctuate because of many risks and events that are outside the financial manager's control. Thus, market values are noisy measures of how well the corporation's management is performing. Third, you can't look up the market value of privately owned companies whose shares are not publicly traded. Nor can you observe the market value of 100-percent-owned subsidiaries, divisions, or plants that are parts of larger companies. You may use market values to satisfy yourself that AstraZeneca as a whole has performed well, but you can't use them to drill down to look at the performance of a specific division. To do this, you need accounting measures of profitability and financial statements for the divisions. We start with economic value added (EVA).

LO2 4.2 ECONOMIC VALUE ADDED AND ACCOUNTING RATES OF RETURN

When accountants draw up an income statement or statement of comprehensive income, they start with revenues and then deduct operating and other costs. But one important cost is not included: the cost of the capital that the company employs. Therefore, to see whether the firm has truly created value, we need to measure whether it has earned a profit after deducting all costs, including the cost of its capital.

Recall from Chapter 2 that the cost of capital is the minimum acceptable rate of return on capital investment. It is an opportunity cost of capital, because it equals the expected rate of return on investment opportunities open to investors in financial markets. The firm creates value only if it can earn more than its cost of capital, that is, more than its investors can earn by investing on their own.

economic value added (EVA) Operating profit minus a charges for the cost of capital employed. Also called *residual income*.

The profit after deducting all costs, including the cost of capital, is called the company's **economic value added** or **EVA**—a term coined by Stern Stewart & Co., which did much to develop and promote the concept. EVA is also called *residual income*.

When calculating EVA, it's customary to take into account all of the capital contributed by investors in the corporations. This means including bonds and other debt as well as equity capital. Total capital, usually called *total capitalization*, is the sum of the firm's debt and shareholders' equity. A simple measure of total capitalization is the interest-bearing debt and shareholders' equity on the firm's statement of financial position. A more detailed measure of total capitalization uses information in other financial statements and in the notes to the financial statements. For example, a firm with a long-term lease contract for renting rooms in a building has committed to paying rent over time so the lease is like debt. Some leases are valued and included in the non-current debt. However, not all leases are on the statement of financial position and some analysts value the lease commitments and include them in the total capitalization. There are other adjustments that can be made but requires more in-depth accounting knowledge.

Using AstraZeneca's statement of financial position, its total capitalization at the end of 2009 (the beginning of 2010) was \$34,970 million. It consisted of the total current and non-current interest-bearing loans and borrowings (\$1,926 + \$9,137 = \$11,063 million), total equity (\$20,660 million), and non-current deferred tax liabilities (\$3,247 million). Deferred tax liabilities are not actual taxes payable but are from income tax expenses on the statement of comprehensive income due to accounting convention. So these taxes reduced equity but aren't payable. Deferred tax liabilities are called *quasi equity*, and including them in capital gives a better measure of the cumulative amount invested by AstraZeneca's debt and equity investors. AstraZeneca's cost of capital was about 6.7 percent.[4] So we can convert the cost of capital into money by multiplying total capitalization by 6.7 percent: $.067 \times \$34{,}970$ million = \$2,343 million. To satisfy its debt and equity investors, AstraZeneca needed to earn income of \$2,343 million.

Now we can compare this figure with the income that AstraZeneca generated in 2010 for its debt and equity investors. In Table 4.1, the 2010 *profit for the period*, \$8,081 million, is the after-tax profit from operations attributable to shareholders.[5] It equals revenues minus operating expenses, minus finance expense, plus finance income and minus taxes and is also called *net earnings* or *net income*. In this chapter, we will call AZN's profit for the period its net income. To measure income generated for both debt and equity holders, add back the after-tax net interest expense to net income. In 2010 finance expense was \$1,033 million and finance income was \$516 million. So the net finance expense was \$1,033 − \$516 = \$517 million. Since this is tax-deductible, the net finance expense reduced AZN's taxes. The after-tax net finance expense is calculated as (1 − tax rate) × net finance expense.[6] Using AstraZeneca's 26 percent tax rate, the after-tax net finance expense is $(1 - .26) \times 517 = \$383$ million.[7] Therefore AstraZeneca's net income + after-tax net interest expense totalled \$8,081 + 383 = \$8,464 million. If you

[4] This is an after-tax weighted-average cost of capital, or WACC. A company's WACC depends on the risk of its business and the mix of debt and equity financing. The WACC is almost the same as the opportunity cost of capital, but with the cost of debt calculated after tax. We will explain WACC and how to calculate it in Chapter 13.

[5] The after-tax other comprehensive income, which capture changes in book value of certain assets and liabilities that are not picked up in net income, because it is not due to operations. By the way, some financial analysts include other comprehensive income when measuring firm's earnings.

[6] Some firms use the term *interest expense*, rather than *finance expense*. Regardless, both are tax-deductible. Remember from Chapter 3 that when a firm pays interest, it reduces its taxable income and therefore its tax bill. This tax saving, or *tax shield*, will vary across firms depending on the amounts of debt financing. But we want to focus here on operating results. To put all firms on a common basis, we subtract the interest tax shield from reported income, or, equivalently, we look at after-tax financing expense. By not including the tax savings from the interest expense, we calculate each firm's income as if had no debt outstanding and shareholders got the (pretax) interest expense. To be consistent, the cost of capital is defined as an after-tax weighted-average cost of capital (WACC). We will have more to say about these issues in Chapters 13 and 16.

[7] The tax rate can be estimated by dividing taxes by taxable income. For AZN, tax rate estimate is taxes/profit before taxes = 2,896/10,977 = .264, or 26 percent.

deduct the dollar cost of capital from this figure, you can see that the company earned \$8,464 − \$2,434 = \$6,121 million *more* than investors required. This was AstraZeneca's EVA or residual income:

$$\begin{aligned}\textbf{EVA} &= \textbf{Net income} + \textbf{after-tax net finance expense} - (\textbf{cost of capital} \\ &\qquad \times \textbf{total capitalization}) \qquad (4.1)\\ &= \$8{,}081 + 383 - \$2{,}343 = \$6{,}121 \textbf{ million}\end{aligned}$$

net operating profit after tax (NOPAT) The after-tax profits from operations, as if the firm had no debt. Equals net income (or net earnings or profit) plus after-tax net finance (or interest) expense.

The sum of net income and after-tax net finance expense is its after-tax operating income and is also called **net operating profit after taxes**, or **NOPAT**. It is what AstraZeneca would earn if it had no debt or could not take finance expense as a tax-deductible expense. NOPAT is what the company would earn if it were all-equity financed and NOPAT = net income + after-tax net interest expense = \$8,081 + 383 = \$8,464 million. Thus EVA also equals:

$$\begin{aligned}\textbf{EVA} &= \textbf{NOPAT} - (\textbf{cost of capital} \times \textbf{total capitalization}) \\ &= \$8{,}464 - \$2{,}343 = \$6{,}121 \textbf{ million}\end{aligned} \qquad (4.2)$$

Of course EVA and its competitors do use debt financing. Nevertheless, EVA comparisons are more useful than net income, because using NOPAT removes the effect of interest tax deductions.

Table 4.4 shows estimates of EVA for our sample of companies, calculated by EVA Dimensions, a consulting firm that is a sophisticated user of financial data. Their calculations of total capitalization and NOPAT are too complex for us to explain and will result in different values than the simple method we used. For example, their measurement of AstraZeneca's total capitalization at the beginning of 2010 was \$40,657 million and NOPAT was \$8,966 million. Using these numbers in equation 4.2 would give EVA = 8,966 − (.067 × 40,657) = \$6,242 million, which is slightly larger than our simpler calculation but not the same as AstraZeneca's EVA in the table. This is because all of the EVA calculations there use the *average* total capitalization for the year, based on the total capitalization at the beginning and end of the year. It is not uncommon to use the average of numbers from the statement of financial position ("snapshot figures") when comparing them to

TABLE 4.4 EVA and ROC, December 30, 2010. Companies are ranked by EVA (US\$ millions).

	1. NOPAT	2. Cost of Capital	3. Average Total Capitalization	4. EVA = 1 − (2 × 3)	ROC = 1/3
AstraZeneca PLC	8,966	6.7%	40,579	6,245	22.09%
GlaxoSmithKline PLC	6,654	6.6%	41,015	3,966	16.22%
Research In Motion Ltd.	3,568	11.0%	9,087	2,571	39.27%
Royal Bank of Canada	4,134	7.2%	36,989	1,467	11.18%
Imperial Oil Ltd.	2,307	5.7%	16,151	1,394	14.28%
Toronto Dominion Bank	3,823	7.2%	34,322	1,349	11.14%
Magna International Inc.	733	5.9%	8,330	238	8.80%
George Weston Ltd.	632	4.9%	8,409	222	7.52%
Loblaw Companies Ltd.	791	5.0%	11,518	220	6.87%
Enbridge Inc.	1,271	4.8%	21,767	218	5.84%
Husky Energy Inc.	1,402	5.5%	22,063	187	6.36%
Suncor Energy Inc.	3,030	5.3%	54,514	127	5.56%

Note: EVAs do not compute exactly because of rounding of numbers.

Source: We are grateful to EVA Dimension for providing these statistics.

EVA, or residual income, is a better measure of a company's performance than accounting profits. Accounting profits are calculated after deducting all costs except the cost of capital. By contrast, EVA recognizes that companies need to cover their opportunity costs before they add value.

numbers from the income statement ("flow figures"). Another possible measure of EVA is to use the total capitalization at the end of the year.

AstraZeneca is at the top of the list, with the largest EVA. GlaxoSmithKline is next and earned about $4 billion more than was needed to cover its cost of capital. Suncor had the lowest EVA, only $127 million, but it was still positive. Even if a company has a positive NOPAT, if its cost of capital is high it can have a negative EVA.

Notice how the cost of capital differs across the firms in Table 4.4. The variation is due to differences in business risk. Relatively safe companies such as Loblaw, a grocery chain, and Enbridge, an oil and gas supplier, have relatively low costs of capital. Riskier companies such as the banks and especially Research In Motion have high costs of capital.

EVA makes the cost of capital visible to operating managers. There is a clear target: earn at least the cost of capital on assets employed. A plant or divisional manager can improve EVA by reducing assets. Evaluating performance by EVA pushes managers to flush out and dispose of underutilized assets. Therefore, a growing number of firms now calculate EVA and tie managers' compensation to it.

Check Point 4.2

Roman Holidays Inc. had $30 million NOPAT on a start-of-the year total capitalization of $188 million. Its cost of capital was 11.5 percent. What was its EVA?

ACCOUNTING RATES OF RETURN

EVA measures how many dollars a business is earning after deducting the cost of capital. Other things equal, the more assets the manager has to work with, the greater the opportunity to generate a large EVA. The manager of a small division may be highly competent, but if that division has few assets, she is unlikely to rank high in the EVA stakes. Therefore, for comparing managers, it can be helpful to measure the firm's profits per dollar of assets. Three common measures are the return on capital (ROC), the return on equity (ROE), and return on assets (ROA). These are called *book rates of return*, because they are based on reported accounting information.

Return on Capital (ROC). The return on capital is equal to NOPAT, net operating profit after taxes, divided by total capitalization. In 2010 AstraZeneca's NOPAT was $8,464 million and started 2010 with total capitalization (debt plus shareholders' equity) of $34,970 million. Therefore its **return on capital (ROC)** was[8]

return on capital (ROC) Net operating profit after taxes (NOPAT) as a percentage of invested capital (debt plus equity).

$$\text{ROC} = \frac{\text{NOPAT}}{\text{total capitalization}} = \frac{8{,}464}{34{,}970} = .242\text{, or } 24.2\% \qquad (4.3)$$

ROC is one prominent accounting or book rate of return. Any book rate of return can be computed in different ways. For example, when we divided AstraZeneca's 2010 NOPAT by its total capitalization at the start of 2010 we have ignored the company's additional financing and investment during that year. If the addition of financing and investment contributed a significant part of the year's NOPAT, it's better to divide by the average of the total capitalization at the beginning and end of the year. The total capitalization at the end of 2010 was $35,777 million, the sum of current and non-current interest-bearing loans and borrowings

[8] The numerator of AZN's ROC is again its after-tax operating profit, NOPAT, calculated by adding back after-tax net finance (interest) expense to net income. Some financial analysts forget that finance expense is tax-deductible, and use pretax finance expense to calculate operating income. This complicates comparisons of ROC for companies that use different fractions of debt financing. It also muddies comparisons of ROC with the after-tax weighted-average cost of capital (WACC). We cover WACC in Chapter 13.

(125 + 9,097 = $9,222 million), total equity ($23,410 million), and non-current deferred tax liabilities ($3,145 million). Using average total assets, AZN's ROC for 2010 decreased slightly to

$$\text{ROC} = \frac{\text{NOPAT}}{\text{average total capitalization}} = \frac{8{,}464}{(34{,}970 + 35{,}777)/2} = .239, \text{ or } 23.9\%$$

As we noted earlier, AZN's cost of capital was about 6.7 percent. This is the return investors might have expected to earn in 2010 if they invested their money in other companies or securities with the same risk as AZN's business. So in 2010 the company earned 23.9 − 6.7 = 17.2 percentage points more than investors required.

Think again about how AZN creates value for its shareholders. It can either make new investments, such as drug R&D or the purchase of new drugs created by another pharmaceutical company, or pay out cash to the shareholders, who can then invest the money for themselves in financial markets. When AZN makes investments it deprives shareholders of the opportunity to invest on their own. The return that shareholders are giving up by keeping their money in the company is called their *cost of equity*, which is included in the calculation of the company's cost of capital. If AZN earns more that the cost of capital, it makes its shareholders better off: it is earning a higher return than they could obtain for themselves. If it earns less than the cost of capital, it makes its investors worse off: they could earn a higher return simply by investing on their own in financial markets. So shareholders want the company to invest only in projects for which the return on capital is at least as great as the cost of capital.

The last column in Table 4.4 shows ROC for our sample of companies. Notice that Research In Motion's return on capital was 39.7 percent, nearly 28 percentage points above its cost of capital. Although RIM had higher return on capital than AstraZeneca, it had a lower EVA. This was partly because RIM was more risky than AstraZeneca and so had a higher cost of capital, but also it had far fewer dollars invested (lower total capitalization) than AstraZeneca.

return on assets (ROA) Net operating profit after taxes (NOPAT) as a percentage of total assets.

Return on Assets. **Return on assets (ROA)** measures the income available to debt and equity investors per dollar of the firm's total assets. Total assets (which equal total liabilities plus shareholders' equity) are greater than total capital, because total capital does not include current liabilities. For AstraZeneca, ROA based on assets at the start of 2010 was

$$\text{Return on assets} = \frac{\text{NOPAT}}{\text{total assets}} = \frac{8{,}464}{54{,}920} = .154, \text{ or } 15.4\%$$

Using average total assets, ROA is slightly smaller:

$$\text{Return on assets} = \frac{\text{NOPAT}}{\text{average total assets}} = \frac{8{,}464}{(54{,}920 + 56{,}127)/2} = .152, \text{ or } 15.2\%$$

For both ROC and ROA, we use after-tax operating income, NOPAT, which is calculated by adding after-tax net finance expense to net income. We are again asking how profitable the company would be if it were all-equity-financed. This what-if calculation is helpful when comparing the profitability of companies with different capital structures. The tax deduction for interest is often ignored, however, and operating income is calculated using pretax finance expense. Some financial analysts take *no* account of interest payments and measure ROA as net income for shareholders divided by total assets. This calculation is *really*—we were about to say "stupid," but don't want to offend anyone. Just using net income in this calculation ignores entirely the income the firm's assets generated for debt investors.

Check Point 4.3

What is the difference between net operating profit after taxes (NOPAT) and net income to a firm's shareholders? How is NOPAT calculated? Why is it useful in calculation of EVA, ROC, and ROA?

return on equity (ROE) Net income as a percentage of shareholders' equity.

Return on Equity. We measure the **return on equity (ROE)** as the income to shareholders per dollar that they have invested. Shareholders' income can be profit (net income) or total comprehensive income, which is the sum of profit and other comprehensive income. So the return on equity can be calculated different ways. To facilitate the comparison with companies using U.S. GAAP accounting standards and to focus on earnings from operations, the most common formula for ROE used by IFRS reports uses profit (and call it net income) rather than total comprehensive income. AstraZeneca PLC plus its subsidiaries had profit of $8,081 million in 2010. Total shareholders' equity of AstraZeneca PLC and its subsidiaries was $20,821 million at the start of the year. So AstraZeneca's ROE was

$$\text{Return on equity} = \frac{\text{net income}}{\text{equity}} = \frac{8{,}081}{20{,}821} = .388, \text{ or } 38.8\%$$

Using average equity, ROE was

$$\text{Return on equity} = \frac{\text{net income}}{\text{average equity}} = \frac{8{,}081}{(20{,}821 + 23{,}410)/2} = .365, \text{ or } 36.5\%$$

If total comprehensive income is used instead of net income, the return on equity is $8,106/[(20,821 + 23,410)/2] = .366 or 36.6%. The inclusion of the other comprehensive income slightly increased ROE but did not make much of change. The key point is that when you are calculating the rate of return earned by shareholders, you must decide whether to use net profit or total comprehensive income.

Check Point 4.4 Explain the differences between ROE, ROC, and ROA.

PROBLEMS WITH EVA AND ACCOUNTING RATES OF RETURN

Rates of return and economic value added have some obvious attractions as measures of performance. Unlike market-value-based measures, they show current performance and are not affected by all the other things that move stock market prices. Also, they can be calculated for an entire company or for a particular plant or division or subsidiary (if the information is available). However, remember that both EVA and accounting rates of return are based on book values for assets, debt, and equity. As we noted in Chapter 3, accountants do not show every asset on the statement of financial position (SFP), yet our calculations take accounting data at face value. For example, we ignored the fact that AstraZeneca has invested large sums in marketing in order to establish its brand name. This brand name is an important asset, but its value is not shown on the SFP. If it were shown, the book values of assets, capital, and equity would increase, and AstraZeneca would not appear to earn such high returns.

EVA Dimensions, which produced the figures in Tables 4.3 and 4.4, does make adjustments to the accounting data. However, it is impossible to include the value of all assets or to judge how rapidly they depreciate. For example, did Research In Motion really earn a return on capital of 39 percent? It's difficult to say, because the value of their research and proprietary technology is not shown in the balance sheet and cannot be measured exactly.

Remember also that the SFP does not show the current market values of all of the firm's assets. As we discussed in Chapter 3, under IFRS companies must select the method for measuring the property, plant, and equipment. If they choose the cost method, the assets are shown at their original cost less accumulated depreciation plus any impact of impairment. However, only the 2010 financial statements of AstraZeneca and GlaxoSmithKline used by EVA Dimension to create Tables 4.3 and 4.4 are based on IFRS. Since the conversion to IFRS in Canada didn't start until January 2011, the financial statements of the other companies in those tables were based on either Canadian or U.S. GAAP. In both cases, the assets in a company's books are valued at their original cost less any depreciation and impairment losses. Older assets may be grossly undervalued in today's market conditions. So a high return on assets indicates that the business has performed well by making profitable investments in the past, but it does not necessarily mean that you could buy the same assets today at their reported book values. Conversely a low return suggests some poor decisions in the past, but it does not always mean that today the assets could be employed better elsewhere.

LO3 4.3 MEASURING EFFICIENCY

We began our analysis of AstraZeneca by calculating how much value that company has added for its shareholders and how much profit the company is earning after deducting the cost of the capital that it employs. We examined AstraZeneca's rates of return on equity, capital, and total assets, which were all impressively high. Our next task is to probe a little deeper to understand the reasons for AstraZeneca's success. What factors contribute to a firm's overall profitability? One factor clearly must be the efficiency with which it uses its many types of assets.

Asset Turnover Ratio. The asset turnover, or sales-to-assets, ratio shows how much sales are generated by each dollar of total assets, and therefore it measures how hard the firm's assets are working. For AstraZeneca, each dollar of assets at the start of 2010 produced about $.61 of sales:

$$\text{Asset turnover} = \frac{\text{revenues}}{\text{total assets at start of year}} = \frac{33{,}269}{54{,}920} = .606$$

Like some of our profitability ratios, the sales-to-assets ratio compares a flow measure (sales over the entire year) to a snapshot measure (assets on one day). Therefore, financial managers and analysts often calculate the ratio of sales over the entire year to the average level of assets over the same period. In this case,

$$\text{Asset turnover} = \frac{\text{revenues}}{\text{average total assets}} = \frac{33{,}269}{(54{,}920 + 56{,}127)/2} = .60$$

The asset turnover ratio measures how efficiently the business is using its entire asset base. But you also might be interested in how intensely particular types of assets are being put to use. Below are a couple of examples.

Inventory Turnover. Efficient firms don't tie up more capital than they need in raw materials and finished goods. They hold only a relatively small level of inventories of raw materials and finished goods, and they turn over those inventories rapidly.

The balance sheet shows the cost of inventories rather than the amount that the finished goods will eventually sell for. So it is usual to compare the average level of inventories with the cost of goods sold (or cost of sales) rather than with revenues. In AstraZeneca's case,

$$\text{Inventory turnover} = \frac{\text{cost of sales}}{\text{average inventories}} = \frac{6{,}389}{(1{,}750 + 1{,}682)/2} = 3.72$$

Another way to express this measure is to look at how many days of output are represented by inventories. This is equal to the level of inventories divided by the daily cost of goods sold (or cost of sales). Daily costs are costs divided by the number of days in the year, 365:

$$\text{Average days in inventories} = \frac{\text{average inventories}}{\text{cost of sales}/365} = \frac{1{,}716}{(6{,}389)/365} = 98 \text{ days}$$

You might say AstraZeneca has sufficient inventories to maintain production for 98 days.[9]

---

[9] This is a loose statement, because it ignores the fact that AstraZeneca may have more than 98 days' supply of some materials and less of others.

In Chapter 20 we will look at how many firms have managed to increase their inventory turnover in recent years. Toyota has been the pioneer in this endeavour. Its just-in-time system ensures that auto parts are delivered exactly when they are needed. Toyota now keeps only about one month's supply of parts and finished cars in inventory and turns over its inventory about 12 times a year.

Receivables Turnover. Sales that have been recorded on the income statement but have not yet been paid are reported on the balance sheet as trade receivables (or accounts receivable). The receivables turnover ratio measures the firm's sales as a multiple of its trade receivables. For AstraZeneca,

$$\text{Receivables turnover} = \frac{\text{revenues}}{\text{average trade receivables}} = \frac{33{,}269}{(5{,}782 + 5{,}864)/2} = 5.7$$

If customers are quick to pay, unpaid bills will be a relatively small proportion of sales and the receivables turnover will be high. Therefore, a comparatively high ratio often indicates an efficient credit department that is quick to follow up on late payers. Sometimes, however, a high ratio might indicate that the firm has an unduly restrictive credit policy and offers credit only to customers who can be relied on to pay promptly.[10]

Another way to measure the efficiency of the credit operation is by calculating the average length of time for customers to pay their bills. The faster the firm turns over its receivables, the shorter the collection period. AstraZeneca's customers pay their bills in about 66 days:

$$\text{Average collection period} = \frac{\text{average trade receivables}}{\text{average daily revenues}} = \frac{5{,}823}{(33{,}269)/365} = 64 \text{ days}$$

Check Point 4.5

The average collection period measures the number of days it takes AstraZeneca to collect its bills. But AstraZeneca also delays paying its own bills. Its unpaid bills for material purchased to produce its goods are recorded as trade payables on the statement of financial position. Use the information in Tables 4.1 and 4.2 to calculate the average number of days that it takes AstraZeneca to pay its bills.

The receivables turnover ratio and the inventory turnover ratio may help to highlight particular areas of inefficiency, but they are not the only possible indicators. For example, a retail chain might compare its sales per square metre with those of its competitors, a steel producer might calculate the cost per tonne of steel produced, an airline might look at revenues per passenger-mile, and a law firm might look at revenues per partner. A little thought and common sense should suggest which measures are likely to produce the most helpful insights into your company's efficiency.

LO4 4.4

ANALYZING THE RETURN ON ASSETS: THE DU PONT SYSTEM

We have seen that every dollar of AstraZeneca's assets at the start of 2010 generated $.61 of sales. But AstraZeneca's success depends not only on the volume of its sales but also on how profitable those sales are. This is measured by AstraZeneca's profit margin.

Profit Margin. The profit margin measures the proportion of sales that finds its way into profits. It is sometimes defined as

$$\text{Profit margin} = \frac{\text{net income}}{\text{sales}} = \frac{8{,}081}{33{,}269} = .243, \text{ or } 24.3\%$$

[10] Where possible, it makes sense to look only at *credit* sales. Otherwise, a high ratio might simply indicate that a small portion of sales is made on credit.

This definition can be misleading. When companies are partly financed by debt, a portion of the revenue produced by sales must be paid as interest to the firm's lenders. So profits from the firm's operations are divided between the debtholders and the shareholders. We would not want to say that a firm is less profitable than its rivals simply because it employs debt finance and pays out part of its income as interest. Therefore, when we are calculating the profit margin, it is common to add back the after-tax debt interest to net income. This gives an alternative measure of profit margin, which is called the **operating profit margin**:

operating profit margin Net operating profit after taxes (NOPAT) as a percentage of sales.

$$\text{Operating profit margin} = \frac{\text{NOPAT}}{\text{sales}} = \frac{8{,}464}{33{,}269} = .2544, \text{ or } 25.44\%$$

THE DU PONT SYSTEM

We calculated earlier that AstraZeneca has earned a return of 15.4 percent on its assets at the beginning of 2010. The following equation shows that this return depends on two factors—the sales that AstraZeneca generates from its assets (asset turnover) and the profit that it earns on each dollar of sales (operating profit margin):

$$\text{ROA} = \frac{\text{NOPAT}}{\text{total assets}} = \underbrace{\frac{\text{sales}}{\text{total assets}}}_{\text{asset turnover}} \times \underbrace{\frac{\text{NOPAT}}{\text{sales}}}_{\text{operating profit margin}} \quad (4.4)$$

Du Pont formula ROA equals the product of the asset turnover and operating profit margin.

This breakdown of ROA into the product of turnover and margin is often called the **Du Pont formula**, after the chemical company that popularized the procedure. In AstraZeneca's case the formula gives the following breakdown of ROA:

$$\text{ROA} = \text{Asset turnover} \times \text{operating profit margin} = .606 \times .2544 = .154, \text{ or } 15.4\%$$

The Du Pont formula is a useful way to think about a company's strategy. For example, a retailer may strive for high asset turnover at the expense of a low operating profit margin (a "Walmart strategy"), or it may seek a high profit margin even if that results in low turnover (a "Bloomingdales strategy"). You would naturally prefer both high operating profit margin and high asset turnover, but life isn't that easy. A high-price and high-margin strategy will typically result in lower sales per dollar of assets, so firms have to make trade-offs between these goals. The Du Pont formula can help sort out which strategy the firm is pursuing.

All firms would like to earn a higher return on their assets, but their ability to do so is limited by competition. The Du Pont formula helps to identify the constraints that firms face. Fast-food chains, which have high asset turnover, tend to operate on low margins. Classy hotels have relatively low turnover ratios but tend to compensate with higher margins.

EXAMPLE 4.1 TURNOVER VERSUS MARGIN

Firms often seek to improve their profit margins by acquiring a supplier. The idea is to capture the supplier's profit as well as their own. Unfortunately, unless they have some special skills in running the new business, they are likely to find that any gain in profit margin is offset by a decline in asset turnover.

A few numbers might help to illustrate this point. Table 4.5 shows the sales, profits and assets of Admiral Motors and its components supplier, Diana Corporation. Both earn a 10 percent return on assets, though Admiral has a lower operating profit margin (20 percent as against Diana's 25 percent). Since all of Diana's output goes to Admiral, Admiral's management reasons that it would be better to merge the two companies. That way, the merged company would capture the profit margin on both the auto components and the assembled car.

The bottom row of Table 4.5 shows the effect of the merger. The merged firm does indeed earn the combined profits. Total sales remain at $20 million, however, because all the components produced by Diana are used within the company. With higher profits and unchanged sales, the profit margin increases. Unfortunately, the asset turnover is reduced by the merger since the merged firm has more assets. This exactly offsets the benefit of the higher profit margin. The return on assets is unchanged.

TABLE 4.5
Merging with suppliers or customers will generally increase the profit margin, but this will be offset by a reduction in asset turnover.

	Millions of Dollars					
	Sales	Profits	Assets	Asset Turnover	Profit Margin	ROA
Admiral Motors	$20	**$4**	$40	.50	20%	10%
Diana Corp.	8	**2**	20	.40	25	10
Diana Motors (the merged firm)	20	**6**	60	.33	30	10

Research has provided evidence of the trade-off between asset turnover and operating profit margin. Industries with high average asset turnover ratios, for example grocery stores, tend to have lower profit margins. Conversely, high operating profit margins are typically associated with low asset turnover. The classic examples are electric or water utilities, which have enormous capital requirements and therefore low asset turnover ratios. However, they have extremely low marginal costs for each unit of additional output and therefore earn high markups, which produce high operating profit margins. Despite the enormous dispersion across industries in both operating profit margin and asset turnover, that variation tends to be offsetting, so for most industries the return on assets lies between 3 and 10 percent.

Check Point 4.6

The Du Pont formula (equation 4.4) seems to suggest that companies with higher asset turnover ratios generally will have high ROAs. Why may this not be so?

LO3 4.5 MEASURING FINANCIAL LEVERAGE

Shareholder value depends not only on good investment decisions and profitable operations but also on sound financing decisions. To explore the quality of financing decisions we look first at measures of financial leverage and then at measures of liquidity.

When a firm borrows money, it promises to make a series of interest payments and then to repay the amount that it has borrowed. If profits rise, the debtholders continue to receive only the fixed interest payment, so all the gains go to the shareholders. Of course, the reverse happens if profits fall. In this case, shareholders bear most of the pain. If times are sufficiently hard, a firm that has borrowed heavily may not be able to pay its debts. The firm is then bankrupt, and shareholders lose most or all of their entire investment.

Because debt increases returns to shareholders in good times and reduces them in bad times, it is said to create financial leverage. Leverage ratios measure how much financial leverage the firm has taken on. CFOs keep an eye on leverage ratios to ensure that lenders are happy to continue to take on the firm's debt.

Debt Ratio. Financial leverage is usually measured by the ratio of long-term debt to total long-term capital. Here "long-term" debt should include not just bonds or other borrowing but also financing from long-term leases.[11] Also, for a complete measure include the current portion

[11] A finance lease is a long-term rental agreement that commits the firm to make regular payments. This commitment is just like the obligation to make payments on an outstanding loan.

of the long-term debt, which is long-term debt due for repayment within the next year. AstraZeneca has no finance leases and no current portion of long-term debt but has \$9,097 million of non-current long term debt, so total long-term debt is \$9,097 million. AstraZeneca also does not have preferred equity. Thus the long-term debt ratio at the end of 2010 is

$$\text{Long-term debt ratio} = \frac{\text{long-term debt} + \text{value of leases}}{\text{long-term debt} + \text{value of leases} + \text{preferred equity} + \text{common equity}}$$

$$= \frac{9{,}097}{9{,}097 + 23{,}410} = .28, \text{ or } 28\%$$

This means that 28 cents of every dollar of long-term capital is in the form of debt.

Leverage is also measured by the debt-equity ratio. For AstraZeneca,

$$\text{Long-term debt-to-equity ratio} = \frac{\text{long-term debt} + \text{value of leases}}{\text{preferred and common equity}} = \frac{9{,}097}{23{,}410} = .39 \text{ or } 39\%$$

Thus for every dollar of equity, AstraZeneca has \$.39 worth of debt. The debt-equity ratio climbs dramatically for highly leveraged companies. A company financed two-thirds with debt and one-third with equity has a long-term debt ratio of 67 percent (2/3) and a debt-equity ratio of 2. Sometimes you see projects such as oil pipelines financed with 90 percent debt and 10 percent equity. In that case the debt-equity ratio is 90/10 = 9.

The long-term debt ratio for the average U.S. manufacturing company is about 30 percent, but some companies deliberately operate at much higher debt levels. For example, in Chapter 23 we will look at leveraged buyouts. Firms acquired in a *leveraged buyout (LBO)* usually issue large amounts of debt. When LBOs first became popular in the 1990s, these companies had average debt ratios of about 90 percent. Many of them flourished and paid back their debtholders in full; others were not so fortunate.

Notice that debt ratios make use of book (accounting) values rather than market values.[12] In principle, lenders should be more interested in the market value of the company, which reflects the actual value of the company's assets and the actual cash flows those assets will produce. If the market value of the company covers its debts, lenders should get their money back. Thus you would expect to see the debt ratio computed using the market values of debt and equity. Yet book debt ratios are used almost universally.

Does use of book rather than market leverage ratios matter much? Perhaps not; after all, the market value of the firm includes the value of intangible assets generated by research and development, advertising, staff training, and so on. These assets are not easy to sell, and if the company falls on hard times, their value may disappear altogether. Thus, when banks demand that a borrower keep within a maximum debt ratio, they usually define that ratio in terms of book values and they ignore the intangible assets that are not shown on the balance sheet.

Notice also that these measures of leverage ignore short-term debt, such as bank borrowings. That probably makes sense if the short-term debt is temporary or is matched by similar holdings of cash, but if the company is a regular short-term borrower, it might be preferable to widen the definition of debt to include all interest-bearing debt, both current and non-current. In this case,

$$\text{Total debt ratio} = \frac{\text{short-term debt} + \text{long-term debt} + \text{value of leases}}{\text{short-term debt} + \text{long-term debt} + \text{value of leases} + \text{preferred equity} + \text{common equity}}$$

$$= \frac{125 + 9{,}097}{125 + 9{,}097 + 23{,}410} = .28, \text{ or } 28\%$$

Therefore, AstraZeneca is financed 28 percent with long- and short-term debt and 72 percent with equity. We could also say that its ratio of total debt to equity is .28/.72 = .39.

[12] In the case of leased assets, accountants estimate the value of the lease commitments. In the case of long-term debt, depending on their accounting policy they might show just the face value, which can be very different from market value.

Another measure of leverage includes all liabilities. Since the sum of liabilities and shareholders' equity equals the firm's total assets, this is the debt-to-assets ratio. For AstraZeneca,

$$\text{Debt-to-asset ratio} = \frac{\text{total liabilities}}{\text{total assets}} = \frac{32{,}717}{56{,}127} = .58, \text{ or } 58\%$$

So liabilities finance 58 percent of AstraZeneca's assets and equity finances 42 percent of the assets. Managers sometimes refer loosely to a company's debt ratio, but we have just seen that the debt ratio may be measured in several different ways. For example, AstraZeneca has a debt ratio of .28 (the long-term debt ratio), also .28 (short-term plus long-term debt ratio), and also .58 (the debt-to-asset ratio). This is not the first time we have come across several ways to define a financial ratio. There is no law stating how a ratio should be defined. So be warned: Do not use a ratio without understanding how it has been calculated.

Times Interest Earned Ratio. Another measure of financial leverage is the extent to which interest obligations are covered by earnings or operating profits. Banks prefer to lend to firms with earnings that cover interest payments with room to spare. Interest coverage is measured by the ratio of earnings before interest and taxes (EBIT) to interest payments (finance expense). To calculate EBIT for AstraZeneca, take the operating profit (which is before the net finance expense), $11,494 million. Then the times interest earned ratio is

$$\text{Times interest earned (TIE)} = \frac{\text{EBIT}}{\text{interest expense}} = \frac{11{,}494}{1{,}033} = 11.1$$

AstraZeneca enjoys an extremely high coverage or times interest earned ratio because it is produces lot of operating profit to cover its interest expense. Sometimes lenders are content with coverage ratios as low as 2 or 3.

The regular interest payment is a hurdle that companies must keep jumping if they are to avoid default. The coverage ratio measures how much clear air there is between hurdle and hurdler. The ratio is only part of the story, however. For example, it doesn't tell us whether AstraZeneca is generating enough cash to repay its debt as it becomes due.

Cash Coverage Ratio. In the previous chapter we pointed out that depreciation and amortization are deducted when calculating the firm's earnings, even though no cash goes out the door. Suppose we add back depreciation to EBIT in order to calculate operating cash flow. Depreciation and amortization is not shown separately on AZN's statement of comprehensive income but is reported on is statement of cash flows, $2,741 million. We then calculate a cash coverage ratio. For AstraZeneca,

$$\text{Cash coverage ratio} = \frac{\text{EBIT} + \text{depreciation and amortization}}{\text{interest expense}} = \frac{11{,}494 + 2{,}741}{1{,}033} = 13.8$$

Check Point 4.7 A firm repays $10 million face value of outstanding debt and issues $10 million of new debt with a lower rate of interest. What happens to its long-term debt ratio? What happens to its times interest earned and cash coverage ratios?

EBITDA

One other measure that is often used companies and analysts is *EBITDA—earnings before interest, depreciation, and amortization*. Although the formula seems quite straightforward, a lot of variations are used, since this is a non-GAAP measure and non-IFRS—meaning that there are no specific rules on how it should be calculated. Items that can be included or excluded based on the analyst's or management's interpretation might include special charges or other unusual gains or expenses and finance income. In addition, often depreciation and amortization is not specifically reported as a line item on the income statement. In this case, we look to the statement of cash flows to find the correct amount. The following is an example of how EBITDA might be calculated for AZN for 2010 (all in millions of US$). Notice that both finance income and finance expenses have been adjusted in this case.

Profit for the period (net income)	$ 8,081
Add back taxes	2,896
Add back finance expense	1,033
Subtract finance income	(516)
Add back depreciation, amortization, and impairment (as disclosed on statement of cash flows)	2,741
EBITDA	$14,235

Why is EBITDA useful? Many companies use EBITDA as a measure of "true" operating performance removing any effect of depreciation and amortization based on accounting methods and assumptions rather than actual performance. At the same time, net finance expenses are removed, since it is a function of how the company manages its capital, rather than performance. And finally, taxes are removed, since the tax expense is based on the jurisdiction where the income is earned and not operating performance. EBITDA allows management or an analyst to compare operating performance on a consistent basis, year over year. It is also often used in some ratios and valuation formulas for similar reasons as discussed above. For example, the cash coverage ratio can be written as EBITDA/interest expense.

LEVERAGE AND THE RETURN ON EQUITY

When the firm raises cash by borrowing, it must make interest payments to its lenders. This reduces net profits. On the other hand, if a firm borrows instead of issuing equity, it has fewer equityholders to share the remaining profits. Which effect dominates? An extended version of the Du Pont formula helps us answer this question. It breaks down the return on equity (ROE) into four parts:

$$\text{ROE} = \frac{\text{net income}}{\text{equity}} = \underset{\substack{\uparrow \\ \text{leverage} \\ \text{ratio}}}{\frac{\text{assets}}{\text{equity}}} \times \underset{\substack{\uparrow \\ \text{asset} \\ \text{turnover}}}{\frac{\text{sales}}{\text{assets}}} \times \underset{\substack{\uparrow \\ \text{operating profit} \\ \text{margin}}}{\frac{\text{NOPAT}}{\text{sales}}} \times \underset{\substack{\uparrow \\ \text{debt burden}}}{\frac{\text{net income}}{\text{NOPAT}}} \quad (4.5)$$

Notice that the product of the two middle terms in equation 4.5 is the return on assets. It depends on the firm's production and marketing skills and is unaffected by the firm's financing mix.[13] However, the first and fourth terms do depend on the debt-equity mix. The first term, assets/equity, which we call the leverage ratio, can be expressed as (equity + liabilities)/equity, which equals 1 + total-debt-to-equity ratio. The last term, which we call the "debt burden," measures the proportion by which interest expense reduces profits.

Suppose that the firm is financed entirely by equity. In this case, both the leverage ratio and the debt burden are equal to 1, and the return on equity is identical to the return on assets. If the firm borrows, however, the leverage ratio is greater than 1 (assets are greater than equity) and the debt burden is less than 1 (part of the profits is absorbed by interest). Thus leverage can either increase or reduce return on equity. In fact, we will see in Chapter 16 that leverage increases ROE when the firm's return on assets is higher than the interest rate on debt. Since AstraZeneca's return on capital exceeds the interest rate that it is paying on its debt, return on equity is higher than return on capital.

---

[13] Again, we are using net operating profit after taxes, which the sum of net income and after-tax net financing expense.

Check Point 4.8

a. Sappy Syrup has a profit margin below the industry average, but its ROA equals the industry average. How is this possible?
b. Sappy Syrup's ROA equals the industry average, but its ROE exceeds the industry average. How is this possible?

LO3

4.6 MEASURING LIQUIDITY

liquidity Access to cash or assets that can be turned into cash on short notice.

If you are extending credit to a customer or making a short-term bank loan, you are interested in more than the company's leverage. You want to know whether the company can lay its hands on the cash to repay you. That is why credit analysts and bankers look at several measures of liquidity. Liquid assets can be converted into cash quickly and cheaply.

Think, for example, what you would do to meet a large unexpected bill. You might have some money in the bank or some investments that are easily sold, but you would not find it so easy to turn your old sweaters into cash. Companies, likewise, own assets with different degrees of liquidity. For example, trade receivables and inventories of finished goods are generally quite liquid. As inventories are sold off and customers pay their bills, money flows into the firm. At the other extreme, real estate may be quite illiquid. It can be hard to find a buyer, negotiate a fair price, and close a deal at short notice.

Managers have another reason to focus on liquid assets: their book (SFP or balance sheet) values are usually reliable. The book value of a blast furnace might be a poor guide to its true value, but at least you know what cash in the bank is worth.

Liquidity ratios also have some less desirable characteristics. Because current assets and liabilities are easily changed, measures of liquidity can rapidly become outdated. You might not know what the blast furnace is worth, but you can be fairly sure that it won't disappear overnight. Cash in the bank can disappear in seconds when used to pay bills.

Also, assets that seem liquid sometimes have a nasty habit of becoming illiquid. This happened during the subprime mortgage crisis in 2007/2008. Some financial institutions had set up funds known as structured investment vehicles (SIVs) that issued short-term debt backed by residential mortgages. As mortgage default rates began to climb, the market for this debt dried up and dealers became very reluctant to quote a price.

Bankers and other short-term lenders applaud firms that have plenty of liquid assets. They know that when they are due to be repaid, the firm will be able to get its hands on the cash. But more liquidity is not always a good thing. For example, efficient firms do not leave excess cash in their bank accounts. They don't allow customers to postpone paying their bills, and they don't leave stocks of raw materials and finished goods littering the warehouse floor. In other words, high levels of liquidity may indicate sloppy use of capital. Here, EVA can help, because it penalizes managers who keep more liquid assets than they really need, since these assets would not be generating any return the longer they sit on the balance sheet.

Net Working Capital to Total Assets Ratio. Current assets include cash and cash equivalents, other current securities, inventories, and trade and other receivables. Current assets are mostly liquid. The difference between current assets and current liabilities is known as *net working capital*. It roughly measures the company's potential net reservoir of cash. Since current assets usually exceed current liabilities, net working capital is usually positive. For AstraZeneca,

$$\text{Net working capital} = \text{current assets} - \text{current liabilities} = 25{,}131 - 16{,}787 = 8{,}344$$

AstraZeneca's net working capital was 15 percent of total assets:

$$\frac{\text{Net working capital}}{\text{Total assets}} = \frac{8{,}344}{56{,}127} = .15$$

Current Ratio. The current ratio is just the ratio of current assets to current liabilities:

$$\text{Current ratio} = \frac{\text{current assets}}{\text{current liabilities}} = \frac{25{,}131}{16{,}787} = 1.5$$

AstraZeneca has $1.50 in current assets for every dollar in current liabilities.

Changes in the current ratio can be misleading. For example, suppose that a company borrows a large sum from the bank and invests it in marketable securities. Current liabilities rise and so do current assets. If nothing else changes, net working capital is unaffected but the current ratio changes. For this reason it is sometimes preferable to net short-term investments against short-term debt when calculating the current ratio.

Quick (Acid-Test) Ratio. Some current assets are closer to cash than others. If trouble comes, inventory may not sell at anything above fire-sale prices. Trouble typically comes because the firm can't sell its inventory of finished products for more than production cost. Also, some other receivables, such as prepaid expenses, are not quickly convertible into cash. Thus managers often exclude inventories and other less liquid components of current assets when comparing current assets to current liabilities. They focus instead on cash, marketable securities, and bills that customers have not yet paid, trade receivables. This results in the quick ratio:

$$\text{Quick ratio} = \frac{\text{cash and cash equivalents} + \text{current other investments} + \text{trade receivables}}{\text{current liabilities}}$$

$$= \frac{11{,}068 + 1{,}491 + 5{,}864}{16{,}787} = 1.1$$

Cash Ratio. A company's most liquid assets are its holdings of cash and cash equivalents. That is why analysts also look at the cash ratio:

$$\text{Cash ratio} = \frac{\text{cash and cash equivalents}}{\text{current liabilities}} = \frac{11{,}068}{16{,}787} = .66$$

A low cash ratio might not matter if the firm can borrow on short notice. Who cares whether the firm has actually borrowed from the bank or whether it has a guaranteed line of credit that lets it borrow whenever it chooses? None of the standard measures of liquidity takes the firm's "reserve borrowing power" into account.

Check Point 4.9

a. A firm has $1.2 million in current assets and $1 million in current liabilities. If it uses $.5 million of cash to pay off some of its accounts payable, what will happen to the current ratio? What happens to net working capital?
b. A firm uses cash on hand to pay for additional inventories. What will happen to the current ratio? To the quick ratio?

LO5 4.7 CALCULATING SUSTAINABLE GROWTH

AstraZeneca's leverage and liquidity ratios are checks on whether its financing policies are safe and sound. But what about the *amount* of financing that is available for investment and growth? To put it another way, how fast could AstraZeneca grow? Would its growth be limited by the availability of financing?

The answer to the last question is in principle no. In well-functioning financial markets, a company's growth is limited not by financing opportunities but by limits to good investment opportunities and by limits to other resources, including trained management and staff. If the company has investment projects that add value, it should be able to issue shares, if necessary, to finance them.

But the window to issue shares may not always be open. For example, a financial manager who believes that investors are unduly pessimistic will be reluctant to issue shares at what he or she sees as a depressed stock price. Therefore, financial managers and analysts are interested in knowing how fast the firm can grow if it relies only on internal financing, keeping the long-term debt ratio constant. They calculate the firm's *sustainable growth rate.*

Mature companies grow mainly by reinvesting earnings. How rapidly they grow depends on the proportion of earnings that is kept in the business and the profits that the company can earn on the new capital.

In 2010 AstraZeneca's net income was $8,081 million and paid $3,494 million in dividends to AstraZeneca PLC shareholders plus $1 million to non-controlling interest. The proportion of earnings (net income) paid out as dividends was, therefore,

$$\text{Payout ratio} = \frac{\text{dividends}}{\text{earnings}} = \frac{3{,}495}{8{,}081} = .43, \text{ or } 43\%$$

The remaining 57 percent of earnings was reinvested and "plowed back into" the business and added to the firm's equity capital. Thus,

$$\text{Plowback ratio} = \frac{\text{earnings} - \text{dividends}}{\text{earnings}} = 1 - \text{payout ratio} = 1 - .43 = .57$$

AstraZeneca's return on equity (ROE) was 38.8 percent. If it continues to reinvest 57 percent of its earnings and to earn 38.8 percent on this investment, both its earnings and its book equity will increase by $.57 \times .388 = .221$ or 22.1 percent a year:

$$\text{Sustainable growth rate} = \text{Growth in equity from plowback} = \frac{\text{earnings} - \text{dividends}}{\text{equity}}$$

$$= \frac{\text{earnings} - \text{dividends}}{\text{earnings}} \times \frac{\text{earnings}}{\text{equity}} = \text{plowback} \times \text{ROE} = .57 \times .388 = .221, \text{ or } 22.1\%$$

sustainable rate of growth The firm's growth rate if it plows back a constant fraction of earnings, maintains constant return on equity, and keeps its debt ratio constant.

This measure is often known as the **sustainable rate of growth.** It assumes that the firm's long-term debt ratio is held constant over time. AZN could grow its assets at a faster rate by borrowing more and more, but that growth strategy would not be sustainable in the long run.

Is this a reasonable long-term prospect? Well, possibly, but it is fairly high. Sometimes the formula for sustainable growth results in huge values, above 30 or even 40 percent. No company could expect to maintain growth rates like this forever. Firms selling products at an early stage of their life tend to have high sustainable growth rates. Competition in these new markets is scarce, return on equity is high, and, with ample opportunity for profitable reinvestment, firms respond with very high plowback ratios. But eventually as a new industry matures, price competition will increase, ROE will decline, and with fewer profitable opportunities for reinvestment, firms will plow back less of their earnings. AS ROE and plowback ratio both decline, growth must also slow. So AZN's high sustainable growth rate is a reflection of the success of its research and development of new drugs to deal with health issues. Thus, provided AZN continues to be successful in its R&D and no other firms come up with same drug solutions, it may be able to assume that its 22 percent sustainable growth is actually sustainable.

LO6 4.8 INTERPRETING FINANCIAL RATIOS

We have shown how to calculate some common summary measures of AstraZeneca's performance and financial condition. These are summarized in Table 4.6.[14]

Now that you have calculated these measures, you need some way to judge whether they are high or low. In some cases there might be a natural benchmark. For example, if a firm has

[14] If you would like to see how we calculated these ratios or to calculate your own, you can use the live Excel spreadsheet available on the Online Learning Centre.

TABLE 4.6
Summary of AstraZeneca's financial ratios.

Performance Measures		
Market value added ($ millions)	Market value of equity/book value of equity	43,208
Market-to-book ratio	Market value of equity/book value of equity	2.86
Profitability Measures		
Return on equity (ROE)	Net income/equity at start of year	38.8%
Return on assets (ROA)	NOPAT/total assets at start of year	15.4%
Return on capital (ROC)	NOPAT/(long-term debt + equity at start of year)	24.2%
EVA ($ millions)	NOPAT − cost of capital × capital	6,121
Operating profit margin	NOPAT/sales	25.4%
Efficiency Measures		
Asset turnover	Revenue/average total assets	.60
Inventory turnover	Cost of sales/average inventories	3.72
Days in inventory	Average inventories/daily cost of sales	98
Receivables turnover	Revenues/average trade receivables	5.7
Average collection period (days)	Average trade receivables/daily revenue	64
Leverage Measures		
Long-term debt ratio	Long-term debt/(long-term debt + equity)	28%
Long-term debt-equity ratio	Long-term debt/equity	39%
Debt-to-asset ratio	Total liabilities/total assets	58%
Times interest earned	EBIT/Interest expense	11.1
Cash coverage ratio	(EBIT + depreciation & amortization)/interest expense	13.8
Liquidity Measures		
Net working capital to total assets	Net working capital/total assets	.15
Current ratio	Current assets/current liabilities	1.5
Quick ratio	(Cash + marketable securities + trade receivables)/current liabilities	1.1
Cash ratio	(Cash + marketable securities)/current liabilities	.66
Growth Measures		
Payout ratio	Dividends/earnings	.43
Sustainable growth	(1 − payout ratio) × ROE	22.1%

Source: Reprinted by permission of Astra Zeneca PLC.

negative value added or a return on capital less than the cost of that capital, it is not creating wealth for its shareholders.

But what about some of the other measures? There is no right level for, say, the asset turnover or profit margin, and if there were, it would almost certainly vary from industry to industry and company to company. For example, you would not expect a soft-drink manufacturer to have the same profit margin as a jeweller or the same leverage as a finance company.

Table 4.7 presents some financial ratios for a sample of Canadian industry groups, based on financial statements constructed using Canadian GAAP. Notice the large variations between industries. Some of these differences may arise from chance; in 2010 the sun shone more kindly on some industries than on others. But the differences also reflect more fundamental industry

TABLE 4.7 Financial ratios for some Canadian industry groups, based on 2010 financial statements.

	Total Debt/ (Total Debt + Equity)	Interest Coverage	Current Ratio	Quick Ratio	Asset Turnover	Net Profit Margin (%)	Return on Assets (%)	Return on Capital (%)	Return on Equity (%)
Food products	.33	10.38	1.86	.6	1.22	5.18	6.59	8.3	9.52
Transportation	.38	4.5	1.01	.83	1.33	12.72	21.49	48.45	5.29
Automobiles and components	.11	40.55	1.82	1.12	1.43	5.27	8.11	11.77	12.61
Chemicals	.35	15.57	1.77	1.04	.79	13.09	10.07	14.24	18.14
Metals and mining	.17	42.81	3.96	3.17	.4	38.43	9.7	12.79	14.66
Retailers	.32	32.82	1.47	.64	1.96	4.59	10.18	14.05	17.92
Media	.38	5.66	1.51	1.2	.59	12.37	6.71	11.37	13.67
Biotechnology	.17	15.11	8.45	7.34	.42	–29.95	–1.74	–3.94	–.09
Capital goods	.46	34.55	2.21	1.24	1.26	1.33	4.05	7.06	5.11
Gold mines	.11	25.31	3.84	2.83	.34	17.9	4.99	5.37	5.06

Note: Ratio definitions are the same as ours except interest coverage = [EBIT + other income(expense)]/interest expense, and net profit margin = net income/revenue.
Source: Industry reports from FPinfomart, **www.fpinfomart.ca.ezproxy.library.yorku.ca**.

factors. For example, notice the high debt ratios of capital goods manufacturers. By contrast, automobile and component manufacturers, biotechnology and goldmine companies scarcely borrow at all. We pointed out earlier that some businesses are able to generate a high level of sales from relatively few assets. For example, you can see that the asset turnover ratio for retailers is nearly three times that for chemical companies. But competition ensures that retailers earn a correspondingly lower margin on their sales. The net effect is that the return on assets is broadly similar for the two groups of companies.

Check Point 4.10

Even within an industry, there can be a considerable difference in the type of business that companies do, and this shows up in their financial ratio. Here are some data on assets, sales, and income for two companies. Calculate for each company the asset turnover, the operating profit margin, and the return on assets. If one of the companies is Walmart and the other is Peoples Jewellers, which is company A and which company B?

	Company A	Company B
Sales	100	100
Assets	40.0	87.3
Net income + after-tax interest	4.0	9.0

When looking for benchmarks to evaluation performance, it usually makes sense to limit the comparison to the firm's major competitors. Table 4.8 sets out some key performance measures for AstraZeneca and GlaxoSmithKline. The two companies are similar in many respects. Both engage in research, development, manufacturing and marketing of pharmaceutical products. Both their headquarters are in the United Kingdom and their sets of financial statements both use IFRS. But although their receivables' average collection periods are almost identical, most of their financial ratios are not the same. Overall, AZN has much better financial performance. Despite the fact that GSK's asset turnover is slightly higher, its ROA is about one-third of AZN's, because GSK's operating profit margin is only one-third AZN's. Part of the reason contributing to these low returns and margins might be the large restructuring plan GSK has been undergoing, costing in excess of $1 billion in 2010 alone. The restructuring included closure of some

TABLE 4.8
Selected 2010 financial measures for AstraZeneca and GlaxoSmithKline.

	AstraZeneca	GlaxoSmithKline
Performance Measures		
Market value added ($ millions)	43,208	88,220
Market-to-book ratio	2.86	7.45
Profitability Measures		
Return on equity (ROE)	38.8%	17.3%
Return on assets (ROA)	15.4%	5.5%
Return on capital (ROC)	24.2%	9.6%
EVA ($ US millions)	6,245	3,966
Operating profit margin	25.4%	8.3%
Efficiency Measures		
Asset turnover	.60	.67
Inventory turnover	3.72	1.92
Days in inventory	98	190
Receivables turnover	5.7	5.6
Average collection period (days)	64	65
Leverage Measures		
Long-term debt ratio	28%	60%
Long-term debt-equity ratio	39%	152%
Debt-to-asset ratio	58%	77%
Times interest earned	11.1	4.6
Cash coverage ratio	13.8	6.6
Liquidity Measures		
Net working capital to total assets	.15	.32
Current ratio	1.5	2.1
Quick ratio	1.1	.86
Cash ratio	.66	.488
Growth Measures		
Payout ratio	.43	**1.79**
Sustainable growth rate	22.1%	**−13.7%**

Source: Reprinted by permission of Astra Zeneca PLC.

manufacturing sites, worker layoffs, and adoption of new research areas. GSK also holds twice as much inventory on hand in comparison to AZN. However, it uses a lot more debt to finance its operations than AZN, which also results in a much lower interest coverage ratio. But GSK does have a higher working capital and current ratio, as a result of the higher inventory and as shown by lower quick and cash ratios. AstraZeneca reinvests more of its earnings. That means less dividends today and the high sustainable growth rate. GSK's negative sustainable growth rate is due to its restructuring process. The company's assets have been decreasing. However, if the restructuring program is successful, future GSK financial performance could be much better.

In addition to comparing financial ratios of competitors, it can also be helpful to look at the ratios over time. If ROA has increased, due to improvements in operating efficiency, you might judge that managers are doing a good job. When looking at ratio history, it is important to look for major business changes, such as acquisitions of other businesses or restructuring, that might cause significant changes to the ratios. For example, GlaxoSmithKline's annual report includes a lot of discussion of the impact of their restructuring strategy on their financial performance.

4.9 THE ROLE OF FINANCIAL RATIOS— AND A FINAL NOTE ON TRANSPARENCY

Whenever two managers get together to talk business and finance, it's a good bet that they will refer to financial ratios. Let's drop in on two conversations.

Conversation 1. The CEO of a Canadian manufacturing firm was musing out loud: "How are we going to finance this expansion? Would the banks be happy to lend us the $30 million that we need?"

"I've been looking into that," the financial manager replies. "Our current ratio of debt to debt plus equity is 30 percent." If we borrow the full cost of the project, the ratio would be about 45 percent. When we took out our last loan from the bank, we agreed that we would not allow our debt ratio to get above 50 percent. So if we borrow to finance this project, we wouldn't have much leeway to respond to possible emergencies. Also, the rating agencies currently give our bonds investment-grade ratings, BBB or higher. They too look at a company's leverage when they rate its bonds. I have a table here [Table 4.9] which shows that when firms are highly leveraged, their bonds receive a lower rating. This table has information about U.S. and European, Middle Eastern and African (EMEA) industrial companies. I've included both because of the differences in their accounting standards. Most of the EMEA companies use IFRS are we have to convert to IFRS. A bond rating agency does not just look at the debt ratio, but lots of other ratios and also the company's operating strategy. I don't know whether the rating agency would downgrade our bonds if our debt ratio increased to 45 percent, but they might. That wouldn't please our existing bondholders, and it might raise the cost of any new borrowing.

"We also need to think about our interest coverage, which is beginning to look a bit thin. Debt interest coverage (EBIT/interest expense) is currently 5 times, and if we borrowed the entire $30 million, interest coverage would fall to about 4 times. You can see the impact of IFRS on the interest coverage. The AA rate EMEA companies have an average EBIT interest coverage of 14.9 but the U.S. companies average is 18.3. We know that our change to IFRS may cause our earnings to fall, because more costs are included on the income statement. One more thing to keep in mind is that we expect to earn additional profits on the new investment, but it could be several years before they come through. If we run into a recession in the meantime, we could find ourselves short of cash."

"Sounds to me as if we should be thinking about a possible equity issue," responded the CEO.

Conversation 2. The CEO was not in the best of moods after his humiliating defeat at the company golf tournament by the manager of the packaging division: "I see our stock was down again yesterday," he growled. "It's now selling below book value, and the stock price is only six

TABLE 4.9 Financial ratios and default risk by rating class, long-term debt—U.S. industrial companies (US) and Europe, Middle East, Africa Companies (EMEA)

Ratios	AAA	AA		A		BBB		BB		B	
	US	US	EMEA	US	EMEA	US	EMEA	US	EMEA	US	EMEA
Return on capital (%)	34.2	25.4	20.8	21.1	15.4	14.1	12.2	12.2	11.4	8.3	8.9
EBIT interest coverage multiple	30.5	18.3	14.9	11.0	6.4	5.8	4.4	3.5	3.2	1.4	1.3
EBITDA interest coverage multiple	33.5	20.5	17.5	14.3	8.8	7.6	6.8	5.2	4.7	2.3	2.6
Funds from operations/total debt (%)	200.7	73.4	87.9	53.0	44.8	34.0	35.3	25.3	23.6	12.0	13.2
Free operating cash flow/total debt (%)	157.8	49.8	42.8	34.0	21.8	17.0	17.2	11.9	7.2	3.2	3.3
Total debt/EBITDA multiple	.4	1.1	.7	1.5	1.7	2.3	2.4	3.0	3.0	5.3	5.0
Total debt/(total debt + equity) (%)	15.1	34.7	28.4	35.7	34.0	44.7	42.5	50.4	51.5	73.1	69.4

Source: Standard & Poor's, "2009 Adjusted Key U.S. and European Industrial and Utility Financial Ratios," 2010. Reproduced by permission of Standard & Poor's, a division of The McGraw-Hill Companies, Inc.

times earnings. I work my socks off for this company; you would think that our stockholders would show a little more gratitude."

"I think I can understand a little of our shareholders' worries," the financial manager replies. "Just look at our return on assets." It's only 6 percent, well below the cost of capital. Sure we are making a profit, but that profit does not cover the cost of the funds that investors provide. Our economic value added is actually negative. Of course, this doesn't necessarily mean that the assets could be used better elsewhere, but we should certainly be looking carefully at whether any of our divisions should be sold off or the assets redeployed.

"In some ways we're in good shape. We have very little short-term debt, and our current assets are three times our current liabilities. But that's not altogether good news because it also suggests that we may have more working capital than we need. I've been looking at our main competitors. They turn over their inventory 12 times a year compared with our figure of just 8 times. Also, their customers take an average of 45 days to pay their bills. Ours take 67. If we could just match their performance on these two measures, we would release $300 million that could be paid out to shareholders."

"Perhaps we could talk more about this tomorrow," said the CEO. "In the meantime I intend to have a word with the production manager about our inventory levels and with the credit manager about our collections policy. You've also got me thinking about whether we should sell off our packaging division. I've always worried about the divisional manager there. He spends too much time practising his backswing and not enough worrying about his return on assets."

TRANSPARENCY

Throughout this chapter we have assumed that financial statements are trustworthy. We assumed that accountants are following the International Financial Reporting Standards, IFRS, and not endorsing misleading numbers. We assumed that managers are not making up good "facts" for the financial statements or covering up bad ones. When these assumptions are correct, we say that the firm is "transparent," because outsiders can assess its value and performance. One big difference between IFRS and U.S. GAAP and former Canadian GAAP is that IFRS requires more detailed disclosure of all changes in asset and liabilities.

Unfortunately, dishonest managers with creamy compensation packages may seek to hide the truth from investors. When the truth comes out, there can be big trouble. Think back to the Enron scandal. Enron was in many ways an empty shell. Its stock price was supported more by investors' enthusiasm than by profitable operating businesses. The company inflated its apparent performance by borrowing aggressively through so-called special-purpose entities (SPEs) and hiding these debts. Much of the SPE borrowing was improperly excluded from Enron's financial statements.

The bad news started to leak out in the last months of 2001. In October, Enron announced a $1 billion write-off of its water and broadband business. In November, it recognized its SPE debt retroactively, which increased its acknowledged indebtedness by $658 million and reduced its claims of past earnings by $591 million. Its public debt was downgraded to junk status, and on December 2 it filed for bankruptcy.

Enron demonstrated the importance of transparency. If Enron had been more transparent to outsiders—that is, if they could have assessed its true profitability and prospects—its problems would have shown up right away in a falling stock price. That in turn would have generated extra scrutiny from security analysts, bond rating agencies, lenders, and investors.

With transparency, corporate troubles generally lead to corrective action. But the top management of a troubled and opaque company may be able to maintain its stock price and postpone the discipline of the market. Market discipline caught up with Enron only a month or two before bankruptcy.

Enron was only one in a series of accounting scandals that came to light in 2001 and 2002. A major goal of the *Sarbanes-Oxley Act* in the United States is to increase transparency and ensure that companies and their accountants provide directors, lenders, and shareholders with the information they need to monitor progress. Among other things, the act set up the Public Company Accounting Oversight Board to oversee auditors; it bans accounting firms from offering their services to companies whose accounts they audit; it prohibits any individual from heading a firm's audit for more than five years; and it requires that the board's audit committee consist of directors who are independent of the company's management. *Sarbanes-Oxley* also requires that management (1) certify that the financial statements present a fair view of the firm's financial position and (2) demonstrate that the firm has adequate controls and procedures for financial reporting.

All this comes at a price. The costs of SOX and the burdens of meeting detailed regulations are pushing some corporations to return to private (rather than public) ownership. Some observers also believe that these added regulatory demands have hurt the international competitiveness of U.S. financial markets.

We stress that transparency in the United States and other developed economies is usually pretty good. Nevertheless, it pays to be careful and critical even in these countries. Take extra care in developing economies, where accounting standards are often lax.

4.10 SUMMARY

1. **How do you measure whether a public corporation has delivered value for its shareholders?** LO1

   For a public corporation, this is relatively easy. Start with market capitalization, which equals price per share times the number of shares outstanding. The difference between market capitalization and the book value of equity measures the market value added by the firm's investments and operations. The book value of equity is the cumulative investment (including reinvested earnings) by shareholders in the company. The ratio of market value to book value is another way of expressing value added.

   For private corporations, financial managers and analysts have to turn to other performance measures, because stock prices are not available.

2. **What measures are used to assess financial performance?** LO2

   Financial managers and analysts track **return on equity (ROE)**, which is the ratio of net income to equity capital. But net income is calculated net of interest expense, so ROE depends on the debt ratio. The **return on capital (ROC)** and the **return on assets (ROA)** are better measures of operating performance. These are ratios of **net operating profit after taxes (NOPAT)** to total capitalization (debt plus shareholders' equity) and to total assets. ROC should be compared with the company's cost of capital. EVA (economic value added or **residual income**) deducts the cost of capital from NOPAT. If EVA is positive, the firm's current operations are adding value for shareholders.

3. **What are the standard measures of profitability, efficiency, leverage, and liquidity?** LO3

   Financial managers and analysts have to condense the enormous volume of information in a company's financial statements. They rely on a handful of ratios to summarize financial performance, operating efficiency, and financial strength. Look back at Table 4.6, which summarizes the most important ratios. Remember that the ratios sometimes appear under different names and may be calculated differently.

   Profitability ratios measure return on investment. Leverage ratios measure how much the firm has borrowed and its obligations to pay interest. Efficiency ratios measure how intensively the firm uses its assets. Liquidity ratios measure how easily the firm can obtain cash.

   Financial ratios crop up repeatedly in financial discussions and contracts. Banks and bondholders usually demand limits on debt ratios or interest coverage.

4. **What determines the return on assets and equity?** LO4

The Du Pont system links financial ratios together to explain the return on assets and equity. Return on assets is the product of asset turnover and operating profit margin. Return on equity is the product of the leverage ratio, asset turnover, operating profit margin, and debt burden.

5. **What is sustainable growth?** LO5

Sustainable growth is the rate at which the firm can grow without changing its leverage ratio. Firms that reinvest more of their earnings can sustain faster growth. The sustainable growth rate is the product of the plowback ratio and return on equity (ROE). (The plowback ratio equals 1 minus the dividend payout ratio.) Of course, this growth rate is really sustainable only if ROE and plowback are maintained at current levels.

6. **What are some pitfalls in financial statement analysis?** LO6

Financial statement analysis will rarely be useful if done mechanically. Financial ratios do not provide final answers, although they should prompt the right questions. In addition, accounting entries do not always reflect current market values, and in rare cases accounting is not transparent, because unscrupulous managers make up good news and hide bad news in financial statements.

You will need a benchmark to assess a company's financial condition. Therefore, we usually compare financial ratios to the company's ratios in earlier years and to ratios of other firms in the same business.

Related Web Links

sedar.com Annual reports and other documents of Canadian public companies

AnnualReports.com Links to financial statements for companies listed on various stock exchanges in the world

annualreports.co.uk Online annual reports

kpmg.com/Ca/en/IssuesAndInsights/ArticlesPublications/Pages/taxrates.aspx KPMG tax site

iasb.org Site of the International Accounting Standards Board

Key Terms

Du Pont formula	110	market value added	100	return on assets (ROA)	106
economic value added (EVA)	103	market-to-book ratio	101	return on capital (ROC)	105
liquidity	115	net operating profit after tax (NOPAT)	104	return on equity (ROE)	107
market capitalization	100	operating profit margin	110	sustainable rate of growth	117

Questions and Problems

connect Practise and learn online with *Connect*. Questions with online Excel templates or datasets are marked with ✎.

BASIC

*1. **Calculating Ratios.** Here are simplified financial statements of phone corporation from a recent year: (LO3)

Income Statement (millions of dollars)

Net sales	13,193
Cost of goods sold	4,060
Other expenses	4,049
Depreciation	2,518
Earnings before interest and taxes (EBIT)	2,566
Interest expenses	685
Income before tax	1,881
Taxes	570
Net income	1,311
Dividends	856

Statement of Financial Position (millions of dollars)

	End of Year	Start of Year
Assets:		
Cash and marketable securities	89	158
Receivables	2,382	2,490
Inventories	187	238
Other current assets	867	932
Total current assets	3,525	3,818
Net property, plant, and equipment	19,973	19,915
Other long-term assets	4,216	3,770
Total assets	27,714	27,503
Liabilities and shareholders' equity:		
Payables	2,564	3,040
Short-term debt	1,419	1,573
Other current liabilities	811	787
Total current liabilities	4,794	5,400
Long-term debt and leases	7,018	6,833
Other long-term liabilities	6,178	6,149
Shareholders' equity	9,724	9,121
Total liabilities and shareholders' equity	27,714	27,503

Write the formulas and calculate the following financial ratios:

a. Long-term debt ratio
b. Total debt ratio
c. Times interest earned
d. Cash coverage ratio
e. Current ratio
f. Quick ratio
g. Operating profit margin
h. Inventory turnover
i. Days in inventory
j. Average collection period
k. Return on equity
l. Return on assets
m. Payout ratio

2. **Market Value Ratios.** Phone Corp. stock price was $84 at the end of the year. There were 205 million shares outstanding. What was the market capitalization and market value added? What was its market-to-book ratio and earnings per share? (LO1)

*3. **EVA.** Phone Corp's cost of capital was 8.3 percent. Estimate the tax rate (taxes/income before taxes) and calculated net operating profit after taxes. What was Phone Corp's economic value added? (LO2)

4. **Measuring Firm Performance.** (LO2)
   a. What would happen to AstraZeneca's economic value added if its cost of equity were 8 percent rather than the 6.7 percent value we assumed?
   b. Would this have any impact on its accounting profits?
   c. Which do you think is a better measure of the firm's performance?

5. **Measuring Firm Performance.** Suppose the broad stock market falls 5 percent in one day and AstraZeneca's stock price also falls by 5 percent. (LO1)
   a. What will happen to our assessment of market value added?
   b. Should this decline affect our assessment of the performance of AstraZeneca's managers?
   c. Would you feel differently about AstraZeneca's managers if the stock market were unchanged and AstraZeneca's stock fell by 5 percent?

6. **Sustainable Growth.** In Table 4.6, we report AstraZeneca's sustainable growth rate as 22.1 percent. (LO5)
   a. What would the sustainable growth rate be if AstraZeneca's payout ratio increased to 70 percent?
   b. What would the sustainable growth rate be if AstraZeneca's return on equity was 30 percent?

7. **Du Pont Analysis.** Use the data for Phone Corp. from question 1 to confirm that ROA = asset turnover × operating profit margin. (LO4)

8. **Du Pont Analysis.** Use the data for Phone Corp. from question 1 to demonstrate that ROE = leverage ratio × asset turnover ratio × operating profit margin × debt burden. (LO4)

INTERMEDIATE

9. **Asset Turnover.** In each case, describe the nature of each business. Choose the firm that you expect to have a higher asset turnover ratio and explain the reason for your choice. (LO3)
   a. Economics Consulting Group or AstraZeneca
   b. Catalog Shopping Network or Mark's Work Wearhouse
   c. Electric Utility Co. or Standard Supermarkets

10. **Economic Value Added.** EVA will be positive whenever ROC is greater than the cost of capital. Explain why this is so. (LO2)

11. **Defining Ratios.** There are no universally accepted definitions of financial ratios, but some of the following

ratios make no sense at all. Substitute correct definitions and then explain what each ratio measures. (LO3)

a. $\text{Debt-equity ratio} = \dfrac{\text{long-term debt}}{\text{long-term debt} + \text{equity}}$

b. $\text{Return on equity} = \dfrac{\text{sales}}{\text{average equity}}$

c. $\text{Operating profit margin} = \dfrac{\text{after-tax operating income}}{\text{sales}}$

d. $\text{Inventory turnover} = \dfrac{\text{total sales}}{\text{average inventory}}$

e. $\text{Current ratio} = \dfrac{\text{current liabilities}}{\text{current assets}}$

f. $\text{Average collection period} = \dfrac{\text{revenues}}{\text{average receivables/365}}$

g. $\text{Quick ratio} = \dfrac{\text{cash and cash equivalents} + \text{current other investments} + \text{trade receivables}}{\text{current liabilities}}$

12. **Current Liabilities.** Suppose that at year-end AstraZeneca had unused lines of credit which would have allowed it to borrow a further $300 million. Suppose also that it used this line of credit to borrow $300 million and invested the proceeds in marketable securities. Would the company have appeared to be (a) more or less liquid or (b) more or less highly leveraged? Calculate the appropriate ratios. (LO3)

13. **Current Ratio.** How would the following actions affect a firm's current ratio? (LO3)
   a. Inventory is sold at cost.
   b. The firm takes out a bank loan to pay its due trade payables.
   c. A customer pays its accounts receivable.
   d. The firm uses cash to purchase additional inventories.

*14. **Liquidity Ratios.** A firm uses $1 million in cash to purchase inventories. What will happen to its current ratio? Its quick ratio? (LO3)

15. **Receivables.** Chik's Chickens has average trade receivables of $6,333. Sales for the year were $9,800. What is its average collection period? (LO3)

*16. **Inventory.** Salad Daze maintains an inventory of produce worth $400. Its total bill for produce over the course of the year was $73,000. How old on average is the lettuce it serves its customers? (LO3)

17. **Inventory Turnover.** If a firm's inventory level of $10,000 represents 30 days' sales, what is the annual cost of goods sold? What is the inventory turnover ratio? (LO3)

*18. **Leverage Ratios.** Lever Age pays an 8 percent rate of interest on $10 million of outstanding debt with face value $10 million. The firm's EBIT was $1 million. (LO3)
   a. What is times interest earned?
   b. If depreciation is $200,000, what is cash coverage?
   c. If the firm must retire $300,000 of debt for the sinking fund each year, what is its "fixed-payment cash-coverage ratio" (the ratio of cash flow to interest plus other fixed debt payments)?

19. **Du Pont Analysis.** Keller Cosmetics maintains an operating profit margin of 5 percent and asset turnover ratio of 3. (LO4)
   a. What is its ROA?
   b. If its debt-equity ratio is 1, its interest payments and taxes are each $8,000, and EBIT is $20,000, what is its ROE?

*20. **Du Pont Analysis.** Torrid Romance Publishers has average receivables of $3,000, which represents 20 days' sales. Average total assets are $75,000. The firm's operating profit margin is 5 percent. Find the firm's ROA and asset turnover ratio and ROA. (LO4)

21. **Leverage.** A firm has a long-term debt-equity ratio of .4. Shareholders' equity is $1 million. Current assets are $200,000, and the current ratio is 2. The only current liabilities are notes payable. What is the total debt ratio? (LO3)

*22. **Leverage Ratios.** A firm has a debt-to-equity ratio of .5 and a market-to-book ratio of 2. What is the ratio of the book value of debt to the market value of equity? (LO3)

23. **Times Interest Earned.** In the past year, TVG had revenues of $3 million, cost of goods sold of $2.5 million, and depreciation expense of $200,000. The firm has a single issue of debt outstanding with book value of $1 million on which it pays an interest rate of 8 percent. What is the firm's times interest earned ratio? (LO3)

24. **Du Pont Analysis.** CFA Corp. has a debt-equity ratio that is lower than the industry average, but its cash coverage ratio is also lower than the industry average. What might explain this seeming contradiction? (LO3)

25. **Leverage.** Suppose that a firm has both floating-rate and fixed-rate debt outstanding. What effect will a decline in market interest rates have on the firm's times interest earned ratio? On the market-value debt-to-equity ratio? On the basis of these answers, would you say that leverage has increased or decreased? (LO3)

*26. **Interpreting Ratios.** In each of the following cases, explain briefly which of the two companies is likely to be characterized by the higher ratio? (LO3)
   a. Debt-equity ratio: a shipping company or a computer software company

b. Payout ratio: Food Producer Inc. or Computer Graphics Inc.
c. Ratio of sales to assets: an integrated pulp and paper mill and manufacturer or a paper mill
d. Average collection period: Regional Electric Power Company or Z-Mart Discount Outlets

27. **Using Financial Ratios.** For each category of financial ratios discussed in this chapter, give examples of who would be likely to examine these ratios and why. (LO6)

CHALLENGE

28. **Financial Statements.** Ink has spilled over some of the entries in the balance sheet and income statement of ABC Corp. Can you use the following information to work out the missing entries? The ratio definitions in table 4.6 were used. (LO3)

Long-term debt ratio	0.4
Times interest earned	6.5
Current ratio	1.4
Quick ratio	1.0
Cash ratio	0.2
Return on assets	18%
Return on equity	20.53%
Inventory turnover	5.4
Average collection period	83.74 days

Income Statement (millions of dollars)

Net sales	. . .
Cost of goods sold	. . .
Selling, general, and administrative expenses	10
Depreciation	20
Earnings before interest and taxes (EBIT)	. . .
Interest expense	. . .
Income before tax	. . .
Tax	. . .
Net income	. . .

Balance Sheet (millions of dollars)

	This Year	Last Year
Assets:		
Cash and marketable securities	. . .	20
Trade Receivables	. . .	34
Inventories	. . .	26
Total current assets	. . .	80
Net property, plant, and equipment	. . .	25
Total assets	. . .	105
Liabilities and shareholders' equity:		
Accounts payable	25	20
Notes payable	30	35
Total current liabilities	. . .	55
Long-term debt	. . .	20
Shareholders' equity	. . .	30
Total liabilities and shareholders' equity	115	105

29. **Interpreting Financial Ratios.** (LO3)
a. Turn back to Table 4.7. For the sample of industries in that table, plot each pair of net profit margin and asset turnover in a scatter diagram. What is the apparent relationship between these two variables? Does this make sense to you?
b. Now plot a scatter diagram of each pair of current ratio versus quick ratio. Do these two measures of liquidity tend to move together? Would you conclude that once you know one of these ratios, there is little to be gained by calculating the other?

30. **Internet.** Log on to **finance.yahoo.com** to find the latest simplified financial statements for AstraZeneca. Recalculate AZN's financial ratios. What have been the main changes from those shown in these tables? If you owned some of AZN's debt, would these changes make you feel more or less happy? (LO3)

Solutions to Check Points

4.1 Market capitalization is $75 × 14.5 million = $1,087.5 million. Market value added is $1,087.5 − $610 = $477.5 million. Market to book is 1,087.5/610 = 1.78. You can also calculate book value per share at $610/14.5 = $42.07, and use price per share to calculate market to book: $75/$42.07 = 1.78.

4.2 The cost of equity in dollars is .115 × $188 million = $21.62 million. EVA is $30 − $21.62 = $8.38 million.

4.3 NOPAT, net operating profit after taxes, is calculated before net finance expense. Net income is calculated after net finance expense. Financial managers usually start with net income, so they add back after-tax net finance expense to get to net operating profit before taxes. NOPAT measures the profitability of the firm's investment and operations. If properly calculated, it is not affected by financing. It is useful in calculating EVA, ROC, and ROA to give measures of operating performance, independently of how the firm is financed.

4.4 ROE measures return to equity as net income divided by the book value of equity. ROC and ROA measure the return to all investors, including interest paid as well as net income to shareholders. ROC measures return versus long-term debt and equity. ROA measures return versus total assets.

4.5 Average daily expenses are cost of sales/365 = 6,389/365 = \$17.5 million. The average trade payables are (2,316 + 2,257)/2 = \$2,287 million. The average payment period is average trade payables/average daily expenses = 2,287/17.5 = 131 days. Wow, 131 days to pay bills? This huge number suggests that some other expenses are not paid right away and get included in trade payables. So, if selling, general, and administrative costs are included as delayed payments, the average payment period is 2,316/[(6,389 + 10,445)/365] = 50.2 days.

4.6 In industries with rapid asset turnover, competition forces prices down, reducing profit margins.

4.7 Nothing will happen to the long-term debt ratio computed using book values, since the face values of the old and new debt are equal. However, times interest earned and cash coverage will increase since the firm will reduce its interest expense.

4.8 a. The firm must compensate for its below-average profit margin with an above-average turnover ratio. Remember that ROA is the product of operating margin × turnover.

b. If ROA equals the industry average but ROE exceeds the industry average, the firm must have above-average leverage. As long as ROA exceeds the borrowing rate, leverage will increase ROE.

4.9 a. The current ratio starts at 1.2/1.0 = 1.2. The transaction will reduce current assets to \$.7 million and current liabilities to \$.5 million. The current ratio increases to .7/.5 = 1.4. Net working capital is unaffected: Current assets and current liabilities fall by equal amounts.

b. The current ratio is unaffected, since the firm merely exchanges one current asset (cash) for another (inventories). However, the quick ratio will fall since inventories are not included among the most liquid assets.

4.10

	Company A	Company B
1. Asset turnover	100/40 = 2.5	100/87.3 = 1.15
2. Operating profit margin, %	4.0/100 = .04, 4%	9/100 = .09, 9%
3. Return on assets, % (1 × 2)	2.5 × 4% = 10%	1.15 × 9% = 10.35%

Walmart, a department store, generates a high volume of sales from its assets but earns a relatively low profit margin on these sales. The reverse is true for Peoples Jewellers, a store that sells jewellery: it has a lower asset turnover but a relatively high profit margin on those sales. So, Walmart is company A and Peoples Jewellers is company B. Asset turnovers and operating profit margins are substantially different for the two companies, but their returns on assets are much less different.

MINI CASE

Burchetts Green had enjoyed the bank training course, but it was good to be starting his first real job in the corporate lending group. Earlier that morning the boss had handed him a set of financial statements for The Hobby Horse Company, Inc. (HH). "Hobby Horse," she said, "has a $45 million loan from us due at the end of September, and it is likely to ask us to roll it over. The company seems to have run into some rough weather recently, and I have asked Furze Platt to go down there this afternoon and see what is happening. It might do you good to go along with her. Before you go, take a look at these financial statements and see what you think the problems are. Here's a chance for you to use some of that stuff they taught you in the training course."

Mr. Green was familiar with the HH story. Founded in 1990, it had rapidly built up a chain of discount stores selling materials for crafts and hobbies. However, last year a number of new store openings coinciding with a poor Christmas season had pushed the company into loss. Management had halted all new construction and put 15 of its existing stores up for sale.

Mr. Green decided to start with the six-year summary of HH's balance sheet and income statement (Table 4.10). Then he turned to examine in more detail the latest position (Tables 4.11 and 4.12).

What appear to be the problem areas in HH? Do the financial ratios suggest questions that Ms. Platt and Mr. Green need to address?

TABLE 4.10 Financial highlights for The Hobby Horse Company, Inc., year ending March 31.

	2011	2010	2009	2008	2007	2006
Net sales	3,351	3,314	2,845	2,796	2,493	2,160
EBIT	−9	312	256	243	212	156
Interest	37	63	65	58	48	46
Taxes (24% tax rate)	3	60	46	43	39	34
Net income	−49	189	145	142	125	76
Earnings per share	−0.15	0.55	0.44	0.42	0.37	0.25
Current assets	669	469	491	435	392	423
Net fixed assets	923	780	753	680	610	536
Total assets	1,592	1,249	1,244	1,115	1,002	959
Current liabilities	680	365	348	302	276	320
Long-term debt	236	159	297	311	319	315
Stockholders' equity	676	725	599	502	407	324
Number of stores	240	221	211	184	170	157
Employees	13,057	11,835	9,810	9,790	9,075	7,825

TABLE 4.11 Income statement for the Hobby Horse Company, Inc., for year ending March 31, 2011 (millions of dollars).

Net sales	3,351
Cost of goods sold	1,990
Selling, general, and administrative expenses	1,211
Depreciation expense	159
Earnings before interest and taxes (EBIT)	−9
Net interest expense	37
Taxable income	−46
Income taxes	3
Net income	−49
Allocation of net income:	
Addition to retained earnings	−49
Dividends	0

Note: Column sums subject to rounding error.

TABLE 4.12
Consolidated statement of financial position for The Hobby Horse Company, Inc. (millions of dollars).

Assets	March 31, 2011	March 31, 2010
Current assets:		
Cash and cash equivalents	14	72
Trade Receivables	176	194
Inventories	479	203
Total current assets	669	469
Non-current assets:		
Property, plant, and equipment (net of depreciation)	1,077	910
Less accumulated depreciation	154	130
Net fixed assets	923	780
Total assets	1,592	1,249
Liabilities and Shareholders' Equity	**March 31, 2011**	**March 31, 2010**
Current liabilities:		
Debt due for repayment	484	222
Trade payables	94	58
Other current liabilities	102	85
Total current liabilities	680	365
Long-term debt	236	159
Stockholders' equity:		
Common stock and other paid-in capital	155	155
Retained earnings	521	570
Total stockholders' equity	676	725
Total liabilities and stockholders' equity	1,592	1,249

Note: Column sums subject to rounding error.

PART 2 Value

5 The Time Value of Money
5.1 Future Values and Compound Interest
5.2 Present Values
5.3 Multiple Cash Flows
5.4 Level Cash Flows: Perpetuities and Annuities
5.5 Inflation and the Time Value of Money
5.6 Effective Annual Interest Rates
5.7 Summary
6 Valuing Bonds
7 Valuing Stocks
8 Net Present Value and Other Investment Criteria
9 Using Discounted Cash Flow Analysis to Make Investment Decisions
10 Project Analysis

CHAPTER 5

The Time Value of Money

LEARNING OBJECTIVES

After studying this chapter, you should be able to:

LO1 Calculate the future value to which money invested at a given interest rate will grow.

LO2 Calculate the present value of a future payment.

LO3 Calculate present and future values of streams of cash payments.

LO4 Find the interest rate implied by the present or future value.

LO5 Explain the difference between real and nominal cash flows and between real and nominal interest rates.

LO6 Explain how we would compare interest rates quoted over different time intervals.

An auto dealer's view of the time value of money. Do you truly understand what these percentages mean? Do you realize that the dealership may not be quoting effective annual interest rates? If the dealership quotes a monthly payment on a 4-year, $10,000 car loan, would you be able to double-check the dealership's calculations?

Companies invest in lots of things. Some are tangible assets—that is, assets you can kick, like factories, machinery, and offices. Others are intangible assets, such as patents or trademarks. In each case the company lays out some money to start in the hopes of receiving even more money later. Individuals also make investments. For example, your university or college tuition may cost you $6,000 per year. That is an investment you hope will pay off in the form of a higher salary later in life. You are sowing now and expecting to reap later.

Companies pay for their investments by raising money and in the process assume liabilities. For example, they may borrow money from a bank and promise to repay it with interest later. You may also have financed your investment in higher education by borrowing money that you plan to pay back out of that fat salary.

All these financial decisions require comparisons of cash payments at different dates. Will your future salary be sufficient to justify the current expenditure on university or college tuition? How much will you have to repay the bank if you borrow to finance your education?

In this chapter we take the first steps toward understanding the relationship between the value of the dollar today and in the future. We start by looking at how funds invested at a specific interest rate will grow over time. We next ask how much you would need to invest today to produce a specified sum of money in the future, and we describe some shortcuts for working out the value of a series of cash payments. Then we consider how inflation affects these financial calculations.

Compare interest rates quoted over different time intervals—for example, monthly versus annual rates. There is nothing complicated about these calculations, but if they are to become second nature, you should read the chapter thoroughly, work carefully through the examples (we have provided plenty), and make sure you tackle the Check Point questions. We are asking you to make an investment now in return for a payoff later.

LO1 5.1 FUTURE VALUES AND COMPOUND INTEREST

You have $100 invested in a bank account. Suppose banks are currently paying an interest rate of 6 percent per year on deposits. So after a year, your account will earn interest of $6:

$$\text{Interest} = \text{interest rate} \times \text{initial investment}$$
$$= .06 \times \$100 = \$6$$

You start the year with $100 and you earn interest of $6, so the value of your investment will grow to $106 by the end of the year:

$$\text{Value of investment after 1 year} = \$100 + \$6 = \$106$$

Notice that the \$100 invested grows by the factor $(1 + .06) = 1.06$. In general, for any interest rate, r, the value of the investment at the end of 1 year is $(1 + r)$ times the initial investment:

$$\text{Value after 1 year} = \text{initial investment} \times (1 + r)$$
$$= \$100 \times (1.06) = \$106$$

What if you leave this money in the bank for a second year? Your balance, now \$106, will continue to earn interest of 6 percent. So

$$\text{Interest in year 2} = .06 \times \$106 = \$6.36$$

You start the second year with \$106 on which you earn interest of \$6.36. So by the end of the year the value of your account will grow to \$106 + \$6.36 = \$112.36.

In the first year your investment of \$100 increases by a factor of 1.06 to \$106; in the second year the \$106 again increases by a factor of 1.06 to \$112.36. Thus the initial \$100 investment grows twice by a factor of 1.06:

$$\text{Value of account after 2 years} = \$100 \times 1.06 \times 1.06$$
$$= \$100 \times (1.06)^2 = \$112.36$$

If you keep your money invested for a third year, your investment multiplies by 1.06 each year for three years. By the end of the third year, it will total $\$100 \times (1.06)^3 = \$119.10$, scarcely enough to put you in the millionaire class, but even millionaires have to start somewhere.

future value (FV) Amount to which an investment will grow after earning interest.

Clearly for an investment horizon of t years, the original \$100 investment will grow to $\$100 \times (1.06)^t$. For an interest rate of r and a horizon of t years, the **future value** of your investment will be

$$\text{Future value of } \$100 = \$100 \times (1 + r)^t$$

compound interest Interest earned on interest.

simple interest Interest earned only on the original investment; no interest is earned on interest.

Notice in our example that your interest income in the first year is \$6 (6 percent of \$100), and in the second year it is \$6.36 (6 percent of \$106). Your income in the second year is higher because you now earn interest on *both* the original \$100 investment and the \$6 of interest earned in the previous year. Earning interest on interest is called *compounding* or **compound interest**. In contrast, if the bank calculated the interest only on your original investment, you would be paid **simple interest**. With simple interest your bank balance is only \$112 after two years, $\$100 + 2 \times \$6$.

Table 5.1 and Figure 5.1 illustrate the mechanics of compound interest. Table 5.1 shows that in each year, you start with a greater balance in your account—your savings have been increased by the previous year's interest. As a result, your interest income also is higher.

Obviously, the higher the rate of interest, the faster your savings will grow. Figure 5.2 shows that a few percentage points added to the (compound) interest rate can dramatically affect the future balance of your savings account. For example, after 10 years \$100 invested at 10 percent will grow to $\$100 \times (1.10)^{10} = \$259.37$. If invested at 5 percent, it will grow to only $\$100 \times (1.05)^{10} = \$162.89$.

The future value, FV, of any investment can be calculated with the future value formula. The formula for the future value of I dollars at r percent interest per period for t periods is

$$\textbf{FMV of \$}I\textbf{ investment} = I \times (1 + r)^t \qquad (5.1)$$

TABLE 5.1
Mechanics of compound interest—interest is earned on previous year's interest.

Year	Balance at Start of Year	Interest Earned During Year	Balance at End of Year
1	\$100.00	.06 × \$100.00 = \$6.00	\$106.00
2	\$106.00	.06 × \$106.00 = \$6.36	\$112.36
3	\$112.36	.06 × \$112.36 = \$6.74	\$119.10
4	\$119.10	.06 × \$119.10 = \$7.15	\$126.25
5	\$126.25	.06 × \$126.25 = \$7.57	\$133.82

FIGURE 5.1
Compound interest. Future value of $100 invested at 6 percent in each of the five years.

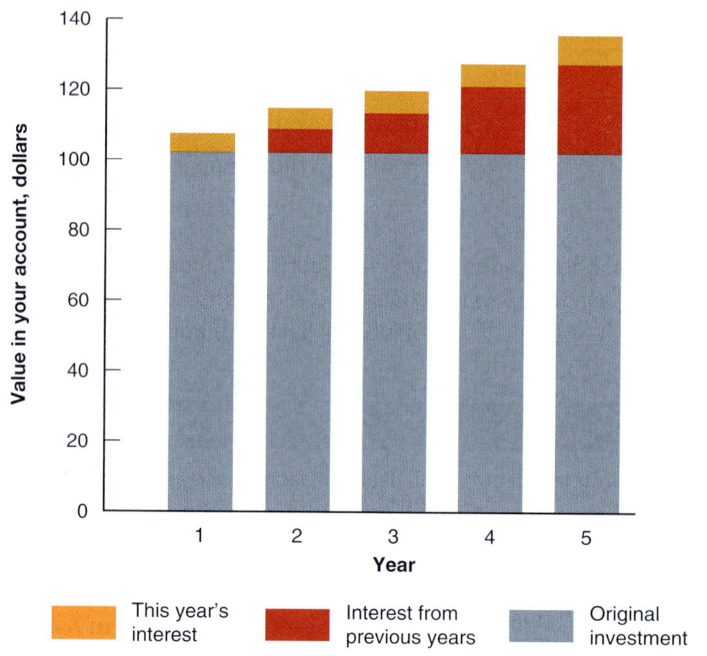

FIGURE 5.2
Future values of $100 invested at various interest rates, with compound interest.

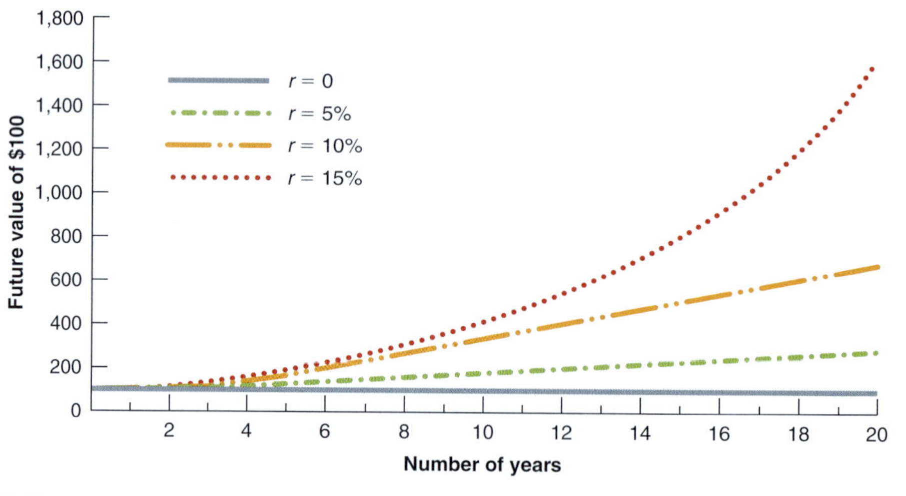

Calculating future values is easy using almost any calculator. If you have patience, you can multiply your initial investment by $1 + r$ once for each period of your investment. A simpler procedure is to use the power key (the y^x key) on your calculator. For example, with a 6 percent interest rate and a 10-year investment, you want to compute (1.06)10. Enter 1.06, press the y^x key, enter 10, press = and discover that the answer is 1.7908. (Try this!)

If you don't have a calculator, you can use a table of future values such as Table 5.2. It shows the future value of a $1 investment for various interest rates and investment periods. We call the

TABLE 5.2
Future value factors—future values of $1, invested at various interest rates for different periods.

Number of Periods	Interest Rate per Period					
	5%	6%	7%	8%	9%	10%
1	1.0500	1.0600	1.0700	1.0800	1.0900	1.1000
2	1.1025	1.1236	1.1449	1.1664	1.1881	1.2100
3	1.1576	1.1910	1.2250	1.2597	1.2950	1.3310
4	1.2155	1.2625	1.3108	1.3605	1.4116	1.4641
5	1.2763	1.3382	1.4026	1.4693	1.5386	1.6105
10	1.6289	1.7908	1.9672	2.1589	2.3674	2.5937
20	2.6533	3.2071	3.8697	4.6610	5.6044	6.7275
30	4.3219	5.7435	7.6123	10.0627	13.2677	17.4494

future value interest factor or **future value factor** Future value of a current cash flow of $1.

future value of a $1 investment at r percent per period for t periods the **future value interest factor** (or just **future value factor**) and write it as FVIF(r, t):

$$\text{Future value factor, FVIF}(r, t) = (1 + r)^t \tag{5.2}$$

You can see that the future value of an investment can be calculated by multiplying the invested amount by the future value factor of a $1 investment for the same time period and interest rate:

$$\text{FV} = I \times \text{future value factor} = I \times \text{FVIF}(r, t) = I \times (1 + r)^t \tag{5.3}$$

Check that you can use Table 5.2 to work out the future value of a 10-year investment of $1 at 6 percent. First find the row corresponding to 10 periods. Now work along that row until you reach the column for a 6 percent interest rate. The entry shows that $1 invested for 10 periods at 6 percent grows to $1.7908. Suppose you invested $20, instead of $1? Multiply the same future value factor by $20 to get its future value of $35.816 (= $20 × 1.7908).

Now try one more example. If you invest $1 for 20 years at 10 percent and do not withdraw any money, what will you have at the end? Your answer should be $6.7275.

Suppose you invest $50? Multiply the future value factor for 10 percent and 20 years by $50 and you end up with $336.375 (= $50 × 6.7275).

Table 5.2 gives future values for only a small selection of years and interest rates. Table A.1 in Appendix A (see the Online Learning Centre) is a bigger version of Table 5.2. It presents the future value of a $1 investment for a wide range of time periods and interest rates.

Future value tables are tedious, and as Table 5.2 demonstrates, they show future values only for a limited set of interest rates and time periods. For example, suppose that you want to calculate future values using an interest rate of 7.835 percent. The power key on your calculator will be faster and easier than future value tables. A third alternative is to use a financial calculator or a spreadsheet. We show you how to do this in several boxes later in the chapter.

How do you calculate future value if interest is paid more often than annually, say monthly? As long as you know the interest per period and the number of periods, the procedure is the same. For example, suppose Money Bank is paying 1 percent per month on deposits. If you invest $500 for 20 months, the future value of your investment is

$$\text{FV} = \$500 \times \text{FVIF}(.01,20) = \$500 \times (1.01)^{20} = \$500 \times 1.2202 = \$610.10$$

Later in the chapter, we will show you how to compare interest rates when they are quoted for different periods, such as weekly or semi-annually.

The power of compounding is not restricted to money. Foresters try to forecast the compound growth rate of trees, demographers the compound growth rate of population. An American social commentator once observed that the number of lawyers in the United States is increasing at a higher compound rate than the population as a whole (3.6 as against .9 percent in the 1980s), and calculated that in about two centuries there will be more lawyers than people! In all these cases, the principle is the same: Compound growth means that value increases each period by the factor (1 + growth rate). The value after t periods will equal the initial value times $(1 + \text{growth rate})^t$. When money is invested at compound interest, the growth rate is the interest rate.

Compound growth means that value increases each period by the factor (1 + growth rate). The value after t periods will equal the initial value times $(1 + \text{growth rate})^t$. When money is invested at compound interest, the growth rate is the interest rate.

EXAMPLE 5.1 MANHATTAN ISLAND

An interesting example of the power of compound interest is the sale of Manhattan Island for \$24 in 1626 to Peter Minuit. Based on New York real estate prices today, it seems that Minuit got a great deal. But consider the future value of that \$24 if it had been invested for 380 years (2006 minus 1626) at an interest rate of 8 percent per year:

$$\$24 \times \text{FVIF}(.08,380) = \$24 \times (1.08)^{380} = \$120{,}569{,}700{,}000{,}000$$
$$= \$120.5697 \text{ trillion}$$

Perhaps the deal wasn't as good as it appeared. The total value of land in Manhattan today is only a fraction of \$121 trillion.

Though entertaining, this analysis is actually somewhat misleading. First, the 8 percent interest rate we've used to compute future values is quite high by historical standards. At a 3.5 percent interest rate, which is more consistent with historical experience, the future value of the \$24 would be *dramatically* lower, only \$24 × (1.035)380 = \$11,416,794! Second, we have understated the returns to Mr. Minuit and his successors: we have ignored the rental income that the island's land has generated over the last three or four centuries.

All things considered, if we had been around in 1626, we would have gladly paid \$24 for the island.

Spreadsheet Questions

5.1 What was the future value of the \$24 paid for Manhattan Island by 1726, that is, after 100 years of compounding? What about by 1826? What was the growth in value during the second 100 years? What was the growth in value in the last 82 years of the "investment"?

5.2 Why is the growth of value so much greater in the later years than in the earlier years?

Check Point 5.1

Suppose that Peter Minuit did not become the first real estate tycoon in New York, but instead had invested his \$24 at a 5 percent interest rate in New Amsterdam Savings Bank. What would have been the balance in his account after five years? 50 years?

Check Point 5.2

Start-up Enterprises had sales last year of only \$0.5 million. However, a stock market analyst is bullish on the company and predicts that sales will double each year for four years. What are projected sales at the end of this period?

LO2, 5 5.2 PRESENT VALUES

A dollar today is worth more than a dollar tomorrow.

Money can be invested to earn interest. If you are offered the choice between \$100,000 now and \$100,000 at the end of the year, you naturally take the money now to get a year's interest. Financial managers make the same point when they say that money in hand today has a time value or perhaps when they quote the most basic financial principle, that a dollar today is worth more than a dollar tomorrow.

present value (PV) Value today of a future cash flow.

We have seen that \$100 invested for 1 year at 6 percent will grow to a future value of 100 × 1.06 = \$106. Let's turn this around: How much do we need to invest now in order to produce \$106 at the end of the year? Financial managers refer to this as the **present value (PV)** of the \$106 payoff.

Future value is calculated by multiplying the present investment by one plus the interest rate, .06, or 1.06. To calculate present value, we simply reverse the process and divide the future value by 1.06:

$$\text{Present value} = \text{PV} = \frac{\text{future value}}{1.06} = \frac{\$106}{1.06} = \$100$$

What is the present value of, say, \$112.36 to be received 2 years from now? Again we ask, how much would we need to invest now to produce \$112.36 after 2 years? The answer is obviously \$100; we've already calculated that at 6 percent \$100 grows to \$112.36:

$$\$100 \times (1.06)^2 = \$112.36$$

However, if we don't know, or forgot the answer, we just divide future value by $(1.06)^2$:

$$\text{Present value} = \text{PV} = \frac{\$112.36}{(1.06)^2} = \$100$$

In general, for a future value or payment t periods away, the present value formula is

$$\textbf{Present value} = \frac{\textbf{future value after } t \textbf{ periods}}{(1 + r)^t} \qquad \textbf{(5.4)}$$

discount rate Interest rate used to compute present values of future cash flows.

In this context the interest rate r is known as the **discount rate**, and the present value is often called the *discounted value* of the future payment. To calculate present value, we discounted the future value at the interest r.

EXAMPLE 5.2 SAVING FOR A FUTURE PURCHASE

Suppose you need \$3,000 next year to buy a new computer. The interest rate is 8 percent per year. How much money should you set aside now in order to pay for the purchase? Just calculate the present value at an 8 percent interest rate of a \$3,000 payment at the end of 1 year. This value is

$$\text{PV} = \frac{\$3{,}000}{1.08} = \$2{,}778$$

Notice that \$2,778 invested for 1 year at 8 percent will provide just enough to buy your computer:

$$\text{Future value} = \$2{,}778 \times 1.08 = \$3{,}000$$

The longer the period before you must make a payment, the less you need to invest today. For example, suppose that you can postpone buying that computer until the end of two years. In this case we calculate the present value of the future payment by dividing \$3,000 by $(1.08)^2$:

$$\text{PV} = \frac{\$3{,}000}{(1.08)^2} = \$2{,}572$$

Thus you need to invest \$2,778 today to provide \$3,000 in 1 year but only \$2,572 to provide the same \$3,000 in 2 years.

To work out how much you will have in the future if you invest for t periods at an interest rate r, multiply the initial investment by $(1 + r)^t$. To find the present value of a future payment, run the process in reverse and divide by $(1 + r)^t$.

We repeat the basic procedure: To work out how much you will have in the future if you invest for t periods at an interest rate r, multiply the initial investment by $(1 + r)^t$. To find the present value of a future payment, run the process in reverse and divide by $(1 + r)^t$.

Present values are always calculated using compound interest. Whereas the ascending lines in Figure 5.2 show the future value of \$100 invested with compound interest, when we calculate present values we move back along the lines from future to present.

Thus present values decline, other things being equal, when future cash payments are delayed. The longer you have to wait for money, the less it's worth today, as we see in Figure 5.3. Notice how very small variations in the interest rate can have a powerful effect on the value of distant cash flows. At an interest rate of 10 percent, a payment of \$100 in Year 20 is worth \$14.86 today.

FIGURE 5.3
Present value of a future cash flow of $100, using various interest rates. Notice that the longer you have to wait for your money, the less it is worth today.

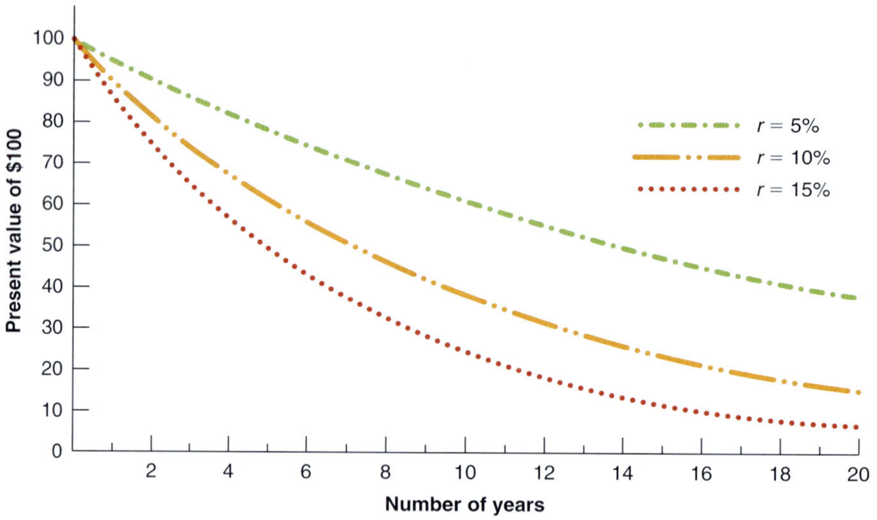

If the interest rate increases to 15 percent, the value of the future payment falls by about 60 percent to $6.11.

The present value formula is sometimes written differently. Instead of dividing the future payment by $(1 + r)^t$, we could just as easily multiply it by $1/(1 + r)^t$:

$$\begin{aligned} \text{PV} &= \frac{\text{future payment}}{(1 + r)^t} \\ &= \text{future payment} \times \frac{1}{(1 + r)^t} \end{aligned} \quad (5.5)$$

discount factor or **present value interest factor** Present value of a $1 future payment.

The expression $1/(1 + r)^t$ is called the **discount factor** or the **present value interest factor**, PVIF(r, t). It measures the present value of $1 to be received in t years from today at a discount rate of r percent. The present value of a future payment of I dollars at r percent per period for t periods can be written as

$$\text{PV} = I \times \text{discount factor} = I \times \text{PVIF}(r, t) = I \times \frac{1}{(1 + r)^t} \quad (5.6)$$

The simplest way to find the discount factor is to use a calculator, but financial managers sometimes find it convenient to use tables of discount factors. For example, Table 5.3 shows discount factors for a small range of years and interest rates. Table A.2 in the online Appendix A provides a set of discount factors for a wide range of years and interest rates.

Try using Table 5.3 to figure out how much to put aside for that $3,000 computer purchase. If the interest rate is 8 percent, the present value of $1 paid at the end of 1 year is $.9259. So the present value of $3,000 is

$$\text{PV} = \$3{,}000 \times \text{PVIF}(.08,1) = \$3{,}000 \times \frac{1}{1.08} = \$3{,}000 \times .9259 = \$2{,}778$$

which matches the value we obtained in Example 5.2.

What if the computer purchase is postponed until the end of two years? Table 5.3 shows that the present value of $1 paid at the end of 2 years is .8573. So the present value of $3,000 is

$$\text{PV} = \$3{,}000 \times \text{PVIF}(.08,2) = \$3{,}000 \times \frac{1}{(1.08)^2} = \$3{,}000 \times .8573 = \$2{,}572$$

as we found in Example 5.2.

TABLE 5.3
Discount factors—present value of $1 for various interest rates and different periods.

Number of Periods	Interest Rate per Period					
	5%	6%	7%	8%	9%	10%
1	.9524	.9434	.9346	.9259	.9174	.9091
2	.9070	.8900	.8734	.8573	.8417	.8264
3	.8638	.8396	.8163	.7938	.7722	.7513
4	.8227	.7921	.7629	.7350	.7084	.6830
5	.7835	.7473	.7130	.6806	.6499	.6209
10	.6139	.5584	.5083	.4632	.4224	.3855
20	.3769	.3118	.2584	.2145	.1784	.1486
30	.2314	.1741	.1314	.0994	.0754	.0573

Notice that as you move along the rows in Table 5.3, moving to higher interest rates, present values decline. As you move down the columns, moving to longer discounting periods, present values again decline. Why does this make sense?

EXAMPLE 5.3 **PUERTO RICO BORROWS SOME CASH**

In 2007, Puerto Rico needed to borrow about $2.6 billion for up to 47 years. It did so by selling IOUs, each of which simply promised to pay the holder $1,000 at the end of that time.[1] The market interest rate at the time was 5.15 percent. How much would you have been prepared to pay for one of these IOUs?

To calculate present value we multiply the $1,000 future payment by the 47-year discount factor:

$$PV = \$1{,}000 \times PVIF(.0515{,}47) = \$1{,}000 \times \frac{1}{(1.0515)^{47}}$$
$$= \$1{,}000 \times .0944 = \$94.40$$

Check Point 5.3

Suppose that Puerto Rico had promised to pay $1,000 at the end of 30 years. If the market interest rate was 5.15 percent, how much would you have been prepared to pay for a 30-year IOU of $1,000?

EXAMPLE 5.4 **FINDING THE VALUE OF FREE CREDIT**

Kangaroo Autos is offering free credit on a $10,000 car. You pay $4,000 down and then the balance at the end of 2 years. Turtle Motors next door does not offer free credit but will give you $500 off the list price. If the interest rate is 10 percent, which company is offering the better deal?

Notice that you pay more in total by buying through Kangaroo, but since part of the payment is postponed, you can keep this money in the bank where it will continue to earn interest. To compare the two offers, you need to calculate the present value of the payments to Kangaroo. The *time line* in Figure 5.4 shows the cash payments to Kangaroo. The first payment, $4,000, takes place today. The second payment, $6,000, takes place at the end of 2 years. To find its present value, we need to multiply by the two-year discount factor. The total present value of the payments to Kangaroo is therefore

$$PV = \$4{,}000 + \$6{,}000 \times PVIF(.10{,}2) = \$4{,}000 + \$6{,}000 \times \frac{1}{(1.10)^2}$$
$$= \$4{,}000 + \$4{,}958.68 = \$8{,}958.68$$

(Continued)

[1] "IOU" means "I owe you." Puerto Rico's IOUs are called *bonds*. Usually, bond investors receive a regular *interest* or *coupon* payment. The Puerto Rico bond will make only a single payment at the end of year 47. It is therefore known as a *zero-coupon bond*. More on this in the next chapter.

FIGURE 5.4
Present value of the cash flows to Kangaroo Autos. Drawing a time line can help with the calculation of the present value of cash flow.

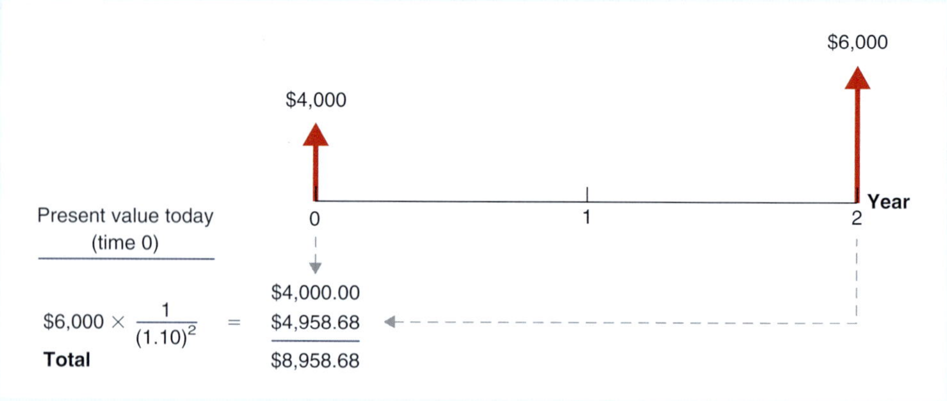

(Concluded)

Suppose you start with $8,958.68. You make a down payment of $4,000 to Kangaroo Autos and invest the balance of $4,958.68. At an interest rate of 10 percent, this will grow over 2 years to $\$4{,}958.68 \times 1.10^2 = \$6{,}000$, just enough to make the final payment on your automobile. The total cost of $8,958.68 is a better deal than the $9,500 charged by Turtle Motors.

These calculations illustrate how important it is to use present values when comparing alternative patterns of cash payment.

> You should never compare cash flows occurring at different times without first discounting them to a common date. By calculating present values, we see how much cash must be set aside today to pay future bills.

FINDING THE INTEREST RATE

When we looked at Puerto Rico's IOUs in Example 5.3, we used the interest rate to compute a fair market price for each IOU. Sometimes you are given the price and have to calculate the interest rate that is being offered.

For example, when Puerto Rico borrowed money, it did not announce an interest rate. It simply offered to sell each IOU for $94.40. Thus we know that

$$\text{PV} = \$1{,}000 \times \frac{1}{(1+r)^{47}} = \$94.40$$

What is the interest rate?

There are several ways to approach this. First, you might use a table of discount factors. You need to find the interest rate for which the 47-year discount factor = .0944.

Second, you might rearrange the equation and use your calculator to solve for r:

$$\$94.40 \times (1+r)^{47} = \$1{,}000$$

$$(1+r)^{47} = \frac{\$1{,}000}{\$94.40} = 10.593$$

$$(1+r) = (10.593)^{1/47} = 1.0515$$

$$r = .0515, \text{ or } 5.15\%$$

Check Point 5.4

You have won a contest and now must decide which prize you want. With prize A, you receive $5,000 today and another $5,500 in one year. Prize B gives you $1,000 today and another $10,000 in one year. The interest rate is 4 percent. Prove to yourself that it does not matter the point in time at which you compare the prizes' cash flows: the better prize has both the bigger present value and future value.

Check Point 5.5

Suppose that Puerto Rico had promised to pay $1,000 at the end of 30 years. If Puerto Rico offers to sell each IOU for $221.68, what is the market interest rate?

In general, this is more accurate. You can also use a financial calculator (see the nearby Financial Calculator box) or a spreadsheet (see Excel Spreadsheet box that follows).

EXAMPLE 5.5 DOUBLE YOUR MONEY

How many times have you heard of an investment advisor who promises to double your money? Is this really an amazing feat? That depends on how long it will take for your money to double. With enough patience, your funds eventually will double even if they earn only a very modest interest rate. Suppose your advisor promises to double your money in eight years? What interest rate is implicitly being promised?

The advisor is promising a future value of $2 for every $1 invested today. Therefore, we find the interest rate by solving for r as follows:

$$\text{Future value} = \text{PV} \times (1 + r)^t$$

$$\$2 = \$1 \times (1 + r)^8$$

$$(1 + r) = 2^{1/8} = 1.0905 = 9.05\%$$

By the way, there is a convenient rule of thumb that one can use to approximate the answer to this problem. The *Rule of 72* states that the time it will take for an investment to double in value equals approximately $72/r$, where r is expressed as a percentage. Therefore, if the doubling period is 8 years, the Rule implies an (approximate) interest rate of 9 percent (since $72/9 = 8$ years). This is quite close to the exact solution of 9.05 percent.

Check Point 5.6

The Rule of 72 works best with relatively low interest rates. Suppose the time it will take for an investment to double in value is 12 years. Find the interest rate. What is the approximate rate implied by the Rule? Now suppose that the doubling period is only two years. Is the approximation better or worse in this case?

FINDING THE INVESTMENT PERIOD

In Example 5.2, we looked at how much money to set aside to pay for a new computer in one year. Suppose instead you have $1,890 but need $3,000 to buy the computer. How long will it take for you to have enough money if the interest rate is 8 percent? We know that

$$\text{PV} = \$3{,}000 \times \frac{1}{(1.08)^t} = \$1{,}890$$

What is the number of periods?

Just as was the case for finding the interest rate, the solution can be found several ways. First, calculate discount factor by rearranging the above equation:

$$\text{PV}(.08,t) = \frac{1}{(1.08)^t} = \frac{\$1{,}890}{\$3{,}000} = .6300$$

Go to Table A.2 in the online Appendix A and look at the column corresponding to 8 percent. You will see that the discount factor for 6 years is .6303, indicating that it will take about 6 years for your savings to grow big enough to buy the computer.

financial calculator

An Introduction to Financial Calculators

Financial calculators are designed with present value and future value formulas already programmed. Therefore, you can readily solve many problems simply by entering the inputs for the problem and punching a key for the solution.

The basic financial calculator uses five keys that correspond to the inputs for common problems involving the time value of money.

n | i | PV | FV | PMT

Each key represents the following input:

- *n* is the number of periods. (We have been using *t* to denote the length of time, or number of periods. Most calculators use *n* for the same concept.)
- *i* is the interest rate per period, expressed as a percentage (not a decimal). For example, if the interest rate is 8 percent, you would enter 8, not .08. On some calculators this key is written I/Y or I/YR. (We have been using *r* to denote the interest rate or discount rate.)
- PV is the present value.
- FV is the future value.
- PMT is the amount of any recurring payment (called an annuity). In single cash-flow problems such as those we have considered so far, PMT is zero.

Given any four of these inputs, the calculator will solve the fifth. We will illustrate with several examples.

Future Values

Recall Example 5.1, where we calculated the future value of Peter Minuit's $24 investment. Enter 24 into the PV register. (You enter the value by typing 24 and then pushing the PV key.) We assumed an interest rate of 8 percent, so enter 8 into the *i* register. Because the $24 had 380 years to compound, enter 380 into the *n* register. Enter 0 into the PMT register because there is no recurring payment involved in the calculation. Now ask the calculator to compute FV. On some calculators you simply press the FV key. On others you need to first press the "compute" key (which may be labelled COMP or CPT), and then press FV. The exact sequence of keystrokes for three popular financial calculators are as follows:*

Hewlett-Packard HP-10B	Sharp EL-738C	Texas Instruments BA II Plus
24 PV	24 PV	24 PV
380 N	380 n	380 N
8 I/YR	8 i	8 I/Y
0 PMT	0 PMT	0 PMT
FV	COMP FV	CPT FV

You should find after hitting the FV key that your calculator shows a value of − 120.5697 trillion, which, except for the minus sign, is the future value of the $24.

Why does the minus sign appear? Most calculators treat cash flows as either inflows (shown as positive numbers) or outflows (negative

You can also rearrange the present value formula and solve[2] for *t* or use a financial calculator or a spreadsheet. The nearby Financial Calculator and Excel Spreadsheet boxes both show you how to solve for the length of an investment.

LO3 5.3 MULTIPLE CASH FLOWS

So far, we have considered problems involving only a single cash flow. This is obviously limiting. Most real-world investments, after all, will involve many cash flows over time. When there are many payments, you'll hear businesspeople refer to a *stream of cash flows*.

FUTURE VALUE OF MULTIPLE CASH FLOWS

Recall the computer you hope to purchase in two years (see Example 5.2). Now suppose that instead of putting aside a lump sum in the bank to finance the purchase, you plan to save a bit

[2] To solve for *t*, rewrite the discount factor as $(1.08)^{-t}$.

$$(1.08)^{-t} = .6300$$
$$\log (1.08)^{-t} = \log .6300$$
$$-t \log 1.08 = \log .6300$$
$$t = -\log .6300/\log 1.08 = 6.003$$

Most calculators have log function key, often labelled LN or LOG.

FINANCIAL CALCULATOR

numbers). For example, if you borrow \$100 today at an interest rate of 12 percent, you receive money now (a *positive* cash flow), but you will have to pay back \$112 in a year, a negative cash flow at that time. Therefore, the calculator displays FV as a negative number. The following time line of cash flows shows the reasoning employed. The final negative cash flow of \$112 has the same present value as the \$100 borrowed today.

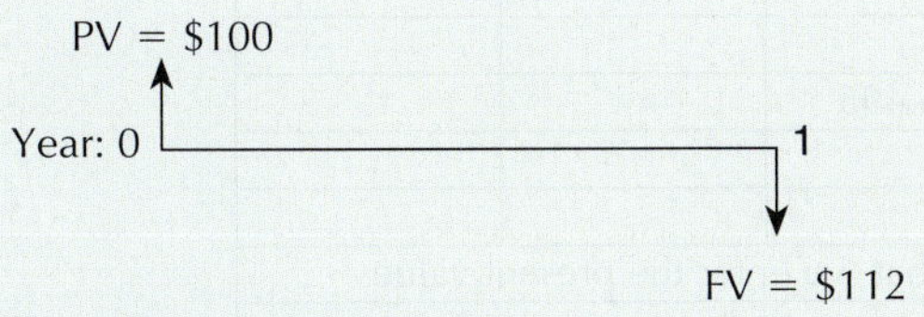

If, instead of borrowing, you were to *invest* \$100 today to reap a future benefit, you would enter PV as a negative number (first press 100, then press the +/− key to make the value negative, and finally press PV to enter the value into the PV register). In this case, FV would appear as a positive number, indicating that you will reap a cash inflow when your investment comes to fruition.

Present Values

Suppose your savings goal is to accumulate \$10,000 by the end of 30 years. If the interest rate is 8 percent, how much would you need to invest today to achieve your goal? Again, there is no recurring payment involved, so PMT is zero. We therefore enter the following: $n = 30$; $i = 8$; FV = 10,000; PMT = 0. Now compute PV, and you should get an answer of −993.77. The answer is displayed as a negative number because you need to make a cash outflow (an investment) of \$993.77 now in order to enjoy a cash inflow of \$10,000 in 30 years.

Finding the Interest Rate

The 47-year IOU from Puerto Rico in Example 5.3 sold at \$94.40 and promised a final payment of \$1,000. We may obtain the market interest rate by entering $n = 47$, FV = 1,000, PV = − 94.40, and PMT = 0. Compute i and you will find that the interest rate is 5.15 percent. This is the value we computed directly (but with more work) in the "Finding the Interest Rate" section earlier.

How Long an Investment?

In Example 5.5, we consider how long it would take for an investment to double in value. This sort of problem is easily solved using a calculator. If the investment is to double, we enter FV = 2 and PV = −1. If the interest rate is 9 percent, enter $i = 9$ and PMT = 0. Compute n and you will find that $n = 8.04$ years. If the interest rate is 9.05 percent, the doubling period falls to 8 years, as we found in the example.

*The BA II Plus calculator requires a little extra work to initialize. When you buy the calculator, it is set to automatically interpret each period as a year and assumes that interest compounds monthly. In our experience, it is best to change the compounding frequency to once per period. To do so, press 2nd {P/Y} 1 ENTER, then press ↓ 1 ENTER and finally press 2nd {*QUIT*} to return to standard calculator mode. You should need to do this only once, even if the calculator is turned off.

of money each year. You might be able to put \$1,200 in the bank now, and another \$1,400 in 1 year. If you earn an 8 percent rate of interest, how much will you be able to spend on a computer in 2 years?

The time line in Figure 5.5 shows how your savings grow. There are two cash inflows into the savings plan. The first cash flow will have 2 years to earn interest and, therefore, will grow to $\$1{,}200 \times (1.08)^2 = \$1{,}399.68$ while the second deposit, which comes a year later, will be invested for only 1 year and will grow to $\$1{,}400 \times (1.08) = \$1{,}512$. Therefore after 2 years, your total savings will be the sum of these two amounts, or \$2,911.68.

FIGURE 5.5
Drawing a time line can help to calculate the future value of your savings.

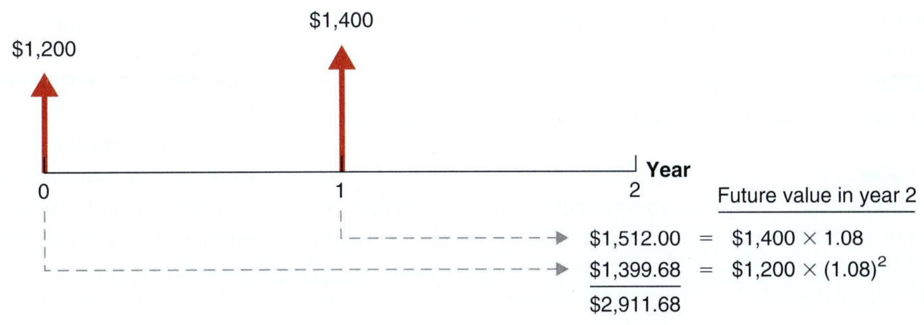

excel spreadsheet

Interest-Rate Functions

	A	B	C	D
1	**Finding the future value of $24 using a spreadsheet**			
2				
3	Present value (*pv*)	24		
4	Interest rate (*rate*)	0.08		
5	Payment (*pmt*)	0		
6	Periods (*nper*)	380		
7				
8	Future value	$120,569,740,656,495		
9				
10				
11	The formula in cell B8 is =FV(B4,B6,B5−B3). Notice that we enter the present value			
12	as the negative of the value in cell B3, since the "purchase price" is a cash outflow.			
13				
14	You can confirm for yourself that changing the entry in cell B4 to .035 will reduce			
15	the value to $11,416,794.			

Just as financial calculators largely replaced interest rate tables in the 1980s, these calculators are today giving way to spreadsheets. Like financial calculators, spreadsheets provide built-in functions that solve the equations linking the five variables in a time-value-of-money problem: the number of periods, the interest rate per period, the present value, the future value, and any recurring payment (the annuity). For single cash flow problems such as the ones we've encountered so far, the recurring payment is zero. We will illustrate the use of these spreadsheets by using Microsoft Excel™.

The four Excel functions relevant for single cash-flow problems are

Future value = FV(*rate, nper, pmt, pv*)
Present value = PV(*rate, nper, pmt, fv*)
Interest rate = RATE(*nper, pmt, pv, fv*)
Number of periods = NPER(*rate, pmt, pv, fv*)

As you can see, each spreadsheet formula requires four inputs—just as financial calculators require four inputs—and provides the solution for the fifth variable. Also like most calculators, the spreadsheet functions interpret cash inflows as positive values and cash outflows as negative values. Unlike financial calculators, however, most spreadsheets require that interest rates be input as decimals rather than whole numbers (for example, .06 rather than 6 percent). Note also the use of = signs in front of the formulas to alert Excel to the fact that these are predefined formulas. In the Financial Calculator box, we saw how to use calculators to solve several problems. Let's see how we would use spreadsheets to solve the same problems.

Future Values

The illustration above shows a spreadsheet that solves Example 5.1 on the future value of the $24 spent to acquire Manhattan Island. The interest rate is entered as a decimal in cell B4. The formula for future value in cell B8 takes as its last input the negative of cell B3, because the $24 purchase price is treated as cash outflow. Note how the spreadsheet shows more digits for future value than the calculator. You can use the Excel ROUND function to ROUND the spreadsheet future value to the calculator value.

Present Values

We next considered an individual who wishes to accumulate a future value of $10,000 by the end of 30 years. If the interest rate is 8 percent, and there is no recurring payment involved, you can find the necessary investment today (the present value) by entering the formula = PV(.08,30,0,10000). If you try this, you will see that the solution is reported as a negative value: the positive future payoff of $10,000 requires an initial payment (cash outflow) of 993.77. (Notice also that, when entering the $10,000 future value, we don't use commas within the number. The spreadsheet would interpret the comma as separating two inputs to the function.)

Finding the Interest Rate

We showed how to use a calculator to find the interest rate on a 47-year $1,000 IOU sold today for $94.40. In Excel, we can compute = RATE(47,0,−94.40,1000) to confirm again that the interest rate is 5.15 percent.

How Long an Investment?

Example 5.5 asks how long it would take an investment to double if it earned interest at a rate of 9 percent. We treat the present value as a $1 investment (cash outflow) and the future value as a $2 cash payback. Therefore, enter = NPER(.09,0,−1,2) to find that the doubling period is 8.04 years.

FIGURE 5.6
To find the future value of a stream of cash flows, calculate the future value of each flow and then add them.

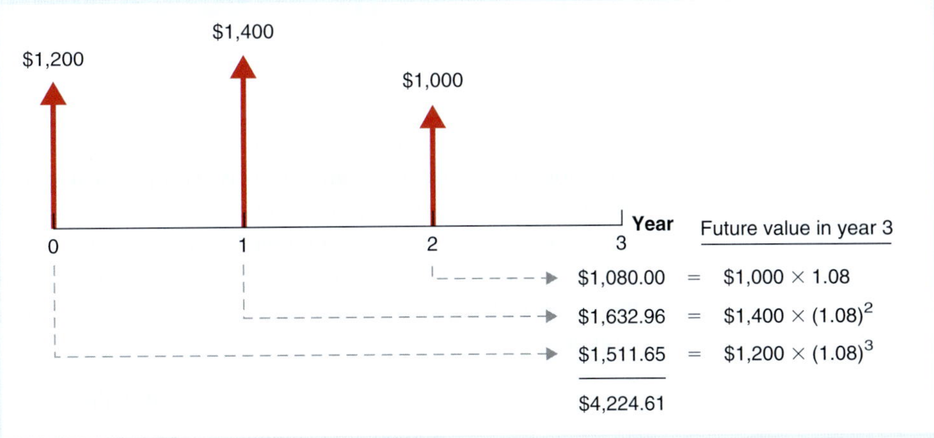

EXAMPLE 5.6 EVEN MORE SAVINGS

Suppose that the computer purchase can be put off for an additional year and that you can make a third deposit of $1,000 at the end of the second year. How much will be available to spend three years from now?

Again we organize our inputs using a time line as in Figure 5.6. The total cash available will be the sum of the future values of all three deposits. Notice that when we save for three years, the first two deposits each have an extra year for interest to compound:

$$\begin{aligned} \$1{,}200 \times (1.08)^3 &= \$1{,}511.65 \\ \$1{,}400 \times (1.08)^2 &= 1{,}632.96 \\ \$1{,}000 \times 1.08 &= \underline{1{,}080.00} \\ \text{Total future value} &= \$4{,}224.61 \end{aligned}$$

Check Point 5.7

Suppose you are planning a one-month European vacation when you graduate two years from now. The cost of the trip will be $3,500. Right now you have $1,500 and will put it into a bank account that pays 6 percent interest. How much more money will you need to deposit one year from now to have enough money for the trip two years from now?

> To find the value at some future date of a stream of cash flows, calculate what each cash flow will be worth at that future date, and then add up these future values.

We conclude that problems involving multiple cash flows are simple extensions of single cash flow analysis. To find the value at some future date of a stream of cash flows, calculate what each cash flow will be worth at that future date, and then add up these future values.

As we will now see, a similar adding-up principle works for present value calculations.

PRESENT VALUE OF MULTIPLE CASH FLOWS

When we calculate the present value of a future cash flow, we are asking how much that cash flow would be worth today. If there is more than one future cash flow, we simply need to work out what each flow would be worth today and then add these present values.

EXAMPLE 5.7 CASH UP FRONT VERSUS AN INSTALMENT PLAN

Suppose your auto dealer gives you a choice between paying $15,500 for a new car or entering into an instalment plan in which you pay $8,000 down today and make payments of $4,000 in each of the next 2 years. Which is the better deal? Before reading this chapter, you might have compared the total payments under the two plans: $15,500 versus $16,000 in the instalment plan. Now, however, you know that this comparison is wrong, because it ignores the time value of money. For example, the last instalment of $4,000 is less costly to you than paying out $4,000 now. The true cost of that last payment is the present value of $4,000.

Assume that the interest rate you can earn on safe investments is 8 percent. Suppose you choose the instalment plan. As the time line in Figure 5.7 illustrates, the present value of the plan's three cash flows is as follows:

	Present Value	
Immediate payment	$8,000	= $ 8,000.00
Second payment	$4,000/1.08	= 3,703.70
Third payment	$4,000/(1.08)^2	= 3,429.36
Total present value		= $15,133.06

Because the present value of the three payments is less than $15,500, the instalment plan is in fact the cheaper alternative.

The instalment plan's present value equals the amount that you would need to invest now to cover the three future payments. Let's check.

Here is how your bank balance would change as you make each payment:

Year	Initial Balance	−	Payment	=	Remaining Balance	+	Interest Earned	=	Balance at Year-End
0	$15,133.06		$8,000		$7,133.06		$570.64		$7,703.70
1	7,703.70		4,000		3,703.70		296.30		4,000.00
2	4,000.00		4,000		0		0		0

If you start with the present value of $15,133.06 in the bank, you could make the first $8,000 payment and be left with $7,133.06. After one year, your savings account would receive an interest payment of $7,133.06 × .08 = $570.64, bringing your account to $7,703.70. Similarly, you would make the second $4,000 payment and be left with $3,703.70. This sum left in the bank would grow with interest to $4,000, just enough to make the last payment.

Spreadsheet Questions

5.3 Find the present value of the three payments at interest rates of 5 and 11 percent. Explain why the values change as they do.

5.4 Total payments over the three years are $16,000. What is the present value if the three payments are instead $6,000, $5,000, $5,000? Why does the present value fall? (Use an interest rate of 8 percent.)

Check Point 5.8

In order to avoid estate taxes, your rich aunt Frederica will pay you $10,000 per year for 4 years, starting 1 year from now. What is the present value of your benefactor's planned gifts? The interest rate is 7 percent. How much will you have 4 years from now if you invest each gift at 7 percent?

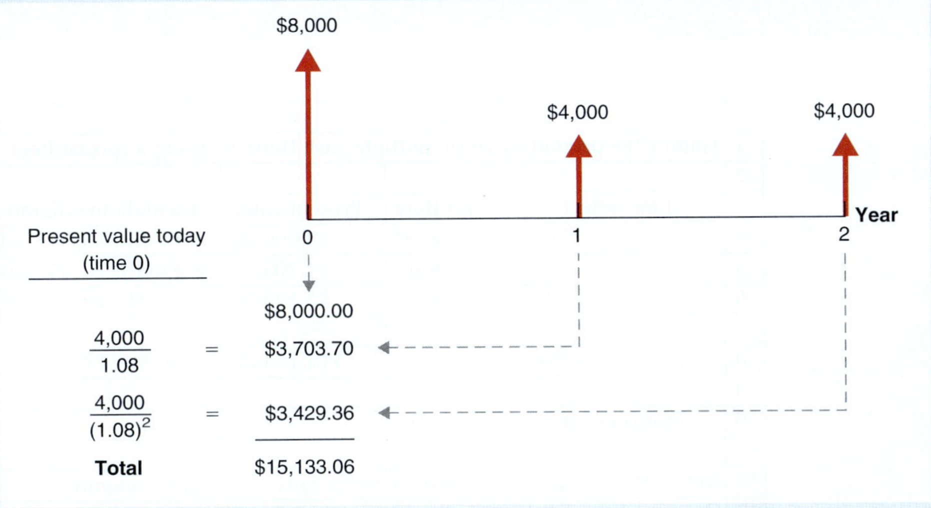

FIGURE 5.7 To find the present value of a stream of cash flows, calculate the present value of each flow and then add them.

LO3 5.4 LEVEL CASH FLOWS: PERPETUITIES AND ANNUITIES

annuity Equally spaced and level stream of cash flows.

perpetuity Stream of level cash payments that never ends.

Frequently, you may need to value a stream of equal cash flows. For example, a home mortgage might require the homeowner to make equal monthly payments for the life of the loan. For a 25-year loan, this would result in 300 equal payments. A 4-year car loan might require 48 equal monthly payments. Any such sequence of equally spaced, level cash flows is called an **annuity**. If the payment stream lasts forever, it is called a **perpetuity**.

HOW TO VALUE PERPETUITIES

Some time ago the British government borrowed by issuing perpetuities. Instead of repaying these loans, the British government pays the investors holding these securities a fixed annual payment in perpetuity.

How might we value such a security? Suppose that you could invest $100 at an interest rate of 10 percent. You would earn annual interest of $.1 \times \$100 = \$10$ per year and could withdraw this amount from your investment account each year without ever running down your balance. In other words, a $100 investment could provide a perpetuity of $10 per year. In general:

$$\text{Cash payment from perpetuity} = \text{interest rate} \times \text{present value}$$

$$C = r \times \text{PV}$$

We can rearrange this relationship to derive the present value of a perpetuity, given the interest rate r and the cash payment C:

$$\textbf{PV of perpetuity} = \frac{C}{r} = \frac{\textbf{cash payment}}{\textbf{interest rate}} \qquad (5.7)$$

Suppose some worthy person wishes to endow a chair in finance at your university. If the rate of interest is 10 percent, and the aim is to provide $100,000 a year forever, the amount that must be set aside today is

$$\text{Present value of perpetuity} = \frac{C}{r} = \frac{\$100{,}000}{.10} = \$1{,}000{,}000$$

excel spreadsheet

Multiple Cash Flows

	A	B	C	D	E
1	**Finding the present value of multiple cash flows by using a spreadsheet**				
2					
3	**Time until CF**	**Cash flow**	**Present value**	**Formula in column C**	
4	0	8000	$8,000.00	= PV($B$10,A4,0,-B4)	
5	1	4000	$3,703.70	= PV($B$10,A5,0,-B5)	
6	2	4000	$3,429.36	= PV($B$10,A6,0,-B6)	
7					
8	SUM:		$15,133.06	= SUM(C4:C6)	
9					
10	**Discount rate:**	0.08			
11					
12	Notice that the time until each payment (*nper*) is found in column A.				
13	Once we enter the formula for present value in cell C4, we can copy it to cells C5 and C6.				
14	The present value for other interest rates can be found by changing the entry in cell B10.				

While uneven cash flow problems are conceptually straightforward, they rapidly become tedious and prone to error due to "typos," even if you use a financial calculator. It really helps to use spreadsheets. The above figure is a spreadsheet solution of Example 5.7.

The spreadsheet uses the present value formula, PV(*rate, nper, pmt, pv*), to calculate the present value of each cash flow. The discount rate (*rate*) is in cell B10. The number of periods until each payment (*nper*) is in column A. With no recurring payment, the value of *pmt* is 0. The values for the cash flow in each future period (*fv*) are entered as negative numbers in the PV formula. The present values (column C) therefore appear as positive numbers.

The present value of a stream of future cash flows is the amount you would have to invest today to generate that stream.

Two warnings about the perpetuity formula. First, at a quick glance you can easily confuse the formula with the present value of a single cash payment. A payment of $1 at the end of one year has a present value $1/(1 + r)$. The perpetuity has a value of $1/r$. These are quite different.

Second, the perpetuity formula tells us the value of a regular stream of payments starting one period from now. Thus an endowment of $1 million would provide the university with its first payment of $100,000 one year hence. If the worthy donor wants to provide the university with an additional payment of $100,000 up front, he or she would need to set aside $1,100,000.

Sometimes you may need to calculate the value of a perpetuity that does not start to make payments for several years. For example, suppose that our philanthropist decides to provide $100,000 a year with the first payment 4 years from now. As the time line in Figure 5.8 shows, we know that in year 3 this endowment will be an ordinary perpetuity with payments starting at the end of 1 year. So our perpetuity formula tells us that in year 3 the endowment will be worth $100,000/*r*. But it is not worth that much now. To find today's value we need to multiply by the three-year discount factor. Thus, the "delayed" perpetuity is worth

$$\$100{,}000 \times \frac{1}{r} \times \frac{1}{(1+r)^3} = \$1{,}000{,}000 \times \frac{1}{(1.10)^3} = \$751{,}315$$

Check Point 5.9

A British government perpetuity pays £4 a year forever and is selling for £48. What is the interest rate?

FIGURE 5.8
Time line for a delayed perpetuity—\$100,000 per year forever, to start in four years.

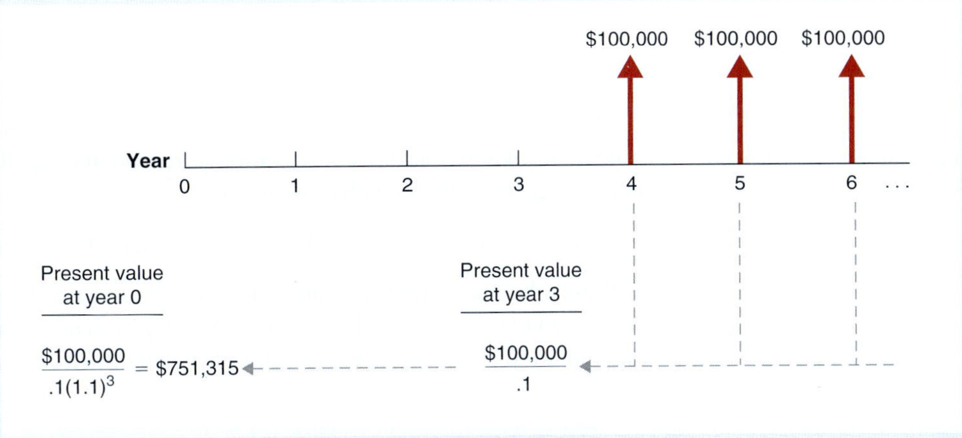

FIGURE 5.9
Valuing an annuity as the difference between an immediate perpetuity (A) and a delayed perpetuity (B).

	Present value (year 0)	Cash flow each year 1	2	3	4	5	6 ...
1. Perpetuity A	$\frac{1}{r}$	\$1	\$1	\$1	\$1	\$1	\$1...
2. Perpetuity B	$\frac{1}{r(1+r)^3}$	0	0	0	\$1	\$1	\$1...
3. Three-year annuity	$\frac{1}{r} - \frac{1}{r(1+r)^3}$	\$1	\$1	\$1			

HOW TO VALUE ANNUITIES

There are two ways to value an annuity, that is, a limited number of cash flows. The slow way is to value each cash flow separately and add up the present values. The quick way is to take advantage of the following simplification. Figure 5.9 shows the cash payments and values of three investments.

Row 1. The investment shown in the first row provides a perpetual stream of \$1 payments starting in Year 1. We have already seen that this perpetuity has a present value of $1/r$.

Row 2. Now look at the investment shown in the second row of Figure 5.9. It also provides a perpetual stream of \$1 payments, but these payments don't start until year 4. This stream of payments is identical to the delayed perpetuity that we just valued. In year 3, the investment will be an ordinary perpetuity with payments starting in one year and will therefore be worth $1/r$ in year 3. To find the value today, we simply multiply this figure by the three-year discount factor. Thus

$$\text{PV} = \frac{1}{r} \times \frac{1}{(1+r)^3} = \frac{1}{r(1+r)^3}$$

Row 3. Finally, look at the investment shown in the third row of Figure 5.9. This provides a level payment of \$1 a year for three years. In other words, it is a three-year annuity. You can also see that, taken together, the investments in rows 2 and 3 provide exactly the same cash payments as the investment in row 1. Thus the value of our annuity (row 3) must be equal to the value of the row 1 perpetuity minus the value of the delayed row 2 perpetuity:

$$\text{Present value of a 3-year \$1 annuity} = \frac{1}{r} - \frac{1}{r(1+r)^3}$$

The general formula for the value of an annuity that pays C dollars a year for each of t years is

$$\text{Present value of } t\text{-year annuity} = C \times \left[\frac{1}{r} - \frac{1}{r(1+r)^t}\right] \tag{5.8}$$

annuity factor Present value of a $1 annuity.

The expression in square brackets shows the present value of a t-year annuity of $1 a year. It is generally known as the t-year **annuity factor** and can be written as PVA(r, t). Therefore, another way to write the value of an annuity is

$$\text{Present value of } t\text{-year annuity} = \text{payment} \times \text{annuity factor} = C \times \text{PVA}(r, t) \tag{5.9}$$

Remembering formulas is about as difficult as remembering other people's birthdays. But as long as you bear in mind that an annuity is equivalent to the difference between an immediate and a delayed perpetuity, you shouldn't have any difficulty.

EXAMPLE 5.8 BACK TO KANGAROO AUTOS

Let us return to Kangaroo Autos for almost the last time. Most instalment plans call for level streams of payments. So let us suppose that this time Kangaroo offers an "easy payment" scheme of $4,000 a year at the end of each of the next three years. First let's do the calculations the slow way; to show that if the interest rate is 10 percent, the present value of the three payments is $9,947.41. The time line in Figure 5.10 shows these calculations. The present value of each cash flow is calculated and then the three present values are summed. The annuity formula, however, is much quicker:

$$\text{Present value} = \$4{,}000 \times \text{PVA}(.10,3) = \$4{,}000 \times \left[\frac{1}{.10} - \frac{1}{.10(1.10)^3}\right]$$

$$= \$4{,}000 \times 2.48685 = \$9{,}947.41$$

You can use a calculator to work out annuity factors or you can use a set of annuity tables. Table 5.4 is an abridged annuity table (an extended version is shown in Table A.3 in the online Appendix A). Check that you can find the three-year annuity factor for an interest rate of 10 percent.

FIGURE 5.10 Time line for Kangaroo Autos' "Easy Payment" scheme of $4,000 a year for three years, Example 5.8. To find the present value of the annuity, calculate the present value of each cash flow. It is usually quicker to use the annuity formula.

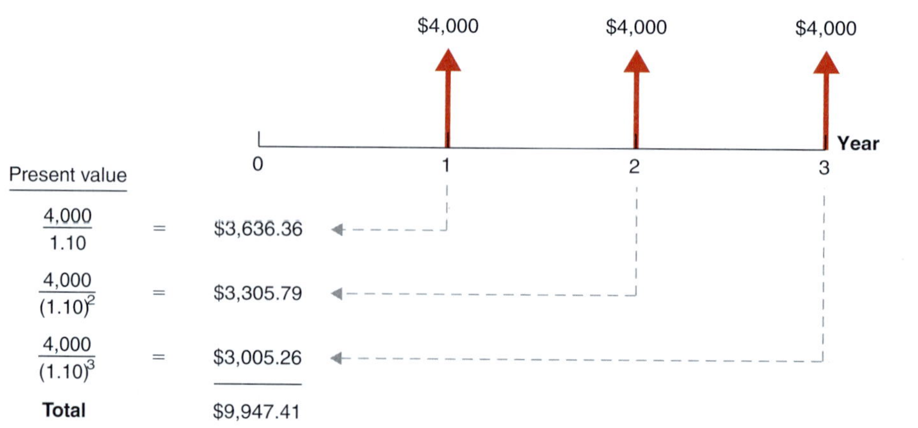

TABLE 5.4
Annuity factors—present value of a $1 received each of *t* periods, at various interest rates.

Number of Periods	Interest Rate per Period					
	5%	6%	7%	8%	9%	10%
1	.9524	.9434	.9346	.9259	.9174	.9091
2	1.8594	1.8334	1.8080	1.7833	1.7591	1.7355
3	2.7232	2.6730	2.6243	2.5771	2.5313	2.4869
4	3.5460	3.4651	3.3872	3.3121	3.2397	3.1699
5	4.3295	4.2124	4.1002	3.9927	3.8897	3.7908
10	7.7217	7.3601	7.0236	6.7101	6.4177	6.1446
20	12.4622	11.4699	1.5940	9.8181	9.1285	8.5136
30	15.3725	13.7648	12.4090	11.2578	1.2737	9.4269

Check Point 5.10

If the interest rate is 8 percent, what is the 4-year discount factor? What is the 4-year annuity factor? What is the relationship between these two numbers? Explain.

EXAMPLE 5.9 WINNING BIG AT A SLOT MACHINE

In January 2007, a 37-year-old Ontario flight attendant put $15 in a Las Vegas slot machine and walked away with $9.37 million. We suspect she received unsolicited congratulations, good wishes, and requests for money from dozens of more or less worthy charities, relatives, and newly devoted friends. In response she could fairly point out that her prize wasn't really worth $9.37 million. That sum was to be paid in 25 annual instalments of $374,800 each. What is the present value of the jackpot? The interest rate at the time was about 5 percent.

The present value of these payments is simply the sum of the present values of each payment. But rather than valuing each payment separately, it is much easier to treat the cash payments as a 25-year annuity. To value this annuity we simply multiply $374,800 by the 25-year annuity factor:

$$PV = \$374{,}800 \times PVA(.05,25)$$

At an interest rate of 5 percent, the annuity factor is

$$PVA(.05,25) = \left[\frac{1}{.05} - \frac{1}{.05(1.05)^{25}}\right] = 14.0939$$

(We also could look up the annuity factor in the online Table A.3.) The present value of the $374,800 annuity is $374,800 × 14.0939 = $5,282,394. That $9.37 million prize has a true value of about $5.3 million.

This present value is the price that investors would be prepared to offer for the series of cash flows. For example, the gambling casino might arrange for an insurance company to actually make the payments to the lucky winner. In this case, the company would charge a bit less than $5.3 million to take over the obligation. With this amount in hand today, it could generate enough interest income to make the 25 payments before running its "account" down to zero. (In case you are wondering, most Canadian casinos and lotteries pay out the stated prize amount as a lump sum.)

EXAMPLE 5.10 HOW MUCH LUXURY AND EXCITEMENT CAN $53 BILLION BUY?

Bill Gates is reputedly the world's richest person, with wealth estimated at $53 billion in 2010. We haven't yet met Mr. Gates, so we cannot fill you in on his plans for allocating the $56 billion between his charitable works and the cost of his life of luxury and excitement (L&E). So to keep things simple, we will just ask the following, entirely hypothetical, question: How much could Mr. Gates spend yearly on 40 more years of L&E if he were to devote the entire $56 billion to those purposes? Assume that his money is invested at 9 percent interest.

The 40-year 9 percent annuity factor is 10.757. Thus

$$\begin{aligned} \text{Present value} &= \text{annual spending} \times \text{PVA}(.09,40) \\ \$53{,}000{,}000{,}000 &= \text{annual spending} \times 10.757 \\ \text{Annual spending} &= \$4{,}927{,}024{,}263 \end{aligned}$$

Warning to Mr. Gates: We haven't considered inflation. The cost of buying L&E will increase, so $4.93 billion won't buy as much L&E in 40 years as it will today. More on that later.

Check Point 5.11

Suppose you retire at age 70. You expect to live 20 more years and to spend $55,000 per year during your retirement. How much money do you need to save by age 70 to support this consumption plan? Assume an interest rate of 7 percent.

EXAMPLE 5.11 HOME MORTGAGES

Sometimes you may need to find the series of cash payments that would provide a given value today. For example, home purchasers typically borrow the bulk of the house price from a lender. The most common loan arrangement is a 25-year loan that is repaid in equal monthly instalments. Suppose that a house costs $150,000, and that the buyer puts down 25 percent of the purchase price, or $37,500, in cash, borrowing the remaining $112,500 from a mortgage lender such as a bank. What is the appropriate monthly mortgage payment?

The borrower repays the loan by making monthly payments over the next 25 years (300 months). The bank needs to set these monthly payments so that they have a present value of $112,500. Thus

$$\begin{aligned} \text{Present value} &= \text{mortgage payment} \times \text{300-month annuity factor} \\ &= \$112{,}500 \\ \text{Mortgage payment} &= \frac{\$112{,}500}{\text{300-month annuity factor}} \end{aligned}$$

Suppose that the interest rate is 1 percent a month. Then

$$\text{Mortgage payment} = \frac{\$112{,}500}{\left[\frac{1}{.01} - \frac{1}{.01(1.01)^{300}}\right]} = \frac{\$112{,}500}{94.9466} = \$1{,}184.88$$

The mortgage loan in Example 5.11 is an example of an *amortizing loan*. "Amortizing" means that part of the monthly payment is used to pay interest on the loan and part is used to reduce the amount of the loan. Table 5.5 illustrates a 4-year amortizing loan of $1,000 with an interest rate of 10 percent and annual payments starting in 1 year. The annual payment (annuity) that would repay the loan is $315.47. (Confirm this for yourself.) At the end of the first year, the interest payment is 10 percent of $1,000, or $100. So $100 of your first payment is used to pay interest, and the remaining $215.47 is used to reduce (or "amortize") the loan balance to $784.53.

TABLE 5.5
An example of an amortizing loan. If you borrow $1,000 at an interest rate of 10 percent, you would need to make an annual payment of $315.47 over four years to repay the loan with interest.

Year	Beginning-of-Year Balance	Year-End Interest Due on Balance	Year-End Payment	Amortization of Loan	End-of-Year Balance
1	$1,000.00	$100.00	$315.47	$215.47	$784.53
2	$ 784.53	$ 78.45	$315.47	$237.02	$547.51
3	$ 547.51	$ 54.75	$315.47	$260.72	$286.79
4	$ 286.79	$ 28.68	$315.47	$286.79	$ 0

Next year, the outstanding balance is lower, so the interest charge is only $78.45. Therefore, $315.47 − $78.45 = $237.02 can be applied to amortization. Amortization in the second year is higher than in the first, because the amount of the loan has declined and therefore less of the payment is taken up in interest. This procedure continues until the last year, when the amortization is just enough to reduce the outstanding balance on the loan to zero.

Because the loan is progressively paid off, the fraction of each payment devoted to interest steadily falls over time, while the fraction used to reduce the loan (the amortization) steadily increases. Figure 5.11 illustrates the amortization of the mortgage loan in Example 5.11. In the early years, almost all of the mortgage payment is for interest. Even after 15 years, the bulk of the monthly payment is interest.

Check Point 5.12

What will the monthly payment be if you take out a $100,000 15-year mortgage at an interest rate of 1 percent per month? How much of the first payment is interest and how much is amortization?

ANNUITIES DUE

The perpetuity and annuity formulas assume that the first payment occurs at the end of the period. They tell you the value of a stream of cash payments starting one period hence.

FIGURE 5.11
Mortgage amortization. This figure shows the breakdown of mortgage payments between interest and amortization. Monthly payments within each year are summed, so the figure shows the annual payment on the mortgage.

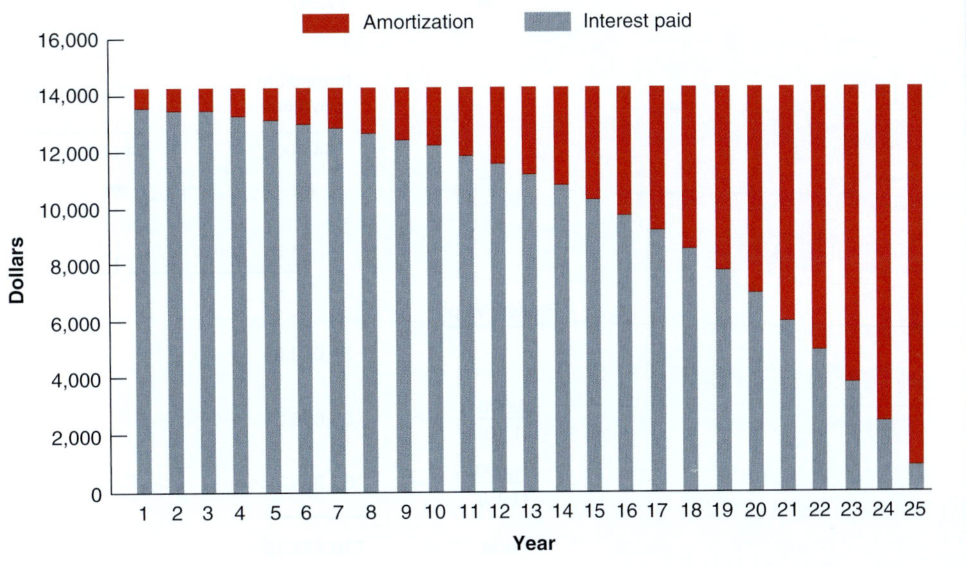

annuity due Level stream of cash flows starting immediately.

However, streams of cash payments often start immediately. For example, Kangaroo Autos in Example 5.8 might have required three annual payments of \$4,000 starting immediately. A level stream of payments starting immediately is known as an **annuity due**.

If Kangaroo's loan was paid as an annuity due, you could think of the three payments as equivalent to an immediate payment of \$4,000, plus an ordinary annuity of \$4,000 for the remaining 2 years. This is made clear in Figure 5.12, which compares the cash flow stream of the Kangaroo Autos loan, treating the three payments as an annuity (panel (a)) and as an annuity due (panel (b)).

In general, the present value of an annuity due of t payments of \$1 per period is the same as \$1 plus the present value of an ordinary annuity providing the remaining $t - 1$ payments. The present value of an annuity due of \$1 for t periods, PVAD(r, t) is therefore

$$\textbf{PV annuity due} = 1 + \textbf{PV ordinary annuity of } t - 1 \textbf{ payments}$$

$$= 1 + \left[\frac{1}{r} - \frac{1}{r(1+r)^{t-1}}\right] \qquad (5.10)$$

By comparing the two panels in Figure 5.12, you can see that each of the three cash flows in the annuity due comes one period earlier than the corresponding cash flow of the ordinary annuity.

FIGURE 5.12
Annuity versus annuity due:
(a) 3-year ordinary annuity;
(b) 3-year annuity due.

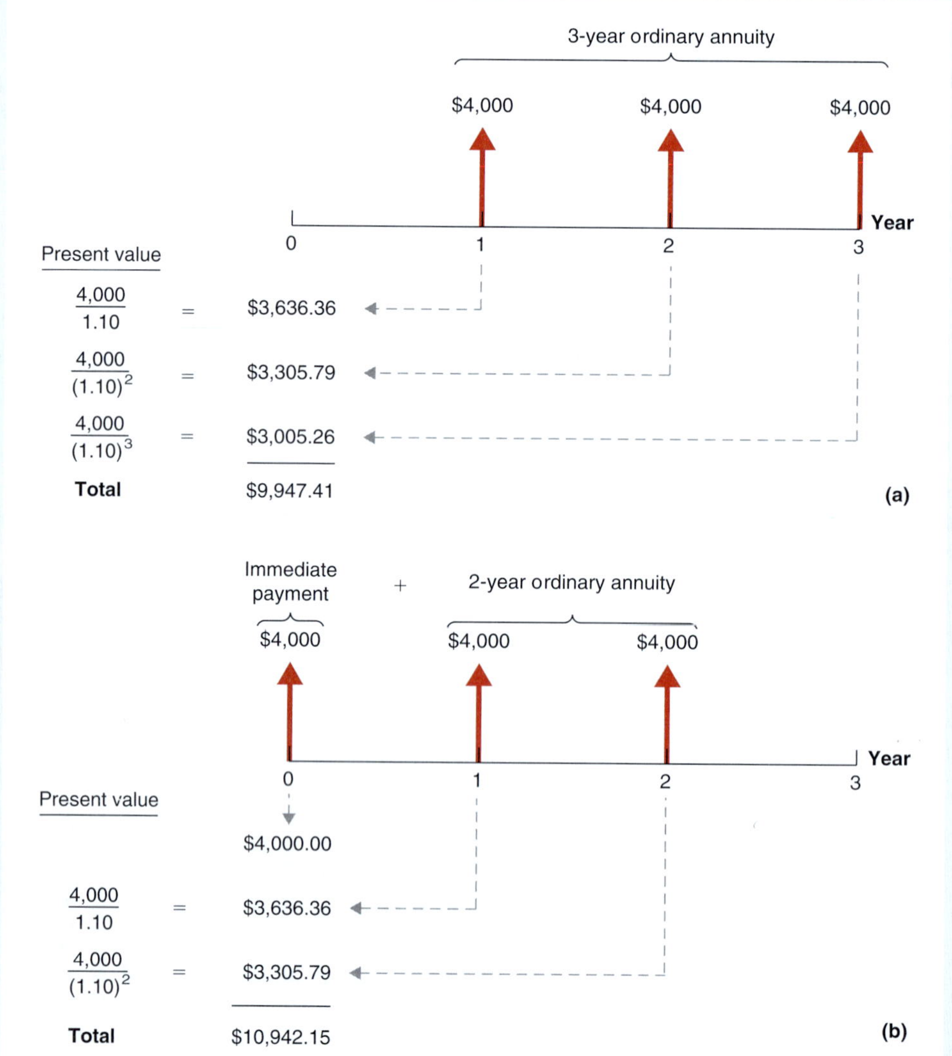

This gives us another way to value an annuity due. The present value of an annuity due is $(1 + r)$ times the present value of an equivalent ordinary annuity.[3] Figure 5.12 shows that bringing the Kangaroo loan payments forward by one year increases their value from \$9,947.41 (as an annuity) to \$10,942.15 (as an annuity due). Notice that \$10,942.15 = \$9,947.41 × 1.10.

Check Point 5.13

When calculating the value of the slot machine winnings in Example 5.9, we assumed that the first of the 25 payments occurs at the end of 1 year. However, the first payment was probably made immediately, with the remaining payments spread over the following 24 years. What is the present value of the \$9.37 million prize?

FUTURE VALUE OF AN ANNUITY

You are back in savings mode again. This time you are setting aside \$3,000 at the end of every year in order to buy a car. If your savings earn interest of 8 percent per year, how much will they be worth at the end of 4 years? We can answer this question with the help of the time line in Figure 5.13. Your first year's savings will earn interest for 3 years, the second will earn interest for 2 years, the third will earn interest for 1 year, and the final savings in year 4 will earn no interest. The sum of the future values of the four payments is

$$(\$3{,}000 \times 1.08^3) + (\$3{,}000 \times 1.08^2) + (\$3{,}000 \times 1.08) + \$3{,}000 = \$13{,}518$$

But wait a minute! We are looking here at a level stream of cash flows—an annuity. We have seen that there is a shortcut formula to calculate the *present* value of an annuity. So there ought to be a similar formula for calculating the *future* value of a level stream of cash flows.

Think first how much your stream of savings is worth today. You are setting aside \$3,000 in each of the next four years. The *present* value of this 4-year annuity is therefore equal to

$$\text{PV} = \$3{,}000 \times \text{4-year annuity factor}$$

$$= \$3{,}000 \times \left[\frac{1}{.08} - \frac{1}{.08(1.08)^4}\right] = \$9{,}936$$

FIGURE 5.13
Future value of a 4-year, \$3,000 per year annuity invested at 8 percent.

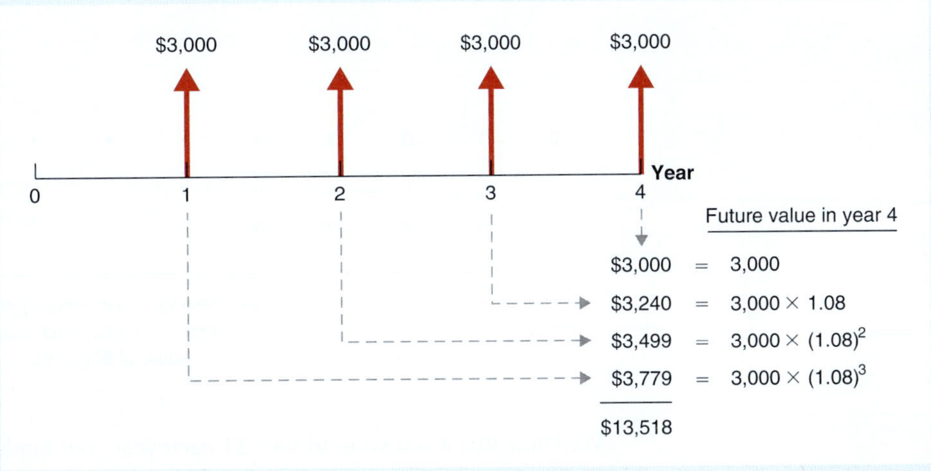

[3] Your financial calculator is equipped to handle annuities due. You simply need to put the calculator in "begin" mode, and the stream of cash flows will be interpreted as starting immediately. The Begin key is labelled BGN or BEG/END. Each time you press the key, the calculator will toggle between ordinary annuity versus annuity DUE mode.

Now think how much you would have after 4 years if you invested \$9,936 today. Simple! Just multiply by $(1.08)^4$:

$$\text{Value at end of year 4} = \$9{,}936 \times 1.08^4 = \$13{,}518$$

We calculated the future value of the annuity by first calculating the present value and then multiplying by $(1 + r)^t$. The general formula for the *future* value of a stream of cash flows of \$1 per year for each of t years, FVA(r, t), is

$$\textbf{Future value of annuity of \$1 per year, FVA}(r, t) = \textbf{present value of annuity of \$1 per year} \times (1 + r)^t$$

$$\text{FVA}(r, t) = \left[\frac{1}{r} - \frac{1}{r(1 + r)^t}\right] \times (1 + r)^t \qquad (5.11)$$

$$\text{FVA}(r, t) = \frac{(1 + r)^t - 1}{r}$$

If you need to find the future value of just four cash flows, as in our example, it is a toss-up whether it is quicker to calculate the future value of each cash flow separately (as we did in Figure 5.13) or to use the annuity formula. If you are faced with a stream of 10 or 20 cash flows, there is no contest.

You can find a table of the future value of an annuity in Table 5.6, or use the more extensive Table A.4 in the online Appendix A. You can see that in the row corresponding to $t = 4$ and the column corresponding to $r = 8\%$, the future value of an annuity of \$1 a year is \$4.5061. Therefore, the future value of the \$3,000 annuity is \$3,000 × 4.5061 = \$13,518.

EXAMPLE 5.12 SAVING FOR RETIREMENT

In only 45 more years, you will retire. Have you started saving yet? Suppose you believe you will need to accumulate \$500,000 by your retirement date in order to support your desired standard of living. How much must you save each year between now and your retirement to meet that future goal? Let's say that the interest rate is 10 percent per year. You need to find how large the annuity in the following figure must be to provide a future value of \$500,000:

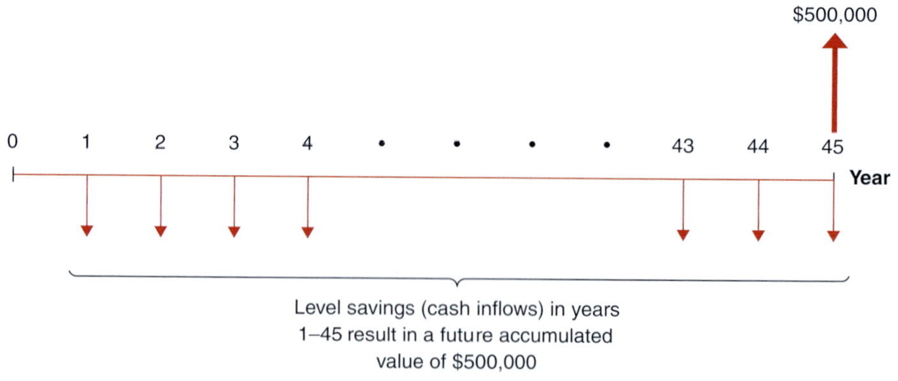

We know that if you were to save \$1 each year your funds would accumulate to

$$\text{Future value of annuity of \$1 a year} = \frac{(1 + r)^t - 1}{r} = \frac{(1.10)^{45} - 1}{.10}$$
$$= \$718.905$$

TABLE 5.6
Future value factors—future value of a $1 annuity invested at various interest rates for different periods.

Number of Periods	Interest Rate per Period					
	5%	6%	7%	8%	9%	10%
1	1.0000	1.0000	1.0000	1.0000	1.0000	1.0000
2	2.0500	2.0600	2.0700	2.0800	2.0900	2.1000
3	3.1525	3.1836	3.2149	3.2464	3.2781	3.3100
4	4.3101	4.3746	4.4399	4.5061	4.5731	4.6410
5	5.5256	5.6371	5.7507	5.8666	5.9847	6.1051
10	12.5779	13.1808	13.8164	14.4866	15.1929	15.9374
20	33.0660	36.7856	40.9955	45.7620	51.1601	57.2750
30	66.4388	79.0582	94.4608	113.2832	136.3075	164.4940

(Rather than compute the future value formula directly, you could look up the future value annuity factor in Table 5.6 or the online Table A.4. In this instance, the future value annuity factor is not provided for a 45-year period. Alternatively, you can use a financial calculator or spreadsheet as we describe in the nearby Financial Calculator and Spreadsheet Solutions boxes.) Therefore, if we save an amount of $\$C$ each year, we will accumulate $\$C \times 718.905$.

We need to choose C to ensure that $\$C \times 718.905 = \$500{,}000$. Thus $C = \$500{,}000/718.905 = \$695.50$. This appears to be surprisingly good news. Saving $695.50 a year does not seem to be an extremely demanding savings program. Don't celebrate yet, however. The news will get worse when we consider the impact of inflation.

Check Point 5.14

What is the required savings level if the interest rate is only 5 percent? Why has the amount increased?

Remember that our ordinary annuity formulas assume that the first cash flow does not occur until the end of the first period. If the first cash flow comes immediately, the future value of the cash flow stream is greater, since each flow has an extra year to earn interest. For example, at an interest rate of 8 percent, the future value of an annuity due would be exactly 8 percent greater than the future value of an ordinary annuity. More generally,

$$\text{Future value of annuity due} = \text{future value of ordinary annuity} \times (1 + r)$$

EXAMPLE 5.13 FUTURE VALUE OF ANNUITIES VERSUS ANNUITIES DUE

In Example 5.12, we showed that an annual savings stream of $695.50 invested for 45 years at 10 percent would satisfy a savings goal of $500,000. What savings stream would be necessary if we invested our money at the beginning rather than the end of each year?

We know from Example 5.12 that the future value of a $1 ordinary 45-year annuity at an interest rate of 10 percent is $718.905. Therefore,

$$\begin{aligned}\text{FV of \$1 annuity due} &= \text{FV of \$1 ordinary annuity} \times (1 + r)\\ &= \$718.905 \times 1.10 = \$790.80\end{aligned}$$

We need to choose C to ensure that $C \times 790.80 = \$500{,}000$. Thus $C = \$632.27$. Notice that $632.27 equals the (ordinary) annuity we found in Example 5.12 divided by 1.10.

CASH FLOWS GROWING AT A CONSTANT RATE—VARIATIONS ON PERPETUITIES AND ANNUITIES

The perpetuity and annuity formulas make valuing streams of equal cash flows easy. Unfortunately, many streams of cash flows are not equal. If, however, the cash flow stream grows at a constant rate, convenient valuation formulas are available. The present value of a perpetual stream of payments growing at a constant rate is

$$\textbf{Present value of a perpetual stream of payments growing at a constant rate} = \frac{C_1}{r - g} \quad \textbf{(5.12)}$$

growing perpetuity An infinite stream of cash flows growing at a constant rate.

where C_1 is the payment to occur at the end of the first period, r is the discount rate, and g is the growth rate of the payments. If the growth rate, g, is zero, the formula becomes the familiar perpetuity formula, C/r. A perpetual stream of cash flows growing at a constant rate is sometimes called a **growing perpetuity**.

EXAMPLE 5.14 VALUING A CONDO

You are considering purchasing a condominium as an investment. Currently, the type of condo you want generates $12,000 in cash flow (rent minus expenses) annually. If the cash flow grows 3 percent per year, the building lasts forever, and the interest rate is 8 percent, what is the present value of the condo's cash flows?

$$\text{Present value} = \frac{\$12{,}000}{.08 - .03} = \$240{,}000$$

Another useful present value formula can be used if the cash flows grow at a constant rate for a limited or finite period. The present value of a finite stream of cash flows growing at a constant rate is

$$\textbf{Present value of a finite stream of payments growing at a constant rate} = \frac{C_1}{r - g}\left(1 - \left[\frac{1 + g}{1 + r}\right]^t\right) \quad \textbf{(5.13)}$$

growing annuity A finite stream of cash flows growing at a constant rate.

where C_1 is the payment to occur at the end of the first period, r is the discount rate, t is the number of payments, and g is the growth rate of the payments. If the growth rate, g, is zero, after a bit of juggling, the formula becomes the familiar present value of an annuity formula. A finite stream of cash flows growing at a constant rate is some times referred to as a **growing annuity**.

EXAMPLE 5.15 ANOTHER LOOK AT THE VALUE OF A CONDO

Upon reflection, the condo in Example 5.14 will not likely be around forever. If the building is torn down in 20 years, what is the present value of the cash flows if the first cash flow is $12,000, the growth rate 3 percent, and the interest rate 8 percent?

$$\text{Present value} = \frac{\$12{,}000}{.08 - .03}\left(1 - \left[\frac{1.03}{1.08}\right]^{20}\right) = \$147{,}000.50$$

We can also calculate the future value of a stream of cash flows that grow at the constant rate for a limited or finite period. We do this the same way as we calculated the future value of an annuity. In other words, we simply multiply the present value of a growing annuity by $(1 + r)^t$. Therefore,

financial calculator

Solving Annuity Problems Using a Financial Calculator

The formulas for both the present value and future value of an annuity are also built into your financial calculator. Again, we can input all but one of the five financial keys, and let the calculator solve for the remaining variable. In these applications, the PMT key is used to either enter or solve for the value of an annuity.

Solving for an Annuity

In Example 5.12, we determined the savings stream that would provide a retirement goal of $500,000 after 45 years of saving at an interest rate of 10 percent. To find the required savings each year, enter $n = 45$, $i = 10$, FV = 500,000, and PV = 0 (because your "savings account" is currently empty). Compute PMT and find that it is −$695.50. Again, your calculator is likely to display the solution as −695.50, since the positive $500,000 cash value in 45 years will require 45 cash payments (outflows) of $695.50.

The sequences of keystrokes necessary to solve this problem on three popular calculators are as follows:

Hewlett-Packard HP-10B	Sharp EL-738C	Texas Instruments BA II Plus
0 PV	0 PV	0 PV
45 n	45 n	45 n
10 I/YR	10 i	10 I/Y
500,000 FV	500,000 FV	500,000 FV
PMT	COMP PMT	CPT PMT

Your calculator displays a negative number, as the 45 cash outflows of $695.50 are necessary to provide for the $500,000 cash value at retirement.

Present Value of an Annuity

In Example 5.11 we considered a 25-year mortgage with monthly payments of $1,184.88 and an interest rate of 1 percent per month. Suppose we didn't know the amount of the mortgage loan. Enter $n = 300$ (months), $i = 1$, PMT = −1,184.88 (we enter the annuity level paid by the borrower to the lender as a negative number since it is a cash outflow), and FV = 0 (the mortgage is paid off after 25 years; there are no final future payments beyond the normal monthly payment). Compute PV to find that the value of the loan is $112,500.

What about the balance left on the mortgage after seven years have passed? This is easy: The monthly payment is still PMT = −1,184.88, and we continue to use $i = 1$ and FV = 0. The only change is that the number of monthly payments remaining has fallen from 300 to 216 (18 years are left on the loan). So enter $n = 216$ and compute PV as 104,675.97. This is the balance remaining on the mortgage.

Future Value of an Annuity

In Figure 5.13, we showed that a 4-year annuity of $3,000 invested at 8 percent would accumulate to a future value of $13,518. To solve this on your calculator, enter $n = 4$, $i = 8$, PMT = −3,000 (we enter the annuity paid by the investor to her savings account as a negative number since it is a cash outflow), and PV = 0 (the account starts with no funds). Compute FV to find that the future value of the savings account after 3 years is $13,518.

Calculator Self-Test Review (answers below)

1. Turn back to Kangaroo Autos in Example 5.8. Can you now solve for the present value of the three instalment payments using your financial calculator? What keystrokes must you use?
2. Now use your calculator to solve for the present value of the three instalment payments if the first payment comes immediately, that is, as an annuity due.
3. Find the annual spending available to Bill Gates using the data in Example 5.10 and your financial calculator.

Solutions to Calculator Self-Test Review Questions

1. Inputs are $n = 3$, $i = 10$, FV = 0, and PMT = 4,000. Compute PV to find the present value of the cash flows as $9,947.41.
2. If you put your calculator in "begin" mode and recalculate PV using the same inputs, you will find that PV has increased by 10 percent to $10,942.15. Alternatively, as depicted in Figure 5.12, you can calculate the value of the $4,000 immediate payment plus the value of a 2-year annuity of $4,000. Inputs for the 2-year annuity are $n = 2$, $i = 10$, FV = 0, and PMT = 4,000. Compute PV to find the present value of the cash flows as $6,942.15. This amount plus the immediate $4,000 payment results in the same total present value: $10,942.15.
3. Inputs are $n = 40$, $i = 9$, FV = 0, PV = − 53,000 million. Compute PMT to find that the 40-year annuity with present value of $56 billion is $4,926.9 million. Slight difference is due to rounding.

Future value of a finite stream of payments growing at a constant rate =

$$= \frac{C_1}{r-g}\left(1 - \left[\frac{1+g}{1+r}\right]^t\right) \times (1+r)^t \qquad (5.14)$$

$$= \frac{C_1}{r-g}([1+r]^t - [1+g]^t)$$

excel spreadsheet

Annuities

By now it should come as no surprise that the *pmt* variable in Excel's time-value-of-money functions denotes the level of an annuity. In addition, Excel provides another function to solve for annuity levels given the values of the other variables: PMT(*rate, nper, pv, fv*). Thus in Example 5.12, we can find the savings stream providing a future retirement goal of $500,000 after 45 years by entering = PMT(.10,45,0,500000), which results in an answer of −$695.50. Notice that we enter 0 for *pv* because our savings account starts with no funds.

Present Value of an Annuity

Example 5.11 examines a 25-year mortgage loan with 300 monthly payments of $1,184.88 each when the interest rate is 1 percent per month. The present value of this annuity = PV(.01,300,1184.88,0), which (except for trivial rounding error) is $112,500. We can also find the balance on the loan after 10 years, when there are 180 remaining payments, as = PV(.01,180,1184.88,0) = $98,726.17.

Future Value of an Annuity

We confirmed on our calculators in the Financial Calculator box that a 4-year annuity of $3,000 invested at 8 percent has a future value of $13,518 (see Figure 5.13). You can also confirm this value on your spreadsheet by entering = FV(.08,4,3000,0).

Annuities Due

Excel will calculate the value of an annuity due rather than an ordinary annuity if you add an extra 1 at the end of the function. For example, we just calculated the present value of 300 monthly mortgage payments. Now assume the first payment comes immediately rather than after one month. In other words, the payments are an annuity due. Then the present value is found as =PV(.01,300,1184.88,0,1), which equals $113,625, exactly 1 percent more than the value of the payments as an ordinary annuity. Similarly, the future value of the 4-year, $3,000 annuity that we just looked at also is higher if the first payment is made immediately. As an annuity due, the future value is =FV(.08,4,3000,0,1) = $14,600, which is 8 percent higher than the future value of the ordinary annuity.

Spreadsheet Self-Test Review

In the previous box, we gave you three self-test review questions for your calculator. Now solve these problems using a spreadsheet program.

EXAMPLE 5.16 **YET ANOTHER LOOK AT THE VALUE OF A CONDO**

Assume you are interested to know the value of the condo in Example 5.15 at the end of 20 years, when the building is torn down. What would be this future value of the cash flows if the first cash flow is $12,000, growth rate is 3 percent, and the interest rate is 8 percent?

$$\text{Future value} = \frac{\$12{,}000}{.08 - .03}\left(1 - \left[\frac{1.03}{1.08}\right]^{20}\right) \times (1.08)^{20}$$

$$= \frac{\$12{,}000}{.08 - .03}(1.08^{20} - 1.03^{20}) = \$685{,}163$$

Using formulas is perhaps the best way to calculate present and future values of growing annuities, as annuity tables cannot be prepared for growing annuities.

LO5 5.5 INFLATION AND THE TIME VALUE OF MONEY

When a bank offers to pay 6 percent on a savings account, it promises to pay interest of $60 for every $1,000 you deposit. The bank fixes the number of dollars that it pays, but it doesn't provide any assurance of how much those dollars will buy. If the value of your investment increases by 6 percent, while the prices of goods and services increase by 10 percent, you actually lose ground in terms of the goods you can buy.

REAL VERSUS NOMINAL CASH FLOWS

inflation Rate at which prices as a whole are increasing.

Prices of goods and services continually change. Textbooks may become more expensive (sorry!) while computers become cheaper. An overall rise in prices is known as **inflation**. If the inflation rate is 5 percent per year, then goods that cost $1 a year ago typically cost $1.05 this

FIGURE 5.14
Consumer price index, 1950–2009.

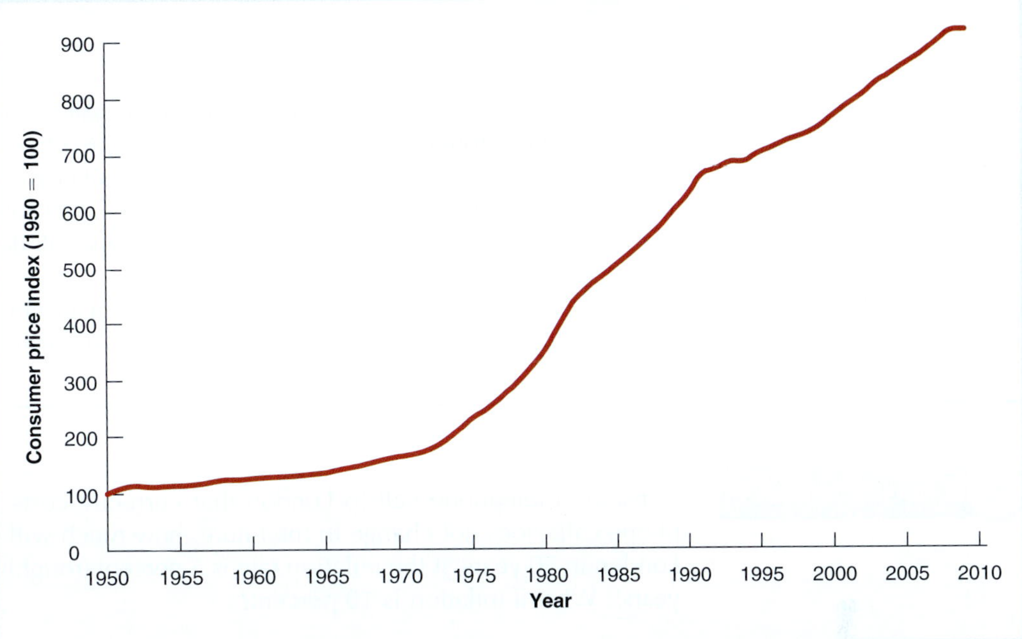

Source: Author's calculations, adapted from Statistics Canada based on annual CPI, CANSIM II Series V41693271.

year. The increase in the general level of prices means that the purchasing power of money has eroded. If a dollar bill bought a loaf of bread last year, the same dollar this year buys only part of a loaf.

Economists track the general level of prices using several different price indexes. The best known of these is the *consumer price index*, or CPI. This measures the number of dollars that it takes to buy a specified basket of goods and services, which is supposed to represent the typical family's purchases.[4] Thus the percentage increase in the CPI from one year to the next measures the rate of inflation.

Figure 5.14 graphs the CPI from 1950 to 2009. We have set the index for the end of 1950 to 100, so the graph shows the price level in each year as a percentage of 1950 prices. For example, the index in 1951 was 110. This means that on average \$110 in 1951 would have bought the same quantity of goods and services as \$100 in 1950. The inflation rate between 1950 and 1951 was therefore 10 percent. By mid-2003, the index was 821, meaning that prices were 8.21 times as high as 1950 prices.[5]

real value of \$1 Purchasing-power-adjusted value of a dollar.

In 2009 the consumer price index was 915 and in 1970 the index was 162. The index had increased 5.65 (915/162) times between 1970 and 2009. A dollar in 2009 would buy only 10.93 percent of the goods it could buy in 1950 (100/915 = .1093). In this case, we would say that the **real value of \$1** declined by 100 − 10.93 = 89.07 percent from 1950 to 2009.

In the first quarter of 2010, inflation in Canada was less than 2 percent per year. Some countries, such as China, were experiencing higher inflation rates because of a more rapid rise in prices. Only a few years earlier some countries experienced falling prices, or deflation, leading some economists to argue (mistakenly, as it turned out) that inflation was dead. In Canada, the Bank of Canada is responsible for setting monetary policy to control inflation. Visit **www.bankofcanada.ca** to learn more about its efforts to manage inflation.

Economists sometimes talk about *current* or *nominal dollars* versus *constant* or *real dollars*. Current or nominal dollars refer to the actual number of dollars of the day; constant or real dollars refer to the amount of purchasing power.

[4] Don't ask how you buy a "basket" of services.

[5] The choice of 100 for the index in 1950 is arbitrary. For example, we could have set the index at 50 in 1950. In this case, the index in 1951 would have been 10 percent higher at 55 (that is, \$50 in 1950 and \$55 in 1951 would have bought the same basket of goods).

EXAMPLE 5.17 **TALK IS CHEAP**

Suppose that in 1970 a telephone call to your Aunt Hilda in London cost $10, while the price to airmail a letter was $.50. By 2009 the price of the phone call had fallen to $3, while that of the airmail letter had risen to $1.55. What was the change in the real cost of communicating with your aunt?

In 2009 the consumer price index was 5.65 (915/162) times its level in 1970. If the price of telephone calls had risen in line with inflation, they would have cost $5.65 \times \$10 = \$56.5$ in 2009. That was the cost of a phone call measured in terms of 2009 dollars rather than 1970 dollars. Thus over the 39 years the real cost of an international phone call declined from $56.5 to $3, a fall of about 95 percent.

What about the cost of sending a letter? If the price of an airmail letter had kept pace with inflation, it would have been $5.65 \times \$.50 = \$2.83$ in 2009. The actual price was only $1.55. So the real cost of letter writing has also declined.

Check Point 5.15

Consider a telephone call to London that currently costs $5. If the real price of telephone calls does not change in the future, how much will it cost you to make a call to London in 50 years, if the inflation rate is 5 percent (roughly its average over the past 33 years)? What if inflation is 10 percent?

Some expenditures are fixed in nominal terms, and therefore *decline* in real terms. Suppose you took out a 25-year house mortgage in 2005. The monthly payment was $800. It was still $800 in 2009, even though the CPI increased by a factor of 1.07 (= 915/856) over those years.

What's the monthly payment for 2009 expressed in real 2005 dollars? The answer is $800/1.07, or $747.7 per month. The real burden of paying the mortgage was less in 2009 than in 1990.

Check Point 5.16

The price index in 2005 was 856. If a family spent $250 a week on their typical purchases in 1950, how much would those purchases cost in 2005? If your salary in 2005 was $30,000 a year, what would be the real value of that salary in terms of 1950 dollars?

INFLATION AND INTEREST RATES

Whenever anyone quotes an interest rate, you can be fairly sure that it is a nominal rate, not a real rate. It sets the actual number of dollars you will be paid with no offset for future inflation.

nominal interest rate Rate at which money invested grows.

If you deposit $1,000 in the bank at a **nominal interest rate** of 6 percent, you will have $1,060 at the end of the year. But this does not mean you are 6 percent better off. Suppose that the inflation rate during the year is also 6 percent. Then the goods that cost $1,000 last year will now cost $\$1{,}000 \times 1.06 = \$1{,}060$, so you've gained nothing:

$$\text{Real future value of investment} = \frac{\$1{,}000 \times (1 + \text{nominal interest rate})}{(1 + \text{inflation rate})}$$

$$= \frac{\$1{,}000 \times 1.06}{1.06} = \$1{,}000$$

real interest rate Rate at which the purchasing power of an investment increases.

In this example, the nominal rate of interest is 6 percent, but the **real interest rate** is zero. The real rate of interest is calculated by

$$1 + \textbf{real interest rate} = \frac{1 + \textbf{nominal interest rate}}{1 + \textbf{inflation rate}} \tag{5.15}$$

In our example, both the nominal interest rate and the inflation rate were 6 percent. So

$$1 + \text{real interest rate} = \frac{1.06}{1.06} = 1$$

$$\text{Real interest rate} = 0$$

What if the nominal interest rate is 6 percent but the inflation rate is only 2 percent? In that case the real interest rate is $1.06/1.02 - 1 = .039$, or 3.9 percent. Imagine that the price of a loaf of bread is $1, so that $1,000 would buy 1,000 loaves today. If you invest that $1,000 at a nominal interest rate of 6 percent, you will have $1,060 at the end of the year. However, if the price of bread has risen in the meantime to $1.02, then your money will buy you only $1{,}060/1.02 = 1{,}039$ loaves. The real rate of interest is 3.9 percent.

Check Point 5.17

a. Suppose that you invest your funds at an interest rate of 8 percent. What will be your real rate of interest if the inflation rate is zero? What if it is 5 percent?
b. Suppose that you demand a real rate of interest of 3 percent on your investments. What nominal interest rate do you need to earn if the inflation rate is zero? If it is 5 percent?

Here is a useful approximation. The real rate approximately equals the difference between the nominal rate and the inflation rate:[6]

$$\textbf{Real interest rate} \approx \textbf{nominal interest rate} - \textbf{inflation rate} \qquad \textbf{(5.16)}$$

Our example used a nominal interest rate of 6 percent, an inflation rate of 2 percent, and a real rate of 3.9 percent. If we round to 4 percent, the approximation gives the same answer:

$$\text{Real interest rate} \approx \text{nominal interest rate} - \text{inflation rate}$$

The approximation works best when both the inflation rate and the real rate are small.[7] When they are not small, throw the approximation away and do it properly.

EXAMPLE 5.18 REAL AND NOMINAL RATES

In Canada in 2010, the interest rate on one-year government borrowing was about 1.0 percent. The inflation rate was 1.6 percent. Therefore, the real rate can be found by computing

$$1 + \text{real interest rate} = \frac{1 + \text{nominal interest rate}}{1 + \text{inflation rate}}$$

$$= \frac{1.01}{1.016} = .9941$$

$$\text{Real interest rate} = -.0059, \text{ or } -.59\%$$

The approximation rule gives a similar value of $1.0 - 1.6 = -.6$ percent. But the approximation would not have worked in the German hyperinflation of 1922/1923, when the inflation rate was well over 100 percent per month (at one point you needed one million marks to mail a letter), or in Peru in 1990, when prices increased by nearly 7,500 percent.

[6] The squiggle (≈) means "is approximately equal to."

[7] When the interest and inflation rates are expressed as decimals (rather than percentages), the approximation error equals the product (real interest rate × inflation rate).

VALUING REAL CASH PAYMENTS

Think again about how to value future cash payments. Earlier in the chapter you learned how to value payments in current dollars by discounting at the nominal interest rate. For example, suppose that the nominal interest rate is 10 percent. How much do you need to invest now to produce \$100 in a year's time? Easy! Calculate the present value of \$100 by discounting by 10 percent:

$$PV = \frac{\$100}{1.10} = \$90.91$$

You get exactly the same result if you discount the *real* payment by the *real interest rate*. For example, assume that you expect inflation of 7 percent over the next year. The real value of that \$100 is therefore only \$100/1.07 = \$93.46. In one year's time your \$100 will buy only as much as \$93.46 today. Also with a 7 percent inflation rate, the real rate of interest is only about 3 percent. We can calculate it exactly from the formula:

$$(1 + \text{real interest rate}) = \frac{1 + \text{nominal interest rate}}{1 + \text{inflation rate}}$$

$$= \frac{1.10}{1.07} = 1.028$$

$$\text{Real interest rate} = .028, \text{ or } 2.8\%$$

If we now discount the \$93.46 real payment by the 2.8 percent real interest rate, we have a present value of \$90.91, just as before:

$$PV = \frac{\$93.46}{1.028} = \$90.91$$

Current dollar cash flows must be discounted by the nominal interest rate; real cash flows must be discounted by the real interest rate.

The two methods should always give the same answer.[8] Remember: Current dollar cash flows must be discounted by the nominal interest rate; real cash flows must be discounted by the real interest rate.

Mixing up nominal cash flows and real discount rates (or real rates and nominal flows) is an unforgivable sin. It is surprising how many sinners one finds.

Check Point 5.18

You are owed \$5,000 by a relative who will pay you back in 1 year. The nominal interest rate is 8 percent and the inflation rate is 5 percent. What is the present value of your relative's IOU? Show that you get the same answer (a) discounting the nominal payment at the nominal rate and (b) discounting the real payment at the real rate.

EXAMPLE 5.19 HOW INFLATION MIGHT AFFECT BILL GATES

We showed earlier (Example 5.10) that at an interest rate of 9 percent, Bill Gates could, if he wished, turn his US\$53 billion wealth into a 40-year annuity of \$4.93 billion per year of luxury and excitement (L&E). Unfortunately L&E expenses inflate just like gasoline and groceries. Thus Mr. Gates would find the purchasing power of that \$4.93 billion steadily declining. If he wants the same luxuries in

[8] If they don't equal there must be an error in your calculations. All we have done in the second calculation is to divide both the numerator (the cash payment) and the denominator (1 plus the nominal interest rate) by the same number (1 plus the inflation rate):

$$PV = \frac{\text{payment in current dollars}}{1 + \text{nominal interest rate}}$$

$$= \frac{(\text{payment in current dollars})/(1 + \text{inflation rate})}{(1 + \text{nominal interest rate})/(1 + \text{inflation rate})}$$

$$= \frac{\text{payment in constant dollars}}{1 + \text{real interest rate}}$$

2050 as in 2010, he'll have to spend less in 2010, and then increase expenditures in line with inflation. How much should he spend in 2010? Assume the long-run inflation rate is 5 percent.

Mr. Gates needs to calculate a 40-year real annuity. The real interest rate is a little less than 4 percent:

$$1 + \text{real interest rate} = \frac{1 + \text{nominal interest rate}}{1 + \text{inflation rate}}$$

$$= \frac{1.09}{1.05} = 1.038$$

so the real rate is 3.8 percent. The 40-year annuity factor at 3.8 percent is 20.396. Therefore, annual spending (in 2010 dollars) should be chosen so that

$$\$53{,}000{,}000{,}000 = \text{annual spending} \times 20.396$$

$$\text{Annual spending} = \$2{,}598{,}548{,}735$$

Mr. Gates could spend that amount on L&E in 2010 and 5 percent more (in line with inflation) in each subsequent year. This is only about half the value we calculated when we ignored inflation. Life has many disappointments, even for tycoons.

Check Point 5.19

You have reached age 60 with a modest fortune of $3 million and are considering early retirement. How much can you spend each year for the next 30 years? Assume that your spending is stable in real terms. The nominal interest rate is 10 percent and the inflation rate is 5 percent.

REAL OR NOMINAL?

Any present value calculation done in nominal terms can also be done in real terms, and vice versa. Most financial analysts forecast in nominal terms and discount at nominal rates. However, in some cases real cash flows are easier to deal with. In our example of Bill Gates, the *real* expenditures were fixed. In this case, it was easiest to use real quantities. On the other hand, if the cash flow stream is fixed in nominal terms (for example, the payments on a loan), it is easiest to use all nominal quantities.

LO6 5.6 EFFECTIVE ANNUAL INTEREST RATES

Thus far in this chapter we have used *annual* interest rates to value a series of *annual* cash flows. But interest rates may be quoted for days, months, years, or any convenient interval. How should we compare rates when they are quoted for different periods, such as monthly versus annually?

Consider your credit card. Suppose you have to pay interest on any unpaid balances at the rate of 1 percent *per month*. What is it going to cost you if you neglect to pay off your unpaid balance for a year?

Don't be put off because the interest rate is quoted per month rather than per year. The important thing is to maintain consistency between the interest rate and the number of periods. If the interest rate is quoted as a percent per month, then we must define the number of periods in our future value calculation as number of months. So if you borrow $100 from the credit card company at 1 percent per month for 12 months, you will need to repay $\$100 \times (1.01)^{12} = \$112.68$. Thus your debt grows after 1 year to $112.68. Therefore, we can say that the interest rate of 1 percent a month is equivalent to an **effective annual interest rate (EAR)**, or *annually compounded rate*, of 12.68 percent.

effective annual interest rate (EAR) Interest rate that is annualized using compound interest.

In general, the effective annual interest rate is defined as the annual growth rate allowing for the effect of compounding. Therefore, the effective annual equivalent to a monthly rate of interest is

$$1 + \text{effective annual rate} = (1 + \text{monthly rate})^{12} \qquad (5.17)$$

When comparing interest rates, it is best to use effective annual rates. This compares interest paid or received over a common period (one year) and allows for possible compounding during the period. Unfortunately, short-term rates are sometimes annualized by multiplying the rate per period by the number of periods in a year. In fact, truth in lending laws in Canada *require* that rates be annualized in this manner. Such rates are called **annual percentage rates (APRs)**.[9] The interest rate on your credit card loan was 1 percent per month. Since there are 12 months in a year, the APR on the loan is 12 × 1% = 12%.

annual percentage rate (APR) Interest rate that is annualized using simple interest.

If the credit card company quotes an APR of 12 percent, how can you find the effective annual interest rate? The solution is simple:

Step 1. Take the quoted APR and divide by the number of compounding periods in a year to recover the rate per period actually charged. In our example, the interest was calculated monthly. So we divide the APR by 12 to obtain the interest rate per month

$$\text{Monthly interest rate} = \frac{\text{APR}}{12} = \frac{12\%}{12} = 1\%, \text{ or } .01$$

Step 2. Now convert to an annually compounded interest rate:

$$1 + \text{effective annual rate} = (1 + \text{monthly rate})^{12} = (1 + .01)^{12} = 1.1268$$

The annual interest rate is .1268, or 12.68 percent.

Putting steps 1 and 2 together gives the formula for converting any APR with m compounding periods in the year into its effective annual equivalent rate:

$$1 + \text{effective annual rate} = \left(1 + \frac{\text{APR}}{m}\right)^{m} \qquad (5.18)$$

The effective annual rate is the rate at which invested funds will grow over the course of a year. It equals the rate of interest per period compounded for the number of periods in a year.

In other words, if you invest at the effective annual rate, the payoff in one year will be the same as investing at the per period rate, APR/m, compounded for the number of periods in the year. For example, a bank loan requiring monthly interest and carrying an APR of 20 percent has an effective annual interest rate of $(1 + .20/12)^{12} - 1 = .2194$, or 21.94 percent. To summarize, the effective annual rate is the rate at which invested funds will grow over the course of a year. It equals the rate of interest per period compounded for the number of periods in a year.

Calculating Effective Annual Rate from Annual Percentage Rate

	A	B	C	D	E
1					
2		Annual Percentage Rate	APR (%)	12%	
3		Number of Compounding Periods	m	12	
4					
5					
6					
7		Effective Annual Rate	EAR	0.126825	=(1+D2/D3)^D3−1
8			**EAR (%)**	**12.6825%**	

How do you calculate a per period rate that is equivalent to an annual rate? Rearrange the effective annual equivalent equation to solve for *APR/m*, which is the per period rate

$$\text{Per-period interest rate} = \frac{\text{APR}}{m} = (1 + \text{effective annual rate})^{1/m} - 1 \qquad (5.19)$$

[9] Although the APR must be disclosed in the loan document, financial institutions typically (though not always) advertise effective rates when marketing their products. APRs are not commonly used or quoted for securities used in the big leagues of finance.

Let's try an example. What is the monthly interest rate equivalent to 8 percent per annum?

$$\text{Monthly interest rate} = \frac{\text{APR}}{m} = (1.08)^{1/12} - 1 = .00643$$

Earning interest of .643 percent per month is the same as earning 8 percent, paid annually. To convert the monthly rate to its APR, multiply by 12, the number of compounding periods in the year: APR = 12 × .643% = 7.716%.

Check Point 5.20

Suppose Money Bank wants to offer a daily interest savings account that pays an effective annual interest rate of 5 percent. What daily interest rate should it pay? What will be the quoted APR for the account?

How can you tell if a rate is an APR or an EAR if it's not specifically stated? It can be difficult but sometimes clues are provided. Generally, if the frequency of payment is mentioned, the rate is likely an APR. For example, if the bank is charging 10 percent interest, payable semi-annually, you should suspect that this is an APR. Interest of 5 percent is charged every 6 months and the EAR is $(1.05)^2 - 1 = .1025$ or 10.25 percent.

Does the frequency of payments matter? Yes, because if interest is paid more frequently, you earn interest on your interest sooner and it builds up over time. Table 5.7 shows how the effective annual rate increases as interest is paid more frequently, even though in each case the APR is 6 percent.

In the limit, interest can be paid in a continuous stream rather than in fixed intervals. With one year's *continuous compounding*, \$1 grows to e^{APR}, where $e = 2.718$ (a figure that may be familiar to you as the base for natural logarithms). Thus if you deposited \$1 in a bank that offered a continuously compounded rate of 6 percent, your investment would grow by the end of the year to $(2.718)^{.06}$ = \$1.061837, just a hair's breadth more than if interest were compounded daily.

Check Point 5.21

A car loan requiring quarterly payments carries an APR of 8 percent. What is the quarterly interest rate? What is the effective annual rate of interest?

EXAMPLE 5.20 FIGURING OUT CANADIAN MORTGAGE INTEREST RATES

In Example 5.11 we showed you how to calculate monthly payments on a mortgage when the interest rate was 1 percent per month. However, before you apply for a job at a bank, you need to know more about Canadian mortgage interest rates. For reasons unclear to us, although mortgage payments are typically made monthly, the mortgage interest rates are APRs quoted with

TABLE 5.7 Compounding frequency and effective annual interest rate (APR = 6%).

Compounding Period	Periods per Year (m)	Per-Period Interest Rate	Growth Factor of Invested Funds	Effective Annual Rate
1 year	1	6%	1.06	6.0000%
Semi-annually	2	3	$1.03^2 = 1.0609$	6.0900
Quarterly	4	1.5	$1.015^4 = 1.061364$	6.1364
Monthly	12	.5	$1.005^{12} = 1.061678$	6.1678
Weekly	52	.11538	$1.0011538^{52} = 1.061800$	6.1800
Daily	365	.01644	$1.0001644^{365} = 1.061831$	6.1831
Continuous			$e^{.06} = 1.061837$	6.1837

semi-annual compounding. For example, if the posted mortgage interest rate is 7.75 percent, this means 7.75 percent, *compounded semi-annually*. In other words, the six-month interest rate is 7.75/2 or 3.875 percent. To get the appropriate discount rate for a mortgage with monthly payments, we need to figure out the equivalent monthly interest rate.

First, convert the quoted APR rate to its effective annual equivalent using Equation 5.18:

$$\text{Effective annual rate} = \left(1 + \frac{\text{APR}}{m}\right)^m - 1 = \left(1 + \frac{.0775}{2}\right)^2 - 1 = .079, \text{ or } 7.9\%$$

Now convert the effective annual rate to its monthly equivalent rate using Equation 5.19:

$$\text{Per-period interest rate} = (1 + \text{effective annual rate})^{1/m} - 1$$
$$= (1.179)^{1/12} - 1 = .00635646163, \text{ or about } .636\%$$

One final point about Canadian mortgages. Typically, the mortgage payment is calculated over an amortization period much longer than the term of the mortgage. For example, a bank commits to lend the money at an APR of 7.75 percent for a term of 5 years but calculates the mortgage payment as if the mortgage will last 25 years. This mortgage has a *term* of 5 years and an *amortization period* of 25 years.

Check Point 5.22

Suppose you arrange a $200,000 mortgage with a 25-year amortization period at the posted mortgage interest rate of 6 percent. What will be your monthly mortgage payment? Check the answer with a mortgage calculator available at any Canadian bank Web site. We went to **www.royalbank.com/mortgage** and clicked on "Mortgage Calculator." Keep in mind that bankers calculate to 10 decimal places.

5.7 SUMMARY

1. **If you invest money at a given interest rate, what will be the future value of your investment? LO1**

   An investment of $1 earning an interest rate of r will increase in value each period by the factor $(1 + r)$. After t periods its value will grow to $\$(1 + r)^t$. This is the **future value** of the $1 investment with compound interest.

2. **What is the present value of a cash flow to be received in the future? LO2**

   The **present value** of a future cash payment is the amount that you would need to invest today to match that future payment. To calculate present value, we divide the cash payment by $(1 + r)^t$ or, equivalently, multiply by the **discount factor** $1/(1 + r)^t$. The discount factor measures the value today of $1 received in period t.

3. **How can we calculate present and future values of streams of cash payments? LO3**

   A level stream of cash payments that continues indefinitely is known as a **perpetuity**; one that continues for a limited number of years is called an **annuity**. The present value of a stream of cash flows is simply the sum of the present value of each cash flow. Similarly, the future value of an annuity is the sum of the future value of each individual cash flow. Shortcut formulas make the calculations for perpetuities and annuities easy. Variations of these formulas make it easy to calculate the present value of cash flows growing at a constant rate.

4. **How can we find the interest rate implied by present and future values? LO4**

The present value equals the discounted value of one or more future cash flows using the appropriate interest rate. Therefore, we solve for the interest rate that makes the discounted value of the future cash flows equal to the given present value. In some cases, this may require trial and error.

5. **What is the difference between real and nominal cash flows and real and nominal interest rates?** LO5

A dollar is a dollar but the amount of goods that a dollar can buy is eroded by **inflation**. If prices double, the **real value of a dollar** halves. Financial managers and economists often find it helpful to re-express future cash flows in terms of real dollars—that is, dollars of constant purchasing power.

Be careful to distinguish the **nominal interest rate** and the **real interest rate**—that is, the rate at which the real value of the investment grows. Discount nominal cash flows (that is, cash flows measured in current dollars) at nominal interest rates. Discount real cash flows (cash flows measured in constant dollars) at real interest rates. *Never* mix and match nominal and real.

6. **How should we compare interest rates quoted over different time intervals—for example, monthly versus annual rates?** LO6

Interest rates for short time periods are often quoted as annual rates by multiplying the per-period rate by the number of periods in a year. These **annual percentage rates** (APRs) do not recognize the effect of compound interest, that is, they annualize, assuming simple interest. The **effective annual rate** (EAR) annualizes using compound interest. It equals the rate of interest per period compounded for the number of periods in a year.

Related Web Links

money.cnn.com Lots of general finance material as well as several interest rate calculations

bankrate.com/can Canadian interest rates for a variety of purposes, some calculators, links to U.S. interest rates

leadfusion.com Calculators for evaluating financial decisions

bankofcanada.ca Canadian interest rates and Canadian monetary policy

rbcroyalbank.com/products/mortgages/index.html Mortgage information and calculator

hsbc.ca Mortgage calculator and other financial calculators

tdcanadatrust.com/mortgages/index.jsp Mortgage calculator

globalfinancialdata.com Data on interest and inflation rates

teachmefinance.com Includes primers on time value, financial calculators, and use of Excel in finance

Key Terms

annual percentage rate (APR)	166	discount rate	137	inflation	160
annuity	147	effective annual interest rate (EAR)	165	nominal interest rate	162
annuity due	154	future value (FV)	133	perpetuity	147
annuity factor	150	future value interest factor *or* future value factor	135	present value (PV)	136
compound interest	133	growing annuity	158	real interest rate	162
discount (or present value interest) factor	138	growing perpetuity	158	real value of $1	161
				simple interest	133

Questions and Problems

connect Practise and learn online with *Connect*. Questions with online Excel templates or datasets are marked with .

*Answers in Appendix B

BASIC

1. **Present Values.** Compute the present value of a $100 cash flow for the following combinations of discount rates and times: (LO2)

*a. r = 8 percent, t = 10 years
b. r = 8 percent, t = 20 years
c. r = 4 percent, t = 10 years
d. r = 4 percent, t = 20 years

*2. **Future Values.** Compute the future value of a $100 cash flow for the same combinations of rates and times as in problem 1. (LO1)

3. **Future Values.** You deposit $1,000 into your bank account. If the bank pays 4 percent simple interest, how much will you accumulate in your account after 10 years? If the bank pays compound interest, how much of your earnings will be interest on interest? (LO1)

*4. **Present Values.** You will require $700 in 5 years. If you earn 5 percent interest on your funds, how much will you need to invest today in order to reach your savings goal? (LO2)

*5. **Calculating Interest Rate.** Find the interest rate implied by the following combinations of present and future values: (LO4)

Present Value	Years	Future Value
$400	11	$684
$183	4	$249
$300	7	$300

6. **Present Values.** Would you rather receive $1,000 per year for 10 years or $800 per year for 15 years if
   a. the interest rate is 5 percent? (LO3)
   b. the interest rate is 20 percent? (LO3)
   c. Why do your answers to parts (a) and (b) differ?

*7. **Present Values.** What is the present value of the following cash flow stream if the interest rate is 5 percent? (LO3)

Year	Cash Flow
1	$200
2	$400
3	$300

8. **Number of Periods.** How long will it take for $400 to grow to $1,000 at the interest rate specified? (LO1)
   *a. 4 percent
   b. 8 percent
   c. 16 percent

*9. **Present Value of Annuities.** Compute the present value of a $100 annual annuity for the same combination of rates and time periods as in problem 1. (LO3)

*10. **Future Value of Annuities.** Compute the future value of a $100 annual annuity for the same combination of rates and time periods as in problem 1. (LO3)

*11. **Calculating Interest Rate.** Find the effective annual interest rate for each case: (LO6)

APR	Compounding Period
12%	1 month
8%	3 months
10%	6 months

*12. **Calculating Interest Rate.** Find the per period rate and the APR (the stated interest rate) for each case: (LO6)

Effective Annual Interest Rate	Compounding Period
10.00%	1 month
6.09%	6 months
8.24%	3 months

*13. **Growth of Funds.** If you earn 8 percent per year on your bank account, how long will it take an account with $100 to double to $200? (LO1)

14. **Comparing Interest Rates.** Suppose you can borrow money at 8.5 percent per year (APR), compounded semi-annually or 8.4 percent per year (APR) compounded monthly. Which is the better deal? (LO6)

*15. **Calculating Interest Rate.** Lenny Loanshark charges "one point" per week (that is, 1 percent per week) on his loans. What APR must he report to consumers? Assume there are exactly 52 weeks in a year. What is the effective annual rate? (LO6)

16. **Compound Interest.** Investments in the stock market have increased at an average compound rate of about 5 percent per year since 1900.
   a. If you invested $1,000 in the stock market in 1900, how much would that investment be worth in 2011? (LO1)
   b. If your investment in 1900 has grown to $1 million in 2011, how much did you invest in 1900? (LO2)

17. **Compound Interest.** Old Time Savings Bank pays 5 percent interest on its savings accounts. If you deposit $1,000 in the bank and leave it there, how much interest will you earn in the first year? The second year? The 10th year? (LO1)

18. **Compound Interest.** New Savings Bank pays 4 percent interest on its deposits. If you deposit $1,000 in the bank and leave it there, will it take more or less than 25 years for your money to double? You should be able to answer this without a calculator or interest rate tables. (LO1)

19. **Calculating Interest Rate.** A zero-coupon bond that will pay $1,000 in 10 years is selling today for $422.41. What interest rate does the bond offer? (LO4)

Unless otherwise stated, assume all cash flows occur at the *end* of each period.

INTERMEDIATE

20. **Loan Payments.** If you take out a 4-year $8,000 car loan that calls for monthly payments at an APR of 10 percent, compounded monthly, what is your monthly payment? What is the effective annual interest rate on the loan? (LO6)

21. **Annuity Values.** (LO3)
    a. What is the present value of a 3-year annuity of $100 if the discount rate is 6 percent?
    b. What is the present value of the annuity in part (a) if you have to wait two years instead of one year for the payment stream to start?

*22. **Annuities and Interest Rates.** Professor's Annuity Corp. offers a lifetime annuity to retiring professors. For a payment of $80,000 at age 65, the firm will pay the retiring professor $600 a month until death.
    a. If the professor's remaining life expectancy is 20 years, what is the monthly rate on this annuity? What is the effective annual rate? What is the APR? (LO4, LO6)
    b. If the monthly interest rate is .5 percent, what monthly annuity payment can the firm offer to the retiring professor? (LO3)

23. **Calculating Interest Rate.** In a discount interest loan, you pay the interest payment up front. For example, if a 1-year loan is stated as $10,000 and the interest rate is 10 percent, the borrower "pays" $.10 \times \$10,000 = \$1,000$ immediately, thereby receiving net funds of $9,000 and repaying $10,000 in a year. (LO6)
    *a. What is the effective interest rate on this loan?
    *b. If you call the discount d (for example, $d = 10\%$ using our numbers), express the effective annual rate on the loan as a function of d.
    c. Why is the effective annual rate always greater than the stated rate d?

24. **Annuity Due.** Recall that an annuity due is like an ordinary annuity except that the first payment is made immediately instead of at the end of the first period. (LO3)
    a. Why is the present value of an annuity due equal to $(1 + r)$ times the present value of an ordinary annuity?
    b. Why is the future value of an annuity due equal to $(1 + r)$ times the future value of an ordinary annuity?

25. **Comprehensive.** You need a $10,000 car loan and are talking to two different banks. (LO6)
    a. Big Bank offers you a $10,000 auto loan requiring 48 monthly payments of $275, paid at the end of each month. What is the APR of the loan? What is the effective annual rate?
    b. Little Bank's loan has four annual year-end instalments, each equal to 12 times the Big Bank monthly loan payments. Should you accept Little Bank's loan?
    c. What annual payment would make the Little Bank loan equivalent to the Big Bank loan? Why is it not simply 12 times the Big Bank monthly payment?

26. **Annuity Value.** Your landscaping company can lease a truck for $8,000 a year (paid at year-end) for 6 years. It can buy the truck for $40,000. The truck will be valueless after six years. (LO3)
    a. If the interest rate your company can earn on its funds is 7 percent, is it cheaper to buy or lease?
    b. If the lease payments are an annuity due, is it cheaper to buy or lease?

27. **Annuity Due.** A store offers two payment plans. Under the instalment plan, you pay 25 percent down and 25 percent of the purchase price in each of the next 3 years. If you pay the entire bill immediately, you can take a 10 percent discount from the purchase price. (LO3)
    a. If you can borrow or lend funds at a 6 percent interest rate, which is the better deal?
    b. If the payments on the 4-year instalment plan do not start for a full year, which plan is a better deal?

*28. **Annuity and Annuity Due Payments.** (LO3)
    a. If you borrow $1,000 and agree to repay the loan in five equal annual payments at an interest rate of 12 percent, what will your payment be?
    b. If you make the first payment on the loan immediately instead of at the end of the first year, what is your payment?

*29. **Valuing Delayed Annuities.** Suppose that you will receive annual payments of $10,000 for a period of 10 years. The first payment will be made four years from now. If the interest rate is 6 percent, what is the present value of this stream of payments? (LO3)

*30. **Mortgage.** You take out a $175,000 Canadian mortgage with a 25-year amortization period, a 5-year term, and a 6 percent posted mortgage interest rate. What is your monthly mortgage payment? When the mortgage expires in five years, what is the unpaid balance? (LO3)

31. **Mortgage.** You are arranging a $350,000 Canadian mortgage with a 25-year amortization period and a 7 percent posted interest rate. What is the monthly mortgage payment? Suppose the bank offers you the opportunity to pay your monthly payments in two equal instalments (pay one-half of the monthly payment every two weeks). How much faster will you pay off your mortgage this way? (LO3)

Unless otherwise stated, assume all cash flows occur at the *end* of each period.

32. **Amortizing Loan.** Consider a four-year amortizing loan. You borrow $1,000 initially, and repay it in four equal annual year-end payments. (LO3)
    a. If the interest rate is 8 percent, show that the annual payment is $301.92.
    b. Fill in the following table, which shows how much of each payment comprises interest versus principal repayment (that is, amortization) and the outstanding balance on the loan at each date.
    c. Show that the loan balance after 1 year is equal to the year-end payment of $301.92 times the 3-year annuity factor.

Time	Loan Balance	Year-End Interest Due on Balance	Year-End Payment	Amortization of Loan
0	$1,000	$80	$301.92	$221.92
1	_____	_____	301.92	_____
2	_____	_____	301.92	_____
3	_____	_____	301.92	_____
4	0	0	_____	_____

33. **Annuity Value.** You've borrowed $4,248.68 and agreed to pay back the loan with monthly payments of $200. If the interest rate is 12 percent stated as an APR, how long will it take you to pay back the loan? What is the effective annual rate on the loan? (LO3, LO6)
34. **Annuity Value.** The $40 million lottery payment that you just won actually pays $2 million per year for 20 years. If the discount rate is 8 percent, and the first payment comes in 1 year, what is the present value of the winnings? What if the first payment comes immediately? (LO3)
*35. **Real Annuities.** A retiree wants level consumption in real terms over a 30-year retirement. If the inflation rate equals the interest rate she earns on her $450,000 of savings, how much can she spend in real terms each year over the rest of her life? (LO5)
36. **EAR Versus APR.** You invest $1,000 at 6 percent compounded monthly. How much will you have in one year? In 1.5 years? (LO6)
37. **Annuity Value.** You just borrowed $100,000 to buy a condo. You will repay the mortgage in equal monthly payments of $804.62 over the next 30 years. What monthly interest rate are you paying on the mortgage? What is the effective annual rate on that mortgage? What rate is the lender more likely to quote on the mortgage? (LO3)
38. **EAR.** If a bank pays 4 percent interest with continuous compounding, what is the effective annual rate? (LO6)
39. **Annuity Values.** You can buy a car that is advertised for $12,000 on the following terms: (a) pay $12,000 and receive a $1,000 rebate from the manufacturer, or (b) pay $250 a month for 4 years, for total payments of $12,000, implying zero percent financing. Which is the better deal if the interest rate is 1 percent per month? (LO3)
40. **Continuous Compounding.** How much will $100 grow to if invested at a continuously compounded interest rate of 10 percent for 6 years? What if it is invested for 10 years at 6 percent? (LO6)
*41. **Future Values.** I now have $20,000 in the bank earning interest of .5 percent per month. I need $30,000 to make a down payment on a house. I can save an additional $100 per month. How long will it take me to accumulate the $30,000? (LO3)
*42. **Perpetuities.** A bank advertises the following deal: "Pay us $100 a year for 10 years and then we will pay you (or your beneficiaries) $100 a year forever." Is this a good deal if the interest rate available on other deposits is 8 percent? (LO3)
43. **Perpetuities.** A bank will pay you $100 a year for your lifetime if you deposit $2,500 in the bank today. If you plan to live forever, what interest rate is the bank paying? (LO4)
44. **Perpetuities.** A property will provide $10,000 a year forever. If its value is $125,000, what must be the discount rate? (LO4)
45. **Calculating Interest Rate.** A store will give you a 3 percent discount on the cost of your purchase if you pay cash today. Otherwise, you will be billed the full price with payment due in one month. What is the implicit effective annual borrowing rate being paid by customers who choose to defer payment for the month? (LO4)
46. **Quoting Rates.** Banks sometimes quote interest rates in the form of "add-on interest." In this case, if a 1-year loan is quoted with a 20 percent interest rate and you borrow $1,000, then you pay back $1,200. But you make these payments in monthly instalments of $100 each. What are the true APR and effective annual rate on this loan? Why should you have known that the true rates must be greater than 20 percent even before doing any calculations? (LO6)
47. **Compound Interest.** Suppose you take out a $1,000, 3-year loan using add-on interest (see previous problem) with a quoted interest rate of 20 percent per year. What will your monthly payments be? (Total payments are $1,000 + $1,000 × .20 × 3 = $1,600.) What are

Unless otherwise stated, assume all cash flows occur at the *end* of each period.

the true APR and effective annual rate on this loan? Are they the same as in the previous problem? (LO6)

48. **Calculating Interest Rate.** What is the effective annual rate on a 1-year loan with an interest rate quoted on a discount basis (see problem 23) of 20 percent? (LO4)

49. **Effective Rates.** First National Bank pays 6.2 percent interest compounded semi-annually. Second National Bank pays 6 percent interest, compounded monthly. Which bank offers the higher effective annual rate? (LO6)

50. **Calculating Interest Rate.** You borrow $1,000 from the bank and agree to repay the loan over the next year in 12 equal monthly payments of $90. However, the bank also charges you a loan-initiation fee of $20, which is taken out of the initial proceeds of the loan. Taking into account the impact of the initiation fee, what is the effective annual interest rate on the loan? (LO4)

51. **Applying Time Value.** A top-ranked quarterback just signed a 5-year contract, providing $3 million per year, payable at the end of each month. A hockey superstar accepts a 5-year contract, with a $4 million signing bonus, payable immediately and $2.1 million per year, payable at the end of each month. The quarterback brags that his contract is better because he is getting $15 million and the hockey player is getting only $14.5 million. Is the quarterback right? The interest rate is 8 percent, EAR. (LO3, LO6)

52. **Applying Time Value.** Bill needs a new car and can afford monthly car payments of $400. The interest rate on new car loans is 7 percent, APR and payments are made at month-end. Bill wonders whether to arrange a 48- or 60-month loan. With either loan, Bill will borrow the maximum amount and buy the most expensive car possible. The average annual rate of depreciation of a car's value is 18 percent. Bill can invest his spare cash in a mutual fund expected to pay 5 percent, compounded monthly. (LO3, LO6)
    a. What is the maximum he can spend on a car if he arranges a 48-month loan? What if he arranges a 60-month loan?
    b. Compare Bill's wealth (the value of his car plus his investments) after 5 years if he arranges a 48-month loan to his wealth if he arranges a 60-month loan.

53. **Applying Time Value.** You can buy property today for $3 million and sell it in 5 years for $4 million. (You earn no rental income on the property.) (LO3)
    a. If the interest rate is 8 percent, what is the present value of the selling price?
    b. Is the property investment attractive to you? Why or why not?
    c. Would your answer to part (b) change if you also could earn $200,000 per year rent on the property?

54. **Applying Time Value.** A factory costs $400,000. You forecast that it will produce cash inflows of $120,000 in year 1, $180,000 in year 2, and $300,000 in year 3. The discount rate is 12 percent. Is the factory a good investment? Explain. (LO3)

*55. **Applying Time Value.** You invest $1,000 today and expect to sell your investment for $2,000 in 10 years. (LO1)
    a. Is this a good deal if the discount rate is 5 percent?
    b. What if the discount rate is 10 percent?

56. **Applying Time Value.** You believe you will need to save $500,000 by the time you retire in 40 years, in order to live comfortably. If the interest rate is 5 percent per year, how much must you save each year to meet your retirement goal? (LO3)

57. **Applying Time Value.** How much would you need in the previous problem if you believe that you will inherit $100,000 in 10 years? (LO3)

*58. **Applying Time Value.** You believe you will spend $40,000 per year for 20 years once you retire in 40 years. If the interest rate is 5 percent per year, how much must you save each year until retirement to meet your retirement goal? (LO3)

*59. **Applying Time Value.** A couple thinking about retirement decide to put aside $3,000 each year in a savings plan that earns 8 percent interest. In 5 years they will receive a gift of $10,000, which can also be invested. (LO3)
    a. How much money will they have accumulated 30 years from now?
    b. If their goal is to retire with $800,000 of savings, how much extra do they need to save every year?

60. **Applying Time Value.** A couple will retire in 50 years; they plan to spend about $30,000 per year in retirement, which should last about 25 years. They believe that they can earn 8 percent interest on retirement savings. (LO3)
    a. If they make annual payments into a savings plan, how much will they need to save each year? Assume the first payment is made in one year.
    b. How would the answer to part (a) change if the couple also realize that in 20 years they will need to spend $60,000 on their child's university or college education?

61. **Integrative.** Acme needs a new $20,000 copier machine and must decide whether to lease or buy it. If the company buys the copier, they expect to sell it for $5,000 in 5 years. The bank has offered a 5-year amortizing loan

Unless otherwise stated, assume all cash flows occur at the *end* of each period.

of $20,000 at 8 percent, compounded monthly. Loan payments will be due at the end of each month. If Acme leases the copier, monthly lease payments will be paid at the beginning of each month and the copier returned to the lessor at the end of five years. Calculate the monthly lease payment that would make the lease equivalent to the loan. (LO3, LO4, LO6)

62. **Real Versus Nominal Dollars.** An engineer in 1950 was earning $6,000 a year. Today, in 2011, she earns $60,000 a year. However, on average, goods today cost 8.2 times what they did in 1950. (LO5)
    a. What is her real income today in terms of constant 1950 dollars?
    b. Calculate her salary's annual inflation rate and the cost of goods annual inflation rate.

*63. **Real Versus Nominal Rates.** If investors are to earn a real interest rate at 4 percent, what nominal interest rate must they earn if the inflation rate is
    a. Zero (LO5)
    b. 4 percent (LO5)
    c. 6 percent (LO5)

64. **Real Rates.** If investors receive an 8 percent interest rate on their bank deposits, what real interest rate will they earn if the inflation rate over the year is
    a. Zero (LO5)
    b. 3 percent (LO5)
    c. 6 percent (LO5)

*65. **Real Versus Nominal Rates.** You will receive $100 from a savings bond in 3 years. The nominal interest rate is 8 percent.
    a. What is the present value of the proceeds from the bond? (LO2)
    b. If the inflation rate over the next few years is expected to be 3 percent, what will the real value of the $100 payoff be in terms of today's dollars? (LO5)
    c. What is the real interest rate? (LO5)
    d. Show that the real payoff from the bond in part (b), discounted at the real interest rate in part (c) gives the same present value for the bond as you found in part (a). (LO5)

66. **Internet.** Go to the Yahoo Finance site (**ca.finance.yahoo.com**) and look up Thomson Reuters Corp. (TRI). Briefly describe its main business activities. Using its annual income statement, calculate the compound annual growth rate over the past three years for sales and net income. Convert these results into real growth rates, using the U.S. inflation rate since Thomson reports in U.S. dollars. Calculate the compound average annual U.S. inflation rate for the past three years by using the "Inflation Calculator" at **www.bls.gov/data/inflation_calculator.htm**. (LO5)

67. **Internet.** Using the Bank of Canada inflation calculator, **www.bankofcanada.ca/en/inflation_calc.htm**, answer the following questions: (LO5)
    a. What annual salary in 2010 was equivalent to $5,000 a year in 1940?
    b. Find the average annual inflation rate from 1914 to the current year.

    Now access the investment calculator by either clicking the button at the bottom of the page or going to **www.bankofcanada.ca/en/rates/investment.htm** and answer these questions:

    c. With the calculator, determine the future value of a five-year investment. Use the average inflation from part (b) and look up the current five-year GIC rate at **www.bankofcanada.ca/en/interest-look.htm**. Verify the calculations made by the calculator. Be sure that you can replicate them all.
    d. Explain the second part of the calculation. Why is it important that the future value entered be the amount of money you want to have in today's dollars (after the effects of inflation have been calculated.)? *Hint:* What interest rate is used by the calculator?

68. **Real Versus Nominal Dollars.** Your consulting firm will produce cash flows of $100,000 this year, and you expect cash flow to keep pace with any increase in the general level of prices. The interest rate currently is 8 percent, and you anticipate inflation of about 3 percent.
    a. What is the present value of your firm's cash flows for years 1 through 5? (LO5)
    b. How would your answer to part (a) change if you anticipated no growth in cash flow? (LO2)

69. **Real Versus Nominal Annuities.** Good news: You will almost certainly be a millionaire by the time you retire in 45 years. Bad news: The inflation rate over your lifetime will average about 3 percent. (LO5)
    a. What will be the real value of $1 million by the time you retire, in terms of today's dollars?
    b. What real annuity (in today's dollars) will $1 million support if the real interest rate at retirement is 2 percent and the annuity must last for 20 years?

*70. **Rule of 72.** Use the Rule of 72 to figure out how long it will take for your money to quadruple in value if the interest rate is 8 percent per year. (LO1)

*71. **Inflation.** Inflation in Brazil in 1992 averaged about 23 percent per month. What was the annual inflation rate? (LO5)

72. **Perpetuities.** British government perpetuities at 4 percent pay £4 interest each year forever. Another bond,

2.5 percent perpetuities, pays £2.50 per year forever. What is the value of 4 percent perpetuities if the long-term interest rate is 6 percent? What is the value of 2.5 percent perpetuities? (LO3)

73. **Internet.** There are dozens of Web sites that provide calculators to help with personal finance decisions. Two good examples are **www.quicken.com** and **www.financialpost.com**. Log on to the *Financial Post* site, and click on "Personal Finance" to find a nice savings calculator. Suppose that you invest $1,000 today. How much will you have after 30 years if the interest rate is 6 percent and you do not save another dime? Check your answer with the savings calculator. Now try the same question assuming that you also save $200 a month. (LO1, LO3)

74. **Internet.** You can buy a car for $20,000 or you can lease it for 36 monthly payments of $350 each, with the first payment due immediately. At the end of the 36 months the car will be worth $10,000. Go to **www.smartmoney.com**, click on "Tools" and go to "Worksheets." Under "Autos" click on "Buy or Lease Calculator." Use this calculator to determine which alternative you should prefer if the interest rate is 10 percent. (LO3)

CHALLENGE

75. **Comprehensive.**
   a. You plan to retire in 30 years and want to accumulate enough by then to have $30,000 per year for 15 years. If the interest rate is 10 percent, how much must you accumulate by the time you retire? (LO3)
   b. How much must you save each year until retirement in order to finance your retirement consumption? (LO3)
   c. You remember that the expected annual inflation rate is 4 percent. If a loaf of bread costs $1 today, what will it cost by the time you retire? (LO5)
   d. You really want to consume $30,000 a year in real dollars during retirement and wish to save an equal real amount each year until then. What is the real amount of savings that you need to accumulate by the time you retire? (LO3, LO5)
   e. Calculate the required preretirement real annual savings necessary to meet your consumption goals. Compare your answer to part (b). Why is there a difference? (LO3, LO5)
   f. What is the nominal value of the amount you need to save during the first year? (Assume the savings are put aside at the end of each year.) The 30th year? (LO1, LO5)

76. **Integrative.** In 1880, five Aboriginal trackers were each promised $1 Australian for helping to capture the notorious outlaw Ned Kelley. In 1993, the granddaughters of two of the trackers claimed that this reward had not been paid. The Australian prime minister stated that if this were the case, the government would be happy to pay them each $1. The granddaughters did not think that $1 was sufficient. As their financial advisor, prepare a counterproposal for the granddaughters to send to the prime minister. You may use the following data for 1880–1993: average annual inflation rate, 3 percent; average annual nominal interest rate paid on savings accounts at Australian commercial banks, 3.2 percent; average annual nominal rate of return on Australian stocks, 9.5 percent. (LO1)

77. **Annuity Value.** What is the value of a perpetuity that pays $100 every 3 months forever? The discount rate quoted on an APR basis is 12 percent. (LO3)

*78. **Changing Interest Rates.** If the interest rate this year is 8 percent and the interest rate next year will be 10 percent, what is the future value of $1 after 2 years? What is the present value of a payment of $1 to be received in 2 years? (LO1, LO2)

79. **Changing Interest Rates.** Your wealthy uncle established a $1,000 bank account for you when you were born. For the first 8 years of your life, the interest rate earned on the account was 8 percent. Since then, rates have been only 6 percent. Now you are 21 years old and ready to cash in. How much is in your account? (LO1)

80. **Applying Time Value.** You would like to travel around the world in a sailboat for two years, leaving five years from now. One year before you leave, you will purchase the sailboat at an expected cost of $150,000. During the pre-trip year, you will learn how to sail the boat. Once the trip is under way, you forecast that your monthly expenses will be $2,200, payable at the start of the month. In addition, you would like to have an emergency fund of $45,000 available on the day you depart. How much do you need to save every month-end for the next five years if you can earn an effective annual interest of 6 percent? (LO3)

81. **Applying Time Value.** You are thinking of buying a used car for $4,000 for driving to school. Your parents are willing to lend you the $4,000 and charge only 2.4 percent APR. They want the loan repaid equally in 48 monthly payments, with the first payment due at the end of the month in which you buy the car. You estimate that the monthly cost of operating the car, including gas, insurance, maintenance, and licence fees, will be $200 and payable at the start of each month. The cost of a monthly bus pass is $80. You expect that the car will be totally worn out in four years, with zero resale

Unless otherwise stated, assume all cash flows occur at the *end* of each period.

value, when you are finished school. Your discount rate is 6 percent, compounded annually. (LO3)

a. If you have three roommates who also need transportation to and from school, how much do you need to charge each of them a month in order to cover all your costs? (You all plan to go to summer school, so you can assume 12 payments a year.)

b. Does it make financial sense to buy the car? Explain your answer.

82. **Applying Time Value.** You and your friend are avid snowboarders and bike racers. Nearly every other weekend you travel to a race in a rented van. Now that both of you have full-time jobs, your friend is pressuring you to purchase a van.

Here's how the conversation goes:

Friend: "Just think of how much we will save on rentals. The rented van costs us $100 a weekend, plus $.50 per kilometre. Most trips are 100 kilometres, one way. With our own van, we will only have to pay for fuel about $.08 per kilometre—and maintenance, about $.25 per kilometre. A used van will only cost about $20,000. Think of the convenience!"

You: "What about insurance? What about depreciation?"

Friend: "Insurance will be only $1,200 per year. The salesperson says the van will depreciate slowly, only 10 percent per year. If we retire from the race circuit in 5 years, the van will still have value. Shouldn't we at least think about it?"

You: "I guess. I think a nominal discount rate of 9 percent is about right."

a. Do you think you should buy the van? Be sure to state your assumptions. (LO3, LO6)

b. What if all costs are subject to a 3 percent annual inflation? Do you change your mind? (LO5)

83. **Applying Time Value.** You are working as a financial planner. A couple has asked you to put together an investment plan for the education of their daughter. She is a bright seven-year-old (her birthday is today), and everyone hopes she will go to university after high school in 10 years, on her 17th birthday. You estimate that today the cost of a year of university is $10,000, including the cost of tuition, books, accommodation, food, and clothing. You forecast that the annual inflation rate will be 4 percent. You may assume that these costs are incurred at the start of each university year. A typical university program lasts four years. The effective annual interest rate is 6 percent and is nominal. (LO3, LO5)

a. Suppose the couple invests money on her birthday, starting today and ending one year before she starts university. How much must they invest each year to have money to send their daughter to university?

b. If the couple waits one year, until their daughter's 8th birthday, how much more do they need to invest annually?

84. **Applying Time Value.** A cottage is for sale for $580,000. Currently it generates annual cash flows, net of all expenses and taxes, of $35,000. If the cottage lasts forever, what rate of growth of the annual cash flows will be necessary for you to earn an 8 percent annual rate of return on your investment? (LO3)

85. **Applying Time Value.** A real estate appraiser is assessing the value of a piece of land in Vancouver. Currently the land is unoccupied but is zoned for commercial use. Plans have been approved to build a five-storey office building. Construction is expected to start in 1 year and will take 2 years to complete, at a total cost of $3 million. For simplicity, assume that the costs are paid in equal amounts at the start of each construction year. (LO3)

a. Suppose a constant annual cash flow of $400,000, net of all taxes and operating costs, is expected at the end of each year of operation, and the building lasts for 50 years. What is the maximum you would be willing to pay for the land if the discount rate is 8 percent? Explain your answer.

b. If the cash flow from the tenants grows at 1.5 percent per year, after the first year of occupancy, recalculate the price you would be willing to pay for the land.

86. **Integrative.** The Smiths are planning to retire in 35 years. They want an annual real income of $45,000, paid at the end of each month of their expected 20-year retirement and to bequeath $500,000, in real dollars, to their son at the end of their retirement. In addition, their son's 4-year university education, to begin in 8 years, is expected to cost $10,000 real dollars per year, due at the start of each year. They recently purchased a house for $250,000, with $50,000 cash and a $200,000, 20-year mortgage, carrying a 7 percent interest rate, compounded monthly and paid monthly. Over the next 55 years, the nominal house value is expected to grow 4 percent annually. The Smiths plan to live in their house for the rest of their lives, and the house will be sold on their demise. The expected annual inflation rate is 3 percent. The Smiths expect to earn 6 percent nominal effective annual interest rate on their retirement savings.

a. How much do they need to save in real dollars at the end of each month, for the next 35 years, on top of their monthly mortgage payment, to meet their financial goals? Clearly state any assumptions you make. (LO1, LO2, LO3, LO5, LO6)

b. What will be the total real and nominal mortgage payment plus savings in the last month of the mortgage? (LO1, LO2, LO3, LO5)

c. How much do they need to save in real and nominal terms in the last month before retirement? (LO1)

87. **RESP Calculator.** The Canadian government is encouraging saving for post-secondary education through registered education savings plans (RESPs) and the Canada Education Savings Grant. Under current rules, the total lifetime maximum savings possible is $50,000. The Canada Education Savings Grant, paid annually by the federal government, is 20 percent of the contribution to a maximum of $500 per year, to a maximum of $7,200. Although the contributions are not tax-deductible, they grow tax-free, and then are taxed at the student's presumably lower tax rate when he or she attends university or college.

Go to **www.mackenziefinancial.com/en/pub/tools/calculators/index.shtml** and click on "RESP calculator." Look at the impact of different interest rates and inflation assumptions on required savings. Create a hypothetical family with a one-year-old child. Prepare a report for the parents outlining how much they should be saving to cover the cost of the child's education. In your report, show them the impact on the needed annual savings of waiting two years before starting the RESP, rather than starting immediately. Be sure to clearly lay out your assumptions, including different inflation and interest rate scenarios. (LO3, LO5)

88. **Internet.** Many banks provide loan and mortgage calculators. (LO6)

a. For example, go to the HSBC Bank of Canada Web site at **www.hsbc.ca** and select "Calculators." A list of different calculators will appear. Select "Loan Payments Calculator." Check that your answer to problem 20 is correct.

b. At the same site, select "Mortgage Payments Calculator." For a $200,000 mortgage, at annual interest of 6 percent and 25-year amortization, compare the payments if you pay monthly, semi-monthly, bi-weekly, or weekly. Can you figure out how the numbers are calculated? Do your own calculations.

c. Go to **www.tdcanadatrust.com** and find another mortgage calculator for the same mortgage as you used in part (b); get the bi-weekly payments. Compare them to HSBC's. Are they the same? What does that tell you about the importance of assumptions in the time value of money calculations and the need to be careful using Internet calculators?

d. U.S. mortgage rates are quoted as the APR of the *monthly* rate. If the mortgage rate is 6 percent, the appropriate monthly rate is 6/12 or .5 percent. Go to **www.smartmoney.com**, click on "Tools" and go to "Worksheets." Under "Real Estate" click on "The Mortgage Calculator." Use this mortgage calculator to figure out the U.S. monthly mortgage payment for the mortgage in part (b). Verify that you can calculate the monthly payment yourself.

Solutions to Check Points

5.1 Value after 5 years would have been $24 \times (1.05)^5 = \$30.63$; after 50 years, $24 \times (1.05)^{50} = \$275.22$.

5.2 When an amount doubles, it increases by 100 percent of itself, giving a growth rate of 100 percent. The future value factor for doubling in 1 year is (1 + 100%), or (1 + 1), which of course is 2. So at the end of the first year, sales will be $.5 million × 2, or $1 million. With 4 years of doubling each year, the future value factor is $(2)^4 = 16$, and projected sales after 4 years are $.5 × 16 = $8 million.

5.3 Multiply the $1,000 payment by the 30-year discount factor:

$$\begin{aligned}PV &= \$1{,}000 \times PVIF(.0515{,}30)\\ &= \$1{,}000 \times \frac{1}{(1.0515)^{30}}\\ &= \$1{,}000 \times .22168 = \$221.68\end{aligned}$$

Instead of using a calculator to find the discount factor, we could use Table A.2 in the online Appendix A. Assuming 5 percent as close enough to 5.15 percent, you can see that the 30-year discount factor is .231 if the interest rate is 5 percent. Therefore, the present value would be $231, a little higher than the exact figure.

5.4 The present value of prize A is $5,000 + $5,500/1.04 = $10,288.46. The present value of prize B is $1,000 + $10,000/1.04 = $10,615.38. Prize B has the highest present value. The future value of prize A is $5,000 × 1.04 + $5,500 = $10,700. The future value of prize B is $1,000 × 1.04 + $10,000 = $11,040. Prize B has the highest future value. It does not matter at which point in time you compare the prizes' value.

5.5 We know that:

$$PV = \$1{,}000 \times \frac{1}{(1 + r)^{30}} = \$221.68$$

Unless otherwise stated, assume all cash flows occur at the *end* of each period.

There are several ways to approach this. First, you can rearrange the equation and use your calculator to solve for r:

$$\$221.68 \times (1 + r)^{30} = \$1{,}000$$

$$(1 + r)^{30} = \frac{\$1{,}000}{\$221.68} = 4.511$$

$$(1 + r) = (4.511)^{1/30} = 1.0515$$

$$r = .0515, \text{ or } 5.15\%$$

In general this is more accurate. Second, you might calculate the discount factor in the equation:

$$\text{Discount factor, PVIF}(r,30) = \frac{\$221.68}{\$1{,}000} = .22168$$

Use a table of discount factors to find the interest rate for which the 30-year discount factor equals .22168. Look at Table A.2 in the online Appendix A and run your finger along the row corresponding to 30 years. You can see that an interest rate of 5 percent gives a close discount factor. Therefore, the interest rate on the Puerto Rico loan is about 5 percent.

5.6 If the doubling time is 12 years, then $(1 + r)^{12} = 2$, which implies that $1 + r = 2^{1/12} = 1.0595$, or $r = 5.95$ percent. The Rule of 72 would imply that a doubling time of 12 years is consistent with an interest rate of 6 percent: 72/6 = 12. Thus the Rule of 72 works quite well in this case. If the doubling period is only 2 years, then the interest rate is determined by $(1 + r)^2 = 2$, which implies that $1 + r = 2^{1/2} = 1.414$, or $r = 41.4$ percent. The Rule of 72 would imply that a doubling time of 2 years is consistent with an interest rate of 36 percent: 72/36 = 2. Thus the Rule of 72 is quite inaccurate when the interest rate is high (or the time to double is short).

5.7 Let D be the unknown deposit to be made in 1 year. The future value of that deposit in 2 years is $D \times 1.06$. It will have only 1 year to grow at 6 percent. We also know that the future value in 2 years of the \$1,500 you have right now will be $\$1{,}500 \times (1.06)^2$. The time line below summarizes all of the information:

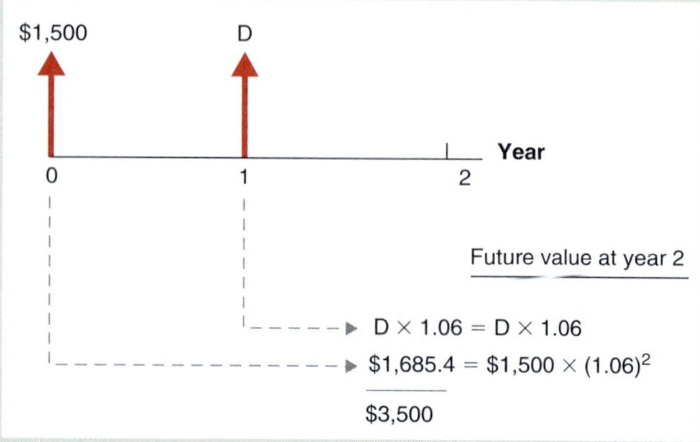

Since the future value of the two deposits must add up to the needed \$3,500, you can rearrange to see that $D \times 1.06 = \$3{,}500 - \$1{,}685.4$. Solving for D gives

$$D = \$1{,}814.6/(1.06) = \$1{,}711.89$$

You will need to deposit about \$1,712 in one year to have enough. Perhaps you better start lobbying your family for a large cash present in one year!

5.8

Gift at Year:	Present Value	
1	$10{,}000/(1.07)$ =	\$ 9,345.79
2	$10{,}000/(1.07)^2$ =	8,734.39
3	$10{,}000/(1.07)^3$ =	8,162.98
4	$10{,}000/(1.07)^4$ =	7,628.95
		\$33,872.11

Gift at Year:	Future Value at Year 4	
1	$10{,}000 \times (1.07)^3$ =	\$12,250.43
2	$10{,}000 \times (1.07)^2$ =	11,449
3	$10{,}000 \times (1.07)$ =	10,700
4	10,000 =	10,000
		\$44,399.43

5.9 The rate is 4/48 = .0833, about 8.3 percent.

5.10 The 4-year discount factor is $1/(1.08)^4 = .735$. The 4-year annuity factor is $[1/.08 - 1/(.08 \times 1.08^4)] = 3.312$. This is the difference between the present value of a \$1 perpetuity starting next year and the present value of a \$1 perpetuity starting in year 5:

$$\text{PV(perpetuity starting next year)} = \frac{1}{.08} = 12.50$$

$$-\text{PV(perpetuity starting year 5)} = \frac{1}{.08} \times \frac{1}{(1.08)^4}$$

$$= 12.50 \times .735 = 9.188$$

$$= \text{PV(4-year annuity)}$$

$$= 12.50 - 9.188 = 3.312$$

5.11 You will need the present value at 7 percent of a 20-year annuity of \$55,000:

Present value = annual spending × annuity factor

The annuity factor is $[1/.07 - 1/(.07 \times 1.07^{20})] = 10.594$. Thus you need $55{,}000 \times 10.594 = \$582{,}670$.

5.12 Fifteen years means 180 months. Then

$$\text{Mortgage payment} = \frac{100{,}000}{\text{180-month annuity factor}}$$

$$= \frac{100{,}000}{83.32}$$

$$= \$1{,}200.17 \text{ per month}$$

$1,000 of the payment is interest. The remainder, $200.17, is amortization.

5.13 Calculate the value of a 24-year annuity, then add the immediate $374,800 payment:

$$24\text{-year annuity factor} = \frac{1}{r} - \frac{1}{r(1+r)^{24}}$$

$$= \frac{1}{.05} - \frac{1}{.05(1.05)^{24}} = 13.7986$$

$$PV = \$374{,}800 \times 13.7956 = \$5{,}171{,}731$$

$$\text{Total value} = \$5{,}171{,}731 + \$374{,}800$$

$$= \$5{,}546{,}531$$

Starting the 25-year cash flow stream immediately, rather than waiting 1 year, increases value by nearly $264,137.

5.14 If the interest rate is 5 percent, the future value of a 45-year, $1 annuity will be

$$\frac{(1.05)^{45} - 1}{.05} = 159.70$$

Therefore, we need to choose the cash flow, C, so that $C \times 159.70 = \$500{,}000$. This requires that $C = \$500{,}000/159.70 = \$3{,}130.87$. This required savings level is much higher than we found in Example 5.12. At a 5 percent interest rate, current savings do not grow as rapidly as when the interest rate was 10 percent; with less of a boost from compound interest, we need to set aside greater amounts in order to reach the target of $500,000.

5.15 The cost in dollars will increase by 5 percent each year to a value of $\$5 \times (1.05)^{50} = \$57.34$. If the inflation rate is 10 percent, the cost will be $\$5 \times (1.10)^{50} = \$586.95$.

5.16 The weekly cost in 2005 is $250 × (856/100) = $2,140. The real value of a 2005 salary of $30,000 expressed in real 1950 dollars is $30,000 × (100/856) = $3,505.

5.17 a. If there's no inflation, real and nominal rates are equal at 8 percent. With 5 percent inflation, the real rate is $(1.08/1.05) - 1 = .02857$, a bit less than 3 percent.

b. If you want a 3 percent *real* interest rate, you need a 3 percent nominal rate if inflation is zero and an 8.15 percent rate if inflation is 5 percent. Note $1.03 \times 1.05 = 1.0815$.

5.18 The present value is

$$PV = \frac{\$5{,}000}{1.08} = \$4{,}629.63$$

The real interest rate is 2.857 percent (see Check Point 5.17(a)). The real cash payment is $5,000/(1.05) = $4,761.90. Thus

$$PV = \frac{\$4{,}761.90}{1.02857} = \$4{,}629.63$$

5.19 Calculate the real annuity. The real interest rate is $1.10/1.05 - 1 = .0476$. We'll round to 4.8 percent. The real annuity is

$$\text{Annual payment} = \frac{\$3{,}000{,}000}{30\text{-year annuity factor}}$$

$$= \frac{\$3{,}000{,}000}{\frac{1}{.048} - \frac{1}{.048(1.048)^{30}}}$$

$$= \frac{\$3{,}000{,}000}{15.73} = \$190{,}728$$

You can spend this much each year in dollars of constant purchasing power. The purchasing power of each dollar will decline at 5 percent per year, so you'll need to spend more in nominal dollars: $\$190{,}728 \times 1.05 = \$200{,}264$ in the second year, $\$190{,}728 \times (1.05)^2 = \$210{,}278$ in the third year, and so on.

5.20 Use equation 5.19 to calculate the daily rate of interest.

$$\text{Per-period rate} = (1 + \text{effective annual rate})^{1/m} - 1$$

$$= (1.05)^{1/365} - 1 = .0001337, \text{ or } .01337\%$$

The annual percentage rate equivalent to .01337 percent per day is

$$APR = m \times \text{per-period rate}$$

$$= 365 \times .0001337$$

$$= .0488, \text{ or } 4.88\%, \text{ compounded daily}$$

5.21 The quarterly rate is 8/4 = 2 percent. The effective annual rate is $(1.02)^4 - 1 = .0824$, or 8.24 percent.

5.22 The posted rate is 6 percent, compounded semi-annually, or 3 percent every 6 months. The effective annual equivalent rate of this is $(1.03)^2 - 1 = .0609$ or 6.09 percent. Now convert this to its equivalent monthly rate:

$$\text{Monthly interest rate} = (1.0609)^{1/12} - 1$$

$$= .004938622, \text{ or } .4938622\%$$

The 300-month, .4938622 percent annuity factor is 156.297225, and your payments will be

$$\text{Monthly mortgage payment} = \frac{\text{mortgage amount}}{\text{annuity factor}}$$

$$= \frac{\$200{,}000}{156.297225} = \$1{,}279.61$$

With a calculator, the inputs are $n = 300$, $i = .4938622$, $PV = -200{,}000$. Compute PMT to find the monthly mortgage payment is $1,279.61.

Solutions to Spreadsheet Questions

5.1

Year	Value	Increase in Value
0	24	
100	52,794	52,770
200	116,134,790	116,081,996
300	255,468,811,638	255,352,676,848
382	140,632,545,501,736	140,377,076,690,098

5.2 The growth of value in the later years is very rapid because you are earning interest on interest—with a lot of compounding already behind you. For example, after 300 years, with accumulated value of $255,468,811,638, just one additional year's interest is .08 × $255,468,811,638 = $2,043,750,493.

5.3

Interest Rate	Present Value
5%	$15,438
8%	15,133
11%	14,850

5.4 $14,916. While the total (undiscounted) payments remain $16,000, part of the first payment in this example has been pushed to the next two years. This reduces present value.

MINI CASE

Alfred Road has reached his 70th birthday and is ready to retire. Mr. Road has no formal training in finance but has saved his money and invested carefully.

Mr. Road owns his home—the mortgage is paid off—and does not want to move. He is a widower, and he wants to bequeath the house and any remaining assets to his daughter.

He has accumulated savings of $180,000, conservatively invested. The investments are yielding 9 percent interest. Mr. Road also has $12,000 in a savings account at 5 percent interest. He wants to keep the savings account intact for unexpected expenses or emergencies.

Mr. Road's basic living expenses now average about $1,500 per month, and he plans to spend $500 per month on travel and hobbies. To maintain this planned standard of living, he will have to rely on his investment portfolio. The interest from the portfolio is $16,200 per year (9 percent of $180,000), or $1,350 per month.

Mr. Road will also receive $750 per month in Canada Pension and Old Age Security payments for the rest of his life. These payments are indexed for inflation. That is, they will be automatically increased in proportion to changes in the consumer price index.

Mr. Road's main concern is with inflation. The inflation rate has been below 3 percent recently, but a 3 percent rate is unusually low by historical standards. His pension payments will increase with inflation, but the interest on his investment portfolio will not.

What advice do you have for Mr. Road? Can he safely spend all the interest from his investment portfolio? How much could he withdraw at year-end from that portfolio if he wants to keep its real value intact?

Suppose Mr. Road will live for 20 more years and is willing to use up all of his investment portfolio over that period. He also wants his monthly spending to increase along with inflation over that period. In other words, he wants his monthly spending to stay the same in real terms. How much can he afford to spend per month?

Assume that the investment portfolio continues to yield a 9 percent rate of return and that the inflation rate is 4 percent.

PART 2 Value

5 The Time Value of Money
6 Valuing Bonds
6.1 Bonds and the Bond Market
6.2 Interest Rates and Bond Prices
6.3 Current Yield and Yield to Maturity
6.4 Bond Rates of Return
6.5 The Yield Curve
6.6 Corporate Bonds and the Risk of Default
6.7 Summary
Appendix 6A A More Detailed Look at the Yield Curve
Appendix 6B Duration: Measuring the Life of a Bond (see the Online Learning Centre)
7 Valuing Stocks
8 Net Present Value and Other Investment Criteria
9 Using Discounted Cash Flow Analysis to Make Investment Decisions
10 Project Analysis

CHAPTER 6

Valuing Bonds

LEARNING OBJECTIVES

After studying this chapter, you should be able to:

LO1 Distinguish among the bond's coupon rate, current yield, and yield to maturity.

LO2 Calculate the market price of a bond given its yield to maturity, calculate a bond's yield given its price, and demonstrate why prices and yields vary inversely.

LO3 Explain what a yield curve is and why expected short-term interest rates affect its shape.

LO4 Show why bonds exhibit interest rate risk and how interest rate risk affects the shape of the yield curve.

LO5 Explain why investors pay attention to bond ratings and demand a higher interest rate for bonds with low ratings.

Investment in a new plant and equipment requires money—often a lot of money. Sometimes firms may be able to generate enough cash from operations to cover the cost of investments, but often they need to raise cash from investors. In broad terms, we can think of two ways to raise new money from investors: borrow the cash or sell additional shares of common stock for cash.

There are many different ways a company can borrow money. Some of the factors determining type of debt a company uses include how long they need the money, amount of money needed, the size of the company, and the riskiness of its business. If a company needs the money for only a short while, they may borrow it from a bank by

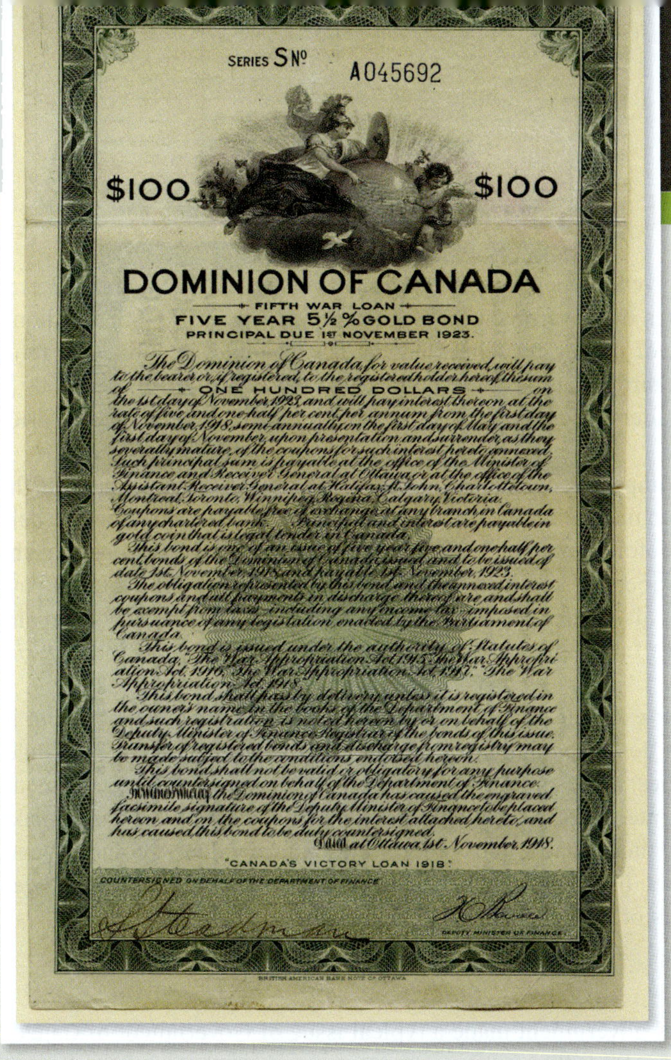

Bondholders used to receive beautifully engraved certificates like this one issued in 1918 by the Dominion of Canada. Today, bond ownership is simply recorded on an electronic database.

arranging a loan. Also, if the company is small and not needing a large amount of cash but making a long-term investment, a bank might be willing to make them a longer loan. If the company is bigger and they need it to make long-term investments, they can issue bonds, which are simply long-term loans sold to investors. When companies issue bonds, they promise to make a series of fixed interest payments and then to repay the debt. As long as the company generates sufficient cash, the payments on a bond are certain. In this case, bond valuation involves straightforward time-value-of-money computations. But there is some chance that even the most well-established, high-quality ("blue chip") company will fall on hard times and will not be able to repay its debts. Investors take this default risk into account when they price the bonds, requiring a higher rate to of return to compensate for default risk.

Companies are not the only bond issuers. Federal, provincial/state and local governments also raise money by selling bonds. There is always some risk that a company, federal government, province, or municipality will not be able to come up with the cash to repay its bonds. However, investors in federal government bonds can be more confident that the federal government will make the promised payments, because they collect tax revenues and can print money. Typically investors regard the risk of default on federal Canada bonds as negligible, and therefore these issues offer a lower rate of interest than corporate bonds. Nevertheless, the interest rates on government bonds provide a benchmark for all interest rates. When government interest rates go up or down, corporate rates follow more or less proportionally. In the first part of this chapter we focus on Canadian government bonds and sidestep the issue of default.

We begin by showing you how to understand the bond pages in the financial press, and we explain what bond dealers mean when they quote yields to maturity. We look at why short-term rates are usually lower (but sometimes higher) than long-term rates and why the longest-term bond prices are most sensitive to fluctuations in interest rates. We distinguish real (inflation-adjusted) interest rates and nominal (money) rates and explain how future inflation can affect interest rates.

Toward the end of the chapter, we look at corporate bonds, which carry a possibility of default. We look at how bond ratings provide a guide to that default risk and how low-grade bonds offer higher promised yields. We will see that corporate bonds are more complex securities than government bonds. Some corporate bonds give the borrower an option to repay early; others can be exchanged for the company's common stock. Such complications affect the "spread" of corporate bond rates over interest rates on government bonds of similar maturities. In Chapter 14 we will look in more detail at the securities that companies issue, and we will look further at some of these variations in bond design. In Chapter 20 we look at different types of short-term loans.

LO1 6.1 BONDS AND THE BOND MARKET

bond Security that obligates the issuer to make specified payments to the bondholder.

Governments and corporations borrow money by selling **bonds** to investors. The bond market is huge. In July 2010 public holdings of Government of Canada bonds was nearly $555 billion.[1] Companies also raise large sums of money by selling bonds. For example, in July 2010 Telus Corporation borrowed $1 billion through an issue of bonds. The market for all these bonds is sophisticated and active. Bond traders frequently make massive trades motivated by tiny price discrepancies.

coupon The interest payment paid to the bondholder.

face value Payment at the maturity of the bond. Also called *par value*, or *maturity value*.

The money governments or companies collect when bonds are issued is the amount of the debt. As borrowers, they promise to make a series of interest payments and then to repay the debt at the maturity date. Years ago, before computers, a typical bond had paper coupons that the investors (*bondholders*) had to clipped off and mail to the bond issuer to claim the interest payment. Thus the interest payment is also called the bond's **coupon**. At maturity, the debt is repaid, when the borrower pays the bond's **face value** (also called the *principal*, *par value*, or *maturity value*) to the bondholders.

Not all bonds are the same. For example, many bonds make a fixed coupon payment, but in other cases the coupon payment is flexible, going up or down as short-term interest rates change. Bonds also have different maturities. For example, the Telus bond has a fixed coupon payment, based on its 5.05 percent coupon rate, and the bond will mature in July 2020. Telus has to make coupon payments for 10 years and then it has to repay the $1 billion face value. A company may need to borrow for only a few years, but there have been a few occasions when bonds have been issued with maturities of 100 years or more.

BOND MARKET DATA

coupon rate Annual interest payment as a percentage of face value.

In June 2008 the Canadian federal government made a typical issue of Government of Canada bonds. It auctioned off to investors $2 billion of 3.5 percent coupon bonds maturing June 1, 2013 and paying interest semi-annually. Each bond has a face value of $1,000. Because the **coupon rate** is 3.5 percent, the government makes total annual coupon payments of 3.5 percent of $1,000, $0.035 \times \$1000 = \$35$ every year. However, the coupons are made in semi-annual instalments of $17.50 ($35/2). The first interest payment of $17.50 was paid on December 1, 2008 and the next one on June 1, 2009. When the bond matures on June 1, 2013, the government must pay the face value of the bond, $1,000, in addition to the final $17.50 coupon payment.

Prices for some government and corporate bonds are reported on the Web sites of major newspapers, such as the *National Post* and *The Globe and Mail*,[2] and are typically for the previous day's trading activity. To get bond price information for all traded Canadian bonds, you can subscribe to a financial data service, such as GlobeInvestor Gold (affiliated with *The Globe and Mail*), or use a bond dealer, such as TD Waterhouse. Table 6.1 shows prices for a small sample of Government of Canada bonds. The entry for the 3.5 percent Canada bonds maturing in June 2013 is bolded.

The prices are the closing prices for June 1, 2010, and are quoted as percentages of face value. For the 2013 3.5 percent bond, the *asked price*—that is, what investors need to pay to buy the bond—is shown as 103.9. This means that the price is 103.9 percent of the $1,000 face value. Therefore, each bond costs $1,039. An investor who already owns the bond and wishes to sell it would receive the *bid price*, which is shown as 103.86, which means $1,038.60. Just as the used-car dealer earns a living by reselling cars at higher prices than he paid for them, so the bond dealer needs to charge a *spread* between the bid and the asked price. The spread for

[1] This figure includes both Treasury bills (bonds maturing in 12 months or less) and bonds maturing in more than a year. Not included is non-traded government debt, such as Canada Savings Bonds.

[2] The Web sites for bond prices are **www.financialpost.com/markets/data/bonds-canadian.html** and **www.globeinvestor.com/servlet/Page/document/v5/data/bonds**.

TABLE 6.1
Sample of Government of Canada bond quotes for June 1, 2010.

Maturity	Coupon Rate	Bid Price	Ask Price	Bid Yield	Ask Yield
2011-06-01	6	104.8	104.82	1.14	1.12
2012-06-01	5.25	106.96	106.98	1.69	1.68
2013-06-01	**3.5**	**103.86**	**103.9**	**2.16**	**2.15**
2013-06-01	0	93.16	93.19	2.38	2.37
2015-06-01	0	86.9	86.94	2.83	2.82
2017-06-01	4	106.46	106.51	2.97	2.96
2018-06-01	4.25	108.16	108.21	3.09	3.08
2019-06-01	3.75	104.35	104.4	3.19	3.18
2020-06-01	3.5	101.8	101.85	3.29	3.28
2025-06-01	9	163.14	163.24	3.54	3.53
2027-06-01	8	154.63	154.73	3.65	3.65
2037-06-01	5	122.05	122.15	3.7	3.7
RRB: 2021-12-01	4.25	131.54	131.74	1.29	1.27
RRB: 2026-12-01	4.25	142.05	142.25	1.39	1.38

Source: GlobeInvestor Gold, "Markets," **www.globeinvestor.com/servlet/Page/document/v5/data/bonds**. Reprinted with permission of *The Globe and Mail*.

these 3.5 percent bonds is \$1,039 − \$1038.6 =\$0.4, or only about .038 percent of the bond's value. Don't you wish that used-car dealers charged such a tiny spread?

The next two columns, *Bid Yield* and *Ask Yield*, stand for *bid yield to maturity* and *ask yield to maturity*. The ask yield measures the rate of return that investors will receive if they buy the bond at the asked price and hold it to maturity in 2013. We will explain shortly how these figures are calculated.

Bonds are traded by a network of bond dealers, who quote bid and ask prices at which they are prepared to buy and sell. In the past, bonds were traded only in an *over-the-counter market*, in which securities are not traded in one central place but over the telephone. However, the development of electronic markets for bond trading, such as CBID (found at **www.pfin.ca**) and CanDeal (**www.candeal.ca**) are changing the operation of the Canadian bond market. Both CBID and CanDeal allow institutional investors, such as pension funds, who trade large dollar values of bonds, to see bond quotes from multiple bond dealers at the same time, rather than having to telephone each dealer for a quote. They can then execute a buy or sell order at the best price. The electronic bond trading platforms increase the competitiveness of the bond market, reducing the spread between the bid and the ask prices. The bond prices reported in newspapers and their Web sites are the prices at which bonds were traded among the dealers and institutional investors.

If you, as a retail investor, wanted to buy the Canada 3.5s of 2013, you would have to contact a bond dealer. Dealers hold inventories of bonds and are typically part of financial institutions such as banks and brokerage houses. For example, TD Waterhouse offers bonds to retail investors through its online brokerage service (**www.tdwaterhouse.ca**). At TD Waterhouse's Web site on August 6, 2010, the quoted ask price for buying the Canada 3.5s of 2013 was 105.372, which therefore was \$1,053.72 per bond. The quoted bid price for selling it was 104.352 percent, or \$1,043.52 per bond. The spread between the bid and ask prices is \$1,053.72 − \$1,043.52 = \$10.2, or about 1 percent of the bond's value. The spread for a retail investor is typically larger than the spread for an institutional investor, because the dollar value of a retail transaction is much smaller.

When you buy a bond, you pay more than the ask price if you do not happen to buy the bond on a coupon payment date. For the Canada 3.5s of 2013, the only days you actually pay the quoted price are June 1 and December 1. The reason is that the buyer has to compensate the seller for the coupon interest earned from the last coupon payment to the settlement date, the date when the buyer must pay the money for the bond. The settlement date for bond is typically three days after the bond deal is executed. This extra payment is called *accrued interest*, and is calculated as

$$\text{Accrued interest} = \text{coupon payment} \times \frac{\text{number of days from last coupon to settlement date}}{\text{number of days in coupon period}} \tag{6.1}$$

accrued interest Coupon interest earned from the last coupon payment to the purchase date of the bond.

clean bond price Bond price excluding accrued interest.

dirty bond price Bond price including accrued interest.

Bond prices are typically quoted without the **accrued interest** and are known as **clean prices**. When the accrued interest is included, the price is referred to as the **dirty price**.

All of the bond prices at TD Waterhouse are clean. So what would be the dirty price for the purchase of a Canada 3.5 of 2013 bond on August 6, 2010? The settlement date, when you have to pay for the bond, would be August 10, 2010. The coupon period is from June 1, 2010, when the last coupon was paid, to December 1, 2010, when the next coupon will be paid, a total of 183 days. The number of days from the last coupon payment to the settlement date is 70 (29 days from June 1 to June 30, 31 days in July, and 10 days in August). So the accrued interest is \$17.5 × 70/183 = \$6.69, making the total cost of buying one bond \$1,053.72 + \$6.69, or \$1,060.41.

Check Point 6.1

Find the Canada 4s of 2017 in Table 6.1.

a. How much does it cost an institutional investor to buy the bond?
b. If the investor already owned the bond, how much would a bond dealer pay for it?
c. What annual interest or coupon payment does the bond make?
d. What is the semi-annual interest payment and when will the payments be made?

LO2 6.2 INTEREST RATES AND BOND PRICES

How is the price of Canada 3.5s of 2013 determined? The value of the bond is the present value of the bond's cash flows. To find this value, you need to identify the bond's cash flows and then calculate the present value of the cash flows using a discount rate that captures the bond's opportunity cost of capital. To keep things simple, for now we will assume that coupon is paid annually. If you bought the bond on June 1, 2010 and plan to hold the bond to maturity, then you will receive the cash flows shown in Figure 6.1. For the first two years,

FIGURE 6.1 Cash flows to an investor in the 3.5 percent annual coupon bond, maturing in the year 2013.

the cash flows equal the 3.5 percent coupon payment, $\$35 = .035 \times \$1{,}000$. Then, when the bond matures in 2013, you receive the $1,000 face value of the bond plus the final coupon payment.

The 3.5s were not the only Canada bonds that matured on June 1, 2013. To select the discount rate for calculating the present value of the bond's cash flows, look for the current rate of interest on similar risk investments. Almost identical bonds maturing at the same time offered a rate of return of about 2.15 percent. So, if the Canada 3.5s of 2013 had offered a lower return than 2.15 percent, no one would have been willing to hold them. Equally, if they had offered a higher return, everyone would have rushed to sell their other bonds and buy the 3.5s. In other words, if investors were on their toes, the 3.5s had to offer the same 2.15 percent rate of interest as similar Canada bonds. You might recognize 2.15 percent as the opportunity cost of the funds invested in the bond, as we discussed in Chapter 2. This is the rate of return investors could earn by placing their funds in similar securities rather than in this bond. The opportunity cost of funds invested in a bond is called the interest rate, or the market interest rate, or the yield and is used as the discount rate in the calculation of the present value of the bond's cash flows.

We can now calculate the present value of 3.5s of 2013 by discounting the cash flows at 2.15 percent:

$$\begin{aligned} PV &= \frac{\$35}{(1+r)} + \frac{\$35}{(1+r)^2} + \frac{\$1{,}035}{(1+r)^3} \\ &= \frac{\$35}{(1.0215)} + \frac{\$35}{(1.0215)^2} + \frac{\$1{,}035}{(1.0215)^3} = \$1{,}038.82 \end{aligned}$$

Bond prices are usually expressed as a percentage of their face value. Thus we can say that our 3.5 percent Canada bond is worth 103.882 percent of face value, and its price would usually be quoted as 103.882.[3]

Did you notice that your bond is like a package of two investments? The first provides a level stream of coupon payments of $35 a year for each of 3 years. The second consists of the final repayment of the $1,000 face value. Therefore, you can use the annunity formula to value the coupon payments and then add on the present value of the final payment of face value:

$$\begin{aligned} \textbf{PV(bond)} &= \textbf{PV(coupons)} + \textbf{PV(face value)} \\ &= \textbf{(coupon} \times \textbf{annuity factor)} + \textbf{(face value} \times \textbf{discount factor)} \\ &= \$35 \times \left[\frac{1}{.0215} - \frac{1}{.0215(1.0215)^3}\right] + 1{,}000 \times \frac{1}{1.0215^3} \qquad (6.2) \\ &= \$100.64 + \$938.18 = \$1{,}038.82 \end{aligned}$$

If you need to value a bond with many years to run before maturity, it is usually easiest to value the coupon payments as an annuity and then add on the present value of the final payment.

Check Point 6.2

Calculate the present value of a 6-year bond with a 9 percent coupon. The discount rate is 5 percent.

[3] The asked price of the bond shown in Table 6.1 is 103.9 percent ($1,039), which is slightly higher than our calculation. The bond's actual coupon is not $35 per year, but $17.50 every six months. In the next example, we'll show how to handle semi-annual coupons.

EXAMPLE 6.1 BOND PRICES AND SEMI-ANNUAL COUPON PAYMENTS

Thus far we've assumed that coupon payments occur annually. But most bonds make coupon payments *semi-annually*. So when you hear that a bond in Canada has a coupon rate of 3.5 percent, you can generally assume that the bond makes a payment of $35/2 = $17.50 every six months. Similarly, when investors in Canada refer to the bond's interest rate, they usually mean the *semi-annually compounded interest rate*. Thus an interest rate quoted at 2.15 percent really means that the 6-month rate is 2.15/2 = 1.075 percent.[4]

FIGURE 6.2
Cash flows to an investor in the 3.5 percent coupon bond, maturing in 2013. The bond pays semi-annual coupons, so there are two payments of $17.50 each year.

The actual cash flows on the Canada bond are illustrated in Figure 6.2. To value the bond more precisely, we should have discounted the series of semi-annual payments by the semi-annual rate of interest as follows:

$$PV = \frac{\$17.5}{(1.01075)} + \frac{\$17.50}{(1.01075)^2} + \frac{\$17.50}{(1.01075)^3} + \frac{\$17.50}{(1.01075)^4} + \frac{\$17.50}{(1.01075)^5} + \frac{\$1{,}017.50}{(1.01075)^6}$$
$$= \$1{,}039.02$$

This is slightly higher than the value of $1,038.82 we obtained when we treated the coupon payments as annual rather than semi-annual,[5] and equals the bond's asked price in Table 6.1. Since semi-annual coupon payments just add to the arithmetic, we will often stick to our simplification and assume annual interest payments.

HOW BOND PRICES VARY WITH INTEREST RATES

Figure 6.3 plots the average interest rates on Government of Canada bonds maturing in 10 or more years, calculated each week from 1957 to 2010. Notice how much the interest rate fluctuates. In 1957 these bonds offered about 4 percent rate of interest. By September 1981 the

[4] You may have noticed that the semi-annually compounded interest rate is also the bond's APR, annual percentage rate, although the APR term is generally not used by bond investors. To find the effective annual rate, we can use a formula we presented in Section 5.6:

$$\text{Effective annual rate} = \left(1 + \frac{\text{APR}}{m}\right)^m - 1$$

where m is the number of payments each year. In the case of our Canada bond,

$$\text{Effective annual rate} = \left(1 + \frac{.0215}{2}\right)^2 - 1 = (1.01075)^2 - 1 = .02162, \text{ or } 2.162\%$$

[5] Why is the present value a bit higher in this case? Because now we recognize that half the annual coupon payment is received six months into the year, rather than at year-end. Because part of the coupon income is received earlier, its present value is higher.

FIGURE 6.3
The average weekly interest rate on Government Canada bonds maturing in 10 or more years.

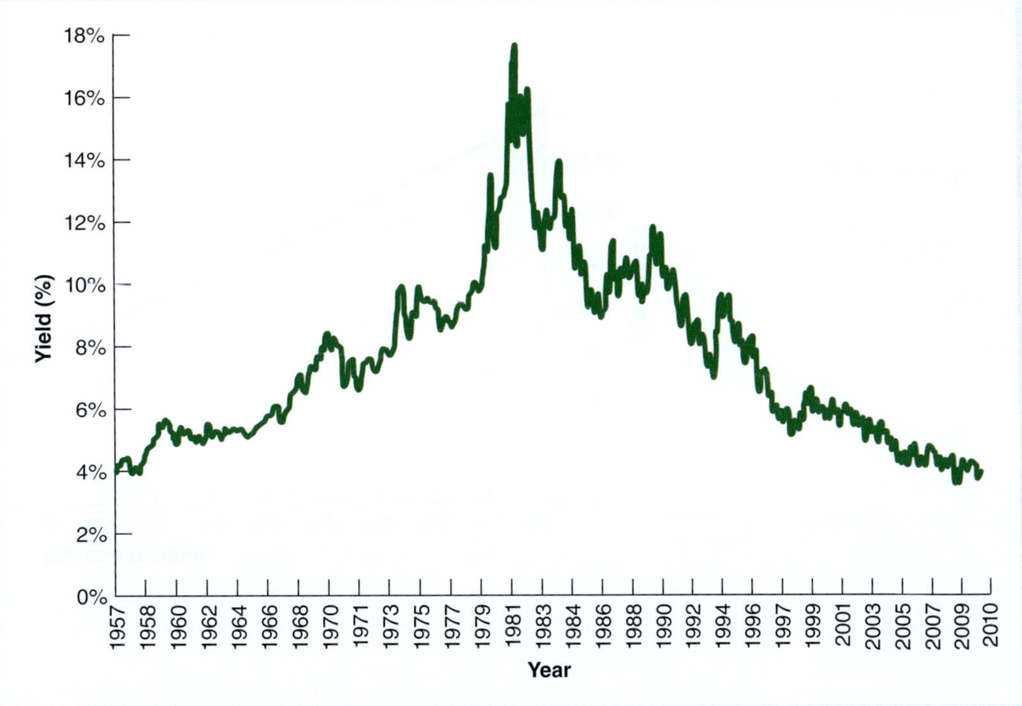

Source: Statistics Canada CANSIM database, Series V121758.

This is a key bond pricing rule. When the market interest rate exceeds the coupon rate, bonds sell for less than face value. When the market interest rate is below the coupon rate, bonds sell for more than face value. When the market rate of interest equals the coupon rate, the bond sells at face value.

interest rate on bonds maturing in 10 plus years had jumped to nearly 18 percent but had fallen to 3.5 percent by the end of 2010.

As interest rates change, so do bond prices. For example, suppose that investors demanded an interest rate of 3.5 percent on 3-year government bonds. What would be the price of the Canada 3.5s of 2013, paying annual coupons? Recalculate Equation 6.2 with a discount rate of $r = .035$:

$$\text{PV at 3.5\%} = \frac{\$35}{(1.035)} + \frac{\$35}{(1.035)^2} + \frac{\$1{,}035}{(1.035)^3} = \$1{,}000$$

Thus when the discount rate is the same as the coupon rate (3.5 percent in our example), the bond sells for its face value.

We first valued the Canada bond with an interest rate (discount rate) of 2.15 percent, which is lower than the 3.5 percent coupon rate. In that case the price of the bond was *higher* than its face value. We then valued it using an interest rate that is equal to the coupon rate and found that bond price equalled face value. You have probably already guessed that when the cash flows are discounted at a rate that is *higher* than the bond's coupon rate, the bond is worth *less* than its face value. The following example confirms that this is the case.

EXAMPLE 6.2 BOND PRICES AND INTEREST RATES

Investors will pay $1,000 for a 3.5 percent annual coupon, 3-year Canada bond, when the interest rate is 3.5 percent. Suppose that the interest rate is higher than the coupon rate at, say, 6 percent. Now what is the value of the bond? Simple! We just repeat our initial calculation but with $r = .06$:

$$\text{PV at 6\%} = \frac{\$35}{(1.06)} + \frac{\$35}{(1.06)^2} + \frac{\$1{,}035}{(1.06)^3} = \$933.17$$

The bond sells for 93.317 percent of face value.

FIGURE 6.4
The value of the 3-year, 3.5 percent annual coupon bond falls as interest rates rise.

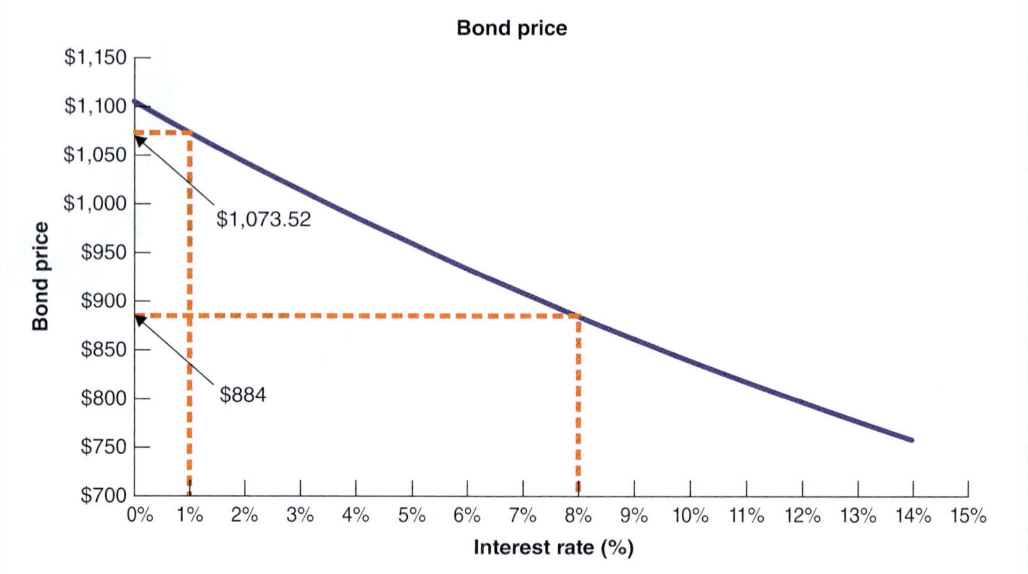

When market interest rate rises, the present value of the payments to be received by the bondholder falls, and bond prices fall. Conversely, declines in the interest rate increase the present value of those payments and result in higher bond prices.

Suppose market interest rates rise. On hearing the news, bond investors appear sad. Why? Don't they like higher interest rates? If you are not sure of the answer, look at Figure 6.4, which shows the present value of the 3.5 percent annual coupon, 3-year Canada bond for different interest rates (discount rates). For example, imagine the interest rate soars from 2.15 to 8 percent. The price of the Canada 3.5s of 2013 would fall from $1,039 to $884.03, creating a loss to bondholders of almost 15 percent. Conversely, bondholders have reason to celebrate when market interest rates fall. You can see this also by looking at Figure 6.4. For instance, if interest rates fall to 1 percent, the value of the 3.5 percent bond would increase to $1,073.52.

Figure 6.4 illustrates a fundamental relationship between interest rates and bond prices: When market interest rate rises, the present value of the payments to be received by the bondholder falls, and bond prices fall. Conversely, declines in the interest rate increase the present value of those payments and result in higher bond prices.

A warning! People sometimes confuse the interest (coupon) *payment* on the bond with the *interest rate*—that is, the return that investors require. The $35 coupon payments on our Canada bond are fixed when the bond is issued. The coupon rate, 3.5 percent, measures the coupon payment ($35) as a percentage of the bond's face value ($1,000) and is therefore also fixed. However, the market interest rate changes from day to day. These changes affect the *present value* of the coupon payments but not the payments themselves. As we will see in the next two sections, changes in the market interest rate causes changes the bond prices and that changes the rate of return earned on the bond.

6.3 CURRENT YIELD AND YIELD TO MATURITY

Suppose you are considering the purchase of a 3-year bond with a coupon rate of 10 percent, paying coupons annually. Your investment advisor quotes a price for the bond. How do you calculate the rate of return the bond offers?

current yield Annual coupon payment divided by current bond price.

premium bond Bond that sells for more than its face value.

discount bond Bond that sells for less than its face value.

yield to maturity Interest rate for which the present value of the bond's payments equals the price.

For bonds priced at face value the answer is easy. The rate of return is the coupon rate. We can check this by setting out the cash flows on your investment:

	Cash Paid to You in Year:			
You Pay:	**1**	**2**	**3**	**Rate of Return**
$1,000	$100	$100	$1,100	10%

Notice that in each year you earn 10 percent on your money ($100/$1,000). In the final year you also get back your original investment of $1,000. Therefore, your total return is 10 percent, the same as the coupon rate.

Now suppose that the market price of the 3-year bond is $1,136.16. Your cash flows are as follows:

	Cash Paid to You in Year:			
You Pay:	**1**	**2**	**3**	**Rate of Return**
$1,136.16	$100	$100	$1,100	?

Because it focuses only on current income and ignores prospective price increases or decreases, the *current* yield does not measure the bond's total rate of return. It overstates the return of premium bonds and understates the return of discount bonds.

What's the rate of return now? Notice that you are paying out $1,136.16 and receiving an annual income of $100. So your income as a proportion of the initial outlay is $100/$1,136.16 = 088, or 8.8 percent. This is sometimes called the bond's **current yield**.

However, total return depends on both interest income and any capital gains or losses. A current yield of 8.8 percent may sound attractive, only until you realize that the bond's price must fall. The price today is $1,136.16, but when the bond matures three years from now, the bond will sell for its face value, or $1,000. A price decline (that is, a *capital loss*) of $136.16 is guaranteed, so the overall return over the next three years must be less than the 8.8 percent current yield.

Let us generalize. A bond that is priced above its face value is said to sell at a *premium* and is called a **premium bond**. Investors who buy a bond at a premium face a capital loss over the life of the bond, so the return on these bonds is always *less* than the bond's current yield. A bond priced below face value sells at a *discount* and is called a **discount bond**. Investors in discount bonds face a capital gain over the life of the bond; the return on these bonds is *greater* than the current yield.

We need a measure of return that takes account of both current yield and the change in a bond's value over its life. The standard measure is called **yield to maturity**. The yield to maturity is the answer to the following question: At what interest rate would the bond be correctly priced?

The yield to maturity is defined as the discount rate that makes the present value of the bond's payments equal to its price.

If you can buy the three-year bond at face value, the yield to maturity is the coupon rate, 10 percent. We can confirm this by noting that when we discount the cash flows at 10 percent, the present value of the bond is equal to its $1,000 face value:

$$\text{PV at 10\%} = \frac{\$100}{(1.10)} + \frac{\$100}{(1.10)^2} + \frac{\$1{,}100}{(1.10)^3} = \$1{,}000$$

But if you have to buy the three-year bond for $1,136.16, the yield to maturity is only 5 percent. At that discount rate, the bond's present value equals its actual market price, $1,136.16:

$$\text{PV at 5\%} = \frac{\$100}{(1.05)} + \frac{\$100}{(1.05)^2} + \frac{\$1{,}100}{(1.05)^3} = \$1{,}136.16$$

EXAMPLE 6.3 CALCULATING YIELD TO MATURITY FOR THE CANADA BOND

We found the value of the 3.5 percent annual coupon Canada bond by discounting at a 2.15 percent interest rate. We could have phrased the question the other way around: If the price of the bond is $1,038.819, what return do investors expect? We need to find the yield to maturity, in other words, the discount rate *r* that solves the following equation:

$$\text{Price} = \frac{\$35}{(1+r)} + \frac{\$35}{(1+r)^2} + \frac{\$1{,}035}{(1+r)^3} = \$1{,}038.819$$

(Continued)

(Concluded)

To find the yield to maturity, most people use a financial calculator or a spreadsheet. For our Canada bond you would enter a PV of $1,038.819.[6] The bond provides a regular payment of $35, entered as PMT = 35. The bond has a future value of $1,000, so FV = 1,000. The bond life is three years, so $n = 3$. Now compute the interest rate, and you will find that the yield to maturity is 2.15 percent. The nearby Financial Calculator and Excel Spreadsheet boxes review the use of the financial calculator and spreadsheets in bond valuation problems.

The yield to maturity is a measure of a bond's total return, including both coupon income and capital gain. If an investor buys the bond today and holds it to maturity, his return will be the yield to maturity. Bond investors often refer loosely to a bond's "yield." It's a safe bet that they are talking about its yield to maturity rather than its current yield.

The only *general* procedure for calculating yield to maturity is trial and error. You guess an interest rate to use as the discount rate and calculate the present value of the bond's payments. If the present value is greater than the actual price, your discount rate must have been too low, so try a higher interest rate (since a higher rate results in a lower PV). Conversely, if PV is less than price, you must reduce the interest rate. In practice, investors use a financial calculator or a computer spreadsheet to do the trial and error for them. The nearby boxes provide examples.

EXAMPLE 6.4 YIELD TO MATURITY WITH SEMI-ANNUAL COUPON PAYMENTS

Let's redo Example 6.3, but this time assume the coupons are paid semi-annually. Instead of three annual coupons of $35, the bond makes six semi-annual payments of $17.50. We can find the *semi-annual* yield to maturity on our calculators by using these inputs: $n = 6$ (semi-annual) periods, PV = −1,038.819, FV = 1,000, PMT = 17.50. We then compute the interest rate to find that it is 1.0784 percent. This of course is a six-month, not an annual, rate. Bond dealers typically annualize the semi-annual rate by doubling it, so the yield to maturity would be quoted as $1.0784 \times 2 = 2.1568$ percent, which rounds to 2.157 percent. In Excel (see nearby Excel Spreadsheet box), you can confirm that =YIELD(DATE(2010,6,1),DATE(2013,6,1),.035,103.88,100,2) = .02157. A better way to annualize would be to account for compound interest. A dollar invested at 1.0784 percent for two 6-month periods would grow to $\$1 \times (1.010784)^2 = \$1.02168$. The *effective* annual yield is therefore 2.168 percent.

Check Point 6.3

A 4-year maturity bond with a 14 percent coupon rate can be bought for $1,200. What is the yield to maturity if the coupon is paid annually? What if it is paid semi-annually? You will need a spreadsheet or a financial calculator to answer this question.

6.4 BOND RATES OF RETURN

The yield to maturity is defined as the discount rate that equates the bond's current price to the present value of all its promised future cash flows. It measures the rate of return that you will earn if you buy the bond today and hold it to maturity. However, as interest rates fluctuate, the return that you earn in the interim may be very different from the yield to maturity. If interest

---

[6] Actually, on most calculators you would enter 1,038.819 as a negative number, (−1038.819), because the purchase of the bond represents a cash *outflow*.

financial calculator

Bond Valuation Using a Financial Calculator

In Chapter 5 we saw that financial calculators can compute the present values of level annuities as well as the present values of one-time future cash flows. Coupon bonds present both of these characteristics: The coupon payments are level annuities and the final payment of face value is an additional one-time payment. Thus for the coupon bond we looked at in Example 6.3, you would treat the periodic payment as PMT = \$35, the final or future one-time payment as FV = \$1,000, the number of periods as $n = 3$ years, and the interest rate as the yield to maturity of the bond, $i = 2.15$ percent. You would thus compute the value of the bond using the following sequence of key strokes. By the way, the order in which the various inputs for the bond valuation problem are entered does not matter.

Hewlett-Packard HP-10B	Sharp EL-738C	Texas Instruments BA II Plus
35 PMT	35 PMT	35 PMT
1000 FV	1000 FV	1000 FV
3 N	3 N	3 N
2.15 I/YR	2.15 I/Y	2.15 I/Y
PV	COMP PV	CPT PV

Your calculator should now display a value of −1,038.81895, which rounds to −1,038.819. The minus sign reminds us that the initial cash flow is negative: You have to pay to buy the bond.

You can also use the calculator to find the yield to maturity of a bond. For example, if you buy this bond for \$1,038.819, you should find that its yield to maturity is 2.15 percent. Let's check that this is so. You enter the PV as \$1,038.81895 because you buy the bond for this price. Thus to solve for the interest rate, use the following keystrokes:

Hewlett-Packard HP-10B	Sharp EL-738C	Texas Instruments BA II Plus
35 PMT	35 PMT	35 PMT
1000 FV	1000 FV	1000 FV
3 N	3 N	3 N
−1038.819 PV	−1038.819 PV	−1038.819 PV
I/YR	COMP I/Y	CPT I/Y

Your calculator should now display 2.14999 percent, which rounds to 2.15 percent, the yield to maturity of the bond.

rates rise in a particular week, month, or year, the price of your bond will fall and your return for that period will be reduced. Conversely, if rates fall, the price of your bond will rise and your return will be increased. Since bond prices change when interest rates change, bonds are said to be subject to interest rate risk. Now we will look at how to calculate the rate of return earned on a bond investment.

Suppose on February 1, 2010, you bought a 5-year, 5.5 percent annual coupon Canada bond, maturing in February 1, 2015, for \$1,114.49. At the time the bond's yield to maturity was 3 percent. On February 1, 2011 you sell the bond for \$1,133.27. The return on your investment is the \$55 annual coupon payment, received February 1, 2011, plus the price change of (\$1,133.27 − \$1,114.49) = \$18.78. The one-year **rate of return** on your investment of \$1,114.49 is

rate of return Total income per period per dollar invested.

$$\text{Rate of return} = \frac{\text{coupon income} + \text{price change}}{\text{investment}} = \frac{18.78 + 55}{1{,}114.49} = .0662, \text{ or } 6.62\% \tag{6.3}$$

When you bought the bond, it was priced such that its yield to maturity was 5.5 percent but the 6.62 percent rate of return you earned over the year is higher than the original yield to maturity.

Check Point 6.4

Suppose that in June 1, 2010 you purchased the 4s of 2013 for \$1,053.20, when they were yielding 2.15 percent. The bonds pay annual coupons. Twelve months later, the bond's yield to maturity had fallen to 1.5 percent. Confirm that the rate of return on your bond would have been greater than the 2.15 percent yield to maturity.

excel spreadsheet

Bond Valuation

	A	B	C	D	E	F
1						
2		**Valuing Bonds Using a Spreadsheet**				
3						
4		**3.5% Coupon**		**6% Coupon 10-Year**		
5		**Maturing June 2013**		**Maturity**		
6						
7	Settlement date	6/1/2010		1/1/2000		
8	Maturity date	6/1/2013		1/1/2010		
9	Annual coupon rate	0.035		0.06		
10	Yield to maturity	0.0215		0.07		
11	Redemption value (% of face value)	100		100		
12	Coupon payments per year	1		1		
13						
14	**Bond price (% of par)**	**103.882**		**92.976**		
15						
16						
17		The formula entered here is: =PRICE(B7,B8,B9,B10,B11,B12)				

Excel and most other spreadsheet programs provide built-in functions to compute bond values and yields. They typically ask you to input both the date you pay for the bond (called the *settlement date*) and the maturity date of the bond.

The Excel function for bond value is

=PRICE(*settlement date, maturity date, annual coupon rate, yield to maturity, final payment, number of coupon payments per year*)

For our 3.5 percent coupon bond, we would enter the values in column B of the spreadsheet above. Alternatively, we could simply enter the following function in Excel:

=PRICE(DATE(2010,06,01),DATE(2013,06,01),.035,.0215,100,1).

The DATE function in Excel, which we use for both the settlement and maturity date, uses the format DATE(*year, month, day*).

Notice that the coupon rate and yield to maturity are expressed as decimals, not percentages. In most cases, final payment will be 100 (that is, 100 percent of face value), and the resulting price will be expressed as a percentage of face value. Occasionally, however, you may encounter bonds that pay off at a premium or discount to face value. One example would be callable bonds, discussed at the end of the chapter.

The value of the bond, assuming annual coupon payments, is 103.882 percent of face value, or $1,038.82. If we wanted to assume semi-annual coupon payments, we would simply change the entry in cell B12 to 2, and the bond value would change to 103.902 percent of face value, as we found in Example 6.1.

In this example, we assume that the first coupon payment comes in exactly one period (either a year or a half-year). In other words, the settlement date is precisely at the beginning of the period. However, the PRICE function will make the necessary adjustments for intraperiod purchase dates.

Suppose now that you wish to find the price of a 10-year maturity bond with a coupon rate of 6 percent (paid annually), selling

When interest rates do not change, the bond price changes with time so that the total return on the bond is equal to the yield to maturity. If the bond's yield to maturity increases, the rate of return during the period will be less than that yield. If the yield decreases, the rate of return will be greater than the yield.

Is there *any* connection between yield to maturity and the rate of return during a particular period? Yes: If the bond's yield to maturity remains unchanged during an investment period, its rate of return will equal that yield. We can check this by assuming that the yield on that 5.5 percent Canada bonds stays at 3 percent. If investors still demand an interest rate of 3 percent as of February 1, 2011, when the bond's maturity is 4 years, the value of the bond will be

$$PV = \frac{\$55}{(1.03)} + \frac{\$55}{(1.03)^2} + \frac{\$55}{(1.03)^3} + \frac{\$1,055}{(1.03)^4} = \$1,092.93$$

At the end of the year you receive a coupon payment of $55 and have a bond worth $1,092.93, somewhat less than you paid for it. Your total profit is $55 + ($1,092.93 − $1,114.49) = $33.44. The return on your investment is therefore $33.44/$1,114.49 = .03, or 3 percent, just equal to the yield to maturity.

	A	B	C	D	E	F	G
1							
2							
3			**Finding Yield to Maturity Using a Spreadsheet**				
4		**June 1, 2013 Maturity Bond, Coupon Rate = 3.5%, Maturity = 3 Years**					
5		**Annual Coupons**		**Semi-annual Coupons**			
6							
7	Settlement date	6/1/2010		6/1/2010			
8	Maturity date	6/1/2013		6/1/2013			
9	Annual coupon rate	0.035		0.035			
10	Bond price	103.882		103.882			
11	Redemption value (% of face value)	100		100			
12	Coupon payments per year	1		2			
13							
14	**Yield to maturity (decimal)**	**0.02150**		**0.02157**			
15							
16							
17		The formula entered here is: =YIELD(B7,B8,B9,B10,B11,B12)					

at a yield to maturity of 7 percent. You are not given a specific settlement or maturity date. You can still use the PRICE function to value the bond. Simply choose an arbitrary settlement date (January 1, 2000 is convenient) and let the maturity date be 10 years hence. The appropriate inputs appear in column D of the spreadsheet on the previous page, with the resulting price, 92.976 percent of face value, appearing in cell D14. You can confirm this value on your calculator using the inputs: $n = 10$, $i = 7$, FV = 1000, PMT = 60.

Excel also provides a function for yield to maturity. It is

= YIELD(*settlement date, maturity date, annual coupon rate, bond price, final payment as percentage of face value, number of coupon payments per year*)

For example, to find the yield to maturity in Example 6.3, we would use column B in the spreadsheet below. If the coupons were paid semi-annually, as in Example 6.4, we would change the entry for payments per year to 2 (see cell D12), and the yield would increase from 2.150 percent to 2.157 percent.

Spreadsheet Questions

6.1 Suppose the yield to maturity on the 3.5 percent annual coupon June 1, 2013 bond increases from 2.15 to 2.5 percent (assume annual coupon payments). What will happen to the bond's price? What is the percentage change in price?

6.2 Now assume the 3.5 percent annual bond matures June 1, 2023. What is the price at an initial yield to maturity of 2.15 percent and the higher yield of 2.5 percent? What is the percentage change in price? Is the price of the longer-maturity bond more or less sensitive to changes in yields than that of the shorter-maturity bond?

6.3 If the price of the 3.5 percent annual coupon June 1, 2013 bond decreases from 103.882 to 102, what happens to its yield to maturity?

Check Point 6.5

Suppose on June 1, 2011, you buy one of the 4s of 2013, for $1,048.90, and hold it for another year, until June 1, 2012. At the end of that time, it has only one more year to maturity. Show that if the bond's yield to maturity as of June 1, 2012, is the same as the yield to maturity as of June 1, 2011, your rate of return will equal the bond's yield to maturity.

The solid curve in Figure 6.5 plots the price of a 30-year maturity, 6 percent Canada bond over time assuming that its yield to maturity remains at 4 percent. The price declines gradually until the maturity date, when it finally reaches face value. In each period, the price decline offsets the coupon income by just enough to reduce total return to 4 percent. The dotted curve in

FIGURE 6.5
Bond prices over time, assuming an unchanged yield to maturity. Prices of both premium and discount bonds approach face value as their maturity date approaches.

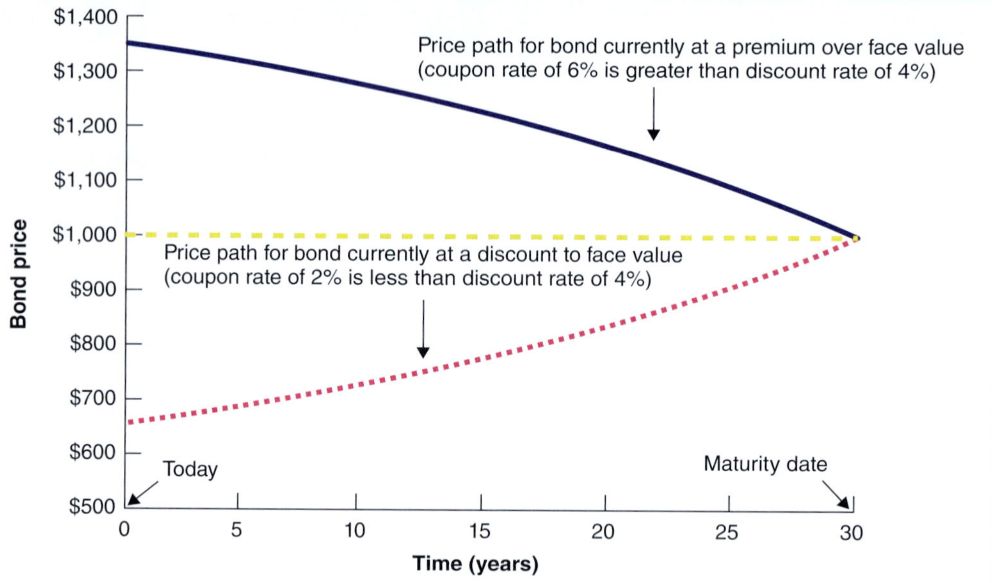

Figure 6.5 shows the corresponding price path for a 30-year maturity, 2 percent coupon Canada bond, also assuming its yield to maturity remains at 4 percent. This low-coupon bond currently sells at a discount to face value. The coupon income provides less than a competitive rate of return, so the bond sells below par. Its price gradually approaches face value, however, and the price gain each year brings its total return up to the market interest rate of 4 percent.

TAXES AND RATES OF RETURN

Taxes reduce the rate of return on an investment. If you bought a 5.5 percent annual coupon bond for $1,024.69 and sold it 1 year later for $1,067.95 the *before-tax* rate of return on your 1-year investment is 9.59 percent, [$55 + ($1,067.95 − $1,024.69)]/$1,024.69. However, as we discussed in Chapter 3, interest income is fully taxable, and 50 percent of capital gains are taxable. To calculate the after-tax rate of return on the investment, convert the cash flows to their after-tax values by subtracting the relevant taxes. If your personal tax rate is 35 percent, the tax on the coupon income of $55 is

$$\text{Tax on coupon income} = \text{personal tax rate} \times \text{coupon income}$$
$$= .35 \times \$55 = \$19.25$$

After taxes, the coupon income is

$$\text{After-tax coupon income} = \text{coupon income} - \text{tax on coupon income}$$
$$= \$55 - \$19.25 = \$35.75$$

The tax on the capital gain is

$$\text{Tax on capital gain} = \text{personal tax rate} \times .5 \times \text{capital gain}$$
$$= .35 \times .5 \times (\$1{,}067.95 - \$1{,}024.69) = \$7.57$$

The after-tax capital gain is

$$\text{After-tax capital gain} = \text{capital gain} - \text{tax on capital gain}$$
$$= (\$1{,}067.95 - \$1{,}024.69) - \$7.57 = \$35.69$$

Your after-tax rate of return is therefore

$$\text{After-tax rate of return} = \frac{\text{after-tax coupon income} + \text{after-tax capital gain}}{\text{investment}}$$

$$= \frac{\$35.75 + \$35.69}{\$1{,}024.69} = .0697, \text{ or } 6.97\%$$

As you can see, taxes have a material effect on the rate of return on your investment! Here, the 9.59 percent before-tax rate of return is only 6.97 percent once you consider the taxes you must pay on your investment income.

Check Point 6.6

Suppose you bought an 8 percent coupon bond for $1,200 and sold it 1 year later for $1,215. Calculate the before-tax and after-tax rate of return on your investment, if your personal tax rate is 40 percent.

MULTIPERIOD RATES OF RETURN

In our examples we have considered only one-year investments. How do you calculate the rate of return if the investment lasts longer than one year? Suppose you buy a 5.5 percent coupon bond for $1,024.69 and sell it in two years for $1,015.5. You receive cash flows at two different points in time: a $55 coupon payment after one year, and then another $55 coupon plus the cash from selling the bond after two years. If you ignore the fact that you received the first $55 early, you can add up all the coupon payments and calculate the rate of return like we did above. This method understates your rate of return—you ignored the value of investing the first coupon during the time of the bond investment. The standard approach to calculating the rate of return is to assume that the first coupon is reinvested for the remaining life of the investment. In other words, calculate the future value of that first coupon payment at the end of the second year.

Suppose when you received the first coupon payment you immediately invested at 4 percent for one year. That coupon payment will be worth $55 × 1.04, or $57.2, one year later. At the end of the two years, the total value of coupon income received is $57.2 + $55, or $112.2. The price change on the bond is a capital loss: $1,015.5 − $1,024.69, or −$9.19. Using Equation 6.3, the rate of return on the investment is

$$\text{Rate of return} = \frac{\text{coupon income} + \text{price change}}{\text{investment}}$$

$$= \frac{\$112.2 - \$9.19}{\$1{,}024.69} = .1005, \text{ or } 10.05\%$$

Did you notice that this is a *two-year* rate of return? Rates of return are normally reported on an annual basis so this two-year rate of return must be converted into its one-year equivalent. The effective annual equivalent is $(1.1005)^{1/2} - 1$, or 4.9 percent. Your *annual* rate of return is 4.9 percent.

How do you know the rate at which the intermediate coupon payments are invested? You can use the actual rates available at the time you received the coupons. Another approach is to use a variation on the yield-to-maturity calculation. Using this method, your rate of return is the discount rate that equates the purchase price to the present value of the coupons and the price you receive when you sell the bond. This assumes that all of the coupons are invested at that discount rate for the remaining time you own the bond. You can use this approach to calculate the after-tax rate of return too—just use the after-tax cash flows. We will see this approach to calculating rates of return again in Chapter 8, but there we will call it the *internal rate of return*.

EXAMPLE 6.5 **CALCULATING THE RATE OF RETURN ON A TWO-YEAR BOND INVESTMENT**

You buy a 5.5 percent bond for $1,024.69 and sell it 2 years later for $1,015.5. What is the annual rate of return on your investment if you use the yield-to-maturity approach? Using a calculator, enter PV = −$1,024.69, PMT = $55, FV = $1,015.5, and n = 2. Now compute the interest rate, which is your rate of return. You should get 4.93 percent.

LO3, LO4 6.5 THE YIELD CURVE

Look back at Table 6.1. The Canada bonds are arranged in order of their maturity. Notice that the longer the maturity, the slightly *higher* the yield. This is usually the case, although sometimes long-term bonds offer *lower* yields.

yield curve or **term structure of interest rates** Graph of the relationship between time to maturity and yield to maturity, for bonds that differ only in their maturity dates.

To properly assess the relationship between yield and years to maturity, known as the **yield curve** or the **term structure of interest rates**, it must be based on yields to maturity of bonds with the same coupon rate and same risk but different maturities. However, very few Canada bonds have the same coupon rate but different maturities. Fortunately, the Bank of Canada uses Canada bond price data to estimate yields to maturities assuming that the Canada bonds had zero coupons and provides the data on the Bank of Canada Web site.[7] Figure 6.6 plots the bond yields and maturities, using data provided on the Bank of Canada site. Each yield curve in the figure is a snapshot of yields for Canada bonds of different maturities and the same coupon on a specific

FIGURE 6.6
The yield curve. A plot of yield to maturity as a function of time to maturity for Government of Canada bills and bonds on various dates.

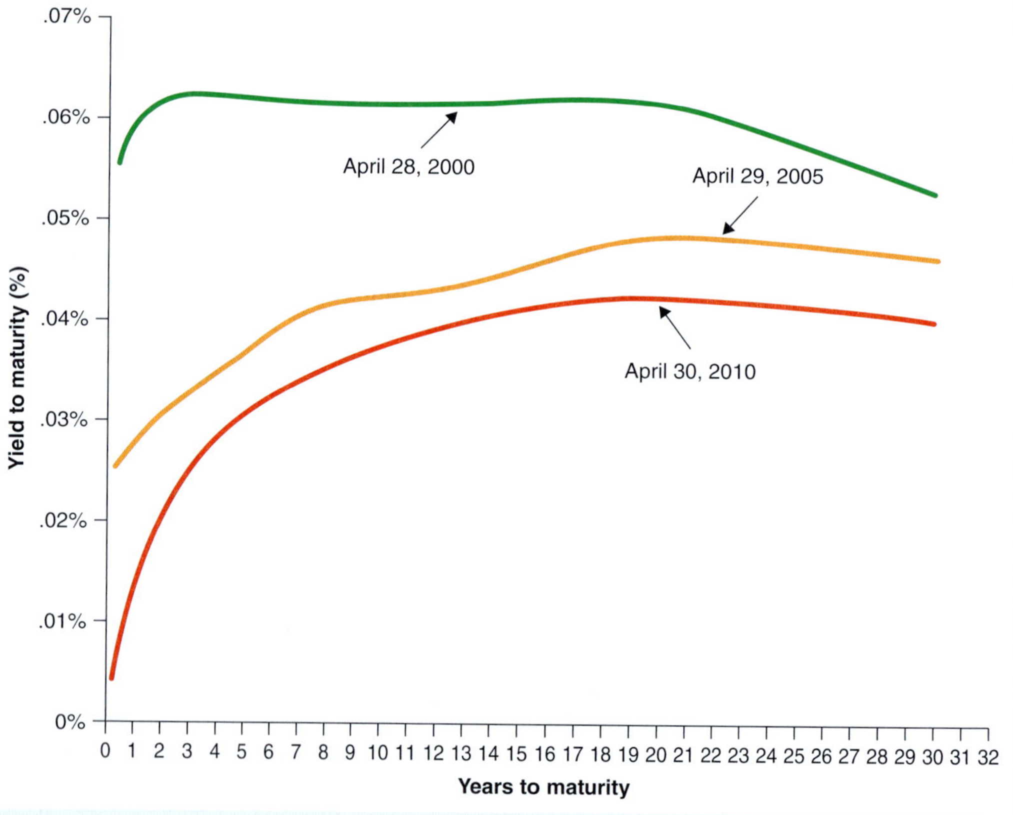

Source: Bank of Canada.

[7] "Yield Curves for Zero-Coupon Bonds," Bank of Canada site, **www.bankofcanada.ca/rates/interest-rates/bond-yield-curves**.

date. The yield curve for April 30, 2010, is the lowest line the graph. It shows that bonds with one year to maturity offered a yield of about 1 percent; those with 10 years to maturity offered 3.7 percent. Compare that curve to the yield curve for five years earlier, April 30, 2005, when one-year bonds were yielding 2.7 percent and 10-year bonds were yielding 4.2 percent. The yield curve for April 30, 2000, is higher than the other two, and the one-year bond yield was 5.9 percent and the 10-year Canada bond yield was 6.1 percent.

Figure 6.6 reveals two important characteristics of interest rates. First, the yields on bonds that differ only in their maturities are not the same. For example, on April 30, 2010, the 10-year bond was earning an extra 2.7 percentage points (= 3.7% − 1%) over the one-year bond. Second, the general level of interest rates changes over time. The April 30, 2010, one-year bond yield was 1.7 percentage points lower than in 2005 and 4.9 percentage points lower than in 2000.

Economists have long sought to explain changes in interest rates, and will continue seeking to explain them for years to come. For now, we can give you some general answers. We will first consider why the general level of interest rates changes over time, affecting the *level* of the yield curve, and then look at factors affecting the *shape* of the yield curve.

NOMINAL AND REAL RATES OF INTEREST

In Chapter 5 we drew a distinction between nominal and real rates of interest. The cash flows on the 3.5 percent Canada bonds are fixed in nominal terms. Investors are sure to receive interest payments of $35 each year, but they do not know what that money will buy them. The *real* interest rate on the bonds depends on the rate of inflation. For example, if the nominal rate of interest is 2.15 percent and the inflation rate is 1 percent, then the real interest rate is calculated as follows:

$$(1 + \text{real interest rate}) = \frac{1 + \text{nominal interest rate}}{1 + \text{inflation rate}} = \frac{1.0215}{1.01} = 1.01139$$

$$\text{Real interest rate} = .01139, \text{ or } 1.14\%$$

real return bond (RRB) Bond with variable nominal coupon payments, determined by a fixed real coupon payment and the inflation rate.

Since the inflation rate is uncertain, so is the real rate of interest on the Canada bonds.

You can nail down a real rate of interest by buying an indexed or **real return bond (RRB)**, whose payments are linked to inflation. The Government of Canada began issuing inflation-indexed or real return bonds, RRBs, in 1991. The real cash flows are fixed, but the nominal cash flows (coupon payments and principal) are increased as the consumer price index increases. For example, the 4.25 percent RRB due December 1, 2026, pays annual real coupons of $42.50. In Table 6.1, the prices and yields of two issues of Government of Canada real return bonds are at the bottom.

To see how the nominal coupon is calculated, suppose the Government of Canada issues a 3 percent, 2-year real return bond. The real cash flows are fixed but the nominal cash flows will depend on the actual increase in the consumer price index. Suppose inflation turns out to be 5 percent in year 1 and 4 percent in year 2. The real and nominal cash flows of the bonds would be:

	Year 1	Year 2
Real cash flows	$30	$1,030
Nominal cash flows	$30 × 1.05 = $31.50	$1,030 × 1.05 × 1.04 = $1,124.76

For the 4.25 percent RRB, the nominal value of each coupon is calculated when the coupon payment is due and reflects the inflation that has occurred since the issue of the bond. We won't know the nominal value of the principal until just before the bond matures in 2026.

In Table 6.1 we can see that the yield to maturity on the 4.25s of 2026 Canada RRBs was about 1.4 percent in June 2010. This yield is a real interest rate. It measures the amount of extra goods your investment will allow you to buy. Table 6.1 also shows that the yield to maturity on the 8s of 2027 Canada bonds was 3.65 percent. An estimate of the expected annual inflation rate used by market participants when discounting future cash flows can be found by rearranging the formula for the real interest rate:

$$(1 + \text{inflation rate}) = \frac{1 + \text{nominal interest rate}}{1 + \text{real interest rate}} = \frac{1.0365}{1.014} = 1.022$$

$$\text{Inflation rate} = .022, \text{ or } 2.2\%$$

If the annual inflation rate proves to be higher than 2.2 percent, you will earn a higher nominal return by holding RRBs; if the inflation rate is lower than 2.2 percent, the reverse will be true.

Inflation-indexed bonds have been issued by other governments and corporations. The United Kingdom has issued indexed bonds since 1982. The United States Treasury began to issue Treasury Inflation-Protected Securities, or TIPs, in 1997 and structured them similarly to the Government of Canada real return bonds. In 2000, 407 International Inc., owner of the largest electronic toll highway in Canada, just north of Toronto, sold real return bonds with a 5.29 percent real coupon rate, maturing in 2039.

What determines the real rate of interest demanded by investors? The classical economist Irving Fisher's answer is that real interest rates depend on the supply of savings and the demand for new investment.[8] As this supply-demand balance changes, real interest rates change. But they do so gradually.

According to Fisher, the nominal interest rate reflects both the real interest rate and the expected inflation. In other words, the nominal interest rate is determined by the real rate of interest and the expected inflation. This is known as the Fisher effect. More formally, the **Fisher effect** is

Fisher effect The nominal interest rate is determined by the real interest rate and the expected rate of inflation.

$$1 + \text{nominal interest rate} = (1 + \text{real interest rate}) \times (1 + \text{expected inflation rate}) \quad (6.4)$$

When inflation and the real interest rate are not high, a reasonable approximation to equation 6.4 is

$$\text{Nominal interest rate} = \text{real interest rate} + \text{expected inflation rate} \quad (6.5)$$

Suppose that investors upwardly revise their forecast of inflation by 1 percent. How will this affect interest rates? According to Fisher, if investors are concerned about the purchasing power of their money, the changed forecast should not affect the real rate of interest. The nominal interest rate must therefore rise by 1 percent to compensate investors for the higher inflation prospects.

How well does Fisher's theory of interest rates work? The gold line in Figure 6.7 shows that the real interest rate on the Government of Canada real return bonds has fluctuated within a relatively narrow range, between 1.4 percent and 5 percent since 1991. The blue line shows the nominal interest rate on ordinary long-term Government of Canada bonds. The nominal rate is more variable than the real rate, ranging between 3.5 percent and 9.5 percent since 1991.

Some economists disagree with Fisher's theory that inflation does not affect the real rate of interest. For example, if inflation causes companies to change their investment activities, the real interest rate will change. Looking at Figure 6.7 you can clearly see the impact of the steady decline in inflation during most of the 1990s. This caused nominal yields to fall but the real yield fell only slightly. In the 2000s, the real yield fell significantly and so did the nominal yield. Unfortunately, no one has yet sorted out the complex relationship between inflation and interest rates. However, a financial manager can use the Fisher effect as a valuable rule of thumb. If the expected inflation rate changes, it is a good bet that there will be a corresponding change in the nominal interest rate.

[8] See Irving Fisher's great book *The Theory of Interest: As Determined by Impatience to Spend Income and Opportunity to Invest It* (New York: August M. Kelley, 1965; orig. pub. 1930).

FIGURE 6.7
The bottom line shows the real yield on long-term Canada Real return bonds. The top line shows the yield on long-term Canada nominal bonds. Notice that the real yield has been much more stable than the nominal yield.

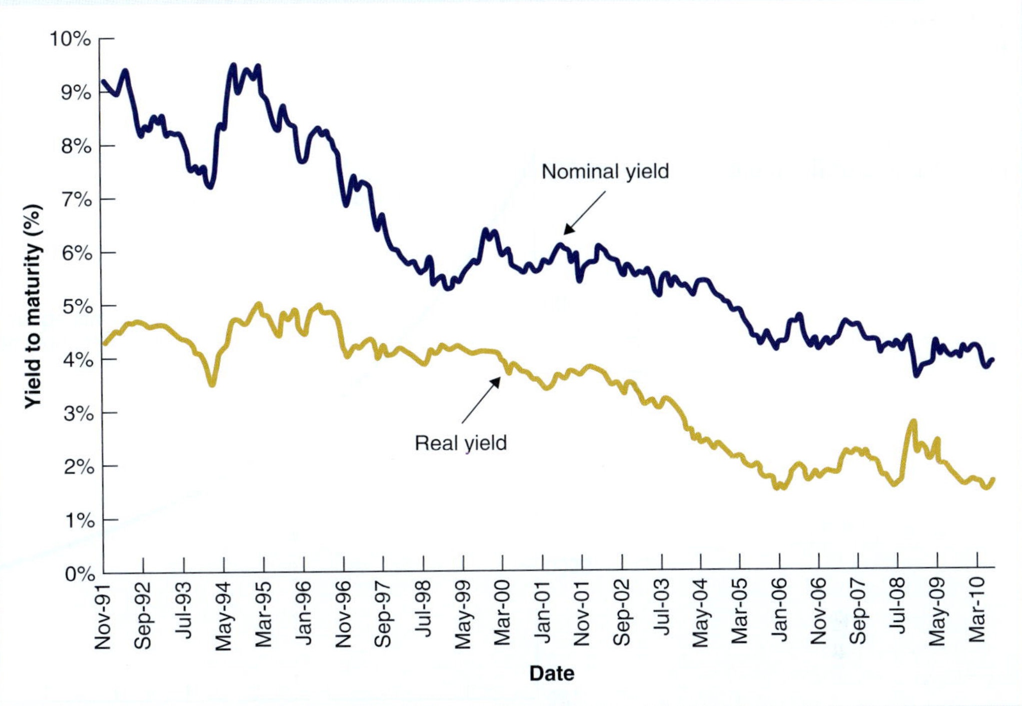

Source: Statistics Canada CANSIM database (**cansim2.statcan.ca**) series V122553 and V122544.

Check Point 6.7 Go back to Figure 6.6. Do you think the inflation rate in 2001 was higher or lower than the 2010 inflation rate? Explain your thinking.

THE DETERMINANTS OF THE YIELD CURVE

We have seen that the general level of interest rates is largely determined by the real interest rate and the expected rate of inflation. But why do long-term bonds offer different yields from short-term bonds? Generally the yield curve is upward-sloping. However, sometimes it is the other way around, with short rates higher than long rates. Sometimes the yield curve is flat or humped, with rising short-term yields followed by lower long-term yields.

EXPECTATIONS THEORY

A major factor determining the shape of the yield curve is expected future interest rates. To see why, consider the following example. Suppose you want to invest your money for two years. You might buy a one-year bond now. A year from now when the bond matures, you reinvest the proceeds in another one-year bond at whatever rate the bond market offers then. Alternatively, you might buy a two-year bond today. According to the expectations theory of interest rates, interest rates will adjust such that you don't care whether you invest in a two-year bond or in two successive one-year bonds. This means an upward-sloping yield curve tells you that investors expect short-term interest rates to rise. Likewise, a downward-sloping yield curve means that investors expect short-term rates to fall.

Why would future short-term interest rates be expected to be higher than today's current short-term rate? As we saw above, expected inflation is a key component of nominal interest rates. So, if investors expect inflation to increase, they will demand higher short-term rates in the future, which tends to result in an upward-sloping yield curve. Expected decreases in future inflation will tend to lead to a downward-sloping yield curve.

FIGURE 6.8
Plots of bond prices as a function of the interest rate. Long-term bond prices are more sensitive to the interest rate than prices of short-term bonds.

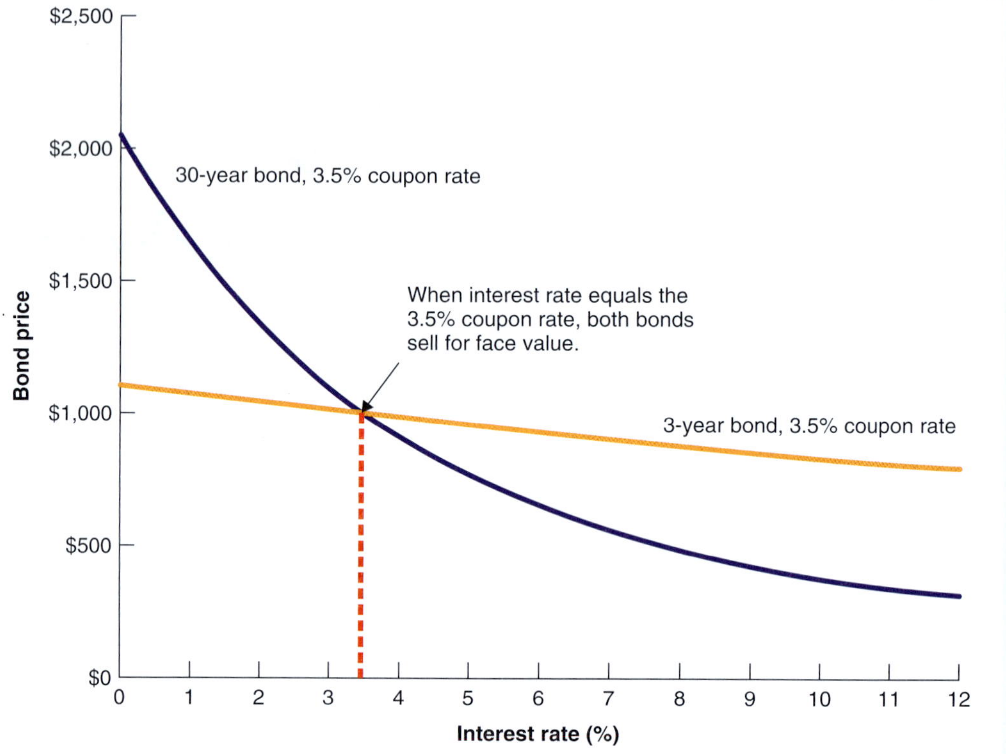

INTEREST RATE RISK AND THE LIQUIDITY PREMIUM

The expectations theory cannot provide a complete explanation of the yield curve, because it does not consider risk.

interest rate risk The risk in bond prices due to fluctuations in interest rates.

We have seen that bond prices fluctuate as interest rates change. In other words, bonds exhibit **interest rate risk**. Bond investors cross their fingers that market interest rates will fall, so that the price of their bond will rise. If they are unlucky and the market interest rate rises, the value of their investment falls.

But all bonds are not equally affected by changing interest rates. Compare the two curves in Figure 6.8. The orange line shows how the value of the 3-year, 3.5 percent coupon bond varies with the level of the interest rate. The blue line shows how the price of a 30-year, 3.5 percent bond varies with the level of interest rates. You can see that the 30-year bond is more sensitive to interest rate fluctuations than the 3-year bond. This should not surprise you. If you buy a three-year bond when the interest rate is 2.15 percent, and rates then rise, you will be stuck with a bad deal—you have just lent your money at a lower interest rate than if you had waited. However, think how much worse it would be if the loan had been for 30 years instead of 3. The longer the period of the loan, the more income you have lost by accepting what turns out to be a low interest rate. This shows that the price of the longer-term bond had a greater decline. Of course, there is a flip side to this effect, which you can also see from Figure 6.8. When interest rates fall, the longer-term bond responds with a greater increase in price.

Check Point 6.8

Suppose that the interest rate rises overnight from 2.15 percent to 5 percent. Calculate the present values of the 3.5 percent annual coupon 3-year bond and of the 3.5 percent annual coupon 30-year bond both before and after this change in interest rates. Confirm that your answers correspond with Figure 6.8. Use your financial calculator or a spreadsheet.

We saw in Figure 6.8 that a longer-term bond has greater interest risk than a short-term bond with the same coupon rate. If two bonds have the same maturity but unequal coupons, the bond with the lower coupon will have the greater interest rate risk. In Appendix 6B, available on the Online Learning Centre, we examine why coupon rates affect bonds' interest rate risk and introduce the important concept of *duration*, a method of measuring a bond's life. We show that bonds with longer duration also have greater interest rate risk.

If investors don't like price fluctuations, they invest their funds in short-term bonds unless they receive a higher yield to maturity on long-term bonds. This extra return has various names, including *liquidity premium*, *maturity risk premium*, and *interest rate risk premium*. According to this theory, known as the *liquidity preference theory*, the yield curve will tend to upward-sloping, because of the liquidity premium needed to induce investors to buy the riskier longer bonds.

The expectations theory and the liquidity preference theory together predict that the yield curve will tend to be upward-sloping, because of both increases in future inflation and the liquidity premium. A downward-sloping yield curve is still possible when future short-term interest rates are expected to fall. However, with the liquidity premium, the declining yield curve will be less steep. In Appendix 6A, at the end of this chapter, we provide a more detailed look at the expectations and liquidity-preference theories.

LO5 6.6 CORPORATE BONDS AND THE RISK OF DEFAULT

Our focus so far has been on Government of Canada bonds. But the federal government is not the only issuer of bonds. Provincial and municipal governments borrow by selling bonds. So do corporations. Canadian governments and corporations borrow in Canada and also borrow in the United States and other countries. So principals are repaid in Canadian dollars, U.S. dollars, and or another currency, such as the British pound or Japanese yen.

There is an important distinction between bonds issued by corporations and those issued by the Government of Canada and other federal governments. Typically, national governments don't go bankrupt if they can print more money or raise taxes. However, if they have borrowed money in a currency that they can't print, such as a foreign currency, and they have a financial crisis, they may not be able to repay the debt. Therefore, when a government borrows in a foreign currency, called *sovereign debt*, investors worry that in some future crisis the government may not be able to come up with enough of the foreign currency to repay the debt. This worry shows up in the yield that investors demand on such debt. For example, in the summer of 2002, concerns about a possible Brazilian default caused yields on the U.S.-dollar bonds issued by the Brazilian government to rise to 13 percentage points above the yields on comparable U.S. Treasury issues.

In Chapter 2 we discussed the fact that the recent financial crisis led governments to raise funds by borrowing. The subsequent recession has left many governments with mountains of debt. Several European countries, Portugal, Ireland, Italy, Greece, and Spain have had big debt problems, and this group has earned the unflattering name "PIIGS," derived from the here-named countries' initials. Although much of the PIIGS countries' borrowing is in euros, the governments cannot simply print more euros to service its debt. Although several of these countries debts were given support, there is still concern that some countries, especially Greece, will default and fail to pay interest and principal. As we write this, there are also concerns about possible U.S. government debt default. Investors currently do not worry that the Canadian government will default on its bonds.

There is always some chance that corporations may get into financial difficulties and may default on their bonds. Corporations have less control over their cash flow than do federal governments. Thus the payments promised to corporate bondholders represent a best-case scenario: the firm will never pay more than the promised cash flows, but in hard times it may pay less.

EXAMPLE 6.6 **PROMISED VERSUS EXPECTED YIELD TO MATURITY**

Bad Bet Inc. issued bonds several years ago with a coupon rate (paid annually) of 10 percent and face value of $1,000. The bonds are due to mature in six years. However, the firm is currently in bankruptcy proceedings, the firm has ceased to pay interest, and the bonds sell for only $200. Based on *promised* cash flow, the yield to maturity on the bond is 63.9 percent. (On your calculator, set PV = −200, FV = 1,000, PMT = 100, n = 6, and compute i.) But this calculation is based on the very unlikely possibility that the firm will resume paying interest and come out of bankruptcy. Suppose that the most likely outcome is that after three years of litigation, during which no interest will be paid, debtholders will receive $.27 on the dollar—that is, $270 for each bond with $1,000 face value. In this case the expected return on the bond is 10.5 percent. (On your calculator, set PV = −200, FV = 270, PMT = 0, n = 3, and compute i.) When default is a real possibility, the promised yield can depart considerably from the expected return. In this example, the default premium is greater than 50 percent.

VARIATIONS IN CORPORATE BONDS

Most corporate bonds are similar to the 3.5 percent Canada bonds we examined earlier in the chapter. In other words, they promise to make a fixed nominal coupon payment for each year until maturity, at which point they also promise to repay the face value. However, you will find that there is greater variety in the design of corporate bonds. We will return to this issue in Chapter 14, but here are a few types of corporate bonds that you may encounter. In the nearby Finance in Action box is an example of a Maple bond, a standard Canadian corporate bond with a twist: the issuer is not in Canada.

Zero-Coupon Bonds. Corporations sometimes issue zero-coupon bonds. In this case, investors receive $1,000 face value at the maturity date but do not receive a regular coupon payment. In other words, the bond has a coupon rate of zero. These bonds are issued at prices considerably below face value, and the investor's return comes from the difference between the purchase price and the payment of face value at maturity.

Strip Bonds. If you buy a five-year Canada 5 percent bond, you get a package of 10 semi-annual coupon payments plus the final repayment of face value. But sometimes it is inconvenient to buy things in packages. For example, perhaps you do not need a regular income of $25 every six months but would prefer to receive the final repayment of $1,000 in five years. That's not a problem. To meet the demand for single-payment bonds, investment dealers split some conventional bonds into a series of mini-bonds, each of which makes a single maturity payment. These single-payment bonds are called *strip bonds*. For example, a five-year Canada bond with a 5 percent coupon rate becomes 11 separate zero-coupon strip bonds. Each of the $25 semi-annual coupon payments is the principal of one of the 10 *strip coupon bonds*, and one bond pays the $1,000 principal payment and is called a *strip bond residual*. So strip bonds are zero-coupon bonds.

Strip bonds are traded like regular bonds, and the prices of strips are available from some online bond data services. All strip bonds sell at a discount to their maturity payments. Table 6.1 shows prices of two Canada strip bonds, with zero coupon rates. The ask price of June 1, 2013, zero-coupon strip bond was 93.19 percent of its maturity payment, and the ask yield was 2.37 percent. Assuming that the maturity payment was $1,000, it would cost $931.90 to buy that bond on June 1, 2010. One advantage of strip bonds is that if you hold them to maturity, the yield to maturity will be the rate of return on your investment. So, if you bought the 2013 strip bond on June 1, 2010, and held it to maturity, the rate of return will be 2.37 percent. The $931.90 investment in bond pays $1,000 in three years, so the rate of return on the investment equals $(1000/931.90)^{1/3} - 1$, or 2.37 percent.

Finance in Action

Maple Bond Sales May Almost Double in 2011 on Loonie Rally: Canada Credit

Sales of Canadian-dollar debt by foreign companies may double this year as borrowers diversify funding sources and take advantage of the nation's strengthening currency.

Issuance of Maple bonds may range from C$7 billion ($7.1 billion) to C$10 billion this year, said Chris Seip, head of Canadian debt capital markets at RBC Capital Markets, the top arranger for Maple bonds last year. That compares with C$4.83 billion in 2010, according to data compiled by Bloomberg.

MetLife Inc. became the first issuer of Maples this year, drawn to the rising loonie, which traded at a two-and-half-year high against the U.S. dollar. Canada is headed toward balancing its budget by 2015, Finance Minister Jim Flaherty said yesterday, which would make it the first Group of Seven country to do so.

"Canada looks like a pretty attractive market for issuers to consider," Seip said in a telephone interview. "What you're seeing is well-branded issuers will continue to have favorable access in 2011."

RBC Capital, the investment-banking unit of Toronto-based Royal Bank of Canada, arranged 11 Maple bonds valued at C$2.01 billion in 2010. Sales for Maples last year were the highest since 2007.

"Demand will continue to be quite hardy," said Seip, 40. "To be able to fill that, investors will look across the spectrum, and Maples are going to be an important component."

The Canadian dollar touched 98.55 cents yesterday, the strongest level since May 2008. One Canadian dollar buys $1.0145. The currency may be worth C$1.05 per U.S. dollar by 2012, according to a Bloomberg survey of foreign exchange forecasts.

Source: Sean B. Pasternak, **Bloomberg.com**, January 13, 2011, **www.bloomberg.com/news/2011-01-13/maple-bond-sales-may-almost-double-in-2011-on-loonie-rally-canada-credit.htm**.

Floating-Rate Bonds. Sometimes the coupon rate can change over time. For example, floating-rate bonds make coupon payments tied to some measure of current market rates. The rate might be reset once a year to the current T-bill rate plus 2 percent. So if the T-bill rate at the start of the year is 4 percent, the bond's coupon rate over the next year would be set at 6 percent. This arrangement means that the bond's coupon rate always approximates current market interest rates.

Convertible Bonds. If you buy a convertible bond, you can choose later to exchange it for a specified number of shares of common stock. For example, a convertible bond that is issued at par value of $1,000 may be convertible into 50 shares of the firm's stock. Because convertible bonds offer the opportunity to participate in any price appreciation of the company's stock, investors will accept lower interest rates on convertible bonds.

Callable Bonds. Suppose that a company issues a 6.5 percent, 30-year bond at a price of $1,000. Five years later, interest rates have fallen to 4 percent and the bond price has risen dramatically. If you were the company's treasurer, wouldn't you like to be able to retire the bond issue and issue some new bonds at the lower interest rate? Well, with some bonds, known as *callable bonds*, the company does have the option to buy them back early for the *call price*. Of course, holders of callable bonds will know that the company will be tempted to buy back the bond if interest rates fall and therefore the price of the bond will not rise above the call price.

Figure 6.10 shows the risk of a call to the bondholder. The blue line is the value of a 30-year, 6.5 percent coupon "straight"—that is, non-callable—bond; the orange line is the value of a bond with the same coupon rate and maturity, but callable at $1,060 (that is, 106 percent of face value). At very high interest rates, the risk of call is negligible, and the values of the bonds are nearly identical. As rates fall, the non-callable bond steadily increases in value, but because call becomes more likely in this region, the value of the callable bond is limited by its call price.

Recognizing this pattern, bond investors calculate yield to call rather than yield to maturity for bonds at high risk of being called. The yield to call is calculated like yield to maturity with time until call replacing time until maturity, and the call price replacing face value.

FIGURE 6.10
Prices of callable versus straight debt. When interest rates fall, bond prices rise. But the price of the callable bond (orange line) is limited by the call price.

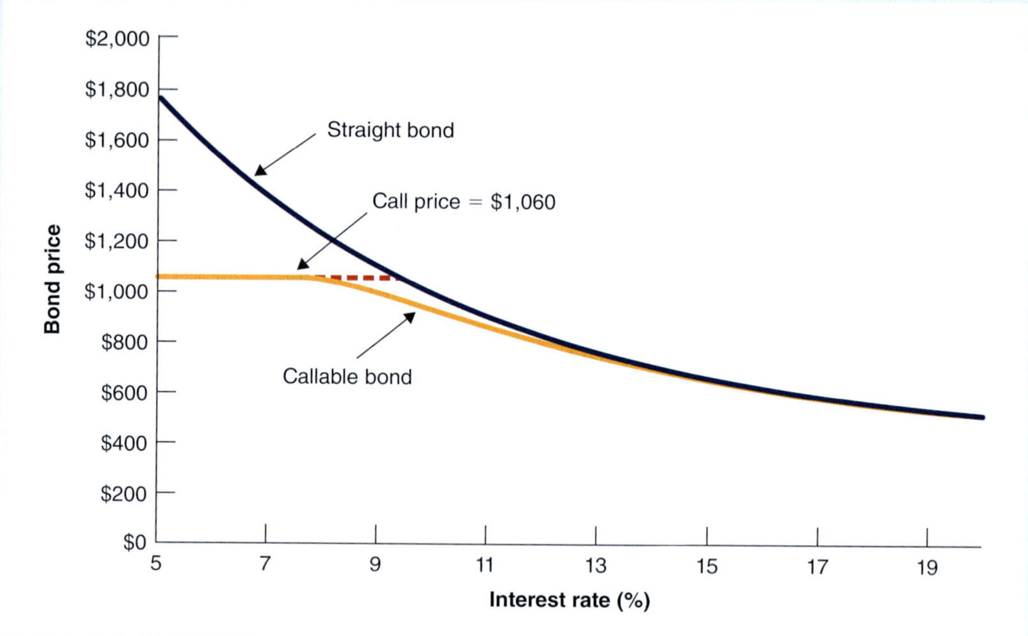

EXAMPLE 6.7 YIELD TO CALL

Suppose a 8.5 percent coupon, 30-year maturity bond (making annual coupon payments) sells for $1,040 and is callable in 10 years at a call price of $1,060. We would calculate its yield to maturity and yield to call on our calculators as follows:

	Calculator Input	Yield to Call	Yield to Maturity
Coupon payment	PMT	85	85
Number of periods	*N*	10	30
Final payment	FV	1,060	1,000
Price	PV	−1,040	−1,040
Answer:	Compute *i*	8.30%	8.14%

In Excel, we could solve for these rates as: yield to call =YIELD(DATE(2000,1,1), DATE(2010,1,1),.085,104,106,1) and yield to maturity =YIELD(DATE(2000,1,1), DATE(2030,1,1),.085,104,100,1). The yield to call is higher because the firm has to pay a premium to call the bonds.

Check Point 6.9 Find the yield to call and yield to maturity of the bond in Example 6.7 if it pays its coupons semi-annually.

Most callable Canadian corporate bonds have a special call feature known as the *Canada call* or the *Doomsday call*. With a Canada call, the call price is not set in advance but is determined at the time of the call. The call price is calculated to generate a specific yield, with par value as the minimum price. A typical Canada call provision states that the call price, referred to as the Canada yield price, must offer an equivalent yield of a Government of Canada bond of the same maturity plus an additional pre-stated amount, for default risk.

With the Canada call, the call price increases as interest rates fall, making it less attractive to call the bond. By contrast, the call price for a conventional call provision is fixed and if interest rates fall enough, it becomes profitable for the issuer to call the bond. You won't be surprised to learn that bonds with a Canada call are rarely called.

EXAMPLE 6.8 CALCULATING THE CANADA YIELD PRICE

A Cameco 4.7 percent bond due September 16, 2015, is callable (redeemable) at any time at the greater of the Canada Yield Price and par. The *Canada Yield Price* is the yield to maturity for a Government of Canada bond with the same maturity date as the Cameco bond. To determine the Canada Yield Price (or *call price*), the remaining cash flows of the Cameco bond are discounted at the Canada Yield plus .22 percent.

Suppose the Cameco bond is trading for $1,031.40 on September 16, 2010, giving a yield to maturity of 4 percent. The coupon rate is greater than the bond's yield. Should the bond be called and replaced with bonds carrying a lower coupon rate? If equivalent-maturity Canada bonds are yielding 3.7 percent, the Canada Price must be calculated with a yield of .037 + .0022, or 3.92 percent, making the call price $1,035.10. (The Cameco bond is five years to maturity, with 10 coupon payments of $23.50 remaining to be paid. On your calculator, set FV = 1,000, PMT = 47/2 = 23.5, n = 10, i = 3.92/2 = 1.96, and compute PV.) The call price is greater than the current market price, and the bond won't be called.

6.7 SUMMARY

1. **What are the differences between the bond's coupon rate, current yield, and yield to maturity? LO1**

   A bond is a long-term debt of a government or corporation. When you own a bond, you receive a fixed interest payment each year until the bond matures. This payment is known as the coupon. The **coupon rate** is the annual coupon payment expressed as a fraction of the bond's **face value**. At maturity the bond's **face value** is repaid. In Canada most bonds have a face value of $1,000. The **current yield** is the annual coupon payment expressed as a fraction of the current bond's price. The **yield to maturity** measures the average rate of return to an investor who purchases the bond and holds it until maturity, accounting for coupon income as well as the difference between purchase price and face value.

2. **How can one find the market price of a bond given its yield to maturity and find a bond's yield given its price? Why do prices and yields vary inversely? LO2**

   Bonds are valued by discounting the coupon payments and the final repayment by the yield to maturity on comparable bonds. The bond payments discounted at the bond's yield to maturity equal the bond price. You may also start with the bond price and ask what interest rate the bond offers. This interest rate that equates the present value of bond payments to the bond price is the yield to maturity. Because present values are lower when discount rates are higher, price and yield to maturity vary inversely.

3. **Why do interest rates change over time and what is a yield curve? LO3**

   The general level of interest rates varies over time with changes in the real rate of interest and expected inflation. The **Fisher effect** says that the nominal interest rate equals the real rate of interest plus expected inflation. The **yield curve** is a snapshot of yields on bonds of different maturities at a point in time. Typically, it is upward-sloping but can also be downward-sloping or humped.

4. **What determines the difference between yields on long-term and short-term bonds? LO4**

According to the *expectations theory*, bonds are priced so that the expected return over any period is independent of the maturity of the bonds held. Consequently, a higher yield on a longer-term bond implies that investors expect future short-term interest rates to rise. However, the expectations theory ignores **interest rate risk**, which arises from the fact that bond prices rise when market rates fall, and fall when market rates rise. Long-term bonds exhibit greater interest rate risk than short-term bonds. According to the *liquidity-preference theory*, long-term bonds earn extra return to compensate for interest rate risk, resulting in higher yields on long-term bonds and a tendency for the yield curve to be upward-sloping.

5. **Why do investors pay attention to bond ratings and demand a higher interest rate for bonds with low ratings? LO5**

Investors demand higher promised yields if there is a high probability that the borrower will run into trouble and default. **Credit risk** implies that the promised yield to maturity on the bond is higher than the expected yield. The additional yield investors require for bearing credit risk is called the **default premium**. Bond ratings measure the bond's credit risk.

Related Web Links

finpipe.com Financial Pipeline, an Internet site dedicated to financial education; see the page on bonds, and ignore the out-of-date Canadian bond market commentary

dbrs.com Web site for Dominion Bond Rating Service

standardpoors.com Standard & Poor's provides information on how it rates securities

bankofcanada.ca Lots of interest rate data

bondsonline.com U.S. bond data

pfin.ca/canadianfixedincome Canadian bond data and bond trading

financialpost.com/markets/data/bonds-canadian.html More Canadian bond data

Key Terms

accrued interest	186	default premium *or* credit spread	204	junk (*or* speculative-grade) bond	204
bond	184	dirty bond price	186	premium bond	191
clean bond price	186	discount bond	191	rate of return	193
coupon	184	face value	184	real return bond (RRB)	199
coupon rate	184	Fisher effect	200	yield curve *or* term structure of interest rates	198
current yield	191	interest rate risk	202	yield to maturity	191
default (*or* credit) risk	204	investment-grade bond	204		

Questions and Problems

connect™ Practise and learn online with *Connect*. Questions with online Excel templates or datasets are marked with a symbol.

*Answers in Appendix B

BASIC

*1. **Bond Yields.** A 30-year Canada bond is issued with par value of $1,000, paying interest of $60 per year. If market yields increase shortly after the bond is issued, what happens to the bond's
   a. Coupon rate (LO1)
   b. Price (LO1)
   c. Yield to maturity (LO1)
   d. Current yield (LO1)

2. **Bond Yields.** If a bond with par value of $1,000 and a coupon rate of 8 percent is selling at a price of $970, is the bond's yield to maturity more or less than 8 percent? What about the current yield? (LO1)

*3. **Bond Yields.** A bond with par value $1,000 has a current yield of 7 percent and a coupon rate of 8 percent. What is the bond's price if it pays interest annually? (LO1)

*4. **Bond Pricing.** A 6-year Circular File bond pays interest of $80 annually and sells for $950. What is its coupon rate, current yield, and yield to maturity? (LO1, LO2)

5. **Bond Pricing.** If Circular File (see previous problem) wants to issue a new 6-year bond at face value, what coupon rate must the bond offer? (LO2)

6. **Bond Yields.** A BCE bond has 10 years until maturity and a coupon rate of 8 percent payable annually, and sells for $1,100.
   a. What is the current yield on the bond? (LO1)
   b. What is the yield to maturity? (LO2)

7. **Coupon Rate.** General Matter's outstanding bond issue has a coupon rate of 7 percent and a current yield of 7.6 percent, and it sells at a yield to maturity of 9.25 percent. The firm wishes to issue additional bonds to the public at par value. What coupon rate must the new bonds offer in order to sell at par? (LO2)

8. **Financial Pages.** Turn back to Table 6.1. What is the current bid yield of the Canada 4.25 percent, June 1, 2018, maturity? What price would you have had to pay to buy the bond that day? (LO1)

*9. **Rate of Return.** You bought a 10-year, 5 percent coupon bond for $1,000 and sold it 1 year later for $1,100. What is the rate of return on your investment if the bond pays interest annually? (LO2)

*10. **After-Tax Rate of Return.** Refer to problem 9. If your marginal tax rate is 30 percent, and 50 percent of capital gains are taxable, what is the after-tax rate of return on your bond investment? (LO2)

INTERMEDIATE

*11. **Bond Prices and Returns.** One bond has a coupon rate of 8 percent, another a coupon rate of 12 percent. Both bonds have 10-year maturities and sell at a yield to maturity of 10 percent. If their yields to maturity next year are still 10 percent, what is the rate of return on each bond? Does the higher coupon bond give a higher rate of return? Assume the bonds pay annual interest. (LO2)

12. **Accrued Interest.** The July 15, 2011, quoted price of a bond with a coupon rate of 4.5 percent, payable semi-annually, maturing on March 1, 2015, is $990. If you buy the bond on July 15, 2011, what is the total price you must pay for the bond? (LO2)

*13. **Bond Returns.**
   a. If the BCE bond in problem 6 has a yield to maturity of 8 percent 1 year from now, what will its price be? (LO2)
   b. What will be your rate of return if you buy it today and sell it in one year? (LO2)
   c. If the inflation rate during the year is 3 percent, what is the real rate of return on the bond? (LO3)

14. **Bond Pricing.** A Metallico bond carries a coupon rate of 8 percent, payable semi-annually, has 9 years until maturity, and sells at a yield to maturity of 9 percent.
   a. What interest payments do bondholders receive each year? (LO1)
   *b. At what price does the bond sell? (LO2)
   c. What will happen to the bond price if the yield to maturity falls to 7 percent? (LO2)

15. **Bond Pricing.** A 30-year maturity bond with $1,000 face value makes annual coupon payments and has a coupon rate of 8 percent. What is the bond's yield to maturity if the bond is selling for
   a. $900? (LO2)
   b. $1,000? (LO2)
   *c. $1,100? (LO2)

16. **Bond Pricing.** Repeat the previous problem if the bond makes semi-annual coupon payments. (LO2)

17. **Bond Pricing.** Fill in the table below for the following zero-coupon bonds. The face value of each bond is $1,000. (LO2)

Price	Maturity (years)	Yield to Maturity
$300	30	—
$300	—	8%
—	10	10%

18. **Consol Bonds.** Perpetual Life Corp. has issued consol bonds with coupon payments of $60. (Consols are perpetuities—they pay interest forever and never mature.) If the required rate of return on these bonds at the time they were issued was 6 percent, at what price were they sold to the public? If the required return today is 10 percent, at what price do the consols sell? (LO2)

*19. **Bond Pricing.** Sure Tea Co. has issued 9 percent annual coupon bonds, which are now selling at a yield to maturity of 10 percent and current yield of 9.8375 percent. What is the remaining maturity of these bonds? (LO2)

20. **Bond Pricing.** Large Industries bonds sell for $1,065.95. The bond life is 9 years, and the yield to maturity is 7 percent. What must be the coupon rate on the bonds? Coupons are paid semi-annually. (LO2)

*21. **Bond Prices and Yields.**
   a. Several years ago, Castles in the Sand, Inc., issued bonds at face value at a yield to maturity of 7 percent. Now, with 8 years left until the maturity of the bonds, the company has run into hard times, and the yield to maturity on the bonds has increased to 15 percent. What has happened to the price of the bond? Coupons are paid semi-annually. (LO2)
   b. Suppose that investors believe that Castles can make good on the promised coupon payments, but

that the company will go bankrupt when the bond matures and the principal comes due. The expectation is that investors will receive only 80 percent of face value at maturity. If they buy the bond today, what yield to maturity do they expect to receive? (LO2)(LO5)

*22. **Bond Returns.** You buy an 8 percent coupon, paid annually, 10-year maturity bond for $980. A year later, the bond price is $1,100.
   a. What is the yield to maturity on the bond today? What is it in one year? (LO2)
   b. What is your rate of return over the year? (LO2)

23. **Bond Returns.** You buy an 8 percent annual coupon, 20-year maturity bond when its yield to maturity is 9 percent. A year later, the yield to maturity is 10 percent. What is your rate of return over the year? (LO4)

24. **Rate of Return.** A 2-year maturity bond with $1,000 face value makes annual coupon payments of $65 and is selling at face value. What will be the rate of return on the bond if its yield to maturity at the end of the year is
   a. 6 percent? (LO4)
   b. 8 percent? (LO4)
   c. 10 percent? (LO4)

25. **Rate of Return.** A bond that pays coupons annually is issued with a coupon rate of 4 percent, maturity of 30 years, and a yield to maturity of 7 percent. What rate of return will be earned by an investor who purchases the bond and holds it for 1 year if the bond's yield to maturity at the end of the year is 8 percent? (LO4)

*26. **Rate of Return.** Five years ago you purchased an 8 percent coupon bond for $975. Today you sold the bond for $1,000. What is your rate of return on the bond in each of the following situations?
   a. All coupons were immediately spent when received. (LO2)
   b. All coupons were reinvested in your bank account, which pays 1 percent interest until the bond is sold. (LO2)
   c. All coupons were reinvested at 8.64 percent until the bond is sold. (LO2)

*27. **Rate of Return.** Looking back at the previous question, use the yield-to-maturity method to compute the rate of return on your bond investment. (LO2)

28. **Bond Pricing.** Are the following statements true or false? Provide simple examples to support your assessment.
   a. If interest rates rise, bond prices rise. (LO2)
   b. If the bond's yield to maturity is greater than its coupon rate, the price is greater than the bond's face value. (LO1)
   c. High-coupon bonds of a given maturity sell for lower prices than otherwise identical low-coupon bonds. (LO2)
   d. If interest rates change, the price of a high-coupon bond changes proportionately more than the price of a low-coupon bond of the same maturity and default risk. (LO2)
   e. A investor who owns a 10 percent, 5-year Canada bond is wealthier if interest rates rise from 4 percent to 5 percent. (LO2)

29. **Internet.** Use historical yield-to-maturity data from the Bank of Canada Web site at **www.bankofcanada.ca** to look at bonds of different types. Go to **www.bankofcanada.ca/rates/interest-rates/lookup-bond-yields** and follow the instructions. Download 60 months of yield-to-maturity data for long-term corporate bonds (series V122518), long-term provincial bonds (V122517), and long-term Canada bonds (series V122544), and put the data into a spreadsheet. Calculate the average spreads of the corporate and provincial bonds over the Canada bonds. Graph the yields to maturity over time. What do you see? Does it make sense? (LO3)

30. **Yield Curve.** The following table shows the prices of strips of Canada bonds in November 2012. Each strip makes a single payment of $100 at maturity.

Maturity	Price ($)
June 2010	96.94
June 2012	91.04
June 2015	80.58
June 2019	65.43
June 2025	45.75

   a. Calculate the annually compounded, yield to maturity (spot interest rate) for each bond. (LO3)
   b. Is the term structure upward- or downward-sloping? (LO3)

31. **Bond Pricing.** Diamond Corporation is planning a bond issue with an escalating coupon rate. The annual coupon rate will be 4 percent for the first 3 years, 5 percent for the subsequent 3 years, and 6 percent for the final 3 years. If bonds of this risk are yielding 5 percent, estimate the bond's current price. (LO2)

32. **Interest Rate Risk.** Consider three bonds with 8 percent coupon rates, all selling at face value. The short-term bond has a maturity of 4 years, the intermediate-term bond has maturity of 8 years, and the long-term bond has maturity of 30 years.
   a. What will happen to the price of each bond if their yields increase to 9 percent? (LO4)
   b. What will happen to the price of each bond if their yields decrease to 7 percent? (LO4)

c. What do you conclude about the relationship between time to maturity and the sensitivity of bond prices to interest rates? (LO4)

*33. **Bond Risk.** A bond's credit rating provides a guide to its risk. Long-term bonds rated AA currently offer yields to maturity of 7.5 percent EAR. A-rated bonds sell at yields of 7.8 percent EAR. If a 10-year bond with a coupon rate of 7 percent, paid semi-annually, is downgraded by DBRS from AA to A rating, calculate the likely effect on the bond price. (LO5)

34. **Internet.** Free online yield-to-maturity and credit spread data for Canadian corporate bonds with different debt ratings is not available. However, old U.S. data is available at **www.bondsonline.com/Todays_Market/Corporate_Bond_Spreads.php**. You will see a table showing credit spreads for corporate bonds of different risk over comparable-term U.S. government bonds from 2006. The spreads are measured in basis points, where 1 basis point equals .01 (1/100) percentage point. Using the 2006 credit spread data and the current yield to maturity for U.S. Treasury bonds, estimate the required rate of return on a 10-year debt issue by a U.S. company with A2/A-rated debt. What if its debt had a B2/B rating? Current yields to maturity on U.S. Treasury bonds are available at **finance.yahoo.com/bonds/composite_bond_rates**. (LO5)

35. **Internet.** From **www.globeinvestor.com/servlet/Page/document/v5/data/bonds**, find five different corporate bonds and find Government of Canada bonds with similar terms to maturity. Look up their ratings at either **www.dbrs.com** or **www.standardandpoors.com**. Compare the bonds' yields to maturity to comparable-term Government of Canada bonds. Do the yields make sense relative to their bond ratings? (LO5)

36. **Real Rate of Interest.** You have been told that the yield to maturity on 3-month Treasury bills is 4 percent and the current inflation rate is 2 percent. Estimate the real rate of interest. (LO3)

37. **Real Returns.** Suppose that you buy a 1-year maturity bond for $1,000 that will pay you $1,000 plus a coupon payment of $60 at the end of the year. What real rate of return will you earn if the inflation rate is
    - *a. 2 percent? (LO3)
    - b. 4 percent? (LO3)
    - c. 6 percent? (LO3)
    - d. 8 percent? (LO3)

38. **Real Returns.** Now suppose that the bond in the previous problem is a real return bond with a coupon rate of 4 percent. What will the cash flow provided by the bond be for each of the four inflation rates? What will be the real and nominal rates of return on the bond in each scenario? (LO3)

39. **Real Returns.** Now suppose the real return bond in the previous problem is a two-year maturity bond. What will be the bondholder's cash flows in each year in each of the inflation scenarios? (LO3)

40. **Yield to Call.** A 6.25 percent 15-year bond, paying interest annually, can be called at 110 percent of par value in 10 years. The bond currently sells for $1,048.
    - a. What is the yield to maturity? (LO2)
    - b. What is the yield to call? (LO2)

41. **Canada Call Price.** A 7 percent corporate bond with 6 years to maturity has a Canada call. The bond's yield to maturity is 4.8 percent. The call price must offer an equivalent yield to a Canada bond plus .35 percent. Currently, six-year Government of Canada bonds are yielding 4 percent. Assume coupons are paid annually.
    - a. What is the current bond price? (LO2)
    - b. What is the current call price? (LO2)

42. **Canada Call.** When ABC Company originally issued its callable 5.5 percent, 10-year bond, it was rated AA and priced to sell at par. The bond is callable at the price that offers an equivalent yield to a Canada bond plus .15 percent. At that time, the credit spread over 10-year Canada bonds was .25 percent. The bond pays interest annually.
    - a. What was the call price at issue? (LO2)

    Now, 5 years later, the bond rating agencies have raised the bond rating to AAA and the bond's yield to maturity is 5 percent. Equivalent-maturity Canada bonds are yielding 4.9 percent.
    - b. What is the current call price? (LO2, LO5)
    - c. Would ABC Company consider calling the bond now? (LO2, LO5)

CHALLENGE

43. **Interest Rate Risk.** Suppose interest rates increase from 8 percent to 9 percent. Which bond will suffer the greater percentage decline in price: a 30-year bond paying annual coupons of 8 percent, or a 30-year zero coupon bond? Can you explain intuitively why the zero exhibits greater interest rate risk even though it has the same maturity as the coupon bond? (LO4)

44. **After-Tax Rate of Return.** Using the information in problem 26, calculate your after-tax rate of return on your bond investment assuming that your marginal tax rate is 35 percent. You pay tax on the interest when it is received. (LO2)

45. **Bond Prices and Yields.** Big Time Company is planning to raise $15 million by selling 10-year bonds. The bond rating agency has advised the company that the

bonds will have an A rating. Currently, the difference between the yield to maturity of A-rated corporate bonds over similar-maturity Government of Canada bonds is 150 basis points (1 basis point equals .01 percentage points). If 10-year Canada bonds are currently priced to yield 5 percent, what coupon rate should Big Time select if the new issue is to sell at par value? (LO2)

46. **Internet.** Go to **www.dbrs.com** and find the bond rating of BCE (BCE) and Agrium (AGU). Which has the higher bond rating (that is, DBRS Issuer Credit Rating)? Then go to **finance.yahoo.com** to learn about the main business activities of each of these companies. Compare their ability to pay their interest obligations by calculating the ratio of EBIT to interest payments. The higher this "times interest earned" ratio, the greater a company's ability to make its interest payments. Also, calculate both companies' indebtedness, as measured by the ratio of debt to equity. The higher the times interest earned and the lower the indebtedness, the more likely a company will be able to make its debt payments. Are the debt ratings consistent with the calculated ratios? (LO5)

Solutions to Check Points

6.1 a. The ask price, your purchase price, is 106.51 percent of face value, or $1,065.1.

b. The bid price, your selling price, is 106.46 percent of face value, or $1,064.6.

c. The annual coupon is 4 percent of face value, or $40, paid in two semi-annual instalments.

d. The semi-annual payment is half of the annual coupon; therefore, the semi-annual payment is $20. The payments will be made every June 1 and December 1 until maturity.

6.2 The coupon is 9 percent of $1,000, or $90, a year. First value the six-year annuity of coupons:

$$\text{PV(coupon)} = \$90 \times (\text{6-year annuity factor})$$

$$= \$90 \times \left[\frac{1}{.05} - \frac{1}{.05(1.05)^6}\right]$$

$$= \$90 \times 5.08 = \$456.81$$

Then value the final payment and add up:

$$\text{PV(face value)} = \frac{\$1,000}{(1.05)^6} = \$746.22$$

$$\text{PV(bond)} = \$456.81 + \$746.22 = \$1,203.03$$

6.3 The yield to maturity assuming annual coupons is about 8 percent, because the present value of the bond's cash returns is $1,199 when discounted at 8 percent:

$$\text{PV(bond)} = \text{PV(coupons)} + \text{PV(face value)}$$

$$= (\text{coupon} \times \text{annuity factor})$$

$$+ (\text{face value} \times \text{discount factor})$$

$$= \$140 \times \left[\frac{1}{.08} - \frac{1}{.08(1.08)^4}\right] + \$1,000 \times \frac{1}{1.08^4}$$

$$= \$463.70 + \$735.03 = \$1,199$$

To obtain a more precise solution on your calculator, these would be your inputs:

	Annual Payments	Semi-annual Payments
n	4	8
PV	−1,200	−1,200
FV	1,000	1,000
PMT	140	70

Compute i to find yield to maturity (annual payments) = 7.97 percent. Yield to maturity (semi-annual payments) = 4.026 percent per 6 months, which would be reported in the financial press as 8.05 percent annual yield.

6.4 The 4 percent coupon bond pays $40 annual coupon and matures June 1, 2013. On June 1, 2010, the bond has 3 years left until maturity. In one year, on June 1, 2011, the bond has only 2 years to maturity and investors demand an interest rate of 1.5 percent. Therefore, the value of the bond on June 1, 2011, is

$$\text{PV} = \frac{\$40}{(1.015)} + \frac{\$1,040}{(1.015)^2} = \$1,048.90$$

You invested $1,053.20. At the end of one year, you receive a coupon payment of $40 and have a bond worth $1,048.90. Your rate of return is therefore

$$\text{Rate of return} = \frac{\$40 + (\$1,048.90 - \$1,053.20)}{\$1,053.20}$$

$$= .0339, \text{ or } 3.39\%$$

The yield to maturity as of June 1, 2010, was 2.15 percent. However, because interest rates fell during the year, the bond price rose and the rate of return for the year was greater than the yield to maturity.

6.5 You can solve for the bond's yield to maturity on June 1, 2011, using a financial calculator, a spreadsheet or by trial and error. The inputs are: $n = 2$, PV $= -1{,}048.90$, FV $= 1000$, PMT $= 40$, resulting in a yield of 1.5 percent. Also, if you noticed that the June 1, 2011, bond price in this Check Point is the same as the June 1, 2011, bond price you calculated in Check Point 6.4, you will know that the yield to maturity is 1.5 percent. In one year, June 1, 2012, the bond will have only 1 year left until maturity. It will make only one more payment of coupon plus face value, so its price will be \$1,040/1.015 = \$1,024.63. The rate of return on the 1-year investment is therefore

$$\frac{\$40 + (\$1{,}024.63 - \$1{,}048.90)}{\$1{,}048.90} = .0150, \text{ or } 1.5\%$$

6.6 The coupon payment is $.08 \times \$1{,}000$, or \$80, before tax. The tax on the coupon interest is $.4 \times \$80$, or \$32. A capital gain of $\$1{,}215 - \$1{,}200 = \$15$ is made. The capital gains tax is $.5 \times .4 \times \$15$, or \$3. The before-tax rate of return is

$$\frac{\$80 + (\$1{,}215 - \$1{,}200)}{\$1{,}200} = .0792, \text{ or } 7.92\%$$

The after-tax rate of return is

$$\frac{\$80 - \$32 + (\$1{,}215 - \$1{,}200) - \$3}{\$1{,}200} = .05, \text{ or } 5.0\%$$

6.7 The general level of nominal interest rates in April 2000 was much higher than in 2010. This suggests that investors were expecting much higher inflation in 2000 than in 2010. The inflation rate in 2000 was about 2.2 percent and was about 1.8 percent in 2010.

6.8 At an interest rate of 2.15 percent, the 3-year bond sells for \$1,024.44. If the interest rate jumps to 5 percent, the bond price falls to \$945.54, a decline of 8.3 percent. The 30-year bond sells for \$1,186.59 when the interest rate is 2.15 percent, but its price falls to \$692.55 at an interest rate of 5 percent, a much larger percentage decline of 71.3 percent.

6.9 The semi-annual coupon is \$42.50. The number of payments will be 20 if the bond is called after 10 years, or 60 if it is held until maturity. Therefore, use these inputs:

	Yield to Call	Yield to Maturity
Coupon payment (PMT)	42.50	42.50
Number of periods (n)	20	60
Final payment (FV)	1,060	1,000
Price (PV)	−1,040	−1,040

The yield to call is 4.15 percent semi-annual, or 8.30 percent annualized. The yield to maturity is 4.07 percent semi-annual, or 8.14 percent annualized. These yields are actually slightly higher than those calculated by using annual payments but are the same to two decimal places.

Solutions to Spreadsheet Questions

6.1

Yield to Maturity	Price (% of face value)
2.15%	103.882
2.50%	102.856

Decline in price is $(102.856/103.882) - 1 = .990123 - 1 = -.009877 = -.9877\%$, just under 1 percent.

6.2

Yield to Maturity	Price (% of face value)
2.15%	115.17
2.50%	110.983

Decline in price is $(110.983/115.17) - 1 = .963645 - 1 = -.03635 = -3.635\%$, just over 3.6 percent.

The price of this 10-year bond is more sensitive to the change in interest rates than is the shorter-maturity, 3-year bond.

6.3

Price (% of face value)	Yield to Maturity
103.883	2.15%
102	2.7957%

Increase in the yield to maturity due to the fall in the bond price: $.027957/.0215 - 1 = .300 = 30$ percent.

A drop in the current bond price causes the yield to maturity to increase.

APPENDIX 6A: A MORE DETAILED LOOK AT THE YIELD CURVE*

*For Appendix 6B, see Online Learning Centre

In June 2010, you could invest in a one-year Government of Canada stripped bond yielding about 1.07 percent. A two-year Canada strip had a yield of about 1.41 percent. These are *spot rates*, interest rates available today on investments today. If you invested in the one-year strip, by June 2011, every dollar invested would have grown to $\$1 \times (1.0107) = \$1.0107$. If instead you invested in the two-year strip, by the end of two years, June 2012, every dollar invested would grow to $\$1 \times (1.0141)^2 = \$1.0284$. By keeping your money invested for the extra year, your savings grow from \$1.0107 to \$1.0284, an increase of 1.75 percent ($= 1.0284/1.0107 - 1$). This extra 1.75 percent that you earn by investing for two years, rather than one, is called a *forward interest rate*.

A forward interest rate is an interest rate calculated using spot rates. Let r_1 be the current one-year spot rate and r_2 be the current two-year spot rate. Invest for one year, each dollar grows to $(1 + r_1)$. Invest for two years in the two-year bond, your investment grows to $(1 + r_2)^2$. The extra rate of return that you earn in the second year is the forward rate, f_2. In our example,

$$f_2 = \frac{(1 + r_2)^2}{(1 + r_1)} - 1 = \frac{(1.0284)}{1.0107} - 1 = .0175\text{, or } 1.75\% \qquad (6A.1)$$

Twist this equation around and you get an expression for the two-year spot rate, r_2, in terms of the one-year spot rate, r_1, and the forward rate, f_2:

$$(1 + r_2)^2 = (1 + r_1) \times (1 + f_2) \qquad (6A.2)$$

In other words, you can think of the two-year investment as earning the one-year spot rate for the first year and the forward rate for the second year.

Forward rates can be calculated for other years, provided that you have the appropriate spot rates. For example, if the 5-year spot rate, r_5, is 6 percent and the 6-year spot rate, r_6, is 6.5 percent, the forward rate for the 6th year, f_6, must satisfy this equation:

$$(1 + r_6)^6 = (1 + r_5)^5 \times (1 + f_6) \qquad (6A.3)$$

In other words, the year 6 forward rate is the extra return for investing for the 6th year. In this case, $f_6 = (1.065)^6/(1.06)^5 - 1$, or 9 percent. Generally, the forward rate for the nth year, f_n, must satisfy the following equation:

$$(1 + r_n)^n = (1 + r_{n-1})^{n-1} \times (1 + f_n) \qquad (6A.4)$$

The Expectations Theory

How attractive is the extra 1.75 percent return for investing for two years compared to one in June 2010? It depends on how you expect interest rates to change over the coming year. Suppose, for example, you expected interest rates to rise, so that by June 2011 the one-year rate will be 2 percent. In that case, rather than investing in a two-year bond and earning the extra 1.75 percent, you would do better if you invested in the one-year bond and, when that matured, reinvested the money for a further year at 2 percent. If all investors thought like you, no one would want to buy the two-year bond. Its price would fall. The price would continue to fall until the extra return on the two-year bond equalled the expected future one-year rate. We use the symbol ${}_1r_2$ to represent the expected future one-year spot rate on a loan maturing at the end of year 2.

According to the expectations theory, in equilibrium the forward rate for year 2, f_2, equals the expected one-year spot rate for year 2, ${}_1r_2$. The expectations theory implies that the *only* reason for an upward-sloping yield curve is that investors expect short-term interest rates to rise.

Likewise, the *only* reason for a downward-sloping yield curve is that investors expect short-term rates to fall.

If the expectations theory is correct, you can use the current spot rates to calculate investors' expected future spot rates. For example, suppose the current one-year spot rate is 3 percent and the current two-year spot rate is 6 percent. What is the expected one-year spot rate for year 2? According to the expectations theory,

$$_1r_2 = f_2 = \frac{(1 + r_2)^2}{(1 + r_1)} - 1 = \frac{(1.06)^2}{1.03} - 1 = .0909, \text{ or } 9.09\%$$

If short-term rates are much lower than long-term rates, it may be tempting to borrow short-term. However, the expectations theory tells us to not be fooled. Long-term rates are connected to short-term rates. If long-term rates are higher, it must be the case that the market is expecting interest rates to rise.

The Liquidity-Preference Theory

The expectations theory implies that investing in a series of one-year bonds earns the same expected return as investing in long-term bonds. However, as we pointed out in Section 6.5, investing in long-term bonds is riskier than short-term bonds, because long-term bond prices are more variable than short-term bond prices. To compensate for the extra risk of lending long, investors demand a liquidity risk premium. With this liquidity premium added to the bond yield, it is no longer the case that the forward rate must equal the expected future spot rate. In fact, the forward rate must be higher than the expected future spot rate to compensate investors for the liquidity risk.

Together, the expectations and liquidity-preference theories can partially explain the shape of yield curves. The yield on a longer-term bond reflects both expectations of future short-term interest rates and the liquidity risk premium. Other theories exist, but they are beyond the scope of this book.

Questions and Problems

6A.1. **Calculating Forward Rates.** The following are the yields to maturity on Canada strip bonds with various years to maturity.

Years to Maturity	Yield to Maturity (%)
1	1.26
2	2.00
3	2.47
4	2.79
5	3.02

a. Calculate the forward rate for each period.

b. Calculate the price today of the following Canada bonds:
   i. 2-year $1000 par value, 5 percent annual coupon, 2-year bond
   ii. 5-year $1000 par value, 5 percent annual coupon, 5-year bond
   iii. 5-year $1000 par value, 10 percent annual coupon, 5-year bond

c. Calculate the yields to maturity on each of the bonds in part (b).

d. Why is the yield to maturity on the 10 percent bond less than the yield on the 5 percent, 5-year bond?

6A.2. **Term Structure Theories.** Refer back to question 6A.1.

a. If the expectations theory of the term structure is correct, what do the forward rates calculated in (a) tell you about expected future short-term interest rates?

b. If the liquidity-preference theory is added, what can you conclude about expected future short-term rates?

6A.3. **Calculating Forward Rates.** Suppose in June 2013, the Canada June 2014 strip was selling for $988.53, the Canada June 2015 strip was selling for $969.15, and the Canada June 2016 strip was selling for $945.51. Each strip pays $1,000 at maturity.

a. Calculate the yield to maturity for each bond.
b. Calculate annually compounded, one-year forward rate of interest at June 2014, June 2015, and June 2016.
c. Using the available information, estimate the June 2013 price of a 5 percent Canada bond maturing June 2016. Explain your assumptions.

6A.4. **Understanding the Yield Curve.** Assume that the term structure is upward-sloping. How would you respond to the following statement? "Given the current yield curve, a company should borrow short-term rather than long-term. It will be cheaper."

PART 2

Value

5 The Time Value of Money

6 Valuing Bonds

7 Valuing Stocks

7.1 Stocks and Stock Markets

7.2 Market Values, Book Values, and Liquidation Values

7.3 Valuing Common Stocks

7.4 Simplifying the Dividend Discount Model

7.5 Growth Stocks and Income Stocks

7.6 There Are No Free Lunches on Bay Street

7.7 Market Anomalies and Behavioural Finance

7.8 Summary

8 Net Present Value and Other Investment Criteria

9 Using Discounted Cash Flow Analysis to Make Investment Decisions

10 Project Analysis

CHAPTER 7

Valuing Stocks

LEARNING OBJECTIVES

After studying this chapter, you should be able to:

LO1 Interpret stock trading information found on financial Web sites.

LO2 Calculate the present value of a stock given forecasts of future dividends and future stock price.

LO3 Use stock valuation formulas to infer the expected rate of return on a common stock.

LO4 Interpret price-earnings ratios.

LO5 Explain what professionals mean when they say that "there are no free lunches on Bay Street."

At the Toronto Stock Exchange and many other stock exchanges, all of the stock trading is done electronically, using computers.

A corporation can raise cash to fund its investments by borrowing or by selling new shares of common stock to investors. If it borrows, it has a fixed obligation to repay the lender. If it issues shares, there is no fixed obligation, but the new stockholders become partial owners of the firm. All existing and new stockholders share in its fortunes, in proportion to the number of shares held. In this chapter, we take a first look at common stocks, the stock market, and the principles of stock valuation.

We start by looking at how stocks are bought and sold. Then we look at what determines stock prices and how stock valuation formulas can be used to infer the rate of return that investors are expecting. We will see how the firm's investment opportunities are reflected in the stock price and why stock market analysts focus so much attention on the price-earnings, or P/E, ratio of the company.

Why should you care how stocks are valued? After all, if you want to know the value of a firm's stock, you can look up the stock price on the Web site of major newspapers, such as *The Globe and Mail*'s **www.reportonbusiness.com**, *The National Post*'s **www.financialpost.com**, or other financial Web sites such as **ca.finance.yahoo.com**. But you need to know what determines prices for at least two reasons. First, you may need to value the common stock of a business that is not traded on a stock exchange. Second, in order to make good capital budgeting decisions, corporations need to have some understanding of how the market values firms. A project is attractive if it increases shareholder wealth. But you can't judge that unless you know how shares are valued.

There may be a third reason you would like to know how stocks are valued. You may be hoping that the knowledge will allow you to make a fortune in the stock market. It's a pleasant thought, but we will see that even professional investors find it difficult to outsmart the competition and earn consistently superior returns.

LO1 7.1 STOCKS AND STOCK MARKETS

In Chapter 1, we saw how RIM (Research In Motion) was founded and how it has grown and thrived. Suppose you're convinced that its best days are yet to come, and you want a piece of the action. What should you do?

common stock or **common equity** or **common shares** Ownership shares in a corporation.

If you want to share in RIM's future, you will want to buy **common stock** (or **common equity** or **common shares**) in the firm. Large firms sell or *issue* shares of stock to the public when they need to raise money, and as the name suggests, shareholders *share* the ownership of the firm in proportion to the number of shares they hold.[1] They benefit if the company prospers, and they suffer losses if it does not. This happens because common stock is entitled to the firm's *residual*

[1] We use the terms "shares," "stock," and "common stock" interchangeably, as we do "shareholders" and "stockholders."

cash flow, the remaining cash flow after employees and all other suppliers, lenders, and the government taxes have been paid.

primary market Market for the sale of new securities issued by corporations.

initial public offering (IPO) First offering of stock to the general public.

seasoned equity offering (SEO) Sale of additional stock by a public company

RIM and other public firms sell new shares only infrequently. Sales of new shares by the firm are said to occur in the **primary market**. There are two types of primary market issues: initial public offerings and seasoned equity offerings. In an **initial public offering**, or **IPO**, a company that has been privately owned sells shares to the public for the first time. RIM did its IPO on October 27, 1998. Now, if RIM were to sell more shares, this would be a **seasoned equity offering, SEO**. In IPOs and SEOs companies raise funds by selling these new shares, but the previous owners now have to share ownership (and profits) of the firm with their new co-owners. In this sense, issuing new shares is like having new partners buy into the firm. To do an IPO or an SEO, companies hire an investment bank, such as Scotia Capital, TD Securities, or RBC Capital Markets, to help them price and sell the new shares. The shares are sold to investors by the securities dealers connected to the investment bank. Many of these new shares are typically sold to institutional investors, organizations with large sums of money such as pension funds; but shares can also be sold to retail investors, individuals.

IPOs are often eagerly anticipated, as they are the first opportunity for the general public to buy shares in hot companies that to date have been owned solely by founders and their private financial backers. For example, a star performer in 2000 was 724 Solutions. Its shares were sold to investors at $37.31 each, and by the end of the first day, they had reached $103.50, a gain of over 277 percent. Within one month, the 724 stock price reached over $330!

However, shares of stock can be risky investments. For example, by 2003 those shares of 724 Solutions had fallen below $1. The company decided to exchange 10 old shares for 1 new share, reducing the number of shares outstanding. By June 2004, the reported share price was about $4.20 or $.42 per original share. 724 Solutions ceased to be a public company in August 2006. The largest shareholder, Austin Ventures, purchased all the shares they did not own for $3.77 (US$3.34) per share, taking the company private. If you had bought a share at the end of the first day of trading in 2000, you had lost over 99 percent of your original investment. You can understand why investors would be unhappy if forced to tie the knot with a particular company forever. So large companies usually arrange for their stocks to be listed on a stock exchange, which allows investors to trade existing stocks among themselves. Exchanges are really markets for secondhand stocks, but they prefer to describe themselves as **secondary markets**.

secondary market Market in which already-issued securities are traded among investors.

The major stock exchange in Canada is the Toronto Stock Exchange, TSX, listing shares of established, large companies. The TSX Venture Exchange, TSX-V, lists new, smaller companies, including those active in natural resource exploration, manufacturing, and technology. Both the TSX and the TSX-V are owned by the TMX Group, **www.tmx.com**. The common ownership of the two stock exchanges makes it easier for successful TSX-V companies to move up to the larger TSX. The Canadian National Stock Exchange, CNSX, **www.cnsx.ca**, is a third Canadian stock exchange, listing very small, new ventures. All Canadian markets are electronic auction markets. Each stock exchange maintains an electronic order book, listing offers to buy and sell, with shares sold to the highest bidder.

The two major exchanges in the United States are the New York Stock Exchange (NYSE) and the Nasdaq market. Of course, there are stock exchanges in many other countries. The major exchanges in cities such as London, Tokyo, and Frankfurt trade vast numbers of shares. But there are also literally hundreds of smaller exchanges throughout the world. For example, the Eastern Caribbean Securities Market was established in 2001 and has grown from 2 to 13 listed stocks. Check out **www.123world.com/stockexchanges** for information about the world's stock exchanges.

It is common for large businesses with global operations to list their shares for trading on stock exchanges in different countries. Stocks listed on more than one stock exchange are called interlisted stocks. The NYSE and Nasdaq are popular U.S. exchanges for Canadian and other foreign companies to list their shares. Go to **www.tmx.com/en/pdf/Interlisted.txt** to see the list of all interlisted TSX stocks. The London Stock Exchange (LSE) is also popular for foreign companies. The TSX is a popular location for foreign companies in the resource industry.

Currently, the London Stock Exchange Group, owner of the LSE, and the TMX group, owner of the TSX and TSX-V, are negotiating a merger of the two companies. It will likely increase the foreign company listings on both exchanges.

Most foreign shares listed on the NYSE are an *American Depositary Receipt, ADR*, which is a certificate representing a specific number of shares of the non-U.S. company. The ADRs are sold by American depositary banks, including JPMorgan, who hold the shares issued by the foreign company. ADRs enable U.S. investors to buy shares in foreign companies without the hazards or inconveniences of cross-border & cross-currency transactions. ADRs carry prices in U.S. dollars, pay dividends in U.S. dollars, and can be traded like the shares of U.S.-based companies. Each ADR has a ratio that how many shares it is worth. For example, U.K. firms Astrazeneca (AZN) and GlaxoSmithKline (GSK) are ADRs on the NYSE. Their ratios are 1 and 2, respectively. So one AZN ADR equals 1 share of AstraZeneca PLC, and 1 GSK ADR equals 2 shares of GlaxoSmithKline PLC. Depositary receipts are also used in countries and have various names, including *Global Depositary Receipts* and *European Depositary Receipts*.

The development of electronic trading has been a major catalyst for change in the world's stock exchanges. An important development in recent years has been the advent of alternative trading systems, ATS, and electronic communication networks, ECNs, which have captured ever-larger shares of trading volume. These are electronic auction houses that match investors' orders to buy and sell shares. Pure Trading, a subsidiary of Canadian National Stock Exchange, and Chi-X Canada are alternative trading systems that offering trading of TSX-listed companies.[2]

Suppose that Ms. Jones, a longtime RIM shareholder, no longer wishes to hold her shares in the company. She has to hire a brokerage firm with trading privileges on a stock exchange listing RIM shares. RIM shares are listed on the TSX and Nasdaq, and also on various ATS. Suppose that Mr. Brown wants to become a RIM shareholder. He has to hire a brokerage firm to execute the purchase. Ms. Jones' RIM shares might be sold to Mr. Brown. The transaction merely transfers (partial) ownership of the firm from one investor to another. No new shares are created, and RIM usually will neither care nor even be aware that such a trade has taken place.[3]

When Ms. Jones and Mr. Brown decide to buy or sell RIM stock, they need to give their brokers instructions about the price at which they are prepared to transact. Ms. Jones, who is anxious to sell quickly, might give her broker a *market order* to sell stock at the best available price. On the other hand, Mr. Brown might give his broker a price limit at which he is willing to buy RIM stock. If his order cannot be executed immediately, it is recorded in the exchange's *limit order book* until it can be executed.

READING STOCK MARKET LISTINGS

If you are thinking about buying shares in Research In Motion, you will wish to see its current price. The Internet provides lots of stock information. For example, if you go to **ca.finance.yahoo.com**, enter Research In Motion's TSX ticker symbol, RIM.TO, and ask to "Get Quotes," you will find recent trading data such as that presented in Table 7.1. Data is reported in Canadian dollars.

The last price at which the stock traded on January 12, 2011, was \$62.69 per share, which was \$.54 higher than its closing price the previous day, \$62.15. RIM's opening price, at the start of day, was \$62.72. The ask price is the price you have to pay to buy the stock and the bid price you can sell your stock. The "1y Target Est" is a forecast of RIM's stock price in a year, provided by stock analysts. The ranges of prices at which the stock traded that day, as well as over the

[2] IIROC, Investment Industry Regulatory Organization of Canada, is the national self-regulatory organization that oversees all investment dealers and trading activity on debt and equity marketplaces in Canada. Listed at **www.iiroc.ca/English/About/OurRole/Pages/MarketplaceWeRegulate.aspx** are links to the three Canadian stock exchanges, TSX, TSX-V, and CNSX, and seven Canadian alternative trading systems.

[3] Eventually, RIM must know to whom it should send notices of shareholder meetings, but this information is needed only when such notices are being prepared. In some cases, RIM might care about a stock transaction, for example, if a large investor is building a big stake in the firm. But this is the exception.

TABLE 7.1
Trading data for Research In Motion, RIM.TO, for January 12, 2011.

Last Trade:	**62.69**	Day's Range:	**62.15–62.93**
Trade Time:	**4:41PM EST**	52wk Range:	**49.38–78.78**
Change:	**↑0.54 (0.87%)**	Volume:	**1,499,036**
Prev Close:	**62.15**	Avg Vol (3m):	**2,037,820**
Open:	**62.72**	Market Cap:	**32.55B**
Bid:	**62.67**	P/E (ttm):	**10.78**
Ask:	**62.7**	EPS (ttm):	**5.82**
1y Target Est:	**83.39**	Div & Yield:	**N/A (N/A)**

Source: Yahoo! Finance, January 12, 2011, **http://ca.finance.yahoo.com/q?s=RIM.TO** Fundamental company data provided by Capital IQ. Historical chart data and daily updates provided by Commodity Systems, Inc. (CSI). International historical chart data, daily updates, fund summary, fund performance, dividend data and Morningstar Index data provided by Morningstar, Inc. Real-Time quotes provided by BATS Exchange. Financials data provided by Edgar Online. International historical chart data, daily updates, fundAnalyst estimates data provided by Thomson Financial Network.

previous 52 weeks, are provided. Yahoo tells us that 1,499,036 shares traded this day, as against average daily volume of 2,037,820 shares over the last three months. RIM's "Market Cap" (shorthand for "market capitalization") is the total value of its outstanding shares of stock, $32.55 billion ($62.69 per share × 519.27 million shares). Traders often refer to firms as *large-cap*, *mid-cap*, or *small-cap*, which is a convenient way to summarize the size of a company. There is no official definition of the size ranges. However, Investopedia Web site suggests that $300 million to $2 billion is the range for a small-cap, $2 billion to $10 billion for a mid-cap, and $10 billion or more for a large-cap firm.

price-earnings multiple or **P/E ratio** Ratio of stock price to earnings per share.

dividend yield A stock's cash dividend divided by its current price.

RIM earned $5.82 per share, EPS, in the past year. (The abbreviation "ttm" in the parentheses stands for "trailing 12 months.") Therefore, the ratio of price per share to earnings per share, known as the **price-earnings multiple** or, equivalently, **P/E ratio**, is 62.69/5.82 or 10.78. The P/E ratio is a key tool of stock market analysts, and we will have much to say about it later in the chapter.

The **dividend yield** tells you how much dividend income you would receive for every $100 invested in the stock. Yahoo reported both Div & Yield as N/A which translates as "not available."[4] In fact, RIM pays no dividends, so its dividend was $0 per share and its yield was $0/$62.69 = 0. Of course, this would not be the total rate of return on your investment, as you would also expect some increase in the stock price. The dividend yield is thus much like the current yield of a bond. Both ignore prospective capital gains or losses. For a technology company such as RIM, where developing new products is essential, cash is reinvested in the firm rather than paid out as dividends and capital gains provide the payoff for investing in the company.

Of course, the price at which you can buy shares in RIM changes day to day and minute to minute. Remember, each share represents partial ownership in the firm, and share values will wax or wane with investors' perceptions of the prospects of the company. Figure 7.1 shows the share price of RIM over a six-month period, starting at $55.83 on July 12, 2010, and rising to $62.69 on January 12, 2011, generating a 12.3 percent return over the six months. However, it fell 19.6 percent in the month from August 12, 2010, to September 13, 2010, then increased again. The lesson? Again, we see that stocks can be risky investments.

The TSX stock listings at **www.financialpost.com/markets/data/market-tsx.html**, report similar data as Yahoo, but in one gigantic Web page. Table 7.2 is an excerpt for January 12, 2011, showing the trading volume, high, low, and closing prices for five stocks on that day.[5]

---

[4] Yahoo Finance uses the symbol N/A when the value is zero but also when Yahoo does not have access to the information. So don't assume that N/A means zero. Yahoo Finance provides the most information for U.S. companies and for non-U.S. companies that list their shares for trading on U.S. stock exchanges. RIMM, the Nasdaq listing for Research In Motion, has RIM's financial statements on Yahoo Finance but no financial statements are provided for RIM.TO, the TSX listing for Research In Motion.

[5] If a stock did not trade on the day, the recorded volume would be "nt" (no trade). In the "High/Ask" column is the ask price, the price at which a dealer is willing to sell the stock to an investor. Likewise, in the "Low/Bid" column would be the dealer's bid price, the price at which the dealer is willing to buy the stock from an investor. In the "Close/Previous" column would the last traded price from some previous day.

FIGURE 7.1
Share Price History for Research In Motion.

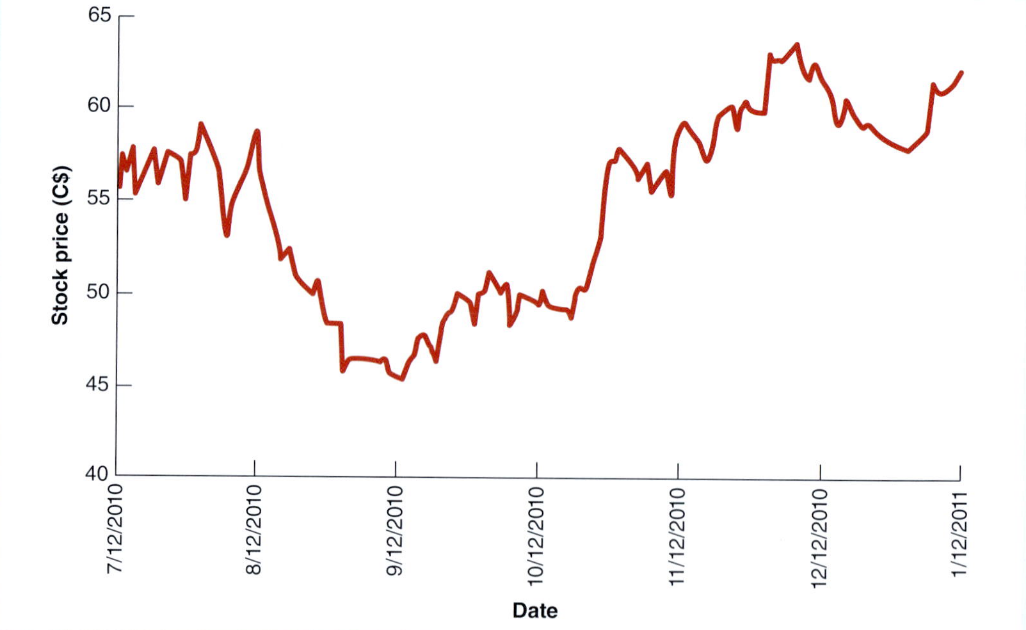

Source: Yahoo! Finance, January 12, 2011, **http://ca.finance.yahoo.com/q?s=RIM.TO** Fundamental company data provided by Capital IQ. Historical chart data and daily updates provided by Commodity Systems, Inc. (CSI). International historical chart data, daily updates, fund summary, fund performance, dividend data and Morningstar Index data provided by Morningstar, Inc. Real-Time quotes provided by BATS Exchange. Financials data provided by Edgar Online. International historical chart data, daily updates, fundAnalyst estimates data provided by Thomson Financial Network.

TABLE 7.2 TSX stock market listings from FinancialPost.com for January 12, 2011.

Stock Description			Daily Trading					52 Weeks		Dividends		Earnings	
Company	Security	Ticker	Volume	High/ Ask	Low/ Bid	Close/ Previous	Net Change	High	Low	Annual Dividends	Yield	P/E	Cumulative
Canadian Tire Corp Ltd.	com	CTC	376	75.5	74.15	75.5	+1.00	76.00	60.00	1.10	1.5	16.7	4.520
Canadian Tire Corp Ltd. v	cl A	CTC.A	209,127	67.32	66.03	66.55	+0.25	68.93	50.86	1.10	1.7	14.7	4.520
Research In Motion Ltd.	com	RIM	1,499,036	62.93	62.15	62.69	+0.54	78.78	44.94	—	—	10.9	US$5.850
Royal Bank of Canada	com	RY	3,544,024	53.04	52.76	53.01	+0.45	62.89	48.85	2.00	3.8	15.2	15.18911
Royal Bank of Canada	pfd 1st ser AA	RY.PR.A	22,173	22.61	22.45	22.59	+0.14	22.88	18.3	1.1125	4.9	—	—

Source: Financial Post site, **www.financialpost.com/markets/data/market-tsx.html**.

The first line of Table 7.2 is for CTC, Canadian Tire Corporation common equity, stock with one vote per share. Next is another Canadian Tire Corporation stock, CTC.A. The "v" at the end of the company name is the method used in the *Financial Post* stock listing to indicate shares with unusual voting rights. CTC.A is Class A non-voting shares. The difference between these two types of equity are the voting rights of each share at shareholders' meetings. At those meetings, an annual event, members of the board of directors are elected, votes occur to approve of committees and initiatives, and presentation about the firm is made by either the CEO or the chair of the board of directors. Each common share gives the shareholder one vote at a shareholder meeting. The CTC non-voting shareholders get to elect three members of the board, but they do not have votes on other issues at the meetings. Typical non-voting shares have no voting rights at shareholders' meetings. Companies issue equity with different numbers of votes per share to help manage control of the corporation.[6]

As of October 2, 2010, there were 78 million CTC Class A non-voting shares outstanding and only 3.4 million CTC common shares. The CTC Class A non-voting shareholders are entitled to $.01 of dividends each year before the CTC common shareholders are paid the same amount. However, the two classes share equally in any further dividends paid. Table 7.2 shows that currently both shares classes receive annual dividends of $1.10 per share. The CTC common shares' high price for the day was $75.5, the low price was $74.15, and they closed at $75.5. The non-voting share, CTC.A, closed at only $66.55. However, the common shares are traded less heavily; only 376 shares as against the 209,127 Class A shares traded on January 12, 2011. This is evidence that a vote is worth money!

The dividend yield, under the heading "Yield," for CTC is 1.10/$75.5 = .015 = 1.5 percent. Therefore, for every $100 invested in the stock, you would receive annual dividend income of $1.50. If you scan Table 7.2, you will see that dividend yields vary across securities. Canadian Tire's non-voting share has a lower price but the same dividend as the common share, generating a higher dividend yield.

preferred stock Stock that takes priority over common stock in regards to dividends.

In addition to common stocks, Table 7.2 shows price for Royal Bank of Canada **preferred stock**, indicated by "PR" in the ticker symbol. Preferred stock typically have fixed dividends that must be paid before the common shareholders receive any dividends. Royal Bank has 17 preferred stocks listed on the TSX. The fixed annual dividend for the 1st Series AA preferred stock is $1.125. Preferred shares can have many different features. We discuss these in more detail in Chapter 14.

Check Point 7.1 Explain the entries for Royal Bank of Canada common stock (RY) in Table 7.2.

7.2 MARKET VALUES, BOOK VALUES, AND LIQUIDATION VALUES

Why were RIM shares selling at $62.69 per share in January 12, 2011, but only $46 in September 2010? And why did it cost $75.5 to buy CTC, Canadian Tire common share? To answer these questions, we need to look at what determines the value.

Finding the value of RIM stock may sound like a simple problem. Each quarter, the company publishes a balance sheet that shows the value of the firm's assets, liabilities, and equity. RIM, like other Canadian companies with global operations and shares listed in the United States, produces its financial statements in U.S. dollars. The simplified balance sheet in Table 7.3 is a snapshot of RIM as of November 27, 2010, but converted to Canadian dollars using the C$/US$ exchange rate for January 12, 2011. The book value of RIM's assets—manufacturing facilities, patents, licences and acquired technology, inventories of materials, cash in the bank, and so on—was $12,038.13 million. RIM's liabilities—money it owes the banks, taxes due to be paid, and the like—amounted to $4,035.03 million. The difference between the value of the assets and the liabilities was $7,973.1 million. This was the **book value** of the firm's equity.[7] Book value records all the money that RIM has raised from its shareholders plus all the earnings that have been plowed back into the firm on the shareholders' behalf.

book value of equity Net worth of the firm according to the balance sheet.

[6] For more information about non-voting shares, go to Chapter 14 and read the common stock section.

[7] "Equity" is yet another word for stock. Thus shareholders are often referred to as "equity investors."

TABLE 7.3
Balance sheet for Research In Motion, November 27, 2010 (C$ millions, converted from US$ as of January 12, 2011).

Assets		Liabilities and Shareholders' Equity	
Plant, equipment, and other assets	12,038.13	Liabilities	4,035.03
		Equity	7,973.10

Note: Shares of stock outstanding: 521.8 million. Book value of equity per share: $7,973.10/521.8 5 $15.28 per share.

Source: Based on information in RIM's 3rd-quarter report, released December 16, 2010. RIM's financial statements are prepared using U.S. GAAP.

TABLE 7.4
Market versus book values based on stock price for January 19, 2011.

Firm	Stock Price ($)	Book Value per Share ($)	Ratio: Price/ Book Value
IMAX	27.67	1.56	17.7
Research In Motion	63.41	15.28	4.2
Saputo	40.78	10.51	3.9
Gildan Activewear	28.06	9.11	3.1
Cameco	39.28	12.88	3.1
Barrick Gold	46.79	17.79	2.6
Canadian Pacific Railway	66.88	29.99	2.2
Royal Bank of Canada	60.66	27.45	2.2
TransCanada	40.01	23.96	1.7
EnCana	30.38	23.37	1.3
Pacific Northern Gas	32.09	25.27	1.3

Source: MSN Finance Web site, **money.ca.msn.com**, Copyright 2011 by MSNBC INTERACTIVE NEWS, LLC. Reproduced with permission of MSNBC INTERACTIVE NEWS, LLC in the format Textbook and E-book via Copyright Clearance Center.

Does the stock price equal book value? In January 2011 RIM shares were selling for a bit more than $63, but as Table 7.3 shows, its book value per share was only $15.28. So the shares were worth about 4.2 times book value. This and the other cases shown in Table 7.4 tell us that investors in the stock market do not just buy and sell at book value per share.

For firms using U.S. GAAP or the former Canadian GAAP, the value of the most assets reported on the firm's balance sheet is equal to their original (or "historical") cost less an allowance for depreciation. But that may not be a good guide to what the firm would need to pay to buy the same assets today. Now that Canadian firms have to use International Financial Reporting Standards, IFRS, the value of assets on the balance sheet, which likely will be called the *statement of financial position*, could be historic cost, or could be fair market value or estimated market value.

liquidation value Net proceeds that would be realized by selling the firm's assets and paying off its creditors.

Well, perhaps stock price equals **liquidation value** per share, that is, the amount of cash per share a company could raise if it sold off all its assets in secondhand markets and paid off all its debts? Wrong again. A successful company ought to be worth more than its liquidation value. That's the goal of bringing all those assets together in the first place.

The difference between a company's actual value and its book or liquidation value is often referred to as *going-concern value*, which refers to three factors:

1. *Extra earning power.* A company may have the ability to earn more than an adequate rate of return on assets. In this case the value of those assets will be higher than their book value or resale (liquidation) value.
2. *Intangible assets.* Accounting rules don't permit firms to put all assets on the balance sheet or statement of financial position, SFP. For example, an amazingly strong marketing staff is not an asset on the SFP. Nevertheless, expertise, experience, and knowledge are crucial assets, and their values do show up in stock prices. RIM, a technology company, continuously works on developing new communication devices. As you can see from Table 7.4, it sells for about 4.2 times book value. Where did all that extra value come from? Largely, it

resulted from the expected success of its extensive research and development (R&D) program. R&D is accounted for as an expense, not as an investment, during the research phase. Once the research has resulted in a viable new product, IFRS provides criteria for capitalizing the expenses to create an intangible assets. U.S. GAAP also has criteria that allows certain costs related to software development be capitalized as a new asset. Successful R&D and the expectation of future successful R&D do show up in stock prices, however.

Market value is not the same as book value or liquidation value; unlike book value and liquidation value, it treats the firm as a going concern.

3. *Value of future investments.* If investors believe a company will have the opportunity to make exceedingly profitable investments in the future, they will pay more for the company's stock today. When Google first sold its stock to investors in 2004, the book value of shareholders' equity was about $2.9 billion. Yet one day after the issue investors valued the equity at over $19 billion. In part, this difference reflected an intangible asset, its unique way of delivery advertising: as being a top search engine on the Internet. But investors also judged that Google was a *growth* company. In other words, they were betting that the company would be able to find other ways to provide services and sell advertising.

It is not surprising that stocks virtually never sell at book or liquidation values. Investors buy shares on the basis of present and *future* earning power. Two key features determine the profits the firm will be able to produce: (1) the earnings that can be generated by the firm's current tangible and intangible assets and (2) the opportunities the firm has to invest in lucrative projects that will increase future earnings.

EXAMPLE 7.1 PACIFIC NORTHERN GAS AND IMAX

IMAX is a growth company. In 2010, its profit was $50.5 million. Yet investors in December 2010 were prepared to pay about 35 times that amount, or $1.77 billion, for IMAX's common stock.

IMAX, headquartered in Mississauga, Ontario, together with its 42 subsidiaries, operates as an entertainment technology company worldwide. It specializes in digital and film-based motion picture technologies. As the company continues to evolve, its potential in the commercial marketplace continues to increase. While IMAX remains committed to its historical roots in museums and science centres, it is rapidly expanding its commercial theatre network. IMAX has forged strategic alliances, relationships, and joint ventures with some of the most prominent exhibitors in the world, including AMC Entertainment, Regal Cinemas, Inc., National Amusements, Odeon & UCI Cinemas, CJ CGV, Wanda Cinema Line Co. Ltd., Tokyu Cinemas, and many more.

Contrast this with Pacific Northern Gas, which distributes natural gas through its pipeline system in northern British Columbia. It is not a growth company; its market is limited to the geographic area it services. More importantly, it is a regulated utility, so its returns on present and future investments are constrained. Pacific Northern Gas's value derives primarily from its existing assets. Therefore, while IMAX shares in 2010 sold for 17.1 times book value, Pacific Northern Gas shares sold at only about 1.3 times book value.

Future investment opportunities are great sources of market value, but they are vulnerable to rapid loss when expectations of the future change. In contrast, earnings from current assets are much more stable. Companies with significant value from growth, such as IMAX, experience wider price swings than those with less value from growth, such as Pacific Northern Gas.

---

market-value balance sheet Financial statement that uses the market value of all assets and liabilities.

Financial executives are not bound by generally accepted accounting principles, and they sometimes construct a firm's **market-value balance sheet**, which helps them think about and evaluate the sources of firm value. Take a look at Table 7.5. A market-value balance sheet contains two classes of assets: (1) assets already in place, both tangible and intangible and (2) opportunities to invest in attractive future ventures. Pacific Northern Gas's stock market value is dominated by tangible assets in place; RIM's by the value of future investment opportunities.

TABLE 7.5
Market-value balance sheet.

Assets	Liabilities and Shareholders' Equity
Assets in place	Market value of debt and other obligations
Investment opportunities	Market value of shareholders' equity

Other firms, such as Microsoft, seem to have it all. Microsoft earns plenty from its current products. These earnings are part of what makes the stock attractive to investors. In addition, investors are willing to pay for the company's ability to invest profitably in new ventures that will increase future earnings.

To summarize:

- *Book value* depends on the accounting rules the firm uses. Either IFRS or U.S. GAAP can result in the book value being what a company has paid for its assets with a simple and often unrealistic deduction for depreciation and no adjustment for inflation. It does not capture the total market value of a business.
- *Liquidation value* is what the company could net by selling its assets and repaying its debts. It does not capture the value of a successful "going concern."
- *Market value* is the amount that investors are willing to pay for the shares of the firm. This depends on the earning power of today's assets and the expected profitability of future investments.

The next question is: What determines market value?

Check Point 7.2

In the 1970s, the computer industry was growing rapidly. In the 1980s, many new competitors entered the market, and computer prices fell. Computer makers in the past decade, including IBM, struggled with thinning profit margins and intense competition. How has the industry's market-value balance sheet changed over time? Have assets in place become proportionately more or less important? Do you think this progression is unique to the computer industry? Think about RIM.

LO2 7.3 VALUING COMMON STOCKS

VALUATION BY COMPARABLES

If book values are unreliable estimates of market value, perhaps there are other, more useful indicators. *Valuation by comparables* is a common first approach. For example, if we were interested in valuing RIM, we would divide its stock price by measures of assets or earnings and then see how these relations stack up against other firms in the same industry.

Look at Table 7.6. In the first row you see that the average stock in the communication services industry sells for 4.1 times its book value. Therefore, as a first stab at valuing RIM, you might estimate that its stock would also sell at 4.1 times book per share. This would give you a value for RIM of $4.1 \times \$15.28 = \$62.65$, a bit lower than its actual market price of \$63.41.

An alternative would be to look at how much investors in the communication services industry are typically prepared to pay for \$1 of earnings. The first row in Table 7.6 shows that the typical price-earnings ratio for these stocks is 11, the same as RIM's. You might therefore presume that RIM stock price is reasonable.

The table sets out the ratios of price-to-book and price-earnings (P/E) for a sample of companies and their industry competitors. Most of the companies' price-to-book ratios are

TABLE 7.6
Price-to-book-value ratios and P/E ratios for selected companies and their competitors.

	Price-to-Book-Value Ratio		Price-Earnings Ratio	
	Company	Industry	Company	Industry
Research In Motion	4.2	4.1	11.0	11.0
IMAX	17.7	17.7	36.7	36.5
Saputo	3.9	3.2	19.4	28.7
Gildan Activewear	3.1	10.6	17.4	38.9
Cameco	3.1	4.0	33.2	15.7
Barrick Gold	2.6	3.5	15.0	23.2
Canadian Pacific Railway	2.2	2.5	17.2	15.3
Royal Bank of Canada	2.2	2.2	16.1	14.2
TransCanada	1.7	1.8	19.1	35.8
EnCana	1.3	1.6	10.8	11.3
Pacific Northern Gas	1.3	3.0	17.8	23.1

fairly close to their industry averages. However, for Gildan Activewear, its price-to-book ratio is substantially less than the industry average. This might be for several reasons. Perhaps Gildan is not doing well compared to its competitors, or its share price is not right. However, it is also possible that the companies in the industry average are not really very similar to Gildan. That is one reason why financial analysts who want to use comparable ratios for valuation will select competitor companies that they assess are similar to the company they are valuing. It is potentially risky to use an industry average when you don't know which firms were used to create the average. Now that Canadian companies financial statements are based on the IFRS rules and American companies financial statements are based on U.S. GAAP rules, the differences in the accounting rules will contribute to variations in comparable ratios.

Price-to-earnings and price-to-book ratios are the most popular rules of thumb for judging the value of a common stock, but financial analysts sometimes look at other multiples (a *multiple* is the ratio of the some value measure to some other firm characteristic). For example, infant firms often do not earn positive profits. So, rather than calculating a price-to-earnings ratio, analysts may look at the price-to-sales ratio for these firms. In the late 1990s, when dot-com companies were growing rapidly but losing lots of money, multiples were often based on revenues divided by the number of subscribers or Web site visits.

There is nothing wrong with rules of thumb if intelligently applied. But all these ratios vary from stock to stock, even for firms in the same line of business; so blind use of industry ratios is unlikely to produce an accurate estimate of the price investors would be prepared to pay for any one stock. To understand why some firms sell at higher multiples than others, we need to dig deeper and look at what determines a stock's value.

PRICE AND INTRINSIC VALUE

In the previous chapter, we saw that the value of a bond is the present value of its coupon payments plus the present value of its final payment of face value. You can think of stocks in a similar way. Instead of receiving coupon payments, investors may receive dividends; and instead of receiving face value, they will receive the stock price at the time they sell their shares.

Consider, for example, an investor who buys a share of Blue Skies Inc. today and plans to sell it in one year. Call the predicted stock price in one year P_1, the expected dividend per share over the year DIV_1, and the discount rate for the stock's expected cash flows r. Then the present value of the cash flows the investor will receive from Blue Skies is

$$V_0 = \frac{DIV_1 + P_1}{1 + r} \tag{7.1}$$

intrinsic value Present value of expected future cash flows from a stock or other security.

We call V_0 the **intrinsic value** of the share. Intrinsic value is just the present value of the cash flows anticipated by the investor in the stock.

To illustrate, suppose investors expect a cash dividend of \$3 over the next year ($DIV_1 = \$3$) and expect the stock to sell for \$81 a year hence ($P_1 = \$81$). If the discount rate is 12 percent, intrinsic value is \$75:

$$V_0 = \frac{3 + 81}{1.12} = \$75$$

You can think of intrinsic value as the "fair" price for the stock. If investors buy the stock for \$75, their expected rate of return will precisely equal the discount rate—in other words, their investment will just compensate them for the opportunity cost of their money.

To confirm this, note that the expected rate of return over the next year is the expected dividend plus the expected increase in price, $P_1 - P_0$, all divided by price at the start of the year, P_0. If the investor buys the shares for intrinsic value, then $P_0 = \$75$ and

$$\text{Expected return} = \frac{DIV_1 + P_1 - P_0}{P_0} = \frac{3 + 81 - 75}{75} = .12, \text{ or } 12\%$$

Notice that this expected return comes in two parts, the dividend and capital gain:

$$\begin{aligned} \textbf{Expected rate of return} &= \textbf{expected dividend yield} + \textbf{expected capital gain} \\ &= \frac{DIV}{P_0} + \frac{P_1 - P_0}{P_0} \\ &= \frac{\$3}{\$75} + \frac{\$81 - \$75}{\$75} \\ &= .04 + .08 = .12, \text{ or } 12\% \end{aligned} \tag{7.2}$$

Of course, the actual return for Blue Skies may turn out to be more or less than investors expect. For example, one of the best-performing stocks on the TSX in 2010 was a producer of oil and gas drilling equipment, Canadian Energy Services & Technology Corp (CEU). Its closing price on December 31, 2010, was \$29.35, up from \$11.90 at the beginning of January. The stock's 2010 dividend was \$.87 so investors earned an actual return of (\$0.87 + \$29.35 − \$11.90)/\$11.90 = 1.539, or 153.9 percent!

CEU's rate of return was almost certainly better than investors expected. At the other extreme, if you had bought shares of Homburg Invest, a company that owns and operates commercial and residential property, on December 31, 2009, you will have paid \$7.51 per share. One year later, the stock was trading from only \$4.10 and had paid no dividends in 2010. The actual rate of return was (\$4.10 − \$7.51)/\$7.51 = −0.45 or −45 percent! Who would buy shares expecting to lose money? Never confuse expected outcomes with actual outcomes.

For many investors, both dividends and capital gains are taxable. Consequently, the investor's *after-tax* rate of return is the best measure of the actual earnings on a stock. To calculate the after-tax rate of return on a stock investment, determine the taxes on dividends and capital gains and use the after-tax cash flows in the return calculation:

$$\textbf{After-tax rate of return} = \frac{DIV_1 - \text{dividend tax}}{P_0} + \frac{\text{capital gain} - \text{capital gains tax}}{P_0} \tag{7.3}$$

EXAMPLE 7.2 **TAXES AND RATE OF RETURN**

You purchased shares of Big Time Toys for \$15 a share and sold them a year later for \$17 each. During the year, you received dividends per share of \$1. Before considering taxes, the rate of return on your investment was (\$1 + \$17 − \$15)/\$15 = .2, or 20 percent. However, your tax rate for dividend income is 20 percent and for capital gains is 16 percent.[8] Thus the dividend tax is \$.20 (= .2 × \$1) and the capital gains tax is \$.32 (= .16 × (\$17 − \$15)). The after-tax rate of return is

$$\text{After-tax rate of return} = \frac{\$1 - \$.2}{\$15} + \frac{\$2 - \$.32}{\$15} = \frac{\$2.48}{\$15} = .1653\text{, or } 16.53\%$$

At each point in time, all securities of the same risk are priced to offer the same expected rate of return. This is a fundamental characteristic of prices in well-functioning markets. It is also common sense.

The dream of every investor is to buy shares at a bargain price, that is, a price less than intrinsic value. But in competitive markets, no price other than intrinsic value could survive for long. To see why, imagine that Blue Skies' current price were above \$75. Then the expected rate of return on Blue Skies stock would be *lower* than that on other securities of equivalent risk. (*Check this!*) Investors would bail out of Blue Skies and move into other securities. In the process they would force down the price of Blue Skies stock. If P_0 were less than \$75, the stock would offer a *higher* expected rate of return than equivalent-risk securities. (*Check this, too!*) Everyone would rush to buy, forcing the price up to \$75. When the stock is priced correctly (that is, price equals present value), the *expected* rate of return on Blue Skies stock is also the rate of return that investors *require* to hold the stock.

Equation 7.1 is just a *definition* of intrinsic value, which works for any discount rate r. Now we can go beyond the definition and identify r as the expected rate of return on all securities at a given level of risk. If a stock is priced correctly, it will offer an expected rate of return equal to that of other equally risky stocks and price will equal intrinsic value:

$$P_0 = \frac{\text{DIV}_1 + P_1}{1 + r} \tag{7.4}$$

Thus, today's price will equal the present value of dividend payments plus the present value of future price. But now we need to take a further step: How do we estimate the future price P_1?

Check Point 7.3

Big Copper Mine is increasing next year's dividend to \$5 per share. The forecast stock price next year is \$105. Equally risky stocks of other companies offer expected rates of return of 10 percent. What should Big Copper's common stock sell for today?

THE DIVIDEND DISCOUNT MODEL

We have managed to explain today's stock price P_0 in terms of the dividend DIV_1 and the expected stock price next year P_1. But future stock prices are not easy to forecast directly, though you may encounter individuals who claim to be able to do so. A formula that requires tomorrow's stock price to explain today's stock price is not generally helpful.

It turns out that we can express a stock's intrinsic value (and, therefore, price) as the present value of all the forecasted future dividends paid by the company to its shareholders without referring to the future stock price. This is the **dividend discount model**:

dividend discount model Discounted cash flow model that states that today's stock price equals the present value of all expected future dividends.

$$P_0 = \text{present value of } (\text{DIV}_1, \text{DIV}_2, \text{DIV}_3, \ldots, \text{DIV}_t, \ldots)$$

$$= \frac{\text{DIV}_1}{1 + r} + \frac{\text{DIV}_2}{(1 + r)^2} + \frac{\text{DIV}_3}{(1 + r)^3} + \cdots + \frac{\text{DIV}_t}{(1 + r)^t} + \cdots$$

[8] Go back to Chapter 3, Section 3.6, for details on the taxation of dividends and capital gains.

How far into the future could we look? In principle, 40, 60, or 100 years or more—corporations are potentially immortal. However, far-distant dividends will not have significant present values. For example, the present value of $1 received in 30 years using a 10 percent discount rate is only $.057. Most of the value of established companies comes from dividends to be paid within a person's working lifetime.

How do we get from the one-period formula $P_0 = (\text{DIV}_1 + P_1)/(1 + r)$ to the dividend discount model? We look at increasingly long investment horizons.

Let's consider investors with different investment horizons. Each investor will value the share of stock as the present value of the dividends that she or he expects to receive plus the present value of the price at which the stock is eventually sold. Unlike bonds, however, the final horizon date for stocks is not specified—stocks do not "mature." Moreover, both dividends and final sales price can be only estimated. But the general valuation approach is the same. For a one-period investor, the valuation formula looks like this:

$$P_0 = \frac{\text{DIV}_1 + P_1}{1 + r}$$

A two-year investor would value the stock as

$$P_0 = \frac{\text{DIV}_1}{1 + r} + \frac{\text{DIV}_2 + P_2}{(1 + r)^2}$$

and a three-year investor would use the formula

$$P_0 = \frac{\text{DIV}_1}{1 + r} + \frac{\text{DIV}_2}{(1 + r)^2} + \frac{\text{DIV}_3 + P_3}{(1 + r)^3}$$

In fact, we can look as far into the future as we like. Suppose we call our horizon date H. Then the stock valuation formula would be

The value of a stock is the present value of the dividends it will pay over the investor's horizon plus the present value of the expected stock price at the end of that horizon.

$$P_0 = \frac{\text{DIV}_1}{1 + r} + \frac{\text{DIV}_2}{(1 + r)^2} + \cdots + \frac{\text{DIV}_H + P_H}{(1 + r)^H} \qquad (7.5)$$

That is, the value of a stock is the present value of the dividends it will pay over the investor's horizon plus the present value of the expected stock price at the end of that horizon.

Does this mean investors of different horizons will all come to different conclusions about the value of the stock? No! Regardless of the investment horizon, the stock value will be the same. This is because the stock price at the horizon date is determined by expectations of dividends from that date forward. Therefore, as long as the investors agree about a firm's prospects, they will also agree on its present value. Let's confirm this with an example.

EXAMPLE 7.3 VALUING BLUE SKIES STOCK

Blue Skies is growing steadily, and investors expect both the stock price and the dividend to increase at 8 percent per year. Now consider three investors: Erste, Zweiter, and Dritter. Erste plans to hold Blue Skies for one year, Zweiter for two, and Dritter for three. Compare their payoffs:

	Year 1	Year 2	Year 3
Erste	$\text{DIV}_1 = 3$ $P_1 = 81$		
Zweiter	$\text{DIV}_1 = 3$	$\text{DIV}_2 = 3.24$ $P_2 = 87.48$	
Dritter	$\text{DIV}_1 = 3$	$\text{DIV}_2 = 3.24$	$\text{DIV}_3 = 3.50$ $P_3 = 94.48$

Remember, we assumed that dividends and stock prices for Blue Skies are expected to grow at a steady 8 percent. Thus $DIV_2 = \$3 \times 1.08 = \$3.24$; $DIV_3 = \$3.24 \times 1.08 = \$3.50$; and so on.

Each investor requires the same 12 percent expected return. So we can calculate present value over Erste's one-year horizon:

$$P_0 = \frac{DIV_1 + P_1}{1 + r} = \frac{\$3 + \$81}{1.12} = \$75$$

or Zweiter's two-year horizon:

$$P_0 = \frac{DIV_1}{1 + r} + \frac{DIV_2 + P_2}{(1 + r)^2}$$
$$= \frac{\$3}{1.12} + \frac{\$3.24 + \$87.48}{(1.12)^2}$$
$$= \$2.68 + \$72.32 = \$75$$

or Dritter's three-year horizon:

$$P_0 = \frac{DIV_1}{1 + r} + \frac{DIV_2}{(1 + r)^2} + \frac{DIV_3 + P_3}{(1 + r)^3}$$
$$= \frac{\$3}{1.12} + \frac{\$3.24}{(1.12)^2} + \frac{\$3.50 + \$94.48}{(1.12)^3}$$
$$= \$2.68 + \$2.58 + \$69.74 = \$75$$

All agree the stock is worth \$75 per share. This illustrates our basic principle: The value of a common stock equals the present value of dividends received out to the investment horizon plus the present value of the forecast stock price at the horizon. Moreover, when you move the horizon date, the stock's present value should not change. The principle holds for horizons of 1, 3, 10, 20, and 50 years or more.

Check Point 7.4

Refer to Check Point 7.3. Assume that Big Copper Mine's dividend and share price are expected to grow at a constant 5 percent rate per year. Calculate the current value of its stock with the dividend discount model using a three-year horizon. You should get the same answer as for Check Point 7.3.

Look at Table 7.7, which continues the Blue Skies example for various time horizons, still assuming that the dividends are expected to increase at a steady 8 percent compound rate. The expected price increases at the same 8 percent rate. Each row in the table represents a present value calculation for a different horizon year. Note that present value does not depend on the

TABLE 7.7
Value of Blue Skies stock for various time horizons, given 8 percent growth of dividends.

Horizon, Years	PV (dividends)	+	PV (terminal price)	=	Value per Share
1	\$ 2.68		\$72.32		\$75.00
2	5.26		69.74		75.00
3	7.75		67.25		75.00
10	22.87		52.13		75.00
20	38.76		36.24		75.00
30	49.81		25.19		75.00
50	62.83		12.17		75.00
100	73.02		1.98		75.00

FIGURE 7.2
Value of Blue Skies for different horizons.

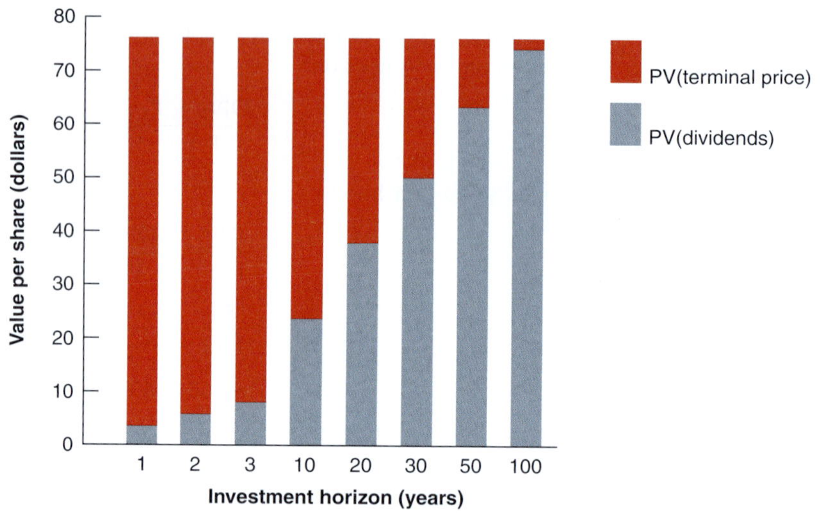

investment horizon. Figure 7.2 presents the same data in a graph. Each column shows the present value of the dividends up to the horizon and the present value of the price at the horizon. As the horizon recedes, the dividend stream accounts for an increasing proportion of present value, but the *total* present value of dividends plus terminal price always equals $75.

If the horizon is infinitely far away, then we can forget about the final horizon price—it has almost no present value—and simply say

$$\text{Stock price} = \text{PV(all future dividends per share)} \tag{7.6}$$

This is the dividend discount model.

LO3 7.4 SIMPLIFYING THE DIVIDEND DISCOUNT MODEL

THE DIVIDEND DISCOUNT MODEL WITH NO GROWTH

Consider a company that pays out all its earnings to its common shareholders. Such a company could not grow because it could not reinvest.[9] Stockholders might enjoy a generous immediate dividend, but they could forecast no increase in future dividends. The company's stock would offer a perpetual stream of equal cash payments, $DIV_1 = DIV_2 = \ldots = DIV_t = \ldots$

The dividend discount model says that these no-growth shares should sell for the present value of a constant, perpetual stream of dividends. We learned how to do that calculation when we valued perpetuities in Chapter 5. Just divide the annual cash payment by the discount rate. The discount rate is the rate of return demanded by investors in other stocks of the same risk:

$$P_0 = \frac{DIV_1}{r} \tag{7.7}$$

Since our company pays out all its earnings as dividends, dividends and earnings are the same, and we might just as well calculate stock value by

$$\text{Value of a no-growth stock} = P_0 = \frac{EPS_1}{r}$$

[9] We assume it does not raise money by issuing new shares.

where EPS_1 represents next year's earnings per share of stock. Thus some people loosely say, "Stock price is the present value of future earnings," and calculate value by this formula. Be careful—this is a special case of no growth. We'll return to the formula later in this chapter.

EXAMPLE 7.4 **PREFERRED SHARES: SHARES WITH NON-GROWING DIVIDENDS**

A preferred share is an example of a share with constant, non-growing dividend. Look back to Table 7.2 at Royal Bank of Canada Utilities 1st series AA preferred share, RY.PR.A, with a promised annual dividend of \$1.1125. The price of this preferred share can be calculated with the no-growth dividend formula, equation 7.7. Assume that rate of return demanded by investors in preferred shares of this risk is 4.925 percent. Given its constant dividend, DIV_1, of \$1.1125, the price of CU.PR.A is

$$P_0 = \frac{DIV_1}{r} = \frac{\$1.1125}{.04925} = \$22.59$$

Where did the discount rate in Example 7.4 come from? We calculated the expected rate of return by rearranging the no-growth formula as

$$r = \frac{DIV}{P_0} = \frac{\$1.1125}{\$22.59} = .04925, \text{ or } 4.925\%$$

You should not be surprised that the price calculated in Example 7.4 equals the price of the preferred share reported in Table 7.2!

Check Point 7.5

Moonshine Industries has produced a barrel per week for the past 20 years, but cannot grow because of certain legal hazards. It earns \$25 per share per year and pays it all out to shareholders. The shareholders have alternative, equivalent-risk ventures yielding 20 percent per year on average. How much is one share of Moonshine worth? Assume the company can keep going indefinitely.

THE CONSTANT-GROWTH DIVIDEND DISCOUNT MODEL

The dividend discount model requires a forecast of dividends for every year into the future, which poses a bit of a problem for stocks with potentially infinite lives. Unless we want to spend a lifetime forecasting dividends, we must use simplifying assumptions to reduce the number of estimates. The easiest simplification assumes a no-growth perpetuity that works for no-growth common shares and most preferred shares.

Here's another simplification that finds a good deal of practical use: Suppose forecast dividends grow at a constant rate into the indefinite future. If dividends grow at a steady rate, then instead of forecasting an infinite number of dividends, we need to forecast only the next dividend and the dividend growth rate.

Recall Blue Skies. It will pay a \$3 dividend in one year. If the dividend grows at a constant rate of $g = .08$ (8 percent) thereafter, dividends in future years will be

$$\begin{aligned} DIV_1 &= \$3 & &= \$3.00 \\ DIV_2 &= \$3 \times (1 + g) = \$3 \times 1.08 & &= \$3.24 \\ DIV_3 &= \$3 \times (1 + g)^2 = \$3 \times 1.08^2 & &= \$3.50 \end{aligned}$$

Plug these forecasts of future dividends into the dividend discount model:

$$P_0 = \frac{\text{DIV}_1}{1+r} + \frac{\text{DIV}_1(1+g)}{(1+r)^2} + \frac{\text{DIV}_1(1+g)^2}{(1+r)^3} + \frac{\text{DIV}_1(1+g)^3}{(1+r)^4} + \cdots$$

$$= \frac{\$3}{1.12} + \frac{\$3.24}{1.12^2} + \frac{\$3.50}{1.12^3} + \frac{\$3.78}{1.12^4} + \cdots$$

$$= \$2.68 + \$2.58 + \$2.49 + \$2.40 + \cdots$$

Although there is an infinite number of terms, each term is proportionately smaller than the preceding one as long as the dividend growth rate, g, is less than the discount rate, r. Because the present value of far-distant dividends will always get closer to zero, the sum of all of these terms is finite despite the fact that an infinite number of dividends will be paid. The sum can be shown to equal

$$P_0 = \frac{\text{DIV}_1}{r-g} \tag{7.8}$$

constant-growth dividend discount model Version of the dividend discount model in which dividends grow at a constant rate.

This equation is called the **constant-growth dividend discount model**, or the *Gordon growth model*, after Myron Gordon, who popularized it.[10]

EXAMPLE 7.5 BLUE SKIES VALUED BY THE CONSTANT-GROWTH MODEL

Let's apply the constant-growth model to Blue Skies. Assume a dividend has just been paid. The next dividend, to be paid in a year, is forecast as $\text{DIV}_1 = \$3$, the growth rate of dividends is $g = 8$ percent, and the discount rate is $r = 12$ percent. Therefore, we solve for the current stock price as

$$P_0 = \frac{\text{DIV}_1}{r-g} = \frac{\$3}{.12-.08} = \$75$$

A stock with a constant-growth dividend will also have a constant-growth stock price. To see this, let's go back to Example 7.5 and calculate Blue Skies' share price in one year. The next dividend, DIV_2, is forecasted as $\text{DIV}_1 \times (1+g) = \$3 \times 1.08 = \$3.24$. The stock price, P_1, is forecasted to be $\$3.24/(.12 - .08) = \$81$. Thus, Blue Skies' stock price is expected to increase $\$81 - \$75/\$75 = .08$, or 8 percent, over the next year. Both the dividend and price of Blue Skies' stocks are growing at 8 percent per year.

The constant-growth formula, equation 7.8, is related to the formula for the present value of a perpetuity. Suppose you forecast no growth in dividends ($g = 0$). Then the dividend stream is a simple perpetuity, and the valuation formula is $P_0 = \text{DIV}_1/r$. This is precisely equation 7.7, the formula you used in Check Point 7.5 to value Moonshine, a no-growth common stock.

In the constant-growth model, a higher g generates a higher stock price. However, the constant-growth formula is valid only when g is less than r. If someone forecasts perpetual dividend growth at a rate greater than investors' required return r, two things happen:

1. The formula explodes. It gives nutty answers. (Try a numerical example.)
2. You know the forecast is wrong because far-distant dividends would have incredibly high present values. (Again, try a numerical example. Calculate the present value of a dividend paid after 100 years, assuming $\text{DIV}_1 = \$3$, $r = .12$, but $g = .20$.)

[10] Notice that the first dividend is assumed to come at the end of the first period and is discounted for a full period. If the stock has just paid dividend D_0, then next year's dividend will be $(1 + g)$ times the dividend just paid. So another way to write the valuation formula is

$$P_0 = \frac{\text{DIV}_1}{r-g} = \frac{\text{DIV}_0 \times (1+g)}{r-g}$$

ESTIMATING EXPECTED RATES OF RETURN

We argued earlier, in Section 7.3, that in competitive markets common stocks with the same risk are priced to offer the same expected rate of return. But how do you figure out what that expected rate of return is?

It's not easy. Consensus estimates of future dividends, stock prices, or overall rates of return are not published in *The Globe and Mail* or reported by TV newscasters. Economists argue about which statistical models give the best estimates. There are nevertheless some useful rules of thumb that can give sensible numbers.

One rule of thumb is based on the constant-growth dividend discount model. Remember that it forecasts a constant growth rate, g, in both future dividends and stock prices. That means expected capital gains equal g per year.

We can calculate the expected rate of return by rearranging the constant-growth formula as

$$r = \frac{\text{DIV}_1}{P_0} + g \qquad (7.9)$$

$$= \text{dividend yield} + \text{growth rate}$$

For Blue Skies from Example 7.5, the expected first-year dividend is \$3 and the growth rate 8 percent. With an initial stock price of \$75, the expected rate of return is

$$r = \frac{\text{DIV}_1}{P_0} + g$$

$$= \frac{\$3}{\$75} + .08 = .04 + .08 = .12, \text{ or } 12\%$$

Suppose we found another stock with the same risk as Blue Skies. It ought to offer the same expected rate of return even if its immediate dividend or expected growth rate is very different. The required rate of return is not the unique property of Blue Skies or any other company; it is set in the worldwide market for common stocks. Blue Skies cannot change its value of r by paying higher or lower dividends, or by growing faster or slower, unless these changes also affect the risk of the stock. When we use the rule-of-thumb formula, $r = \text{DIV}_1/P_0 + g$, we are *not* saying that r, the expected rate of return, is *determined* by DIV_1 or g. It is determined by the rate of return offered by other equally risky stocks. That return determines how much investors are willing to pay for Blue Skies' forecast future dividends:

$$\underbrace{\frac{\text{DIV}_1}{P_0} + g}_{\substack{\text{Given DIV}_1\text{ and}\\ g\text{, investors set}\\ \text{the stock price}}} = r = \underbrace{\text{expected rate of return offered by other equally risky stocks}}_{\substack{\text{so that Blue Skies offers an}\\ \text{adequate expected rate of return, } r}}$$

EXAMPLE 7.6 BLUE SKIES GETS A WINDFALL

Blue Skies has won a lawsuit against its archrival, Nasty Manufacturing, which forces Nasty Manufacturing to withdraw as a competitor in a key market. As a result Blue Skies is able to generate 9 percent per year future growth without sacrificing immediate dividends. Will that increase r, the expected rate of return?

This is very good news for Blue Skies shareholders. The stock price will jump to

$$P_0 = \frac{\text{DIV}_1}{r - g} = \frac{\$3}{.12 - .09} = \$100$$

(Continued)

(Concluded)

But at the new price Blue Skies will offer the same 12 percent expected return:

$$r = \frac{\text{DIV}_1}{P_0} + g$$

$$= \frac{\$3}{\$100} + .09 = .12, \text{ or } 12\%$$

Blue Skies' good news is reflected in a higher stock price today, not in a higher expected rate of return in the future. The unchanged expected rate of return corresponds to Blue Skies' unchanged risk.

Check Point 7.6

Big Copper Mine can grow at 5 percent per year indefinitely. It's selling at $100, and next year's dividend is $5. What is the expected rate of return from investing in Carrabasset Mining common stock? Carrabasset and Big Copper shares are equally risky.

Few real companies are expected to grow in such a regular and convenient way as Blue Skies or Big Copper Mine. Nevertheless, in some mature industries, growth is reasonably stable and the constant-growth model approximately valid. In such cases the model can be turned around to infer the rate of return expected by investors.

NON-CONSTANT GROWTH

Many companies grow at rapid or irregular rates for several years before finally settling down. Obviously we can't use the constant-growth dividend discount model in such cases. However, there is an alternative approach. Set the *investment horizon* (year H) at the future year by which you expect the company's growth to settle down. Calculate the present value of dividends from now to the horizon year. Forecast the stock price in that year and discount it also to present value. Then add it up to get the total present value of dividends plus the ending stock price. The formula is

$$P_0 = \underbrace{\frac{\text{DIV}_1}{1+r} + \frac{\text{DIV}_2}{(1+r)^2} + \cdots + \frac{\text{DIV}_H}{(1+r)^H}}_{\text{PV of dividends from year 1 to horizon}} + \underbrace{\frac{P_H}{(1+r)^H}}_{\text{PV of stock price at horizon}} \qquad (7.10)$$

The stock price in the horizon year is often called *terminal value*.

EXAMPLE 7.7 ESTIMATING THE VALUE OF SAPUTO STOCK

Saputo is Canada's largest cheese producer and is among the top three dairy processors in the United States and top 12 in the world. In January 2011 the price of Saputo's stock was about $41. The company's annual dividend was currently $.64 a share. So Saputo was selling at a dividend yield of $.64/$41 = .0156, or 1.56 percent. Let's use the dividend discount model to see if we can make sense of this stock value.

Earnings per share in 2010 were $2.1, making the payout ratio $\text{DIV}_0/\text{EPS}_0$ = $.64/$2.1 = .305 or 30.5 percent. In 2011, financial analysts were optimistic about the prospects for Saputo and were forecasting that earnings would grow over the next 5 years by 10 percent a year.[11] This growth rate is almost certainly higher than the return, *r*, that investors required from Saputo stock, and it is unrealistic

---

[11] Consensus analysts' forecasts were from at **ca.finance.yahoo.com**. They were provided there by Thomson Financial Network.

to suppose that such rapid growth could continue indefinitely. Therefore, we cannot use the simple perpetual-growth formula to value Saputo. Instead, we will break the problem down into three steps:

Step 1. Value Saputo's dividends over the period of rapid growth.

Step 2. Estimate Saputo's stock price at the horizon year, when growth should have settled down.

Step 3. Calculate the present value of Saputo stock by summing the present value of dividends up to the horizon year and the present value of the stock price at the horizon.

Step 1: Our first task is to value Saputo's dividends over the next five years. If dividends keep pace with the 10 percent growth in earnings, then forecasted earnings and dividends are as follows:

Year	**1**	**2**	**3**	**4**	**5**
Earnings per share	2.31	2.54	2.80	3.07	3.38
Dividends per share (30.50% of earnings)	.70	.78	.85	.94	1.03

We estimate that in 2011 investors required a return of about 6 percent from Saputo's stock.[12] In this case the present value of the forecast dividends for years 1 to 5 was

$$\text{PV of dividends years 1 to 5} = \frac{\$.70}{1.06} + \frac{\$.78}{1.06^2} + \frac{\$.85}{1.06^3} + \frac{\$.94}{1.06^4} + \frac{\$1.03}{1.06^5} = \$3.58$$

Step 2: The trickier task is to estimate the price of Saputo stock in the horizon year 5. The most likely scenario is that after year 5 growth will gradually settle down to a sustainable rate, but to keep life simple, we will assume that in year 6 the growth rate falls *immediately* to 4.17 percent a year.[13] Thus the forecast dividend in year 6 is

$$\text{DIV}_6 = 1.0417 \times \text{DIV}_5 = 1.0417 \times \$1.03 = \$1.073$$

and the expected price at the end of year 5 is the present value of the expected dividends from year 6 to infinity:

$$P_5 = \frac{\text{DIV}_6}{r - g} = \frac{\$1.073}{.06 - .0417} = \$58.63$$

Step 3: The value of Saputo today is equal to the present value of forecast dividends up to the horizon date plus the present value of the price at the horizon, the end of year 5. Thus,

$$P_0 = \text{PV(dividends years 1–5)} + \text{PV(price at end of year 5)}$$

$$= \$3.58 + \frac{\$58.63}{(1.06)^5} = \$47.39$$

A Valuation Check. Our estimate of Saputo's value in Example 7.7 looks somewhat reasonable, but the estimate is bigger than Saputo's actual market price. But does it make you nervous to note that the estimate of the terminal price accounts for such a large proportion of the stock's value? It should. Only very minor changes in your assumptions about growth beyond year 5 could change the estimate of this terminal price by 10, 20, or 30 percent.

In the case of Saputo we *know* what the market price really was in January 2011, but suppose you are using the dividend discount model to value a company going public for the first time, or

[12] For now, you can take this value purely as an assumption. In Chapter 12, we will show how to estimate required returns.

[13] We will show shortly that if a company plows back a constant proportion of earnings and earns a constant rate of return on these new investments, then earnings and dividends will grow by g = plowback ratio × return on new investment. Thus, if from year 5 onward, Saputo continues to reinvest 69.5 percent (plowback ratio = 1 − payout ratio = 1 − .305) of its earnings but earns only its cost of capital on this investment, earnings and dividends will grow by .695 × .06 = .0417.

that you are wondering whether to buy Blue Skies' Concatenator division. In such cases you do not have the luxury of looking up the market price at **www.globeinvestor.com**. A valuation error of 30 percent could amount to serious money. Wise managers, therefore, check that their estimate of value is in the ballpark by looking at what the market is prepared to pay for similar businesses. For example, suppose you can find mature, public companies whose scale, risk, and growth prospects today roughly match those projected for Saputo at the investment horizon. You discover that their stocks tend to sell at multiples of 18 times recent earnings. Then you can reasonably guess that Saputo's value in year 5 will be about 15 times current earnings, that is, $17 \times \$3.38 = \$57.46$. This is not too far from the \$58.63 horizon value we obtained from the dividend discount model.

Of course, these checks using price-earnings or price-to-book ratios are just an application of the *valuation by comparables* method introduced earlier in the chapter. One other way to check the value is use another valuation method. A common one is to value the business (assets) and then subtract the market value of the debt to estimate the value of the equity. There are various business valuation methods. A comparable business valuation measure similar to price-earnings ratio is to use ratio of value of a comparable business to its earnings before interest, depreciation and amortization (EV/EBITDA). A business valuation method similar to the dividend discount model is to calculate the present value of the firm's expected free cash flows (see Chapter 4), which is the cash flow available to pay to shareholders and bondholders. We provide more details about this valuation method in Chapter 13.

Check Point 7.7

Suppose you decide on further analysis that, after year 5, Saputo's earnings and dividends will grow by a constant 5 percent a year. How does this affect your estimate of the value of Saputo stock at year 0?

Not all companies list their stocks for trading on stock exchanges. This is especially the case for small companies. Listing is costly and also public companies must regularly release financial information. Some companies are not public so they can keep their information private. However, these valuation models can also be used to value the shares of a private company. If owner of a private company wants to sell his shares to someone else, he needs to value the equity. Comparables are often used to give a quick assessment of the value of private company. Find a public company that is similar to the private company and calculate its price-to-book and P/E ratios and use them to value the equity of the private company. As a shareholder of a private company, you receive the same type of cash payments as the shareholder of public company: dividends. So the dividend model can also be used to estimate the value of the equity. Because private equity is not easy to sell, typically the estimated price is reduced to capture the impact of the illiquidity of the shares, relative to liquidity of public shares.

LO4 7.5 GROWTH STOCKS AND INCOME STOCKS

We often hear investors speak of *growth stocks* and *income stocks*. They buy growth stocks primarily in the expectation of capital gains, and they are interested in the future growth of earnings rather than in next year's dividends. On the other hand, they buy income stocks principally for the cash dividends. Let us see whether these distinctions make sense.

Think back once more to Blue Skies. It is expected to pay a dividend next year of \$3 ($DIV_1 = 3$), and this dividend is expected to grow at a steady rate of 8 percent a year ($g = .08$). If investors require a return of 12 percent ($r = .12$), then the price of Blue Skies should be $DIV_1/(r - g) = \$3/(.12 - .08) = \$75$.

But what determines the rate of dividend growth? Let's check. Suppose that Blue Skies starts year 1 with book equity of $25 a share and earns a return on this equity of 20 percent a year. Then Blue Skies' earnings per share are

$$\text{Earnings per share} = \text{initial book equity per share} \times \text{return on equity} = \$25 \times .20 = \$5$$

payout ratio Fraction of earnings paid out as dividends.

plowback ratio Fraction of earnings retained by the firm. Also called *retention ratio*.

sustainable growth rate Steady rate at which a firm can grow; return on equity × plowback ratio.

Blue Skies proposes to pay a dividend in year 1 of $DIV_1 = \$3$ a share, which leaves $2 a share to be plowed back in new plant and equipment. The company's **payout ratio** (the fraction of earnings paid out as dividends) is therefore $3/$5 = .60, and its **plowback ratio** (the fraction of earnings reinvested in the firm) is $2/$5 = .40.

After reinvesting 40 percent of its earnings, Blue Skies will start year 2 with additional equity per share of

$$\begin{aligned}&\text{Earnings per share in year 1} \times \text{plowback ratio}\\&= \text{initial equity per share} \times \text{return on equity} \times \text{plowback ratio}\end{aligned}$$

Since Blue Skies started with assets of $25 a share, the growth in Blue Skies' equity is $2/$25 = .08, or 8 percent. The growth rate is

$$\text{Growth rate} = \text{return on equity} \times \text{plowback ratio}$$

If a company earns a constant return on its equity and plows back a constant proportion of earnings, then

g = sustainable growth rate = return on equity × plowback ratio

For example, for Blue Skies, the growth rate equals .20 × .40 = .08, or 8 percent.

If Blue Skies continues to earn a return of 20 percent on its equity and plows back 40 percent of its earnings in new plant and equipment, earnings and dividends will also continue to grow by 8 percent. Financial managers sometimes refer to this as the company's **sustainable growth rate**, because it is the rate of growth the company can sustain from reinvested earnings without changing its leverage.

What if Blue Skies did not plow back *any* of its earnings into new plant and equipment? In that case it would pay out all of its earnings, $5 a share, but would forgo any further growth in earnings and dividends:

$$g = \text{sustainable growth rate} = \text{return on equity} \times \text{plowback ratio} = .20 \times 0 = 0$$

We could recalculate the stock value with $DIV_1 = EPS_1 = \$5$ and $g = 0$:

$$P_0 = \frac{DIV_1}{r - g} = \frac{\$5}{.12 - 0} = \$41.67$$

Plowing earnings back into new investments may result in growth in earnings and dividends, but it does not add to the current stock price if that money is expected to earn only the return that investors require. Plowing earnings back *does* add to value if investors believe that the reinvested earnings will earn a higher rate of return than investors require.

Thus, if Blue Skies did not reinvest any of its earnings, its stock price would not be $75 but $41.67. The $41.67 represents the value of earnings from assets that are already in place. The rest of the stock price ($75 − $41.67 = $33.33) is the net present value of the *future* investments that Blue Skies is expected to make.

What if Blue Skies kept to its policy of reinvesting 40 percent of its profits but the forecast return on new investments was only 12 percent? In that case the sustainable growth rate would also be lower:

$$\begin{aligned}g &= \text{sustainable growth rate} = \text{return on equity} \times \text{plowback ratio}\\&= .12 \times .40 = .048, \text{ or } 4.8\%\end{aligned}$$

If we plug this new figure into our valuation formula, we come up again with a value of $41.67 for Blue Skies stock:

$$P_0 = \frac{DIV_1}{r - g} = \frac{\$3}{.12 - .048} = \$41.67$$

To repeat, if Blue Skies did not reinvest any of its earnings, the value of its stock would simply derive from the stream of earnings from the existing assets:

$$P_0 = \frac{DIV_1}{r} = \frac{EPS_1}{r} = \frac{\$5}{.12} = \$41.67$$

Finance in Action

Valuing Growth Opportunities

In April 2004 Google, the Internet search-engine provider, announced plans to go public. Rather than selling shares at a fixed price, it proposed to auction them to investors. Stock would be allotted to investors who were prepared to pay the most, but all those receiving stock would pay the same price.

The popularity of Google's sophisticated search technology created enormous interest in the issue, and investment managers and their advisors began to debate how much the stock was worth. Google's preliminary prospectus suggested a value of between \$108 and \$135 a share, which would have valued the equity at \$29 billion to \$36 billion.

If Google stock were sold at these prices, book value per share would amount to less than \$10 and earnings per share would be about \$1. Clearly a stock price of \$108 or more could not be justified by the stream of earnings generated by existing assets; it would make sense only if investors believed that Google had very valuable growth opportunities that would allow it to earn high returns on future investments. As *The Wall Street Journal* commented, "Sure, the company is making money hand over fist, and it has juicy margins and profits that are expanding rapidly. But . . . in the long run, Google likely will have to prove that it can continue to come up with new ways to profit from its dominant position in the Web-search business for its shares to be big winners."

It is notoriously difficult to guess what future opportunities might become available to a high-tech company. Rather than attempting to make detailed growth forecasts, many investors simply compared Google with rival companies such as Yahoo, whose stock was also trading at a price of around 100 times recent earnings.

As the date of the issue approached, a number of financial analysts expressed reservations about Google's suggested price range, and the company announced that it was reducing the number of shares on offer and cutting its estimate of the issue price to \$85 to \$95 a share. The auction took place in August, and after investors had submitted their bids, Google announced a sale price of \$85, somewhat below the point at which the supply of shares equalled demand. It seemed that the pessimists had been right in their criticisms of the price range Google had originally suggested. However, once trading started, investors rushed to buy. Google stock opened for trading at \$100, and within five months the price had doubled to just over \$200; in early 2008 the stock was selling at around \$600. It seems that valuing growth stocks is far from an exact science.

Equally, if the company *did* reinvest each year but earned only the return that investors require, those new investments would not add any value; the price of the stock would still be \$41.67. Fortunately, investors believe that Blue Skies has the opportunity to earn 20 percent on its new investments, well above the 12 percent return that investors require. This is reflected in the \$75 that investors are prepared to pay for the stock. The total value of Blue Skies stock is equal to the value of its assets in place *plus* the **present value of its growth opportunities**, or **PVGO**:

present value of growth opportunities (PVGO) Net present value of a firm's future investments.

Value of assets in place	\$41.67
+ Present value of growth opportunities (PVGO)	33.33
= Total value of Blue Skies stock	\$75.00

The superior prospects of Blue Skies are reflected in its price-earnings ratio. With a stock price of \$75 and earnings of \$5, the P/E ratio is \$75/\$5 = 15. If Blue Skies had no growth opportunities, its stock price would be only \$41.67 and its P/E would be \$41.67/\$5 = 8.33. The P/E ratio is, therefore, an indicator of Blue Skies' rosy prospects.

Does this mean that the financial manager should celebrate if the firm's stock sells at a high P/E? The answer is usually yes. The high P/E suggests that investors think that the firm has good growth opportunities. However, firms can have high P/E ratios not because the price is high but because earnings are temporarily depressed. A firm that earns *nothing* in a particular period will have an *infinite* P/E.

Of course, valuing stocks is always harder in practice than in principle. Forecasting cash flows and settling on an appropriate discount rate require skill and judgment. The difficulties are often greatest in the case of companies like Blue Skies, whose value comes largely from growth opportunities rather than assets that are already in place. As the Finance in Action box here shows, in these cases there is plenty of room for disagreement about value.

Check Point 7.8

Suppose that instead of plowing money back into lucrative ventures, Blue Skies' management is investing at an expected return on equity of 10 percent, which is below the return of 12 percent that investors could expect to get from comparable securities.

a. Find the sustainable growth rate of dividends and earnings in the above circumstances. Assume a 60 percent payout ratio.
b. Find the new value of its investment opportunities. Explain why this value is negative despite the positive growth rate of earnings and dividends.
c. If you were a corporate raider, would Blue Skies be a good candidate for an attempted takeover?

LO5 7.6 THERE ARE NO FREE LUNCHES ON BAY STREET

We have explained how common stocks are valued. Does that mean that we have just given the game away and told you how to make an instant fortune on the stock market? We are sorry to disappoint you. It is not so easy to beat the market, and even highly paid pros find it very difficult to do so with any consistency.

Look, for example, at Figure 7.3, which shows the average performance of general equity mutual funds over three decades compared to that of the Standard & Poor's S&P 500 Index. You can see that in some years these mutual funds did beat the market, but just as often it was the other way around. Of course, it would be surprising if some of the managers were not smarter than others and were able to earn superior returns; but it seems hard to spot the smart ones, and the top-performing managers one year have about an average chance of falling on their face the next year.

FIGURE 7.3
Annual returns on the S&P 500 Index versus general equity mutual funds.

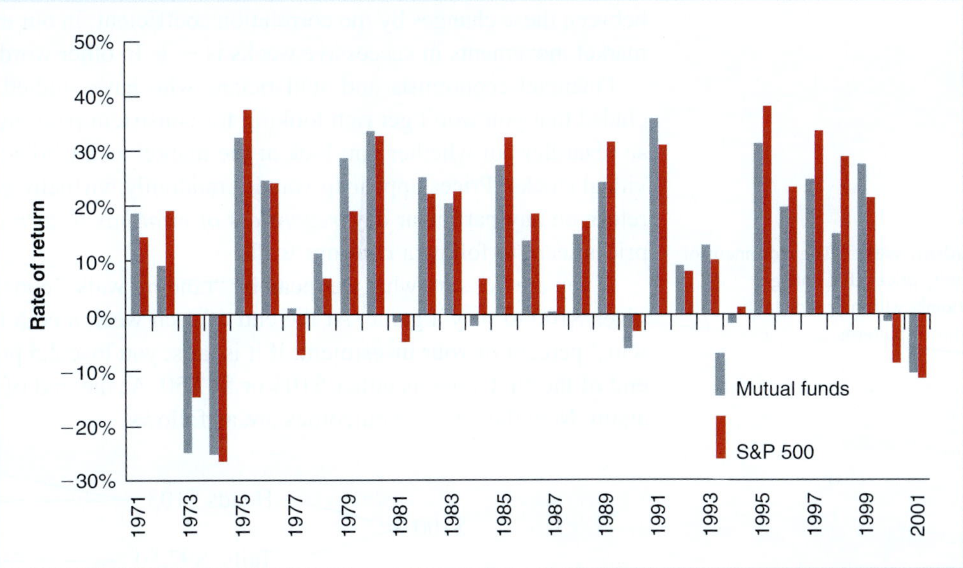

EXAMPLE 7.8 **PERFORMANCE OF MONEY MANAGERS**

Forbes Magazine, a widely read investment magazine, publishes annually an "honour roll" of the most consistently successful mutual funds. Suppose that every year, starting in 1975, you invested an equal sum in each of these successful funds when *Forbes* announced its honour roll. You would have outperformed the market in only five of the following 16 years and your average annual return would have been more than 1 percent below the return on the market.[14]

As this kind of discouraging evidence has accumulated, many investors have given up the search for superior investment returns. They simply buy and hold index funds or exchange-traded portfolios (ETFs) that track the entire stock market. We discussed index funds and ETFs in Chapter 2. Recall that they provide maximum diversification, with very low management fees. Why pay higher fees to managers who attempt to "beat the market" but can't do so consistently? Corporate pension funds now invest over one-quarter of their equity holdings in index funds.

Why is it so difficult to beat the market consistently? Let's look at two possible ways that you might attempt to do so.

METHOD 1: TECHNICAL ANALYSIS

technical analysts Investors who attempt to identify undervalued stocks by searching for patterns in past stock prices.

Some investors try to achieve superior returns by spotting and exploiting patterns in stock prices. These investors are known as **technical analysts**.

Technical analysis sounds plausible. For example, you might hope to beat the market by buying stocks when they are on their way up and by selling them on their way down. Unfortunately, it turns out that such simple rules don't work. A large price rise in one period may be followed by a further rise in the next period, but it is just as likely to be followed by a fall.

Look, for example, at Figure 7.4. The horizontal axis shows the return on the TSX Composite Index in one week (five business days), while the vertical axis shows the return in the following week.

Each point in the chart represents a different week between January 1990 and December 2010. If a market rise one week tended to be followed by a rise the next week, the points in the chart would plot along an upward-sloping line. But you can see that there was no such tendency; the points are scattered randomly across the chart. Statisticians sometimes measure the relationship between these changes by the correlation coefficient. In our example, the correlation between the market movements in successive weeks is −.1. In other words, almost zero.

Financial economists and statisticians who have studied stock price movements have concluded that you won't get rich looking for consistent patterns in price changes. This seems to be so regardless of whether you look at the market as a whole (as we did in Figure 7.4) or at individual stocks. Prices appear to wander randomly, virtually equally likely to offer a high or low return on any particular day, *regardless of what has occurred on previous days*. In other words, prices seem to follow a **random walk**.

random walk The movement of security prices that change randomly, with no predictable trends or patterns.

If you are not sure what we mean by "random walk," consider the following example. You are given $100 to play a game. At the end of each week a coin is tossed. If it comes up heads, you win 3 percent of your investment; if it is tails, you lose 2.5 percent. Therefore, your payoff at the end of the first week is either $103 or $97.50. At the end of the second week the coin is tossed again. Now the possible outcomes are as follows:

$100 → Heads $103 → Heads $106.09 / Tails $100.43

$100 → Tails $97.50 → Heads $100.43 / Tails $95.06

---

[14] See B.G. Malkiel, "Returns from Investing in Equity Mutual Funds 1971 to 1991," *Journal of Finance* 50 (June 1995): 549–72.

FIGURE 7.4
Each dot shows the returns on the TSX Composite Index on two successive weeks between January 1990 and December 2010. The circled dot shows a weekly return of +4.27%, followed by −5.36% in the next week. The scatter diagram shows no significant relationship between returns on successive weeks.

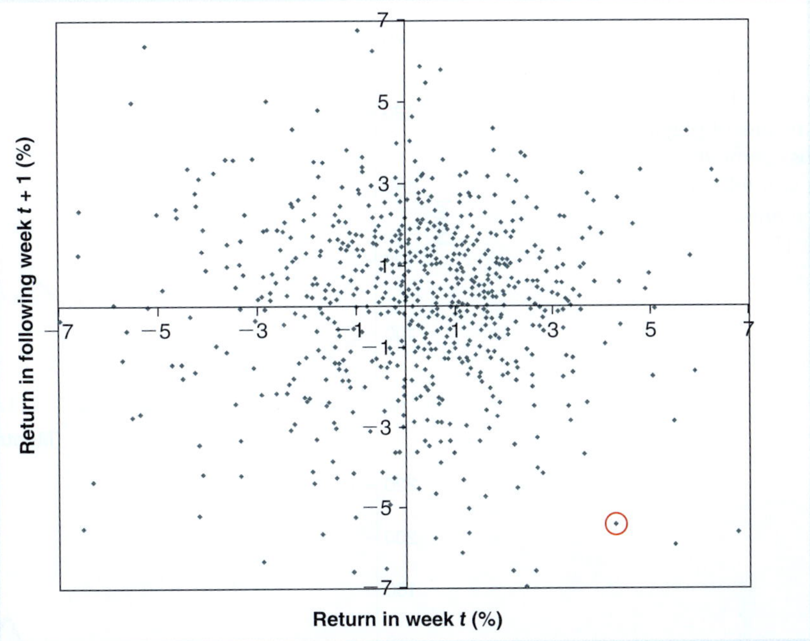

Source: Author's calculations using TSX Composite Index.

This process is a random walk because successive changes in the value of your stake are independent. That is, the odds of making money each week are the same, regardless of the value at the start of the week or the pattern of heads or tails in the previous weeks.

If a stock's price follows a random walk, the odds of an increase or decrease during any day, month, or year do not depend at all on the stock's previous price moves. The historical path of prices gives no useful information about the future—just as a long series of recorded heads and tails gives no information about the next toss.

If you find it difficult to believe that stock prices could behave like our coin-tossing game, look at the two charts in Figure 7.5. One of these charts shows the outcome from playing our game for five years; the other shows the actual performance of the TSX Composite's Index for a five-year period. Can you tell which is which?[15]

Does it surprise you that stocks seem to follow a random walk? If so, imagine that it were not the case and that changes in stock prices were expected to persist for several months. Figure 7.6 provides a hypothetical example of such a predictable cycle. You can see that an upswing in the market started last month when the index was 1,100 and is expected to carry the price to 1,300 next month. What will happen when investors perceive this bonanza? Since stocks are a bargain at their current level, investors will rush to buy. They will stop buying only when stocks are fairly priced. Thus, as soon as a cycle becomes apparent to investors, they immediately eliminate it by their trading.

Check Point 7.9

True or false: If stock prices follow a random walk,

a. Successive stock prices are not related.
b. Successive stock price changes are not related.
c. Stock prices fluctuate above and below a normal long-run price.
d. The history of stock prices cannot be used to predict future returns to investors.

[15] The top chart in Figure 7.5 shows the real TSX Composite's index for the years 1994 through 1998. The bottom chart was generated by a series of random numbers. You may be among the 50 percent of our readers who guess right, but we bet it was just a guess.

FIGURE 7.5
One of these charts shows the TSX Composite's Index for a five-year period. The other shows the results of playing our coin-toss game for five years. Can you tell which is which? (The answer is given in footnote 15.)

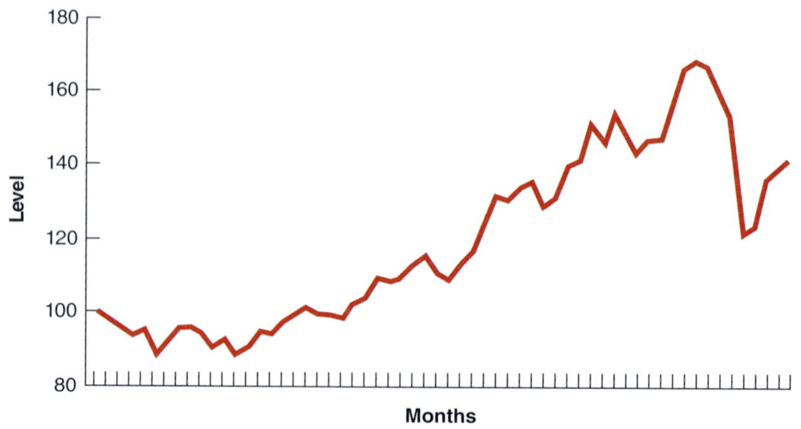

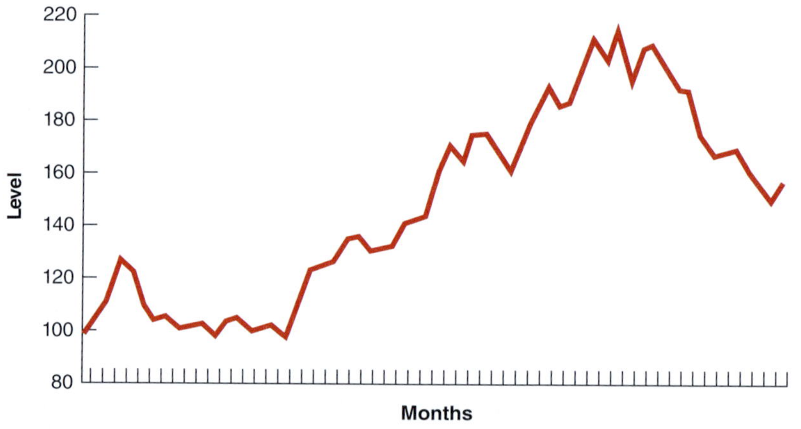

FIGURE 7.6
Cycles self-destruct as soon as they are recognized by investors. The stock price instantaneously jumps to the present value of the expected future price.

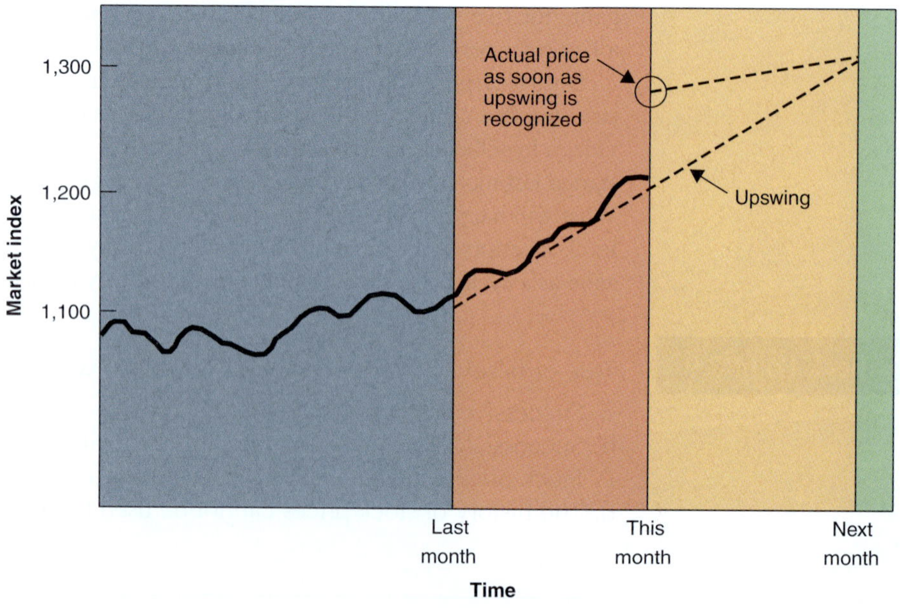

METHOD 2: FUNDAMENTAL ANALYSIS

You may not be able to earn superior returns just by studying past stock prices, but what about other types of information? After all, most investors don't just look at past stock prices. Instead they try to gauge a firm's business prospects by studying the financial and trade press, the company's financial accounts, the president's annual statements, and other items of news. These investors are called **fundamental analysts**, in contrast to technical analysts, who focus on past stock price movements.

fundamental analysts Investors who attempt to find mispriced securities by analyzing fundamental information, such as accounting data and business prospects.

Fundamental analysts are paid to uncover stocks for which price does *not* equal intrinsic value. If intrinsic value exceeds price, for example, the stock is a bargain and will offer a superior expected return. But what happens if there are many talented and competitive fundamental analysts? If one of them uncovers a stock that appears to be a bargain, it stands to reason that others will as well, and there will be a wave of buying that pushes up the price. In the end, their actions will eliminate the original bargain opportunity. To profit, your insights must be *different* from those of your competitors, and you must act *faster* than they can. This is a tall order.

To illustrate the challenge facing stock market analysts, look at Figure 7.7, which shows how stock prices react to one particular item of news—the announcement of a takeover. In most takeovers the acquiring company is willing to pay a hefty premium to induce the shareholders of the target company to give up their shares. You can see from the figure that the stock price of the target company typically jumps up on the day the public becomes aware of a takeover attempt (day 0 in the graph). However, this adjustment in the stock price is immediate; thereafter there is no further drift in the stock price, either upward or downward. By the time the acquisition has been made public, it is too late to buy.

Researchers have looked at the stock price reaction to many other types of news, such as earnings and dividend announcements, and plans to issue additional stock or repurchase existing stock. All this information seems to be rapidly and accurately reflected in the price of the stock, so that it is impossible to make superior returns by buying or selling after the announcement.

inside information Relevant information about a company known by its board of directors, management and/or employees, and other insiders but not by the public.

insider Member of the board of directors, management, employees, and others with a close relationship to a company, including lawyers, financial advisors, and accountants.

What if you get the news about the corporate event *before* it is released to the market? You might be able to act on it and make a lot of money before other market participants figure out what is going on. However, if that information is **inside information**, information about a company from an **insider** and not yet publicly announced, it is illegal to use it. Insiders include members of the board, management, employees, and those with a close relationship with the company, such as

FIGURE 7.7
The performance of the stocks of target companies compared with that of the market. The prices of target stocks jump up on the announcement day, but from then on there are no unusual price movements. The announcement of the takeover attempt seems to be fully reflected in the stock price on the announcement day.

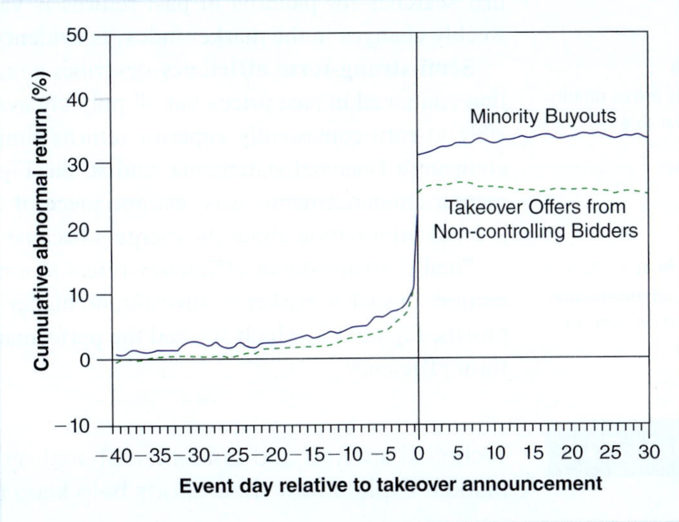

Source: B. Smith and B. Amoako-Adu, "Minority Buyouts and Ownership Characteristics: Evidence from the Toronto Stock Exchange," *Financial Management* 21 (Summer 1992). Reproduced with permission of Blackwell Publishing Ltd.

insider trading Illegal trading of securities, including stocks, bonds, and options, by insiders or those tipped by insiders, on the basis of inside information.

lawyers, financial advisors, and accountants. If you receive information from an insider, you are a *tippee* and also not allowed to trade on the information. Investors guilty of **insider trading** face heavy financial penalties and possible jail time. It can be difficult to catch insider traders, but it does happen.

EXAMPLE 7.9 **THE PERILS OF TRADING ON INSIDE INFORMATION**

In April 2005, Joanne Chang, the former head of investor relations at ATI Technologies Inc. and her husband, David Stone, agreed to pay nearly $1.5 million to settle insider trading charges brought by the Ontario Securities Commission. Chang was also banned from trading in the market for 20 years, and Stone was banned for life. Both the accused sold shares just before ATI released unexpected news about poor financial performance. The news caused ATI's stock price to fall 53 percent in two days. The chair of the OSC panel was quoted as saying, "You have both admitted your conduct in this matter was wrong and illegal. It's an activity that erodes public confidence in the market. This, I'm sure, has been a severe lesson for both of you."[16]

Insider trading laws are needed to help create a market in which investors have confidence they are not being taken advantage of by better-informed market participants. In the ATI insider trading case, Chang and Stone were able to sell their shares at a price substantially higher than the full-information price. The buyers of the shares they sold paid much more for the shares than they were worth when the inside information was revealed. In addition to the prohibition against insider trading, companies are required to make timely disclosure of news expected to have a material impact on their stock price. With up-to-date information flowing to the market, and no one trading on inside information, the stock market can work well.

A THEORY TO FIT THE FACTS

efficient market Market in which prices reflect all available information.

Economists often refer to the stock market as an **efficient market**. By this they mean that the competition to find misvalued stocks is intense. So, when new information comes out, investors rush to take advantage of it and thereby eliminate any profit opportunities. Professional investors express the same idea when they say that there are no free lunches on Bay Street.

weak-form efficiency Market prices rapidly reflect all information contained in the history of past prices.

It is useful to distinguish three types of information and three degrees of efficiency. The term **weak-form efficiency** describes a market in which prices already reflect all the information contained in past prices. In such a market, share price changes are random and technical analysis that searches for patterns in past returns is valueless. Figure 7.4, which looked at successive weekly changes in the market index, is evidence in favour of weak-form efficiency.

semi-strong-form efficiency Market prices rapidly reflect all publicly available information.

Semi-strong-form efficiency describes a market in which prices reflect not just the information contained in past prices but all publicly available information. In such a market it is impossible to earn consistently superior returns simply by reading the financial press, studying the company's financial statements, and so on. Figure 7.7, which looked at the market reaction to merger announcements, was just one piece of evidence in favour of semi-strong efficiency. As soon as information about the mergers became public, the stock prices jumped.

strong-form efficiency Market prices rapidly reflect all information that could in principle be used to determine true value.

Finally, **strong-form efficiency** refers to a market where prices impound all available information. In such a market no investor, no matter how hard working, could expect to earn superior profits. Figure 7.3, which showed the performance of mutual funds, was consistent with strong-form efficiency.

Check Point 7.10

Technical analysts and fundamental analysts all try to earn superior returns in the stock market. Explain how their efforts help keep the market efficient.

[16] Simon Avery, "ATI Insider, Husband to Pay $1.5-Million; Cease-Trading Order, Directorship Ban Also Part of Settling OSC Charges," *The Globe and Mail*, April 12, 2005, B2.

7.7 MARKET ANOMALIES AND BEHAVIOURAL FINANCE

MARKET ANOMALIES

Few simple economic theories are as well supported by the evidence as the efficient market theory. However, no theory this simple can be universally true; there are always some puzzles or apparent exceptions. Let us look at two examples.

The Earnings Announcement Puzzle. In an efficient stock market, a company's stock price should react instantly at the announcement of unexpectedly good or bad earnings. But, in fact, stocks with the best earnings news typically outperform the stocks with the worst earnings news. Figure 7.8 shows stock performance following the announcement of unexpectedly good or bad earnings during the years 1972 to 2001. The 10 percent of the stocks of firms with the best earnings news outperform those with the worst news by about 1 percent per month over the six-month period following the announcement. It seems that investors underreact to the earnings announcement and become aware of the full significance only as further information arrives.

The New-Issue Puzzle. When firms issue stock to the public, investors typically rush to buy. On average, those lucky enough to receive stock receive an immediate capital gain. However, researchers have found that these early gains often turn into losses. For example, suppose that you bought stock immediately following each initial public offering and then held that stock for five years. Over the period 1970 to 2003 your average annual return would have been 4.1 percent less than the return on a portfolio of similar-sized stocks. [17]

The jury is still out on these studies of longer-term anomalies. We can't be sure whether they are important exceptions to the efficient market theory or a coincidence that stems from the efforts of many researchers to find interesting patterns in the data. There may also be other explanations. Take, for example, the new-issue puzzle. Most new issues during the past 30 years have involved

FIGURE 7.8
Average stock returns over the six months following announcements of quarterly earnings. The 10 percent of stocks with the best earnings news (portfolio 10) outperform those with the worst news (portfolio 1) by about 1 percent per month.

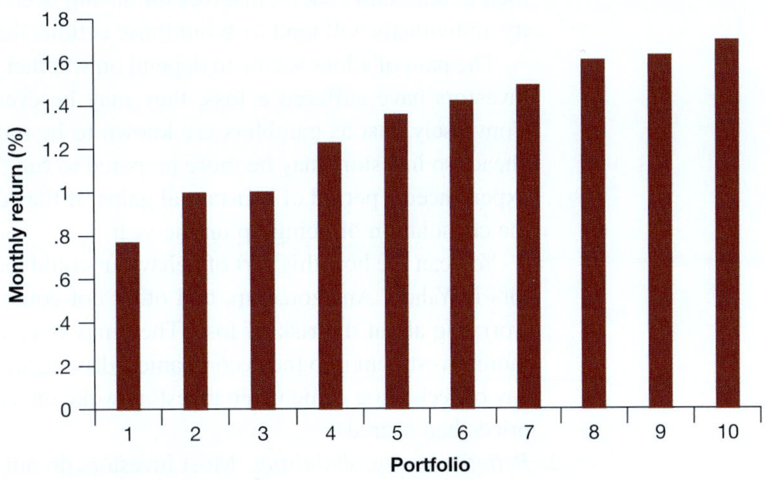

Source: T. Chordia and L. Shivakumar, "Inflation Illusion and the Post-Earnings Announcement Drift," *Accounting Research* 43 (2005): 521–556.

[17] An excellent resource for data and analysis of initial public offerings is Professor Jay Ritter's Web page, **bear.cba.ufl.edu/ritter**.

growth stocks with high market values and limited book assets. Perhaps the stocks performed badly, not because they had just been issued, but because all growth stock happened to perform badly during this period. Of course, if that is true, we need to address another question: Why have growth stocks performed poorly over such a long period of time? We will come back to this question in Chapter 12.

BEHAVIOURAL FINANCE

Investors in technology stocks in the 1990s saw an extraordinary run-up in the value of their holdings. The Nasdaq market index, which is heavily weighted toward high-tech stocks, rose 580 percent from the start of 1995 to March 2000. But then, even more rapidly than it began, the boom ended. By October 2002 the Nasdaq index had fallen 78 percent.

Some of the largest price gains and losses were experienced by the new "dot-com" stocks. For example, Yahoo shares, which began trading in April 1996, appreciated by 1,400 percent in just four years. At this point Yahoo stock was valued at $124 billion, more than that of General Motors, Heinz, and Boeing combined. It was not to last, however; just over a year later Yahoo's market capitalization was little more than $6 billion.

One tech stock high flyer was Nortel Networks, a Canadian multinational telecommunications equipment manufacturer. At its peak of $123.10 in July 2000, Nortel accounted for 40 percent of the TSX Composite Index. However, by the fall of 2002, its stock was worth less than $1, and in 2009 Nortel went bankrupt.

What caused the boom in high-tech stocks? Had there been a sharp improvement in the prospects for dividend growth? Or had investors decided that they did not need such high returns from common stocks? Neither explanation seemed capable of explaining the prices investors had been prepared to pay. Might it be that the theory of efficient markets was another casualty of the rise and fall of the dot-coms?

Some believe the answers lie in behavioural psychology. People are not 100 percent rational 100 percent of the time. This shows up in two broad areas—their attitudes to risk and how they assess probabilities.

1. *Attitudes toward risk.* Psychologists have observed that, when making risky decisions, people are particularly loath to incur losses, even if those losses are small. Losers are liable to regret their actions and kick themselves for having been so foolish. To avoid this unpleasant possibility, individuals will tend to avoid those actions that may result in loss.

   The pain of a loss seems to depend on whether it comes on the heels of earlier losses. Once investors have suffered a loss, they may be even more cautious not to risk a further loss. Conversely, just as gamblers are known to be more willing to take large bets when they are ahead, so investors may be more prepared to run the risk of a stock market dip after they have experienced a period of substantial gains. If they do then suffer a small loss, they at least have the consolation of being up on the year.

   You can see how this sort of behaviour could lead to a stock-price "bubble." The early investors in Yahoo, Amazon.com, and other dot-coms were big winners. They may have stopped worrying about the risk of loss. They may have thrown caution to the winds and piled even more investment into these companies, driving stock prices far above fundamental values. The day of reckoning came when investors woke up and realized how far above fundamental value prices had soared.
2. *Beliefs about probabilities.* Most investors do not have a Ph.D. in probability theory and may make common errors in assessing the probability of uncertain outcomes. Psychologists have found that, when judging the possible future outcomes, individuals commonly look back to what has happened in recent periods and then assume that this is representative of what may occur in the future. The temptation is to project recent experience into the future and to forget the lessons learned from the more distant past. For example, an investor who places too much weight on recent events may judge that glamorous growth companies are very likely to continue to grow rapidly, even though very high rates of growth cannot persist indefinitely.

A second common bias is that of overconfidence. Most of us believe we are better-than-average drivers, and most investors think they are better-than-average stockpickers. We know that two speculators who trade with one another cannot both make money from the deal; for every winner there must be a loser. But presumably investors are prepared to continue trading because each is confident that it is the other one who is the patsy.

You can see how such behaviour may have reinforced the dot-com boom. As the bull market developed, it generated increased optimism about the future and stimulated demand for shares. The more investors racked up profits on their stocks, the more confident they became in their views and the more willing they became to bear the risk that next month might not be so good.

Now, it is not difficult to believe your Uncle Harry or Aunt Hetty could have got caught up in a scatty whirl of irrational exuberance,[18] but why didn't hard-headed professional investors bail out of the overpriced stocks and force their prices down to fair value? Perhaps they felt that it was too difficult to predict when the boom would end and that their jobs would be at risk if they moved aggressively into cash when others were raking in profits. In this case, sales of stock by the pros were simply not large enough to stem the tide of optimism.

It is too early to say how far behavioural finance scholars can help sort out some of the puzzles and explain events like the dot-com boom. One thing, however, seems clear: it is relatively easy for statisticians to spot anomalies with the benefit of hindsight and for psychologists to provide an explanation for them. It is much more difficult for investment managers who are at the sharp end to spot and invest in mispriced securities. And that is the basic message of the efficient market theory.

---

[18] The term "irrational exuberance" was coined by Alan Greenspan, chairman of the Federal Reserve Board, to describe the dot-com boom. It was also the title of a book by Robert Shiller that examined the boom. See R. Shiller, *Irrational Exuberance* (New York: Broadway Books, 2001). For another view of the dot-com boom, check out John Cassidy's book *Dot.con: How America Lost Its Mind and Money in the Internet Era* (New York: Perennial Currents, 2003).

7.8 SUMMARY

1. **What information about company stocks is regularly reported in the financial Web sites of newspapers and online financial services?** LO1

Firms that wish to raise new capital may either borrow money or bring new "partners" into the business by selling shares of **common stock**. Large companies usually arrange for their stocks to be traded on a stock exchange. The stock listings report the stock's price, price change, trading volume, **dividend yield**, and price-earnings (P/E) ratio.

2. **How can one calculate the present value of a stock given forecasts of future dividends and future stock price?** LO2

Shareholders generally expect to receive (1) cash **dividends** and (2) capital gains or losses. The rate of return that they expect over the next year is defined as the expected dividend per share DIV_1 plus the expected increase in price $P_1 - P_0$, all divided by the price at the start of the year P_0.

Unlike the fixed interest payments that the firm promises to bondholders, the dividends paid to shareholders depend on the fortunes of the firm. That's why a company's common stock is riskier than its debt. The return that investors expect on any one stock is also the return that they demand on all stocks subject to the same degree of risk. The present value of a stock equals the present value of the forecast future dividends and future stock price, using that expected return as the discount rate.

The present value of a share is equal to the stream of expected dividends per share up to some horizon date plus the expected price at this date, all discounted at the return that investors require. If the horizon date is far away, we simply say that stock price equals the present value of all future dividends per share. This is the **dividend discount model**.

3. **How can stock valuation formulas be used to infer the expected rate of return on a common stock? LO3**

   If dividends are expected to grow forever at a constant rate g, the expected return on the stock is equal to the dividend yield (DIV_1/P_0) plus the expected rate of dividend growth. The value of the stock according to this **constant-growth dividend discount model** is $P_0 = DIV_1/(r - g)$.

4. **How should investors interpret price-earnings ratios? LO4**

   You can think of a share's value as the sum of two parts—the value of the assets in place and the **present value of growth opportunities**, that is, of future opportunities for the firm to invest in high-return projects. The **price-earnings (P/E) ratio** reflects the market's assessment of the firm's growth opportunities.

5. **How does competition among investors lead to efficient markets? LO5**

   Competition between investors will tend to produce an **efficient market**—that is, a market in which prices rapidly reflect new information, and investors have difficulty making consistently superior returns. Of course, we all hope to beat the market, but, if the market is efficient, all we can rationally expect is a return that is sufficient on average to compensate for the time value of money and for the risks we bear.

   The efficient market theory comes in three flavours. The **weak form** states that prices reflect all the information contained in the past series of stock prices. In this case it is impossible to earn superior profits simply by looking for past patterns in stock prices. The **semi-strong form** of the theory states that prices reflect all published information, so that it is impossible to make consistently superior returns just by reading the newspaper, looking at the company's annual accounts, and so on. The **strong form** states that stock prices effectively impound all available information. This form tells us that private information is hard to come by, because in pursuing it you are in competition with thousands—perhaps millions—of active and intelligent investors. The best you can do in this case is to assume that securities are fairly priced.

   The evidence for market efficiency is voluminous, and there is little doubt that skilled professional investors find it difficult to win consistently. Nevertheless, there remain some puzzling instances in which markets do not seem to be efficient. Some financial economists attribute these anomalies to behavioural foibles.

Related Web Links

tmx.com Site of the Toronto Stock Exchange and the TSX Venture Exchange

cnsx.ca Site of CNSX, Canada's new stock exchange

nasdaq.com Web site of Nasdaq stock market

nyse.com Web site of the New York Stock Exchange

123world.com/stockexchanges Links to exchanges

world-exchanges.org Web site of World Federation of Exchanges

globeinvestor.com and **financialpost.com** Information about Canadian companies and their share prices provided by major Canadian newspapers

ca.finance.yahoo.com and **finance.yahoo.com** Canadian and U.S. company and market information

fool.com/School/HowtoValueStocks.htm How investors value firms

valuepro.net Software for estimating stock values

Key Terms

book value of equity 225
common stock *or* equity *or* shares 220
constant-growth dividend discount model 236
dividend discount model 231
dividend yield 223
efficient market 248
fundamental analysts 247
initial public offering (IPO) 221
inside information 247
insider 247
insider trading 248
intrinsic value 230
liquidation value 226
market-value balance sheet 227
payout ratio 241
plowback ratio 241
preferred stock 225
present value of growth opportunities (PVGO) 242
price-earnings multiple *or* P/E ratio 223
primary market 221
random walk 244
seasoned equity offering (SEO) 221
secondary market 221
semi-strong-form efficiency 248
strong-form efficiency 248
sustainable growth rate 241
technical analysts 244
weak-form efficiency 248

Questions and Problems

connect Practise and learn online with *Connect*. Questions with online Excel templates or datasets are marked with .

*Answers in Appendix B

BASIC

1. **Dividend Discount Model.** Research In Motion has never paid a dividend, but in January 2011 its share price was $63. Does this invalidate the dividend discount model? (LO2)

2. **Dividend Yield.** Favoured stock will pay a dividend this year of $2.40 per share. Its dividend yield is 8 percent. At what price is the stock selling? (LO1)

*3. **Preferred Stock.** Preferred Products has issued preferred stock with a $8 annual dividend that will be paid in perpetuity. (LO2)
   a. If the discount rate is 12 percent, at what price should the preferred sell?
   b. At what price should the stock sell one year from now?
   c. What is the dividend yield, the capital gains yield, and the expected rate of return of the stock?

4. **Constant-Growth Model.** Waterworks has a dividend yield of 8 percent. If its dividend is expected to grow at a constant rate of 5 percent, what must be the expected rate of return on the company's stock? (LO3)

5. **Dividend Discount Model.** How can we say that price equals the present value of all future dividends when many investors may be seeking capital gains and planning to hold their shares for only a year or two? Explain. (LO2)

*6. **Rate of Return.** Steady As She Goes, Inc., will pay a year-end dividend of $3 per share. Investors expect the dividend to grow at a rate of 4 percent indefinitely.
   a. If the stock currently sells for $30 per share, what is the expected rate of return on the stock? (LO3)
   b. If the expected rate of return on the stock is 16.5 percent, what is the stock price? (LO2)

7. **Dividend Yield.** BMM Industries pays a dividend of $2 per quarter. The dividend yield on its stock is reported at 4.8 percent. What price is the stock selling at? (LO1)

*8. **Forms of Efficient Markets.** Supply the missing words in the paragraph that follows, using the following list: *fundamental, semi-strong, strong, technical, weak*. (LO5)

   There are three forms of the efficient market theory. Tests that have found there are no patterns in share price changes provide evidence for the _____ form of the theory. Evidence for the _____ form of the theory is provided by tests that look at how rapidly markets respond to new public information, and evidence for the _____ form of the theory is provided by tests that look at the performance of professionally managed portfolios. Market efficiency results from competition between investors. Many investors search for information about the company's business that would help them to value the stock more accurately. This is known as _____ analysis. Such research helps to ensure that prices reflect all available information. Other investors study past stock prices for recurrent patterns that would allow them to make superior profits. This is known as _____ analysis. Such research helps to eliminate any patterns.

9. **Information and Efficient Markets.** "It's competition for information that makes securities markets efficient." Is this statement correct? Explain. (LO5)

10. **Behavioural Finance.** Some finance scholars cite well-documented behavioural biases to explain apparent cases of market inefficiency. Describe some of these biases. (LO5)

INTERMEDIATE

*11. **Stock Values.** Integrated Potato Chips paid a $1 per share dividend *yesterday*. You expect the dividend to grow steadily at a rate of 4 percent per year. (LO2)
   a. What is the expected dividend in each of the next three years?
   b. If the discount rate for the stock is 12 percent, at what price will the stock sell?
   c. What is the expected stock price three years from now?
   d. If you buy the stock and plan to hold it for three years, what payments will you receive? What is the present value of those payments? Compare your answer to part (b).

12. **Constant-Growth Model.** A stock sells for $40. The next dividend will be $4 per share. If the rate of return earned on reinvested funds is 15 percent and the company reinvests 40 percent of earnings in the firm, what must be the discount rate? (LO3)

*13. **Constant-Growth Model.** Gentleman Gym just paid its annual dividend of $3 per share, and it is widely expected that the dividend will increase by 5 percent per year indefinitely. (LO2)

a. What price should the stock sell at? The discount rate is 15 percent.
b. How would your answer change if the discount rate were only 12 percent? Why does the answer change?
c. What is the estimated stock price if the dividend is expected to decrease by 5 percent per year indefinitely and the discount rate is 15 percent?

14. **Constant-Growth Model.** Arts and Crafts, Inc., will pay a dividend of $5 per share in 1 year. It sells at $50 a share, and firms in the same industry provide an expected rate of return of 14 percent. What must be the expected growth rate of the company's dividends? (LO2)

*15. **Constant-Growth Model.** Eastern Electric's recent annual dividend was $1.64 per share and currently sells for about $27 per share. (LO3)
a. If investors believe the growth rate of dividends is 3 percent per year, what rate of return do they expect to earn on the stock?
b. If investors' required rate of return is 10 percent, what must be the growth rate they expect of the firm?
c. If the sustainable growth rate is 5 percent and the plowback ratio is .4, what must be the rate of return earned by the firm on its new investments?

16. **Constant-Growth Model.** Currently, Non-Stick Gum Inc. pays no dividend. However, analysts forecast that in 4 years Non-Stick will pay its first annual dividend of $0.50 and dividends will grow at 6 percent per year thereafter. If stocks with similar risk to the equity of Non-Stick Gum Inc. currently earn a return of 12 percent, estimate the current share price of Non-Stick Gum. (LO2)

17. **Negative Growth.** Horse and Buggy Inc. is in a declining industry. Sales, earnings, and dividends are all shrinking at a rate of 10 percent per year.
a. If r = 15 percent and DIV_1 = $3, what is the value of a share? (LO2)
b. What price do you forecast for the stock next year? (LO2)
c. What is the expected rate of return on the stock? (LO3)
d. Can you distinguish between "bad stocks" and "bad companies"? Does the fact that the industry is declining mean that the stock is a bad buy? (LO2)

*18. **Constant-Growth Model.** Metatrend's stock will generate earnings of $5 per share this year. The discount rate for the stock is 15 percent and the rate of return on reinvested earnings is also 15 percent. (LO2)
a. Find both the growth rate of dividends and the price of the stock if the company reinvests the following fraction of its earnings in the firm: (1) 0 percent, (2) 40 percent, (3) 60 percent.
b. Redo part (a) now assuming that the rate of return on reinvested earnings is 20 percent. What is the present value of growth opportunities for each reinvestment rate?
c. Considering your answers to parts (a) and (b), can you briefly state the difference between companies experiencing growth versus companies with growth opportunities?

19. **Internet.** The major stock exchanges are members of the World Federation of Exchanges, found at **www.world-exchanges.org**. Click on "Member Exchanges," tour the world, and select three stock exchanges by clicking on their pins. Note the number of listed companies, the types of securities traded (click on "View More Information"), and visit their Web sites. Compare what you find to the Toronto Stock Exchange. (LO1)

20. **Internet.** Do you think that all stock exchanges trade stocks? Check out the Hollywood Stock exchange on **www.hsx.com**. Buy shares in your favourite actors, movies, and music artists and watch their values rise or fall based on the success of their careers and personal life. Join and play for free. It's 90 percent fun but it will also get you used to some stock market jargon. Real stock values are established with "votes," just like on the HSX, but the votes cost real money. (LO1)

*21. **Sustainable Growth.** Computer Corp. reinvests 60 percent of its earnings in the firm. The stock sells for $50, and the next dividend will be $2.50 per share. The discount rate is 15 percent. What is the rate of return on the company's reinvested funds? (LO3)

*22. **Non-constant Growth.** You expect a share of stock to pay dividends of $1, $1.25, and $1.50 in each of the next 3 years. You believe the stock will sell for $20 at the end of the third year.
a. What is the stock price if the discount rate for the stock is 10 percent? (LO2)
b. What is the dividend yield? (LO3)

23. **Constant-Growth Model.** Here are recent data on two stocks, both of which have discount rates of 15 percent: (LO2)

	Stock A	Stock B
Return on equity	15%	10%
Earnings per share	$2.00	$1.50
Dividends per share	$1.00	$1.00

a. What are the dividend payout ratios for each firm?
b. What are the expected dividend growth rates for each firm?
c. Estimate the stock price for each firm.

*24. **P/E Ratios.** Web Cites Research projects a rate of return of 20 percent on new projects. Management plans to plow back 30 percent of all earnings into the firm. Earnings this year will be $2 per share, and investors expect a 12 percent rate of return on the stock.
   a. What is the sustainable growth rate? (LO4)
   b. What is the stock price? (LO2)
   c. What is the present value of growth opportunities? (LO2)
   d. What is the P/E ratio? (LO4)
   e. What would the price and P/E ratio be if the firm paid out all earnings as dividends? (LO2, LO4)
   f. What do you conclude about the relationship between growth opportunities and P/E ratios? (LO4)

25. **Constant-Growth Model.** Fincorp will pay a year-end dividend of $2.40 per share, which is expected to grow at a 4 percent rate indefinitely. The discount rate is 12 percent.
   a. What is the stock selling for? (LO2)
   b. If earnings are $3.10 a share, what is the implied value of the firm's growth opportunities? (LO2)

*26. **P/E Ratios.** No-Growth Industries pays out all of its earnings as dividends. It will pay its next $4 per share dividend in a year. The discount rate is 12 percent. (LO4)
   a. What is the price-earnings ratio of the company?
   b. What would the P/E ratio be if the discount rate were 10 percent?

27. **Growth Opportunities.** Stormy Weather has no attractive investment opportunities. Its return on equity equals the discount rate, which is 10 percent. Its expected earnings this year are $3 per share. Find the stock price, P/E ratio, and growth rate of dividends for plowback ratios of
   a. Zero (LO2)
   b. .40 (LO2)
   c. .80 (LO2)

*28. **Growth Opportunities.** Trend-line Inc. has been growing at a rate of 6 percent per year and is expected to continue to do so indefinitely. The next dividend is expected to be $5 per share. (LO2)
   a. If the market expects a 10 percent rate of return on Trend-line, at what price must it be selling?
   b. If Trend-line's earnings per share will be $8, what part of Trend-line's value is due to assets in place, and what part to growth opportunities?

29. **P/E Ratios.** Castles in the Sand generates a rate of return of 20 percent on its investments and maintains a plowback ratio of .30. Its earnings this year will be $2 per share. Investors expect a 12 percent rate of return on the stock.
   a. Find the price and P/E ratio of the firm. (LO2)
   b. What happens to the P/E ratio if the plowback ratio is reduced to .20? Why? (LO4)
   c. Show that if plowback equals zero, the earnings-price ratio, E/P, falls to the expected rate of return on the stock. (LO4)

30. **Dividend Growth.** Grandiose Growth has a dividend growth rate of 20 percent. The discount rate is 10 percent. The end-of-year dividend will be $2 per share. (LO2)
   a. What is the present value of the dividend to be paid in year 1? Year 2? Year 3?
   b. Could anyone rationally expect this growth rate to continue indefinitely?

*31. **Stock Valuation.** Start-up Industries is a new firm, which has raised $100 million by selling shares of stock. Management expects to earn a 24 percent rate of return on equity, which is more than the 15 percent rate of return available on comparable-risk investments. Half of all earnings will be reinvested in the firm. (LO2)
   a. What will be Start-up's ratio of market value to book value?
   b. How would that ratio change if the firm can earn only a 10 percent rate of return on its investments?

32. **Stock Valuation.** Telus, a Canadian wireless communications company, earned $3.38 per share in 2010 and paid dividends of $1.70 per share. Analysts forecast an annual earnings growth rate of 7 percent for the next 5 years. Based on similar-risk companies, the estimated required rate of return on Telus stock is 8.9 percent. It is assumed that after 2015 onward, Telus will maintain its current reinvestment rate but earn only its cost of capital on new investments. Estimate Telus' current stock price at the beginning of 2011. (LO2)

33. **Non-constant Growth.** Planned Obsolescence has a product that will be in vogue for three years, at which point the firm will close up shop and liquidate the assets. As a result, forecast dividends are DIV_1 = $2, DIV_2 = $2.50, and DIV_3 = $18. What is the stock price if the discount rate is 12 percent? (LO2)

34. **Non-constant Growth.** Tattletale News Corp. has been growing at a rate of 20 percent per year, and you expect this growth rate in earnings and dividends to continue for another 3 years.
   a. If the last dividend paid was $2, what will the next dividend be? (LO2)
   b. If the discount rate is 15 percent and the steady growth rate after 3 years is 4 percent, what should the stock price be today? (LO2)
   c. What is your prediction for the stock price in one year? (LO2)
   d. Show that the expected rate of return equals the discount rate. (LO3)

35. **Non-constant Growth.** ToyTime's common stock's annual dividend for the next 3 years is expected to be $.50. Thereafter, the dividend is expected to grow 4 percent per year. Stocks of ToyTime's risk are expected to earn 11 percent per annum.
    a. Calculate the share price today and at the beginning of each of the next four years. (LO2)
    b. Calculate the dividend yield and capital gains yield for each year. Does the dividend yield plus the capital gains yield equal the expected return each year? (LO3)

36. **Non-constant Growth.** Earnings per common share of ABC Industries for the current year are expected to be $3 and to grow 10 percent per year over the next 4 years. At the end of the 5 years, earnings growth rate is expected to fall to 5 percent and continue at that rate for the foreseeable future. ABC's dividend payout ratio is 40 percent. If the expected return on ABC's common shares is 15 percent, calculate the current share price. (LO2)

37. **Internet.**
    a. Create a list of preferred shares traded on the TSX using the Globe Investor filter at **www.globeinvestor.com/v5/content/filters**. Select "Preferred" from the "Security" menu. Find BCE's Series T preferred shares, which pays an annual dividend of $1.1255. Use the current share price to calculate the expected rate of return on the share. (LO1, LO3)
    b. Go to **www.cibc.com/ca/investor-relations/share-info/preferred-shares.html** and download the list of CIBC preferred shares. Using the Globe Investor filter in (a), see if you can match the listed preferred shares of CIBC with their trading prices. Using the dividend discount model, calculate the discount rate for each preferred share. (LO1, LO3)

38. **Internet.** Go **ca.finance.yahoo.com**, enter MB.TO, and click "Go." Click on "Company Snapshot" and find out what the company does and visit its Web site. What type of information is provided to its investors? Repeat for SRF.TO. Compare and contrast the information provided to shareholders. (LO1)

*39. **After-Tax Rate of Return.** One year ago you purchased 100 shares of Dog Bites common stock for $25. You received dividends of $.70 per share and just sold the shares for $26.25 each. What are your before- and after-tax rates of return? Your marginal personal tax rate is 40 percent, your dividend tax rate is 30 percent, and capital gains are taxed at 50 percent of your personal rate. (LO3)

40. **Interpreting the Efficient Market Theory.** How would you respond to the following comments? (LO5)
    a. "Efficient market, my eye! I know lots of investors who do crazy things."
    b. "Efficient market? Balderdash! I know at least a dozen people who have made a bundle in the stock market."
    c. "The trouble with the efficient market theory is that it ignores investors' psychology."

41. **Investment Performance.** It seems that every month we read an article in *The Globe and Mail* or *National Post* about a stockpicker with a marvellous track record. Do these examples mean that financial markets are not efficient? (LO5)

*42. **Implications of Efficient Markets.** The president of Good Fortunes, Inc., states at a press conference that the company has a 30-year history of ever-increasing dividend payments. Good Fortunes is widely regarded as one of the best-run firms in its industry. Does this make the firm's stock a good buy? Explain. (LO5)

43. **Implications of Efficient Markets.** "Long-term interest rates are at record highs. Most companies, therefore, find it cheaper to finance with common stock or relatively inexpensive short-term bank loans." Discuss. (LO5)

44. **Expectations and Efficient Markets.** Geothermal Corp. just announced good news: its earnings have increased by 20 percent. Most investors had anticipated an increase of 25 percent. Will Geothermal's stock price increase or decrease when the announcement is made? (LO5)

CHALLENGE

45. **Non-constant Growth.** Compost Science Inc. (CSI) is in the business of converting Calgary's sewage sludge into fertilizer. The business is not in itself very profitable. However, to induce CSI to remain in business, the Metropolitan District Commission (MDC) has agreed to pay whatever amount is necessary to yield CSI a 10 percent return on investment. At the end of the year, CSI is expected to pay a $4 dividend. It has been reinvesting 40 percent of earnings and growing at 4 percent a year.
    a. Suppose CSI continues on this growth trend. What is the expected rate of return from purchasing the stock at $100? (LO3)
    b. What part of the $100 price is attributable to the present value of growth opportunities? (LO2)
    c. Now the MDC announces a plan for CSI to treat Edmonton sewage. CSI's plant will therefore be expanded gradually over five years. This means that CSI will have to reinvest 80 percent of its earnings for 5 years. Starting in year 6, however, it will again be able to pay out 60 percent of earnings. What will be CSI's stock price once this announcement is made and its consequences for CSI are known? (LO2, LO5)

46. **Non-constant Growth.** Better Mousetraps has come out with an improved product, and the world is beating a path to its door. As a result, the firm projects growth of 20 percent per year for 4 years. By then, other firms will have copycat technology, competition will drive down profit margins, and the sustainable growth rate will fall to 5 percent. The most recent annual dividend was $DIV_0 = \$1$ per share.
    a. What are the expected values of DIV_1, DIV_2, DIV_3, and DIV_4? (LO2)
    b. What is the expected stock price four years from now? The discount rate is 10 percent. (LO2)
    c. What is the stock price today? (LO2)
    d. Find the dividend yield, DIV_1/P_0. (LO3)
    e. What will next year's stock price, P_1, be? (LO2)
    f. What is the expected rate of return to an investor who buys the stock now and sells it in one year? (LO3)

47. **After-Tax Rate of Return.** You live in British Columbia and your marginal federal tax rate is 22 percent, your marginal provincial tax rate is 11.9 percent, the dividend gross-up factor is 125 percent, the federal dividend tax credit is 13.33 percent of grossed-up dividends, and the provincial dividend tax credit is 6.6 percent of grossed-up dividends. If you bought shares of Mighty Mixer for \$50, received dividends of \$2, and sold the shares for \$53 one year after you bought them, what are your before- and after-tax rates of return? (LO3)

48. **After-Tax Rate of Return.** Refer back to problem 47. Suppose you bought the shares of Mighty Mixer for \$50, received annual dividends of \$2, and sold the shares for \$55 three years after you bought them. What are your before- and after-tax rates of return on your investment? *Hint:* You will need to make an assumption about what happens to the \$2 dividends received in year 1 and year 2. (LO3)

49. **After-Tax Rate of Return.** You have \$10,000 to invest and are considering either a consol (a perpetual bond) or preferred shares of Canada Leasing. The consol has a \$1,000 par value, an annual coupon rate of 4 percent, and never matures. The preferred share pays fixed dividends of \$6 and is expected to continue indefinitely. Currently, the consol is selling for \$800 and the preferred share for \$120. (LO3)
    a. What is the before-tax expected rate of return on each of the investments?
    b. If your personal tax rate is 35 percent, your dividend tax rate is 29 percent, and capital gains are taxed at 50 percent of the personal tax rate, what is the after-tax expected rate of return on each investment?
    c. What is the expected rate of return on each investment to a Canadian corporation with a corporate tax rate of 35 percent?
    d. Why do you think that many of the preferred shares sold by Canadian corporations are purchased by other Canadian corporations?

50. **Non-constant Growth.** City Garden Suppliers paid a \$1 dividend yesterday. It is expected that the dividend will grow at 10 percent per year for 4 years, 8 percent per year for 10 years, and then at 5 percent per year thereafter. If the investors' expected rate of return is 12 percent, what is the stock worth today? *Hint:* Use the present value formula for a growing annuity from Chapter 5. (LO2)

51. **Non-constant Growth.** Golddigger, a gold exploration and development company, currently pays no dividends. Using the company's assay reports, analysts have determined the following possible outcomes of Goldigger's exploration efforts in one year:

Event	Probability	Annual Dividend per Share
High-quality gold vein	40%	\$8
Medium-quality gold vein	50	2
No gold	10	0

If gold is found, the mine is expected to operate for 20 years and then be exhausted. If investors expect to earn 9 percent on gold mining stocks, what will be the price of the stock today? (LO2)

52. **Non-constant Growth.** ABC Manufacturing pays dividends annually. Dividends have been growing 4 percent a year. Today is May 1, 2006. Its next dividend, to be paid one year from today, will be \$1.20 per share. The company is involved in a research and development (R&D) program to develop a new widget. The results are expected in one year. The discount rate is 10 percent.
    a. *Scenario 1.* It is May 1, 2007 and the company announces the new widget is a great success. ABC pays its previously announced \$1.20 dividend and announces the 2008 dividend will be \$2.50 per share. What will be the stock price on May 1, 2007, if dividends beyond 2008 are expected to grow at 6 percent in perpetuity? (LO2)
    b. *Scenario 2.* It is May 1, 2007, and the company announces that the widget program has been ended and that the next annual dividend will be \$1.248, 4 percent larger than the dividend it just paid. What is the stock price May 1, 2007? (LO2)
    c. If the probability of success of the R&D (scenario 1) is 30 percent, what price would you expect the stock to be today? (LO2)
    d. Suppose you bought the stock for the price you calculated in part (c) and the research and development

program is successful. What will be the one-year rate of return on your investment? What will be the one-year rate of return on your investment if the R&D is not successful? What is the expected rate of return? (LO3)

53. **Yield Curve and EMH.** If the yield curve is downward-sloping, meaning that long-term interest rates are lower than current short-term rates, what might investors believe about *future* short-term interest rates? (LO5)

54. **Implications of EMH.** Suppose that a company *splits* its stock two-for-one, meaning it doubles the number of shares outstanding. Each shareholder is given a new share for each one previously held, so that the number of shares held doubles. The split is not associated with any change in the firm's investment policy. (LO5)
    a. Has the firm acquired any new assets as a result of the split?
    b. Has anything happened to the value of the firm's real assets (its projects)?
    c. What will happen to earnings per share?
    d. What should happen to the firm's stock price?
    e. What should happen to the dollar value of the shareholder's stock? Has investor wealth changed?

55. **Internet.** Go to **money.ca.msn.com** to get data to update each firm's information in Table 7.4. Type each firm name in the "Name or Symbol" box and click on "Go." Record the previous close stock price and click on "Highlights" to get book value per share. Then calculate the price-to-book-value ratio. Now compare the new data to the data in Table 7.4. Which stock price has changed by the greatest percentage since 2011, when the table was created? Have the book values for any firm changed much? How much have the price/book value ratios changed? Which seems to be more stable, stock price, book value per share, or price/book value? What do you think causes the variability of these measures to differ? (LO1, LO4)

56. **Internet.** Go to **finance.yahoo.com** and obtain the price-earnings ratios of Adobe Systems (ADBE) and American Electric Power (AEP). Which of these two firms seem to more of a "growth stock"? Now obtain a forecast of each firm's expected earnings per share in the coming year. You can find earnings forecasts on yahoo.com under "Analysts Estimates." What is the present value of growth opportunities for each firm as a fraction of its stock price? (Assume, for simplicity, that the required rate of return on the stock is $r = 8$ percent.) Are the relative values you obtain for PVGO consistent with the P/E ratios? (LO1, LO2, LO3)

57. **Integrative.** At Green Construction, earnings before interest and taxes (EBIT) for the year just ended were \$70 million and are not expected to grow. The company pays \$10 million in interest each year on its perpetual bonds. The expected rate of return on its bonds is 5 percent and on its stocks is 11 percent. Last year, interest rates were higher and the bond's expected rate of return was 6 percent. Green's corporate tax rate is 30 percent. Green's dividend payout ratio is 100 percent. Green has 15 million shares outstanding and 150,000 bonds with \$1,000 par value. Calculate Green's current share price and its current bond price. (LO2)

Solutions to Check Points

7.1 RY's trading volume was 3,544,024 shares. The highest price at which the shares traded during the day was \$53.04, the lowest was \$52.76, and the closing price was \$53.01, which was \$.45 higher than the previous day's close. RY's high and low prices over the past 52 weeks have been \$62.89 and \$48.85 per share. The annual dividend is \$2 per share, dividend yield was 3.8 percent, and P/E ratio was 15.2.

7.2 IBM's forecast future profitability has fallen. Thus the value of future investment opportunities has fallen relative to the value of assets in place. This happens in all growth industries sooner or later, as competition increases and profitable new investment opportunities shrink. RIM has experienced a similar shift, its assets in place increasing relative to its growth opportunities. By July 2005, RIM's price-to-book ratio had fallen to 6.7.

7.3 $$P_0 = \frac{\text{DIV}_1 + P_1}{1 + r} = \frac{\$5 + \$105}{1.10} = \$100$$

7.4 Since dividends and share price grow at 5 percent,

$$\text{DIV}_2 = \$5 \times 1.05 = \$5.25, \quad \text{DIV}_3 = \$5 \times 1.05^2 = \$5.51$$

$$P_3 = \$100 \times 1.05^3 = \$115.76$$

$$P_0 = \frac{\text{DIV}_1}{1 + r} + \frac{\text{DIV}_2}{(1 + r)^2} + \frac{\text{DIV}_3 + P_3}{(1 + r)^3}$$

$$= \frac{\$5}{1.10} + \frac{\$5.25}{1.10^2} + \frac{\$5.51 + \$115.76}{1.10^3} = \$100$$

7.5 $$P_0 = \frac{\text{DIV}}{r} = \frac{\$25}{.20} = \$125$$

7.6 The two firms have equal risk, so we can use the data for Big Copper to find the expected return on either stock:

$$r = \frac{\text{DIV}_1}{P_0} + g = \frac{\$5}{\$100} + .05 = .10, \text{ or } 10\%$$

7.7 We've already calculated the present value of dividends through year 5 as \$2.63. We can also forecast the dividend in year 6 as

$$\text{DIV}_6 = 1.05 \times \text{DIV}_5 = 1.05 \times \$.81 = \$.8505$$

Price in year 5 is

$$P_5 = \frac{\$.8505}{.066 - .05} = \$53.16$$

Price in year 0 is

$$P_0 = \text{PV(dividends years 1–5)} + \text{PV}(P_5)$$

$$= \$2.63 + \frac{\$53.16}{1.066^5}$$

$$= \$2.63 + \$38.62 = \$41.25$$

7.8 a. The sustainable growth rate is

$$g = \text{return on equity} \times \text{plowback ratio}$$

$$= .10 \times .40 = .04, \text{ or } 4\%$$

b. First value the company. At a 60 percent payout ratio, DIV_1 = \$3 as before. Using the constant-growth model,

$$P_0 = \frac{\$3}{.12 - .04} = \$37.50$$

which is \$4.17 per share less than the company's no-growth value of \$41.67. In this example Blue Skies is throwing away \$4.17 of potential value by investing in projects with unattractive rates of return.

c. Sure. A raider could take over the company and generate a profit of \$4.17 per share just by halting all investments offering less than the 12 percent rate of return demanded by investors. This assumes the raider could buy the shares for \$37.50.

7.9 a. False. The *levels* of successive stock prices are related. If a stock is selling for \$100 per share today, the best guess of its price tomorrow is \$100.

b. True. *Changes* in stock prices are unrelated. Whether a stock price increases or decreases today has no bearing on whether it will do so tomorrow.

c. False. There is no such thing as a "normal" price. If there were, you could make easy profits by buying shares selling below their normal prices (which would tend to be rising back toward those normal levels) and selling shares currently selling above their normal prices. Under a random walk, prices are equally likely to rise or fall.

d. True. Under a random walk, prices are equally likely to rise or fall regardless of their past history.

7.10 Fundamental analysts ensure that stock prices reflect all publicly available information about the underlying value of the firm. If share prices deviate from their fundamental values, such analysts will generate buying or selling pressure that will return prices to their proper levels. Similarly, technical analysts ensure that if there is useful information in stock price history, it will be reflected in current share prices.

MINI CASE

Terence Breezeway, the CEO of Prairie Home Stores, wondered what retirement would be like. It was almost 20 years to the day since his uncle Jacob Breezeway, Prairie Home's founder, had asked him to take responsibility for managing the company. Now it was time to spend more time riding and fishing on the old Lazy Beta Ranch.

Under Mr. Breezeway's leadership Prairie Home had grown slowly but steadily and was solidly profitable. (Table 7.8 shows earnings, dividends, and book asset values for the last five years.) Most of the company's supermarkets had been modernized and its brand name was well known.

Mr. Breezeway was proud of this record, although he wished that Prairie Home could have grown more rapidly. He had passed up several opportunities to build new stores in adjacent counties. Prairie Home was still just a family company. Its common stock was distributed among 15 grandchildren and nephews of Jacob Breezeway, most of whom had come to depend on generous regular dividends. The commitment to high-dividend payout[19] had reduced the earnings available for reinvestment and thereby constrained growth.

Mr. Breezeway believed the time had come to take Prairie Home public. Once its shares were traded in the public market, the Breezeway descendants who needed (or just wanted) more cash to spend could sell off part of their holdings. Others with more interest in the business could hold on to their shares and be rewarded by higher future earnings and stock prices.

But if Prairie Home did go public, what should its shares sell for? Mr. Breezeway worried that shares would be sold, either by Breezeway family members or by the company itself, at too low a price. One relative was about to accept a private offer for $200, the current book value per share, but Mr. Breezeway had intervened and convinced the would-be seller to wait.

Prairie Home's value did not just depend on its current book value or earnings, but on its future prospects, which were good. One financial projection (shown in the top panel of Table 7.9) called for growth in earnings of over 100 percent by 2018. Unfortunately this plan would require reinvestment of all Prairie Home's earnings from 2013 to 2018. After that the company could resume its normal dividend payout and growth rate. Mr. Breezeway believed this plan was feasible.

He was determined to step aside for the next generation of top management. But before retiring he had to decide whether to recommend that Prairie Home Stores "go public"—and before that decision, he had to know what the company was worth.

The next morning he rode to work thoughtfully. He left his horse at the south corral and ambled down the dusty street to Mike Gordon's Saloon, where Francine Firewater, the company's CFO, was having her usual steak-and-beans breakfast. He asked Ms. Firewater to prepare a formal report to Prairie Home shareholders, valuing the company on the assumption that its shares were publicly traded.

Ms. Firewater asked two questions immediately: First, what should she assume about investment and growth? Mr. Breezeway suggested two valuations: one assuming more rapid expansion (as in the top panel of Table 7.9) and another just projecting past growth (as in the bottom panel of Table 7.9).

Second, what rate of return should she use? Mr. Breezeway said that 15 percent, Prairie Home's usual return on book equity, sounded right to him, but he referred her to an article in *The Journal of Finance* indicating that investors in rural supermarket chains, with risks similar to Prairie Home Stores, expected to earn about 11 percent on average.

TABLE 7.8 Financial data for Prairie Home Stores, 2008–2012 ($ millions).

	2008	2009	2010	2011	2012
Book value, start of year	$62.7	$66.1	$69.0	$73.9	$76.5
Earnings	9.7	9.5	11.8	11.0	11.2
Dividends	6.3	6.6	6.9	7.4	7.7
Addition to retained earnings	3.4	2.9	4.9	2.6	3.5
Book value, end of year	66.1	69.0	73.9	76.5	80.0

Notes:
1. Prairie Home Stores has 400,000 common shares.
2. The company's policy is to pay cash dividends equal to 10 percent of start-of-year book value.

[19] The company traditionally paid out cash dividends equal to 10 percent of start-of-period book value. See Table 7.8.

TABLE 7.9
Financial projections for Prairie Home Stores, 2013–2018 ($ millions).

	2013	2014	2015	2016	2017	2018
Rapid-Growth Scenario						
Book value, start of year	$80	$ 92	$105.8	$121.7	$140.0	$147.0
Earnings	12	13.8	15.9	18.3	21.0	22.0
Dividends	0	0	0	0	14	14.7
Addition to retained earnings	12	13.8	15.9	18.3	7.0	7.3
Book value, end of year	92	105.8	121.7	140.0	147.0	154.3
Constant-Growth Scenario						
Book value, start of year	$80	$ 84	$ 88.2	$ 92.6	$ 97.2	$102.1
Earnings	12	12.6	13.2	13.9	14.6	15.3
Dividends	8	8.4	8.8	9.3	9.7	10.2
Addition to retained earnings	4	4.2	4.4	4.6	4.9	5.1
Book value, end of year	84	88.2	92.6	97.2	102.1	107.2

Notes:
1. Both panels assume earnings equal to 15 percent of start-of-year book value. This profitability rate is constant.
2. The top panel assumes all earnings are reinvested from the start of 2013 to the end of 2017. At the end of 2018 and later years, two-thirds of earnings are paid out as dividends and one-third reinvested.
3. The bottom panel assumes two-thirds of earnings are paid out as dividends in all years.

PART 2 Value

5 The Time Value of Money

6 Valuing Bonds

7 Valuing Stocks

8 Net Present Value and Other Investment Criteria

8.1 Net Present Value

8.2 Other Investment Criteria

8.3 More Examples of Mutually Exclusive Projects

8.4 Capital Rationing

8.5 A Last Look

8.6 Summary

9 Using Discounted Cash Flow Analysis to Make Investment Decisions

10 Project Analysis

CHAPTER 8

Net Present Value and Other Investment Criteria

LEARNING OBJECTIVES

After studying this chapter, you should be able to:

LO1 Calculate the net present value of an investment.

LO2 Calculate the internal rate of return of a project and know what to look out for when using the internal rate of return rule.

LO3 Explain why the payback and discounted payback rules *don't* always make shareholders better off.

LO4 Use the net present value rule to analyze three common problems that involve competing projects: (a) when to postpone an investment expenditure, (b) how to choose between projects with unequal lives, and (c) when to replace equipment.

LO5 Calculate the profitability index and use it to choose between projects when funds are limited.

The investment decision, also known as *capital budgeting*, is central to the success of the company. We have already seen that capital investments sometimes absorb substantial amounts of cash; they also have very long-term consequences. The assets you buy today may determine the business you are in many years hence.

Calculating NPV can be hard work. But you've got to sweat the details and learn to do it right.

Royalty-Free/Corbis.

For some investment projects "substantial" is an understatement. Consider the following examples:

- By 2007, Verizon had already spent $18 billion rolling out its fibre-optic network, FiOS. Toyota's research and development costs for its hybrid gas-electric engine have been about US$6 billion.
- Capital spending by Canadian Oil Sands Trust on Oil Sands projects in 2004 alone totalled $942 million.
- ExxonMobilis developing the Sakhalin Island oil and gas field in eastern Russia involve a likely outlay of US$20 billion.
- Production and merchandising costs for the movie *Spider-Man 3* were almost $500 million.
- The cost of bringing one new prescription drug to market was estimated to be at least US$800 million.
- The development costs of the Airbus A380 jumbo jet are estimated at around $15 billion.
- The 13-kilometre-long Confederation Bridge linking New Brunswick and Prince Edward Island cost $1 billion.
- The Sable Island Offshore Energy Project, which will bring natural gas to the Atlantic Provinces and northeastern United States through hundreds of kilometres of pipelines, is estimated to have cost over US$2 billion in its first phase.

Notice from these examples of big capital projects that many projects require heavy investment in intangible assets. The costs of drug development are almost all research and testing, for example, and much of the development of the hybrid auto is for design and testing. Any expenditure made in the hope of generating more cash later can be called a *capital investment project*, regardless of whether the cash outlay goes to tangible or intangible assets.

A company's shareholders prefer to be rich rather than poor. Therefore, they want the firm to invest in every project that is worth more than it costs. The difference between a project's value and its cost is termed the net present value. Companies can best help their shareholders by investing in projects with a positive net present value.

We start this chapter by showing how to calculate the net present value of a simple investment project. We also examine other criteria that companies sometimes consider when evaluating investments. One of these, the payback period is little better than a rule of thumb. Although there is a place for rules of thumb in this world, an engineer needs something more accurate when designing a 100-storey building, and a financial manager needs more than a rule of thumb when making a substantial capital investment decision.

Instead of calculating a project's net present value, companies sometimes compare the expected rate of return from investing in a project with the return that shareholders might earn on equivalent-risk investments in the capital market. Companies accept only those projects that provide a higher return than shareholders could earn for themselves. This rate of return rule generally gives the same answers as the net present value rule, but as we shall see, it has some pitfalls.

We then turn to more complex issues such as project interactions. These occur when a company is obliged to *choose* between two or more competing proposals; if it accepts one proposal, it cannot take the other. For example, a company may need to choose between buying an expensive, durable machine or a cheap and short-lived one. We will show how the net present value criterion can be used to make such choices.

Sometimes the firm may be forced to make choices because it does not have enough money to take on every project that it would like. We will explain how to maximize shareholder wealth when capital is rationed. It turns out that the solution is to pick the projects that have the highest net present value per dollar invested. This measure is known as the *profitability index*.

LO1 8.1 NET PRESENT VALUE

In Chapter 5 you learned how to discount future cash payments to find their present value. We now apply these ideas to evaluate a simple investment proposal.

Suppose that you are in the real estate business. You are considering construction of an office block. The land would cost \$50,000 and construction would cost a further \$300,000. You foresee a shortage of office space and predict that a year from now you will be able to sell the building for \$400,000. Thus you would be investing \$350,000 now in the expectation of realizing \$400,000 at the end of the year. Therefore, projected cash flows may be summarized in a simple time line as follows:

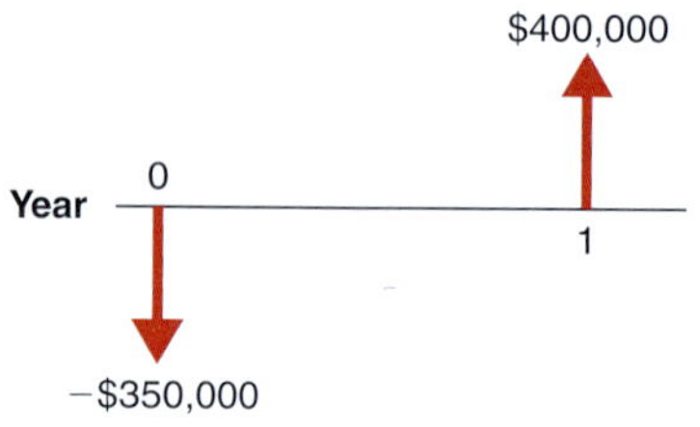

You should go ahead if the present value of the \$400,000 payoff is greater than the investment of \$350,000.

Assume for the moment that the \$400,000 payoff is a sure thing. The office building is not the only way to obtain \$400,000 a year from now; you could invest in a one-year Treasury bill. Suppose the T-bill offers interest of 7 percent. How much would you have to invest in it in order to receive \$400,000 at the end of the year? That's easy: you would have to invest

$$\$400{,}000 \times \frac{1}{1.07} = \$400{,}000 \times .935 = \$373{,}832$$

Let's assume that as soon as you have purchased the land and laid out the money for construction, you decide to cash in on your project. How much could you sell it for? Since the property will be worth \$400,000 in a year, investors would be willing to pay at most \$373,832 for it now. That's all it would cost them to get the same \$400,000 payoff by investing in a government security. Of course, you could always sell your property for less, but why sell for less than the market will bear?

Therefore, at an interest rate of 7 percent, the present value of the \$400,000 payoff from the office building is \$373,832.

The \$373,832 present value is the only price that satisfies both buyer and seller. In general, the present value is the only feasible price, and the present value of the property is also its *market price* or *market value.*

To calculate present value, we discounted the expected future payoff by the rate of return offered by comparable investment alternatives. The discount rate—7 percent in our example—is often known as the **opportunity cost of capital**. It is called the opportunity cost because it is the return being given up by investing in the project.

opportunity cost of capital Expected rate of return given up by investing in a project.

The building is worth \$373,832, but this does not mean that you are \$373,832 better off. You committed \$350,000, and therefore your **net present value (NPV)** is \$23,832. Net present value is found by subtracting the required initial investment from the present value of the project cash flows:

net present value (NPV) Present value of cash flows minus initial investment.

$$\begin{aligned}\text{NPV} &= \text{PV} - \text{required investment} \\ &= \$373{,}832 - \$350{,}000 = \$23{,}832\end{aligned} \tag{8.1}$$

In other words, your office development is worth more than it costs—it makes a net contribution to value.

The net present value rule states that managers increase shareholders' wealth by accepting all projects that are worth more than they cost. Therefore, they should accept all projects with a positive net present value.

A COMMENT ON RISK AND PRESENT VALUE

In our discussion of the office development, we assumed we knew the value of the completed project. Of course, you will never be certain about the future values of office buildings. The $400,000 represents the best *forecast*, but it is not a sure thing.

Therefore, our initial conclusion about how much investors would pay for the building is wrong. Since they could achieve $400,000 risk-free by investing in $373,832 worth of T-bills, they would not buy your building for that amount. You would have to cut your asking price to attract investors' interest.

Here we can invoke a basic financial principle: A risky dollar is worth less than a safe one.

A risky dollar is worth less than a safe one.

Most investors avoid risk when they can do so without sacrificing return. However, the concepts of present value and the opportunity cost of capital still apply to risky investments. It is still proper to discount the payoff by the rate of return offered by a comparable investment. But we have to think of *expected* payoffs and the *expected* rates of return on other investments.

Not all investments are equally risky. The office development is riskier than a T-bill, but is probably less risky than investing in a start-up biotech company. Suppose you believe the office development is as risky as an investment in the stock market and that you forecast a 12 percent rate of return for stock market investments. Then 12 percent would be the appropriate opportunity cost of capital. That is what you are giving up by not investing in comparable securities. You can now recompute NPV:

$$\text{PV} = \$400{,}000 \times \frac{1}{1.12} = \$400{,}000 \times .893 = \$357{,}143$$

$$\text{NPV} = \text{PV} - \$350{,}000 = \$7{,}143$$

If other investors agree with your forecast of a $400,000 payoff and with your assessment of a 12 percent opportunity cost of capital, then the property ought to be worth $357,143 once construction is under way. If you tried to sell for more than that, there would be no takers, because the property would then offer a lower expected rate of return than the 12 percent available in the stock market. The office building still makes a net contribution to value, but it is much smaller than our earlier calculations indicated.

Check Point 8.1

What is the office development's NPV if construction costs increase to $355,000? Assume the opportunity cost of capital is 12 percent. Is the development still a worthwhile investment? How high can development costs be before the project is no longer attractive? Now suppose that the opportunity cost of capital is 20 percent with construction costs of $355,000. Why is the office development no longer an attractive investment?

VALUING LONG-LIVED PROJECTS

The net present value rule works for projects of any length. For example, suppose that you have identified a possible tenant who would be prepared to rent your office block for three years at a fixed annual rent of $16,000. You forecast that after you have collected the third year's rent the building could be sold for $450,000. The projected cash flows (denoted C) in each year are now:

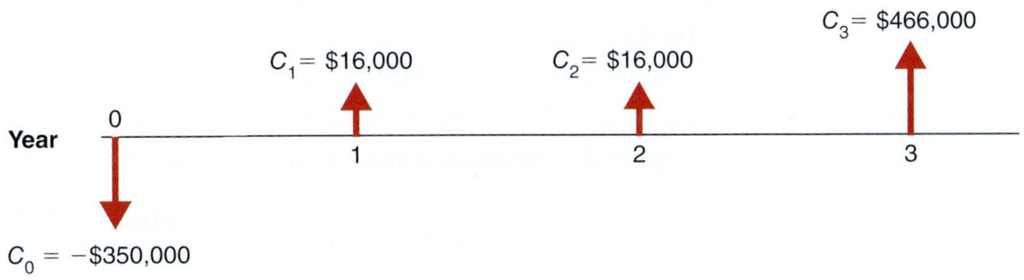

FIGURE 8.1
Cash flows and their present values for the office block project. Final cash flow of \$466,000 is the sum of the rental income in year 3 plus the forecast sales price for the building.

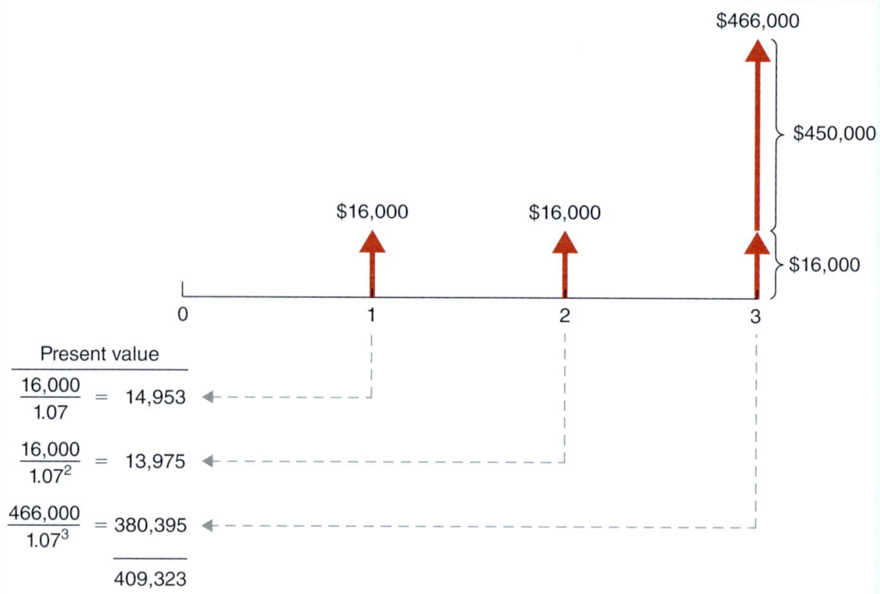

For simplicity, we will again assume that these cash flows are certain and that the opportunity cost of capital is $r = 7$ percent.

Figure 8.1 shows a time line of these cash flows and their present values. To find the present values, we discount the future cash flows at the 7 percent opportunity cost of capital:

$$\text{PV} = \frac{C_1}{1+r} + \frac{C_2}{(1+r)^2} + \frac{C_3}{(1+r)^3}$$

$$= \frac{\$16{,}000}{1.07} + \frac{\$16{,}000}{(1.07)^2} + \frac{\$466{,}000}{(1.07)^3} = \$409{,}323$$

The net present value of the revised project is NPV = \$409,323 − \$350,000 = \$59,323. Constructing the office block and renting it for three years makes a greater addition to your wealth than selling the office block at the end of the first year.

Of course, rather than subtracting the initial investment from the project's present value, you might calculate NPV directly, as in the following equation, where C_0 denotes the initial cash outflow required to build the office block. (Notice that C_0 is negative, reflecting the fact that it is a cash outflow.)

$$\text{NPV} = C_0 + \frac{C_1}{1+r} + \frac{C_2}{(1+r)^2} + \frac{C_3}{(1+r)^3}$$

$$= -\$350{,}000 + \frac{\$16{,}000}{1.07} + \frac{\$16{,}000}{(1.07)^2} + \frac{\$466{,}000}{(1.07)^3} = \$59{,}323$$

Let's check that the owners of this project really are better off. Suppose you put up \$350,000 of your own money, commit to build the office building, and sign a lease that will bring in \$16,000 a year for 3 years. Now you can cash in by selling the project to someone else.

Suppose you sell 1,000 shares in the project. Each share represents a claim to 1/1,000 of the future cash flows. Since the cash flows are sure things, and the interest rate offered by other sure things is 7 percent, investors will value the shares for

$$\text{Price per share} = P = \frac{\$16}{1.07} + \frac{\$16}{(1.07)^2} + \frac{\$466}{(1.07)^3} = \$409.32$$

Thus you can sell the project to outside investors for 1,000 × \$409.32 = \$409,320, which, save for rounding, is exactly the present value we calculated earlier. Your net gain is

$$\text{Net gain} = \$409{,}320 - \$350{,}000 = \$59{,}320$$

which is the project's NPV. This equivalence should be no surprise, since the present value calculation is designed to calculate the value of future cash flows to investors in the capital markets.

Notice that in principle there could be a different opportunity cost of capital for each period's cash flow. In that case, we would discount C_1 by r_1, the discount rate for one-year cash flows; C_2 would be discounted by r_2; and so on. Here we assume that the cost of capital is the same regardless of the date of the cash flow. We do this for one reason only—simplicity. But we are in good company: with only rare exceptions, firms decide on an appropriate discount rate and then use it to discount all project cash flows.

EXAMPLE 8.1 VALUING A NEW COMPUTER SYSTEM

Obsolete Technologies is considering the purchase of a new computer system to help handle its warehouse inventories. The system costs \$50,000, is expected to last 4 years, and should reduce the cost of managing inventories by \$22,000 a year. The opportunity cost of capital is 10 percent. Should Obsolete proceed?

Don't be put off by the fact that the computer system does not generate any sales. If the expected cost savings are realized, the company's cash flows will be \$22,000 a year higher as a result of buying the computer. Thus we might say the computer increases cash flows by \$22,000 a year for each of 4 years. To calculate present value, you can discount each of these cash flows by 10 percent. However, it is smarter to recognize that the cash flows are level and therefore you can use the annuity formula to calculate the present value:

$$\text{PV} = \text{cash flow} \times \text{annuity factor} = \$22{,}000 \times \left[\frac{1}{.10} - \frac{1}{.10(1.10)^4}\right]$$

$$= \$22{,}000 \times 3.170 = \$69{,}740$$

The net present value is

$$\text{NPV} = -\$50{,}000 + \$69{,}740 = \$19{,}740$$

The project has a positive NPV of \$19,740. Undertaking it would increase the value of the firm by that amount.

The first two steps in calculating NPVs—forecasting the cash flows and estimating the opportunity cost of capital—are tricky, and we will have a lot more to say about them in later chapters. But once you have assembled the data, the calculation of present value and net present value should be routine. Here is another example.

EXAMPLE 8.2 CALCULATING EUROTUNNEL'S NPV

One of the world's largest commercial investment projects was construction of the Channel Tunnel by the Anglo-French company Eurotunnel. Here is a chance to put yourself in the shoes of Eurotunnel's financial manager and find out whether the project looked like a good deal for shareholders. The figures in the column headed "cash flow" in Table 8.1 are based on the forecasts of construction costs and revenues that the company provided to investors in 1986.

(Continued)

TABLE 8.1
Forecast cash flows and present values in 1986 for the Channel Tunnel. The investment at the time appeared to have a small positive NPV of £249.8 million (figures in £ millions).

	A	B	C	D	E
1			**Cash Flow**		
2	**Year**	**Time**	**(£ million)**	**PV at 13%**	**Formula in Column D**
3	1986	0	−457	−457.0	=C3/1.13^B3
4	1987	1	−476	−421.2	=C4/1.13^B4
5	1988	2	−497	−389.2	=C5/1.13^B5
6	1989	3	−522	−361.8	=C6/1.13^B6
7	1990	4	−551	−337.9	=C7/1.13^B7
8	1991	5	−584	−317.0	=C8/1.13^B8
9	1992	6	−619	−297.3	=C9/1.13^B9
10	1993	7	211	89.7	=C10/1.13^B10
11	1994	8	489	183.9	=C11/1.13^B11
12	1995	9	455	151.5	=C12/1.13^B12
13	1996	10	502	147.9	=C13/1.13^B13
14	1997	11	530	138.2	=C14/1.13^B14
15	1998	12	544	125.5	=C15/1.13^B15
16	1999	13	636	129.8	=C16/1.13^B16
17	2000	14	594	107.3	=C17/1.13^B17
18	2001	15	689	110.2	=C18/1.13^B18
19	2002	16	729	103.2	=C19/1.13^B19
20	2003	17	796	99.7	=C20/1.13^B20
21	2004	18	859	95.2	=C21/1.13^B21
22	2005	19	923	90.5	=C22/1.13^B22
23	2006	20	983	85.3	=C23/1.13^B23
24	2007	21	1,050	80.6	=C24/1.13^B24
25	2008	22	1,113	75.6	=C25/1.13^B25
26	2009	23	1,177	70.8	=C26/1.13^B26
27	2010	24	17,781	946.4	=C27/1.13^B27
28					
29	**SUM:**			**249.8**	=SUM(D3:D27)
30					
31	Instead, use Excel's NPV function			**249.8**	=NPV(0.13,C4:C27) + C3

Note: Cash flow for 2010 includes the value in 2010 of forecast cash flows in all subsequent years. Some of these figures involve guesswork, because the prospectus reported accumulated construction costs including interest expenses.

Source: Eurotunnel Equity II prospectus, October 1986. Reprinted with permission.

(Concluded)

The Channel Tunnel project was not a safe investment. Indeed, the prospectus to the Channel Tunnel share issue cautioned investors that the project "involves significant risk and should be regarded at this stage as speculative. If for any reason the Project is abandoned or Eurotunnel is unable to raise the necessary finance, it is likely that equity investors will lose some or all of their money."

To be induced to invest in the project, investors needed a higher prospective rate of return than they could get on safe government bonds. Suppose investors expected a return of 13 percent from investments in the capital market that had a degree of risk similar to that of the Channel Tunnel. That was what investors were giving up when they provided the capital for the tunnel. To find the project's NPV, we therefore discount the cash flows in Table 8.1 at 13 percent.

Since the tunnel was expected to take about seven years to build, there are seven years of negative cash flows in Table 8.1. To calculate NPV you just discount all the cash flows, positive and negative, at 13 percent and sum the results. Call 1986 year 0, 1987 year 1, and so on. Then

$$
\begin{aligned}
\text{NPV} &= C_0 + \frac{C_1}{1+r} + \frac{C_2}{(1+r)^2} + \cdots + \frac{C_{24}}{(1+r)^{24}} \\
&= -£457 + \frac{-£476}{1.13} + \frac{-£497}{(1.13)^2} + \cdots + \frac{£17{,}781}{(1.13)^{24}} = £249.8 \text{ million}
\end{aligned}
$$

(Concluded)

We present the calculations in column D. (The nearby Excel spreadsheet box provides additional discussion of how to calculate present values by using spreadsheets.) The net present value of the forecast cash flows is £249.8 million, making the tunnel a worthwhile project, though not by a wide margin considering the planned investment of nearly £4 billion.

---

mutually exclusive projects Two or more projects that cannot be pursued simultaneously.

Of course, NPV calculations are only as good as the underlying cash-flow forecasts. The well-known "Pentagon Law of Large Projects" states that anything big takes longer and costs more than you were originally led to believe. As the law predicted, the tunnel proved much more expensive to build than anticipated in 1986, and the opening was delayed by more than a year. Revenues also have been below forecast, and Eurotunnel has not even generated enough profits to pay the interest on its debt. Thus, in hindsight, the tunnel was a costly negative-NPV venture. By 2007, Eurotunnel was operating under French bankruptcy law and had to be restructured. Eventually, the firm was reorganized into a new company called Groupe Eurotunnel.

The spreadsheet box nearby further describes the Eurotunnel problem illustrated in Table 8.1.

> When you need to choose between mutually exclusive projects, calculate the NPV of each project and, from those options that have a positive NPV, choose the one whose NPV is highest.

USING THE NPV RULE TO CHOOSE AMONG PROJECTS

The simple projects we have considered so far involve take-it-or-leave-it decisions. But almost all real-world decisions are either-or choices. You might build an apartment block, rather than the office block, on that vacant lot. You might build a 7-storey office building or a 10-storey one. You might heat it with oil or with natural gas. You might build it today or wait a year to start construction. Such choices are said to be **mutually exclusive**.

When you need to choose between mutually exclusive projects, the decision rule is simple. Calculate the NPV of each project and, from those options that have a positive NPV, choose the one whose NPV is highest.

EXAMPLE 8.3 CHOOSING BETWEEN TWO PROJECTS

It has been several years since your office last upgraded its office networking software. Two competing systems have been proposed. Both have an expected useful life of three years, at which point it will be time for another upgrade. One proposal is for an expensive, cutting-edge system, which will cost $800,000 and increase firm cash flows by $350,000 a year through increased productivity. The other proposal is for a cheaper, somewhat slower system. This system would cost only $700,000 but would increase cash flows by only $300,000 a year. If the cost of capital is 7 percent, which is the better option?

The following table summarizes the cash flows and the NPVs of the two proposals:

Cash Flows (thousands of dollars)				
System	C_0	C_1	C_2	NPV at 7%
Faster	−800	+350	+350	+350
Slower	−700	+300	+300	+350

In both cases, the software systems are worth more than they cost, but the faster system would make the greater contribution to value and therefore should be your preferred choice.

LO2, 3 8.2 OTHER INVESTMENT CRITERIA

A project with a positive net present value is worth more than it costs. So, whenever a firm invests in such a project, it is making its shareholders better off.

These days almost every large corporation calculates the NPV of proposed investments, but management may also consider other criteria when making investment decisions. Most commonly, they may look at the project's payback or discounted payback and its internal rate of return.

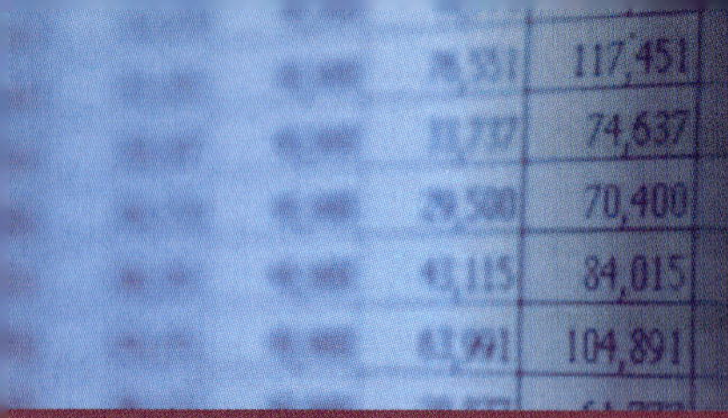

excel spreadsheet

Computer spreadsheets are tailor-made to calculate the present value of a series of cash flows. For example, the spreadsheet in Table 8.1 sets up the Eurotunnel problem as an Excel spreadsheet. Cells D3 to D27 calculate the present value of each year's cash flows by discounting at 13 percent for the length of time given in Column B. Cell D29 shows the sum of these separate present values.

Excel also provides a built-in function to calculate net present values. The formula is =NPV(*rate, list of cash flows*). So, instead of computing the present value of each cash flow separately and then summing, we could have used the NPV function in cell D31. The first entry in the function is the discount rate expressed as a decimal, in this case .13. That is followed by a list of the cash flows that appear in column C.

Why is the first entry in the cash-flow list cell C4 rather than C3, which contains the immediate cash flow, −457? It turns out that Excel always assumes the first cash flow comes after one period, the next after two periods, and so on. If the first cash flow actually comes immediately, as in our example, we do not want it discounted, nor do we want the other cash flows discounted for an extra period. Therefore, we don't include the immediate cash flow in the NPV function, instead adding it undiscounted to the present value of the other cash flows (see cells D31 and E31).

Spreadsheet Questions

8.1. Try calculating Eurotunnel's NPV using the function =NPV(0.13,C3:C27). What do you find?

8.2. The value for NPV in Table 8.1 is exactly 1.13 times as large as the answer you should find for the previous question. Why does this make sense?

In this section, we introduce three of these alternative investment criteria: payback and discounted payback periods and internal rate of return. As we describe these measures, you will see that payback and its improved version, discounted payback, are no better than being very rough guides to an investment's worth. On the other hand, when properly used, the internal rate of return will lead to the same decisions as net present value.

PAYBACK

We suspect you have often heard conversations that go something like this: "A washing machine costs about $400. But we are currently spending $3 a week, or around $150 a year, at the laundromat. So the washing machine should pay for itself in less than three years." You have just encountered the payback rule.

payback period Time until cash flows recover the initial investment of the project.

A project's **payback period** is the length of time before you recover your initial investment. For the washing machine the payback period was just under three years.

The payback rule states that a project should be accepted if its payback period is less than a specified cutoff period. For example, if the cutoff period is four years, the washing machine makes the grade; if the cutoff is two years, it doesn't.

The payback rule states that a project should be accepted if its payback period is less than a specified cutoff period.

As a rule of thumb the payback rule may be adequate, but it is easy to see that it can lead to nonsensical decisions. For example, compare projects A and B. Project A has a two-year Excel Spreadsheet payback and a large positive NPV. Project B also has a two-year payback but a negative NPV. Project A is clearly superior, but the payback rule ranks them equally. This is because payback does not consider any cash flows that arrive after the payback period. A firm that uses the payback criterion with a cutoff of two or more years would accept both A and B despite the fact that only A would increase shareholder wealth.

	Cash Flows, $					
Project	C_0	C_1	C_2	C_3	**Payback Period, Years**	**NPV at 10%**
A	−2,000	+1,000	+1,000	+10,000	2	$7,249
B	−2,000	+1,000	+1,000	0	2	−264
C	−2,000	0	+2,000	0	2	−347

A second problem with payback is that it gives equal weight to all cash flows arriving *before* the cutoff period despite the fact that the more distant flows are less valuable. For example, look at project C. It also has a payback period of 2 years but it has an even lower NPV than project B. Why? Because its cash flows arrive later within the payback period.

To use the payback rule a firm has to decide on an appropriate cutoff period. If it uses the same cutoff regardless of project life, it will tend to accept too many short-lived projects and reject too many long-lived ones. The payback rule will bias the firm against accepting long-term projects, because cash flows that arrive after the payback period are ignored.

Earlier in the chapter we evaluated the Channel Tunnel project. Large construction projects of this kind inevitably have long payback periods. The cash flows that we presented in Table 8.1 implied a payback period of just under 14 years. But most firms that employ the payback rule use a much shorter cutoff period than this. If they used the payback rule mechanically, long-lived projects like the Channel Tunnel wouldn't have a chance.

In our example, the payback works out to be exactly two years for all three projects. Suppose the numbers don't work out exactly, as in project D below:

	Project D Cash Flow $				**Payback**
Year	**0**	**1**	**2**	**3**	**Period, Years**
Cash flow	−2,000	+1,000	+500	+1,000	
Cumulative cash flow	−2,000	−1,000	−500	+500	2.5

We see that the initial investment is $2,000, whereas the cash inflows over years 1 to 3 are $2,500. The cumulative cash flows are negative until year 2 but they become positive by year 3. This means that the project pays back sometime in the third year. If we assume that cash inflows occur uniformly across time, we can figure out the fractional year. We see that out of the total cash flow of $1,000 in year 3, the first $500 comes in by 500/1,000 = .5 years. The payback is therefore 2.5 years.

The primary attraction of the payback criterion is its simplicity. But remember that the hard part of project evaluation is forecasting the cash flows, not doing the arithmetic. Today's spreadsheets make discounting a trivial exercise. Therefore, the payback rule saves you only the easy part of the analysis.

We have had little good to say about payback. So why do many large companies continue to use it? Senior managers don't truly believe that all cash flows after the payback period are irrelevant. It seems more likely (and more charitable to those managers) that payback survives because the deficiencies are relatively unimportant or because there are offsetting benefits. Thus, managers might point out that payback is the simplest way to *communicate* an idea of project desirability. Investment decisions require discussion and negotiation between people from all parts of the firm, and it is important to have a measure that everyone can understand. Perhaps, also, managers favour quick payback projects even when they have lower NPVs, because they believe that quicker profits mean quicker promotion. That takes us back to Chapter 1 where we discussed the need to align the objectives of managers with those of the shareholders.

discounted payback period The time until discounted cash flows recover the initial investment in the project.

In practice, payback is most commonly used when the capital investment is small or when the merits of the project are so obvious that more formal analysis is unnecessary. For example, if a project is expected to produce constant cash flows for 10 years and the payback period is only 2 years, the project in all likelihood has a positive NPV.

The discounted payback rule asks: How long must the project last in order to offer a positive net present value?

DISCOUNTED PAYBACK

Sometimes managers calculate the **discounted payback period**. This is the number of periods before the present value of prospective cash flows equals or exceeds the initial investment.

This surmounts the objection that equal weight is given to all cash flows before the cutoff date. However, the discounted payback rule still takes no account of cash flows after the cutoff date.

Project A			
Year	**Cash Flows, $**	**Discounted Cash Flows at 10%, $**	**Cumulative Discounted Cash Flows, $**
0	−2,000	−2,000	−2,000
1	+1,000	909	−1,091
2	+1,000	827	−264
3	+10,000	7,513	+7,249
		NPV = 7,249	

To show how this would work, suppose we look at the cash flows for project A once again. These cash flows are discounted at 10 percent; the total discounted cash flows represent the project's NPV of $7,249. The cumulative discounted cash flows are negative until year 2 but sizably positive by year 3. This means the project pays back sometime in the third year. Once again, assuming uniform cash inflows across time, we can figure out the fractional year. We see that out of the total discounted cash flow of $7,513 in year 3, the first $264 comes in by 264/7,513 = 0.04 years. The discounted payback is therefore 2.04 years.

The discounted payback does offer one important advantage over the normal payback criterion. If a project meets a discounted payback cutoff, it must have a positive NPV because the cash flows that accrue up to the discounted payback period are (by definition) just sufficient to provide a present value equal to the initial investment. Any cash flows after that date tip the balance and ensure positive NPV.

Despite this advantage, the discounted payback rule has little to recommend it. It still ignores all cash flows occurring after the arbitrary cutoff date and, therefore, will incorrectly reject some positive NPV opportunities. It is no easier to use than the NPV rule because both project cash flows and an appropriate discount rate must be determined. The best that can be said is it is a better criterion than the (even more unsatisfactory) payback rule. See the Excel spreadsheet nearby.

Check Point 8.2

A project costs $3,000 and will generate annual cash flows of $660 for 7 years. What is the payback period? If the interest rate is 6 percent, what is (a) the discounted payback period, and (b) the project NPV? Should the project be accepted?

INTERNAL RATE OF RETURN

Instead of calculating a project's net present value, companies often prefer to ask whether the project's return is higher or lower than the opportunity cost of capital. For example, think back to the original proposal to build the office block. You planned to invest $350,000 to get back a cash flow of C_1 = $400,000 in one year. Therefore, you forecast a profit on the venture of $400,000 − $350,000 = $50,000. In a one-period project like this one, it is easy to calculate the rate of return. Simply compute end-of-year profit per dollar invested in the project:

$$\text{Rate of return} = \frac{\text{profit}}{\text{investment}} = \frac{C_1 - \text{investment}}{\text{investment}} = \frac{\$400{,}000 - \$350{,}000}{\$350{,}000}$$

$$= .1429, \text{ or about } 14.3\%$$

excel spreadsheet

Discounted Payback Period

	A	B	C	D	E	F
1	**Year**	**Time**	**Cash Flow**	**PV at 13%**	**Cumulative PV**	**Formula for Column E**
2	1986	0	−457	−457	−457	=D2
3	1987	1	−476	−421	−878	=E2+D3
4	1988	2	−497	−389	−1267	=E3+D4
5	1989	3	−522	−362	−1629	=E4+D5
6	1990	4	−551	−338	−1967	=E5+D6
7	1991	5	−584	−317	−2284	=E6+D7
8	1992	6	−619	−297	−2581	=E7+D8
9	1993	7	211	90	−2492	=E8+D9
10	1994	8	489	184	−2308	=E9+D10
11	1995	9	455	151	−2156	=E10+D11
12	1996	10	502	148	−2008	=E11+D12
13	1997	11	530	138	−1870	=E12+D13
14	1998	12	544	126	−1745	=E13+D14
15	1999	13	636	130	−1615	=E14+D15
16	2000	14	594	107	−1508	=E15+D16
17	2001	15	689	110	−1397	=E16+D17
18	2002	16	729	103	−1294	=E17+D18
19	2003	17	796	100	−1195	=E18+D19
20	2004	18	859	95	−1099	=E19+D20
21	2005	19	923	91	−1009	=E20+D21
22	2006	20	983	85	−924	=E21+D22
23	2007	21	1,050	81	−843	=E22+D23
24	2008	22	1,113	76	−767	=E23+D24
25	2009	23	1,177	71	−697	=E24+D25
26	2010	24	17,781	946	250	=E25+D26
27	**SUM:**			**250**		
28						
29				**23.7360** = Discounted Payback {= 23 +(−E25/D26)}		

Once we have the cumulative present values in place, calculating the discounted payback period is quite easy in Excel. The discounted payback period for the Channel Tunnel project is provided in cell E29. The period is returned as a decimal.

The alternative of investing in a T-bill would provide a return of only 7 percent. Thus, the return on your office building is higher than the opportunity cost of capital.[1]

This suggests two rules for deciding whether to proceed with an investment project:

1. *The NPV rule.* Invest in any project that has a positive NPV when its cash flows are discounted at the opportunity cost of capital.
2. *The rate of return rule.* Invest in any project offering a rate of return that is higher than the opportunity cost of capital.

The two rules set the same cutoff point. An investment on the knife edge, with an NPV of zero, will also have a rate of return just equal to the cost of capital.

[1] Recall that we are assuming the profit on the office building is risk-free. Therefore, the opportunity cost of capital is the rate of return on other risk-free investments.

FIGURE 8.2
The value of the office project is lower when the discount rate is higher. The project has positive NPV if the discount rate is less than 14.3 percent.

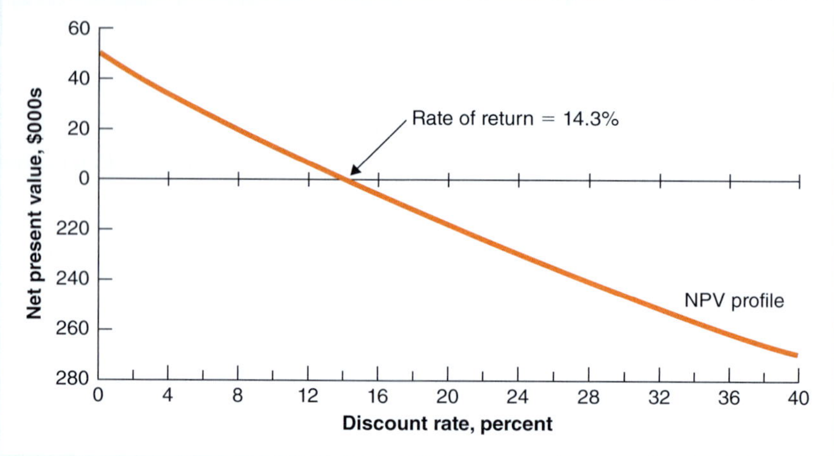

Suppose that the rate of interest on T-bills is not 7 percent but 14.3 percent. Since your office project also offers a return of 14.3 percent, the rate of return rule suggests that there is now nothing to choose between taking the project and leaving your money in T-bills.

The NPV rule also tells you that if the interest rate is 14.3 percent, the project is evenly balanced with an NPV of zero:[2]

$$\text{NPV} = C_0 + \frac{C_1}{1+r} = -\$350{,}000 + \frac{\$400{,}000}{1.143} = 0$$

The project would make you neither richer nor poorer; it is worth what it costs. Thus, the NPV rule and the rate of return rule give the same decision on accepting the project.

A CLOSER LOOK AT THE RATE OF RETURN RULE

We know that if the office project's cash flows are discounted at a rate of 7 percent the project has a net present value of $23,832. If they are discounted at a rate of 14.3 percent, it has an NPV of zero. In Figure 8.2 the project's NPV for a variety of discount rates is plotted. This is often called the *NPV profile* of the project. Notice two important things about Figure 8.2:

1. The project rate of return (in our example, 14.3 percent) is also the discount rate that would give the project a zero NPV. This gives us a useful definition: *The rate of return is the discount rate at which NPV equals zero.*[3]
2. If the opportunity cost of capital is less than the project rate of return, then the NPV of your project is positive. If the cost of capital is greater than the project rate of return, then NPV is negative. Thus, the rate of return rule and the NPV rule are equivalent.

CALCULATING THE RATE OF RETURN FOR LONG-LIVED PROJECTS

There is no ambiguity in calculating the rate of return for an investment that generates a single payoff after one period. Remember that C_0, the time 0 cash flow corresponding to the initial investment, is negative. Thus

$$\text{Rate of return} = \frac{\text{profit}}{\text{investment}} = \frac{C_1 - \text{investment}}{\text{investment}} = \frac{C_1 + C_0}{-C_0}$$

[2] Notice that the initial cash flow C_0 is negative. The investment in the project is therefore $-C_0 = -(-\$350{,}000)$, or $350,000.

[3] Check it for yourself. If NPV $= C_0 + C_1/(1 + r) = 0$, then rate of return $= (C_1 + C_0)/ - C_0 = r$.

FIGURE 8.3
The internal rate of return is the discount rate for which NPV equals zero.

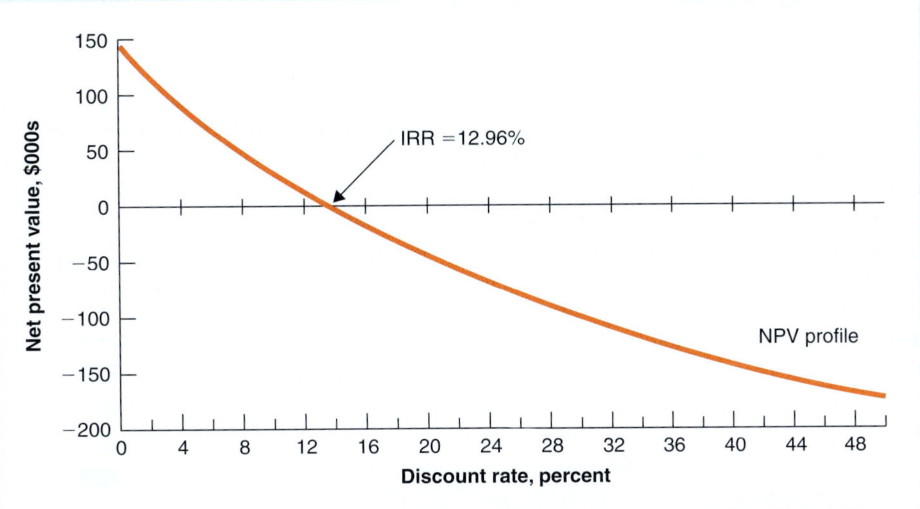

But how do we calculate return when the project generates cash flows in several periods? Go back to the definition that we just introduced—*the project rate of return is also the discount rate that gives the project a zero NPV*. Managers usually refer to this figure as the project's **internal rate of return**, or **IRR**.[4] It is also known as the *discounted cash flow (DCF) rate of return*.

internal rate of return (IRR) The discount rate at which a project NPV = 0.

Let's calculate the IRR for the revised office project. If you rent out the office block for three years, the cash flows are as follows:

Year	**0**	**1**	**2**	**3**
Cash flows	−$350,000	+16,000	+16,000	+466,000

The IRR is the discount rate at which these cash flows would have zero NPV. Thus,

$$\text{NPV} = -\$350{,}000 + \frac{\$16{,}000}{1 + \text{IRR}} + \frac{\$16{,}000}{(1 + \text{IRR})^2} + \frac{\$466{,}000}{(1 + \text{IRR})^3} = 0$$

There is no simple general method for solving this equation. You have to rely on a little trial and error. Let us arbitrarily try a zero discount rate. This gives an NPV of $148,000:

$$\text{NPV} = -\$350{,}000 + \frac{\$16{,}000}{1.0} + \frac{\$16{,}000}{(1.0)^2} + \frac{\$466{,}000}{(1.0)^3} = \$148{,}000$$

With a zero discount rate the NPV is positive. So the IRR must be greater than zero.

The next step might be to try a discount rate of 50 percent. In this case NPV is −$194,000:

$$\text{NPV} = -\$350{,}000 + \frac{\$16{,}000}{1.50} + \frac{\$16{,}000}{(1.50)^2} + \frac{\$466{,}000}{(1.50)^3} = -\$194{,}000$$

The rate of return rule tells you to accept a project if the rate of return exceeds the opportunity cost of capital.

NPV is now negative. So the IRR must lie somewhere between zero and 50 percent. In Figure 8.3 we have plotted the net present values for a range of discount rates. You can see that a discount rate of 12.96 percent gives an NPV of zero. Therefore, the IRR is 12.96 percent.[5] You can always find the IRR by plotting an NPV profile, as in Figure 8.3, but it is quicker and more accurate to let a computer or specially programmed financial calculator do the trial and error for you. The nearby Financial Calculator and Excel spreadsheet boxes illustrate how to do so.

[4] In Chapter 6 you learned how to calculate the yield to maturity on a bond. A bond's yield to maturity is just its internal rate of return.

[5] You can find an appropriate answer for IRR by trial and error and interpolation. By interpolating, after a few trials, one can usually arrive at a reasonably close answer. See end-of-chapter problem 44 if you wish to try out the interpolation technique for solving for IRR.

financial calculator

Using Financial Calculators to Find NPV and IRR

We saw in Chapter 5 that the formulas for the present and future values of level annuities and one-time cash flows are built into financial calculators. However, as the example of the office block illustrates, most investment projects entail multiple cash flows that cannot be expected to remain level over time. Fortunately, many calculators are equipped to handle problems involving a sequence of uneven cash flows. In general, the procedure is quite simple. You enter the cash flows one by one into the calculator, and then you press the IRR key to find the project's internal rate of return. The first cash flow you enter is interpreted as coming immediately, the next cash flow is interpreted as coming at the end of one period, and so on. We illustrate using the office block as an example. To find the project IRR, you would use the following sequence of keystrokes:

Hewlett-Packard HP-10B	Sharp EL-738C	Texas Instruments BA II Plus
−350,000 CFj	−350,000 CFj	CF
16,000 CFj	16,000 CFj	2nd {CLR WORK}
16,000 CFj	16,000 CFj	−350,000 ENTER ↓
466,000 CFj	466,000 CFj	16,000 ENTER ↓
		16,000 ENTER ↓
		466,000 ENTER ↓
■ {IRR/YR}	IRR	IRR
		CPT

The calculator should display the value 12.96, the project's internal rate of return.

To calculate project NPV, the procedure is similar. You need to enter the discount rate in addition to the project cash flows, and then simply press the NPV key. Here is the specific sequence of keystrokes, assuming that the opportunity cost of capital is 7 percent:

Hewlett-Packard HP-10B	Sharp EL-738C	Texas Instruments BA II Plus
−350,000 CFj	−350,000 CFj	CF
16,000 CFj	16,000 CFj	2nd {CLR WORK}
16,000 CFj	16,000 CFj	−350,000 ENTER ↓
466,000 CFj	466,000 CFj	16,000 ENTER ↓
7 I/YR	7 i	16,000 ENTER ↓
		466,000 ENTER ↓
■ {NPV}	NPV	NPV
		7 ENTER
		↓ CPT

The calculator should display the value 59,323, the project's NPV when the discount rate is 7 percent.

By the way, you can check the accuracy of our earlier calculations using your calculator. Enter 50 percent for the discount rate (press 50, then press *i*) and then press the NPV key to find that NPV = −194,148. Enter 12.96 (the project's IRR) as the discount rate and you will find that NPV is just about zero (it is not exactly zero because we are rounding off the IRR to only two decimal places).

The rate of return rule will give the same answer as the NPV rule as long as the NPV of a project declines smoothly as the discount rate increases.

You can see from Figure 8.3 why this makes sense. Because the NPV profile is downward-sloping, the project has a positive NPV as long as the opportunity cost of capital is less than the project's 12.96 percent IRR. If the opportunity cost of capital is higher than the 12.96 percent IRR, NPV is negative. Therefore, when we compare the project IRR with the opportunity cost of capital, we are effectively asking whether the project has a positive NPV. This was true for our one-period office project. It is also true for our three-period office project. We conclude that the rate of return rule will give the same answer as the NPV rule *as long as the NPV of a project declines smoothly as the discount rate increases.*

The usual agreement between the net present value and internal rate of return rules should not come as a surprise. Both are *discounted cash flow* methods of choosing between projects. Both are concerned with identifying those projects that make shareholders better off and both recognize that companies always have a choice: they can invest in a project or, if the project is not sufficiently attractive, they can give the money back to shareholders and let them invest it for themselves in the capital market.

excel spreadsheet

Internal Rate of Return

	A	B	C	D	E	F
1		Calculating IRR by Using a Spreadsheet				
2						
3	Year	Cash Flow				Formula
4	0	−350,000		IRR =	0.1296	=IRR(B4:B7)
5	1	16,000				
6	2	16,000				
7	3	466,000				

Calculating internal rate of return in Excel is as easy as listing the project cash flows. For example, to calculate the IRR of the office-block project, you could simply type in its cash flows as in the spreadsheet (left), and then calculate IRR as we do in cell E4. As always, the interest rate is returned as a decimal.

Check Point 8.3

Suppose the cash flow in year 3 is only $416,000. Redraw Figure 8.3. How would the IRR change?

Check Point 8.4

Suppose that a company invests $60,000 in a project. The project generates a cash inflow of $30,000 a year for each of three years and nothing thereafter. For simplicity, we assume there are no taxes.

Calculate the project's internal rate of return. (If you do not have a financial calculator or spreadsheet program, this will require a little trial and error.)

A WORD OF CAUTION

Some people confuse the internal rate of return on a project with the opportunity cost of capital. Remember that the project IRR measures the profitability of the project. It is an *internal rate* of return in the sense that it depends only on the project's own cash flows. The opportunity cost of capital is the standard for deciding whether to accept the project. It is equal to the return offered by equivalent-risk investments in the capital market.

SOME PITFALLS OF THE IRR RULE

Many firms use the internal rate of return rule instead of net present value. We think this is a pity. Used properly, the two rules head to the same decision, but the rate of return rule has several pitfalls that can trap the unwary. Here are a couple of examples.

Pitfall 1: Lending or Borrowing? Remember our condition for the IRR rule to work: the project's NPV must fall as the discount rate increases. Now consider the following projects:

	Cash Flows, $			
Project	C_0	C_1	**IRR, %**	**NPV at 10%**
J	−100	+150	+50	+$36.4
K	+100	−150	+50	−$36.4

Each project has an IRR of 50 percent. In other words, if you discount the cash flows at 50 percent, both of them would have zero NPV.

Does this mean that the two projects are equally attractive? Clearly not. In the case of J, we are paying out $100 now, and getting $150 back at the end of the year. That is better than any bank account. But what about K? Here we are getting paid $100 now, but we have to pay out $150 at the end of the year. That is equivalent to borrowing money at 50 percent.

If someone asked you whether 50 percent was a good rate of interest, you could not answer unless you also knew whether that person was proposing to lend or borrow at that rate. Lending money at 50 percent is great (as long as the borrower does not flee the country), but borrowing at 50 percent is not usually a good deal (unless of course you plan to flee the country). When you lend money, you want a *high* rate of return; when you borrow, you want a *low* rate of return.

When NPV is higher as the discount rate increases, a project is acceptable only if its internal rate of return is less than the opportunity cost of capital.

If you plot a graph like Figure 8.2 for project K, you will find the NPV increases as the discount rate increases. (Try it!) Obviously, the rate of return rule will not work in this case.

Project K is a fairly obvious trap, but if you want to make sure you don't fall into it, calculate the project's NPV. For example, suppose that the cost of capital is 10 percent. Then the NPV of project J is +$36.4 and the NPV of project K is −$36.4. The NPV rule correctly warns us away from a project that is equivalent to borrowing money at 50 percent.

When NPV rises as the interest rate rises, the rate of return rule is reversed: when NPV is higher as the discount rate increases, a project is acceptable only if its internal rate of return is less than the opportunity cost of capital.

Pitfall 2: Multiple Rates of Return. Here is a trickier problem. King Coal Corporation is considering a project to strip-mine coal. The project requires an investment of $22 million and is expected to produce a cash inflow of $15 million in each of years 1 through 4. However, the company is obliged in year 5 to reclaim the land at a cost of $40 million. At a 10 percent opportunity cost of capital the project has an NPV of $.7 million.

To find the IRR, we have calculated the NPV for various discount rates and plotted the results in Figure 8.4. You can see that there are two discount rates at which NPV = 0. That is, *each* of the following statements holds:

$$\text{NPV} = -22 + \frac{15}{1.06} + \frac{15}{1.06^2} + \frac{15}{1.06^3} + \frac{15}{1.06^4} - \frac{40}{1.06^5} = 0$$

and

$$\text{NPV} = -22 + \frac{15}{1.28} + \frac{15}{1.28^2} + \frac{15}{1.28^3} + \frac{15}{1.28^4} - \frac{40}{1.28^5} = 0$$

In other words, the investment has an IRR of both 6 and 28 percent. The reason for this is the double change in the sign of the cash flows. There can be as many different internal rates of return as there are changes in the sign of the cash-flow stream.[6]

Is the coal mine worth developing? The simple IRR rule—accept if the IRR is greater than the cost of capital—won't help. For example, you can see from Figure 8.4 that with a low cost

[6] There may be *fewer* IRRs than the number of sign changes. You may even encounter projects for which there is *no* IRR. For example, there is no IRR for a project that has cash flows of +$1,000 in year 0, −$3,000 in year 1, and +$2,500 in year 2. If you don't believe us, try plotting NPV for different discount rates. Can such a project ever have a negative NPV?

FIGURE 8.4
King Coal's project has two internal rates of return. NPV = 0 when the discount rate is either 6 percent or 28 percent.

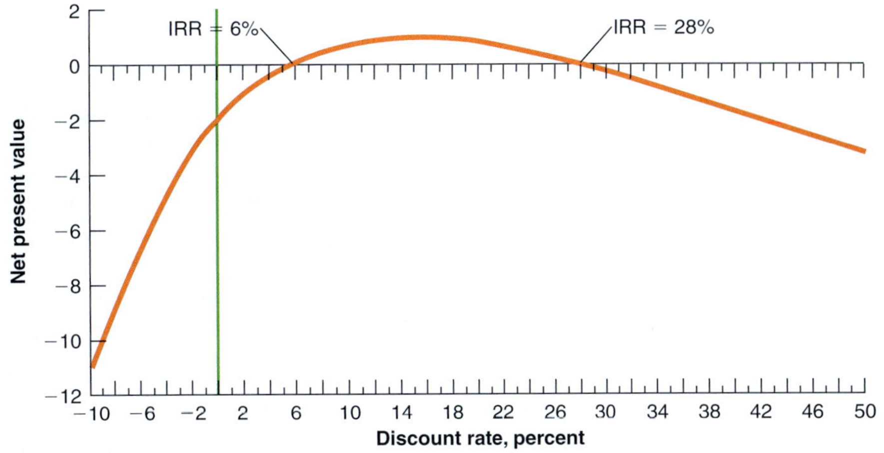

of capital (less than 6 percent) the project has a negative NPV. It has a positive NPV only if the cost of capital is between 6 percent and 28 percent.[7]

Decommissioning and cleanup costs, which make King Coal's final cash flow negative, can sometimes be huge. Phillips Petroleum has estimated that it will need to spend $1 billion to remove its Norwegian offshore oil platforms. It can cost over $300 million to decommission a nuclear power plant. These are obvious examples where cash flows go from positive to negative, but you can probably think of a number of other cases where the company needs to plan for later expenditures. Ships periodically need to go into dry dock for a refit, hotels may receive a major facelift, machine parts may need replacement, and so on.

When there are multiple changes in the sign of the cash flows, the IRR rule does not work, but the NPV rule always does.

Whenever the cash-flow stream is expected to change sign more than once, the project typically has more than one IRR and there is no simple IRR rule. Companies sometimes get around the problem of multiple rates of return by successively combining the later cash flows into one present value until there remains only one change in sign. A *modified internal rate of return (MIRR)* can be calculated from this revised series. We illustrate by continuing the King Coal example.

EXAMPLE 8.4 MODIFIED IRR

The cash flows for King Coal are as follows:

Year:	**0**	**1**	**2**	**3**	**4**	**5**
Cash flows	−$22	$15	$15	$15	$15	−$40

First try combining the last two cash flows into one PV calculated as of year 4. Use the 10 percent cost of capital to discount.

$$15 - \frac{40}{1.10} = -21.36$$

This PV is still negative, and therefore the project still entails two changes in sign. So we step back an additional year and combine the last *three* cash flows into a single PV calculated as of year 3:

$$15 + \frac{15}{1.10} - \frac{40}{(1.10)^2} = -4.42$$

(Continued)

[7] We will examine more pitfalls in Section 8.3 when we reevaluate the IRR rule in the context of mutually exclusive projects.

(Concluded)

This is still negative. So we step back yet another year and combine last *four* cash flows into a PV calculated as of time 2:

$$15 + \frac{15}{1.10} + \frac{15}{(1.10)^2} - \frac{40}{(1.10)^3} = 10.98$$

This value is finally positive, so if we use it in place of the last four cash flows, we will have only one change of sign. Now we can compute IRR using the *modified* cash-flow sequence:

Year:	**0**	**1**	**2**	**3**	**4**	**5**
Modified cash flows	−$22	$15	$10.98			

IRR is the discount rate at which net present value is zero:

$$-22 + \frac{15}{1 + \text{IRR}} + \frac{10.98}{(1 + \text{IRR})^2} = 0$$

We solve to find that modified IRR = .1253, or 12.53 percent, which is greater than the cost of capital, 10 percent. The project has a positive NPV when valued at the cost of capital.

Of course, it would be much easier in cases like this one to abandon the IRR rule and just calculate project NPV.

Pitfall 3: Mutually Exclusive Projects. We have seen that firms are seldom faced with take-it-or-leave-it projects. Usually they need to choose from a number of mutually exclusive alternatives.

But what about the rate of return rule? Would it make sense to just choose the project that offers the highest internal rate of return? Unfortunately, no. Mutually exclusive projects involve an additional pitfall for users of the IRR rule.

Think once more about the two office-block proposals from Section 8.1. You initially intended to invest $350,000 in the building and then sell it at the end of the year for $400,000. Under the revised proposal, you plan to rent out the offices for three years at a fixed annual rent of $16,000 and then sell the building for $450,000. Here are the cash flows, their IRRs, and their NPVs:

	Cash Flows, $000s					
Project	C_0	C_1	C_2	C_3	**IRR, %**	**NPV at 7%**
H: Initial proposal	−350	+400			+14.29	+$24,000
I: Revised proposal	−350	+16	+16	+466	+12.96	+$59,000

Both projects are good investments; both offer a positive NPV. But the revised proposal has the higher net present value and therefore is the better choice. Unfortunately, the superiority of the revised proposal doesn't show up as a higher rate of return. The IRR rule seems to say you should go for the initial proposal because it has the higher IRR. If you follow the IRR rule, you have the satisfaction of earning a 14.29 percent rate of return; if you use NPV, you are $59,000 richer.

Remember, a high IRR is not an end in itself. You want projects that increase the value of the firm. Projects that earn a good rate of return for a long time often have higher NPVs than those that offer high percentage rates of return but die young.

Figure 8.5 shows why the IRR rule gives the wrong signal. The figure plots the NPV of each project as a function of the discount rate. These two NPV profiles cross at an interest rate of 12.26 percent. So if the opportunity cost of capital is higher than 12.26 percent, the initial proposal, with its rapid cash inflow, is the superior investment. If the cost of capital is lower than 12.26 percent, then the revised proposal dominates. Depending on the discount rate, either proposal may be superior. For the 7 percent cost of capital that we have assumed, the revised proposal is the better choice.

Now consider the IRR of each proposal. The IRR is simply the discount rate at which NPV equals zero, that is, the discount rate at which the NPV profile crosses the horizontal axis in Figure 8.5. As noted, these rates are 14.29 percent for the initial proposal and 12.96 percent for the revised proposal. However, as you can see from Figure 8.5, the higher IRR for the initial proposal does not mean that it has a higher NPV.

In our example both projects involved the same outlay, but the revised proposal had the longer life. The IRR rule mistakenly favoured the quick-payback project, with the high percentage return but the lower NPV.

FIGURE 8.5
The initial proposal offers a higher IRR than the revised proposal, but its NPV is lower if the discount rate is less than 12.26 percent.

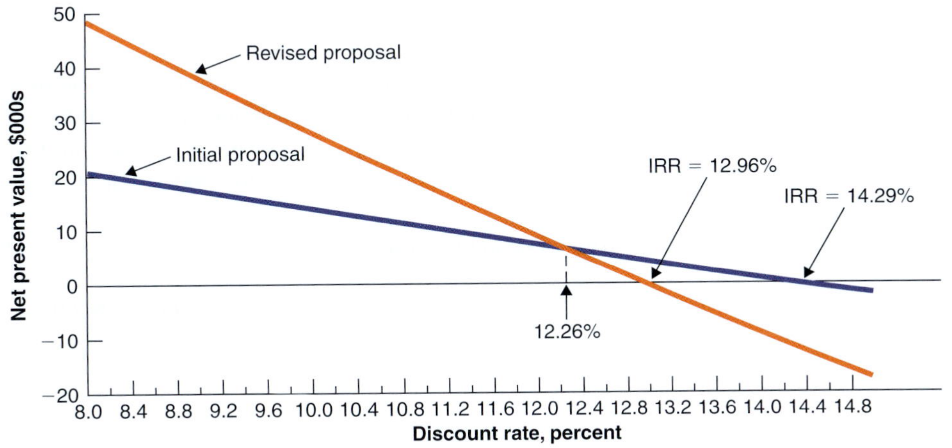

Check Point 8.5

A rich, friendly, and probably slightly unbalanced benefactor offers you the opportunity to invest $1 million in two mutually exclusive ways. The payoffs are

a. $2 million after 1 year, a 100 percent return
b. $300,000 a year forever

Neither investment is risky, and safe securities are yielding 7.5 percent. Which investment will you take? You can't take both, so the choices are mutually exclusive. Do you want to earn a high percentage return or do you want to be rich? By the way, if you really had this investment opportunity, you'd have no trouble borrowing the money to undertake it.

Pitfall 3a: Mutually Exclusive Projects Involving Different Outlays. A similar misranking may also occur when comparing projects with the same lives but different outlays. In this case the IRR may mistakenly favour small projects with high rates of return but low NPVs.

Check Point 8.6

Your wacky benefactor now offers you the choice of two opportunities:

a. Invest $1,000 today and quadruple your money—a 300 percent return—in one year, with no risk.
b. Invest $1 million for one year at a guaranteed 50 percent return.

Which will you take? Do you want to earn a wonderful rate of return (300 percent) or do you want to be rich? Safe securities still yield 7.5 percent.

LO4 8.3 MORE EXAMPLES OF MUTUALLY EXCLUSIVE PROJECTS

Although the IRR rule can quickly lead you astray when choosing among mutually exclusive projects, the choice is easy using the NPV rule, at least in principle. As long as at least one project has positive NPV, simply choose the project with the highest NPV. Let us look at an example.

EXAMPLE 8.5 **CHOOSING BETWEEN TWO PROJECTS**

It has been several years since your office last upgraded its office networking software. Two competing systems have been proposed. Both have an expected useful life of three years, at which point it will be time for another upgrade. One proposal is for an expensive cutting-edge system, which will cost $800,000 and increase firm cash flows by $350,000 a year through increased productivity. The other proposal is for a cheaper, somewhat slower system. This system would cost only $700,000 but would increase cash flows by only $300,000 a year. If the cost of capital is 7 percent, which is the better option?

The following table summarizes the cash flows and the NPVs of the two proposals:

	Cash Flows, $000s				
System	C_0	C_1	C_2	C_3	**NPV at 7%**
Faster	−800	+350	+350	+350	+118.5
Slower	−700	+300	+300	+300	+87.3

In both cases, the software systems are worth more than they cost, but the faster system would make the greater contribution to value and therefore should be your preferred choice.

Mutually exclusive projects, such as our two proposals to update the networking system, involve a project interaction, since taking one project forecloses the other. Unfortunately, not every project interaction is as simple to evaluate as the choice between the two networking projects, but we will explain how to tackle three important, but often challenging, decisions:

- *The investment timing decision.* Should you buy a computer now or wait and think again next year? (Here today's investment is competing with possible future investments.)
- *The choice between long- and short-lived equipment.* Should the company save money today by installing cheaper machinery that will not last as long? (Here today's decision would accelerate a later investment in machine replacement.)
- *The replacement decision.* When should existing machinery be replaced? (Using it another year could delay investment in machine replacement.)

INVESTMENT TIMING

Let us return to Example 8.1, where Obsolete Technologies was contemplating the purchase of a new computer system. The proposed investment has a net present value of almost $20,000, so it appears that the cost savings would easily justify the expense of the system. However, the financial manager is not persuaded. She reasons that the price of computers is continually falling and therefore proposes postponing the purchase, arguing that the NPV of the system will be even higher if the firm waits until the following year. Unfortunately, she has been making the same argument for 10 years and the company is steadily losing business to competitors with more efficient systems. Is there a flaw in her reasoning?

This is a problem in investment timing. When is it best to commit to a positive-NPV investment? Investment timing problems all involve choices among mutually exclusive investments. You can either proceed with the project now, or you can do so later. You can't do both.

Table 8.2 lays out the basic data for Obsolete. You can see that the cost of the computer is expected to decline from $50,000 today to $45,000 next year, and so on. The new computer system is expected to last for four years from the time it is installed. The present value of the savings *at the time of installation* is expected to be $70,000. Thus if Obsolete invests today, it achieves an NPV of $70,000 − $50,000 = $20,000; if it invests next year, it will have an NPV of $70,000 − $45,000 = $25,000.

TABLE 8.2
Obsolete Technologies: The gain from purchase of a computer is rising, but the NPV today is highest if the computer is purchased in year 3 ($000s).

Year of Purchase	Cost of Computer	PV Savings	NPV at Year of Purchase (r = 10%)	NPV Today
0	$50	$70	$20	$20.0
1	45	70	25	22.7
2	40	70	30	24.8
3	36	70	34	25.5 ←Optimal purchase date
4	33	70	37	25.3
5	31	70	39	24.2

Isn't a gain of $25,000 better than one of $20,000? Well, not necessarily—you may prefer to be $20,000 richer *today* rather than $25,000 richer *next year*. The better choice depends on the cost of capital. The fifth column of Table 8.2 shows the value today (year 0) of those net present values at a 10 percent cost of capital. For example, you can see that the discounted value of that $25,000 gain is $25,000/1.10 = $22,700. The financial manager has a point. It is worth postponing investment in the computer, but it should not be postponed indefinitely. You maximize net present value today by buying the computer in year 3.

The decision rule for investment timing is to choose the investment date that results in the highest net present value today.

Notice that you are involved in a trade-off. The sooner you can capture the $70,000 savings the better, but if it costs you less to realize those savings by postponing the investment, it may pay you to do so. If you postpone the purchase by one year, the gain from buying a computer rises from $20,000 to $25,000, an increase of 25 percent. Since the cost of capital is only 10 percent, it pays to postpone at least until year 1. If you postpone from year 3 to year 4, the gain rises from $34,000 to $37,000, a rise of just under 9 percent. Since this is less than the cost of capital, it is not worth waiting any longer.

Check Point 8.7

Unfortunately, Obsolete Technology's business is shrinking as the company dithers and dawdles. Its chief financial officer realizes that the savings from installing the new computer will likewise shrink by $4,000 per year, from a present value of $70,000 now to $66,000 next year, then to $62,000, and so on. Redo Table 8.2 with this new information. When should Obsolete buy the new computer?

LONG-VERSUS SHORT-LIVED EQUIPMENT

Suppose the firm is forced to choose between two machines, D and E. The two machines are designed differently but have identical capacity and do exactly the same job. Machine D costs $15,000 and will last 3 years. It costs $4,000 per year to run. Machine E is an "economy" model, costing only $10,000, but it will last only 2 years and costs $6,000 per year to run.

Because the two machines produce exactly the same product, the only way to choose between them is on the basis of cost. Suppose we compute the present value of the costs:

	Costs, $000s				
Year:	**0**	**1**	**2**	**3**	**PV at 6%**
Machine D	15	4	4	4	25.69
Machine E	10	6	6	—	21.00

Should we take machine E, the one with the lower present value of costs? Not necessarily. All we have shown is that machine E offers two years of service for a lower cost than three years of service from machine D. But is the annual cost of using E lower than that of D?

Suppose the financial manager agrees to buy machine D and pay for its operating costs out of his budget. He then charges the plant manager an annual amount for use of the machine. There will be three equal payments starting in year 1. Obviously, he has to make sure that the present value of these payments equals the present value of the costs of machine D, \$25,690. The payment stream with such a present value when the discount rate is 6 percent turns out to be \$9,610 a year. In other words, the cost of buying and operating machine D is equivalent to an annual charge of \$9,610 a year for three years. This figure is therefore termed the **equivalent annual cost** of machine D.

equivalent annual cost The cost per period with the same present value as the cost of buying and operating a machine.

	Costs, \$000s				
Year:	**0**	**1**	**2**	**3**	**PV at 6%**
Machine D	15	4	4	4	25.69
Equivalent annual cost		9.61	9.61	9.61	25.69

How did we know that an annual charge of \$9,610 has a present value of \$25,690? The annual charge is a three-year annuity. So we calculate the value of this annuity and set it equal to \$25,690:

$$\text{Equivalent annual cost} \times \text{3-year annuity factor} = \text{PV cost of D} = \$25{,}690$$

If the cost of capital is 6 percent, the 3-year annuity factor is 2.673. So

$$\textbf{Equivalent annual cost} = \frac{\textbf{present value of costs}}{\textbf{annuity factor}} \tag{8.2}$$

$$= \frac{\$25{,}690}{\text{3-year annuity factor}} = \frac{\$25{,}690}{2.673} = \$9{,}610$$

If we make a similar calculation of costs for machine E, we get this:

	Costs, \$000s			
Year:	**0**	**1**	**2**	**PV at 6%**
Machine E	10	6	6	21.00
Equivalent 2-year annuity		11.45	11.45	21.00

Rule for comparing assets of different lives: Select the machine that has the lowest equivalent annual cost.

We see now that machine D is better, because its equivalent annual cost is less (\$9,610 for D versus \$11,450 for E). In other words, the financial manager could afford to set a lower *annual* charge for the use of D. We thus have a rule for comparing assets of different lives: Select the machine that has the lowest equivalent annual cost.

Think of the equivalent annual cost as the level annual charge[8] necessary to recover the present value of investment outlays and operating costs. The annual charge continues for the life of the equipment. Calculate equivalent annual cost by dividing the appropriate present value by the annuity factor.

EXAMPLE 8.6 EQUIVALENT ANNUAL COST

You need a new car. You can either purchase one outright for \$15,000 or lease one for 7 years for \$3,000 a year. If you buy the car, it will be worth \$500 to you in 7 years. The discount rate is 10 percent. Should you buy or lease? What is the maximum lease you would be willing to pay?

The present value of the cost of purchasing is

$$PV = \$15{,}000 - \frac{\$500}{(1.10)^7} = \$14{,}743$$

[8] We have implicitly assumed that inflation is zero. If that is not the case, it would be better to calculate the equivalent annuities for machines D and E in real terms, using the real rate of interest to calculate the annuity factor.

The equivalent annual cost of purchasing the car is therefore the annuity with this present value:

$$\text{Equivalent annual cost} \times \frac{\text{7-year annuity}}{\text{factor at 10\%}} = \frac{\text{PV cost}}{\text{of buying}} = \$14{,}743$$

$$\text{Equivalent annual cost} = \frac{\$14{,}743}{\text{7-year annuity factor}} = \frac{\$14{,}743}{4.8684} = \$3{,}028$$

Therefore, the annual lease payment of $3,000 is less than the equivalent annual cost of buying the car. You should be willing to pay up to $3,028 annually to lease.

EXAMPLE 8.7 ANOTHER EQUIVALENT ANNUAL ANNUITY

Low-energy light bulbs typically cost $3.50, have a life of 9 years, and use about $1.60 of electricity a year. Conventional light bulbs are cheaper to buy, for they cost only $.50. On the other hand, they last only about a year and use about $6.60 of energy. If the real discount rate is 5 percent, what is the relative cost of the two products?

To answer this question, you need first to convert the initial cost of each bulb to an annual figure and then to add in the annual energy cost.[9] The following table sets out the calculations.

	Low-Energy Bulb	Conventional Bulb
1. Initial cost, $	3.50	.50
2. Estimated life, years	9	1
3. Annuity factor at 5%	7.1078	.9524
4. Equivalent annual annuity, $, = (1)/(3)	.49	.52
5. Annual energy cost, $	1.60	6.60
6. Total annual cost, $, = (4) + (5)	2.09	7.12

Note: It is assumed that energy costs are incurred at the end of each year.

It seems that a low-energy light bulb provides an annual saving of about $7.12 − $2.09 = $5.03.

REPLACING AN OLD MACHINE

The previous example took the life of each machine as fixed. In practice, the point at which equipment is replaced reflects economics, not physical collapse. *We* usually decide when to replace. The machine will rarely decide for us.

Here is a common problem. You are operating an old machine that will last two more years before it gives up the ghost. It costs $12,000 per year to operate. You can replace it now with a new machine, which costs $25,000 but is much more efficient ($8,000 per year in operating costs) and will last for five years. Should you replace it now or wait a year? The opportunity cost of capital is 6 percent.

We can calculate the NPV of the new machine and its equivalent annual cost, that is, the five-year annuity that has the same present value.

	Costs, $000s						
Year:	**0**	**1**	**2**	**3**	**4**	**5**	**PV at 6%**
New machine	25	8	8	8	8	8	58.70
Equivalent 5-year annuity		13.93	13.93	13.93	13.93	13.93	58.70

[9] Our calculations ignore any environmental costs.

The cash flows of the new machine are equivalent to an annuity of $13,930 per year. So we can equally well ask at what point we would want to replace our old machine, which costs $12,000 a year to run, with a new one costing $13,930 a year. When the question is posed this way, the answer is obvious. As long as your old machine costs only $12,000 a year, why replace it with a new machine that costs $1,930 more?[10]

Check Point 8.8

Machines F and G are mutually exclusive and have the following investment and operating costs. Note that machine F lasts for only two years:

Year:	0	1	2	3
F	10,000	1,100	1,200	—
G	12,000	1,100	1,200	1,300

Calculate the equivalent annual cost of each investment using a discount rate of 10 percent. Which machine is the better buy?

Now suppose you have an existing machine. You can keep it going for only one more year, but it will cost $2,500 in repairs and $1,800 in operating costs. Is it worth replacing now with either F or G?

LO5 8.4 CAPITAL RATIONING

A firm maximizes its shareholders' wealth by accepting every project that has a positive net present value. But this assumes that the firm can raise the funds needed to pay for these investments. This is usually a good assumption, particularly for major firms that can raise very large sums of money on fair terms and short notice. Why then does top management sometimes tell subordinates that capital is limited and that they may not exceed a specified amount of capital spending? There are two reasons.

SOFT RATIONING

capital rationing Limit set on the amount of funds available for investment.

For many firms the limits on capital funds are "soft." By this we mean that the **capital rationing** is not imposed by investors. Instead the limits are imposed by top management. For example, suppose that you are an ambitious, upwardly mobile junior manager. You are keen to expand your part of the business and, as a result, you tend to overstate the investment opportunities. Rather than trying to determine which of your many bright ideas really are worthwhile, upper management may find it simpler to impose a limit on the amount that you and other junior managers can spend. This limit forces you to set your own priorities.

Even if capital is not rationed, other resources may be. For example, very rapid growth can place considerable strains on management and the organization. A somewhat rough-and-ready response to this problem is to ration the amount of capital that the firm spends.

HARD RATIONING

Soft rationing should never cost the firm anything. If the limits on investment become so tight that truly good projects are being passed up, then upper management should raise more money and relax the limits it has imposed on capital spending.

[10] In our discussion, we have ignored tax-law implications, such as those applicable to the amortization of assets. We will take up this discussion in Chapter 9 when we will examine Canada's capital cost allowance system in detail.

But what if there is "hard rationing," meaning that the firm actually cannot raise the money it needs? In that case, it may be forced to pass up positive-NPV projects.

With hard rationing you may still be interested in net present value, but you now need to select the package of projects that is within the company's resources and yet gives the highest net present value.

Let us illustrate. Suppose that the opportunity cost of capital is 10 percent, that the company has total resources of $20 million, and that it is presented with the following project proposals:

	Cash Flows, $ Millions				
Project	C_0	C_1	C_2	**PV at 10%**	**NPV**
L	−3	+2.2	+2.42	$4	$1
M	−5	+2.2	+4.84	6	1
N	−7	+6.6	+4.84	10	3
O	−6	+3.3	+6.05	8	2
P	−4	+1.1	+4.84	5	1

All five projects have a positive NPV. Therefore, if there were no shortage of capital, the firm would like to accept all five proposals. But with only $20 million available, the firm needs to find the package that gives the highest possible NPV within the budget.

profitability index Ratio of net present value to initial investment.

The solution is to pick the projects that give the highest net present value per dollar of investment. The ratio of net present value to initial investment is known as the **profitability index.**[11]

$$\textbf{Profitability index} = \frac{\textbf{net present value}}{\textbf{initial investment}} \tag{8.3}$$

For our five projects the profitability index is calculated as follows:

Project	PV	Investment	NPV	Profitability Index
L	$4	$3	1	1/3 = .33
M	6	5	1	1/5 = .20
N	10	7	3	3/7 = .43
O	8	6	2	2/6 = .33
P	5	4	1	1/4 = .25

Project N offers the highest ratio of net present value to investment (.43), and therefore N is picked first. Next come projects L and O, which tie with a ratio of .33, and after them comes P. These four projects use up exactly the $20 million budget. Between them they offer shareholders the highest attainable gain in wealth.[12]

Check Point 8.9 Which projects should the firm accept if its capital budget is only $10 million?

[11] Sometimes the profitability index is defined as the ratio of present value to required investment. By this definition, all the profitability indexes calculated below are increased by 1.0. For example, project L's index would be PV/investment = 4/3 = 1.33. Note that project rankings under either definition are identical.

[12] Unfortunately, when capital is rationed in more than one period, or when personnel, production capacity, or other resources are rationed in addition to capital, it isn't always possible to get the NPV-maximizing package just by ranking projects on their profitability index. Tedious trial and error may be called for, or linear programming methods may be used.

PITFALLS OF THE PROFITABILITY INDEX

The profitability index is sometimes used to rank projects even when there is no soft or hard capital rationing. In this case the unwary user may be led to favour small projects over larger projects with higher NPVs. The profitability index was designed to select the projects with the most bang per buck—the greatest NPV per dollar spent. That's the right objective when bucks are limited. When they are not, a bigger bang is always better than a smaller one, even when more bucks are spent. Check Point 8.10 is a numerical example.

Check Point 8.10 Calculate the profitability indexes of the two pairs of mutually exclusive investments in Check Points 8.5 and 8.6. Use a 7.5 percent discount rate. Does the profitability index give the right ranking in each case?

8.5 A LAST LOOK

We've covered several investment criteria, each with its own nuances. If your head is spinning, you might want to take a look at Table 8.3, which gives an overview and summary of these decision rules.

Clearly, NPV is the gold standard. It is designed to tell you whether an investment will increase the value of the firm and by how much it will do so. It is the only rule that consistently can be used to rank and choose among mutually exclusive investments. The only instance in which

TABLE 8.3 A comparison of investment decision rules.

Criterion	Definition	Investment Rule	Comments
Net present value (NPV)	Present value of cash inflows minus present value of cash outflows	Accept project if NPV is positive. For mutually exclusive projects, choose the one with the highest (positive) NPV.	The "gold standard" of investment criteria. Only criterion necessarily consistent with maximizing the value of the firm. Provides proper rule for choosing among mutually exclusive investments. Only pitfall involves capital rationing, when one cannot accept all positive-NPV projects.
Internal rate of return (IRR)	The discount rate at which project NPV equals zero	Accept project if IRR is greater than opportunity cost of capital.	Results in same accept/reject decision as NPV in the absence of project interactions. However, beware of the following pitfalls: IRR cannot rank mutually exclusive projects—the project with higher IRR may have lower NPV; IRR rule cannot be used in cases of multiple IRRs or upward-sloping NPV profile.
Payback period	Time until sum of project cash flows equals the initial investment	Accept project if payback period is less than some specified number of years.	A quick and dirty rule of thumb, with several critical pitfalls. Ignores cash flows beyond the acceptable payback period. Ignores discounting. tends to improperly reject long-lived projects.
Discounted payback period	Time until sum of project's discounted cash flow equals the initial investment	Accept project if discounted payback period is less than some specified number of years.	Discounting cash flows is an improvement on the payback period. the other critical pitfalls of the payback period still remain.
Profitability index	Ratio of net present value to initial investment	Accept project if profitability index is greater than 0. In case of capital rationing, accept projects with highest profitability index.	Results in same accept/reject decision as NPV in the absence of project interactions. Useful for ranking projects in case of capital rationing, but misleading in the presence of interactions. Cannot rank mutually exclusive projects.

TABLE 8.4
Capital budgeting techniques used in practice.

Investment Criterion	Percentage of Firms That Always or Almost Always Use the Criterion	Average Score on 0–4 Scale (0 = never use; 4 = always use)		
		All Firms	Small Firms	Large Firms
Internal rate of return	76	3.1	2.9	3.4
Net present value	75	3.1	2.8	3.4
Payback period	57	2.5	2.7	2.3
Profitability index	12	.8	.9	.8

Source: J.R. Graham and C.R. Harvey, "The Theory and Practice of Corporate Finance: Evidence from the Field," *Journal of Financial Economics* 60(2/3) (May 2001): 187–243. © 2001 with permission from Elsevier Science.

NPV fails as a decision rule is when the firm faces capital rationing. In this case, it may not be possible to take every project with positive NPV, and the firm must then rank projects by profitability ratio, that is, net present value per dollar invested.

IRR is a handy and widely used measure that indicates rate of return on investment. Despite its pitfalls, it will generally give the correct answer about project viability.

A recent survey of large U.S. and Canadian firms found that for managers in the field, discounted cash-flow analysis is in fact the dominant tool for project evaluation. Table 8.4 provides a sample of the results of this large survey of CFOs. Notice that 75 percent of firms either always or almost always use both NPV and IRR to evaluate projects. The dominance of these criteria is even stronger among larger, presumably more sophisticated, firms. Despite the clear advantages of discounted cash-flow methods, however, firms do use other investment criteria to evaluate projects. For example, just over half of corporations always or almost always compute a project's payback period. Profitability index is routinely computed by about 12 percent of firms.

What explains such wide use of presumably inferior decision rules? To some extent, these rules present rough reality checks on the project. As we noted in the introduction to the chapter, managers might want to consider some simple ways to describe project profitability, even if they pre sent obvious pitfalls. For example, managers talk casually about quick-payback projects in the same way that investors talk about high-P/E stocks. The fact that they talk about payback does not mean that the payback rule governs their decisions.

8.6 SUMMARY

1. **What is the net present value of an investment, and how do you calculate it? LO1**

The **net present value** of a project measures the difference between its value and cost. NPV is therefore the amount that the project will add to shareholder wealth. A company maximizes shareholder wealth by accepting all projects that have a positive NPV.

2. **How is the internal rate of return of a project calculated, and what must one look out for when using the internal rate of return rule? LO2**

Instead of asking whether a project has a positive NPV, many businesses prefer to ask whether it offers a higher return than shareholders could expect to get by investing in the capital market. Return is usually defined as the discount rate that would result in a zero NPV. This is known as the **internal rate of return**, or IRR. The project is attractive if the IRR exceeds the **opportunity cost of capital**.

There are pitfalls in using the internal rate of return rule. Be careful about using the IRR when (1) the early cash flows are positive, (2) there is more than one change in the sign of the cash flows, or (3) you need to choose between two **mutually exclusive projects**.

3. **Why don't the payback and discounted payback rules always make shareholders better off?** LO3

The net present value rule properly reflects the time value of money. But companies sometimes use rules of thumb to judge projects. One is the payback rule, which states that a project is acceptable if you get your money back within a specified period. The payback rule takes no account of any cash flows that arrive after the payback period and fails to discount cash flows within the payback period.

The discounted payback rule improves upon the payback rule by examining discounted cash flows. It states that a project is acceptable if the discounted cash flows recover your initial investment within a specified period.

4. **How can the net present value rule be used to analyze three common problems that involve competing projects: when to postpone an investment expenditure; how to choose between projects with unequal lives; and when to replace equipment?** LO4

Sometimes a project may have a positive NPV if undertaken today but an even higher NPV if the investment is delayed. Choose between these alternatives by comparing their NPVs *today*.

When you have to choose between projects with different lives, you should put them on an equal footing by comparing the **equivalent annual cost** or benefit of the two projects. When you are considering whether to replace an aging machine with a new one, you should compare the cost of operating the old one with the equivalent annual cost of the new one.

5. **How is the profitability index calculated, and how can it be used to choose between projects when funds are limited?** LO5

If there is a shortage of capital, companies need to choose projects that offer the highest net present value per dollar of investment. This measure is known as the **profitability index**.

Related Web Links

tbs-sct.gc.ca/fin/sigs/Revolving_Funds/bcag/BCA2_E.asp A cost–benefit analysis guide prepared by the Treasury Board of Canada Secretariat

datadynamica.com/FinCalc/FinHome.htm NPV, IRR, and other financial calculators are available at this site

Key Terms

capital rationing	286	internal rate of return (IRR)	275	opportunity cost of capital	264
discounted payback period	271	mutually exclusive projects	269	payback period	270
equivalent annual cost	284	net present value (NPV)	264	profitability index	287

Questions and Problems

connect Practise and learn online with *Connect*. Questions with online Excel templates or datasets are marked with .

*Answers in Appendix B

BASIC

Problems 1–9 refer to two projects with the following cash flows:

Year	Project A	Project B
0	−\$100	−\$100
1	40	50
2	40	50
3	40	50
4	40	

*1. **IRR/NPV.** If the opportunity cost of capital is 11 percent, which of these projects is worth pursuing? (LO1)

2. **Mutually Exclusive Investments.** Suppose that you can choose only one of these projects. Which would you choose? The discount rate is still 11 percent. (LO5)

*3. **IRR/NPV.** Which project would you choose if the opportunity cost of capital were 16 percent? (LO1)

4. **IRR.** What are the internal rates of return on projects A and B? (LO1)

*5. **Investment Criteria.** In the light of your answers to problems 2 to 4, is there any reason to believe the project with the higher IRR is the better one? (LO2)

6. **Profitability Index.** If the opportunity cost of capital is 11 percent, what is the profitability index for each project? Does the profitability index rank the projects correctly? (LO5)

*7. **Payback.** What is the payback period of each project? (LO3)

8. **Discounted Payback.** What is the discounted payback for each project if the opportunity cost of capital is 11 percent? (LO3)

9. **Investment Criteria.** Considering your answers to problems 2, 3, and 7, is there any reason to believe that the project with the lower payback period is the better project? LO3)

10. **NPV and IRR.** A project that costs \$3,000 to install will provide annual cash flows of \$800 for each of the next 6 years. Is this project worth pursuing if the discount rate is 10 percent? How high can the discount rate be before you would reject the project? (LO1)

11. **Payback.** A project that costs \$2,500 to install will provide annual cash flows of \$600 for the next 6 years. The firm accepts projects with payback periods of less than five years. Will the project be accepted? (LO3)

*12. **Profitability Index.** What is the profitability index of a project that costs \$10,000 and provides cash flows of \$3,000 in years 1 and 2 and \$5,000 in years 3 and 4? The discount rate is 10 percent. (LO5)

13. **Discounted Payback.** A project that costs \$3,000 to install will provide annual cash flows of \$800 for each of the next 6 years. The firm accepts projects with a discounted payback of 5 years or less. Should this project be pursued if the discount rate is 2 percent? What if the discount rate is 12 percent? Will the firm's decision change as the discount rate changes? (LO3)

14. **NPV.** A proposed nuclear power plant will cost \$2.2 billion to build and then will produce cash flows of \$300 million a year for 15 years. After that period (in year 15), it must be decommissioned at a cost of \$900 million. What is project NPV if the discount rate is 6 percent? What if it is 16 percent? (LO1)

INTERMEDIATE

*15. **NPV/IRR.** Consider projects A and B:

	Cash Flows, \$			
Project	C_0	C_1	C_2	**NPV at 10%**
A	−30,000	21,000	21,000	+\$6,446
B	−50,000	33,000	33,000	+\$7,273

Calculate IRRs for A and B. Which project does the IRR rule suggest is best? Which project is really best? (LO2)

*16. **IRR.** You have the chance to participate in a project that produces the following cash flows:

C_0	C_1	C_2
+\$5,000	+\$4,000	−\$11,000

The internal rate of return is 13.6 percent. If the opportunity cost of capital is 12 percent, would you accept the offer? (LO2)

*17. **NPV/IRR.**

a. Calculate the net present value of the following project for discount rates of 0, 50, and 100 percent: (LO1)

C_0	C_1	C_2
+\$6,750	+\$4,500	−\$18,000

b. What is the IRR of the project? (LO2)

18. **IRR.** Marielle Machinery Works forecasts the following cash flows on a project under consideration. It uses the internal rate of return rule to accept or reject projects. Should this project be accepted if the required return is 12 percent? (LO2)

C_0	C_1	C_2	C_2
+\$10,000	0	−\$7,500	−\$8,500

*19. **NPV/IRR.** A new computer system will require an initial outlay of \$20,000 but it will increase the firm's cash flows by \$4,000 a year for each of the next 8 years. Is the system worth installing if the required rate of return is 9 percent? What if it is 14 percent? How high can the discount rate be before you would reject the project? (LO1)

20. **Investment Criteria.** If you insulate your office for \$1,000, you will save \$100 a year in heating expenses. These savings will last forever.

a. What is the NPV of the investment when the cost of capital is 8 percent? 10 percent? (LO1)
b. What is the IRR of the investment? (LO2)
c. What is the payback period on this investment? (LO3)
d. What is the discounted payback period on this investment when the cost of capital is 8 percent? 10 percent? (LO3)

21. **NPV Versus IRR.** Here are the cash flows for two mutually exclusive projects:

Project	C_0	C_1	C_2	C_3
A	−\$20,000	+\$8,000	\$8,000	+\$8,000
B	−\$20,000	0	0	\$25,000

a. At what interest rates would you prefer project A to B? *Hint:* Try drawing the NPV profile of each project. (LO1, LO2)
b. What is the IRR of each project? (LO2)

*22. **Payback and NPV.** A project has a life of 10 years and a payback period of 10 years. What must be true of project NPV? (LO1, LO3)

23. **IRR/NPV.** Consider this project with an internal rate of return of 13.1 percent. Should you accept or reject the project if the discount rate is 12 percent? (LO2)

Year	Cash Flow
0	+\$100
1	−60
2	−60

*24. **Payback, Discounted Payback, and NPV.** A firm is considering the following projects. Its opportunity cost of capital is 10 percent.

		Cash Flows, \$			
Project	Time: 0	1	2	3	4
A	−5,000	+1,000	+1,000	+3,000	0
B	−1,000	0	+1,000	+2,000	+3,000
C	−5,000	+1,000	+1,000	+3,000	+5,000

a. What are the payback period and discounted payback period on each project? (LO3)
b. Given that you wish to use the payback rule with a cutoff period of two years, which projects would you accept? (LO3)
c. If you use a cutoff period of three years with the discounted payback rule, which projects would you accept? (LO3)
d. Which projects have positive NPVs? (LO1)
e. "Payback gives too much weight to cash flows that occur after the cutoff date." True or false? (LO3)

25. **NPV.** Consider these data on a proposed project: (LO1)

Original investment = \$200
Straight-line depreciation of \$50 a year for 4 years
Project life = 4 years

Year:	0	1	2	3	4
Sales	—	100	110	120	130
Costs	—	30	35	40	45
Depreciation	—	—	—	—	—
Net income	—	—	—	—	—

a. Fill in the blanks in the table.
b. Find project NPV if the discount rate is 20 percent.

26. **NPV.** A project requires an initial investment of \$10,000, and over its 5-year life it will generate annual cash revenues of \$5,000 and cash expenses of \$2,000. The firm will use straight-line depreciation, but it does not pay taxes. (LO1)

*a. Is the project worth pursuing if the opportunity cost of capital is 8 percent?
b. Suppose now there is a new accounting treatment whereby half the initial \$10,000 outlay were treated as an expense instead of a capital investment. Does NPV change as a result of this different accounting treatment? *Hint:* Instead of depreciating all of the \$10,000, treat \$5,000 as an expense in the first year.

27. **Profitability Index.** Consider the following projects:

Project	C_1	C_2	C_3
A	−$2,100	+$2,000	+$1,200
B	−2,100	+1,440	+1,728

a. Calculate the profitability index for A and B assuming a 20 percent opportunity cost of capital. (LO5)
b. Use the profitability index rule to determine which project(s) you should accept (1) if you could undertake both and (2) if you could undertake only one. (LO5)

28. **Capital Rationing.** You are a manager with an investment budget of $8 million. You may invest in the following projects. Investment and cash-flow figures are in millions of dollars. (LO5)

Project	Discount Rate, %	Investment	Annual Cash Flow	Project Life, Years
A	10	3	1	5
B	12	4	1	8
C	8	5	2	4
D	8	3	1.5	3
E	12	3	1	6

a. Why might these projects have different discount rates? (LO1)
b. Which projects should the manager choose? (LO5)
c. Which projects will be chosen if there is no capital rationing? (LO4, LO5)

29. **Profitability Index Versus NPV.** Consider these two projects:

Project	C_0	C_1	C_2	C_3
A	−$18	+$10	+$10	+$10
B	−$50	+$25	+$25	+$25

a. Which project has the higher NPV if the discount rate is 10 percent? (LO1)
b. Which has the higher profitability index? (LO5)
c. Which project is most attractive to a firm that can raise an unlimited amount of funds to pay for its investment projects? Which project is most attractive to a firm that is limited in the funds it can raise? (LO4, LO5)

*30. **Mutually Exclusive Investments.** Here are the cash-flow forecasts for two mutually exclusive projects: (LO1)

	Cash Flows, $	
Year	Project A	Project B
0	−$100	−$100
1	30	49
2	50	49
3	70	49

a. Which project would you choose if the opportunity cost of capital is 2 percent?
b. Which would you choose if the opportunity cost of capital is 12 percent?
c. Why does your answer change?

31. **Investment Criteria.** Elm City Electronics is considering two mutually exclusive projects that differ greatly on the required investment and projected cash flows. The initial investment required for project I is $250,000 while for project II it is $25,000. Projected after-tax cash flows are shown below: (LO1, LO2, LO3, LO4, LO5)

	Cash Flows, $	
Year	Project I	Project II
1	12,000	15,000
2	18,000	8,000
3	18,000	6,000
4	30,000	6,000
5	250,000	500

The opportunity cost of capital for Elm City is 6 percent.

a. Decide which project you would choose by applying each of the following decision criteria separately. Explain your reasoning in each case: (1) payback period, (2) discounted payback period, (3) NPV, (4) IRR, and (5) profitability index.
b. Which project would you eventually choose? Explain your answer.

*32. **Equivalent Annual Cost.** A precision lathe costs $10,000 and will cost $20,000 a year to operate and maintain. If the discount rate is 12 percent and the lathe will last for 5 years, what is the equivalent annual cost of the tool? (LO4)

33. **Equivalent Annual Cost.** A firm can lease a truck for 4 years at a cost of $30,000 annually. It can instead buy a truck at a cost of $80,000, with annual maintenance expenses of $10,000. The truck will be sold at the end of 4 years for $20,000. Which is the better option if the discount rate is 12 percent? (LO4)

34. **Multiple IRR.** Consider the following cash flows: (LO2)

C_0	C_1	C_2	C_3	C_4
−22	+20	+20	+20	−40

a. Confirm that one internal rate of return on this project is (a shade above) 7 percent, and that the other is (a shade below) 34 percent.
*b. Is the project attractive if the discount rate is 5 percent?
*c. What if it is 20 percent? 40 percent?
d. Why is the project attractive at mid-range discount rates but not at very high or very low rates?

35. **Equivalent Annual Cost.** Econo-cool air conditioners cost $300 to purchase, result in electricity bills of $150 per year, and last for 5 years. Luxury Air models cost $500, result in electricity bills of $100 per year, and last for 8 years. The discount rate is 21 percent. (LO4)
   a. What are the equivalent annual costs of the Econo-cool and Luxury Air models?
   b. Which model is more cost-effective?
   c. Now you remember that the inflation rate is expected to be 10 percent per year for the foreseeable future. Redo parts (a) and (b).

36. **Investment Timing.** You can purchase an optical scanner today for $400. The scanner provides benefits worth $60 a year. The expected life of the scanner is 10 years. Scanners are expected to decrease in price by 20 percent per year. Suppose the discount rate is 10 percent. Should you purchase the scanner today or wait to purchase? When is the best purchase time? (LO4)

37. **Replacement Decision.** You are operating an old machine that is expected to produce a cash inflow of $5,000 in each of the next 3 years before it fails. You can replace it now with a new machine that costs $20,000 but is much more efficient and will provide a cash flow of $10,000 a year for 4 years. Should you replace your equipment now? The discount rate is 15 percent. (LO4)

*38. **Replacement Decision.** A forklift will last for only two more years. It costs $5,000 a year to maintain. For $20,000 you can buy a new lift that can last for 10 years and should require maintenance costs of only $2,000 a year. (LO4)
   a. If the discount rate is 5 percent per year, should you replace the forklift?
   b. If the discount rate is 10 percent per year? Why does your answer change?

39. **Internet.** Go to the Statistics Canada Web site at **www.statcan.gc.ca** and click on the "The Daily." You will be able to reach a number of publications providing analyses and statistics on a wide range of economic, demographic, trade-related, and other issues. From these publications, can you find the amount of business investment in machinery and equipment for the most recent period? Also, what is the percentage capacity utilization of different industry sectors such as food, paper, plastic and rubber products, and machinery in the most recent period? From which publications did you obtain the information? Does the percentage capacity utilization provide an indicator of the likelihood of future capital spending? (LO1, LO4)

CHALLENGE

40. **NPV/IRR.** Growth Enterprises believes its latest project, which will cost $80,000 to install, will generate a perpetual growing stream of cash flows. Cash flow at the end of this year will be $5,000, and cash flows in future years are expected to grow indefinitely at an annual rate of 5 percent.
   a. If the discount rate for this project is 10 percent, what is the project NPV? (LO1)
   b. What is the project IRR? (LO3)

41. **Investment Timing.** A classic problem in management of forests is determining when it is most economically advantageous to cut a tree for lumber. When the tree is young, it grows very rapidly. As it ages, its growth slows. Why is the NPV-maximizing rule to cut the tree when its growth rate equals the discount rate? (LO4)

42. **Multiple IRRs.** Strip Mining, Inc., can develop a new mine at an initial cost of $5 million. The mine will provide a cash flow of $30 million in 1 year. The land then must be reclaimed at a cost of $28 million in the second year.
   a. What are the IRRs of this project? (LO3)
   b. Should the firm develop the mine if the discount rate is 10 percent? 20 percent? 350 percent? 400 percent? (LO1)

43. **Replacement Decision.** The Faculty of Business at Old Renowned University wishes to buy new personal computers for its 20 full-time faculty members. The university is a nonprofit institution and does not pay any taxes. The Faculty can buy 20 Ultra Fast PCs, each costing $2,500. It is estimated that the annual cost of each PC will be $150. The Ultra Fast PCs will be scheduled for replacement at the end of 5 years, at which time they can be resold for $450 each. As an alternative to the Ultra Fast brand, the Faculty can also buy the more moderately priced Medium Fast PC for $2,000 apiece with annual servicing cost of $300 each. If the Faculty does decide on the Medium Fast PC, it will buy 25 units for all its full and part-time faculty members. The Medium Fast PCs are expected to be replaced at the end of 4 years with an estimated resale value of $250 each.

    The Dean of the Faculty of Business has approached you to conduct an analysis and make a recommendation. You have been informed that the opportunity cost of funds to the Faculty for investments of this nature is 12 percent. (LO4)
   a. Based on your analysis, would you recommend buying the Ultra Fast or the Medium Fast brand?
   b. Suppose now that the PCs will not be resold at the time of replacement but will instead be donated for free to an international charitable organization. Rework your analysis to see whether your recommendation will change on the basis of this new information.

c. The Dean has informed you that if a new, superior model, the Hyper 3MM, appears on the market in the near future, it will be the preferred choice for replacement purposes. In this case, the Faculty will replace all its existing PCs with the Hyper brand at the end of four years. Would you now recommend the Ultra Fast or the Medium Fast brand until the end of year 4?

44. **Comprehensive.** Visionary Inc. is examining two projects, A and B. Project A has a lower initial investment than project B and is expected to generate a steady stream of cash flows over its economic life. Project B is expected to generate lower cash flows in earlier years and higher cash flows in later years relative to project A. Details regarding the initial investment projected at time 0 and subsequent cash flows for the two projects are provided below:

	Cash Flows, $	
Year	**Project A**	**Project B**
0	−10,000	−15,000
1	6,000	3,000
2	6,000	5,000
3	6,000	7,000
4	6,000	8,000

Assume that the cost of capital for both projects is 10 percent.

a. Calculate the payback and discounted payback period for each project. Which project appears to be preferable using these methods? Give reasons. What are the major flaws in these methods? (LO3)
b. Calculate the net present value of each project. Which project is preferable using this method? (LO1)
c. Calculate the profitability index for each project. Which project would you select using this method? (LO5)
d. Calculate the IRR for each project. Which project would you choose using the IRR rule? Try to calculate the IRR for project B using interpolation and see whether you are able get an answer close to the one you would get using a financial calculator or a software package. (LO2)
e. Does the question provide sufficient information to help us determine whether the projects are independent or mutually exclusive? How would you distinguish between the two categories? (LO4)
f. Are you able to reach the same decision by applying the different decision criteria? If not, which criterion would you rely on? Why? (LO1, LO2, LO3, LO4, LO5)

45. **Comprehensive.** You wish to start a new line of software. Your initial investment in the project will be $100,000. You do not expect to generate any cash flows for the first two years. However, cash flows in year 3 are expected to be $16,000 and are expected to increase by 15 percent every year till year 7, after which time they will decline by 2 percent until year 9. You do not expect any growth in cash flows beyond year 9. However, you expect your business to generate constant cash flows into the foreseeable future. (LO1, LO2, LO3, LO4, LO5)

a. Assuming that your cost of capital is 8 percent per year, should you pursue the project if your objective is to accept projects only when they are worth more than their cost?
b. Explain your answer to part (a) above. What technique did you use in your answer to part (a)?
c. By what time frame do you expect to recover your initial investment in the project: (1) ignoring the time value of money and (2) taking into account the time value of money? Name the techniques you have used for your computation. What are the benefits and drawbacks to these techniques?
d. Can you find the IRR for this project?

46. **Comprehensive.** You have joined the Projects division of GrowMore Inc. Your first job is to analyze two projects, which you have code-named "alpha" and "beta." Both projects will require the same initial investment of $100,000 and are expected to generate the following cash flows over an expected economic life of 4 years. (LO1, LO2, LO3, LO4, LO5)

Year	Project "Alpha," $	Project "Beta," $
1	70,000	40,000
2	32,000	40,000
3	32,000	40,000
4	9,000	40,000

Assuming that GrowMore Inc.'s cost of capital for these projects is 10 percent:

a. Calculate its (1) payback period and (2) discounted payback period. Which project would you select under these methods? Explain your answer.
b. Calculate net present values for each project and indicate which one you would undertake using this decision rule.
c. Calculate internal rates of return for each project. Which project would you select using the IRR rule?
d. Calculate the profitability index for each project and indicate your decision using this rule.
e. Can you think of any situations in which, because of a change in the cost of capital, you might be confronted with conflicting decisions using the NPV and IRR rules? Show how this might happen.

47. **Replacement.** You are thinking of purchasing a new machine (NEW) for your business operations and replacing the existing machine (OLD), which you have used for the past 3 years. The new machine will cost \$75,000 and will be useful to your business for 5 years after which it can be sold to fetch a salvage value of \$9,000. The new machine will be depreciated straight-line to 0 over 5 years. The old machine was purchased for \$70,000 and is also being depreciated straight-line to 0 over 5 years. The old machine can be sold today for \$30,000, but if you waited for 5 years it will be worth only \$6,500 at that time.

The new machine is expected to significantly boost the efficiency of your business operations. Annual savings in operating costs are expected to be \$12,000. Also, your net working capital requirement will decline annually by \$4,000. Your business pays tax at the rate of 35 percent and has a cost of capital rate of 12 percent. Does it make sense for you to replace the OLD machine with the NEW machine? (LO1, LO4)

Solutions to Check Points

8.1 Even if construction costs are \$355,000, NPV is still positive:

$$\text{NPV} = \text{PV} - \$355{,}000 = \$357{,}143 - \$355{,}000 = \$2{,}143$$

Therefore, the project is still worth pursuing. The project is viable as long as construction costs are less than the PV of the future cash flow, that is, as long as construction costs are less than \$357,143. However, if the opportunity cost of capital is 20 percent, the PV of the \$400,000 sales price is lower and NPV is negative:

$$\text{PV} = \$400{,}000 \times \frac{1}{1.20} = \$333{,}333$$

$$\text{NPV} = \text{PV} - \$355{,}000 = -\$21{,}667$$

The present value of the future cash flow is not as high when the opportunity cost of capital is higher. The project would need to provide a higher payoff in order to be viable in the face of the higher opportunity cost of capital.

8.2 The payback period is \$3,000/\$660 = 4.6 years. We find the discounted payback period and NPV as follows:

Year	Cash Flows	Discount Factor	Discounted Cash Flows	Cumulative Discounted Cash Flows
0	−3,000	1.0000	−3,000	
1	660	.9434	623	−2,377
2	660	.8900	587	−1,790
3	660	.8396	554	−1,236
4	660	.7921	523	−713
5	660	.7473	493	−220
6	660	.7050	465	245
7	660	.6651	439	**684** ↓ NPV

Notice the cumulative discounted cash flows are negative until year 5 and positive from year 6. This means that the discounted payback period = 5 years + 220/465 = 5.5 years. The cumulative discounted cash flow for year 7 is also the NPV, \$684.

You can also calculate NPV by taking the present value of a \$660 annuity for 7 years at 6 percent:

$$\text{PV annuity} = \$3{,}684$$

$$\text{NPV} = -\$3{,}000 + \$3{,}684 = \$684$$

The project should be accepted.

8.3 The IRR is now about 8.9 percent, because

$$\text{NPV} = -\$350{,}000 + \frac{\$16{,}000}{1.089} + \frac{\$16{,}000}{(1.089)^2} + \frac{\$416{,}000}{(1.089)^3} = 0$$

Note in Figure 8.6 that NPV falls to zero as the discount rate reaches 8.9 percent.

8.4 IRR = 23% (that is, $-60 + 30/1.23 + 30/(1.23)^2 + 30/(1.23)^3 = 0$)

8.5 You want to be rich. The NPV of the long-lived investment is much larger.

$$\text{Short: NPV} = -\$1 + \frac{\$2}{1.07z} = +\$.8605 \text{ million}$$

$$\text{Long: NPV} = -\$1 + \frac{\$.3}{.075} = +\$3 \text{ million}$$

8.6 You want to be rich. The second alternative generates greater value at any reasonable discount rate. For example, other risk-free investments offer 7.5 percent. Then

$$\text{NPV} = -\$1{,}000 + \frac{\$4{,}000}{1.075} = +\$2{,}721$$

$$\text{NPV} = -\$1{,}000{,}000 + \frac{\$1{,}500{,}000}{1.075} = +\$395{,}349$$

FIGURE 8.6
NPV falls to zero at an interest rate of 8.9 percent.

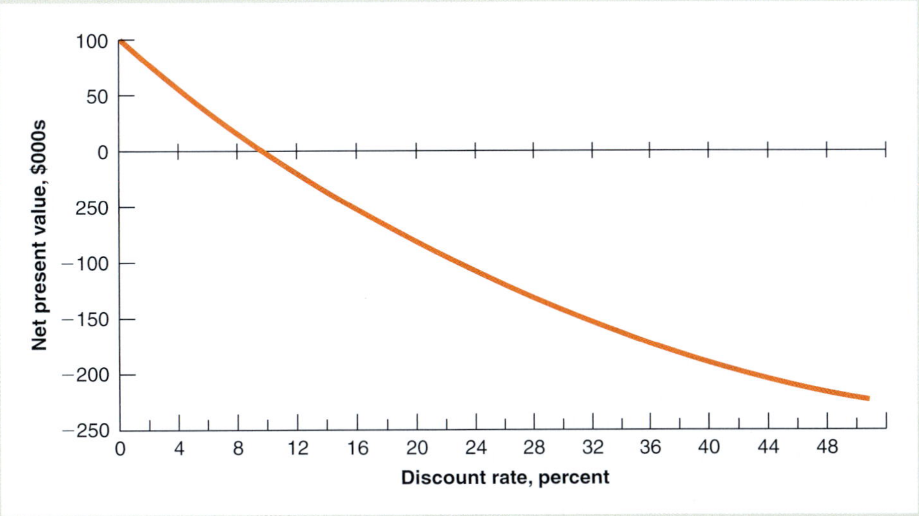

8.7

Year of Purchase	Cost of Computer	PV Savings	NPV at Year of Purchase	NPV Today
0	50	70	20	20
1	45	66	21	19.1
2	40	62	22	18.2
3	36	58	22	16.5
4	33	54	21	14.3
5	31	50	19	11.8

Purchase the new computer now.

8.8

Year:	0	1	2	3	PV of Costs
F. Cash flows	10,000	1,100	1,200		11,992
Equivalent annual cost		6,910	6,910		11,992
G. Cash flows	12,000	1,100	1,200	1,300	14,968
Equivalent annual cost		6,019	6,019	6,019	14,968

Machine G is the better buy. However, it's still better to keep the old machine going one more year. That costs $4,300, which is less than G's equivalent annual cost, $6,019.

8.9 Rank each project in order of profitability index as in the following table:

Project	Profitability Index	Investment
N	.43	$7
L	.33	3
O	.33	6
P	.25	4
M	.20	5

Starting from the top, we run out of funds after accepting projects N and L. While L and O have equal profitability indexes, project O could not be chosen because it would force total investment above the limit of $10 million.

8.10 The profitability index gives the correct ranking for the first pair, the wrong ranking for the second:

Project	PV	Investment	NPV	Profitability Index (NPV/investment)
Short	$1,860,500	$1,000,000	$ 860,500	.86
Long	4,000,000	1,000,000	3,000,000	3.0
Small	$ 3,721	$ 1,000	$ 2,721	2.7
Large	1,395,349	1,000,000	395,349	.395

Solutions to Spreadsheet Questions

8.1 NPV would be calculated as £221.08 million.

8.2 This value, £221.08 million, is 1.13 times as great as the value in Table 8.1, because each cash flow is discounted for one fewer period. The Excel NPV function assumes the first cash flow comes after one period. In this example, the first cash flow actually comes immediately.

MINI CASE

Flowton Products enjoys a steady demand for stainless steel infiltrators used in a number of chemical processes. Revenues from the infiltrator division are $50 million a year and production costs are $47.5 million. However, the 10 high-precision Munster stamping machines used in the production process are coming to the end of their useful life. One possibility is simply to replace each existing machine with a new Munster. These machines would cost $800,000 each and would not involve any additional operating costs. The alternative is to buy 10 centrally controlled Skilboro stampers. Skilboros cost $1.25 million each, but unlike the Munster they would produce a total saving in operator and material costs of $500,000 a year. Moreover, the Skilboro is sturdily built and would last 10 years, as against an estimated seven-year life for the Munster.

Analysts in the infiltrator division have produced the summary table shown here, which shows the forecast total cash flows from the infiltrator business over the life of each machine. Flowton's standard procedures for appraising capital investments involve calculating net present value, internal rate of return, and payback, and these measures are also shown in the table.

As usual, Emily Balsam arrived early at Flowton's head office. She had never regretted joining Flowton. Everything about the place, from the mirror windows to the bell fountain in the atrium, suggested a classy outfit. Ms. Balsam sighed happily and reached for the envelope at the top of her in-tray. It was an analysis from the infiltrator division of the replacement options for the stamper machines. Pinned to the paper was the summary table of cash flows and a note from the CFO, which read, "Emily, I have read through 20 pages of excruciating detail and I still don't know which of these machines we should buy. The NPV calculation seems to indicate that the Skilboro is best, while IRR and payback suggest the opposite. Would you take a look and tell me what we should do and why."

Can you help Ms. Balsam by writing a memo to the CFO? You need to justify your solution and also to explain why some or all of the measures in the summary tables are inappropriate

	Cash Flows, Millions of Dollars				
Year:	**0**	**1–7**	**8**	**9**	**10**
Munster					
Investment	−8.0				
Revenues		50.0	0	0	0
Costs		47.5	0	0	0
Net cash flow	−8.0	2.5	0	0	0
NPV at 15%	$2.40 million				
IRR	24.5%				
Payback period	3.2 years				
Skilboro					
Investment	−12.5				
Revenues		50.0	50.0	50.0	50.0
Costs		47.0	47.0	47.0	47.0
Net cash flow	−12.5	3.0	3.0	3.0	3.0
NPV at 15%	$2.56 million				
IRR	20.2%				
Payback period	4.2 years				

PART 2

Value

5 The Time Value of Money
6 Valuing Bonds
7 Valuing Stocks
8 Net Present Value and Other Investment Criteria
9 Using Discounted Cash Flow Analysis to Make Investment Decisions
- 9.1 Identifying Cash Flows
- 9.2 Calculating Cash Flows
- 9.3 Business Taxes in Canada and the Capital Budgeting Decision
- 9.4 Example: Blooper Industries
- 9.5 Summary
- Appendix 9A Deriving the CCA Tax Shield (see the Online Learning Centre)

0 Project Analysis

CHAPTER 9

Using Discounted Cash Flow Analysis to Make Investment Decisions

LEARNING OBJECTIVES

After studying this chapter, you should be able to:

LO1 Identify the cash flows properly attributable to a proposed new project.

LO2 Calculate the cash flows of a project from standard financial statements.

LO3 Explain how the company's tax bill is affected by depreciation and how this affects project value.

LO4 Explain how changes in working capital affect project cash flows.

A working magnoosium mine. But how do you find its net present value?

Think of the problems that Toyota's management faces when considering whether to introduce a new model. How much will we need to invest in new plant and equipment? What will it cost to market and promote the new car? How soon can we get the car into production? What is the projected production cost? What do we need in the way of inventories of raw materials and finished cars? How many cars can we expect to sell each year and at what price? What credit arrangements will we need to give our dealers? How long will the model stay in production? What happens at the end of that time? Can we use the plant and equipment elsewhere in the company? All of these issues affect the level and timing of project cash flows. In this chapter we continue our analysis of the capital budgeting decision by turning our focus to how the financial manager should prepare cash flow estimates for use in net present value analysis.

In Chapter 8 we used the net present value rule to make a simple capital budgeting decision. We tackled the problem in four steps:

Step 1: Forecast the project cash flows.

Step 2: Estimate the opportunity cost of capital—that is, the rate of return that your shareholders could expect to earn if they invested their money in the capital market.

Step 3: Use the opportunity cost of capital to discount the future cash flows. The project's present value (PV) is equal to the sum of the discounted future cash flows.

Step 4: Net present value (NPV) measures whether the project is worth more than it costs. To calculate NPV, you need to subtract the required investment from the present value of the future payoffs:

$$\text{NPV} = \text{PV} - \text{required investment}$$

You should proceed with the project if it has a positive NPV.

We now need to consider how to apply the net present value rule to practical investment problems. The first step is to decide what to discount. We know the answer in principle: discount cash flows. This is why capital budgeting is often referred to as *discounted cash flow*, or *DCF*, analysis. But useful forecasts of cash flows do not arrive on a silver platter. Often the financial manager has to make do with raw data supplied by specialists in product design, production, marketing, and so on, and must adjust such data before they are useful. In addition, most financial forecasts are prepared in accordance with accounting principles that do not necessarily recognize cash flows when they occur. These forecasts must also be adjusted.

We look first at what cash flows should be discounted. We then present an example designed to show how standard accounting information can be used to compute those cash flows and why cash flows and accounting income usually differ. The example will lead us to various further points, including the links between depreciation and taxes, and the importance of tracking investments in working capital.

LO1 9.1 IDENTIFYING CASH FLOWS

DISCOUNT CASH FLOWS, NOT PROFITS

Up to this point we have been concerned mainly with the mechanics of discounting and with the various methods of project appraisal. We have had almost nothing to say about the problem of what you should discount. The first and most important point is this: to calculate net present value you need to discount cash flows, *not* accounting profits.

We stressed the difference between cash flows and profits in Chapter 3. Here we stress it again. Income statements are intended to show how well the firm has performed. They do not track cash flows.

If the firm lays out a large amount of money on a big capital project, you would not conclude that the firm performed poorly that year, even though a lot of cash is going out the door. Therefore, the accountant does not deduct capital expenditure when calculating the year's income but instead depreciates it over several years.

That is fine for computing year-by-year profits, but it could get you into trouble when working out net present value. For example, suppose that you are analyzing an investment proposal. It costs \$2,000 and is expected to bring in a cash flow of \$1,500 in the first year and \$500 in the second. You think that the opportunity cost of capital is 10 percent, and so calculate the present value of the cash flows as follows:

$$\text{PV} = \frac{\$1{,}500}{1.10} + \frac{\$500}{(1.10)^2} = \$1{,}776.86$$

The project is worth less than it costs; it has a negative NPV:

$$\text{NPV} = \$1{,}776.86 - \$2{,}000 = -\$223.14$$

The project costs \$2,000 today, but accountants would not treat that outlay as an immediate expense. They would depreciate that \$2,000 over two years and deduct the depreciation from the cash flow to obtain accounting income:

	Year 1	Year 2
Cash inflow	+ \$1,500	+\$ 500
Less depreciation	− 1,000	− 1,000
Accounting income	+ 500	− 500

When calculating NPV, recognize investment expenditures when they occur, not later when they show up as depreciation. Projects are financially attractive because of the cash they generate, either for distribution to shareholders or for reinvestment in the firm. Therefore, the focus of capital budgeting must be on cash flow, not profits.

Thus an accountant would forecast income of \$500 in year 1 and an accounting loss of \$500 in year 2.

Suppose you were given this forecast income and loss and naively discounted them. Now NPV *looks* positive:

$$\text{Apparent NPV} = \frac{\$500}{1.10} + \frac{-\$500}{(1.10)^2} = \$41.32$$

Of course, we know this is nonsense. The project is obviously a loser; we are spending money today (\$2,000 cash outflow) and we are simply getting our money back (\$1,500 in year 1 and \$500 in year 2). We are earning a zero return when we could get a 10 percent return by investing our money in the capital market.

The message of the example is as stated in the margin here.

We saw another example of the distinction between cash flow and accounting profit in Chapter 3. Here is yet another example of the distinction between cash flow and accounting profits. Accountants try to show profit as it is earned, rather than when the company and the customer get around to paying their bills. For example, an income statement will recognize revenue when the sale is made, even if the bill is not paid for months. This practice also results in a difference between accounting profits and cash flow. The sale generates immediate profits, but the cash flow comes later.

EXAMPLE 9.1 **SALES BEFORE CASH**

Reggie Hotspur, ace computer salesperson, closed a $500,000 sale on December 15, just in time to count it toward his annual bonus. How did he do it? Well, for one thing he gave the customer 180 days to pay. The income statement will recognize Hotspur's sale in December, even though cash will not arrive until June. But a financial analyst tracking cash flows would concentrate on the latter event.

The accountant takes care of the timing difference by adding $500,000 to accounts receivable in December, then reducing accounts receivable when the money arrives in June. (The total of accounts receivable is just the sum of all cash due from customers.)

You can think of the increase in accounts receivable as an investment—it's effectively a 180-day loan to the customer—and therefore a cash outflow. That investment is recovered when the customer pays. Thus financial analysts often find it convenient to calculate cash flow as follows:

December		June	
Sales	$500,000	Sales	0
Less investment in accounts receivable	−$500,000	Plus recovery of accounts receivable	+$500,000
Cash flow	0	Cash flow	$500,000

Note that this procedure gives the correct cash flow of $500,000 in June.

It is not always easy to translate accounting data back into actual dollars. If you are in doubt about what is a cash flow, simply count the dollars coming in and take away the dollars going out.

Check Point 9.1

A regional supermarket chain is deciding whether to install a tewgit machine in each of its stores. Each machine costs $250,000. Projected income per machine is as follows:

Year:	1	2	3	4	5
Sales	$250,000	$300,000	$300,000	$250,000	$250,000
Operating expenses	200,000	200,000	200,000	200,000	200,000
Depreciation	50,000	50,000	50,000	50,000	50,000
Accounting income	0	50,000	50,000	0	0

Why would the stores continue to operate a machine in years 4 and 5 if it produces no profits? What are the cash flows from investing in a machine? Assume each tewgit machine is completely depreciated and has no salvage value at the end of its five-year life.

DISCOUNT INCREMENTAL CASH FLOWS

A project's present value depends on the extra cash flows that it produces. Forecast the firm's cash flows first if you proceed with the project. Then forecast the cash flows if you don't accept the project. Take the difference and you have the extra (or incremental) cash flows produced by the project:

$$\textbf{Incremental cash flow} = \textbf{cash flow with project} - \textbf{cash flow without project} \qquad (9.1)$$

EXAMPLE 9.2 LAUNCHING A NEW PRODUCT

Consider the decision by Microsoft to develop Windows 7, its new operating system. But are these profits all incremental cash flows? Certainly not. Our with-versus-without principle reminds us that we also need to think about what the cash flows would be without the new system. If Microsoft went ahead with Windows 7, demand for its older operating system, Vista, would be reduced. The incremental cash flows are therefore

Cash flow with Windows 7 (including lower cash flow from Vista) − cash flow without Windows 7 (with higher cash flow from Vista)

The trick in capital budgeting is to trace all the incremental flows from a proposed project. Here are some things to look out for.

INCLUDE ALL INDIRECT EFFECTS

To forecast incremental cash flow, you must trace out all indirect effects of accepting the project.

Microsoft's new operating system illustrates a common indirect effect. New products often damage sales of an existing product. Of course, companies frequently introduce new products anyway, usually because they believe that their existing product line is under threat from competition. Even if you don't go ahead with a new product, there is no guarantee sales of the existing product line will continue at their present level. Sooner or later they will decline.

Sometimes a new project will *help* the firm's existing business. Suppose you are the financial manager of an airline considering opening a new short-haul route from Prince George, B.C., to Vancouver International Airport. Considered in isolation, the new route may have a negative NPV. But once you allow for the additional business the new route brings to your other traffic out of Vancouver, it may be a very worthwhile investment.

Some capital investments have very long lives once all indirect effects are recognized. Consider the introduction of a new jet engine. Engine manufacturers often offer attractive pricing to achieve early sales, because once an engine is installed, 15 years' sales of replacement parts are almost assured. Also, since airlines prefer to reduce the number of different engines in their fleet, selling jet engines today improves sales tomorrow as well. Later sales will generate further demand for replacement parts. Thus the string of incremental effects from the first sales of a new model engine can run out 20 years or more.

FORGET SUNK COSTS

Sunk costs are like spilled milk: they are past and irreversible outflows. For instance, if a firm has spent $50,000 on a market study to determine the feasibility of a project, it would be a sunk cost. If the project is found to be unattractive, the project should be rejected and the sunk cost should not be a consideration in this decision.

Unfortunately, often managers are influenced by sunk costs. For example, in 1971 Lockheed sought a federal guarantee for a bank loan to continue development of the Tristar airplane. Lockheed and its supporters argued that it would be foolish to abandon a project on which nearly $1 billion had already been spent. This was a poor argument, however, because the $1 billion was sunk. The relevant questions were how much more needed to be invested and whether the finished product warranted the incremental investment.

Sunk costs remain the same whether or not you accept the project. Therefore, they do not affect project NPV.

Lockheed's supporters were not the only ones to appeal to sunk costs. Some of its critics claimed that it would be foolish to continue with a project that offered no prospect of a satisfactory return on that $1 billion. This argument too was faulty. The $1 billion was gone, and the decision to continue with the project should have depended only on the return on the incremental investment.

INCLUDE OPPORTUNITY COSTS

Resources are almost never free, even when no cash changes hands. For example, suppose a new manufacturing operation uses land that could otherwise be sold for $100,000. This resource is costly; by using the land you pass up the opportunity to sell it. There is no out-of-pocket cost, but there is an **opportunity cost**, that is, the value of the forgone alternative use of the land.

opportunity cost Benefit or cash flow forgone as a result of an action.

This example prompts us to warn you against judging projects "before versus after" rather than "with versus without." A manager comparing before versus after might not assign any value to the land because the firm owns it both before and after:

Before	Take Project	After	Cash Flow, Before Versus After
Firm owns land	⟶	Firm still owns land	0

The proper comparison, *with versus without*, is as follows:

Before	Take Project	After	Cash Flow, with Project
Firm owns land	⟶	Firm still owns land	0

Before	Do Not Take Project	After	Cash Flow, Without Project
Firm owns land	⟶	Firm sells land for $100,000	$100,000

Comparing the cash flows with and without the project, we see that $100,000 is given up by undertaking the project. The original cost of purchasing the land is irrelevant—that cost is sunk.

The opportunity cost equals the cash that could be realized from selling the land now, and therefore is a relevant cash flow for project evaluation.

When the resource can be freely traded, its opportunity cost is simply the market price.[1] However, sometimes opportunity costs are difficult to estimate. Suppose that you go ahead with a project to develop Computer Nouveau, pulling your software team off their work on a new operating system that some existing customers are not-so-patiently awaiting. The exact cost of infuriating those customers may be impossible to calculate, but you'll think twice about the opportunity cost of moving the software team to Computer Nouveau.

RECOGNIZE THE INVESTMENT IN WORKING CAPITAL

net working capital Current assets minus current liabilities.

Net working capital (often referred to simply as *working capital*) is the difference between a company's short-term assets and liabilities. The principal short-term assets are cash, accounts receivable (customers' unpaid bills), and inventories of raw materials and finished goods. The principal short-term liabilities are accounts payable (bills that you have not paid), notes payable,

[1] If the value of the land to the firm were less than the market price, the firm would sell it. On the other hand, the opportunity cost of using land in a particular project cannot exceed the cost of buying an equivalent parcel to replace it.

Investments in working capital, just like investments in plant and equipment, result in cash outflows.

and accruals (liabilities for items such as wages or taxes that have recently been incurred but have not yet been paid).

Most projects entail an additional investment in working capital. For example, before you can start production, you need to invest in inventories of raw materials. Then, when you deliver the finished product, customers may be slow to pay and accounts receivable will increase. (Remember Reggie Hotspur's computer sale, described in Example 9.1. It required a $500,000, six-month investment in accounts receivable.) Next year, as business builds up, you may need a larger stock of raw materials and you may have even more unpaid bills.

We find that working capital is one of the most common sources of confusion in forecasting project cash flows.[2] Here are the most common mistakes:

1. *Forgetting about working capital entirely.* We hope that you never fall into that trap.
2. *Forgetting that working capital may change during the life of the project.* Imagine that you sell $100,000 of goods per year and customers pay on average six months late. You will therefore have $50,000 of unpaid bills. Now you increase prices by 10 percent, so that revenues increase to $110,000. If customers continue to pay six months late, unpaid bills increase to $55,000, and therefore, you need to make an *additional* investment in working capital of $5,000.
3. *Forgetting that working capital is recovered at the end of the project.* When the project comes to an end, inventories are run down, any unpaid bills are (you hope) paid off, and you can recover your investment in working capital. This generates a cash *inflow*.

A project may generate extra overhead costs, but then again, it may not. We should be cautious about assuming that the accountant's allocation of overhead costs represents the *incremental* cash flow that would be incurred by accepting the project.

REMEMBER SHUTDOWN CASH FLOWS

The end of a project almost always brings additional cash flows. For example, nuclear power plants need to be decommissioned at costs measured in the hundreds of millions of dollars. Coal mines need to be closed down, and their surrounding environments often need rehabilitation. On the other hand, not all shutdown cash flows are negative. Once the project is complete, you might be able to sell some of the plant, equipment, or real estate that was dedicated to it. Also, as we just mentioned, you may recover some of your investment in working capital as you sell off inventories of finished goods and collect on outstanding accounts receivable. The important point is not to overlook these incremental cash flows.

BEWARE OF ALLOCATED OVERHEAD COSTS

We have already mentioned that the accountant's objective in gathering data is not always the same as the investment analyst's. A case in point is the allocation of overhead costs such as rent, heat, or electricity. These overhead costs may not be related to a particular project, but they must be paid for nevertheless. Therefore, when the accountant assigns costs to the firm's projects, a charge for overhead is usually made. But our principle of incremental cash flows says that in investment appraisal we should include only the extra expenses that would result from the project.

Check Point 9.2

A firm is considering an investment in a new manufacturing plant. The site is already owned by the company, but existing buildings would need to be demolished. Which of the following should be treated as incremental cash flows?

a. The market value of the site
b. The market value of the existing buildings
c. Demolition costs and site clearance
d. The cost of a new access road put in last year
e. Lost cash flows on other projects due to executive time spent on the new facility
f. Future depreciation of the new plant

[2] If you are not clear why working capital affects cash flow, look back to Chapter 3, where we gave a primer on working capital and a couple of simple examples.

DISCOUNT NOMINAL CASH FLOWS BY THE NOMINAL COST OF CAPITAL

The distinction between nominal and real cash flows and interest rates is crucial in capital budgeting. Interest rates are usually quoted in *nominal* terms. If you invest $100 in a bank deposit offering 6 percent interest, then the bank promises to pay you $106 at the end of the year. It makes no promises about what that $106 will buy. The real rate of interest on the bank deposit depends on inflation. If inflation is 2 percent, that $106 will buy you only 4 percent more goods at the end of the year than your $100 could buy today. The real rate of interest is therefore about 4 percent.[3]

You cannot mix and match real and nominal quantities. Real cash flows must be discounted at a real discount rate, nominal cash flows at a nominal rate. Discounting real cash flows at a nominal rate is a big mistake.

If the discount rate is nominal, consistency requires that cash flows be estimated in nominal terms as well, taking into account trends in selling price, labour and materials costs, and so on. This calls for more than simply applying a single assumed inflation rate to all components of cash flow. Some costs or prices increase faster than inflation, some slower. For example, perhaps you have entered into a five-year fixed-price contract with a supplier. No matter what happens to inflation over this period, this part of your costs is fixed in nominal terms.

Of course, there is nothing wrong with discounting real cash flows at the real interest rate, although this is not commonly done. We saw in Chapter 5 that real cash flows discounted at the real discount rate give exactly the same present values as nominal cash flows discounted at the nominal rate. It should go without saying that you cannot mix and match real and nominal quantities. Real cash flows must be discounted at a real discount rate, nominal cash flows at a nominal rate. Discounting real cash flows at a nominal rate is a big mistake.

While the need to maintain consistency may seem obvious, analysts sometimes forget to account for the effects of inflation when forecasting future cash flows. As a result, they end up discounting real cash flows at a nominal interest rate. This can grossly understate project values.

EXAMPLE 9.3 CASH FLOWS AND INFLATION

City Consulting Services is considering moving into a new office building. The cost of a one-year lease is $8,000, but this cost will increase in future years at the annual inflation rate of 3 percent. The firm believes that it will remain in the building for four years. What is the present value of its rental costs if the discount rate is 10 percent?

The present value can be obtained by discounting the nominal cash flows at the 10 percent discount rate as follows:

Year	Cash Flow	Present Value at 10% Discount Rate	
1	8,000	8,000/1.10 =	7,272.73
2	$8,000 \times 1.03 = 8,240$	$8,240/1.10^2$ =	6,809.92
3	$8,000 \times 1.03^2 = 8,487.20$	$8,487.20/1.10^3$ =	6,376.56
4	$8,000 \times 1.03^3 = 8,741.82$	$8,741.82/1.10^4$ =	5,970.78
			$26,429.99

[3] Remember from Chapter 5,

$$\text{Real rate of interest} \approx \text{nominal rate of interest} - \text{inflation rate}$$

The exact formula is

$$1 + \text{real rate of interest} = \frac{1 + \text{nominal rate of interest}}{1 + \text{inflation rate}}$$

$$= \frac{1.06}{1.02} = 1.0392$$

Therefore, the real interest rate is .0392, or 3.92 percent.

Alternatively, the real discount rate can be calculated as 1.10/1.03 − 1 = .067961 = 6.7961 percent. The present value of the cash flows can also be computed by discounting the real cash flows at the real discount rate as follows:

Year	Real Cash Flow	Present Value at 6.7961% Discount Rate
1	$8{,}000/1.03 = 7{,}766.99$	$7{,}766.99/1.067961 = 7{,}272.73$
2	$8{,}240/1.03^2 = 7{,}766.99$	$7{,}766.99/1.067961^2 = 6{,}809.92$
3	$8{,}487.20/1.03^3 = 7{,}766.99$	$7{,}766.99/1.067961^3 = 6{,}376.56$
4	$8{,}741.82/1.03^4 = 7{,}766.99$	$7{,}766.99/1.067961^4 = 5{,}970.78$
		$26,429.99

Notice the real cash flow is a constant, since the lease payment increases at the rate of inflation. The present value of *each* cash flow is the same regardless of the method used to discount. The sum of the present values is also identical, of course.

Check Point 9.3

Nasty Industries is closing down an outmoded factory and throwing all of its workers out on the street. Nasty's CEO, Cruella DeLuxe, is enraged to learn that it must continue to pay for workers' health insurance for four years. The cost per worker next year will be $2,400 per year, but the inflation rate is 4 percent, and health costs have been increasing at 3 percentage points faster than inflation. What is the present value of this obligation? The (nominal) discount rate is 10 percent.

SEPARATE INVESTMENT AND FINANCING DECISIONS

When we calculate the cash flows from a project, we ignore how that project is financed. The company may decide to finance partly by debt, but even if it did, we would neither subtract the debt proceeds from the required investment nor recognize the interest and principal payments as cash outflows. Regardless of the actual financing, we should view the project as if it were all-equity-financed, treating all cash outflows required for the project as coming from shareholders and all cash inflows as going to them.

This procedure focuses exclusively on the *project* cash flows, not the cash flows associated with alternative financing schemes. It therefore allows you to separate the analysis of the investment decision from that of the financing decision. First, you ask whether the project has a positive net present value, assuming all-equity financing. Then, if the project is viable, you can undertake a separate analysis of the best financing strategy. Financing decisions are considered later in the text.

LO1, 2 9.2 CALCULATING CASH FLOWS

It is helpful to think of a project's cash flow as composed of three elements:

Total cash flow = cash flow from investment in plant and equipment
+ cash flow from investment in working capital **(9.2)**
+ cash flow from operations

We will look at each of these components in turn.

CAPITAL INVESTMENT

To get a project off the ground, a company will typically need to make considerable up-front investments in plant, equipment, research, marketing, and so on. For example, development of Boeing's 787 Dreamliner is estimated to top $10 billion. This $10 billion is a negative cash flow—negative because cash goes out the door.

When the 787 program finally comes to an end, Boeing can either sell the plant and equipment or redeploy the assets elsewhere in the business. This salvage value (net of any taxes if the equipment is sold) represents a positive cash flow to the firm.

Final cash flows may also be *negative* if there are significant shutdown costs. For example, the U.S. mining firm Phelps Dodge has earmarked over US$300 million to cover the future costs of closing its New Mexico copper mines.

EXAMPLE 9.4 CASH FLOW FROM INVESTMENTS

Gillette's competitor, Slick, invests $800 million to develop the Mock4 razor blade. The specialized blade factory will run for 7 years, until it is replaced by more advanced technology. At that point, the machinery will be sold for scrap metal, for a price of $50 million. Taxes of $10 million will be assessed on the sale.

Therefore, the initial cash flow from investment is −$800 million, and in 7 years, the cash flow from the disinvestment in the production line will be $50 million − $10 million = $40 million.

INVESTMENT IN WORKING CAPITAL

We pointed out earlier in the chapter that when a company builds up inventories of raw materials or finished product, the company's cash is reduced; the reduction in cash reflects the firm's investment in inventories. Similarly, cash is reduced when customers are slow to pay their bills—in this case, the firm makes an investment in accounts receivable. Investment in working capital, just like investment in plant and equipment, represents a negative cash flow. On the other hand, later in the life of a project, when inventories are sold off and accounts receivable are collected, the firm's investment in working capital is reduced as it converts these assets into cash.

EXAMPLE 9.5 CASH FLOW FROM INVESTMENTS IN WORKING CAPITAL

Slick makes an initial (year 0) investment of $10 million in inventories of plastic and steel for its blade plant. Then in year 1 it accumulates an additional $20 million of raw materials. The total level of inventories is now $10 million + $20 million = $30 million, but the cash expenditure in year 1 is simply the $20 million addition to inventory. The $20 million investment in additional inventory results in a cash flow of −$20 million. Notice that the increase in working capital is an *investment* in the project. Like other investments, a buildup of working capital requires cash. Increases in the *level* of working capital therefore show up as *negative* cash flows.

Later on, say in year 5, the company begins planning for the next-generation blade. At this point, it decides to reduce its inventory of raw material from $20 million to $15 million. This reduction in inventory investment frees up $5 million of cash, which is a positive cash flow. Therefore, the cash flows from inventory investment are −$10 million in year 0, −$20 million in year 1, and +$5 million in year 5.

These calculations can be summarized in a simple table, as follows:

Year:	**0**	**1**	**2**	**3**	**4**	**5**
1. Total working capital, year-end ($ million)	10	30	30	30	30	25
2. Investment in working capital ($ million)	10	20	0	0	0	− 5
3. Cash flow from investments in working capital	−10	−20	0	0	0	+ 5

An *increase* in working capital is an investment, and therefore implies a *negative* cash flow; a decrease implies a positive cash flow. The cash flow is measured by the change in working capital, not the *level* of working capital.

In years 0 and 1, there is a net investment in working capital (line 2), corresponding to a negative cash flow (line 3), and an increase in the *level* of total working capital (line 1). In years 2 to 4, there is no investment in working capital, so its level remains unchanged at $30 million. But in year 5, as the firm begins to disinvest in working capital, the total declines, which provides a positive cash flow.

In general, an *increase* in working capital is an investment, and therefore implies a *negative* cash flow; a decrease implies a positive cash flow. The cash flow is measured by the change in working capital, not the *level* of working capital.

OPERATING CASH FLOW

Think back to Boeing's decision to develop the Dreamliner or Slick's decision to produce a new razor blade. In each case, operating cash flow consists of revenues from the sale of the new product less the costs of production and any taxes:

$$\text{Operating cash flow} = \text{revenues} - \text{costs} - \text{taxes}$$

Undoubtedly, both Boeing and Slick expect the revenues to outweigh the costs, and both therefore look forward to positive operating cash flows.

Many investments do not result in additional revenues; they are simply designed to reduce the costs of the company's existing operations. For example, a new computer system may provide labour savings, or a new heating system may be more energy-efficient than the one it replaces. Such projects also contribute to the operating cash flow of the firm—not by increasing revenues but by reducing costs. These cost savings therefore represent a positive cash flow.

Here is another matter you need to look out for when calculating cash flow. When the firm calculates its taxable income, it makes a deduction for depreciation. This depreciation charge is an accounting entry. It affects the tax that the company pays, but it is not a cash expense and should not be deducted when calculating operating cash flow. (Remember from our earlier discussion that you want to discount cash flows, not profits.)

When you work out a project's cash flows, there are three possible ways to deal with depreciation.

Method 1: Dollars In Minus Dollars Out. Take only the items from the income statement that represent cash flows. We start with cash revenues and subtract cash expenses and taxes paid. We do not, however, subtract a charge for depreciation because depreciation is an accounting entry, not a cash expense. Thus

$$\text{Operating cash flow} = \text{revenues} - \text{cash expenses} - \text{taxes}$$

Method 2: Adjusted Accounting Profits. Alternatively, you can start with after-tax accounting profits and add back any deductions that were made for non-cash expenses such as depreciation. (Remember from our earlier discussion that you want to discount cash flows, not profits.) By this reasoning,

$$\text{Operating cash flow} = \text{after-tax profit} + \text{depreciation}$$

Method 3: Tax Shields. Although the depreciation deduction is not a cash expense, it does affect net profits and therefore taxes paid, which is a cash item.[4] For example, if the firm's tax bracket is 35 percent, each additional dollar of depreciation reduces taxable income by $1. Tax payments therefore fall by $.35, and cash flow increases by the same amount. The total **depreciation tax shield** equals the product of depreciation and the tax rate:

depreciation tax shield Reduction in taxes attributable to the depreciation allowance.

$$\textbf{Depreciation tax shield} = \textbf{depreciation} \times \textbf{tax rate} \qquad \textbf{(9.3)}$$

[4] The discussion here is general, without reference to the tax laws of any country. In Section 9.3 we will examine the treatment of depreciation in Canadian tax law.

This suggests a third way to calculate operating cash flow. First, calculate net profit *assuming* zero depreciation. This item would be (revenues − cash expenses) × (1 − tax rate). Now add back the tax shield created by depreciation. We then calculate operating cash flow as follows:

$$\text{Cash flow from operations} = (\text{revenues} - \text{cash expenses}) \times (1 - \text{tax rate}) + (\text{depreciation} \times \text{tax rate})$$

At this point, it would be worthwhile to pause and review some generally accepted terminology. The term *depreciation* is often used by accountants in reference to the periodic charge against revenue for the cost of tangible assets. When capital assets include tangible and intangible assets as well as natural resources and long-term deferred charges, the more appropriate all-encompassing term is *amortization*.[5] Since our discussion mostly deals with tangible assets, we will continue to use the term *depreciation* in this and other chapters on capital budgeting.

The following example confirms that the three methods for estimating operating cash flow all give the same answer.

EXAMPLE 9.6 OPERATING CASH FLOW

A project generates revenues of $1,000, cash expenses of $600, and depreciation charges of $200 in a particular year. The firm's tax bracket is 35 percent. Net income is calculated as follows:

Revenues	$1000
− Cash expenses	600
− Depreciation expense	200
= Profit before tax	200
− Tax at 35%	70
= Net income	130

Methods 1, 2, and 3 all show that operating cash flow is $330:

Method 1: Operating cash flow = revenues − cash expenses − taxes
= 1,000 − 600 − 70 = 330

Method 2: Operating cash flow = net profit + depreciation
= 130 + 200 = 330

Method 3: Operating cash flow = (revenues − cash expenses) × (1 − tax rate
+ (depreciation × tax rate)
=(1,000 – 600) × (1 − .35) + (200 × .35) = 330

Check Point 9.4

A project generates revenues of $600, expenses of $300, and depreciation charges of $200 in a particular year. The firm's tax bracket is 35 percent. Find the operating cash flow of the project using all three approaches.

In many cases, a project will seek to improve efficiency or cut costs. A new computer system may provide labour savings. A new heating system may be more energy efficient than the one it replaces. These projects also contribute to the operating cash flow of the firm—not by increasing revenue, but by reducing costs. As the next example illustrates, we calculate the addition to operating cash flow on cost-cutting projects just as we would for projects that increase revenues.

[5] For a good exposition of these issues, you may refer to T.H. Beechy and J.E.D. Conrad, *Intermediate Accounting: Volume One*, 3rd ed. (Toronto: McGraw-Hill Ryerson, 2005).

EXAMPLE 9.7 OPERATING CASH FLOW ON COST-CUTTING PROJECTS

Suppose the new heating system costs $100,000 but reduces heating expenditures by $30,000 a year. The system will be depreciated straight-line over a 5-year period, so the annual depreciation charge will be $20,000. The firm's tax rate is 35 percent. We calculate the incremental effects on revenues, expenses, and depreciation charges as follows. Notice that the reduction in expenses increases revenues minus cash expenses.

Increase in (revenues − cash expense)	$30,000
− Additional depreciation expense	− 20,000
= Incremental profit before tax	= 10,000
− Incremental tax at 35%	− 3,500
= Change in net income	= 6,500

Therefore, the increment to operating cash flow can be calculated by method 1 as

$$\begin{aligned}&\text{Increase in (revenues} - \text{cash expenses)} - \text{taxes}\\&= \$30{,}000 - \$3{,}500\\&= \$26{,}500\end{aligned}$$

or by method 2 as

$$\begin{aligned}&\text{Increase in net profit} + \text{additional depreciation}\\&= \$6500 + \$20{,}000\\&= \$26{,}500\end{aligned}$$

or by method 3 as

$$\begin{aligned}&\text{Increase in (revenues} - \text{cash expenses)} \times (1 - \text{tax rate}) + (\text{additional depreciation} \times \text{tax rate})\\&= \$30{,}000 \times (1 - .35) + (\$20{,}000 \times .35)\\&= \$26{,}500\end{aligned}$$

LO3, 4 9.3 BUSINESS TAXES IN CANADA AND THE CAPITAL BUDGETING DECISION

DEPRECIATION AND CAPITAL COST ALLOWANCE

capital cost allowance (CCA) The amount of write-off on depreciable assets allowed by Canada Revenue Agency (CRA) against taxable income.

undepreciated capital cost (UCC) The balance remaining in an asset class that has not yet been depreciated in that year.

CCA tax shield Tax savings arising from the capital cost allowance charge.

While calculating profit before tax, or taxable income, the business is allowed to deduct an amount for depreciation on its depreciable assets. This deduction, called the **capital cost allowance (CCA)** in Canada, enables the business to recover the original amount invested in the asset over a period of time, free of tax. In a general sense,

$$\text{Taxable income} = \text{revenues} - \text{expenses} - \text{CCA} \quad (9.4)$$

The CCA for each year is calculated by multiplying the balance on the asset, called the **undepreciated capital cost (UCC)**, by the appropriate tax rate.[6] Although the CCA itself is a non-cash charge, it does affect cash flow to the extent that it reduces the taxes paid. This tax saving, called the **CCA tax shield**, or sometimes the *depreciation tax shield*, is discussed in more detail later in the chapter.

It is important to remember that although the terms *depreciation* and *CCA* are often used interchangeably, they are not necessarily the same. In fact, the depreciation figure shown in a

[6] We can define UCC as the total cost of all assets in an asset class minus the accumulated CCA in that class. It is similar to the concept of "net fixed assets" under GAAP.

company's income statement is often calculated in a different manner than the CCA it reports to Canada Revenue Agency (CRA). We should note that only the CCA amount has an effect on the company's cash flows since it determines its tax bill.

THE ASSET CLASS SYSTEM

asset class Eligible depreciable assets are grouped into specified asset classes by CRA. Each asset class has a prescribed CCA rate.

All eligible depreciable assets are grouped into one of over 30 CCA **asset classes**. Each asset class has been assigned a CCA rate by CRA. Table 9.1 provides details regarding some of the asset classes. We note that buildings are generally included in Classes 1 and 3 and allowed a lower CCA rate. For instance, most buildings acquired after 1987 would fall into Class 1, and a firm that owned such buildings would be entitled to a CCA amount equal to 4 percent of the value of this class. At the other extreme, chinaware, cutlery, most computer software, and videotape cassettes used for rental purposes fall into Class 12, which is allowed a 100 percent CCA rate. CCA rate can change periodically. For instance, in 2004, changes were made to CCA rates

TABLE 9.1 Some of the most common capital cost allowance (CCA) classes.

Class Number	Description	CCA Rate
1	Most buildings bought after 1987 and the cost of certain additions or alterations made after 1987.	4%
3	Most buildings acquired before 1988. Also included is the cost of additions or alterations made after 1987.	5%
7*	Canoes, rowboats, and most other vessels, including their motors, furniture, and fittings.	15%
8	Property not included in any other class. Also included is data network infrastructure equipment and systems software for that equipment acquired before March 23, 2004.	20%
9*	Aircraft, including furniture, fittings, or equipment attached, and their spare parts.	25%
10	General-purpose electronic data processing equipment (commonly called computer hardware) and systems software for that equipment acquired before March 23, 2004, or after March 22, 2004, and before 2005 if you made an election.	
	Motor vehicles, automobiles, and some passenger vehicles.	30%
12	Chinaware, cutlery, linen, uniforms, dies, jigs, moulds, or lasts, computer software (except systems software), cutting or shaping parts of a machine, certain production costs associated with making a motion picture film, such as apparel or costumes and videotape cassettes.	100%
13	Property that is leasehold interest (the maximum CCA rate depends on the type of the leasehold and the terms of the lease).	N/A
17	Roads, parking lots, sidewalks, airplane runways, storage areas, or similar surface construction.	8%
22*	Most power-operated movable equipment bought before 1988 and used for excavating, moving, placing, or compacting earth, rock, concrete, or asphalt.	50%
38*	Most power-operated movable equipment acquired after 1987 used for moving, excavating, placing, or compacting earth, rock, concrete, or asphalt.	30%
45	General-purpose electronic data processing equipment (commonly called computer hardware) and systems software for that equipment acquired after March 22, 2004, and before March 19, 2007.	45%
46	Data network infrastructure equipment acquired after March 22, 2004.	30%
50	General-purpose electronic data processing equipment (commonly called computer hardware) and systems software for that equipment, including ancillary data processing equipment acquired after March 18, 2007.	55%
52	General-purpose electronic data processing equipment (commonly called computer hardware) and systems software for that equipment, including ancillary data processing equipment acquired after January 27, 2009, and before February 2011.	100%

*These asset classes have been extracted from the Income Tax Regulations (C.R.C., c. 945), Department of Justice Canada Web site, **laws.justice.gc.ca/eng/C.R.C.-c.945/index.html**, accessed October 4, 2010.

Source: Author's calculations based on Canada Revenue Agency Web site, **www.cra-arc.gc.ca**, accessed August 17, 2010. Reproduced with permission of the Canada Revenue Agency and the Minister of Public Works and Government Services Canada, 2011.

pertaining to information and communications technology equipment. The CCA rate applicable to computer equipment was raised from 30 to 45 percent in Class 45. Also, the CCA rate applicable to broadband Internet and other data network infrastructure equipment was raised from 20 to 30 percent. These assets are grouped under Class 46. For up-to-date information on CCA rates, you might check out Canada Revenue Agency's Web site at **www.ccra-adrc.gc.ca**. For most assets, CCA is calculated by applying the appropriate asset class rate against the declining asset balance (UCC amount). Intangible assets such as leasehold improvements (a Class 13 asset) or patents (a Class 14 asset) follow the **straight-line depreciation** method for computing CCA. For such assets, CCA essentially represents an annuity series.

straight-line depreciation Constant depreciation for each year of the asset's accounting life.

Under the asset class system, all assets within a particular CCA class are depreciated for tax purposes as if they were a single asset. To understand how the asset class system works, suppose that you have started a business as a tour bus operator and have invested $100,000 in a new bus. This would be a Class 10 asset for which the CCA is computed using a **declining balance depreciation** method, and the applicable CCA rate is 30 percent. Suppose, in the second year, you decide to expand your business and buy another bus for $100,000. To keep things simple, let us ignore the **half-year rule** for now.[7] Your CCA claims at the end of the first and second years are provided in Table 9.2.

declining balance depreciation This is computed by applying the depreciation rate to the asset balance for each year.

half-year rule Only one-half of the purchase cost of the asset is added to the asset class and used to compute CCA in the year of purchase.

You would reduce your taxable income in the first year by $30,000. You begin the next year with an undepreciated balance (the *undepreciated capital cost, UCC*) of $70,000, to which you would add the purchase cost of the second bus of $100,000 for a total UCC amounting to $170,000. In the second year you would be entitled to a CCA deduction from your taxable income of $51,000. The UCC remaining at the end of the second year is $119,000.

Let us now introduce the half-year rule for the illustration above. As is shown in Table 9.3, the CCA for asset Class 10 is $15,000 in year 1 and $40,500 in year 2. Taxable income is reduced by these amounts in the two years. In the first year, CCA is calculated on one-half of the purchase cost of the asset or .5 × $100,000 × .30. In the second year, the total CCA of $40,500 for the asset class is calculated as follows: for the asset purchased in the first year, CCA computed on the UCC balance is $85,000 × .30, or $25,500, whereas the half-year rule applies to the second year's purchase, and the eligible CCA is .5 × $100,000 × .30, or $15,000. Notice that, for year 3, if you do not make any further additions to this asset class, CCA will be calculated on the UCC balance of $144,500 at the applicable rate of 30 percent.

TABLE 9.2
Undepreciated capital cost (UCC) and capital cost allowance (CCA) (without the half-year rule).

Year	Cost of Buses	Beginning of Year UCC	CCA	End of Year UCC
1	$100,000	$100,000	$30,000*	$ 70,000
2	$100,000	$170,000	$51,000	$119,000

*$100,000 × .30.

Source: Author's calculations based on Canada Revenue Agency Web site: **http://www.cra-arc.gc.ca**. Reproduced with permission of the Canada Revenue Agency and the Minister of Public Works and Government Services Canada, 2011.

TABLE 9.3
Undepreciated capital cost (UCC) and capital cost allowance (CCA) (with the half-year rule).

Year	Cost of Buses	Beginning of Year UCC	CCA	End of Year UCC
1	$100,000	$100,000	$15,000	$ 85,000
2	$100,000	$185,000	$40,500	$144,500

Source: Author's calculations based on Canada Revenue Agency Web site: **http://www.cra-arc.gc.ca**. Reproduced with permission of the Canada Revenue Agency and the Minister of Public Works and Government Services Canada, 2011.

[7] The half-year rule, which applies to most assets, will allow your firm to include one-half of the purchase cost of the asset for calculating the year's CCA in that asset class in the year the asset is purchased. This is the case regardless of what part of the year the asset is purchased. The remaining half of the purchase cost is added to the asset class in the next year.

SALE OF ASSETS

A company is entitled to a CCA as long as it owns at least one asset in the asset class. When a depreciable asset is sold, the undepreciated capital cost of its asset class is reduced by either the asset's sale price or its initial cost, whichever is less. The result is called the *adjusted cost of disposal*. In the example in Table 9.3, if the bus purchased in year 1 for $100,000 is sold in year 3 for $80,000, the adjusted cost of disposal is $80,000 and gets deducted from the UCC of Class 10 in year 3.

In any given year, the company may buy new assets and sell old assets from within the same asset class. In this case, we would apply the *net acquisitions rule*. That is, we would determine the total cost of all additions to an asset class and then subtract the adjusted cost of disposal of all assets in that class. If the net acquisition is positive, we would apply the half-year rule and calculate CCA as shown earlier. Continuing with our tour bus operator example, suppose in year 3, in addition to selling the bus bought in year 1 for $80,000, we buy another luxury coach for $150,000. Our net acquisition in year 3 will be $150,000 − $80,000, or $70,000. To calculate CCA for year 3, we will apply the half-year rule on $70,000. This result will be added to the CCA computed on the UCC balance of $144,500 to get the overall CCA for year 3. If, on the other hand, the net acquisition is negative, we do not adjust for the half-year rule. Instead, we will subtract the negative net acquisition amount from the beginning UCC balance of the asset class. CCA for the year will be calculated by applying the CCA rate on this net amount.

Check Point 9.5

In year 1 of your new business as a boat rental company, you have bought a motorboat for $100,000 and a sailboat for $80,000. In year 2, you sell the motorboat for $110,000 and the sailboat for $75,000. You also buy a speedboat in year 2 for $150,000. For CCA purposes, the boats are grouped in Class 7, which carries a 15 percent CCA rate. Calculate the CCA for years 1 and 2. What is the UCC balance at the end of year 2?

TERMINATION OF ASSET POOL

terminal loss The positive balance following the disposal of all assets in the class. The UCC of the asset class is set to zero after a terminal loss is recognized.

recaptured depreciation The negative balance that is caused in an asset class by the sale of an asset. Recaptured depreciation is added to taxable income.

What happens if the company disposes of its entire pool of assets in an asset class? Once again, we determine the adjusted cost of disposal (as the lower of the sale proceeds or the initial cost of this pool of assets) and subtract this amount from the undepreciated capital cost of the asset class. If this leaves a positive balance in the asset class and there are *no other assets remaining* in the class, this remaining balance is called a **terminal loss** and is deducted from taxable income. Also, the UCC then becomes zero, and the asset class ceases to generate CCA tax shields.[8]

If, on the other hand, we arrive at a negative balance after deducting the adjusted cost of disposal from the UCC of the asset class, this amount is called **recaptured depreciation** and is added back to taxable income. Once again, the undepreciated capital cost of the asset class becomes zero.

When an asset is sold for more than its initial cost, the difference between the sale price and initial cost is called a *capital gain*. Presently capital gains, net of any capital losses, are taxed at 50 percent of the firm's applicable marginal tax rate.

EXAMPLE 9.8 **RECAPTURED DEPRECIATION**

Remember our example where you bought two buses in years 1 and 2, respectively, each costing $100,000. To calculate CCA, the buses fall into Class 10 and are eligible for a 30 percent CCA rate. From Table 9.3, we saw that after taking two years of CCA, the undepreciated capital cost in the asset class is $144,500. Suppose you now decide to end your career as a tour bus operator and terminate the pool of assets in this class by selling both buses. You sell each bus for $120,000 for a total sale value of $240,000. Notice that because the sale price of the buses exceeds their purchase cost, they have actually appreciated in value instead of depreciating. The adjusted cost of disposal is their total purchase cost

[8] We should note that if the asset pool is not completely terminated—that is, there are other assets remaining in the asset class—then a positive balance would simply become the UCC of the class and continue to generate CCA tax shields.

of \$200,000. In such a situation, CRA will determine that you have taken \$200,000 − \$144,500 = \$55,500 depreciation that did not reflect the economic depreciation on the assets. Therefore, this amount (\$55,500) will be "recaptured" and added to your income to calculate tax. In addition, you have a capital gain of \$240,000 − \$200,000 = \$40,000. The capital gain will be taxed at 50 percent of your firm's applicable marginal tax rate.

Suppose that instead of selling the two buses, you sell only one bus for \$120,000 and continue running your business using the other bus. Notice that because one bus still remains in the asset class, the asset pool is not terminated. The UCC of \$144,500 gets reduced by the adjusted cost of disposal of \$100,000,[9] but it is still a positive amount of \$44,500 and so there is no recaptured depreciation. You have also made a capital gain on the sale of \$120,000 − \$100,000 = \$20,000.

Check Point 9.6

Think again about Example 9.8. Suppose that instead of selling the two buses for \$120,000 each, you sell the bus bought in year 1 for \$65,000 and the one bought in year 2 for \$70,000. What are the tax consequences of this transaction, assuming that the firm has no other Class 10 assets?

PRESENT VALUES OF CCA TAX SHIELDS

We start a new asset class by buying an asset. We'll use the following notation for our subsequent discussion:

C = Capital cost of an asset acquired at the beginning of year 1

d = CCA rate for the asset class to which the asset belongs

UCC_t = Undepreciated capital cost in year t after deducting CCA for the year

T_c = The firm's tax rate

r = Discount rate

S = Salvage amount from the sale of the asset at the end of year t

To evaluate a project properly and calculate its present value, we need to compute the present value of the CCA tax shields accruing from capital investments in the project. As we show later in our discussion of Example 9.9, an asset can continue to generate CCA tax shields for the firm even after it is sold, provided there are other assets remaining in its class and the total UCC balance for the asset class is positive. This suggests that the CCA tax shield from investing in an asset can continue in perpetuity, since we are essentially deducting a fraction of the remaining UCC balance over an infinite period. Equation 9.5 below can be used to compute the present value of a perpetual tax shield.[10]

$$\frac{CdT_c}{r + d}\left[\frac{1 + .5r}{1 + r}\right] \tag{9.5}$$

Let us now introduce a residual or salvage value arising from the sale of an asset into the discussion. We would deduct this salvage value from the UCC of the asset class, and thereby reduce the CCA deductions and CCA tax shields for later years. Let us assume that other assets remain in the asset class and the total UCC exceeds the salvage value.[11] If the asset is sold at the end of year t for a salvage amount, S, then the total tax shield lost is a perpetuity with a present value at the end of year t of

$$\frac{SdT_c}{r + d}$$

---

[9] This amount, representing the initial purchase cost, is lower than the sale price of \$120,000.

[10] A detailed discussion of how this equation is obtained can be found in Appendix 9A at the Online Learning Centre.

[11] Notice that, otherwise, we may have to consider recapture of CCA and capital gains or terminal losses.

When we discount this back to the present, we get the present value of lost CCA tax shields due to salvage value:

$$\left[\frac{SdT_c}{r + d}\right]\left[\frac{1}{(1 + r)^t}\right] \tag{9.6}$$

Combining equations 9.5 and 9.6 enables us to provide a general formula for the present value of the CCA tax shield:

$$\textbf{Present value of CCA tax shield} = \left[\frac{CdT_c}{r + d}\right]\left[\frac{1 + .5r}{1 + r}\right] - \left[\frac{SdT_c}{r + d}\right]\left[\frac{1}{(1 + r)^t}\right] \tag{9.7}$$

We can now look at an example of how to get the present value of the tax shields. Keep in mind that we are looking for incremental changes in CCA and UCC that arise because of the purchase (or sale) of assets for the project. From Chapter 3, we know that the combined federal and provincial tax rate varies from province to province. Also, the tax rate could be different depending on whether the firm is a large corporation or a small business, and also whether it is in manufacturing and processing or some other industry. To illustrate the calculation of taxes, we will assume that the company pays a total of 35 percent of its taxable income to the federal and provincial government.

EXAMPLE 9.9 PV OF CCA TAX SHIELDS

Suppose that in year 1 you buy equipment for aircraft used in your business operations for an amount C of \$250,000. The equipment belongs to asset Class 9 with a CCA rate $d = .25$. You intend to sell the equipment in year 8 for a salvage value, S, of \$8,000. At the time of sale, you still anticipate having other assets in the class and a UCC that exceeds the salvage value of the asset, so you will not have to deal with recaptured CCA or a terminal loss. Your tax rate is 35 percent and your discount rate is 12 percent. You want to know the present value of the incremental tax shields generated from owning and eventually selling the asset.

To calculate the present value of such incremental tax shields, we would have to reduce the present value of CCA tax shields by the present value of the tax shields lost due to the sale of the asset in year 8.

$$\begin{aligned}
\text{PV of CCA tax shields} &= \begin{array}{c}\text{PV of perpetual tax}\\ \text{shield on assets acquired}\\ \text{in year 1}\end{array} - \begin{array}{c}\text{PV of perpetual tax}\\ \text{shield on salvage}\\ \text{value in year 8}\end{array}\\
&= \left[\frac{CdT_c}{r + d}\right]\left[\frac{1 + .5r}{1 + r}\right] - \left[\frac{SdT_c}{r + d}\right]\left[\frac{1}{(1 + r)^t}\right]\\
&= \left[\frac{250{,}000 \times .25 \times .35}{.12 + .25}\right]\left[\frac{1 + (.5 \times .12)}{1 + .12}\right]\\
&\quad - \left[\frac{8{,}000 \times .25 \times .35}{.12 + .25}\right]\left[\frac{1}{(1 + .12)^8}\right]\\
&= \left[\frac{21{,}875}{.37}\right]\left[\frac{1.06}{1.12}\right] - \left[\frac{700}{.37}\right]\left[\frac{1}{2.48}\right]\\
&= 55{,}954 - 763 = 55{,}191
\end{aligned}$$

From Table 9.4, note that the UCC generated by the equipment after eight years of CCA tax shields is \$29,200. Even *after* selling the equipment in year 8, you will continue to depreciate \$29,200 − \$8,000 = \$21,200 over future years. This example shows us a unique feature of Canadian tax law, that it is possible for an asset to generate CCA tax shields for the firm even after it is sold. Notice that two basic conditions have to be met for this to happen: (1) there are other assets remaining in its class and (2) the proceeds from disposing of any such assets are less than the total UCC for the asset class.

TABLE 9.4
CCA and UCC generated by the aircraft equipment until year 8.

Year	1	2	3	4	5	6	7	8
C	250,000							
CCA	31,250	54,688	41,016	30,762	23,071	17,303	12,978	9,732
UCC	218,750	164,062	123,046	92,284	69,213	51,910	38,932	29,200

Source: Author's calculations based on Canada Revenue Agency Web site: **http://www.cra-arc.gc.ca**. Reproduced with permission of the Canada Revenue Agency and the Minister of Public Works and Government Services Canada, 2011.

Check Point 9.7

You are evaluating a project that requires an investment of $5,000 and generates revenues of $3,000 and expenses of $1,500. CCA on the project will be based on a declining balance system with an applicable rate of 15 percent. The project will last for 5 years, at which time the machinery will be worthless and the firm will no longer produce cash flows. The firm's tax bracket is 35 percent.

a. Find the relevant cash flows for the first 5 years.
b. Assume that depreciation is on a straight-line basis over 5 years. What is the yearly depreciation charge? How would this change the cash flows for the first 5 years?

9.4 EXAMPLE: BLOOPER INDUSTRIES

Now that we have examined many of the pieces of a cash flow analysis, let's try to put them together into a coherent whole. As the newly appointed financial manager of Blooper Industries, you are about to analyze a proposal for mining and selling a small deposit of high-grade magnoosium ore.[12] You are given the forecasts shown in Table 9.5. We will walk through the lines in the table.

Capital Investment (line 1). The project requires an investment of $10 million in mining machinery. At the end of five years the machinery has no further value. The machinery falls into asset Class 38, which has a CCA rate of 30 percent. The company owns other assets that also fall into this asset class. These other assets will remain in the asset class even after the magnoosium project ceases to exist after five years.

Working Capital (lines 2 and 3). Line 2 shows the level of working capital. As the project gears up in the early years, working capital increases, but later in the project's life, the investment in working capital is recovered.

Line 3 shows the change in working capital from year to year. Notice that in years 1 to 4 the change is positive; in these years the project requires a continuing investment in working capital. Starting in year 5 the change is negative; there is a disinvestment as working capital is recovered.

Revenues (line 4). The company expects to be able to sell 750,000 kilograms of magnoosium a year at a price of $20 a kilogram in year 1. That points to initial revenues of $750{,}000 \times 20 = \$15{,}000{,}000$. But be careful: inflation is running at about 5 percent a year. If magnoosium prices keep pace with inflation, you should up your forecast of the second-year revenues by 5 percent. Third-year revenues should increase by a further 5 percent, and so on. Line 4 in Table 9.5 shows revenues rising in line with inflation.

The sales forecasts in Table 9.5 are cut off after five years. That makes sense if the ore deposit will run out at that time. But if Blooper could make sales for year 6, you should include them in your forecasts. We have sometimes encountered financial managers who assume a project life of (say) five years, even when they confidently expect revenues for 10 years or more. When asked

[12] Readers have inquired whether magnoosium is a real substance. Here, now, are the facts. Magnoosium was created in the early days of TV, when a splendid-sounding announcer closed a variety show by saying, "This program has been brought to you by Blooper Industries, proud producer of aleemium, magnoosium, and stool." We forget the company, but the blooper really happened.

TABLE 9.5
Financial projections for Blooper's magnoosium mine ($000s).

Year:	0	1	2	3	4	5	6
1. Capital investment	10,000						
2. Working capital	1,500	4,075	4,279	4,493	4,717	3,039	0
3. Change in working capital	1,500	2,575	204	214	224	−1,678	−3,039
4. Revenues		15,000	15,750	16,538	17,364	18,233	
5. Expenses		10,000	10,500	11,025	11,576	12,155	
6. CCA of mining equipment (asset Class 38, $d = 30\%$)		1,500*	2,550	1,785	1,250	875	612 ...
7. Pretax profit		3,500	2,700	3,728	4,538	5,203	
8. Tax (35%)		1,225	945	1,305	1,588	1,821	
9. Profit after tax		2,275	1,755	2,423	2,950	3,382	

*In the first year, CCA is computed using the half-year rule.

Note: Some entries are subject to rounding error.

the reason, they explain that forecasting beyond five years is too hazardous. We sympathize, but you just have to do your best. Do not arbitrarily truncate a project's life.

Expenses (line 5). We assume that the expenses of mining and refining also increase in line with inflation at 5 percent per year.

CCA (line 6). Mining equipment falls in asset Class 38, which has a CCA rate of 30 percent. We compute CCA using the declining balance method, which is prescribed by CRA for this asset class. Notice from Table 9.6 that, even though the magnoosium mine stops producing in year 5, an undepreciated capital cost (UCC) balance of $2.04 million remains at the end of year 5. This suggests that the initial investment has not been completely depreciated. In fact, computing with the declining balance system will continue to provide smaller CCA values each year over an infinite period. To get around this problem, we will use a method of computing the present value of the CCA tax shields under the declining balance system we described with equation 9.7. Even after the magnoosium mine shuts its operations in year 5, we assume that the company has other assets in Class 38 and that the asset pool will not be terminated.

Pretax Profits (line 7). Profit after depreciation equals (revenues − expenses − CCA).

Tax (line 8). Company taxes are 35 percent of pretax profits. For example, in year 1,

$$\text{Tax} = .35 \times 3{,}500 = 1{,}225, \text{ or } \$1{,}225{,}000$$

Profit After Tax (line 9). Profit after tax is simply equal to pretax profit less taxes.

CALCULATING BLOOPER'S PROJECT CASH FLOWS

Table 9.5 provides most of the information you need to figure out the cash flows on the magnoosium project. These cash flows are the sum of three broad components: investment in plant and equipment, investment in working capital, and cash flows from operations. In turn, cash flows

TABLE 9.6
Computation of CCA and UCC balances for Blooper's magnoosium mine ($000s).

Year	Capital Investment UCC	CCA	End of Year (UCC)
1	10,000	1,500	8,500
2	8,500	2,550	5,950
3	5,950	1,785	4,165
4	4,165	1,250	2,915
5	2,915	875	2,040
6	2,040	612	1,428

from operations comprise (1) operating cash flows excluding depreciation (CCA) and (2) the CCA tax shield.

Cash flow from investment in plant and equipment
+ Cash flow from investment in working capital
+ Cash flow from operations, including
- Operating cash flows
- CCA tax shield

= Total project cash flows

Table 9.7 provides calculations for yearly operating cash flows excluding CCA tax shields, Table 9.8 sets out the project cash flows excluding the CCA tax shield, and Table 9.9 provides details by year regarding the CCA tax shield. First, let's see where these figures come from.

Capital Investment. Investment in plant and equipment is taken from line 1 of Table 9.5. Blooper's initial investment is a negative cash flow of −$10 million shown in line 1 of Table 9.8.

Investment in Working Capital. We've seen that investment in working capital, just like investment in plant and equipment, produces a negative cash flow. For instance, when the company builds up inventories of refined magnoosium, the company's cash is reduced, or when customers are slow to pay their bills, cash is reduced. An increase in working capital implies a negative cash flow; a decrease implies a positive cash flow.

The numbers required for these calculations come from lines 2 and 3 of Table 9.5. Line 2 shows the amount or level of working capital whereas line 3 shows the change in working capital. Notice the cash flow is measured by the *change* in working capital, not the level of working capital. For

TABLE 9.7 Operating cash flows excluding CCA tax shields for Blooper's magnoosium mine ($000s).

Year:	0	1	2	3	4	5	6
Revenues		15,000	15,750	16,538	17,364	18,233	
− Expenses		10,000	10,500	11,025	11,576	12,155	
= Profit before tax		5,000	5,250	5,513	5,788	6,078	
− Tax at 35%		1,750	1,838	1,930	2,026	2,127	
= Operating cash flows (excluding CCA tax shield)		3,250	3,412	3,583	3,762	3,951	

TABLE 9.8 Cash flows for Blooper's magnoosium mine ($000s).

Year:	0	1	2	3	4	5	6
1. Capital investment	−10,000						
2. Change in working capital	−1,500	−2,575	−204	−214	−224	1,678	3,039
3. Cash flows from operations (excluding CCA tax shield)		3,250	3,412	3,583	3,762	3,951	
4. Total cash flows (excluding CCA tax shield)	−11,500	675	3,208	3,369	3,538	5,629	3,039

TABLE 9.9 Computation by year of CCA tax shields for Blooper's magnoosium mine ($000s).

Year:	0	1	2	3	4	5	6
CCA		1,500	2,550	1,785	1,250	875	612
× Tax rate		.35	.35	.35	.35	.35	.35
= CCA tax shield		525	893	625	438	306	214

instance, from Table 9.5, line 2, we see that Blooper makes an initial (year 0) investment of \$1,500,000 in working capital, which goes up to \$4,075,000 in year 1. This *total* level of working capital in year 1 is arrived at by an additional investment in working capital of \$2,575,000 in year 1 to year 0's investment, that is, \$1,500,000 + \$2,575,000 = \$4,075,000. The additional investment in year 1 of \$2,575,000 is shown in line 3, Table 9.5, and results in a negative cash flow by this amount (line 2, Table 9.8).

Operating Cash Flows. The third component of project cash flows is operating cash flow. As we have discussed earlier, we can segregate this component into two parts: (1) operating cash flows, excluding CCA, and (2) the CCA tax shield. Let us discuss these one by one.

- *Operating cash flows, excluding CCA.* Table 9.5 has the necessary data to calculate such operating cash flows. The details, in thousands of dollars, are provided in Table 9.7.

  The cash flow amounts for Blooper's magnoosium mine are in line 3 of Table 9.8. Line 4 provides the yearly total cash flows excluding the CCA tax shield. Notice that the table does not fully capture the entire amount of cash flows for the project since the CCA tax shield is not included. Let us now examine the CCA tax shield.

- *CCA tax shield.* In Section 9.3, we saw that CCA has an important effect on cash flows because it reduces taxable income and the firm's tax bill. For any year, this tax shield is calculated as the product of the CCA and the tax rate.

$$\text{CCA tax shield} = \text{CCA} + \text{tax rate} \qquad (9.8)$$

For Blooper, which pays tax at a rate of 35 percent, this means that each additional dollar of CCA reduces taxable income by \$1 and taxes owed by 35 cents. Table 9.9 provides details regarding the CCA tax shields for Blooper. Notice that both the CCA and the CCA tax shield increase between years 1 and 2, but thereafter are represented by a series of declining balances. This is because in year 1 when Blooper purchases the machine, the half-year rule applies, but all subsequent CCA tax shield calculations use a declining balance system. Also, CCA tax shields from the project will continue to be generated beyond year 5, assuming that Blooper will have other assets in Class 38 after the magnoosium mine is shut down.

CALCULATING THE NPV OF BLOOPER'S PROJECT

Table 9.10 sets out the calculations for the total present value of cash flows excluding the CCA tax shield. Assume that investors expect a return of 12 percent from investments in the capital market with the same risk as the magnoosium project. This is the opportunity cost of the shareholders' money that Blooper is proposing to invest in the project. Therefore, to calculate NPV you need to discount the cash flows at 12 percent. Remember that to calculate the present value of a cash flow in year t you can divide the cash flow by $(1 + r)^t$ or you can multiply by a discount factor that is equal to $1/(1 + r)^t$.

The total present value in Table 9.10 is not the net present value of the project, because we still have to deal with the CCA tax shield. We deal with the tax shields separately because even though the magnoosium project terminates in year 5 and we have computed cash flows till year 6, from Table 9.6 we have noted that there is still a UCC balance at the end of year 6 on

TABLE 9.10
Cash flows and total present value of Blooper's project excluding the CCA tax shield (\$000s).

Year:	0	1	2	3	4	5	6
Total cash flow excluding tax shields	−11,500	675	3,208	3,369	3,538	5,629	3,039
Discount factor	1.0000	.8929	.7972	.7118	.6355	.5674	.5066
Present value (excluding CCA tax shields)	−11,500	603	2,557	2,398	2,248	3,194	1,540
Total present value (excluding CCA tax shields)	1,040						

which CCA can be computed for future years.[13] To compute the present value of the CCA tax shield, we use equation 9.7. Notice that in the example we have assumed a zero salvage value, S, at the end of the project's life.

$$\text{PV of CCA tax shield} = \left[\frac{CdT_c}{r+d}\right]\left[\frac{1+.5r}{1+r}\right] - \left[\frac{SdT_c}{r+d}\right] \times \left[\frac{1}{(1+r)^t}\right]$$

$$= \left[\frac{10{,}000 \times .3 \times .35}{.12+.3}\right]\left[\frac{1+(.5\times .12)}{1+.12}\right] - \left[\frac{0 \times .3 \times .35}{.12+.3}\right]\left[\frac{1}{(1+.12)^6}\right]$$

$$= \$2{,}366$$

We now have all the necessary information to determine the net present value of Blooper's magnoosium project. It is the sum of the total present value excluding CCA tax shields in Table 9.10 and the present value of the CCA tax shield, that is,

$$\text{NPV} = \text{Total PV excluding CCA tax shields} + \text{PV of CCA tax shield}$$
$$= \$1{,}040 + \$2{,}366 = \$3{,}406$$

We see that when all cash flows are discounted and added up, the magnoosium project offers a positive net present value of about $3.4 million.

Now let's consider a small point that often causes confusion. To calculate the present value of the first year's cash flow, we divide by $(1 + r) = 1.12$. Strictly speaking, this makes sense only if all the sales and all the costs occur exactly 365 days, 0 hours, and 0 minutes from now. But, of course, the year's sales don't all take place on the stroke of midnight December 31. However, when making capital budgeting decisions, companies are usually happy to pretend that all cash flows occur at one-year intervals, for one reason only—simplicity. When sales forecasts are sometimes little more than intelligent guesses, it may be pointless to inquire how the sales are likely to be spread out during the year.[14]

FURTHER NOTES AND WRINKLES ARISING FROM BLOOPER'S PROJECT

Before we leave Blooper and its magnoosium project, we should cover a few extra wrinkles.

How to Deal with Salvage Value. So far, we have assumed that Blooper will not receive any salvage value from the mining equipment when the magnoosium mine is closed. But suppose Blooper forecasts that the equipment can be sold for $1.5 million in year 6.

You recorded the initial $10 million investment as a negative cash flow. Now, in year 6, you have a forecast return of $1.5 million of that investment. That is a positive cash flow estimate, which has a present value of

$$\frac{S}{(1+r)^6} = \frac{1.5}{(1.12)^6} = .76$$

The salvage value will also reduce future tax shields, and therefore the present value of the CCA tax shield, as follows:[15]

$$\frac{1}{(1+r)^6} \times \frac{SdT_c}{(r+d)} = \frac{1}{(1.12)^6} \times \frac{1.5 \times .3 \times .35}{(.12+.3)} = .19$$

---

[13] Of course, this assumes that the firm has other assets in the asset class.

[14] Financial managers sometimes assume cash flows arrive in the middle of the calendar year, that is, the end of June. This also makes NPV a mid-year number. If you are standing at the start of the year, the NPV must be discounted for a further half-year. To do this, divide the mid-year NPV by the square root of $(1 + r)$. This mid-year convention is roughly equivalent to assuming cash flows are distributed evenly throughout the year. This is a bad assumption for some industries. In retailing, for example, most of the cash flow comes late in the year as the holiday season approaches.

[15] Remember that we have assumed that Blooper has other machines in this asset class, so the sale will not close out the asset class.

excel spreadsheet

A Spreadsheet Model for Blooper (Formula Inserts)

	A	B	C	D	E	F	G	H
1	Year:	0	1	2	3	4	5	6
2	Capital investment	10,000						
3	Working capital	=0.15*C6+2/12*B5	=0.15*D6+2/12*C5	=0.15*E6+2/12*D5	=0.15*F6+2/12*E5	=0.15*G6+2/12*F5	=0.15*H6+2/12*G5	=0.15*I6+2/12*H5
4	Change in working capital	=B3	=C3−B3	=D3−C3	=E3−D3	=F3−E3	=G3−F3	=H3−G3
5	Revenues		15000	=C5*1.05	=D5*1.05	=E5*1.05	=F5*1.05	
6	Expenses		10000	=C6*1.05	=D6*1.05	=E6*1.05	=F6*1.05	
7	Profit before tax (excluding CCA tax shield)		=C5−C6	=D5−D6	=E5−E6	=F5−F6	=G5−G6	
8	Tax (35%)		=C7*0.35	=D7*0.35	=E7*0.35	=F7*0.35	=G7*0.35	
9	Operating cash flows (excluding CCA tax shield)		=C7−C8	=D7−D8	=E7−E8	=F7−F8	=G7−G8	
10	Salvage value							0
11	Total cash flow (excluding CCA tax shield)	=−B2−B4	=C2−C4+C9	=D2−D4+D9	=E2−E4+E9	=F2−F4+F9	=G2−G4+G9	=H2−H4+H9+H10
12	PV of cash flow (excluding CCA tax shield)	=B11/(1.12)^B1	=C11/(1.12)^C1	=D11/(1.12)^D1	=E11/(1.12)^E1	=F11/(1.12)^F1	=G11/(1.12)^G1	=H11/(1.12)^H1
13	Total present value (excluding CCA tax shield) (A)	=SUM(B12:H12)						
14	CCA		=0.5*B2*0.3	=(B2−C14)*0.3	=D14*0.7	=E14*0.7	=F14*0.7	=G14*0.7
15	CCA tax shield		=10000*0.3/2*0.35	=8500*0.3*0.35	=5950*0.3*0.35	=4165*0.3*0.35	=2916*0.3*0.35	=2041*0.3*0.35
16	PV of CCA tax shield (B)	=(B2*0.3*0.35/(0.12+0.3))*((1+(0.5*0.12))/(1+0.12))−(H10*0.3*0.35/(0.3+0.12)*(1/(1+0.12)^H1))						
17	Total net present value (A) + (B)	=(B13+B16)						

You might have guessed that discounted cash flow analysis such as that of the Blooper case is tailor-made for spreadsheets. The worksheet directly above shows the formulas from the Excel spreadsheet that we used to generate the Blooper example. The first spreadsheet shows the resulting values, which appear in the text in Tables 9.5 through 9.10. This model assumes that there is no salvage value on Blooper's equipment. We have also included a spreadsheet model in which we assume a salvage value of $1.5 million in year 6.

The assumed values are the capital investment (cell B2), the initial level of revenues (cell C5), and expenses (cell C6). Rows 5 and 6 show that each entry for revenues and expenses equals the previous value times (1 + inflation rate), or 1.05. Row 3, which is the amount of working capital, is the sum of inventories and accounts receivable. To capture the fact that inventories tend to rise with production, we set working capital equal to .15 times the following year's expenses. Similarly, accounts receivable rise with sales, so we assumed that accounts receivable would be 1/6 times the current year's revenues. Each entry in row 3 is the sum of these two quantities.[16] Net investment in working capital (row 4) is the increase in working capital from one year to the next. Total cash flow excluding the CCA tax shield (row 11) is capital investment plus change in working capital plus profit after tax, which we have called operating cash flows. Cell H10 includes a provision for salvage value in year 6 that is set at zero in the first spreadsheet model and $1.5 million in the second model. In row 12, we discount the cash flow amounts at a 12 percent discount rate and in cell B13 we add the present value of each cash flow to find the total present value excluding the CCA tax shield. Row 14 includes CCA values. Notice that the first year's CCA in cell C14 is computed using the half-year rule, whereas the subsequent CCA amounts follow the declining balance system. Row 15 includes the yearly CCA tax shields and row 16 incorporates the present value of the CCA tax shield. The project's net present value is provided in cell B17 as the sum of the total present value excluding the CCA tax shield (cell B13) and the present value of the CCA tax shield (cell B16).

Once the spreadsheet is up and running, it is easy to do various sorts of "what if" analysis. Also, we can do some comparative analysis involving straight-line and declining balance calculations. Keep in mind that so far we have used declining balance CCA. But what if we used straight-line depreciation instead? Here are a few questions to try your hand.

***Spreadsheet Questions** (answers in Appendix 9A, found at the Online Learning Centre)*

9.1 Suppose the firm can economize on working capital by managing inventories more efficiently. If the firm can reduce inventories from 15 percent to 10 percent of next year's cost of goods sold, what will be the effect on project NPV?

9.2 What happens to NPV if the inflation rate falls from 5 percent to zero and the discount rate falls from 12 percent to 7 percent? Given that the real discount rate is almost unchanged, why does project NPV increase?

9.3 Suppose that Blooper's mining equipment could be depreciated on a five-year, straight-line basis. What is the present value of the depreciation tax shield? What happens to cash flow in each year and to the project NPV?

[16] For convenience we assume that Blooper pays all its bills immediately and therefore accounts payable equals zero. If it didn't, working capital would be reduced by the amount of the payables.

A Spreadsheet Model for Blooper (Without Salvage Value)[1]

	A	B	C	D	E	F	G	H	I
1	Year:	0	1	2	3	4	5	6	… ∞
2	Capital investment	10,000							
3	Working capital	1,500	4,075	4,279	4,493	4,717	3,039	0	
4	Change in working capital	1,500	2,575	204	214	225	−1,679	−3,039	
5	Revenues		15,000	15,750	16,538	17,364	18,233		
6	Expenses		10,000	10,500	11,025	11,576	12,155		
7	Profit before tax (excluding CCA tax shield)		5,000	5,250	5,513	5,788	6,078		
8	Tax (35%)		1,750	1,838	1,930	2,026	2,127		
9	Operating cash flows (excluding CCA tax shield)		3,250	3,412	3,583	3,762	3,950		
10	Salvage value							0	
11	Total cash flow (excluding CCA tax shield)	−11,500	675	3,208	3,369	3,538	5,629	3,039	
12	PV of cash flow (excluding CCA tax shield)	−11,500	603	2,558	2,398	2,248	3,194	1,540	
13	Total present value (excluding CCA tax shield) (A)	1,041							
14	CCA[2]		1,500	2,550	1,785	1,250	875	612	'0
15	CCA tax shield[2]		525	893	625	437	306	214	'0
16	PV of CCA tax shield[2] (B)	2,366							
17	Total net present value (A) + (B)	3,407							

Notes: [1] Some entries in this table may differ from those in Tables 9.5 to 9.10 due to rounding error.
[2] The CCA and the CCA tax shield (lines 14 and 15) will continue even after year 6. The PV of the CCA tax shield (line 16) has been calculated assuming that the CCA and the CCA tax shield will continue in perpetuity.

A Spreadsheet Model for Blooper (with Salvage Value)[1]

	A	B	C	D	E	F	G	H	I
1	Year:	0	1	2	3	4	5	6	… ∞
2	Capital investment	10,000							
3	Working capital	1,500	4,075	4,279	4,493	4,717	3,039	0	
4	Change in working capital	1,500	2,575	204	214	225	−1,679	−3,039	
5	Revenues		15,000	15,750	16,538	17,364	18,233		
6	Expenses		10,000	10,500	11,025	11,576	12,155		
7	Profit before tax (excluding CCA tax shield)		5,000	5,250	5,513	5,788	6,078		
8	Tax (35%)		1,750	1,838	1,930	2,026	2,127		
9	Operating cash flows (excluding CCA tax shield)		3,250	3,412	3,583	3,762	3,950		
10	Salvage value							1500	
11	Total cash flow (excluding CCA tax shield)	−11,500	675	3,208	3,369	3,538	5,629	4,539	
12	PV of cash flow (excluding CCA tax shield)	−11,500	603	2,558	2,398	2,248	3,194	2,299	
13	Total present value (excluding CCA tax shield) (A)	1,801							
14	CCA[2]		1,500	2,550	1,785	1,250	875	612	'0
15	CCA tax shield[2]		525	893	625	437	306	214	'0
16	PV of CCA tax shield[2] (B)	2,176							
17	Total net present value (A) + (B)	3,977							

Notes: [1] Some entries in this table may differ from those in Tables 9.5 to 9.10 due to rounding error.
[2] The CCA and the CCA tax shield (lines 14 and 15) will continue even after year 6. The PV of the CCA tax shield (line 16) has been calculated assuming that the CCA and the CCA tax shield will continue in perpetuity.

So we see that while the sale of the mining equipment increases the net present value of the project by $760,000, the present value of the lost tax shield from the salvage will reduce net present value by $190,000. Overall, net present value of the project will increase by $760,000 − $190,000 = $570,000.

A Further Note on CCA. We warned you earlier not to assume that all cash flows are likely to increase with inflation. The CCA tax shield is a case in point because CRA lets companies depreciate only the amount of the original investment. For example, if you go back to CRA to explain that inflation mushroomed since you made the investment and you should be allowed to depreciate more, CRA won't listen. The *nominal* amount of CCA is fixed, and therefore, the higher the rate of inflation, the lower the *real* value of the CCA that you can claim.

9.5 SUMMARY

1. **How should the cash flows properly attributable to a proposed new project be calculated? LO1**

Here is a checklist to bear in mind when forecasting a project's cash flows:

- Discount cash flows, not profits.
- Estimate the project's incremental cash flows—that is, the difference between the cash flows with the project and those without the project.
- Include all indirect effects of the project, such as its impact on the sales of the firm's other products.
- Forget sunk costs.
- Include **opportunity costs**, such as the value of land that you could otherwise sell.
- Beware allocated overhead charges for heat, light, and so on. These may not reflect the incremental effects of the project on these costs.
- Remember the investment in working capital. As sales increase, the firm may need to make additional investments in working capital and, as the project finally comes to an end, it will recover these investments.
- Do not include debt interest or the cost of repaying a loan. When calculating NPV, assume that the project is financed entirely by the shareholders and that they receive all the cash flows. This isolates the investment decision from the financing decision.

2. **How can the cash flows of a project be computed from standard financial statements? LO2**

Project cash flow does not equal profit. You must allow for changes in working capital as well as non-cash expenses such as depreciation. Also, if you use a nominal cost of capital, consistency requires that you forecast *nominal* cash flows—that is, cash flows that recognize the effect of inflation.

3. **How is the company's tax bill affected by capital cost allowance (CCA) and how does this affect project value? LO3**

CCA is not a cash flow. However, because CCA reduces taxable income, it reduces taxes. This tax reduction is called the **CCA tax shield**. For computing tax depreciation in Canada, assets are assigned into different **asset classes**, which have specified CCA rates. Most asset classes follow a declining balance system for computing CCA, and, therefore, most assets continue to generate CCA tax shields over an infinite time frame. Because of this, we find the present value of operating cash flows separately from the present value of the CCA tax shields to determine the net present value of a project.

4. **How do changes in working capital affect project cash flows? LO4**

Increases in **net working capital**, such as accounts receivable or inventory, are investments and, therefore, use cash. That is, they reduce the net cash flow provided by the project in that period. When working capital is run down, cash is freed up, so cash flow increases.

Related Web Links

4pm.com/articles/palette.html An online demonstration that you should try in order to see how good business judgment is used to formulate cash flow projections

acfa-cashflow.com Web site of the American Cash Flow Association, which manages the infrastructure of the cash flow industry in the United States and Canada

acfi-online.com Web site of the American Cash Flow Institute, which provides training on cash flows and income streams

cra-arc.gc.ca Canada Revenue Agency Web site; provides tax information including information on CCA regulations and rates

irs.ustreas.gov/businesses/index.html Web Site maintained by the U.S. Internal Revenue Service; provides tax information for businesses from the U.S. standpoint

Key Terms

asset class	312	depreciation tax shield	309	recaptured depreciation	314
capital cost allowance (CCA)	311	half-year rule	313	straight-line depreciation	313
CCA tax shield	311	net working capital	304	terminal loss	314
declining balance depreciation	313	opportunity cost	304	undepreciated capital cost (UCC)	311

Questions and Problems

connect™ Practise and learn online with *Connect*. Questions with online Excel templates or datasets are marked with .

*Answers in Appendix B

BASIC

1. **Cash Flows.** A new project will generate sales of $74 million, costs of $42 million, and depreciation expense of $10 million in the coming year. The firm's tax rate is 35 percent. Calculate cash flows for the year using all three methods discussed in the chapter and confirm that they are equal. (LO2)

2. **Cash Flows.** Canyon Tours showed the following components of working capital last year: (LO2)

	Beginning	End of Year
Accounts receivable	$24,000	$22,500
Inventory	12,000	13,000
Accounts payable	14,500	16,500

a. What was the change in net working capital during the year?

b. If sales were $36,000 and costs were $24,000, what was cash flow for the year? Ignore taxes.

*3. **Cash Flows.** Tubby Toys estimates that its new line of rubber ducks will generate sales of $7 million, operating costs of $4 million, and a depreciation expense of $1 million. If the tax rate is 40 percent, what is the firm's operating cash flow? Show that you get the same answer using all three methods to calculate operating cash flow. (LO2)

4. **Cash Flows.** We've emphasized that the firm should pay attention only to cash flows when assessing the net present value of proposed projects. Depreciation is a non-cash expense. Why then does it matter whether we assume straight-line depreciation or declining balance CCA depreciation when we assess project NPV? (LO3)

*5. **Proper Cash Flows.** Quick Computing currently sells 10 million computer chips every year at $20 per chip. It is about to introduce a new chip, and it forecasts annual sales of 12 million of these improved chips at a price of $25 each. However, demand for the old chip will decrease and sales of the old chip are expected to fall to 3 million per year. The old chip costs $6 each to manufacture, and the new ones will cost $8 each. What is the proper cash flow to use to evaluate the present value of the introduction of the new chip? (LO1)

6. **Calculating Net Income.** The owner of a bicycle repair shop forecasts revenues of $160,000 a year. Variable costs will be $45,000, and rental costs for the shop are $35,000 a year. Depreciation on the repair tools will be

$10,000. Prepare an income statement for the shop based on these estimates. The tax rate is 35 percent. (LO2)

7. **Cash Flows.** Calculate the operating cash flow for the repair shop in the previous problem using all three methods suggested in the chapter: (a) net income plus depreciation; (b) cash inflow/cash outflow analysis; and (c) the depreciation tax shield approach. Confirm that all three approaches result in the same value for cash flow. (LO2)

*8. **Cash Flows and Working Capital.** A house-painting business had revenues of $16,000 and expenses of $9,000. There were no depreciation expenses. However, the business reported the following changes in various components of working capital:

	Beginning	End
Accounts receivable	$1,200	$4,500
Accounts payable	600	200

Calculate net cash flow for the business for this period. (LO4)

9. **Incremental Cash Flows.** A corporation donates a valuable painting from its private collection to an art museum. Which of the following are incremental cash flows associated with the donation? (LO1)
   a. The price the firm paid for the painting
   b. The current market value of the painting
   c. The deduction from income that it declares for its charitable gift
   d. The reduction in taxes due to its declared tax deduction

*10. **Operating Cash Flows.** Laurel's Lawn Care, Ltd., has a new mower line that can generate revenues of $120,000 per year. Direct production costs are $40,000 and the fixed costs of maintaining the lawn mower factory are $15,000 a year. The factory originally cost $1 million and is included in an asset class with a CCA rate of 5 percent. Calculate the operating cash flows of the project for the next 6 years if the firm's tax bracket is 35 percent. (LO2)

INTERMEDIATE

*11. **Operating Cash Flows.** Talia's Tutus bought some equipment for a data network for $40,000 that will be depreciated in asset Class 46, which has a CCA rate of 30 percent. This firm's tax bracket is 35 percent. (LO2)
   a. Find the CCA amount each year for the next three years.
   b. If the equipment is sold after 3 years for $20,000, what will be the after-tax proceeds on the sale if the firm's tax bracket is 35 percent? Assume that Talia's Tutus has other assets in Class 46.
   c. Now rework your calculations assuming that Talia's Tutus has no other assets in Class 46 and the asset class will be terminated upon the sale of the equipment in year 3.

12. **Proper Cash Flows.** Conference Services Inc. has leased a large office building for $4 million per year. The building is larger than the company needs: two of the building's eight stories are almost empty. A manager wants to expand one of her projects, but this will require using one of the empty floors. In calculating the net present value of the proposed expansion, upper management allocates one-eighth of $4 million of building rental costs (that is, $.5 million) to the project expansion, reasoning that the project will use one-eighth of the building's capacity. (LO1)
   a. Is this a reasonable procedure for the purposes of calculating NPV?
   b. Can you suggest a better way to assess the cost of the office space used by the project?

13. **Cash Flows and Working Capital.** A firm had net income last year of $1.2 million. Its depreciation expenses were $.5 million, and its total cash flow was $1.2 million. What happened to net working capital during the year? (LO4)

14. **Cash Flows and Working Capital.** The only capital investment required for a small project is investment in inventory. Profits this year were $10,000, and inventory increased from $4,000 to $5,000. What was the cash flow from the project? (LO4)

15. **Cash Flows and Working Capital.** A firm's balance sheets for year-ends 2009 and 2010 contain the following data. What happened to investment in net working capital during 2008? All items are in millions of dollars. (LO4)

	Dec. 31, 2009	Dec. 31, 2010
Accounts receivable	32	35
Inventories	25	30
Accounts payable	12	25

*16. **Salvage Value.** Quick Computing (from problem 5) installed its previous generation of computer chip manufacturing equipment three years ago. Some of that older equipment will become unnecessary when the company goes into production of its new product. The obsolete equipment, which originally cost $40 million, has been depreciated straight-line over an assumed tax life of 5 years, but it can now be sold for $18 million. The firm's tax rate is 35 percent. What is the after-tax cash flow from the sale of the equipment? (LO2)

17. **Salvage Value.** Your firm purchased machinery for $10 million. The machinery falls into an asset class that has a CCA rate of 25 percent. The project will end after

five years. If the equipment can be sold for $4 million at the completion of the project and your firm's tax rate is 35 percent, what is the after-tax cash flow from the sale of the machinery? Assume that the firm has no other assets in the class, and that the asset class will be terminated upon the sale of the machinery. (LO2)

*18. **CCA, Depreciation, and Project Value.** Bottoms Up Diaper Service is considering the purchase of a new industrial washer. It can purchase the washer for $6,000 and sell its old washer for $2,000. The new washer will last for 6 years and save $1,500 a year in expenses. If the old washer is retained, it will also last for 6 more years after which it will have to be junked. The washers fall into an asset class with a CCA rate of 30 percent. Bottoms Up owns other washing machines that also fall into this asset class. The opportunity cost of capital is 15 percent, and the firm's tax rate is 40 percent. (LO3)
   a. If the salvage value of the washer is expected to be zero at the end of its six-year life, what are the cash flows of the project in years 0 to 6?
   b. What is the project NPV?
   c. What will the NPV and IRR be if the firm uses straight-line depreciation with a 6-year tax life?

19. **Equivalent Annual Cost.** What is the equivalent annual cost of the washer in the previous problem if the firm uses straight-line depreciation? (LO2)

20. **Cash Flows and NPV.** Johnny's Lunches is considering purchasing a new, energy-efficient grill. The grill will cost $20,000 and will be depreciated in an asset class that carries a CCA rate of 30 percent. It will be sold for scrap metal after 3 years for $5,000. The grill will have no effect on revenues but will save Johnny's $10,000 in energy expenses. The firm has other assets in this asset class. The tax rate is 35 percent. (LO2)
   a. What are the operating cash flows in years 1 to 3?
   b. What are total cash flows in years 1 to 3?
   c. If the discount rate is 12 percent, should the grill be purchased?

21. **Project Evaluation.** Revenues generated by a new fad product are forecast as follows:

Year	Revenues
1	$40,000
2	30,000
3	20,000
4	10,000
Thereafter	0

Expenses are expected to be 40 percent of revenues, and working capital required in each year is expected to be 20 percent of revenues in the following year. The product requires an immediate investment of $50,000 in plant and equipment. (LO2)
   a. What is the initial investment in the product? Remember working capital.
   b. If the plant and equipment are in an asset class that has a CCA rate of 25 percent, and the firm's tax rate is 40 percent, what are the project cash flows in each year?
   c. If the opportunity cost of capital is 10 percent, what is the project NPV?

22. **Buy Versus Lease.** You can buy a car for $25,000 and sell it in 5 years for $5,000, or you can lease the car for 5 years for $5,000 a year. The discount rate is 10 percent per year. (LO2)
   a. Which option do you prefer?
   b. What is the maximum amount you should be willing to pay to lease rather than buy the car?

*23. **Project Evaluation.** Kinky Copies may buy a high-volume copier. The machine costs $100,000 and will be depreciated straight-line over 5 years to a salvage value of $20,000. Kinky anticipates that the machine can be sold in 5 years for $30,000. The machine will save $20,000 a year in labour costs but will require an increase in working capital, mainly paper supplies, of $10,000. The firm's marginal tax rate is 35 percent. Ignore the CCA system and assume that the straight-line depreciation method adopted by Kinky Copies will suffice for tax purposes. Should Kinky buy the machine? The discount rate is 8 percent. (LO2)

24. **Project Evaluation.** Fireplaces Etc. is about to launch a new range of wood stoves, priced at $110 per unit. The unit cost of the wood stoves is $65. The firm expects to sell the wood stoves over the next five years. The venture will require an initial investment in plant and equipment of $25,000. Assume that the investment will be in an asset class with a CCA rate of 15 percent. At the end of 5 years, the plant and equipment will have a zero salvage value, but Fireplaces Etc. will continue to have other assets in this asset class. Sales projections for the wood stoves are as follows:

Year	Unit Sales
1	300
2	350
3	400
4	500
5	500

The net working capital requirement (including the initial working capital needed in year 0) is expected to be 20 percent of the following year's sales. The firm's tax rate is 35 percent. Using a discount rate of 15 percent, calculate the net present value of the project. (LO4)

*25. **Project Evaluation.** Blooper Industries must replace its magnoosium purification system. Quick & Dirty Systems sells a relatively cheap purification system for $10 million. The system will last 5 years. Do-It-Right sells a sturdier but more expensive system for $12 million; it will last for 8 years. Both systems entail $1 million in operating costs; both will be depreciated in an asset class that has a CCA rate of 30 percent; neither will have any salvage value at the end of its life. The firm's tax rate is 35 percent, and the discount rate is 12 percent. Which system should Blooper install? (LO2)

26. **Project Evaluation.** The following table presents sales forecasts for Golden Gelt Giftware. The unit price is $40. The unit cost of the giftware is $25.

Year	Unit Sales
1	22,000
2	30,000
3	14,000
4	5,000
Thereafter	0

It is expected that net working capital will amount to 25 percent of sales in the following year. For example, the store will need an initial (year 0) investment in working capital of .25 × 22,000 × $40 = $220,000. Plant and equipment necessary to establish the giftware business will require an additional investment of $200,000. This investment will be depreciated in an asset class with a CCA rate of 25 percent. We will assume that the firm has other assets in this asset class. After four years, the equipment will have an economic and book value of zero. The firm's tax rate is 35 percent. The discount rate is 20 percent. What is the net present value of the project? (LO4)

*27. **Project Evaluation.** Ilana Industries, Inc., needs a new lathe. It can buy a new high-speed lathe for $1 million. The lathe will cost $35,000 to run, will save the firm $125,000 in labour costs, and will be useful for 10 years. Suppose that for tax purposes, the lathe will be in an asset class with a CCA rate of 25 percent. Ilana has many other assets in this asset class. The lathe is expected to have a 10-year life with a salvage value of $100,000. The actual market value of the lathe at that time will also be $100,000. The discount rate is 10 percent and the corporate tax rate is 35 percent. What is the NPV of buying the new lathe? (LO2)

28. **Internet.** Go to the Canada Revenue Agency Web site at **www.cra-arc.gc.ca/menu-eng.html** and try to get to relevant documents describing the Capital Cost Allowance system. One quick way is to do a search on the site on the keywords "Capital Cost Allowance." Read the prescribed rules and regulations that govern capital cost allowance. How many asset classes are there? What are the minimum and maximum eligible CCA rates? Most asset classes have declining balance rates. Can you identify the asset classes that involve straight-line computation? Why do you think the rate structure is not declining balance for these asset classes? (LO3)

29. **Internet.** Go to the Investors Relations section of the Rogers Communications site, **www.rogers.com**. From the annual reports find the net capital expenditures, capital expenditures less sales of plant and equipment, and total sales for the last three years. What were the ratios of net capital expenditure to sales for the past 3 years? What were the sales and net capital expenditures relative to total assets? Did the company make an investment or disinvestment in working capital in each of the 3 years? (LO4)

CHALLENGE

30. **Project Evaluation.** The efficiency gains resulting from a just-in-time inventory management system will allow a firm to reduce its level of inventories permanently by $250,000. What is the most the firm should be willing to pay for installing the system? (LO4)

31. **Project Evaluation.** You are considering investing in a new line of entertainment products. The project has an estimated economic life of 5 years. You anticipate some immediate startup costs amounting to $25,000. In addition, you will be investing $100,000 in new plant and equipment. Assume, for tax purposes, that the machinery and equipment will be depreciated straight-line over its economic life. Also assume that the initial startup costs are fully tax-deductible.

In the first year of operation you are anticipating sales revenues of $60,000. These revenues are expected to grow by 5 percent per year until year 4; however, the revenues are expected to decline by 5 percent in the fifth year. First-year operating costs will be $10,000; in subsequent years, these are expected to grow in proportion to sales revenues. The tax rate applicable to your business will be 34 percent. Also, at the end of the project's economic life, your plant and equipment will not have any salvage value. Your cost of capital is 12 percent.

Assuming that you will be able to expense the project's startup costs,

a. Calculate its payback period, discounted payback period, internal rate of return, net present value, and profitability index. (LO2)
b. Using the net present value and internal rate of return criteria, do you think it is worthwhile for you to pursue this project? Explain your answer. (LO2)
c. Now, assume that for CCA purposes, your plant and equipment belong to asset Class 39. which carries a CCA rate of 25 percent. Recompute the project's net

present value, assuming that you have other assets in asset Class 39 that will be continued even after the economic life of this project is over. Work out your calculations separately assuming (1) a zero salvage value and (2) a $10,000 salvage value, at the end of the project's economic life. Would you pursue the project under these new conditions? Explain your answer. (LO3)

*32. **Project Evaluation.** Better Mousetraps has developed a new trap. It can go into production for an initial investment in equipment of $6 million. The equipment will be depreciated straight-line over 5 years to a value of zero, but in fact it can be sold after 5 years for $500,000. The firm believes that working capital at each date must be maintained at a level of 10 percent of next year's forecast sales. The firm estimates production costs equal to $1.50 per trap and believes that the traps can be sold for $4 each. Sales forecasts are given in the following table. The project will come to an end in 5 years, when the trap becomes technologically obsolete. The firm's tax bracket is 35 percent, and the required rate of return on the project is 12 percent. What is project NPV? (LO2)

Year:	0	1	2	3	4	5	Thereafter
Sales (millions of traps)	0	.5	.6	1.0	1.0	.6	0

33. **Working Capital Management.** Return to the previous problem. Suppose the firm can cut its requirements for working capital in half by using better inventory control systems. By how much will this increase project NPV? (LO4)

34. **Project Evaluation.** PC Shopping Network may upgrade its modem pool. It last upgraded 2 years ago, when it spent $115 million on equipment with an assumed life of 5 years and an assumed salvage value of $15 million for tax purposes. The firm uses straight-line depreciation. The old equipment can be sold today for $80 million. A new modem pool can be installed today for $150 million. This will have a 3-year life, and will be depreciated to zero using straight-line depreciation. The new equipment will enable the firm to increase sales by $25 million per year and decrease operating costs by $10 million per year. At the end of 3 years, the new equipment will be worthless. Assume the firm's tax rate is 35 percent and the discount rate for projects of this sort is 12 percent.
   a. What is the net cash flow at time 0 if the old equipment is replaced? (LO2)
   b. What are the incremental cash flows in years 1, 2, and 3? (LO2)
   *c. What are the NPV and IRR of the replacement project? (LO2)
   *d. Now ignore straight-line depreciation and assume that both new and old equipment are in an asset class with a CCA rate of 30 percent. PC Shopping Network has other assets in this asset class. What is the NPV of the replacement project? For this part, assume that the new equipment will have a salvage value of $30 million at the end of 3 years. (LO3)

35. **Integrative.** You are exploring the possibility of starting a project involving production of an assortment of spicy curried pickles. You had approached a marketing consultant to conduct market research and do a one-year feasibility study for $25,000. The recommendations of the study are positive, and you have decided to begin work on the project. You expect the life of the project to be 6 years. (LO1, LO2, LO3, LO4)

   The initial investment in the project is expected to be as follows:

   - Land: $150,000
   - Buildings: $350,000
   - Manufacturing equipment: $250,000
   - Net working capital: $40,000

   For CCA computation, the buildings belong to asset Class 1 and the manufacturing equipment is in Class 39, with applicable CCA rates of 4 percent and 25 percent, respectively. At the end of the project's economic life, you expect to be able to sell the buildings and land for $450,000 (the value of the land is expected to remain unchanged). The manufacturing equipment is, however, expected to have a salvage value of only $125,000. Net working capital requirements for each year are expected to increase by 10 percent from the previous year. Your business will be taxed at 35 percent.

   In the first year, you expect to sell 30,000 units of the gourmet pickles in bottled jars. In each subsequent year, unit sales are expected to increase by 4 percent. You have decided to price the pickles at $8.50 for each jar in the first year. You intend to adjust the price in subsequent years to keep up with inflation, which you expect to be about 1.5 percent per year over the life of the project. Variable costs are expected to be $16,000 in the first year and are expected to grow in proportion to sales in each subsequent year. Fixed costs are estimated at $40,000 per year.

   On the basis of your estimates of the cost of financing the project, you have decided that the appropriate discount rate to evaluate the project's cash flows should be 12 percent. Conduct an NPV analysis to determine whether your decision to go ahead with the project is correct.

36. **Project Evaluation.** Virtual Printing Inc. has devised a new technology based on which it plans to launch a new line of print media products. The firm intends to spend $160,000 in new plant and equipment and $40,000 in expanding its building facilities to house the project.

The project has an estimated economic life of eight years. Assume, for tax purposes, that the machinery and equipment and building will be depreciated straight-line over its economic life.

In the first year of operation, Virtual Printing expects to generate sales revenues of $60,000. These revenues are expected to stay at the same level until year 3, but they are subsequently expected to grow by 10 percent annually until year 6, after which the revenues are expected to decline by 5 percent per year. First-year operating costs will be $15,000; in subsequent years, these are expected to grow in proportion to sales revenues. The tax rate applicable to Virtual Printing's business will be 34 percent. Also, at the end of the project's economic life, the plant and equipment will not have any salvage value. The expanded building facilities also cannot be sold, leased, or rented to another business entity without compromising the firm's existing operations. Virtual Printing's cost of capital is 12 percent.

a. Should Virtual Printing's finance manager recommend accepting the project if the firm's objective is to accept projects only when they are worth more than their cost? (LO2)
b. Explain your answer to part (a) above. What technique did you use in that answer? (LO2)
c. By what time frame can Virtual Printing expect to recover its initial investment in the project: (1) ignoring the time value of money and (2) taking into account the time value of money? Name the techniques you have used for your computation. What are the benefits and drawbacks to these techniques? (LO2)
d. What is the IRR for this project? (LO2)
e. Now, assume that for CCA purposes the plant and equipment actually belong to Class 39 and the buildings belong to Class 1, with applicable CCA rates of 25 percent and 4 percent, respectively. Recompute the project's net present value, assuming that Virtual Printing has other assets in both asset classes that will be continued even after the economic life of this project is over. Work out your calculations assuming a zero salvage value for the building expansion and a $10,000 salvage value for the plant and equipment, at the end of the project's economic life. Would you pursue the project under these new conditions? Explain your answer. (LO3)

Solutions to Check Points

9.1 Remember, discount cash flows, not profits. Each tewgit machine costs $250,000 right away; recognize that outlay, but forget accounting depreciation. Cash flows per machine are as in the table below.

Year:	0	1	2	3	4	5
Investment (outflow)	−250,000					
Sales		250,000	300,000	300,000	250,000	250,000
Operating expenses		−200,000	−200,000	−200,000	−200,000	−200,000
Cash flow	−250,000	+ 50,000	+100,000	+100,000	+ 50,000	+ 50,000

Each machine is forecast to generate $50,000 of cash flow in years 4 and 5. Thus it makes sense to keep operating for five years.

9.2 a. b. The site and buildings could have been sold or put to another use. Their values are opportunity costs, which should be treated as incremental cash outflows.
c. Demolition costs are incremental cash outflows.
d. The cost of the access road is sunk and not incremental.
e. Lost cash flows from other projects are incremental cash outflows.
f. Depreciation is not a cash expense and should not be included, except as it affects taxes. (Taxes are discussed later in this chapter.)

9.3 Actual health costs will be increasing at about 7 percent a year.

Year:	1	2	3	4
Cost per worker	$2,400	$2,568	$2,748	$2,940

The present value at 10 percent is $9,214 if the first payment is made immediately. If it is delayed a year, present value falls to $8,377.

9.4 The tax rate is $T = 35$ percent. Taxes paid will be

$$T \times (\text{revenue} - \text{expenses} - \text{depreciation}) = .35 \times (600 - 300 - 200) = \$35$$

Operating cash flow can be calculated as follows.

a. Revenue − expenses − taxes = 600 − 300 − 35 = \$265

b. Net profit + depreciation = (600 − 300 − 200 − 35) + 200 = 65 + 200 = \$265

c. (Revenues − cash expenses) × (1 − tax rate) + (depreciation × tax rate) = (600 − 300) × (1 − .35) + (200 × .35) = \$265

9.5

	Year 1	Year 2
Beginning UCC	—	\$166,500
Net acquisition	\$180,000	(25,000)
CCA	13,500	21,225
Ending UCC	166,500	120,275

Calculations:

Year 1: CCA = \$180,000 × .5 × .15 = \$13,500

Year 2: Adjusted cost of disposal = \$100,000 + 75,000 = \$175,000

Net acquisition = total cost of additions − adjusted cost of disposal = \$150,000 − \$175,000 = −\$25,000

CCA = \$141,500 × .15 = \$21,225

Ending UCC = \$141,500 − \$21,225 = \$120,275

9.6 Adjusted cost of disposal = \$65,000 + \$70,000 = \$135,000. UCC is reduced by this amount to \$144,500 − \$135,000 = \$9,500. If the firm has no other assets in Class 10, then the asset pool will be terminated, and the amount of \$9,500 will be treated as a terminal loss.

9.7 a.

	(All figures in dollars)					
Year:	0	1	2	3	4	5
1. Capital investment	−5,000					
2. Revenues		3,000	3,000	3,000	3,000	3,000
3. Expenses		1,500	1,500	1,500	1,500	1,500
4. Profit before tax (2 − 3)		1,500	1,500	1,500	1,500	1,500
5. Tax at 35%		525	525	525	525	525
6. Operating cash flow excluding CCA tax shield (4 − 5)		975	975	975	975	975
7. UCC		4,625	3,931	3,341	2,840	2,414
8. CCA		375	694	590	501	426
9. CCA tax shield (.35 × 8)		131	243	207	175	149
10. Total yearly cash flows including CCA tax shield (1 + 6 + 9)	−5,000	1,106	1,218	1,182	1,150	1,124

Notice that the amounts in row 10 do not reflect all cash flows, since there remains a UCC balance of \$2,414 in year 5, which should continue to provide CCA tax shields beyond year 5 if there are other assets in the asset class.

b. If depreciation is on a straight-line basis over 5 years, we would change items 8, 9, and 10 of the table in part (a) above as follows:

	(All figures in dollars)					
Year:	0	1	2	3	4	5
8. Depreciation		1,000	1,000	1,000	1,000	1,000
9. Depreciation tax shield (.35 × 8)		350	350	350	350	350
10. Total yearly cash flows including depreciation tax shield (1 + 6 + 9)	−5,000	1,325	1,325	1,325	1,325	1,325

MINI CASE

Jack Tar, CFO of Sheetbend & Halyard, Inc., opened the company confidential envelope. It contained a draft of a competitive bid for a contract to supply duffel canvas to the Canadian Armed Forces. The cover memo from Sheetbend's CEO asked Mr. Tar to review the bid before it was submitted.

The bid and its supporting documents had been prepared by Sheetbend's sales staff. It called for Sheetbend to supply 100,000 yards of duffel canvas per year for 5 years. The proposed selling price was fixed at $30 per yard.

Mr. Tar was not usually involved in sales, but this bid was unusual in at least two respects. First, if accepted by the forces, it would commit Sheetbend to a fixed-price, long-term contract. Second, producing the duffel canvas would require an investment of $1.5 million to purchase machinery and to refurbish Sheetbend's plant in Saint John, New Brunswick.

Mr. Tar set to work and by the end of the week had collected the following facts and assumptions:

- The plant in Saint John was built in the early 1900s and is now idle. The plant was fully depreciated on Sheetbend's books, except for the purchase cost of the land (in 1947) of $10,000.
- Now that the land was valuable shorefront property, Mr. Tar thought the land and the idle plant could be sold, immediately or in the future, for $600,000.
- Refurbishing the plant would cost $500,000. This investment would be depreciated for tax purposes in an asset class that has a CCA rate of 5 percent.
- The new machinery would cost $1 million. This investment could be depreciated in an asset class that has a CCA rate of 30 percent.
- The refurbished plant and new machinery would last for many years. However, the remaining market for duffel canvas was small, and it was not clear that additional orders could be obtained once the Forces contract was finished. The machinery was custom-built and could be used only for duffel canvas. Its second-hand value at the end of five years was probably zero.
- Table 9.11 shows the sales staff's forecasts of income from the navy contract. Mr. Tar reviewed this forecast and decided that its assumptions were reasonable, except that the forecast used book, not tax, depreciation.
- But the forecast income statement contained no mention of working capital. Mr. Tar thought that working capital would average about 10 percent of sales.

Armed with this information, Mr. Tar constructed a spreadsheet to calculate the NPV of the duffel canvas project, assuming that Sheetbend's bid would be accepted by the Forces.

He had just finished debugging the spreadsheet when another confidential envelope arrived from Sheetbend's CEO. It contained a firm offer from a New Brunswick real estate developer to purchase Sheetbend's Saint John land and plant for $1.5 million in cash.

Should Mr. Tar recommend submitting the bid to the Forces at the proposed price of $30 per yard? The discount rate for this project is 12 percent.

TABLE 9.11
Forecast income statement for the navy duffel canvas project (dollar figures in thousands, except price per yard).

Year:	1	2	3	4	5
1. Yards sold	100.00	100.00	100.00	100.00	100.00
2. Price per yard	30.00	30.00	30.00	30.00	30.00
3. Revenue (1 × 2)	3,000.00	3,000.00	3,000.00	3,000.00	3,000.00
4. Cost of goods sold	2,100.00	2,184.00	2,271.36	2,362.21	2,456.70
5. Operating cash flow (3 − 4)	900.00	816.00	728.64	637.79	543.30
6. Depreciation	250.00	250.00	250.00	250.00	250.00
7. Income (5 − 6)	650.00	566.00	478.64	387.79	293.30
8. Tax at 35%	227.50	198.10	167.52	135.73	102.66
9. Net income (7 − 8)	$ 422.50	$ 367.90	$ 311.12	$ 252.06	$ 190.64

Notes:
1. Yards sold and price per yard would be fixed by contract.
2. Cost of goods includes fixed cost of $300,000 per year plus variable costs of $18 per yard. Costs are expected to increase at the inflation rate of 4 percent per year.
3. Depreciation: A $1 million investment in machinery is depreciated straight-line over 5 years ($200,000 per year). The $500,000 cost of refurbishing the Saint John plant is depreciated straight-line over 10 years ($50,000 per year).

PART 2

Value

5 The Time Value of Money
6 Valuing Bonds
7 Valuing Stocks
8 Net Present Value and Other Investment Criteria
9 Using Discounted Cash Flow Analysis to Make Investment Decisions
10 Project Analysis
10.1 How Firms Organize the Investment Process
10.2 Some "What If" Questions
10.3 Break-Even Analysis
10.4 Real Options and the Value of Flexibility
10.5 Summary

CHAPTER 10

Project Analysis

LEARNING OBJECTIVES

After studying this chapter, you should be able to:

LO1 Describe the practical problems of capital budgeting in large corporations.

LO2 Use sensitivity, scenario, and break-even analyses to see how project profitability would be affected by an error in your forecasts.

LO3 Explain why an overestimate of sales is more serious for projects with high operating leverage.

LO4 Recognize the importance of managerial flexibility in capital budgeting.

When understanding capital investments, good managers try to keep maximum flexibility.

© Mark Andersen/Getty Images.

It helps to use discounted cash-flow techniques to value new projects, but good investment decisions also require good data. Therefore, we start this chapter by thinking about how firms organize the capital budgeting operation to get the kind of information they need. In addition, we look at how they try to ensure that everyone involved works together toward a common goal.

Project evaluation should never be a mechanical exercise in which the financial manager takes a set of cash-flow forecasts and cranks out a net present value. Cash-flow estimates are just that—estimates. Financial managers need to look behind the forecasts to try to understand what makes the project tick and what might go wrong with it. A number of techniques have been developed to help managers identify the key assumptions in their analysis. These techniques involve asking a number of "what if" questions. What if your market share turns out to be higher or lower than you forecast? What if interest rates rise during the life of the project? In the second part of this chapter we show how managers use the techniques of sensitivity analysis, scenario analysis, and break-even analysis to help answer these "what if" questions.

Books about capital budgeting sometimes create the impression that once the manager has made an investment decision, there is nothing to do but sit back and watch the cash flows develop. But since cash flows rarely proceed as anticipated, companies constantly need to modify their operations. If cash flows are better than anticipated, the project may be expanded; if they are worse, it may be scaled back or abandoned altogether. In the third section of this chapter we describe how good managers take account of these options when they analyze a project and why they are willing to pay money today to build in future flexibility.

LO1 10.1 HOW FIRMS ORGANIZE THE INVESTMENT PROCESS

In the previous chapter you learned how to evaluate a proposed investment such as the Blooper project. But potential projects and accurate cash-flow forecasts don't fall from the sky. Promising investment opportunities have to be identified, and they have to fit in with the firm's strategic goals. To evaluate these opportunities properly, financial managers need unbiased cash-flow forecasts that have not been skewed to "sell" a project to upper management. Large firms in particular need to establish systems that facilitate effective communication across different parts of the organization.

For most sizable firms, investments are evaluated in two separate stages.

STAGE 1: THE CAPITAL BUDGET

capital budget List of planned investment projects.

Once a year, the head office generally asks each of its divisions and plants to provide a list of the investments that they would like to make.[1] These are gathered into a proposed **capital budget**.

This budget is then reviewed and pruned by senior management and other staff specializing in planning and financial analysis. Usually there are negotiations between the firm's senior management and its divisional management, and there may also be special analyses of major outlays or ventures into new areas. Once the budget has been approved, it generally remains the basis for planning over the ensuing year.

Many investment proposals bubble up from the bottom of the organization. But sometimes the ideas are likely to come from higher up. For example, the managers of plants A and B cannot be expected to see the potential benefits of closing their plants and consolidating production at a new plant C. We expect divisional management to propose plant C. Similarly, divisions 1 and 2 may not be eager to give up their own data processing operations to a large central computer. That proposal would come from senior management.

Senior management's concern is to see that the capital budget matches the firm's strategic plans. It needs to ensure that the firm is concentrating its efforts in areas where it has a real competitive advantage. As part of this effort, management must also identify declining businesses that should be sold or allowed to run down.

The firm's capital investment choices should reflect both "bottom-up" and "top-down" processes—capital budgeting and strategic planning, respectively. The two processes should complement each other. Plant and division managers, who do most of the work in bottom-up capital budgeting, may not see the forest for the trees. Strategic planners may have a mistaken view of the forest because they do not look at the trees.

STAGE 2: PROJECT AUTHORIZATIONS

The annual budget is important because it allows everybody to exchange ideas before attitudes have hardened and personal commitments have been made. However, the fact that your pet project has been included in the annual budget doesn't mean you have permission to go ahead with it. At a later stage you will need to draw up a detailed proposal describing particulars of the project, engineering analyses, cash-flow forecasts, and present value calculations. If your project is large, this proposal may have to pass a number of hurdles before it is finally approved.

The type of backup information that you need to provide depends on the project category. For example, some firms use a fourfold breakdown:

1. *Outlays required by law or company policy; for example, for pollution control equipment.* These outlays do not need to be justified on financial grounds. The main issue is whether requirements are satisfied at the lowest possible cost. The decision is therefore likely to hinge on engineering analyses of alternative technologies.
2. *Maintenance or cost reduction, such as machine replacement.* Engineering analysis is also important in machine replacement, but new machines have to pay their own way. In this category of the proposal the firm faces the classical capital budgeting problems described in Chapters 8 and 9.
3. *Capacity expansion in existing businesses.* Projects in this category are less straightforward; these decisions may hinge on forecasts of demand, possible shifts in technology, and the reactions of competitors.

[1] Large firms may be divided into several divisions. For example, International Paper has divisions that specialize in printing paper, packaging, specialty products, and forest products. Each of these divisions may be responsible for a number of plants.

4. *Investment for new products.* Projects in this category are most likely to depend on strategic decisions. The first projects in a new area may not have positive NPVs if considered in isolation, but they may give the firm a valuable option to undertake follow-up projects. More about this later in the chapter.

PROBLEMS AND SOME SOLUTIONS

Valuing capital investment opportunities is hard enough when you can do the entire job yourself. In most firms, however, capital budgeting is a cooperative effort, and this brings with it some challenges.

Ensuring That Forecasts Are Consistent. Inconsistent assumptions often creep into investment proposals. For example, suppose that the manager of the furniture division is bullish (optimistic) on housing starts but the manager of the appliance division is bearish (pessimistic). This inconsistency makes the projects proposed by the furniture division look more attractive than those of the appliance division.

To ensure consistency, many firms begin the capital budgeting process by establishing forecasts of economic indicators, such as inflation and the growth in national income, as well as forecasts of particular items that are important to the firm's business, such as housing starts or the price of raw materials. These forecasts can then be used as the basis for all project analyses.

Eliminating Conflicts of Interest. In Chapter 1 we pointed out that while managers want to do a good job, they are also concerned about their own futures. If the interests of managers conflict with those of shareholders, the result is likely to be poor investment decisions. For example, new plant managers naturally want to demonstrate good performance right away. To this end, they might propose quick-payback projects even if NPV is sacrificed. Unfortunately, many firms measure performance and reward managers in ways that encourage such behaviour. If the firm always demands quick results, it is unlikely that plant managers will concentrate only on NPV.

Reducing Forecast Bias. Someone who is keen to get a project proposal accepted is also likely to look on the bright side when forecasting the project's cash flows. Such overriding optimism is a common feature in financial forecasts. For example, think of large public expenditure proposals. How often have you heard of a new missile, dam, or highway that actually cost less than was originally forecast? Think back to the Eurotunnel project introduced in Chapter 8. The final cost of the project was about 50 percent higher than initial forecasts. It is probably impossible to ever eliminate bias completely, but if senior management is aware of why bias occurs, it is at least part way to solving the problem.

Project sponsors are likely to overstate their case deliberately only if the head office encourages them to do so. For example, if middle managers believe that success depends on having the largest division rather than the most profitable one, they will propose large expansion projects that they do not believe have the largest possible net present value. Or if divisions must compete for limited resources, they will try to outbid each other for those resources. The fault in such cases is with top management—if lower-level managers are not rewarded based on net present value and contribution to firm value, it should not be surprising that they focus their efforts elsewhere.

Other problems stem from sponsors' eagerness to obtain approval for their favourite projects. As the proposal travels up the organization, alliances are formed. Thus once a division has screened its own plants' proposals, the plants in that division unite in competing against outsiders. The result is that the head office may receive several thousand investment proposals each year, all essentially sales documents presented by united fronts and designed to persuade. The forecasts have been doctored to ensure that NPV appears positive.

Since it is difficult for senior management to evaluate each specific assumption in an investment proposal, capital investment decisions are effectively decentralized whatever the rules say. Some firms accept this; others rely on head office staff to check capital investment proposals.

Sorting the Wheat from the Chaff. Senior managers are continually bombarded with requests for funds for capital expenditures. All these requests are supported with detailed analyses showing that the projects have positive NPVs. How then can managers ensure that only worthwhile projects make the grade? One response of senior managers to the problem of poor information is to impose rigid expenditure limits on individual plants or divisions. These limits force the subunits to choose among projects. The firm ends up using capital rationing, not because capital is unobtainable but as a way of decentralizing decisions.[2]

Senior managers might also ask some searching questions about why the project has a positive NPV. After all, if the project is so attractive, why hasn't someone already undertaken it? Will others copy your idea if it is so profitable? Positive NPVs are plausible only if your company has some competitive advantage.

Such an advantage can arise in several ways. You may be smart enough or lucky enough to be the first to the market with a new or improved product for which customers will pay premium prices. Your competitors eventually will enter the market and squeeze out excess profits, but it may take them several years to do so. Or you may have a proprietary technology or production cost advantage that competitors cannot easily match. You may have a contractual advantage such as the distributorship for a particular region. Or your advantage may be as simple as a good reputation and an established customer list.

Analyzing competitive advantage can also help ferret out projects that incorrectly appear to have a negative NPV. If you are the lowest cost producer of a profitable product in a growing market, then you should invest to expand along with the market. If your calculations show a negative NPV for such an expansion, then you have probably made a mistake.

LO2, 3 10.2 SOME "WHAT IF" QUESTIONS

"What if" questions ask what will happen to a project in various circumstances. For example, what will happen if the economy enters a recession? What if a competitor enters the market? What if costs turn out to be higher than anticipated?

You might wonder why one would bother with these sorts of questions. For instance, suppose your project seems to have a positive NPV based on the best available forecasts that have already factored in the chances of both positive and negative surprises. Won't you commit to this project regardless of possible future surprises? If things later don't work out as you had hoped, that is too bad, but would it have changed any of your decisions?

In fact, what-if analysis is crucial to capital budgeting. First recall that cash-flow estimates are just that—estimates. You often have the opportunity to improve on those estimates if you are willing to commit additional resources to the effort. For example, if you wish to improve the precision of an estimate of the demand for a product, you might conduct additional market research. Or if cost uncertainty is a concern, you might commission additional engineering studies to evaluate the feasibility of a novel production process. But how do you know when to keep sharpening your forecasts or where it is best to devote your efforts? What-if analysis can help identify the inputs that are most worth refining before you commit to a project. These will be the ones that have the greatest potential to alter project NPV.

Moreover, managers don't simply turn a key to start a project and then walk away and let the cash flows roll in. There are always surprises, adjustments, and refinements. What-if analysis alerts managers to where the most likely need for adjustments will arise and where to devote the most effort toward contingency planning. In this section, therefore, we examine some of the standard tools managers use when considering important types of what-if questions.

SENSITIVITY ANALYSIS

sensitivity analysis Analysis of the effects of changes in sales, costs, and so on, on project profitability.

Uncertainty means that more things can happen than *will* happen. Therefore, whenever managers are given a cash flow forecast, they try to determine what else might happen and the implications of those possible events. This is called **sensitivity analysis**.

[2] We discussed capital rationing in Chapter 8.

TABLE 10.1
Cash-flow forecasts for Finefodder's superstore.

	A	B	C	D
1		**Year 0**	**Years 1–12**	**Formula in Column C**
2	Initial investment	−5,400,000		
3	1. Sales		16,000,000	16000000
4	2. Variable costs		13,000,000	=$C$12*C3
5	3. Fixed costs		2,000,000	2000000
6	4. Depreciation		450,000	=−B2/12
7	5. Pretax profit		550,000	=C3−C4−C5−C6
8	6. Taxes (at 40%)		220,000	=0.4*C7
9	7. Profit after tax		330,000	=C7−C8
10	8. Cash flow from operations		780,000	=C6+C9
11				
12	Variable costs as % of sales		0.8125	0.8125
13	Discount rate		8%	0.08
14	12-year annuity factor		7.5361	=(1/Rate)*(1−1 /(1+Rate)^12)
15	Net present value		478,141	=B2+C10*C14

Put yourself in the well-heeled shoes of the financial manager of the Finefodder supermarket chain. Finefodder is considering opening a new superstore in Gravenstein, and your staff members have prepared the figures shown in Table 10.1. The figures are fairly typical for a new supermarket, except that to keep the example simple we have assumed no inflation. We have also assumed that the entire investment can be depreciated straight-line for tax purposes, we have neglected the working capital requirement, and we have ignored the fact that at the end of the 12 years you could sell off the land and buildings.

fixed costs Costs that do not depend on the level of output.

Some of the costs of running a supermarket are fixed. For example, regardless of the level of output, you still have to heat and light the store and pay the store manager. These **fixed costs** are forecast to be $2 million per year.

variable costs Costs that change as the level of output changes.

Other costs vary with the level of sales. In particular, the lower the sales, the less food you need to buy. Also, if sales are lower than forecast, you can operate a lower number of checkouts and reduce the staff needed to restock the shelves. The new superstore's variable costs are estimated at 81.25 percent of sales. Thus **variable costs** = .8125 × $16 million = $13 million (see cells C4 and D4).

The initial investment of $5.4 million will be depreciated on a straight-line basis over the 12-year period, resulting in annual depreciation of $450,000. Profits are taxed at a rate of 40 percent.

Given these inputs, we add after-tax profit plus depreciation to obtain cash flow in periods 1 to 12 of $780,000 (cell C10). As an experienced financial manager, you recognize immediately that these cash flows constitute an annuity, and therefore you calculate the 12-year annuity factor in cell C14. The net present value of the project is calculated in cell C15 as

$$\text{NPV} = -\$5{,}400{,}000 + \$780{,}000 \times \text{12-year annuity factor} = \$478{,}141$$

It appears that the project is in fact viable, with a positive net present value. Before you agree to go ahead, however, you want to delve behind these forecasts and identify the key variables that will determine whether the project succeeds or fails.

You seem to have taken account of the important factors that will determine success or failure, but look out for things you may have forgotten. Perhaps there will be delays in obtaining planning permission, or perhaps you will need to undertake costly landscaping. The greatest dangers often lie in these *unknown* unknowns, or "unk-unks," as scientists call them.

Having found no unk-unks (no doubt you'll find them later), you look at how NPV may be affected if you have made a wrong forecast of sales, costs, and so on. To do this, you first obtain optimistic and pessimistic estimates for the underlying variables. These are set out in the left-hand columns of Table 10.2.

TABLE 10.2 Sensitivity analysis for superstore project.

Variable	Range			NPV		
	Pessimistic	Expected	Optimistic	Pessimistic	Expected	Optimistic
Investment	6,200,000	5,400,000	5,000,000	− 120,897	+478,141	+ 777,660
Sales	14,000,000	16,000,000	18,000,000	−1,217,477	+478,141	+2,173,758
Variable cost as percent of sales	83	81.25	80	− 787,920	+478,141	+1,382,470
Fixed cost	2,100,000	2,000,000	1,900,000	+ 25,976	+478,141	+ 930,306

Next you see what happens to NPV under the optimistic or pessimistic forecasts for each of these variables. You recalculate project NPV under these various forecasts to determine which variables are most critical to NPV.

EXAMPLE 10.1 SENSITIVITY ANALYSIS

The right-hand side of Table 10.2 shows the project's net present value if the variables are set *one at a time* to their optimistic and pessimistic values. For example, suppose fixed costs are $1.9 million rather than the forecast $2 million. To find NPV in this case, we simply substitute $1,900,000 in cell C5 of the spreadsheet, and discover that NPV rises to $930,306—a gain of approximately $452,000. The other entries in the three columns on the right in Table 10.2 similarly show how the NPV of the project changes when each input is changed.

Your project is by no means a sure thing. The principal uncertainties appear to be sales and variable costs. For example, if sales are only $14 million rather than the forecast $16 million (and all other forecasts are unchanged), then the project has an NPV of −$1.217 million. If variable costs are 83 percent of sales (and all other forecasts are unchanged), then the project has an NPV of −$787,920.

Check Point 10.1 Recalculate cash flow as in Table 10.1 if variable costs are 83 percent of sales. Confirm that NPV will be $787,900.

Value of Information. Now that you know the project could be thrown badly off course by a poor estimate of sales, you might like to see whether it is possible to resolve some of this uncertainty. Perhaps your worry is that the store will fail to attract sufficient shoppers from neighbouring towns. In that case, additional survey data and more careful analysis of travel times may be worthwhile.

On the other hand, there is less value to gathering additional information about fixed costs. Because the project is marginally profitable even under pessimistic assumptions about fixed costs, you are unlikely to be in trouble if you have estimated that variable incorrectly.

Limits to Sensitivity Analysis. Your analysis of the forecasts for Finefodder's new superstore is known as a *sensitivity analysis*. Sensitivity analysis expresses cash flows in terms of unknown variables and then calculates the consequences of incorrectly estimating those variables. It forces the manager to identify the underlying factors, indicates where additional information would be most useful, and helps to expose confused or inappropriate forecasts.

Of course, there is no law stating which variables you should consider in your sensitivity analysis. For example, you may wish to look separately at labour costs and the costs of the goods sold. Or, if you are concerned about a possible change in the corporate tax rate, you may wish to look at the effect of such a change on the project's NPV.

One drawback to sensitivity analysis is that it gives somewhat ambiguous results. For example, what exactly do *optimistic* and *pessimistic* mean? One department may be interpreting the terms in a different way from another. Ten years from now, after hundreds of projects, hindsight may show that one department's pessimistic limit was exceeded twice as often as the other's, but hindsight won't help you now while you're making the investment decision.

Another problem with sensitivity analysis is that the underlying variables are likely to be interrelated. For example, if sales exceed expectations, demand will likely be stronger than you anticipated and your profit margins will be wider. Or, if wages are higher than your forecast, both variable costs and fixed costs are likely to be at the upper end of your range.

Because of these connections, you cannot push one-at-a-time sensitivity analysis too far. It is impossible to obtain expected, optimistic, and pessimistic values for total project cash flows from the information in Table 10.2. Still, it does give a sense of which variables should be most closely monitored.

SCENARIO ANALYSIS

scenario analysis Project analysis given a particular combination of assumptions.

When variables are interrelated, managers often find it helpful to look at how their project would fare under different scenarios. **Scenario analysis** allows them to look at different but *consistent* combinations of variables. Forecasters generally prefer to give an estimate of revenues or costs under a particular scenario rather than giving some absolute optimistic or pessimistic value.

EXAMPLE 10.2 SCENARIO ANALYSIS

You are worried that Stop and Scoff may decide to build a new store in nearby Salome. That would reduce sales in your Gravenstein store by 15 percent and you might be forced into a price war to keep the remaining business. Prices might be reduced to the point that variable costs equal 82 percent of revenue. Table 10.3 shows that under this scenario of lower sales and smaller margins your new venture would no longer be worthwhile.

TABLE 10.3
Scenario analysis comparing NPV of superstore with and without competing store.

	A	B	C	D
1			**Cash flows in years 1–12**	
2		**Year 0**	**Base Case**	**Competing Store Scenario**
3	Initial investment	−5,400,000		
4	1. Sales		16,000,000	13,600,000
5	2. Variable costs		13,000,000	11,152,000
6	3. Fixed costs		2,000,000	2,000,000
7	4. Depreciation		450,000	450,000
8	5. Pretax profit		550,000	−2,000
9	6. Taxes (at 40%)		220,000	−800
10	7. Profit after tax		330,000	−1,200
11	8. Cash flow from operations		780,000	448,800
12				
13	Variable costs as % of sales		0.8125	0.8200
14	Discount rate		8%	8%
15	12-year annuity factor		7.5361	7.5361
16	Net present value		478,141	−2,017,808
17				
18	*Assumptions:* Competing store causes (1) a 15 percent decline in sales and (2) variable costs			
19	to increase to 82 percent of sales.			

simulation analysis Estimation of the probabilities of different possible outcomes—for example, from an investment project.

An extension of scenario analysis is called **simulation analysis**. Here, instead of specifying a relatively small number of scenarios, a computer generates several hundred or thousand possible combinations of variables according to probability distributions specified by the analyst. Each combination of variables corresponds to one scenario. Project NPV and other outcomes of interest can be calculated for each combination of variables, and the entire probability distribution of outcomes can be constructed from the simulation results.

Check Point 10.2 What is the basic difference between sensitivity analysis and scenario analysis?

LO2, 3 **10.3**

BREAK-EVEN ANALYSIS

break-even analysis Analysis of the level of sales at which the company breaks even.

When we undertake a sensitivity analysis of a project or when we look at alternative scenarios, we are asking how serious it would be if we misestimated sales or costs. Managers sometimes prefer to rephrase this question and ask how far off the estimates could be before the project begins to lose money. This exercise is known as **break-even analysis**.

For many projects, the make-or-break variable is sales volume. Therefore, managers most often focus on the break-even level of sales. However, you might also look at other variables, for example, at how high costs could be before the project goes into the red.

As it turns out, "losing money" can be defined in more than one way. Most often, the break-even condition is defined in terms of accounting profits. More properly, however, it should be defined in terms of net present value. We will start with accounting break-even, show that it can lead you astray, and then show how NPV break-even can be used as an alternative.

ACCOUNTING BREAK-EVEN ANALYSIS

The *accounting break-even* point is the level of sales at which profits are zero or, equivalently, at which total revenues equal total costs. As we have seen, some costs are fixed regardless of the level of output. Other costs vary with the level of output.

When you first analyzed the superstore project, you came up with the following estimates:

Sales	$16	million
Variable cost	13	million
Fixed costs	2	million
Depreciation	.45	million

Notice that variable costs are 81.25 percent of sales. So, for each additional dollar of sales, costs increase by only $.8125. We can easily determine how much business the superstore needs to attract to avoid losses. If the store sells nothing, the income statement will show fixed costs of $2 million and depreciation of $450,000. Thus there will be a loss of $2.45 million. Each dollar of sales reduces this loss by $1 − $.8125 = $.1875. Therefore, to cover fixed costs plus depreciation, you need sales of 2.45 million/.1875 = $13.067 million. At this sales level, the firm will break even. More generally,

$$\text{Break-even level of revenues} = \frac{\text{fixed costs including depreciation}}{\text{additional profit from each additional dollar of sales}} \tag{10.1}$$

Table 10.4 shows how the income statement looks with only $13.067 million of sales.

TABLE 10.4
Income statement, break-even sales volume.

Item	$000s	
Revenues	13,067	
Variable costs	10,617	(81.25% of sales)
Fixed costs	2,000	
Depreciation	450	
Pretax profit	0	
Taxes	0	
Profit after tax	0	

A project that simply breaks even on an accounting basis gives you your money back but does not cover the opportunity cost of the capital tied up in the project. A project that breaks even in accounting terms will surely have a negative NPV.

Figure 10.1 shows how the break-even point is determined. The 45-degree line shows accounting revenues. The cost line shows how costs vary with sales. If the store doesn't sell a cent, it still incurs fixed costs and depreciation amounting to $2.45 million. Each extra dollar of sales adds $.8125 to these costs. When sales are $13.067 million, the two lines cross, indicating that costs equal revenues. For lower sales, revenues are less than costs and the project is in the red; for higher sales, revenues exceed costs and the project moves into the black.

Is a project that breaks even in accounting terms an acceptable investment? If you are not sure about the answer, this may be an easier question: Would you be happy about an investment in a stock that after five years gave you a total rate of return of zero? We hope not. You might break even on such a stock but a zero return does not compensate you for the time value of money or the risk that you have taken.

Let's check this with the superstore project. Suppose that in each year the store has sales of $13.067 million—just enough to break even on an accounting basis. What would be the cash flow from operations?

$$\text{Cash flow from operations} = \text{profit after tax} + \text{depreciation}$$
$$= 0 + \$450{,}000 = \$450{,}000$$

The initial investment is $5.4 million. In each of the next 12 years, the firm receives a cash flow of $450,000. So the firm gets its money back:

$$\text{Total cash flow from operations} = \text{initial investment}$$
$$12 \times \$450{,}000 = \$5.4 \text{ million}$$

FIGURE 10.1
Accounting break-even analysis.

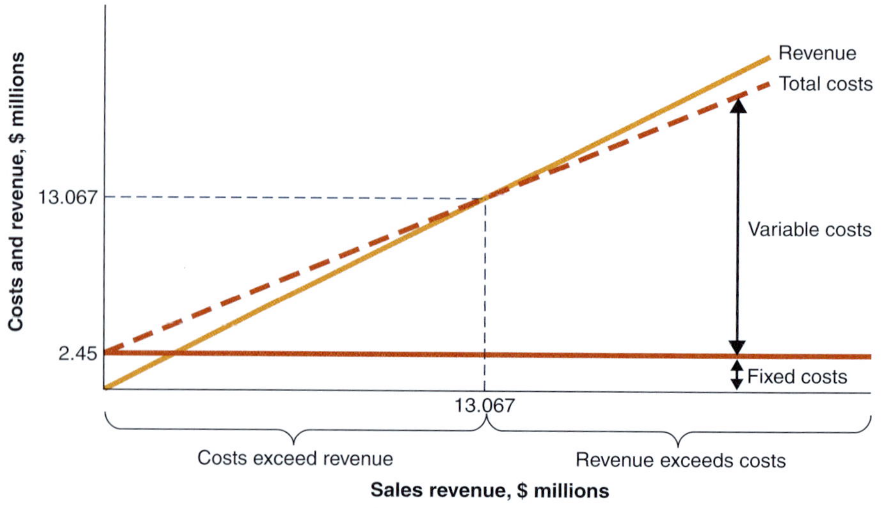

But revenues are not sufficient to repay the opportunity cost of that \$5.4 million investment. NPV is negative.

NPV BREAK-EVEN ANALYSIS

NPV break-even point The level of sales at which NPV is zero.

A manager who calculates an accounting-based measure of break-even may be tempted to think that any project that earns more than this figure will help shareholders. But projects that break even on an accounting basis are really making a loss—they are failing to cover the costs of capital employed. Managers who accept such projects are not helping their shareholders. Therefore, instead of asking what sales must be to produce an accounting profit, it is more useful to focus on the point at which NPV switches from negative to positive. This is called the **NPV break-even point**.

The cash flows of the superstore project in each year will depend on sales as follows:

(1) Variable costs	81.25% of sales
(2) Fixed costs	\$2 million
(3) Depreciation	\$450,000
(4) Pretax profit	$(.1875 \times \text{sales}) - \$2.45$ million
(5) Tax (at 40%)	$.40 \times (.1875 \times \text{sales} - \$2.45$ million)
(6) Profit after tax	$.60 \times (.1875 \times \text{sales} - \$2.45$ million)
(7) Cash flow, (3) + (6)	$\$450{,}000 + .6 \times (.1875 \times \text{sales} - \$2.45$ million) $= .1125 \times \text{sales} - \$1.02$ million

This cash flow will last for 12 years. So to find its present value we multiply by the 12-year annuity factor. With a discount rate of 8 percent, the present value of \$1 a year for each of 12 years is \$7.536. Thus the present value of the cash flows is

$$\text{PV (cash flows)} = 7.536(.1125 \times \text{sales} - \$1.02 \text{ million})$$

The project breaks even in present value terms (that is, has a zero NPV) if the present value of these cash flows is equal to the initial \$5.4 million investment. Therefore, break-even occurs when

$$\begin{aligned} \text{PV(cash flows)} &= \text{investment} \\ 7.536 \times (.1125 \times \text{sales} - \$1.02 \text{ million}) &= \$5.4 \text{ million} \\ .8478 \times \text{sales} - \$7.69 \text{ million} &= \$5.4 \text{ million} \\ \text{Sales} = (5.4 + 7.69)/.8478 &= \$15.4 \text{ million} \end{aligned}$$

Therefore, the store needs sales of \$15.4 million a year for the investment to have a zero NPV. This is more than 18 percent higher than the point at which the project has zero profit.

Figure 10.2 is a plot of the present value of the inflows and outflows from the superstore as a function of annual sales. The two lines cross when sales are \$15.4 million. This is the point at which the project has zero NPV. As long as sales are greater than this, the present value of the inflows exceeds the present value of the outflows and the project has a positive NPV.[3]

Check Point 10.3

What would be the NPV break-even level of sales if the capital investment was only \$5 million?

[3] Think back to our discussion of economic value added (EVA) in Chapter 4. A project that breaks even on a present value basis will have a positive accounting profit but zero economic value added. In other words, it will just cover *all* its costs including the cost of capital.

FIGURE 10.2
NPV break-even analysis.

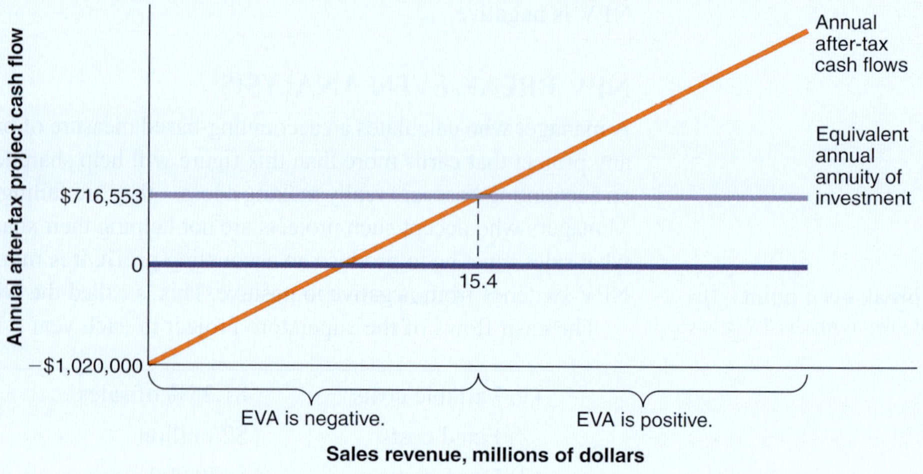

EXAMPLE 10.3 BREAK-EVEN ANALYSIS

We have said that projects that break even on an accounting basis are really making a loss—they are losing the opportunity cost of their investment. Here is a dramatic example. Lophead Aviation is contemplating investment in a new passenger aircraft, code-named the Trinova. Lophead's financial staff has gathered the following estimates:

1. The cost of developing the Trinova is forecast at $900 million, and this investment can be depreciated in six equal annual amounts.
2. Production of the plane is expected to take place at a steady annual rate over the following six years.
3. The average price of the Trinova is expected to be $15.5 million.
4. Fixed costs are forecast at $175 million a year.
5. Variable costs are forecast at $8.5 million a plane.
6. The tax rate is 50 percent.
7. The cost of capital is 10 percent.

Lophead's financial manager has used this information to construct a forecast of the profitability of the Trinova program. This is shown in rows 1 to 7 of Table 10.5 (ignore row 8 for a moment).

TABLE 10.5
Forecast profitability for production of the Trinova airliner (figures in $ millions).

	Year 0	Years 1–6
Investment	$900	
(1) Sales		15.5 × planes sold
(2) Variable costs		8.5 × planes sold
(3) Fixed costs		175
(4) Depreciation		900/6 = 150
(5) Pretax profit (1) − (2) − (3) − (4)		(7 × planes sold) − 325
(6) Taxes (at 50%)		(3.5 × planes sold) − 162.5
(7) Net profit (5) − (6)		(3.5 × planes sold) − 162.5
(8) Net cash flow (4) + (7)	−$900	(3.5 × planes sold) − 12.5

How many aircraft does Lophead need to sell to break even? The answer depends on what is meant by "break even." In accounting terms the venture will break even when net profit (row 7 in the table) is zero. In this case

$$(3.5 \times \text{planes sold}) - 162.5 = 0$$
$$\text{Planes sold} = 162.5/3.5 = 46.4$$

Thus Lophead needs to sell about 46 planes a year, or a total of 280 planes over the 6 years to show a profit. With a price of \$15.5 million a plane, Lophead will break even in accounting terms with annual revenues of 46.4 × \$15.5 million = \$719 million.

We would have arrived at the same answer if we had used our formula to calculate the break-even level of revenues. Notice that the variable cost of each plane is \$8.5 million, which is 54.8 percent of the \$15.5 million sale price. Therefore, each dollar of sales increases pretax profits by \$1 − \$.548 = \$.452. Now we use the formula for the accounting break-even point:

$$\text{Break-even revenues} = \frac{\text{fixed costs including depreciation}}{\text{additional profit from each additional dollar of sales}}$$
$$= \frac{\$325 \text{ million}}{.452} = \$719 \text{ million}$$

If Lophead sells about 46 planes a year, it will recover its original investment, but it will not earn any return on the capital tied up in the project. Companies that earn a zero return on their capital can expect some unhappy shareholders. Shareholders will be content only if the company's investments earn at least the cost of the capital invested. True break-even occurs when the projects have zero economic value added.

How many planes must Lophead sell to break even in terms of net present value? Development of the Trinova costs \$900 million. If the cost of capital is 10%, the 6-year annuity factor is 4.3553. The last row of Table 10.5 shows that net cash flow (in millions of dollars) in years 1–6 equals (3.5 × planes sold − 12.5). We can now find the annual plane sales necessary to break even in terms of NPV:

$$4.3553(3.5 \times \text{planes sold} - 12.5) = 900$$
$$15.2436 \times \text{planes sold} - 54.44 = 900$$
$$\text{Planes sold} = 954.44/15.2436 = 62.6$$

Thus, while Lophead will break even in terms of accounting profits with sales of 46.4 planes a year (about 280 in total), it needs to sell 62.6 a year (or about 375 in total) to also recover the opportunity cost of the capital invested in the project and break even in terms of NPV.

Our example may seem fanciful, but it is based loosely on reality. In 1971 Lockheed was in the middle of a major program to bring out the L-1011 TriStar airliner. This program was to bring Lockheed to the brink of failure and it tipped Rolls-Royce (supplier of the TriStar engine) over the brink. In giving evidence to the U.S. Congress, Lockheed argued that the TriStar program was commercially attractive and that sales would eventually exceed the break-even point of about 200 aircraft. But in calculating this break-even point Lockheed appears to have ignored the opportunity cost of the huge capital investment in the project. Lockheed probably needed to sell about 500 aircraft to reach a zero net present value.[4]

Check Point 10.4 What is the basic difference between sensitivity analysis and break-even analysis?

[4] The true break-even point for the TriStar program is estimated in U.E. Reinhardt, "Break-Even Analysis for Lockheed's TriStar: An Application of Financial Theory," *Journal of Finance* 28 (September 1973): 821–38.

OPERATING LEVERAGE

A project's break-even point depends on both its *fixed costs*, which do not vary with sales, and the profit on each extra sale. Managers often face a trade-off between these variables. For example, we typically think of rental expenses as fixed costs. But supermarket companies sometimes rent stores with contingent rent agreements. This means that the amount of rent the company pays is tied to the level of sales from the store. Rent rises and falls along with sales. The store thus replaces a fixed cost with a *variable cost* that rises along with sales. Because a greater proportion of the company's expenses will fall when its sales fall, its break-even point is reduced.

Of course, a high proportion of fixed costs is not all bad. The firm whose costs are largely fixed fares poorly when demand is low, but it may make a killing during a boom. Let us illustrate.

Finefodder has a policy of hiring long-term employees who will not be laid off except in the most dire circumstances. For all intents and purposes, these salaries are fixed costs. Its rival, Stop and Scoff, has a much smaller permanent labour force and uses expensive temporary help whenever demand for its product requires extra staff. A greater proportion of its labour expenses are therefore variable costs.

Suppose that if Finefodder adopted its rival's policy, fixed costs in its new superstore would fall from \$2 million to \$1.56 million but variable costs would rise from 81.25 to 84 percent of sales. Table 10.6 shows that with the normal level of sales, the two policies fare equally. In a slump a store that relies on temporary labour does better, since its costs fall along with revenue. In a boom the reverse is true, and the store with the higher proportion of fixed costs has the advantage.

If Finefodder follows its normal policy of hiring long-term employees, each extra dollar of sales increases pre-tax profits by \$1 − \$.8125 = \$.1875. If it uses temporary labour, an extra dollar of sales increases profits by only \$1 − \$.84 = \$.16. As a result, a store with high fixed costs is said to have high **operating leverage**. High operating leverage magnifies the effect on profits of a fluctuation in sales.

operating leverage Degree to which costs are fixed.

We can measure a business's operating leverage by asking how much profits change for each 1 percent change in sales. The **degree of operating leverage**, often abbreviated as **DOL**, is this measure.

degree of operating leverage (DOL) Percentage change in profits given a 1 percent change in sales.

$$\text{DOL} = \frac{\text{percentage change in profits}}{\text{percentage change in sales}}$$

For example, Table 10.6 shows that as the store moves from normal conditions to boom, sales increase from \$16 million to \$19 million, a rise of 18.75 percent. For the policy with high fixed costs, profits increase from \$550,000 to \$1,112,000, a rise of 102.2 percent. Therefore,

$$\text{DOL} = \frac{102.2}{18.75} = 5.45$$

The percentage change in sales is magnified more than fivefold in terms of the percentage impact on profits.

TABLE 10.6
A store with high operating leverage performs relatively badly in a slump but flourishes in a boom (figures in \$000s).

	High Fixed Costs			High Variable Costs		
	Slump	Normal	Boom	Slump	Normal	Boom
Sales	13,000	16,000	19,000	13,000	16,000	19,000
− Variable costs	10,563	13,000	15,438	10,920	13,440	15,960
− Fixed costs	2,000	2,000	2,000	1,560	1,560	1,560
− Depreciation	450	450	450	450	450	450
= Pretax profit	−13	550	1,112	70	550	1,030

Now look at the operating leverage of the store if it uses the policy with low fixed costs but high variable costs. As the store moves from normal times to boom, profits increase from \$550,000 to \$1,030,000, a rise of 87.3 percent. Therefore,

$$\text{DOL} = \frac{87.3}{18.75} = 4.65$$

Because some costs remain fixed, a change in sales still generates a large percentage change in profits, but the degree of operating leverage is lower.

In fact, one can show that degree of operating leverage depends on fixed charges (including depreciation) in the following manner:[5]

$$\text{DOL} = 1 + \frac{\text{fixed costs}}{\text{profits}}$$

This relationship makes it clear that operating leverage increases with fixed costs.

EXAMPLE 10.4 OPERATING LEVERAGE

Suppose the firm adopts the high-fixed-cost policy. Then fixed costs including depreciation will be \$2 million + \$.45 million = \$2.45 million. Since the store produces profits of \$.55 million at a normal level of sales, DOL should be

$$\text{DOL} = 1 + \frac{\text{fixed costs}}{\text{profits}} = 1 + \frac{2.45}{.55} = 5.45$$

This value matches the one we obtained by comparing the actual percentage changes in sales and profits.

The risk of a project depends on operating leverage. If a large proportion of costs is fixed, a shortfall in sales has a magnified effect on profits.

Notice that operating leverage will affect the risk of a project. For example, if the degree of operating leverage is 5.45, every 1 percent drop in sales will decrease profits by 5.45 percent. The greater the degree of operating leverage, the greater the sensitivity of profits to variation in sales. Some companies have much higher fixed costs than others. For instance, steel producers may have high fixed costs relative to food producers.

The risk of a project depends on operating leverage. If a large proportion of costs is fixed, a shortfall in sales has a magnified effect on profits. We will have more to say about risk in the next three chapters.

Check Point 10.5

Suppose that sales increase by 10 percent from the values in the normal scenario. Compute the percentage change in pretax profits from the normal level for both policies in Table 10.6. Compare your answers to the values predicted by the DOL formula.

---

[5] This formula for DOL can be derived as follows. If sales increase by 1 percent, then variable costs also should increase by 1 percent, and profits will increase by .01 × (sales − variable costs) = .01 × (profits + fixed costs). Now recall the definition of DOL:

$$\begin{aligned}\text{DOL} &= \frac{\text{percentage change in profits}}{\text{percentage change in sales}} = \frac{\text{change in profits/level of profits}}{.01}\\ &= 100 \times \frac{\text{change in profits}}{\text{level of profits}} = 100 \times \frac{.01 \times (\text{profits} + \text{fixed costs})}{\text{level of profits}}\\ &= 1 + \frac{\text{fixed costs}}{\text{profits}}\end{aligned}$$

Finance in Action

Unexpected Cost Overruns in a Large Capital Budgeting Project

The future of yet another major gold project is in question after a study projected massive capital spending to bring it to production.

NovaGold Resources Inc. said that the Donlin Creek project in Alaska, which it co-owns with Barrick Gold Corp., will cost an estimated US$4.48-billion to construct. It is a gigantic number that is more than double what Nova-Gold projected in 2006, and is further proof that miners are struggling with sky-high costs despite talk that they are coming down.

"Four billion is atrocious for a gold mining company," said Ron Coll, an analyst at Jennings Capital.

"This isn't Big Oil; it's mining. It's a different league. I think that they'd have to go back and rejig this somehow to come up with a program and a project that isn't going to cripple the partners."

The cost figure, while not a shock, is not welcome news for either company.

Just a few weeks ago, Barrick learned from partner Kinross Gold Corp. that its Cerro Casale project in Chile is expected to cost US$3.6-billion, above what many experts were looking for.

Donlin adds additional billions of dollars in potential spending to the company's pipeline.

Vancouver-based Nova-Gold, meanwhile, only had $78.8-million in cash at the end of the first quarter, and would somehow have to come up with more than US$2-billion to fund its 50% portion of the project.

Capital-cost escalation is nothing new for NovaGold, which had to shelve its Galore Creek project in 2007 when costs ballooned 127% to about US$5-billion in just a year.

NovaGold did note that estimates on Donlin Creek were completed in the latter half of 2008, a point when mining costs hit their absolute peak. That was due to massive escalation in fuel, labour and heavy equipment expenses.

Since then, prices for inputs such as fuel and steel have plummeted, and the company said it may update the project economics later this year to account for lower costs.

Analysts have projected that industry-wide costs could be down about 15% from the peak.

But even if they come down substantially, experts said the Donlin mine plan will probably be re-worked before the partners consider developing it. The project is not a priority for Barrick.

"Given this [feasibility] study and the current commodity price, I don't think the internal rate of return after tax would justify the development of Donlin Creek just yet," said Haytham Hodaly, an analyst at Salman Partners.

Barrick spokesman Vince Borg said that the company suspected for a couple of years that Donlin Creek could cost more than US$4-billion. He added that the partners will meet in early May to discuss the future of the project.

A spokesperson for Nova-Gold was unavailable.

David Haughton, an analyst at BMO Capital Markets, wrote that Barrick should "consider acquisitions to replace this high-cost organic growth project."

Source: Excerpted from Peter Koven, "Donlin Gold Mine in Doubt: Development Cost Soars to US$4.48-Billion," *Financial Post*, April 29, 2009, FP5. Material reprinted with the express permission of National Post, a division of Postmedia Network Inc.

A SECOND REAL OPTION: THE OPTION TO ABANDON

If the option to expand has value, what about the decision to bail out? Projects don't just go on until assets expire of old age. The decision to terminate a project is usually taken by management, not by nature. Once the project is no longer profitable, the company will cut its losses and exercise its option to abandon the project.

Some assets are simpler to bail out of than others. Tangible assets are usually easier to sell than intangible ones. It helps to have active secondhand markets, which really exist only for standardized items. Real estate, airplanes, trucks, and certain machine tools are likely to be relatively easy to sell. On the other hand, the knowledge accumulated by a software company's research and development program is a specialized intangible asset and probably would not have significant abandonment value. (Some assets, such as old mattresses, even have *negative* abandonment value; you have to pay to get rid of them. It is costly to decommission nuclear power plants or to reclaim land that has been strip-mined.)

EXAMPLE 10.5 ABANDONMENT OPTION

Suppose that the Widgeon Company must choose between two technologies for the manufacture of a new product, a Wankel-engined outboard motor:

1. Technology A uses custom-designed machinery to produce the complex shapes required for Wankel engines at low cost. But if the Wankel engine doesn't sell, this equipment will be worthless.

2. Technology B uses standard machine tools. Labour costs are much higher, but the tools can easily be sold if the motor doesn't sell.

Technology A looks better in an NPV analysis of the new product, because it is designed to have the lowest possible cost at the planned production volume. Yet you can sense the advantage of technology B's flexibility if you are unsure whether the new outboard will sink or swim in the marketplace.

Check Point 10.7

Draw a decision tree showing how the choices open to the Widgeon Company depend on demand for the new product. Pick some plausible numbers to illustrate why it might make sense to adopt the more expensive technology B.

Check Point 10.8

Consider a firm operating a copper mine that incurs both variable and fixed costs of production. Suppose the mine can be shut down temporarily if copper prices fall below the variable cost of mining copper. Why is this a valuable operating option? How does it increase the NPV of the mine to the operator?

A THIRD REAL OPTION: THE TIMING OPTION

When you are unsure about the success of a venture, you might wish to choose a flexible technology with a good resale market to preserve the option to abandon the project at low cost.

Suppose that you have a project that could be a big winner or a big loser. The project's upside potential outweighs its downside potential, and it has a positive NPV if undertaken today. However, the project is not "now or never." So should you invest right away or wait? It's hard to say. If the project turns out to be a winner, waiting means the loss or deferral of its early cash flows. But if it turns out to be a loser, it may pay to wait and get a better fix on the likely demand.

You can think of any project proposal as giving you the *option* to invest today. You don't have to exercise that option immediately. Instead you need to weigh the value of the cash flows lost by delaying against the possibility that you will pick up some valuable information. Suppose, for example, you are considering development of a new oil field. At current oil prices the investment has a small positive NPV. But oil prices are highly volatile, occasionally halving or doubling in the space of a couple of years. If a small decline in crude prices could push your project into the red, it might be better to wait a little before investing.

Our example illustrates why companies sometimes turn down apparently profitable projects. For example, suppose you approach your boss with a proposed project. It involves spending $1 million and has an NPV of $1,000. You explain to him how carefully you have analyzed the project, but nothing seems to convince him that the company should invest. Is he being irrational to turn down a positive-NPV project?

Faced by such marginal projects, it often makes sense to wait. One year later you may have much better information about the prospects for the project and it may become clear whether it is really a winner or a loser. In the former case you can go ahead with confidence, but, if it looks like a loser, the delay will have helped you to avoid a bad mistake.[6]

[6] Does this conclusion contradict our earlier dictum (see Chapter 8) that the firm should accept all positive-NPV projects? No. Notice that the investment timing problem involves a choice among mutually exclusive alternatives. You can build the project today or next year, but not both. In such cases, we have seen that the right choice is the one with the *highest* NPV. The NPV of the project today, even if positive, may well be less than the NPV of deferring investment and keeping alive the option to invest later.

A FOURTH REAL OPTION: FLEXIBLE PRODUCTION FACILITIES

A sheep is not a flexible production facility. It produces mutton and wool in roughly fixed proportions. If the price of mutton suddenly rises and that of wool falls, there is little the farmer with a flock of sheep can do about it. Many manufacturing operations are different, for they have built-in flexibility to vary their output mix as demand changes. Since we have mentioned sheep, we might point to the knitwear industry as a case in which manufacturing flexibility has become particularly important in recent years. Fashion changes have made the pattern of demand in the knitwear industry notoriously difficult to predict, and firms have increasingly invested in computer-controlled knitting machines, which provide an option to vary the product mix as demand changes.

Companies also try to avoid becoming dependent on a single source of raw materials. For example, at current prices gas-fired industrial boilers may be cheaper to operate than oil-fired ones. Yet most companies prefer to buy boilers that can use *either* oil or natural gas, even though these dual-fired boilers cost more than a gas-fired boiler. The reason is obvious. If gas prices rise relative to oil prices, the dual-fired boiler gives the company a valuable option to exchange one asset (an oil-fired boiler) for another (a gas-fired boiler).

Check Point 10.9

Investments in new products or production capacity often include an option to expand. What are the other major types of option encountered in capital investment decisions?

10.5 SUMMARY

1. **How do large corporations go about selecting positive-NPV projects? LO1**

   For most large corporations there are two stages in the investment process: the preparation of the **capital budget**, which is a list of planned investments, and the authorization process for individual projects. This process is usually a cooperative effort.

   Investment projects should never be selected through a purely mechanical process. Managers need to ask why a project should have a positive NPV. A positive NPV is plausible only if the company has some competitive advantage that prevents its rivals from stealing most of the gains.

2. **How are sensitivity, scenario, and break-even analyses used to see the effects of forecasting errors on project profitability? LO2**

   Good managers realize that the forecasts behind NPV calculations are imperfect. Therefore, they explore the consequences of a poor forecast and check whether it is worth doing some more homework. They use the following principal tools to answer these "what if" questions:

   - **Sensitivity analysis**, in which one variable at a time is changed.
   - **Scenario analysis**, in which the manager looks at the project under alternative scenarios.
   - **Simulation analysis**, an extension of scenario analysis in which a computer generates hundreds or thousands of possible combinations of variables.
   - **Break-even analysis**, in which the focus is on how far sales could fall before the project begins to lose money. Often the phrase "lose money" is defined in terms of accounting losses, but it makes more sense to define it as "failing to cover the opportunity cost of capital"—in other words, as a negative NPV.

3. **Why is an overestimate of sales more serious for projects with high operating leverage? LO3**

   Operating leverage, the degree to which costs are fixed. A project's break-even point will be affected by the extent to which costs can be reduced as sales decline. If the project has mostly **fixed costs**, it is said to have *high operating leverage*. High operating leverage implies that profits are more sensitive to changes in sales.

4. Why is managerial flexibility important in capital budgeting? LO4

Some projects may take on added value because they give the firm the option to bail out if things go wrong or to capitalize on success by expanding. These options are known as **real options**, which include options to expand, abandon, delay investment, or make use of flexible production facilities. We showed how **decision trees** may be used to set out the possible choices.

Related Web Links

palisade.com Software for Monte Carlo analysis

suncor.com Web site of Suncor Energy

lockheedmartin.com Web site of Lockheed Martin

Key Terms

break-even analysis	341	fixed costs	338	sensitivity analysis	337
capital budget	335	NPV break-even point	343	simulation analysis	341
decision tree	348	operating leverage	346	variable costs	338
degree of operating leverage (DOL)	346	real options	349		
		scenario analysis	340		

Questions and Problems

connect Practise and learn online with *Connect*. Questions with online Excel templates or datasets are marked with .

*Answers in Appendix B

BASIC

*1. **Fixed and Variable Costs.** In a slow year, Wimpy's Burgers will produce 1 million hamburgers at a total cost of $1.75 million. In a good year, it can produce 2 million hamburgers at a total cost of $2.25 million. What are the fixed and variable costs of hamburger production? (LO2)

2. **Average Cost.** Reconsider Wimpy's Burgers from problem 1. (LO2)
   a. What is the average cost per burger when the firm produces 1 million hamburgers?
   b. What is average cost when the firm produces 2 million hamburgers?
   c. Why is average cost lower when more burgers are produced?

3. **Sensitivity Analysis.** A project currently generates sales of $10 million, variable costs equal to 50 percent of sales, and fixed costs of $2 million. The firm's tax rate is 35 percent. What are the effects of the following changes on after-tax profits and cash flows? (LO2)
   a. Sales increase from $10 million to $11 million.
   b. Variable costs increase to 60 percent of sales.

INTERMEDIATE

4. **Sensitivity Analysis.** The project in problem 3 will last for 10 years. The discount rate is 12 percent. (LO2)
   a. What is the effect on project NPV of each of the changes considered in the problem?
   b. If project NPV under the base-case scenario is $2 million, how much can fixed costs increase before NPV turns negative?
   c. How much can fixed costs increase before accounting profits turn negative?

*5. **Sensitivity Analysis.** Emperor's Clothes Fashions can invest $5 million in a new plant for producing invisible makeup. The plant has an expected life of 5 years, and expected sales are 6 million jars of makeup a year. Fixed costs are $2 million a year, and variable costs are $1 per jar. The product will be priced at $2 per jar. The plant will be depreciated straight-line over five years to a salvage value of zero. The opportunity cost of capital is 12 percent, and the tax rate is 40 percent. (LO2)
   a. What is project NPV under these base-case assumptions?

b. What is NPV if variable costs turn out to be $1.20 per jar?
c. What is NPV if fixed costs turn out to be $1.5 million per year?
d. At what price per jar would the project NPV equal zero?

6. **Scenario Analysis.** The most likely outcomes for a particular project are estimated as follows:

Unit price:	$50
Variable cost:	$30
Fixed cost:	$300,000
Expected sales:	30,000 units per year

However, you recognize that some of these estimates are subject to error. Suppose that each variable may turn out to be either 10 percent higher or 10 percent lower than the initial estimate. The project will last for 10 years and requires an initial investment of $1 million, which will be depreciated straight-line over the project life to a final value of zero. The firm's tax rate is 35 percent and the required rate of return is 14 percent. What is project NPV in the "best case" scenario, that is, assuming all variables take on the best possible value? What about the "worst case" scenario? (LO2)

7. **Scenario Analysis.** Reconsider the best- and worst-case scenarios in the previous problem. In terms of the combination of variables, do the best- and worst-case outcomes seem reasonable when each variable is treated independently? For example, if price is higher than predicted, is it more or less likely that cost is higher than predicted? What other relationships may exist among the variables? (LO2)

8. **Break-Even.** The following estimates have been prepared for a project under consideration:

Fixed costs:	$20,000
Depreciation:	$10,000
Price:	$2
Accounting break-even:	60,000 units

What must be the variable cost per unit? (LO2)

*9. **Break-Even.** Dime a Dozen Diamonds makes synthetic diamonds by treating carbon. Each diamond can be sold for $100. The materials cost for a standard diamond is $30. The fixed costs incurred each year for factory upkeep and administrative expenses are $200,000. The machinery costs $1 million and is depreciated straight-line over 10 years to a salvage value of zero. (LO2)
a. What is the accounting break-even level of sales in terms of number of diamonds sold?
b. What is the NPV break-even level of sales assuming a tax rate of 35 percent, a 10-year project life, and a discount rate of 12 percent?

10. **Break-Even.** Turn back to problem 9. (LO2)
a. Would the accounting break-even point in the first year of operation increase or decrease if the machinery were depreciated over a five-year period?
b. Would the NPV break-even point increase or decrease if the machinery were depreciated over a five-year period?

*11. **Break-Even.** You are evaluating a project that will require an investment of $10 million that will be depreciated over a period of seven years. You are concerned that the corporate tax rate will increase during the life of the project. Would such an increase affect the accounting break-even point? Would it affect the NPV break-even point? (LO2)

*12. **Break-Even.** Define the *cash-flow break-even point* as the sales volume (in dollars) at which cash flow equals zero. Is the cash-flow break-even level of sales higher or lower than the zero-profit break-even point? (LO2)

13. **Break-Even and NPV.** If a project operates at cash-flow break-even (see problem 12) for its entire life, what must be true of the project's NPV? (LO2)

14. **Break-Even.** Modern Artifacts can produce keepsakes that will be sold for $80 each. Non-depreciated fixed costs are $1,000 per year and variable costs are $60 per unit. (LO2)
a. If the project requires an initial investment of $3,000 and is expected to last for 5 years and the firm pays no taxes, what are the accounting and NPV break-even levels of sales? The initial investment will be depreciated straight-line over 5 years to a final value of zero, and the discount rate is 10 percent.
b. How do your answers change if the firm's tax rate is 40 percent?

*15. **Break-Even.** A financial analyst based in the United States has computed both accounting and NPV break-even sales levels for a project under consideration using straight-line depreciation over a six-year period. The project manager wants to know what will happen to these estimates if the firm uses depreciation calculated on the basis of the Modified Accelerated Cost Recovery System (MACRS). Firms in the United States are allowed by the Internal Revenue Service to depreciate their equipment for tax purposes using this system. The capital investment will be in a 5-year recovery period class under MACRS rules. Under the rules, applicable percentage depreciation rates over years 1 to 6 will be 20, 32, 19.20, 11.52, 11.52, and 5.76, so the firm will be able to use higher rates in earlier years. The firm is in a 35 percent tax bracket. (LO2)
a. What (qualitatively) will happen to the accounting break-even level of sales in the first years of the project?
b. What (qualitatively) will happen to the NPV break-even level of sales?

c. If you were advising the analyst, would the answer to (a) or (b) be important to you? Specifically, would you say that the switch to MACRS makes the project more or less attractive?

16. **Break-Even.** Reconsider Finefodder's new superstore. Suppose that by initially investing an additional $600,000 in more efficient checkout equipment, Finefodder could reduce variable costs to 80 percent of sales. (LO2)
   a. Using the base-case assumptions (Table 10.1), find the NPV of this alternative scheme. *Hint:* Remember to focus on the *incremental* cash flows from the project.
   b. At what level of sales will accounting profits be unchanged if the firm invests in the new equipment? Assume the equipment receives the same 12-year straight-line depreciation treatment as in the original example. *Hint:* Focus on the project's *incremental* effects on fixed and variable costs.
   c. What is the NPV break-even point?

*17. **Break-Even and NPV.** If the superstore project (see the previous problem) operates at accounting break-even, will net present value be positive or negative? (LO2)

18. **Operating Leverage.** You estimate that your cattle farm will generate $1 million of profits on sales of $4 million under normal economic conditions, and that the degree of operating leverage is 7.5. What will profits be if sales turn out to be $3.5 million? What if they are $4.5 million? (LO3)

19. **Operating Leverage.** (LO3)
   a. What is the degree of operating leverage of Modern Artifacts (in problem 14) when sales are $8,000?
   b. What is the degree of operating leverage when sales are $10,000?
   c. Why is operating leverage different at these two levels of sales?

*20. **Operating Leverage.** What is the lowest possible value for the degree of operating leverage for a profitable firm? Show with a numerical example that if Modern Artifacts from problem 14(a) has zero fixed costs, then DOL = 1, and in fact sales and profits are directly proportional, so that a 1 percent change in sales results in a 1 percent change in profits. (LO3)

21. **Operating Leverage.** A project has fixed costs of $1,000 per year, depreciation charges of $500 a year, revenue of $6,000 a year, and variable costs equal to two-thirds of revenues. (LO3)
   a. If sales increase by 5 percent, what will be the increase in pretax profits?
   b. What is the degree of operating leverage of this project?
   c. Confirm that the percentage change in profits equals DOL times the percentage change in sales.

22. **Project Options.** Your midrange guess as to the amount of oil in a prospective field is 10 million barrels, but in fact there is a 50 percent chance that the amount of oil is 15 million barrels and a 50 percent chance of 5 million barrels. If the actual amount of oil is 15 million barrels, the present value of the cash flows from drilling will be $8 million. If the amount is only 5 million barrels, the present value will be only $2 million. It costs $3 million to drill the well. Suppose that a seismic test that costs $100,000 can verify the amount of oil under the ground. Is it worth paying for the test? Use a decision tree to justify your answer. (LO4)

*23. **Project Options.** A silver mine can yield 10,000 ounces of silver at a variable cost of $8 per ounce. The fixed costs of operating the mine are $10,000 per year. In half the years, silver can be sold for $12 per ounce; in the other years, silver can be sold for only $6 per ounce. Ignore taxes. (LO4)
   a. What is the average cash flow you will receive from the mine if it is always kept in operation and the silver is always sold in the year it is mined?
   b. Now suppose you can shut down the mine in years of low silver prices. What happens to the average cash flow from the mine?

24. **Project Options.** An auto plant that costs $100 million to build can produce a new line of cars that will produce cash flows with a present value of $140 million if the line is successful, but only $50 million if it is unsuccessful. You believe that the probability of success is only about 50 percent. (LO4)
   a. Would you build the plant?
   b. Suppose that the plant can be sold for $90 million to another automaker if the auto line is not successful. Now would you build the plant?
   c. Illustrate the option to abandon in (b) using a decision tree.

25. **Production Options.** Explain why options to expand or contract production are most valuable when forecasts about future business conditions are most uncertain. (LO4)

CHALLENGE

26. **Internet.** Go to Yahoo Finance (**ca.finance.yahoo.com**). (LO3)
   a. Can you guess Dell's incremental cost for producing one computer? You probably have that amount in your wallet or purse! Let's estimate the sales break-even point and degree of operating leverage for Dell Computer (DELL). Go to the annual income statement. With reference to Table 10.4, treating S&GA, research and development (R&D), and depreciation expense as our proxy for fixed costs, and costs of goods sold as variable costs, estimate the break-even level of sales for Dell for the last year (annual).
   b. Estimate Dell's degree of operating leverage (DOL) by calculating the percentage change in operating profits compared to the previous year and dividing that by the percentage change in sales. How does

that compare to the result you would obtain for operating leverage using the formula DOL = 1 + fixed costs/profits? Why is there a difference when using these two approaches?

27. **Decision Tree.** Zoom Technologies, Inc., is considering expanding its operations into digital music devices. Zoom anticipates an initial investment of $1.3 million and, at best, an operational life of 3 years for the project. Zoom's management team has considered several probable outcomes over the life of the project, which it has labelled as either "successes" or "failures." Accordingly, Zoom anticipates that in the first year of operations there is a 65 percent chance of "success," with after-tax cash flow of $800,000, or a 35 percent chance of "failure," with a meagre $1,000 cash flow after tax.

If the project "succeeds" in the first year, Zoom expects three probable outcomes regarding net cash flows after tax in the second year. These outcomes are $2.2 million, $1.8 million, or $1.5 million, with probabilities of .3, .5, and .2, respectively. In the third and final year of operation, the net cash flows after tax are expected to be either $35,000 more or $55,000 less than they were in year 2, with an equal chance of occurrence.

If, on the other hand, the project "fails" in year 1, there is a 60 percent chance that it will produce net cash flows after tax of only $1,500 in years 2 and 3. There is also a 40 percent chance that it will really fail and Zoom will earn nothing in year 2, and will get out of this line of business, terminating the project and resulting in no net cash flows after tax in year 3.

The opportunity cost of capital for Zoom Technologies is 10 percent. (LO4)

a. Construct a decision tree representing the possible outcomes.
b. Determine the joint probability of each possible sequence of events.
c. What is the project's expected NPV?

*28. **Abandonment Option.** Hit or Miss Sports is introducing a new product this year. If its see-at-night soccer balls are a hit, the firm expects to be able to sell 50,000 units a year at a price of $60 each. If the new product is a bust, only 30,000 units can be sold at a price of $55. The variable cost of each ball is $30 and fixed costs are zero. The cost of the manufacturing equipment is $6 million, and the project life is estimated at 10 years. The firm will use straight-line depreciation over the 10-year life of the project. The firm's tax rate is 35 percent and the discount rate is 12 percent. (LO4)

a. If each outcome is equally likely, what is the expected NPV? Will the firm accept the project?
b. Suppose now that the firm can abandon the project and sell off the manufacturing equipment for $5.4 million if demand for the balls turns out to be weak. The firm will make the decision to continue or abandon after the first year of sales. Does the option to abandon change the firm's decision to accept the project?

29. **Expansion Option.** Now suppose that Hit or Miss Sports from the previous problem can expand production if the project is successful. By paying its workers overtime, it can increase production by 20,000 units; the variable cost of each ball will be higher, equal to $35 per unit. By how much does this option to expand production increase the NPV of the project? (LO4)

Solutions to Check Points

10.1 Cash flow forecasts for Finefodder's new superstore:

	Year 0	Years 1–12
Investment	−5,400,000	
(1) Sales		16,000,000
(2) Variable costs		13,280,000
(3) Fixed costs		2,000,000
(4) Depreciation		450,000
(5) Pretax profit (1) − (2) − (3) − (4)		270,000
(6) Taxes (at 40%)		108,000
(7) Profit after tax		162,000
(8) Cash flow from operations (4) + (7)		612,000
Net cash flow	−5,400,000	612,000

NPV = −$5.4 million + (7.536 × $612,000) = −$787,968

10.2 Both calculate how NPV depends on input assumptions. Sensitivity analysis changes inputs one at a time, whereas scenario analysis changes several variables at once. The changes should add up to a consistent scenario for the project as a whole.

10.3 With the lower initial investment, depreciation is also lower; it now equals $417,000 per year. Cash flow is now as follows:

(1) Variable costs	81.25 percent of sales
(2) Fixed costs	$2 million
(3) Depreciation	$417,000
(4) Pretax profit	(.1875 × sales) − $2.417 million
(5) Tax (at 40%)	.4 × (.1875 × sales − $2.417 million)
(6) Profit after tax	.6 × (.1875 × sales − $2.417 million)
(7) Cash flow (3) + (6)	.6 × (.1875 × sales − $2.417 million) + $417,000 = .1125 × sales − $1.033 million

Break-even occurs when

PV(cash inflows) = Investment

7.536(.1125 × sales −\$1.033 million) = \$5.0 million, and

Sales = \$15.08 million

10.4 Break-even analysis finds the level of sales or revenue at which NPV = 0. Sensitivity analysis changes these and other input variables to optimistic and pessimistic values and recalculates NPV.

10.5 Reworking Table 10.6 for the normal level of sales and 10 percent higher sales gives the result shown in the table below.

For the high-fixed-cost policy, profits increase by 54.5 percent, from \$550,000 to \$850,000. For the low-fixed-cost policy, profits increase by 46.5 percent. In both cases the percentage increase in profits equals DOL times the percentage increase in sales. This illustrates that DOL measures the sensitivity of profits to changes in sales.

	High Fixed Costs		High Variable Costs	
	Normal	**10% Higher Sales**	**Normal**	**10% Sales Higher**
Sales	16,000	17,600	16,000	17,600
− Variable costs	13,000	14,300	13,440	14,784
− Fixed costs	2,000	2,000	1,560	1,560
− Depreciation	450	450	450	450
= Pretax profit	550	850	550	806

10.6 A decision tree model for Goody Foods' Choc-O-Spice cookie project is provided below:

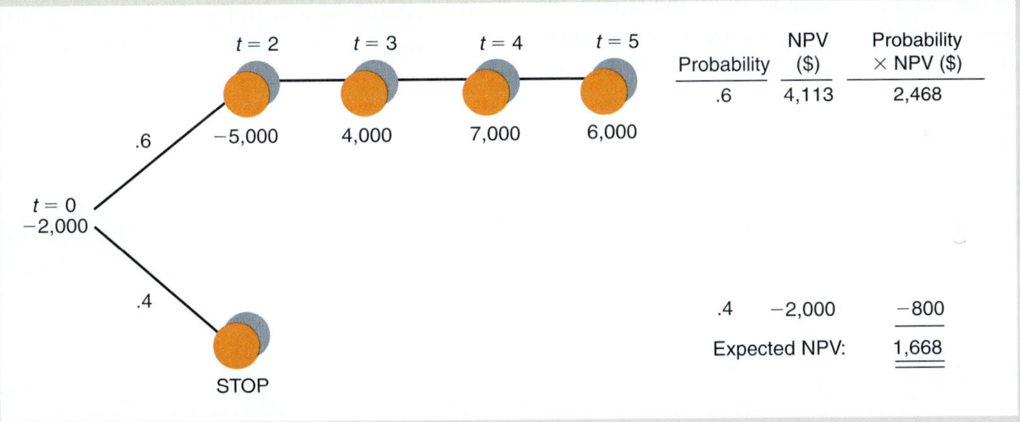

NPV Analysis for Satisfactory Outcome (\$000s)

Year	Cash Flows (\$)	Present Value = $1/(1.14)^t$	Discounted Cash Flows (\$)
0	−2,000	1.0000	−2,000
1	—	.8772	
2	−5,000	.7695	−3,848
3	4,000	.6750	2,700
4	7,000	.5921	4,145
5	6,000	.5194	3,116
			NPV 4,113

Expected NPV of \$1,668 is greater than zero, so the company should go forward with the project.

10.7 See Figure 10.4. Note that while technology A delivers the higher NPV if demand is high, technology B has the advantage of a higher salvage value if demand is unexpectedly low.

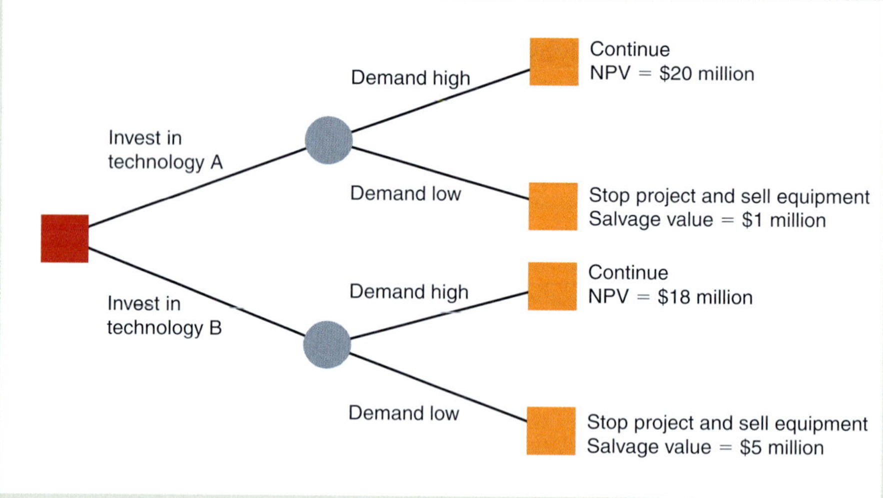

FIGURE 10.4
Example of a decision tree for Widgeon Company.

10.8 The option to shut down is valuable because the mine operator can avoid incurring losses when copper prices are low. If the shut-down option were not available, cash flow in the low-price periods would be negative. With the option, the worst cash flow is zero. By allowing managers to respond to market conditions, the option makes the worst-case cash flow better than it would be otherwise. The average cash flow (that is, averaging over all possible scenarios) therefore must improve, which increases project NPV.

10.9 Abandonment options, options due to flexible production facilities, and investment timing options.

MINI CASE

Maxine Peru, the CEO of Peru Resources, hardly noticed the plate of savoury quenelles de brochet and the glass of Corton Charlemagne '94 on the table before her. She was absorbed by the engineering report handed to her just as she entered the executive dining room.

The report described a proposed new mine on the North Ridge of Mt. Zircon. A vein of transcendental zirconium ore had been discovered there on land owned by Peru's company. Test borings indicated sufficient reserves to produce 340 tonnes per year of transcendental zirconium over a 7-year period.

The vein probably also contained hydrated zircon gemstones. The amount and quality of these zircons were hard to predict, since they tended to occur in "pockets." The new mine might come across one, two, or dozens of pockets. The mining engineer guessed that 150 pounds per year might be found. The current price for high-quality hydrated zircon gemstones was $3,300 per pound.

Peru Resources was a family-owned business with total assets of $45 million, including cash reserves of $4 million. The outlay required for the new mine would be a major commitment. Fortunately, Peru Resources was conservatively financed, and CEO Peru believed that the company could borrow up to $9 million at an interest rate of about 8 percent.

The mine's operating costs were projected at $900,000 per year, including $400,000 of fixed costs and $500,000 of variable costs. Peru thought these forecasts were accurate. The big question marks seemed to be the initial cost of the mine and the selling price of transcendental zirconium.

Opening the mine, and providing the necessary machinery and ore-crunching facilities, was supposed to cost $10 million, but cost overruns of 10 percent or 15 percent were common in the mining business. In addition, new environmental regulations, if enacted, could increase the cost of the mine by $1.5 million.

There was a cheaper design for the mine, which would reduce its cost by $1.7 million and eliminate much of the uncertainty about cost overruns. Unfortunately, this design would require much higher fixed operating costs. Fixed costs would increase to $850,000 per year at planned production levels.

The current price of transcendental zirconium was $10,000 per tonne, but there was no consensus about future prices.[7] Some experts were projecting rapid price increases to as much as $14,000 per tonne. On the other hand, there were pessimists saying that prices could be as low as $7,500 per tonne. Peru did not have strong views either way: her best guess was that price would just increase with inflation at about 3.5 percent per year. (Mine operating costs would also increase with inflation.)

Peru had wide experience in the mining business, and she knew that investors in similar projects usually wanted a forecast nominal rate of return of at least 14 percent.

You have been asked to assist Peru in evaluating this project. Lay out the base-case NPV analysis and undertake sensitivity, scenario, or break-even analyses as appropriate. Assume that Peru Resources pays tax at a 35 percent rate. For simplicity, also assume that the investment in the mine could be depreciated for tax purposes straight-line over seven years.

What forecasts or scenarios should worry Peru the most? Where would additional information be most helpful? Is there a case for delaying construction of the new mine?

[7] There were no traded forward or futures contracts on transcendental zirconium. See Chapter 26.

PART 3

Risk

11 Introduction to Risk, Return, and the Opportunity Cost of Capital

11.1 Rates of Return: A Review

11.2 Eighty-Five Years of Capital Market History

11.3 Measuring Risk

11.4 Risk and Diversification

11.5 Thinking About Risk

11.6 Summary

12 Risk, Return, and Capital Budgeting

13 The Weighted-Average Cost of Capital and Company Valuation

CHAPTER 11

Introduction to Risk, Return, and the Opportunity Cost of Capital

LEARNING OBJECTIVES

After studying this chapter, you should be able to:

LO1 Estimate the opportunity cost of capital for an "average risk" project.

LO2 Calculate returns and standard deviation of returns for individual common stocks and for a stock portfolio.

LO3 Explain why diversification reduces risk.

LO4 Distinguish between unique risk, which can be diversified away, and market risk, which cannot.

Investing in risky assets is not the same as gambling.

In previous chapters we skirted the issue of project risk; now it is time to confront it head-on. We can no longer be satisfied with vague statements like "The opportunity cost of capital depends on the risk of the project." We need to know how to measure risk and we need to understand the relationship between risk and the cost of capital. These are the topics of the next two chapters.

Think for a moment what the cost of capital for a project means. It is the rate of return that shareholders could expect to earn if they invested in equally risky securities. So one way to estimate the project's cost of capital is to find securities that have the same risk as the project and then estimate the expected rate of return on these securities.

We start our analysis by looking at the rates of return earned in the past from different investments in securities, concentrating on the *extra* return that investors have received for investing in risky rather than safe securities. We then show how to measure the risk of a portfolio of securities by calculating its standard deviation and we look again at past history to find out how risky it is to invest in the stock market.

Finally, we explore the concept of diversification. Most investors do not put all their eggs into one basket—they diversify. Thus investors are not concerned with the risk of each security in isolation; instead they are concerned with how much it contributes to the risk of a diversified portfolio. We therefore need to distinguish between the risk that can be eliminated by diversification and the risk that cannot be eliminated.

11.1 RATES OF RETURN: A REVIEW

When investors buy a stock or a bond, their return comes in two forms: (1) a dividend or interest payment and (2) a capital gain or a capital loss. For example, suppose you bought the stock of Canadian Pacific Railway (CP) December 31, 2009, when its price was \$56.79 a share. One year later, December 31, 2010, the value of that investment had appreciated to \$64.62, giving a capital gain of \$64.62 − 56.79 = \$7.83. In addition, in 2010 Canadian Pacific paid a dividend of \$1.035 per share.

The *percentage* return on your investment was therefore

$$\textbf{Percentage return} = \frac{\textbf{capital gain + dividend}}{\textbf{initial share price}} \qquad \textbf{(11.1)}$$

$$= \frac{\$7.83 + \$1.035}{\$56.79} = .1561, \text{ or } 15.61\%$$

The percentage return can also be expressed as the sum of the dividend yield and percentage capital gain. The dividend yield is the dividend expressed as a percentage of the stock price at the beginning of the year:

$$\textbf{Dividend yield} = \frac{\textbf{dividend}}{\textbf{initial share price}} \qquad \textbf{(11.2)}$$

$$= \frac{\$1.035}{\$56.79} = .0182, \text{ or } 1.82\%$$

Similarly, the percentage capital gain is

$$\textbf{Percentage capital gain} = \frac{\textbf{capital gain}}{\textbf{initial share price}} \qquad \textbf{(11.3)}$$

$$= \frac{\$7.83}{\$56.79} = .1379, \text{ or } 13.79\%$$

Thus the total return is the sum of 1.82% + 13.79% = 15.61%.

EXAMPLE 11.1

COMPARING RATES OF RETURN USING EQUIVALENT ANNUAL RATES OF RETURN

Rates of return can be calculated over any time period—a day, a month, years. For example, suppose you bought a share for \$50 at the beginning of 2010 and sold it 3 months later at the beginning of April 2010, when the stock was at \$52 per share. The capital gain was \$52 − \$50 or \$2. One dividend of \$.25 was paid. The percentage rate of return was (\$2 + \$.25)/\$50 or 4.5 percent. This is a 3-month rate of return. How does it compare with the 15.61 percent earned on Canadian Pacific over 12 months? As we saw in Chapter 5, to compare rates measured over different time period you calculate the *effective annual interest rate*, EAR. To convert the three-month return to its annual equivalent rate, first, calculate the monthly equivalent rate: $(1 + 3 \text{ month rate})^{1/3} - 1 = (1.045)^{1/3} - 1 = .01478$. Next, convert the monthly rate to its equivalent annual rate: $(1 + 1 \text{ month rate})^{12} - 1 = (1.01478)^{12} - 1 = .1925$, or 19.25 percent per year.[1] We have not compared the riskiness of the two stocks, so we can't say which investment was better.

In Chapter 5 we made a distinction between the *nominal* rate of return and the *real* rate of return. The nominal return measures how much more money you will have at the end of the year if you invest today. The 2010 return that we just calculated for Canadian Pacific stock is therefore a nominal return. The real rate of return tells you how much more you will be able to *buy* with your money at the end of the year. To convert from a nominal to a real rate of return, we use the following relationship:

$$\textbf{1 + real rate of return} = \frac{\textbf{1 + nominal rate of return}}{\textbf{1 + inflation rate}} \qquad \textbf{(11.4)}$$

The real rate of return is less than the nominal rate of return when the inflation rate is positive. In 2010, inflation was 2 percent. So we calculate the real rate of return on Canadian Pacific stock as follows:

$$1 + \text{real rate of return} = \frac{1.1561}{1.02} = 1.1334$$

Therefore, the real rate of return equals .1334, or 13.34 percent. Fortunately, inflation in 2010 was moderate; the real return was only slightly less than the nominal return.

Check Point 11.1

Suppose you buy a bond for \$1,020 with a 15-year maturity paying an annual coupon of \$80. A year later interest rates have dropped and the bond's price has increased to \$1,050. What are your nominal and real rates of return? Assume the inflation rate is 4 percent.

---

[1] We could have jumped directly to the annual equivalent rate by recognizing that a year has four three-month periods (12/3 = 4) making the annual equivalent rate equal to $(1.045)^4 - 1$, or 19.25 percent.

LO1 11.2 EIGHTY-FIVE YEARS OF CAPITAL MARKET HISTORY

When you invest in a stock, you don't know what return you will earn. But by looking at the history of security returns, you can get some idea of the return that investors might reasonably expect from investments in different types of securities and of the risks that they face. Let us look, therefore, at the risks and returns that investors have experienced in the past.

MARKET INDEXES

Investors can choose from an enormous number of different securities. Common shares, preferred shares, income trust units, and convertible debentures of more than 1,500 large, established companies are listed for trading on the Toronto Stock Exchange (TSX, **www.tsx.com**). Common shares of about 2,385 new and smaller companies trade on the TSX Venture Exchange. In addition, Canadian investors are free to cross-border-shop in the United States and overseas markets. Also, since 2005, the foreign content restriction for an individual's registered retirement savings plans (RRSP) has been removed. The New York Stock Exchange (NYSE), the major U.S. stock exchange, lists about 2,800 common stocks and another 3,100 common stocks are traded on the Nasdaq Stock Market. The London Stock Exchange lists common shares of about 2,800 companies; it is Europe's largest stock exchange. In today's global economy, many companies list their shares on more than one stock exchange. So the total number of securities listed on each stock exchange includes securities listed on other exchanges too.

market index Measure of the investment performance of the overall market.

S&P/TSX Composite Index Index of the investment performance of a portfolio of the major stocks listed on the Toronto Stock Exchange. Also called the *TSX index*. Formerly called the *TSE 300*.

S&P/TSX Composite Total Return Index (TSXT) Measure of the Composite Index based on the prices plus dividends paid by the stocks in the S&P/TSX Composite Index.

Financial analysts can't track every stock, so they rely on **market indexes** to summarize the return on different classes of securities. The primary stock market index in Canada is the **S&P/TSX Composite Index** (TSX index), based on a portfolio of the largest TSX stocks. To be included in the index, stocks must meet size and trading activity minimums. In January 2011 the index was based on 245 stocks. It is a *value-weighted* index, measuring the performance of a portfolio calculated as if all shares of each stock are owned. Thus, weight on each stock equals the ratio of its market capitalization (number shares times the price per share) to the sum of the market capitalization of all stocks in the portfolio. An *equal-weighted* index measures the performance of a portfolio consisting of one share of each stock. Weighting shares by their relative market value rather than giving equal weight per share is a better way to measure market performance. A value-weighted index shows the *average* performance of investors in the stocks.[2]

Every day, the index is calculated by multiplying the current share prices by the number of outstanding shares.[3] The number is then divided by the original value of the index, arbitrarily taken from January 1975, and multiplied by 1,000. An index value of 8,000 says that the TSX stocks have increased 8 times from their 1975 value. If the index rises by 80 points to end the day at 8,080, the portfolio makes a capital gain of 80/8,000 = .01, or 1 percent.

To know the total rate of return (capital gains plus dividends) on the TSX index stocks, use the **S&P/TSX Composite Total Return Index (TSXT)**, which includes dividends paid to stocks in the index. For example, in January 2011, TSX decreased from 13,443.221 to 13,258.57 points,

---

[2] In January 2011 there were about 1,425 million Royal Bank common shares outstanding and 172 million common shares of Tim Hortons, and their stock prices at the beginning of January were $52.32 and $41.4. So, on average, investors did *not* hold the same number of shares of the two firms. The market cap of Royal Bank stock was about $74,556 million ($52.32/share × 1,425 million shares) and for Tim Hortons was $7,120.8 million. The Royal Bank's TSX index weight was 4.83 percent and Tim Hortons's weight was 0.46 percent. The fact that Royal Bank's index weight was 10.5 times Tim Hortons's (4.83/.46) reflects the fact that Royal Bank's market cap was 10.5 times greater than Tim Hortons's market cap ($74,556/$7,120.8).

[3] For some stocks, a portion of shares is not available to investors for trading, such as shares held by a control group, founding family, another company, or a government. If 20 percent or more of the shares are held by controlling shareholders, these shares are subtracted from the total number of shares to determine the *float* shares. The weights for the S&P/TSX index stocks are based on the number of float shares. For example, in 2011 about 64 percent of Loblaw Company's 276 million common shares were owned by George Weston Inc. Loblaw's weight in the index is based on the 99 million shares held outside of the George Weston control block.

a −1.39 percent return (a capital loss). Over the same period, the TSXT decreased from 36,480.62 to 36,004.33 points, a −1.32 percent return. The less negative rate of return on the TSXT, the total return index, comes from dividends earned during the month, offsetting the drop in the stock prices. Use the TSXT rate of return when comparing the total rate of return on a stock to the market's return.

Dow Jones Industrial Average U.S. index of the investment performance of a portfolio of 30 "blue-chip" stocks.

The best-known stock market index in the United States is the **Dow Jones Industrial Average**, generally known as the *Dow*. The Dow tracks the performance of a portfolio that holds one share in each of 30 large firms. The stock of such high-quality, stable firms is sometimes referred to as "blue-chip."

However, the Dow is far from the best measure of the performance of the U.S. stock market. First, with only 30 large industrial stocks, it is not representative of the performance of stocks generally. Second, unlike the TSX, it is an *equal-weighted* index. Despite the fact that in 2010 there were 10.1 billion shares in General Electric and just under 1 billion shares of DuPont, the index gave equal weight to each company. An equal-weighted portfolio cannot reflect the average performance of investors in the stocks.

Standard & Poor's Composite Index U.S. index of the investment performance of a portfolio of 500 large stocks. Also called the *S&P 500*.

The **Standard & Poor's Composite Index**, better known as the *S&P 500*, includes the stocks of 500 major U.S. companies and is therefore a more comprehensive index than the Dow. Like the TSX index, it measures the performance of a portfolio that holds shares in each firm in proportion to the value of shares that have been issued to investors.[4]

Only a small proportion of the thousands of publicly traded companies are represented in the TSX or the S&P 500. However, these firms are among the largest in Canada and the United States, respectively, and they account for roughly 70 percent of the stocks traded. Therefore, success for professional investors usually means "beating the TSX" or "beating the S&P."

Market indexes track performance of stock markets around the world. The main index of the London Stock Exchange is the Financial Times Stock Exchange Index, FTSE 100, or the "footsie." The Tokyo Stock Exchange market index is the Nikkei 225. Many other indexes have been created to measure performance of special groups of stock, such as the S&P/TSX SmallCap Index based on smaller companies listed on the TSX. Morgan Stanley Capital International (MSCI) computes the MSCI World Index, covering 24 countries and Standard & Poor's produces many indexes for markets around the world. Visit the MSCI Web site at **www.mscibarra.com** and the S&P Web site at **www.standardandpoors.com** (click on "indices") to learn more about global indexes.

THE HISTORICAL RECORD

The historical returns of stock or bond market indexes can give us an idea of the typical performance of different investments. Using data prepared by the Canadian Institute of Actuaries and Statistics Canada (CANSIM),[5] we can measure the investment performance of three portfolios of securities since 1925:

1. A portfolio of 91-day government securities, known as Treasury bills[6]
2. A portfolio of long-term Canadian government bonds
3. A portfolio of stocks of large Canadian companies[7]

---

[4] The S&P 500 and all other U.S. S&P stock indexes are calculated on the basis of the number of float shares (shares outside control groups), similar to the way the TSX index is calculated. Also, there are total return versions of these indexes, such as the S&P 500 Total Return Index, which include dividends.

[5] The main data source is the Canadian Institute of Actuaries Report on Canadian Economic Statistics 1924–2003, retrieved May 18, 2004. Index values for 2004–2010 are calculated by the authors using Government of Canada Long Bond yields (v122487) and 91-day Treasury Bill yields (v122541), from Statistics Canada CANSIM database, and TSX Total Return Index values, from **www.globeinvestorgold.com**, all retrieved on January 18, 2011.

[6] Canada did not have Treasury bills until 1934. We used U.S. Treasury bill data from Ibbotson Associates adjusted for the U.S.–Canada exchange rate for the years 1926 to 1933.

[7] Stock data used in the *Report on Canadian Economic Statistics* comes from different sources. A stock index from M.C. Urquhart and K.A.H. Buckley, *Historical Statistics of Canada* (Toronto: Macmillan, 1965), is used for 1926 to 1934. The TSE Industrial Index is used for 1935 to 1956. In 1956, the TSE 300 index began and then was replaced by S&P/TSX index in 2002. For convenience, we refer to this portfolio as the TSX Index.

These portfolios are not equally risky. Treasury bills are about as safe an investment as you can make. Because they are issued by the federal government, you can be sure that you will get your money back. Their short-term maturity means that their prices are relatively stable. In fact, investors who wish to lend money for three months can achieve a certain payoff by buying three-month Treasury bills. Of course, they can't be sure what that money will buy; there is still some uncertainty about inflation.

Long-term government bonds are also certain to be repaid when they mature, but the prices of these bonds fluctuate more as interest rates vary. When interest rates fall, the value of long-term bonds rises; when rates rise, the value of the bonds falls.

Common stocks are the riskiest of the three groups of securities. When you invest in common stocks, there is no promise that you will get your money back. As a part-owner of the corporation, you receive whatever is left over after the bonds and any other debts have been repaid.

Figure 11.1 shows the performance of the three groups of securities assuming that all dividend or interest income had been reinvested in the portfolio. You can see that the performance of the portfolios fits our intuitive risk ranking. Common stocks were the riskiest investment but they also offered the greatest gains. One dollar invested at the end of 1925 in a portfolio of common stocks would have grown to $2,787.25 by the end of 2010. At the other end of the spectrum, an investment of $1 in a Treasury bill would have accumulated to only $41.79.

Table 11.1 shows the average of the annual returns from each of these portfolios. These rates of return are comparable to the return that we calculated for Canadian Pacific. In other words, they include (1) dividends or interest and (2) any capital gains or losses.

maturity premium Extra average return from investing in long-term bonds versus short-term Treasury securities.

The safest investment, Treasury bills, had the lowest rates of return—they averaged 4.6 percent a year. Long-term government bonds gave somewhat higher returns than Treasury bills. This difference is called the **maturity premium**. Common stocks were in a class by themselves. Investors who accepted the risk of common stocks received on average an extra return of

FIGURE 11.1
The value to which a $1 investment made at the end of 1925 in each of three different portfolios of securities would have grown by the end of 2010 (index values plotted on log scale).

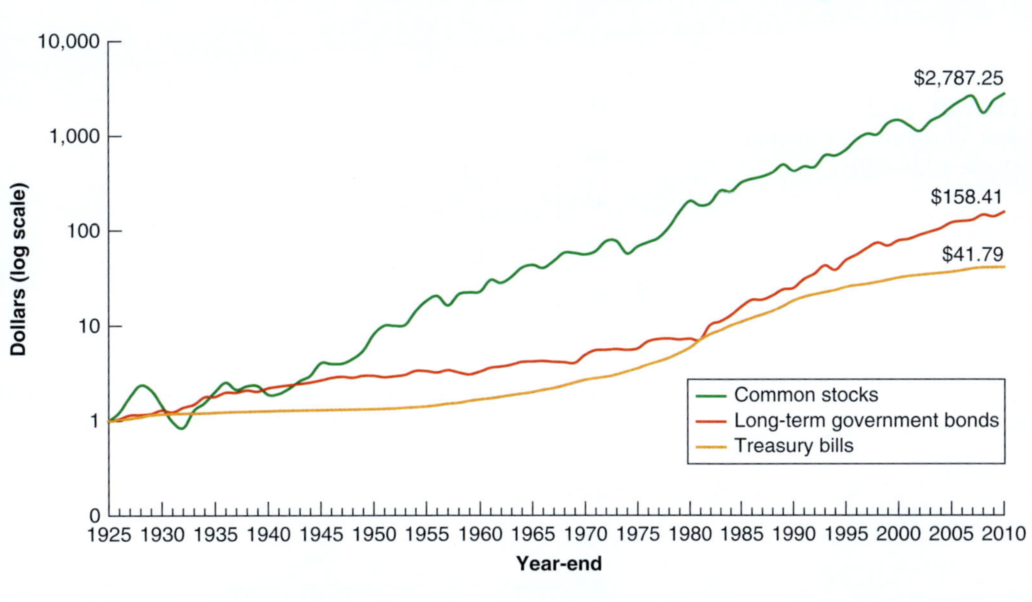

Sources: Authors' calculations using data from Canadian Institute of Actuaries, *Report on Canadian Economic Statistics 1924–2003*, augmented with values for 2004–2010 calculated with data from Statistics Canada CANSIM database, Series v122487 and v122541, **cansim2.statcan.ca**, and S&P/TSX Composite Total Return Index, **www.globeinvestorgold.com**. Courtesy of the Bank of Canada.

TABLE 11.1
Average rates of return on Treasury bills, government bonds, and common stocks, 1926–2010 (percent per year).

Portfolio	Average Annual Rate of Return	Average Risk Premium (extra return versus Treasury bills)
Treasury bills	4.6	
Long-term government bonds	6.5	1.9
Common stocks	11.5	6.9

Source: Author's calculations using data from Canadian Institute of Actuaries, *Report on Canadian Economic Statistics 1924–2003*, augmented with values for 2004–2010 calculated with data from Statistics Canada CANSIM database, Series v122487 and v122541, **cansim2.statcan.ca**, and S&P/TSX Composite Total Return Index, **www.globeinvestorgold.com**. Courtesy of the Bank of Canada.

6.9 percent a year over the return on Treasury bills. This compensation for taking on the risk of common stock ownership is known as the market **risk premium**:

risk premium Expected return in excess of risk-free return as compensation for risk.

$$\text{Rate of return on common stocks} = \text{interest rate on Treasury bills} + \text{market risk premium} \qquad (11.5)$$

The historical average risk premium for long-term government bonds portfolio is only 1.9, which is substantially less than 6.9 historical common stock portfolio risk premium. This is consistent with the fact that a bond portfolio is less risky than a stock portfolio.

The historical record shows that investors have received a risk premium for holding risky assets. Average returns on high-risk assets are higher than those on low-risk assets.

You might ask why we look back over such a long period to measure average rates of return. The reason is that annual rates of return for common stocks fluctuate so much that averages taken over short periods are extremely unreliable. In some years investors in common stocks had a disagreeable shock and received a substantially lower return than they expected. In other years they had a pleasant surprise and received a higher-than-expected return. By averaging the returns across both the rough years and the smooth ones, we should get a fair idea of the typical return that investors might justifiably expect.

While common stocks have offered the highest average returns, they have also been riskier investments. Figure 11.2 shows the 85 annual rates of return for the stock portfolio. The fluctuations in year-to-year returns on common stocks are remarkably wide. In 1933 and 1950 investors earned a return of around 50 percent. However, Figure 11.2 shows that you can also lose money

FIGURE 11.2
Rate of return on common stock, 1926–2010.

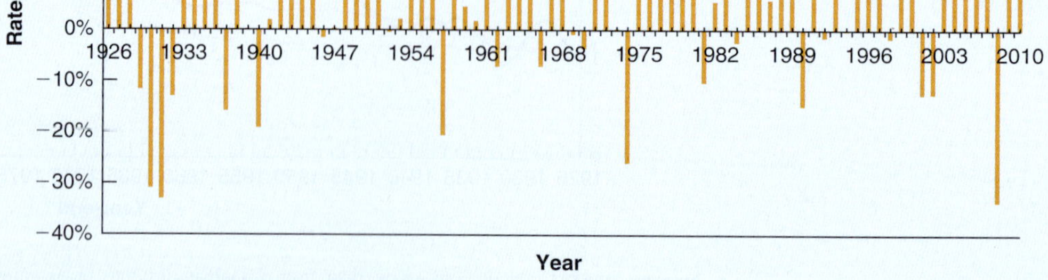

Source: Author's calculations using data from the Bank of Canada, Canadian Institute of Actuaries, *Report on Canadian Economic Statistics 1924–2003*, augmented with values for 2004–2010 calculated with data from Statistics Canada CANSIM database, Series v122487 and v122541, **cansim2.statcan.ca**, and S&P/TSX Composite Total Return Index, **www.globeinvestorgold.com**.

by investing in the stock market. The most dramatic case was the world stock market crash of 1929/1932. Between 1929 and 1932, the Canadian stock markets fell 64 percent and the U.S. stock market fell almost 90 percent.

You don't have to look that far back to see that the stock market is a risky place. Investors who bought S&P/TSX Composite Index at the beginning of 2008 experienced a 33 percent loss by the end of year, due to the financial market crisis. But the market recovered in 2009, with a 35 percent gain in the index.

Bond prices also fluctuate, but far less than stock prices. The worst year for investors in our long-term bond portfolio was 1994; their return that year was −10.5 percent.

Check Point 11.2

Here are the average rates of return for common stocks, government bonds, and Treasury bills for three different periods:

	1926–1949	1950–1975	1976–2007
Stocks	9.8%	11.6%	12.5%
Government bonds	4.8	2.7	10.4
Treasury bills	1.2	3.9	7.4

What were the risk premium on stocks and the maturity premium on government bonds for each period?

USING HISTORICAL EVIDENCE TO ESTIMATE TODAY'S COST OF CAPITAL

Think back now to Chapter 8, where we showed how firms calculate the present value of a new project by discounting the expected cash flows by the opportunity cost of capital. The opportunity cost of capital is the return that is given up by investing in the project rather than in comparable risk alternatives.

Measuring the cost of capital is easy if the project is a sure thing. Since investing in a Government of Canada Treasury bill provides a sure-fire payoff, the firm should invest in a risk-free project only if it can at least match the rate of interest on such a loan. If the project is risky—and most projects are—then the firm needs to at least match the return that could expected to be earned if they invested in securities of similar risk. It is not easy to put a precise figure on this, but our skim through history provides an idea of the average return an investor might expect to earn from an investment in risky common stocks.

Suppose there is an investment project that you *know*—don't ask how—has the same risk as an investment in a diversified portfolio of all Canadian stocks. We will call this the *market portfolio*. We will say that the investment project has the same degree of risk as the market portfolio. Although the S&P/TSX Composite Index does not include all stocks, we will use it as a proxy for the market portfolio.

Instead of investing in the project, you might invest directly in this market portfolio. In this case, the opportunity cost of capital for your project is the return expected to be earned on the market portfolio. This measures what is given up by investing money in your project.

Estimating this project's cost of capital boils down to estimating the currently expected rate of return on the market portfolio. You might be tempted to estimate the expected market return by assuming that the future will be like the past and that today's investors expect to receive the average rates of return shown in Table 11.1. In this case, you would judge that the expected market return today is 11.5 percent, the average of past market returns.

Unfortunately, this is *not* the way to do it. Investors are not likely to demand the same return every year on an investment in common stocks. For example, we know that the interest rate on safe Treasury bills varies over time. At their peak in 1981, Treasury bills offered a return of 20 percent, more than 15 percentage points[8] above the historical 4.6 percent average return on bills shown in Table 11.1.

What if you were called upon to estimate the expected return on common stocks in 1981? Would you have said 11.5 percent? That doesn't make sense. Who would invest in the risky stock market for an expected return of 11.5 percent when you could get a safe 20 percent from Treasury bills?

A better procedure is to take the current interest rate on Treasury bills plus 7 percentage points, the average *risk premium* shown in Table 11.1. In 1981, when the rate on Treasury bills was 20 percent, that would have given the expected return on common stock as:

The expected return on an investment provides compensation to investors both for waiting (the time value of money) and for worrying (the risk of the particular asset).

$$\text{Expected market return (1981)} = \text{interest rate on Treasury bills (1981)} + \text{normal risk premium}$$
$$= 20\% + 7\% = 27\%$$

The first term on the right-hand side tells us the time value of money in 1981; the second term measures the compensation for risk.

What about today? As we write this in early 2011, 91-day Treasury bills offer a return of only 1 percent. This suggests that investors in common stocks are looking for a return of around 8 percent:

$$\text{Expected market return (2011)} = \text{interest rate on Treasury bills (2011)} + \text{normal risk premium}$$
$$= 1\% + 7\% = 8\%$$

These calculations assume that there is a normal, stable risk premium on the market portfolio, so that the expected *future* risk premium can be measured by the average past risk premium. But, even with 85 years of data, we cannot estimate the market risk premium exactly; moreover, we cannot be sure that investors today are demanding the same reward for risk that they were in the 1940s. All this leaves plenty of room for argument about what the risk premium *really* is. One other issue is the use of the TSX index as the market portfolio for measuring the historical risk premium. If data for all Canadian stocks was used to construct the market index, the historical risk premium might be smaller. Since we don't have that data, we use historical TSX index return data to estimate the market risk premium.[9]

Many financial managers and economists believe that long-run historical returns are the best measure available and therefore settle on a risk premium of about 7 percentage points over the Treasury bill rate. Others have a gut instinct that investors don't need such a large risk premium to persuade them to hold common stocks and so shade downward their estimate of the expected future risk premium. Another source of disagreement is which government security to use as the risk-free security. When firms consider investments in long-lived projects, they usually think about risk premiums relative to long-term government bonds, rather than Treasury bills. Looking back at Table 11.1, common stocks have earned an average of 5 percentage points, 11.5% − 6.5%, over the portfolio of long-term government bonds. The current average yield on long-term Government of Canada bonds is about 3.7 percent. The expected market rate of return is estimated as 3.7% + 5%, or 8.7 percent, if the long-term government bond is used as the risk-free security. Whenever you talk about the risk premium, remember to state your chosen "risk-free" security.

[8] The term *percentage points* is used when measuring the *difference* in percentages, to avoid confusion with percentage change. Had we measured the *percentage change* in the returns, we would have calculated (20% − 4.7%)/4.7% = 3.26 or 326 percent, and said, "The 1981 Treasury bill rate was 326 percent bigger than the historical average Treasury bill rate of return." Related to percentage points are *basis points, bp.* One hundred bp equals one percentage point.

[9] Some researchers gather stock data for many years to calculate a bigger market portfolio to estimate the historical portfolio return. If you are interested in learning more about historical market risk premium for various countries, read the book E. Dimson, P.R. Marsh, and M. Staunton, *Triumph of the Optimists: 101 Years of Global Investment Returns* (Princeton, NJ: Princeton University Press, 2002).

LO2 11.3 MEASURING RISK

You now have some benchmarks. You know that the opportunity cost of capital for safe projects must be the rate of return offered by safe Treasury bills and you know that the opportunity cost of capital for "average risk" projects must be the expected return on the market portfolio. But you *don't* know how to estimate the cost of capital for projects that do not fit these two simple cases. Before you can do this you need to understand more about investment risk.

The average fuse time for army hand grenades is seven seconds, but that average hides a lot of potentially relevant information. If you are in the business of throwing grenades, you need some measure of the variation around the average fuse time.[10] Similarly, if you are in the business of investing in securities, you need some measure of how far the returns may differ from the average.

One way to present the spread of possible investment returns is by using histograms, such as the ones in Figure 11.3. The bars in each histogram show the number of years between 1926 and 2010 that the investment's return fell within a specific range. Look first at the performance of common stocks. Their risk shows up in the wide spread of outcomes. For example, you can see that in one year the return was between +50 and +55 percent but in three other years, investors lost between 30 and 35 percent.

The corresponding histograms for government bonds and Treasury bills show that unusually high or low returns are much less common. Investors in these securities face a smaller range of outcomes than do investors in common stocks.

VARIANCE AND STANDARD DEVIATION

Investment risk depends on the dispersion or spread of possible outcomes. For example, Figure 11.3 shows that on past evidence there is a greater uncertainty about the possible returns from common stocks than about the returns from Treasury bills or bonds. Sometimes a picture like Figure 11.3 tells you all you need to know about (past) dispersion. But in general, pictures do not suffice. The financial manager needs a numerical measure of dispersion. The standard measures are **variance** and **standard deviation**. More variable returns imply greater investment risk. This suggests that some measure of dispersion will provide a reasonable measure of risk, and dispersion is precisely what is measured by variance and standard deviation.

variance Average value of squared deviations from mean. A measure of volatility.

standard deviation Square root of variance. Another measure of volatility.

Here is a very simple example showing how variance and standard deviation are calculated. Suppose that you are offered the chance to play the following game. You start by investing \$100. Then two coins are flipped simultaneously. For each head that comes up your starting balance will be *increased* by 20 percent, and for each tail that comes up your starting balance will be *reduced* by 10 percent. There are four equally likely outcomes of the simultaneous flips of the 2 coins:

- Head & head: You make 20 + 20 = 40%
- Head & tail: You make 20 − 10 = 10%
- Tail & head: You make −10 + 20 = 10%
- Tail & tail: You make −10 − 10 = −20%

There is a chance of 1 in 4, or .25, that you will make 40 percent; a chance of 2 in 4, or .5, that you will make 10 percent; and a chance of 1 in 4, or .25, that you will lose 20 percent. The game's expected return is therefore a weighted average of the possible outcomes:

$$\textbf{Expected return} = \textbf{probability-weighted average of possible outcomes} \qquad (11.6)$$

$$= (.25 \times 40\%) + (.5 \times 10\%) + (.25 \times -20\%) = +10\%$$

If you play the game a very large number of times, your average return should be 10 percent.

[10] We assure you, the variation around the standard fuse time is very small.

FIGURE 11.3
Historical returns on major asset classes, 1926–2010.

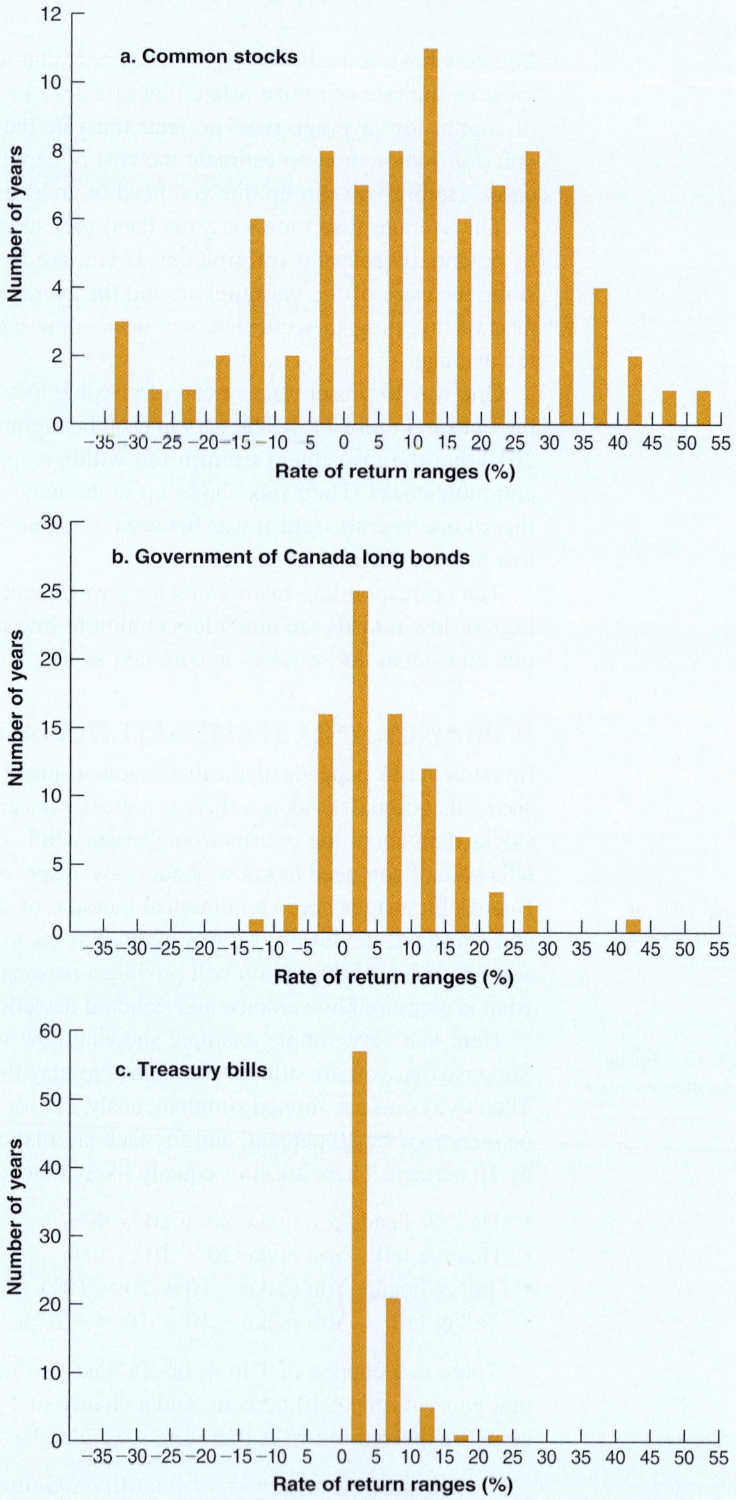

Source: Authors' calculations using data from Canadian Institute of Actuaries, *Report on Canadian Economic Statistics 1924–2003*, augmented with values for 2004–2010 calculated with data from Statistics Canada CANSIM database, Series v122487 and v122541, **cansim2.statcan.ca**, and S&P/TSX Composite Total Return Index, **www.globeinvestorgold.com**. Courtesy of the Bank of Canada.

TABLE 11.2
The coin-toss game: calculating variance and standard deviation when there are equal probabilities of each outcome.

(1) Percent Rate of Return	(2) Deviation from Expected Return	(3) Squared Deviation
+40	+30	900
+10	0	0
+10	0	0
−20	−30	900

Variance = average of squared deviations = 1,800/4 = 450.
Standard deviation = square root of variance = $\sqrt{450}$ = 21.2, about 21%.

Table 11.2 shows how to calculate the variance and standard deviation of the returns on your game. Column 1 shows the four equally likely outcomes. In column 2 we calculate the difference between each possible outcome and the expected outcome. You can see that at best the return could be 30 percentage points higher than expected; at worst it could be 30 percentage points lower.

These deviations in column 2 illustrate the spread of possible returns. But if we want a measure of this spread, it is no use just averaging the deviations in column 2—the average is always going to be zero. To get around this problem, we square the deviations in column 2 before averaging them. These squared deviations are shown in column 3. The variance is the weighted average of the squared deviations, where the weights are the probabilities. It is a useful measure of dispersion.

$$\textbf{Variance} = \textbf{probability-weighted average of squared deviations around the expected return} \quad \textbf{(11.7)}$$

$$= (.25 \times 900) + (.25 \times 0) + (.25 \times 0) + (.25 \times 900) = 450$$

When each of the outcomes is equally likely, the variance is just the average of the squared deviations. Taking the average of the squared deviations in column 3 of Table 11.2, you get 1,800/4 or 450.

When we squared the deviations from the expected return, we changed the units of measurement from *percentages* to *percentages squared*. Our last step is to get back to percentages by taking the square root of the variance. This is the standard deviation:

$$\textbf{Standard deviation} = \textbf{square root of variance} \quad \textbf{(11.8)}$$

$$= \sqrt{450} = 21\%$$

Because standard deviation is simply the square root of variance, it too is a natural measure of risk. If the outcome of the game had been certain, the standard deviation would have been zero because there would then be no deviations from the expected outcome. The actual standard deviation is positive because we *don't* know what will happen.

Now think of a second game. It is the same as the first except that each head means a 35 percent gain and each tail means a 25 percent loss. Again there are four equally likely outcomes:

- Head + head: You gain 70%
- Head + tail: You gain 10%
- Tail + head: You gain 10%
- Tail + tail: You lose 50%

For this game, the expected return is 10 percent, the same as that of the first game, but it is more risky. For example, in the first game, the worst possible outcome is a loss of 20 percent, which is 30 percentage points worse than the expected outcome. In the second game the downside is a loss of 50 percent, or 60 percentage points below the expected return. This increased spread of outcomes shows up in the standard deviation, which is double that of the first game, 42 percent versus 21 percent. By this measure the second game is twice as risky as the first.

A NOTE ON CALCULATING VARIANCE

When we calculated variance in Table 11.2 we recorded each of the four possible outcomes separately. An alternative would have been to recognize that in two of the cases the outcomes were the same. Thus there was a 50 percent chance of a 10 percent return from the game, a 25 percent chance of a 40 percent return, and a 25 percent chance of a −20 percent return. We calculate variance by weighting each squared deviation by the probability and then summing the results. Table 11.3 confirms that this method gives the same answer.

Check Point 11.3

Calculate the expected return, the variance, and the standard deviation of the second (higher-risk) coin-toss game in the same formats as Tables 11.2 and 11.3.

MEASURING THE VARIATION IN STOCK RETURNS

When estimating the spread of possible outcomes from investing in the stock market, most financial analysts start by assuming that the spread of returns in the past is a reasonable indication of what could happen in the future. Therefore, they calculate the variance and standard deviation of past returns. However, this situation is not the same as the previous coin-toss example, where the probability of each possible outcome was known, and variance was calculated as the probability-weighted average of the squared deviations. In the coin-toss example, we calculated the *population* variance and the *population* standard deviation. When you have a sample of observed rates of return, the probability of each possible return is unknown.[11] For a sample of observations, we calculate the *sample variance*. As before, the squared deviations from the average rate of return are calculated. The sample variance is the sum of the squared deviations around the estimated average rate of return, divided by the number of observations minus one:

$$\frac{\text{Variance based on}}{\text{sample of observations}} \quad \text{Variance based on sample of observations} = \frac{\text{sum of squared deviations from average return}}{\text{number of observations} - 1} \tag{11.9}$$

The sample standard deviation is the square root of the sample variance.

Although there are two different definitions of variance, people often call them both variance. However, you can always tell which variance is being used. If you know the probability of each possible value, you have the population variance, as in the coin-toss example. If you have a group of observed values, the sample variance is calculated using the formula above. The sample variance is also sometimes called the *estimated* variance.

To illustrate, suppose that you were given the stock market returns shown in Table 11.4. The average return over the 6 years from 2005 to 2010 was 11.8 percent. This is just the sum of the returns over the 6 years divided by 6 (70.9/6 = 11.8 percent).

TABLE 11.3 The coin-toss game: calculating variance and standard deviation when there are different probabilities of each outcome.

(1) Percent Rate of Return	(2) Probability of Return	(3) Deviation from Expected Return	(4) Probability × Squared Deviation
+40	.25	+30	.25 × 900 = 225
+10	.50	0	.50 × 0 = 0
−20	.25	−30	.25 × 900 = 225

Variance = sum of squared deviations weighted by probabilities = 225 + 0 + 225 = 450.
Standard deviation = square root of variance = $\sqrt{450}$ = 21.2, about 21%.

[11] In terms of statistics, we are drawing a distinction between *calculating* the variance of a population, where you know the probability of every possible outcome (the coin-toss example), and *estimating* the variance of a population using a sample of observations. We use the sample variance to infer the true but unknown variance of the population. That is why the sample variance is also called the *estimated* variance of the population.

TABLE 11.4
The average return and standard deviation of stock market returns, 2005–2010.

Year	Rate of Return	Deviation from Average Return	Squared Deviation
2005	24.4	12.6	158.76
2006	17.0	5.2	27.04
2007	9.8	−2.0	4.00
2008	−33.0	−44.8	2,007.04
2009	35.1	23.3	542.98
2010	17.6	5.8	33.64
Total	70.9		2,773.37

Average rate of return = 70.9/6 = 11.8%.

Variance = sum of squared deviations/(number of observations − 1) = 2,773.37/(6 − 1) = 554.7.

Standard deviation = square root of variance = $\sqrt{544.7}$ = 23.3%.

Source: Authors' calculations using data from Canadian Institute of Actuaries, *Report on Canadian Economic Statistics 1924–2003*, augmented with values for 2004–2010 calculated with data from Statistics Canada, Series v122487 and v122541, CANSIM database **cansim2.statcan.ca**, and S&P/TSX Composite Total Return Index, **www.globeinvestorgold.com**. Courtesy of the Bank of Canada.

Column 2 in Table 11.4 shows the difference between each year's return and the average return. For example, in 2005 the return of 24.4 percent on common stocks was above the six-year average by 12.6 percentage points, 24.4 − 11.8. In column 3 we square these deviations from the average. Using equation 11.9, the variance is the sum of these squared deviations divided by the number of observations minus one:

$$\text{Sample variance} = \text{sum of squared deviations}/(\text{number of observations} - 1)$$

$$= \frac{2{,}773.37}{6 - 1} = 544.7$$

Since standard deviation is the square root of the variance,

$$\text{Sample standard deviation} = \text{square root of sample variance}$$

$$= \sqrt{544.7} = 23.3\%$$

With Excel, sample variance and standard deviation can be quickly calculated using the VAR and STDEV functions. If the six stock returns from Table 11.4 were in cells A1 to A6, the variance and standard deviations of the returns would be calculated as VAR(A1:A6) and STDEV(A1:A6).

It is inadequate to estimate the risk of securities on the basis of just six past outcomes. Therefore, Table 11.5 lists the annual standard deviations for our three portfolios of securities over the period from 1926 to 2010. As expected, Treasury bills were the least variable security and common stocks were the most variable. Long-term government bonds hold the middle ground.

Of course, there is no reason to believe that the market's variability should stay the same over many years. Indeed, many people believe that in recent years the stock market has become more volatile due to irresponsible speculation by some investors. Figure 11.4 provides a chart of the volatility of the Canadian and U.S. stock markets for each year from 1950 to 2010. The U.S.

TABLE 11.5
Standard deviation of rates of return, 1926–2010.

Portfolio	Standard Deviation, %
Treasury bills	4.1
Long-term government bonds	8.8
Common stocks	18.9

Source: Authors' calculations using data from Canadian Institute of Actuaries, *Report on Canadian Economic Statistics 1924–2003*, augmented with values for 2004–2010 calculated with data from Statistics Canada CANSIM database, Series v122487 and v122541, **cansim2.statcan.ca**, and S&P/TSX Composite Total Return Index, **www.globeinvestorgold.com**. Courtesy of the Bank of Canada.

FIGURE 11.4
Canadian and U.S. stock market volatility, 1950–2010, based on annualized monthly standard deviation of monthly rates of return on each index.

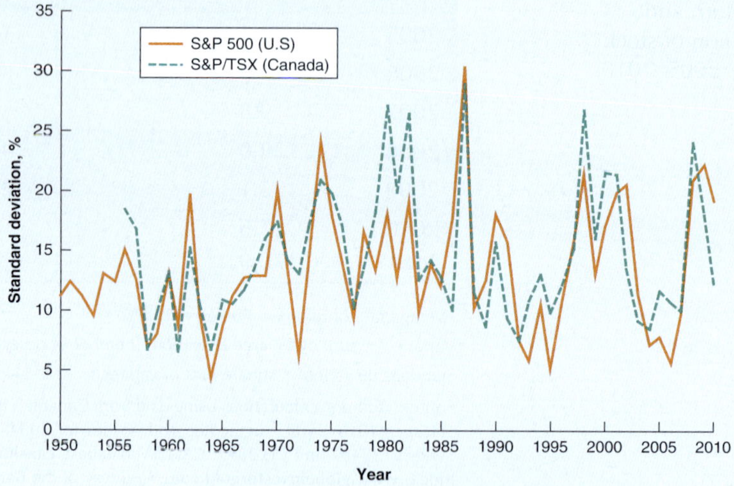

Source: Authors' calculations using monthly S&P 500 Index prices and S&P/TSX Composite Index prices.

stock market volatility is based on the sample standard deviation of the S&P 500 monthly index returns and the Canadian stock market volatility is based on standard deviation of the S&P/TSX composite index monthly returns.[12] You can see that there are periods of unusually high variability, with high annual standard deviation. In 1987 there was a major market crash and also significant recovery, and the annual standard deviations of both the S&P 500 and S&P/TSX index were about 30 percent. The recent financial market crisis, which began in 2007, also caused higher variability of the stock indexes, but the Canadian market index volatility has reduced more than the United States'. The main point is that there is no long-term upward trend in either U.S. or Canadian stock market volatility.

LO3 11.4 RISK AND DIVERSIFICATION

DIVERSIFICATION

We can calculate our measures of variability equally well for individual securities and portfolios of securities. Of course, the level of variability over 85 years is less interesting for specific companies than for the market portfolio because it is a rare company that faces the same business risks today as it did in 1926.

Table 11.6 presents estimated standard deviations for the common stocks of nine Canadian companies for a recent five-year period, 2006 to 2010.[13] The average of these nine standard deviations is 36.3 percent. Do these standard deviations look high to you? They should. The annual standard deviation of the market portfolio over the period from 1926 to 2010, reported in Table 11.5 was 18.9 percent. Also, at the bottom of Table 11.6 is the standard deviation of the S&P/TSX Composite Total Return Index, measured over 2006 to 2010 and is only 16.8 percent. Of our individual stocks, only TransCanada had a standard deviation of less than 16.8 percent! Most stocks are substantially more variable than the market portfolio; only a handful are less variable.

---

[12] We calculated the monthly variance for each year using each year's monthly rates of return. Then converted the monthly variance for each year to an annual variance by multiplying by 12. In other words, the variance of annual returns is 12 times that of monthly returns. Then, the annual standard deviation is the square root of the annual variance. The longer you hold a security, the more risk you have to bear. Monthly data for the TSX index begins in 1956.

[13] We pointed out earlier that six annual observations are insufficient to give a reliable estimate of variability. Therefore, these estimates are derived from 60 monthly rates of return and then the monthly variance is multiplied by 12 and then the square root is calculated to give the estimated annual standard deviation.

TABLE 11.6
Standard deviations of stock rates of return for selected common stocks, January 2006–December 2010.

Stock	Standard Deviation, %
IMAX	64.0
Research In Motion	55.2
Gildan Activewear	46.3
Barrick Gold	39.1
Cameco	36.9
Canadian Pacific Railway	24.8
Royal Bank	22.5
Loblaw	22.3
TransCanada Corp	15.4
S&P/TSX Composite Total Return Index	16.8

Source: Author's calculations using 2006–2009 monthly return data from TSX-CFMRC database, augmented with 2010 monthly returns calculated with stock prices from **www.globeinvestorgold.com** and dividend data from Financial Post Advisor.

diversification Strategy designed to reduce risk by spreading the portfolio across many investments.

This raises an important question: The market portfolio comprises individual stocks, so why isn't its variability equal to the average variability of its components? The answer is that **diversification** reduces variability.

Selling umbrellas is a risky business; you might make a fortune when it rains, but you are likely to lose your shirt in a heat wave. Selling ice cream is no safer; you do well in a heat wave, but business is poor in the rain or snow. Suppose, however, that you invest in both an umbrella shop and an ice cream shop. By diversifying your investment across the two businesses you make an average level of profit rain or shine.

Portfolio diversification works because prices of different stocks do not move exactly together. Statisticians make the same point when they say that stock price changes are less than perfectly correlated. Diversification works best when the returns are negatively correlated, as is the case for our umbrella and ice cream businesses. When one business does well, the other does badly. Unfortunately, in practice, stocks that are negatively correlated are extremely rare.

ASSET VERSUS PORTFOLIO RISK

The history of returns on different asset classes provides compelling evidence of a risk–return trade-off and suggests that the variability of the rates of return on each asset class is a useful measure of risk. However, volatility of returns can be a misleading measure of risk for an individual asset held as part of a portfolio. To see why, consider the following example.

Suppose there are three equally likely outcomes, or *scenarios*, for the economy: a recession, normal growth, and a boom. An investment in an auto stock will have a rate of return of −8 percent in a recession, 5 percent in a normal period, and 18 percent in a boom. Auto firms are cyclical: they do well when the economy does well. In contrast, gold firms are often said to be *countercyclical*, meaning that they do well when other firms do poorly. Suppose that stock in a gold mining firm will provide a rate of return of 20 percent in a recession, 3 percent in a normal period, and −20 percent in a boom. These assumptions are summarized in Table 11.7.

It appears that gold is the more volatile investment. The difference in return across the boom and bust scenarios is 40 percentage points (−20 percent in a boom versus +20 percent in a recession) compared to a spread of only 26 percentage points for the auto stock. In fact, we can confirm the higher volatility by measuring the variance or standard deviation of returns of the two assets. The calculations are set out in Table 11.8.

Since all three scenarios are equally likely, the expected return on each stock is simply the average of the three possible outcomes.[14] For the auto stock the expected return is 5 percent; for

[14] If the probabilities were not equal, we would need to weight each outcome by its probability in calculating the expected outcome and the variance.

TABLE 11.7

Rate of return assumptions for two stocks.

Scenario	Probability	Rate of Return, %: Auto Stock	Rate of Return, %: Gold Stock
Recession	1/3	− 8	+20
Normal	1/3	+ 5	+ 3
Boom	1/3	+18	−20

TABLE 11.8

Expected return and volatility for two stocks.

	Auto Stock			Gold Stock		
Scenario	Rate of Return, %	Deviation from Expected Return, %	Squared Deviation	Rate of Return, %	Deviation from Expected Return, %	Squared Deviation
Recession	−8	−13	169	+20	+19	361
Normal	+5	0	0	+ 3	+ 2	4
Boom	+18	+13	169	−20	−21	441
Expected return	$\frac{1}{3}(-8 + 5 + 18) = 5\%$			$\frac{1}{3}(+20 + 3 - 20) = 1\%$		
Variance[a]	$\frac{1}{3}(169 + 0 + 169) = 112.7$			$\frac{1}{3}(361 + 4 + 441) = 268.7$		
Standard deviation ($= \sqrt{\text{variance}}$)	$\sqrt{112.7} = 10.6\%$			$\sqrt{268.7} = 16.4\%$		
Covariance[b]	$= \frac{1}{3}(-13 \times 19) + \frac{1}{3}(0 \times 2) + \frac{1}{3}(13 \times -21) = -173.3$					
Correlation[c]	$= \frac{-173.3}{(10.6)(16.4)} = -.997$, or about -1					

[a] Variance = probability-weighted average of squared deviations from the expected value.

[b] Covariance = probability-weighted average of the product of each stock's deviation from its expected value, for each possible scenario.

[c] Correlation $= \frac{\text{covariance}}{\text{standard deviation of auto} \times \text{standard deviation of gold}}$.

the gold stock it is 1 percent. The variance is the average of the squared deviations from the expected return and the standard deviation is the square root of the variance.

Check Point 11.4

Suppose the probabilities of the recession or boom are .30, while the probability of a normal period is .40. Would you expect the variance of returns on these two investments to be higher or lower? Why? Confirm by calculating the standard deviation of the auto stock.

The gold mining stock offers a lower expected rate of return than the auto stock, and *more* volatility—a loser on both counts, right? Would anyone be willing to hold gold mining stocks in an investment portfolio? The answer is a resounding *yes*.

To see why, suppose you do believe that gold is a lousy asset, and therefore, hold your entire portfolio in the auto stock. Your expected return is 5 percent and your standard deviation is 11.6 percent. We'll compare that portfolio to a partially diversified one, invested 75 percent in autos and 25 percent in gold. For example, if you have a $10,000 portfolio, you could put $7,500 in autos and $2,500 in gold.

First, we need to calculate the return on this portfolio in each scenario. The portfolio return is the weighted average of returns on the individual assets with weights equal to the proportion of the portfolio invested in each asset. For a portfolio formed from only two assets,

$$\begin{aligned}\text{Portfolio rate of return} &= \left(\begin{array}{c}\text{fraction of portfolio}\\\text{in first asset}\end{array} \times \begin{array}{c}\text{rate of return}\\\text{on first asset}\end{array}\right)\\ &+ \left(\begin{array}{c}\text{fraction of portfolio}\\\text{in second asset}\end{array} \times \begin{array}{c}\text{rate of return}\\\text{on second asset}\end{array}\right)\end{aligned} \tag{11.10}$$

For example, autos have a weight of .75 and a rate of return of −8 percent in the recession, and gold has a weight of .25 and a return of 20 percent in a recession. Therefore, the portfolio return in the recession is the following weighted average:[15]

$$\begin{aligned}\text{Portfolio return in recession} &= [.75 \times (-8\%)] + [.25 \times 20\%]\\ &= -1\%\end{aligned}$$

Table 11.9 expands Table 11.7 to include the portfolio of the auto and gold mining stocks. The expected returns and volatility measures are summarized at the bottom of the table. The surprising finding is this: When you shift funds from the auto stock to the more volatile gold mining stock, your portfolio variability actually *decreases*. In fact, the volatility of the auto-plus-gold stock portfolio is considerably less than the volatility of either stock separately. The standard deviation of the portfolio return is only 3.9 percent, less than the standard deviations of either the auto or gold stocks. This is the payoff for diversification.

We can understand this more clearly by focusing on asset returns in the two extreme scenarios, boom and recession. In the boom, when auto stocks do best, the poor return on gold reduces the performance of the overall portfolio. However, when auto stocks are stalling in a recession, gold shines, providing a substantial positive return that boosts portfolio performance. The gold stock offsets the swings in the performance of the auto stock, reducing the best-case return but improving the worst-case return. The inverse relationship between the returns on the two stocks means that the addition of the gold mining stock to an all-auto portfolio stabilizes returns.

A gold stock is really a *negative-risk* asset to an investor starting with an all-auto portfolio. Adding it to the portfolio reduces the volatility of returns. The *incremental* risk of the gold stock (that is, the *change* in overall risk when gold is added to the portfolio) is negative despite the fact that gold returns are highly volatile.

TABLE 11.9
Rates of return for two stocks and a portfolio.

	Rate of Return, %			
Scenario	Probability	Auto Stock	Gold Stock	Portfolio Return, %[a]
Recession	1/3	−8	+20	−1%
Normal	1/3	+5	+3	+4.5
Boom	1/3	+18	−20	+8.5
Expected return		5%	1%	4%
Variance		112.7	268.7	15.2
Standard deviation		10.6%	16.4%	3.9%

[a] Portfolio return = (.75 × auto stock return) + (.25 × gold stock return).

[15] Let's confirm this. Suppose you invest $7,500 in autos and $2,500 in gold. If the recession hits, the rate of return on autos will be −8 percent, and the value of the auto investment will fall by 8 percent to $6,900. The rate of return on gold will be 20 percent, and the value of the gold investment will rise 20 percent to $3,000. The value of the total portfolio falls from its original value of $10,000 to $6,900 + $3,000 = $9,900, which is a rate of return of −1 percent. This matches the rate of return given by the formula for the weighted average.

In general, the incremental risk of a stock depends on whether its returns tend to vary with or against the returns of the other assets in the portfolio. Incremental risk does not just depend on a stock's volatility. If returns do not move closely with those of the rest of the portfolio, the stock will reduce the volatility of portfolio returns.

We can summarize as follows:

1. Investors care about the expected return and risk of their *portfolio* of assets. The risk of the overall portfolio can be measured by the volatility of the portfolio returns, that is, the variance or standard deviation.
2. The standard deviation of the returns of an individual security measures how risky that security would be if held in isolation. But an investor who holds a portfolio of securities is interested only in how each security affects the risk of the entire portfolio. The contribution of a security to the risk of the portfolio depends on how the security's returns vary with the investor's other holdings. Thus a security that is risky if held in isolation may nevertheless serve to reduce the variability of the portfolio, as long as its returns vary inversely with those of the rest of the portfolio.

COVARIANCE AND CORRELATION

We have given you an intuitive idea of how diversification reduces risk. Combining assets into a portfolio reduces risk because the assets' prices do not move in lockstep, and so the rates of return are different. When the auto stock is doing poorly, the gold stock does well, helping to offset the negative impact of the auto stock on the portfolio return. The next step is to measure the degree to which the returns on two stocks are related. The *covariance* of the returns on the two stocks is a statistical concept that measures how much the returns of the two stocks move together. Covariance is equal to the probability-weighted average of the product of each variable's difference from its expected return, for each possible future event. If the covariance is positive you know that the stock returns move together. Negative covariance means that they vary inversely.

To calculate the covariance of the auto and gold stock returns, the first step is to calculate the deviation from expected return for each stock. The deviations from expected return are the same calculations made to calculate each stock's variance, and are shown in Table 11.8. For example, in a recession the deviation from expected return is –13 percent of auto stock and is +19 percent for gold stock. The next step is to multiply together the deviations for each scenario and then calculate the probability-weighted average of the product of the deviations. The covariance between the return on the auto and gold stocks is:

$$\text{Covariance} = \text{probability-weighted average of the products of each deviation for each scenario} \quad (11.11)$$

$$= \frac{1}{3}(-13 \times 19) + \frac{1}{3}(0 \times 2) + \frac{1}{3}(13 \times -21) = -173.3$$

The covariance is negative, statistical proof that the auto and gold stock returns move differently in the boom and recession scenarios.

Once you've calculate the covariance between the returns and also the variance of each stock return, you can calculate the correlation coefficient. The correlation coefficient is an easier statistic to use to measure how stock returns vary relative to each other. The correlation coefficient formula is the covariance between the two stock returns, x and y, divided by the product of their standard deviations:

$$\text{Correlation between and } x \text{ and } y = \frac{\text{covariance between } x \text{ and } y}{\text{standard deviation of } x \times \text{standard deviation of } y} \quad (11.12)$$

So the correlation coefficient between the auto and gold returns is $-173.3/(10.6 \times 16.4) = -0.997$ or about -1.

correlation coefficient Measure of how closely two variables move together.

The **correlation coefficient**, which is always a number between -1 and 1, measures the degree to which two variables move together. If the correlation coefficient is greater than zero, the two variables tend to move in the same direction; they are *positively* correlated. The higher the correlation coefficient, the stronger the relationship between the two variables. When the correlation coefficient equals 1, the variables are perfectly positively correlated and the variables move in lockstep. On the other hand, if the correlation coefficient is less than zero, the two variables tend to move in the opposite direction; they are *negatively* correlated. With a correlation coefficient equal to −1, the variables are perfectly negatively correlated. If the correlation coefficient equals zero, a change in one variable does not tell you anything about the likely change in the other; the variables are said to be *uncorrelated*.

Check Point 11.5

Are each of the following pairs of variables likely to be positively correlated, negatively correlated, or uncorrelated? Briefly explain why.

a. The number of hours of sunshine per day and the average daily air temperature.
b. The number of hours of television you watch per day and your grade on your finance final exam.
c. The flying time from Vancouver to St. John's and the quality of the in-flight movie.
d. The level of interest rates in the United States and the level of interest rates in Canada.

CORRELATION AND PORTFOLIO DIVERSIFICATION

The degree of correlation among assets determines the extent to which risk is reduced through portfolio diversification. To illustrate, we will create a portfolio of two stocks, Steelco (S), a manufacturer of construction steel, and Gold Bear (G), a gold mine and refinery. The expected return on Steelco shares, r_S, is 15 percent, and the expected return on Gold Bear shares, r_G, is 9 percent. The standard deviation of return on Steelco is 12 percent and the standard deviation of return on Gold Bear is 18 percent. What are the expected return and standard deviation of return for a portfolio of these two stocks?

The expected return on the portfolio of Steelco and Gold Bear stocks will depend on the fraction of funds invested in each. Let x_S be the fraction of the total funds invested in shares of Steelco and x_G be the fraction invested in shares of Gold Bear Mine. The expected return on the portfolio is the weighted average of the expected returns on the two stocks, where the weights equal the fraction invested in each, so

$$r_p = x_S \times 15\% + x_G \times 9\%$$

If 100 percent of the funds are invested in Steelco, $x_S = 1$ and $x_G = 0$, the portfolio expected return is 15 percent, the expected return on Steelco. If 25 percent of the funds are invested in Steelco ($x_S = .25$) and 75 percent are invested in Gold Bear ($x_G = .75$), the expected portfolio return is

$$r_p = .25 \times 15\% + .75 \times 9\% = 10.5\%$$

The general formula for expected return of a portfolio is simply the weighted average of the expected return on the assets in the portfolio, where the weights are the fractions invested in each stock:

$$\text{Portfolio expected return} = r_p = x_S r_S + x_G r_G$$

Is the portfolio standard deviation equal to the weighted average of the standard deviations of assets in the portfolio? The answer depends on the correlation between the assets in the portfolio. If the assets' returns are perfectly positively correlated, there is no benefit from diversification and the portfolio standard deviation is simply the weighted average of the individual stocks' standard deviations. However, if the stocks are less than perfectly correlated, diversification reduces portfolio risk—the portfolio standard deviation will be less than the weighted average of the assets' standard deviations.

To show you how this works, we need a bit of notation. The commonly used symbol for standard deviation is the Greek letter σ ("sigma"). Thus the standard deviation of the return on Steelco is σ_S, and for Gold Bear, σ_G. We use the Greek letter ρ ("rho") to represent the

TABLE 11.10
Relationship between correlation and portfolio standard deviation.

Correlation Coefficient, ρ_{SG}	Portfolio Standard Deviation $= \sigma_p = \sqrt{x_S^2\sigma_S^2 + x_G^2\sigma_G^2 + 2x_Sx_G\rho_{SG}\sigma_S\sigma_G}$ $= \sqrt{(.25)^2(.12)^2 + (.75)^2(.18)^2 + 2(.25)(.75)\rho_{SG}(.12)(.18)}$
1.0	.165
0.8	.160
0.2	.144
0	.138
−0.3	.129
−0.7	.116
−1.0	.105

correlation coefficient. Thus ρ_{SG} is the correlation coefficient for Steelco and Big Bear. The formula for the standard deviation of a portfolio with two stocks is

$$\text{Portfolio standard deviation} = \sigma_p = \sqrt{x_S^2\sigma_S^2 + x_G^2\sigma_G^2 + 2x_Sx_Gr_{SG}\sigma_S\sigma_G} \quad (11.13)$$

Notice that the portfolio standard deviation depends on the individual stocks' standard deviations and also on their correlation to one another.

Suppose the returns on Steelco and Gold Bear are perfectly positively correlated, $\rho_{SG} = 1$. The standard deviation of a portfolio with 25 percent invested in Steelco ($x_S = .25$) and 75 percent in Gold Bear ($x_G = .75$) is

$$\sigma_p = \sqrt{(.25)^2(.12)^2 + (.75)^2(.18)^2 + 2(.25)(.75)(1)(.12)(.18)} = .165$$

This is also the weighted average of Steelco's and Gold Bear's standard deviations: $(.25)(.12) + (.75)(.18) = .165$. Only if the stocks are perfectly positively correlated, $\rho_{SG} = 1$, will there be no benefit from diversification. Table 11.10 shows portfolio standard deviation for other possible correlation coefficients. Notice that with lower correlation, the benefit of diversification increases, seen as lower portfolio standard deviation. Can portfolio risk (portfolio standard deviation) be reduced to zero through diversification? If some assets are negatively correlated with the others, it is mathematically possible to reduce the portfolio risk to zero. In our example, if the correlation coefficient was −.3, and you invested about 65 percent in Steelco and 35 percent in Gold Bear, the portfolio standard deviation would be close to zero.

Unfortunately, assets with negative correlation with the economy are hard to find. Although some assets have low correlation with other assets (gold, for instance), all assets' returns tend to be positively correlated. Portfolio diversification can reduce risk up to a point but cannot remove all risks.

EXAMPLE 11.2 LOBLAW AND TRANSCANADA PORTFOLIOS

Our example of the auto and gold mining stocks was entirely based on made-up numbers. But we can look at the benefits of diversification using real companies. Suppose at the end of August 2007 you invested $100 in the stock of Loblaw (LOB). The value of the Loblaw portfolio at the end of each month equals the value at the start of the month times 1 plus Loblaw's rate of return for that month. Loblaw's rate of return for September 2007 was −8.8 percent. So the value of the Loblaw portfolio at the end of September was $100 × (1 − .088) or $91.2. The blue (lower) line in Figure 11.5 shows how the value of your investment would have fluctuated over the following 40 months. The portfolio started at $100 and was worth only $89.52 at the end of December, 2010, 40 months later. The risk causes variation in the monthly returns and shows up in the variation in the value of the portfolio. In 21 out of 40 months, you would have had a negative return. You can see the impact of the 2008 financial crisis. The value of the portfolio fell between June and October, 2008 and the lowest monthly rate of return was –23.8 percent in December 2008, during the peak of the financial market

FIGURE 11.5
The values of investments in the Loblaw and TransCanada stocks have been very variable. But the two stocks have not moved in lockstep. Investors could have reduced variability by dividing their money equally between the two stocks.

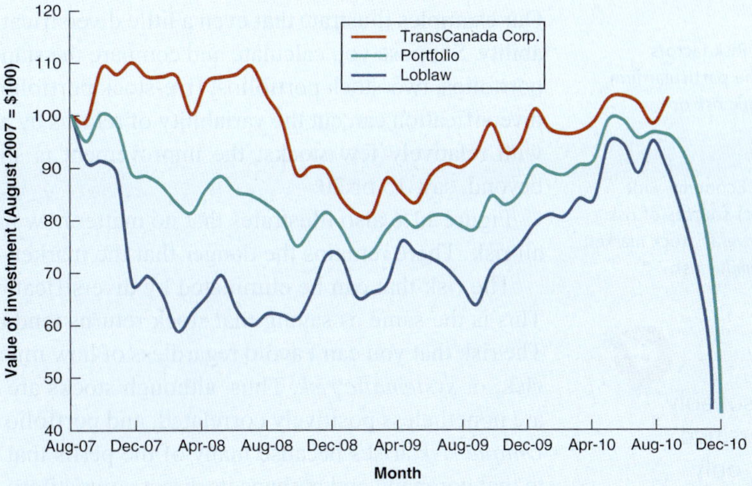

crisis. The Loblaw's rates of return turned positive and the portfolio value increased. The standard deviation of LOB's monthly rates of return during this period was about 7.1 percent. This was calculated with monthly rates of return using the Excel variance function, STDEV. Converted to an annual standard deviation: $[12 \times (.071)^2]^{1/2} = .246$ or 25 percent.

The red line (top) in Figure 11.5 shows a picture of the performance of $100 invested in TransCanada Corporation (TRP) stock over the same period. In 19 out of 40 months, you would have had a negative return. The value of the TransCanada portfolio also fell during the financial market crisis. Its worst monthly return was –10 percent in November, 2008. The portfolio started at $100 and was worth $103.23 at the end of December, 2010. The standard deviation of TRP's monthly returns during this period was 4.4 percent. Convert to an annual basis, the standard deviation is $[12 \times (.044)^2]^{1/2} = .1524$ or 15 percent. The fluctuations in TRP were slightly smaller than those of Loblaw.

Although both stocks had their ups and downs, the two stocks did not move in lockstep. Despite the fact that both stocks were affected by the financial crisis, there were times when the value of the TransCanada investment increased when the value of the Loblaw investment fell. So if you split your savings and put 50 percent in TRP and the other 50 percent in LOB, you would have reduced the monthly fluctuations in the value of your savings. You can see from the green line in Figure 11.5 (the middle line) which shows the value of a portfolio that started with $50 invested in Loblaw and $50 invested in Canadian Pacific. The value of this portfolio is between the other two portfolios. There were more months when the combined return was less extreme. By diversifying between the two stocks, you would have reduced the standard deviation of the monthly returns on your investment to 4.1 percent, which is slightly lower than the monthly standard deviation of either Loblaw's or TransCanada's stock returns. The annual equivalent of the monthly standard deviation is 14 percent. This is lower than the weighted average of the standard deviation of both LOB and TRP, $.5 \times .246 + .5 \times .1524 = .1992$. As we saw in equation 11.13, this lower portfolio standard deviation implies that the correlation coefficient for the returns on LOB and TRP must be less than one.

Using the Excel correlation function CORREL, we calculated the correlation coefficient between the rate of return on Loblaw and TransCanada. The estimated correlation coefficient is .028. This implies that the tendency is that when the Loblaw stock return is positive, the TransCanada stock return is positive but not always. This is a very low positive correlation. That is why the variability of the portfolio of the two stocks is less than the variability of each of the individual stocks. You can see this in Figure 11.5. The tendency is that when the value of the Loblaw portfolio goes up, the value of the Canadian Pacific portfolio goes up too but not always. Although they were both affected by the financial market crisis in 2008, the major stock reactions were in different months. So the return on portfolio of the two stocks is less variable than that of the two individual stocks.

MARKET RISK VERSUS UNIQUE RISK

unique risk Risk factors affecting only the particular firm. Also called *specific risk* or *diversifiable risk.*

market risk Economy-wide (macroeconomic) sources of risk that affect the overall stock market. Also called *systematic risk.*

For a reasonably well-diversified portfolio, only market risk matters.

Our examples illustrate that even a little diversification can provide a substantial reduction in variability. Suppose you calculate and compare the standard deviations of randomly chosen one-stock portfolios, two-stock portfolios, five-stock portfolios, and so on. You can see from Figure 11.6 that diversification can cut the variability of returns by about half. But you can get most of this benefit with relatively few stocks: the improvement is slight when the number of stocks is increased beyond, say, 15 or 20.

Figure 11.6 also illustrates that no matter how many securities you hold, you cannot eliminate all risk. There remains the danger that the market—including your portfolio—will plummet.

The risk that can be eliminated by diversification is called **unique risk** or *firm-specific risk.* This is the same as saying that stock returns tend to be less than perfectly positively correlated. The risk that you can't avoid regardless of how much you diversify is generally known as **market risk**, or *systematic risk.* Thus, although stocks are less than perfectly positively correlated, they are nonetheless positively correlated, and portfolio standard deviation cannot be reduced to zero. *Unique risk* arises because many of the perils that surround an individual company are specific to that company and perhaps its direct competitors. Market risk stems from economy-wide perils that threaten all businesses. *Market risk* explains why stocks have a tendency to move together, so that even well-diversified portfolios are exposed to market movements.

Figure 11.7 divides risk into its two parts—unique risk and market risk. If you have only a single stock, unique risk is very important; but once you have a portfolio of 30 or more stocks, diversification has done most of what it can to eliminate risk.

FIGURE 11.6
Diversification reduces portfolio risk (standard deviation) rapidly at first, then more slowly.

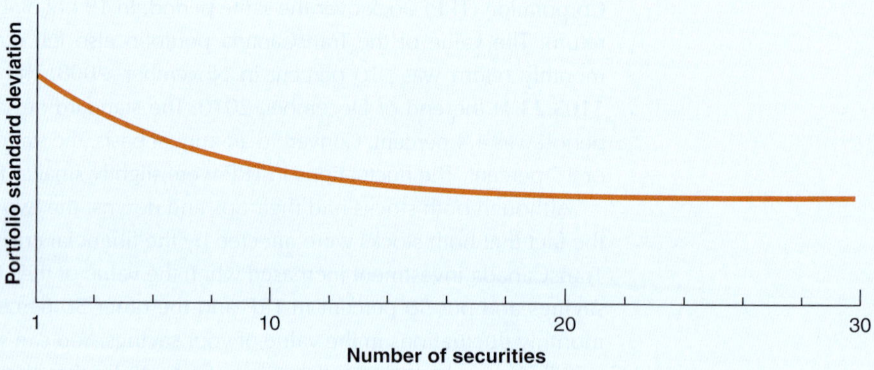

FIGURE 11.7
Diversification eliminates unique risk. But diversification cannot eliminate market risk.

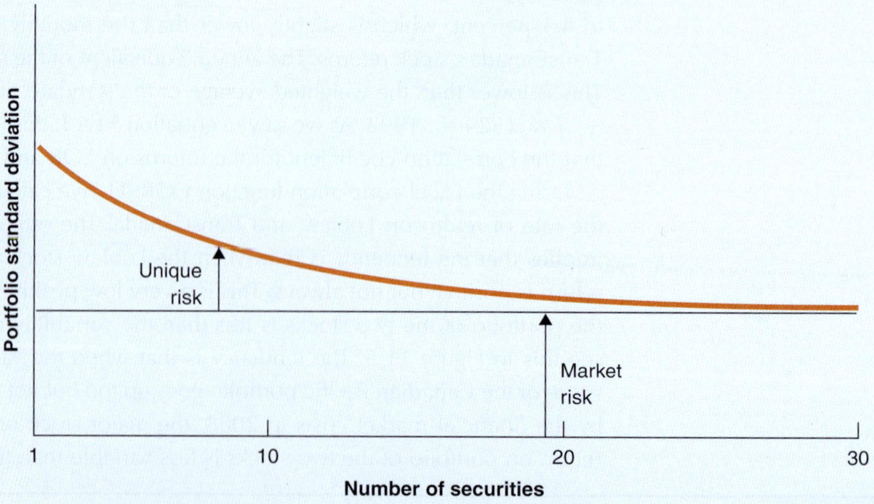

EXAMPLE 11.3 **INTERNATIONAL PORTFOLIO DIVERSIFICATION**

If holding a portfolio of Canadian stocks reduces investors' risk without sacrificing return, holding a portfolio of Canadian and foreign stocks should further reduce risk. Investing internationally yields benefits to investors from increased diversification. The portfolio standard deviation is decreased by including an international component. The ability to reduce risk without sacrificing return arises because not all markets move up or down all at the same time. Due to this less than perfect positive correlation between the Canadian financial markets and financial markets in other countries, losses in the domestic market can often be offset by gains in those foreign markets that have a low correlation to our markets. By diversifying internationally, the investor hopes to have international investments that are doing well when the Canadian portion of the portfolio is not, and vice versa.

Look back at Figure 11.4. You will see that the standard deviations of the TSX and the S&P 500 tend to move together but not perfectly. The correlation coefficient between the annual rates of return of the two market indexes over the period 1956 to 2007 is about 70 percent. By holding both stock indexes, you can reduce portfolio risk, since the markets are not perfectly correlated. But the high degree of integration between the U.S. and Canadian economies and stock markets means that the correlation coefficient is far from zero, reflecting the common market risk.

You can add stocks from other countries to further reduce the portfolio risk, provided their returns are less than perfectly correlated with the U.S. and Canadian markets. However, the recent financial crisis has demonstrated that an international portfolio cannot eliminate all market risk. Stock markets around the world crashed in 2008. Research on correlation of various market indexes has found that the correlation coefficient between foreign stocks and the U.S. S&P have risen from an average of about .5 or .6 in the late 1980s to current levels around .8 or .9. Global markets are more connected. Investing in many different countries and in a wide variety of financial securities, including stocks, bonds and real estate can still reduce portfolio variance.

LO4 11.5 THINKING ABOUT RISK

How can you tell which risks are unique and diversifiable? Where do market risks come from? Here are three messages to help you think clearly about risk.

MESSAGE 1: SOME RISKS LOOK BIG AND DANGEROUS BUT REALLY ARE DIVERSIFIABLE

Managers confront risks "up close and personal." They must make decisions about particular investments. The failure of such an investment could cost a promotion, bonus, or a steady job. Yet that same investment may not seem risky to an investor who can stand back and combine it in a diversified portfolio with many other assets or securities.

EXAMPLE 11.4 **WILDCAT OIL WELLS**

You have just been promoted to director of exploration, Western Hemisphere, of MPS Oil. The manager of your exploration team in far-off Costaguana has appealed for $20 million extra to drill in an even steamier part of the Costaguanan jungle. The manager thinks there may be an "elephant" field worth $500 million or more hidden there. But the chance of finding it is at best one in 10, and yesterday, MPS's CEO sourly commented on the $100 million already "wasted" on Costaguanan exploration.

Is this a risky investment? For you it probably is; you may be a hero if oil is found, and a goat otherwise. But MPS drills hundreds of wells worldwide; for the company as a whole, it's the *average*

(Continued)

(Concluded) success rate that matters. Geologic risks (is there oil or not?) should average out. The risk of a worldwide drilling program is much less than the apparent risk of any single wildcat well.

Step back and think of the investors who buy MPS stock. The investors may hold other oil companies, too, as well as companies producing steel, computers, clothing, cement, and breakfast cereal. They naturally—and realistically—assume that your successes and failures in drilling oil wells will average out with the thousands of independent bets made by the companies in their portfolio.

Therefore, the risks you face in Costaguana do not affect the rate of return they demand for investing in MPS Oil. Diversified investors in MPS stock will be happy if you find that elephant field, but they are unlikely to notice if you fail and lose your job. In any case, they will not demand a higher *average* rate of return for worrying about geologic risks in Costaguana.

EXAMPLE 11.5 **FIRE INSURANCE**

Would you be willing to write a $100,000 fire insurance policy on your neighbour's house? The neighbour is willing to pay you $100 for a year's protection, and experience shows that the chance of fire damage in a given year is substantially less than one in a thousand. But if your neighbour's house is damaged by fire, you would have to pay up.

Few of us have deep enough pockets to insure our neighbours, even if the odds of fire damage are very low. Insurance seems a risky business if you think policy by policy. But a large insurance company, which may issue a million policies, is concerned only with average losses, which can be predicted with excellent accuracy.

Check Point 11.6

Imagine a laboratory at IBM, late at night. One scientist speaks to another.

"You're right, Watson, I admit this experiment will consume all the rest of this year's budget. I don't know what we'll do if it fails. But if this yttrium–magnoosium alloy superconducts, the patents will be worth millions."

Would this be a good or bad investment for IBM? Can't say. But from the ultimate investors' viewpoint this is *not* a risky investment. Explain why.

MESSAGE 2: MARKET RISKS ARE MACRO RISKS

We have seen that diversified portfolios are not exposed to the unique risks of individual stocks, but that they are exposed to the uncertain events affecting the entire securities market and economy. These are macroeconomic, or "macro," factors such as changes in interest rates, industrial production, inflation, foreign exchange rates, and energy costs. They affect most firms' earnings and stock prices. When the relevant macro risks turn generally favourable, stock prices rise and investors do well; when the same variables go the other way, investors suffer.

You can often assess relative market risks just by thinking through exposures to the business cycle and other macro variables. The following businesses have substantial macro and market risks:

- *Airlines.* Because business travel falls during a recession and individuals postpone vacations and other discretionary travel, the airline industry is subject to the swings of the business cycle. On the positive side, airline profits really take off when business is booming and personal incomes are rising.
- *Machine tool manufacturers.* These businesses are especially exposed to the business cycle. Manufacturing companies that have excess capacity rarely buy new machine tools to expand. During recessions, excess capacity can be quite high.

Here, on the other hand, are two industries with less than average macro exposures:

- *Food companies.* Companies selling staples, such as breakfast cereal, flour, and dog food, find that demand for their products is relatively stable in good times and bad.
- *Electric utilities.* Business demand for electric power varies somewhat across the business cycle, but by much less than demand for air travel or machine tools. Also, many electric utilities' profits are regulated. Regulation cuts off upside profit potential but also gives the utilities the opportunity to increase prices when demand is slack. Remember, investors holding diversified portfolios are mostly concerned with macroeconomic risks. They do not worry about microeconomic risks peculiar to a particular company or investment project. Micro risks wash out in diversified portfolios. Company managers may worry about both macro and micro risks, but only the former affect the cost of capital.

Check Point 11.7

Which company of each of the following pairs would you expect to be more exposed to macro risks?

a. A luxury Montréal restaurant or an established Burger Queen franchise?
b. A paint company that sells through small paint and hardware stores to do-it-yourselfers, or a paint company that sells in large volumes to Ford, GM, and Honda?

MESSAGE 3: RISK CAN BE MEASURED

Air Canada clearly has more exposure to macro risks than food companies such as Weston or Kraft. These are easy cases. But is IBM stock a riskier investment than Imperial Oil? That's not an easy question to reason through. We can, however, *measure* the risk of IBM and Imperial Oil by looking at how their stock prices fluctuate.

We've already hinted at how to do this. Remember that diversified investors are concerned with market risks. The movements of the stock market sum up the net effects of all relevant macroeconomic uncertainties. If the market portfolio of all traded stocks is up in a particular month, we conclude that the net effect of macroeconomic news is positive. Remember, the performance of the market is barely affected by a firm-specific event. These cancel out across thousands of stocks in the market.

How do we measure the risk of a single stock, such as IBM or Imperial Oil? We do not look at the stocks in isolation, because the risks that loom when you're up close to a single company are often diversifiable. Instead we measure the individual stock's sensitivity to the fluctuations of the overall stock market. We will show you how this works in the next chapter.

11.6 SUMMARY

1. **How can one estimate the opportunity cost of capital for an "average risk" project? LO1**

Over the past 85 years the calculated return on a large portfolio of Canadian common stocks has averaged about 7 percentage points a year higher than the return on safe Treasury bills. This is the risk premium that investors have received for taking on the risk of investing in stocks. Long-term bonds have offered a higher return than Treasury bills but less than stocks.

If the risk premium in the past is a guide to the future, we can estimate the expected return on the market today by adding that 7 percentage point expected risk premium to today's interest rate on Treasury bills. This would be the opportunity cost of capital for an average-risk project, that is, one with the same risk as a typical share of common stock.

2. **How is the standard deviation of returns for individual common stocks or a stock portfolio calculated? LO2**

The spread of outcomes on different investments is commonly measured by the variance or standard deviation of the possible outcomes. The variance is the average of the squared deviations around the average outcome, and the standard deviation is the square root of the variance. The standard deviation of the returns on a market portfolio of common stocks has averaged about 17 percent per year.

3. **Why does diversification reduce risk? LO3**

The standard deviation of returns is generally higher on individual stocks than it is on the market. Because individual stocks do not move in lockstep, much of their risk can be diversified away. Stock returns are less than perfectly correlated. By spreading your portfolio across many investments you smooth out the risk of your overall position. The risk that can be eliminated through diversification is known as unique risk.

4. **What is the difference between unique risk, which can be diversified away, and market risk, which cannot? LO4**

Even if you hold a well-diversified portfolio, you will not eliminate all risk. You will still be exposed to macroeconomic changes that affect most stocks and the overall stock market. This means that stock returns are positively correlated. These macro risks combine to create market risk—that is, the risk that the market as a whole will slump.

Stocks are not all equally risky. But what do we mean by a "high risk" stock? We don't mean a stock that is risky if held in isolation; we mean a stock that makes an above-average contribution to the risk of a diversified portfolio. In other words, investors don't need to worry much about the risk that they can diversify away; they do need to worry about risk that can't be diversified. This depends on the stock's sensitivity to macroeconomic conditions.

Related Web Links

bankofcanada.ca Current and historical Canadian government Treasury bills and bond rates of return

stern.nyu.edu/~adamodar New York University site containing historical data on market risk and return

tsx.com Toronto Stock Exchange and TSX Venture Exchange

nyse.com New York Stock Exchange

spglobal.com and **mscibarra.com** Web sites for many stock market indexes

Key Terms

correlation coefficient 378
diversification 375
Dow Jones Industrial Average 364
market index 363
market risk 382
maturity premium 365
risk premium 366
S&P/TSX Composite Index 363
S&P/TSX Composite Total Return Index (TSXT) 363
Standard & Poor's Composite Index 364
standard deviation 369
unique risk 382
variance 369

Questions and Problems

connect Practise and learn online with *Connect*. Questions with online Excel templates or datasets are marked with .

*Answers in Appendix B

BASIC

*1. **Rate of Return.** A stock is selling today for $40 per share. At the end of the year, it pays a dividend of $2 per share and sells for $44. What is the total rate of return on the stock? What are the dividend yield and capital gains yield? (LO2)

2. **Rate of Return.** Return to problem 1. Suppose the year-end stock price after the dividend is paid is $36. What are the dividend yield and capital gains yield in this case? Why is the dividend yield unaffected? (LO2)

3. **Real Versus Nominal Returns.** You purchase 100 shares of stock for $40 a share. The stock pays a $2 per share dividend at year-end. What is the rate of return on your investment for these end-of-year stock prices? What is your real (inflation-adjusted) rate of return? Assume an inflation rate of 3 percent. (LO2)

*a. $38
b. $40
c. $42

4. **Real Versus Nominal Returns.** The Costaguanan stock market provided a rate of return of 95 percent. The inflation rate in Costaguana during the year was 80 percent. In Canada, in contrast, the stock market return was only 14 percent, but the inflation rate was only 3 percent. Which country's stock market provided the higher *real* rate of return? (LO2)

*5. **Real Versus Nominal Returns.** The inflation rate in Canada between 1926 and 2010 averaged 3.2 percent. What was the average real rate of return on Treasury bills, government bonds, and common stocks in that period? Use the data in Table 11.1. (LO2)

6. **Real Versus Nominal Returns.** Do you think it is possible for risk-free Treasury bills to offer a negative nominal interest rate? Might they offer a negative *real* expected rate of return? (LO2)

7. **Market Indexes.** The accompanying table shows quarterly stock prices on the Dar es Salaam Stock Exchange for 2005–2009. Construct two stock market indexes, one using equal weights, as in the Dow Jones Industrial Average, the other using market-value weights, as in the S&P/TSX Composite Index. (LO2)

	San Tome Mining, 184 Million*	Sulaco Market, 42 Million*	National Central Railway, 64 Million*	Minerva Shipping, 38 Million*	Azuera, Inc., 16 Million*
2005	55.10	80.00	21.45	82.50	135.00
2006	58.15	144.62	24.04	115.52	151.22
2007	58.45	135.93	26.53	138.90	166.99
2008	52.43	74.61	23.53	212.02	149.42
2009	52.50	75.01	32.46	174.62	177.27

*Number of shares outstanding.

8. **Stock Market History.** Using the data in problem 7, calculate the average rate of return and standard deviation of return for each stock as well as for an equal-weighted portfolio of all the stocks using Excel. Do you observe any benefits from diversification? (LO2, LO3)

INTERMEDIATE

9. **Risk Premiums.** Here are annual stock market, Government of Canada bond, and Treasury bill rates of return from 2006 to 2010:

Year	TSX Return	T-Bill Return	Government Long Bond Return
2006	0.1701	0.0397	0.1505
2007	0.0983	0.0428	0.0322
2008	−0.3300	0.0264	0.0330
2009	0.3505	0.0046	0.136
2010	0.1761	0.0049	−0.043

a. What were the risk premiums on the TSX and on long-term government bonds in each year? (LO1)
*b. What were the average risk premiums for the TSX and long-term government bonds? (LO1)
*c. Calculate the standard deviation of each risk premium using the approach in Table 11.4. Do they make sense? (LO2)

10. **Market Indexes.** In 1990, the S&P/TSX Composite Index was at a level of about 3,400. In 2010, it was about 13,000. Would you expect the S&P/TSX in 2010 to be more or less likely to move up or down by more than 40 points in a day than in 1990? Does this mean the market was riskier in 2010 than it was in 1990? (LO2)

11. **Maturity Premiums.** Investments in long-term government bonds produced a negative average return during the period 1977–1981. How should we interpret this? Did bond investors in 1977 expect to earn a negative maturity premium? What do these five years of bond returns tell us about the normal future maturity premium? (LO1)

12. **Risk Premiums.** What will happen to the opportunity cost of capital if investors suddenly become especially conservative and less willing to bear investment risk? (LO1)

13. **Risk Premiums and Discount Rates.** You believe that a stock with the same market risk as the S&P/TSX will sell at year-end at a price of $50. The stock will pay a dividend at year-end of $2. What price will you be

willing to pay for the stock today? *Hint:* Start by checking today's three-month Treasury bill rate. (LO1)

*14. **Scenario Analysis.** The common stock of Leaning Tower of Pita, Inc., a restaurant chain, will generate the following payoffs to investors next year:

	Probability	Dividend	Stock Price
Boom	.3	$5	$195
Normal economy	.5	2	100
Recession	.2	0	0

The company goes out of business if a recession hits. Calculate the expected rate of return and standard deviation of return to Leaning Tower of Pita shareholders. The stock is selling today for $90. (LO1)

15. **Portfolio Risk.** Who would view the stock of Leaning Tower of Pita (see problem 14) as a risk-reducing investment—the owner of a gambling casino or a successful bankruptcy lawyer? Explain. (LO3)

16. **Scenario Analysis.** The common stock of Escapist Films sells for $25 a share and offers the following payoffs next year:

	Probability	Dividend	Stock Price
Boom	.3	$0	$18
Normal economy	.5	1	26
Recession	.2	3	34

Calculate the expected return and standard deviation of Escapist. Then calculate the expected return and standard deviation of a portfolio half invested in Escapist and half in Leaning Tower of Pita (from problem 14). Show that the portfolio standard deviation is lower than either stock's. Explain why this happens. (LO3)

17. **Scenario Analysis.** Consider the following scenario analysis:

		Rate of Return	
Scenario	**Probability**	**Stocks**	**Bonds**
Recession	.2	−5%	+14%
Normal economy	.6	+15	+8
Boom	.2	+25	+4

a. Is it reasonable to assume that bonds will provide higher returns in recessions than in booms? (LO2)

*b. Calculate the expected rate of return and standard deviation for each investment. (LO2)

c. Which investment would you prefer? (LO1)

18. **Portfolio Analysis.** Use the data in the previous problem and consider a portfolio with weights of .60 in stocks and .40 in bonds. (LO3)

a. What is the rate of return on the portfolio in each scenario?

b. What are the expected rate of return and standard deviation of the portfolio?

c. Would you prefer to invest in the portfolio, in stocks only, or in bonds only?

d. Calculate the correlation coefficient for the bond and stock returns.

19. **Risk Premium.** If the stock market return in 2011 turns out to be −20 percent, what will happen to our estimate of the "normal" risk premium? Does this make sense? (LO1)

20. **Diversification.** In which of the following situations would you get the largest reduction in risk by spreading your portfolio across two stocks? In each case, is the correlation less than, greater than, or equal to zero? (LO3)

a. The stock returns vary with each other.

b. The stock returns are independent.

c. The stock returns vary against each other.

*21. **Market Risk.** Which firm from each pair would you expect to have greater market risk? Explain your choice. (LO4)

a. General Steel or General Food Supplies

b. Exotic World Tours Agency or General Cinemas

22. **Risk and Return.** A stock will provide a rate of return of either −20 percent or +30 percent.

a. If both possibilities are equally likely, calculate the expected return and standard deviation. (LO2)

b. If Treasury bills yield 5 percent, and investors believe that the stock offers a satisfactory expected return, what must be the market risk of the stock? (LO4)

23. **Unique Versus Market Risk.** Sassafras Oil is staking all its remaining capital on wildcat exploration off the Côte d'Huile. There is a 10 percent chance of discovering a field with reserves of 50 million barrels. If it finds oil, it will immediately sell the reserves to Big Oil, at a price depending on the state of the economy. Thus the possible payoffs are as follows:

	Value of Reserves, per Barrel	Value of Reserves, 50 Million Barrels	Value of Dryholes
Boom	$4	$200,000,000	0
Normal economy	$5	$250,000,000	0
Recession	$6	$300,000,000	0

Is Sassafras Oil a risky investment for a diversified investor in the stock market—compared, say, to the stock of Leaning Tower of Pita, described in problem 14? Explain. (LO4)

24. **Portfolio Risk and Return.** The expected return on Big Time Toys is 9 percent and its standard deviation is 20 percent. The expected return on Chemical Industries is 8 percent and its standard deviation is 25 percent.
   a. Suppose the correlation coefficient for the two stocks' returns is .2. What are the expected return and standard deviation of a portfolio with 30 percent invested in Big Time Toys and the rest in Chemical Industries? (LO2)
   b. If the correlation coefficient is .7, recalculate the portfolio expected return and standard deviation, assuming the portfolio weights are unchanged. (LO2)
   c. Explain the difference between your answers to (a) and (b). (LO3)

*25. **Portfolio Risk and Return.** Using the data in problem 9,
   a. Calculate the average rate of return and standard deviation of return for the TSX, government bonds, and Treasury bills between 2006 and 2010. (LO2)
   b. Form a portfolio with one-third in each of the three securities and calculate its average rate of return and standard deviation. Can you see any benefit from diversification? (LO3)

26. **Correlation.** Using the Excel function CORREL, calculate the correlation between the return on San Tome Mining and each of the other four stocks mentioned in problem 7. Which stock offers the best diversification benefit? (LO3)

27. **Internet.** Rates of return on U.S. stock, bond, and bill indexes are available to download for free at **pages.stern.nyu.edu/~adamodar**. Click on "Updated Data" and look for "Historical Returns on Stocks, Bonds and Bills—US" and download the spreadsheet. Calculate the average market risk premium for the NYSE stocks, using the Treasury bill as the risk-free security for successive 10-year periods and for the entire period. Repeat, using the long-term government bond as the risk-free security.
   a. Is the overall market risk premium bigger or smaller when the risk-free security is the Treasury bill or the long-term government bond? (LO1)
   b. Compare the risk premiums over time. Do you think the results suggest that the risk premium may have been changing? Explain. (LO1)

28. **Internet.** A large variety of mutual funds are available to Canadian investors. Some, called "sector funds," specialize in particular industries; others, known as "index funds," simply invest in the market index. Go to **www.theglobeandmail.com/globe-investor/funds-and-etfs/fund-lookup**, look up "AGF Canada Class" and click on its name to find its three-year risk (the standard deviation of its monthly return). Now find the three-year risk (standard deviation) for four other mutual funds for different industry (sector) funds. Are they larger or smaller than the Index fund? Read the information on their page. How do you interpret your results? (LO4)

29. **Internet.** Using Finance.Yahoo.com, download monthly stock prices for Magna International (MGA) by clicking on historical prices, then on Monthly Data. Find the December closing stock price the most recent four years. Then click on "Dividends Only" button and download the per-share dividends paid in the same year. Calculate the annual dividend yield, capital gains yield, and rate of return for each year. Repeat for the Ford Motor Company (F) and Microsoft (MSFT). Read each company's profile, and describe the main business activities of these companies. Compare their rates of return, dividend yields, and capital gains yields and try to explain the differences between the companies. (LO4)

30. **Internet.** Using ca.Finance.Yahoo.com, download the monthly prices over a five-year period for five Canadian companies of your choice. Calculate the monthly rates of return for each stock using "Adj. Close" (which includes dividends and stock splits).
   a. Using the Excel functions for average (AVERAGE) and sample standard deviation (STDEV), calculate the average and the standard deviation of the returns for each of the firms. (LO2)
   b. Using Excel's correlation function (CORREL), find the correlations between each pair of five stocks. What are the highest and lowest correlations? (LO3)
   c. Pick one more stock that is in the same industry of one of your other stock. Find correlations between pairs of stocks in the same industry. Are the correlations higher than those you found in part (b)? Is this surprising? (LO3)

31. **Internet.** Use the monthly returns of the five companies you chose in the previous question to look at the return on an equally weighted portfolio of the five stocks (that is, a portfolio with equal investment in each stock each month). The portfolio rate of return each month is the equal-weighted average of the stocks' rates of return. Use Excel to calculate the portfolio's average return and standard deviation. Compare the portfolio statistics that of those of the stocks. What evidence of portfolio diversification do you find? (LO3)

32. **Internet.** Repeat problem 31, but for a value-weighted portfolio. Use the data from problem 30 to create a portfolio in which you invest \$100 in each stock. Calculate the value of each stock investment each month (\$100 × [1 + monthly rate of return]) and the value of the portfolio each month (sum of the value of each stock investment each month). Calculate the monthly rate of return on your portfolio. Using that data, calculate portfolio rate of return, calculate its statistics and compare them to the stocks. Compare the results to those in problem 31. (LO3)

Solutions to Check Points

11.1 The bond price at the end of the year is \$1,050. Therefore, the capital gain on each bond is \$1,050 − \$1,020 = \$30. Your dollar return is the sum of the income from the bond, \$80, plus the capital gain, \$30, or \$110. The rate of return is

$$\frac{\text{Income plus capital gain}}{\text{Original price}} = \frac{80 + 30}{1{,}020} = .108, \text{ or } 10.8\%$$

Real rate of return is

$$\frac{1 + \text{nominal return}}{1 + \text{inflation rate}} - 1 = \frac{1.108}{1.04} - 1 = .065, \text{ or } 6.5\%$$

11.2 The risk premium on stocks is the average return in excess of Treasury bills. It was 8.6 percentage points in period 1, 7.7 percentage points in period 2, and 5.1 percentage points in period 3. The maturity premium is the average return on Canada long bonds minus the return on Treasury bills. It was 3.6 percentage points in period 1, −1.2 percentage points in period 2, and 3 percentage points in period 3.

11.3 Expected return = (.25 × 70) + (.5 × 10) + (.25 × −50) = +10%

Variance and standard deviation calculation with equal probabilities:

Rate of Return	Deviation	Squared Deviation
+70%	+60%	3,600
+10	0	0
+10	0	0
−50	−60	3,600

Variance = average of squared deviations = 7,200/4 = 1,800.

Standard deviation = square root of variance = $\sqrt{1{,}800}$ = 42.4, or about 42%.

Variance and standard deviation calculation with unequal probabilities:

(1) Rate of Return (%)	(2) Probability of Return	(3) Deviations from Expected Return (%)	(4) Probability × Squared Deviation
+70	.25	+60	.25 × 3,600 = 900
+10	.50	0	.50 × 0 = 0
−50	.25	−60	.25 × 3,600 = 900

Variance = sum of squared deviations weighted by probabilities = 900 + 0 + 900 = 1,800.

Standard deviation = square root of variance = $\sqrt{1{,}800}$ = 42.4, or about 42%.

11.4 The standard deviation should decrease because there is now a lower probability of the more extreme outcomes. The expected rate of return on the auto stock is now

$$[.3 \times (-8\%)] + [.4 \times 5\%] + [.3 \times 18\%] = 5\%$$

The variance is

$$[.3 \times (-8 - 5)^2] + [.4 \times (5 - 5)^2] + [.3 \times (18 - 5)^2] = 101.4$$

The standard deviation is $\sqrt{101.4}$ = 10.07 percent, which is lower than the value assuming equal probabilities of each scenario.

11.5 a. Since sunshine heats the air, the number of hours of sunshine per day and average daily temperature will be positively correlated. However, they will not be perfectly positively correlated because other factors affect air temperature such as latitude, altitude, and season.

b. The more television watched, the less time you have to study and the lower will be your grade in finance. Thus these two variables will be negatively correlated.

c. The quality of the in-flight movie has no relationship with the flying time. Thus these two variables are uncorrelated. Of course, if the movie is boring, the trip will *seem* to take longer!

d. The connectedness of the Canadian and U.S. economies and financial markets leads to a positive correlation between interest rates in Canada and the United States.

11.6 The success of this project depends on the experiment. Success does *not* depend on the performance of the overall economy. The experiment creates a diversifiable risk. A portfolio of many stocks will embody "bets" on many such unique risks. Some bets will work out and some will fail. Because the outcomes of these risks do not depend on common factors, such as the overall state of the economy, the risks will tend to cancel out in a well-diversified portfolio.

11.7 a. The luxury restaurant will be more sensitive to the state of the economy because expense account meals will be curtailed in a recession. Burger Queen meals should be relatively recession-proof.

b. The paint company that sells to the auto producers will be more sensitive to the state of the economy. In a downturn, auto sales fall dramatically as consumers stretch the lives of their cars. In contrast, in a recession, more people "do it themselves," which makes paint sales through small stores more stable and less sensitive to the economy.

PART 3 Risk

11 Introduction to Risk, Return, and the Opportunity Cost of Capital

12 Risk, Return, and Capital Budgeting

12.1 Measuring Market Risk

12.2 Risk and Return and Capital Asset Pricing Model, CAPM

12.3 Capital Budgeting and Project Risk

12.4 Summary

13 The Weighted-Average Cost of Capital and Company Valuation

CHAPTER 12

Risk, Return, and Capital Budgeting

LEARNING OBJECTIVES

After studying this chapter, you should be able to:

LO1 Measure and interpret the market risk, or beta, of a security.

LO2 Calculate the beta of a portfolio.

LO3 Relate the market risk of a security to the rate of return that investors demand. Explain the capital asset pricing model, CAPM, and use the CAPM to estimate a security's expected return.

LO4 Calculate the opportunity cost of capital for a project.

Professor William F. Sharpe receiving the Nobel Prize in economics. The prize was awarded for Sharpe's development of the capital asset pricing model. This model shows how risk should be measured and provides a formula relating risk to the opportunity cost of capital.

In Chapter 11 we began to come to grips with the topic of risk. We made the distinction between *unique risk* and macro, or *market*, risk. Unique risk arises from events that affect only the individual firm or its immediate competitors; it can be eliminated by diversification. But regardless of how much you diversify, you cannot avoid the macroeconomic events that create market risk. This is why investors do not require a higher rate of return to compensate for unique risk but do need a higher return to persuade them to take on market risk.

How can you measure the market risk of a security or a project? We will see that market risk is usually measured by the sensitivity of the investment's returns to fluctuations in the market, called beta. We will also see that the risk premium investors demand should be proportional to this sensitivity. This relationship between risk and return is a useful way to estimate the return that investors expect from investing in common stocks.

Finally, we will distinguish between the risk of the company's securities and the risk of an individual project. We will also consider what managers should do when the risk of the project is different from that of the company's existing business.

LO1, 2 12.1 MEASURING MARKET RISK

market portfolio Portfolio of all assets in the economy. In practice, a broad stock market index, such as the S&P/TSX or S&P 500 Composite Index, is used to represent the market.

Changes in interest rates, government spending, monetary policy, oil prices, foreign exchange rates, and other macroeconomic events affect almost all companies and the returns on almost all stocks. We can therefore assess the impact of "macro" news by tracking the rate of return on a **market portfolio** of all securities. If the market is up on a particular day, then the net impact of macroeconomic changes must be positive. We know the performance of the market reflects only macro events, because firm-specific events—that is, unique risks—average out when we look at the combined performance of thousands of companies and securities.

In principle, the market portfolio should contain all assets in the world economy—not just stocks, but bonds, foreign securities, real estate, and so on to achieve the greatest diversification. In practice, however, financial analysts make do with indexes of the stock market, such as the S&P/TSX Composite Index (TSX) or the Standard & Poor's Composite Index (the S&P 500).[1]

beta Sensitivity of a stock's return to the return on the market portfolio.

Our task here is to define and measure the risk of *individual* common stocks. You can probably see where we are headed. Risk depends on exposure to macroeconomic events and can be measured as the sensitivity of a stock's returns to fluctuations in returns on the market portfolio. This sensitivity is called the stock's **beta**. Beta is often written as the Greek letter β.

Aggressive stocks have high betas, betas greater than 1.0, meaning that their returns tend to respond more than one-for-one to changes in the return of the overall market. The betas of defensive stocks are less than 1.0. The returns of these stocks vary less than one-for-one with market returns. The average beta of all stocks is—no surprises here—1.0 exactly.

MEASURING BETA

In Chapter 11 we looked at the variability of individual securities. IMAX had the highest standard deviation and TransCanada the lowest. If you had held IMAX on its own, your returns would have varied over four times as much as if you had held TransCanada. But wise investors don't put all their eggs in just one basket: they reduce their risk by diversification. An investor with a diversified portfolio will be interested in the effect each stock has on the risk of the entire portfolio.

Diversification can eliminate the risk that is unique to individual stocks, but not the risk that the market as a whole may decline, carrying your stocks with it.

Some stocks are less affected than others by market fluctuations. The average beta of all stocks is 1.0. Investment managers talk about "defensive" and "aggressive" stocks. Defensive stocks are not very sensitive to market fluctuations, so their betas are less than 1.0. In contrast, aggressive stocks amplify any market movements, so their betas are greater than 1.0. If the market goes up, it is good to be in aggressive stocks; if it goes down, it is better to be in defensive stocks (and even better to have your money in the bank). Unfortunately, you don't know which way the market is going to move.

Now we'll show you how betas are measured.

EXAMPLE 12.1 MEASURING BETA FOR TURBOT-CHARGED SEAFOODS

Suppose we look back at the trading history of Turbot-Charged Seafoods and pick out six months when the return on the market portfolio was plus or minus 1 percent.

Month	Market Return, %	Turbot-Charged Seafoods' Return, %	
1	+1	+ .8	Average = +.8%
2	+1	+1.8	
3	+1	− .2	
4	−1	−1.8	Average = −.8%
5	−1	+ .2	
6	−1	− .8	

Look at Figure 12.1, in which these observations are plotted. We've drawn a line through the average performance of Turbot when the market is up or down by 1 percent. *The slope of this line is Turbot's beta*. You can see right away that the beta is .8, because on average Turbot stock gains or loses .8 percent when the market is up or down by 1 percent. Notice that a 2-percentage-point difference in the market return (−1 to +1) generates on average a 1.6-percentage-point difference for Turbot shareholders (−.8 to +.8). The ratio, 1.6/2 = .8, is beta.

In four months, Turbot's returns lie above or below the line in Figure 12.1. The distance from the line shows the response of Turbot's stock returns to news or events that affected Turbot but did not

[1] We discussed the most popular stock market indexes in Section 11.2. In our calculations we use the total return version of TSX, the S&P/TSX Composite Total Return Index which includes dividends as well as capital gain.

FIGURE 12.1
This figure is a plot of the data presented in the table from Example 12.1. Each point shows the performance of Turbot-Charged Seafoods stock when the overall market is either up or down by 1 percent. On average, Turbot-Charged moves in the same direction as the market, but not as far. Therefore, Turbot-Charged's beta is less than 1.0. We can measure beta by the slope of a line fitted to the points in the figure. In this case it is .8.

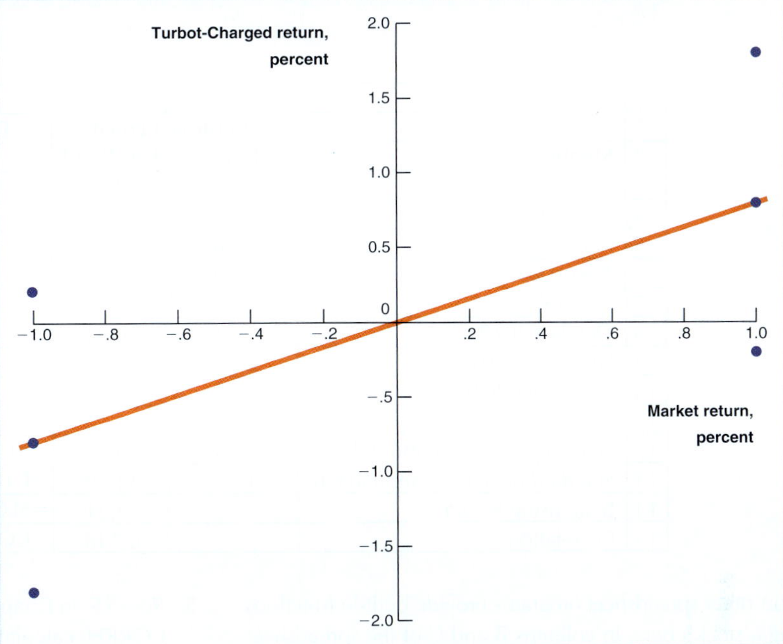

affect the overall market. For example, in month 2, investors in Turbot stock benefited from good macroeconomic news (the market was up 1 percent) and also from some favourable news specific to Turbot. The market rise gave a boost of .8 percent to Turbot stock (beta of .8 times the 1 percent market return). Then firm-specific news gave Turbot shareholders an extra 1 percent return, for a total return that month of 1.8 percent.

As this example illustrates, we can break down common stock returns into two parts: the part explained by market returns and the firm's beta, and the part due to news that is specific to the firm. Fluctuations in the first part reflect market risk; fluctuations in the second part reflect unique risk. Of course, diversification can get rid of the unique risks. That's why wise investors, who don't put all their eggs in one basket, will look to Turbot's less-than-average beta and call its stock "defensive."

Check Point 12.1

Here are six months' returns to shareholders in the Anchovy Queen restaurant chain:

Month	Market Return, %	Anchovy Queen Return, %
1	+1	+2
2	+1	+0
3	+1	+1
4	−1	−1
5	−1	+0
6	−1	−2

Draw a figure like Figure 12.1 and check the slope of the fitted line. What is Anchovy Queen's beta?

excel spreadsheet

Calculating Risk

	A	B	C	D
1		Returns, Percent		Formulas Used in
2	**Month**	**TSX**	**CAMECO**	**Column C**
3	May 2010	−3.48	2.84	
4	June 2010	−3.71	−11.81	
5	July 2010	3.96	15.64	
6	August 2010	1.90	−0.61	
7	September 2010	4.09	10.18	
8	October 2010	2.71	10.31	
9	November 2010	2.37	17.78	
10	December 2010	4.09	18.64	
11				
12	Standard deviation (monthly)	3.25	9.58	=STDEV(C3:C10)
13	Standard deviation, annualized	11.25	33.19	=C10*SQRT(12)
14	Beta, using SLOPE		2.21	=SLOPE(C3:C10,B3:B10)
15	Correlation		0.748	=CORREL(B3:B10,C3:C10)

Excel and most other spreadsheet programs provide built-in functions for computing a stock's beta. In columns B and C of the spreadsheet above we have entered returns for S&P/TSX Composite Total Return Index and Cameco for 8 months in 2010. (In practice, estimates based on just eight months would be *very* unreliable. Most estimates of standard deviation and beta use something like five years of monthly data.)

Here are some points to note about the spreadsheet:

1. *Columns B and C.* Notice that these columns show monthly rates of *returns* for the market index and the stock. Sometimes people mistakenly enter prices instead of returns and get nonsensical results.
2. *Row 12.* In Chapter 11 we discussed how to calculate sample variance, equation 11.9, and standard deviation, equation 11.8. The Excel calculates the sample variance and standard deviation using these formulas.
3. *Row 13.* We have converted monthly standard deviations to annual figures by multiplying by the square root of 12 (the number of months in a year).
4. *Row 14.* In calculating beta, enter first the addresses for the stock returns (C3:C10) and then those for the market returns (B3:B10).
5. *Row 15.* In Chapter 11 we discussed the correlation coefficient. CORREL calculates the correlation coefficient of Cameco and TSX stock returns.

Spreadsheet Questions

12.1. Suppose that Cameco's return in June 2010 had been −8 percent, and its return in September 2010 had been 8 percent. Would you expect its beta to be more or less than the value obtained in the original spreadsheet? Reestimate beta with these new data, and confirm your intuition.

12.2. Suppose that Cameco's return in each month had been 1 percent higher than the values presented in the original spreadsheet. Would Cameco's beta differ from the value obtained in the spreadsheet? Reestimate beta with these new data, and confirm your intuition.

12.3. Suppose you add one more month of data to the original spreadsheet data and find that in January 2011, Cameco was down 5 percent while the market was up 5 percent. Would you expect Cameco's beta to be more or less than the value obtained in the spreadsheet? Reestimate beta with this new data point, and confirm your intuition.

Real life doesn't serve up numbers quite as convenient as those in our examples so far. However, the procedure for measuring real companies' betas is exactly the same:

1. Observe rates of return, usually monthly, for the stock and the market.
2. Plot the observations as in Figure 12.1.
3. Fit a line showing the average return to the stock at different market returns.

Beta is the slope of the fitted line.

This might sound like a lot of work, but in practice computers do it for you. The nearby Excel Spreadsheet box shows how to use the SLOPE function in Excel to calculate a beta.

You can also calculate the beta of a stock if you know the correlation of the stock's return with the market's return, and the standard deviations of the stock and market returns. Using the notation from Chapter 11, let ρ_{jm} be the correlation coefficient for the return on stock j with the market; σ_j the standard deviation of the return on stock j; and σ_m the standard deviation of the return on the market. The beta of stock j is the correlation coefficient times the stock's standard deviation, divided by the market's standard deviation:

$$\textbf{Beta of stock } j = \beta_j = \frac{\rho_{jm}\sigma_j}{\sigma_m} \quad \textbf{(12.1)}$$

Using the return data for Cameco stock, its correlation coefficient with the market is .748, its stock return's standard deviation is 9.58 percent, and the market return's standard deviation is 3.25 percent. The beta of the stock is (.748 × 9.58)/3.25 = 2.2048, which almost rounds to 2.21. If Cameco's correlation with the market were only .3, its beta will be much lower: (.3 × 9.58)/3.25 = .88.

Another way to measure the relatedness of changes in one random variable with another is *covariance*. The correlation between two variables equals their covariance divided by the product of their standard deviations: $\rho_{jm} = \text{cov}(r_j, r_m)/\sigma_j\sigma_m$. If we replace correlation with this expression, we get another expression for beta: covariance between the return on the stock, r_j, and the market return, r_m, divided by the variance of the market return, σ_m^2:

$$\textbf{Beta of stock } j = \beta_j = \frac{\text{cov}(r_j, r_m)}{\sigma_m^2} \quad \textbf{(12.2)}$$

This formula for beta is consistent with our estimation of beta as the slope of the fitted line. Consult any basic statistics text and you will see that the slope of a fitted line can be expressed in terms of covariance and variance.

Here are two real examples of how to estimate stock betas.

BETAS FOR CAMECO AND ROYAL BANK

Each point in Figure 12.2(a) shows the return on Cameco stock and the return on the S&P/TSX Composite Total Return Index in the same month, from January 2006 to December 2010. For example, the circled point shows that in the month of January 2006, Cameco stock price rose by 22.1 percent, whereas the market index rose by 5.8 percent. Notice that more often than not Cameco outperformed the market when the index rose and underperformed the market when the index fell. Thus Cameco was a relatively aggressive, high-beta stock.

We have drawn a line of best fit through the points in the figure.[2] The slope of this line is 1.5. For each extra 1 percent rise in the market, Cameco stock price moved on average an extra 1.51 percent. For each extra 1 percent fall in the market, Cameco stock price fell an extra 1.51 percent. Thus Cameco's beta was 1.51.

Of course, Cameco's stock returns are not perfectly related to market returns. The company was also subject to unique risk, which shows up in the scatter of points around the line. Sometimes Cameco stock flew south while the market went north, or vice versa.

Figure 12.2(b) shows a similar plot of the monthly returns for Royal Bank. In contrast to Cameco, Royal Bank was a defensive, low-beta stock. It was not highly sensitive to market movements, usually lagging when the market rose and yet doing better (or not as badly) when the market fell. The slope of the line of best fit shows that on average an extra 1 percent change in the index resulted in an extra .63 percent change in the price of Royal Bank stock. Thus Royal Bank's beta was .63.

Estimates of beta can be accessed online for some stocks. For example, for stocks trading in the U.S., they are listed at **finance.yahoo.com**. Click on "Key Statistics" and you will find a beta. However, the Canadian version, **ca.finance.yahoo.com**, lists stock trading in Canada does not always have betas. Table 12.1 shows how past market movements have affected the stocks from Table 11.6.

[2] The line of best fit is usually known as a *regression* line. The slope of the line can be calculated using *ordinary least squares* regression. The dependent variable is the return on the stock (Cameco). The independent variable is the return on the S&P/TSX Composite Total Return Index.

FIGURE 12.2

(a) Each point in this figure shows the returns on Cameco common stock and the overall market in a particular month. Sixty months are plotted in all. Cameco's beta is the slope of the line fitted to these points. Cameco has a relatively high beta of 1.51.

(b) In this plot of 60 months' returns for Royal Bank and the overall market, the slope of the fitted line is much less than Cameco's beta in (a). Royal Bank has a relatively low beta of .63.

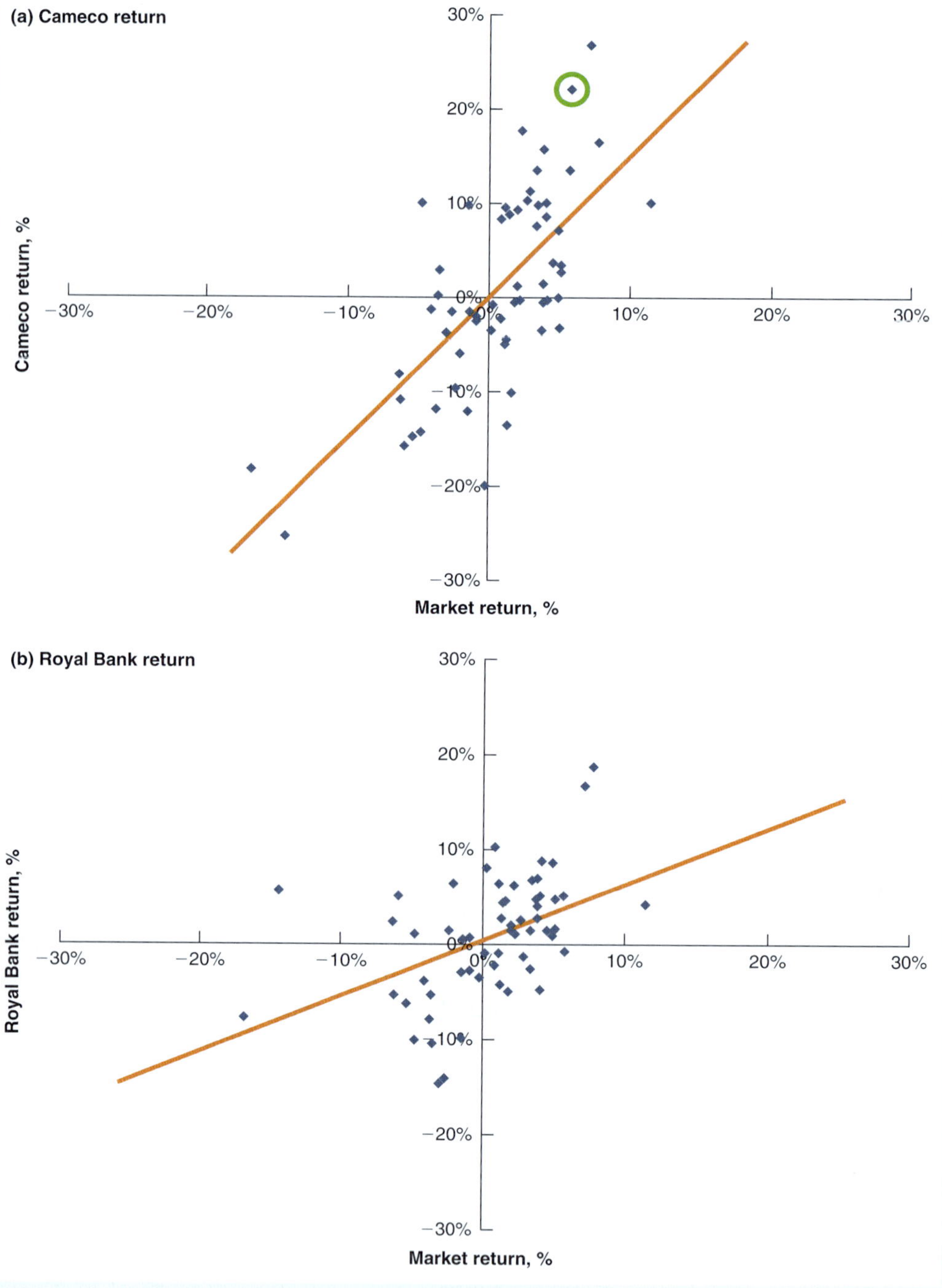

Source: Author's calculations using 2006–2010 monthly return data from TSX-CFMRC database, augmented with 2010 monthly returns calculated with stock prices from **www.globeinvestorgold.com** and dividend data from Financial Post Advisor.

TOTAL RISK AND MARKET RISK

The stocks in Table 12.1 are sorted by the standard deviation of their return, not by beta. Table 12.1 shows that high variability of returns does not necessarily imply high sensitivity to market movements. Total risk is not the same as market risk. Some stocks with high variability of return have below-average betas and vice versa.

IMAX, with the highest standard deviation of 64 percent, has an average beta of 1.06. Since its beta is just about 1, IMAX stock return is about as sensitive as the average stock to market movements. Much of IMAX stock variability is from unique risk, uncorrelated with the market,

TABLE 12.1
Betas and standard deviations of stock returns for selected Canadian common stocks, January 2006–December 2010.

Stock	Standard Deviation, %	Beta
IMAX	64.0	1.06
Research In Motion	55.2	1.64
Gildan Activewear	46.3	1.04
Barrick Gold	39.1	.45
Cameco	36.9	1.51
Canadian Pacific Railway	24.8	.82
Royal Bank	22.5	.63
Loblaw	22.3	.39
TransCanada Corp	15.4	.40

Note: Betas are calculated with five years of monthly returns.

Source: Author's calculations using 2006–2010 monthly return data from TSX-CFMRC database, augmented with 2010 monthly returns calculated with stock prices from **www.globeinvestorgold.com** and dividend data from Financial Post Advisor and the S&P/TSX Composite Total Return Index.

resulting in an average beta. RIM has the highest beta, 1.64. Its returns are 1.64 times as sensitive as the average stock market movements. But it also has high variability of its stock returns. So it has both high total risk and high market risk.

Consider, for example, Barrick Gold. Barrick Gold is large gold producer. A major risk is the variation in the price of gold. This creates variation in revenues but the price of gold tends to have low correlation with the economy. When the economy is weak, the gold prices tend to rise. So although the stock has above-average volatility, 39 percent it has a relatively low beta, .45.

Check Point 12.2

Compare the standard deviation and beta of Loblaw to the numbers for the other companies in Table 12.1. Try to explain the reasons for Loblaw's numbers.

PORTFOLIO BETAS

Diversification decreases variability from unique risk but not from market risk. The beta of a portfolio is just the weighted average of the betas of the securities in the portfolio. The weight for each security is its fraction of the portfolio value. For example, a portfolio comprising only two stocks would have a beta as follows:

$$\text{Beta of portfolio} = (\text{fraction of portfolio in first stock} \times \text{beta of first stock}) + (\text{fraction of portfolio in second stock} \times \text{beta of second stock}) \quad (12.3)$$

Thus, a portfolio invested 50-50 in Cameco and Royal Bank would have a beta of $(.5 \times 1.51) + (.5 \times .63) = 1.07$.

A well-diversified portfolio of stocks each with betas of 1.51, such as Cameco, would still have a portfolio beta of 1.51. However, most of the individual stocks' unique risk would be diversified away. The market risk would remain, and such a portfolio would end up 1.51 times as variable as the market. For example, if the market has an annual standard deviation of 19 percent (about the historical average reported in Table 11.5, Chapter 11), a fully diversified portfolio with beta of 1.518 has a standard deviation of 1.51×19 percent = 28.7 percent.

Portfolios with betas between 0 and 1.0 tend to move in the same direction as the market but not as far. A well-diversified portfolio of low-beta stocks like Royal Bank, all with betas of .59, has almost no unique risk and is relatively unaffected by market movements. Such a portfolio is .59 times as variable as the market, $.59 \times 19$ percent = 11.2 percent.

Of course, on average, stocks have a beta of 1. A well-diversified portfolio including all kinds of stocks, with an average beta of 1, has the same variability as the market index.

Check Point 12.3 Say you invested an equal amount in each of the stocks shown in Table 12.1. Calculate the beta of your portfolio.

EXAMPLE 12.2 **HOW RISKY ARE MUTUAL FUNDS AND EXCHANGE-TRADED FUNDS (ETFs)?**

You don't have to be wealthy to own a diversified portfolio. You can buy shares or units in one of the more than 9,500 Canadian mutual funds and 198 Canadian exchange-traded funds (ETFs).

Investors buy shares of the funds, and the funds use the money to buy portfolios of securities. The returns on the portfolios are passed back to the funds' owners in proportion to their shareholdings. Therefore, the funds act like investment cooperatives, offering even the smallest investors diversification and professional management at low cost.

Let's look at the betas of two funds that invest in stocks. Figure 12.3(a) plots the monthly returns of Front Street Canadian Energy fund and the S&P/TSX Composite Total Return Index from January 2006 to December 2010. You can see that the stocks in the fund had above-average sensitivity to market changes: on average they had a beta of 1.63.

If the Front Street Canadian Energy fund had no unique risk, its portfolio would have been 1.63 times as variable as the market portfolio. But the fund had not diversified away quite all the unique risk; there is still some scatter about the line in Figure 12.3(a). As a result, the variability of the fund was more than 1.63 times that of the market.

Figure 12.3(b) shows the same sort of plot for iShares S&P/TSX Capped Composite Index fund, an exchange-traded fund. Notice that this fund has a beta of .99, which rounds to 1.0 and had a low residual of unique risk—the fitted line fits almost exactly because an *index fund* is designed to track the market as closely as possible. The fund matches the S&P/TSX Capped Composite Index. The capped index has the same stocks as the S&P/TSX Composite Return Index, but limits each stock to be no more than 10 percent of the fund. However, currently, the two indexes are virtually the same. The managers of the fund do not attempt to pick good stocks; they just work to achieve full diversification at very low cost. The index fund is *fully diversified*. Investors in this fund buy the market as a whole and don't have to worry at all about unique risk. The iShares S&P/TSX Capped Composite Index fund is managed for an annual fee of .25 percent of the fund's assets. By contrast, the annual management fee for the Front Street Canadian Energy mutual fund is 2.00 percent.

Check Point 12.4 Suppose you could achieve full diversification in a portfolio constructed from stocks with an average beta of .5. If the standard deviation of the market is 20 percent per year, what is the standard deviation of the portfolio return?

LO3 12.2 RISK AND RETURN AND CAPITAL ASSET PRICING MODEL, CAPM

In Chapter 11 we looked at past returns on selected investments. The least risky investment was Treasury bills. Since the return on Treasury bills is fixed, it is unaffected by what happens to the market. Thus the beta of Treasury bills is zero. The most risky investment that we considered was the market portfolio of common stocks. This has average market risk: its beta is 1.0.

Wise investors don't invest and take risks just for fun. They are playing with real money and therefore require compensation for both tying up their money in the investments and for taking on risk. Investors expect to earn the risk-free rate of return on Treasury bills because they demand compensation for the time value of money. They expect a higher return from the market portfolio than from Treasury bills to compensate for the added risk. The difference between the

FIGURE 12.3
(a) The slope of the fitted line shows that investors in the Front Street Canadian Energy fund bore more market risk than that of the S&P/TSX portfolio. Front Street Canadian Energy's beta was 1.63. This was the average beta of the individual common stocks held by the fund. They also bore some unique risk, however: note the scatter of Front Street Canadian Energy's returns above and below the fitted line.

(b) The iShares S&P/TSX Capped Composite Index Fund is a fully diversified index exchange-traded fund (ETF) designed to track the performance of the market. Note the fund's beta of 0.99 and the very low unique risk. The fund's returns lie very close to the fitted line, relating its returns to those of the TSX portfolio.

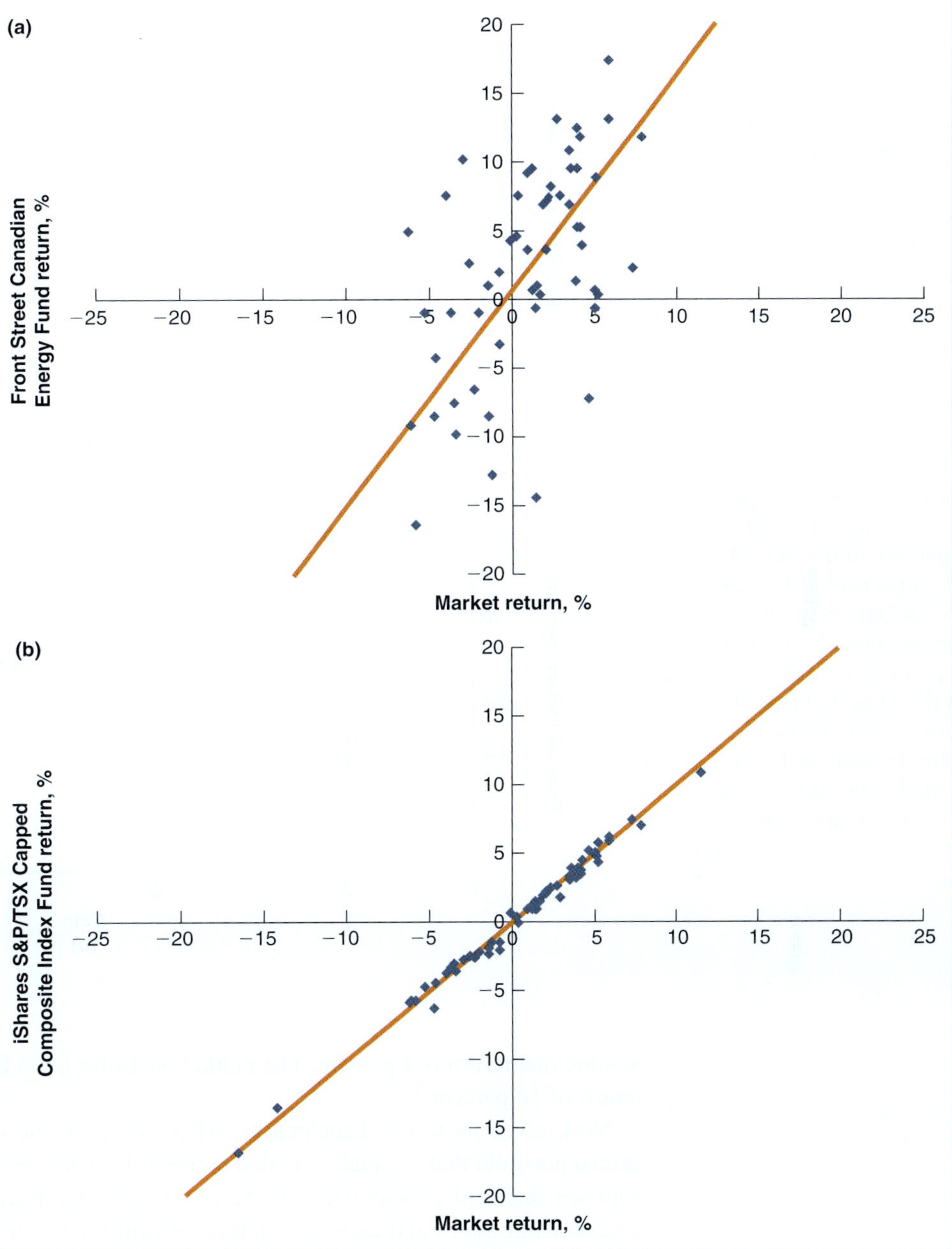

Source: Author's calculations, using data from **www.globeinvestorgold.com**, retrieved February 11, 2011.

market risk premium, MRP
Risk premium of market portfolio. Expected extra return on the market portfolio relative to the return on risk-free Treasury bills.

expected return on the market portfolio and the interest rate on Treasury bills is termed the **market risk premium, MRP**. The challenge is to estimate the expected market risk premium. As we saw in Chapter 11, over the past 85 years the average Canadian market risk premium has been about 7 percent a year. Of course, there is plenty of scope for argument about whether the past 85 years constitute a typical period, but we will just assume here that 7 percent is the normal market risk premium. Thus, the additional return an investor might reasonably expect from investing in the stock market portfolio rather than Treasury bills is estimated using the using the historic average market risk premium.

In Figure 12.4(a) we plotted the risk (beta) and expected return from Treasury bills and the market portfolio. You can see that Treasury bills have a beta of zero and a risk-free return; we'll

FIGURE 12.4
(a) Here we begin the plot of expected rate of return against beta. The first benchmarks are Treasury bills (beta = 0) and the market portfolio (beta = 1.0). We assume a Treasury bill rate of 3 percent and a market return of 10 percent. The market risk premium is 10 − 3 = 7 percent.

(b) A portfolio split evenly between Treasury bills and the market will have beta = .5 and an expected return of 6.5 percent (point X). A portfolio invested 20 percent in the market and 80 percent in Treasury bills has beta = .2 and an expected rate of return of 4.4 percent (point Y). Note that the expected rate of return on any portfolio mixing Treasury bills and the market lies on a straight line. The risk premium is proportional to the portfolio beta.

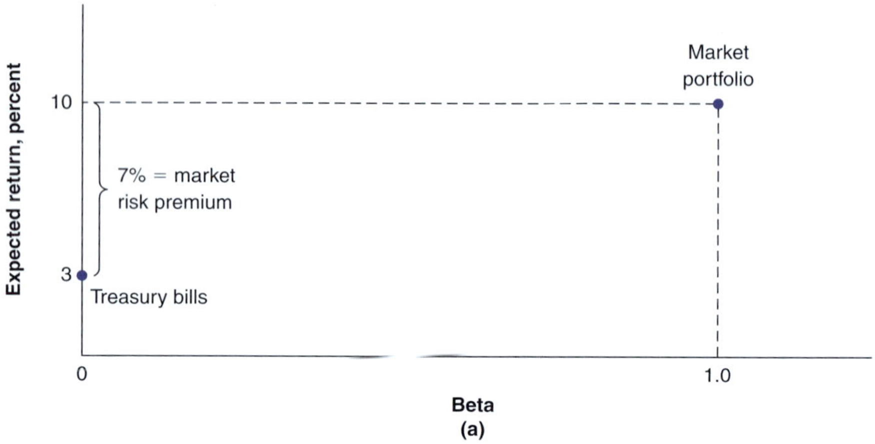

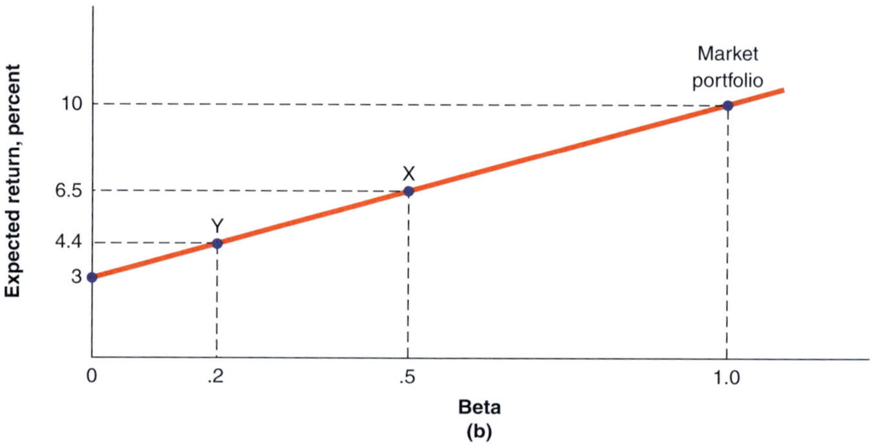

assume that return is 3 percent. The market portfolio has a beta of 1.0 and an assumed expected return of 10 percent.[3]

Now, given these two benchmarks, what expected rate of return should an investor require from a portfolio that is equally divided between Treasury bills and the market portfolio? Halfway between them, of course. Thus, in Figure 12.4(b) we have drawn a straight line through the Treasury bill return and expected market portfolio return to show the relationship between beta and expected return. The portfolio (marked with an X) would have a beta of .5 and an expected return of 6.5 percent. This includes a risk premium of 3.5 percent above the Treasury bill return of 3 percent. Sure enough, that's half of the 7 percent market risk premium.

You can calculate this return as follows. Start with the difference between the expected market return, r_m, and the Treasury bill rate, r_f. This is the expected market risk premium.

$$\text{Expected market risk premium} = r_m - r_f = 10\% - 3\% = 7\%$$

Beta measures the riskiness of a security by calculating its variability relative to the market. If the security's beta were 1, it would have the same risk as the market portfolio and its risk premium would also be the market risk premium. Therefore, the expected risk premium on any security equals its beta times the market risk premium:

$$\textbf{Risk premium on any security} = \textbf{security's beta} \times \textbf{expected market risk premium} = \beta \times (r_m - r_f) \qquad \textbf{(12.4)}$$

[3] On past evidence the risk premium on the market is 7 percentage points. With a 3 percent Treasury bill rate, the expected market return would be 3 + 7 = 10 percent.

With a beta of .5 and a market risk premium of 7 percent, a security's risk premium is

$$\text{Risk premium} = \beta(r_m - r_f) = .5 \times 7 = 3.5\%$$

The total expected rate of return on a security is the sum of the risk-free rate and the security's risk premium:

$$\textbf{Security's expected return} = \textbf{risk-free rate} + \textbf{security's risk premium} \quad (12.5)$$

$$r = r_f + \beta(r_m - r_f)$$
$$= 3\% + 3.5\% = 6.5\%$$

You could have calculated the security's expected rate of return in one step from this formula:

$$\text{Security's expected return} = r = r_f + \beta(r_m - r_f)$$
$$= 3\% + .5\% \times 7\% = 6.5\%$$

capital asset pricing model (CAPM) Theory of the relationship between risk and return that states that the expected risk premium on any security equals its beta times the market risk premium.

This formula states the basic risk–return relationship called the **capital asset pricing model**, or **CAPM**. It can be rewritten using the symbol MRP to represent the expected market risk premium:

$$\textbf{Security's expected return} = r = r_f + \beta \times (r_m - r_f) = r_f + \beta \times \text{MRP} \quad (12.6)$$

The CAPM has a simple interpretation: The expected rate of return demanded by investors depends on two things: (1) compensation for the time value of money (the risk-free rate, r_f) and (2) a risk premium, which depends on beta and the market risk premium. The beta of a security measures the *quantity* of risk and the market risk premium determines the extra return per unit of risk. Together, beta 3 market risk premium determine the extra compensation for the security's risk, its risk premium. The theoretical definition of the market risk premium is the difference between the expected return on the most diversified portfolio (called the market portfolio) and the rate of return on the risk-free security. To use the CAPM formula, the market risk premium must be estimated. We estimated the market risk premium using the historic average difference between the return on a stock market portfolio and Treasury bill, based on 85 years.

Note that the expected rate of return on an asset with $\beta = 1.0$ is just the expected market return. With a risk-free rate of 3 percent and market risk premium, MRP, of 7 percent, the stock's expected rate of return is

$$r = r_f + \beta \times \text{MRP}$$
$$= 3\% + (1 \times 7\%) = 10\%$$

Check Point 12.5

What are the risk premium and expected rate of return on a stock with $\beta = 1.5$? Assume a Treasury bill rate of 6 percent and a market risk premium of 7 percent.

WHY THE CAPM MAKES SENSE

The CAPM assumes that the stock market is dominated by well-diversified investors who are concerned only with market risk. That makes sense in a stock market where trading is dominated by large institutions and even small fry can diversify at very low cost. Thus the only risk that matters is the risk that cannot be diversified away, beta. Investors can only expect to be compensated for taking on "beta" risk. Their expected rate of return on an investment equals the risk-free

EXAMPLE 12.3 HOW WOULD YOU INVEST $1 MILLION?

Have you ever dreamed about winning a lottery and receiving a $1 million cheque, no strings attached? Let's daydream about how you would invest it.

We have two good candidates: Treasury bills, which offer an absolutely safe return, and the market portfolio (possibly via the iShares S&P/TSX Capped Composite Index fund discussed earlier in this chapter). The market has generated superior returns on average, but those returns have fluctuated a lot. (Look back to Figure 11.3 in Chapter 11.) So your investment policy will depend on your tolerance for risk.

(Continued)

(Concluded)

If you're a cautious soul, you might invest only part of your money in the market portfolio and lend the remainder to the government by buying Treasury bills. Suppose that you invest 20 percent of your money in the market portfolio and put the other 80 percent in Treasury bills. Then the beta of your portfolio will be a mixture of the beta of the market ($\beta_{market} = 1.0$) and the beta of the Treasury bills ($\beta_{T\text{-}bills} = 0$):

$$\text{Beta of portfolio} = \left(\begin{array}{c}\text{proportion}\\ \text{in market}\end{array} \times \begin{array}{c}\text{beta of}\\ \text{market}\end{array}\right) + \left(\begin{array}{c}\text{proportion}\\ \text{in T-bills}\end{array} \times \begin{array}{c}\text{beta of}\\ \text{T-bills}\end{array}\right)$$

$$\beta = (.2 \times \beta_{market}) + (.8 \times \beta_{T\text{-}bills})$$
$$= (.2 \times 1.0) + (.8 \times 0) = .2$$

The fraction of funds you invest in the market also affects your return. If you invest your entire million in the market portfolio, you earn the full market risk premium. But if you invest only 20 percent of your money in the market, you earn only 20 percent of the risk premium.

$$\begin{array}{l}\text{Expected}\\ \text{risk premium}\\ \text{on portfolio}\end{array} = \left(\begin{array}{c}\text{proportion}\\ \text{in market}\end{array} \times \begin{array}{c}\text{expected market}\\ \text{risk premium}\end{array}\right) + \left(\begin{array}{c}\text{proportion}\\ \text{in T-bills}\end{array} \times \begin{array}{c}\text{risk premium}\\ \text{on T-bills}\end{array}\right)$$
$$= (.2 \times \text{expected market risk premium}) + (.8 \times 0)$$
$$= .2 \times \text{expected market risk premium}$$
$$= .2 \times 7 = 1.4\%$$

The expected return on your portfolio is equal to the risk-free interest rate plus the expected risk premium:

$$\text{Expected portfolio return} = r_{portfolio} = 3 + 1.4 = 4.4\%$$

In Figure 12.4(b) we show the beta and expected return on this portfolio by the letter *Y*.

---

rate plus the investment's beta times the expected market risk premium. Investors will invest in securities only if they offer the same expected return as other equally risky securities.

When securities are properly priced, the return that investors can expect from their investments is also the return that they *require*. The terms *expected return* and *required return* are used interchangeably. The following example shows why in this case the CAPM makes sense.

THE SECURITY MARKET LINE

security market line Relationship between expected return and beta.

Example 12.3 illustrates a general point: by investing some proportion of your money in the market portfolio and lending (or borrowing) the balance, you can obtain any combination of risk and expected return along the sloping line in Figure 12.5.[4] This line is generally known as the **security market line**.

Check Point 12.6

How would you construct a portfolio with a beta of .25? What is the expected return to this strategy? Assume Treasury bills yield 6 percent and the market risk premium is 7 percent.

The security market line describes the expected returns and risks from investing different fractions of your funds in the market. It also sets a standard for other investments.

(continued on p. 405)

Look back to Figure 12.4(b), which asserts that an individual common stock with $\beta = .5$ must offer a 6.5 percent expected rate of return when Treasury bills yield 3 percent and the market risk

[4] Notice that the security market line extends above the market return at $\beta = 1$. How would you generate a portfolio with, say, $\beta = 2$? It's easy, but it's risky. Suppose you borrow \$1 million at the risk-free rate and invest the loan plus \$1 million in the market portfolio. That gives you \$2 million invested and a \$1 million liability. Your portfolio now has a beta of 2:

$$\text{Beta of portfolio} = (\text{proportion in market} \times \text{beta of market}) + (\text{proportion in loan} \times \text{beta of loan})$$
$$\beta = (2 \times \beta_{market}) + (-1 \times \beta_{loan})$$
$$= (2 \times 1.0) + (-1 \times 0) = 2$$

Notice that the proportion in the loan is negative because you are borrowing, not lending, money.

By the way, borrowing from a bank or stockbroker would not be difficult or unduly expensive as long as you put up your \$2 million stock portfolio as security for the loan.

Can you calculate the risk premium and the expected rate of return on this borrow-and-invest strategy?

FIGURE 12.5
The security market line shows how expected rate of return depends on beta. According to the capital asset pricing model, expected rates of return for all securities and all portfolios lie on this line.

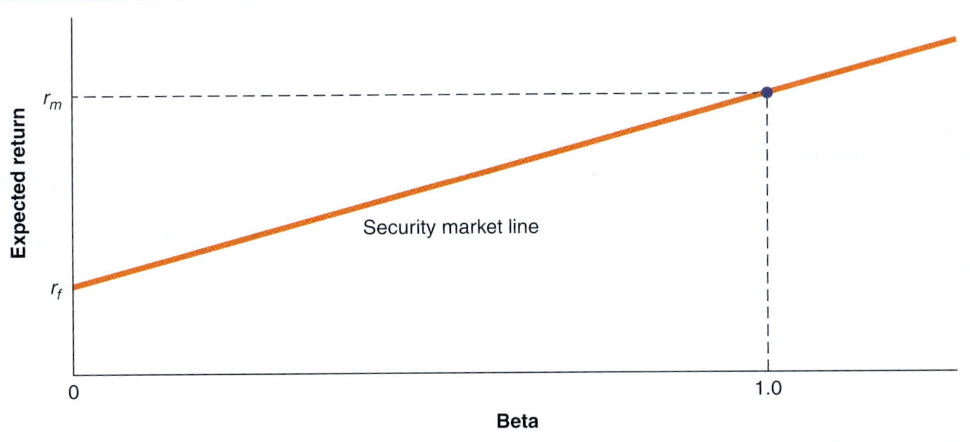

premium is 7 percent. You can now see why this has to be so. If that stock offered a lower rate of return, nobody would buy even a little of it—they could get 6.5 percent just by investing 50-50 in Treasury bills and the market. And if nobody wants to hold the stock, its price has to drop. A lower price means a better buy for investors, that is, a higher rate of return. The price will fall until the stock's expected rate of return is pushed up to 6.5 percent. At that price and expected return the CAPM holds.

If, on the other hand, our stock offered more than 6.5 percent return, diversified investors would want to buy more of it. That would push the price up and the expected return down to the levels predicted by the CAPM.

This reasoning holds for stocks with any beta. That's why the CAPM makes sense, and why the expected risk premium on an investment should be proportional to its beta.

Check Point 12.7

Suppose you invest $400,000 in Treasury bills and $600,000 in the market portfolio. What is the return on your portfolio if Treasury bills yield 6 percent and the expected return on the market is 14 percent? Under these assumptions, what is the current expected market risk premium? What is the beta of this portfolio? What does the return on this portfolio imply for the expected return on individual stocks with betas of .6?

(Concluded)

Investors will be willing to hold other investments only if they offer equally good prospects. Thus, the required risk premium for *any* investment is given by the security market line:

Risk premium on investment = investment's beta × expected market risk premium

HOW WELL DOES THE CAPM WORK?

The basic idea behind the capital asset pricing model is that investors expect a reward for both waiting and worrying. The greater the worry, the greater the expected return. If you invest in a risk-free Treasury bill, you just receive the rate of interest. That's the reward for waiting. When you invest in risky stocks, you can expect an extra return or risk premium for worrying. The capital asset pricing model states that this risk premium is equal to the stock's beta times the market risk premium. Therefore,

$$\text{Expected return on stock} = \text{risk-free interest rate} + \left[\text{stock's beta} \times \text{expected market risk premium}\right]$$

$$r = r_f + \beta(r_m - r_f) = r_f + \beta \times \text{MRP}$$

How well does the CAPM work in practice? Do the returns on stocks with betas of .5 on average lie halfway between the return on the market portfolio and the interest rate on Treasury bills? Unfortunately, the evidence is conflicting. Let's look back to the actual returns earned by investors in low-beta stocks and in high-beta stocks.

Imagine that, in 1931, ten investors gathered together in a Wall Street bar and agreed to establish investment trust funds for their children. Each investor decided to follow a different strategy.

FIGURE 12.6
The capital asset pricing model states that the expected risk premium from any investment should lie on the security market line. The dots show the actual average risk premiums from portfolios with different betas. The high-beta portfolios generated higher average returns, just as predicted by the CAPM. But the high-beta portfolios plotted below the security market line, and four of the five low-beta portfolios plotted above. A line fitted to the 10 portfolio returns would be flatter than the market line.

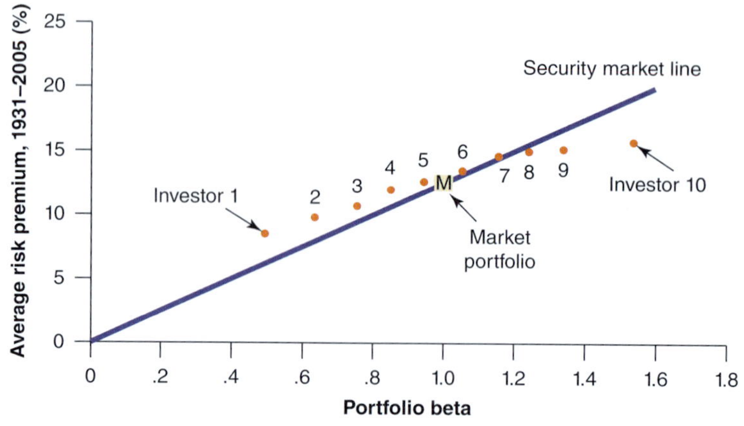

Source: F. Black, "Beta and Return," *Journal of Portfolio Management* 20 (Fall 1993). We are grateful to Adam Kolasinski for recalculating and extending the plots.

Investor 1 opted to buy the 10 percent of the New York Stock Exchange stocks with the lowest estimated betas; investor 2 chose the 10 percent with the next-lowest betas; and so on, up to investor 10, who bought the stocks with the highest betas. They also planned that at the end of each year they would reestimate the betas of all NYSE stocks and reconstitute their portfolios to keep their target betas. And so they parted with much cordiality and good wishes.

In time the 10 investors all passed away, but their children agreed to meet in early 2006 in the same bar to compare the performance of their portfolios. Figure 12.6 shows how they fared. Investor 1's portfolio, based on the stock with the lowest estimated betas, turned out to be much less risky than the market; its beta was only .49. However, investor 1 also realized the lowest return, 8.5 percent above the risk-free rate of interest. At the other extreme, the beta of investor 10's portfolio was 1.53, about three times that of investor 1's portfolio. But investor 10 was rewarded with the highest return, averaging 15.6 percent a year above the interest rate. So over this 75-year period returns did indeed increase with beta.

As you can see from Figure 12.6, the market portfolio over the same 75-year period provided an average return of 12.5 percent above the interest rate[5] and (of course) had a beta of 1.0. The CAPM predicts that the risk premium should increase in proportion to beta, so the returns of each portfolio should lie on the upward-sloping security market line in Figure 12.6. Since the market provided a risk premium of 12.5 percent, investor 1's portfolio, with a beta of .49, should have provided a risk premium of about 6 percent ($\beta \times \text{MRP} = .49 \times 12.5\% = 6.1$ percent) and investor 10's portfolio, with a beta of 1.53, should have given a premium of over 19 percent ($\beta \times \text{MRP} = 1.53 \times 12.5\% = 19.1$ percent). You can see that, while high-beta stocks performed better than low-beta stocks, the difference was not as great as the CAPM predicts.

Figure 12.6 provides broad support for the CAPM, though it suggests that the line relating return to beta has been too flat. But recent years have been less kind to the CAPM. For example, if the 10 friends had invested their cash in 1966 rather than 1931, there would have been very little relation between their portfolio returns and beta. During this later period, the returns to investors 1 to 7 did increase in line with beta. However, the highest-beta portfolios, 8 to 10, performed poorly. Does this imply that there has been a fundamental change in the relation

[5] In Figure 12.6 the stocks in the "market portfolio" are weighted equally. Since the stocks of small firms have provided higher average returns than those of large firms, the risk premium on an equally weighted index is higher than on a value-weighted index. This is one reason for the difference between the 12.5 percent market risk premium in Figure 12.6 and the 7 percent premium reported in Table 11.1. Also, this study is based on U.S. market data and covers a different time period than we used in Chapter 11.

FIGURE 12.7
The blue line shows the cumulative difference between the returns on small-firm and large-firm stocks from 1926 to 2007. The orange line shows the cumulative difference between the returns on high-book-to-market-value stocks and low-book-to-market-value stocks.

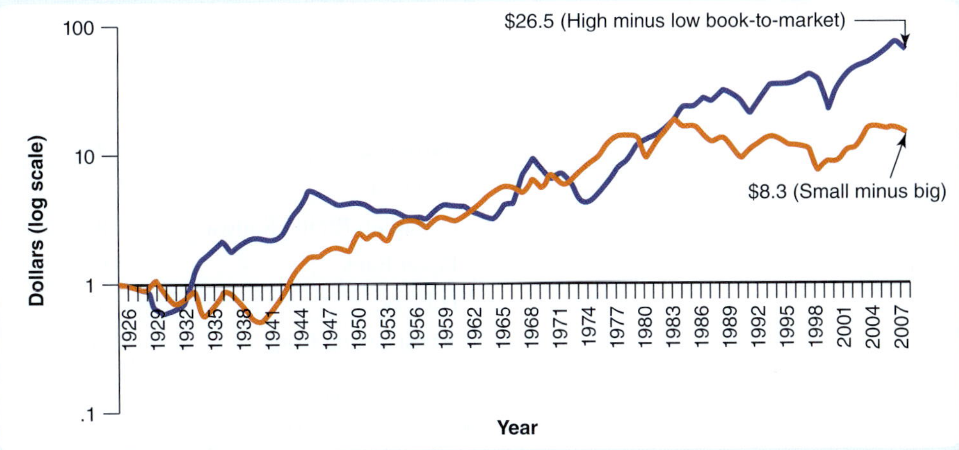

Source: Professor Kenneth R. French faculty page at Dartmouth College, **mba.tuck.dartmouth.edu/pages/faculty/ken.french/data_library.html**. Used by permission.

between risk and return in the last 40 years or so, or did high-beta stocks just happen to perform worse during these years than investors expected? It is hard to be sure.

There is little doubt that the CAPM is too simple to capture everything that is going on in the stock market. For example, look at Figure 12.7. The orange line shows the cumulative difference between the returns on small-firm stocks and large-firm stocks. If you had bought the shares with the smallest market capitalizations and sold those with the largest capitalizations, this is how your wealth would have changed. You can see that small-cap stocks did not always do well, but over the long haul their owners have made substantially higher returns. Since the end of 1926 the average annual difference between the returns on the two groups of stocks has been 3.9 percent. Now look at the purple line in Figure 12.7, which shows the cumulative difference between the returns on value stocks and growth stocks. Value stocks here are defined as those with high ratios of book value to market value. Growth stocks are those with low ratios of book to market. Notice that value stocks have provided a higher long-run return than growth stocks. Since 1926 the average annual difference between returns on value and growth stocks has been 4.5 percent.

The superior performance of small-firm stocks and value stocks does not fit well with the CAPM, which predicts that beta is the *only* reason that expected returns differ. If investors *expected* the returns to depend on firm size or book-to-market ratios, then the simple version of the capital asset pricing model cannot be the whole truth.

What's going on here? It is hard to say. Defenders of the capital asset pricing model emphasize that it is concerned with *expected* returns, whereas we can observe only actual returns. Actual returns reflect expectations, but they also embody lots of "noise"—the steady flow of surprises that conceal whether on average investors have received the returns that they expected. Thus, when we observe that in the past small-firm stocks and value stocks have provided superior performance, we can't be sure whether this was simply a coincidence or whether investors have required a higher return to hold these stocks.

Such debates have prompted headlines like "Is Beta Dead?" in the business and academic press. It is not the first time that beta has been declared dead, but the CAPM remains the leading model for estimating required returns. Only strong theories can have more than one funeral.

The CAPM is not the only model of risk and return. It has several brothers, sisters, and cousins. These other models, including the multi-factor CAPM and Arbitrage Pricing Theory (APT), argue that the risk of a stock depends on more than its correlation with the market portfolio. Although much of a stock's risk does depend on the general movement of the market, stock risk may also be affected by the growth rate of GDP, the yield spread between long-term and

TABLE 12.2
Expected rates of return.

Stock	Beta	Expected Return, %
IMAX	1.06	8.9
Research In Motion	1.64	12.9
Gildan Activewear	1.04	8.8
Barrick Gold	.45	4.6
Cameco	1.51	12.1
Canadian Pacific Railway	.82	7.2
Royal Bank	.63	5.9
Loblaw	.39	4.2
TransCanada Corp	.40	4.3

Note: Expected return = $r = r_f + \beta \times \text{MRP} = 1.5\% + (\beta \times 7\%)$.

Source: Authors' calculations using 2006–2009 monthly return data from TSX-CFMRC database, augmented with 2010 monthly returns calculated with stock prices from **www.globeinvestorgold.com** and dividend data from Financial Post Advisor.

short-term bonds, and relative firm size.[6] Researchers have examined these other factors and some believe that beta and the CAPM are not enough to capture all the systematic (non-diversifiable) risks. However, the CAPM captures two fundamental ideas in a simple way. First, almost everyone agrees that investors require some extra return for taking on risk. Second, investors appear to be concerned principally with the market risk that they cannot eliminate by diversification. That is why financial managers rely on the capital asset pricing model as a good rule of thumb.

USING THE CAPM TO ESTIMATE EXPECTED RETURNS

To calculate the returns that investors are expecting from a particular stock, we need three numbers—the risk-free interest rate, the expected market risk premium, and the stock's beta. Suppose that the interest rate on Treasury bills is about 1.5 percent and that the market risk premium is about 7 percent. Now, go back to Table 12.1, where we gave you betas of several stocks. Table 12.2 puts these numbers together to give an estimate of the expected return from each stock. Let's take Cameco as an example:

$$\text{Expected return on Cameco's stock} = \text{risk-free interest rate} + \left(\text{beta} \times \begin{array}{c}\text{expected market}\\ \text{risk premium}\end{array}\right)$$

$$r = 1.5\% + (1.51 \times 7\%) = 12.1\%$$

Of our same sample of companies, Research In Motion had the highest betas. Investors in RIM stocks required compensation for taking on the extra market risk. Table 12.2 suggests that the expected rate of return from Research In Motion was around 12.9 percent, three times the figure for Loblaw, the company with the lowest expected rate of return and lowest beta in Table 12.2.

LO4 12.3 CAPITAL BUDGETING AND PROJECT RISK

We have seen that the firm faces a trade-off. It can either buy new plant and equipment or return cash to its shareholders, who can then invest the money for themselves in the capital market. When the company invests the cash, shareholders can't invest these funds in the capital market. The return that shareholders give up by keeping their money in the company is therefore called the *opportunity cost of capital*. Shareholders need the company to earn at least the opportunity cost of capital on its investments.

---

[6] To learn more about models of stock returns, see Z. Bodie, A. Kane, A.J. Marcus, S. Perrakis, and P. Ryan, *Investments*, 7th Canadian ed. (Toronto: McGraw-Hill Ryerson, 2011).

We have referred loosely to the return that investors could expect to earn by buying securities. But there are thousands of different securities that investors can buy. The expected return on each of these securities depends on its risk. So we need to redefine the opportunity cost of capital for a project, r, as the expected return on a security that has a similar level of risk to that of the project. The capital asset pricing model tells us how to calculate this.

COMPANY RISK VERSUS PROJECT RISK

company cost of capital Expected rate of return demanded by investors in a company, determined by the average risk of the company's assets and operations.

Many companies estimate the rate of return required by investors in their securities and use this **company cost of capital** to discount the cash flows on all new projects. Since investors require a higher rate of return from a risky company, risky firms will have a higher company cost of capital and will set a higher discount rate for their new investment opportunities. For example, we showed in Table 12.2 that on past evidence IMAX has a beta of 1.06 and the corresponding expected rate of return (see Table 12.2) is about 8.9 percent. According to the company cost of capital rule, IMAX should use an 8.9 percent cost of capital to calculate project NPVs.

This is a step in the right direction, but we must take care when the firm has issued securities other than equity.[7] Moreover, this approach can get a firm in trouble if its new projects do not have the same risk as its existing business. IMAX's beta reflects investors' estimate of the risk of business, and its company cost of capital is the return that investors require for taking on this risk. If IMAX is considering an expansion of its regular business, it makes sense to discount the forecast cash flows by the company cost of capital. But suppose that IMAX is wondering whether to branch out into the grocery business. Its beta tells us nothing about the **project cost of capital**. That depends on the risk of the grocery business and the return that shareholders require from investing in such a business.

project cost of capital Minimum acceptable expected rate of return on a project given its risk.

Check Point 12.8

IMAX is contemplating an expansion of its existing business. The investment forecast to produce cash flows of $50 million a year for each of 10 years. What is its present value? Use data from Table 12.2.

The project cost of capital depends on the use to which that capital is put. Therefore, it depends on the risk of the project and not on the risk of the company. If a company invests in a low-risk project, it should discount the cash flows at a correspondingly low cost of capital. If it invests in a high-risk project, those cash flows should be discounted at a high cost of capital.

The project cost of capital depends on the use to which that capital (money) is put. Therefore, it depends on the risk of the project, not the risk of company. However, sometimes managers seriously miscalculate a project's required rate of return because they ignore the fact that the project's risk is very different than the firm's overall risk. To avoid that mistake, ask yourself: If this project were a mini-firm, separate from our company, what rate of return would investors require to be willing to invest in it? When a firm evaluates an investment, it must use a required rate of return that corresponds to the risk of the investment.

The principle of assessing the required rate of return on the basis of the risk of the investment applies to your own investment activities. Suppose you take money from your savings account, which is currently paying 1 percent annual interest, and invest in shares of Cameco. You would not be happy if your expected return on the Cameco shares was only 1 percent. You would expect to earn a higher rate of return to compensate for the substantially higher market risk associated with Cameco, right? The same applies to a firm's investment decisions: the project's required rate of return depends on the project's risk.

[7] We could ignore this complication in the case of IMAX, because IMAX is currently almost completely financed by common stock. Therefore, the risk of its assets equals the risk of its stock. But most companies issue a mix of debt and common stock. In Chapter 13 you will learn how to incorporate other securities into the cost of capital.

EXAMPLE 12.4 **ESTIMATING THE OPPORTUNITY COST OF CAPITAL FOR A PROJECT**

Suppose that RIM is contemplating investment in a new project. You have forecast the cash flows on a project and calculated that its internal rate of return is 12 percent. Suppose that Treasury bills offer a return of 1.5 percent and the expected market risk premium is 7 percent. Should you go ahead with the project?

To answer this question you need to figure out the opportunity cost of capital r. You start with the *project's* beta. For example, if the project is a sure thing, the beta is zero and the cost of capital equals the interest rate on Treasury bills:

$$r = 1.5 + (0 \times 7) = 1.5\%$$

If the project offers a return of 12 percent when the cost of capital is 1.5 percent, RIM should obviously go ahead.[8] But if you had compare this project's return with RIM's 12.9 percent *company* cost of capital, you would have wrongly concluded that it was not worthwhile.

Sure-fire projects rarely occur outside finance texts. So let's think about the cost of capital if the project has the same risk as the market portfolio. In this case beta is 1 and the cost of capital is the expected return on the market:

$$r = 1.5 + (1 \times 7) = 8.5\%$$

The project looks less attractive than before, but still worth doing.

Check Point 12.9

The company cost of capital for IMAX is about 8.9 percent (see Table 12.2); for Loblaw it is about 4.2 percent. What would be the more reasonable discount rate for IMAX to use for its proposed move into the grocery business? Why?

The security market line provides a standard for project acceptance. If the project's return lies above the security market line, then the return is higher than investors might expect to get by investing their funds in the capital market, and therefore it is an attractive investment opportunity.

The project in Example 12.4 is attractive because, as Figure 12.8 shows, its expected rate of return, 12 percent, lies above the security market line. The project offers a higher return than investors can reasonably expect elsewhere on equally risky investments, beta equal 1. Therefore it is a positive NPV investment.

DETERMINANTS OF PROJECT RISK

We have seen that the company cost of capital is the correct discount rate for projects that have the same risk as the company's existing business, but *not* for those projects that are safer or riskier than the company's average. How do we know whether a project is unusually risky? Estimating project risk is never going to be an exact science, but here are a few things to bear in mind.

First, we saw in Chapter 10 that operating leverage increases the risk of a project. When a large fraction of your costs is fixed, any change in revenues can have a dramatic effect on earnings. Therefore, projects that involve high fixed costs tend to have higher betas.

Second, many people intuitively associate risk with the variability of earnings. But much of this variability reflects diversifiable risk. Lone prospectors in search of gold look forward to extremely uncertain future earnings, but whether they strike it rich is not likely to depend on the performance of the rest of the economy. These investments have a high standard deviation but a low beta.

pure-play approach
Estimating project cost of capital using the cost of capital of another company involved exclusively in the same type of project.

Third, look at the risk and required rate of return of a similar risk project outside the firm. (We saw this in Check Point 12.9.) IMAX uses the required rate of return of a company already in the grocery industry—Loblaw—to assess its investment in a communications division. Using Loblaw's cost of capital is an application of the **pure-play approach** to determine project risk. *Pure play* is a term used by investors to refer to companies exclusively involved in a single line

[8] In Chapter 8 we described some special cases in which you should prefer projects that offer a *lower* internal rate of return than the cost of capital. We assume here that your project is a "normal" one, and that you prefer high IRRs to low ones.

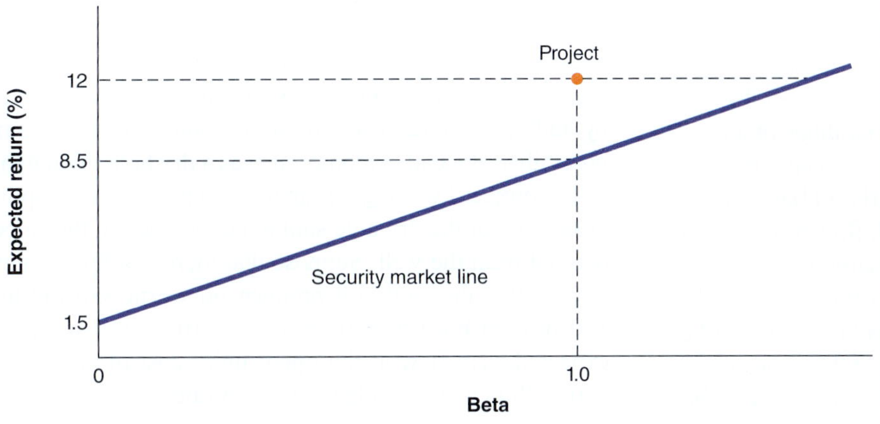

FIGURE 12.8
The expected return of this project is more than the expected return one could earn on stock market investments with the same market risk (beta). Therefore, the project's expected return-risk combination lies above the security market line, and the project should be accepted.

The beta risk of a firm is driven by the strength of the relationship between the firm's earnings and the aggregate earnings of all firms. Thus cyclical businesses, whose revenues and earnings are strongly dependent on the state of the economy, tend to have high betas and a high cost of capital. By contrast, businesses that produce essentials, such as food, beer, and cosmetics, are less affected by the state of the economy. They tend to have low betas and a low cost of capital.

of business. If you wanted a pure play in silver, you would invest in a silver mining company and not in diversified company that owns a silver mine.

The key to the pure-play approach is finding the beta and market-required rate of return of a company exclusively involved in the type of project under consideration. If the comparable company is publicly traded, its beta may be available on a financial information site such as **finance.yahoo.com** or from a company specializing in financial analysis such as Bloomberg or Ibbotson. You can also estimate the beta yourself using the stock's monthly rates of return, as we did for Figure 12.2. Don't be surprised if a stock's beta is different at the various Web sites and not the same as your estimate. A beta estimated with stock returns from the most recent 60 months will likely be different from the one estimated with returns for a different time period. Also, the market rate of return depends on the selected market portfolio and the estimation procedure. State your assumptions and use your judgment when selecting a beta.

It may be difficult to find a suitable pure play for comparison. Many companies are involved in several different businesses and hence their betas reflect the risks of all of the businesses. Like any portfolio, the beta of a company is the sum of the betas of its businesses, each weighted by its fraction of the firm's total value. Even if a comparable company is found, determining the appropriate risk and discount rate may be complicated by a different capital structure. We will have more to say about this in Chapter 13.

You cannot hope to measure the systematic risk of a project with high precision, but good managers examine any project from a variety of angles and look for clues to its riskiness. They know that high market risk is a characteristic of cyclical ventures and of ventures with high fixed costs. They think about the major uncertainties affecting the economy and how projects are affected by these uncertainties. Experience at assessing risks plays an important role too. Regrettably, we have no magic formula for determining a project's risk. On the other hand, if such a formula existed, no one would pay financial managers handsomely for their expertise.

DON'T ADD FUDGE FACTORS TO DISCOUNT RATES

Risk to an investor arises because an investment adds to the spread of possible portfolio returns. To a diversified investor, risk is predominantly market risk. But in everyday usage risk simply means "bad outcome." People think of the "risks" of a project as the things that can go wrong. For example,

- A geologist looking for oil worries about the risk of a dry hole.
- A pharmaceutical manufacturer worries about the risk that a new drug that reverses balding may not be approved by Health Canada.
- The owner of a hotel in a politically unstable part of the world worries about the political risk of expropriation.

Expected cash flow forecasts should already reflect the probabilities of all possible outcomes, good and bad. If the cash flow forecasts are prepared properly, the discount rate should reflect only the market risk of the project. It should not have to be fudged to offset errors or biases in the cash flow forecast.

Managers sometimes add fudge factors to discount rates to account for worries such as these.

This sort of adjustment makes us nervous. First, the bad outcomes we cited appear to reflect diversifiable risks that would not affect the expected rate of return demanded by investors. Second, the need for an adjustment in the discount rate usually arises because managers fail to give bad outcomes their due weight in cash flow forecasts. They then try to offset that mistake by adding a fudge factor to the discount rate. For example, if a manager is worried about the possibility of a bad outcome, such as a dry hole in oil exploration, he or she may reduce the value of the project by using a higher discount rate. This approach is unsound, however. Instead, the possibility of the dry hole should be included in the calculation of the expected cash flows to be derived from the well. Suppose that there is a 50 percent chance of a dry hole and a 50 percent chance that the well will produce oil worth $20 million. Then the *expected* cash flow is not $20 million but $(.5 \times 0) + (.5 \times 20) = \$10$ million. You should discount the $10 million expected cash flow at the opportunity cost of capital: it does not make sense to discount the $20 million using a fudged discount rate.

12.4 SUMMARY

1. **How can you measure and interpret the market risk, or beta, of a security? LO1**

   The contribution of a security to the risk of a diversified portfolio depends on its market risk. But not all securities are equally affected by fluctuations in the market. The sensitivity of a stock to market movement is known as **beta**. Stocks with a beta greater than 1.0 are particularly sensitive to market fluctuations. Those with a beta of less than 1.0 are not so sensitive to such movements. The average beta of all stocks is 1.0.

2. **How do you calculate the beta of a portfolio? LO3**

   The relevant risk of any security is its beta, the sensitivity of its return to the return on the market portfolio. The beta of a portfolio, a group of securities, is the weighted average of the betas of each security, where each security's weight is its fraction of the portfolio value.

3. **What is the relationship between the market risk of a security and the rate of return that investors demand of that security? LO2**

   The extra return that investors require for taking risk is known as the risk premium. The Canadian **market risk premium**—that is, the risk premium on the **market portfolio**—averaged 7 percent between 1926 and 2010. The **capital asset pricing model** states that the expected risk premium of an investment should be proportional to both its beta and the market risk premium. The expected rate of return from any investment is equal to the risk-free interest rate plus the risk premium, so the **CAPM** boils down to

   $$r = r_f + \beta(r_m - r_f)$$

   The **security market line** is the graphical representation of the CAPM equation. The security market line relates the expected return investors demand of a security to the beta.

4. **How can a manager calculate the opportunity cost of capital for a project? LO4**

   The opportunity cost of capital is the return investors give up by investing in the project rather than in securities of equivalent risk. Financial managers use the capital asset pricing model to estimate the opportunity cost of capital. The **company cost of capital** is the expected rate of return demanded by investors in a company, determined by the average risk of the company's assets and operations.

   The opportunity cost of capital depends on the use to which the capital is put. Therefore, required rates of return are determined by the risk of the project, not by the risk of the firm's existing business. The **project cost of capital** is the minimum acceptable expected rate of return on a project given its risk.

   Your cash flow forecasts should already factor in the chances of pleasant and unpleasant surprises. Potential bad outcomes should be reflected in the discount rate only to the extent that they affect beta.

Related Web Links

globeinvestor.com Up-to-date investing news and analysis.

finance.yahoo.com Includes stock betas as well as other risk measures and company profiles

Key Terms

beta	394	market portfolio	393	pure-play approach	410
capital asset pricing model (CAPM)	403	market risk premium (MRP)	401	security market line	404
company cost of capital	409	project cost of capital	409		

Questions and Problems

connect™ Practise and learn online with *Connect*. Questions with online Excel templates or datasets are marked with [icon].

*Answers in Appendix B

BASIC

*1. **Risk and Return.** True or false? Explain or qualify as necessary.
   a. Investors demand higher expected rates of return on stocks with more variable rates of return. (LO3)
   b. The capital asset pricing model predicts that a security with a beta of zero will provide an expected return of zero. (LO3)
   c. An investor who puts $10,000 in Treasury bills and $20,000 in the market portfolio will have a portfolio beta of 2. (LO2)
   d. Investors demand higher expected rates of return from stocks with returns that are highly exposed to macroeconomic changes. (LO3)
   e. Investors demand higher expected rates of return from stocks with returns that are very sensitive to fluctuations in the stock market. (LO3)

2. **Diversifiable Risk.** In the light of what you've learned about market versus diversifiable (unique) risks, explain why an insurance company has no problem selling life insurance to individuals but is reluctant to issue policies insuring against flood damage to residents of coastal areas. Why don't the insurance companies simply charge coastal residents a premium that reflects the actuarial probability of damage from hurricanes and other storms? (LO1)

3. **Unique Versus Market Risk.** Figure 12.9 plots monthly rates of return from 2006 to 2020 for the Snake Oil mutual fund and the S&P/TSX Composite Total Return Index. Was this fund well diversified? Explain. (LO1)

4. **Risk and Return.** Suppose that the risk premium on stocks and other securities did in fact rise with total risk (that is, the variability of returns) rather than just market risk. Explain how investors could exploit the situation to create portfolios with high expected rates of return but low levels of risk. (LO3)

FIGURE 12.9
Monthly rates of return for the Snake Oil mutual fund and the S&P/TSX Composite Total Return Index (see problem 3).

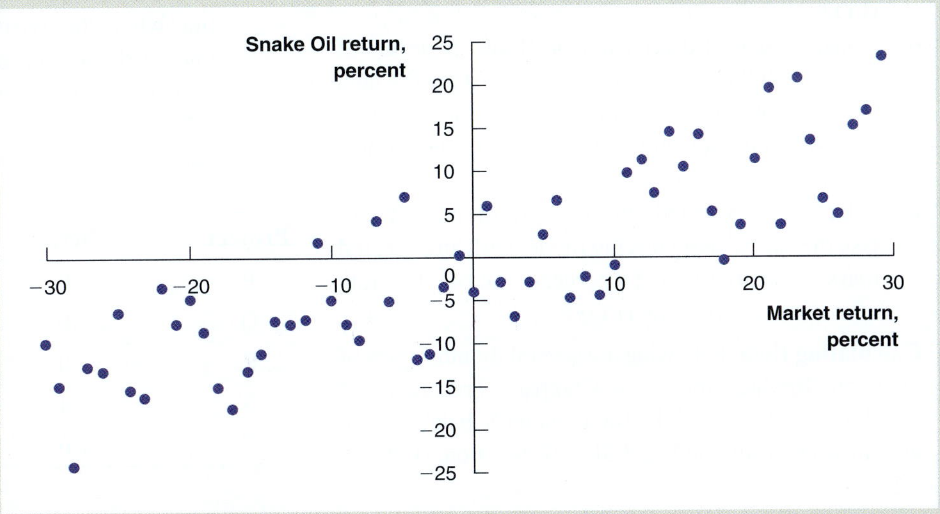

5. **CAPM and Hurdle Rates.** A project under consideration has an internal rate of return of 14 percent and a beta of .6. The risk-free rate is 4 percent and the expected rate of return on the market portfolio is 11 percent. (LO4)
   a. Should the project be accepted?
   b. Should the project be accepted if its beta is 1.6?
   c. Does your answer change? Why or why not?

INTERMEDIATE

6. **CAPM and Valuation.** You are considering acquiring a firm that you believe can generate expected cash flows of $10,000 a year forever. However, you recognize that those cash flows are uncertain. (LO3)
   a. Suppose you believe that the beta of the firm is .4. How much is the firm worth if the risk-free rate is 5 percent and the expected market risk premium is 7 percent?
   b. By how much will you misvalue the firm if its beta is actually .6?

*7. **CAPM and Expected Return.** If the risk-free rate is 4 percent and the expected market risk premium is 7 percent, is a security with a beta of 1.25 and an expected rate of return of 11 percent overpriced or underpriced? (LO3)

8. **Using Beta.** Investors expect the market rate of return this year to be 14 percent. A stock with a beta of .8 has an expected rate of return of 12 percent. If the market return this year turns out to be 10 percent, what is your best guess as to the rate of return on the stock? (LO1)

*9. **Unique Versus Market Risk.** Figure 12.10 shows plots of monthly rates of return on three stocks versus the stock market index. The beta and standard deviation of each stock is given beside its plot.
   a. Which stock is riskiest to a diversified investor? (LO1)
   b. Which stock is riskiest to an undiversified investor who puts all her funds in one of these stocks? (LO1)
   c. Consider a portfolio with equal investments in each stock. What would this portfolio's beta have been? (LO2)
   d. Consider a well-diversified portfolio made up of stocks with the same beta as Ford. What are the beta and standard deviation of this portfolio's return? The standard deviation of the market portfolio's return is 20 percent. (LO2)
   e. What is the expected rate of return on each stock? Use the capital asset pricing model with an expected market risk premium of 8 percent. The risk-free rate of interest is 4 percent. (LO3)

10. **Calculating Beta.** Following are several months' rates of return for Tumblehome Canoe Company. Prepare a plot like Figure 12.1. What is Tumblehome's beta? Check your answers using the Excel SLOPE function. (LO1)

Month	Market Return, %	Tumblehome Return, %
1	0	+1
2	0	−1
3	−1	−2.5
4	−1	−0.5
5	+1	+2
6	+1	+1
7	+2	+4
8	+2	+2
9	−2	−2
10	−2	−4

*11. **Expected Returns.** An economy has two scenarios: boom or bust. The returns in each scenario for the market portfolio, an aggressive stock A, and a defensive stock D are in this chart.

	Rate of Return		
Scenario	Market	Aggressive Stock A	Defensive Stock D
Bust	−8%	−10%	−6%
Boom	32	38	24

   a. Find the beta of each stock. In what way is stock D defensive? (LO1)
   b. If each scenario is equally likely, calculate the expected rate of return on the market portfolio and on each stock.
   c. If the Treasury bill rate is 4 percent, what does the CAPM say about the fair expected rate of return on the two stocks? (LO3)
   d. Which stock seems to be a better buy based on your answers to (a) through (c)? (LO3)

12. **CAPM and Cost of Capital.** Draw the security market line when the Treasury bill rate is 4 percent and the market risk premium is 7 percent. What are the project costs of capital for new ventures with betas of .75 and 1.75? Which of the following capital investments have positive NPVs? (LO4)

Project	Beta	Internal Rate of Return, %
P	1.0	14
Q	.0	6
R	2.0	18
S	.4	7
T	1.6	20

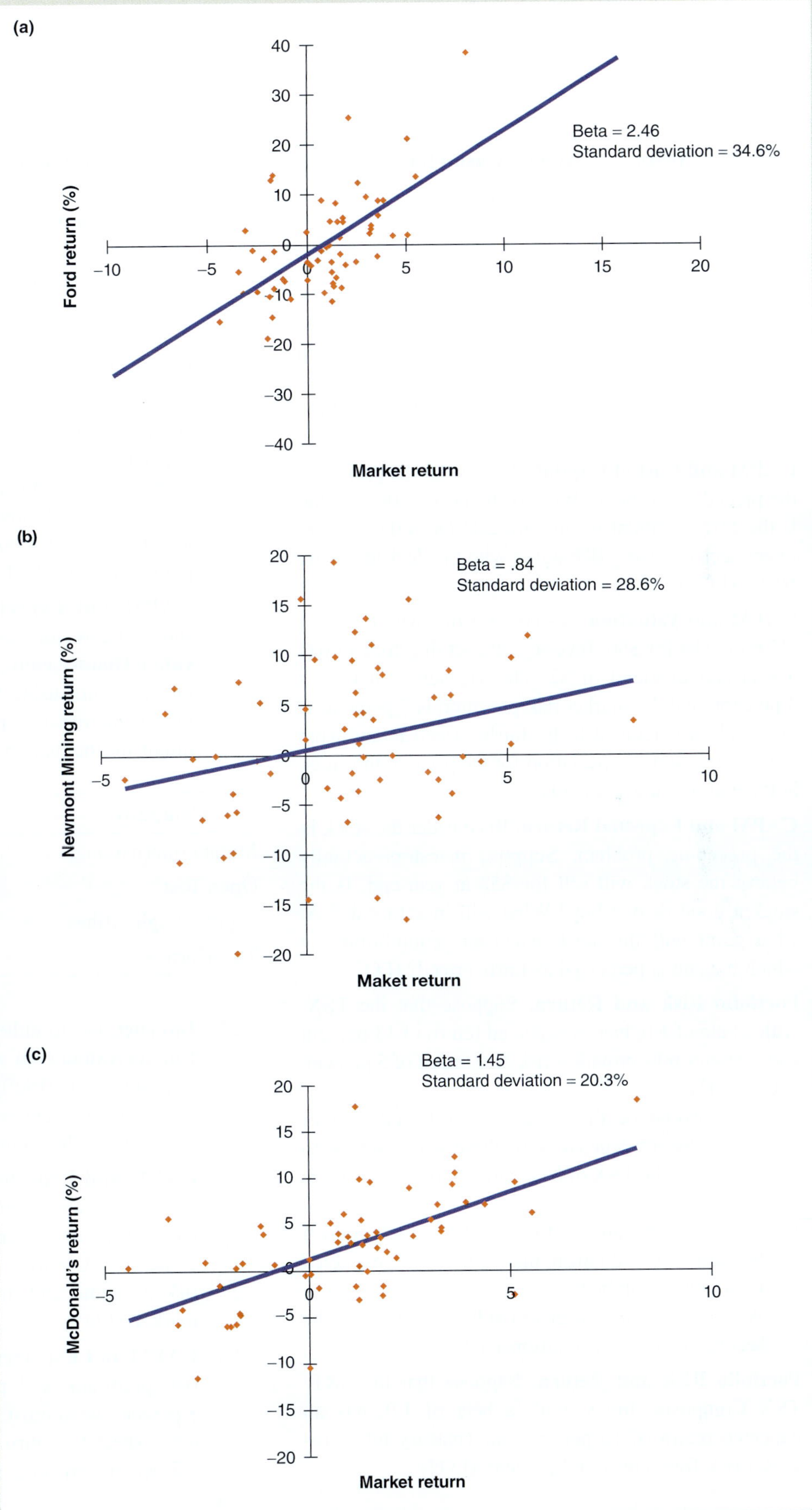

FIGURE 12.10 These plots show monthly rates of return for (a) Ford, (b) Newmont Mining, and (c) McDonalds, plus the market portfolio. See problem 9.

*13. **CAPM and Valuation.** You are a consultant to a firm evaluating an expansion of its current business. The annual cash flow forecasts (in millions of dollars) for the project are: (LO4)

Years	Annual Cash Flow
0	−100
1−10	+15

Based on the behaviour of the firm's stock, you believe that the beta of the firm is 1.4. Assuming that the rate of return available on risk-free investments is 4 percent and that the expected rate of return on the market portfolio is 12 percent, what is the net present value of the project?

14. **CAPM and Cost of Capital.** Reconsider the project in the preceding problem. What is the project IRR? What is the cost of capital for the project? Does the accept–reject decision using IRR agree with the decision using NPV? (LO4)

*15. **CAPM and Valuation.** A share of stock with a beta of .75 now sells for $50. Investors expect the stock to pay a year-end dividend of $2. The Treasury bill rate is 4 percent, and the market risk premium is 7 percent. If the stock is perceived to be fairly priced today, what must be investors' expectation for the price of the stock at the end of the year? (LO3)

16. **CAPM and Expected Return.** Reconsider the stock in the preceding problem. Suppose investors actually believe the stock will sell for $52 at year-end. Is the stock a good or bad buy? What will investors do? At what point will the stock reach an "equilibrium" at which it again is perceived as fairly priced? (LO3)

17. **Portfolio Risk and Return.** Suppose that the TSX, with a beta of 1.0, has an expected return of 13 percent and Treasury bills provide a risk-free return of 5 percent. (LO2, LO3)
   a. What would be the expected return and beta of portfolios constructed from these two assets with weights in the TSX of (i) 0; (ii) .25; (iii) .5; (iv) .75; (v) 1.0?
   b. Based on your answer to (a), what is the trade-off between risk and return, that is, how does expected return vary with beta?
   c. What does your answer to (b) have to do with the security market line relationship?

18. **Portfolio Risk and Return.** Suppose that the S&P/TSX Composite Index, with a beta of 1.0, has an expected return of 10 percent and Treasury bills provide a risk-free return of 4 percent. (LO2)
   a. Construct a portfolio from these two assets with an expected return of 8 percent. What is the beta of this portfolio?
   b. Construct a portfolio from these two assets with a beta of .4. Calculate the portfolio's expected return.
   c. Show that the risk premiums of the portfolios in (a) and (b) are proportional to their betas.

*19. **CAPM and Valuation.** You are considering the purchase of real estate that will provide perpetual income that should average $50,000 per year. How much will you pay for the property if you believe its market risk is the same as the market portfolio's? The Treasury bill rate is 5 percent, and the expected market risk premium is 7 percent. (LO4)

20. **Risk and Return.** According to the CAPM, would the expected rate of return on a security with a beta less than zero be more or less than the risk-free interest rate? Why would investors be willing to invest in such a security? *Hint:* Look back to the auto and gold example in Chapter 11. (LO3)

21. **CAPM and Expected Return.** The following table shows betas for several Canadian companies from **yahoo.finance.com**. Calculate each stock's expected rate of return using the CAPM. Assume the risk-free rate of interest is 2 percent. Use a 7 percent risk premium for the market portfolio. (LO3)

Company	Listing	Beta
Magna International	TSX, NYSE	1.33
Open Text	TSX, Nasdaq	.62
Agnico-Eagle Mines	TSX, NYSE	.79
Tim Hortons	TSX, NYSE	.77

22. **Internet.** Go to either **www.globeinvestor.com** or **ca.finance.yahoo.com** and look up the companies listed in problem 21. Briefly describe the main businesses of each company. Do you think that beta estimates make sense, given the nature of the businesses? (LO1)

23. **CAPM and Expected Return.** Stock A has a beta of .5 and investors expect it to return 5 percent. Stock B has a beta of 1.5 and investors expect it to return 13 percent. Use the CAPM to find the expected market risk premium and the expected rate of return on the market. (LO3)

*24. **CAPM and Expected Return.** If the expected market risk premium is 7 percent and Treasury bills yield 3 percent, what must be the betas of a stock that investors expect to return 13.6 percent and a bond with a 5.5 percent expected return? (LO3)

25. **Internet.** Free online betas are hard to find for Canadian stocks unless they are also listed on a U.S. stock exchange such as the NYSE, or Nasdaq. To find Canadian stocks listed on the NYSE, go to **www.nyse.com/about/listed/lc_all_region_1.html**. For Nasdaq-listed companies, go to **www.nasdaq.com/screening/company-list.aspx**.

    For a Canadian U.S.-listed company's beta, go to **finance.yahoo.com**, enter the stock's ticker symbol, then click on "Key Statistics" to find the beta. If you have access to Financial Post Advisor, betas of Canadian companies are found in Corporate Analyzer (click on "market data"). Using one of these methods, find the beta estimates for five different Canadian stocks and estimate their required rates of return. Use the current 3-month Treasury bill yield, available at **www.bankofcanada.ca/rates/interest-rates/t-bill-yields**, as the risk-free rate and a 7 percent market risk premium. Also, record the main business activities of the firms. (LO3)
26. **Internet.** Using Internet resources such as **www.globeinvestor.com** or **ca.finance.yahoo.com**, look up the companies listed in Table 12.2. What are the main businesses of each? On what stock exchanges are they listed? Do their betas make sense? (LO1)
27. **Project Cost of Capital.** Suppose Cara Operations, **www.cara.com**, is considering opening a chain of coffee shops. Which of the betas shown in problem 21 is most relevant in determining the required rate of return for this venture? Explain why the others are *not* appropriate. (LO4)
28. **Risk and Return.** True or false? Explain or qualify as necessary. (LO3)
    a. The expected rate of return on an investment with a beta of 2 is twice as high as the expected rate of return of the market portfolio.
    b. The contribution of a stock to the risk of a diversified portfolio depends on the market risk of the stock.
    c. If a stock's expected rate of return plots below the security market line, it is underpriced.
    d. A diversified portfolio with a beta of 2 is twice as volatile as the market portfolio.
    e. An undiversified portfolio with a beta of 2 is twice as volatile as the market portfolio.
29. **CAPM and Expected Return.** A mutual fund manager expects her portfolio to earn a rate of return of 11 percent this year. The beta of her portfolio is .8. If the rate of return available on risk-free assets is 4 percent and you expect the rate of return on the market portfolio to be 14 percent, should you invest in this mutual fund? (LO3)
30. **Required Rate of Return.** Reconsider the mutual fund manager in the previous problem. Explain how you would use a stock index mutual fund and a risk-free position in Treasury bills (or a money market mutual fund) to create a portfolio with the same risk as the manager's but with a higher expected rate of return. What is the rate of return on that portfolio? (LO2, LO3)
31. **Required Rate of Return.** In view of your answer to the preceding problem, explain why a mutual fund must be able to provide an expected rate of return in excess of that predicted by the security market line for investors to consider the fund an attractive investment opportunity. (LO3)
32. **CAPM.** We Do Bankruptcies is a law firm that specializes in providing advice to firms in financial distress. It prospers in recessions when other firms are struggling. Consequently, its beta is negative, −.2.
    a. If the interest rate on Treasury bills is 5 percent and the expected return on the market portfolio is 12 percent, what is the expected return on the shares of the law firm according to the CAPM? (LO3)
    b. Suppose you invested 90 percent of your wealth in the market portfolio and the remainder of your wealth in the shares in the law firm. What would be the beta of your portfolio? (LO2)

CHALLENGE

33. **Leverage and Portfolio Risk.** Footnote 4 in the chapter asks you to consider a borrow-and-invest strategy in which you use $1 million of your own money and borrow another $1 million at the risk-free rate to invest $2 million in a market index fund. If the risk-free interest rate is 4 percent and the expected rate of return on the market index fund is 12 percent, what is the risk premium and expected rate of return on the borrow-and-invest strategy? Why is the risk of this strategy twice that of simply investing your $1 million in the market index fund? (LO3)
34. **Integrative.** BigCo has a market value of $1 billion and a beta of .9. It has three divisions: chemical processing, oil and gas distribution, and plastic products. The company is thinking about buying another chemical producer, ChemCo. ChemCo is expected to earn cash flows of $9 million this year and cash flows are expected to grow 4 percent per year thereafter. The beta of ChemCo is 1.4. Currently, the risk-free rate is 4 percent and the expected rate of return on the market portfolio is 11 percent. (LO4)
    a. What is the expected rate of return for BigCo?
    b. What discount rate should BigCo use to evaluate ChemCo and why?
    c. How much is ChemCo worth?
    d. Suppose BigCo acquires ChemCo for the price in (c). What will be BigCo's new beta after adding ChemCo?

35. **Integrative.** Food Express is a well-established grocery chain. Computer Power is an up-and-coming computer software developer for business. Bridge Steel is an integrated steel producer, focusing on steel for buildings and bridges. Some information about the companies was provided by an investment banking company as follows:

		Expected Cash Flow	Expected Cash Flow Growth Rate	
Firm	**Beta**	**Year 1**	**Years 2 to 5**	**Year 6 and On**
Food Express	.85	$ 7 million	3%	3%
Computer Power	.95	2 million	8%	4%
Bridge Steel	1.3	10 million	2%	3%

a. If the risk-free rate is 4 percent and the expected market risk premium is 7 percent, what is each firm worth? (LO3)

b. If you owned all three companies, what would be the beta of your stock portfolio? (LO2)

36. **Comprehensive.** Conglomerated Industries has four divisions, each worth about one quarter of the firm's market value. The following chart summarizes the possible returns on the divisions as well as on the market portfolio. (LO3)

		Division Internal Rates of Return				
State of the Economy	**Probability**	**A**	**B**	**C**	**D**	**Market Portfolio**
Recession	.20	8%	−10%	−1%	−4%	−3%
Normal	.60	8%	15%	7%	15%	11%
Boom	.20	9%	30%	10%	20%	22%
Correlation with the market portfolio		.730	.995	.970	.945	1

a. Calculate the expected rate of return and standard deviation of return for each division, the firm, and the market.

b. What is the beta of the divisions, the firm, and the market? (LO1)

c. According to the CAPM, what rate of return do investors require for each division, if the risk-free rate is 4 percent and the expected rate of return for the market is as calculated in (a)? (LO3)

d. If the company was thinking of selling the underperforming divisions, which one(s) should it consider selling? Explain your answer. (LO4)

Solutions to Check Points

12.1 See Figure 12.11. Anchovy Queen's beta is 1.

12.2 Loblaw has the lowest beta, 0.39, but not the lowest standard deviation of its stock returns. Loblaw is the largest food retailer in Canada. The low beta, the low sensitivity of the stock price to market fluctuations, reflects the fact that people need to eat food regardless of the state of the economy. So Loblaw's revenues are not very sensitive to macroeconomic factors which contribute to its low stock beta. But there is still variability in revenues and earnings, most due to the impact of competitors because the grocery industry is competitive. So Loblaw does not have the lowest standard deviation of its stock return.

12.3 A portfolio's beta is just a weighted average of the betas of the securities in the portfolio. In this case the weights are equal, since an equal amount is assumed invested in each of the stocks in Table 12.1. The average beta of these stocks is $(1.06 + 1.64 + 1.04 + .45 + 1.51 + .82 + .63 + .39 + .40)/9 = .88$.

12.4 The standard deviation of a fully diversified portfolio's return is proportional to its beta. The standard deviation in this case is $.5 \times 20 = 10$ percent.

FIGURE 12.11
Each point shows the performance of Anchovy Queen stock when the market is up or down by 1 percent. On average, Anchovy Queen stock follows the market; it has a beta of 1.

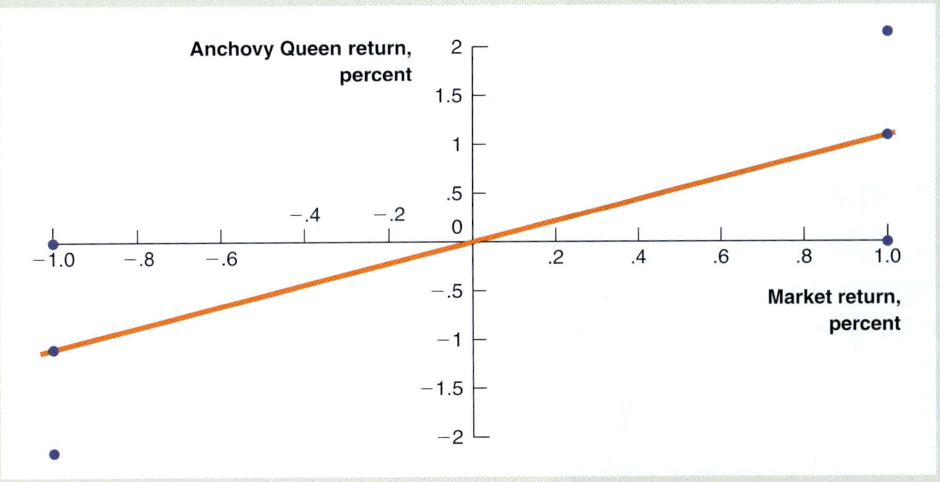

12.5 Risk premium is $\beta(r_m - r_f) = 1.5 \times 7 = 10.5\%$. Expected rate of return is

$$r = r_f + \beta\,(r_m - r_f)$$
$$= 6 + (1.5 \times 7) = 16.5\%$$

12.6 Put 25 percent of your money in the market portfolio ($\beta = 1$) and remaining 75 percent in Treasury bills ($\beta = 0$). So the portfolio beta is $.25 \times 1 + .75 \times 0 = .25$. The expected market return is $6\% + 1 \times 7\% = 13\%$. The portfolio's beta is .25 and its expected return is

$$r_{\text{portfolio}} = (.75 \times 6) + (.25 \times 13) = 7.75\%$$

12.7 $r_{\text{portfolio}} = (.4 \times 6\%) + (.6 \times 14\%) = 10.8\%$. The expected market risk premium is $r_m - r_f = 14 - 6 = 8$ percentage points. This portfolio's beta is .6, since $600,000, which is 60 percent of the investment, is in the market portfolio. Investors would not buy a stock with a beta of .6 it unless it also offered a rate of return of 10.8 percent, and would rush to buy if it offered more. The stock price would adjust until the stock's expected rate of return was 10.8 percent.

12.8 Present value = $50 million × 10-year annuity factor at 8.9% = $748.6 million.

12.9 IMAX should use Loblaw's cost of capital. IMAX's cost of capital tells us what expected rate of return investors demand from the movie theatre industry. This is not the appropriate project cost of capital for IMAX's venture into food retail industry. Note that we have ignored the fact that Loblaw is financed with a mix of debt and equity. And we have not considered whether IMAX's proposed new venture makes any business sense. We shall deal with these issues in Chapter 13.

Solutions to Spreadsheet Questions

12.1 We would expect beta to fall from the value obtained in the spreadsheet. Cameco's return in June (when the market fell) is not as bad as originally assumed, and its return in September (when the market rose) is not as good as originally assumed. In both cases, Cameco's returns are less responsive to the market. In fact, beta falls to 1.86.

12.2 Cameco's beta is precisely the same as the original value. Increasing the assumed return in each month by a constant does not change the typical *responsiveness* of Cameco to variation in the return of the market index.

12.3 If in the additional month of data Cameco is down 5 percent while the market is up 5 percent, we would expect beta to fall. This is because the stock moved in opposition to the market index. Adding this observation therefore reduces our estimate of Cameco's typical response to market movements. In fact, beta falls to 1.49.

PART 3 Risk

11 Introduction to Risk, Return, and the Opportunity Cost of Capital

12 Risk, Return, and Capital Budgeting

13 The Weighted-Average Cost of Capital and Company Valuation

13.1 Geothermal's Cost of Capital

13.2 The Weighted-Average Cost of Capital

13.3 Measuring Capital Structure

13.4 Calculating Required Rates of Return

13.5 Calculating the Weighted-Average Cost of Capital

13.6 Interpreting the Weighted-Average Cost of Capital

13.7 Valuing Entire Businesses

13.8 Summary

CHAPTER 13

The Weighted-Average Cost of Capital and Company Valuation

LEARNING OBJECTIVES

After studying this chapter, you should be able to:

LO1 Explain the concept of the weighted average cost of capital, WACC.

LO2 Calculate a firm's capital structure.

LO3 Estimate the required rates of return on the securities issued by the firm.

LO4 Calculate the weighted-average cost of capital.

LO5 State when the weighted-average cost of capital is or isn't the appropriate discount rate for a new project.

LO6 Use the weighted-average cost of capital to value a business given forecasts of its future cash flows.

Jo Ann Cox explains the cost of capital to Geothermal's top management.

In the previous chapter you learned how to use the capital asset pricing model to estimate the expected return on a company's common stock. If the firm is financed wholly by common stock, the shareholders own all the firm's assets and are entitled to all the cash flows. In this case, the expected return required by investors in the common stock equals the company cost of capital.[1]

Most companies, however, are financed by a mixture of securities, including common stock, bonds, preferred stock or other securities. Each of these securities has different risks and therefore people who invest in them look for different rates of return. In these circumstances, the company cost of capital is no longer the same as the expected return on the common stock. It depends on the expected return from all the securities that the company has issued.

The cost of capital also depends on taxes, because interest payments made by a corporation are tax-deductible expenses. Therefore, the company cost of capital is usually calculated as a weighted average of the *after-tax* interest cost of debt financing and the "cost of equity"—that is, the expected rate of return on the firm's common stock. The weights are the fractions of debt and equity in the firm's capital structure. Managers refer to the firm's *weighted-average cost of capital*, or *WACC* (rhymes with "quack").

Managers use the weighted-average cost of capital to evaluate average-risk capital investment projects. "Average risk" means that the project's risk matches the risk of the firm's existing assets and operations. This chapter explains how the weighted-average cost of capital is calculated in practice.

Managers calculating WACC can get bogged down in formulas. We want you to understand *why* WACC works, not just how to calculate it. Let's start with "why?" We'll listen in as a young financial manager struggles to recall the rationale for project discount rates.

LO1 13.1 GEOTHERMAL'S COST OF CAPITAL

Jo Ann Cox, a recent graduate of a Canadian business school, poured a third cup of black coffee and tried again to remember what she once knew about project hurdle rates. Why hadn't she paid more attention in Finance 101? Why had she sold her finance text the day after passing the finance final?

Costas Thermopolis, her boss and CEO of Geothermal Corporation, had told her to prepare a financial evaluation of a proposed expansion of Geothermal's production. She was to report

[1] Investors will invest in the firm's securities only if they offer the same expected return as that of other equally risky securities. When securities are properly priced, the return that investors can *expect* from their investments is therefore also the return that they *require*. The terms "expected rate of return" and "required rate of return" are used interchangeably.

at 9 o'clock Monday morning. Thermopolis, whose background was geophysics, not finance, not only expected a numerical analysis, but also expected her to explain it to him.

Thermopolis had founded Geothermal in 1996 to produce electricity from geothermal energy trapped deep under Alberta. The company had pioneered this business and had been able to obtain perpetual production rights for a large tract of land on favourable terms from the Canadian government. When the 2011 oil shock drove up energy prices worldwide, Geothermal became an exceptionally profitable company. It was currently reporting a rate of return on book assets of 25 percent per year.

Now, in 2014, production rights are no longer cheap. The proposed expansion would cost $30 million and should generate a perpetual after-tax cash flow of $4.5 million annually. The projected rate of return is 4.5/30 = .15, or 15 percent, much less than the profitability of Geothermal's existing assets. However, once the new project is up and running, it will be no riskier than Geothermal's existing business.

Jo Ann realized that 15 percent is not necessarily a bad return—though, of course, 25 percent would have been better. Fifteen percent might still exceed Geothermal's cost of capital, that is, exceed the expected rate of return that outside investors would demand to invest money in the project. If the cost of capital was less than the 15 percent expected return, expansion would be a good deal and would generate net value for Geothermal and its shareholders.

Jo Ann remembered how to calculate the cost of capital for companies that use only common stock financing. Briefly she sketched the argument.

"I need the expected rate of return investors would require from Geothermal's real assets—the wells, pumps, generators, etc. That rate of return depends on the assets' risk. However, the assets aren't traded in the stock market, so I can't observe how risky they have been. I can observe only the risk of Geothermal's common stock.

"But if Geothermal issues only stock—no debt—then owning the stock means owning the assets, and the expected return demanded by investors in the stock must also be the cost of capital for the assets." She jotted down the following identities for a business with no debt:

$$\text{Value of business} = \text{value of stock}$$

$$\text{Risk of business} = \text{risk of stock}$$

$$\text{Rate of return on business} = \text{rate of return on stock}$$

$$\text{Investors' required return from business} = \text{investors' required return from stock}$$

Unfortunately, Geothermal had borrowed a substantial amount of money; its shareholders did *not* have unencumbered ownership of Geothermal's assets. The expansion project would also justify some extra debt finance. Jo Ann realized that she would have to look at Geothermal's **capital structure**—its mix of debt and equity financing—and consider the required rates of return of debt as well as equity investors.

capital structure A firm's mix of debt and equity financing.

Geothermal had issued 22.65 million shares, now trading at $20 each. Thus shareholders valued Geothermal's equity at $20 × 22.65 million = $453 million. In addition, the company had issued bonds with a market value of $194 million. The market value of the company's debt and equity was therefore $194 + $453 = $647 million. Debt was 194/647 = .3, or 30 percent of the total.

"Geothermal's worth more to investors than either its debt or its equity," Jo Ann mused. "But I ought to be able to find the overall value of Geothermal's business by adding up the debt and equity." She sketched a rough market-value balance sheet:

Assets		**Liabilities and Shareholders' Equity**		
Market value of assets = value of Geothermal's existing business	$647	Market value of debt	$194	(30%)
		Market value of equity	$453	(70%)
Total value	$647	Total value	$647	(100%)

"Holy Toledo, I've got it!" Jo Ann exclaimed. "If I bought all the securities issued by Geothermal, debt as well as equity, I'd own the entire business. That means . . ." She jotted again:

$$\text{Value of business} = \text{value of portfolio of all the firm's debt and equity securities} \quad (13.1)$$

$$\text{Risk of business} = \text{risk of portfolio} \quad (13.2)$$

$$\text{Rate of return on business} = \text{rate of return on portfolio} \quad (13.3)$$

$$\text{Investors' required return on business (company cost of capital)} = \text{investors' required return on portfolio} \quad (13.4)$$

"All I have to do is calculate the expected rate of return on a portfolio of all the firm's securities. That's easy. The debt's yielding 8 percent, and Fred, the banker, says that equity investors want 14 percent. Suppose he's right. The portfolio would contain 30 percent debt and 70 percent equity, so . . ."

$$\text{Portfolio return} = (.3 \times 8\%) + (.7 \times 14\%) = 12.2\%$$

It was all coming back to her now. The company cost of capital is just a weighted average of returns on debt and equity, with weights depending on relative market values of the two securities.

"But there's one more thing. Interest is tax-deductible. If Geothermal pays $1 of interest, taxable income is reduced by $1, and the firm's tax bill drops by 35 cents, assuming a 35 percent tax rate. The net cost is only 65 cents. So the after-tax cost of debt is not 8 percent, but $(1 - .35) \times 8 = .65 \times 8 = 5.2$ percent.

"Now I can finally calculate the weighted-average cost of capital:

$$\text{WACC} = (.3 \times 5.2\%) + (.7 \times 14\%) = 11.4\%$$

"Looks like the expansion's a good deal. Fifteen's better than 11.4. But I sure need a break."

13.2 THE WEIGHTED-AVERAGE COST OF CAPITAL

Jo Ann's conclusions were important. It should be obvious by now that the choice of the discount rate can be crucial, especially when the project involves large capital expenditures or is long-lived. The nearby Finance in Action box describes how a major investment in a power station—an investment with both a large capital expenditure and very long life—turned on the choice of the discount rate.

Think again what the company cost of capital is, and what it is used for. We *define* it as the opportunity cost of capital for the firm's existing assets; we *use* it to value new assets that have the same risk as the old ones. The company cost of capital is the minimum acceptable rate of return when the firm expands by investing in average-risk projects.

We first introduced the opportunity cost of capital in Chapter 2. "Opportunity cost" is a shorthand reminder that, when the firm invests rather than returning cash to shareholders, the shareholders lose the opportunity to invest in financial markets. If the corporation acts in the shareholders' interests, it will invest their money only if it can find projects that offer higher rates of return than investors could achieve on their own. Therefore, the expected rates of return on investments in financial markets determine the cost of capital for corporate investments.

The company cost of capital is the opportunity cost of capital for the company as a whole. We discussed the company cost of capital in Chapter 12, but did not explain how to measure it when the firm has raised different types of debt and equity financing or how to adjust it for the tax-deductibility of interest payments. The weighted-average cost of capital formula handles these complications.

Finance in Action

Choosing the Discount Rate

Shortly before the British government began to sell off the electricity industry to private investors, controversy erupted over the industry's proposal to build a 1,200-megawatt nuclear power station known as Hinkley Point C. The government argued that a nuclear station would both diversify the sources of electricity generation and reduce sulphur dioxide and carbon dioxide emissions. Protesters emphasized the dangers of nuclear accidents and attacked the proposal as "bizarre, dated, and irrelevant."

At the public inquiry held to consider the proposal, opponents produced some powerful evidence that the nuclear station was also a very high cost option. Their principal witness, Professor Elroy Dimson, argued that the government-owned power company had employed an unrealistically low figure for the opportunity cost of capital. Had the government-owned industry used a more plausible figure, the cost of building and operating the nuclear station would have been higher than that of a comparable station based on fossil fuels.

The reason why the choice of discount rate was so important was that nuclear stations are expensive to build but cheap to operate. If capital is cheap (that is, the discount rate is low), then the high up-front cost is less serious. But if the cost of capital is high, the high initial cost of nuclear stations made them uneconomic.

Evidence produced at the inquiry suggested that the construction cost of a nuclear station was £1,527 million (or about $2.3 billion), while the cost of a comparable non-nuclear station was only £895 million. However, power stations last about 40 years and, once built, nuclear stations cost much less to operate than non-nuclear stations. If operated at 75 percent of theoretical capacity, the running costs of the nuclear station would be about £63 million a year, compared with running costs of £168 million a year for the non-nuclear station.

The following table shows the cost advantage of the nuclear power station at different (real) discount rates. At a 5 percent discount rate, which was the figure used by the government, the present value of the costs of the nuclear option was nearly £1 billion lower than that of a station based on fossil fuels. But with a discount rate of 16 percent, which was the figure favoured by Professor Dimson, the position was almost exactly reversed, so that the government could save nearly £1 billion by refusing the power company permission to build Hinkley Point C and relying instead on new fossil-fuel power stations.

Present Value of the Cost Advantage to a Nuclear Rather Than a Fossil-Fuel Station

Real Discount Rate	Present Value of the Cost Advantage of the Nuclear Station (billions of pounds)
5%	.9
8	.2
10	−.1
12	−.4
14	−.7
16	−.9
18	−1.2

Thirteen years after the inquiry, the proposal to construct Hinkley Point C has not been implemented. However, British Energy, the privatized electric utility, has suggested that it is time to build new nuclear power stations. To do so, they need the approval of the British government—and more hearings may take place—which means discussion may well resume about the appropriate discount rate for the project.

Technical Notes

1. Present values are measured at the date that the power station comes into operation.
2. The above table assumes for simplicity that construction costs for nuclear stations are spread evenly over the eight years before the station comes into operation, while the costs for fossil-fuel stations are assumed to be spread evenly over the four years before operation. As a result, the present value of the costs of the two stations may differ slightly from the more precise estimates produced by Professor Dimson.

Source: Adapted from E. Dimson, "The Discount Rate for a Power Station," *Energy Economics* 11(3) (Oxford: Elsevier Science Ltd., July 1989): 175–180. © 1989, with permission from Elsevier.

CALCULATING COMPANY COST OF CAPITAL AS A WEIGHTED AVERAGE

Calculating the company cost of capital is straightforward, though not always easy, when only common stock is outstanding. For example, a financial manager could estimate beta and calculate shareholders' required rate of return using the capital asset pricing model (CAPM). This would be the expected rate of return investors require on the company's existing assets and operations and also the expected return they will require on new investments that do not change the company's market risk.

But most companies issue debt as well as equity. So their cost of capital depends on both the cost of debt and the cost of equity. In this case, the company cost of capital is a weighted average of the returns demanded by the debt and equity investors.

Let's review Jo Ann Cox's calculations for Geothermal. To avoid complications, we'll ignore taxes for the next couple of pages. The total market value of Geothermal, which we denote as V, is the sum

The company cost of capital is a *weighted average* of the returns demanded by debt and equity investors. The weighted average is the expected rate of return investors would demand on a portfolio of all the firm's outstanding securities.

of the market values of the outstanding debt D and the equity E. Thus firm value is $V = D + E$ = \$194 million + \$453 million = \$647 million. Debt accounts for 30 percent of the value and equity accounts for the remaining 70 percent. If you held all the shares and all the debt, your investment in Geothermal would be V = \$647 million. Between them, the debt and equity holders own all the firm's assets. So V is also the value of these assets—the value of Geothermal's existing business.

Suppose that Geothermal's equity investors require a 14 percent rate of return on their investment in the stock. What rate of return must a new project provide in order that all investors—both debtholders and shareholders—earn a fair rate of return? The debtholders require a rate of return of r_{debt} = 8 percent. So each year the firm will need to pay interest of $r_{\text{debt}} \times D = .08 \times \$194$ million = \$15.52 million. The shareholders, who have invested in a riskier security, require a return of r_{equity} = 14 percent on their investment of \$453 million. Thus in order to keep shareholders happy, the company needs additional income of $r_{\text{equity}} \times E = .14 \times \$453$ million = \$63.42 million. To satisfy both the debtholders and the shareholders, Geothermal needs to earn \$15.52 million + \$63.42 million = \$78.94 million. This is equivalent to earning a return of $r_{\text{assets}} = 78.94/647 = .122$, or 12.2 percent.

Figure 13.1 illustrates the reasoning behind our calculations. The figure shows the amount of income needed to satisfy the debt and equity investors. Notice that debtholders account for 30 percent of Geothermal's capital structure but receive less than 30 percent of its expected income. On the other hand, they bear less than a 30 percent share of risk, since they have first cut at the company's income, and also first claim on its assets if the company gets in trouble. Shareholders expect a return of more than 70 percent of Geothermal's income because they bear correspondingly more risk.

However, if you buy *all* Geothermal's debt and equity, you own its assets lock, stock, and barrel. You receive all the income and bear all the risks. The expected rate of return you would require on this portfolio of securities is the same return you would require from unencumbered ownership of the business. This rate of return—12.2 percent, ignoring taxes—is therefore the company cost of capital and the required rate of return from an equal-risk expansion of the business.

The bottom line (still ignoring taxes) is

Company cost of capital = weighted average of debt and equity returns **(13.5)**

The underlying algebra is simple. Debtholders need income of $(r_{\text{debt}} \times D)$ and the equity investors need income of $(r_{\text{equity}} \times E)$. The *total* income that is needed is $(r_{\text{debt}} \times D) + (r_{\text{equity}} \times E)$.

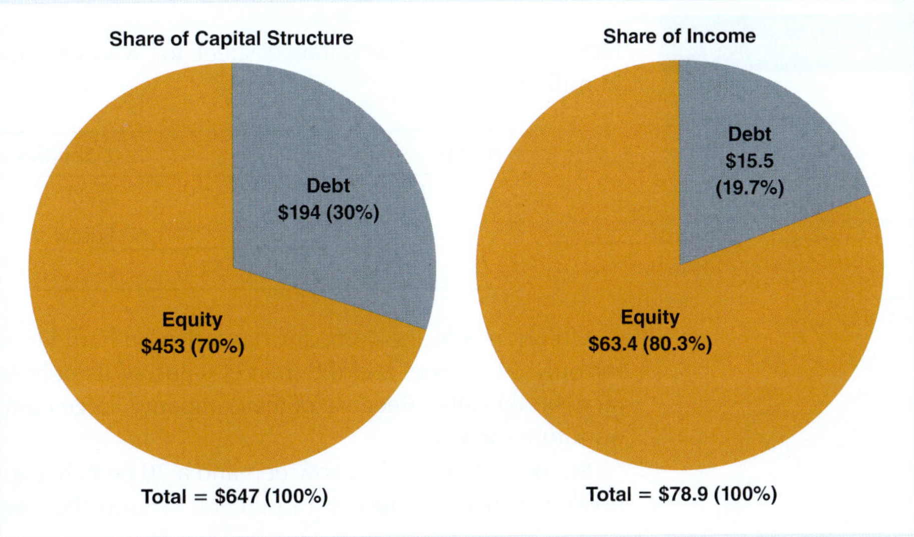

FIGURE 13.1
Geothermal's debtholders account for 30 percent of the company's capital structure, but they get a smaller share of income because their return is guaranteed by the company. Geothermal's shareholders bear more risk and receive, on average, greater return. Of course, if you buy all the debt and all the equity, you get all the income.

The amount of their combined existing investment in the company is V. So to calculate the return that is needed on the assets, we simply divide the income by the investment:

$$r_{\text{assets}} = \frac{\textbf{total income}}{\textbf{value of investment}}$$

$$= \frac{(D \times r_{\text{debt}}) + (E \times r_{\text{equity}})}{V} = \left(\frac{D}{V} \times r_{\text{debt}}\right) + \left(\frac{E}{V} \times r_{\text{equity}}\right) \quad \textbf{(13.6)}$$

For Geothermal,

$$r_{\text{assets}} = (.30 \times 8\%) + (.70 \times 14\%) = 12.2\%$$

This figure is the expected return demanded by investors in the firm's assets.

Check Point 13.1

Hot Rocks Corp., one of Geothermal's competitors, has issued long-term bonds with a market value of $50 million and an expected return of 9 percent. It has 4 million shares outstanding trading for $10 each. At this price the shares offer an expected return of 17 percent. What is the weighted-average cost of capital for Hot Rocks's assets and operations? Assume Hot Rocks pays no taxes.

USE MARKET WEIGHTS, NOT BOOK WEIGHTS

The cost of capital must be based on what investors are actually willing to pay for the company's outstanding securities—that is, based on the securities' *market* values.

The company cost of capital is the expected rate of return that investors demand from the company's assets and operations.

Market values often differ from the values recorded by accountants in the company's books. The book value of Geothermal's equity reflects money raised in the past from shareholders and earnings reinvested by the firm on their behalf. If investors recognize Geothermal's excellent prospects, the market value of equity may be much higher than book value, and the debt ratio will be lower when measured in terms of market values rather than book values.

Financial managers use book debt-to-value ratios for various other purposes, and sometimes they unthinkingly look to the book ratios when calculating weights for the company cost of capital. That's a mistake, because the company cost of capital measures what investors want from the company, and it depends on how *they* value the company's securities. That value depends on future profits and cash flows, not on accounting history. Book values, while useful for many other purposes, measure only net cumulative historical outlays; they don't generally measure market values accurately.

Check Point 13.2

Here is a book-value balance sheet for Rhodes Construction Company. Figures are in millions.

Assets		**Liabilities and Shareholders' Equity**	
Assets (book value)	$75	Debt	$25
		Equity	50
	$75		$75

Unfortunately, the company has fallen on hard times. The 6 million shares are trading for only $4 apiece, and the market value of its debt securities is 20 percent below the face (book) value. Because of the company's large cumulative losses, it will pay no taxes on future income.

Suppose shareholders now demand a 20 percent expected rate of return and the bondholders' expected return is 14 percent. What is the weighted-average cost of capital?

TAXES AND THE WEIGHTED-AVERAGE COST OF CAPITAL

Thus far in this chapter our examples have ignored taxes. When you calculate a project's NPV, you need to discount the cash flows *after* tax because the after-tax cash flows are the relevant project cash flows.

Taxes are also important because most companies are financed by both equity and debt. The interest payments on the debt are deducted from income before tax is calculated. Therefore, the cost to the company of an interest payment is reduced by the amount of this tax saving.

The interest rate on Geothermal's debt is $r_{\text{debt}} = 8$ percent. However, with a corporate tax rate of $T_c = .35$, the government bears 35 percent of the cost of the interest payments. The government doesn't send the firm a cheque for this amount, but the income tax that the firm pays is reduced by 35 percent of its interest expense.

Therefore, Geothermal's after-tax cost of debt is only 100 − 35 = 65 percent of the 8 percent pretax cost:

$$\begin{aligned}\textbf{After-tax cost of debt} &= \mathbf{(1 - \text{tax rate}) \times \text{pretax cost}} \\ &= \mathbf{(1 - T_c) \times r_{\text{debt}}} \\ &= (1 - .35) \times 8\% = 5.2\%\end{aligned} \qquad \textbf{(13.7)}$$

We can now adjust our calculation of Geothermal's cost of capital to recognize the tax saving associated with interest payments:

$$\text{Company cost of capital, after tax} = (.3 \times 5.2\%) + (.7 \times 14\%) = 11.4\%$$

Check Point 13.3

Criss-Cross Industries has earnings before interest and taxes (EBIT) of $10 million. Interest payments are $2 million and the corporate tax rate is 35 percent. Construct a simple income statement to show that the debt interest reduces the taxes the firm owes to the government. How much more tax would Criss-Cross pay if it were financed solely by equity?

weighted-average cost of capital (WACC) Expected rate of return on a portfolio of all the firm's securities, adjusted for tax savings due to interest payments.

Now we're back to the **weighted-average cost of capital**, or **WACC**. The general formula is

$$\textbf{WACC} = \left[\frac{D}{V} \times (1 - T_c) r_{\text{debt}}\right] + \left[\frac{E}{V} \times r_{\text{equity}}\right] \qquad \textbf{(13.8)}$$

EXAMPLE 13.1 WEIGHTED-AVERAGE COST OF CAPITAL FOR CANADIAN PACIFIC RAILWAY

In Chapter 12 we showed how the capital asset pricing model can be used to estimate the expected return on Canadian Pacific's common stock. We will now use this estimate to figure out the company's weighted average cost of capital.

Step 1. Calculate the value of each source of financing as a proportion of firm value. The company has outstanding 169.1 million common shares, which at the beginning of 2011 had a market value of about $67 each. The total market value of CP's equity was $E = 169.1 \times \$67 = \$11{,}329.7$ million. The company's latest balance sheet showed that it had borrowed $D = \$4{,}389$ million, which was very close to its market value. So the total value of Canadian Pacific's securities is $V = D + E = \$4{,}389 + \$11{,}329.7 = \$15{,}718.7$ million. Debt as a proportion of total value is $D/V = \$4{,}389/\$15{,}718.7 = .279$, and equity as a proportion of the total is $\$11{,}329.7/\$15{,}718.7 = .721$.

Step 2. Determine the required rate of return for each source of financing. In Chapter 12, we estimated that CP's shareholders required a return of 7.2 percent. The current required rate of return on CP debt is about 5 percent.

(Continued)

(Concluded)

Step 3. Calculate the weighted average of the after-tax return on the debt and the return on equity. The weighted-average cost of capital is

$$\text{WACC} = \left[\frac{D}{V} \times (1 - T_c) r_{\text{debt}}\right] + \left[\frac{E}{V} \times r_{\text{equity}}\right]$$

$$= .279 \times (1 - .35) \times 5\% + .721 \times 7.2\% = 6.1\%$$

Check Point 13.4 Calculate WACC for Hot Rocks (Check Point 13.1) and Rhodes Construction (Check Point 13.2) assuming the companies face a 35 percent corporate income tax rate.

WHAT IF THERE ARE THREE (OR MORE) SOURCES OF FINANCING?

We have simplified our discussion of the cost of capital by assuming the firm has only two classes of securities: debt and common stock. Even if the firm has issued other classes of securities, our general approach to calculating WACC remains unchanged. We simply calculate the weighted-average after-tax return of each security type.

For example, suppose the firm also has outstanding preferred stock. Preferred stock has some of the characteristics of both common stock and fixed-income securities. Like bonds, preferred stock promises to pay a given, usually level, stream of dividends. Unlike bonds, however, there is no maturity date for the preferred stock. The promised dividends constitute a perpetuity as long as the firm stays in business. Moreover, a failure to come up with the cash to pay the dividends does not push the firm into bankruptcy. Instead, unpaid dividends simply cumulate; the common shareholders do not receive dividends until the accumulated preferred dividends have been paid. Finally, unlike interest payments, preferred stock dividends are not considered tax-deductible expenses.

How would we calculate WACC for a firm with preferred stock as well as common stock and bonds outstanding?[2] Using P to denote the value of preferred stock, we simply generalize the formula for WACC as follows:

$$\text{WACC} = \left[\frac{D}{V} \times (1 - T_c) r_{\text{debt}}\right] + \left[\frac{P}{V} \times r_{\text{preferred}}\right] + \left[\frac{E}{V} \times r_{\text{equity}}\right] \quad (13.9)$$

WRAPPING UP GEOTHERMAL

We now turn one last time to Jo Ann Cox and Geothermal's proposed expansion. We want to make sure that she—and you—know how to *use* the weighted-average cost of capital.

Remember that the proposed expansion cost $30 million and should generate a perpetual cash flow of $4.5 million per year. A simple cash flow worksheet might look like this:[3]

Revenue	$10.00 million
− Operating expenses	− 3.08
= Pretax operating cash flow	6.92
− Tax at 35%	− 2.42
After-tax cash flow	$ 4.50 million

Note that these cash flows do not include the tax benefits of using debt.

[2] Financial managers often use "equity" to refer to *common* stock, even though a firm's equity includes both common and preferred stocks. We continue to use r_{equity} to refer specifically to the expected return on the common stock.

[3] For this example we ignore depreciation, a non-cash but tax-deductible expense. (If the project were really perpetual, why depreciate?)

Geothermal's managers and engineers forecast revenues, costs, and taxes as if the project was to be all-equity financed. The interest tax shields generated by the project's actual debt financing are not forgotten, however. They are accounted for by using the *after-tax* cost of debt in the weighted-average cost of capital.

Project net present value is calculated by discounting the cash flow (which is a perpetuity) at Geothermal's 11.4 percent weighted-average cost of capital:

$$\text{NPV} = -30 + \frac{4.5}{.114} = +\$9.5 \text{ million}$$

Expansion will thus add $9.5 million to the net wealth of the owners of Geothermal's assets: Geothermal's debtholders and shareholders.

CHECKING OUR LOGIC

Any project offering a rate of return more than 11.4 percent will have a positive NPV, assuming that the project has the same risk and financing as Geothermal's business. A project offering exactly 11.4 percent would be just break-even; it would generate just enough cash to satisfy both debtholders and shareholders.

Let's check that out. Suppose the proposed expansion had revenues of only $8.34 million and after-tax cash flows of $3.42 million:

Revenue	$8.34 million
− Operating expenses	−3.08
= Pretax operating cash flow	5.26
− Tax at 35%	−1.84
After-tax cash flow	$3.42 million

With an investment of $30 million, the internal rate of return on this perpetuity is exactly 11.4 percent:

$$\text{Rate of return} = \frac{3.42}{30} = .114, \text{ or } 11.4\%$$

NPV is exactly zero:

$$\text{NPV} = -30 + \frac{3.42}{.114} = 0$$

If a project has zero NPV when the expected cash flows are discounted at the weighted-average cost of capital, then the project's cash flows are just sufficient to give debtholders and shareholders the returns they require.

When we calculated Geothermal's weighted-average cost of capital, we recognized that the company's debt ratio was 30 percent. When Geothermal's analysts use the weighted-average cost of capital to evaluate the new project, they are assuming that the $30 million additional investment would support the issue of additional debt equal to 30 percent of the investment, or $9 million. The remaining $21 million is provided by the shareholders.

The following table shows how the cash flows would be shared between the debtholders and shareholders. We start with the pretax operating cash flow of $5.26 million:

Cash flow before tax and interest	$5.26 million
− Interest payment (.08 × $9 million)	−.72
= Pretax cash flow	4.54
− Tax at 35%	−1.59
Cash flow after tax	$2.95 million

Project cash flows before tax and interest are forecast to be \$5.26 million. Out of this figure, Geothermal needs to pay interest of 8 percent of \$9 million, which comes to \$.72 million. This leaves a pretax cash flow of \$4.54 million, on which the company must pay tax. Taxes equal $.35 \times 4.54 = \$1.59$ million. Shareholders are left with \$2.95 million, just enough to give them the 14 percent return that they need on their \$21 million investment. (Note that $2.95/21 = .14$, or 14 percent.) Therefore, everything checks out.

LO2 13.3 MEASURING CAPITAL STRUCTURE

We have explained the formula for calculating the weighted-average cost of capital. We will now look at some of the practical problems in applying that formula. Suppose that the financial manager of Big Oil has asked you to estimate the firm's weighted-average cost of capital. Big Oil is an integrated oil and gas company. Integrated means that it explores for oil and gas and also refines the oil and gas into petroleum products which it sells through its distribution channels, including gas stations. Your first step is to work out Big Oil's capital structure as of the date you want to calculate the WACC. But where do you get the data?

Financial managers usually start with the company's financial accounts, which show the book value of debt and equity, whereas the weighted-average cost of capital formula calls for their *market* values. A little work and a dash of judgment are needed to go from one to the other.

The company's financial accounts include various accounting entries, many of which are not relevant to determining the company's capital structure. Look for financing that the company has raised. The key items to identify are the interest-bearing debt and the equity. Many of the items listed on balance sheets, such as accounts payable, taxes payable and future taxes, are the consequence of the accounting system used and not explicit financing that the company has raised. Ignore these items.

Table 13.1 is an excerpt from Big Oil's balance sheet, showing the debt and equity issued by Big Oil. The firm has borrowed \$200 million from banks and has issued a further \$200 million of long-term bonds. These bonds have a coupon rate of 8 percent and mature at the end of 12 years. The firm has 7.5 million shares of preferred stock outstanding, with \$20 par value and dividend yield of 8 percent, payable semi-annually. The book value of the preferred stock is \$20/share $\times$ 7.5 million shares = \$150 million. Finally, there are 100 million shares of common stock outstanding, originally issued at \$1.00 per share. But the accounts also recognize that Big Oil has in past years plowed back into the firm \$300 million of retained earnings. The total book value of the common equity shown in the accounts is the sum of common stock and retained earnings, \$100 million + \$300 million = \$400 million.

The figures shown in Table 13.1 are taken from Big Oil's annual accounts and are therefore book values. Sometimes the differences between book values and market values are negligible. For example, consider the \$200 million that Big Oil owes the bank. The interest rate on bank loans is usually a *floating rate*, meaning that the rate charged is linked to the general level of interest rates. Thus, if interest rates rise, the rate charged on Big Oil's loan also rises to maintain the loan's value. The market value of floating rate debt is typically equal to its book value. As long as Big Oil is reasonably sure to repay the loan, the loan is worth close to \$200 million. Most financial managers are usually willing to accept the book value of bank debt as a fair approximation of its market value.

TABLE 13.1 The book value of Big Oil's debt and equity (\$ millions).

Bank debt	\$200	21.05%
Long-term bonds (12-year maturity, 8% coupon)	200	21.05
preferred stock (7.5 million shares, \$20 par value, 8% dividend yield)	150	15.79
Common stock (100 million shares)	100	10.53
Retained earnings	300	31.58
Total	\$950	100.00%

What about Big Oil's long-term bonds? If the bonds are publicly traded, you can look up their price.[4] But many bonds are not traded regularly, and in such cases you need to infer their price by calculating the bond's value using the yield offered by similar bonds. If you know the bond's rating, you can estimate the bond's yield by using the credit spread on comparable bonds.

For example, Big Oil's bonds are rated BBB and currently long-term BBB-rated bonds yield about 2.50 percentage points over long-term government bonds. The current yield on long-term government bonds is 6.5 percent. So, the estimated yield to maturity on Big Oil's bonds is $6.5 + 2.5 = 9$ percent.

With the yield to maturity, we can calculate the value today of each Big Oil bond as follows. Since coupons are paid semi-annually, there are 24 coupon payments of $.08/2 \times 200 = \$8$ million, and then repayment of face value of \$200 12 years out. All the bond's cash flows are discounted back at the *current* interest rate of 9 percent. We assume that 9 percent rate is an effective annual rate. Thus the 6-month discount rate is $(1.09)^{1/2} - 1 = 0.044$. The present value of the bond is

$$\text{PV} = \frac{8}{1.044} + \frac{8}{(1.044)^2} + \frac{8}{(1.044)^3} + \cdots + \frac{8}{(1.044)^{24}} + \frac{200}{(1.044)^{24}} = \$188.3$$

Therefore, the bonds are worth \$188.3 million, 94.2 percent of their face value.

If you used the book value of Big Oil's long-term debt rather than its market value, you would be a little bit off in your calculation of the weighted-average cost of capital, but probably not seriously so.

The really big errors are likely to arise if you use the book value of equity rather than its market value. The \$400 million book value of Big Oil's common equity measures the total amount of cash that the firm has raised from common shareholders in the past plus earnings retained and invested on their behalf. But perhaps Big Oil has been able to find projects that were worth more than they originally cost or perhaps the value of the assets has increased with inflation. Perhaps investors see great future investment opportunities for the company. All these considerations determine what investors are willing to pay for Big Oil's common stock.

Currently, Big Oil stock is \$12 a share, giving the total *market value* of the common stock as

$$\text{Number of common shares} \times \text{common share price} = 100 \text{ million} \times \$12 = \$1{,}200 \text{ million}$$

The preferred shares of Big Oil have been trading at \$16 per share. The market value of the preferred stock is

$$\text{Number of preferred shares} \times \text{preferred share price} = 7.5 \text{ million} \times \$16 = \$120 \text{ million}$$

In Table 13.2 we show the market value of Big Oil's debt and preferred and common equity. You can see that debt accounts for 22.7 percent of company value ($D/V = .227$), preferred equity accounts for 7.0 percent ($P/V = .07$) and common equity accounts for 70.3 percent ($E/V = .703$). These are the proportions to use when calculating the weighted-average cost of capital. Notice that if you looked only at the book values shown in the company accounts, you would mistakenly

TABLE 13.2
The market value of Big Oil's debt and equity (\$ millions).

Bank debt	\$ 200	11.7%
Long-term bonds	188.3	11.0
Total debt	388.3	22.7
Preferred stock, 7.5 million shares at \$16	120	7.0
Common stock, 100 million shares at \$12	1,200	70.3
Total	\$1,708.3	100.0%

[4] Some corporate bond prices are available on several Web sites including **www.globeinvestor.com/servlet/Page/document/v5/data/bonds** and **www.pfin.ca/canadianfixedincome**.

conclude that debt accounted for 42.1 percent, preferred equity for 15.8 percent and common equity for only 42.1 percent of value.

Check Point 13.5

Here is the capital structure shown in Executive Fruit's *book* balance sheet:

Debt	$4.1 million	45%
Preferred stock	2.2	24.2
Common stock	2.8	30.8
Total	$9.1 million	100.0%

Explain why the percentage weights given above should *not* be used in calculating Executive Fruit's WACC.

LO3 13.4 CALCULATING REQUIRED RATES OF RETURN

To calculate Big Oil's weighted-average cost of capital, you also need the rate of return that investors require from each security.

THE EXPECTED RETURN ON BONDS

We know that Big Oil's bonds offer a yield to maturity of 9 percent. As long as the company does not go belly-up, that is the rate of return investors can expect to earn from holding Big Oil's bonds. If there is any chance that the firm may be unable to repay the debt, however, the yield to maturity of 9 percent represents the most favourable outcome and the *expected* return is lower than 9 percent.

For most large and healthy firms, the probability of bankruptcy is sufficiently low that financial managers are content to take the promised yield to maturity on the bonds as a measure of the expected return. But if a company has financial difficulties, bondholders might not receive their promised coupons and principal, resulting in lower expected cash flows and the expected rate of return will be less than the calculated yield to maturity. Look back to Example 6.5 in Chapter 6 to see an example of the difference between the promised yield to maturity and the expected rate of return.

THE EXPECTED RETURN ON COMMON STOCK

Estimates Based on the Capital Asset Pricing Model In Chapter 12 we showed you how to use the capital asset pricing model to estimate the expected rate of return on common stock. The capital asset pricing model tells us that investors demand a higher rate of return from stocks with high betas. The formula is

$$\begin{matrix}\text{Expected return} \\ \text{on stock}\end{matrix} = \begin{matrix}\text{risk-free} \\ \text{interest rate}\end{matrix} + \left[\begin{matrix}\text{stock's} \\ \text{beta}\end{matrix} \times \begin{matrix}\text{expected market} \\ \text{risk premium}\end{matrix}\right]$$

To implement the CAPM you need the stock's beta, the current risk-free interest rate and an estimate of the market risk premium. In Chapter 12 we used government Treasury bill as the risk-free security. The expected market risk premium was estimated as the historic average of the difference between the return on the stock portfolio and government Treasury bill based on 85 years of capital market history. The data used to estimate the historic market risk premium was in Chapter 11, Table 11.1. The difference between the historic average return on common stocks, 11.5 percent, and the historic average return on government Treasury bills, 4.6 percent, is 11.5 − 4.6 = 6.9%, or about 7 percent.

Let's suppose Big Oil's common stock beta is estimated at .85, the risk-free security is Treasury bill and its interest rate of r_f is 6 percent. The expected market risk premium $(r_m - r_f)$ based on the historic difference between the return on stock portfolio and Treasury bill is 7 percent. Then the CAPM would put Big Oil's cost of equity at

$$\begin{aligned}\text{Cost of equity} &= r_{\text{equity}} = r_f + \beta(r_m - r_f)\\ &= 6\% + .85(7\%) = 11.95\%\end{aligned}$$

Of course, no one can estimate expected rates of return to two decimal places, so we'll just round to 12 percent.

Check Point 13.6

Jo Ann Cox decides to check whether Fred, the banker, was correct in claiming that Geothermal's cost of equity is 14 percent. She estimates Geothermal's beta at 1.2. The risk-free interest rate in 2014 is 6 percent, and the long-run average market risk premium is 7 percent. What is the expected rate of return on Geothermal's common stock, assuming of course that the CAPM is true? Recalculate Geothermal's weighted-average cost of capital.

Estimates Based on the Dividend Discount Model Whenever you are given an estimate of the expected return on a common stock, always look for ways to check whether it is reasonable. One crucial check is that the cost of equity must be greater than the cost of debt because the equity of a firm is riskier than any of its debt. One other check on the estimates provided by the CAPM can be obtained from the dividend discount model (DDM). In Chapter 7 we showed you how to use the constant-growth DDM formula to estimate the return that investors expect from different common stocks. Remember the formula: If dividends are expected to grow indefinitely at a constant rate g, then the price of the stock is equal to

$$P_0 = \frac{\text{DIV}_1}{r_{\text{equity}} - g}$$

where P_0 is the current stock price, DIV_1 is the forecast dividend at the end of the year, and r_{equity} is the expected return from the stock. We can rearrange this formula to provide an estimate of r_{equity}.

$$r_{\text{equity}} = \frac{\text{DIV}_1}{P_0} + g \tag{13.10}$$

The constant-growth formula will get you into trouble if you apply it to firms with very high current rates of growth. Such growth cannot be sustained indefinitely.

In other words, the expected return on equity is equal to the dividend yield (DIV_1/P_0) plus the expected perpetual growth rate in dividends (g).

This constant-growth dividend discount model is widely used in estimating expected rates of return on common stocks of public utilities. Utility stocks have a fairly stable growth pattern and are therefore tailor-made for the constant-growth formula. Remember that the constant-growth formula will get you into trouble if you apply it to firms with very high current rates of growth. Such growth cannot be sustained indefinitely. Using the formula in these circumstances of currently extreme growth will lead to an overestimate of the expected return.

Beware of False Precision Do not expect estimates of the cost of equity to be precise. In practice you can't know whether the capital asset pricing model fully explains expected returns or whether the assumptions of the dividend discount model hold exactly. Even if your formulas were right, the required inputs would be "noisy" and subject to error. Thus a financial analyst who can confidently locate the cost of equity in a band of two or three percentage points is doing pretty well. In this endeavour it is perfectly OK to conclude that the cost of equity is, say, "about 15 percent" or "somewhere between 14 and 16 percent."[5]

[5] The calculations in this chapter have been done to one or two decimal places only to avoid confusion from rounding.

Sometimes accuracy can be improved by estimating the cost of equity or WACC for an industry or a group of comparable companies. This cuts down the "noise" that plagues single-company estimates. Suppose, for example, that Jo Ann Cox is able to identify three companies with investments and operations similar to Geothermal's. The average WACC for these three companies would be a valuable check on her estimate of WACC for Geothermal alone.

Or suppose that Geothermal is contemplating an investment in oil refining. For this venture, Geothermal's existing WACC is probably not right; it needs a discount rate reflecting the risks of the refining business. It could therefore try to estimate WACC for a sample of oil refining companies. If too few "pure-play" refining companies were available—most oil companies invest in production and marketing as well as refining—an industry WACC for a sample of large oil companies could be a useful check or benchmark.

THE EXPECTED RETURN ON PRFFERRED STOCK

Preferred stock that pays a fixed annual dividend can be valued from the perpetuity formula:

$$\text{Price of preferred} = \frac{\text{dividend}}{r_{\text{preferred}}}$$

where $r_{\text{preferred}}$ is the appropriate discount rate for the preferred stock. Therefore, we can infer the required rate of return on preferred stock by rearranging the valuation formula to

$$r_{\text{preferred}} = \frac{\text{dividend}}{\text{price of preferred}} \tag{13.11}$$

For Big Oil's preferred stock, the annual dividend is 8 percent of its par value, .08 × \$20= \$1.60. The shares sell for \$16 per share, making the expected return on preferred stock $r_{\text{preferred}}$ = \$1.60 / \$16 = 10 percent, which is also the current dividend yield.

LO4 13.5 CALCULATING THE WEIGHTED-AVERAGE COST OF CAPITAL

Now that you have worked out Big Oil's capital structure and estimated the cost (required rate of return) of its securities, you need only simple arithmetic to calculate the weighted-average cost of capital. Table 13.3 summarizes the necessary data. We have combined the bank debt with the bonds, assuming that both have a 9 percent required rate of return.[6]

You might find it easier to put the data into a table such as Table 13.4, calculate the component cost (market value weight × after-tax cost) of each type of financing, and add them up to get the WACC.

Suppose that Big Oil needed to evaluate a project with the same risk as its existing business that would also support 22.7 percent debt. Its weighted-average cost of capital, rounded to 10.5 percent, would be the appropriate discount rate for the cash flows.

TABLE 13.3 Data needed to calculate Big Oil's weighted-average cost of capital (\$ millions).

Security Type	Capital Structure		Required Rate of return
Debt	D = \$ 388.3	D/V = .227	r_{debt} =.09, or 9%
Preferred stock	P = \$ 120	P/V = .07	$r_{\text{preferred}}$ =.10, or 10%
Common stock	E = \$1,200	E/V = .703	r_{equity} =.12, or 12%
Total	V = \$1,788.3		

Note: Corporate tax rate T_c = .35.

[6] If the debt beta is not zero, the equation for the unlevered beta is

$$\beta_u = \frac{\beta_{\text{levered}} + \beta_{\text{debt}} \times (1 - T_c) \times D/E}{1 + (1 - T_c) \times D/E}$$

TABLE 13.4 Calculating Big Oil's weighted-average cost of capital.

Source of Financing	Weight	After-Tax Cost	Component Cost = Weight × After-Tax Cost
Debt	.227	(1 − .35) × 9% = 5.85%	.227 × 5.85% = 1.32%
Preferred stock	.07	10%	.07 × 10% = .7%
Common stock	.703	12%	.703 × 12% = 8.44%
Total	1.00		WACC = 10.46%

REAL COMPANY WACC

Big Oil is an entirely hypothetical company, but the steps taken to estimate its WACC are actually what you would do: (1) identify the capital structure and estimates the market value of each source of financing; (2) estimate the required rates of return on each type of financing; and (3) calculate the WACC using the weights, costs, and tax rate.

One practical issue is the choice of the risk-free security when implementing the CAPM. Up to now, we have used government Treasury bill as the risk-free security. However, financial managers frequently use a long-term government bond as the risk-free security because they want a WACC to evaluate a long-term investment. Because the Canadian federal government can print money, the risk of the government not paying principal and interest on a long-term government bond is essentially zero. Now, if a long-term government bond is chosen as the risk-free security, the appropriate market risk premium must be the difference between the expected return on the market portfolio and the long-term government bond. Look back at Chapter 11, Table 11.1, and you will see that the historic average annual rate of return on long-term government bonds, over the past 85 years is 6.5 percent. The difference between the historic average returns on common stock portfolio and the long-term government bond portfolio is 11.5 − 6.5 = 5 percent. This suggests that if a long-term government bond is used as the risk-free security, the expected market risk premium is about 5 percent.

Typically long-term government bond interest rates are higher than Treasury bill rates. In January 2011, Treasury bill rates were about 1.5 percent and the interest rate for government bonds with maturity of 10 plus years was about 3.8 percent. In Chapter 6 the discussion of the shape of the yield curve covered two reasons why the bonds with longer maturities tend to have higher yields: expected inflation and higher interest rate risk. The main reason to use a long-term government bond as the risk-free security is to capture expected inflation into the equity cost of capital.

The cost of equity for Canadian Pacific Railway in Example 13.1 was calculated with Treasury bill as the risk-free security. The risk-free rate was 1.5 percent, the market risk premium was 7 percent, and the stock beta was .82. Thus, the estimated cost of equity was 1.5% + .82 × 7% = 7.24 percent. If Canadian Pacific's weighted average cost of capital is to be used to evaluate a 10-year or longer investment, it would make sense to use the long-term government bond as the risk-free security in the cost of equity calculation. With the long-term Government of Canada bond as the risk-free security, Canadian Pacific's estimated cost of equity would be 3.8% + .82 × 5% = 7.9 percent.

LO5 13.6 INTERPRETING THE WEIGHTED-AVERAGE COST OF CAPITAL

WHEN YOU CAN AND CAN'T USE WACC

When we discussed the company cost of capital in Chapter 12, we did not know how to measure the company cost of capital when the firm issues different types of securities or how to adjust for the tax-deductibility of interest payments. The weighted-average cost of capital formula solves those problems.

A company's weighted-average cost of capital is the rate of return that the firm must expect to earn on its average-risk investments in order to provide a fair expected return to all its security holders. We use it to value new assets that have the same risk as the old ones and that support the same ratio of debt. Strictly speaking, the weighted-average cost of capital is an appropriate discount rate only for a project that is a carbon copy of the firm's existing business. It is also used to calculate the company's economic value added, EVA, which is shown in Chapter 4. But often it is used as a company-wide benchmark discount rate; the benchmark is adjusted upward for unusually risky projects and downward for unusually safe ones.

There is a good musical analogy here. Most of us, lacking perfect pitch, need a well-defined reference point, such as middle C, before we can sing on key. But anyone who can carry a tune gets *relative* pitches right. Businesspeople have good intuition about *relative* risks (at least in industries they are used to) but not about absolute risk or required rates of return. Therefore, they set a company- or industry-wide cost of capital as a benchmark. This is not the right hurdle rate for everything the company does, but good-judgment adjustments can be used to make for more or less risky ventures.

SOME COMMON MISTAKES

> There are actually two costs of debt finance. The explicit cost of debt is the rate of interest that bondholders demand. But there is also an implicit cost, because borrowing increases the required return to equity.

One danger with the weighted-average formula is that it tempts people to make logical errors. Think back to your estimate of the cost of capital for Big Oil:

$$\text{WACC} = \left[\frac{D}{V} \times (1 - T_c) r_{\text{debt}}\right] + \left[\frac{P}{V} \times r_{\text{preferred}}\right] + \left[\frac{E}{V} \times r_{\text{equity}}\right]$$

$$= [.227 \times (1 - .35)9\%] + [.07 \times 10\%] + [.703 \times 12\%] = 10.46\%$$

Now, you might be tempted to say to yourself, "Aha! Big Oil has a good credit rating. It could easily push up its debt ratio to 50 percent. If the interest rate is 9 percent and the required return on equity is 12 percent, the weighted-average cost of capital would be

$$\text{WACC} = [.50 \times (1 - .35)9\%] + [.07 \times 10\%] + [.43 \times 12\%] = 8.8\%$$

At a discount rate of 8.8 percent, we can justify a lot more investment."

That reasoning will get you into trouble. First, if Big Oil increased its borrowing, the lenders would almost certainly demand a higher rate of interest on the debt. Second, as the borrowing increased, the risk of the common stock would also increase and therefore the shareholders would demand a higher return.

When you jumped to the conclusion that Big Oil could lower its weighted-average cost of capital to 8.8 percent by borrowing more, you were recognizing only the explicit cost of debt and not the implicit cost.

Check Point 13.7

Jo Ann Cox's boss has pointed out that Geothermal proposes to finance its expansion entirely by borrowing at an interest rate of 8 percent. He argues that this is therefore the appropriate discount rate for the project's cash flows. Is he right?

HOW CHANGING CAPITAL STRUCTURE AFFECTS WACC WHEN THE CORPORATE TAX RATE IS ZERO

We will illustrate how changes in capital structure affect WACC and expected returns by focusing on the simplest possible case, where the corporate tax rate, T_c, is zero.

Think back to our earlier example of Geothermal. Geothermal, you may remember, has the following market-value balance sheet:

Assets		**Liabilities and Shareholders' Equity**		
Assets = value of Geothermal's existing business	$647	Debt	$194	(30%)
		Equity	$453	(70%)
Total value	$647	Value	$647	(100%)

Geothermal's debtholders require a return of 8 percent and the shareholders require a return of 14 percent. Since we assume here that Geothermal pays no corporate tax, its weighted-average cost of capital is simply the expected return on the firm's assets:

$$\text{WACC} = r_{\text{assets}} = (.3 \times 8\%) + (.7 \times 14\%) = 12.2\%$$

This is the return you would expect if you held all Geothermal's securities and therefore owned all its assets.

Now think what will happen if Geothermal borrows an additional \$97 million and uses the cash to buy back and retire \$97 million of its common stock. The revised market-value balance sheet is:

Assets		Liabilities and Shareholders' Equity		
Assets = value of Geothermal's existing business	\$647	Debt	\$291	(45%)
	____	Equity	\$356	(55%)
Total value	\$647	Value	\$647	(100%)

Geothermal's leverage (debt/total value) has risen from 30 percent to 45 percent. If there are no corporate taxes and the change in capital structure has no impact on Geothermal's operating activities or on its assets, the total cash that Geothermal pays out to its security holders and the risk of those cash flows, the *business risk*, are unchanged. Therefore, if investors require a return of 12.2 percent on the total package of debt and equity before the financing, they must require the same 12.2 percent return on the package afterward. The weighted-average cost of capital is therefore unaffected by the change in the capital structure with no corporate taxes. More on this topic appears in Chapter 16.

HOW CHANGING CAPITAL STRUCTURE AFFECTS DEBT AND EQUITY WHEN THE CORPORATE TAX RATE IS ZERO

We just saw that the required return on the *package* of the debt and equity is unaffected by the change in capital structure when the corporate tax rate is zero. The change in capital structure does not change the assets, or their cash flow or their risk. However, the change in capital structure does affect the required returns on the individual securities. If leverage is increased, the debt is riskier. Debtholders are likely to demand a higher return. Increasing leverage also makes the equity riskier, because shareholders are paid only after the debtholders, increasing the shareholders' required rate of return.

Since the shareholders and debtholders receive the cash flow produced by the company's assets, they also share the risk of that cash flow. The weighted average of the debt risk, β_{debt}, and equity risk, β_{equity}, must add up to the risk of the assets, the asset beta, β_{asset}:

$$\beta_{\text{assets}} = \frac{D}{V} \times \beta_{\text{debt}} + \frac{E}{V} \times \beta_{\text{equity}} \qquad (13.12)$$

Debtholders bear less risk than shareholders. Interest and principal payments are made to debtholders before shareholders are paid dividends. If the company fails to pay the promised interest and principal payments, the debtholders have the right to force the company into bankruptcy and can take over the company. The risk of the debt of large blue chip firms is close to zero—close enough that many financial analysts assume that beta of the debt, β_{debt}, is zero.

Think back to our original Geothermal example, when the firm was 30 percent debt-financed. Assume that the risk-free rate of interest is 6 percent and the expected market risk premium is 7 percent. If Geothermal's debtholders require an 8 percent return and shareholders require 14 percent, what are the debt and equity betas? Rearranging the CAPM equation,

$$\text{Stock's beta} = \frac{\text{expected return on stock} - \text{risk-free rate}}{\text{expected market risk premium}} = \frac{14\% - 6\%}{7\%} = 1.14$$

$$\text{Debt's beta} = \frac{\text{expected return on debt} - \text{risk-free rate}}{\text{expected market risk premium}} = \frac{8\% - 6\%}{7\%} = .29$$

Geothermal's asset beta is the weighted average of the debt and equity betas:

$$\beta_{assets} = (.3 \times .29) + (.7 \times 1.14) = .89$$

What happens after the proposed refinancing, where Geothermal borrows an additional \$97 million and retires \$97 million of equity? The company's assets and their expected cash flows are unchanged and thus the beta of the assets is unchanged. Thus the risk of the package of debt and equity is unaffected but how that risk is shared between the debt and equity is changed. Suppose that the debt beta increases to .3. We can work out what the new equity beta must be:

$$\beta_{assets} = \frac{D}{V} \times \beta_{debt} + \frac{E}{V} \times \beta_{equity}$$

$$.89 = .45 \times .3 + (.55 \times \beta_{equity})$$

$$\beta_{equity} = 1.37$$

The equity beta has increased from 1.14 to 1.37 due to the additional leverage. Shareholders bear not only business risk but also financial risk. Financial risk exists because shareholders are paid dividends only after debtholders receive their promised interest and principal. By rearranging equation 13.12, the beta of a firm's equity, in the absence of corporate taxes, can be expressed as

$$\beta_{equity} = \beta_{assets} + (\beta_{assets} - \beta_{debt})\frac{D}{E} \qquad \textbf{(13.13)}$$

Often it is reasonable to assume that the beta of debt is zero, and equation 13.13 reduces to

$$\beta_{equity} = \beta_{assets} + \left(\beta_{assets}\frac{D}{E}\right) = \beta_{assets} \times \left(1 + \frac{D}{E}\right) \qquad \textbf{(13.14)}$$

These formulas for the equity beta show the two sources of risk: the business risk, measured by the asset beta, and the financial risk, reflecting the impact of leverage, dependent on the debt/equity ratio, *D*/*E*. Increasing leverage raises the debt-equity ratio and increases the financial risk to shareholders. If the firm is unlevered (debt-free), *D*/*V* is zero and the shareholders bear only the business risk and no financial risk.

If the corporate tax rate is zero, you can use equation 13.13 or 13.14 to assess the effect of a change in capital structure on the riskiness of equity.

Check Point 13.8

Tollbar Cookies Inc. is 80 percent equity-financed, its common stock beta, β_{equity}, is .8, and its debt beta, β_{debt}, is .1. The corporate tax rate is zero. The risk-free rate is 4 percent and the market risk premium is 7 percent. What will be the equity beta if Tollbar is 50 percent debt-financed? Assume the debt beta is .14 at 50 percent debt. Calculate Tollbar's WACC for both capital structures. Explain what you find.

WHAT HAPPENS IF CAPITAL STRUCTURE CHANGES AND THE CORPORATE TAX RATE IS NOT ZERO?

We have shown that when there are no corporate taxes both the weighted-average cost of capital and the beta of the assets are unaffected by a change in capital structure. Adding corporate taxes complicates the picture. Since interest paid on the debt is tax-deductible, increasing leverage reduces the company's tax bill and hence increases the company's total cash flows. In this situation, changing the capital structure of the firm can change the value of the firm's assets and also their risk. We will show you the details in Chapter 16. For now, we will show you the implications for the asset and equity betas.

unlevered beta Beta of equity of a debt-free firm, reflecting the risk arising from the firm's operating activities.

We start by defining the asset beta of the debt-free ("unlevered") firm, **unlevered beta**, β_u. The unlevered beta measures the business risk, the risk arising from the firm's operating activities and not by its financing choices. Since the firm has no debt, the unlevered asset beta is also the unlevered equity beta. With leverage, the shareholders not only bear business risk but also the added

levered equity beta Beta of equity of a firm that has debt, reflecting both the risk arising from the firm's operating activities and the risk created by the leverage (debtholders are entitled to be paid principal and interest before shareholders are paid dividends).

risk from financial leverage. The equity beta for the firm with debt is the **levered equity beta**, $\beta_{levered}$. The levered equity beta is a function of the unlevered beta, β_u, the beta of the debt, β_{debt}, the degree of financial leverage, D/E, and the tax rate, T_c:

$$\beta_{levered} = \beta_u + (\beta_u - \beta_{debt})(1 - T_c)\frac{D}{E} \tag{13.15}$$

If it is reasonable to assume that the debt is riskless, the debt beta is zero and the equation becomes

$$\beta_{levered} = \beta_u \times \left[1 + (1 - T_c)\frac{D}{E}\right] \tag{13.16}$$

A word of warning: These formulas are based on assumptions that you will learn more about in Chapter 16. However, analysts and investment bankers often use them to unlever and relever equity betas when assessing the impact of a change in capital structure. In Example 13.2, we show you how to do it, and in the next section we will show you how unlevering and relevering betas can be useful when hunting for the appropriate beta for a project.

EXAMPLE 13.2 SUPER BIKES'S CAPITAL STRUCTURE AND EQUITY BETA

Super Bikes, a bicycle manufacturer, is currently 30 percent debt-financed. Its current equity beta is 1.1 and its debt beta is 0. What would be the impact on the riskiness of its equity if debt financing is increased to be 50 percent of the firm value? Assume the debt beta remains 0. The company's tax rate is 35 percent.

First rearrange equation 13.16 to find Super Bikes's unlevered beta:[7]

$$\beta_u = \frac{\beta_{levered}}{1 + (1 - T_c)\frac{D}{E}} \tag{13.17}$$

$$= \frac{1.1}{1 + (1 - .35) \times \left(\frac{.3}{.7}\right)} = .86$$

Without the added risk from leverage, the unlevered beta is .86. When leverage is increased to 50 percent the new levered equity beta is:

$$\beta_{levered} = \beta_u \times \left[1 + (1 - T_c)\frac{D}{E}\right] = .86 \times \left[1 + (1 - .35)\frac{.5}{.5}\right] = 1.42$$

We see that by increasing the leverage from 30 percent debt to 50 percent debt the levered equity beta increases from 1.1 to 1.42.

To summarize, you should remember:

- A company's weighted-average cost of capital is the right discount rate for average-risk capital investment projects.
- The weighted-average cost of capital is the return the company needs to earn on its investments, after tax, in order to satisfy all its security holders.
- If the firm increases its debt ratio, both the debt and the equity will become more risky. The debtholders and equity holders require higher rates of return to compensate for the increased risk. Exactly how the risk increases depends on whether or not the company pays taxes.

---

[7] You can plug the data into the weighted-average cost of capital formula, equation 13.9.

REVISITING THE PROJECT COST OF CAPITAL

In Chapter 12 we introduced the project cost of capital: the minimum acceptable expected rate of return on a project, given its risks. When funds are invested in a project, the required rate of return on the investment depends on the project's *risk*, not the source of funds. In Chapter 12 we discussed ways of finding a suitable estimate of a project's cost of capital. We now must extend that analysis to consider a project's weighted-average cost of capital.

We use the weighted-average cost of capital because, typically, firms are financed by a mix of securities. The weighted-average cost of capital depends on the expected return on all of the securities issued by the company. In our analysis so far, we have not answered an important question: Why are firms financed this way? We have shown that when there are no corporate taxes, a company's cost of capital is unaffected by how it is financed. With taxes, the analysis is more complex. We will deal with the details in Chapter 16. In the meantime we can say that a firm selects its capital structure to maximize the firm's or project's value. Consequently, the determination of the cost of capital appropriate for a project has two components. First, the risks of the project's cash flows must be assessed; that is, the project's unlevered beta must be determined. Second, the best financing mix must be selected. This will determine the added financial risk for shareholders and the levered equity beta. The project's weighted-average cost of capital will reflect the project's overall risk and the best securities mix for the project.

We now know that the pure-play approach to assessing the project's risk is complicated by the choice of capital structure. As a first step, you may want to use the pure-play company's weighted-average cost of capital as a proxy for the project's weighted-average cost of capital. This assumes that the pure-play company's choice of financing mix is also the best mix of financing for the project. However, you can also use the formula for levered equity beta to change the pure-play equity beta to your chosen capital structure. Of course, this presupposes that you have picked the appropriate capital structure for the project.

EXAMPLE 13.3 ESTIMATING THE COST OF CAPITAL FOR A NEW VENTURE

Snow Fun Inc., a manufacturer of skis and snowboards, is contemplating entering a new line of business: bicycle manufacturing. The company's analysts have estimated the project's cash flows but need to determine the project cost of capital. Snow Fun analysts assess that the capital structure for their new bicycle division will be 40 percent debt.

Super Bike, in Example 13.2, is a pure play in bicycle manufacturing and is 30 percent debt-financed. Analysts at Snow Fun use Super Bike's unlevered equity of .86 and relever it to their chosen capital structure:

$$\beta_{\text{levered}} = \beta_u \times \left[1 + (1 - T_c)\frac{D}{E}\right] = .86 \times \left[1 + (1 - .35)\frac{.4}{.6}\right] = 1.23$$

Given that the cost of debt is 6 percent, the risk-free rate is 4 percent, and the market risk premium is 7 percent, the project cost of equity is

$$r_{\text{equity}} = r_f + \beta_{\text{levered}} \times \text{market risk premium} = 4\% + 1.23 \times 7\% = 12.61\%$$

The project cost of capital is

$$\text{Project cost of capital} = \frac{D}{V} \times (1 - T_c)r_{\text{debt}} + \frac{E}{V} \times r_{\text{equity}}$$

$$= .4 \times (1 - .35) \times 6\% + .6 \times 12.61\% = 9.13\%, \text{ or about } 9.1\%$$

LO6 13.7 VALUING ENTIRE BUSINESSES

Investors routinely buy and sell shares of common stock. Companies frequently buy and sell entire businesses. Do the discounted cash-flow formulas that we used in Chapter 7 to value Blue Skies stock also work for entire businesses?

TABLE 13.5 Forecasts of operating cash flow and investment for the concatenator division (thousands of dollars). Rapid expansion means that free cash flow is negative in the early years, because investment outstrips the cash flow from operations. Free cash flow turns positive when growth slows down.

	Year					
	1	2	3	4	5	6
(1) Sales	1,189	1,421	1,700	2,020	2,391	2,510
(2) Costs	1,070	1,279	1,530	1,818	2,152	2,260
(3) Earnings before interest, taxes, depreciation, and amortization (EBITDA) = (1) − (2)	119	142	170	202	239	250
(4) Depreciation	45	59	76	99	128	136
(5) Earnings before interest and taxes (EBIT) = (3) − (4)	74	83	94	103	111	114
(6) Tax at 35%	25.9	29.05	32.9	36.05	38.85	39.9
(7) Earnings after tax = (5) − (6)	48.1	54.0	61.1	67.0	72.2	74.1
(8) Operating cash flow = (4) + (7)	93.1	113.0	137.1	166.0	200.2	210.1
(9) Investment in long-term assets and net working capital	166.7	200	240	200	160	130.6
(10) Free cash flow = (8) − (9)	−73.6	−87.1	−102.9	−34.1	40.2	79.5

Sure! As long as the company's debt ratio is expected to remain fairly constant, you can treat the company as one big project and discount its cash flows by the weighted-average cost of capital. The result is the combined value of the company's debt and equity. If you want to know just the value of the equity, you must remember to subtract the value of the debt from the company's total value.

Suppose that you are interested in buying Establishment Industry's concatenator manufacturing operation. The problem is how to figure out what it is worth. Table 13.5 sets out your forecasts for the next six years. Row 8 shows the expected cash flow from operations. This is equal to the expected earnings before interest and tax, EBIT, minus taxes plus depreciation.[8] Remember, depreciation is not a cash outflow, and therefore you need to add it back when calculating the operating cash flow. Row 9 in the table shows the forecasted investments in long-term assets and working capital.

free cash flow Cash flow that is not required for investment in fixed assets or working capital and is therefore available to investors.

The operating cash flow less investment expenditures is the amount of cash that the business can pay out to investors after paying for all investments necessary for growth. This is the concatenator division's **free cash flow** (row 10 in the table). Notice that the free cash flow is negative in the early years. Is that a bad sign? Not really. The business is running a cash deficit not because it is unprofitable but because it is growing so fast. Rapid growth is good news, not bad, as long as the business is earning more than the cost of capital on its investments.

The forecast cash flows in Table 13.5 did not include a deduction for debt interest. But we will not forget that acquisition of the concatenator business will support additional debt. We will recognize that fact by discounting the free cash flows by the weighted-average cost of capital, which reflects both the firm's capital structure and the tax deductibility of its interest payments.

Suppose that a sensible capital structure for the concatenator operation is 60 percent equity and 40 percent debt.[9] You estimate that the required rate of return on the equity is 12 percent and that the business could borrow at an interest rate of 5 percent. The weighted-average cost of capital is therefore

$$\text{WACC} = \frac{D}{V} \times (1 - T_c)r_{\text{debt}} + \frac{E}{V} \times r_{\text{equity}}$$

$$= [.4 \times (1 - .35)5\%] + (.6 \times 12\%) = 8.5\%$$

[8] Technically, we should be subtracting the capital cost allowance, CCA, to calculate taxable income. We are assuming that depreciation is the same as CCA. Look back to Chapter 9 for a review of CCA.

[9] By this we mean that it makes sense to finance 40 percent of the present value of the business by debt. Remember that we use market-value weights to compute WACC. Debt as a proportion of book value may be more or less than 40 percent.

CALCULATING THE VALUE OF THE CONCATENATOR BUSINESS

The value of the concatenator operation is equal to the discounted value of the free cash flows (FCFs) out to a horizon year plus the forecasted value of the business at the horizon, also discounted back to the present. That is,

$$PV = \underbrace{\frac{FCF_1}{1+WACC} + \frac{FCF_2}{(1+WACC)^2} + \cdots + \frac{FCF_H}{(1+WACC)^H}}_{\text{PV(free cash flows for years 1 to } H)} + \underbrace{\frac{PV_H}{(1+WACC)^H}}_{+\text{PV(horizon value)}}$$

Of course, the concatenator business will continue to grow after the horizon, but it's not practical to forecast free cash flow year by year to infinity. PV_H stands in for the value of free cash flows in periods $H+1$, $H+2$, and so on.

Horizon years are often chosen arbitrarily. Sometimes the boss tells everybody to use 10 years because that's a nice round number. We have picked year 5 as the horizon, because the business is expected to settle down to steady growth of 5 percent a year from then on.

There are several common formulas or rules of thumb for estimating horizon value. Let's try the constant-growth formula that we introduced in Chapter 7:

$$\text{Horizon value} = \frac{\text{free cash flow in year 6}}{r-g} = \frac{79.5}{.085-.05} = \$2{,}271.4 \text{ thousand}$$

We now have all we need to calculate the value of the concatenator business today. We add up the present values of the free cash flows in the first five years and that of the horizon value:

$$\begin{aligned}\text{PV(business)} &= \text{PV(free cash flows years 1–5)} + \text{PV(horizon value)}\\ &= -\frac{73.6}{1.085} - \frac{87.1}{(1.085)^2} - \frac{102.9}{(1.085)^3} - \frac{34.1}{(1.085)^4} + \frac{40.2}{(1.085)^5} + \frac{2{,}271.4}{(1.085)^5}\\ &= \$1{,}290.3 \text{ thousand}\end{aligned}$$

Notice that when we use the weighted-average cost of capital to value a company, we are asking, "What is the combined value of the company's debt and equity?" If you need to value the equity, you must subtract the value of any outstanding debt. Suppose that the concatenator business has been partly financed with \$516,000 of debt, 40 percent of the overall value of about \$1,290,000. Then the equity in the business is worth only \$1,290,000 − 516,000 = \$774,000.

Check Point 13.9

Managers often use rules of thumb to check their estimates of horizon value. Suppose you observe that the value of the debt plus equity of a typical mature concatenator producer is 9 times its EBITDA. (EBITDA is defined at line 3 of Table 13.5.) If your operation sold in year 5 at a similar multiple of EBITDA, how would your estimate of the present value of the operation change?

Before we end this chapter, we want to deal with a few other issues about the appropriate WACC for valuations. First, when doing a valuation of business, the WACC is typically used to discount many years of cash flows. This is why that many practitioners calculate the cost of equity using the long-term government bond as the risk-free security. The current interest rate on a long-term bond reflects the market's expectation of future interest rates. The fact that the interest rate on a long-term bond is affected by expected future interest rates is discussed in Chapter 6 in Section 6.5, "The Yield Curve," and also in Appendix 6A, "A More Detailed Look at the Yield Curve."

Some people question whether short-term debt should be included in WACC. Remember, the free cash flows are cash flows available for investors, and that includes both lenders of short-term and long-term debt. So, include short-term interest-bearing debt in WACC. Some firms are permanent short-term borrowers. When the current short-term debt matures, the firm borrows again. So another issue is: What is the cost of short-term debt? The current cost of short-term debt can be used. However, if the WACC is being used to discount many years of cash flows, it might make sense to use a long-term equivalent of the short-term interest rate. So, if the debt rating of the short-term debt is BBB, the current interest rate for long-term BBB debt can be used as the cost of the short-term debt. Again, this helps makes the WACC relevant for discounting future cash flows.

Another issue is calculating the WACC to use if valuing a privately held corporation. With no public equity, there is no stock return data available to estimate the firm's beta. Therefore, the beta of a public company assessed to have similar risk can be used. But as we discussed above, you also have to assess whether the capital structure of the comparable company is appropriate for the private company. It might be necessary to calculate the unlevered equity beta and then relever it to reflect the capital structure of the private company. The relevered beta is used to calculate the cost of equity for the WACC. One other issue that is often dealt with is the lack of liquidity of the private corporation. The cost of equity based on a public company's beta might be lower than if the company was private. So a liquidity premium is sometimes added to the estimated WACC to capture the cost of the lack of liquidity.

Finally, one more issue is the appropriate WACC used to calculate a firm's economic value added, EVA, a concept from Chapter 4. The current WACC, based on the current cost of all sources of financing, is needed because WACC is used to calculate the current charge for the capital employed. In this case, use the Treasury bill as the risk-free interest rate and the current cost of all sources of debt.

13.8 SUMMARY

1. **Why do managers compute their company's weighted-average cost of capital?** LO1

Managers need a standard discount rate for evaluating average-risk projects. An "average risk" project is one that has the same risk as the firm's existing assets and operations.

2. **What about projects that are not average?** LO5

A **weighted-average cost of capital** can still be used as a benchmark. The appropriate benchmark (or project cost of capital) must use the cost of equity that reflects the risk of the project and incorporate the appropriate mix of debt and equity financing for the project.

3. **How do firms compute weighted-average costs of capital?** LO2, LO4

Here's the WACC formula one more time:

$$\text{WACC} = \frac{D}{V} \times (1 - T_c)r_{\text{debt}} + \frac{E}{V} \times r_{\text{equity}}$$

The WACC is the expected rate of return on the portfolio of debt and equity securities issued by the firm. The required rate of return on each security is weighted by its proportion of the firm's total market value (not book value). Since interest payments reduce the firm's income tax bill, the required rate of return on debt is measured after tax, as $(1 - T_c)\, r_{\text{debt}}$.

This WACC formula is usually written assuming the firm's capital structure includes just two classes of securities: debt and equity. If there is another class, say preferred stock, the formula expands to include it. In other words, we would estimate $r_{\text{preferred}}$, the rate of return demanded by preferred shareholders, determine P/V, the fraction of market value accounted for by preferred, and add $r_{\text{preferred}} \times P/V$ to the equation. Of course, the weights in the WACC formula always add up to 1.0. In this case, $D/V + P/V + E/V = 1.0$.

4. **How are the costs of debt and equity calculated?** LO3

The cost of debt (r_{debt}) is the market interest rate demanded by bondholders. In other words, it is the rate that the company would pay on new debt issued to finance its investment projects. The cost of preferred ($r_{\text{preferred}}$) is just the preferred dividend divided by the market price of a preferred share.

The tricky part is estimating the cost of equity (r_{equity}), the expected rate of return on the firm's shares. Financial managers use the capital asset pricing model to estimate expected return. But for mature, steady-growth companies, it can also make sense to use the constant-growth dividend discount model. Remember, estimates of expected return are less reliable for a single firm's stock than for a sample of comparable-risk firms. Therefore, some managers also consider WACCs calculated for industries.

5. **What happens when capital structure changes?** LO5
The rates of return on debt and equity will change. For example, increasing the debt ratio will increase the risk borne by both debt and equity investors and cause them to demand higher returns. However, this does not necessarily mean that the overall WACC will increase, because more weight is put on the cost of debt, which is less than the cost of equity. In fact, if we ignore taxes, the overall cost of capital will stay constant as the fractions of debt and equity change. For firms that pay corporate taxes, increasing the debt ratio creates a tax saving. This is discussed further in Chapter 16.

6. **Can WACC be used to value an entire business?** LO6
Just think of the business as a very large project. Forecast the business's operating cash flows (after-tax profits plus depreciation), and subtract the future investments in plant and equipment and in net working capital. The resulting *free cash flows* can then be discounted back to the present at the weighted-average cost of capital. The appropriate WACC reflects the riskiness of the firm and the selected capital structure. Of course, the cash flows from a company may stretch far into the future. Financial managers therefore typically produce detailed cash flows only up to some horizon date and then estimate the remaining value of the business at the horizon.

Related Web Links

valuepro.net Software and data for estimating the weighted-average cost of capital and valuing companies

pages.stern.nyu.edu/~adamodar Professor Aswath Damodaran's home page, which includes estimates of industry asset betas and costs of capital

Key Terms

capital structure	422	levered equity beta	439	weighted-average cost of capital (WACC)	427
free cash flow	441	unlevered beta	438		

Questions and Problems

connect Practise and learn online with *Connect*. Questions with online Excel templates or datasets are marked with ✎.

*Answers in Appendix B

BASIC

*1. **Cost of Debt.** Micro Spinoffs, Inc., issued 20-year debt a year ago at par value, with a coupon rate of 9 percent paid annually. Today, the debt is selling at $1,050. If the firm's tax bracket is 30 percent, what is its after-tax cost of debt? (LO3)

2. **Cost of Preferred Stock.** Micro Spinoffs also has preferred stock outstanding. The stock pays a dividend of $4 per share and the stock sells for $40. What is the cost of preferred stock? (LO3)

*3. **Calculating WACC.** Suppose Micro Spinoffs's cost of equity is 12.5 percent. What is its WACC if equity is 50 percent, preferred stock is 20 percent, and debt is 30 percent of total capital? (LO4)

*4. **Cost of Equity.** Reliable Electric is a regulated public utility, and it is expected to provide steady growth of dividends of 5 percent per year for the indefinite future. Its last dividend was $5 per share; the stock sold for $60 per share just after the dividend was paid. What is the company's cost of equity? (LO3)

5. **Calculating WACC.** Reactive Industries has the following capital structure. Its corporate tax rate is 35 percent. What is its WACC? (LO4)

Security	Market Value	Required Rate of Return
Debt	$20 million	6%
Preferred stock	$10 million	8%
Common stock	$50 million	12%

*6. **Company Versus Project Discount Rates.** Geothermal's WACC is 11.4 percent. Executive Fruit's WACC is 12.3 percent. Now Executive Fruit is considering an investment in geothermal power production. Should it discount project cash flows at 12.3 percent? Why or why not? (LO5)

7. **Company Valuation.** Icarus Airlines is proposing to go public, and you have been given the task of estimating the value of its equity. Management plans to maintain debt at 30 percent of the company's present value, and you believe that at this capital structure the company's debtholders will demand a return of 6 percent and stockholders will require 11 percent. The company is forecasting that next year's operating cash flow (depreciation plus profit after tax at 40 percent) will be $68 million and that investment expenditures will be $30 million. Thereafter, operating cash flows and investment expenditures are forecast to grow by 4 percent a year.
   a. What is the total value of Icarus? (LO6)
   b. What is the value of the company's equity? (LO6)

INTERMEDIATE

*8. **WACC.** The common stock of Buildwell Conservation & Construction, Inc. (BCCI), has a beta of .8. The Treasury bill rate is 4 percent and the market risk premium is estimated at 7 percent. BCCI's capital structure is 30 percent debt paying a 5 percent interest rate, and 70 percent equity. What is BCCI's cost of equity capital and its WACC? Buildwell's tax rate is 35 percent. (LO4)

9. **WACC and NPV.** BCCI (see problem 8) is evaluating a project with an internal rate of return of 12 percent. Should it accept the project? If the project will generate a cash flow of $100,000 per year for 7 years, what is the most BCCI should be willing to pay to initiate the project? (LO1, LO6)

10. **Company Valuation.** You need to estimate the value of BCCI (see problem 8). You have the following forecasts (in millions of dollars) of Buildwell's earnings and of its future investments in new plant and working capital:

	Year			
	1	2	3	4 . . .
Earnings before interest, taxes, depreciation, and amortization (EBITDA)	80	100	115	120
Depreciation	20	30	35	40
EBIT	60	70	80	80
Investment in plant and working capital	12	15	18	20

From year 5 onward, EBITDA, depreciation, and investment are expected to remain unchanged at year-4 levels. Estimate the company's total value and the separate values of its debt and equity. (LO6)

*11. **Calculating WACC.** Find the WACC of William Tell Computers. The total book value of the firm's equity is $10 million; book value per share is $20. The stock sells for a price of $30 per share, and the cost of equity is 15 percent. The firm's bonds have a par value of $5 million and sell at a price of 110 percent of par. The yield to maturity on the bonds is 9 percent and the firm's tax rate is 30 percent. (LO4)

12. **WACC.** Nodebt, Inc., is a firm with all-equity financing. Its equity beta is .8. The Treasury bill rate is 5 percent and the market risk premium is expected to be 10 percent. What is Nodebt's asset beta? What is Nodebt's weighted-average cost of capital? The firm is exempt from paying taxes. (LO4)

13. **Cost of Capital.** A financial analyst at Dawn Chemical notes that the firm's total interest payments this year were $10 million while total debt outstanding was $80 million, and he concludes that the cost of debt was 12.5 percent. What is wrong with this conclusion? (LO3)

14. **Cost of Equity.** Bunkhouse Electronics is a recently incorporated firm that makes electronic entertainment systems. Its earnings and dividends have been growing at a rate of 30 percent per year, and the current dividend yield is 2 percent. Its beta is 1.2, the market risk premium is 8 percent, and the risk-free rate is 4 percent.
   a. Calculate two estimates of the firm's cost of equity. (LO3)
   b. Which estimate seems more reasonable to you? Why? (LO3)

15. **Cost of Debt.** Olympic Sports has two issues of debt outstanding. One is a 9 percent coupon bond with a face value of $20 million, a maturity of 10 years, and a yield to maturity of 10 percent. The coupons are paid annually. The other bond issue has a maturity of 15 years, with coupons also paid annually, and a coupon rate of 10 percent. The face value of the issue is $25 million and the issue sells for 92.8 percent of par value. The firm's tax rate is 30 percent.
   *a. What is the before-tax cost of debt for Olympic? (LO3)
   b. What is Olympic's after-tax cost of debt? (LO3)

16. Capital Structure. Examine the following book-value balance sheet for University Products, Inc. What is the capital structure of the firm based on market values? The preferred stock currently sells for $15 per share and the common stock for $20 per share. There are one million common shares outstanding. (LO2)

Book Value Balance Sheet ($ millions)

Assets		Liabilities and Net Worth	
Cash and short-term securities	$ 1	Bonds, coupon = 8%, paid annually (maturity = 10 years, current yield to maturity = 9%)	$10
Accounts receivable	3	Preferred stock (par value $20 per share)	2
Inventories	7	Common stock	10
Plant and equipment	21	Retained earnings	10
Total	$32	Total	$32

*17. **Calculating WACC.** Turn back to University Products's balance sheet from problem 16. If the preferred stock pays a dividend of $2 per share, the beta of the common stock is 1.5, the market risk premium is 7 percent, the risk-free rate is 4 percent, and the firm's tax rate is 40 percent, what is University's weighted-average cost of capital? (LO4)

18. **Integrative.** University Products is evaluating a new venture into home computer systems (see problems 16 and 17). The internal rate of return on the new venture is estimated at 13.4 percent. WACCs of firms in the personal computer industry tend to average around 14 percent. Should the new project be pursued? What assumptions must valid to make discounting the cash flows from the proposed venture at University Products's WACC the correct decision? On the other hand, what assumptions must be valid to making discounting the cash flows from the proposed venture at the average WACC of firms in the personal computer industry the correct decision? (LO1, LO5)

19. **Comprehensive.** The total market value of Muskoka Real Estate Company is $6 million and the total value of its debt is $2 million. The treasurer estimates that the beta of the stock is currently 1.5 and that the expected risk premium on the market is 7 percent. The Treasury bill rate is 4 percent.
   a. What is the required rate of return on Muskoka stock? (LO3)
   b. What is the beta of the company's existing portfolio of assets? The debt is perceived to be virtually risk-free. (LO3)
   c. Estimate the weighted-average cost of capital assuming a tax rate of 40 percent. (LO4)
   d. Estimate the discount rate for an expansion of the company's present business. (LO5)
   e. Suppose the company wants to diversify into the manufacture of rose-coloured glasses. The beta of optical manufacturers with no debt outstanding is 1.2. What is the required rate of return on Muskoka's new venture? (LO4)

20. **Integrative.** Big Door Company has 10 million shares outstanding, which are currently trading for about $15 per share and have an equity beta of 1.2. Big Door has 20,000 outstanding bonds, with a 6 percent coupon rate, payable semi-annually and due in 10 years. The bonds are rated BBB. Currently the credit spread for BBB is 150 basis points over equivalent-maturity Government of Canada debt. The current yield on 10-year Canada bonds is 4 percent, compounded semi-annually. The risk-free interest rate is 2.5 percent, and the market risk premium is 6.5 percent. The company has a 35 percent tax rate.
   a. Calculate Big Door's WACC. (LO4)
   b. Calculate Big Door's unlevered beta, using the formula in footnote 6. (LO3)
   c. If Big Door was 50 percent debt-financed, what would be its WACC? Assume that the beta of its debt is unchanged by the capital structure change. (LO4)

21. **Comprehensive.** Two ambitious business graduates, Boris and Isabelle, are considering purchasing Premier Pizza, a frozen pizza manufacturer. Forecasted annual sales for the coming year are $10 million, with operating costs equal to 70 percent of sales, depreciation is 5 percent of sales, the tax rate is 35 percent, and required annual investment in equipment is 5 percent of sales. Sales, costs, and investments are expected to grow 4 percent in perpetuity. On the basis of their analysis of

the industry, Boris and Isabelle anticipate financing their company with 25 percent debt. The required rate of return on the debt will be 6 percent and the required rate of return on the equity will be 15 percent. Premier Pizza's corporate tax rate is 35 percent. The risk-free interest rate is 3 percent and the market risk premium is 7 percent.

a. What is the maximum price Boris and Isabelle should be willing to pay for Premier Pizza? Explain your answer. (LO4, LO6)

b. A national grocery chain, Fresh Foods, is also considering making an offer for Premier Pizza. The levered equity beta of the grocery chain is .8, its cost of debt is 5 percent, it is 40 percent debt-financed, and it has a 35 percent tax rate. What is the maximum price that Fresh Foods should be willing to pay for Premier Pizza? Assume that Fresh Foods's forecast for Premier's cash flows is the same as Boris and Isabelle's. Explain your answer. (LO5, LO6)

CHALLENGE

22. **Expected Cost of Debt.** Risky Business's outstanding debt are 6 percent bonds, paying interest annually and maturing one year from today. The bonds currently sell for $569 per $1,000 par value. The company is experiencing severe financial difficulties and analysts predict that there is a 60 percent probability that the company will go bankrupt within the year. If bankruptcy occurs, bondholders are predicted to receive only 30 percent of the promised cash flow (principal plus coupon).

a. What is the current promised yield to maturity (assuming that bondholders receive all promised)? (LO3)

b. What is the current yield to maturity assuming that default occurs? (LO3)

c. What is the current expected yield to maturity? Explain why the promised yield to maturity is not a good measure of a bond's expected return when the probability of default is not low. (LO3)

23. **Changes in Capital Structure.** Look again at our calculation of Big Oil's WACC. Suppose Big Oil is excused from paying taxes. How would its WACC change? Now suppose Big Oil makes a large stock issue and uses the proceeds to pay off all its debt. How would the cost of equity change? (LO3)

24. **Changes in Capital Structure.** Refer back to problem 23. Suppose Big Oil starts from the financing mix in Table 12.3, and then borrows an additional $200 million from the bank. It then pays out a special $200 million dividend, leaving its assets and operations unchanged. What happens to Big Oil's WACC, still assuming it pays no taxes? What happens to the cost of equity? (LO2, LO3)

25. **WACC and Taxes.** "The after-tax cost of debt is lower when the firm's tax rate is higher; therefore, the WACC falls when the tax rate rises. Thus, with a lower discount rate, the firm must be worth more if its tax rate is higher." Explain why this argument is wrong. (LO6)

26. **Cost of Capital.** An analyst at Dawn Chemical notes that its cost of debt is far below that of equity. He concludes that it is important for the firm to maintain the ability to increase its borrowing because if it cannot borrow, it will be forced to use more expensive equity to finance some projects. This might lead it to reject some projects that would have seemed attractive if evaluated at the lower cost of debt. Comment on this reasoning. (LO5)

27. **Internet.** Use the required rates of return calculated in Chapter 12, problem 25, to estimate the weighted-average cost of capital for the five companies. For their capital structures, go to **finance.yahoo.com**, click on "Key Statistics" and record the "Market Cap," the current market value of equity, and the book value of debt, near the bottom of the page. Estimating the yield on the debt is trickier. If you are lucky, the bonds are rated at **www.moodys.com**, **www.dbrs.com**, or **www.standardandpoors.com**. If you cannot find a debt rating, assume that the debt is BBB-rated. Assume that each company's debt has an average maturity of seven years. Assume that the credit spread (that is, the extra yield over the equivalent-term government bond) for AA-rated debt is 44 basis points, for A-rated debt is 71 basis points, for BBB-rated debt is 125 basis points, and for BB-rated debt is 265 basis points. (One basis point is .01 percentage points.) Add each spread to the current yield on 7-year Government of Canada bonds, found at **www.bankofcanada.ca/rates/interest-rates/canadian-bonds**. Assume that the companies have a 30 percent corporate tax rate. Now calculate the WACCs. (LO4)

Solutions to Check Points

13.1 Hot Rocks' 4 million common shares are worth $40 million.

$$\text{WACC} = (.56 \times 9\%) + (.44 \times 17\%) = 12.5\%$$

We use Hot Rocks' pretax return on debt because the company pays no taxes.

Its market value balance sheet is:

Assets		Liabilities and Shareholders' Equity	
Assets	$90	Debt	$50 (56%)
		Equity	40 (44%)
Value	$90	Value	$90

13.2 Rhodes's 6 million shares are now worth only 6 million $\times$ \$4 = \$24 million. The debt is selling for 80 percent of book, or \$20 million. The market value balance sheet is:

Assets		Liabilities and Shareholders' Equity	
Assets	\$44	Debt	\$20 (45%)
	___	Equity	24 (55%)
Value	\$44	Value	\$44

$$\text{WACC} = (.45 \times 14\%) + (.55 \times 20\%) = 17.3\%$$

Note that this question ignores taxes because the company does not anticipate paying any taxes.

13.3 Compare the two income statements (\$ millions), one for Criss-Cross Industries as it currently is and the other for Criss-Cross with no debt in its capital structure.

	Criss-Cross	Criss-Cross with No Debt
EBIT	\$10.0	\$10.0
Interest expense	2.0	0.0
Taxable income	8.0	10.0
Taxes owed	2.8	3.5
Net income	5.2	6.5
Total income accruing to debt and equity holders	7.2	6.5

Notice that Criss-Cross with no debt pays \$.7 million (= 3.5 million − 2.8 million) more in taxes than it does with debt. Total income accruing to debtholders and shareholders is interest expense and net income, respectively. Accordingly, the total income available to debt and equity holders is \$.7 million higher when Criss-Cross is financed with both debt and equity (7.2 − 6.5).

13.4 For Hot Rocks,

$$\text{WACC} = [.56 \times 9\% \times (1 - .35)] + (.44 \times 17\%) = 10.76\%$$

For Rhodes Construction,

$$\text{WACC} = [.45 \times 14\% \times (1 - .35)] + (.55 \times 20\%) = 15.1\%$$

13.5 WACC measures the expected rate of return demanded by debt and equity investors in the firm (plus a tax adjustment capturing the tax-deductibility of interest payments). Thus the calculation must be based on what investors are actually paying for the firm's debt and equity securities. In other words, it must be based on market values.

13.6 From the CAPM:

$$r_{\text{equity}} = r_f + \beta_{\text{equity}}(r_m - r_f)$$
$$= 6\% + 1.2(7\%) = 14.4\%$$
$$\text{WACC} = .3(1 - .35)8\% + .7(14.4\%) = 11.64\%$$

13.7 Jo Ann's boss is wrong for two reasons. The ability to borrow at 8 percent does not mean that the firm's cost of capital is 8 percent. You can't ignore the shareholders' required rate of return. If the firm undertakes a new investment, it must generate enough cash flow to pay both bondholders' and shareholders' required rates of return; thus, it must earn at least the company's cost of capital. Furthermore, this analysis ignores the side effects of the borrowing—for example, that at the higher indebtedness of the firm the equity will be riskier, and therefore the equityholders will demand a higher rate of return on their investment.

13.8 Using equation 13.12, find Tollbar's asset beta:

$$\beta_{\text{assets}} = \frac{D}{V} \times \beta_{\text{debt}} + \frac{E}{V} \times \beta_{\text{equity}}$$
$$= .2 \times .1 + .8 \times .8 = .66$$

Using equation 13.13, if Tollbar is 50 percent debt-financed, its new equity beta will be

$$\beta_{\text{equity}} = \beta_{\text{assets}} + (\beta_{\text{assets}} - \beta_{\text{debt}})\frac{D}{E}$$
$$= .66 + (.66 - .14)\frac{.5}{.5} = 1.18$$

WACC at original capital structure:

$$r_{\text{debt}} = r_f + \beta_{\text{debt}} \times \text{MRP} = 4\% + .1 \times 7\% = 4.7\%$$
$$r_{\text{equity}} = r_f + \beta_{\text{equity}} \times \text{MRP} = 4\% + .8 \times 7\% = 9.6\%$$
$$\text{WACC} = \frac{D}{V} \times r_{\text{debt}} + \frac{E}{V} \times r_{\text{equity}}$$
$$= .2 \times 4.7\% + .8 \times 9.6\% = 8.62\%$$

WACC at new capital structure:

$$r_{\text{debt}} = r_f + \beta_{\text{debt}} \times \text{MRP}$$
$$= 4\% + .14 \times 7\% = 4.98\%$$
$$r_{\text{equity}} = r_f + \beta_{\text{equity}} \times \text{MRP}$$
$$= 4\% + 1.18 \times 7\% = 12.26\%$$
$$\text{WACC} = \frac{D}{V} \times r_{\text{debt}} + \frac{E}{V} \times r_{\text{equity}}$$
$$= .5 \times 4.98\% + .5 \times 12.26\% = 8.62\%$$

As expected, with no corporate taxes, the WACC of the firm does not change when its capital structure is changed.

13.9 Estimated horizon value for the concatenator business is 9 $\times$ year-5 EBITDA = 9 $\times$ 239 = \$2,151 thousand. PV (horizon value) is \$2,151/(1.085)^5 = \$1,430.5 thousand. Adding in the PV of free cash flows for years 1 to 5 gives a present value for the business of \$1,210.3 thousand.

Bernice Mountaindog was glad to be back at Sea Shore Salt. Employees were treated well. When she had asked a year ago for a leave of absence to complete her degree in finance, top management promptly agreed. When she returned with an honours degree, she was promoted from administrative assistant (she had been secretary to Joe-Bob Brinepool, the president) to treasury analyst.

Bernice thought the company's prospects were good. Sure, table salt was a mature business, but Sea Shore Salt had grown steadily at the expense of its less well-known competitors. The company's brand name was an important advantage, despite the difficulty most customers had in pronouncing it rapidly.

Bernice started work on January 2, 2012. The first two weeks went smoothly. Then Mr. Brinepool's cost of capital memo (see Figure 13.2) assigned her to explain Sea Shore Salt's weighted-average cost of capital to other managers. The assignment came as a surprise to Bernice, so she stayed late to prepare for the questions that would surely come the next day.

Bernice first examined Sea Shore Salt's most recent balance sheet, summarized in Table 13.6. Then she jotted down the following additional points:

- The company's bank charged interest at current market rates, and the long-term debt had just been issued. Book and market values could not differ by much.
- But the preferred stock had been issued 35 years ago, when interest rates were much lower. The preferred stock was now trading for only \$70 per share.
- The common stock traded for \$40 per share. Next year's earnings per share would be about \$4.00 and dividends per share, probably \$2. Sea Shore Salt had traditionally paid out 50 percent of earnings as dividends and plowed back the rest.
- Earnings and dividends had grown steadily at 6 to 7 percent per year, in line with the company's sustainable growth rate:

$$\text{Sustainable growth rate} = \text{return on equity} \times \text{plowback ratio}$$
$$= 4.00/30 \times .5$$
$$= .067, \text{ or } 6.7\%$$

- Sea Shore Salt's beta had averaged about .5, which made sense, Bernice thought, for a stable, steady-growth business. She made a quick cost-of-equity calculation using the capital asset pricing model (CAPM). With current interest rates of about 7 percent, and a market risk premium of 7 percent,

$$\text{CAPM cost of equity} = r_E = r_f + \beta(r_m - r_f)$$
$$= 7\% + .5(7\%) = 10.5\%$$

This cost of equity was significantly less than the 16 percent decreed in Mr. Brinepool's memo. Bernice scanned her notes apprehensively. What if Mr. Brinepool's cost of equity was wrong? Was there some other way to estimate the cost of equity as a check on the CAPM calculation? Could there be other errors in his calculations?

Bernice resolved to complete her analysis that night. If necessary, she would try to speak with Mr. Brinepool when he arrived at his office the next morning. Her job was not just finding the right number. She also had to figure out how to explain it all to Mr. Brinepool.

TABLE 13.6
Sea Shore Salt's balance sheet, taken from the company's 2011 balance sheet (\$ millions).

Assets		Liabilities and Net Worth	
Working capital	\$200	Bank loan	\$120
Plant and equipment	360	Long-term debt	80
Other assets	40	Preferred stock	100
		Common stock, including retained earnings	300
Total	\$600	Total	\$600

Notes:
1. At year-end 2011, Sea Shore Salt had 10 million common shares outstanding.
2. The company had also issued 1 million preferred shares with book value of \$100 per share. Each share receives an annual dividend of \$6.

FIGURE 13.2
Mr. Brinepool's cost of capital memo.

Sea Shore Salt Company
Salt Spring Island, British Columbia

CONFIDENTIAL MEMORANDUM

DATE: January 15, 2012
TO: S.S.S. Management
FROM: Joe-Bob Brinepool, President
SUBJECT: Cost of Capital

This memo states and clarifies our company's long-standing policy regarding hurdle rates for capital investment decisions. There have been many recent questions, and some evident confusion, on this matter.

Sea Shore Salt evaluates replacement and expansion investments by discounted cash flow. The discount or hurdle rate is the company's after-tax weighted-average cost of capital.

The weighted-average cost of capital is simply a blend of the rates of return expected by investors in our company. These investors include banks, bondholders, and preferred stock investors in addition to common shareholders. Of course, many of you are, or soon will be, shareholders of our company.

The following table summarizes the composition of Sea Shore Salt's financing:

	Amount ($ millions)	Percent of Total	Rate of Return (%)
Bank loan	$120	20%	7.75%
Bond issue	80	13.3	8
Preferred stock	100	16.7	6
Common stock	300	50	16
	$600	100%	

The rates of return on the bank loan and bond issue are, of course, just the interest rates we pay. However, interest is tax-deductible, so the after-tax interest rates are lower than shown above. For example, the after-tax cost of our bond financing, given our 35 percent tax rate, is 8(1 − .35) = 5.2 percent.

The rate of return on preferred stock is 6 percent. Sea Shore Salt pays a $6 dividend on each $100 preferred share.

Our target rate of return on equity has been 16 percent for many years. I know that some newcomers think this target is too high for the safe and mature salt business. But we must all aspire to superior profitability.

Once this background is absorbed, the calculation of Sea Shore Salt's weighted-average cost of capital (WACC) is elementary:

$$\text{WACC} = 7.75(1 - .35)(.2) + 8(1 - .35)(.133) + 6(.167) + 16(.50) = 10.7\%$$

The official corporate hurdle rate is therefore 10.7 percent.

If you have further questions about these calculations, please direct them to our new treasury analyst, Bernice Mountaindog. It is a pleasure to have Bernice back at Sea Shore Salt after a year's leave of absence to complete her degree in finance.

PART 4

Financing

4 Introduction to Corporate Financing and Governance

14.1 Creating Value with Financing Decisions

14.2 Common Stock

14.3 Preferred Stock

14.4 Corporate Debt

14.5 Convertible Securities

14.6 Patterns of Corporate Financing

14.7 Summary

Appendix 14A: The Bond Refunding Decision

5 Venture Capital, IPOs, and Seasoned Offerings

CHAPTER 14

Introduction to Corporate Financing and Governance

LEARNING OBJECTIVES

After studying this chapter, you should be able to:

LO1 Explain why managers should assume the securities they issue are fairly priced.

LO2 Describe major sources of information contained in the shareholders' equity account in the firm's financial statements.

LO3 Describe the major classes of securities sold by firms.

LO4 Summarize the changing ways Canadian firms have financed their growth.

There are more than 57 different kinds of securities that a company can issue.

Up to this point we have concentrated almost exclusively on the firm's capital expenditure decisions. Now we move to the other side of the balance sheet to look at how the firm can finance those capital expenditures. To put it crudely, you have learned how to spend money; now you must learn how to raise it. In this chapter and the next, therefore, we assume that the firm has already decided on which investment projects to accept, and we focus on the best way to finance these projects.

You will find that in some ways financing decisions are more complicated than investment decisions. You'll learn about the wide variety of securities that companies can issue and the financial institutions that may buy these securities. But there are also ways in which financing decisions are easier than investment decisions. For example, financing decisions do not have the same degree of finality as investment decisions. When Ford Motor Company decides to issue a bond, it knows that it can buy it back later if second thoughts arise. It would be far more difficult for Ford to dismantle or sell an auto factory that is no longer needed.

In later chapters we will look at some of the classic finance problems, such as how much firms should borrow and what dividends they should pay their shareholders. In this chapter we set the scene with a brief overview of the types of long-term finance.

We begin our discussion of financing with a basic conceptual point. It is easier to make shareholders wealthier through your investment decisions than through your financing decisions. As we explain, competition between investors makes it difficult to find misvalued securities.

We then introduce you to the principal sources of finance and we show how they are used by corporations. It is customary to classify these sources of finance as debt or equity. However, we will see that a simple division of sources of finance into debt and equity would miss the enormous variety of financing instruments that companies use today. For example, Table 14.1 shows the many long-term securities issued by George Weston Ltd. Yet George Weston has not come close to exhausting the menu of possible securities.

TABLE 14.1
Large firms use many different kinds of securities. Look at the variety of securities issued by George Weston Limited Ltd.

Equity	Debt
Common stock	Debentures
Preferred stock	Medium-term notes
Exchangeable debentures	Fixed-rate notes
	Notes payable
	Commercial paper
	Capital lease
	Bank loan
	Independent funding trust loan

Note: You can also retrieve this annual report at **www.sedar.com**. The Web site for the System for Electronic Document Analysis and Retrieval (SEDAR) provides a variety of information including annual reports and proxy forms for most publicly traded Canadian companies.

Source: Adapted from George Weston Limited annual report, 2009.

LO1 **14.1**

CREATING VALUE WITH FINANCING DECISIONS

Smart investment decisions make shareholders wealthier. So do smart financing decisions. For example, if your company can borrow at 3 percent when the going rate is 4 percent, you have done your shareholders a good turn.

Unfortunately, this is more easily said than done. The problem is that competition in financial markets is more intense than in most product markets. In product markets, companies regularly find competitive advantages that allow positive-NPV investments. For example, a company may have only a few competitors that specialize in the same line of business in the same geographical area. Or it may be able to capitalize on patents or technology or on customer recognition and loyalty. All this opens up the opportunity to make superior profits and find projects with positive NPVs.

But there are few protected niches in *financial* markets. You can't patent the design of a new security. Moreover, in these markets you always face fast-moving competition, including all the other corporations seeking funds, to say nothing of the provincial, local, and federal governments, financial institutions, individuals, and foreign firms and governments that also come to Toronto, New York, London, or Tokyo for financing. The investors who supply financing are numerous, and they are savvy. Most likely, these investors can assess values of securities at least as well as you can.

Of course, when you borrow, you would like to pay less than the going rate of interest. But if the loan is a good deal for your shareholders, it must be a bad one for the lenders. So what are the chances your firm might consistently trick investors into overpaying for its securities? In general, firms should assume that the securities they issue sell for their true values.

But what do we mean by *true value*? This is a potentially slippery phrase. True value does not mean ultimate future value—we do not expect investors to be fortune-tellers. It means a price that incorporates all the information *currently* available to investors. We came across this idea in Chapter 7, when we introduced the concept of *efficient capital markets* and showed how difficult it is for investors to obtain consistently superior performance. In an efficient capital market all securities are fairly priced given the information available to investors. In that case the sale of securities at their market price can never be a positive-NPV transaction.

All this means that it's harder to make or lose money by smart or stupid financing strategies. It is difficult to make money—that is, to find cheap financing—because the investors who supply the financing demand fair terms. At the same time, it's harder to lose money because competition among investors prevents any one of them from demanding more than fair terms.

Just remember as you read the following chapters: There are no free lunches on Bay Street and no easy answers for the financial manager who must decide which securities to issue.

LO2 14.2 COMMON STOCK

We will illustrate the characteristics of different securities by looking at how George Weston has financed its capital expenditures.

Most major corporations are far too large to be owned by one investor. For example, you would need to lay your hands on over $20 billion if you wanted to own all of George Weston Ltd. (GW).

GW is owned by 930 different investors, each of whom holds a number of shares of common stock. These investors are therefore known as *shareholders* or *stockholders*. Altogether GW has outstanding about 129 million shares of common stock. Thus, if you were to buy one GW share, you would own 1/129,073,662, or about .0000008 percent of the company. Of course, a large pension fund, such as the Ontario Teachers' Pension Plan, might hold many thousands of GW shares.

issued shares Shares that have been issued by the company.

outstanding shares Shares that have been issued by the company and are held by investors.

authorized share capital Maximum number of shares that the company is permitted to issue as specified in the firm's articles of incorporation.

par value Value of security shown on certificate.

additional paid-in capital Difference between issue price and par value of stock, also called *capital surplus*.

retained earnings Earnings not paid out as dividends.

The 129 million shares held by investors at the end of 2009 represents the number of outstanding or **issued** and **outstanding shares** of GW.[1] If GW wishes to raise more money, it can sell more shares. The maximum number of shares that can be issued is known as the **authorized share capital**; looking at Table 14.2, for GW, this is unlimited. However, many firms set a limit to their authorized share capital, which is specified in the firm's articles of incorporation and can be changed only with the permission of the shareholders. Votes on proposed changes to the *articles of incorporation* occur at shareholders' meetings.

Table 14.2 shows how the investment by GW's shareholders is recorded in the company's books. The value of new shares issued by GW is shown in the common shares account. As of December 31, 2009, this is $133 million. In the past, a company issuing new shares would specify a monetary value, called **par value**, for such shares. The par value was an arbitrarily set number and almost always lower than the actual sale price of the new shares. The difference was recorded as **additional paid-in capital**, *paid-in surplus*, *capital surplus*, or *contributed surplus*. The *Canada Business Corporations Act* has since been changed to stop this practice, and today common shares mostly do not have a par value.[2]

Besides buying new stock, shareholders also indirectly contribute new capital to the firm whenever profits that could be paid out as dividends are instead plowed back into the company. Table 14.2 shows that the cumulative amount of such **retained earnings** is about $6,084 million.

A negative amount of $92 million is shown in Table 14.2 for "Accumulated other comprehensive loss," representing currency translation losses from GW's foreign operations, cash flow hedges, and available-for-sale assets. In this chapter we will ignore foreign exchange accounting and cash flow hedging.

The sum of common shares, retained earnings, and foreign currency translation adjustment gains is known as the *net common equity* of the firm. It equals the total amount contributed

TABLE 14.2 Book value of common stockholders' equity of George Weston Ltd., December 31, 2009 (figures in millions).

Common shares	$133
Retained earnings	6,084
Accumulated other comprehensive loss	(92)
Net common equity	6,125
Note:	
Authorized shares	Unlimited
Issued shares	129

Source: Adapted from George Weston Limited annual report, 2009, retrieved December 27, 2010.

[1] Of course, only about 48 million of these common shares are available for public trading. The remaining shares are closely held.

[2] The practice of setting par value and using the additional paid-in capital account is still followed in the United States.

directly by common shareholders when the firm issued new stock, and indirectly, when it plowed back part of its earnings.

During 2009, GW did not repurchase any of its shares although it had done so in the past.[3] For instance, in 2003 GW had repurchased a little over 2.8 million of its shares. In the United States, when a company repurchases some of its shares, it can continue to hold them as its own stock. These shares would appear in the balance sheet as treasury stock. In Canada treasury stock is not allowed. Instead, any shares repurchased must be cancelled. This is done by reducing the company's net equity account to the extent of the amount paid for any shares repurchased.[4] The common shares account is reduced by the average issue price. Any amount in excess of the average issue price is subtracted from retained earnings or, sometimes, from the paid-in surplus account. For example, suppose 1,000 shares are repurchased for $30 per share and the average issue price was $25 per share. To cancel the repurchased shares, the overall net equity account is reduced by $30 × $1,000 = $30,000. This comprises a reduction to the common shares account by $25 × $1,000 = $25,000 and a reduction to retained earnings by the remaining $5,000. In 2003, the repurchase of the 2.8 million shares cost GW $275 million. It cancelled these shares by charging $2 million to its common shares account and about $273 million to its retained earnings account.

Check Point 14.1

Generic Products has had one stock issue in which it sold 100,000 shares to the public at $15 per share. Can you fill in the following table?

Common shares	______
Retained earnings	______
Common equity	$3,000,000

Book value is a backward-looking measure. It tells us how much capital the firm has raised from shareholders in the past. It does not measure the value that investors put on those shares today. The market value of the firm is forward-looking; it depends on the future dividends that shareholders expect to receive.

BOOK VALUE VERSUS MARKET VALUE

We discussed the distinction between book and market value in Chapters 3 and 7, but it bears repeating.

GW's common equity has a book value of $6,125 million. With 129 million shares outstanding, this translates to a book value of $6,125/129 million = $47.48 per share. But on December 31, 2009, GW shares were priced at about $66.92 each. So the total *market* value of the common stock was 129 million shares × $66.92 per share = $8,633 million, nearly 141 percent more than the book value.

Market value is usually greater than book value. This is partly because inflation has driven the value of many assets above what they originally cost. Also, firms raise capital to invest in projects with present values that exceed initial cost. These positive-NPV projects make the shareholders better off. So we would expect the market value of the firm to be higher than the amount of money put up by the shareholders.

However, sometimes projects do go awry and companies fall on hard times. In this case, market value can fall below book value.

Check Point 14.2

No-Name News can be established by investing $10 million in a printing press. The newspaper is expected to generate a cash flow of $2 million a year for 20 years. If the cost of capital is 10 percent, is the firm's market or book value greater? What if the cost of capital is 20 percent?

[3] We will look into why companies repurchase their shares in Chapter 17.

[4] For this reason, in Canada, the number of shares issued always equals the number outstanding.

DIVIDENDS

Shareholders hope to receive a series of dividends on their investment. However, the company is not obliged to pay any dividends and the decision is up to the board of directors. In Chapter 17, we will discuss how that decision affects the value of the stock.

Because dividends are discretionary, they are not considered to be a business expense. Therefore, companies are not allowed to deduct dividend payments when they calculate their taxable income.

OWNERSHIP OF THE CORPORATION

A corporation is owned by its common shareholders. While a large proportion of stock is held directly by individual investors and unincorporated businesses, as we saw in Chapter 2, insurance companies, trusteed pension plans, mutual funds, and banks also have sizable investments in shares.

What do we mean when we say that the shareholders *own* the corporation? First, the shareholders are entitled to whatever profits are left over after the lenders have received their entitlement. Usually the company pays out part of these profits as dividends and plows back the remainder into new investments. Shareholders hope that these investments will enable the company to earn higher profits and pay higher dividends in the future.

Second, shareholders have control of the company's affairs. Occasionally companies need shareholder approval before they can take certain actions. For example, they need approval to increase the authorized capital or to merge with another company.

On most other matters, shareholder control boils down to the right to vote on appointments to the board of directors.

The board usually consists of the company's top management as well as *non-executive directors*, who are not employed by the firm. In principle, the board is elected as an agent of the shareholders. It appoints and oversees the management of the firm and meets to vote on such matters as new share issues. Most of the time the board will go along with management, but in crisis situations it can be very independent. For example, when management of RJR Nabisco, the giant American tobacco and food company, announced that it wanted to take over the company, the outside directors stepped in to make sure that the company was sold to the highest bidder. When serious accounting and managerial irregularities were found with Livent, the Toronto-based production company, which had staged such hits as *Phantom of the Opera*, its board of directors fired the company's two co-founders and also filed a multimillion-dollar civil suit against them. Chicago-based Hollinger International filed a US$1.25 billion lawsuit against its former chairman and CEO as well as its former chief operating officer for improperly taking millions of dollars in management fees and other payments from the company. Unfortunately, many of the recent corporate scandals have occurred in companies in which boards have not been sufficiently independent but have instead acquiesced to errant management decisions.

VOTING PROCEDURES

majority voting Voting system in which each director is voted on separately.

cumulative voting Voting system in which all the votes one shareholder is allowed to cast can be cast for one candidate for the board of directors.

In most companies shareholders elect directors by a system of **majority voting**. In this case each director is voted on separately, and shareholders can cast one vote for each share they own. In some companies directors are elected by **cumulative voting**. The directors are then voted on jointly and the shareholders can, if they choose, cast all their votes for just one candidate. For example, suppose there are five directors to be elected and you own 100 shares. You therefore have a total of $5 \times 100 = 500$ votes. Under majority voting you can cast a maximum of 100 votes for any one candidate. With a cumulative voting system, you can cast all 500 votes for your favourite candidate. Cumulative voting makes it easier for a minority group of the shareholders to elect a director to represent their interests. That is why minority groups devote so much effort to campaigning for cumulative voting.

On many issues, a simple majority of the votes cast is enough to carry the day, but some decisions require a "supermajority" of between two-thirds and 80 percent of those eligible to vote. For example, a supermajority vote of two-thirds of the shareholders of record is usually needed to approve a merger. This requirement makes it difficult for the firm to be taken over and therefore helps to protect the incumbent management.

proxy contest Takeover attempt in which outsiders compete with management for shareholders' votes.

Shareholders can either vote in person or appoint a proxy to vote. The issues on which they are asked to vote are rarely contested, particularly in the case of large, publicly traded firms. Occasionally, however, there are **proxy contests** in which outsiders compete with the firm's existing management and directors for control of the corporation. But the cards are stacked against the outsiders, because the insiders can get the firm to pay all the costs of presenting their case and obtaining votes.

In some special situations involving important corporate decisions such as mergers, or selling the firm's assets, the votes of most of the minority shareholders must be received. For example, the Ontario Securities Commission has introduced regulations intended to give the minority shareholders the opportunity to prevent majority shareholders and management from making deals that reduce the value of the minority shareholders' shares. Sometimes powerful minority shareholders can successfully prevent takeover decisions made by the company's management or majority shareholders.

In 2000, a deal valued at $5.7 billion was struck to sell the Montréal-based cable company Groupe Videotron Ltée to Rogers Communications, Inc., of Toronto. The powerful Caisse de dépôt et placement du Québec, Canada's biggest pension fund manager, which held a 10 percent minority voting stake in Videotron, opposed the deal, because it wanted Videotron to remain in Québec. Caisse de dépôt broke ranks with the Chagnon family, which had built Videotron into Québec's largest cable operator and held 71 percent of its votes. Instead, Caisse de dépôt engineered a competing bid with Montréal-based printing and publishing giant Quebecor, Inc., worth $5.9 billion. Videotron was eventually acquired by Quebecor.

CLASSES OF STOCK

Many companies issue just one class of common stock. Sometimes, however, a firm may have two or more classes outstanding, which differ in their right to vote or receive dividends.[5] Suppose that a firm needs fresh capital but its present shareholders do not want to give up control of the firm. The existing shares could be labelled Class A, and then Class B shares could be issued to outside investors. The Class B shares could have limited voting rights, although they would probably sell for less as a result.

For instance, in January 2010, Bombardier had listed about 316 million Class A shares and over 1,438 million Class B shares on the Toronto Stock Exchange. The Class A shares carry 10 votes per share, whereas the Class B shares carry only one. The Bombardier family controlled, through holding companies, over 78 percent of the Class A shares, or about 54 percent of the total voting rights.

Common shares without full voting rights are called *restricted shares*. There are various types of restricted shares. If the restricted shares have no votes, they are called *non-voting*. If the restricted shares have fewer votes per share than another class of common shares, they are called *subordinate voting*. You can also own *limited voting* shares that also carry fewer voting rights relative to another class of common shares. As of February 2009, 95 different classes of restricted shares were trading on the TSX. These included 35 non-voting shares, 50 subordinate-voting shares, 4 limited-voting shares, 2 restricted-voting shares, and 4 variable-voting shares. The class of any given share is denoted by abbreviations: *nv* stands for non-voting, *sv* subordinate-voting, *lv* limited-voting, and *rv* restricted-voting. In addition to Bombardier, other large Canadian companies, such as Canadian Tire, Power Corporation, Quebecor, Inc., and Magna International, have also issued restricted-voting shares. For instance, Canadian Tire has issued non-voting shares, and Power Corporation subordinate-voting shares. Table 14.3 shows some large multivoting-share Canadian companies. From Table 14.3, notice that Rogers Communication Inc.'s Class A shares carry 50 votes per share. Only shareholders holding this category of shares are eligible to vote. The company also has a large number of Class B non-voting shares. Similarly, only the common

[5] In the United States, most companies issue one class of common stock and follow the practice of "one share, one vote."

TABLE 14.3 Some large multivoting share companies in Canada in 2008.

	Other Share Class	Votes per Share	Major Shareholder	% of Total Shares	% of Total Votes
Power Corp. of Canada	Partic. Pref.	10	Paul Desmarais	26.4	62.2
Onex Corp.	Multiple	60%*	Gerald W. Schwartz	20.3	68.1
Magna International Inc.	Class B	300	M. Unicar Inc.†	1.2	66.3
Bombardier Inc.	Class A	10	Bombardier family	14.3	54.1
Alimentation Couche-Tard Inc.	Multiple	10	Dev. Orano; Metro Inc.	25.8	66.8
Empire Co. Ltd.	Class B	1	Sobey family	51.7	88.1
Rogers Communications Inc.	Class A	50	Rogers family	16.3	90.9
Canadian Tire Corp. Ltd.	Common	1	Martha and Owen Billes	2.6	61.4
Fairfax Financial Holdings Ltd.	Multiple	10	V. Prem Watsa	10.2	48.2
Teck Cominco Ltd.	Class A	100	Sumitomo; Keevil; Caisse	1.8	53.2

*Multiple-voting shares hold 60% of aggregate votes.
†Owned by Stronach Trust (92.4%) and five Magna executives (7.6%).

Source: Excerpted from *Financial Post Magazine*, June 2009 (FP500), 76, retrieved January 3, 2010. Material reprinted with the express permission of National Post, a division of Postmedia Network Inc.

shares at Canadian Tire carry voting rights—albeit at one vote per share—although the company has a large issue of non-voting Class A shares outstanding.[6]

Canadian securities regulators are also making it more difficult for a firm to convert an existing common share class into two share classes with different voting rights. In order to convert, most of the minority shareholders must approve. Also, the stock exchanges will not list a new class of non-voting or subordinate voting shares unless the shares have the right to participate in takeover bids. This right is called a *coattail provision*.

The following example illustrates how coattail provisions may be valuable.[7] In 1986 a group of independent dealers from Canadian Tire stores offered to purchase 49 percent of Canadian Tire common (voting) shares for $160.24 each, which were then trading at $40, while making no offer for the Class A non-voting stock, which traded at about $14.50. This offer, if accepted, would give them control of the firm, since they already owned about 17 percent of the voting stock. However, the Class A non-voting stock had a coattail provision in place, which stated that in the event of a bid for all or substantially all of the voting common shares, the Class A shareholders would be entitled to tender their shares to the bidder as well. The Class A non-voting shareholders felt that a bid for 49 percent of the common stock meant "substantially all" of the voting shares, so the coattail provision should be triggered. Therefore, they took the view that they should also be allowed to sell their shares for $160.24 per share. The Ontario Securities Commission disallowed the transaction after a hearing. Their decision, in favour of the Class A non-voting shareholders, was later upheld by the court and the takeover bid was withdrawn.

CORPORATE GOVERNANCE IN CANADA AND ELSEWHERE

In many large corporations, shareholders own the company but they don't manage it. For instance, the large international gold mining company, Barrick Gold Corporation is owned by 19,830 different shareholders. Management is delegated to a team of professional managers. Each shareholder owns only a small fraction of Barrick Gold's shares and can exert little

---

[6] For two interesting studies on dual class shares, see Brian Smith and Ben Amoako-Adu, "Relative Prices of Dual Class Shares," *Journal of Financial and Quantitative Analysis* 30(2) (June 1995): 223–239, and Ben Amoako-Adu and Brian Smith, "Dual Class Firms: Capitalization, Ownership Structure, and Recapitalization Back into Single Class," *Journal of Banking and Finance*, June 2001: 1083–1111.

[7] See also E. Maynes, C. Robinson, and A. White, "How Much Is a Share Vote Worth," *Canadian Investment Review* III (Spring 1990): 49–55.

influence on the way the company is run. If shareholders do not like the policies the management team pursues, they can try to vote in another board of directors who will bring about a change in policy. But such attempts are rarely successful and the shareholders' simplest solution is to sell the shares.

The separation between ownership and management in major Canadian corporations creates a potential conflict between shareholders (the principals who own the company) and managers (their agents who make the decisions). We noted in Chapter 1 several mechanisms that have evolved to mitigate this conflict:

- Shareholders elect a board of directors, which then appoints the managers, oversees them, and, on occasion, fires them.
- Managers' remuneration is tied to their performance.
- Poorly performing companies are taken over and the management is replaced by a new team.[8]

These mechanisms work only when there is sufficient transparency that outsiders can judge how well the company is performing. Unfortunately, dishonest managers with creamy option packages may seek to hide the truth from investors. When investors eventually learn the true state of affairs, there can be big trouble. Consider, for example, the case of the telecom giant, WorldCom. Bernie Ebbers, its CEO of Canadian origin, was on a generous compensation package that earned him US$10 million in bonuses in 2001. Ebbers also owned 17 million shares of WorldCom stock and 8.3 million options, and therefore had a strong incentive to ensure that the company performed well. Unfortunately, he also had a strong incentive to pump up the price of the stock when the company was not performing so well. In 2002 it emerged that WorldCom had overstated its income over a 3-year period by US$11 billion and in the meantime had piled up US$41 billion of debt. When the company's true profitability was discovered, it was bankrupt within a month—the largest U.S. bankruptcy ever.

WorldCom has had plenty of company in recent years. In October and November 2001 Enron revealed that it had overstated its earnings by more than US$1 billion and had hidden more than US$8 billion of debt. By year-end it had become the second-largest bankruptcy ever. In Canada, Nortel Networks came under scrutiny for overstating profits. Elsewhere, the Italian food processor Parmalat revealed that billions of dollars in assets had simply gone missing, while in Holland the supermarket group Ahold confessed to heavily overstating its profits.

Such scandals led the U.S. Congress to pass the *Sarbanes-Oxley Act*, which aims to ensure that companies and their accountants provide directors, lenders, and shareholders with the information that they need to monitor progress. Among other things, the act set up the Public Company Accounting Oversight Board to oversee auditors; banned accounting firms from offering other services to companies whose accounts they audit; prohibited any individual from heading a firm's audit for more than five years; and required that the board's audit committee consist of directors who are independent of the company's management. *Sarbanes-Oxley* also required that management (1) certify that the financial statements present a fair view of the firm's financial position and (2) demonstrate that the firm has adequate controls and procedures for financial reporting. All this comes at a price. For example, the CEO of Tennant Company, a midsized producer of cleaning products, estimated that complying with the act has led to a doubling of audit fees and added nearly US$1 million of other costs.

A few years ago, Ontario introduced legislation to improve corporate governance and disclosure practices under an enactment popularly known as Bill C-198 or "Canada's *Sarbanes-Oxley*."[9]

---

[8] Lately, corporate governance has been a popular theme of study among academic researchers, particularly in the United States. A recent study of large Canadian firms finds little evidence of a relationship between corporate governance and firm performance, and indeed between performance and CEO pay, which appears to be associated more with firm size. See V. Jog and S. Dutta, "Searching for the Governance Trail: Is There a Link Between the Quality of Corporate Governance and a Firm's Performance or CEO Compensation?" *Canadian Investment Review* 17(1) (Spring 2004): 33–43.

[9] Actually the omnibus bill introduced by the Ontario government was titled *Keeping the Promise for a Strong Economy Act (Budget Measures), 2002*.

situation, the company may not pay dividends on common shares or redeem any preferred shares until all arrears are paid. If, on the other hand, a preferred share is *non-cumulative* then the investor is entitled to payment of a dividend only if the board of directors declares a dividend. Arrears do not accrue on non-cumulative preferred shares.

Like common stock, preferred stock usually does not have a final repayment. However, a sizable number of issues tend to be *redeemable*. This means the company has the right to acquire the shares at a set amount known as the *call price*. GW's preferred shares are redeemable at $26 per share. Sometimes, preferred shares can also be *retractable*, in which case the investor can force the company to buy back the share at a specified date.

Some preferred shares are *convertible*, which means that the shares can be converted into another class of shares—usually common shares—at a predetermined price (the exercise price) and for a certain period of time. For example, Loblaw Companies has issued non-voting second preferred shares, Series A, which will be convertible into a specified number of common shares on or after July 31, 2013. To discourage investors from simply buying convertible preferred shares and immediately converting them, such shares usually trade at a premium. Investors like the convertibility option especially when the company's common stock has the potential for price appreciation, since investors will want to convert if the price of the common shares rises above the exercise price.

How do you tell whether a share is common or preferred? This is fairly easy to do, because usually the stock symbols for preferred shares will have a special extension. For example, when preferred shares are listed on the TSX, the stock symbol ends in ".PR."

Preferred stock rarely confers full voting privileges. This is an advantage to firms that want to raise new money without sharing control of the firm with the new shareholders. However, if there is any matter that affects their place in the queue, preferred shareholders usually get to vote on it. Most issues also provide the holder with some voting power if the preferred dividend is skipped.

Companies cannot deduct preferred dividends when they calculate taxable income. However, dividend income is generally not taxed when received by Canadian corporations, and is taxed at reduced rates when received by individuals who are eligible to a dividend tax credit.[11] Thus, in Canada, corporations tend to invest more in preferred shares than individual investors. Firms paying little or no tax could have a tax-based incentive to issue preferred shares rather than debt. For example, suppose XYZ Company pays no tax. The company wishes to obtain financing from a bank that has offered it a loan at an 8 percent annual interest rate. If the bank's marginal tax rate is 35 percent, after paying tax on the interest the bank will receive a net return of $(1 - .35) \times 8\% = 5.2$ percent. The bank can earn the same return by buying XYZ's preferred shares with a dividend yield of 5.2 percent, since the bank pays no tax on the preferred share dividends. Now consider XYZ's point of view. The company cannot use the interest deduction from the bank loan to reduce its tax since it pays no tax, so its before- and after-tax costs of the bank loan are 8 percent. On the other hand, if it sells preferred shares with a 5.2 percent dividend yield, it has reduced its cost of funds from 8 percent to 5.2 percent. It is much cheaper for XYZ to raise the needed money by selling preferred shares than by borrowing.

The Government of Canada has made it more difficult for banks to buy preferred stock from other corporations. For instance, in 1987, the federal government introduced measures to reduce the tax loophole by requiring issuers of preferred shares to pay a 40 percent tax on preferred dividends.[12] The tax is refunded if the issuer is taxable.

Individual U.S. investors do not have the dividend tax credit of Canadian investors, and must pay the full personal tax on dividend income. U.S. corporations enjoy some tax relief on dividend income. If one corporation buys another's stock, only 30 percent of the dividends it receives are

---

[11] We discussed this issue in Chapter 3 and will also discuss it later in Chapter 18.

[12] See I. Fooladi, P.A. McGraw, and G.S. Roberts, "Preferred Share Rule Freezes Out the Individual Investor," *CA Magazine*, April 11, 1988, 38–41.

taxed. This rule applies to both common and preferred stock; but it is most important for preferred, for which returns are dominated by dividends rather than capital gains. Also, regulated American public utilities, which can take tax payments into account when negotiating the rates they charge to customers, can effectively pass the tax disadvantage of preferred stock on to the consumer. As a result, a large fraction of the dollar value of American offerings of non-convertible preferred stock consists of issues by utilities. Overall, preferred share financing is used less in the United States than in Canada, due to lower tax incentives.

If you invest your firm's spare cash in a preferred stock, you will want to make sure that when it is time to sell the stock it won't have plummeted in value. One problem with garden-variety preferred stock that pays a fixed dividend is that the preferreds' market prices go up and down as interest rates change (because present values fall when rates rise). So one ingenious banker had an idea: Why not link the dividend on the preferred stock to interest rates so that it goes up when interest rates rise, and vice versa? The result is known as floating-rate preferred. If you own **floating-rate preferred**, the dividend rate could be tied to the prime rate of interest. You know that any change in interest rates will be counterbalanced by a change in the dividend payment, so the value of your investment is protected. For instance, Bombardier's Series 2 preferred shares carry floating dividend rates.

floating-rate preferred Preferred stock paying dividends that vary with short-term interest rates.

Check Point 14.4

A company in a 35 percent tax bracket can buy a bond yielding 10 percent or a preferred stock of the same firm priced to yield 8 percent. Which will provide the higher after-tax yield? What if the purchaser is a private individual in a 35 percent tax bracket? The dividend on preferred stock would receive a tax credit of 18.97 percent after being grossed up by 45 percent.

LO3 14.4 CORPORATE DEBT

When companies borrow money, they promise to make regular interest payments and to repay the principal (that is, the original amount borrowed). However, corporations have limited liability. By this we mean that the promise to repay the debt is not always kept. If the company gets into deep water, the company has the right to default on the debt and hand over the company's assets to the lenders.

> Corporations have limited liability. By this we mean that the promise to repay the debt is not always kept. If the company gets into deep water, the company has the right to default on the debt and hand over the company's assets to the lenders.

Clearly the company will choose bankruptcy only if the value of the assets is less than the amount of the debt. In practice, when companies go bankrupt, this handover of assets is far from straightforward. For example, when Eaton's, the venerated department store, went into bankruptcy, there were a large number of creditors all jostling for a place in the queue. Some fashion companies reportedly sent their employees to the store locations to seize their merchandise. Sorting out these problems is left to the bankruptcy court.

Because lenders are not regarded as owners of the firm, they don't normally have any voting power. Also, the company's payments of interest are regarded as a cost and are therefore deducted from taxable income. Thus interest is paid out of *before-tax* income, whereas dividends on common and preferred stock are paid out of *after-tax* income. This means that the government provides a tax subsidy on the use of debt which it does not provide on stock.

DEBT COMES IN MANY FORMS

An orderly scheme of classification is essential to cope with the almost endless variety of debt issues. We will walk you through the major distinguishing characteristics.

Interest Rate The interest payment, or *coupon*, on most long-term loans is fixed at the time of issue. If a $1,000 bond is issued with a coupon of 10 percent, the firm continues to pay $100 a year regardless of how interest rates change. As we pointed out in Chapters 5 and 6, you sometimes encounter zero-coupon bonds. In this case the firm does not make a regular interest payment. It just makes a single payment at maturity. Obviously, investors pay less for zero-coupon bonds.

prime rate Benchmark interest rate charged by banks.

Most loans from a bank and some long-term loans carry a *floating interest rate*. For example, your firm may be offered a loan at "1 percent over prime." The **prime rate** is the benchmark interest rate charged by banks to large customers with good to excellent credit. (But the largest and most creditworthy corporations can, and do, borrow at less than prime.) The prime rate is adjusted up and down with the general level of interest rates. When the prime rate changes, the interest on your floating-rate loan also changes.

Floating-rate loans are not always tied to the prime rate. Often they are tied to the rate at which international banks lend to one another. This is known as the *London Interbank Offered Rate*, or *LIBOR*.

Check Point 14.5

Would you expect the price of a 10-year floating-rate bond to be more or less sensitive to changes in interest rates than the price of a 10-year maturity fixed-rate bond?

funded debt Debt with more than one year remaining to maturity.

Maturity **Funded debt** is any debt repayable more than one year from the date of issue. Debt due in less than a year is termed *unfunded* and is carried on the balance sheet as a current liability. Short-term debt is often described as unfunded debt, and long-term debt is described as funded, although it is clearly artificial to call a 364-day debt short-term and a 366-day debt long-term.

There are corporate bonds of nearly every conceivable maturity. For example, Bristol-Myers Squibb has issued bonds that do not mature until 2097. Before it broke up into separately traded companies, Canadian Pacific Railway had issued perpetual debentures—that is, bonds that may survive forever. Of course, the survival of the debentures depended on the survival of the company. At the other extreme we find firms borrowing literally overnight.

sinking fund Fund established to retire debt before maturity.

Repayment Provisions Long-term loans are commonly repaid in a steady regular way, perhaps after an initial grace period. For bonds that are publicly traded, this is done by means of a **sinking fund**. Every year the firm puts aside a sum of cash into a sinking fund that is then used to buy back the bonds. When there is a sinking fund, investors are prepared to lend at a lower rate of interest. They know that they are more likely to be repaid if the company sets aside cash every year than if the entire loan has to be repaid on a specific day.

callable bond Bond that may be repurchased by the firm before maturity at a specified call price.

Suppose that a company issues a 6 percent, 30-year bond at a price of $1,000. Five years later interest rates have fallen to 4 percent, and the price of the bond has risen dramatically. If you were the company's treasurer, wouldn't you like to be able to retire the bonds and issue some new bonds at the lower interest rate? Well, with some bonds, known as **callable bonds**, the company does have the option to buy them back for the *call price*.[13] Of course, holders of these callable bonds know that the company will wish to buy the issue back if interest rates fall, and therefore the price of the bond will not rise above the call price.

Figure 14.1 shows the risk of a call to the bondholder. The purple line is the value of a 30-year, 6.5 percent "straight," that is, non-callable, bond; the orange line is the value of a bond with the same coupon rate and maturity but callable at $1,060 (that is, 106 percent of face value). At very high interest rates, the risk that the company will call the bonds is negligible, and the values of the two bonds are nearly identical. As rates fall, the straight bond continues to increase steadily in value, but since the capital appreciation of the callable bond is limited by the call price, its capital appreciation will lag behind that of the straight bond.

[13] Sometimes callable bonds specify a period during which the firm is not allowed to call the bond if the purpose is simply to issue another bond at a lower interest rate.

FIGURE 14.1
Prices of callable versus straight debt. When interest rates fall, bond prices rise. But the price of the callable bond (orange line) is limited by the call price.

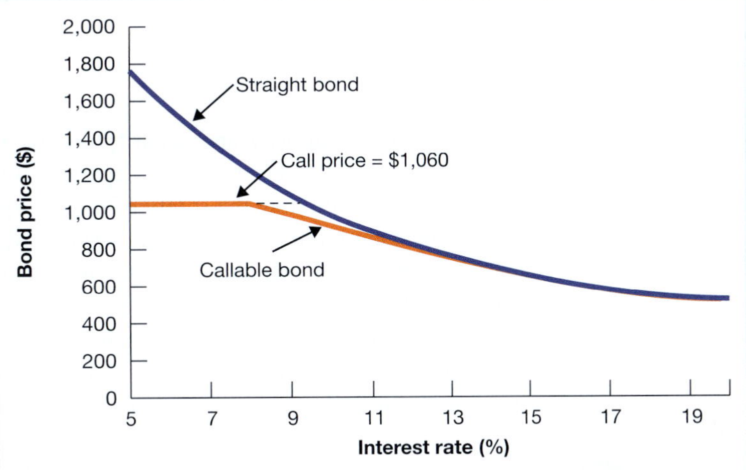

A callable bond gives the *company* the option to retire the bonds early. The price at which the firm can call the bonds is set at the time that the bonds are issued. Call provisions usually come into effect after several years have elapsed since the bond issue. For instance, a bond issue may stipulate that it remain *call-protected* during its first five years, in which case, the company may not issue a call during this time frame.

This option to call the bond is attractive to the issuer. If interest rates decline and bond prices rise, the issuer may repay the bonds at the specified call price and borrow the money back at a lower rate of interest. This would be a bond **refunding** decision by the company and would be made by looking at present values of the costs associated with calling the existing bond and the benefits associated with lower coupon payments on the new bond. The analysis would be conducted using a net present value framework. We will discuss the bond refunding decision later in Appendix 14A.

refunding Replacing an old bond issue with a new one by the firm. Often done when interest rates decline, and the firm can save on the interest cost of the new issue.

Some bonds give the *investor* the right to demand early repayment. During the 1990s many loans to Asian companies gave the lenders a repayment option. Consequently, when the Asian crisis struck in 1997, these companies were faced by a flood of lenders demanding their money back. Needless to say, companies already struggling to survive did not appreciate this additional burden.

Check Point 14.6

Suppose GW is considering two issues of 20-year maturity coupon bonds; one issue will be callable, the other not. For a given coupon rate, will the callable or non-callable bond sell at the higher price? If both the bonds are to be sold to the public at par value, which bond must have the higher coupon rate?

subordinated debt Debt that may be repaid in bankruptcy only after senior debt is paid.

Seniority Some debts are **subordinated**. In the event of default, the subordinated lender has to get in line behind the firm's general creditors; it holds a junior claim and is paid only after all senior creditors are satisfied.

When you lend money to a firm, you may assume you hold a senior claim unless the debt agreement says otherwise. However, this does not always put you at the front of the line, because the firm may have set aside some of its assets specifically for the protection of other lenders. This brings us to our next classification.

Security When you borrow to buy your home, the bank or trust company will take out a mortgage on the house. The mortgage acts as security for the loan. If you default on the loan payments, the bank can seize your home.

secured debt Debt that has first claim on specified collateral in the event of default.

When companies borrow, they also may set aside certain assets as security for the loan. These assets are termed *collateral* and the debt is said to be **secured**. In the event of default, the secured lender has first claim on the collateral; unsecured lenders have a general claim on the rest of the firm's assets but only a junior claim on the collateral.

Default Risk Seniority and security do not guarantee payment. A debt can be senior and secured but still extremely risky—it depends on the value and the risk of the firm's assets. In Chapter 6 we showed how the safety of most corporate bonds can be judged from bond ratings provided by Dominion Bond Rating Service, Moody's, and Standard & Poor's. Bonds rated AAA, or triple-A, seldom default. At the other extreme, many speculative-grade bonds (or junk bonds) may be teetering on the brink.

As you would expect, investors demand a high return from low-rated bonds. We saw evidence of this in Chapter 6, where Figure 6.9 showed yields on Canadian long-term bonds. The lower-rated bonds did, in fact, offer higher promised yields to maturity.

Country and Currency These days capital markets know few national boundaries and many large firms, in particular, those with sizable foreign operations, borrow abroad. For example, a Canadian company may choose to finance a new plant in Switzerland by borrowing Swiss francs from a Swiss bank, or it may expand its Dutch operation by issuing a bond in Holland.

eurodollars Dollars held on deposit in a bank outside the United States.

In addition to these national capital markets, there is also an international capital market centred mainly in London. There are about 500 banks in London from over 70 different countries, which include such giants as Citicorp, UBS, BNP Paribas, Deutsche Bank, Bank of Tokyo–Mitsubishi, and HSBC. One reason they are there is to collect deposits in the major currencies. For example, suppose an Arab sheikh has just received payment in dollars for a large sale of oil to the United States. Rather than depositing the cheque in the United States, he may choose to open a U.S. dollar account with a bank in London. Dollars held in a bank outside the United States came to be known as **eurodollars**. Similarly, yen held outside Japan were termed *euroyen*, and so on. When the new European currency was named the *euro*, the term *eurodollars* became confusing. Doubtless, in time, bankers will dream up a new name for dollars held outside the United States; until they do, we'll just call them *international dollars*.

The London bank branch holding the sheikh's U.S. dollar deposit may temporarily lend those dollars to a company in the same way that a bank in the United States may re-lend U.S. dollars that have been deposited with it. Thus, a company can either borrow U.S. dollars from a bank in the United States or borrow U.S. dollars from a bank in London.[14]

eurobond Bond that is denominated in the currency of one country but issued to investors in other countries.

If a firm wants to make an issue of long-term bonds, it can choose to do so in Canada. Alternatively, it can sell the bonds to investors in several countries. These bonds have traditionally been known as **eurobonds**, but *international bonds* may be a less misleading term. Although these bonds are sold to investors in different countries, they are typically denominated in the currency of the issuer. For example, a Canadian company could issue bonds denominated in Canadian dollars to investors in other countries. The payments on these bonds may be fixed in dollars, euros, or any other major currency. Companies usually sell these bonds to the London branches of the major international banks, which then resell them to investors throughout the world.

foreign bond Bond issued in the currency of its country but the borrower is from another country.

Sometimes companies may issue **foreign bonds**, which are issued in another country and denominated in the currency of that country. For instance, Alcan has long-term debt issues in several different currencies including US dollars, Swiss francs, and euros.

private placement Sale of securities to a limited number of investors without a public offering.

Public Versus Private Placements Publicly issued bonds are sold to anyone who wishes to buy, and once they have been issued, they can be freely traded in the securities markets. In a **private placement**, the issue is sold directly to a small number of banks, insurance companies,

[14] Because the Federal Reserve requires banks in the United States to keep interest-free reserves, there is a tax on U.S. dollar deposits in the United States. Such deposits made overseas are free of this tax, and therefore banks can afford to charge the borrower slightly lower interest rates.

Finance in Action

Marriott Plan Enrages Holders of Its Bonds

Marriott Corp. has infuriated bond investors with a restructuring plan that may be a new way for companies to pull the rug out from under bondholders.

Prices of Marriott's existing bonds have plunged as much as 30 percent in the past two days in the wake of the hotel and food-services company's announcement that it plans to separate into two companies, one burdened with virtually all of Marriott's debt.

On Monday, Marriott said that it will divide its operations into two separate businesses. One, Marriott International, Inc., is a healthy company that will manage Marriott's vast hotel chain; it will get most of the old company's revenue, a larger share of the cash flow and will be nearly debt-free.

The second business, called Host Marriott Corp., is a debt-laden company that will own Marriott hotels along with other real estate and retain essentially all of the old Marriott's $3 billion of debt.

The announcement stunned and infuriated bondholders, who watched nervously as the value of their Marriott bonds tumbled and as Moody's Investors Service, Inc., downgraded the bond to the junk-bond category from investment grade.

Price Plunge

In trading, Marriott's 10 percent bonds that mature in 2012, which Marriott sold to investors just six months ago, were quoted yesterday at about $.80 on the dollar, down from $1.10 Friday. The price decline translates into a stunning loss of $300 for a bond with a $1,000 face amount.

Marriott officials concede that the company's spinoff plan penalizes bondholders. However, the company notes that, like all public corporations, its fiduciary duty is to stockholders not bondholders. Indeed, Marriott's stock jumped 12 percent Monday. (It fell a bit yesterday.)

Bond investors and analysts worry that if the Marriott spinoff goes through, other companies will soon follow suit by separating debt-laden units from the rest of the company. "Any company that fears it has underperforming divisions that are dragging down its stock price is a possible candidate" for such a restructuring, says Dorothy K. Lee, an assistant vice president at Moody's.

If the trend heats up, investors said, the Marriott restructuring could be the worst news for corporate bondholders since RJR Nabisco, Inc.'s managers shocked investors in 1987 by announcing they were taking the company private in a record $25 billion leveraged buy-out. The move, which loaded RJR with debt and tanked the value of RJR bonds, triggered a deep slump in prices of many investment-grade corporate bonds as investors backed away from the market.

Strong Covenants May Re-emerge

Some analysts say the move by Marriott may trigger the re-emergence of strong covenants, or written protections, in future corporate bond issues to protect bondholders against such restructurings as the one being engineered by Marriott. In the wake of the RJR buy-out, many investors demanded stronger covenants in new corporate bond issues.

Some investors blame themselves for not demanding stronger covenants. "It's our own fault," said Robert Hickey, a bond fund manager at Van Kampen Merritt. In their rush to buy bonds in an effort to lock in yields, many investors have allowed companies to sell bonds with covenants that have been "slim to none," Mr. Hickey said.

or other investment institutions. Privately placed bonds generally cannot be resold to individuals in Canada but only to other qualified institutional investors. However, there is increasingly active trading among these investors.

There is more information about the difference between public issues and private placements in the next chapter.

Protective Covenants When investors lend to a company, they know that they might not get their money back. But they expect that the company will use their money well and not take unreasonable risks. To help ensure this, lenders usually impose a number of conditions, or **protective covenants**, on companies that borrow from them. An honest firm is willing to accept these conditions, because it knows that they enable the firm to borrow at a reasonable rate of interest.

protective covenant
Restriction on a firm to protect bondholders.

Companies that borrow in moderation are less likely to get into difficulties than those that are deep in debt; lenders therefore usually restrict the amount of extra debt that the firm can issue. They are also eager to prevent others from pushing ahead of them in the queue if trouble occurs, so they will not allow the company to create new debt senior to theirs or put aside assets for other lenders.

In June 2006 Heinz announced plans to raise its dividend and buy back US$1 billion of its shares. Holders of Heinz's bonds were unhappy with the news, since it meant there would be less cash available to service their debt. By August the price of Heinz's bonds had drifted down by 5 percent. Debtholders are aware that bumper payments to shareholders can reduce the value of their debt, and they often protect themselves by limiting the amount of cash that can be paid out as dividends or repurchases.

The story of Marriott in the nearby box is a more dramatic example of what can happen when bondholders are not sufficiently careful about the conditions they impose.

Check Point 14.7

In 1987, RJR Nabisco, the food and tobacco giant, had US$5 billion of A-rated debt outstanding. In that year the company was taken over, and US$19 billion of debt was issued and used to buy back equity. The debt ratio skyrocketed, and the debt was downgraded to a BB rating. The holders of the previously issued debt were furious, and one filed a lawsuit claiming that RJR had violated an implicit obligation not to undertake major financing changes at the expense of existing bondholders. Why did these bondholders believe they had been harmed by the massive issue of new debt? What type of explicit restriction would you have wanted if you had been one of the original bondholders?

A Debt by Any Other Name The word *debt* sounds straightforward, but companies enter into a number of financial arrangements that look suspiciously like debt yet are treated differently in the accounts. Some of these obligations are easily identifiable. For example, accounts payable are simply obligations to pay for goods that have already been delivered and are therefore like short-term debt.

lease Long-term rental agreement.

Other arrangements are not so easy to spot. For example, instead of borrowing money to buy equipment, many companies **lease** or rent it on a long-term basis. In this case the firm promises to make a series of payments to the lessor (the owner of the equipment). This is just like the obligation to make payments on an outstanding loan. What if the firm can't make the payments? The lessor can then take back the equipment, which is precisely what would happen if the firm had *borrowed* money from the lessor, using the equipment as collateral for the loan. We will discuss the analysis of leasing in detail in Chapter 17.

EXAMPLE 14.1 **THE TERMS OF RIO-TINTO ALCAN'S BOND ISSUE**

Now that you are familiar with some of the jargon, you might like to look at an example of a bond issue. Table 14.4 is a summary of the terms of a bond which was originally issued by Alcan. Alcan was recently acquired by the Rio Tinto Group for over US$38 billion. The combined company is now called Rio-Tinto Alcan and has its headquarters in Montréal. We have added some explanatory notes on the bond issue.

INNOVATION IN THE DEBT MARKET

We have discussed domestic bonds and eurobonds, fixed-rate and floating-rate loans, secured and unsecured loans, senior and junior loans, and much more. You might think that this gives you all the options you need. Yet almost every day, companies and their advisors dream up a new type of debt. Here are some examples of unusual bonds.

Indexed Bonds We saw in Chapter 6 how the Canadian government has issued bonds whose payments rise in line with inflation. Occasionally borrowers have linked the payments on their bonds to the price of a particular commodity. For example, Mexico, which is a large oil producer, has issued billions of dollars worth of bonds that provide an extra payoff if oil prices rise. Mexico reasons that oil-linked bonds reduce its risk. If the price of oil is high, it can afford the higher payments on the bond. If oil prices are low, its interest payments will also be lower.

Asset-Backed Bonds The rock star David Bowie earns royalties from a number of successful albums such as *The Rise and Fall of Ziggy Stardust and the Spiders from Mars* and *Diamond Dogs*.

TABLE 14.4 Rio-Tinto Alcan's bond issue ($US).

Comments	Description of Bond
1. A debenture is an unsecured bond.	**Alcan Aluminum, Ltd., 6.450% debentures, due 2011**
2. Coupon is 6.450 percent. Thus, each bond makes an annual interest payment of .0645 × US$1,000 = US$64.50.	
3. Moody's bond rating is A2 and Standard and Poor's is A−.	**Rating: A2 and A−**
4. Alcan has issued and has outstanding US$400 million of the bonds.	Outstanding: US$400,000,000.
5. The bond was issued in March 2001 and is to be repaid In March 2011.	Dated: March 23, 2001. Due: March 15, 2011.
6. Interest is payable at six-month intervals on March and September 15.	Interest: March and September 15.
7. The bonds can be held in multiples of US$1,000.	Denomination: US$1,000 and integral multiples thereof.
8. Unlike some bond issues, this issue does not give the company an option to call (that is, repurchase) the bonds before maturity at specific prices. Thus the bond is not redeemable prior to maturity.	Early redemption: The debentures are not redeemable prior to maturity.
9. The bonds are not secured; that is, no assets have been set aside to protect the bondholders in the event of default.	Security: Not secured.
10. The bonds were sold at a price of 99.748 percent of face value. The company will have to deduct the payment to the underwriters before it receives any money from the bond issue.	Offered: US$400,000,000 debenture offerings are priced at 99.748% of their principal amount to yield 6.485%. Morgan Stanley & Co. Inc., Credit Suisse First Boston Corporation, RBC Dominion Securities Corporation, Salomon Smith Barney, Inc., Scotia Capital (U.S.), Inc., CIBC World Markets Corp., and Toronto Dominion Securities (U.S.) are co-underwriters of the offerings, which are to be made by prospectus only.
11. A trustee is appointed to look after the bondholder's interest.	
12. The bonds are registered. The registrar keeps a record of who owns the bonds.	

Sources: **www.bondsonline.com**; *Financial Post* historical reports, **www.fpdata.finpost.com**; **www.alcan.com**.

But instead of waiting to receive these royalties, Bowie decided that he would prefer the money upfront. The solution was to issue $55 million 10-year bonds and to set aside the future royalty payments from the singer's albums to make the payments on these bonds. Such bonds are known as *asset-backed securities*; the borrower sets aside a group of assets and the income from these assets is then used to service the debt.

The Bowie bonds are an unusual example of an asset-backed security, but billions of dollars of house and commercial mortgages, credit card loans, personal lines of credit, and receivables are packaged every year, or *securitized*, and resold as asset-backed bonds. As of September 30, 2010, Canada's outstanding asset-backed securities stood at about $98.3 billion compared with about $116 billion in 2007. For the most part, these securities comprised assets financed by short-term unsecured debt such as commercial paper.[15] Investors in asset-backed securities include money market mutual funds, pension funds, corporations, financial institutions, and governments. Securitization can be done through multiseller or single-seller programs that are typically offered by large investment dealers such as BMO Nesbitt Burns, TD Securities, or CIBC World Markets. For instance, a multiseller program that securitizes receivables may pool such receivables from a variety of providers and then finance those purchases by issuing commercial paper securities.

[15] We will discuss commercial paper in more detail in Chapter 20.

Finance in Action

Is There a Subprime Crisis in Canada?

Rod and Joyce Marentette bought their house in Chatham, Ont., a month before getting married in 2005. The economy was booming and credit was plentiful, so even though they didn't have a down payment and Rod had recently gone through a bankruptcy, there were plenty of mortgage companies willing to lend to them.

The house was $98,000 and with the additional legal fees the total price came to $100,000, all of which they were able to borrow from the mortgage company.

Things took a turn for the worse when Rod, who is 39, suffered a workplace injury and had to leave his job as a factory supervisor. But Joyce, 40, was determined to hold on to the house, taking on extra work to make ends meet. When Rod finally recovered two years later, he found a new job with a construction company. While the paycheque was lower, it took the financial pressure off.

That's when they got the call from the mortgage company. It was the year the credit crunch hit. The economy was in a tailspin and lenders around the world were scrambling for liquidity. The mortgage, they were informed, could not be renewed and as the company was closing its subprime business, they would have to find another lender.

But the little lenders who had been so eager for their business back in 2005 had disappeared. That left the big banks and insurance companies, but they wouldn't lend either and the Marentettes quickly realized their dream of owning a home was about to become a nightmare.

It ends up that despite its squeaky-clean financial image, Canada does indeed have its own subprime-mortgage mess.

Industry insiders say that over the next few years the Marentettes' story will play out over and over again across Canada, as an estimated 30,000 so-called "orphan mortgages" reach maturity. Unless the government takes action, this may trigger a flood of foreclosures.

In the wake of the financial crisis, the business of subprime loans has dried up. Prior to 2007, there were at least a dozen subprime lenders in Canada and it was the fastest-growing sector of the entire mortgage market, says Benjamin Tal, senior economist at CIBC World Markets, who pegged it at about 5% of the total market.

But most of those lenders, including players such as Xceed Mortgage Corp., GMAC Residential Lending and Wells Fargo, have either changed their business or closed up shop.

Meanwhile, the rules around home loans have been tightened. Earlier this year, the federal government raised the minimum down payment required for Canada Mortgage and Housing Corp. insurance.

The mortgage industry clearly has a problem on its hands.

"This thing is a wave and it's just starting," says Eric Putnam, formerly with a subprime lender, now managing director of Debt Coach Canada, a company that provides financial and bankruptcy advice to consumers.

Estimates vary on the total value of the subprime market in Canada.

But according to Ivan Wahl, chief executive of Xceed, one of the biggest players in Canada until it recently converted to a bank, the subprime market in this country grew to about $11-billion in 2006, the year before things started to implode.

Given that the total mortgages outstanding in Canada amount to around $1-trillion today, the subprime portion is not a huge slice.

But the vast majority were made toward the middle of the decade with terms of three and five years and they're coming due over the next two years.

Similarly, commercial mortgage-backed securities can be securitized as single-asset and multi-asset offerings, the former involving one building and the latter involving several buildings. Brookfield Properties, a large Canadian real estate company, raised US$432 million from refinancing its One Liberty Plaza building in New York and a further US$500 million from refinancing another Manhattan building. In both deals, investors purchased securities known as *multiclass mortgage pass-through* certificates, which ranged from being AAA rated to just investment-grade (BBB-).[16]

Only a few years ago, asset-backed securities were considered high-quality investments with good credit ratings. In recent years, the sector has gone through very difficult times all over the world. The problem began with a meltdown in the market for subprime mortgages in the United States. Subprime mortgages were typically provided to less creditworthy borrowers who were charged higher interest rates for such relatively risky loans. The lenders assumed that the buoyant housing market and a general climate for low interest rates in the United States would enable such borrowers to sustain their mortgage payments. Such predictions proved wrong, however, with a slowdown in the U.S. housing markets and rising interest rates. Subprime borrowers began defaulting on their loans in large numbers, causing the insolvency of many lenders.

---

[16] See also B. Critchley, "Asset-Backed Market Soaring: Value of Securities Up Eightfold from Five Years Ago," *Financial Post*, March 21, 2001, D3. See also B. Critchley, "Brookfield Taps into U.S. MBS Market: Raises US$932 Million with New York Refinancings," *Financial Post*, March 19, 2001, C8. Following the tragic events of September 11, 2001, at New York's World Trade Center, the One Liberty Plaza complex had to be temporarily vacated. The building has since been reopened to tenants.

"Given the current environment it will be very difficult to finance these [people]," says Mr. Tal, who calls it "a big problem for specific borrowers but not one from a macro perspective."

But the industry is so concerned about the situation that it recently approached the federal government with a request for a bailout.

According to Mr. Putnam and others, it wants the federal government to participate in a $1-billion fund to help finance the coming flood of orphan mortgages.

During the credit bubble, subprime lenders funded themselves through the asset-backed commercial paper market.

The loans they made were packaged up and sold to securitization pools and then to investors in the form of ABCP.

But when the commercial paper market froze up in the financial crisis, lenders were suddenly left without a way to fund their businesses.

"Investors are no longer willing to continue on and these mortgages were not insured by the Canada Mortgage and Housing Corp., so the borrowers are not going to be able to move to another lender in today's environment," Mr. Putnam says.

The definition of subprime depends on who you ask, but for practical purposes the term generally refers to high-interest loans made to people who are unable to get a better deal at one of the big banks. Many such borrowers are simply self employed entrepreneurs but a good part are people with ugly credit histories.

In the United States the subprime market took off in the run-up to the crisis, growing to more than 20% of total mortgages outstanding as the loans were packaged up into complex securities and sold to investors around the world. When home prices finally started to crumble the value of the securities cratered, ultimately destabilizing the global financial system.

Analysts say it's difficult to draw comparisons between the U.S. subprime market and what happened in Canada. The market here never grew to more than a sliver of the total and, more important, the type of loans offered by Canadian players were more conservative than those offered by their peers south of the border.

But there are nevertheless some disturbing parallels between the two markets. "Compared to what was going on in the U.S., it never got to the same level here, but having said that, they were going down the same slippery slope," says Mr. Putnam.

"The Canadian population wanted to buy a home, that was the No. 1 goal. People were taking on high debt loads, stretching the amortization out as long as possible and lenders were looking at all the opportunities. It made sense when the market was hot, but of course, no one could foresee the problems. "

Exacerbating the situation, the early part of the decade saw the arrival of a number of U.S. players looking to get in on the Canadian market and increasing competition.

Because many of the players were not deposit-taking institutions, they qualified for looser regulations than banks and other traditional players.

That meant, for instance, that they didn't need insurance for risky loans and they could lend in excess of the value of the property. Borrowers loved it at the time but in today's post-crisis world, such loans are almost impossible to renew.

Source: Excerpted from John Greenwood, "Subprime Mortgages Alive Here: 'Orphan Mortgages' Begin to Surface," *Financial Post*, April 1, 2010, online section. Material reprinted with the express permission of National Post, a division of Postmedia Network Inc.

Subprime lenders had sold their loans to other investors, including financial institutions such as commercial banks, hedge funds, and pension funds looking to earn high returns. When large numbers of subprime borrowers began defaulting, these investments suddenly became bad and hit many financial institutions hard. For instance, Citigroup had over US$37 billion invested in this sector and had to write off about US$30 billion in losses. Canadian Imperial Bank of Commerce also had to write off about US$10 billion in losses due to exposure to the U.S. subprime mortgages. As investor losses mounted, they refused further loans or began asking for much higher interest rates, causing a global credit crunch. While the resultant credit crunch has had a far-reaching impact on the U.S. economy, the nearby Finance in Action box shows that the Canadian financial sector and economy have not been immune either.

The next Finance in Action box shows that several banks and brokerage houses were accused by regulators of improperly selling asset-backed commercial paper and were required to pay millions of dollars in fines and penalties.

Reverse Floaters Floating-rate bonds that pay a higher rate of interest when other interest rates fall and a lower rate when other rates rise are called *reverse floaters*. They are riskier than normal bonds. When interest rates rise, the prices of all bonds fall, but the prices of reverse floaters suffer a double whammy, because the coupon payments on the bonds fall as the discount rate rises. In 1994, Orange County, California, learned this the hard way when it invested heavily in reverse floaters. Robert Citron, the treasurer, was betting that interest rates would fall. He was wrong; interest rates rose sharply and partly because of its investment in reverse floaters, the county lost US$1.7 billion.

Finance in Action
Banks and Brokerages Agree to Pay Hefty Penalties

Canadian Imperial Bank of Commerce, National Bank of Canada and brokerages agreed to pay a total of $134 million in fines and penalties to settle regulators' claims they improperly sold asset-backed commercial paper in Canada just before the market collapsed in 2007.

National Bank was fined $70 million by Québec regulators and will pay $1 million for the cost of the investigation, while CIBC, Canada's fifth-biggest bank, was fined by Ontario regulators $21.7 million and will pay $300,000 in costs.

Bank of Nova Scotia's Scotia Capital unit will pay a total of $29.3 million, according to an agreement approved by the Investment Industry Regulatory Organization of Canada. Laurentian Bank will pay $3.2 million.

The banks agreed to settle for their roles in selling commercial paper in late July and early August of 2007, before the market collapsed on concern about ties to U.S. subprime mortgages. About $32 billion of the debt became insolvent, leading to a court-ordered plan in which the short-term debt was swapped for longer-term notes in Canada's biggest restructuring.

The settlement "reflects the failure of a small number of employees, handling a small number of large trades," Scotiabank said in an e-mailed statement. The bank is "taking additional measures to prevent this from happening again."

Securities regulators in Ontario, Québec, and B.C. have been collaborating on a probe with the Investment Industry Regulatory Organization of Canada, OSC spokeswoman Carolyn Shaw-Rimmington said in July. The investigation focused on the actions of firms selling the debt after Coventree Inc., Canada's biggest commercial paper administrator at the time, warned bank-owned dealers of ties to risky U.S. loans.

The OSC also approved a settlement with HSBC Bank of Canada under which the bank agreed to pay a fine of $5.925 million and $75,000 in costs. Canaccord Financial Ltd., a brokerage based in Vancouver, agreed to pay IIROC a fine and costs of $3.1 million and Credential Securities Inc. will pay $200,000 in fines and costs.

In a July 2007 e-mail, Coventree alerted the dealers that some of its debt funds had ties to U.S. subprime mortgages, according to court filings. The market collapsed three weeks late. CIBC kept selling the paper until Aug. 3, when it became concerned over its liquidity, according to the settlement.

Source: Excerpted from Doug Alexander and Joe Schneider, "Banks and Brokerages to Pay Hefty Penalties; CIBC, National Bank Settle with Regulators in Subprime Probe," *Times Colonist (Victoria)*, December 22, 2009, B7.

These three examples illustrate the great variety of potential security designs. As long as you can convince investors of its attractions, you can issue, say, a callable, subordinated, floating-rate bond denominated in euros. Or, rather than combining features of existing securities, you might create an entirely new one. For example, a copper mining company might issue preferred shares whose dividend fluctuates with the world copper price. We know of no such security, but it would perfectly legal, and just might generate considerable interest among investors.

Variety is intrinsically good. People have different tastes, wealth, tax rates, and so on. Why not offer a choice? Of course, one must consider the expense of designing and marketing new securities. But if you have reason to think some new security will appeal to investors, you can always issue it on especially favourable terms, and thus increase the value of your company.

LO3 14.5 CONVERTIBLE SECURITIES

warrant Right to buy shares from a company at a stipulated price before a set date.

We have seen that companies sometimes have the option to repay an issue of bonds before maturity. There are also cases in which investors have an option. The most dramatic case is provided by a **warrant**, which really is an option. Companies often issue warrants and bonds in a package.

EXAMPLE 14.2 WARRANTS

Macaw Bill wishes to make a bond issue, which might include some warrants as a "sweetener." Each warrant might allow you to purchase one share of Macaw stock at a price of $50 any time during the next five years. If Macaw's stock performs well, that option could turn out to be very valuable. For instance, if the stock price at the end of the five years is $80, you pay the company $50 and receive in exchange a share worth $80. Of course, an investment in warrants has its perils. If the price of Macaw stock fails to rise above $50, the warrants expire and are worthless.

convertible bond Bond that the holder may exchange for a specified amount of another security.

A **convertible bond** gives its owner the option to exchange the bond for a predetermined number of common shares. The convertible bondholder hopes that the company's share price will zoom up so that the bond can be converted at a big profit. But if the shares zoom down, there is no obligation to convert; the bondholder remains just that. Not surprisingly, investors value this option to keep the bond or exchange it for shares, and therefore a convertible bond sells at a higher price than a comparable bond that is not convertible.

The convertible is like a package of a bond and a warrant. But there is an important difference: when the owners of a convertible wish to exercise their options to buy shares, they do not pay cash—they just exchange the bond for shares of the stock.

Companies may also issue convertible preferred stock. In this case the investor receives preferred stock with fixed dividend payments, but has the option to exchange this preferred stock for the company's common stock. The preferred stock issued by the Bank of Montreal is convertible into common stock. In February 2009, 124 convertible preferred stock issues were listed on the TSX.

These examples do not exhaust the options encountered by the financial manager. In fact, once you read Chapter 25 and learn how to analyze options, you will find they are all around you.

LO4 14.6 PATTERNS OF CORPORATE FINANCING

Firms have two broad sources of cash: they can raise money from external sources by an issue of shares or debt or they can plow back part of their profits. Shareholders are happy for companies to plow this money back into the firm, so long as it goes to positive-NPV investments. Every positive-NPV investment generates a higher price for their shares.

internally generated funds Cash reinvested in the firm: depreciation plus earnings not paid out as dividends.

Figure 14.2 summarizes the sources of capital for Canadian corporations. The most striking aspect of this figure is the dominance of **internally generated funds**, defined as depreciation plus earnings that are not paid out as dividends.[17] For much of this period, over half of the total funding requirement of corporations was met from internally generated funds.

FIGURE 14.2
Sources of financing for non-financial private corporations.

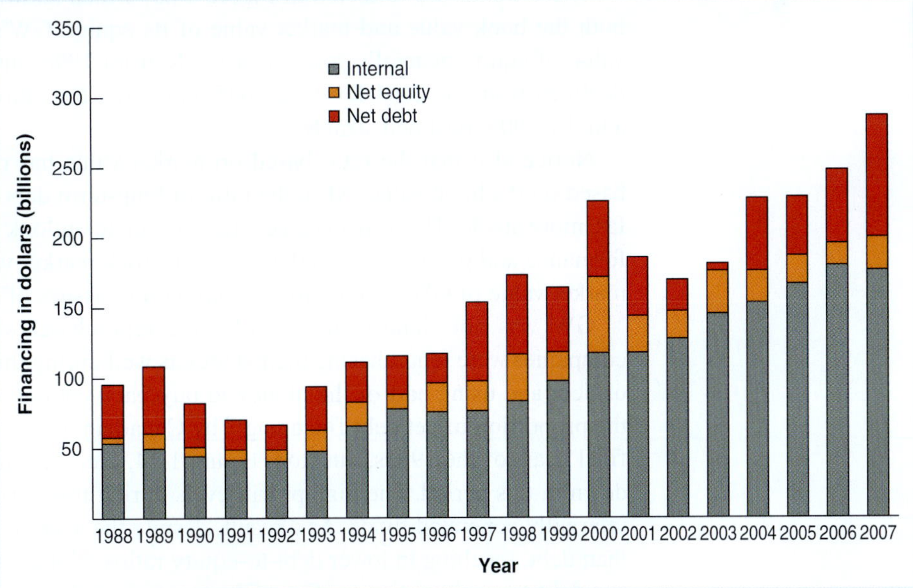

Source: Adapted from Statistics Canada CANSIM database, Table 378-0021, v52219976, v52220000, v52220001, v52220002, v52220003, v52220004, v52220005, v52220006, and v52220007, **cansim2.statcan.gc.ca**. Computations, use, and interpretation of these data are entirely those of the author.

[17] Remember that depreciation is a non-cash expense.

DO FIRMS RELY TOO HEAVILY ON INTERNAL FUNDS?

Some observers worry that companies rely so much on internal funds. They argue that managers might think more carefully about spending money if they had to ask investors for it. Think back to Chapter 1, where we pointed out that a firm is a team, consisting of shareholders, debtholders, managers, and so on. Shareholders and debtholders want to make sure management it is pulling its weight and truly maximizing market value. But it is costly for individual investors to keep checks on management, and large financial institutions are specialists in monitoring—when the firm goes to the bank for a large loan or makes a public issue of stocks or bonds, managers had better have all the answers. Which is why they often avoid going to the capital market to raise money, and they will retain sufficient earnings to be able to meet unanticipated demands for cash.

Not that managers are generally loafers; there might be good reasons for relying on internally generated funds. The costs of new securities are avoided, for example. Moreover, the announcement of a new equity issue is usually bad news for investors, who worry that the decision signals lower profits.[18] Raising equity capital from internal sources avoids the costs and the bad omens associated with equity issues.

Check Point 14.8

"Since internal funds provide the bulk of industry's needs for capital, the securities markets serve little function." Does the speaker have a point?

EXTERNAL SOURCES OF CAPITAL

Of course, firms don't rely exclusively on internal funds. They also issue securities and retire them, sometimes in large volume. For example, from the mid-1990s to 2003, GW steadily increased its reliance on new debt by issuing considerable numbers of bonds. Between 2000 and 2001, its outstanding long-term debt increased by about 64 percent. In the same period, GW consistently bought back shares from the public. So, for instance, over the period 1995–1999, and between 2002 and 2003, GW had *negative* net stock issues. In recent years GW has increased its equity and reduced long-term debt somewhat.

These trends are reflected in Figure 14.3, which shows the ratio of GW's long-term debt to both the book value and market value of its equity. GW's ratio of long-term debt to the book value of equity generally rose consistently from 1996 until 2004, barring 2002 when the ratio declined from the 2001 level. In 2005 and 2006, the ratio has come down from the 2004 level and, by 2009, declined sizably.

Notice also that the ratio based on market value has consistently been lower than the ratio based on the book value. Also, the ratio of long-term debt to the market value of equity was, by far, more stable. This reflects a general optimistic outlook of investors about the company's performance and prospects as well as a rise in stock market values in the 1990s, which allowed the market value of GW's equity to keep up with its issues of long-term debt.

GW was not alone in its use of share repurchases since the mid-1990s. Other Canadian companies were repurchasing their shares as well during this period, often by making large issues of debt and using part of the money to buy back common stock. We see from Figure 14.2 that the proportion of net debt financing[19] by Canadian non-financial firms generally went up in the final years of the 1990s, but from Figure 14.4, their average debt-to-equity ratios actually came down in this period. The high profit levels during this period resulted in record-setting levels of internally generated funds. As a result, despite the share repurchases, common equity rose more than debt, resulting in lower debt-to-equity ratios. Notice, from Figure 14.4, an increase in average debt-to-equity ratios for Canadian non-financial enterprises in 2001 and 2002; this was also

[18] Managers do have insiders' insights and naturally are tempted to issue stock when the stock price looks good to them, that is, when they are less optimistic than outside investors. The outside investors realize this and will buy a new issue only at a discount from the pre-announcement price. Stock issues are discussed further in the next chapter.

[19] This includes long-term and short-term debt.

FIGURE 14.3
Long-term debt-to-equity ratios for George Weston Limited.

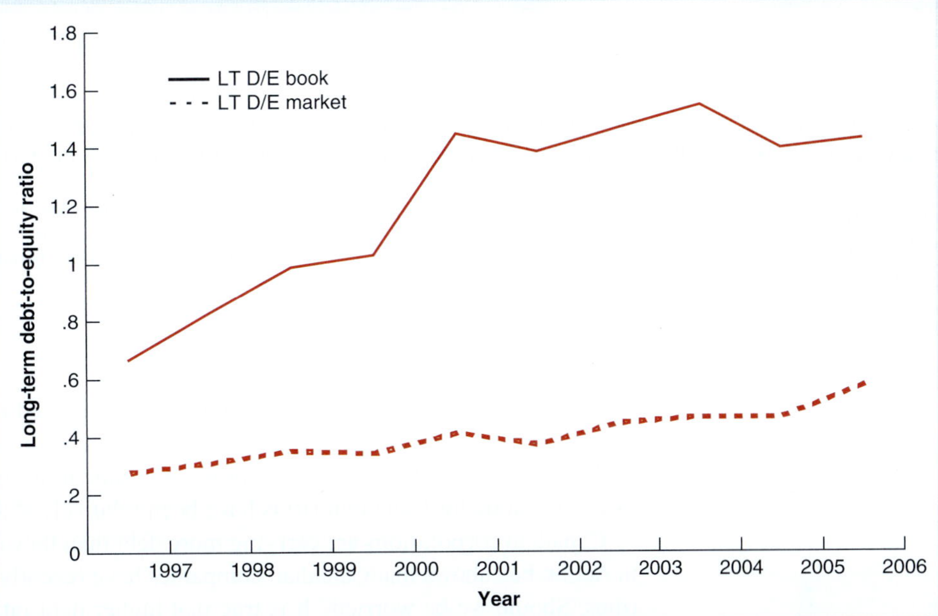

Notes:
1. LT D/E ratio (book) = long-term debt/common shareholder's equity.
2. LT D/E ratio (market) = long-term debt/average number of common shares × average stock prices.

Source: *Financial Post Online Historical Reports and FP Analyzer*, **www.fpinfomart.ca** (FP Corporate Analyzer), retrieved December 29, 2010. Material reprinted with the express permission of National Post, a division of Postmedia Network Inc.

FIGURE 14.4
Average debt-to-equity ratio, Canadian non-financial enterprises, 1993–2009.

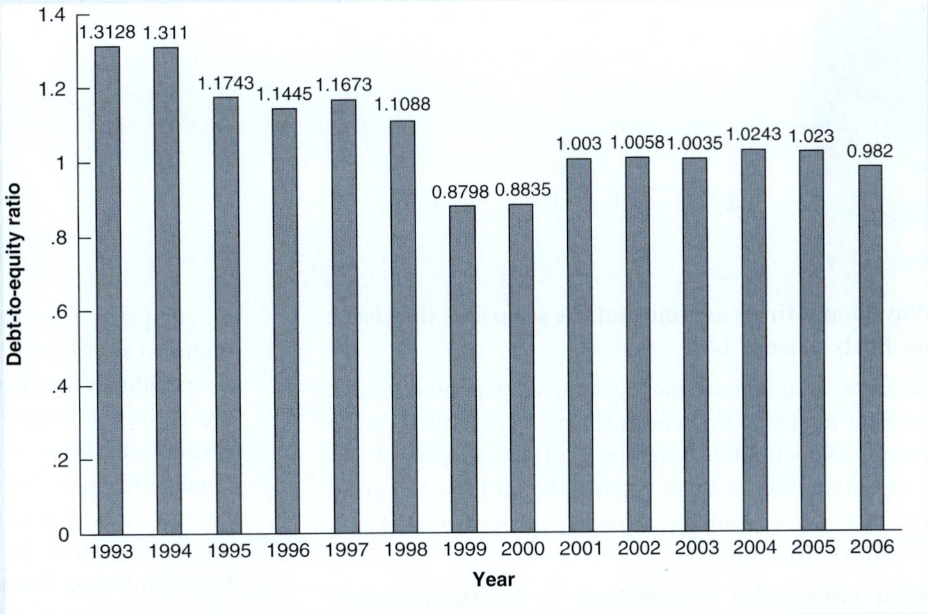

Notes:
1. The annual debt-to-equity ratios were calculated by taking the average of the quarterly debt-to-equity ratios reported for each year. Debt includes loans and accounts with affiliates plus borrowings. Equity is total equity.
2. Debt-to-equity ratios were calculated using the latest available data; for instance, where possible, the first quarter report of a subsequent year was used to calculate the average debt-to-equity ratio for a given year.

Sources: Adapted from Statistics Canada, *Quarterly Financial Statistics for Enterprises*, Catalogue No. 61-008, Table 3-1, 1993–2009, **www.statcan.gc.ca/pub/61-008-x/61-008-x2010003-eng.pdf**, accessed December 30, 2010; also issues 61-008-x2009001.pdf, 61-008-x2008001.pdf, 61-008-x2007001.pdf, 61-008-XIE2005004.pdf, 61-008-XIE2006002.pdf, 61-008-XIE2006003.pdf, 61-008-XIE2006004.pdf, 0010361-008-XIE.pdf, 0010461-008-XIE.pdf, and 0010561-008-XIE.pdf. Computations, use, and interpretation of these data are entirely those of the author.

Finance in Action

Upturn in Corporate Financing

After slim pickings in the first quarter of the year, corporate finance activity bounced back in the second quarter as Canadian companies raised a very healthy $31.1-billion in 157 deals. That's up from 108 deals worth $21.4-billion in the first quarter of 2009.

The 157 deals is also the highest number since the second quarter of 2008, suggesting the worst of the economic storm is over and capital markets are slowly recovering.

The debt markets played an important role for underwriters, with 38 deals worth $13.9.– billion, while 114 equity deals accounted for $12.4-billion of the $31.1-billion.

Source: Excerpted from Jim Middlemiss, "Upturn in Corporate Financing: "The Quality Names Are Still Attractive," *Financial Post*, July 22, 2009, FP6. Material reprinted with the express permission of National Post, a division of Postmedia Network Inc.

the period when corporate profits and internally generated funds declined somewhat. Since 2006 average debt-to-equity ratios declined until 2008 and went up again in 2009.

The net effect of these financing policies is shown in Figure 14.4, which confirms that debt-to-equity ratios for Canadian firms have been relatively stable in book-value terms.

Canadian corporations are carrying more debt than they did 30 years ago. The nearby Finance in Action box shows that Canadian companies have recently issued high levels of new debt securities. Should we be worried? It is true that higher debt ratios mean more companies are likely to fall into financial distress when a serious recession hits the economy. But all companies live with this risk to some degree, and it does not follow that less risk is better. Finding the optimal debt ratio is like finding the optimal speed limit: we can agree that accidents at 60 kilometres per hour are less dangerous, other things being equal, than accidents at 100 kilometres per hour, but we do not therefore set the national speed limit at 60. Speed has benefits as well as risks. So does debt, as we will see in Chapter 16.

14.7 SUMMARY

1. **Why should firms assume that the securities they issue are fairly priced? LO1**

   Managers want to raise money at the lowest possible cost, but their ability to find cheap financing is limited by the intense competition between investors. As a result of this competition, securities are likely to be fairly priced given the information available to investors. Such a market is said to be **efficient**.

2. **What information is contained in the shareholders' equity account in the firm's financial statements? LO2**

   The shareholders' equity account breaks down the book value of equity into **paid-in capital** and **retained earnings**. The total number of shares issued as well as shares repurchased by the company are also shown.

3. **What are the major classes of securities issued by firms to raise capital? LO3**

   A company can issue a variety of securities such as common shares, preferred shares, and bonds. The **common shareholders** own the company. By this we mean that they are entitled to whatever profits are left over after other investors have been paid and that they have the ultimate control over how the company is run. Because shareholdings in many Canadian companies are widely dispersed, managers get to make most of the decisions. Managers may be given strong financial incentives to perform well, and their actions are monitored by the board of directors.

   Preferred stock offers a fixed dividend but the company has the discretion not to pay it. It cannot, however, then pay a dividend on the common stock. Despite its name, preferred stock is not a popular source of finance, but it is useful in special situations.

   When companies issue **bonds**, they promise to make a series of interest payments and to repay the principal.

However, this liability is limited. Shareholders have the right to default on their obligation and to hand over the assets to the debtholders. Unlike dividends on common stock and preferred stock, the interest payments on debt are regarded as a cost and therefore they are paid out of before-tax income. Here are some forms of debt:

- Fixed-rate and floating-rate debt
- Long-term (funded) and short-term (unfunded) debt
- Callable and sinking-fund debt
- Senior and subordinated debt
- Secured and unsecured debt
- Investment grade and junk debt
- Domestic and international debt
- Publicly traded debt and private placements

The fourth source of finance consists of options and option-like securities. The simplest option is a warrant, which gives its holder the right to buy a share from the firm at a set price by a set date. Warrants are often sold in combination with other securities. **Convertible bonds** give the holder the right to convert the bond to shares. They therefore resemble a package of straight debt and a warrant.

4. **What are recent trends in firms' use of different sources of finance?** LO4

Internally generated cash is the principal source of company funds. Some people worry about that, thinking that if management does not go to the trouble of raising money, it may be profligate with it.

In recent years, net equity issues were negative; that is, companies repurchased more equity than they issued. At the same time, companies issued large quantities of debt. However, large levels of **internally generated funds** in this period allowed book equity to increase despite the share repurchases, with the result that the ratio of long-term debt to book value of equity was fairly stable.

Related Web Links

finpipe.com Information under "Bonds"

hoovers.com Information about corporations and corporate financing

lacaisse.com Caisse de dépôt et placement du Québec

canadiantire.ca Canadian Tire

weston.ca George Weston

cpr.ca Canadian Pacific

osc.gov.on.ca Ontario Securities Commission

bondsonline.com Informative Web site on bonds

riotintoalcan.com Rio Tinto Alcan

soxlaw.com Financial and accounting disclosure information at the *Sarbanes-Oxley* Web site

Key Terms

additional paid-in capital	454	internally generated funds	473	protective covenant	467
authorized share capital	454	issued shares	454	proxy contest	457
callable bond	464	lease	468	refunding	465
convertible bond	473	majority voting	456	retained earnings	454
cumulative voting	456	net worth	461	secured debt	466
eurobond	466	outstanding shares	454	sinking fund	464
eurodollars	466	par value	454	subordinated debt	465
floating-rate preferred	463	preferred stock	461	warrant	472
foreign bond	466	prime rate	464		
funded debt	464	private placement	466		

Questions and Problems

connect — Practise and learn online with *Connect*. Questions with online Excel templates or datasets are marked with ✎.

*Answers in Appendix B

BASIC

*1. **Equity Accounts.** The authorized share capital of the Alfred Cake Company is 100,000 shares. Currently 20,000 shares are issued and outstanding. The equity is currently shown in the company's books as follows: (LO2)

Common stock	$60,000
Retained earnings	30,000
Common equity	90,000

a. How many more shares can be issued without the approval of shareholders?

b. If the company issues 10,000 shares at $5 a share, show how this will appear in the company's books.

2. **Equity Accounts.** Look back at problem 1. What would happen to the company's books if instead it bought back 1,000 shares at $5 per share? The average issue price of these shares was $5. (LO2)

3. **Financing Terms.** Fill in the blanks by choosing the appropriate term from the following list: lease, funded, floating-rate, eurobond, convertible, subordinated, call, sinking fund, prime rate, private placement, public issue, senior, unfunded, eurodollar rate, warrant, debentures, term loan. (LO3)

*a. Debt maturing in more than one year is often called ________ debt.

*b. An issue of bonds that is sold simultaneously in several countries is traditionally called a(n) ________.

c. If a lender ranks behind the firm's general creditors in the event of default, the loan is said to be ________.

*d. In many cases a firm is obliged to make regular contributions to a(n) ________, which is then used to repurchase bonds.

e. Most bonds give the firm the right to repurchase or ________ the bonds at specified prices.

*f. The benchmark interest rate that banks charge to their customers with good to excellent credit is generally termed the ________.

*g. The interest rate on bank loans is often tied to short-term interest rates. These loans are usually called ________ loans.

*h. Where there is a(n) ________, securities are sold directly to a small group of institutional investors. These securities cannot be resold to individual investors. In the case of a(n) ________, debt can be freely bought and sold by individual investors.

i. A long-term rental agreement is called a(n) ________.

j. A(n) ________ bond can be exchanged for shares of the issuing corporation.

k. A(n) ________ gives its owner the right to buy shares in the issuing company at a predetermined price.

4. **Financing Trends.** Are the following statements true or false? Explain. (LO4)

a. In several recent years, non-financial corporations in Canada have repurchased more stock than they have issued.

b. A Canadian corporation pays tax on only 30 percent of the common or preferred dividends it receives from other corporations.

c. Because of the tax advantage, a large fraction of preferred shares is held by corporations.

5. **Preferred Stock.** In what ways is preferred stock like long-term debt? In what ways is it like common stock? (LO3)

INTERMEDIATE

*6. **Voting for Directors.** If there are 10 directors to be elected and a shareholder owns 90 shares, indicate the maximum number of votes that he or she can cast for a favourite candidate under

a. Majority voting (LO2)

b. Cumulative voting (LO2)

*7. **Voting for Directors.** The shareholders of the Pickwick Paper Company need to elect five directors. There are 400,000 shares outstanding. How many shares do you need to own to ensure that you can elect at least one director if the company has

a. Majority voting? (LO2)

b. Cumulative voting? (LO2)

Hint: How many votes in total will be cast? How many votes are required to ensure that at least a fifth of votes are cast for your choice?

8. **Equity Accounts.** Look back at Table 14.2. (LO2)

a. Suppose that George Weston issues 10 million shares at $55 a share. Rework the table to show the company's equity after the issue.

b. Suppose that George Weston *subsequently* repurchased 500,000 shares at $60 a share. Rework part (a) to show the effect of the further change. Take the average issue price of the shares to be $30.

9. **Protective Covenants.** Why might a bond agreement limit the amount of assets that the firm can lease? (LO3)

10. **Bond Yields.** Other things being equal, will the following provisions increase or decrease the yield to maturity at which a firm can issue a bond? (LO3)

a. A call provision

b. A restriction on further borrowing

c. A provision of specific collateral for the bond

d. An option to convert the bonds into shares

*11. **Income Bonds.** *Income bonds* are unusual. Interest payments on such bonds may be skipped or deferred if the firm's income is insufficient to make the payment. In what way are these bonds like preferred stock? Why might a firm choose to issue an income bond instead of preferred stock? (LO3)

12. **Preferred Stock.** Preferred stock of financially strong firms sometimes sells at lower yields than the bonds of those firms. For weaker firms, the preferred stock has a higher yield. What might explain this pattern? (LO3)

13. **Internet.** In Table 14.1, we showed examples of securities issued by George Weston Ltd. Try to construct a similar table for another company, say Enbridge Inc., by looking up its annual report on the Web. An easy way to do this is to go to Enbridge's Web site at **www.enbridge.com**, click on "Investor Relations," and see a variety of information about the company, including its annual reports. You can also retrieve Enbridge's annual report at **www.sedar.com**. (LO4)

14. **Internet.** Now try to retrieve the annual report of another large company, Bell Canada Inc., by either going to its Web site or through the SEDAR site. You can always search and find the Web site of Bell Canada through a search engine such as Yahoo (**www.yahoo.com**) or Google (**www.google.com**). How many issued and outstanding common shares did the company have in 2008 and 2009? Has the company in the past raised more money by new issues of shares or by plowing back earnings? Is that typical of Canadian public companies? (LO4)

15. **Internet.** In Figure 14.3, we calculated the book and market long-term debt-to-equity ratios of George Weston Ltd. Using Enbridge's annual report calculate the company's book long-term debt-to-equity ratio for 2008 and 2009. See if you can use other resources on the Web (*Hint:* Try the Yahoo Finance site) to calculate a recent market long-term debt-to-equity ratio estimate for the company. (LO4)

16. **Internet.** Retrieve the annual reports of Research In Motion Ltd. and Aastra Technologies Ltd. from their Web sites. Compare the major sources and uses of funds (annual cash flow report and balance sheet) for the two companies. What factors might explain the differences in financing patterns for these companies? (LO4)

CHALLENGE

17. **Comprehensive.** (LO4)
    a. Retrieve the annual report of Heineken International by going to the "Investors" section of its Web site (**www.heinekeninternational.com/investors.aspx**). Examine Heineken's internal and external sources of funds and then compare your findings with Figure 14.2 in this chapter. (See Heineken's annual cash flow statement.) What was Heineken's primary use of funds?
    b. Using book values, find the balance sheet debt ratios for Heineken in 2008 and 2009. How has the debt ratio changed if one calculates debt ratios using the market value of equity? You can use Yahoo Finance Web site to retrieve historical stock prices for Heineken International (HEIA.AS).
    c. Locate a Canadian company, preferably in the same industry as Heineken, and redo the calculations required in parts (a) and (b) for this company. What insights do you get when you compare the results for this company with that of Heineken?

Solutions to Check Points

14.1 The paid-in capital to the extent of common shares sold to the public is $15 × 100,000 shares = $1,500,000. Since book value is $3,000,000, retained earnings must be $1,500,000. Therefore, the accounts look like this:

Paid-in capital	$1,500,000
Retained earnings	1,500,000
Common equity	3,000,000

14.2 Book value is $10 million. At a discount rate of 10 percent, the market value of the firm ought to be $2 million × 20-year annuity factor at 10 percent = $17 million, which exceeds book value. At a discount rate of 20 percent, market value falls to $9.7 million, which is below book value.

14.3 The *Sarbanes-Oxley Act* tried to prevent damaging conflicts of interest. If auditing firms earn substantial business from other services to their clients, they may be more forgiving about the firm's transgressions. (For example, many believe that Enron's auditors, Arthur Andersen, might have been tougher on the company had it not also earned substantial fees from providing Enron with accounting services.) The requirement for rotation of auditors is prompted by the view that the relationship between company and auditor may become unduly cozy.

14.4 The corporation's after-tax yield on the bonds is 10% − (.35 × 10%) = 6.5 percent. The after-tax yield on the preferred stock is 8 percent. The preferred stock provides the higher after-tax return despite its lower before-tax rate. For the individual, the after-tax yield on the bonds is 10% − (.35 × 10%) = 6.5 percent. For the preferred stock, the dividend is grossed up 45% to 1.45 × 8% = 11.6 percent. The tax is .35 × 11.6% = 4.06 percent, but with a tax credit of 18.97 percent of the grossed-up dividend, it is reduced by $.1897 \times 11.6\% = 2.20$ to 1.86 percent. The after-tax return is, therefore, $8 - 1.86 = 6.14$ percent, providing a lower after-tax yield than the bonds. The bonds provide the higher after-tax yield.

14.5 Because the coupon on floating-rate debt adjusts periodically to current market conditions, the bondholder is less vulnerable to changes in market yields. The coupon rate paid by the bond is not locked in for as long a period of time. Therefore, prices of floaters should be less sensitive to changes in market interest rates.

14.6 The callable bond will sell at a lower price. Investors will not pay as much for the callable bond since they know that the firm may call it away from them if interest rates fall. Thus they know that their capital gains potential is limited, which makes the bond less valuable. If both bonds are to sell at par value, the callable bond must pay a higher coupon rate as compensation to the investor for the firm's right to call the bond.

14.7 The extra debt makes it more likely that the firm will not be able to make good on its promised payments to its creditors. If the new debt is not junior to the already-issued debt, the original bondholders suffer a loss when their bonds become more susceptible to default risk. A protective covenant limiting the amount of new debt that the firm can issue would have prevented this problem. Investors, having witnessed the problems of the RJR bondholders, generally demanded the covenant on future debt issues.

14.8 Capital markets provide liquidity for investors. Because individual shareholders can always lay their hands on cash by selling shares, they are prepared to invest in companies that retain earnings rather than pay them out as dividends. Well-functioning capital markets allow the firm to serve all its shareholders simply by maximizing value. Capital markets also provide managers with information. Without this information, it would be very difficult to determine opportunity costs of capital or to assess financial performance.

APPENDIX 14A: THE BOND REFUNDING DECISION

We saw in Section 14.4 that corporate bonds often include a call provision that allows the company to pay back the debt early. If interest rates fall and bond prices rise, the option to buy back the bond at a fixed price can be very attractive to the company. It can buy back the existing bond and issue a new one at a higher price and a lower interest rate.

The refunding decision would involve an analysis of whether it is profitable for the firm to replace an existing issue of higher-interest cost bonds with a new issue of lower-interest cost bonds.[20] The approach used is similar to the analysis done in a replacement capital budgeting situation. This involves determining the net present value (NPV) of the proposed refunding after considering incremental after-tax cash flows from the new issue relative to the old issue. The analysis will typically be conducted for the period remaining until the maturity of the existing issue. A refunding project yielding a positive net present value would be taken up, while a negative NPV project will be rejected.

Let us examine the issues involved in a refunding project through the analysis conducted by the finance manager of Strike-a-Deal, Inc.

EXAMPLE 14A

The finance manager of Strike-a-Deal, Inc., has been closely watching interest rates with a view to refunding the company's 20-year, $100 million outstanding callable bonds, which were issued at par 5 years ago but still have 15 years remaining to maturity. The bonds have a par value of $1,000 and carry a 10 percent coupon interest rate. Flotation costs of $3 million were incurred when the bonds were issued. The bonds carry a call premium of 10 percent. The finance manager feels that because of a drop in long-term interest rates, the firm can sell an additional $100 million of new 15-year bonds at a coupon interest rate of 7.7 percent. To ensure the availability of funds to refund the outstanding bonds, the new bonds will have to be sold one month before the old issue is called. The finance manager is well aware that interest will have to be paid on both issues for one month, but feels that the proceeds of the new issue can be invested for this period in money market funds to yield 5 percent annually. The estimated flotation cost on the new issue is $2.5 million. Strike-a-Deal's marginal tax rate is 35 percent. Should it refund its outstanding bonds?

As we have mentioned earlier, to determine the NPV of the proposed refunding, we would look at incremental after-tax cash flows from the new issue. To do this, we would compare, in present-value terms, the net investment required to refund the bond issue with the incremental savings generated from lower interest payments on the new issue. To arrive at present values, we would discount all such after-tax cash flows by the after-tax cost of the new issue. This would be the appropriate discount rate. Refunding projects are of low risk to the firm, since they involve only the replacement of one issue by another, so using the higher weighted average cost of capital rate would not be appropriate.

NET INVESTMENT COSTS ASSOCIATED WITH REFUNDING

Let us first look at the incremental investment required to refund the bond issue. For Strike-a-Deal, this will include the call premium to be paid on the old bonds, flotation costs, and net additional interest costs for the overlapping month when both new and old bond issues are in place. Tax implications of such incremental costs will also have to be considered, so our objective will be to arrive at the overall after-tax investment costs.

Call Premium. This works out to $.1 \times \$100,000,000 = \$10,000,000$. The call premium is not a tax-deductible expense to the firm.

[20] The refunding decision can also be applied to preferred stock issues. For instance, a company may decide to replace an existing issue of preferred stock with a new issue carrying a lower dividend rate.

Flotation Costs. For tax purposes, flotation costs must be amortized over the life of the new bond or five years, whichever is less. The flotation cost on the old bond would have been amortized by now. However, the annual tax deduction on the flotation cost on the new bond issue will have to be computed. So

$$\text{Annual tax deduction on flotation cost of new issue} = \$2{,}500{,}000/5 = \$500{,}000$$

Using Strike-a-Deal's marginal tax rate of 35 percent, the tax savings in each of the five years will be $.35 \times \$500{,}000 = \$175{,}000$. This represents an annuity series over the five-year period. The present value of these deductions will have to be computed. As discussed earlier, the appropriate discount rate here is the after-tax cost of the new debt issue:

$$\begin{aligned}\text{After-tax cost of new debt} &= 7.7\%\ (1 - \text{tax rate})\\ &= 7.7\%\ (1 - .35)\\ &= 5.005\%\end{aligned}$$

We compute the present value of the tax saving by applying the annuity formula that we studied in Chapter 5:

$$\$175{,}000\left[\frac{1 - [1/(1.05005)^5]}{.05005}\right] = \$757{,}554$$

When, from the gross flotation cost, we subtract the present value of the tax saving from amortizing such costs, we get the net after-tax flotation cost on the new issue:

Gross flotation costs on new issue	\$2,500,000
Less: Present value of associated tax savings	−757,554
Net after-tax flotation cost on new issue	\$1,742,446

Additional Interest. The new bond issue will have to be sold one month before the old bonds are replaced, so for this month Strike-a-Deal will have to incur interest costs on both issues. The additional cost during this month will be the interest that will have to be paid on the old issue. Because this interest is tax-deductible, we will consider the after-tax interest cost on the old issue.

$$\begin{aligned}\text{After-tax interest cost} &= \text{dollar amount of old issue}\\ &\quad \times (1/12 \times \text{old interest rate})(1 - T)\\ &= \$100{,}000{,}000 \times (1/12 \times .1)(1 - .35)\\ &= \$541{,}667\end{aligned}$$

Keep in mind that the proceeds of the new issue can also be invested for a month. Strike-a-Deal has decided to invest in the money market for this period. Because any interest earned on this investment will incur tax, we compute the after-tax interest earned:

$$\begin{aligned}\text{After-tax interest earned} &= \text{dollar amount of new issue}\\ &\quad \times (1/12 \times \text{new interest rate})(1 - T)\\ &= \$100{,}000{,}000 \times (1/12 \times .05)(1 - .35)\\ &= \$270{,}833\end{aligned}$$

The net after-tax additional interest cost to Strike-a-Deal is the difference between the after-tax additional interest paid on the old issue and the after-tax interest earned on the new issue, or

$$\$541{,}667 - \$270{,}833 = \$270{,}834$$

Total After-Tax Investment Costs. We have now figured out the different after-tax component costs. When we add them up, we arrive at the total present value of net investments costs associated with the refunding decision.

Call premium	\$10,000,000
Net after-tax flotation cost on new issue	1,742,446
Net after-tax additional interest	270,834
Total present value of net investment costs	\$12,013,280

NET SAVINGS ASSOCIATED WITH REFUNDING

If Strike-a-Deal goes forward with the refunding, it will save every year on lower interest payments on the new issue. To determine the extent of the annual savings, we will have to take the difference between the yearly after-tax interest costs on the two issues. These savings will continue to be generated every year over the life of the new issue and can, therefore, be represented by a 15-year annuity.

The annual after-tax interest cost on the old issue is $100,000,000 × .10 × (1 − .35) = $6,500,000. For the new issue, the annual after-tax interest cost is $100,000,000 × .077 × (1 − .35) = $5,005,000. So the yearly interest savings from going forward with refunding is $6,500,000 − $5,005,000 = $1,495,000. To find the present value of this stream of yearly savings, we, once again, discount the annuity by the after-tax interest cost of the new issue:

$$\$1{,}495{,}000\left[\frac{1 - 1/(1.05005)^{15}}{.05005}\right] = \$15{,}512{,}346$$

The present value of the net savings from refunding is therefore $15,512,346.

NET PRESENT VALUE ASSOCIATED WITH REFUNDING

Having figured out, in present value terms, the net savings and investment costs, we are now in a position to compute the NPV of the proposed refunding:

$$\begin{aligned}\text{NPV of refunding} &= \text{present value of net savings} - \text{net investment cost}\\ &= \$15{,}512{,}346 - 12{,}013{,}280 = \$3{,}499{,}066\end{aligned}$$

Since NPV is positive, the finance manager of Strike-a-Deal concludes that it will be profitable for the company to refund the existing bond issue.

You may have noticed that the analysis of bond refunding is tailor-made for spreadsheets. Spreadsheet A here recreates our analysis of Strike-a-Deal's proposed bond refunding. Spreadsheet B shows the formulas that were used to generate relevant values for the spreadsheet. Once we have the spreadsheet, we can try various sorts of "what-if analysis" to aid in our decision.

A. SPREADSHEET MODEL FOR STRIKE-A-DEAL'S PROPOSED BOND REFUNDING WITH CONVENTIONAL CALL

	A	B	C	D
1		**Rate**	**Time Period (years)**	**Dollar Amount ($)**
2	Outstanding bond issue		0	100,000,000
3	Coupon interest rate on old issue	10%		
4	New bond issue		0	100,000,000
5	Coupon interest rate on new issue	7.7%		
6	After-tax coupon interest rate on new issue	5.0%		
7	Short-term money market investment yield	5.0%		
8	Marginal tax rate	35%		
9	**Present Value of Net Investment Costs**			
10	Call premium on outstanding bond issue	10%	0	10,000,000
11	Flotation cost on new issue		0	2,500,000
12	Flotation cost amortized for tax purposes		1–5	500,000
13	Annual tax savings on amortized flotation cost		1–5	175,000
14	PV of tax savings on flotation cost		0	757,554
15	Net after-tax flotation cost on new issue		0	1,742,446
16	Additional interest cost on old issue		0	541,667
17	Interest earned on short-term investment of new issue (after tax)		0	270,833
18	Net after-tax additional interest		0	270,833
19	Total PV of after-tax investment costs (D10 + D15 + D18)		0	12,013,280
20	**Net Savings from Refunding**			
21	Annual after-tax interest on old issue		1–15	6,500,000
22	Annual after-tax interest on new issue		1–15	5,005,000
23	Net annual savings in interest cost		1–15	1,495,000
24	PV of total interest cost savings over 15 years		0	15,512,346
25	**Net Present Value (NPV) from Bond Refunding** (D24 − D19)		0	**3,499,066**

B. FORMULA INSERTS FOR STRIKE-A-DEAL'S PROPOSED BOND REFUNDING SPREADSHEET MODEL WITH CONVENTIONAL CALL

	A	B	C	D
1		**Rate**	**Time Period (years)**	**Dollar Amount ($)**
2	Outstanding bond issue		0	100,000,000
3	Coupon interest rate on old issue	.1		
4	New bond issue		0	100,000,000
5	Coupon interest rate on new issue	.077		
6	After-tax coupon interest rate on new issue	=B5*(1−B8)		
7	Short-term money market investment yield	.05		
8	Marginal tax rate	.35		
9	**Present Value of Net Investment Costs**			
10	Call premium on outstanding bond issue	.1	0	=D2*B10
11	Flotation cost on new issue		0	2,500,000
12	Flotation cost amortized for tax purposes		1−5	=D11/5
13	Annual tax savings on amortized flotation cost		1−5	=D12*BB
14	PV of tax savings on flotation cost		0	=D13*(1−(1/(B6+1)^5))/B6
15	Net after-tax flotation cost on new issue		0	=D11−D14
16	Additional interest cost on old issue		0	=D2*(1/12*B3)(1−B8)
17	Interest earned on short-term investment of new issue (after tax)		0	=D4*(1/12*B7)(1−B8)
18	Net after-tax additional interest		0	=D16−D17
19	Total PV of after-tax investment costs (D10 + D15 + D18)		0	=D10+D15+D18
20	**Net Savings from Refunding**			
21	Annual after-tax interest on old issue		1−15	=D2*B3*(1−B8)
22	Annual after-tax interest on new issue		1−15	=D4*B5*(1−B8)
23	Net annual savings in interest cost		1−15	=D21−D22
24	PV of total interest cost savings over 15 years		0	=D23*(1−(1/(B6+1)^15))/B6
25	**Net Present Value (NPV) from Bond Refunding** (D24 − D19)		0	**=D24−D19**

BOND REFUNDING WITH THE CANADA CALL OR DOOMSDAY CALL FEATURE

Our example above assumed a fixed call price based on a conventional call provision. In this situation, a sufficient decline in interest rates will make refunding profitable to the issuer. However, as we saw in Chapter 6, in Canada corporate bonds seldom have conventional call provisions. Callable bonds in Canada often come with a feature known as a "Canada call" or "Doomsday call." With this feature, if a bond is called back by the issuer before its maturity, it can be redeemed at a price set to provide a yield equivalent to that on a Canada bond of the same maturity plus a premium for default risk determined at the time of the issue. The bondholder is paid the Canada yield price, which is the higher of (a) the price calculated on the basis of the Canada bond yield plus default risk premium and (b) its par value. When interest rates fall, the call price goes up, resulting in a higher call premium. With the Canada call feature, therefore, any savings to the issuer from refunding associated with a decline in interest rates is offset by a higher call price. No wonder, then, that bonds with Canada calls rarely get called.

To see why the Canada call makes refunding less attractive, let us rework Example 14A assuming now that Strike-a-Deal's bonds are redeemable at the greater of Canada Yield Price (Canada Yield plus .7 percent) and par. You will recall, from Chapter 6, that the Canada Yield is the yield to maturity for a Government of Canada bond with the same maturity date as the Strike-a-Deal bond. At the time the finance manager is contemplating refunding the bond issue, the yield to maturity of 15-year Canada bonds is 7 percent. To determine the call price on Strike-a-Deal's bonds, its remaining cash flows will have to be discounted at the Canada yield plus .7 percent. On our calculator, we set FV = 1,000, PMT = 100, n = 15, and I = 7.7, and compute PV = 1200.526. The call price is therefore $1,200.526. Given a par value of $1,000, the call premium per bond is now $1,200.526 − $1,000 = $200.526. With 100,000 bonds outstanding, the total call premium is 100,000 × \$200.526 = \$20,052,600. Notice that the call premium is now \$10,052,600 higher than the call premium with the conventional call. When we add this additional call premium to the total present value of net investment costs that we computed earlier for the conventional call, we get \$10,052,600 + 12,013,280 = \$22,065,880.

$$\text{NPV of refunding} = \text{present value of savings} - \text{present value of net investment costs}$$
$$= \$15{,}512{,}346 - 22{,}065{,}880 = -\$6{,}553{,}534$$

Notice that, with the Canada call feature, NPV is now negative, and refunding the bonds is no longer worthwhile for Strike-a-Deal.

C. SPREADSHEET MODEL FOR STRIKE-A-DEAL'S PROPOSED BOND REFUNDING WITH CANADA CALL FEATURE

	A	B	C	D
1		**Rate**	**Time Period (years)**	**Dollar Amount ($)**
2	Outstanding bond issue		0	100,000,000
3	Par value per bond			1,000
4	Coupon interest rate on old issue	10%		
5	New bond issue		0	100,000,000
6	Coupon interest rate on new issue	7.7%		
7	After-tax coupon interest rate on new issue	5.005%		
8	Short-term money market investment yield	5.0%		
9	Marginal tax rate	35%		
10	**Present Value of Net Investment Costs**			
11	Call price per bond			1200.526
12	Call premium per bond			200.526
13	Call premium on outstanding bond issue			20,052,600
14	Flotation cost on new issue		0	2,500,000
15	Flotation cost amortized for tax purposes		1–5	500,000
16	Annual tax savings on amortized flotation cost		1–5	175,000
17	PV of tax savings on flotation cost		0	757,554
18	Net after-tax flotation cost on new issue			1,742,446
19	Additional interest cost on old issue		0	541,667
20	Interest earned on short-term investment of new issue (after tax)		0	270,833
21	Net after-tax additional interest		0	270,833
22	Total PV of after-tax investment costs (D13 + D18 + D21)		0	22,065,880
23	**Net Savings from Refunding**			
24	Annual after-tax interest on old issue		1–15	6,500,000
25	Annual after-tax interest on new issue		1–15	5,005,000
26	Net annual savings in interest cost		1–15	1,495,000
27	PV of total interest cost savings over 15 years		0	15,512,346
28	**Net Present Value (NPV) from Bond Refunding** (D27 – D22)		0	**–6,553,534**

D. FORMULA INSERTS FOR STRIKE-A-DEAL'S PROPOSED BOND REFUNDING SPREADSHEET WITH CANADA CALL FEATURE

	A	B	C	D
1		**Rate**	**Time Period (years)**	**Dollar Amount ($)**
2	Outstanding bond issue		0	100,000,000
3	Par value per bond			1,000
4	Coupon interest rate on old issue	.1		
5	New bond issue		0	100,000,000
6	Coupon interest rate on new issue	.077		
7	After-tax coupon interest rate on new issue	=B6*(1−B9)		
8	Short-term money market investment yield	.05		
9	Marginal tax rate	.35		
10	**Present Value of Net Investment Costs**			
11	Call price per bond			=100*(1−1/1.077)^15/0.077)+1,000/(1.077)^15
12	Call premium per bond			=D11−D3
13	Call premium on outstanding bond issue			=D12*D2/D3
14	Flotation cost on new issue		0	2,500,000
15	Flotation cost amortized for tax purposes		1−5	=D14/5
16	Annual tax savings on amortized flotation cost		1−5	=D15*B9
17	PV of tax savings on flotation cost		0	=D16*(1−(1/(B7+1)^5)/B7
18	Net after-tax flotation cost on new issue		0	=D14−D17
19	Additional interest cost on old issue		0	=D2*(1/12*B4)*(1−B9)
20	Interest earned on S-T investment of new issue (after tax)		0	=D5*(1/12*B8)*(1−B9)
21	Net after-tax additional interest		0	=D19−D20
22	Total PV of after-tax investment costs (D13 + D18 + D21)		0	=D13+D18+D21
23	**Net Savings from Refunding**			
24	Annual after-tax interest on old issue		1−15	=D2*B4*(1−B9)
25	Annual after-tax interest on new issue		1−15	=D5*B6*(1−B9)
26	Net annual savings in interest cost		1−15	=D24−D25
27	PV of total interest cost savings over 15 years		0	=D26*(1−(1/(B7+1)^15)/B7
28	**Net Present Value (NPV) from Bond Refunding** (D27 − D22)		0	**=D27−D22**

Questions and Problems

INTERMEDIATE

14A.1. **Bond Refunding.** E-Books.com currently has a 10-year $1 million bond issue outstanding (5 years remaining to maturity) with an 11 percent coupon interest rate and a $1,000 par value. The call premium on these bonds is 5 percent. Because of a decline in interest rates, the firm would be able to refund the issue with a $1 million issue of 9 percent 5-year bonds. The flotation costs for refunding the issue are $25,000. The new bonds will have to be issued one month before the old bonds are called. The present return on short-term government securities is 5 percent annually. E-books has a marginal tax rate of 25 percent. Assume that there are no other costs associated with refunding. Should the firm refund the bond issue?

14A.2. **Bond Refunding.** Food-Galore, Inc., has a $10 million outstanding bond issue, carrying a 12 percent coupon interest rate with 20 years remaining to maturity. This issue was sold 5 years ago and can be called by the company at a premium of 7 percent over its par value. Currently new 20-year bonds can be floated at a coupon interest rate of 9 percent. To ensure the availability of funds to pay off the old debt, the new bonds would be sold one month before the old issue is called, so for one month interest would have to be paid on both issues. Flotation costs, comprising mainly issuing and underwriting expenses, for the new debt would be $150,000. Currently, short-term interest rates are at 10 percent per annum. Food-Galore's marginal tax rate is 35 percent. Based on discounted cash flow analysis, should refunding take place?

CHALLENGE

14A.3. **Bond Refunding.** Universal Heavy Equipment is looking into the possibility of refunding its 30-year $100 million outstanding bond issue, carrying a 14 percent coupon rate, which was sold 10 years ago. If the company goes ahead with the refunding, it can sell a new 20-year issue at a lower coupon rate of 10 percent, given current low interest rates in the economy. A call premium of 12 percent will have to be paid to retire the old bonds, while flotation costs on the new issue are expected to be $5 million. The company's marginal tax rate is 35 percent. The new bonds will have to be issued one month before the old bonds are called. Short-term government securities are currently providing a return of 6 percent annually. Universal's management is aware that the low interest rates may not last for very long, and may in fact go up if the economy continues to grow very rapidly and creates inflationary pressures.

1. Provide a complete bond refunding analysis and compute the NPV of the proposed refunding.
2. Create a spreadsheet model of your analysis and also provide detailed formula inserts.
3. Now assume that the bonds have a Canada call feature and are callable at the greater of Canada Yield Price (Canada Yield plus 0.50 percent) and par. The yield to maturity on a 20-year Government of Canada bond is 9.5 percent. Rework the bond refunding analysis. How does the Canada Call feature affect the NPV of the proposed refunding? Create a new spreadsheet model for this analysis and provide detailed formula inserts.

PART 4 Financing

14 Introduction to Corporate Financing and Governance

15 Venture Capital, IPOs, and Seasoned Offerings

15.1 Venture Capital

15.2 The Initial Public Offering

15.3 The Underwriters

15.4 Listing on the Stock Market

15.5 Rights Issues and General Cash Offers by Public Companies

15.6 The Private Placement

15.7 Summary

Appendix 15A The Financing of New and Small Enterprises

Appendix 15B Hotch Pot's New Issue Prospectus

CHAPTER 15

Venture Capital, IPOs, and Seasoned Offerings

LEARNING OBJECTIVES

After studying this chapter, you should be able to:

LO1 Explain how venture capital firms design successful deals.

LO2 Explain how firms make initial public offerings and the costs of such offerings.

LO3 State what is involved when established firms make a general cash offer or a private placement of securities.

LO4 Explain the role of the underwriter in an issue of securities.

LO5 Discuss some of the significant questions that arise when established firms make a rights issue, a general cash offer, or a private placement of securities.

Ontario Premier Dalton McGuinty opens the Toronto Stock Exchange (TSX) for trading Wednesday, November 14, 2007, in Toronto.

Courtesy of the Toronto Stock Exchange.

Bill Gates and Paul Allen founded Microsoft in 1975 when they were both around 20. Eleven years later, Microsoft shares were sold to the public for $21 a share and immediately zoomed to $35. The largest shareholder was Bill Gates, whose shares in Microsoft then were worth US$350 million.

In 1976 two college dropouts, Steve Jobs and Steve Wozniak, sold their most valuable possessions, a van and a couple of calculators, and used the cash to start manufacturing computers in a garage. In 1980 when Apple Computer went public, the shares were offered to investors at $22 and jumped to $36. At that point, the shares owned by the company's two founders were worth US$414 million.

In 1996 two Stanford computer science students, Larry Page and Sergey Brin, decided to collaborate to develop a Web search engine. To help turn their idea into a commercial product, the two friends succeeded in raising almost $1 million from several wealthy investors (known as *angel*), and this was later supplemented by funding from two venture capital firms that specialized in helping young startup businesses. The company, now named Google, went public in 2004 at a price of $85 a share, putting a value on the enterprise of $23 billion.

Mike Lazardis quit his studies in electrical engineering at the University of Waterloo at 23.[1] In 1984 he started Research In Motion (RIM) with two friends. RIM went public in 1997, offering 13.8 million common shares at $7.25 each on the Toronto Stock Exchange. RIM's product, the BlackBerry e-mail pager-cum-computer, was such a success that by early 2000 its shares were trading at $260. Mike Lazardis became a billionaire and recently shared an Academy Award for technical achievement with a co-worker for designing a device that quickened the pace of film editing.

Such stories illustrate that the most important asset of a new firm may be a good idea. But that is not all you need. To take an idea from the drawing board to a prototype and through to large-scale production requires ever greater amounts of capital.

To get a new company off the ground, entrepreneurs may rely on their own savings and personal bank loans. But this is unlikely to be sufficient to build a successful enterprise. Venture capital firms specialize in providing new equity capital to help firms over the awkward-adolescent period before they are large enough to "go public." In the first part of this chapter, we will explain how venture capital firms do this.

If the firm continues to be successful, there will likely come a time when it needs to tap a wider source of capital. At this point it will make its first public issue of common stock. This is known as an *initial public offering*, or IPO. In the second section of the chapter we will describe what is involved in an IPO.

A company's initial public offering is seldom its last. In Chapter 14 we saw that internally generated cash is not usually sufficient to satisfy the firm's needs. Established companies make up the deficit by issuing more equity or debt. The remainder of this chapter looks at this process.

[1] While it is true that some of these highly successful entrepreneurs dropped out of college or university, we do not want to give the impression that quitting school had anything to do with their success.

LO1 15.1 VENTURE CAPITAL

You have taken a big step. With a couple of friends, you have formed a corporation to open a number of fast-food outlets, offering innovative combinations of international dishes such as sushi with sauerkraut, curry Bolognese, and chow mein with Yorkshire pudding. Breaking into the fast-food business costs money, but after pooling your savings and borrowing to the hilt from the bank, you have raised $100,000 and purchased one million shares in the new company. At this *zero-stage* investment, your company's assets are $100,000 plus the *idea* for your new product.

That $100,000 is enough to get the business off the ground, but if the idea takes off, you will need more capital to pay for new restaurants. You therefore decide to look for an investor prepared to back an untried company in return for part of the profits. Equity capital in young businesses is known as **venture capital**, and it is provided by specialized venture capital firms, financial and investment institutions such as banks and pension funds, and government agencies. If you need very-early-stage financing for your new enterprise, you may seek out an **angel** investor—a wealthy individual investor that can play a critical role in the creation of new ventures by making small-scale investments in local startups and early-stage ventures. Angels also bring a significant hands-on contribution to such business ventures. We will describe these venture capital providers in more detail in Appendix 15A.

venture capital Money invested to finance a new firm.

angel A wealthy individual investor in early-stage ventures.

Most entrepreneurs can spin a plausible yarn about their company. But it is as hard to convince a venture capitalist to invest in your business as it is to get a first novel published. Your first step is to prepare a *business plan*. This describes your product, the potential market, the production method, and the resources—time, money, employees, facilities, and equipment—needed for success. It helps if you can point out that you are prepared to put your money where your mouth is. By staking all your savings in the company, you *signal* your faith in the business.

The venture capital company knows that the success of a new business depends on the effort its managers put in. Therefore, it will try to structure a deal in which you have a strong incentive to work hard. For example, if you agree to accept a modest salary (and look forward instead to increasing the value of your investment in the company's stock), the venture capital company knows you will be committed to working hard. However, if you insist on a watertight employment contract and a fat salary, you won't find it easy to raise venture capital.

You are unlikely to persuade a venture capitalist to give you as much money as you need all at once. Rather, the firm will probably give you enough to reach the first major checkpoint. Suppose you can convince the venture capital company to buy one million new shares for $.50 each. This means it owns half of the firm: it owns one million shares, and you and your friends also own one million shares. Because the venture capitalist is paying $500,000 for a claim to half your firm, it is placing a $1 million value on the business. After this *first-stage* financing, your company's balance sheet looks like this:

First-Stage Market-Value Balance Sheet ($ millions)

Assets		Liabilities and Shareholders' Equity	
Cash from new equity	$ .5	New equity from venture capital	$ .5
Other assets	.5	Your original equity	.5
Value	$1.0	Value	$1.0

Check Point 15.1

Why might the venture capital company prefer to put up only part of the funds up front? Would this affect the amount of effort put in by you, the entrepreneur? Is your willingness to accept only part of the venture capital that will eventually be needed a good signal of the likely success of the venture?

Suppose that two years later your business has grown to the point that it needs a further injection of equity. This *second-stage* financing might involve the issue of another one million shares at $1 each. Some of these shares might be bought by the original backers and some by other venture capital firms. The balance sheet after the new financing would then be as follows:

Second-Stage Market-Value Balance Sheet ($ millions)

Assets		Liabilities and Shareholders' Equity	
Cash from new equity	$1.0	New equity from second-stage financing	$1.0
Other assets	2.0	Equity from first stage	1.0
		Your original equity	1.0
Value	$3.0	Value	$3.0

Notice that the value of the initial one million shares owned by you and your friends has now been marked up to $1 million. Is this beginning to sound like a money machine? It works only if you have made a success of the business and new investors are prepared to pay $1 to buy a share in the business. When you started out, it wasn't clear that sushi and sauerkraut would catch on. If it hadn't caught on, the venture capital firm might have refused to put up more funds.

You are not yet in a position to cash in on your investment, but your gain is real. The second-stage investors have paid $1 million for a one-third share in the company. (There are now three million shares outstanding, and the second-stage investors hold one million shares.) Therefore, at least these impartial observers—who are willing to back up their opinions with a large investment—must have decided that the company was worth at least $3 million. Your one-third share is therefore also worth $1 million.

VENTURE CAPITAL COMPANIES

While some young companies grow with the aid of angels, many others raise capital from specialist venture capital firms, which pool funds from a variety of investors, seek out fledgling companies to invest in, and then work with these companies as they try to grow. In addition, some large technology firms such as Intel, Johnson & Johnson, and Sun Microsystems, act as *corporate venturers* by providing capital to new innovative companies.

Most venture capital funds are organized as limited private partnerships with a fixed life of about 10 years. Pension funds and other investors are the limited partners. The management company, which is the general partner, is responsible for making and overseeing the investments and, in return, receives a fixed fee as well as a share of the profits. You will find that these venture capital partnerships are often lumped together with similar partnerships that provide funds for companies in distress or that buy out whole companies and then take them private. The general term for these activities is *private equity investing*.

Venture capital firms are not passive investors. They are usually represented on each company's board of directors, they help to recruit senior managers for the company, and they provide ongoing advice that can be very valuable to businesses in their early years and help them bring their products more quickly to market.

For every 10 first-stage venture capital investments, only two or three may survive as successful, self-sufficient businesses, and only one may pay off big. From these statistics come two rules of success in venture capital investment. First, don't shy away from uncertainty; accept a low probability of success. But don't buy into a business unless you can see the *chance* of a big, public company in a profitable market. There's no sense taking a big risk unless the reward is big if you win. Second, cut your losses; identify losers early, and if you can't fix the problem—by replacing management, for example—don't throw good money after bad.

The same advice holds for any backer of a risky startup—after all, only a fraction of new businesses are funded by card-carrying venture capitalists. Some are funded directly by managers or by friends and family. Some grow using bank loans and reinvested earnings. But if your startup combines high risk, sophisticated technology, and substantial investment, you will probably try to find venture capital financing.

LO2 15.2 THE INITIAL PUBLIC OFFERING

Very few new businesses make it big, but those that do can be very profitable. For example, an investor who provided $1,000 of first-stage financing for Intel would have reaped over $25 million by 2007. So venture capitalists keep sane by reminding themselves of the success stories[2]—those who got in on the ground floor of firms like Genentech, Sun Microsystems, Federal Express, and Research In Motion.

For many successful startups there comes a time when they need more capital than can comfortably be provided by a small number of individuals or venture capitalists. At this point one solution is to sell the business to a larger firm. But many entrepreneurs do not easily fit into a corporate bureaucracy and would prefer instead to remain the boss. In this case, the company may choose to raise money by selling shares to the public. A firm is said to "go public" when it sells its first issue of shares in a general offering to investors. This first sale of stock is called an **initial public offering**, or **IPO**.

initial public offering (IPO) First offering of stock to the general public.

A firm is said to "go public" when it sells its first issue of shares in a general offering to investors. This first sale of stock is called an *initial public offering (IPO)*.

An IPO is called a *primary* offering when new shares are sold to raise additional cash for the company. It is a *secondary* offering when the company's founders and the venture capitalist cash in on some of their gains by selling shares. A secondary offer, therefore, is no more than a sale of shares from the early investors to new investors, and the cash raised in a secondary offer does not flow to the company. Of course, IPOs can be, and commonly are, both primary and secondary: the firm raises new cash at the same time that some of the already-existing shares in the firm are sold to the public. Some of the biggest secondary offerings have involved governments selling off stock in nationalized enterprises. For example, the Japanese government raised US$12.6 billion by selling its stock in Nippon Telegraph and Telephone, and the British government took in US$9 billion from its sale of British Gas. The Canadian government received about $2.2 billion in 1996 in the biggest initial public offering in Canadian history—when 84 million shares of the newly privatized Canadian National Railway hit the stock market. The world's largest IPO took place in 2010 when the Chinese Government raised US$22.1 billion from the sale of shares in the state-owned Agricultural Bank of China.

We have seen that companies may make an IPO to raise new capital or to enable the existing shareholders to cash out, but there may be other benefits to going public. For example, the company's stock price provides a readily available yardstick of performance and allows the firm to reward the management team with stock options. And, because information about the company becomes more widely available, the firm can diversify its sources of finance and reduce its borrowing cost.

While there are advantages to having a market for your shares, we should not give the impression that firms everywhere aim to go public. In many countries it is common for businesses to remain privately owned. Even in Canada and the United States many firms choose to remain as private, unlisted companies. They include some very large operations, such as McCain Foods in Canada and Bechtel and Levi Strauss in the United States. Also, you should not think of the issue process in the United States as a one-way street; public firms often go into reverse and return to being privately owned. For a somewhat extreme example, consider the food service company Aramark. It began life in 1936 as a private company and went public in 1960. In 1984 the management bought out the company and took it private, and it remained private until 2001, when it had its second public offering. But the experiment did not last long, for six years later Aramark was the object of yet another buyout that took the company private once again.

Managers often chafe at the red tape involved in running a public company and at the unrelenting pressure from shareholders to report increasing earnings. These complaints have become more vocal since the passages of Bill C-198 in Ontario and the *Sarbanes-Oxley Act* in the United States. This act has sought to prevent a repeat of the corporate scandals that brought about the collapse of Enron and WorldCom, but a consequence has been an increased reporting burden on

[2] Fortunately, the successes have outweighed the failures. The National Venture Capital Association (NVCA) estimated that net returns on venture capital funds averaged about 20 percent a year for the 10 years ending June 2007.

small public companies and a rise in the number of companies reverting to private ownership. Following the recent global financial crisis, the United States enacted the *Dodd-Frank Wall Street Reform and Consumer Protection Act* of 2010. The act has sought to bring in a wide range of financial regulatory reform. Time will tell about the efficacy of these measures.

ARRANGING A PUBLIC ISSUE

underwriter Investment dealer that buys an issue of securities from a company and resells it to the public.

Once a firm decides to go public, the first task is to select the **underwriters**—investment dealers that act as financial "midwives" to a new issue. Usually they play a triple role—first providing the company with procedural and financial advice, then buying the stock, and finally reselling it to the public.

A small IPO may have only one underwriter, but larger issues usually requires a syndicate of underwriters who buy the issue and resell it. For example, the initial public offering by Microsoft involved a total of 114 underwriters.

spread Difference between public offer price and price paid by underwriter.

In the typical underwriting arrangement, called a *firm commitment*, the underwriters buy the securities from the firm and then resell them to the public. The underwriters receive payment in the form of a **spread**—that is, they are allowed to sell the shares at a slightly higher price than they paid for them. But the underwriters also accept the risk that they won't be able to sell the stock at the agreed offering price. If that happens, they will be stuck with unsold shares and must get the best price they can for them. In the more risky cases, the underwriter may not be willing to enter into a firm commitment and will handle the issue on a *best-efforts* basis. In this case the underwriter agrees to sell as much of the issue as possible but does not guarantee the sale of the entire issue. Because fees tend to be less in a best-efforts distribution, it might also be favoured by a high-quality issuer wishing to reduce issuing expenses. Investment dealers prefer to include a *lockup period* clause in underwriting agreements. Such a clause prevents the existing equity holders such as the company founders and other private equity investors from flooding the market by selling their shares and cashing out up to a given period of time.

Before any stock can be sold to the public, the company must satisfy the requirements of provincial securities laws and regulations.[3] Each province and territory in Canada has a securities commission or related authority and its own piece of securities legislation. The stock may have to be registered with an appropriate securities commission. For instance, companies listed on the Toronto Stock Exchange (TSX) come under the purview of the Ontario Securities Commission (OSC), which administers the *Ontario Securities Act*. Generally, securities laws tend to be similar across provinces with the OSC playing a leadership role, given the overall importance of the TSX.

prospectus Formal summary that provides information on an issue of securities.

The first part of the registration statement is distributed to the public in the form of a preliminary **prospectus**. The preliminary prospectus contains some financial information that will also be included in the final prospectus, the company's history and its plans for the future, but it does not provide the price at which the security will be offered. It is sometimes called a *red herring*, because it contains a printed disclaimer in red letters, which claims that it is not a final document and is subject to amendments because the securities commission has neither approved nor disapproved the registration statement.

One function of the prospectus is to warn investors about the risks involved in any investment in the firm. Some investors have joked that if they read prospectuses carefully, they would never dare buy a new issue. Appendix 15B is an example prospectus for your fast-food business.

The securities commission, while reviewing the preliminary prospectus, may require it to be revised before approving it. Recent Canadian prospectuses can be found at the System for Electronic Documents and Retrieval (SEDAR) site (**www.sedar.com**).

The company and its underwriters also need to set the issue price. To gauge how much the stock is worth, they may undertake discounted cash flow calculations like those described in Chapter 7. They also look at the price-earnings ratios of the shares of the firm's principal competitors.

[3] In contrast, in the United States, all securities regulation is handled at the federal level by the Securities and Exchange Commission (SEC).

Before settling on the issue price, the underwriters might arrange a "roadshow," which gives the underwriters and the company's management an opportunity to talk to potential investors. These investors may then offer their reaction to the issue, suggest what they think is a fair price, and indicate how much stock they would be prepared to buy. This allows the underwriters to build up a book of likely orders. Although investors are not bound by their indications, they know that if they want to remain in the underwriters' good books, they must be careful not to renege on their expressions of interest.

underpricing Issuing securities at an offering price set below the true value of the security.

The managers of the firm are eager to secure the highest possible price for their stock, but the underwriters are likely to be cautious because they will be left with any unsold stock if they overestimate investor demand. As a result, underwriters typically try to underprice the initial public offering. **Underpricing**, they argue, is needed to tempt investors to buy stock and to reduce the cost of marketing the issue to customers. Underpricing represents a cost to the existing owners, since the new investors are allowed to buy shares in the firm at a favourable price. The cost of underpricing may be very large.

> Underpricing represents a cost to the existing owners, since the new investors are allowed to buy shares in the firm at a favourable price. The cost of underpricing may be very large.

It is common to see the stock price increase substantially from the issue price in the days following an issue. Such immediate price jumps indicate the amount by which the shares were underpriced compared to what investors were willing to pay for them. For example, one study of new issues between 1990 and 2007 found an average first-day price rise of 23 percent.[4] Sometimes new issues are dramatically underpriced. In January 2000, for example, six million shares in 724 Solutions were sold in an IPO simultaneously on the Toronto and Nasdaq stock exchanges, priced at $37.29 and US$26, respectively, per share. When the issue opened, the stock started trading at $108 on the TSX and US$73 on Nasdaq. Greg Wolfond, the co-founder of 724 Solutions, owned eight million shares in the company and ended the day US$828 million richer than when he woke up that morning. Unfortunately, the bonanza did not last. By July 2001, the stock price had fallen to a little over $10 on the TSX.

EXAMPLE 15.1 UNDERPRICING OF IPOs

Suppose an IPO is a secondary issue, and the firm's founders sell part of their holding to investors. Clearly, if the shares are sold for less than their true worth, the founders will suffer an opportunity loss.

But what if the IPO is a primary issue that raises new cash for the company? Do the founders care whether the shares are sold for less than their market value? The following example illustrates that they do care.

Suppose Cosmos.com has two million shares outstanding and now offers a further one million shares to investors at $50. On the first day of trading, the share price jumps to $80, so that the shares that the company sold for $50 million are now worth $80 million. The total market capitalization of the company is 3 million × $80 = $240 million.

The value of the founders' shares is equal to the total value of the company less the value of the shares that have been sold to the public—in other words, $240 − $80 = $160 million. The founders might justifiably rejoice at their good fortune. However, if the company had issued shares at a higher price, it would have needed to sell fewer shares to raise the $50 million that it needs, and the founders would have retained a larger share of the company. For example, suppose that the outside investors, who put up $50 million, received shares that were *worth* only $50 million. In that case the value of the founders' shares would be $240 − $50 = $190 million.

The effect of selling shares below their true value is to transfer $30 million of value from the founders to the investors who buy the new shares.

Unfortunately, underpricing does not mean that anyone can become wealthy by buying stock in IPOs. If an issue is underpriced, everybody will want to buy it and the underwriters will not have enough stock to go around. You are therefore likely to get only a small share of these hot issues. If it is overpriced, other investors are unlikely to want it, and the underwriter will be only

[4] These figures are provided on Professor Jay Ritter's home page, **bear.cba.ufl.edu/ritter**.

too delighted to sell it to you. This phenomenon is known as the *winner's curse*.[5] It implies that, unless you can spot which issues are underpriced, you are likely to receive a small proportion of the cheap issues and a large proportion of the expensive ones. Since the dice are loaded against uninformed investors, they will play the game only if there is substantial underpricing on average. An unsavoury explanation for the underpricing phenomenon is *spinning*, through which the underwriter may allocate shares in an initial public offering to preferred clients who, in turn, are able to reap windfall profits by selling the shares. In the late 1990s during the time of the Internet bubble, this practice enabled some investment dealers to provide favours to clients.

EXAMPLE 15.2 UNDERPRICING OF IPOs AND INVESTOR RETURNS

Suppose that an investor will earn an immediate 10 percent return on underpriced IPOs and lose 5 percent on overpriced IPOs. But because of high demand, you may get only half the shares you bid for when the issue is underpriced. Suppose you bid for \$1,000 of shares in two issues, one overpriced and the other underpriced. You are awarded the full \$1,000 of the overpriced issue, but only \$500 worth of shares in the underpriced issue. The net gain on your two investments is $(.10 \times \$500) - (.05 \times \$1{,}000) = 0$. Your net profit is zero, despite the fact that on average, IPOs are underpriced. You have suffered the winner's curse: You "win" a larger allotment of shares when they are overpriced.

Check Point 15.2 What is the percentage profit earned by an investor who can identify the underpriced issues in Example 15.2? Who are such investors likely to be?

flotation costs The costs incurred when a firm issues new securities to the public.

The costs of a new issue are termed **flotation costs**. Underpricing is not the only flotation cost. In fact, when people talk about the cost of a new issue, they often think only of the *direct costs* of the issue. For example, preparation of the registration statement and prospectus involves management, legal counsel, and accountants, as well as underwriters and their advisors. There is also the underwriting spread. (Remember, underwriters make their profit by selling the issue at a higher price than they paid for it.)

According to the Toronto Stock Exchange, Canadian companies raised over \$60 billion in new equity financing in 2009, including almost \$5 billion through 60 initial public offerings. Figure 15.1 summarizes the results of a study that compared the direct costs of going public, expressed as a percentage of total proceeds for IPOs on the TSX, Nasdaq, and NYSE over the period January 1, 1998, to September 30, 1999.[6] Direct costs include underwriting commissions, legal, accounting, and other administrative costs. In general, larger IPO issues have lower direct costs as a percentage of total proceeds. For a small IPO of no more than \$10 million, the underwriting spread and administrative costs are likely to absorb over 11 to 17 percent of the proceeds from the issue depending on the exchange. For the very largest IPOs, these direct costs may amount to only 3.5 percent of the proceeds.

Figure 15.2 details the extent of underpricing on the three exchanges for a subsample of the group of IPOs discussed above. This is estimated by calculating the percentage difference between the offer price of the share and its closing price after the first day of trading. For the TSX, the simple average of the underpricing was 10 percent while the weighted average was 5.8 percent. For the American exchanges, the numbers were found to be higher.

[5] The highest bidder in an auction is the participant who places the highest value on the auctioned object. Therefore, it is likely that the winning bidder has an overly optimistic assessment of true value. Winning the auction suggests that you have overpaid for the object—this is the winner's curse. In the case of IPOs, your ability to "win" an allotment of shares may signal that the stock is overpriced.

[6] For complete details of the study, see T. Shutt and H. Williams, "Going to Market: The Costs of IPOs in Canada and the United States" (Conference Board of Canada, June 2000), 1–4.

FIGURE 15.1
Direct cost as a percentage of total proceeds (by size category, figures in millions, U.S. dollars).

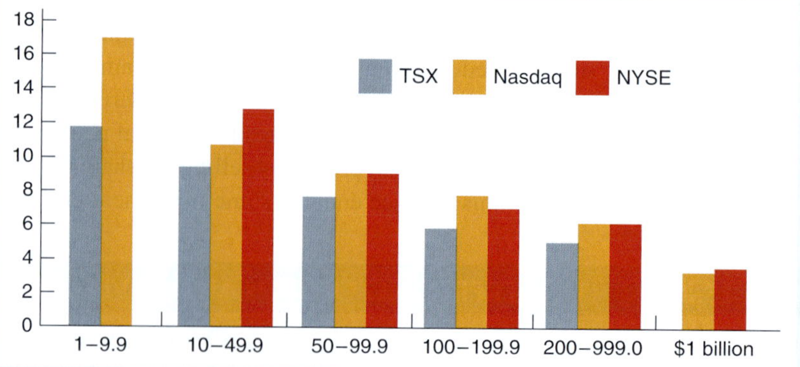

Source: Financial Post DataGroup, Securities Data Company. Excerpted from T. Shutt and H. Williams, "Going to Market: The Cost of IPOs in Canada and the United States" (Ottawa: Conference Board of Canada, June 2000), 1–4.

FIGURE 15.2
Degree of underpricing.

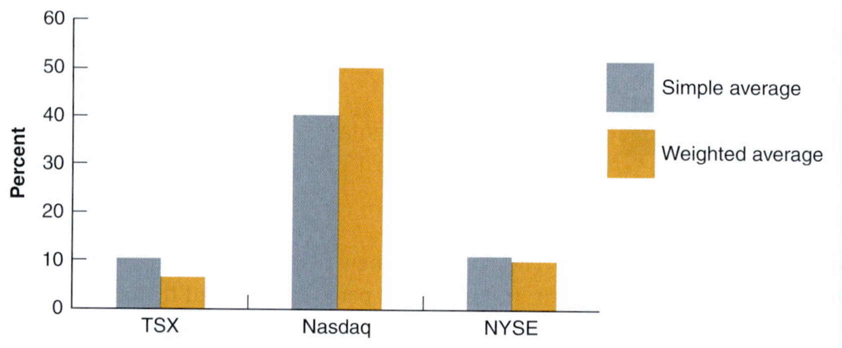

Source: Financial Post DataGroup, Securities Data Company. Excerpted from T. Shutt and H. Williams, "Going to Market: The Cost of IPOs in Canada and the United States" (Ottawa: Conference Board of Canada, June 2000), 1–4.

EXAMPLE 15.3 COSTS OF AN IPO

When the American investment bank Goldman Sachs went public in 1999, the sale was partly a primary issue (the company sold new shares to raise cash) and partly a secondary one (two large existing shareholders cashed in some of their shares). The underwriters acquired a total of 69 million Goldman Sachs shares for US$50.75 each and sold them to the public at an offering price of $53.[7] The underwriters' spread was therefore $53 − $50.75 = $2.25. The firm and its shareholders also paid a total of US$9.2 million in legal fees and other costs. By the end of the first day's trading, Goldman's stock price had risen to US$70.

Here are the direct costs of the Goldman Sachs issue:

Direct Expenses	(US$ in millions)
Underwriting spread	69 million × $2.25 = $155.25
Other expenses	9.2
Total direct expenses	$164.45

[7] No prizes for guessing which investment bank acted as lead underwriter.

The total amount of money raised by the issue was 69 million × \$53 = \$3,657 million. Of this sum, 4.5 percent was absorbed by direct expenses (that is, 164.45/3,657 = .045).

In addition to these direct costs, there was underpricing. The market valued each share of Goldman Sachs at US\$70, so the cost of underpricing was 69 million × (\$70 − \$53) = \$1,173 million, resulting in total costs of \$164.45 + \$1,173 = \$1,337.45 million. Therefore, while the total market value of the issued shares was 69 million × \$70 = \$4,830 million, direct costs and the costs of underpricing absorbed nearly 28 percent of the market value of the shares.

Check Point 15.3

Suppose that the underwriters acquired Goldman Sachs shares for US\$60 and sold them to the public at an offering price of \$64. If all other features of the offer were unchanged (and investors still valued the stock at \$70 a share), what would have been the direct costs of the issue and the costs of underpricing? What would have been the total costs as a proportion of the market value of the shares?

LO3 15.3 THE UNDERWRITERS

We have described underwriters as playing a triple role—providing advice, buying a new issue from the company, and reselling it to investors. Underwriters don't just help the company make its initial public offering; they are called in whenever a company wishes to raise cash by selling securities to the public.

Most companies raise capital only occasionally, but underwriters are in the business all the time. Established underwriters are careful of their reputation and will not handle a new issue unless they believe the facts have been presented fairly to investors. Thus, in addition to handling the sale of an issue, the underwriters, in effect, give it their seal of approval. This implied endorsement may be worth quite a bit to a company that is coming to the market for the first time.

For large issues, a group of underwriters called a *syndicate* or *banking group* will usually be formed to handle the sale. Syndication helps to market and distribute the issue more widely and also to spread its risks. The principal underwriter acts as the lead manager to the issue while other underwriters in the group are also responsible for buying and reselling the security, but play *non-lead roles*.

Underwriting is not always fun. On October 15, 1987, the British government finalized arrangements to sell its holding of British Petroleum (BP) shares at £3.30 a share. This huge issue involving more than US\$12 billion was underwritten by an international group of underwriters and simultaneously marketed in a number of countries. Four days after the underwriting arrangement was finalized, the October stock market crash occurred and stock prices nosedived. The underwriters appealed to the British government to cancel the issue, but the government hardened its heart and pointed out that the underwriters knew the risks when they agreed to handle the sale.[8] By the closing date of the offer, the price of BP stock had fallen to £2.96, and the underwriters had lost more than US\$1 billion. Needless to say, the business is very competitive, resulting, at times, in participants being accused of unethical behaviour. As the nearby Finance in Action box describes, this is what happened when Canadian Imperial Bank of Commerce (CIBC) recently sued some high-profile former employees who defected from the bank to form Genuity Capital Markets, a new investment banking firm. CIBC alleged that the employees had taken with them privileged information from the bank when they left.

Companies get to make only one IPO, but underwriters are in the business all the time. Wise underwriters, therefore, realize that their reputation is on the line and will not handle an issue

[8] The government's only concession was to put a floor on the underwriters' losses by giving them the option to resell their stock to the government at £2.80 a share. The BP offering is described and analyzed in C. Muscarella and M. Vetsuypens, "The British Petroleum Stock Offering: An Application of Option Pricing," *Journal of Applied Corporate Finance* 1 (1989): 74–80.

Finance in Action

Allegations of Unethical Conduct: The Controversy Surrounding Ex-Employees of CIBC and Genuity Capital Markets

CIBC is suing Genuity Capital Markets, a new Toronto-based investment management firm established by six former CIBC employees. The lawsuit centres around CIBC's allegation that these former employees used their BlackBerrys to improperly recruit their colleagues while still working at the bank.

The case against Genuity was established through CIBC's probing of the alleged conspirators' e-mail for evidence, including those of David Kassie, CIBC's one-time vice-chairman and a 25-year veteran employee with the firm who resigned in February of 2004. Mr. Kassie, an aggressive dealmaker once regarded as the heir successor to CIBC chief executive officer John Hunkin, was ousted as head of CIBC World Markets in 2004 as the bank attempted to overhaul its culture and lower its risk profile following a settlement with U.S. regulators over its involvement with disgraced Enron Corp.

CIBC filed a statement of claim against Genuity late Friday, and added David Morrison, Ted Hirst, and Gunnar Eggertson to its original list of defendants. The bitter legal battle erupted this month when CIBC sued six former employees, including star investment banker David Kassie and several other top dealmakers, for allegedly taking confidential information from the bank and planning a "scheme" to lure co-workers to Genuity. The bank is asking for $10 million in damages, plus costs, any compensation paid while employees were planning Genuity, all of Genuity's revenue, and the right to inspect the IT equipment of ex-employees.

Mr. Morrison was head of institutional equity sales at CIBC World Markets Inc. before he resigned from the bank's brokerage arm in mid-December, shortly after year-end bonuses were paid. Mr. Hirst and Mr. Eggertson are a Vancouver-based investment-banking team specializing in the mining sector, and are among the more than 20 CIBC traders, analysts, and bankers who have already left for Genuity.

Genuity's founders have denied CIBC's allegations.

CIBC argues that the former employees named in the suit, who all went to Genuity after leaving the bank in early 2004, had agreed not to "directly or indirectly solicit" their former colleagues for 21 months; however, their e-mail records indicated that they were recruiting for Genuity during the summer of 2004. These records were culled from the supposedly secure BlackBerry PIN messages.

In a recent interview, Mr. Kassie insisted he did not recruit former colleagues or spirit away confidential information from the bank, pointing out that potential employees signed confidentiality agreements with Genuity in which they confirmed they had not been solicited. However, the bank is still seeking a court-imposed injunction that would prevent Genuity from soliciting any of its staff.

Genuity officially opened for business earlier this month, and is regarded as the largest startup investment-banking boutique in Bay Street history. Last week it unveiled its first major deal: an advisory role on Cedara Software Corp.'s planned $477 million merger with Merge Technologies Inc. of Milwaukee.

In addition to Mr. Kassie, CIBC is suing Phil Evershed, who was the bank's head of mergers and acquisitions; Dan Daviau, a high-ranking investment banker specializing in technology and media; former vice-chair Earl Rotman, one of the architects of CIBC's push into income trusts; and John Esteireiro, who ran the trading operations.

On the legal side, this case is significant in that it marks one of the first times (if not the first time) an employer has used PIN-forwarded e-mails against former employees in a public court battle.

Sources: Sinclair Stewart, "CIBC Names Three More in Lawsuit," *The Globe and Mail*, January 24, 2005; Javad Heydary, "Is Your Boss Monitoring Your Blackberry?" *E-Commerce Times*, May 26, 2005, **www.technewsworld.com/story/security/43376.html**, accessed December 6, 2011; "Canada Rocked by Recruiting Scandal: CIBC Sues Genuity for Recruiting Its Employees," *Canadian Headhunter*, January 9, 2009, **canadianheadhunter.blogspot.com/2005/01/canada-rocked-by-recruiting-scandal.html**, accessed December 6, 2011.

unless they believe the facts have been presented fairly to investors. If a new issue goes wrong and the stock price crashes, the underwriters can find themselves very unpopular with their clients. For example, in 1999 the software company VA Linux went public at $30 a share. The next day trading opened at $299 a share, but then the price began to sag. Within two years it had fallen below $2. Disgruntled VA Linux investors sued the underwriters for overhyping the issue. VA Linux investors were not the only ones to feel aggrieved. As the next Finance in Action box explains, investment banks soon found themselves embroiled in a major scandal as evidence emerged that they had deliberately oversold many of the issues that they underwrote during the dot-com boom years. The underwriter's seal of approval for a new issue no longer seemed as valuable as it once had.

WHO ARE THE UNDERWRITERS?

Since underwriters play such a crucial role in new issues, we should look at who they are. Several hundred investment banks, security dealers, and brokers are, at least, sporadically involved in underwriting. However, the market for the larger issues is dominated by the major investment

Finance in Action

How Scandal Hit the Investment Banking Industry

For investment banks, 1999 looked like a wonderful year. Not only did they underwrite a near-record number of IPOs, but the stocks that they sold leaped by an average of 71 percent on their first day of trading, earning the underwriters some very grateful clients. Just three years later the same investment banks were in disgrace. Probing by the New York State attorney general, Eliot Spitzer, uncovered a chronicle of unethical and shameful behaviour during the boom years.

As the dot-com stock market boom developed, investment banking analysts had begun to take on the additional role of promoters of the shares they analyzed, in the process becoming celebrities with salaries to match. The early run-up in the stock price of dot-com IPOs therefore owed much to hype by the underwriters' analysts, who strongly promoted stocks that they sometimes privately thought were overpriced. One superstar Internet analyst was revealed in internal e-mails to have believed that stocks he was peddling to investors were "junk" and "a piece of crap." In many cases the stocks were indeed junk, and the underwriters who had puffed the IPOs soon found themselves sued by disgruntled investors who had bought at the inflated prices.

The underwriters' troubles deepened further when it was disclosed that in a number of cases they had allocated stock in hot new issues to the personal brokerage accounts of the CEOs of major corporate clients. This stock could then be sold, or "spun," for quick profits. Five senior executives of leading telecom companies were disclosed to have received a total of $28 million in profits from their allocation of stocks in IPOs underwritten by one bank. Over the same period the bank received over $100 million of business from these five companies. Eliot Spitzer argued that such lucrative perks were really attempts by the banks to buy future business and that the profits therefore belonged to the companies' shareholders rather than the executives. Soon top executives of several other companies were facing demands from disgruntled shareholders that they return to their companies the profits they had pocketed from hot initial public offerings.

These scandals that engulfed the investment banking industry resulted in a $1.4 billion payout by the banks and an agreement to separate investment banking and research departments, hire independent consultants, and select independent research providers. But the revelations also raised troubling questions about ethical standards and the pressures that can lead employees to unscrupulous behaviour.

dealers, which specialize in underwriting new issues, dealing in securities, and arranging mergers. These firms enjoy great prestige, experience, and financial muscle.

Table 15.1 lists some of the largest Canadian firms, ranked by total value of issues in 2009. Notice that each of the firms has acted as a lead underwriter and also in a non-lead capacity within a syndicate. RBC Capital Markets, the winner, raised a total of $58,540 million.

Of course, only a small proportion of these issues was for companies that were coming to the market for the first time. Table 15.2 lists the top 10 Canadian corporate equity issues in 2008.

Some of the largest debt and equity issues are in the United States. In Chapter 14, we pointed out that instead of issuing bonds in Canada, corporations can issue eurobonds in London, which are then sold to investors outside Canada. In addition, new equity issues by large multinational companies are increasingly marketed to investors throughout the world. Since these securities are

TABLE 15.1
Canada's top underwriters for equity and debt, 2009 (dollar figures in millions).

Underwriter	Total Number	Total Amount
1 RBC Capital Markets	242	58,540
2 TD Securities Inc.	137	37,336
3 CIBC World Markets Inc.	180	36,339
4 Scotia Capital Inc.	128	27,524
5 BMO Capital Markets	125	20,929
6 Bank of America Securities LLC	38	19,079
7 National Bank Financial Inc.	85	15,426
8 J.P. Morgan Securities Inc.	18	10,210
9 HSBC Securities (Canada) Inc.	33	9,220
10 Credit Suisse Securities (USA) LLC	25	6,192

Source: **FPinfomart.ca**, *National Post*, October 11, 2010, retrieved October 11, 2010. Material reprinted with the express permission of *National Post*, a division of Postmedia Network Inc.

TABLE 15.2
Top 10 IPO issues in 2008.

Rank 2008	Gross Proceeds Raised ($000s)	Lead Underwriter(s)
1 Sprott Inc.	200,000	Cormark Securities Inc.; TD Securities Inc.
2 Seacliff Construction Corp.	100,000	Raymond James Ltd
3 Orbit Garant Drilling Inc.	60,000	CIBC World Markets Inc.
4 Pristine Power Inc.	55,000	Haywood Securities Inc.
5 Davie Yards Inc.	47,312	Dundee Securities Corp.
6 Sea Dragon Energy Inc.	35,000	Salman Partners Inc.
7 Angle Energy Inc.	31,000	GMP Securities LP
8 Fluid Music Canada Inc.	27,000	Blackmont Capital Inc.
9 Colossus Minerals Inc.	24,332	GMP Securities LP
10 Timbercreek Mortgage Investment Corp.	23,004	Manulife Securities Inc.

Source: *National Post Business*, June 2009 (FP500), 105, retrieved October 27, 2010. Material reprinted with the express permission of National Post, a division of Postmedia Network Inc.

TABLE 15.3
Top ten underwriters of debt, equity, and equity-related issues in 2009 (US$ millions).

Global		
Underwriter	**Proceeds**	**No. of Issues**
J.P. Morgan	614,658.2	1,702
Barclays Capital	475,619.6	1,133
Bank of America Merrill Lynch	447,514.0	1,338
Citigroup	408,197.7	1,220
Deutsche Bank AG	381,219.8	1,174
Goldman Sachs & Co	357,299.1	911
Morgan Stanley	339,859.7	984
Credit Suisse	311,610.5	952
HSBC Holding PLC	268,234.2	920
RBS	258,930.6	854
Top ten total	**3,863,143.4**	**11,188**
Industry total	**6,446,889.6**	**17,072**

Source: Thomson Reuters, "Equity Capital Market Review," Fourth Quarter 2009, p. 3, **www.thomsonreuters.com/league**, retrieved October 11, 2010.

sold in a number of countries, many of the major international banks are involved in underwriting the issues. Have a look at Table 15.3. It shows the names of principal underwriters of global debt and equity issues in 2009.

15.4 LISTING ON THE STOCK MARKET

When a firm decides on an initial public offering of its stocks, it has to decide where its newly issued shares should be traded. As we have discussed in Chapters 2 and 7, stock markets can be either organized exchanges with centralized physical locations or over-the-counter markets consisting of a network of security dealers who trade with each other over the phone and increasingly over electronic networks. Most trading in the shares of large Canadian corporations takes place on the Toronto Stock Exchange (TMX), while shares of smaller and emerging companies are traded through the TSX Venture Exchange (TMXV). Electronic trading in shares can also be done through Nasdaq Canada, which has operations in Montréal for the purpose of trading in shares listed on the Nasdaq stock market. Table 15.4 provides details regarding the trading activity for September 2010 of the Toronto Stock Exchange and the TMX Venture Exchange.

In order to list its stock issue on a stock exchange, the firm will have to meet the exchange's listing requirements and pay the requisite listing fee. These tend to vary; generally, the larger and more prestigious stock exchanges also tend to have stricter listing requirements and higher listing fees. Table 15.5 summarizes major listing requirements of the TMX for profitable industrial companies.

TABLE 15.4
Trading activity on Canadian stock exchanges.

	Trading Activity, September 2010	
Stock Exchange	Value of Shares (millions of dollars)	Volume of Shares (millions of shares)
Toronto Stock Exchange	131,436	9,687
TSX Venture Exchange	3,736	6,812

Source: "Monthly Trading Statistics," September 2010, **www.tmx.com**.

TABLE 15.5
Toronto Stock Exchange: major listing requirements for profitable industrial companies[a]

(i) *Assets:* Net tangible assets of $7,500,000.
(ii) *Earnings:* Earnings from ongoing operations of at least $300,000 before taxes and extraordinary items in the fiscal year immediately preceding the filing of the listing application.
(iii) *Cash Flow:* Pretax cash flow of $700,000 in the immediately preceding fiscal year.
(iv) *Working Capital and Capital Structure:* Adequate working capital to carry on the business and an appropriate capital structure.
(v) *Public Distribution:* At least 1,000,000 freely tradeable shares having an aggregate market value of $4,000,000 must be held by at least 300 public holders, each holding one board lot or more shares.[b]
(vi) *Management:* Management (including the company's board of directors) should have adequate experience and technical expertise relevant to the company's business and industry and adequate public company experience. Companies will be required to have at least two independent directors.

[a] The requirements vary with the type of industrial company, that is, profitable companies, companies forecasting profitability, technology companies, or research and development companies. Different requirements also exist for mining and for oil and gas companies. Requirements may also change from time to time. Complete details regarding all listing requirements are provided on the TMX site at **www.tmx.com**.
[b] A board lot comprises 100 shares for securities selling at $1 and more. See **www.tmx.com**.

Source: **www.tmx.com**.

LO4, 5 15.5 RIGHTS ISSUES AND GENERAL CASH OFFERS BY PUBLIC COMPANIES

seasoned offering Sale of securities by a firm that is already publicly traded.

rights issue Issue of securities offered only to current shareholders.

After the initial public offering, a successful firm will continue to grow and from time to time it will need to raise more money by issuing stock or bonds. An issue of additional stock by a company whose stock already is publicly traded is called a **seasoned offering**. Any issue of securities needs to be formally approved by the firm's board of directors. If a stock issue requires an increase in the company's authorized capital, it also needs the consent of the shareholders.

Public companies can issue securities either by making a general cash offer to investors at large or by making a **rights issue**, which is limited to existing shareholders. Let us first concentrate on the mechanics of the rights issue.

RIGHTS ISSUES

In a rights issue, the company offers the shareholders the opportunity, or *right*, to buy more shares at an "attractive" subscription price. For example, if the current stock price is $100, the company might offer investors an additional share at $50 for each share they hold. Suppose that before the issue an investor has one share worth $100 and $50 in the bank. If the investor takes up the offer of a new share, that $50 of cash is transferred from the investor's bank account to the company's. The investor now has two shares that are a claim on the original assets worth $100 and on the $50 cash that the company has raised. So the two shares are worth a total of $150, or $75 each.

By directly offering a new share issue to existing shareholders, a company could hope to save on issuing and underwriting expenses. Also, shareholders do not run a risk of dilution of their proportional shareholding and are able to retain their voting position on the company's major business decisions. Of course, shareholders will have an incentive to exercise their rights only if the subscription price stays below the market price of the shares. Otherwise, if the share price falls, the full issue of new shares may not be taken up. To protect against this possibility, the firm may enter into a **standby underwriting agreement** with an investment dealer. Under this arrangement, the underwriter stands ready to purchase any unsold shares and receives a *standby fee* and possible additional amounts depending on the extent of unsold shares. Also, the company may give its shareholders an **oversubscription privilege** under which they will be able to purchase any unsold shares at the subscription price. Of course, a small proportion of shareholders may not exercise their rights, perhaps because they are away on vacation or for other personal reasons.

standby underwriting agreement An underwriting agreement in which underwriter stands ready to purchase any unsold shares.

oversubscription privilege A privilege given to shareholders in a rights issue, enabling them to purchase any unsold shares at the subscription price.

In some countries, rights issues are the most common or only method for issuing common stock. In Canada, they are less common. Sometimes, a preemptive right is contained in the firm's articles of incorporation, in which case, the firm has to offer any new issue of common stock to its existing shareholders.

In a rights offering, existing shareholders receive one right for each share of stock held. To take advantage of the rights offering, shareholders will have to exercise the right within a specified period of time by submitting a completed subscription form to the company's subscription agent. If rights are not exercised within the period stipulated, they expire.

EXAMPLE 15.4 RIGHTS ISSUES

In 2007 banks around the world were battered by heavy losses on their real estate loans. The Royal Bank of Scotland, the U.K.'s second-largest bank, was no exception, and in April 2008 it announced that to rebuild its capital it would raise a record £12.22 billion (or about US$24 billion) by an equity rights issue. If you were a shareholder of RBS, you received the right to buy 11 additional shares for every 18 shares that you initially owned. The purchase price was set at £2 a share.

Before the issue, the bank had approximately 10 billion shares outstanding, which were priced at £3.725 each. So investors valued the bank at $10 \times £3.725 = £37.25$ billion. The new issue increased the total number of shares by $10 \times 11/18 = 6.11$ billion and therefore raised $6.11 \times £2 = £12.22$ billion. In effect, the issue increased the total value of the bank to $37.25 + 12.22 = £49.47$ billion and reduced the value of each share to $£49.47/16.11 = £3.071$.

The standard procedure for issuing rights involves the firm announcing the issue and setting a **holder-of-record date**, the date on which existing shareholders, as listed in the company's records, are entitled to the stock rights. Actually, to comply with stock exchange rules, the stock will usually go *ex-rights* four trading days before the holder-of-record date. If the stock is sold before this date, the new owner will receive the rights, and so its value will be with *rights*, *rights-on*, or *cum-rights*. If the stock is sold after the **ex-rights date**, the buyer will no longer be entitled to the rights.

holder-of-record date The date on which shareholders appearing on company records are entitled to receive the stock rights.

ex-rights date This date is usually four business days before the holder-of-record date.

Since rights offerings enable shareholders to buy shares at a favourable price, they clearly have value. How would you arrive at the value of a right? Notice that the existing shareholder can buy 18 new shares at the purchase price of £2 for 11 shares held, or approximately 1.64 new shares for each old share. However, the market price of the share after the rights issue, that is the ex-rights price, is £3.071. We can, therefore, formulate an equation that will give the theoretical value of a right:

$$\text{Value of one right} = \frac{\text{market value of share, ex-rights} - \text{subscription price}}{\text{number of rights required to purchase a share}}$$

$$= \frac{£3.071 - £2}{1.64} = \frac{£1.071}{1.64} = £.65$$

You can also arrive at the theoretical value of a right by using the price of the stock during the cum-rights period:

$$\text{Value of one right} = \frac{\text{market value of share, rights on} - \text{subscription price}}{\text{number of rights required to purchase a share} + 1}$$

$$= \frac{£3.725 - £2}{1.64 + 1} = \frac{£1.725}{2.64} = £.65$$

Suppose that you owned 18 shares in the bank before the issue. Your holding would have been worth $18 \times £3.725 = £67.05$. If you decided to take up the rights offer, you would have needed to lay out $11 \times £2 = £22$ and the value of your shareholding would have increased by exactly £22 to $29 \times £3.071 = £89.05$. The rights-on price of the shares is £3.725. After the rights offering, it drops to the ex-rights price of £3.071. Notice that the share price drops by £.65, that is, to the extent of the value of a right.

GENERAL CASH OFFERS

general cash offer Sale of securities open to all investors by an already-public company.

When a public company makes a **general cash offer** of debt or equity, it essentially follows the same procedure used when it first went public. This means that it must first register the issue in compliance with the regulations of relevant provincial commissions. The issue is then sold to an underwriter under a firm-commitment arrangement or on a best-efforts basis.[9] The underwriter (or syndicate of underwriters), in turn, offers the securities to the public.

bought deal An arrangement in which the underwriter buys securities from the issuing company and sells them to investors.

Many underwriting agreements, including those involving firm commitments, may contain a *market-out clause or disaster-out clause*, which limits the underwriters' risk. Such a clause can enable the underwriter to terminate the underwriting agreement without penalty under extraordinary circumstances or even if the underwriter judges that the state of the financial market is not good for the security issue. Another well-known practice is for underwriting contracts to have an *overallotment* or *green-shoe* option. This option allows the underwriter to buy more shares from the issuer if the need arises because of strong investor demand.[10] In Canada, competition for lucrative underwriting deals and a dislike of the market-out clause among investors has created an environment for **bought deals**, which are often used by large, well-known companies for their seasoned equity issues. Here, the investment dealer buys the entire offering from the issuing company and then decides how to sell it to investors. This is advantageous to the company because it is able to obtain a relatively quick and firm commitment on its securities. Bought deals are not commonly used in the United States.

prompt offering prospectus (POP) system Allows qualified firms quicker access to capital markets by enabling them to use a short-form filing process rather than a full prospectus.

shelf registration A procedure followed in the United States that allows firms to file one registration statement for several issues of the same security.

Usually the large issuers in Canada who go for bought deals can also take advantage of the **prompt offering prospectus (POP) system**, which allows short-form filing since much of the information contained in the regular prospectus is already expected to have been filed annually. Thus, under the POP system, only material changes and financial statements have to be provided to regulators who are able to give their clearance within about five days—instead of several weeks required for a full prospectus. The investing public must still be provided with a regular prospectus. In the United States, companies can take advantage of **shelf registration**, which

[9] A large issue will typically be handled by a syndicate of underwriters.

[10] Typically, the overallotment option allows the underwriter to buy up to 15 percent more shares.

allows them to file a single registration statement covering financing plans for up to two years into the future. Within this time period, companies do not need to prepare a separate registration statement every time they issue new securities.

COSTS OF THE GENERAL CASH OFFER

Whenever a firm makes a cash offer, it incurs substantial administrative costs. Also, the firm needs to compensate the underwriters by selling them securities below the price that they expect to receive from investors. Figure 15.3 shows the average underwriting spread and administrative costs for several types of security issues in the United States.[11] The figure clearly shows the economies of scale in issuing securities. Costs may absorb 15 percent of a small IPO or seasoned equity issue of no more than US$10 million. This occurs because a large part of the issue cost is fixed. The costs are similar in Canada.[12] Figure 15.3 shows that issue costs are higher for equity than for debt securities—the costs for both types of securities, however, show the same economies of scale. Issue costs are higher for equity than for debt because administrative costs are somewhat higher, and also because underwriting stock is riskier than underwriting bonds. The underwriters demand additional compensation for the greater risk they take in buying and reselling equity.

Check Point 15.4

Use Figure 15.3 to compare the costs of 10 issues of US$15 million of stock in a seasoned offering versus one issue of US$150 million.

MARKET REACTION TO STOCK ISSUES

Because stock issues usually throw a sizable number of new shares onto the market, it is widely believed that they must temporarily depress the stock price. If the proposed issue is very large, this price pressure may, it is thought, be so severe as to make it almost impossible to raise money.

FIGURE 15.3 Total direct costs as a percentage of gross proceeds. The total direct costs for initial public offerings (IPOs), seasoned equity offerings (SEOs), convertible bonds, and straight bonds are composed of underwriter spreads and other direct expenses.

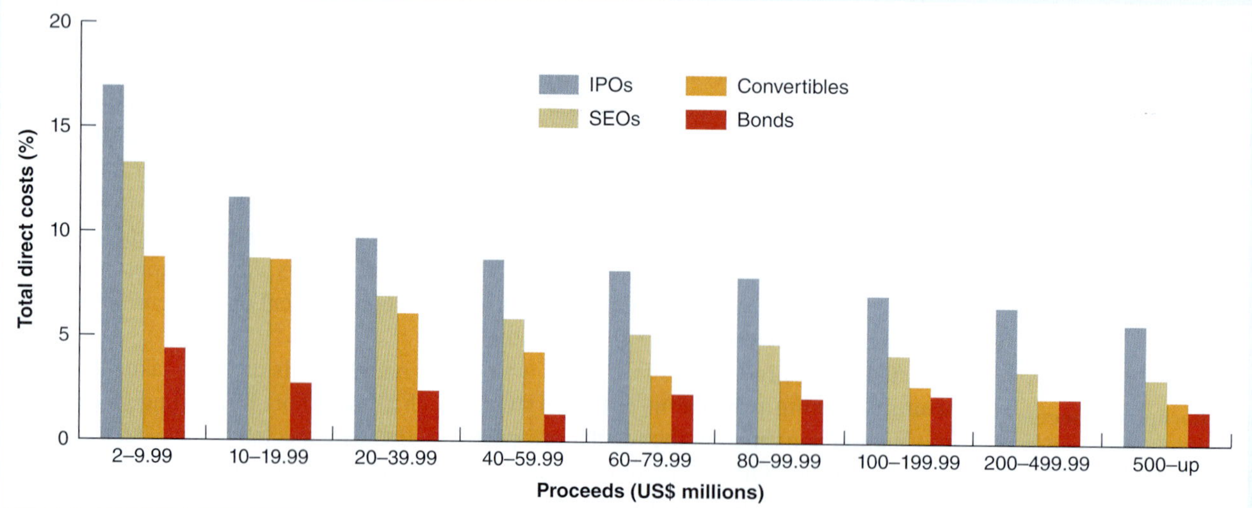

Source: I. Lee, S. Lochhead, J. Ritter, and Q. Zhao, "The Costs of Raising Capital," *Journal of Financial Research* 19 (Spring 1996): 59–74.

[11] These figures do not capture all administrative costs. For example, they do not include management time spent on the issue.

[12] A study finds that average Canadian underwriter fees for medium-sized IPOs ($10 to 50 million) average 6 percent, as against a U.S. average of 7 percent. See L. Kryzanowski and I. Rakita, "Is the US 7 Percent Solution Equivalent to the Canadian 6 Percent Solution?" *Canadian Investment Review* 2 (Fall 1999): 27–34.

This belief in price pressure implies that a new issue depresses the stock price temporarily below its true value. However, that view doesn't appear to fit very well with the notion of market efficiency. If the stock price falls solely because of increased supply, then that stock would offer a higher return than comparable stocks, and investors would be attracted to it like ants to a picnic.

Economists who have studied new issues of common stock have generally found that the announcement of the issue *does* result in a decline in the stock price. For industrial issues in the United States, this decline amounts to about 3 percent.[13] While this may not sound overwhelming, such a price drop can be a large fraction of the money raised. Suppose that a company with a market value of equity of \$5 billion announces its intention to issue \$500 million of additional equity and thereby causes the stock price to drop by 3 percent. The loss in value is .03 × \$5 billion, or \$150 million. That's 30 percent of the amount of money raised (.30 × \$500 million = \$150 million).

What's going on here? Is the price of the stock simply depressed by the prospect of the additional supply? Possibly, but here is an alternative explanation.

Suppose managers (who have better information about the firm than outside investors) know that their stock is undervalued. If the company sells new stock at this low price, it will give the new shareholders a good deal at the expense of the old shareholders. In these circumstances managers might be prepared to forgo the new investment rather than sell shares at too low a price.

If managers know that the stock is overvalued, the position is reversed. If the company sells new shares at the high price, it will help its existing shareholders at the expense of the new ones. Managers might be prepared to issue stock even if the new cash were just put in the bank.

Of course, investors are not stupid. They can predict that managers are more likely to issue stock when they think it is overvalued, and they mark the price of the stock down accordingly.

The tendency for stock prices to decline at the time of an issue may have nothing to do with increased supply. Instead, the stock issue may simply be a signal that well-informed managers believe the market has overpriced the stock.[14]

15.6 THE PRIVATE PLACEMENT

private placement Sale of securities to a limited number of investors without a public offering.

Whenever a company makes a public offering, it must register the issue with the relevant provincial commission. It could avoid this costly process by selling the issue privately. There are no hard-and-fast definitions of a **private placement**. Most private sales of debt and equity are to exempt institutions such as large pension funds or insurance companies, which are considered to be knowledgeable buyers and will not require all the information provided in a regular prospectus. Currently, the minimum investment requirement for a private placement is \$150,000, which effectively shuts out average investors, although some wealthy individuals do participate as buyers.

One disadvantage of a private placement is that the investor cannot easily resell the security. This is less important to institutions such as insurance companies, which invest huge sums of money in corporate debt for the long haul.

As you would expect, it costs less to arrange a private placement than to make a public issue. That might not be so important for the very large issues where costs are less significant, but it is a particular advantage for companies making smaller issues.

Another advantage of the private placement is that the debt contract can be custom-tailored for firms with special problems or opportunities. Also, if the firm wishes later to change the terms of the debt, it is much simpler to do this with a private placement where only a few investors are involved.

[13] See, for example, P. Asquith and D.W. Mullins, "Equity Issues and Offering Dilution," *Journal of Financial Economics* 15 (January/February 1986): 61–90; R.W. Masulis and A.N. Korwar, "Seasoned Equity Offerings: An Empirical Investigation," *Journal of Financial Economics* 15 (January/February 1986): 91–118; W.H. Mikkelson and M.M. Partch, "Valuation Effects of Security Offerings and the Issuance Process," *Journal of Financial Economics* 15 (January/February 1986): 31–60. There appears to be a smaller price decline for utility issues. Also, a smaller decline for rights issues in the United Kingdom has been observed; see P.R. Marsh, "Equity Rights Issues and the Efficiency of the UK Stock Market," *Journal of Finance* 34 (September 1979): 839–862.

[14] This explanation was developed in S.C. Myers and N.S. Majluf's "Corporate Financing and Investment Decisions When Firms Have Information That Investors Do Not Have," *Journal of Financial Economics* 13 (1984): 187–222.

Therefore, it is not surprising that private placements occupy a particular niche in the corporate debt market, namely, loans to small- and medium-sized firms. These are the firms that face the highest costs in public issues, that require the most detailed investigation, and that may require specialized, flexible loan arrangements.

We do not mean that large, safe, and conventional firms should rule out private placements. Enormous amounts of capital are sometimes raised by this method. For example, in July 2010 Laricina Energy Inc., a private oil company looking to establish a presence in Alberta's oil sands, completed a $250 million private placement of equity to the Canada Pension Plan Investment Board. The deal represents a 17.1 percent equity interest in Laricina Energy Inc. Nevertheless, the advantages of private placement—avoiding registration costs and establishing a direct relationship with the lender—are generally more important to smaller firms.

Of course, these advantages are not free. Lenders in private placements have to be compensated for the risks they face and for the costs of research and negotiation. They also have to be compensated for holding an asset that is not easily resold. All these factors are rolled into the interest rate paid by the firm. It is difficult to generalize about the differences in interest rates between private placements and public issues, but a typical yield differential might be on the order of half a percentage point.

15.7 SUMMARY

1. **How do venture capital firms design successful deals? LO1**

   Infant companies raise **venture capital** to carry them through to the point where they can make their first public issue of stock. More established publicly traded companies can issue additional securities in a **general cash offer**. Financing choices should be designed to avoid conflicts of interest. This is especially important in the case of a young company that is raising venture capital. If both managers and investors have an important equity stake in the company, they are likely to pull in the same direction. The willingness to take that stake also signals management's confidence in the new company's future. Therefore, most deals require that the entrepreneur maintain large stakes in the firm. In addition, most venture financing is done in stages that keep the firm on a short leash and force it to prove, at several crucial points, that it is worthy of additional investment.

2. **How do firms make initial public offerings and what are the costs of such offerings? LO2**

   The **initial public offering** is the first sale of shares in a general offering to investors. The sale of the securities is usually managed by an underwriting firm that buys the shares from the company and resells them to the public. The **underwriter** helps to prepare a **prospectus**, which describes the company and its prospects. The costs of an IPO include direct costs such as legal and administrative fees as well as the underwriting spread—the difference between the price the underwriter pays to acquire the shares from the firm and the price the public pays the underwriter for those shares. Another major implicit cost is the **underpricing** of the issue—that is, shares are typically sold to the public somewhat below the true value of the security. This discount is reflected in abnormally high average returns to new issues on the first day of trading.

3. **What is the role of the underwriter in an issue of securities? LO3**

   The underwriter manages the sale of the securities for the issuing company. The underwriting firms have expertise in such sales because they are in the business all the time, whereas the company raises capital only occasionally. Moreover, the underwriters may give an implicit seal of approval to the offering. Because the underwriters will not want to squander their reputation by misrepresenting facts to the public, the implied endorsement may be quite important to a firm coming to the market for the first time.

4. **What is a rights issue?** LO4

Unlike a general cash offering, a rights issue is an offer to buy shares that is made only to existing shareholders. The shares are priced at a substantial discount to current market value, which ensures that the shareholders will either exercise the rights themselves or sell them to other investors. In either case, the firm raises funds when the right is exercised.

5. **What are some of the significant issues that arise when established firms make a rights issue, a general cash offer, or a private placement of securities?** LO5

There are always economies of scale in issuing securities. It is cheaper to go to the market once for $100 million than to make two trips for $50 million each. Consequently, firms "bunch" security issues. This may mean relying on short-term financing until a large issue is justified. Or it may mean issuing more than is needed at the moment to avoid another issue later.

A **seasoned offering** may depress the stock price. The extent of this price decline varies, but for issues of common stocks by industrial firms, the fall in the value of the existing stock may amount to a significant proportion of the money raised. The likely explanation for this pressure is the information the market reads into the company's decision to issue stock.

The **prompt offering prospectus (POP) system** often makes sense for equity or debt issues by well-established companies. It allows short-form filing to regulators and, thereby, reduces the time taken to arrange a new issue.

Private placements are well suited for small, risky, or unusual firms. Of course, established and conventional firms also often raise large sums of capital by this method. The special advantages of private placement stem from avoiding registration expenses and getting a more direct relationship with the lender.

Related Web Links

renaissancecapital.com News and statistics on the IPO market

marketwatch.com Information on new IPOs in the United States

thomsonreuters.com/league Information on underwriting activity

FreeEDGAR.com Information on registration of new securities offerings in the United States

cob.ohio-state.edu/~fin/resources_education/credit.htm The changing mix of corporate financing

vnpartners.com Venture capital as a source of project financing

strategis.ic.gc.ca Industry Canada

bdc.ca Business Development Bank of Canada

rim.com Research In Motion

osc.gov.on.ca Ontario Securities Commission

sedar.com Information on document filings by Canadian companies including for new securities

724.com 724 Solutions

cvca.ca Canadian Venture Capital Association (CVCA)

canadavc.com Venture capital information; Web site of Thomson Financial (acquired from Macdonald and Associates Ltd.)

iclub.com Products and services targeted at investment clubs

canadait.com Venture capital and angel investor information

bear.cba.ufl.edu/ritter Web page of Jay Ritter, the well-known finance professor; includes some great data on IPOs

aboutus.org/VentureEconomics.com News and statistics on the U.S. venture capital industry

nvca.org Home page of the National Venture Capital Association, based in the United States

Key Terms

angel 490
bought deal 503
ex-rights date 502
flotation costs 495
general cash offer 503
holder-of-record date 502
initial public offering (IPO) 492
oversubscription privilege 502
private placement 505
prompt offering prospectus (POP) system 503
prospectus 493
rights issue 501
seasoned offering 501
shelf registration 503
spread 493
standby underwriting agreement 502
underpricing 494
underwriter 493
venture capital 490

Questions and Problems

connect Practise and learn online with *Connect*. Questions with online Excel templates or datasets are marked with .

*Answers in Appendix B

BASIC

*1. **Underwriting.** (LO3)
   a. Is a rights issue more likely to be used for an initial public offering or for subsequent issues of stock?
   b. Is a private placement more likely to be used for issues of seasoned stock or seasoned bonds by an industrial company?
   c. Is the prompt offering prospectus (POP) system more likely to be used for issues of unseasoned stocks or bonds by a large industrial company?

2. **Underwriting.** Each of the following terms is associated with one of the events beneath. Can you match them up? (LO4)
   a. Red herring
   b. Firm commitment
   c. Rights issue
   A. The underwriter agrees to buy the issue from the company at a fixed price.
   B. The company offers to sell stock to existing stockholders.
   C. The company issues a preliminary prospectus for distribution to the public.

*3. **Underwriting Costs.** For each of the following pairs of issues state which of the two you would expect to involve the lower proportionate underwriting and administrative costs, other things being equal: (LO3)
   a. A large issue/a small issue
   b. A bond issue/a common stock issue
   c. A small private placement of bonds/a small general cash offer of bonds

*4. **IPO Costs.** Why are the issue costs for debt issues generally less than those for equity issues? (LO2)

5. **Venture Capital.** Why do venture capital companies prefer to advance money in stages? (LO1)

6. **IPOs.** Your broker calls and says that you can get 500 shares of an imminent IPO at the offering price. Should you buy? Are you worried about the fact that your broker called you? (LO2)

INTERMEDIATE

*7. **IPO Underpricing.** Having heard about IPO underpricing, I put in an order to my broker for 1,000 shares of every IPO he can get for me. After three months, my investment record is as follows: (LO2)

IPO	Shares Allocated to Me	Price per Share	Initial Return
A	500	$10	7%
B	200	20	12
C	1,000	8	−2
D	0	12	23

   a. What is the average underpricing of this sample of IPOs?
   b. What is the average initial return on my "portfolio" of shares purchased from the four IPOs I bid on? Calculate the average initial return, weighting by the amount of money invested in each issue.
   c. Why have I performed so poorly relative to the average initial return on the full sample of IPOs? What lessons do you draw from my experience?

8. **IPO Costs.** Moonscape has just completed an initial public offering. The firm sold three million shares at an offer price of $8 per share. The underwriting spread was $.50 a share. The price of the stock closed at $11 per share at the end of the first day of trading. The firm incurred $100,000 in legal, administrative, and other costs. What were flotation costs as a fraction of funds raised? (LO2)

9. **IPO Costs.** Look at the illustrative new-issue prospectus in Appendix 15B. (LO2)
   a. Is this issue a primary offering, a secondary offering, or both?
   b. What are the direct costs of the issue as a percentage of the total proceeds? Are these more than the average for an issue of this size?
   c. Suppose that on the first day of trading the price of Hotch Pot's stock is $15 a share. What are the *total* costs of the issue as a percentage of the market price?
   d. After paying her share of the expenses, how much will the firm's president, Emma Lucullus, receive from the sale? What will be the value of the shares that she retains in the company?

*10. **Flotation Costs.** "For small issues of common stock, the costs of flotation amount to about 15 percent of the proceeds. This means that the opportunity cost of external equity capital is about 15 percentage points higher than that of retained earnings." Does this make sense? (LO2)

11. **Flotation Costs.** When Microsoft went public, the company sold two million new shares (the primary issue). In addition, existing shareholders sold .8 million shares (the secondary issue) and kept 21.1 million shares. The new shares were offered to the public at $21 and the underwriters received a spread of $1.31 a share. At the end of the first day's trading, the market price was $35 a share. (LO2)
    a. How much money did the company receive before paying its portion of the direct costs?
    b. How much did the existing shareholders receive from the sale before paying their portion of the direct costs?
    c. If the issue had been sold to the underwriters for $30 a share, how many shares would the company have needed to sell to raise the same amount of cash?
    d. How much better off would the existing shareholders have been?

*12. **Flotation Costs.** The market value of the marketing research firm Fax Facts is $600 million. The firm issues an additional $100 million of stock, but as a result the stock price falls by 2 percent. What is the cost of the price drop to existing shareholders as a fraction of the funds raised? (LO2)

13. **Flotation Costs.** Young Corporation stock currently sells for $30 per share. There are one million shares currently outstanding. The company announces plans to raise $3 million by offering shares to the public at a price of $30 per share. (LO2)
    a. If the underwriting spread is 8 percent, how many shares will the company need to issue in order to be left with net proceeds of $3 million?
    b. If other administrative costs are $60,000, what is the dollar value of the total direct costs of the issue?
    c. If the share price falls by 3 percent at the announcement of the plans to proceed with a seasoned offering, what is the dollar cost of the announcement effect?

14. **Private Placements.** You need to choose between the following types of issues: (LO3)
    i. *A public issue of $10 million face value of 10-year debt.* The interest rate on the debt would be 8.5 percent and the debt would be issued at face value. The underwriting spread would be 1.5 percent and other expenses would be $80,000.
    ii. *A private placement of $10 million face value of 10-year debt.* The interest rate on the private placement would be 9 percent, but the total issuing expenses would be only $30,000.
    a. What is the difference in the proceeds to the company net of expenses?
    b. Other things being equal, which is the better deal?
    c. What other factors beyond the interest rate and issue costs would you wish to consider before deciding between the two offers?

*15. **Rights.** In 2010, Pandora, Inc., makes a rights issue at a subscription price of $5 a share. One new share can be purchased for every four shares held. Before the issue there were 10 million shares outstanding, and the share price was $6. (LO5)
    a. What is the total amount of new money raised?
    b. What is the expected stock price after the rights are issued?

16. **Rights.** Problem 15 contains details of a rights offering by Pandora. Suppose that the company had decided to issue the new stock at $4 instead of $5 a share. How many new shares would it have needed to raise the same sum of money? Recalculate the answers to problem 15. Show that Pandora's shareholders are just as well off if it issues the shares at $4 a share rather than $5. (LO5)

17. **Rights.** Consolidated Jewels needs to raise $2 million to pay for its Diamonds in the Rough campaign. It will raise the funds by offering 200,000 rights, each of which entitles the owner to buy one new share. The company currently has one million shares outstanding priced at $20 each. (LO5)
    *a. What must be the subscription price on the rights the company plans to offer?
    *b. What will be the share price after the rights issue?
    *c. What is the value of a right to buy one share?
    *d. How many rights would be issued to an investor who currently owns 1,000 shares?
    e. Show that the investor who currently holds 1,000 shares is unaffected by the rights issue. Specifically, show that the value of the rights plus the value of the 1,000 shares after the rights issue equals the value of the 1,000 shares before the rights issue.

18. **Rights.** (LO5) Associated Breweries is planning to market unleaded beer. To finance the venture it proposes to make a rights issue with a subscription price of $10. One new share can be purchased for each two shares held. The company currently has 100,000 shares outstanding priced at $40 a share. Assuming that the new money is invested to earn a fair return, give values for the
    a. Number of new shares
    b. Amount of new investment
    c. Total value of company after issue
    d. Total number of shares after issue
    e. Share price after the issue

CHALLENGE

19. **Globe and Mail Investor.** Go to Globe and Mail Investor Web site (**www.theglobeandmail.com/globe-investor**). Search for the Telus Corp. (T) and Shaw Communications Inc. (SJR). Which company has the higher price-earnings ratio? What variables (for example, financial ratios or growth rates) might explain the P/E differential? (LO2)
20. **Internet.** Jay Ritter's home page (**bear.cba.ufl.edu/ritter**) is a gold mine of information on IPOs. Look up the number of IPOs during the 1999–2000 period and compare this with the number of IPOs during the 2009–2010 period. What is the average first-day return on IPOs and money left on the table for the two periods? From his table of "money-left-on-the-table," which company provided the greatest one-day dollar gains to investors? (LO2)
21. **Venture Capital.** Here is an especially difficult question. Pickwick Electronics is a new high-tech company financed entirely by one million ordinary shares, all of which are owned by George Pickwick. The firm needs to raise $1 million now for stage one and, assuming all goes well, a further $1 million at the end of 5 years for stage two. (LO1)

    First Cookham Venture Partners is considering two possible financing schemes:

    1. Buying two million shares now at their current valuation of $1
    2. Buying one million shares at the current valuation and investing a further $1 million at the end of 5 years at whatever the shares are worth

    The outlook for Pickwick is uncertain, but as long as the company can secure the additional financing for stage two, it will be worth either $2 million or $12 million after completing stage two. (The company will be valueless if it cannot raise the funds for stage two.) Show the possible payoffs for Mr. Pickwick and First Cookham and explain why one scheme might be preferred. Assume an interest rate of zero.
22. **Internet.** In Appendix 15B we provide a flavour of an IPO prospectus, but you can see what an actual prospectus or registration statement looks like by using the System for Electronic Document Analysis and Retrieval (SEDAR) site at **www.sedar.com** for Canadian companies or the SEC's huge database on **www.freeedgar.com** for U.S. companies. You can also log in to **www.nasdaq.com**, click on "IPOs" to find a company, and then click on "Filings," which will take you to the correct SEC form. Pick a recent prospectus filing of a Canadian company from **www.sedar.com**. On the basis of this prospectus, do you think the stock looks like an attractive investment? Which parts of the statement look most useful? Least useful? (LO2)

Solutions to Check Points

15.1 Unless the firm can secure second-stage financing, it is unlikely to succeed. If the entrepreneur will reap any reward on his own investment, he needs to put in enough effort to get further financing. By accepting only part of the necessary venture capital, management increases its own risk and reduces that of the venture capitalist. This decision would be costly and foolish if management lacked confidence that the project would be successful enough to get past the first stage. A credible signal by management is one that only managers who are truly confident can afford to provide. However, words are cheap and there is little to be lost by *saying* you are confident (although if you are proved wrong, you might find it difficult to raise money a second time).

15.2 If an investor can distinguish between overpriced and underpriced issues, she will bid only on the underpriced ones. In this case she will purchase only issues that provide a 10 percent gain. However, the ability to distinguish these issues requires considerable insight and research. The return to the informed IPO participant may be viewed as a return on the resources expended to become informed.

15.3

Direct Expenses ($ millions)	
Underwriting spread = 69 million × $4	276.0
Other expenses	9.2
Total direct expenses	285.2
Underpricing = 69 million × ($70 − $64)	414.0
Total expenses	699.2
Market value of issue = 69 million × $70	4,830.0

Expenses as proportion of market value 699.2/4,830 = .145 = 14.5 percent.

15.4 Ten issues of $15 million each will cost about 9 percent of proceeds, or .09 × $150 million = $13.5 million. One issue of $150 million will cost only 4 percent of $150 million, or $6 million.

MINI CASE

Mutt.Com was founded in 2008 by two graduates of the University of Wisconsin with help from Georgina Sloberg, who had built up an enviable reputation for backing new startup businesses. Mutt.com's user-friendly system was designed to find buyers for unwanted pets. Within three years the company was generating revenues of $3.4 million a year, and despite racking up sizable losses, was regarded by investors as one of the hottest new e-commerce businesses. The news that the company was preparing to go public therefore generated considerable excitement.

The company's entire equity capital of 1.5 million shares was owned by the two founders and Ms. Sloberg. The initial public offering involved the sale of 500,000 shares by the three existing shareholders, together with the sale of a further 750,000 shares by the company in order to provide funds for expansion.

The company estimated that the issue would involve legal fees, auditing, printing, and other expenses of $1.3 million, which would be shared proportionately between the selling shareholders and the company. In addition, the company agreed to pay the underwriters a spread of $1.25 per share.

The roadshow had confirmed the high level of interest in the issue, and indications from investors suggested that the entire issue could be sold at a price of $24 a share. The underwriters, however, cautioned about being too greedy on price. They pointed out that indications from investors were not the same as firm orders. Also, they argued, it was much more important to have a successful issue than to have a group of disgruntled shareholders. They therefore suggested an issue price of $18 a share.

That evening Mutt.com's financial manager decided to run through some calculations. First she worked out the net receipts to the company and the existing shareholders, assuming that the stock was sold for $18 a share. Next she looked at the various costs of the IPO and tried to judge how they stacked up against the typical costs for similar IPOs. That brought her up against the question of underpricing. When she had raised the matter with the underwriters that morning, they had dismissed the notion that the initial day's return on an IPO should be considered part of the issue costs. One of the members of the underwriting team had asked: "The underwriters want to see a high return and a high stock price. Would Mutt.com prefer a low stock price? Would that make the issue less costly?" Mutt.com's financial manager was not convinced but felt that she should have a good answer. She wondered whether underpricing was a problem only because the existing shareholders were selling part of their holdings. Perhaps the issue price would not matter if they had not planned to sell.

APPENDIX 15A: THE FINANCING OF NEW AND SMALL ENTERPRISES

VENTURE CAPITAL IN CANADA

We saw in Section 15.1 that venture capital is an important source of equity for startup companies that have the potential to develop into significant economic contributors. Venture capitalists make risky investments with the expectation of earning high rewards if the young ventures become successful. Often, their investments pay off handsomely, as in the case of companies such as Microsoft, Intel, or Research In Motion, which are today established leaders in their respective industries. Of course, venture capitalists may seek to lessen the risk of venture investing in a number of ways. For instance, before making investment decisions, they try to screen the technical and business merits of the proposed company carefully and usually end up investing in only a small percentage of the businesses they review. They also like to work actively with managements of companies they invest in by contributing their business knowledge and experience, gained from helping other companies with similar growth challenges. Often, they diversify their investments by developing a portfolio of young companies in a single venture fund. Many times they will co-invest with other professional venture capital firms in syndicated investment arrangements. In addition, many venture capitalists manage multiple funds together. Table 15A.1 lists some of the important attributes of classic venture capital investing.

TYPES OF VENTURE CAPITAL FUNDS

In Canada, venture capital activity has grown significantly since 1990. For instance, in 1990 there were 34 venture funds with $3.3 billion worth of capital under management. By 2006, the number of venture capital investment firms had grown to 1,200. Together, these funds had over $50 billion worth of capital under management. However, in the aftermath of the financial crisis, venture capital activity has declined in 2008 and 2009.

Canada's venture capital funds can be grouped into one of five categories: private independent, labour-sponsored, corporate, government and hybrid.[15] *Private independent firms*

TABLE 15A.1
Attributes of classic venture capital investing.

1. Create new businesses or expand or revitalize existing ones.
2. The investor, usually the venture capital (VC) fund's general manager and associates, are involved in the management of their portfolio companies, providing a great deal of "value added" to their companies.
3. The *potential* return from the investment is quite large due to investing in high-risk/high-reward situations.
4. Only a few investments are made each year after many candidates have been screened and a handful have been fully analyzed.
5. Negotiate appropriate financial structures using individualized investment instruments.
6. Take a long-term orientation toward their portfolio companies because of the illiquidity of their investments.
7. Try to maximize the growth of their funds since the VC receives, as incentive, compensation as a percentage of the capital gains after return of capital.
8. Venture capitalists often diversify their risk by syndicating their investment with other VC funds.

Source: A. Best and D. Mitra, "The Venture Capital Industry in Canada," *Journal of Small Business Management* 35(2) (April 1997): 105–110. Based on information in K.W. Rind, "The Role of Venture Capital in Corporate Development," *Strategic Management Journal*, April–June 1981: 169–180.

[15] These classifications are used by Canada's Venture Capital and Private Equity Association (CVCA) to provide periodic reports on venture capital activity. The reports are available on its site at **www.cvca.ca**. Data for these reports is often compiled by Macdonald and Associates Ltd., the best-known data source on Canadian venture capital activity.

typically have no affiliations with any other financial institution. Some large private independent funds have been very active although in recent years the level of activity of this category of funds has slowed somewhat. For instance, in 2009, about $995 million of new capital flowed into the industry across all fund types, with private independent funds attracting $527 million of new capital, about a 27 percent decline from the $719 million raised by such funds in 2008. Fund raising was generally quite sluggish in 2009, down from the $1 billion of 2008.

Labour-sponsored funds, or retail funds, are venture capital pools formed with the help of provincial and federal governments. These funds were mostly introduced in the late 1980s to facilitate business and economic growth. By 2000, these had about 50 percent of the money invested in the venture capital industry, mainly because of generous tax incentives given to investors in such funds. Despite a decline in investment activity in recent years, these funds were the largest investors when compared with all other categories until 2003. However, by 2006, their share of the total investment activity of venture capital firms had dropped to second place at 22 percent. In 2009, labour-sponsored and other retail funds raised $331 million of new commitments, roughly 33 percent of the total. Currently, investors receive a 15 percent tax credit from both the federal government and participating provincial governments. Moreover, the investment is registered retirement savings plan (RRSP)–eligible, and, therefore, provides the investor an additional tax benefit in the form of a tax deferral depending on her income level. Labour-sponsored funds are structured in a similar fashion to mutual funds. Individuals are able to buy shares in the fund, allowing investment by those who are not wealthy. The fund pools the money with the objective of investing in enterprises that have yet to go public instead of purchasing stocks and bonds. Two large and active labour-sponsored funds are GrowthWorks and Fonds de Solidarité de le Fédération des Travailleurs du Québec. A number of *corporate venture capital funds* also exist in Canada. These might include financial corporation funds, which tend to be venture capital affiliates or subsidiaries set up by large Canadian banks. For instance, RBC Capital Partners is a subsidiary of the RBC Financial Group. The financial institution can provide a range of financial services to entrepreneurs and enhance their credibility with suppliers and customers. You might also have subsidiaries of large manufacturing companies such as Dow Chemical Corporate Venture Capital, or subsidiaries of utility and power corporations such as Hydro-Québec Capitech Inc. Goals of corporate venture capital funds tend to be strategically tied to the parent organization; they often prefer to invest in ventures that will give them access to new technologies or provide a competitive advantage. For instance, Chrysalix Energy LP is an early to mid-stage venture capital firm focusing on fuel cell and related fuelling technology companies and was formed jointly by Ballard Power Systems and several large multinational companies such as Boeing, Mitsubishi Corporation, and Shell Hydrogen.

Federal or provincial governments run government funds by employing professional venture capital fund managers. For instance, the federal Business Development Corporation (BDC) has an active venture capital division that, for the end of fiscal year March 2010, had a total commitment of venture capital investments of $362 million. The BDC has focused on using venture capital to generate growth in new economy industries such as biotechnology, medical/health-related, information technology, and electronics. Much of the financing goes to companies in early stages of development and considered to be high-risk. Some Crown corporations, such as Export Development Canada, have venture capital operations as well. Provincial governments have also sponsored their own funds with goals of nurturing small businesses and also providing financing to high-technology firms, such as Crown Investments Corporation of Saskatchewan.

Pension funds, insurance companies or large endowments also may form venture capital funds. Teachers' Private Capital which is the venture capital arm of Ontario Teachers' Pension Plan is an example of one such *institutional fund*. Government and institutional funds have profit-maximizing objectives similar to those private and labour-sponsored funds. Table 15A.2 lists some Canadian venture capital funds and describes their investment preferences.

TABLE 15A.2
Some representative Canadian venture capital firms.

Firm	Type of Firm	Capital Under Management ($ millions)	Geographic Preference	Industry Preference
GrowthWorks[a]	Labour-sponsored venture capital fund	$800	Canada	Information technology and life sciences
Société Innovatech Québec[b]	Corporate investor	$150	Canada	Information technology and telecommunications, biotechnology, and advanced applied technologies
32 Degrees Capital[c]	Private venture capital fund	$ 70	Canada	Other technologies
Clairvest Group Inc.[d]	Private equity investor	$589	Canada, United States	All industries
Ventures West Capital LTD.[e]	Private venture capital fund	$485	Canada	Biotechnology, cleantech, and communications

[a] GrowthWorks site, **www.growthworks.ca/aboutus**, accessed October 11, 2010.
[b] Société Innovatech Québec site, **www.innovatechquebec.com/www/home.html**, accessed October 11, 2010.
[c] 32 Degrees Capital site, **www.32degrees.ca**, accessed October 11, 2010.
[d] Clairvest Group Inc. site, **www.clairvest.com/index.php/about**, accessed October 11, 2010.
[e] Ventures West Capital Ltd. site, **www.ventureswest.com**, accessed October 11, 2010.

Source: CVCA—Canada Venture Capital & Private Equity Association, **www.cvca.ca/membership/directory**, accessed October 11, 2010.

STAGES OF DEVELOPMENT FINANCED BY CANADIAN VENTURE CAPITAL FIRMS

New enterprises can be at different stages of development. Described below are some of the stages firms may go through after they are started.

- *Seed stage.* The very early stage when the new enterprise may seek to test a concept or build a product prototype and develop a product.
- *Startup stage.* The enterprise may have a product being developed, but not yet marketed and sold commercially.
- *Expansion stage.* The firm requires significant capital for plant expansion, marketing, and initiation of full commercial production and sales.
- *Acquisition/buyout stage.* The management of the firm acquires a product line, a division, or a company.
- *Turnaround stage.* The firm was once profitable but is now earning less than its cost of capital.

Generally the seed and startup stages are considered the early stages of development. During their life cycle, all firms will go through the seed, startup, and expansion stages, but not all will experience the buyout or turnaround stages. From Table 15A.3, we see that Canadian venture

TABLE 15A.3
Venture capital investment activity by stage of development in 2008 and 2009.

Stage	2009		2008	
	Amount ($ million)	Percentage of Total	Amount ($ million)	Percentage of Total
Early stage	$ 449	45%	$ 553	42%
Expansion	$ 478	47%	$ 701	53%
Acquisition/buyout	$ 17	2%	$ 46	4%
Turnaround	$ 14	1%	$ 10	0%
Other	$ 51	5%	$ 15	1%
Total	**$1,009**	**100%**	**$1,325**	**100%**

Source: Canada's Venture Capital & Private Equity Association and Macdonald & Associates Ltd., **www.cvca.ca**.

capital firms tend to finance enterprises across different stages of development. Over $449 million, or roughly 45 percent of all investments, went to financing 150 early-stage enterprises including seed, startup, and other early-stage firms in 2009, which represents a three-year high. Some recent examples of big early-stage deals include NowPublic.com, Shopify, and Coveo Solutions Inc. Follow-on and expansion-stage investments amounted to about $560 million, or 55 percent of all disbursements in 2009.

RECENT VENTURE CAPITAL INVESTMENT ACTIVITY

Just a few years ago, Canada's venture capital firms had been very active, with record investments of $5.8 billion in 2000 disbursed to 1,006 companies.[16] Since then, investment activity has considerably declined and, in 2009, $1.009 billion was disbursed to 371 firms. Table 15A.4 provides sector-wise details regarding where the venture capital firms invested in 2009. We see that 81.2 percent of the investing has focussed on large deals involving technology companies, particularly in life sciences, computer and Internet-related sectors, communications, and electronics. Topping the list were firms in the information technology sector, accounting for 129 companies that absorbed about $489 million or 48.4 percent of total disbursement. In this sector, firms in software and semiconductor-related sectors received $214 million, followed by those in the communications industry with $182 million, while firms in the electronics and computer hardware industry received $45 million. Biotechnology and health science firms received 21.3 percent representing 39 firms. Companies in traditional industries such as manufacturing or consumer-related received 18.7 percent of venture capital investments.

Table 15A.5 provides details on the top 10 venture capital deals for 2008. Notice the very large amounts invested in some life science firms. However, there were only a few such mega

TABLE 15A.4
Venture capital investment activity by sector.

Industry	2009 Amount ($ million)	2009 Percentage of Total	2008 Amount ($ million)	2008 Percentage of Total
Technology				
Biopharmaceuticals	179	17.6	287	21.7
Medical/health-related	40	4.1	70	5.3
Communications and networking	182	18.0	142	10.7
Electronics and computer hardware	45	4.5	120	9.1
Internet focus	53	5.3	117	8.8
Semiconductors and software	214	21.2	247	18.6
Energy and environmental technologies	102	10.1	186	14.0
Other IT services	4	0.4	34	2.6
Total	**819**	**81.2**	**1203**	**90.8**
Traditional				
Consumer-related	87	8.6	67	5.1
Manufacturing	67	6.6	22	1.6
Miscellaneous	36	3.6	33	2.5
Total	190	18.8	122	9.2
Total	**1,009**	**100.0**	**1,325**	**100.0**

Source: Canada's Venture Capital & Private Equity Association and Macdonald & Associates Ltd., **www.cvca.ca**.

[16] In contrast, the American venture capital industry reported a 10 percent increase in investment activity in 2006 from the previous year, with investments totalling US$25.5 billion disbursed to 3,416 company deals. For more information on venture capital activity in the United States, go the National Venture Capital Association site at **www.nvca.org**.

TABLE 15A.5
Top 10 venture capital deals in 2008.

Rank 2007	Invested $000s	Business Description	Investors
1 Cytochroma Inc	45,000	Pharmaceutical firm specializing in vitamin D deficiency	BDC Venture, GrowthWorks, Novo A/S, others
2 Gemin X Pharmaceuticals Inc.	38,000	Development of target-based cancer therapeutics	BDC Venture, Caxton-Iseman, FTQ, others
3 Sonco Gaming New Brunswick Ltd.	32,000	Selected for New Brunswick Destination Casino Project	Clairvest Equity Partners III LP, others
4 Kleer Semiconductor Corp.	28,496	Developer of wireless audio technology	BDC Venture, TL Ventures, U.S. Venture Partners, others
5 Inimex Pharmaceuticals Inc.	22,829	Medicines using the innate immune response	Advantage, Astellas Venture, BDC Venture, others
6 6N Silicon Inc.	20,558	Supplier of solar-grade silicon to the solar industry	Good Energies, Ventures West 8, Yaletown Ventures I LP, others
7 Natrix Separations Inc.	19,000	Supplier of disposable chromatography products	BDC Venture, Cdn. Med. Discoveries Fund, D.E., others
8 NxtGen Emission Controls Inc.	18,337	Syngas technology for clean-diesel and combustion engines	Altira Group LLC, Yaletown Ventures I LP, others
9 BTI Photonic Systems Inc.	17,727	Amplification and monitoring for optical networks	EDC Equity Fund, others
10 D-Wave Systems Inc.	17,000	Developer of commercial quantum computers	BDC Venture, BCIMC, Harris & Harris, others

Source: *National Post Business*, June 2009 (FP500), 106, retrieved October 27, 2010. Material reprinted with the express permission of National Post, a division of Postmedia Network Inc.

deals in 2008. Venture Capital activity in Canada slowed significantly in 2008, reaching its lowest level in years. A total of $1.3 billion was invested in that year, a 36 percent decline from the $2.1 billion invested in 2007. On average, the size of financing was much less, at $3.6 million in 2008. In general, the average amount invested per company was 30 percent higher than the $5.0 million average of 2007. About $570 million, or 44 percent of the total invested, went to 119 Ontario-based firms. Québec-based companies captured the second largest portion of total spending—about 27 percent at $349 million.

VENTURE CAPITAL EXITS

Venture capitalists provide a combination of unique services to companies in which they invest. In addition to financial capital they also help with a variety of advisory services. The investee firm also benefits indirectly when a reputed venture capital organization invests in it. By making the investment, the venture capitalist is, in a sense, signalling its approval of the firm's business plan, growth and profit potential, and future prospects. Once information gets out about the venture capitalist's interest in the firm, other service providers such as advertisement agencies or accounting firms also become eager to do business with the firm and are, often, willing to provide significant discounts on fees and other charges during its early-growth phase. As the investee firm matures and becomes more established, the value of services provided to it by the venture capitalist diminishes. It becomes important, therefore, for the venture capitalist to exit from the firm and to recycle its investment into another young venture.[17]

[17] For further discussion, see B.S. Black and R.J. Gilson, "Venture Capital and the Structure of Capital Markets: Banks Versus Stock Markets," *Journal of Financial Economics* 47 (1998): 243–277.

The venture capitalist can exit from an investment through a variety of means, including (a) acquisition by a third party, (b) company buyback by the entrepreneur, (c) initial public offering, (d) merger with another entity, and, in the event that all other options fail, (e) write-off. According to a recent study, company buybacks by entrepreneur/managers from venture capitalists appear to be the predominant mode of venture capital exits in Canada followed by initial public offerings.[18] Acquisition by a third party is also a popular exit route. Unfortunately, a sizeable number of exits occur through write-offs as well. The average duration of successful venture capital investments before exiting through a company buyback or an initial public offering is close to six years. Venture capitalists appear to be able to spot failures earlier on; the average duration of investments that are written off is a little over four years.

ANGEL INVESTING

Although the organized venture capital industry plays an important role in the creation of new ventures, those seeking very early-stage financing for small and new enterprises often have to resort to informal financing sources. In this context, wealthy individual investors, known as angels, can play a critical role by making small-scale investments in local startups and early-stage ventures, and by bringing a significant hands-on contribution to such business ventures.

The angel investor, typically a millionaire or a multimillionaire, may invest on average between $100,000 and $250,000 in a startup, and prefers to be involved with the project. According to some estimates, there are about 200,000 angel investors in Canada.[19] Angels can play either *active* or *passive* roles in the investee firms. "Active" angels are often highly motivated ex-entrepreneurs who are skilled at picking good management teams and good ideas. They help companies arrange additional financing, hire top management, and recruit knowledgeable board members. "Passive" angels provide only money and rarely monitor the firm closely; they are often part of an informal network led by one or more active angels who find deals and manage the investments. A number of organized services exist that are designed to match angel investors with entrepreneurs looking to fund their new ventures. These angel-network services include Ottawa Capital Network, VentureDrive.com, the Montréal-based InvestAngel Network, the Ottawa-based eValhalla.com, and Angel Investors Canada, which is the Toronto chapter of the International Angel Investors Group.

OTHER SOURCES OF SMALL BUSINESS FINANCING

FINANCING UNDER THE *CANADA SMALL BUSINESS FINANCING ACT*[20]

This type of financing comprises term loans and capital leases of up to 10 years available through all chartered banks, most credit unions and caisses populaires, and many trust and insurance companies, and are guaranteed by the federal government if taken for specific purposes and limits. The loans or leases are available under the federal government's *Canada Small Business Financing Act* (CSBFA) to small businesses in Canada that have gross revenues of $5 million or less in the year of application for the loan. The loans can be used to finance up to 90 percent of the purchase or improvement of eligible assets such as land, premises, and equipment. The loans cannot be used to buy shares or provide working capital. Capital leases (with an option to purchase) can be used to finance the cost of a variety of new and used equipment including vehicles, hotel and restaurant equipment, medical and health services equipment, computer hardware and

---

[18] See D.J. Cummings and J.G. MacIntosh, "A Cross-Country Comparison of Full and Partial Venture Capital Exits," *Journal of Banking and Finance* 27 (2003): 511–548.

[19] See, for instance, "Startups Angle for Angels," *The Globe and Mail*, June 29, 2000, T1.

[20] Details are available at the Industry Canada site, **strategis.ic.gc.ca**.

software, telecommunications, and manufacturing equipment. CSBFA loans and leases are made to small businesses in a variety of industries such as communication, construction, manufacturing, transportation, and wholesale trade. The loans and leases are not available to farming, charitable, or religious enterprises.

BUSINESS DEVELOPMENT BANK OF CANADA

The Business Development Bank of Canada (BDC) is a Crown financial institution that specializes in providing financial and other support services to small- and medium-sized businesses in Canada. BDC's major activities include term lending, giving loan guarantees, and providing venture capital financing. It is also involved in lease financing and providing consultancy services. As of the fiscal year ending March 2009, BDC had over 29,000 customers to whom the total financing committed exceeded $21 billion. During the fiscal year March 2009, total financing authorized had reached a record $4.4 billion. In recent years, BDC supports new ventures in fields such as medical technologies, telecommunications, information technology etc. BDC continued to provide financing in support of new ventures with direct investment of $59.5 million as of the fiscal year ending March 2009. It also plays an active role in the First Peoples' market and in supporting female entrepreneurs.

REGIONAL AND PROVINCIAL LENDING PROGRAMS

There are a number of regional agencies across Canada that have lending and other assistance programs, designed to nurture and grow small businesses. Some of the important regional agencies and initiatives include Atlantic Canada Opportunities Agency (ACOA), Federal Economic Development Initiative in Northern Ontario (FedNor), Canada Economic Development for Québec Regions: Financing, and Western Economic Diversification Canada: Financing. For descriptions of such agencies and details regarding the services provided by them, go to the Industry Canada site at **strategis.ic.gc.ca**.

Practice Problems

1. **Internet.** This chapter has provided Web site information for several venture capital sources and angel investing networks. Use the Internet to explore these sites. Also, see whether you can identify other interesting sites that will provide useful information on venture capital and angel investing activity.
2. **Venture Capital.** Based on your Internet research in problem 1, can you answer the following?
   a. We described different types of venture capital funds that exist in Canada. What are the main differences in investment goals and characteristics between these funds? Do some types of funds appear to participate more in earlier stage financing than others?
   b. Do some venture capitalists appear to specialize by investing in only a few selected industries, while others are more diversified in their investment activity? Can you think of some good reasons for firms pursuing either of the two strategies?
   c. Venture capitalists have geographical preferences for their investment activity. Can you discern some common motivations for such preferences?
3. **Venture Capital and Angel Investing.** Venture capitalists and many angel investors are often actively involved with the ventures in which they invest. How does this benefit the entrepreneur? Does this benefit the venture capitalist and angel investor as well?
4. **Internet.** To find out what is happening in the venture capital industry in the United States, look at the National Venture Capital Association website (**www.nvca.org**). Now find the NVCA's *Yearbook 2010* in the "Resources/Publications & Products" section of the Web site and look at the recent U.S. national data. How does the level of deals compare with the boom year of 2000? Which industries are attracting the most venture capital? Is the money going into new startups or expansion of existing businesses?

APPENDIX 15B: HOTCH POT'S NEW ISSUE PROSPECTUS[21]

PROSPECTUS

800,000 Shares
Hotch Pot, Inc.
Common Stock

Of the 800,000 shares of Common Stock offered hereby, 500,000 shares are being sold by the Company and 300,000 shares are being sold by the Selling Shareholders. See "Principal and Selling Shareholders." The Company will not receive any of the proceeds from the sale of shares by the Selling Shareholders.

Before this offering there has been no public market for the Common Stock. **These securities involve a high degree of risk. See "Certain Factors."**

THESE SECURITIES HAVE NOT BEEN APPROVED OR DISAPPROVED BY A SECURITIES COMMISSION, NOR HAS ANY COMMISSION PASSED ON THE ACCURACY OR ADEQUACY OF THIS PROSPECTUS. ANY REPRESENTATION TO THE CONTRARY IS A CRIMINAL OFFENSE.

	Price to Public	Underwriting Discount	Proceeds to Company*	Proceeds to Selling Shareholders
Per share	$12.00	$1.30	$10.70	$10.70
Total	$9,600,000	$1,040,000	$5,350,000	$3,210,000

*Before deducting expenses payable by the Company estimated at $400,000, of which $250,000 will be paid by the Company and $150,000 by the Selling Stockholders.

The Common Shares are offered, subject to prior sale, when, as, and if delivered to and accepted by the Underwriters and subject to approval of certain legal matters by their counsel and by counsel for the Company and the Selling Shareholders. The Underwriters reserve the right to withdraw, cancel, or modify such offers and reject orders in whole or in part.

Silverman Pinch Inc. **April 1, 2011**

No person has been authorized to give any information or to make any representations, other than as contained therein, in connection with the offer contained in this Prospectus, and, if given or made, such information or representations must not be relied upon. This Prospectus does not constitute an offer of any securities other than the registered securities to which it relates or an offer to any person in any jurisdiction where such an offer would be unlawful. The delivery of this Prospectus at any time does not imply that information herein is correct as of any time subsequent to its date.

IN CONNECTION WITH THIS OFFERING, THE UNDERWRITER MAY OVER ALLOT OR EFFECT TRANSACTIONS WHICH STABILIZE OR MAINTAIN THE MARKET PRICE OF THE COMMON SHARES OF THE COMPANY AT A LEVEL ABOVE THAT WHICH MIGHT OTHERWISE PREVAIL IN THE OPEN MARKET. SUCH STABILIZING, IF COMMENCED, MAY BE DISCONTINUED AT ANY TIME.

[21] Most prospectuses have content similar to that of the Hotch Pot prospectus, but go into considerably more detail. Also, we have omitted from this prospectus the company's financial statements. You can get a better impression of the contents of a prospectus by looking at some real ones. These are available at the System for Electronic Document Analysis and Retrieval (SEDAR) site at **www.sedar.com**. For instance, you might read the preliminary prospectus of Ripple Lake Diamonds Inc., which was filed on August 26, 2004.

PROSPECTUS SUMMARY

The following summary information is qualified in its entirety by the detailed information and financial statements appearing elsewhere in this Prospectus.

The Company: Hotch Pot, Inc., operates a chain of 140 fast-food outlets in Canada, offering unusual combinations of dishes.

The Offering: Common Shares offered by the Company 500,000 shares;
Common Shares offered by the Selling Shareholders 300,000 shares;
Common Shares to be outstanding after this offering 3,500,000 shares.

Use of Proceeds: For the construction of new restaurants and to provide working capital.

THE COMPANY

Hotch Pot, Inc., operates a chain of 140 fast-food outlets in Ontario, Québec, and British Columbia. These restaurants specialize in offering an unusual combination of foreign dishes.

The Company was organized in Ontario in 2000.

USE OF PROCEEDS

The Company intends to use the net proceeds from the sale of 500,000 shares of Common Stock offered hereby, estimated at approximately $5 million, to open new outlets in the Atlantic provinces and to provide additional working capital. It has no immediate plans to use any of the net proceeds of the offering for any other specific investment.

DIVIDEND POLICY

The company has not paid cash dividends on its Common Stock and does not anticipate that dividends will be paid on the Common Stock in the foreseeable future.

CERTAIN FACTORS

Investment in the Common Stock involves a high degree of risk. The following factors should be carefully considered in evaluating the Company:

- **Substantial Capital Needs.** The Company will require additional financing to continue its expansion policy. The Company believes that its relations with its lenders are good, but there can be no assurance that additional financing will be available in the future.
- **Competition.** The Company is in competition with a number of restaurant chains supplying fast food. Many of these companies are substantially larger and better capitalized than the Company.

CAPITALIZATION

The following table sets forth the capitalization of the Company as of December 31, 2011, and is adjusted to reflect the sale of 500,000 shares of Common Stock by the Company.

	Actual	As Adjusted
	($000s)	
Long-term debt	$ —	$ —
Stockholders' equity		
Common shares: 3,000,000 shares outstanding, 3,500,000 shares outstanding, as adjusted	2,000	7,350
Retained earnings	3,200	3,200
Total shareholders' equity	5,200	10,550
Total capitalization	$5,200	$10,550

SELECTED FINANCIAL DATA

[The Prospectus typically includes a summary income statement and balance sheet.]

MANAGEMENT'S ANALYSIS OF RESULTS OF OPERATIONS AND FINANCIAL CONDITION

Revenue growth for the year ended December 31, 2011, resulted from the opening of 10 new restaurants in the Company's existing geographic area and from sales of a new range of desserts, notably crêpe suzette with custard. Sales per customer increased by 20% and this contributed to the improvement in margins.

During the year the Company borrowed $600,000 from its banks at an interest rate of 2% above the prime rate.

BUSINESS

Hotch Pot, Inc., operates a chain of 140 fast-food outlets in Ontario, Québec, and British Columbia. These restaurants specialize in offering an unusual combination of international dishes. Fifty percent of the company's revenues were derived from the sale of two dishes, sushi and sauerkraut, and curry bolognese. All dishes are prepared in three regional centres and then frozen and distributed to the individual restaurants.

MANAGEMENT

The following table sets forth information regarding the Company's directors, executive officers, and key employees:

Name	Age	Position
Emma Lucullus	38	President, Chief Executive Officer, and Director
Ed Lucullus	43	Treasurer & Director

Emma Lucullus Emma Lucullus established the Company in 2000 and has been its Chief Executive Officer since that date.

Ed Lucullus Ed Lucullus has been employed by the Company since 2000.

EXECUTIVE COMPENSATION

The following table sets forth the cash compensation paid for services rendered for the year 2007 by the executive officers:

Name	Capacity	Cash Compensation
Emma Lucullus	President and Chief Executive Officer	$130,000
Ed Lucullus	Treasurer	$ 95,000

CERTAIN TRANSACTIONS

At various times between 2000 and 2010, First Cookham Venture Partners invested a total of $1.5 million in the Company. In connection with this investment, First Cookham Venture Partners was granted certain rights to registration under the *Ontario Securities Act*, including the right to have their shares of Common Stock registered at the Company's expense with the Ontario Securities Commission.

PRINCIPAL AND SELLING STOCKHOLDERS

The following table sets forth certain information regarding the beneficial ownership of the Company's voting Common Stock as of the date of this prospectus by (i) each person known by the Company to be the beneficial owner of more than 5% of its voting Common Stock and

(ii) each director of the Company who beneficially owns voting Common Stock. Unless otherwise indicated, each owner has sole voting and dispositive power over his or her shares.

Name of Beneficial Owner	Shares Beneficially Owned Prior to Offering		Shares to Be Sold	Shares Beneficially Owned After Offering	
	Number	Percent		Number	Percent
Emma Lucullus	400,000	13.3	25,000	375,000	10.7
Ed Lucullus	400,000	13.3	25,000	375,000	10.7
First Cookham Venture Partners	1,700,000	56.7	250,000	1,450,000	41.4
Hermione Kraft	200,000	6.7	—	200,000	5.7

DESCRIPTION OF CAPITAL STOCK

The Company's authorized capital stock consists of 10,000,000 shares of voting Common Stock.

As of the date of this Prospectus, there are four holders of record of the Common Stock.

Under the terms of one of the Company's loan agreements, the Company may not pay cash dividends on Common Stock except from net profits without the written consent of the lender.

UNDERWRITING

Subject to the terms and conditions set forth in the Underwriting Agreement, the Underwriter, Silverman Pinch, Inc., has agreed to purchase from the Company and the Selling Stockholders 800,000 shares of Common Stock.

There is no public market for the Common Stock. The price to the public for the Common Stock was determined by negotiation between the Company and the Underwriter, and was based on, among other things, the Company's financial and operating history and condition, its prospects, and the prospects for its industry in general, the management of the Company, and the market prices of securities for companies in businesses similar to that of the Company.

LEGAL MATTERS

The validity of the shares of Common Stock offered by the Prospectus is being passed on for the Company by Blair, Kohl, and Chirac, and for the Underwriter by Chretien Howard.

LEGAL PROCEEDINGS

Hotch Pot was served in January 2011 with a summons and complaint in an action commenced by a customer who alleged that consumption of the Company's products caused severe nausea and loss of feeling in both feet. The Company believes that the complaint is without foundation.

EXPERTS

The consolidated financial statements of the Company have been so included in reliance on the reports of Hooper Firebrand, independent accountants, given on the authority of that firm as experts in auditing and accounting.

FINANCIAL STATEMENTS

[Text and tables omitted.]

PART 5

Debt and Payout Policy

16 Debt Policy
16.1 How Borrowing Affects Value in a Tax-Free Economy
16.2 Capital Structure and Corporate Taxes
16.3 Costs of Financial Distress
16.4 Explaining Financing Choices
16.5 Bankruptcy Procedures
16.6 Summary
17 Leasing
18 Payout Policy

CHAPTER 16

Debt Policy

LEARNING OBJECTIVES

After studying this chapter, you should be able to:

LO1 Show why capital structure does not affect firm value in perfect capital markets.

LO2 Show why the tax system encourages debt finance, and derive the value of interest tax shields.

LO3 Show how costs of financial distress can lead to an optimal capital structure.

LO4 Explain why financial slack is valuable and might influence optimal capital structure.

LO5 Summarize bankruptcy procedures for firms that cannot pay their creditors.

"Neither a borrower nor a lender be." So says Polonius in Shakespeare's *Hamlet*. Is this sound advice for the modern corporation?

Everett Collection.

A firm's basic financial resource is the stream of cash flows produced by its assets and operations. When the firm is financed entirely by common stock, all those cash flows belong to the shareholders. When it issues both debt and equity, the firm splits the cash flows into two streams, a relatively safe stream that goes to the debtholders and a more risky one that goes to the shareholders.

The firm's mix of securities is known as its capital structure. Look at Table 16.6 in this chapter. You can see that in some industries companies borrow much more heavily than in others. Most high-tech firms, such as Research In Motion, rely almost wholly on equity finance, as do most biotech, software, and Internet companies. At the other extreme, debt accounts for a substantial part of the market value of retailers, utilities, and banks. For instance, Rogers Communications' total debt is higher than its total equity.

Capital structure is not immutable. Firms change their capital structure, sometimes almost overnight. For instance, Alliance Atlantis Communications recently announced a $131.5 million offering of Class B non-voting common shares that will be used to pay down some of the firm's debt. In the 1990s, DuPont Canada generated large amounts of cash flows and used the money to pay off its long-term debt. Later in the chapter you will see how an American company, Sealed Air Corporation, benefited from changing its capital structure.

Shareholders want management to choose the mix of securities that maximizes firm value. But does this optimal capital structure exist? We must consider the possibility that no combination has any greater appeal than any other. Perhaps the really important decisions concern the company's assets, and decisions about capital structure are mere details—matters to be attended to but not worried about.

In the first part of the chapter, we will look at examples in which capital structure doesn't matter. After that we will put back some of the things that *do* make a difference, such as taxes, bankruptcy, and the signals that your financing decisions may send to investors. We will then draw up a checklist for financial managers who need to decide on the firm's capital structure. We conclude the chapter with a brief discussion of what happens when firms cannot pay their debts and enter bankruptcy proceedings.

LO1 16.1

HOW BORROWING AFFECTS VALUE IN A TAX-FREE ECONOMY

It is after the ball game and the pizza man is delivering a pizza to Yogi Berra. "Should I cut it into four slices as usual, Yogi?" asks the pizza man. "No," replies Yogi, "Cut it into eight; I'm hungry tonight."

capital structure A firm's mix of long-term financing.

If you understand why more slices won't sate Yogi's appetite, you will have no difficulty understanding why a company's choice of **capital structure** can't increase the underlying value of the cash flows generated by its real assets and operations.

Think of a simple balance sheet with all entries expressed as current market values:

Assets	**Liabilities and Stockholders' Equity**
Value of cash flows from the firm's real assets and operations	Market value of debt Market value of equity
Value of firm	Value of firm

The right-hand and left-hand sides of a balance sheet are always equal. (Balance sheets have to balance!) Therefore, if you add up the market value of all the firm's debt and equity securities, you can calculate the value of the future cash flows from the real assets and operations.

In fact the value of those cash flows *determines* the value of the firm, and therefore determines the aggregate value of all the firm's outstanding debt and equity securities. If the firm changes its capital structure, say by using more debt and less equity financing, overall value should not change.

Think of the left-hand side of the balance sheet as the size of the pizza; the right-hand side determines how it is sliced. A company can slice its cash flow into as many parts as it likes, but the value of those parts will always sum back to the value of the unsliced cash flow. (Of course, we have to make sure that none of the cash flow stream is lost in the slicing. We cannot say that the value of a pizza is independent of how it is sliced if the slicer is also a nibbler.)

When there are no taxes and well-functioning capital markets exist, the market value of a company does not depend on its capital structure. In other words, financial managers cannot increase value by changing the mix of securities used to finance the company.

The basic idea here (the value of a pizza does not depend on how it is sliced) has various applications. Yogi Berra got friendly chuckles for his misapplication. Franco Modigliani and Merton Miller received Nobel prizes for applying it to corporate financing. Modigliani and Miller, always referred to as "MM," showed in 1958 that the value of a firm does not depend on how its cash flows are "sliced." More precisely, they demonstrated the following proposition: When there are no taxes and well-functioning capital markets exist, the market value of a company does not depend on its capital structure. In other words, financial managers cannot increase value by changing the mix of securities used to finance the company.

Of course, this MM proposition rests on some important simplifying assumptions. For example, capital markets have to be "well functioning." That means that investors can trade securities without restrictions and can borrow or lend on the same terms as the firm. It also means that capital markets are efficient, so that securities are fairly priced given the information available to investors. (We discussed market efficiency in Chapter 7.) MM's proposition also assumes that there are no distorting taxes, and it ignores the costs encountered if a firm borrows too much and lands in financial distress.

The firm's capital structure decision can matter if these assumptions are not true or if other practical complications are encountered. But the best way to start thinking about capital structure is to work through MM's argument. *To keep things as simple as possible, in the following discussion we will ignore taxes until further notice.*

MM'S ARGUMENT

Cleo, the president of River Cruises, is reviewing the firm's capital structure with Antony, the financial manager. Table 16.1 shows the current position. The company has no debt and all its operating income is paid as dividends to the shareholders. The *expected* earnings and dividends per share are $1.25, but this figure is by no means certain—it could turn out to be more or less than $1.25. For example, earnings could fall to $.75 in a slump, or they could jump to $1.75 in a boom.

The price of each share is $10. The firm expects to produce a level stream of earnings and dividends in perpetuity. With no growth forecast, shareholders' expected return is equal to the dividend yield—that is, the expected dividend per share divided by the price, $1.25/$10 = .125, or 12.5 percent.

Cleo has come to the conclusion that shareholders would be better off if the company had equal proportions of debt and equity. She therefore proposes to issue $500,000 of debt at an interest rate of 10 percent and to use the proceeds to repurchase 50,000 shares. This is called a **restructuring**. Notice that the $500,000 raised by the new borrowing does not stay in the firm. It goes right out the door to shareholders in order to repurchase and retire 50,000 shares. Therefore, the assets and investment policy of the firm are not affected. Only the financing mix changes.

restructuring Process of changing the firm's capital structure without changing its assets.

What would MM say about this new capital structure? Suppose the change is made. Operating income is the same, so the value of the "pie" is fixed at $1 million. With $500,000 in new debt outstanding, the remaining common shares must be worth $500,000, that is, 50,000 shares at $10 per share. The total value of the debt and equity is still $1 million.

Since the value of the firm is the same, common shareholders are no better or worse off than before. River Cruises' shares still trade at $10 each. The overall value of River Cruises' equity falls from $1 million to $500,000, but shareholders have also received $500,000 in cash.

Antony points all this out. "The restructuring doesn't make our shareholders any richer or poorer, Cleo. Why bother? Capital structure doesn't matter."

Check Point 16.1

Suppose River Cruises issues $350,000 of new debt (rather than $500,000) and uses the proceeds to repurchase and retire common stock. How does this affect price per share? How many shares will be left outstanding?

HOW BORROWING AFFECTS EARNINGS PER SHARE

Cleo is unconvinced. She prepares Table 16.2 and Figure 16.1 to show how borrowing $500,000 could increase earnings per share. Comparison of Tables 16.1 and 16.2 shows that "normal" earnings per share increase to $1.50 (versus $1.25) after the restructuring.

TABLE 16.1
River Cruises is entirely equity-financed. Although it expects to have an income of $125,000 in perpetuity, this income is not certain. This table shows the return to the shareholders under different assumptions about operating income. No taxes are assumed.

Data				
Number of shares	100,000			
Price per share	$10			
Market value of shares	$1 million			
		State of the Economy		
		Slump	Normal	Boom
Operating income		$75,000	125,000	175,000
Earnings per share		$.75	1.25	1.75
Return on shares		7.5%	12.5%	17.5%
			Expected outcome	

TABLE 16.2
River Cruises is wondering whether to issue $500,000 of debt at an interest rate of 10 percent and repurchase 50,000 shares. This table shows the return to the shareholder under different assumptions about operating income. Returns to shareholders are increased in normal and boom times but fall in slumps.

Data			
Number of shares	50,000		
Price per share	$10		
Market value of shares	$500,000		
Market value of debt	$500,000		
	State of the Economy		
	Slump	Normal	Boom
Operating income	$75,000	125,000	175,000
Interest	$50,000	50,000	50,000
Equity earnings	$25,000	75,000	125,000
Earnings per share	$.50	1.50	2.50
Return on shares	5%	15%	25%
		Expected outcome	

FIGURE 16.1
Borrowing increases River Cruises' earnings per share (EPS) when operating income is greater than $100,000, but reduces it when operating income is less than $100,000. Expected EPS rises from $1.25 to $1.50.

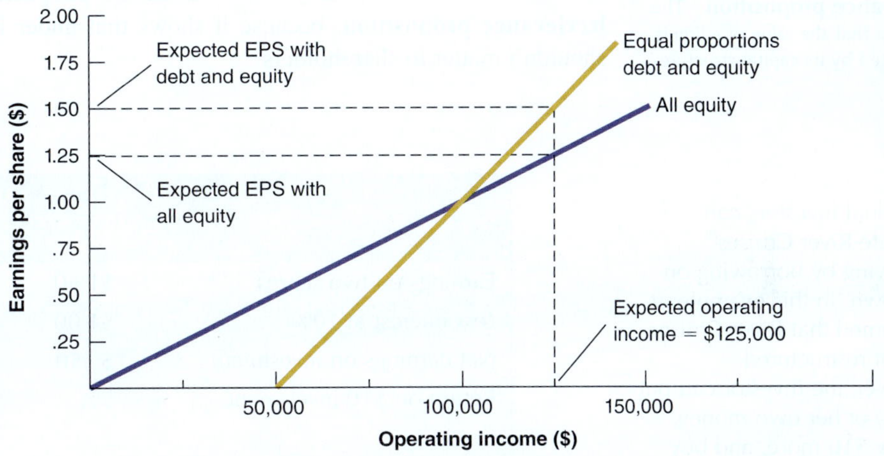

Table 16.2 also shows more "upside" (earnings per share of $2.50 versus $1.75) and more "downside" ($.50 versus $.75).

The blue line in Figure 16.1 shows how earnings per share would vary with operating income under the firm's current all-equity financing. It is therefore simply a plot of the data in Table 16.1. The gold line shows how earnings per share would vary if the company moves to equal proportions of debt and equity. It is therefore a plot of the data in Table 16.2.

Cleo reasons as follows: "It is clear that debt could either increase or reduce the return to the equityholder. In a slump the return to the equityholder is reduced by the use of debt, but otherwise it is increased. We could be heading for a recession, but it doesn't look likely. Maybe we could help our shareholders by going ahead with the debt issue."

As financial manager, Antony replies as follows: "I agree that borrowing will increase earnings per share as long as there's no slump. But we're not really doing anything for shareholders that they can't do on their own. Suppose River Cruises does not borrow. In that case an investor could go to the bank, borrow $10, and then invest $20 in two shares. Such an investor would put up only $10 of her own money. (Table 16.3 shows how the payoffs on this $10 investment vary with River Cruises' operating income.) You can see that these payoffs are exactly the same as the investor would get by buying one share in the company after the restructuring. (Compare the last two lines of Tables 16.2 and 16.3.) It makes no difference whether shareholders borrow directly or whether River Cruises borrows on their behalf. Therefore, if River Cruises goes ahead and borrows, it will not allow investors to do anything that they could not do already, and so it cannot increase the value of the firm."

"We can run the same argument in reverse and show that investors won't be worse off after the restructuring either. Imagine an investor who owns two shares in the company before the restructuring. If River Cruises borrows money, there is some chance that the return on the shares will be lower than before. If that possibility is not to our investor's taste, he can buy one share in the restructured company and also invest $10 in the firm's debt. (Table 16.4 shows how the payoff on this investment varies with River Cruises' operating income.) You can see that these payoffs are exactly the same as the investor got before the restructuring. (Compare the last lines of Tables 16.1 and 16.4.) By lending half of his capital (by investing in River Cruises' debt), the investor offsets the company's borrowing exactly. So if River Cruises goes ahead and borrows, it won't *stop* investors from doing anything that they could previously do."

The value of the firm must be unaffected by its capital structure.

This recreates MM's original argument.[1] As long as investors can borrow or lend on their own account on the same terms as the firm, they are not going to pay more for a firm that has borrowed on their behalf. The value of the firm after the restructuring must be the same as before. In other words, the value of the firm must be unaffected by its capital structure.

MM's proposition I or **debt-irrelevance proposition** The principle that the value of a firm is unaffected by its capital structure.

This conclusion is widely known as **MM's proposition I**. It is also called the **MM debt-irrelevance proposition**, because it shows that under ideal conditions the firm's debt policy shouldn't matter to shareholders.

TABLE 16.3 Individual investors can replicate River Cruises' borrowing by borrowing on their own. In this example, it is assumed that River Cruises has not restructured. However, the investor can put up $10 of her own money, borrow $10 more, and buy two shares at $10 apiece. This generates the same rates of return as in Table 16.2.

	State of the Economy		
	Slump	Normal	Boom
Earnings on two shares	$1.50	2.50	3.50
Less interest at 10%	$1.00	1.00	1.00
Net earnings on investment	$ .50	1.50	2.50
Return on $10 investment	5%	15%	25%
		Expected outcome	

TABLE 16.4 Individual investors can also undo the effects of River Cruises' borrowing. Here the investor buys one share for $10 and lends out $10 more. Compare these rates of return to the original returns of River Cruises in Table 16.1.

	State of the Economy		
	Slump	Normal	Boom
Earnings on one share	$ .50	1.50	2.50
Plus interest at 10%	$1.00	1.00	1.00
Net earnings on investment	$1.50	2.50	3.50
Return on $20 investment	7.5%	12.5%	17.5%
		Expected outcome	

[1] There are many more general—and technical—proofs of the MM proposition. We will not pursue them here.

Check Point 16.2

Suppose that River Cruises issues $750,000 of debt and uses the proceeds to buy back stock.

a. What would be the impact of a $50,000 change in operating income on earnings per share?
b. Show how a conservative investor might "undo" the change in River Cruises' capital structure by varying the investment strategy shown in Table 16.4. *Hint:* The investor will have to lend $3 for every dollar invested in River Cruises' stock.

HOW BORROWING AFFECTS RISK AND RETURN

Figure 16.2 summarizes the implications of MM's debt-irrelevance proposition for River Cruises. The upper circles represent firm value, the lower circles expected, or "normal," operating income. Restructuring does not affect the size of the circles, because the amount and risk of operating income are unchanged. Thus if the firm raises $500,000 in debt and uses the proceeds to repurchase and retire shares, the remaining shares *must* be worth $500,000, and the total value of debt and equity must stay at $1 million.

The two bottom circles in Figure 16.2 are also the same size. But notice that the bottom right circle shows that shareholders can expect to earn more than half of River Cruises' normal operating income. They get more than half of the expected "income pie." Does that mean shareholders are better off? MM say no. Why not? The answer is that shareholders bear more risk.

operating risk or **business risk** Risk in a firm's operating income.

Look again at Tables 16.1 and 16.2. Restructuring does not affect operating income, regardless of the state of the economy. Therefore, debt financing does not affect the **operating risk** or, equivalently, the **business risk** of the firm. But with less equity outstanding, a change in operating income has a greater impact on earnings per share. Suppose operating income drops from $125,000 to $75,000. Under all-equity financing, there are 100,000 shares; so earnings per share fall by $.50. With 50 percent debt, there are only 50,000 shares outstanding; so the same drop in operating income reduces earnings per share by $1.

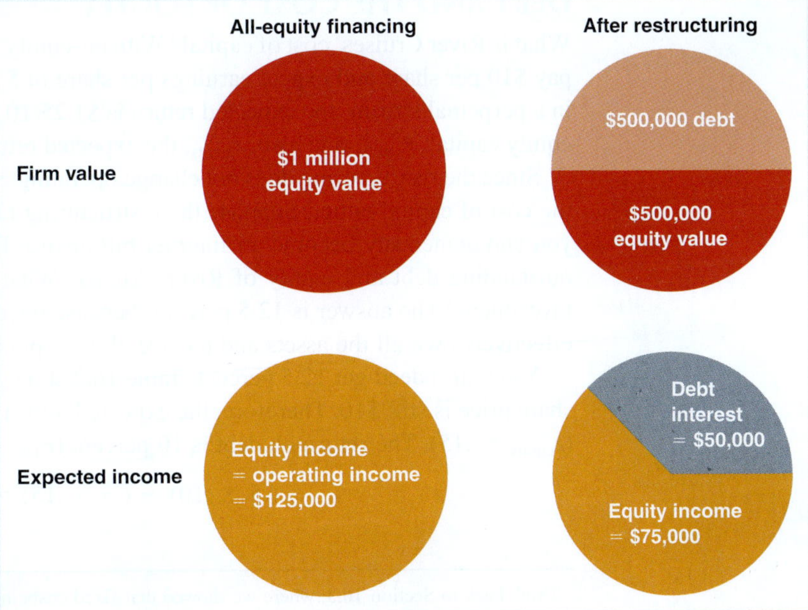

FIGURE 16.2 "Slicing the pie" for River Cruises. The circles on the left assume the company has no debt. The circles on the right reflect the proposed restructuring. The restructuring splits firm value (top circles) 50-50. Shareholders get more than 50 percent of expected, or "normal," operating income (bottom circles), but only because they bear financial risk. Note that restructuring does not affect total firm value or operating income.

financial leverage Debt financing to amplify the effects of changes in operating income on the returns to stockholders.

financial risk Risk to shareholders resulting from the use of debt.

You can see now why the use of debt finance is known as **financial leverage**, and a firm that has issued debt is described as a *levered firm*. The debt increases the uncertainty about percentage stock returns. If the firm is financed entirely by equity, a decline of $50,000 in operating income reduces the return on the shares by 5 percent. If the firm issues debt, then the same decline of $50,000 in operating income reduces the return on the shares by 10 percent. (Compare Tables 16.1 and 16.2.) In other words, the effect of leverage is to double the magnitude of the upside and downside in the return on River Cruises' shares. Whatever the beta of the firm's shares before the restructuring, it would be twice as high afterward.

Debt finance does not affect the operating risk, but it does add **financial risk**. With only half the equity to absorb the same amount of operating risk, risk per share must double.[2]

Consider now the implications of MM's proposition I for the expected return on River Cruises' stock. Before the proposed debt issue, the expected stream of earnings and dividends per share is $1.25. Since investment in the shares is risky, the shareholders require a return of 12.5 percent, or 2.5 percent above the interest rate. So the share price (which for a perpetuity is equal to the expected dividends divided by the required return) is $1.25/.125 = $10. The good news is that after the debt issue, expected earnings and dividends rise to $1.50. The bad news is that the risk of the shares has now doubled. So instead of being content with a return of 2.5 percent above the interest rate, shareholders now demand a return of 5 percent more than the interest rate—that is, a required return of 10 + 5 = 15 percent. The benefit from the rise in dividends is exactly cancelled out by the rise in the required return. The share price after the debt issue is $1.50/.15 = $10—exactly the same as before.

	Current Structure: All Equity	Proposed Structure: Equal Debt and Equity
Expected earnings per share	$1.25	$1.50
Share price	$10	$10
Expected return on share	12.5%	15.0%

Thus leverage increases the expected return to shareholders but it also increases the risk. The two effects cancel each other out, leaving shareholder value unchanged.

DEBT AND THE COST OF EQUITY

What is River Cruises' cost of capital? With all-equity financing, the answer is easy. Shareholders pay $10 per share and expect earnings per share of $1.25. If the earnings per share are paid out in a perpetual stream, the expected return is $1.25/10 = .125, or 12.5 percent. This is the cost of equity capital, r_{equity}, and also, r_{assets}, the expected return and cost of capital for the firm's assets.

Since the restructuring does not change operating earnings or firm value, it should not change the cost of capital either. Suppose the restructuring takes place. Also, by a grand stroke of luck you simultaneously become an Internet billionaire. Flush with cash, you decide to buy all the outstanding debt and equity of River Cruises. What rate of return should you expect on this investment? The answer is 12.5 percent, because once you own all the debt and equity, you will effectively own all the assets and receive all the operating income.

You will indeed get 12.5 percent. Table 16.2 shows expected earnings per share of $1.50, and share price is still $10. Therefore, the expected return on equity is $1.50/10 = .15, or 15 percent ($r_{\text{equity}} = .15$). The return on debt is 10 percent ($r_{\text{debt}} = .10$). Your overall return is

$$(.5 \times .10) + (.5 \times .15) = .125 = r_{\text{assets}}$$

[2] Think back to Section 10.3, where we showed that fixed costs increase the variability in a firm's profits. These fixed costs are said to provide *operating leverage*. It is exactly the same with debt. Debt interest is a fixed cost and therefore debt magnifies the variability of profits after interest. These fixed interest charges create financial leverage.

There is obviously a general principle here: The appropriate weighted average of r_{debt} and r_{equity} takes you to r_{assets}, the opportunity cost of capital for the company's assets. The formula is

$$r_{assets} = (r_{debt} \times D/V) + (r_{equity} \times E/V)$$

where D and E are the amounts of outstanding debt and equity and V equals overall firm value, the sum of D and E. Remember that D, E, and V are market values, not book values.

This formula does not match the weighted-average cost of capital (WACC) formula presented in Chapter 13.[3] Don't worry, we'll get to WACC in a moment. (Remember, we're still ignoring taxes.) First let's look at the implications of MM's debt-irrelevance proposition for the cost of equity.

MM's proposition I states that the firm's choice of capital structure does not affect the firm's operating income or the value of its assets. So r_{assets}, the expected return on the package of debt and equity, is unaffected.

However, we have just seen that leverage does increase the risk of the equity and the return that shareholders demand. To see how the expected return on equity varies with leverage, we simply rearrange the formula for the company cost of capital as follows:

$$r_{equity} = r_{assets} + \frac{D}{E}(r_{assets} - r_{debt})$$

which in words says that

$$\text{Expected return on equity} = \text{expected return on assets} + \left[\text{debt-equity ratio} \times \left(\text{expected return on assets} - \text{expected return on debt}\right)\right] \quad \textbf{(16.1)}$$

MM's proposition II The principle that the required rate of return on equity increases as the firm's debt-equity ratio increases.

This is **MM's proposition II**. It states that the expected rate of return on the common stock of a leveraged firm increases in proportion to the debt-equity ratio (D/E), expressed in market values. Note that $r_{equity} = r_{assets}$ if the firm has no debt.

EXAMPLE 16.1 RIVER CRUISES' COST OF EQUITY

We can check out MM's proposition II for River Cruises. Before the decision to borrow,

$$r_{equity} = r_{assets} = \frac{\text{expected operating income}}{\text{market value of all securities}}$$

$$= \frac{125{,}000}{1{,}000{,}000} = .125, \text{ or } 12.5\%$$

If the firm goes ahead with its plan to borrow, the expected return on assets, r_{assets}, is still 12.5 percent. So the expected return on equity is

$$r_{equity} = r_{assets} + \frac{D}{E}(r_{assets} - r_{debt})$$

$$= .125 + \frac{500{,}000}{500{,}000} \times (.125 - .10)$$

$$= .15, \text{ or } 15\%$$

We pointed out in Chapter 13 that you might think of a debt issue as having an explicit cost and an implicit cost. The explicit cost is the rate of interest charged on the firm's debt. Debt also increases financial risk and causes shareholders to demand a higher return on their investment. Once you recognize this implicit cost, debt is no cheaper than equity—the return that investors require on their assets is unaffected by the firm's borrowing decision.

[3] See Sections 13.1 and 13.2.

Check Point 16.3 When the firm issues debt, why does r_{assets}, the company cost of capital, remain fixed, while the expected return on equity, r_{equity}, changes? Why is it not the other way around?

Debt increases financial risk and causes shareholders to demand a higher return on their investment. Once you recognize this implicit cost, debt is no cheaper than equity—the return that investors require on their assets is unaffected by the firm's borrowing decision.

The implications of MM's proposition II are shown in Figure 16.3. No matter how much the firm borrows, the expected return on the package of debt and equity, r_{assets}, is unchanged, but the expected rate of return on the separate parts of the package does change. How is this possible? Because the proportions of debt and equity in the package are also changing. More debt means that the cost of equity increases, but at the same time the amount of equity is less.

In Figure 16.3 we have drawn the rate of interest on the debt as constant no matter how much the firm borrows. That is not wholly realistic. It is true that most large, conservative companies could borrow a little more or less without noticeably affecting the interest rate that they pay. But at higher debt levels, lenders become concerned that they may not get their money back, and they demand higher rates of interest. Figure 16.4 modifies Figure 16.3 to take account of this. You can see that as the firm borrows more, the risk of default increases and the firm has to pay higher rates of interest. Proposition II continues to predict that the expected return on the package of debt and equity does not change. However, the slope of the r_{equity} line now tapers off as D/E increases. Why? Essentially because holders of risky debt begin to bear part of the firm's operating risk. As the firm borrows more, more of that risk is transferred from shareholders to bondholders.

Figures 16.3 and 16.4 wrap up our discussion of MM's leverage-irrelevance proposition. Because overall firm value is constant, the average return on the firm's debt and equity securities is also constant, regardless of the fraction of debt financing. This result follows from MM's assumptions that capital markets are well-functioning and taxes are absent. Now it's time to put taxes back into the picture.

FIGURE 16.3
MM's proposition II with a fixed interest rate on debt. The expected return on River Cruises' equity rises in line with the debt-equity ratio. The weighted average of the expected returns on debt and equity is constant, equal to the expected return on assets.

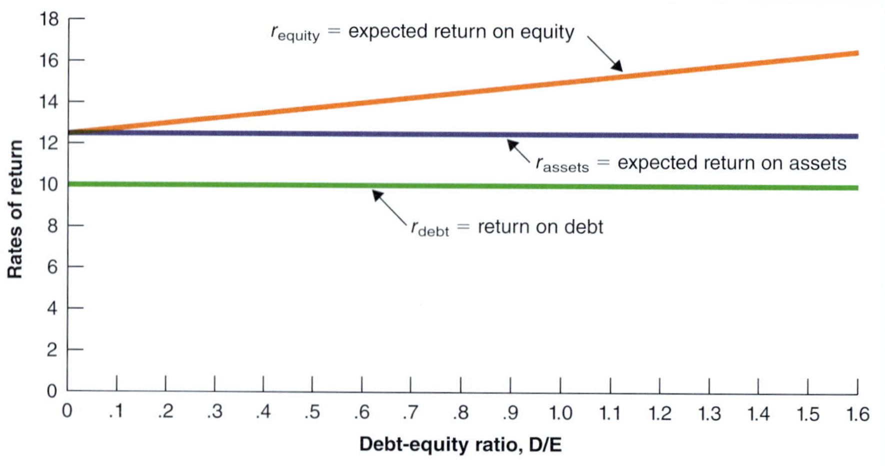

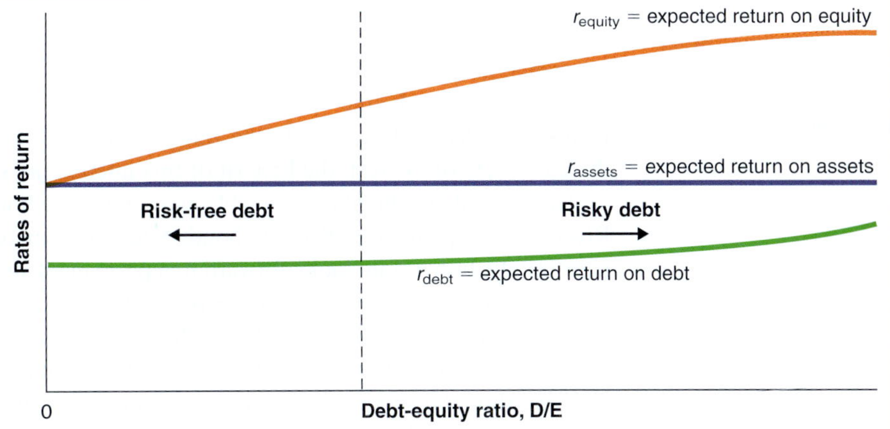

FIGURE 16.4 MM's proposition II, when debt is not risk-free. As the debt-equity ratio increases, debtholders demand a higher expected rate of return to compensate for the risk of default. The expected return on equity increases more slowly when debt is risky because the debtholders take on part of the risk. The expected return on the package of debt and equity, r_{assets}, remains constant.

LO2 16.2 CAPITAL STRUCTURE AND CORPORATE TAXES

The MM propositions suggest that debt policy should not matter. Yet financial managers do worry about debt policy, and for good reasons. Now we are ready to see why.

If debt policy were *completely* irrelevant, actual debt ratios would vary randomly from firm to firm and from industry to industry. Yet almost all airlines, utilities, banks, and real estate development companies rely heavily on debt. And so do many firms in capital-intensive industries like steel, aluminum, chemicals, petroleum, and mining. On the other hand, it is rare to find a drug company or advertising agency that is not predominantly equity-financed. Glamorous growth companies seldom use much debt, despite rapid expansion and often heavy requirements for capital.

The explanation of these patterns lies partly in the things that we have so far left out of our discussion. Now we will put all these things back in, starting with taxes.

DEBT AND TAXES AT RIVER CRUISES

Debt financing has one important advantage. The interest that the company pays is a tax-deductible expense but equity income is subject to corporate tax.

To see the advantage of debt finance, let's look once again at River Cruises. Table 16.5 shows how expected income is reduced if profits are taxed at a rate of 35 percent. The left-hand column sets out the position if River Cruises is financed entirely by equity. The right-hand column shows what happens if the firm issues \$500,000 of debt at an interest rate of 10 percent.

TABLE 16.5 Since debt interest is tax-deductible, River Cruises' debtholders and equityholders expect to receive a higher combined income when the firm is leveraged.

	Zero Debt	\$500,000 of Debt
Expected operating income	\$125,000	\$125,000
Debt interest at 10%	0	50,000
Before-tax income	125,000	75,000
Tax at 35%	43,750	26,250
After-tax income	81,250	48,750
Combined debt and equity income (debt interest + after-tax income)	81,250	98,750

Notice that the combined income of the debtholders and equityholders is higher by \$17,500 when the firm is levered. This is because the interest payments are tax-deductible. Thus every dollar of interest reduces taxes by \$.35. The total amount of tax savings is simply .35 × interest payments. In the case of River Cruises, the **interest tax shield** is .35 × \$50,000 = \$17,500 each year. In other words, the "pie" of after-tax income to be shared by debt and equity investors increases by \$17,500 relative to the zero-debt case. Since the debtholders receive no more than the going rate of interest, the benefit of this interest tax shield is captured by the shareholders.

interest tax shield Tax savings resulting from deductibility of interest payments.

The interest tax shield is a valuable asset. Let's see how much it could be worth. Suppose that River Cruises plans to replace its bonds when they mature and to keep "rolling over" the debt indefinitely. It therefore looks forward to a permanent stream of tax savings of \$17,500 per year. These savings depend only on the corporate tax rate and on the ability of River Cruises to earn enough to cover interest payments. So the risk of the tax shield is likely to be small. Therefore, if we wish to compute the present value of all the future tax savings associated with permanent debt, we should discount the interest tax shields at a relatively low rate.

But what rate? The most common assumption is that the risk of the tax shields is the same as that of the interest payments generating them. Thus we discount at 10 percent the expected rate of return demanded by investors who are holding the firm's debt. If the debt is permanent, then the firm can look forward to an annual savings of \$17,500 in perpetuity. Their present value is

$$\text{PV tax shield} = \frac{\$17{,}500}{.10} = \$175{,}000$$

This is what the tax savings are worth to River Cruises.

How does company value change? We continue to assume that if the firm is all-equity financed, the shareholders will demand a 12.5 percent return and, therefore, the company will be valued at \$81,250/.125 = \$650,000.[4] But if River Cruises issues \$500,000 of permanent debt, the package of all the firm's securities increases by the value of the tax shield to \$650,000 + \$175,000 = \$825,000.

Let us generalize. The interest payment each year equals the rate of interest times the amount borrowed, or $r_{\text{debt}} \times D$. The annual tax savings is the corporate tax rate, T_c, times the interest payment. Therefore,

$$\begin{aligned}\text{Annual tax shield} &= \text{corporate tax rate} \times \text{interest payment} \\ &= T_c \times (r_{\text{debt}} \times D)\end{aligned}$$

If the tax shield is perpetual, we use the perpetuity formula to calculate its present value:

$$\textbf{PV tax shields} = \frac{\text{annual tax shield}}{r_{\text{debt}}} = \frac{T_c \times (r_{\text{debt}} \times D)}{r_{\text{debt}}} = T_c D \qquad \textbf{(16.2)}$$

Of course, the present value of the tax shield is less if the firm does not plan to borrow permanently or if it may not be able to use the tax shields in the future.[5] This present value (T_cD) is actually the maximum possible value. However, we will continue to use this value in the rest of this chapter in order to keep the argument and illustrations simple.

Check Point 16.4

In 2006, BCE, Inc., paid out \$952 million as debt interest. How much more tax would BCE have paid if the firm was entirely equity-financed? What is the present value of BCE's interest tax shield if BCE planned to keep its borrowing permanently at the 2006 level? Assume an interest rate of 8 percent and a corporate tax rate of 35 percent.

---

[4] The firm was worth \$1 million when the corporate tax rate was zero (see Table 16.1). It is worth only \$650,000 when all-equity-financed because 35 percent of income is lost to taxes.

[5] The value of the interest tax shield is also reduced if the future level of debt is not fixed, but it is increased when the firm does well and paid down when it does poorly. In this case the future interest tax shields are correlated with the firm's performance and are therefore risky.

HOW INTEREST TAX SHIELDS CONTRIBUTE TO THE VALUE OF SHAREHOLDERS' EQUITY

MM's proposition I amounts to saying, "The value of the pizza does not depend on how it is sliced." The pizza is the firm's assets, and the slices are the debt and equity claims. If we hold the pizza constant, then a dollar more of debt means a dollar less of equity value.

But there is really a third slice—the government's. MM would still say that the value of the pizza—in this case the company value *before taxes*—is not changed by slicing. But anything the firm can do to reduce the size of the government's slice obviously leaves more for the others. One way to do this is to borrow money. This reduces the firm's tax bill and increases the cash payments to the investors. The value of their investment goes up by the present value of the tax savings.

In a no-tax world, MM's proposition I states that the value of the firm is unaffected by capital structure. But MM also modified proposition I to recognize corporate taxes:

Value of levered firm = value if all-equity-financed + present value of tax shield

In the special case of permanent debt,

$$\textbf{Value of levered firm} = \textbf{value if all-equity-financed} + T_c D$$

This "corrected" formula is illustrated in Figure 16.5. It implies that borrowing increases firm value and shareholders' wealth.

CORPORATE TAXES AND THE WEIGHTED-AVERAGE COST OF CAPITAL

We have shown that when there are corporate taxes, debt provides the company with a valuable tax shield. Few companies explicitly calculate the present value of interest tax shields associated with a particular borrowing policy. The tax shields are not forgotten, however, because they show up in the discount rate used to evaluate capital investments.

Since debt interest is tax-deductible, the government in effect pays 35 percent of the interest cost. So to keep its investors happy, the firm has to earn the *after-tax* rate of interest on its debt and the return required by shareholders. Once we recognize the tax benefit of debt, the weighted-average cost of capital formula (see Chapter 13 for a review if you need one) becomes

$$\text{WACC} = (1 - T_c) r_{\text{debt}} \left(\frac{D}{D+E}\right) + r_{\text{equity}} \left(\frac{E}{D+E}\right) \tag{16.3}$$

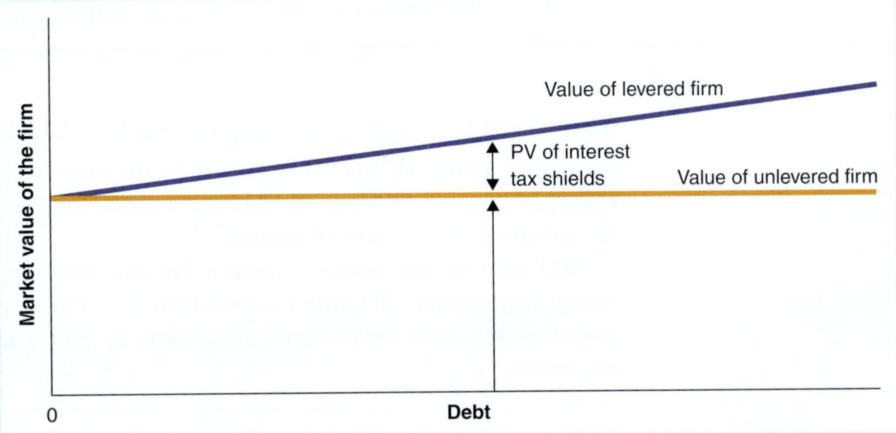

FIGURE 16.5
The blue line shows how the availability of interest tax shields affects the market value of the firm. Additional borrowing decreases corporate income tax payments and increases the cash flows available to lenders and shareholders; thus, market value increases.

Notice that when we allow for the tax advantage of debt, the weighted-average cost of capital depends on the *after-tax* rate of interest, $(1 - T_c) \times r_{debt}$.

EXAMPLE 16.2 WACC AND DEBT POLICY

We can use the weighted-average cost of capital formula to see how leverage affects River Cruises' cost of capital if the company pays corporate tax. When a company has no debt, the weighted-average cost of capital and the return required by shareholders are identical. In the case of River Cruises, the WACC with all-equity financing is 12.5 percent, and the value of the firm is $650,000.

Now let us calculate the weighted-average cost of capital if River Cruises issues $500,000 of permanent debt ($D = \$500{,}000$). Company value increases by PV tax shield = $175,000, from $650,000 to $825,000 (meaning that $D + E = \$825{,}000$). Therefore the value of equity must be $\$825{,}000 - \$500{,}000 = \$325{,}000$ ($E = \$325{,}000$).

To calculate River Cruises' weighted-average cost of capital, we would need to know its cost of equity after issuing debt. We can take some guidance from MM proposition II with corporate taxes, which tells us that for a levered firm the expected rate of return to shareholders, or the cost of equity, should be

$$r_{equity} = r_{assets} + (D/E)(1 - T_c)(r_{assets} - r_{debt})$$

We get $r_{equity} = .125 + (500{,}000/325{,}000)(1 - .35)(.125 - .10) = .15$.

Table 16.5 shows that when River Cruises borrows, the expected equity income is $48,750. So the expected return to shareholders is $48,750/$325,000 = 15 percent ($r_{equity} = .15$).[6] The interest rate is 10 percent ($r_{debt} = .10$) and the corporate tax rate is 35 percent ($T_c = .35$). This is all the information we need to see how leverage affects River Cruises' weighted-average cost of capital:

$$\text{WACC} = (1 - T_c)r_{debt}\left(\frac{D}{D+E}\right) + r_{equity}\left(\frac{E}{D+E}\right)$$
$$= (1 - .35) \times .10\left(\frac{500{,}000}{825{,}000}\right) + .15\left(\frac{325{,}000}{825{,}000}\right) = .0985, \text{ or } 9.85\%$$

We saw earlier that if there are no corporate taxes, the weighted-average cost of capital is unaffected by borrowing. But when there are corporate taxes, debt provides the company with a new benefit—the interest tax shield. In this case leverage reduces the weighted-average cost of capital (in River Cruises' case from 12.5 percent to 9.85 percent).

Figure 16.6 repeats Figure 16.3, except that now we have allowed for the effect of taxes on River Cruises' cost of capital. You can see that as the company borrows more, the expected return on equity rises, but the rise is less rapid than in the absence of taxes. The after-tax cost of debt is only 6.5 percent. As a result, the weighted-average cost of capital declines. For example, if the company has debt of $500,000, the equity is worth $325,000, and the debt-equity ratio (D/E) is $500,000/$325,000 = 1.54. Figure 16.6 shows that with this amount of debt the weighted-average cost of capital is 9.85 percent, the same figure that we calculated above.

THE IMPLICATIONS OF CORPORATE TAXES FOR CAPITAL STRUCTURE

If borrowing provides an interest tax shield, the implied optimal debt policy appears to be embarrassingly extreme: All firms should borrow to the hilt. This maximizes firm value and minimizes the weighted-average cost of capital.

MM were not that fanatical about it. No one would expect the gains to apply at extreme debt ratios. For example, if a firm borrows heavily, all its operating income may go to pay interest, and, therefore, there are no corporate taxes to be paid. There is no point in such firms borrowing any more.

[6] This is consistent with our result obtained from using the equation based on MM proposition II with corporate taxes.

FIGURE 16.6
Changes in River Cruises' cost of capital with increased leverage, when there are corporate taxes. The after-tax cost of debt is assumed to be constant at (1 − .35)10 = 6.5 percent. With increased borrowing the cost of equity rises, but more slowly than in the no-tax case (see Figure 16.3). The weighted-average cost of capital (WACC) declines as the firm borrows more.

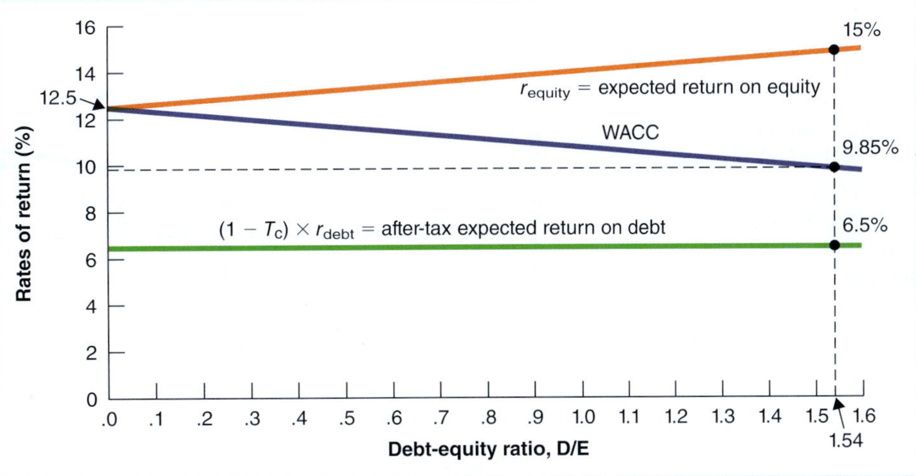

There might also be tax *disadvantages* to borrowing because bondholders have to pay personal income tax on any interest they receive. Shareholders, on the other hand, can get a tax break, because some of their returns come as capital gains. Capital gains are not taxed until the stock is sold and, currently, only 50 percent of such capital gains are taxed.[7]

All this suggests that there may come a point at which the tax savings from debt level off and may even decline. But it doesn't explain why highly profitable companies with large tax bills often thrive with little or no debt. There are clearly factors besides tax to consider. One such factor is the likelihood of financial distress.

LO3 16.3 COSTS OF FINANCIAL DISTRESS

Financial distress occurs when promises to creditors are broken or honoured with difficulty. Sometimes financial distress leads to bankruptcy. Sometimes it only means skating on thin ice.

As we will see, financial distress is costly. Investors know that levered firms may run into financial difficulty, and they worry about the **costs of financial distress**. That worry is reflected in the current market value of the levered firm's securities. Even if the firm is not now in financial distress, investors factor the potential for future distress into their assessment of current value. This means that the overall value of the firm is

costs of financial distress
Costs arising from bankruptcy or distorted business decisions before bankruptcy.

$$\text{Overall market value} = \text{value of all-equity-financed} + \text{PV tax shield} - \text{PV costs of financial distress} \quad (16.4)$$

The present value of the costs of financial distress depends both on the probability of distress and on the magnitude of the costs encountered if distress occurs.

Figure 16.7 shows how the trade-off between the tax benefits of debt and the costs of distress determines optimal capital structure. Think of a firm like River Cruises, which starts with no debt but considers moving to higher and higher debt levels, holding its assets and operations constant.

[7] Recall from Chapter 3 that combined federal and provincial tax rates on ordinary income can be close to 50 percent in most provinces. But, as we have just discussed, capital gains are taxed at one-half of the regular personal tax rate.

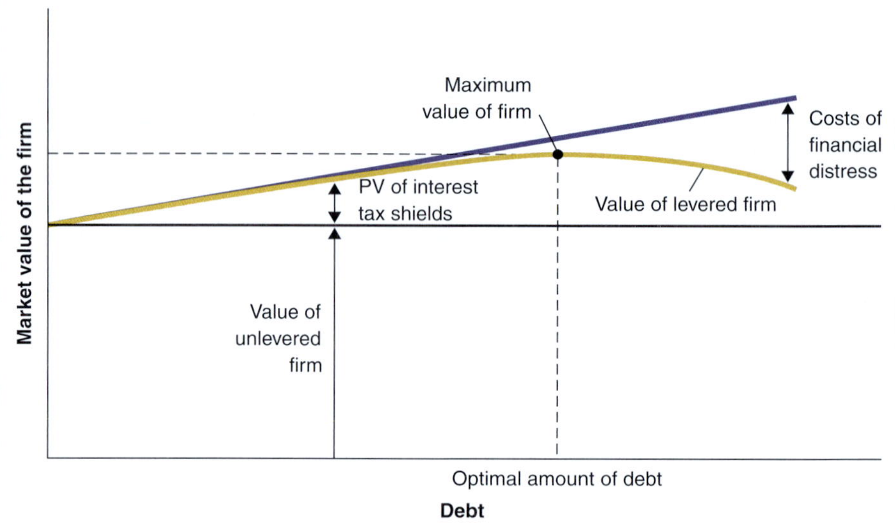

FIGURE 16.7
The trade-off theory of capital structure. The curved gold line shows how the market value of the firm initially increases as the firm borrows but decreases as the costs of financial distress become more and more important. The optimal capital structure balances the costs of financial distress against the value of the interest tax shields generated by borrowing.

trade-off theory The idea that debt levels are chosen to balance interest tax shields against the costs of financial distress.

At moderate debt levels, the probability of financial distress is trivial and therefore the tax advantages of debt dominate. But at some point the probability of financial distress increases rapidly with additional borrowing, and the potential costs of distress begin to take a substantial bite out of firm value. The theoretical optimum is reached when the present value of tax savings due to additional borrowing is just offset by increases in the present value of costs of distress.

At moderate debt levels, the probability of financial distress is trivial and therefore the tax advantages of debt dominate. But at some point the probability of financial distress increases rapidly with additional borrowing, and the potential costs of distress begin to take a substantial bite out of firm value. The theoretical optimum is reached when the present value of tax savings due to additional borrowing is just offset by increases in the present value of costs of distress. This is called the **trade-off theory** of optimal capital structure. It says that managers will try to increase debt levels to the point where the value of additional interest tax shields is offset by the additional costs of financial distress exactly.

An enterprise that maximizes firm value should also minimize its weighted-average cost of capital. It follows that a particular debt-to-equity ratio represents the *optimal capital structure* if it results in the lowest possible weighted-average cost of capital, keeping in mind the potential costs of financial distress and bankruptcy that can result from excessive debt. We see this in Figure 16.8.

Now let's take a closer look at financial distress.

BANKRUPTCY COSTS

In principle, bankruptcy is merely a legal mechanism for allowing creditors (that is, lenders) to take over the firm when the decline in the value of its assets triggers a default on outstanding debt. If the company cannot pay its debts, the company is turned over to the creditors, who become the new owners; the old shareholders are left with nothing. Bankruptcy is not the *cause* of the decline in the value of the firm. It is the result.

In practice, of course, anything involving courts and lawyers cannot be free. The fees involved in a bankruptcy proceeding are paid out of the remaining value of the firm's assets. Creditors end up with only what is left after paying the lawyers and other court expenses. If there is a possibility of bankruptcy, the current market value of the firm is reduced by the present value of these potential costs.

It is easy to see how increased leverage affects the costs of financial distress. The more the firm owes, the higher the chance of default and therefore the greater the expected value of the associated costs. This reduces the current market value of the firm.

Creditors foresee the costs and realize that if default occurs, the bankruptcy costs will come out of the value of the firm. For this they demand compensation in advance in the form of a

FIGURE 16.8
The figure shows that an optimal capital structure is consistent with a minimum WACC for the firm.

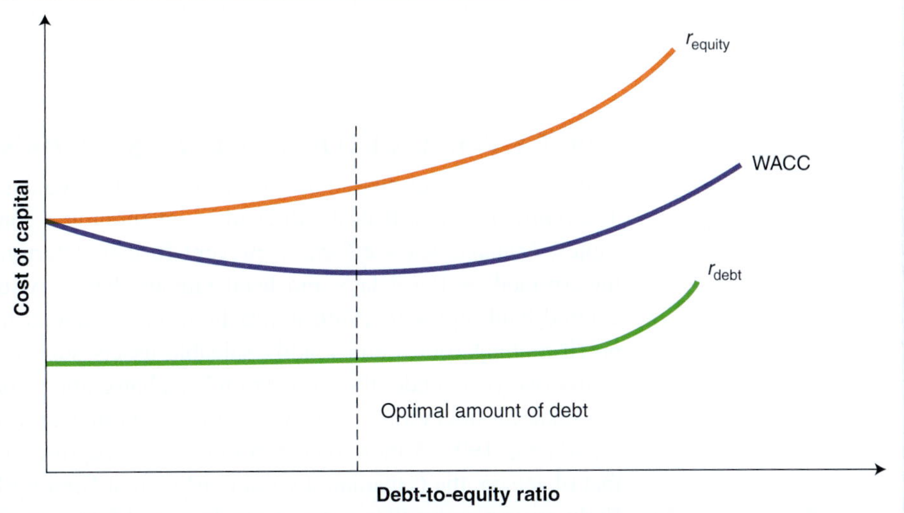

higher promised interest rate. This reduces the possible payoffs to shareholders and reduces the current market value of their shares.

Check Point 16.5

Suppose investors foresee $2 million of legal costs if the firm defaults on its bonds. How does this affect the value of the firm's bonds if bankruptcy occurs? How does the possibility of default affect the interest rate demanded by bondholders today? How does this possibility affect today's value of the firm's common stock?

EVIDENCE ON BANKRUPTCY COSTS

When large firms file for bankruptcy, they usually do so under regulations provided in the *Bankruptcy and Insolvency Act of 1992*. Some companies are also governed by the *Companies' Creditors Arrangement Act* and the *Winding-Up and Restructuring Act*. The purpose of these statutes is to nurse the firm back to health and enable it to face the world again. This requires approval of a reorganization plan for who gets what; under the plan each class of creditors needs to give up its claim in exchange for new securities or a mixture of new securities and cash. The challenge is to design a new capital structure that will satisfy the creditors and allow the firm to solve the business problems that got it into trouble in the first place. Sometimes it proves possible to satisfy both demands and the patient emerges fit and healthy. Often, however, the proceedings involve costly delays and legal tangles and the business continues to deteriorate.

Bankruptcy costs can add up fast. Failed energy giant Enron estimated that its total legal and accounting costs since entering bankruptcy would reach $1 billion by 2006. And WorldCom paid between $800 million and $1 billion in fees during the 21 months that it spent putting together a reorganization plan under the protection of Chapter 11 of the U.S. *Bankruptcy Reform Act*.[9]

[9] See "Enron Bankruptcy Specialist to File for Additional Payment," *Wall Street Journal*, September 3, 2004, A2, and "Weil Gotshal Leads Pack as Firms Gobble $50 Million MCI Fees," *The Lawyer*, April 26, 2004, 5.

Daunting as such numbers seem, they may not be a large *percentage* of the total pre-bankruptcy value of the firm. A recent study of troubled, highly leveraged firms found costs of financial distress amounting to 10 to 20 percent of pre-distress market value.[10] But the percentage costs can be much higher when smaller companies get into trouble.

DIRECT VERSUS INDIRECT COSTS OF BANKRUPTCY

Thus far, we have discussed only the *direct* (that is, legal and administrative) costs of bankruptcy. The *indirect* costs reflect the difficulties of running a company while it is going through bankruptcy. Management's efforts to prevent further deterioration in the firm's business are often undermined by the delays and legal tangles that go with bankruptcy. When Eastern Airlines entered bankruptcy in 1989, it was in severe financial trouble, but it still had some valuable, profit-making routes and readily saleable assets such as planes and terminal facilities. After nearly two years under the "protection" of a bankruptcy court, which allowed Eastern to continue loss-making operations, there was hardly anything of value left when it was finally forced to liquidate in 1991. A more recent example of disruptions and costs associated with bankruptcy is that of Jetsgo, the Canadian discount airline that filed for bankruptcy protection in March 2005. Eight airport authorities across Canada joined forces in a bid to recoup nearly $3 million owed to them by the insolvent carrier.

We don't know how much these indirect costs add to the expenses of bankruptcy. We suspect it is a significant amount, particularly when bankruptcy proceedings are prolonged. Perhaps the best evidence is the reluctance of creditors to force a firm into bankruptcy. In principle, they would be better off to end the agony and seize the assets as soon as possible. But instead creditors often overlook defaults in the hope of nursing the firm over a difficult period. They do this in part to avoid the costs of bankruptcy. There is an old financial saying, "Borrow $1,000 and you've got a banker. Borrow $10,000,000 and you've got a partner."

FINANCIAL DISTRESS WITHOUT BANKRUPTCY

Not every firm that gets into trouble goes bankrupt. As long as the firm can scrape up enough cash to pay the interest on its debt, it may be able to postpone bankruptcy for many years. Eventually the firm may recover, pay off its debt, and escape bankruptcy altogether.

A narrow escape from bankruptcy does not mean that costs of financial distress are avoided. When a firm is in trouble, suppliers worry that they may not be paid, potential customers fear that the firm will not be able to honour its warranties, and employees start contemplating their next job. While all firms suffer in times of financial trouble, manufacturers of relatively expensive, durable products requiring regular after-sales service, such as automobile or computer companies, can have particularly high costs associated with financial distress. Similarly, the perception that an airline company is in financial trouble may scare away customers concerned about the maintenance and safety of the aircraft and its ability to honour frequent flyer programs. For instance, before Canadian Airlines was taken over by Air Canada, concerns about its growing financial difficulties caused business travellers to switch to other airlines.

In 2004, Air Canada's own financial woes caused similar concerns among travellers as the troubled airline struggled to restructure itself under court-ordered bankruptcy protection. Indeed, there is good reason for concern because an insolvent airline can cause a lot of turmoil for its customers, suppliers, and generally anyone doing business with it. Once again, take the case of Jetsgo. In March 2005, the discount airline sought bankruptcy protection and, without any warning, cancelled all its flights. An estimated 17,000 passengers, including many travelling on spring break, found that their tickets were no good and were left stranded. Many of these passengers were forced to make alternative arrangements with other carriers, providing brisk business to competitors such as Air Canada and WestJet.

---

[10] G. Andrade and S.N. Kaplan, "How Costly Is Financial (Not Economic) Distress? Evidence from Highly Leveraged Transactions That Became Distressed," *Journal of Finance* 53 (October 1998): 1443–1493.

Financial distress is costly when conflicts get in the way of running the business. Shareholders are tempted to forsake the usual objective of maximizing the overall market value of the firm; they pursue their self-interests instead. They are tempted to play games at the expense of their creditors. These games add to the costs of financial distress.

The firm's bondholders and stockholders both want the company to recover, but in other respects their interests may be in conflict. In times of financial distress the security holders are like many political parties—united on generalities but threatened by squabbling on any particular issue. Financial distress is costly when conflicts get in the way of running the business. Shareholders are tempted to forsake the usual objective of maximizing the overall market value of the firm; they pursue their self-interests instead. They are tempted to play games at the expense of their creditors. These games add to the costs of financial distress.

Think of a company—call it Double-R Nutting—teetering on the brink of bankruptcy. It has large debts and large losses. Double-R's assets have little value, and if its debts were due today, Double-R would default, leaving the firm bankrupt. The assets would then be sold off, the debtholders would perhaps receive a few cents on the dollar, and the shareholders would be left with nothing.

But suppose the debts are not due yet. That grace period explains why Double-R's shares still have value. Some stroke of luck might rescue the firm and allow it to pay off its debts with something left over. It's a long shot—unless firm value increases sharply, the stock will be valueless. But the owners have a secret weapon: they control investment and operating strategy.

The First Game: Bet the Bank's Money Suppose Double-R has the opportunity to take a wild gamble. If it can't pull it off, the shareholders will be no worse off, the company will probably go under anyway. But if the gamble does succeed, there will be more than enough assets to pay off the debt, and the surplus will go into the shareholders' pockets. You can see why management might want to take the chance. In taking the gamble, they are essentially betting the debtholders' money, but if Double-R does hit the jackpot, the equityholders get most of the loot.

One owner-manager of a small bankrupt company called KenDavis Industries put it this way: "Everyone agrees there is no shareholder equity—so *we've* got *nothing* to lose. The *banks* have it all on the line now—not us." In another case, the managers of the failing firm took the incentive to gamble literally. They went to Las Vegas and bet the company's money, hoping to win enough to pay off the creditors. The effects of such distorted incentives to take on risk are usually not this blatant, but the results can be the same. For example, Sambo's Restaurants borrowed against unencumbered assets while in bankruptcy proceedings and used the funds to pay for a risky marketing initiative, changing the name and concept of its restaurants. When the gamble failed, unsecured creditors suffered most of the loss, getting only $.11 of each dollar owed to them.[11]

These kinds of warped capital investment strategies clearly are costly for the bondholders and for the firm as a whole. Why do we say they create costs of financial distress? Because the temptation to follow such strategies is strongest when the odds of default are high. A healthy firm would never invest in Double-R's negative-NPV gamble, since it would be gambling with its own money, not the bondholders'. A healthy firm's creditors would not be vulnerable to this type of game.

The Second Game: Don't Bet Your Own Money We have just seen how shareholders, acting in self-interest, may take on risky, unprofitable projects. These are errors of commission. We will now illustrate how conflicts of interest may also lead to errors of omission.

Suppose Double-R uncovers a relatively safe project with a positive NPV. Unfortunately, the project requires a substantial investment. Double-R will need to raise this extra cash from its shareholders. Although the project has a positive NPV, the profits may not be sufficient to rescue the company from bankruptcy. If that is so, all the profits from the new project will be used to help pay off the company's debt and the shareholders will get no return on the cash they put up. Although it is in the firm's interest to go ahead with the project, it is not in the owners' interest, and the project will be passed up.

[11] These cases are cited in Lynn M. LoPucki, "The Trouble with Chapter 11," *Wisconsin Law Review*, 1993: 729–760.

If the probability of default is high, managers and shareholders will be tempted to take excessively risky projects. At the same time, shareholders might refuse to contribute more equity capital even if the firm has safe, positive-NPV opportunities. Shareholders would rather take money out of the firm than put new money in.

Again, our example illustrates a general point. The value of any investment opportunity to the firm's *shareholders* is reduced because project benefits must be shared with the bondholders. Thus it may not be in the shareholders' interest to contribute fresh equity capital even if that means forgoing positive-NPV opportunities.

These two games illustrate potential conflicts of interest between shareholders and debtholders. These conflicts, which theoretically affect all levered firms, become much more serious when firms are staring bankruptcy in the face. If the probability of default is high, managers and shareholders will be tempted to take on excessively risky projects. At the same time, shareholders might refuse to contribute more equity capital even if the firm has safe, positive-NPV opportunities. Shareholders would rather take money out of the firm than put new money in.

The company knows lenders will demand a higher rate of interest if they are worried that games will be played at their expense. So to reassure lenders that its intentions are honourable, the firm will commonly agree to **loan covenants**. It might promise to limit future borrowing and not to pay excessive dividends. Of course, no amount of fine print can cover every possible game the company might play. For instance, no contract can ensure that companies will accept all positive-NPV investments and reject negative ones.

We do not mean to leave the impression that managers and shareholders always succumb to temptation unless restrained. Usually they refrain voluntarily, not only from a sense of fair play but also on pragmatic grounds: a firm or individual that makes a killing today at the expense of a creditor will be coldly received when the time comes to borrow again. Aggressive game playing is done only by out-and-out crooks and by firms in extreme financial distress. Firms limit borrowing precisely because they don't wish to be in distress and exposed to the temptation to play.

Check Point 16.6

We have described two games that might be played by firms in financial distress. Why are the games costly? How does the possibility that the game might be played at some point in the future affect today's capital structure decisions?

loan covenant Agreement between firm and lender requiring the firm to fulfill certain conditions to safeguard the loan.

COSTS OF DISTRESS VARY WITH TYPE OF ASSET

Suppose your firm's only asset is a large downtown hotel, Heartbreak Hotel, mortgaged to the hilt. A recession hits, occupancy rates fall, and the mortgage payments cannot be met. The lender takes over and sells the hotel to a new owner and operator. The stock is worthless and you use the firm's stock certificates for wallpaper.

What is the cost of bankruptcy? In this example, probably very little. The value of the hotel is, of course, much less than you hoped, but that is due to the lack of guests not bankruptcy. Bankruptcy does not damage the hotel itself. The direct bankruptcy costs are restricted to items such as legal and court fees, real estate commissions, and the time the lender spends sorting things out.

Suppose we repeat the story of Heartbreak Hotel for Fledgling Electronics. Everything is the same, except for the underlying assets. Fledgling is a high-tech going concern and much of its value reflects investors' beliefs that its research team will come up with profitable ideas. Fledgling is a "people business"; its most important assets go down in the elevator and into the parking lot every night.

If Fledgling gets into trouble, the shareholders might be reluctant to put up money to cash in on those profitable ideas—why should they put up cash that will simply go to pay off the banks? Failure to invest is likely to be much more serious for Fledgling than for a company like Heartbreak Hotel.

If Fledgling finally defaults on its debt, the lender would find it much more difficult to cash in by selling off the assets. In fact, if trouble comes, many of those assets may ride off into the sunset and never return.

Don't think only about whether borrowing is likely to bring trouble. Think also of the value that may be lost if trouble comes.

Some assets, such as good commercial real estate, can pass through bankruptcy and reorganization largely unscathed; the values of other assets are likely to be considerably diminished. The losses are greatest for intangible assets linked to the continuing prosperity of the firm. An important determinant of debt capacity is the availability of collateral. When a firm faces financial distress, certain assets such as plants, land, and equipment are more readily valued and sold than patents, brand names, and other intangibles. That might be why debt ratios are low in the pharmaceutical industry, in which company values depend on continued success in research and development. It might also explain the low debt ratios in many service companies, whose main asset is their skilled labour. On the other hand, capital-intensive manufacturing firms or wholesale and retail businesses with sizable tangible assets tend to have higher debt ratios. Table 16.6 provides debt-to-equity ratios for some representative Canadian firms in different industries as well as industry average debt-to-equity ratios. Notice the very low debt-to-equity ratio of the communications equipment company, Research In Motion, Ltd., but the relatively high debt-to-equity ratio of Loblaw, the large grocery chain. The moral of these examples is: Don't think only about whether borrowing is likely to bring trouble. Think also of the value that may be lost if trouble comes.

Check Point 16.7

For which of the following companies would the costs of financial distress be most serious? Why?

- A three-year-old biotech company. So far the company has no products approved for sale, but its scientists are hard at work developing a breakthrough drug.
- An oil production company with 50 producing wells and 20 million barrels of existing oil reserves.

We have now completed our review of the building blocks of the trade-off theory of optimal capital structure. In the next section we will sum up that theory and briefly cover a competing "pecking order" theory.

TABLE 16.6
Debt-to-equity ratio for a sample of Canadian firms and industries in 2009.

Firm	Debt-to-Equity Ratio	Industry	Industry Average Debt-to-Equity Ratio
QLT, Inc.	.00	Biotechnology	.37
Stantec, Inc.	.43	Commercial Services & Supply	1.84
Research In Motion, Inc.	.00	Communications equipment	.04
Gildan Activewear, Inc.	.00	Consumer durable and apparel	1.14
Power Financial Corp.	.35	Insurance	.48
Maple Leaf Foods, Inc.	.82	Food, beverage, and tobacco	.38
Loblaw Companies, Ltd.	.72	Food and staples retailing	.47
Barrick Gold Corporation	.40	Gold	.14
Rogers Communications, Inc.	1.98	Telecommunication Services	.88
Imperial Oil, Ltd.	.01	Oil, gas, and consumable fuels	.47
Canadian National Railway Company	.58	Transportation	.93
ATCO, Ltd.	.90	Utilities	1.24

Source: *Financial Post Analyzer, Industry Reports and Corporate Analyzer*, retrieved October 29, 2010 from **www.fpinfomart.ca**. Material reprinted with the express permission of National Post, a division of Postmedia Network Inc.

LO4 16.4 EXPLAINING FINANCING CHOICES

THE TRADE-OFF THEORY

Financial managers often think of the firm's debt-equity decision as a trade-off between interest tax shields and the costs of financial distress. Of course, there is controversy about how valuable interest tax shields are and what kinds of financial trouble are most threatening, but these disagreements are only variations on a theme. Thus Figure 16.7 illustrates the debt-equity trade-off.

This trade-off theory predicts that target debt ratios will vary from firm to firm. Companies with safe, tangible assets and plenty of taxable income to shield should have high target ratios. Unprofitable companies with risky, intangible assets should rely primarily on equity financing.

All in all, the theory tells a comforting story. It avoids extreme predictions and rationalizes moderate debt ratios. But what are the facts? Can the theory explain how companies actually behave?

The answer is yes and no. On the yes side, the trade-off theory successfully explains many industry differences in capital structure. For example, high-tech growth companies, whose assets are risky and mostly intangible, normally use relatively little debt. Utilities or retailers can and do borrow heavily because their assets are tangible and relatively safe. From Table 16.6, compare the low debt-to-equity ratio of the high-tech company Research In Motion with the much higher debt-to-equity ratio of the utility company, ATCO. Notice that in general, the company ratios are consistent with their respective industry averages.

On the no side, there are other things the trade-off theory cannot explain. It cannot explain why some of the most successful companies thrive with little debt. Consider, for example, the large American pharmaceutical company Johnson & Johnson, which is basically all-equity-financed. Granted, Johnson & Johnson's most valuable assets are intangible—the fruits of its research and development. We know that intangible assets and conservative capital structures should go together. But Johnson & Johnson also has a very large corporate income tax bill ($3.5 billion in 2009) and the highest possible credit rating. It could borrow enough to save tens of millions of tax dollars without raising a whisker of concern about possible financial distress.

Our example illustrates an odd fact about real-life capital structures: the most profitable companies generally borrow the least. Here the trade-off theory fails, because it predicts exactly the reverse. Under the trade-off theory, high profits should mean more debt-servicing capacity and more taxable income to shield and therefore should give a higher debt ratio.

Check Point 16.8 Rank these industries in order of predicted debt ratios under the trade-off theory of capital structure: (1) Internet software, (2) auto manufacturing, and (3) regulated electric utilities.

A PECKING-ORDER THEORY

There is an alternative theory that could explain why profitable companies borrow less. It is based on *asymmetric information*—managers know more than outside investors about the profitability and prospects of their firm. Thus investors may not be able to assess the true value of a new issue of securities by the firm. They may be especially reluctant to buy newly issued common stock because they worry that the new shares will turn out to be overpriced.

Such worries can explain why the announcement of a stock issue can drive down the stock price.[12] If managers know more than outside investors, they will be tempted to time stock issues when their companies' stock is overpriced—in other words, when the managers are relatively pessimistic. On the other hand, optimistic managers will see their companies' shares as underpriced and decide not to issue. You can see why investors would learn to interpret the

[12] We described this "announcement effect" in Chapter 15.

announcement of a stock issue as a "pessimistic manager" signal and mark down the stock price accordingly. You can also see why optimistic financial managers—and most managers are optimistic!—would view a common stock issue as a relatively expensive source of financing.

All these problems are avoided if the company can finance with internal funds, that is, with earnings retained and reinvested. But if external financing is required, the path of least resistance is debt, not equity. Issuing debt seems to have a trifling effect on stock prices. There is less scope for debt to be misvalued and therefore a debt issue is a less worrisome signal to investors.

pecking-order theory Firms prefer to issue debt rather than equity if internal finance is insufficient.

These observations suggest a **pecking-order theory** of capital structure. It goes like this:

1. Firms prefer internal finance, because these funds are raised without sending any adverse signals that may lower the stock price.
2. If external finance is required, firms issue debt first and issue equity only as a last resort. This pecking order arises because an issue of debt is less likely than an equity issue to be interpreted by investors as a bad omen.

In this story, there is no clear target debt-equity mix, because there are two kinds of equity, internal and external. The first is at the top of the pecking order and the second is at the bottom. The pecking order explains why the most profitable firms generally borrow less; it is not because they have low target debt-ratios but because they don't need outside money. Less profitable firms issue debt, because they do not have sufficient internal funds for their capital investment program and because debt is first in the pecking order for *external* finance.

The pecking order theory does not deny that taxes and financial distress can be important factors in the choice of capital structure. However, the theory says that these factors are less important than managers' preference for internal over external funds and for debt financing over new issues of common stock.

We saw in Chapter 14 that for most Canadian corporations, internal funds finance the majority of new investment and most external financing comes from debt. These aggregate financing patterns are consistent with the pecking-order theory. Yet the pecking order seems to work best for mature firms. Fast-growing high-tech firms often resort to a series of common stock issues to finance their investments. For this type of firm, common stock often comes at the *top* of the pecking order. The reasons the pecking-order theory works for some firms and not others are not well understood.

THE TWO FACES OF FINANCIAL SLACK

Other things being equal, it's better to be at the top of the pecking order than at the bottom. Firms that have worked down the pecking order and need external equity may end up living with excessive debt or bypassing good investments because shares can't be sold at what managers consider a fair price.

Asked what factors are uppermost in their minds when they think about debt policy, financial managers commonly mention the tax advantage of debt and the importance of maintaining the firm's credit rating. But they place even greater emphasis on the need to retain flexibility so that the company has access to funds for pursuing new projects when they come along.[13] In other words, they put a high value on **financial slack**. Having financial slack means having cash, marketable securities, and ready access to the debt markets or to bank financing. Ready access basically requires conservative financing so that potential lenders see the company's debt as a safe investment.

financial slack Ready access to cash or debt financing.

In the long run, a company's value rests more on its capital investment and operating decisions than on financing. Therefore, you want to make sure your firm has sufficient financial slack so that financing is quickly available for good investments. Financial slack is most valuable to firms with plenty of positive-NPV growth opportunities. That is another reason growth companies usually aspire to conservative capital structures.

---

[13] J.R. Graham and C.R. Harvey, "The Theory and Practice of Corporate Finance: Evidence from the Field," *Journal of Financial Economics* 61 (2001): 187–243.

Finance in Action

How Sealed Air's Change in Capital Structure Acted as a Catalyst to Organizational Change

Sealed Air Corporation manufactures a wide variety of packaging materials such as plastic packing bubbles and Jiffy padded envelopes.

As it entered 1989, Sealed Air was very conservatively financed with $33 million in total debt and over $54 million in cash. Thus, rather than borrowing cash, the company was actually a net lender. However, in June of that year, Sealed Air dramatically changed its capital structure by paying a special one-time dividend of $40 a share. With about 8.25 million shares trading, the total cash payout amounted to almost $330 million, or close to 90 percent of the total market value of the firm's common stock. To help finance this special dividend, the company borrowed a total of $307 million. The company went overnight from being a net lender to being a very heavy borrower. Debt now amounted to 125 percent of the book value of the assets and 65 percent of their market value.

Until the change in capital structure, Sealed Air's performance was no better than that of the industry as a whole. But the change was a prelude to a sharp improvement in the company's operating performance. In the following five years, operating profit increased by 70 percent while the asset base grew by only 9 percent. This improvement in profitability was more than matched by the company's stock market performance. The initial effect of Sealed Air's announced change in capital structure was a jump of 10 percent in the stock price. Over the next 5.5 years the stock outperformed the market by 400 percent.

What, then, motivated the change in capital structure and what role, if any, did this change play in the company's subsequent performance?

Some of the gains from the change in capital structure may have come from the fact that the company was able to offset the interest payments against tax. But this does not appear to have been a primary motive. Instead, the change appears to have been management's response to the realization that life at Sealed Air was in many respects too comfortable. For years patents had insulated the company from competition. Cash was plentiful. So the company never needed to think hard about requests to invest in new projects, and there was no sense of urgency in removing inefficiencies. In the management's view, it would take nothing less than a crisis to shake employees out of their complacency. The change in capital structure was just such a crisis.

The sharp increase in debt levels meant that cash was no longer abundant for it was now needed to pay the debtholders and was literally essential to the company's survival. Managers now felt under pressure to make those efficiency gains that previously had not seemed worthwhile. As employees became aware of the need for more effective operations, it was possible to decentralize decision making within the company and to install a more effective system of performance measurement and compensation. The result was a sharp increase in profit margins and a reduction in the working capital and fixed assets employed to generate each dollar of sales. It seemed that the capital structure change had succeeded in kick-starting a remarkable improvement in Sealed Air's performance.

Source: Adapted from K.H. Wruck, "Financial Policy as a Catalyst for Organizational Change: Sealed Air Corporation's Leveraged Special Dividend," *Journal of Applied Corporate Finance* 7 (Winter 1995): 20–37.

There is also a dark side to financial slack. Too much of it may encourage managers to take it easy, expand their perks, or empire-build with cash that should be paid back to shareholders. Michael Jensen has stressed the tendency of managers with ample free cash flow (or unnecessary financial slack) to plow too much cash into mature businesses or ill-advised acquisitions. "The problem," Jensen says, "is how to motivate managers to disgorge the cash rather than investing it below the cost of capital or wasting it in organizational inefficiencies."[14]

If that's the problem, maybe debt is an answer. Scheduled interest and principal payments are contractual obligations of the firm. Debt forces the firm to pay out cash. Perhaps the best debt level would leave just enough cash in the bank after debt service to finance all positive-NPV projects, with not a penny left over.

We do not recommend this degree of fine-tuning, but the idea is valid and important. For some firms, the threat of financial distress may have a good effect on managers' incentives. After all, skating on thin ice can be useful if it makes the skater concentrate. Likewise, managers of highly levered firms are more likely to work harder, run a leaner operation, and think more carefully before they spend money.

The nearby Finance in Action box tells the story of how Sealed Air Corporation borrowed more than US$300 million, using the proceeds of the loan to pay a special cash dividend to

[14] M.C. Jensen, "Agency Costs of Free Cash Flow, Corporate Finance and Takeovers," *American Economic Review* 26 (May 1986): 323.

Finance in Action

The Canadian Income Trust Boom and Bust

Raising the leverage of a firm can create value by increasing the interest tax shield and by reducing the "free cash flow problem," since interest payments reduce management's opportunity to waste the company's excess cash on negative net present value projects. On the other hand, increasing leverage also increases the probability of financial distress, increasing the costs of financial distress. What if a business could be set up to take advantage of the tax-deductibility of interest, reduce the free cash flow problem without significantly increasing the probability of financial distress? Clever lawyers and financial advisors figured out a way to make that happen: have the debt and equity of the corporation owned by an *income trust*.

An income trust is an investment fund, legally known as a *mutual fund trust*. Mutual fund trusts sell units to investors to raise money to purchase shares and debt of operating businesses. Mutual fund trusts are not operating companies but are *flow-through entities*, where the earnings on the investments are not taxed at the fund level but passed to the unitholders, who pay tax on the earnings. Unlike typical investment funds, which invest in many different companies, an income trust invests in only one company, making a unit similar to a share. The creative innovation of the income trust is to have the trust own both the shares and the debt of the corporation. This creates an opportunity for the underlying corporation to have higher leverage than if it were a regular corporation, increasing the tax shield, increasing payouts without causing the same increase in the costs of financial distress.

To understand how this works, keep in mind that some of the costs of financial distress are due to the conflict of interest between debtholders and shareholders. As we saw in Section 16.3, shareholders can try to make money at the expense of the debtholders, especially in times of financial trouble. But if shareholders are also the debtholders, they cannot benefit from these activities because what they gain as a shareholder they lose as a debtholder. Furthermore, as both shareholders and bondholders, the income trust is less likely to rush the company into bankruptcy. Thus, the corporation, owned by an income trust, is able to operate with more leverage than if it were a regular corporation.

With the corporation owned by the trust, the corporation pays out more of its earnings as interest than as dividends. Thus trust unitholders receive more interest than dividends, whereas they would have only received dividends as shareholders. As we saw in Chapter 3, the personal tax rate on interest income is higher than on dividend income. Until a tax change in 2006, the tax savings at the corporate level, due to the deductibility of the interest from corporate income, more than offset the impact of receiving interest rather than dividends, at the investor level. Thus, the income trust structure reduced the total taxes paid by the corporation and investors, increasing the total after-tax cash flow. This is why income trusts were said to be "tax-efficient."

A second type of income trust developed, known as royalty trusts. In the case of Boston Pizza, the trust owns the trademark "Boston Pizza" and the operating company pays a percentage of revenues to the trust for use of the trademark. This creates a tax deduction for the operating business, similar to an interest payment, reducing taxes. The unitholders receive the royalty, which is taxed at the same rate as interest income. Again, the total taxes of the business and investors is lower with the trust structure than it would be if the business had been set up without the trust. The advantage of the royalty trust is that the tax deduction increases with revenues, allowing the tax savings to grow with the business, avoiding the problem of the fixed interest payment.

Attracted by the tax-efficiency of income trusts, Canadian business embraced the trust structure. Initially trusts were limited to real estate assets, *real estate investment trusts* (REITs), and oil and gas assets, *Oil and Gas Royalty Trusts*, but gradually the trust structure was moved into other businesses. This third category, known as *business trusts*, grew rapidly from the late 1990s. Income trusts became very popular, with some corporations converting to the trust structures and other businesses going public as trusts. In 2006, when the trust market hit its peak, more than 250 trusts traded on the TSX, with market capitalization over $200 billion.

In September 2006, it appeared that one of Canada's largest businesses, BCE, was about to convert into an income trust. On October 31, 2006, the Canadian federal government, fearing significant loss of tax revenue, abruptly changed the rules for the taxation of income trusts, taking away their tax advantage and the income trust boom came to a sudden end. The market value of income trusts dropped, and many angry investors tried to persuade the federal government reverse its decision. Some trusts converted into corporations and others were bought out in takeovers. By 2008, fewer than 200 income trusts remained.

Sources: Michael King, *Income Trusts—Understanding the Issues*, Bank of Canada, Working Paper 2003–25; Sonita Horvitch, "Best Trusts Survived Darwinian Shakeout," *National Post*, May 8, 2008; **en.wikipedia.org/wiki/income_ trust#the_ conservatives_propose_new_rules_for_income_trusts**.

shareholders. The net effect was to increase debt from a trivial level to a full 65 percent of the total value of the firm. The dramatic increase in debt committed the firm to pay out large sums of money as interest, leaving it with little opportunity to fritter its cash away in pursuit of a comfortable life. Sealed Air showed great improvements in efficiency after the change in capital structure.

The next Finance in Action box gives the story of the boom and bust of income trusts in Canada. Similarly to the Sealed Air story, the income trust boom was driven by taxes and the power of leverage as a discipline on management. The boom came to an abrupt end on October 31, 2006, when the Canadian government changed the taxation rules of income trusts. See the box for details.

LO5 16.5 BANKRUPTCY PROCEDURES

bankruptcy The reorganization or liquidation of a firm that cannot pay its debts.

According to the Office of the Superintendent of Bankruptcy (OSB), over 6,700 businesses filed for **bankruptcy** in 2009, with liabilities that were in excess of $6.9 billion. Table 16.7 provides details regarding business bankruptcies by type of industry in 2009.

TABLE 16.7
Business bankruptcy reported in the calendar year 2009, by type of industry.

Type of Industry	Number of Cases	Total Assets, $	Total Liabilities, $	Total Deficiency
Agriculture, forestry, fishing, and hunting	250	68,108,238	209,442,437	141,334,199
Mining and oil and gas extraction	69	167,317,387	626,631,549	459,314,162
Utilities	21	1,150,015	8,906,860	7,756,845
Construction	999	158,262,602	658,789,521	500,526,919
Manufacturing	759	239,568,158	1,240,997,526	1,001,429,368
Wholesale trade	370	100,169,209	435,177,667	335,008,458
Retail trade	946	120,421,264	541,282,241	420,860,977
Transportation and warehousing	597	57,558,218	214,325,095	156,766,877
Information and cultural industries	116	11,846,286	144,922,801	133,076,515
Finance and insurance	144	33,678,947	1,221,218,462	1,187,539,515
Real estate and rental and leasing	213	101,916,838	295,386,144	193,469,306
Professional, scientific, and technical services	423	39,578,290	439,494,731	399,916,441
Management of companies and enterprises	41	14,306,889	118,544,071	104,237,172
Administrative and support, waste management and remediation services	296	25,327,426	126,488,824	101,161,398
Educational services	44	1,978,684	25,333,276	23,354,592
Health care and social assistance	79	9,854,825	92,783,355	82,928,530
Arts, entertainment, and recreation	137	17,648,437	56,262,387	38,613,947
Accommodation and food services	815	168,116,970	340,957,185	172,840,215
Other services (except public administration)	403	38,169,689	116,651,500	78,481,811
Public administration	6	277,211	1,326,960	1,049,749
Total	6,729	1,375,288,094	6,915,785,385	5,540,497,291

Source: Table 4: Insolvencies by NAICS Economic Sector, Canada, URL: **http://www.ic.gc.ca/eic/site/bsf-osb.nsf/eng/br02690.html#tbl4** Table NAICS produced by the Office of the Superintendent of Bankruptcy Canada, Industry Canada. Reproduced with the permission of the Minister of Public Works and Government Services, 2011.

workout Agreement between a company and its creditors establishing the steps the company must take to avoid bankruptcy.

A corporation that cannot pay its debts will often try to come to an informal agreement with its creditors. This is known as a **workout**. A workout may take several forms. For example, the firm might negotiate an *extension*, that is, an agreement with its creditors to delay payments. Or it might negotiate a *composition*, in which it makes partial payments to its creditors in exchange for relief of its debts.

The advantage of a negotiated agreement is that the costs and delays of formal bankruptcy are avoided. However, the larger the firm, and the more complicated its capital structure, the less likely it is that a negotiated settlement can be reached. (For example, the American firm Wickes Corp. tried—and failed—to reach a negotiated settlement with its 250,000 creditors.)

liquidation Sale of a bankrupt firm's assets.

Regulations pertaining to bankruptcies are provided in the *Bankruptcy and Insolvency Act, 1992*. Some companies are also governed by the *Companies' Creditors Arrangement Act* and the *Winding-Up and Restructuring Act*. These laws provide mechanisms by which the firm's assets can be **liquidated**—that is, sold—and the proceeds used to pay creditors. Liquidation usually involves a process wherein a petition is first filed in a federal court, either voluntarily by the debtor company, or involuntarily if it is filed on behalf of the company by its creditors. A trustee in bankruptcy is then elected by the creditors to take over and liquidate the assets of the company. Proceeds from the liquidation are distributed among the creditors after paying bankruptcy administration costs. If any assets remain after meeting expenses and payments to creditors, they are distributed to preferred and common shareholders. This priority for distribution of claims might not always be followed, at the discretion of the courts. Secured creditors are paid from the proceeds of sales of assets to which they have title, while unsecured creditors share in what is left over. If, however, the sale of the secured property does not generate sufficient cash to cover the amount owed, the secured creditors join with the unsecured creditors in dividing the liquidated value of the remaining assets. In contrast, if secured assets are liquidated for proceeds greater than the secured claim, the net proceeds are used to pay unsecured creditors and others. In large bankruptcies involving numerous secured and unsecured claimants, creditors sometimes take controversial actions in their attempt at securing a piece of a shrinking asset pool. The nearby Finance in Action box describes the controversy surrounding Enron, the energy giant, and one of its large lenders, Citigroup, after Enron's bankruptcy filing.

There is also a pecking order of unsecured creditors. First come claims for expenses that arise after bankruptcy is filed, such as attorneys' fees or employees' compensation earned after the filing. If such post-filing claims did not receive priority, no firm in bankruptcy proceedings could continue to operate. Next come claims for wages and employee benefits earned in the period immediately prior to the filing. Taxes are next in line, together with debts to some government agencies such as the Workers' Compensation Board. Finally, there are the general unsecured claims such as bonds or unsecured trade debt. The nearby Finance in Action box describes the situation of some former Nortel employees seeking to challenge the loss of their long-term disability benefits following Nortel's restructuring.

reorganization Restructuring of financial claims on a failing firm to allow it to keep operating.

The alternative to liquidation is to seek a **reorganization**, which keeps the firm as a going concern and usually compensates creditors with new securities, often including equity, in the reorganized firm. Such reorganizations are generally in the shareholders' interests—they have little to lose if things deteriorate further and everything to gain if the firm recovers.

Firms attempting reorganization may seek refuge under specific provisions of the *Bankruptcy and Insolvency Act, 1992*, the *Companies' Creditors Arrangement Act*, or the *Winding-Up and Restructuring Act*. Such provisions are designed to keep the firm alive and operating and to protect the value of its assets while a plan of reorganization is being worked out. During this period, other proceedings against the firm are halted and the company is operated by existing management or by a court-appointed trustee.

Recently, Ivaco, Inc., a leading Canadian steel manufacturer, filed for and obtained protection under the *Companies' Creditors Arrangement Act* from the Ontario Superior Court, effectively putting its creditors on hold. Although such court-ordered reorganization keeps creditors at bay, shareholders may not always feel that protection under the *Companies' Creditors Arrangement Act* is in their best interest. This happened in the case of Stelco, Inc., another large Canadian

Finance in Action

Dissenting Nortel Group Loses Bid on Restructuring

TORONTO—A group of former Nortel Networks Corp. employees receiving long-term disability benefits have lost a bid before the Supreme Court of Canada to challenge Nortel's restructuring.

A three-judge panel of the high court dismissed the appeal without costs. As is customary, the court provided no reasons why it will not hear the appeal.

The group, described in the litigation as the Dissenting Nortel LTD Beneficiaries, had previously lost a bid to appeal the original Ontario court ruling to the Ontario Court of Appeal. The dissenting beneficiaries disagreed with a 2010 Ontario Superior Court of Justice decision in the Nortel restructuring case.

Greg McAvoy, one of the former Nortel former employees, said in a statement: "While we were aware that only a limited number of leave applications are allowed by the Supreme Court, we were hopeful that the gravity of the situation facing the disabled and the broad legal issues raised by the motion judge's decision would have caught the attention of the country's highest Court."

A court-appointed monitor, Ernst & Young Inc., recommended a plan for the allocation of funds in Nortel's Health and Welfare Trust.

The plan called for future pensioner life benefits to be included in distributions of the trust. The dissenters believed the monitor's plan would have the effect of diluting the existing claims of the disabled by $30-million.

The Ontario court approved that plan, and now two appellate courts have upheld the decision.

Aided by independent financial analyst Diane Urquhart, the group continues to call for the federal government to amend bankruptcy legislation to protect employees in similar situations.

As well, in a complaint to the Ontario Consumer Services Bureau, four of the dissenting Nortel employees allege that Nortel and Sun Life Financial Inc. made false, misleading or deceptive representations to Nortel's employees about its disability insurance.

Source: Drew Hasselback, "Dissenting Nortel Group Loses Bid on Restructuring," *Financial Post*, June 10, 2011. Material reprinted with the express permission of National Post, a division of Postmedia Network Inc.

steel maker, which had been trying to restructure itself under protection from the *Companies' Creditors Arrangement Act* when there was a general glut in steel prices. However, a subsequent increase in the price of steel led some shareholders to question the need for such court-ordered protection.

The responsibility for developing a plan of reorganization may fall on the debtor firm. Otherwise, a plan may also be submitted by others—for example, a trustee, if appointed, or a committee of creditors.

The reorganization plan is basically a statement of who gets what; each class of creditors gives up its claim in exchange for new securities. (Sometimes creditors receive cash as well.) The problem is to design a new capital structure for the firm that will (1) satisfy the creditors and (2) allow the firm to solve the *business* problems that got the firm into trouble in the first place. Sometimes only a plan of baroque complexity can satisfy these two requirements. When the Penn Central Corporation was finally reorganized in the United States in 1978 (seven years after it became the largest railroad bankruptcy ever), more than a dozen new securities were created and parcelled out among 15 classes of creditors.

The reorganization plan goes into effect if it is accepted by creditors and confirmed by the court. Acceptance requires approval by a majority of each class of creditor. Once a plan is accepted, the court normally approves it, provided that *each* class of creditors has approved it and that the creditors will be better off under the plan than if the firm's assets were liquidated and distributed. The court may, under certain conditions, confirm a plan even if one or more classes of creditors vote against it. This is known as a *cram-down*. The terms of a cram-down are open to negotiation among all parties. For example, unsecured creditors may threaten to slow the process as a way of extracting concessions from secured creditors. The secured creditors may take less than 100 cents on the dollar and give something to unsecured creditors in order to expedite the process and reach an agreement.

Restructuring efforts under court protection are often successful, and the patient emerges fit and healthy. But in other cases, cures prove impossible and the assets are sold or liquidated. Sometimes the firm may emerge from bankruptcy protection for a brief period before it is once again submerged by disaster and back in bankruptcy. For example, the American airline company

TWA came out of Chapter 11 bankruptcy at the end of 1993 and was back again less than two years later, prompting jokes about "Chapter 22." The once successful Canadian clothing retailer Dylex emerged from bankruptcy protection in 1995. Five years later, the company was once again on the brink of bankruptcy and had sold most of its well-known retail outlets, such as BiWay, Tip Top Tailors, Thriftys, and Braemar.

THE CHOICE BETWEEN LIQUIDATION AND REORGANIZATION

Here is an idealized view of the bankruptcy decision. Whenever a payment is due to creditors, management checks the value of the firm. If the firm is worth more than the promised payment, the firm pays up (if necessary, raising the cash by an issue of shares). If not, the equity is worthless and the firm defaults on its debt and petitions for bankruptcy. If in the court's judgment the assets of the bankrupt firm can be put to better use elsewhere, the firm is liquidated and the proceeds are used to pay off the creditors. Otherwise, the creditors simply become the new owners and the firm continues to operate.

In practice, matters are rarely so simple. For example, we observe that firms often petition for bankruptcy even when the equity has a positive value. And firms are often reorganized even when the assets could be used more efficiently elsewhere. There are several reasons.

First, although the reorganized firm is legally a new entity, it is entitled to any tax-loss carry-forwards belonging to the old firm. If the firm is liquidated rather than reorganized, any tax-loss carry-forwards disappear. Thus, there is an incentive to continue in operation even if assets are better used by another firm.

Second, if the firm's assets are sold off, it is easy to determine what is available to pay the creditors. However, when the company is reorganized, it needs to conserve cash as far as possible. Therefore, claimants are generally paid in a mixture of cash and securities. This makes it less easy to judge whether they have received their entitlement. For example, each bondholder may be offered \$300 in cash and \$700 in a new bond, which pays no interest for the first two years and a low rate of interest thereafter. A bond of this kind in a company struggling to survive may not be worth much, but the bankruptcy court usually looks at the face value of the new bonds and might decide that the bondholders have received as much as they would have if the firm was liquidated, and therefore regard them as paid in full.

Senior creditors who know they are likely to get a raw deal in a reorganization are likely to press for a liquidation. Shareholders and junior creditors prefer a reorganization. They hope that the court will not interpret the pecking order too strictly and that they will receive some crumbs.

Third, although shareholders and junior creditors are at the bottom of the pecking order, they have a secret weapon: playing for time. Bankruptcies of large companies often take several years before a plan is presented to the court and agreed to by each class of creditor. The bankruptcy proceedings of the Missouri Pacific Railroad took a total of 22 years. When they use delaying tactics, the junior claimants are betting on a turn of fortune that will rescue their investment. On the other hand, the senior creditors know that time is working against them, so they may be prepared to accept a smaller payoff as part of the price for getting a plan accepted. Also, prolonged bankruptcy cases are costly (while their cases are extreme, we have seen that the WorldCom and Enron bankruptcies each generated about US\$1 billion in legal and administrative costs while the liquidators handling the Eaton's bankruptcy reportedly received \$80 million). Senior claimants may see their money seeping into lawyers' pockets and therefore decide to settle quickly.

Fourth, while a reorganization plan is being drawn up, the company is allowed to buy goods on credit and borrow money. Post-petition creditors (those who extend credit to a firm already in bankruptcy proceedings) have priority over the old creditors, and their debt may even be secured by assets that are already mortgaged to existing debtholders. This also gives the pre-petition creditors an incentive to settle quickly, before their claim on assets is diluted by the new debt.

Finally, profitable companies may file for bankruptcy to protect themselves against "burdensome" suits. For example, in 1982, Manville Corporation was threatened by 16,000 damage suits alleging injury from asbestos. Manville filed for bankruptcy under Chapter 11 of the *Bankruptcy Reform Act* in the United States, and the bankruptcy judge agreed to put the damage suits on hold until the company was reorganized. This took six years. Of course, legislators worry that these actions are contrary to the original intent of the bankruptcy acts.

16.6 SUMMARY

1. What is the goal of the capital structure decision? What is the financial manager trying to do? LO1

The goal is to maximize the overall market value of all the securities issued by the firm. Think of the financial manager as taking all the firm's real assets and selling them to investors as a package of securities. Some financial managers choose the simplest package possible: all-equity financing. Others end up issuing dozens of types of debt and equity securities. The financial manager must try to find the particular combination that maximizes the market value of the firm. If firm value increases, common shareholders will benefit.

But capital structure does not necessarily affect firm value. Modigliani and Miller's (MM's) famous **debt-irrelevance proposition** states that firm value can't be increased by changing **capital structure**. Therefore, the proportions of debt and equity financing don't matter. **Financial leverage** does increase the expected rate of return to shareholders, but the risk of their shares increases proportionally. MM show that the extra return and extra risk balance out, leaving shareholders no better or worse off.

Of course, MM's argument rests on simplifying assumptions. For example, the argument assumes efficient, well-functioning capital markets, and ignores taxes and costs of financial distress. But even if these assumptions are incorrect in practice, MM's proposition is important. It exposes logical traps that financial managers sometimes fall into, particularly the idea that debt is "cheap financing" because the explicit cost of debt (the interest rate) is less than the cost of equity. Debt has an implicit cost too, because increased borrowing increases **financial risk** and the cost of equity. When both costs are considered, debt is not cheaper than equity. MM show that if there are no corporate income taxes, the firm's weighted-average cost of capital does not depend on the amount of debt financing.

2. How do corporate income taxes modify MM's leverage-irrelevance proposition? LO2

Debt interest is a tax-deductible expense. Thus borrowing creates an **interest tax shield**, which equals the marginal corporate tax rate, T_c, times the interest payment $r_{\text{debt}} \times D$. Future interest tax shields are usually valued by discounting at the borrowing rate r_{debt}. In the special case of permanent debt,

$$\text{PV tax shield} = \frac{T_c \times (r_{\text{debt}} \times D)}{r_{\text{debt}}} = T_c D$$

Of course, interest tax shields are valuable only for companies that are making profits and paying taxes.

3. If interest tax shields are valuable, why don't all tax-paying firms borrow as much as possible? LO3

The more they borrow, the higher the odds of financial distress. The **costs of financial distress** can be broken down as follows:

- Direct bankruptcy costs, primarily legal and administrative costs
- Indirect bankruptcy costs, reflecting the difficulty of managing a company when it is in bankruptcy proceedings
- Costs of the threat of bankruptcy, such as poor investment decisions resulting from conflicts of interest between debtholders and shareholders

Combining interest tax shields and costs of financial distress leads to a **trade-off theory** of optimal capital structure. The trade-off theory says that financial managers should increase debt to the point where the value of additional interest tax shields is just offset by additional costs of possible financial distress.

The trade-off theory says that firms with safe, tangible assets and plenty of taxable income should operate at high debt levels. Less profitable firms, or firms with risky, intangible assets, should borrow less.

4. **What's the pecking-order theory?** LO4

The **pecking-order theory** says that firms prefer internal financing (that is, earnings retained and reinvested) over external financing. If external financing is needed, they prefer to issue debt rather than issue new shares. The pecking-order theory starts with the observation that managers know more than outside investors about the firm's value and prospects. Therefore, investors find it difficult to value new security issues, particularly issues of common stock. Internal financing avoids this problem. If external financing is necessary, debt is the first choice.

The pecking-order theory says that the amount of debt a firm issues will depend on its need for external financing. The theory also suggests that financial managers should try to maintain at least some **financial slack**, that is, a reserve of ready cash or unused borrowing capacity.

On the other hand, too much financial slack may lead to slack managers. High debt levels (and the threat of financial distress) can create strong incentives for managers to work harder, conserve cash, and avoid negative-NPV investments.

5. **Is there a rule for finding optimal capital structure?** LO3, LO4

No, there are no simple answers for capital structure decisions. Debt may be better than equity in some cases, worse in others. But there are at least four dimensions for the financial manager to think about.

- *Taxes.* How valuable are interest tax shields? Is the firm likely to continue paying taxes over the full life of a debt issue? Safe, consistently profitable firms are most likely to stay in a tax-paying position.
- *Risk.* Financial distress is costly even if the firm survives it. Other things being equal, financial distress is more likely for firms with high business risk. That is why risky firms typically issue less debt.
- *Asset type.* If distress does occur, the costs are generally greatest for firms whose value depends on intangible assets. Such firms generally borrow less than firms with safe, tangible assets.
- *Financial slack.* How much is enough? More slack makes it easy to finance future investments, but it may weaken incentives for managers. More debt, and therefore less slack, increases the odds that the firm may have to issue stock to finance future investments.

6. **What happens when firms cannot pay their creditors?** LO5

A firm that cannot meet obligations may try to arrange a **workout** with its creditors to enable it to settle its debts. If this is unsuccessful, the firm may file for **bankruptcy**, in which case the business may be liquidated or reorganized. **Liquidation** means that the firm's assets are sold and the proceeds used to pay creditors. **Reorganization** means that the firm is maintained as an ongoing concern, and creditors are compensated with securities in the reorganized firm. Ideally, reorganization should be chosen over liquidation when the firm as a going concern is worth more than its liquidation value. However, the conflicting interests of the different parties can result in violations of this principle.

Related Web Links

investinginbonds.com Bond Market Association site with extensive information about bond markets and bond pricing

bondsonline.com/Bond_Ratings_Definitions.php Information on bond ratings from a variety of sources

finance.yahoo.com Information on the capital structure of individual firms and industries

ic.gc.ca/eic/site/bsf-osb.nsf/Intro Site of the Office of the Superintendent of Bankruptcy, providing a variety of information, including statistics on personal and business bankruptcies, relevant acts and laws, etc.

bankrupt.com Resources for firms that have made some bad decisions

strategis.gc.ca Maintained by Industry Canada, providing a variety of trade, business, and consumer information

insolvency.ca The Insolvency Institute of Canada

abiworld.org, bankruptcydata.com For useful statistics and information on bankruptcy procedures

Key Terms

bankruptcy	548	financial risk	530	loan covenant	542
capital structure	525	financial slack	545	MM's proposition I *or* debt-irrelevance proposition	528
costs of financial distress	537	interest tax shield	534	MM's proposition II	531
financial leverage	530	liquidation	549		

operating risk *or* business risk	529	reorganization	549	trade-off theory	538
pecking-order theory	545	restructuring	526	workout	549

Questions and Problems

connect Practise and learn online with *Connect*. Questions with online Excel templates or datasets are marked with .

*Answers in Appendix B

BASIC

1. **MM's Leverage-Irrelevance Proposition.** True or false? MM's leverage-irrelevance proposition says that (LO1)
   a. The value of the firm does not depend on the fraction of debt versus equity financing.
   b. As financial leverage increases, the value of the firm increases by just enough to affect the additional financial risk absorbed by equity.
   c. The cost of equity increases with financial leverage only when the risk of financial distress is high.
   d. If the firm pays no taxes, the weighted-average cost of capital does not depend on the debt ratio.
2. **Effects of Leverage.** Increasing financial leverage can increase both the cost of debt, (r_{debt}), and the cost of equity, (r_{equity}). How can the overall cost of capital stay constant? (Assume the firm pays no taxes.) (LO1)
3. **Tax Shields.** What is an interest tax shield? How does it increase the "pie" of after-tax income to shareholders? Explain. *Hint:* Construct a simple numerical example showing how financial leverage affects the total cash flow available to debt and equity investors. Be sure to hold pretax operating income constant. (LO2)

*4. **Value of Tax Shields.** Establishment Industries borrows $800 million at an interest rate of 7.6 percent. It expects to maintain this debt level into the far future. What is the present value of interest tax shields? Establishment will pay tax at an effective rate of 37 percent. (LO2)

5. **Trade-Off Theory.** What is the trade-off theory of optimal capital structure? How does it define the optimal debt ratio? (LO3)
6. **Financial Distress.** Give three examples of the types of costs incurred by firms in financial distress. (LO3)
7. **Pecking-Order Theory.** What is the pecking-order theory of optimal capital structure? If the theory is correct, what types of firms would you expect to operate at high debt levels? (LO4)
8. **Financial Slack.** Why is financial slack valuable? *Hint:* What does the pecking-order theory say about financial slack? Are there circumstances where too much financial slack might actually reduce the market value of the firm? (LO4)
9. **Earnings and Leverage.** Suppose that River Cruises, which currently is all-equity-financed, issues $250,000 of debt and uses the proceeds to repurchase 25,000 shares. Assume the firm pays no taxes and that debt finance has no impact on its market value. Rework Table 16.2 to show how earnings per share and share return now vary with operating income. (LO1)
10. **Debt-Irrelevance.** Suppose an investor is unhappy with River Cruises' decision to borrow $250,000 (see the previous problem). What modifications can she make to her own investment portfolio to offset the effects of the firm's additional borrowing? (LO1)

*11. **Leverage and P/E Ratio.** Calculate the ratio of price to expected earnings for River Cruises both before and after it borrows the $250,000. Why does the P/E ratio fall after the increase in leverage? (LO1)

12. **Tax Shields.** Now suppose that the corporate tax rate is $T_c = .35$. Demonstrate that when River Cruises borrows the $250,000, the combined after-tax income of its debtholders and equityholders increases (compared to all-equity financing) by 35 percent of the firm's interest expense regardless of the state of the economy. (LO2)
13. **Bankruptcy.** True or false? (LO5)
   a. It makes sense to evaluate the credit manager's performance by looking at the proportion of bad debts.
   *b. When a company becomes bankrupt, it is usually in the interests of the equityholders to seek a liquidation rather than a reorganization.
   *c. A reorganization plan must be presented for approval by each class of creditor.
   d. Canada Revenue Agency has first claim on the company's assets in the event of bankruptcy.
   e. In a reorganization, creditors may be paid off with a mixture of cash and securities.
   f. When a company is liquidated, one of the most valuable assets to be sold is often the tax-loss carry-forward.

INTERMEDIATE

14. **Equity Return and Leverage.** The common stock and debt of Northern Sludge are valued at $70 million and $30 million, respectively. Investors currently require a 16 percent return on the common stock and an 8 percent return on the debt. If Northern Sludge issues an additional $10 million of common stock and uses this money to retire debt, what happens to the expected return on the stock? Assume that the change in capital structure does not affect the risk of the debt and that there are no taxes. (LO1)

15. **Earnings and Leverage.** Reliable Gearing currently is all-equity-financed. It has 10,000 shares of equity outstanding, selling at $100 a share. The firm is considering a capital restructuring. The low-debt plan calls for a debt issue of $200,000 with the proceeds used to buy back stock. The high-debt plan would exchange $400,000 of debt for equity. The debt will pay an interest rate of 10 percent. The firm pays no taxes. (LO1)
    a. What will be the debt-to-equity ratio after each possible restructuring?
    b. If earnings before interest and tax (EBIT) will be either $90,000 or $130,000, what will earnings per share be for each financing mix for both possible values of EBIT? If both scenarios are equally likely, what is expected (that is, average) EPS under each financing mix? Is the high-debt mix preferable?
    c. Suppose that EBIT is $100,000. What is EPS under each financing mix? Why are they the same in this particular case?

16. **Leverage and Risk Premiums.** Schuldenfrei A.G. is financed entirely by common stock and has a beta of 1.0. The firm pays no taxes. The stock has a price-earnings multiple of 10 and is priced to offer a 10 percent expected return. The company decides to repurchase half the common stock and substitute an equal value of debt. If the debt yields a risk-free 5 percent, calculate (LO1)
    a. The beta of the common stock after the refinancing
    b. The required return and risk premium on the common stock before the refinancing
    c. The required return and risk premium on the common stock after the refinancing
    d. The required return on the debt
    e. The required return on the company (that is, stock and debt combined) after the refinancing

    Assume that the operating profit of the firm is expected to remain constant. Give
    f. the percentage increase in earnings per share after the refinancing
    g. The new price-earnings multiple. *Hint:* Has anything happened to the stock price?

*17. **Leverage and Capital Costs.** Hubbard's Pet Foods is financed 80 percent by common stock and 20 percent by bonds. The expected return on the common stock is 12 percent and the rate of interest on the bonds is 6 percent. Assume that the bonds are default-free and that there are no taxes. Now assume that Hubbard's issues more debt and uses the proceeds to retire equity. The new financing mix is 40 percent equity and 60 percent debt. If the debt is still default-free, what happens to the expected rate of return on equity? What happens to the expected return on the package of common stock and bonds? (LO2)

18. **Leverage and Capital Costs.** "MM totally ignore the fact that as you borrow more, you have to pay higher rates of interest." Explain carefully whether this is a valid objection. (LO1)

19. **Debt-Irrelevance.** What's wrong with the following arguments? (LO1)
    a. As the firm borrows more and debt becomes risky, both share- and bondholders demand higher rates of return. Thus by *reducing* the debt ratio we can reduce both the cost of debt and the cost of equity, making everybody better off.
    b. Moderate borrowing doesn't significantly affect the probability of financial distress or bankruptcy. Consequently, moderate borrowing won't increase the expected rate of return demanded by shareholders.
    c. A capital investment opportunity offering a 10 percent internal rate of return is an attractive project if it can be 100 percent debt-financed at an 8 percent interest rate.
    d. The more debt the firm issues, the higher the interest rate it must pay. That is one important reason firms should operate at conservative debt levels.

20. **Leverage and Capital Costs.** A firm currently has a debt-equity ratio of 1/2. The debt, which is virtually riskless, pays an interest rate of 6 percent. The expected rate of return on the equity is 12 percent. What would happen to the expected rate of return on equity if the firm reduced its debt-equity ratio to 1/3? Assume the firm pays no taxes. (LO1)

21. **Leverage and Capital Costs.** If an increase in the debt-equity ratio makes both debt and equity more risky, how can the cost of capital remain unchanged? (LO1)

22. **Tax Shields.** Look back to Table 3.2 in Chapter 3, where we provided a summary 2010 income statement for AstraZeneca PLC. If the tax rate is 35 percent, what is AstraZeneca' annual interest tax shield? What is the present value of the annual tax shield if the company plans to maintain its current debt level indefinitely? Assume a discount rate of 8 percent. (LO2)

*23. **WACC.** Here is Establishment Industries' market-value balance sheet ($ millions):

Net working capital	$ 550	Debt	$ 800
Long-term assets	$2,150	Equity	$1,900
Value of firm	$2,700		$2,700

The debt is yielding 7.6 percent and the cost of equity is 14 percent. The tax rate is 37 percent. Investors expect this level of debt to be permanent. (LO2)

a. What is Establishment's WACC?
b. Write out a market-value balance sheet assuming Establishment has no debt. Use your answer to problem 4.

*24. **Tax Shields and WACC.** Here are book- and market-value balance sheets of the United Frypan Company: (LO2)

Book-Value Balance Sheet			
Net working capital	$ 20	Debt	$ 40
Long-term assets	80	Equity	60
	$100		$100

Market-Value Balance Sheet			
Net working capital	$ 20	Debt	$ 40
Long-term assets	140	Equity	120
	$160		$160

Assume that MM's theory holds except for taxes. There is no growth and the $40 of debt is expected to be permanent. Assume a 35 percent corporate tax rate.

a. How much of the firm's value is accounted for by the debt-generated tax shield?
b. What is United Frypan's after-tax weighted-average cost of capital (WACC)?
c. Now suppose that Parliament passes a law that eliminates the deductibility of interest for tax purposes after a grace period of 5 years. What will be the new value of the firm, other things being equal? Assume an 8 percent borrowing rate.

*25. **Bankruptcy.** What are the drawbacks of operating a firm that is close to bankruptcy? Give some examples. (LO5)

26. **Costs of Financial Distress.** The Salad Oil Storage Company (SOS) has financed a large part of its facilities with long-term debt. There is a significant risk of default, but the company is not on the ropes yet. Explain why (LO3)

a. SOS shareholders could lose by investing in a positive-NPV project financed by an equity issue.
b. SOS shareholders could gain by investing in a highly risky, negative-NPV project.

27. **Financial Distress.** Explain how financial distress can lead to conflicts of interest between debt and equity investors. Then explain how these conflicts can lead to costs of financial distress. (LO3)

28. **Bankruptcy.** Explain why equity can sometimes have a positive value even when companies petition for bankruptcy. (LO5)

29. **Costs of Financial Distress.** For which of the following firms would you expect the costs of financial distress to be highest? Explain briefly. (LO3)

a. A computer software company that depends on skilled programmers to produce new products
b. A shipping company that operates a fleet of modern oil tankers

30. **Trade-Off Theory.** Smoke and Mirrors currently has EBIT of $25,000 and is all-equity-financed. EBIT is expected to stay at this level indefinitely. The firm pays corporate taxes equal to 35 percent of taxable income. The discount rate for the firm's projects is 10 percent. (LO3)

a. What is the market value of the firm?
b. Now assume the firm issues $50,000 of debt paying interest of 6 percent per year and uses the proceeds to retire equity. The debt is expected to be permanent. What will happen to the total value of the firm (debt plus equity)?
c. Recompute your answer to part (b) under the following assumptions: the debt issue raises the possibility of bankruptcy; the firm has a 30 percent chance of going bankrupt after 3 years; if it does go bankrupt, it will incur bankruptcy costs of $200,000. The discount rate is 10 percent. Should the firm issue the debt?

31. **Pecking-Order Theory.** Alpha Corp. and Beta Corp. both produce turbo encabulators. Both companies' assets and operations are growing at the same rate and their annual capital expenditures are about the same. However, Alpha Corp. is the more efficient producer and is consistently more profitable. According to the pecking-order theory, which company should have the higher debt ratio? Explain. (LO4)

32. **Financial Slack.** Look back to the Sealed Air example in the first Finance in Action box. What was the value of financial slack to Sealed Air before its restructuring? What does the success of the restructuring say about

optimal capital structure? Would you recommend that all firms restructure as Sealed Air did? (LO4)

33. **Internet.** Log in to **ca.finance.yahoo.com** and find the profile for Magna International (MGA). Construct the debt ratio, debt/(debt + equity), for the firm. Now calculate Magna's debt ratio by using the market value of equity, but assuming that book value of debt approximates its market value. How does debt as a proportion of firm value change as you switch from book to market value? (LO2)

34. **Internet.** Go to Nasdaq site at **www.nasdaq.com**. Review the financial ratios under the "Financial" section of "Fundamentals" for one or more of the following companies: Hertz Global Holdings (HTZ), Sprint Nextel (S), and Rite Aid Corp. (RAD). Do you see a trend toward financial distress for these companies? If so, what factors seem to be associated with their financial distress? (LO3)

CHALLENGE

35. **Internet.**
    a. Go to **finance.yahoo.com** and find the profiles for PepsiCo (PEP) and IBM (IBM) and then look at each firm's annual balance sheet and income statement under "Financials." Calculate the present value of the interest tax shield contributed by each company's long-term debt. Assume a 34 percent tax rate for both companies. Now suppose that each issues $3 billion more of long-term debt and uses the proceeds to repurchase equity. How would the interest tax shield change? (LO2)
    b. While you are logged in to the Yahoo page for PepsiCo or IBM, move down and click on "Industry" in the left-hand column. This will give you a table of financial ratios for different industries in the United States. Compare the debt-equity ratios for different industries. Can you account for the differences? Are they better explained by the trade-off theory or the pecking-order theory? (LO3, LO4)

*36. **Costs of Financial Distress.** Let's go back to the Double-R Nutting Company. Suppose that Double-R's bonds have a face value of $50. Its current market-value balance sheet is as follows:

Assets		**Liabilities and Equity**	
Net working capital	$20	Bonds outstanding	$25
Fixed assets	10	Common stock	5
Total assets	$30	Total liabilities and shareholders' equity	$30

Who would gain or lose from the following manoeuvres? (LO3)

a. Double-R pays a $10 cash dividend.
b. Double-R halts operations, sells its fixed assets for $6, and converts net working-capital into $20 cash. It invests its $26 in Treasury bills.
c. Double-R encounters an investment opportunity requiring a $10 initial investment with NPV = $0. It borrows $10 to finance the project by issuing more bonds with the same security, seniority, and so on, as the existing bonds.
d. Double-R finances the investment opportunity in part (c) by issuing more common stock.

37. **Trade-Off Theory.** Ronald Masulis[15] has analyzed the stock price impact of *exchange offers* of debt for equity, or vice versa. In an exchange offer, the firm offers to trade freshly issued securities for seasoned securities in the hands of investors. Thus, a firm that wanted to move to a higher debt ratio could offer to trade new debt for outstanding shares. A firm that wanted to move to a more conservative capital structure could offer to trade new shares for outstanding debt securities. Masulis found that debt-for-equity exchanges were good news (stock price increased on announcement) and equity-for-debt exchanges were bad news. (LO4)
    a. Are these results consistent with the trade-off theory of capital structure?
    b. Are the results consistent with the evidence that investors regard announcements of (1) stock issues as bad news, (2) stock repurchases as good news, and (3) debt issues as no news, or at most trifling disappointments?

38. **Pecking-Order Theory.** Construct a simple example to show that a firm's existing shareholders gain if they can sell overpriced stock to new investors and invest the cash in a zero-NPV project. Who loses from these actions? If investors are aware that managers are likely to issue stock when it is overpriced, what will happen to the stock price when the issue is announced? (LO4)

39. **Pecking-Order Theory.** When companies announce an issue of common stock, the share price typically falls. When they announce an issue of debt, there is typically only a negligible change in the stock price. Can you explain why? (LO4)

40. **Taxes.** MM's proposition I suggests that in the absence of taxes it makes no difference whether the firm borrows on behalf of its shareholders or whether they

[15] R.W. Masulis, "The Effects of Capital Structure Change on Security Prices: A Study of Exchange Offers," *Journal of Financial Economics* 8 (June 1980): 139–177, and "The Impact of Capital Structure Change on Firm Value," *Journal of Finance* 38 (March 1983): 107–126.

borrow directly. However, if there are corporate taxes, this is no longer the case. Construct a simple example to show that with taxes it is better for the firm to borrow than for the shareholders to do so. (LO2)

41. **Taxes.** MM's proposition I, when modified to recognize corporate taxes, suggests that there is a tax advantage to firm borrowing. If there is a tax advantage to firm borrowing, there is also a tax disadvantage to firm lending. Explain why. (LO2)

Solutions to Check Points

16.1 Price per share will stay at $10, so with $350,000, River Cruises can repurchase 35,000 shares, leaving 65,000 outstanding. The remaining value of equity will be $650,000. Overall firm value stays at $1 million. Shareholders' wealth is unchanged: they start with shares worth $1 million, receive $350,000, and retain shares worth $650,000.

16.2 a. Data:

Number of shares	25,000
Price per share	$ 10
Market value of shares	$250,000
Market value of debt	$750,000

	State of the Economy		
	Slump	Normal	Boom
Operating income	$75,000	125,000	175,000
Interest	$75,000	75,000	75,000
Equity earnings	$ 0	50,000	100,000
Earnings per share	$ 0	2	4
Return on shares	0%	20%	40%

Every change of $50,000 in operating income leads to a change in the return to equityholders of 20 percent. This is double the swing in equity returns when debt was only $500,000.

b. The shareholder should lend out $3 for every $1 invested in River Cruises' stock. For example, he could buy one share for $10 and then lend $30. The payoffs are

	State of the Economy		
	Slump	Normal	Boom
Earnings on one share	$0	2	4
Plus interest at 10%	$3	3	3
Net earnings	$3	5	7
Return on $40 investment	7.5%	12.5%	17.5%

16.3 Business risk is unaffected by capital structure. As the financing mix changes, whatever equity is outstanding must absorb the fixed business risk of the firm. The less equity, the more risk absorbed per share. Therefore, as capital structure changes, r_{assets} is held fixed while r_{equity} adjusts.

16.4 BCE's borrowing reduced taxable profits by $952 million. With a tax rate of 35 percent, tax was reduced by $.35 \times \$952 = \$333.2$ million. If the borrowing is permanent, BCE will save this amount of tax each year. The present value of the tax saving would be $\$333.2/.08 = \$4,165$ million.

16.5 In bankruptcy bondholders will receive $2 million less. This lowers the expected cash flow from the bond and reduces its present value. Therefore, the bonds will be priced lower and must offer a higher interest rate. This higher rate is paid by the firm today. It comes out of shareholders' income. Thus common stock value falls.

16.6 The conflicts are costly because they lead to poor investment decisions. The more debt the firm has today, the greater the chance of poor decisions in the future. Investors foresee this possibility and reduce today's market value of the firm.

16.7 Financial distress would be most costly for the biotech company. Its assets are all intangible. If bankruptcy threatens and the best scientists accept job offers from other firms, there may not be much value remaining for the biotech company's debt and equity investors. On the other hand, bankruptcy would have little or no effect on the value of 50 producing oil wells and of the oil reserves still in the ground.

16.8 The electric utility has the most stable cash flow. It also has the highest reliance on tangible assets that would not be impaired by a bankruptcy. It should have the highest debt ratio. The software firm has the least dependence on tangible assets and the most on assets that have value only if the firm continues as an ongoing concern. It probably also has the most unpredictable cash flows. It should have the lowest debt ratio.

MINI CASE

In March 2011, the management team of Londonderry Air (LA) met to discuss a proposal to purchase five short-haul aircraft at a total cost of $25 million. There was general enthusiasm for the investment, and the new aircraft were expected to generate an annual cash flow of $4 million for 20 years.

The focus of the meeting was on how to finance the purchase. LA had $20 million in cash and marketable securities (see Table 16.8 below), but Ed Johnson, the chief financial officer, pointed out that the company needed at least $10 million in cash to meet normal outflow and as a contingency reserve. This meant that there would be a cash deficiency of $15 million, which the firm would need to cover either by the sale of common stock or by additional borrowing. While admitting that the arguments were finely balanced, Johnson recommended an issue of stock. He pointed out that the airline industry was subject to wide swings in profits, and the firm should be careful to avoid the risk of excessive borrowing. He estimated that in market-value terms the long-term debt ratio was about 62 percent, and that a further debt issue would raise the ratio to 64 percent.

Johnson's only doubt about making a stock issue was that investors might jump to the conclusion that management believed the stock was overpriced, in which case the announcement might prompt an unjustified selloff by investors. He stressed therefore that the company needed to explain carefully the reasons for the issue. Also, he suggested that demand for the issue would be enhanced if at the same time LA increased its dividend payment. This would provide a tangible indication of management's confidence in the future.

These arguments cut little ice with LA's chief executive. "Ed," she said, "I know you're the expert on all this, but everything you say flies in the face of common sense. Why should we want to sell more equity when our stock has fallen over the past year by nearly a fifth? Our stock is currently offering a dividend yield of 6.5 percent, which makes equity an expensive source of capital. Increasing the dividend would simply make it more expensive. What's more, I don't see the point of paying out more money to the shareholders at the same time that we are asking *them* for cash. If we hike the dividend, we will need to increase the amount of the stock issue; so we will just be paying the higher dividend out of the shareholders' own pockets. You're also ignoring the question of dilution. Our equity currently has a book value of $12 a share; it's not playing fair by our existing shareholders if we now issue stock for around $10 a share.

"Look at the alternative. We can borrow today at 5 percent. We get a tax break on the interest, so the after-tax cost of borrowing is $.65 \times 5 = 3.25$ percent. That's about half the cost of equity. We expect to earn a return of 15 percent on these new aircraft. If we can raise money at 3.25 percent and invest it at 15 percent, that's a good deal in my book.

"You finance guys are always talking about risk, but as long as we don't go bankrupt, borrowing doesn't add any risk at all. In any case, my calculations show that the debt ratio is only 45 percent, which doesn't sound excessive to me.

"Ed, I don't want to push my views on this—after all, you're the expert. We don't need to make a firm recommendation to the board until next month. In the meantime, why don't you get one of your new business graduates to look at the whole issue of how we should finance the deal and what return we need to earn on these planes."

TABLE 16.8
Summary financial statements for Londonderry Air, 2010 (book values, $ millions)

Balance Sheet			
Cash	$ 20	Bank debt	$ 50
Other current assets	20	Other current liabilities	20
Fixed assets	250	10% bond, due 2023*	100
		Stockholders' equity**	120
Total assets	$290	Total liabilities	$290
Income Statement			
Gross profit	57.5		
Depreciation	20.0		
Interest	7.5		
Pretax profit	30.0		
Tax	10.5		
Net profit	19.5		
Dividend	6.5		

*The yield to maturity on LA debt currently is 5 percent.
**LA has 10 million shares outstanding and a market price of $10 a share. LA's equity beta is estimated at 1.25, the market risk premium is 8 percent, and the Treasury bill rate is 4 percent.

PART 5

Debt and Payout Policy

16 Debt Policy
17 Leasing
17.1 What Is a Lease?
17.2 Why Lease?
17.3 Valuing Leases
17.4 When Do Financial Leases Pay?
17.5 Summary
18 Payout Policy

CHAPTER 17

Leasing

LEARNING OBJECTIVES

After studying this chapter, you should be able to:

LO1 Explain the different kinds of leases and some of the reasons for their use.

LO2 Determine the net present value of a long-term lease.

LO3 Explain how a long-term lease is an alternative to debt financing.

LO4 Explain the implication of tax rates for the benefits of leasing to the lessor and lessee.

Should Greenfield Construction lease or buy the new backhoe loader?

© iStockphoto/1001 Nights.

Most of us occasionally rent a car, bicycle, or boat, and usually these kinds of rentals are short-term—we rent them for a day or a week or so. But in corporate finance longer-term rentals are common. A rental agreement that extends for a year or more and involves a series of fixed payments is called a **lease**.[1]

Firms often lease as an alternative to buying capital equipment. Computers are often leased; so are trucks, railroad cars, aircraft, and ships. Just about every kind of asset has been leased some time by somebody, including electric and nuclear power plants, handball courts, and even horses.

Every lease involves two parties. The *user* of the asset is called the **lessee**. The lessee makes periodic payments to the *owner* of the asset, who is called the **lessor**. For example, if you sign an agreement to rent an apartment for a year, you are the lessee and the owner is the lessor.

Firms lease assets for a variety of reasons. One reason firms lease is for convenience, if the asset is needed only for a short period of time. Another reason is for the flexibility of cancelling the lease if the asset is no longer needed. However, tax reduction is the main reason for long-term leasing. Companies pay fewer taxes if they acquire the asset by leasing rather than borrowing. The tax savings occur because in a lease arrangement, it is the asset owner not the asset user who can deduct the asset's capital cost allowance (CCA) from its taxable income. By transferring the CCA from a lower-taxed user to a higher-taxed owner, total taxes are lowered and both parties are better off.

LO1 17.1 WHAT IS A LEASE?

lease Rental agreement for the use of an asset extending for more than one year and involving a series of fixed payments.

lessee User of the asset in a lease. Responsible for making regular payments to lessor.

lessor Owner of the asset in a lease. Receives regular payments from lessee.

operating lease Short-term, cancellable lease.

Leases come in many forms, but in all cases the **lessee** (user) promises to make a series of payments to the **lessor** (owner). The lease contract specifies the monthly or semi-annual payments; the first payment is usually due as soon as the contract is signed. The payments are usually level, but their time pattern can be tailored to the user's needs. For example, suppose that a manufacturer leases a machine to produce a complex new product. There will be a year's "shakedown" period before volume production starts. In this case, it might be possible to arrange for lower payments during the first year of the lease.

When a lease is terminated, the leased equipment reverts to the lessor. However, the agreement often gives the user the option to purchase the equipment or take out a new lease.

Some leases provide for the *temporary* use of an asset. Generally known as **operating leases**, these leases are either short term or cancellable during the contract period at the option of the

[1] Our discussion of leasing is drawn, in part, from Chap. 25 of R. Brealey and S. Myers, *Principles of Corporate Finance*, 6th ed. (Boston: McGraw-Hill, 2000).

financial lease Long-term, non-cancellable lease. Also known as *capital* or *full-payout* lease.

lessee. On the other hand, a **financial lease** provides for *long-term* use of an asset. With a financial lease, the lessee has the asset for most of its estimated economic life, and the lease cannot be cancelled, or can be cancelled only if the lessor is reimbursed for any losses. This type of lease is also called a *capital* or *full-payout lease*.[2]

Financial leases are a *source of financing*. Signing a financial lease contract is like borrowing money. There is an immediate cash inflow because the lessee is relieved of having to pay for the asset. But the lessee also assumes a binding obligation to make the payments specified in the lease contract. The user could have borrowed the full purchase price of the asset by accepting a binding obligation to make interest and principal payments to the lender. Thus the cash flow consequences of leasing and borrowing are similar. In either case, the firm raises cash now and pays it back later. A large part of this chapter will be devoted to comparing leases and borrowing as financing alternatives.

Leases also differ in the services provided by the lessor. Under a *full-service* or *rental lease*, the lessor promises to maintain and insure the equipment and to pay any property taxes due on it. In a *net* lease, the lessee agrees to maintain the asset, insure it, and pay any property taxes. Financial leases are usually net leases.

Most financial leases are arranged for brand-new assets. The lessee identifies the equipment, arranges for the leasing company to buy it from the manufacturer, and signs a contract with the leasing company. This is called a *direct lease*. In other cases, the firm sells an asset it already owns and leases it back from the buyer. These *sale and lease-back* arrangements are common in real estate. For example, a company might wish to raise cash by selling its factory, but still retain use of it. It could do this by selling the factory for cash to a leasing company and simultaneously signing a long-term lease for the factory. Legal ownership of the factory passes to the leasing company, but the right to use it stays with the company.

You may also encounter *leveraged* leases. These are financial leases in which the lessor borrows part of the purchase price of the leased asset, using the lease contract as security for the loan. This does not change the lessee's obligations, but it can complicate the lessor's analysis considerably.

LEASING INDUSTRY

Leasing has grown substantially since the 1950s when the first independent leasing companies, completely separate from the manufacturers, were established. Now, leasing provides significant amounts of financing to businesses worldwide. In Canada, it is estimated that 20 to 25 percent of total business investment in machinery and equipment is financed by asset-based financing and leasing. In 2009, the total value of assets under lease in Canada was estimated at $89.5 billion.[3]

The leasing industry comprises various types of companies that are in the business of providing leases. Some of the largest individual lessors are equipment manufacturers. For example, IBM is a large lessor of computers, and Xerox is a large lessor of copiers. By offering leasing, they are able to sell more products.

The major providers of lease finance are finance companies, which are non-deposit-taking financial institutions. For example, GE Capital, a large finance company, operates in many different countries and leases a wide range of assets. Its subsidiary, GE Capital Aviation Services, owned and leased out about 1,800 commercial aircraft in 2010. A large fraction of the world's airlines rely entirely on leasing to finance their fleet.

Statistics Canada estimates that finance companies provided 45 percent of Canadian lease financing in 2008. Leasing companies, businesses that specialize exclusively in providing lease

---

[2] In the shipping industry, a financial lease is called a *bareboat charter* or a *demise hire*.

[3] See **www.cfla-acfl.ca/files/public/CFLA2009-2010_Annual_Report.pdf** from the Canadian Finance and Leasing Association (CFLA).

financing, accounted for 26 percent of the outstanding leases in 2008. Although Canadian banks are not permitted to engage in consumer car leasing, they are active in other types of leasing. Banks provided about 17 percent of lease financing in 2008.[4]

EXAMPLE 17.1 OPERATING AND FINANCIAL LESSORS

GE Capital is a major global, diversified financial services company. Its businesses include providing operating and financial leases for many different types of assets including cars, trucks and trailers, jets, and commercial equipment. As an operating lessor, GE Capital has a significant number of "off-lease assets"—assets available to be leased but currently not leased. Sometimes off-lease assets are sold, rather than leased again. At **www.geasset.com**, GE Capital has a long list of off-lease assets for sale. Items for sale include corporate aircraft, construction and forestry equipment, and plastic machinery and equipment.

By contrast, lessors specializing in providing financial leases do not end up with off-lease assets. Typically, at the end of the financial lease, the lessee purchases the asset from the lessor. TD Asset Finance primarily offers financial leases and supplies relatively few operating leases; TD does not want to be in the used-equipment business.

LO1 17.2 WHY LEASE?

You hear many suggestions about why companies should lease equipment rather than buy it. Let us look at some sensible reasons and then at four more dubious ones.

SENSIBLE REASONS FOR LEASING

Short-Term Leases Are Convenient Suppose you are flying to Nova Scotia for a week's vacation and want the use of a car for the week. You could buy a car and sell it seven days later, but that would be silly. Apart from the fact that registering ownership is a nuisance, you would spend time selecting a car, negotiating its purchase, and arranging insurance. Then at the end of the week you would negotiate resale and cancel the registration and insurance. When you need a car for only a short time, it clearly makes more sense to rent it. You save the trouble of registering ownership, and you know the effective cost. In the same way, it pays a company to lease equipment that it needs for only a year or two. This kind of lease is an operating lease.

Sometimes the cost of short-term rentals may seem prohibitively high, or you may find it difficult to rent at any price. This can happen for equipment that is easily damaged by careless use. The owner knows that short-term users are unlikely to take the same care they would with their own equipment. When the danger of abuse becomes too high, short-term rental markets do not survive. Thus, it is easy enough to buy a Lamborghini Diablo, a high-end sports car, provided your pockets are deep enough, but nearly impossible to rent one.

Cancellation Options Are Valuable Some leases that *look* expensive actually look fairly priced once the option to cancel is recognized.

Maintenance Is Provided Under a full-service lease, the user receives maintenance and other services. Many lessors are well equipped to provide efficient maintenance. However, bear in mind that these benefits will be reflected in higher lease payments.

[4] See **www.statcan.gc.ca/daily-quotidien/091211/dq091211d-eng.htm**.

EXAMPLE 17.2 **LEASING A HORSE**

Did you know you can lease a horse? Doing so is a good way to find out if you are ready to own one without the long-term commitment of purchasing it. It can also make sense for meeting the changing needs of growing teenagers whose horseback-riding skills are improving. Rather than buying and selling a succession of horses, it might be cheaper to lease. Leases can include the cost of board, vet, and farrier (someone who puts shoes on the horse) on top of the lease fee. The terms of the lease might include how often the horse can be ridden, what feed it gets, and who pays if the horse gets hurt. Like other short-term leases, a horse lease is more expensive than buying the horse itself. If you think you might want the animal for many years, you would be better off buying it.

Standardization Leads to Low Administrative and Transaction Costs Suppose that you operate a leasing company that specializes in financial leases for trucks. You are effectively lending money to a large number of firms (lessees), which may differ considerably in size and risk. But because the underlying asset is, in each case, the same saleable item (a truck), you can safely "lend" the money (lease the truck) without conducting a detailed analysis of each firm's business. You can also use a simple, standard lease contract. This standardization makes it possible to "lend" small sums of money without incurring large investigative, administrative, or legal costs.

For these reasons leasing is often a relatively cheap source of cash for a small company. It offers financing on a flexible, piecemeal basis and has lower transaction costs than either a private placement or a public offering of debt or equity.

Tax Shields Can Be Used The lessor owns the leased asset and deducts the asset's capital cost allowance (CCA) from taxable income. If the lessor can make better use of CCA tax shields than an asset's user can, it may make sense for the leasing company to own the equipment and pass on some of the tax benefits to the lessee in the form of lower lease payments.

SOME DUBIOUS REASONS FOR LEASING

Leasing Avoids Capital Expenditure Controls In many companies lease proposals are scrutinized as carefully as capital expenditure proposals, but in others, leasing may enable an operating manager to avoid the elaborate approval procedures needed to buy an asset. Although this is a dubious reason for leasing, it may be influential, particularly in the public sector. For example, hospitals have sometimes found it politically more convenient to lease their medical equipment than to ask the government to provide funds for purchase.

Leasing Preserves Capital Leasing companies provide "100 percent financing"; they advance the full cost of the leased asset. Consequently, they often claim that leasing preserves capital, allowing the firm to save its cash for other things.

But the firm can also "preserve capital" by borrowing money. If Greenfield Construction leases a $100,000 backhoe rather than buying it, it conserves $100,000 cash. It might also (1) buy the backhoe for cash and (2) borrow $100,000, using the backhoe as security. Its bank balance ends up the same whether it leases or buys and borrows. It has the backhoe in either case, and it incurs a $100,000 liability in either case. What's so special about leasing?

Leases May Be Off-Balance-Sheet Financing The rules for reporting leases in a firm's financial statements vary internationally. In some countries, financial leases are **off-balance-sheet financing**; that is, a firm can acquire an asset, finance it through a financial lease, and show neither the asset nor the lease contract on its balance sheet. All lease payments are recognized as an expense of the lessee and reported as lease income by the lessor.

off-balance-sheet financing Financing that is not shown as a liability on a company's balance sheet.

No distinction is made between operating leases, which give temporary use of an asset, and financial leases, which are commitments of the lessee to use and pay for the asset over the bulk of the asset's economic life.

Both the Canadian Accounting Standards Board (AcSB) and the U.S. Financial Accounting Standards Board (FASB) require that leases be accounted for according to who bears the risks and rewards of ownership of the assets. In an operating lease, the lessor bears the risks and rewards of ownership because the lease is short term. At the end of the lease period, the lessor gets the asset back and bears the risk of finding another lessee. The asset stays on the lessor's balance sheet and the lessor reports lease payments as income. Likewise, the lessee is just a temporary user of the asset and the lease payments are another business expense.

With a financial lease, although the lessor is the legal owner of the leased assets, the lessee bears essentially all of the risk and rewards of ownership. As we noted, a financial lease is primarily a means of providing financing so that the lessee can acquire the asset without actually buying it up front. Canadian and U.S. accounting rules require that the financial statements reflect the true economic consequences of a financial lease. In other words, the leased assets are reported along with the other assets on the balance sheet of the lessee. Likewise, the lease financing shows up as a liability on the lessee's balance sheet. To do this, the lease is *capitalized.*

To capitalize a lease, the present value of the lease payments is calculated and listed along with debt on the right-hand side of the balance sheet. The same amount is shown as an asset on the left-hand side. This leased asset would typically be included with other fixed assets and is amortized over the life of the lease. The amortization is deducted from book income, just as depreciation is deducted for a purchased asset.

According to the *CICA Handbook*, a lease is normally considered to be a financial lease when at least one of the following conditions is present at the start of the lease:[5]

1. There is reasonable assurance that the lessee will obtain ownership of the leased property at the end of the lease term. This would occur if the lease provides for automatic transfer of title to the lessee at the end of the lease, or if the lessee is entitled to purchase the asset at a bargain price (below its expected value) at the end of the lease.
2. The lessee will receive all of the economic benefits expected to be derived through the use of the leased asset. Since assets are most productive in the earlier years of their lives, this condition is presumed to be satisfied if the lease term is at least 75 percent of the asset's economic life.
3. The lessor is assured of recovering the investment in the leased asset plus a return on its investment over the lease term. This condition is presumed to be satisfied if the present value of the lease payments is equal to at least 90 percent of the fair value of the asset at the inception of the lease.

The Canadian criteria are similar to those used in the United States. In Canada and the United States, all other leases are operating leases as far as accountants are concerned.

Many financial managers have tried to take advantage of this arbitrary boundary between operating and financial leases. Suppose that you want to finance a computer-controlled machine tool costing $1 million. The machine tool's life is expected to be 12 years. You could sign a lease contract for 8 years, 11 months (just missing requirement 2) with lease payments having a present value of $899,000 (just missing requirement 3). You could also make sure the lease contract avoids requirement 1. Result? You have off-balance-sheet financing. This lease would not have to be capitalized, although it is clearly a long-term fixed obligation.

When a firm obtains off-balance-sheet financing, the conventional measures of financial leverage, such as the debt-equity ratio, understate the true degree of financial leverage. Some

[5] These criteria are from *CICA Handbook*, para. 3065.06, as summarized in T.H. Beechy and J.E.D. Conrod, *Intermediate Accounting, Volume 2* (Toronto: McGraw-Hill Ryerson, 2005), 1032. CICA, the Canadian Institute of Chartered Accountants, is the professional association and regulator of Canadian chartered accountants.

Finance in Action

Off-Balance-Sheet Leases: Capitalization and Ratings Implications

Out of Sight but Not out of Mind

Should creditors to a company engaged in off-balance-sheet leases be concerned about the existence of these transactions? The argument is that leases are secured by their own assets and could effectively be ignored for the purpose of analyzing on-balance-sheet debt. However, we beg to differ, and firmly believe that leases represent use of a company's debt capacity and could meaningfully impact the recovery prospects of a balance sheet creditor in a stress scenario.

Debt capacity may be loosely defined as a company's ability to incur *additional* debt. Simply put, a use of debt capacity and a corresponding increase in leverage arises from any transaction that stakes a claim to a company's cash flow.

It is not difficult to see why leases do utilize a company's debt capacity. Lease agreements are contractual obligations, resulting in a claim on cash flow through fixed lease payments over the life of the lease. Failure to comply with the terms of the lease agreement would constitute default. Besides, in the absence of a lease financing option, the company would likely borrow the money and buy the asset.

Our discussion will focus on operating lease transactions. Our objectives are two-fold: to accurately depict a firm's effective leverage and to achieve comparability in analyzing firms employing different financing tools (e.g., lease vs. buy). The choice of capitalization method is ultimately a judgement call, though we believe the present value approach (or variations thereof) may be the lesser of the evils. We calculate the net present value of the future minimum lease payments using an appropriate discount rate.

Once an "appropriate" capitalization amount [for the operating leases] is determined we may incorporate it into the analysis and rating of the various debt issues. It is more meaningful to incorporate capitalized lease if the amount is significant and the leased assets are essential to the business.

Source: Moody's Investors Service, "Off–Balance Sheet Leases: Capitalization and Rating Implications" (Boston: Global Credit Research, October 1999).

believe that financial analysts do not always notice off-balance-sheet lease obligations (which are still referred to in footnotes) or the greater volatility of earnings that result from the fixed lease payments. They may be right, but we would not expect such an imperfection to be widespread.

When a company borrows money, it must usually consent to certain restrictions on future borrowing. Early bond indentures did not include any restrictions on financial leases. Therefore leasing was seen as a way to circumvent restrictive covenants. Loopholes such as these are easily stopped, and most bond indentures now include limits on leasing.

Long-term lease obligations ought to be regarded as debt whether or not they appear on the balance sheet. Financial analysts may overlook moderate leasing activity, just as they overlook minor debts. But major lease obligations are generally recognized and taken into account.

Debt-rating agencies, such as Moody's and Standard & Poor's, do not ignore operating leases when assessing a company's financial leverage. In the nearby Finance in Action box, you can read about Moody's treatment of operating leases.

Recognizing that the existing accounting standards for leasing have created distortions in companies' financial statements, FASB and IASB are engaged in a joint project to consider requiring all leases to be recognized on the balance sheet. The next two Finance in Action boxes report on the impact of such a change on retailers and transport companies, who are big users of operating leases.

Leasing Affects Book Income Leasing can make the firm's balance sheet and income statement *look* better by increasing book income or decreasing book asset value, or both.

A lease that qualifies as off-balance-sheet financing affects book income in only one way: the lease payments are an expense. If the firm buys the asset instead and borrows to finance it, both depreciation and interest expense are deducted. Leases are usually set up so that payments in the early years are less than depreciation plus interest under the buy-and-borrow alternative. Consequently, leasing increases book income in the early years of an asset's life. The book rate of return can increase even more dramatically, because the book value of assets (the denominator

Finance in Action

Implications of IFRS on the Retail Industry

As their lenders, suppliers, customers and competitors switch to international financial reporting standards, even privately-owned retailers will be affected. David Bromley, partner at PricewaterhouseCoopers, discusses some of the special considerations for retailers, such as leases and loyalty programs.

Q Who does IFRS apply to in the retail sector?

A IFRS is relevant to all publicly listed retail companies. But a Canadian retailer that is private could also be interested in IFRS. For fiscal years beginning on or after Jan. 1, 2011, retailers in the private sector will have to choose either to adopt IFRS or Canadian GAAP for Private Enterprises. IFRS may be the best alternative if you are considering going public in the future, have an exit strategy that could involve acquisition by an IFRS reporter or private-equity interest, or have banking institutions that require IFRS-compliant financial statements.

Q Are there any aspects of IFRS that impact retailers differently from other businesses or issues unique to retail that affect the transition in any way?

A Retail companies normally have a significant number of leased locations across the country. That means retailers are going to have to focus on identifying differences between Canadian GAAP and IFRS pertaining to lease accounting. This will include reviewing the accounting treatment of pre-opening costs, rent-free periods, step rent, other lease incentives, contingent rental payments, as well as asset retirement obligations. Under IFRS, the classification of leases is determined using guidelines that are more qualitative in nature and require more professional judgment. In addition, a new IFRS standard on leases is expected to be issued in the coming years, which may require all leases to be capitalized on the balance sheet. This could have a significant impact on the financial statements of retail companies.

Q I've heard IFRS referred to as standing for, "I feel really stressed." Do you have a sense of how well prepared retailers are for this?

A PricewaterhouseCoopers LLP conducted a survey with the Canadian Financial Executives Research Foundation during April 2009 to gauge the progress of Canadian companies in their conversion to IFRS. Of the 147 public companies that were surveyed, 80% indicated they remained short of the halfway mark in their overall conversion process.

Source: Excerpted from Hollie Shaw, "Rebalancing the Financials: Retail," *Financial Post*, September 24, 2009, FP14.

in the book-rate-of-return calculation) is understated if the leased asset never appears on the firm's balance sheet.

Leasing's impact on book income should in itself have no effect on firm value. In efficient capital markets, investors will look through the firm's accounting results to the true value of the asset and the liability incurred to finance it.

LO2, 3 17.3 VALUING LEASES

Typically, any analysis of leasing an asset involves examining the costs and benefits of this option relative to the alternative: buying the asset. In this section, we discuss how operating and financial leases are valued.

OPERATING LEASES

Leases can be attractive for a variety of reasons. However, the decision to lease requires careful calculation of the cash inflows and outflows from the lease. If you are considering an *operating lease*, decide whether it is cheaper to lease the asset for the time that you need it or to buy it. Figure out the *equivalent annual cost*[6] of buying the asset and compare it to the annual lease payment charged by the lessor. In other words, can you "lease" the asset to yourself more cheaply than you can lease it from a lessor? Generally, the longer you need the asset, the more sense it makes to buy it rather than arranging an operating lease.

[6] Look back at Chapter 8 for a review of equivalent annual cost and an example of the analysis of an operating lease.

Finance in Action

Business as Usual for Transportation with IFRS

For Canadian transportation companies like airlines and railways, the move to new accounting standards will mean their financial statements will be more detailed. It will also make a big difference in how they account for leased equipment. The *Financial Post* asked Peter Barr, national consumer business leader for Deloitte, to explain further.

Q Are there any specific issues that you see arising for the transportation sector?

A Under transportation, in particular airlines and to some extent railways, one of the big issues is that lease accounting is quite different and these types of organizations tend to finance a lot of their equipment acquisitions through leasing. In Canadian and U.S. GAAP, you used to be able to account for a leasing transaction under specific circumstances, which is easy to create through the way you write the lease, as though you bought the equipment and you've taken out the loan. So, you get to put the asset on the balance sheet and you put a loan on your balance sheet and you amortize it, so what you record over time is really the financing charge, the interest charged. Whereas with IFRS, most of those leases will not be accounted for that way, which means all of the lease payments are going to hit the [profit and loss].

Q What will be the impact?

A That will have some impact on the apparent profitability of these organizations. They will have fewer assets on the balance sheets as a result, and of course, there will be the proverbial off-balance-sheet financing. There will not be—other than a note to the financial statement that describes the amount of lease payments and commitments they have out there—a loan on the balance sheet related to the acquisition of those assets.

Q Are there other issues that might arise?

A Generally speaking, capital asset accounting under IFRS is far more complex than it has been in the Canadian GAAP. So, you're going to end up with scenarios where you have what I would call "componentization." If you had a building in Canadian GAAP, you depreciated the building at 5% declining balance over a number of years or 40% for 40 years, whatever your choice was. Under IFRS, you need to break down and depreciate the different components of the buildings, the roofs, the building itself, whatever. While that doesn't necessarily have a big impact on what the financial statements are going to look like to the user, it has a big impact on how the organization does its accounting.

Source: Excerpted from Scott Deveau, "Business Won't Change," Transportation, *Financial Post*, September 24, 2009, FP15. Material reprinted with the express permission of National Post, a division of Postmedia Network Inc.

An attractive feature of an operating lease is the option to cancel the lease, avoiding the risks of obsolescence. The options embedded in an operating lease can be very valuable but are rather tricky to assess and are beyond this book. In general, operating leases make sense when the user needs the equipment for a short time, when the lessor is better able to bear the risks of obsolescence, or when the lessor can offer a good deal on maintenance.

FINANCIAL LEASES

When you are considering a *financial* lease, the decision amounts to "lease versus borrow." Financial leases extend over most of the economic life of the lease equipment. They are not cancellable. The lease payments are fixed obligations equivalent to *debt service*, the sum of interest and principal repayment on the debt.

Financial leases make sense when the company is prepared to take on the business risks of owning and operating the leased asset. Suppose a company is thinking about getting a stretch limousine. If managers aren't sure whether they will use it enough, they will want to consider an operating lease to give them the option of cancelling the lease: They will avoid the risk of owning the limo. If the company signs a financial lease, it is stuck with the limo for a long time. The financial lease is just another way of borrowing to pay for the asset.

Financial leases do offer special advantages to some firms in some circumstances. However, there is no point in discussing this further until you know how to value financial lease contracts.

CASH FLOWS OF A FINANCIAL LEASE

Jane Jones, president of Greenfield Construction, has to decide whether to lease or borrow to finance the acquisition of a new backhoe loader. Greenfield Construction builds residential housing in Busy Town and has always owned its construction equipment. Jane is now reconsidering this policy. The new backhoe loader costs $100,000 and will last seven years before going to the scrap yard. The net present value of purchasing the backhoe is positive, convincing Jane that the investment in the additional equipment is worthwhile. The equipment manufacturer is willing to lease the backhoe to Greenfield for seven annual payments of $18,500, payable at the start of each year. Greenfield would remain responsible for all maintenance, insurance, and operating expenses.

Table 17.1 shows the direct cash flow consequences of signing the lease contract rather than purchasing the backhoe. (An important indirect effect is considered later.) The consequences are:

1. Greenfield does not have to pay for the backhoe. This is equivalent to a cash inflow of $100,000.
2. Greenfield would not own the backhoe, and so it cannot claim any CCA. Therefore it gives up a valuable CCA tax shield. Calculation of the tax shield is shown in Table 17.1. We assume that the backhoe is a Class 38 asset with a 30 percent CCA rate. To simplify the calculations, we assume that Greenfield is able to hold this asset alone in its own asset pool. After seven years of operation, the backhoe is scrapped and a terminal loss equal to the remaining undepreciated capital cost is taken.[7]
3. Greenfield must pay $18,500 per year for seven years to the lessor. The first payment is due immediately.
4. However, these lease payments are fully tax-deductible. At a 35 percent marginal tax rate, each lease payment generates an annual tax shield of .35 × $18,500, or $6,475. The after-tax lease payment is $18,500 − $6,475, or $12,025. This can also be calculated as: lease payment × (1 − tax rate).

TABLE 17.1 Cash flow consequences to Greenfield Construction by accepting the lease contract rather than purchasing the backhoe loader (figures in dollars; some columns may not add up due to rounding).

	Year							
Lease Cash Flows	0	1	2	3	4	5	6	7
Saved cost of a new backhoe loader	+100,000							
Lost CCA tax shield (calculated below)	− 5,250	− 8,925	− 6,248	− 4,373	− 3,061	− 2,143	− 1,500	−3,500
Lease payment	− 18,500	−18,500	−18,500	−18,500	−18,500	−18,500	−18,500	
Lease payment tax shield	+ 6,475	+ 6,475	+ 6,475	+ 6,475	+ 6,475	+ 6,475	+ 6,475	
Cash flow of lease	82,725	−20,950	−18,273	−16,398	−15,086	−14,168	−13,525	−3,500
Tax Shield Calculation								
UCC	100,000	85,000	59,500	41,650	29,155	20,409	14,286	10,000
CCA (CCA rate = 30%)*	15,000	25,500	17,850	12,495	8,747	6,123	4,286	
CCA tax shield (tax rate = 35%)†	5,250	8,925	6,248	4,373	3,061	2,143	1,500	3,500

*The half-year rule is in effect. See Chapter 9 for details.
†At the very end of year 7 the backhoe is scrapped, generating a terminal loss of $10,000, equal to the undepreciated capital cost. The terminal loss creates a tax savings of .35 × $10,000, or $3,500.

[7] This assumption allows us to ignore any tax saving from CCA beyond year 7. See Example 17.4 for the case where the asset pool is not closed.

In Table 17.1, the first CCA deduction occurs at year 0, because we assume that the backhoe is purchased at the end of year 0.[8] The table also assumes that the backhoe will be worthless when it goes to the scrap yard at the end of year 7. Otherwise, there would be an entry for salvage value lost, and the undepreciated capital cost would have been reduced by the salvage value before we took the terminal loss.

Check Point 17.1

Suppose the backhoe loader costs $85,000, has zero-expected salvage value, and the annual lease payments are $15,000, payable in advance. If the lease is for seven years, what are Greenfield's after-tax cash flows from leasing, rather than buying the backhoe, assuming everything else is unchanged?

WHO REALLY OWNS THE LEASED ASSET?

To a lawyer or a tax accountant, that would be a silly question. The lessor is clearly the legal owner. That is why the lessor is allowed to deduct depreciation from taxable income.

From an *economic* point of view, you might say that the *user* is the real owner, because in a *financial* lease, the user faces the risks and receives the rewards of ownership. Greenfield cannot cancel a financial lease. If the new backhoe turns out be hopelessly expensive and unsuited for Greenfield, that is Greenfield's problem, not the lessor's. If it turns out to be a great success, the profit goes to Greenfield, not the lessor. The success or failure of the firm's business operations does not depend on whether the backhoes are financed by leasing or some other financial instrument.

In many respects, a financial lease is equivalent to a secured loan. The lessee must make a series of fixed payments; if the lessee fails to do so, the lessor can repossess the asset. Thus we can think of a balance sheet like this:

Greenfield Construction ($000s)

Backhoe loader	100	100	Loan secured by backhoe loader
All other assets	1,000	450	Other loans
	____	550	Equity
Total assets	1,100	1,100	Total liabilities

as economically equivalent to a balance sheet like this:

Greenfield Construction ($000s)

Backhoe loader	100	100	Financial lease
All other assets	1,000	450	Other loans
	____	550	Equity
Total assets	1,100	1,100	Total liabilities

Having said this, we must immediately add two qualifications. First, legal ownership can make a big difference when a financial lease expires because the lessor gets the salvage value of the asset. Once a secured loan is paid off, the user owns the asset free and clear.

[8] In Chapter 9, the first CCA deduction always occurred in year 1 because we implicitly assumed that the asset was purchased in year 1. However, it is only an assumption—the asset could have been purchased at the end of year 0 and the first CCA deduction taken in year 0. In practice, a company will think about the tax consequences of the timing of significant asset purchases.

Second, whether you are a lessor or a secured creditor makes a difference in bankruptcy or reorganization. When a lessee fails to make a lease payment, the lessor is entitled to take back its asset. However, what if the value of that asset is much less than the present value of the future lease payments the lessee had promised to pay? The lessor loses. The lessor can try to recover its loss from the firm but the lessor is only an unsecured creditor.

By contrast, if the firm defaults on a secured lender, the secured lender is entitled to receive the full amount of the principal and unpaid interest, secured by the asset. In default, the lender can sell the asset to recover the full amount owed. If this asset is worth less than the amount the lender is owed, the lender is entitled to make a claim for the full amount of the difference. This claim has priority over the unsecured lenders of the firm.

Of course, neither the lessor nor the secured lender can be sure it will be paid the full amount owed. Our point is that lessors and secured creditors have different rights if the asset user gets into financial trouble.

LEASING AND THE CANADA REVENUE AGENCY (CRA)

We have already noted that the lessee loses the capital cost allowance (CCA) of the leased asset but can deduct the lease payment in full. The *lessor*, as legal owner, uses the CCA tax shield but must report the lease payments as taxable rental income.

However, the Canada Revenue Agency (CRA) is suspicious by nature and will not allow the lessee to deduct the entire lease payment unless it is satisfied the arrangement is a genuine lease and not a disguised instalment purchase or secured loan agreement. Here are examples of lease provisions that will arouse its suspicion:[9]

1. The lessee is given the option to acquire the asset, say for $1, when the lease expires. Such a provision would effectively give the asset's salvage value to the lessee.
2. The lessee automatically acquires title to the property after payment of a specified amount in lease payments.
3. The lessee is required to buy the asset at the end of lease contract.

FIRST PASS AT VALUING A FINANCIAL LEASE CONTRACT

When we left Jane Jones, president of Greenfield Construction, she was thinking about leasing rather than buying the required new backhoe loader. She had set down in Table 17.1 the incremental cash flows from leasing the backhoe rather than purchasing it. To recap, by leasing and not purchasing the equipment, Greenfield does not pay up front for the backhoe. However, in each of the subsequent years, the lease payments must be made and the CCA tax shields are forgone. If leasing is preferred to purchasing, the net present value of these lease cash flows must be positive. In other words, the cash saved up front must be greater than the present value of the future cash outflows required to service the lease obligation. If the NPV is negative, Greenfield pays out more in future cash flows than the cash saved initially. In this case, shareholders of Greenfield are worse off by leasing than purchasing the backhoe.

What is the appropriate discount rate to use in calculating the NPV of the lease? That depends on the nature of the risks of the cash flows. The lease cash flows are typically assumed to be about as safe as the interest and principal payments on a secured loan issued by the lessee. This assumption is reasonable for the lease payments because the lessor is effectively lending money to the lessee. But the various tax shields might carry enough risk to deserve a higher discount rate. For example, Greenfield might be confident that it could make the lease payments but not confident that it could earn enough taxable income to use these tax shields. In that case the cash flows generated by the tax shields would probably deserve a higher discount rate than the borrowing rate used for the lease payments.

[9] This list is based on information contained in *CRA Interpretation Bulletin* IT 233-R. However, this publication was cancelled in June 2001 because it was being misused. CRA stated that whether a contract is a lease or sale, it is based on the legal relationship created by the terms of the agreement.

A lessee might, in principle, end up using a separate discount rate for each line of Table 17.1, each rate chosen to fit the risk of that line's cash flow. But established, profitable firms usually find it reasonable to simplify by discounting the types of flows shown in Table 17.1 at a single rate based on the rate of interest the firm would pay if it borrowed rather than leased. We will assume Greenfield's borrowing rate is 10 percent.

We have determined that the risk of the lease cash flows is equal to the risk of its secured debt. However, we have to make one further adjustment: the discount rate has to be the firm's *after-tax* cost of its secured debt, because we are valuing *after-tax* cash flows arising from the lease. Since Greenfield can borrow at 10 percent, we should discount the lease cash flows at $r_D(1 - T) = .10(1 - .35) = .065$, or 6.5 percent. This gives

$$\text{NPV lease} = 82{,}725 - \frac{20{,}950}{1.065} - \frac{18{,}273}{(1.065)^2} - \frac{16{,}398}{(1.065)^3} - \frac{15{,}086}{(1.065)^4} - \frac{14{,}168}{(1.065)^5} - \frac{13{,}525}{(1.065)^6} - \frac{3{,}500}{(1.065)^7} = -221, \text{ or } -\$221$$

Since the lease has a negative NPV, Greenfield is better off buying the backhoe.

Check Point 17.2 What is the NPV of the lease in Check Point 17.1? Assume that Greenfield can borrow at 10 percent, before tax.

A positive or negative NPV is not an abstract concept; in this case, Greenfield's shareholders are really \$221 poorer if the company leases. Let's now check how this situation comes about.

The lease cash outflows are contractual obligations like the principal and interest payments, or debt service, on secured debt. The cash inflow in year 0 of the lease is like the amount of money borrowed through the loan. This gives us another way to examine the attractiveness of the lease. Let's compare it to an **equivalent loan**, a loan with identical annual cash outflows as the lease.

equivalent loan Present value of the lease cash outflows, discounted at the after-tax cost of borrowing.

Suppose Jane went to the bank and asked, "How much would you lend me today if I promised to make the following after-tax loan payments?" (principal and interest):

Year	1	2	3	4	5	6	7
Payments	−20,950	−18,273	−16,398	−15,086	−14,168	−13,525	−3,500

Note that Greenfield's loan payments are identical to the lease cash flows shown in years 1 to 7 of Table 17.1. This equivalent loan would carry a 10 percent interest rate, Greenfield's borrowing rate. The bank would be willing to lend Jane an amount equal to the present value of the lease cash outflows, discounted at Greenfield's after-tax borrowing rate:

$$\begin{aligned}\text{Equivalent loan} &= \text{present value of lease cash outflows in years 1 to 7}\\ &= \frac{20{,}950}{1.065} + \frac{18{,}273}{(1.065)^2} + \frac{16{,}398}{(1.065)^3} + \frac{15{,}086}{(1.065)^4} + \frac{14{,}168}{(1.065)^5}\\ &\quad + \frac{13{,}525}{(1.065)^6} + \frac{3{,}500}{(1.065)^7} = 82{,}946, \text{ or } \$82{,}946\end{aligned}$$

Table 17.2 shows the details of a loan for \$82,946 at 10 percent interest rate with exactly the same annual cash outflows as the lease. At the end of each year, interest on the outstanding loan amount is paid. Also, Greenfield repays part of the loan principal to make that year's total loan payment equal to the lease cash flow the company would have paid had it leased the equipment. For example, at the end of the first year, Greenfield would need to pay interest of $.10 \times \$82{,}946$,

TABLE 17.2 Details of equivalent loan offered to Greenfield Construction (figures in dollars; some columns may not add up due to rounding).

	Year							
	0	1	2	3	4	5	6	7
Amount borrowed at year-end	82,946	67,388	53,495	40,574	28,125	15,785	3,286	0
Interest paid at 10%		− 8,295	− 6,739	− 5,350	− 4,057	− 2,813	− 1,579	− 329
Interest tax shield (35% tax rate)		2,903	2,359	1,872	1,420	984	552	115
Interest paid after tax*		− 5,391	− 4,380	− 3,477	− 2,637	− 1,828	− 1,026	− 214
Principal repaid		−15,559	−13,892	−12,921	−12,449	−12,340	−12,499	−3,286
Net cash flow of equivalent loan†	82,946	−20,950	−18,273	−16,398	−15,086	−14,168	−13,525	−3,500

*Interest paid after tax = interest paid + interest tax shield.
†Net cash flow of equivalent loan = interest paid after tax + principal repaid.

or \$8,295. Greenfield would receive a tax shield on this interest of .35 × 8,295, or \$2,903. In other words, its after-tax interest expense is \$8,295 − \$2,903, or \$5,391. Greenfield could then repay \$15,559 of the loan principal, giving a net cash outflow of \$5,391 + \$15,559 = \$20,950, exactly the same as the cash outflow in the first year of the lease. The loan amount outstanding at the start of year 2 is now the original amount borrowed less the principal repaid in year 1, \$82,946 − \$15,559, or \$67,387. We repeat the calculation of interest owed and pay down the principal of the loan such that the total cash outflow in year 2 is \$18,273, exactly equal to year 2's lease cash flow.

Check Point 17.3

Look again at Table 17.2. Explain the calculations for the equivalent loan payments made in year 2.

Check Point 17.4

The bank receives interest before Greenfield pays tax. What is the present value of the cash flows received by the bank, discounting the cash flows at the required 10 percent? Does it equal the equivalent loan amount of \$82,946?

As you walk through the calculations in Table 17.2, you see that it costs exactly the same to service a loan that brings an immediate cash flow of \$82,946 as it does to service the lease, which brings in only \$82,725. The lease is not as attractive as the loan. The difference between the cash inflow of the lease and cash inflow of an equivalent loan equals the net present value of the lease: \$82,725 − \$82,946 = −\$221. If Greenfield leases the backhoe rather than raising an equivalent loan,[10] there will be \$221 less in Greenfield's bank account.

Our example illustrates two general points about leases and equivalent loans. First, if you can devise a borrowing plan that gives the same cash flow as the lease in every future period but a higher immediate cash flow, then you should not lease. If, however, the equivalent loan results in the same future cash outflows as the lease but a lower immediate inflow, then leasing is the better choice.

[10] When we compare the lease to its equivalent loan, we do not mean to imply that the backhoe alone could support all of the loan. Some part of the loan would be supported by Greenfield's other assets. Some part of the lease would likewise be supported by the other assets.

Second, our example suggests two ways to value a lease:

1. *Hard way.* Construct a table like Table 17.2 showing the equivalent loan.
2. *Easy way.* Discount the lease cash flows at the after-tax interest rate that the firm would pay on an equivalent loan. Both methods give the same answer—in our case an NPV of −\$221.

FINANCIAL LEASE EVALUATION

We concluded that the lease contract offered to Greenfield Construction was not attractive because the lease provided \$221 less financing than the equivalent loan. The underlying principle is as follows: A financial lease is superior to buying and borrowing if the financing provided by the lease exceeds the financing generated by the equivalent loan.

The principle implies this formula:

$$\text{Net value of lease} = \text{initial financing provided} - \text{value of equivalent loan}$$

Initial financing provided equals the cost of the leased asset minus any immediate lease payment or other cash outflow attributable to the lease.

Notice that the value of the lease is its incremental value relative to borrowing via an equivalent loan. A positive lease value means that *if* you acquire the asset, lease financing is advantageous. It does not prove you should acquire the asset.

However, sometimes favourable lease terms rescue a capital investment project. Suppose that Greenfield had decided *against* buying a new backhoe because the NPV of the \$100,000 investment was −\$5,000 assuming normal financing. The equipment manufacturer could rescue the deal by offering a lease with a value of, say, +\$8,000. By offering such a lease, the manufacturer would in effect cut the price of the backhoe to \$92,000, giving the backhoe-lease package a positive value to Greenfield. The total NPV of acquiring the backhoe is the sum of the NPV of the investment in a new backhoe, assuming normal financing, plus the NPV of the lease:

$$\begin{aligned}\text{NPV of backhoe investment} + \text{lease financing} &= \text{NPV of project} + \text{NPV of lease}\\ &= -5{,}000 + 8{,}000 = +\$3{,}000\end{aligned}$$

Notice also that this approach applies to *net* financial leases. Any insurance, maintenance, and other operating costs picked up by the lessor have to be evaluated separately and added to the value of the lease. If the asset has salvage value at the end of the lease, that value should be taken into account also.

USING FORMULAS TO EVALUATE FINANCIAL LEASES

In Table 17.1 we laid out all of the incremental cash flows for each year, added them up, and calculated the present value of those annual cash flows to determine the net present value of leasing rather than buying the asset. Alternatively, the lease value can be calculated using formulas for each cash-flow stream, taking advantage of the annuity formulas and the CCA tax shield formulas. Following this approach, the lease NPV is

$$\begin{aligned}\textbf{NPV}_{\textbf{lease}} = \ &\textbf{cost of leased asset} - \textbf{PV(after-tax lease payments)}\\ &- \textbf{PV(CCA tax shield)} - \textbf{PV(salvage value)}\\ &+ \textbf{PV(saved maintenance costs, if any)}\end{aligned} \tag{17.1}$$

Be sure to use the annuity formula that matches the timing of the cash flows. Following the notation in Chapter 5, the expression PVAD(r, t) represents the present value of \$1 paid at the beginning of each period (an *annuity due*), for t periods, when the discount rate is r. The deferred annuity formula, for cash flows at the end of each period, is represented as PVA(r, t). If done correctly, the lease value is the same whether you sum up the present value of each year's cash flows or calculate the present value of the different types of payments and then add them up.

In Example 17.3, we use present value formulas to calculate the value of several changes to the lease under consideration at Greenfield Construction. Example 17.4 illustrates the use of the formula approach to calculate the net present value of a lease.

EXAMPLE 17.3 LEASE VARIATIONS: A NET FINANCIAL LEASE AND ASSET SALVAGE VALUE

The backhoe manufacturer includes routine maintenance that would otherwise cost Greenfield \$2,000 per year after tax. Also, new information indicates that the backhoe will probably be worth \$10,000 after seven years, rather than nothing. The value of the lease increases by the present value of the maintenance savings and decreases by the present value of the lost salvage value. In addition, the lost tax savings from giving up the terminal loss (or future CCA) will also be lower if the machine has a positive salvage value.

Maintenance and salvage value are harder to predict than the cash flows shown in Table 17.1, and so they normally deserve a higher discount rate. Suppose that Ms. Jones uses 12 percent, the project's (after-tax) discount rate. The maintenance expenses are paid at the end of each year and the salvage value is measured at the end of year 7. Recognizing that the maintenance savings are a seven-year deferred annuity, the present value of the maintenance savings are

$$\$2{,}000 \times \text{PVA}(12\%,7) = \$2{,}000\left[\frac{1}{.12} - \frac{1}{.12(1.12)^7}\right] = \$9{,}128$$

The lost salvage is worth $\$10{,}000/(1.12)^7$, or \$4,523. If Greenfield owned the backhoe, the salvage value would also be subtracted from the asset pool and any balance remaining would be taken as a terminal loss (assuming that the asset pool is closed). From Table 17.1, you see that at the end of year 7, the backhoe's undepreciated capital cost was \$10,000. Once the asset is sold, the asset pool is empty and there is no terminal loss. Originally, when salvage value was assumed to be 0, there was a tax shield from the terminal loss worth \$3,500 (.35 × \$10,000) and it had a present value of $\$3{,}500/(1.065)^7$, or \$2,252. By leasing, Greenfield gave up the tax savings from this terminal loss. Now, with the \$10,000 salvage value, there is no terminal loss and no lost tax savings.

The original lease was worth −\$221. We add the value of the maintenance to be provided by the lessor, \$9,128, but subtract the salvage value given up by not owning the backhoe, \$4,523. We also add back the tax savings from the terminal loss originally expected when the salvage value was zero, \$2,252. The revised value is therefore −\$221 + \$9,128 − \$4,523 + \$2,252 = \$6,636. Now the lease looks like a good deal.

EXAMPLE 17.4 EVALUATING A LEASE USING FORMULAS

Food Express, a grocery chain, needs new electronic cash registers. The cost to purchase them is \$150,000. They will last four years and be scrapped with zero value. The allowable CCA is 30 percent and the company has many assets of this type. Thus, if Food Express buys the cash registers, the asset pool will not be closed when the cash registers are scrapped. If it buys the equipment, the CCA tax savings will start at the end of the first year. The equipment manufacturer is offering to lease the cash registers for \$42,000 a year, payable in advance. The tax rate is 35 percent and the company's cost of borrowing is 8 percent, giving an after-tax cost of debt of .08(1 − .35) = .052. Should it lease or buy the cash registers? Determine the value of each component in equation 17.1:

$$\text{Cost of leased asset} = \$150{,}000$$

$$\begin{aligned}\text{PV(after-tax lease payments)} &= \text{annual lease payment} \times (1 - \text{tax rate}) \times \text{PVAD}(r, t)\\ &= \$42{,}000 \times (1 - .35) \times \text{PVAD}(.052,4)\\ &= \$27{,}300\left[1 + \frac{1}{.052} - \frac{1}{.052(1.052)^3}\right] = \$27{,}300 \times 3.7131 = \$101{,}368\end{aligned}$$

(Continued)

(Concluded)

Since the Chapter 9 formulas for calculating CCA tax shields are based on the assumption that the first CCA tax saving occurs at the *end* of the first year, we use one of them to calculate the lost CCA tax shield. With zero salvage value and an asset pool that does not close, we can use equation 8.1 from Chapter 8 to calculate the present value of the CCA tax savings:

$$\text{PV(CCA tax shield)} = \frac{\text{asset cost} \times \text{CCA rate} \times \text{tax rate}}{\text{CCA rate} + \text{interest rate}}\left[\frac{1 + .5 \times \text{interest rate}}{1 + \text{interest rate}}\right]$$

$$= \frac{\$150{,}000 \times .3 \times .35}{.3 + .052}\left[\frac{1 + .5 \times .052}{1 + .052}\right] = \$43{,}638$$

The net present value of leasing rather than buying the cash registers is:

$$\text{NPV}_{\text{lease}} = \$150{,}000 - \$101{,}368 - \$43{,}638 = \$4{,}994$$

The net present value of leasing rather than buying the cash registers is \$4,994. By leasing, Food Express will increase the company's value by \$4,994.

LO4 17.4 WHEN DO FINANCIAL LEASES PAY?

We have examined the value of a lease from the viewpoint of the lessee. However, the lessor's criterion is simply the reverse. As long as lessor and lessee are in the same tax bracket, every cash outflow to the lessee is an inflow to the lessor, and vice versa. In our numerical example, the backhoe manufacturer would project cash flows in a table like Table 17.1, but with the signs reversed. The value of the lease to the backhoe manufacturer would be

$$\text{Value of lease to lessor} = -82{,}725 + \frac{20{,}950}{1.065} + \frac{18{,}273}{(1.065)^2} + \frac{16{,}398}{(1.065)^3} + \frac{15{,}086}{(1.065)^4}$$
$$+ \frac{14{,}168}{(1.065)^5} + \frac{13{,}525}{(1.065)^6} + \frac{3{,}500}{(1.065)^7}$$
$$= +221, \text{ or } \$221$$

In this case, the values to lessee and lessor offset exactly. The lessor can win only at the lessee's expense.

But both lessee and lessor can win if their tax rates differ. Suppose that Greenfield paid no tax ($T_C = 0$). Then the only cash flows of the equipment lease would be

Year	0	1	2	3	4	5	6
Cost of new backhoe	+100,000						
Lease payment	−18,500	−18,500	−18,500	−18,500	−18,500	−18,500	−18,500

These flows would be discounted at 10 percent, because $r_D(1 - T_C) = r_D$ when $T_C = 0$. The value of the lease is

$$\text{Value of lease} = +100{,}000 - 18{,}500 \times \text{PVAD}(10\%,7)$$
$$= +100{,}000 - 18{,}500\left[1 + \frac{1}{.1} - \frac{1}{.1(1.1)^6}\right] = 928, \text{ or } \$928$$

In this case there is a net gain of \$221 to the lessor (who has the 35 percent tax rate) *and* a net gain of \$928 to the lessee (who pays zero tax). This mutual gain is at the expense of the government. On one hand, the government gains from the lease contract because it can tax the lease payments. On the other hand, the contract allows the lessor to take advantage of CCA and interest tax shields that are of no use to the lessee. However, because the CCA is accelerated and the interest rate is positive, the government suffers a net loss in the present value of its tax receipts as a result of the lease.

Now you should begin to understand the circumstances in which the government incurs a loss on the lease and the other two parties gain. Other things being equal, the potential gains to lessor and lessee are highest when

- The lessor's tax rate is substantially higher than the lessee's.
- The CCA tax shield is received early in the lease period.
- The lease period is long and the lease payments are concentrated toward the end of the period.
- The interest rate, r_D, is high; if it were zero, there would be no advantage in present value terms to postponing tax.

17.5 SUMMARY

1. **What is a lease? LO1**

A lease is just an extended rental agreement. The owner of the equipment (the **lessor**) allows the user (the **lessee**) to operate the equipment in exchange for regular lease payments.

There is a wide variety of possible arrangements. Short-term, cancellable leases are known as **operating leases**. In these leases the lessor bears the risks of ownership. Long-term, non-cancellable leases are called full-payout, **financial**, or capital leases. In these leases the lessee bears the risks. Financial leases are **sources of financing** for assets the firm wishes to acquire and use for an extended period.

Many vehicle or office equipment leases include insurance and maintenance. They are full-service leases. If the lessee is responsible for insurance and maintenance, the lease is a net lease.

Frequently the lessor acquires the asset directly from the manufacturer. This is a direct lease. Sometimes the lessor acquires the asset from the user and then leases it back to the user. This is a sale and lease-back.

2. **How do you value an operating lease? LO2, LO3**

Operating leases are attractive to equipment users if the lease payment is less than the user's equivalent annual cost of buying the equipment. Operating leases make sense when the user needs the equipment only for a short time, when the lessor is better able to bear the risks of obsolescence, or when the lessor can offer a good deal on maintenance. Remember too that operating leases often have valuable options attached.

3. **How do you value a financial lease? LO2, LO3**

A financial lease extends over most of the economic life of the leased asset and cannot be cancelled by the lessee. Signing a financial lease is like signing a secured loan to finance purchase of the leased asset. With financial leases, the choice is not "lease versus buy" but "lease versus borrow."

Many companies have sound reasons for financing via leases. For example, companies that are not paying taxes can usually strike a favourable deal with a tax-paying lessor. Also, it may be less costly and time consuming to sign a standardized lease contract than to negotiate a long-term secured loan.

When a firm borrows money, it pays the after-tax rate of interest on its debt. Therefore, the opportunity cost of lease financing is the after-tax rate of interest on the firm's bonds. To value a financial lease, we need to discount the incremental cash flows from leasing by the after-tax interest rate.

An equivalent loan is one that commits the firm to exactly the same future cash flow as a financial lease. When we calculate the net present value of the lease, we are measuring the difference between the amount of financing provided by the lease and the financing provided by the equivalent loan:

$$\text{Net present value of lease} = \text{financing provided by lease} - \text{value of equivalent loan}$$

4. What are the implications of tax rates on the gains from leasing to the lessor and lessee? LO4

We can also analyze leases from the lessor's side of the transaction using the same approaches we developed for the lessee. If lessee and lessor are in the same tax bracket, they will receive exactly the same cash flows but with signs reversed. Thus, the lessee can gain only at the lessor's expense, and vice versa. However, if the lessee's tax rate is lower than the lessor's, then both can gain at the government's expense.

Related Web Links

cfla-acfl.ca The Web site of the Canadian Finance and Leasing Association

executivecaliber.ws/sys-tmpl/door Lots of information on leasing, especially U.S. accounting issues

leasingcanada.com Information on leasing in Canada

gecapitalsolutions.ca/en/product/asset.asp Major Canadian equipment lessor

Key Terms

equivalent loan	572	lessee	561	operating lease	561
financial lease	562	lessor	561		
lease	561	off-balance-sheet financing	564		

Questions and Problems

connect Practise and learn online with *Connect*. Questions with online Excel templates or datasets are marked with .

*Answers in Appendix B

BASIC

1. **Lease Terms.** The following terms are often used to describe leases: (LO1)
   i. Direct
   ii. Full-service
   iii. Operating
   iv. Financial
   v. Rental
   vi. Net
   vii. Leveraged
   viii. Sale and lease-back
   ix. Full-payout

   Match one or more of these terms with each of the following statements:
   a. The initial lease period is shorter than the economic life of the asset.
   b. The initial lease period is long enough for the lessor to recover the cost of the asset.
   c. The lessor provides maintenance and insurance.
   d. The lessee provides maintenance and insurance.
   e. The lessor buys the equipment from the manufacturer.
   f. The lessor buys the equipment from the prospective lessee.
   g. The lessor finances the lease contract by issuing debt and equity claims against it.

*2. **Why Lease?** Some of the following reasons for leasing are rational. Others are irrational or assume imperfect or inefficient capital markets. Which of the following reasons are the rational ones? (LO1)
   a. The lessee's need for the leased asset is only temporary.
   b. Specialized lessors are better able to bear the risk of obsolescence.
   c. Leasing provides 100 percent financing and thus preserves capital.
   d. Leasing allows firms with low tax rates to "sell" CCA tax shields.
   e. Leasing increases earnings per share.
   f. Leasing reduces the transaction cost of obtaining external financing.
   g. Leasing avoids restrictions on capital expenditures.

3. **Reasons to Lease.** True or False? Explain your answers. (LO1)
   a. It makes sense to enter into an operating lease if you are sure that you want to keep the asset for a long time.
   b. Leasing is advantageous because it provides a company with off-balance-sheet financing, allowing it to hide its financial obligations.
4. **Understanding Leases.** True or false? (LO1)
   a. Lease payments are usually made at the start of each period. Thus the first payment is usually made as soon as the lease contract is signed.
   b. Financial leases can still provide off-balance-sheet financing.
   c. The cost of capital for a financial lease is the interest rate the company would pay on a bank loan.
   d. An equivalent loan's principal plus after-tax interest payments exactly match the after-tax cash flows of the lease.
   e. A financial lease should not be undertaken unless it provides more financing than the equivalent loan.
   f. It makes sense for firms that pay no taxes to lease from firms that do.
   g. Other things being equal, the net tax advantage of leasing increases as nominal interest rates increase.

*5. **Lease Valuation.** Suppose that National Waferonics has before it a proposal for a four-year financial lease. The firm constructs a table like Table 17.1. The bottom line of its table shows the lease cash flows:

Year	0	1	2	3
Lease cash flow	+62,000	−26,800	−22,200	−17,600

These flows reflect the cost of the machine, CCA tax shields, and the after-tax lease payments. Ignore salvage value. Assume the firm could borrow at 10 percent and faces a 30 percent marginal tax rate. (LO2, LO3)
   a. What is the value of the equivalent loan?
   b. What is the value of the lease?
   c. Suppose the machine's NPV under normal financing is −$5,000. Should National Waferonics invest? Should it sign the lease?

INTERMEDIATE

6. **Lease as Financing.** A lessee does not have to pay to buy the leased asset. Thus it's said that "leases provide 100 percent financing." Explain why this is not a true advantage to the lessee. (LO1)

*7. **Lease Valuation.** ABC Brickworks proposes to lease a $75,000 forklift. Five annual lease payments of $15,000 are due in advance. ABC's tax rate is 35 percent. If it purchases the forklift, it will be in its own 25 percent CCA class. The half-year rule applies, the first CCA tax deduction is taken in year 0 and after five years, the forklift will be worthless. The interest rate is 9 percent. (LO2, LO3)
   a. Using Table 17.1 as a guide, determine the cash flows of leasing rather than purchasing the forklift.
   b. What are the equivalent loan and NPV of the lease?
   c. If the forklift is expected to have a $10,000 salvage value after 5 years and the project's discount rate is 12 percent, what is the NPV of the lease?

8. **Lease Valuation.** Printing World thinks it may need a new colour printing press. The press will cost $500,000 but will substantially reduce annual operating costs by $215,000 a year, before tax. The press has a 30 percent CCA rate and will be in its own asset pool. The first CCA deduction is made in year 0. The press will operate for 4 years and then be worthless. The cost of equity for Printing World is 12 percent, the cost of debt is 8 percent, and the company's target debt-equity ratio is .5. The company's tax rate is 30 percent. (LO2, LO3, LO4)
   a. What is the NPV of buying the press?
   b. The equipment manufacturer is offering to lease the press for $112,000 a year, for 4 years, payable in advance. Should Printing World accept the offer?

9. **Lease Valuation Using Formulas.** BigCo is considering leasing the new equipment that it requires, for $155,000 a year, payable in advance. The cost of the equipment is $900,000, has a CCA rate of 25 percent and will last for 6 years. The expected scrap value is $150,000. Assume that the first CCA tax deduction would be taken at the end of the first year. BigCo has lots of other equipment in this asset pool. The tax rate is 30 percent and the cost of debt is 7 percent. (LO2, LO3)
   a. Should BigCo lease or buy the equipment?
   b. What is the maximum lease payment that would make BigCo indifferent between leasing or buying?

10. **Lease Valuation.** Use the information in problem 9 to create a table similar to Table 17.1 and value the lease. Is it the same value found in problem 9? It should be! (LO2, LO3)

11. **Why Lease?** Why do you think that leasing of trucks, airplanes, and computers is such big business? What efficiencies offset the costs of running these leasing operations? (LO1)

12. **Operating Lease.** Financial leases make sense when the lessee faces a lower marginal tax rate than the lessor. Does this tax advantage carry over to operating leases? (LO2, LO3)

The following questions all apply to financial leases.

*13. **Lease Valuation.** Look again at the backhoe-loader lease described in Table 17.1 Consider each question separately. (LO2, LO3)

a. What is the value of the lease if Greenfield's tax rate is 20 percent?

b. What would the lease value be if Greenfield's first CCA deduction was taken at the end of year 1? Use the formula approach to calculate the value of leasing.

c. What would the lease value be if Greenfield had many other assets in the equipment asset pool? In this case, the equipment asset pool would not be closed.

*14. **Setting Lease Payments.** In Section 17.4 we showed that the lease offered to Greenfield Construction had a positive NPV of $928 if Greenfield paid no tax and a +$221 NPV to a lessor paying 35 percent tax. (LO2, LO3)

a. What is the minimum lease payment the lessor could accept under these circumstances?

b. What is the maximum amount that Greenfield could pay?

15. **Gains from Leasing.** In Section 17.4 we listed four circumstances in which there are potential gains from leasing. Check them out by conducting a sensitivity analysis on the Greenfield Construction lease, assuming that Greenfield does not pay tax. Try, in turn, (a) a lessor tax rate of 50 percent (rather than 35 percent), (b) a CCA rate of 35 percent rather than 30 percent, (c) a 4-year lease with four annual payments (rather than a 7-year lease), and (d) an interest rate of 20 percent (rather than 10 percent). In each case, find the minimum rental that would satisfy the lessor and calculate the NPV to the lessee. (LO2, LO3)

16. **Taxes and Leasing.** In Section 17.4 we stated that if the interest rate were zero, there would be no advantage in postponing tax and therefore no advantage in leasing. Value the Greenfield Construction lease with an interest rate of zero. Assume that Greenfield does not pay tax. Can you devise any lease terms that would make both a lessee and a lessor happy? (LO2, LO3, LO4)

*17. **Comprehensive.** Nodhead College needs a new computer. It can either buy it for $250,000 or lease it from Compulease. The lease terms require Nodhead to make six annual payments (prepaid) of $55,000. Nodhead pays no tax. Compulease pays tax at 35 percent. Compulease can depreciate the computer for tax purposes at a CCA rate of 30 percent, and will close the asset pool at the end of the 6th year. The computer will have no residual value at the end of year 5. The interest rate is 8 percent. (LO2, LO3, LO4)

a. What is the NPV of the lease for Nodhead College?

b. What is the NPV for Compulease?

c. What is the overall gain from leasing?

18. **Integrative.** The Safety Razor Company has a large tax-loss carryforward and does not expect to pay taxes for another 10 years. The company is therefore proposing to lease $100,000 of new machinery. The lease terms consist of eight equal lease payments prepaid annually. The lessor will take CCA on the machinery at a 30 percent rate and the pool will never close. The first CCA tax deduction is assumed to occur at the end of the first year. There is no salvage value at the end of the machinery's economic life. The tax rate is 35 percent, and the rate of interest is 10 percent. Wilbur Occam, the president of Safety Razor, wants to know the minimum lease payment that the lessor is likely to accept. Can you help him? (LO2, LO3, LO4)

19. **Lease Rate of Return.** A company can calculate the internal rate of return of the incremental after-tax cash flows from financial leases when evaluating a lease. Calculate the IRR of the lease cash flows in question 5. To what rate should this IRR be compared? How does a company decide whether to lease the assets when they calculate the lease rate of return? (LO2, LO3)

20. **Why Lease?** Discuss the following two opposite statements. Which do you think makes more sense? (LO1)

a. "Leasing is tax avoidance and should be legislated against."

b. "Leasing ensures that the government's investment incentives work. It does so by allowing companies in non-tax-paying positions to take advantage of CCA deductions."

21. **Internet.** Visit GE Capital's Asset Seller Web site, **www.geasset.com** to see off-lease assets for sale. Pick two asset categories, select five items, and compare the average asking prices. (LO1)

CHALLENGE

22. **Comprehensive.** Magna Charter has been asked to operate a Beaver bush plane for a mining company exploring in Yukon. Magna will have a one-year contract with the mining company and expects that the contract will be renewed after 1 year, for the remaining 4 years of the exploration program. If the mining company renews after 1 year, it will commit to use the plane for 4 more years. (LO2, LO3, LO4)

Magna Charter has the following choices:

- Buy the plane for $500,000
- Arrange a 5-year, non-cancellable, net financial lease at a rate of $75,000 per year, paid in advance

How would you advise Agnes Magna, the charter company's CEO? Assume that the CCA rate is 25 percent and Magna has many other airplanes in its asset pool. The first CCA deduction is made at the end of the first year. The company's tax rate is 35 percent. The weighted-average cost of capital for the bush plane business is 14 percent, but Magna can borrow at 9 percent.

Ms. Magna thinks the plane will be worth $300,000 after 5 years. She also thinks that there is a 20 percent chance that the contract will not be renewed at year 1. If the contract is not renewed, the plane will have to be sold on short notice for $400,000.

If Magna Charters takes the 5-year financial lease and the mining company cancels at year 1, Magna can sublet the plane, that is, rent it out to another user.

Make additional assumptions as necessary.

23. **Lease NPV.** Recalculate the value of the lease to Greenfield Construction if the company pays no taxes until year 3. Calculate the lease cash flows by modifying Table 17.1. Remember that the after-tax borrowing rate for years 1 and 2 differs from the rate for years 3 through 7. (LO2, LO3)

24. **Internet.** Retrieve the most recent annual reports of Walmart and Abercrombie & Fitch from their Web sites. Compare the leverage ratios of two retailers for the past two years. Can you guess which company relies more heavily on operating leases? Look carefully in the notes to the financial statements. Why are operating leases relatively more important to one of the companies? (LO1)

25. **Internet.** Canadian Capital Leasing's Web site at **www.leasingcanada.com** has information about leasing in Canada. Click on "LeaseGuide" and then on "Your Guide to Leasing Terms." Identify the terms that deal with the possibility of terminating (or not terminating) a lease. Likewise, identify the various ways the asset can be disposed of at the end of lease. (LO1)

26. **Internet.** In the same Web site as for problem 25, click on "Leasing for Business," and read the arguments about why businesses should consider leasing. What do you think about the arguments? (LO1)

27. **Internet.** The "Lease or Buy Calculator" at **www.canadabusiness.ca/eng/page/calc**, the Web site of *Canada Business*, shows the cash flows of a lease versus a loan. This calculator assumes that the asset pool is not closed at the end of the lease. A neat feature of this calculator is that it allows you to look up the CCA rate for the asset you are purchasing. Suppose the lease is for a $100,000 Class 38 asset that will have zero salvage value and last for 3 years. The company's tax rate is 40 percent and the cost of debt is 10 percent. If the loan is also three years, can you figure out what the monthly lease payment must be to be indifferent between borrowing and leasing? See if you can figure out the numbers the calculator produces. (LO2, LO3)

Solutions to Check Points

17.1 The lease cash flows are in Table 17.3.

17.2

$$\text{NVP lease} = 70{,}787 - \frac{17{,}336}{1.065} - \frac{15{,}060}{(1.065)^2} - \frac{13{,}467}{(1.065)^3} - \frac{12{,}352}{(1.065)^4} - \frac{11{,}571}{(1.065)^5} - \frac{11{,}025}{(1.065)^6} - \frac{2{,}975}{(1.065)^7}$$

$$= \$2{,}565$$

17.3 Interest paid in year 2 is 10 percent of the amount borrowed during the year $.1 \times 67{,}388 = \$6{,}739$. However, Greenfield gets an interest tax shield of 35 percent of the interest paid, $.35 \times \$6{,}739 = \$2{,}359$, so the interest paid after tax is $\$6{,}739 - \$2{,}359 = \$4{,}380$. To match the year 2 lease cash outflow of $18,273, Greenfield can repay principal equal to $\$18{,}273 - \$4{,}380$, or $13,893. Due to rounding, this calculated principal repayment is a dollar less than the amount reported in Table 17.2—don't worry about it.

17.4 The cash flows received by the bank are the interest paid and the principal repayments. For example, in year 1 the bank is paid $\$8{,}295 + \$15{,}559 = \$23{,}854$. The present value of the cash flows received by the bank is

$$\frac{23{,}854}{1.1} + \frac{20{,}631}{(1.1)^2} + \frac{18{,}271}{(1.1)^3} + \frac{16{,}506}{(1.1)^4} + \frac{15{,}153}{(1.1)^5} + \frac{14{,}078}{(1.1)^6} + \frac{3{,}615}{(1.1)^7} = \$82{,}947$$

According to these numbers, the bank would be willing to lend $82,947 to Greenfield in return for receiving the interest and principal repayments. If the numbers in Table 17.2 had been reported with more decimal places, the present value of the cash flows to the bank would have equalled $82,946 exactly.

TABLE 17.3 Lease cash flows for Check Point 17.1.

Lease Cash Flows	Year 0	1	2	3	4	5	6	7
Saved cost of a new backhoe loader	+85,000							
Lost CCA tax shield (calculated below)	− 4,463	− 7,586	− 5,310	− 3,717	− 2,602	− 1,821	− 1,275	−2,975
Lease payment	−15,000	−15,000	−15,000	−15,000	−15,000	−15,000	−15,000	
Lease payment tax shield	+ 5,250	+ 5,250	+ 5,250	+ 5,250	+ 5,250	+ 5,250	+ 5,250	
Cash flow of lease	70,787	−17,336	−15,060	−13,467	−12,352	−11,571	−11,025	−2,975
Tax Shield Calculation								
UCC	85,000	72,250	50,575	35,403	24,782	17,347	12,143	8,500
CCA (CCA rate = 30%)	12,750	21,675	15,173	10,621	7,435	5,204	3,643	
CCA tax shield (tax rate = 35%)	4,463	7,586	5,310	3,717	2,602	1,821	1,275	2,975

MINI CASE

Rachel Gold, a newly recruited financial analyst at Halverton Corporation, had just been asked to analyze a proposal to acquire a new dredger.

She reviewed the capital appropriation request. The dredger would cost $3.5 million and was expected to generate cash flows of $470,000 a year for 9 years. After that point, the dredger would almost surely be obsolete and have no significant salvage value. The company's weighted-average cost of capital was 16 percent.

Rachel proposed a standard DCF analysis, but this suggestion was brushed off by Halverton's top management. They seemed to be convinced of the merits of the investment but were unsure of the best ways to finance it. Halverton could raise the money by issuing a secured 8-year note at an interest rate of 12 percent. However, Halverton had large tax-loss carryforwards from a disastrous foray into foreign exchange options. As a result, the company was unlikely to be in a tax-paying position for many years. Halverton's CEO thought it might be better to lease the dredger rather than to buy it.

Rachel's first step was to invite two leasing companies, Mount Zircon Finance and First Cookham Bank, to submit proposals. Both companies were in a tax-paying position and could claim CCA on the dredger. The dredger is a Class 38 asset with a 30 percent CCA rate.

Rachel received the following letters, the first from Mount Zircon Finance:

March 31, 2010

Dear Rachel,

We appreciated the opportunity to meet you the other day and to discuss the possibility of providing lease finance for your proposed new JLT4 dredger. As you know, Mount Zircon has extensive experience in this field, and because of our large volumes and low borrowing costs, we are able to offer very attractive terms.

We would envisage offering a 9-year lease with 10 annual payments of $550,000, with the initial lease payment due on entering into the lease contract. This is equivalent to a borrowing cost of 11.8 percent per annum (i.e., 10 payments of $550,000 paid at the beginning of each year discounted at 11.8 percent amounts to $3,500,000).

We hope that you agree with us that this is an attractive rate. It is well below your company's overall cost of capital. Our leasing proposal will cover the entire $3.5 million cost of the dredger, thereby preserving Halverton's capital for other uses. Leasing will also allow a very attractive return on equity from your company's acquisition of this new equipment.

This proposal is subject to a routine credit check and review of Halverton's financial statements. We expect no difficulties on that score, but you will understand the need for due diligence.

Thank you for contacting Mount Zircon Finance. We look forward to hearing your response.

Sincerely yours,

Henry Attinger
For and on behalf of Mount Zircon Finance

The next letter was from First Cookham.

March 31, 2010

Dear Rachel,

It was an honour to meet you the other day and to discuss how First Cookham Bank can help your company to finance its new dredger. First Cookham has a small specialized leasing operation. This enables us to tailor our proposals to our clients' needs.

We recommend that Halverton consider leasing the dredger on a 7-year term. Subject to documentation and routine review of Halverton's financial statements, we could offer a 7-year lease on the basis of eight payments of $619,400 due at the beginning of each year. This is equivalent to a loan at an interest rate of 11.41 percent.

We expect that this lease payment will be higher than quoted by the large, mass-market leasing companies, but our financial analysts have determined that by offering a shorter lease, we can quote a lower interest rate.

We are confident that this is a highly competitive offer, and we look forward to your response.

Yours sincerely,

George Bucknall
First Cookham Bank

Both proposals looked attractive. However, Rachel realized the need to undertake careful calculations before deciding whether leasing made sense and which firm was offering the better deal. She also wondered whether the terms offered were really as attractive as the two lessors claimed. Perhaps she could persuade them to cut their prices.

PART 5

Debt and Payout Policy

16 Debt Policy
17 Leasing
18 Payout Policy
18.1 How Dividends Are Paid
18.2 Share Repurchase
18.3 How Do Companies Decide on How Much to Pay Out?
18.4 Why Payout Policy Should Not Matter
18.5 Why Dividends May Increase Firm Value
18.6 Why Dividends May Reduce Firm Value
18.7 Summary

CHAPTER 18

Payout Policy

LEARNING OBJECTIVES

After studying this chapter, you should be able to:

LO1 Describe how dividends are paid and how companies decide on dividend payments.

LO2 Explain how share repurchases are used to distribute cash to shareholders.

LO3 Explain why dividend increases and repurchases are good news for investors and why dividend cuts are bad news. Explain why payout policy would not affect firm value in an ideal world.

LO4 Show how differences in the tax treatment of dividends and capital gains might affect dividend policy.

LO5 Explain why dividends may be used by management to signal the prospects of the firm.

This investor is obviously delighted with his extra cash, but can companies increase share value simply by increasing their dividend payout?

Everett Collection.

In this chapter we explain how companies set their payout policy, and discuss the controversial question of how dividend policy affects value.

Shareholders invest in the company when they buy newly issued shares and when the company reinvests earnings on the shareholders' behalf. The shareholders do not usually demand a prompt cash return on their investment. Some long-established companies have never yet paid a cash dividend. Sooner or later, however, most corporations do pay out cash to their shareholders. They pay dividends, or they use cash to buy back previously issued shares.

How much should a company pay out in a given year? Should the payout come as dividends or share repurchases? The answers to these two questions are the corporation's *payout policy*.

We start the chapter with a discussion of how dividends are paid. We then show that in an ideal world, the value of a firm would be independent of its dividend policy. This demonstration is in the same spirit as the Modigliani and Miller debt-irrelevance proposition of Chapter 16.

That leads us to look at the real-world complications that might favour one dividend policy over another. These complications include transaction costs, taxes, and the signals that investors might read into the firm's payout announcement.

LO1 18.1 HOW DIVIDENDS ARE PAID

CASH DIVIDENDS

cash dividend Payment of cash by the firm to its shareholders.

On February 23, 2011, Maple Leaf Foods Inc. (MFI) announced a regular quarterly **cash dividend** of $.04 per share, making a total payment of $.16 for the year; soon after, its board of directors met and approved the decision. The term *regular* indicates that MFI expected to maintain the payment in the future. If it did not want to give that kind of assurance, it could have declared both a regular and an *extra dividend*. In July 2004, Microsoft did just that. The cash-rich software giant declared a whopping US$32 billion *special dividend*, because it could not find any other way to spend its sizeable cash flows. The company also declared a US$3.5 billion regular quarterly dividend and still had $20 billion cash on hand. Investors realize that extra dividends are less likely to be repeated.[1] The nearby Finance in Action box discusses the aftermath of a special dividend declared by another cash-rich company, George Weston.

Who receives the MFI dividend? That may seem an obvious question, but because shares trade constantly, the firm's records of who owns its shares can never be fully up to date. So MFI announced that it would send a dividend cheque to all shareholders recorded in its books on March 10, 2011. This is known as the *record date*.

[1] Companies also use the term "special dividend" for payments that are unlikely to be repeated.

Finance in Action

Special Dividend Drives Grocer George Weston Shares Up 5%

George Weston Ltd. (WN/ TSX) rose 5% to $83.36 at midday on the Toronto Stock Exchange after the company announced it will pay a special one-time dividend of $1-billion. That represents $7.74751 per common share, which will be paid on Jan. 25, 2011 to shareholders of record on Jan. 18, 2011.

Shares lost a sliver by the end of the day, closing at $82.86, up $3.48, or 4.4%.

"Capital markets have come through some very turbulent times and the corporation took a conservative position holding excess cash," said Chairman and President W. Galen Weston.

The company has two main divisions—bakery operations and Loblaw grocery stores.

Despite a number of companies looking to divest their frozen bakery operations, management at the food company is having difficulty finding attractive acquisitions at reasonable prices, says Robert Gibson, analyst at Octagon Capital. "Weston was getting a minimal amount of interest on its cash," he told clients. "Without the prospect of growth through acquisition, investors may start to discount Weston's cash."

Mr. Gibson maintained a "hold" rating on the stock and said his long-term price target will fall to $73.50 on Jan. 19, 2011 from $81.30 currently.

Source: Jonathan Ratner, "Special Dividend Drives Grocer George Weston Shares Up 5%," *National Post*, December 17, 2010, accessed at **www.financialpost.com/news/Special+dividend+drives+grocer+George+Weston+shares/3990795/story.html**. Material reprinted with the express permission of National Post, a division of Postmedia Network Inc.

The *payment date* for MFI's dividend was March 31. On that date the dividend cheques were mailed to investors. If MFI's records were not up to date, some of those cheques would be sent to the wrong investor. To handle this problem, stock exchanges fix a cut-off date, called the **ex-dividend date**, two business days prior to the record date. If you owned MFI stock on the *with-dividend date*, which in this case was March 7, you were entitled to the dividend. If MFI mistakenly sent that dividend to someone else, that person was obliged to pass it on to you. If you acquired the stock after March 7, you were not entitled to the dividend. If MFI sent you that dividend by mistake, you had to send it on to the previous owner.

ex-dividend date Date that determines whether a stockholder is entitled to a dividend payment; anyone holding stock before this date is entitled to a dividend.

Through March 7, MFI stock was said to be trading "with dividend" or "cum dividend." Beginning on March 8, the stock traded "ex dividend." The only difference between buying MFI before and after the ex-dividend date is that in the second case you miss out on the dividend. Other things being equal, the stock is worth more when it is with dividend. Thus when the stock "goes ex," we would expect the stock price to drop by the amount of the dividend.

Figure 18.1 illustrates the sequence of the key dividend dates. This sequence is the same whenever companies pay a dividend (though of course the actual dates will differ).

Some of MFI's shareholders may have desired the cash payment, but others preferred to reinvest the dividend in the company. To help these investors, MFI had an automatic dividend reinvestment plan. If a shareholder belonged to this plan, his or her dividends were automatically used to buy additional shares.[2]

FIGURE 18.1
The key dates for Maple Leaf Foods Inc. quarterly dividend.

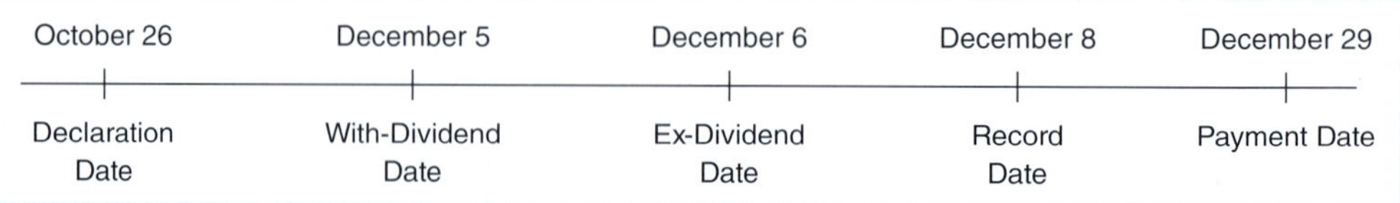

Note: Maple Leaf Foods' present dividend rate is $.16 per common share per annum paid in regular quarterly payments of $.04 per share. The above time line is for MFI's fourth-quarter payment of 2010.

Source: "FP Dividends," *Financial Post Online*, **www.fpinfomart.ca**, retrieved March 23, 2011. Material reprinted with the express permission of National Post, a division of Postmedia Network Inc.

[2] Often the new shares in an automatic dividend investment plan are issued at a small discount from the market price; the firm offers this sweetener because it saves the underwriting costs of a regular share issue. Sometimes 10 percent or more of total dividends will be reinvested under such plans.

Check Point 18.1 Mick Milekin buys 100 shares of Junk Bombs, Inc., on Tuesday, June 2. The company has declared a dividend of $1 per share payable on June 30 to shareholders on record as of Wednesday, June 3. If the ex-dividend date is June 1, is Mick entitled to the dividend? When will the cheques go out in the mail?

SOME LEGAL LIMITATIONS ON DIVIDENDS

Suppose that an unscrupulous board decided to sell all the firm's assets and distribute the money as dividends. That would not leave anything in the kitty to pay the company's debts. Therefore, bondholders often guard against this danger by placing limits on dividend payments.

Federal law under the *Canadian Business Corporations Act* as well as provincial acts may include provisions prohibiting firms from paying dividends under certain conditions. The intent of such provisions is to protect the firm's creditors against excessive dividend payments, which could push the firm toward insolvency. For example, payment of dividends could be prohibited if it results in the firm being unable to pay its liabilities when they become due, or if such liabilities exceed the firm's assets. Similarly, restrictions may be imposed when the dividend exceeds retained earnings, or when the dividend would be paid from the firm's invested capital.[3] Essentially, the spirit of such regulations is that dividends should be paid from retained earnings. Under certain conditions, firms are allowed to pay a "liquidating dividend." The laws give most corporations a large degree of flexibility in deciding what to pay out, but they help prevent unscrupulous managers from gutting the firm by paying out all its assets as dividends and then escaping creditors.

STOCK DIVIDENDS, STOCK SPLITS, AND REVERSE SPLITS

stock dividend Distribution of additional shares to a firm's shareholders.

stock split Issue of additional shares to firm's shareholders.

MFI's dividend was in the form of cash, but companies often declare **stock dividends**. For example, the firm could declare a stock dividend of 10 percent. In this case, it would send shareholders 1 additional share for every 10 currently owned. The Royal Bank of Canada declared a 100 percent stock dividend in 2006, doubling the number of common shares.

A stock dividend is very much like a **stock split**. In both cases the shareholder is given a fixed number of new shares for each share held. For example, in a two-for-one split, each investor would receive one additional share for each share already held. The investor ends up with two shares rather than one. For instance, a recent two-for-one stock split by Canadian Natural Resources Ltd. is therefore like a 100 percent stock dividend.[4] Both result in a doubling of the number of outstanding shares, but neither changes the total assets held by the firm. In both cases, therefore, we would expect the stock price to fall by half, leaving the total market value of the firm (price per share times shares outstanding) unchanged.[5]

More often than not, however, the announcement of a stock split does result in a rise in the market value of the firm, even though investors are aware that the company's assets and business are not affected. The reason: Investors take the decision to split as a signal of management's confidence in the company's propects.[6]

---

[3] Invested capital consists of part or all the receipts from the issue of shares.

[4] The Bank of Montreal's stock dividend effectively achieved a two-for-one stock split.

[5] One American survey of managers indicated that 93.7 percent of splits are motivated by the desire to bring the stock price into an acceptable "trading range." They seem to believe that if the price is too high, investors won't be able to afford to buy a "round lot" of 100 shares. Of course that might be a problem for you or us, but it isn't a worry for the Prudential or GM pension funds. See J. Lakonishok and B. Lev, "Stock Splits and Stock Dividends: Why, Who, and When," *Journal of Finance* 42 (September 1987): 913–932.

[6] The insight that stock splits provide a signal to investors was proposed in E.F. Fama, L. Fisher, M. Jensen, and R. Roll, "The Adjustment of Stock Prices to New Information," *International Economic Review* 10 (February 1969): 1–21. For evidence that companies that split their stock have above-average earnings prospects, see P. Asquith, P. Healy, and K. Palepu, "Earnings and Stock Splits," *Accounting Review* 64 (July 1989): 387–403.

EXAMPLE 18.1 **STOCK DIVIDENDS AND SPLITS**

Amoeba Products has issued two million shares currently selling at $15 each. Thus investors place a total market value on Amoeba of $30 million. The company now declares a 50 percent stock dividend. This means that each shareholder will receive one new share for every two shares currently held. So the total number of Amoeba shares will increase from two million to three million. The company's assets are not changed by this paper transaction and are still worth $30 million. The value of each share after the stock dividend is therefore $30/3 = $10.

If Amoeba split its stock three-for-two, the effect would be the same.[7] In this case two shares would split into three. (Amoeba's motto is "divide and conquer.") So each shareholder has 50 percent more shares with the same total value. Share price must decline by a third.

There are other types of noncash dividends. For example, companies sometimes send shareholders a sample of their product. The British company Dundee Crematorium once offered its more substantial shareholders a discount cremation. Needless to say, you were not *required* to receive this dividend.

reverse split Issue of new shares in exchange for old shares, which results in the reduction of outstanding shares.

Sometimes a firm may decide to opt for a **reverse split**, which would effectively reduce its number of outstanding shares. For instance, in a one-for-two reverse split, shareholders would exchange two existing shares for one new share. Reverse splits occur much more infrequently than stock splits. An important consideration in a reverse-split decision appears to be an expectation of the resultant increase in share price. A company may wish to achieve such a share price increase in order to maintain minimum price per share requirements of the stock exchange (or exchanges) listing its stock. Also, for a low-priced stock, bringing the share price up to a higher, more acceptable trading range could increase its market participation and improve its liquidity. A more dubious reason could be to ease out minority shareholders who may end up with less than a required minimum number of shares following the reverse split.

DIVIDEND REINVESTMENT PLANS AND SHARE PURCHASE PLANS

dividend reinvestment plan Enables shareholders to reinvest dividends into additional new shares.

share purchase plan Allows shareholders to make cash contributions toward the acquisition of new shares.

Nowadays many firms offer their shareholders additional means of investing in new shares through **dividend reinvestment plans** and **share purchase plans**. Shareholders have the choice of reinvesting their dividend receipts into additional shares of the firm through a *dividend reinvestment plan (DRIP)*. The reinvested proceeds may initially translate only into new fractional shares; however, those shareholders who continue to reinvest over a period of time could acquire sizeable amounts of new shares. Notice that DRIPs can be useful to firms looking for ways to finance valuable investment opportunities, which is why companies may sometimes offer discounts on the cost of acquiring additional shares through DRIPs. One should note that by investing through a DRIP, the shareholder does not necessarily get any tax advantage since reinvested amounts are treated on par with cash dividends for tax purposes and taxed as ordinary income. Firms also provide shareholders the choice of acquiring additional shares through *share purchase plans (SPP)* into which they can make cash contributions. By investing through DRIPs or SPPs, investors are able to save on brokerage costs. Also, costs associated with administering the plans are typically borne by the firms.

LO2 18.2 SHARE REPURCHASE

share repurchase Firm buys back stock from its shareholders.

When a firm wants to pay cash to its shareholders, it usually declares a cash dividend. But an alternative and increasingly popular method is for the firm to repurchase its own stock. In a **share repurchase**, the company pays cash to repurchase shares from its shareholders.

[7] The distinction between stock dividends and stock splits is a technical one. A stock dividend is shown on the balance sheet as a transfer from retained earnings to par value and additional paid-in capital, whereas a split is shown as a proportional reduction in the par value of each share. Neither affects the total book value of shareholders' equity.

There are four main ways to implement a stock repurchase.

1. *Open-market repurchase.* The firm announces that it plans to buy stock in the secondary market, just like any other investor. This is by far the most common method. There are limits on how many of its own shares a firm can purchase on a given day, so repurchases are spread out over several months or years.
2. *Tender offer.* The firm offers to buy back a stated number of shares at a fixed price. If enough shareholders accept the offer, the deal is done.
3. *Auction.* The firm states a range of prices at which it is prepared to repurchase. Shareholders submit offers declaring how many shares they are prepared to sell at each price, and the firm calculates the lowest price at which it can buy the desired number of shares.
4. *Direct negotiation.* The firm may negotiate repurchase of a block of shares from a major shareholder. The most notorious examples are *greenmail transactions*, in which the target of an attempted takeover buys out the hostile bidder. "Greenmail" means that the shares are repurchased at a generous price that makes the bidder happy to leave the target alone.

WHY REPURCHASES ARE LIKE DIVIDENDS

To see why share repurchase is similar to a dividend, look at panel A of Table 18.1, which shows the market value of Hewlard Pocket's assets and liabilities. Shareholders hold 100,000 shares worth, in total, \$1 million, so price per share equals \$1 million/100,000 = \$10.

Pocket is proposing to pay a dividend of \$1 per share. With 100,000 shares outstanding, that amounts to a total payout of \$100,000. Panel B shows the effect of this dividend payment. The cash account is reduced by \$100,000, and the market value of the firm's assets falls to \$900,000. Since there are still 100,000 shares outstanding, share price falls to \$9. Suppose that before the dividend payment you owned 1,000 shares of Pocket worth \$10,000. After the payment you would have \$1,000 in cash and 1,000 shares worth \$9,000.

TABLE 18.1
Cash dividend versus share repurchase. Hewlard Pocket's market-value balance sheet.

Assets		Liabilities and Shareholders' Equity	
A. Original balance sheet			
Cash	\$ 150,000	Debt	\$ 0
Other assets	850,000	Equity	1,000,000
Value of firm	\$1,000,000	Value of firm	\$1,000,000
Shares outstanding = 100,000			
Price per share = \$1,000,000/100,000 = \$10			
B. After-cash dividend			
Cash	\$ 50,000	Debt	\$ 0
Other assets	850,000	Equity	900,000
Value of firm	\$ 900,000	Value of firm	\$ 900,000
Shares outstanding = 100,000			
Price per share = \$900,000/100,000 = \$9			
C. After-stock repurchase			
Cash	\$ 50,000	Debt	\$ 0
Other assets	850,000	Equity	900,000
Value of firm	\$ 900,000	Value of firm	\$ 900,000
Shares outstanding = 90,000			
Price per share = \$900,000/90,000 = \$10			

Rather than paying out \$100,000 as a dividend, Pocket could use the cash to buy back 10,000 shares at \$10 each. Panel C shows what happens. The firm's assets fall to \$900,000 just as in panel B, but only 90,000 shares remain outstanding, so price per share remains at \$10. If you owned 1,000 shares before the repurchase, you would own 1 percent of the company. If you then sold 100 of your shares to Pocket, you would still own 1 percent of the company. Your sale would put \$1,000 cash in your pocket and you would keep 900 shares worth \$9,000. This is precisely the position that you would have been in if Pocket had paid a dividend of \$1 per share.

It is not surprising that a cash dividend and a share repurchase are equivalent transactions. In both cases, the firm pays out some of its cash, which then goes into the shareholders' pockets. The assets that are left in the company are the same regardless of whether that cash was used to pay a dividend or to buy back shares. Later, however, we will see that how the company chooses to pay out cash may affect the tax that the investor is obliged to pay.

Check Point 18.2

What would Table 18.1 look like if the dividend changes to \$1.50 per share and the share repurchase to \$150,000?

REPURCHASES AND SHARE VALUATION

Now here is a question that often causes confusion. We stated in Chapter 7 that the value of a share is equal to the discounted value of the stream of dividends paid on that stock. If companies also hand back cash to their shareholders in the form of repurchases, does our simple dividend discount model still hold?

The answer is yes, but we need to explain why. Suppose that you hold one share. As long as you continue to hold it, you will be entitled to receive any dividend that the company pays. However, if you sell your share either to another investor or to the company itself, you receive cash from the sale, but of course you lose out on any *subsequent* dividends that the company may pay. You can, therefore, either value the share by assuming that you continue to hold it (that is, discount a continuing stream of dividends) or by assuming that you sell the share back to the company (that is, discount both the dividend stream *up to the time of sale* and the price at which the share is sold). As long as the company buys your share at a fair price, the two methods are equivalent.

Here is a simple example. Company X has outstanding 100,000 shares and pays a dividend of \$10 a share. Investors expect this dividend to be maintained indefinitely and require a return of 10 percent on their investment. Therefore share price today is

$$\text{PV(share)} = 10/1.10 + 10/1.10^2 + \cdots = 10/.10 = \$100$$

Since the dividend stream is not expected to grow, the share price is forecast to remain at \$100.

Now suppose that the company announces that it plans to repurchase 1,000 shares in the market just after it has paid the next dividend. The announcement does not change investors' forecast of future dividends per share. So those shareholders who do not plan to sell their shares back to the company can continue to look forward to dividends of \$10 per share each year and will be happy to pay \$100 today for the share. But what about those shareholders who *do* plan to sell their shares? They will receive at the end of the year an expected dividend of \$10, plus the \$100 that the company must pay to repurchase their shares. The value of the shares today for these shareholders is $(10 + 100)/1.10 = \$100$. Thus, it does not matter whether we consider the cash flows for the shareholder who continues to hold the shares or the cash flows for the shareholder who resells her shares to the company. As long as the company pays a fair price for the share, both methods give the same value. It would, however, be double-counting to assume that a shareholder could both sell her share *and* continue to receive dividends.

As long as X's announcement does not lead investors to revise their view of company prospects, it will not affect today's company value. But after the repurchase has taken place, there will be 1,000 fewer shares outstanding. Since each share is worth \$100, the *total* value of the company's shares will fall by $1{,}000 \times \$100 = \$100{,}000$.

LO3 18.3 HOW DO COMPANIES DECIDE ON HOW MUCH TO PAY OUT?

In 2004 a survey asked senior executives about their firms' dividend policies.[8] Figure 18.2 summarizes the executives' responses. Three features stand out:

1. Managers are reluctant to make dividend changes that may have to be reversed, and they are willing to raise new financing if necessary to maintain payout.
2. Managers "smooth" dividends and hate to cut them back. Dividends tend to follow trends in long-run, sustainable earnings. Transitory fluctuations in earnings rarely affect dividend payouts. Firms appear to have long-run target **dividend payout ratios**. This ratio is the fraction of earnings paid out as dividends.
3. Managers focus more on dividend *changes* than on absolute levels. Thus paying a $2 dividend is an important financial decision if last year's dividend was $1, but it's no big deal if last year's dividend was $2.

dividend payout ratio Percentage of earnings paid out as dividends.

Corporations that pay regular dividends sometimes act as though they have a *target payout ratio*, say 40 percent of earnings. A 40 percent target ratio does *not* imply that each year's dividends equal 40 percent of each year's earnings, however. Dividends in that case would be just as volatile as earnings. We know, on the contrary, that dividends are smoothed.

Think instead of the *target dividend* as a percentage of *expected* or *normal* earnings, not this year's actual earnings. For example, suppose that the financial manager forecasts average income of $5 per share over the next two or three years. If the target payout ratio is 40 percent, the target dividend is 40 percent of $5, or $2.

If the current dividend is less than the target, then the dividend is increased gradually toward the target. But what if the firm hits hard times and expected earnings fall, leaving the current dividend *higher* than the target dividend? In this case, the dividend would probably not be cut immediately, but just be left alone. Financial managers don't cut regular dividends unless the cut is forced by heavy losses or dangerously high debt.

Consider Figure 18.3, which plots the dividends and earnings per share of MFI. While earnings per share fluctuate quite erratically, dividends per share do not. Since 1997, dividends have remained

FIGURE 18.2 A survey of financial executives suggested that their firms were reluctant to cut the dividend and tried to maintain a smooth series of payments.

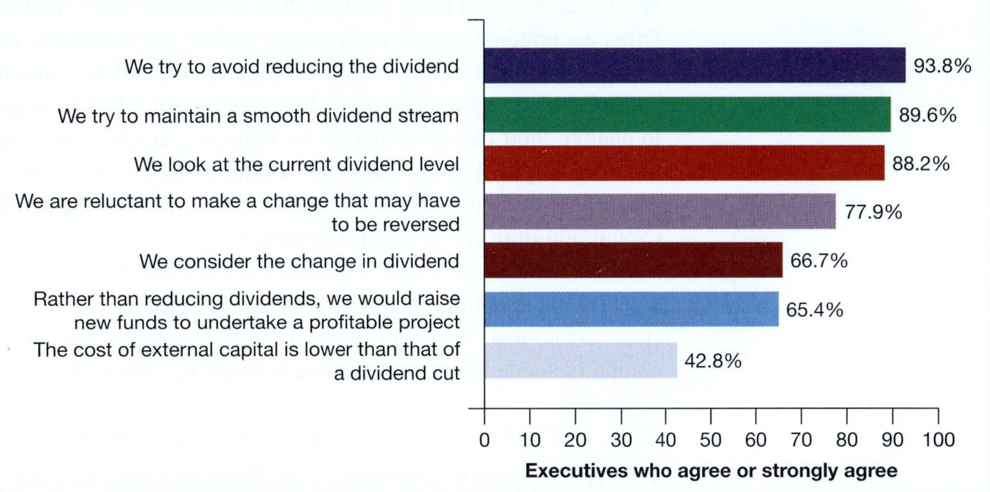

Source: A. Brav, J.R. Graham, C.R. Harvey, and R. Michaely, "Payout Policy in the 21st Century," *Journal of Financial Economics* 77 (September 2005): 483–527. © 2005 Elsevier Science, with permission.

[8] See A. Brav, J.R. Graham, C.R. Harvey, and R. Michaely, "Payout Policy in the 21st Century," *Journal of Financial Economics* 77 (September 2005): 483–527.

FIGURE 18.3
Maple Leaf Foods Inc.: Earnings and dividends per common share.

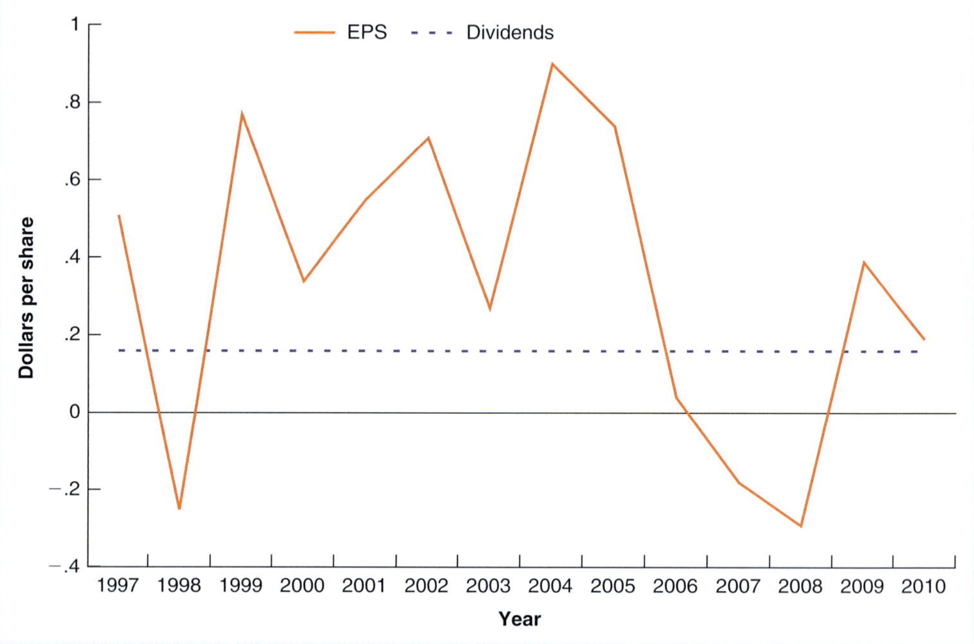

Source: *Financial Post Advisor*, FP analyzer database at **www.fpinfomart.ca**, retrieved March 23, 2011. Material reprinted with the express permission of National Post, a division of Postmedia Network Inc.

steady at \$.16 per share right through to 2010. Notice that management continued to pay a dividend of \$.16 per share in 1998 and again in 2007 and 2008 despite losses incurred in those years.

THE ROLE OF SHARE REPURCHASE DECISIONS

Repurchases are like special or bumper dividends; they cause large amounts of cash to be paid to investors. But they don't *substitute* for dividends. Most companies that repurchase stock are mature, profitable companies that also pay dividends. When a company announces a repurchase program, it is not making a long-term commitment to distribute more cash. Repurchases are therefore much more volatile than dividends. They tend to mushroom during boom times as firms accumulate excess cash and to wither in recessions. Firms occasionally use share repurchases when their cash resources have outrun good investment opportunities.

Firms repurchase stock when they have accumulated a large amount of unwanted cash or wish to change their capital structure by replacing equity with debt. For example, in February 2011, the third-largest U.S oil company, ConocoPhillips, announced plans to spend US\$10 billion to repurchase company stock. The repurchase plan was expected to reduce ConocoPhillips' cost of capital and improve its capital structure.

Shareholders often worry that excess cash will be frittered away on unprofitable ventures. So, when firms announce that they will use the cash to repurchase shares, the stock price generally rises. Of course, investors would be less thrilled if the management of their favourite growth company suddenly announced that it could not think of anything better to do with the cash.

THE INFORMATION CONTENT OF DIVIDENDS AND REPURCHASES

When a corporation announces a dividend increase, its stock price usually jumps. For example, Healy and Palepu found that the announcement of a company's first dividend caused an immediate price increase of 4 percent on average.[9] Such announcements are obviously good news

[9] See P. Healy and K. Palepu, "Earnings Information Conveyed by Dividend Initiations and Omissions," *Journal of Financial Economics* 21 (1988): 149–175.

Finance in Action

The Dividend Cut Heard 'Round the World

On May 9, 1994, FPL Group, the parent company of Florida Power & Light Company, announced a 32 percent reduction in its quarterly dividend payout, from $.62 per share to $.42. This was the first-ever dividend cut by a healthy utility. A number of utilities had reduced their dividends in the past, but only after cash flow problems—often associated with heavy investment in nuclear plants—had given them no choice.

In its announcement, FPL stressed that it had studied the situation carefully and that, given the prospect of increased competition in the electric utility industry, the company's high-dividend payout ratio (which had averaged 90 percent in the past four years) was no longer in the shareholders' best interests. The new policy resulted in a dividend payout of about 60 percent of the prior year's earnings. Management also announced that, starting in 1995, the dividend payout would be reviewed in February instead of May to reinforce the linkage between dividends and annual earnings. In doing so, the company wanted to minimize unintended "signalling effects" from any future changes in the dividend.

At the same time it announced this change in dividend policy, FPL Group's board authorized the repurchase of up to 10 million shares of common stock over the next three years. FPL's management said that four million shares would be repurchased over the next 12 months, depending on market conditions. In adopting this strategy, the company noted that changes in the U.S. tax code since 1990 had made capital gains more attractive than dividends to shareholders.

Besides providing a more tax-efficient means of distributing excess capital to its shareholders, FPL's substitution of stock repurchases for dividends was also designed to increase the company's financial flexibility in preparation for a new era of deregulation and heightened competition among utilities. Although much of the cash savings from the dividend cut would be returned to investors in the form of stock repurchases, the rest would be used to retire debt at Florida Power & Light and so reduce the company's leverage ratio. This deleveraging and strengthening of FPL's financial condition were intended to prepare the company for an increase in business risk and to provide the financial resources to take advantage of future growth opportunities.

The stock market's initial reaction to FPL's announcement was negative. On the day of the announcement, the company's stock price fell from $31.88 to $27.50, a drop of nearly 14 percent. But, as analysts digested the news and considered the reasons for the reduction, they concluded that the action was not a signal of financial distress but rather a strategic decision that would improve the company's long-term financial flexibility and prospects for growth. This view spread throughout the financial community, and FPL's stock began to recover.

On May 31, less than a month after the announcement, FPL's stock closed at $32.17 (adjusted for the quarterly dividend of $.42), or about $.30 higher than the pre-announcement price. By the middle of June, at least 15 major brokerage houses had placed FPL's common stock on their "buy" lists. On May 9, 1995—exactly one year after the announcement of the cut—FPL's stock price closed at $37.75, giving shareholders a one-year post-announcement return (including dividends) of 23.8 percent, more than double the 11.2 percent of the S&P Index and well above the 14.2 percent of the S&P utilities index over the same period.

Source: Adapted from D. Soter, E. Brigham, and P. Evanson, "The Dividend Cut 'Heard 'Round the World': The Case of FPL," *Journal of Applied Corporate Finance* 9 (Spring 1996): 4–15.

for investors. The news is good, not because investors simply "like dividends," but because announcements of dividend increases send positive signals about future income. Managers don't increase dividends unless they are confident that income will be high enough to cover the dividend with room to spare. A dividend increase conveys that confidence to investors. A dividend cut, on the other hand, conveys *lack* of confidence.

It is no surprise, therefore, to find that announcements of dividend cuts are usually taken as bad news (stock price typically falls) and that dividend increases are good news (stock price rises). This is called the **information content of dividends**. The stock price responses to dividend cuts or increases do not mean that investors like dividends for their own sake. A dividend initiation or increase may be welcomed only as a sign that the company is doing well. Even investors who otherwise prefer low-payout policies might find that a cut in the dividend is unwelcome news about the firm's prospects.

information content of dividends Dividend increases send good news about future cash flow and earnings. Dividend cuts send bad news.

Notice that investors do not get excited about the *level* of a company's dividend; they worry about the *change*, which they view as an important indicator of the company's ability to generate cash. The nearby box illustrates how an unexpected change in dividends can cause the stock price to bounce back and forth as investors struggle to interpret its significance.

Check Point 18.3

In January 2004 GATX, a specialized leasing company, announced that although earnings for the latest quarter were higher than a year earlier, it was cutting its regular quarterly dividend from $.32 a share to $.20. It pointed out that this new dividend level better reflected current earnings and recovery expectations. The next day, 10 times the normal number of shares changed hands and the stock price fell by 16 percent. Why would the dividend cut result in such a sharp fall in price?

Announcements of share repurchase programs are also good news for investors. But repurchase programs are short-lived and may not be repeated, unlike dividend increases, which imply a longer-run commitment. Therefore, the information content of a repurchase program can be different from the information content of dividends. For example, a repurchase announcement may signal only that the manager thinks that the firm's stock is undervalued and a "good buy."

Companies repurchase shares when they have accumulated more cash than they can invest profitably or when they undertake to substitute debt for equity. Shareholders are often relieved to see companies paying out the excess cash rather than frittering it away on unprofitable investments. Of course, investors would be less thrilled if their favourite growth company suddenly announced a repurchase program because its managers could not think of anything better to do with its cash.

LO4 18.4 WHY PAYOUT POLICY SHOULD NOT MATTER

Franco Modigliani and Merton Miller (MM), who proved that financing doesn't matter in perfect financial markets, also proved that dividend policy doesn't matter in perfect financial markets.[10] We have already seen the common sense of MM's argument in Table 18.1, which shows that investors should not care whether a firm distributes cash by dividends or share repurchases.

MM would admit that payout policy *may* matter, not just because of the information content of dividends and repurchases but also because of taxes and market imperfections. But first we take a more thorough look at **MM's dividend-irrelevance proposition**.

MM's dividend-irrelevance proposition Under ideal conditions, the value of the firm is unaffected by dividend policy.

Payout decisions are often intertwined with other financing or investment decisions. Some firms pay out little cash because management is optimistic about the firm's future and wishes to retain earnings for expansion. In this case the payout decision is a by-product of the firm's capital budgeting decision. Another firm might finance capital expenditures largely by borrowing. This frees up cash that can be paid out to shareholders. In this case the payout decision is a by-product of the borrowing decision.

We wish to isolate payout policy from other problems of financial management. The precise question we should ask is, What is the effect of a change in payout policy, *given the firm's capital budgeting and borrowing decisions*?

Suppose that the firm proposes to increase its dividend. The cash to finance that dividend increase has to come from somewhere. If we fix the firm's investment outlays and borrowing, there is only one possible source—an issue of stock. What if the firm decides to reduce its dividend? In that case it would have extra cash. If investment outlays and borrowing are fixed, there is only one possible way that this cash can be used—to repurchase stock. We define *payout policy* as the trade-off between higher or lower cash dividends and the issue or repurchase of shares.

---

[10] M.H. Miller and F. Modigliani, "Dividend Policy, Growth and the Valuation of Shares," *Journal of Business* 34 (October 1961): 411–433.

One nice feature of economics is that it can accommodate not just two, but three opposing points of view—and so it is with dividend policy. On one side there is a group that believes high dividends increase firm value. On the other side there is a group that believes high dividends bring high taxes and therefore reduce firm value. And in the centre there is a middle-of-the-road party that believes dividend policy makes no difference.

PAYOUT POLICY IS IRRELEVANT IN EFFICIENT FINANCIAL MARKETS

We can illustrate MM's views about dividend policy by considering the Pickwick Paper Company, which had set aside $100 million in cash to construct a new paper mill. But Pickwick's directors now propose to use the $100 million to increase the dividend payment. If Pickwick is to continue to build its new mill, that cash needs to be replaced. If the borrowing is fixed, there is only one place the money can come from, and that is the sale of new shares. The combination of the dividend payment and the new issue of shares leaves Pickwick and its shareholders in exactly the same position they started from. All that has happened is that Pickwick has put an extra $100 million in investors' pockets (the dividend payment) and then taken it out again (the share issue). In other words, Pickwick is simply recycling cash. To suggest that this makes investors better off is like advising the cook to cool the kitchen by leaving the refrigerator door open.

After Pickwick pays the additional dividend and replaces the cash by selling new shares, the company value is unchanged. The old shareholders now have an extra $100 million cash in their pockets, but they have given up a stake in the firm to those investors who buy the newly issued shares. The new shareholders are putting up $100 million and therefore will demand to receive shares *worth* $100 million. Since the total value of the company is the same, the value of the old shareholders' stake in the company falls by this $100 million. Thus the extra dividend that the old shareholders receive just offsets the loss in the value of the shares that they hold.

> Because investors do not need dividends to convert their shares to cash, they will not pay higher prices for firms with higher dividend payouts. In other words, payout policy will have no impact on the value of the firm. This is MM's argument.

Does it make any difference to the old shareholders that they receive an extra dividend payment plus an offsetting capital loss? It might if that were the only way they could get their hands on the cash. But as long as there are efficient capital markets, they can raise cash by selling shares. Thus Pickwick's old shareholders can "cash in" either by persuading the management to pay a higher dividend or by selling some of their shares. In either case there will be the same transfer of value from the old to the new shareholders.

The example of the Pickwick Paper Company showed that the firm cannot make shareholders better off simply by increasing the proportion of earnings paid out as dividends. But the same argument also works in reverse: if investment and borrowing are held constant, any *reduction* in dividends must be balanced by a *purchase* of stock. For example, suppose that Old Curiosity Shops has $100 million surplus cash which it had been proposing to pay out to shareholders as a dividend. If Old Curiosity now decides not to pay this dividend, then the surplus cash can be used only to buy back some of the company's shares. The shareholders miss out on $100 million of dividend payments but they receive $100 million from the sale to the company of part of their shareholdings. Thus MM's irrelevance argument holds both for increases in dividends and for reductions.

> As these examples illustrate, payout policy is a trade-off between cash dividends and the issue or repurchase of common shares. In a perfect capital market, dividend choice would have no impact on firm value.

These examples may seem artificial at first because we do not observe firms scheduling a stock issue with every dividend payment. But there are many firms that pay dividends and also issue stock from time to time. They could avoid the stock issues by paying lower dividends and retaining more funds in the firm. Many other firms restrict dividends so that they *do not* have to issue shares. They could instead issue shares occasionally and increase the dividend.

Of course, our demonstrations of dividend-irrelevance have ignored taxes, issue costs, and a variety of other real-world complications. We will turn to these intricacies shortly, but before we do, we note that the crucial assumption in our proof is that the sale or purchase of shares occurs at a fair price. The shares that Pickwick sells to raise $100,000 must actually be worth $100,000; those that Old Curiosity buys for $100,000 must also be worth that figure. In other words, dividend-irrelevance assumes efficient capital markets.

EXAMPLE 18.2 DIVIDEND-IRRELEVANCE

The columns labelled "Old Dividend Plan" in Table 18.2 show that Consolidated Pasta is expected to pay annual dividends of $10 per share in perpetuity. Shareholders expect a 10 percent rate of return from Consolidated stock, and therefore the value of each share is

$$\text{PV} = \frac{10}{1.10} + \frac{10}{1.10^2} + \frac{10}{1.10^3} + \ldots = \frac{10}{.10} = \$100$$

Consolidated has issued one million shares. So the total forecast dividend payment in each year is 1 million × $10 = $10 million, and the total value of Consolidated Pasta equity is 1 million × $100 = $100 million. The president, Al Dente, has read that the value of a share depends on the dividends it pays. That suggests an easy way to keep shareholders happy—increase next year's dividend to $20 per share. That way, he reasons, share price should rise by the present value of the increase in the first-year dividend to a new value of

$$\text{PV} = \frac{20}{1.10} + \frac{10}{1.10^2} + \frac{10}{1.10^3} + \ldots + \frac{10}{1.10} + \frac{10}{.10} = \$109.91$$

The president's heart is obviously in the right place. Unfortunately, his head isn't. Let's see why.

Consolidated is proposing to pay out an extra $10 million in dividends. It can't do that and earn the same profits in the future, unless it also replaces the lost cash by an issue of shares. The new shareholders who provide this cash will require a return of 10 percent on their investment. So Consolidated will need to pay $1 million per year of dividends to the new shares ($1 million/$10 million = .10, or 10 percent). This is shown in the last line of Table 18.2.

As long as the company replaces the extra cash it pays out, it will continue to earn the same profits and to pay out $10 million of dividends each year from year 2. However, $1 million of this total will be needed to satisfy the new shareholders, leaving only $9 million (or $9 per share) for the original shareholders. Now recalculate the value of the original shares under the revised dividend plan:

$$\text{PV} = \frac{20}{1.10} + \frac{9}{1.10^2} + \frac{9}{1.10^3} + \ldots = \frac{11}{1.10} + \frac{9}{.10} = \$100$$

The value of the shares is unchanged. The extra cash dividend in year 1 is exactly offset by the reduction of dividends per share in later years. This reduction is necessary because some of the money paid out as dividends in later years is diverted to the new shareholders.[11]

TABLE 18.2

Consolidated Pasta is currently expected to pay a dividend of $10 million in perpetuity. However, the president is proposing to pay a one-time bumper dividend of $20 million in year 1. To replace the lost cash, the firm will need to issue more shares, and the dividends that will need to be diverted to the new shareholders will exactly offset the effect of the higher dividend in year 1.

	Old Dividend Plan		Revised Dividend Plan	
	Year 1	From Year 2 On	Year 1	From Year 2 On
Total dividend payments ($ million)	10	10	20	10
Total dividends paid to old shareholders ($ million)	10	10	20	9
Total dividends paid to new shareholders ($ million)	—	—	—	1

Note: New shareholders are putting up $10 million cash at the end of year 1. Since they require a return of 10 percent, the total dividends paid to the new shares (starting in year 2) must be 10 percent of $10 million, or $1 million.

[11] Notice that at the end of year 1, when the new shareholders purchase their shares, the dividend per share they can look forward to receiving will be $9; since this dividend is expected to be a perpetuity, the share price at that time will be $9/.10 = $90. So the new shareholders will receive $10,000,000/$90 = 111,111 shares. Consistently with Table 18.2, the new shareholders therefore will receive total dividend payments of 111,111 × $9 = $1 million, and the old shareholders will receive total dividend payments of 1 million × $9 = $9 million. Notice also that after the extra $10 million dividend is paid in year 1, the share price falls to $90, and the value of the shares held by the original shareholders falls by exactly $10 million to $90 million.

Check Point 18.4 Suppose that Consolidated Pasta had issued $10 million in preferred stock rather than common stock to pay the extra dividend. What would be the stock price?

THE ASSUMPTIONS BEHIND DIVIDEND-IRRELEVANCE

Many shareholders and businesspeople find it difficult to accept the suggestion that dividend policy is irrelevant. When faced with MM's argument, they often reply that dividends are cash in hand while capital gains are at best in the bush. It may be true, they say, that the recipient of an extra cash dividend forgoes an equal capital gain, but if the dividend is safe and the capital gain is risky, isn't the shareholder ahead?

It's correct that dividends are more predictable than capital gains. Managers can stabilize dividends but they cannot control stock price. From this it seems a small step to conclude that increased dividends make the firm less risky.[12] But the important point is, once again, that as long as investment policy and borrowing are held constant, a firm's *overall* cash flows are the same regardless of payout policy. The risks borne by *all* the firm's shareholders are likewise fixed by its investment and borrowing policies and unaffected by dividend policy.

If we really believed that existing shareholders are better off by trading a risky asset for cash, then we would also have to argue that the new shareholders—those who trade cash for the newly issued shares—are worse off. But this doesn't make sense. The new shareholders are bearing risk, but they are getting paid for it. They are willing to buy because the new shares are priced to offer an expected return adequate to compensate for the risk.

MM's argument for the irrelevance of dividend policy does not assume a world of certainty; it assumes an efficient capital market. Market efficiency means that the transfers of ownership created by shifts in dividend policy are carried out on fair terms. And since the overall value of (old and new) shareholders' equity is unaffected, nobody gains or loses.

LO5 18.5 WHY DIVIDENDS MAY INCREASE FIRM VALUE

MARKET IMPERFECTIONS

Most economists believe that MM's conclusions are correct, given their assumptions of perfect and efficient capital markets. However, nobody claims their model is an exact description of the so-called real world. Thus the impact of dividend policy finally boils down to arguments about imperfections and inefficiencies.

> There are natural clienteles for high-payout stocks, but it does not follow that any particular firm can benefit by increasing its dividends. The high-dividend clienteles already have plenty of high-dividend stocks to choose from.

Those who believe that dividends are good argue that some investors have a natural preference for high-payout stocks. For example, some financial institutions are legally restricted from holding stocks lacking established dividend records. Trusts and endowment funds may prefer high-dividend stocks because dividends are regarded as spendable "income," whereas capital gains are "additions to principal," which may not be spent.[13]

In addition, there is a natural clientele of investors, including the elderly, who look to their stock portfolios for a steady source of cash to live on. In principle this cash can be generated from stocks paying no dividends at all; the investors can just sell off a small fraction of their holdings from time to time. But that can be inconvenient and lead to heavy transaction costs.

Behavioural psychology may also help to explain why some investors prefer to receive regular dividends rather than sell small amounts of stock. We are all liable to succumb to temptation. Some of us may hanker after fattening foods, while others may crave a drink. We could seek to control these cravings by willpower, but that can be a painful struggle. Instead, it may be easier to set

---

[12] In that case one might also argue that interest payments are even more predictable, so that a company's risk would be reduced by increasing the proportion of profits paid out as interest. How would you respond to that suggestion?

[13] Many colleges and universities are legally free to spend capital gains from their endowments, but this is rarely done.

simple rules for ourselves ("cut out chocolate" or "wine only with meals"). In just the same way, we may benefit from the self-discipline that comes from limiting our spending to dividend income, allowing us to avoid making the difficult decision of how much we should dip into capital.

All this is undoubtedly true, but it does not follow that you can increase the value of your firm by increasing the dividend payout. Smart managers already have recognized that there is a clientele of investors who would be prepared to pay a premium for high-payout stocks. High-payout fans already have a wide variety of stocks to choose from.

You don't hear businesspeople argue that because there is a clientele of car buyers, their company should manufacture cars. So why should you believe that because there is a clientele of investors who like high payouts, your company can increase value by manufacturing a high payout? That clientele was probably satisfied long ago.

Check Point 18.5

Suppose an investor in BCE does not need a regular income. What could she do to offset BCE's "overly generous" payout policy? If there were no trading costs, would she have any reason to care about BCE's dividend payout policy? What if there is a brokerage fee on the purchase of new shares? What if BCE has a dividend reinvestment plan that allows the investor to buy shares at a 5 percent discount?

18.6 WHY DIVIDENDS MAY REDUCE FIRM VALUE

The low-dividend creed is simple. Companies can convert dividends into capital gains by shifting their dividend policy. If dividends are taxed more heavily than capital gains, such financial alchemy should be welcomed by any taxpaying investor. Firms should pay the lowest cash dividend they can get away with. Surplus cash should be used to repurchase shares.

Table 18.3 illustrates this. It assumes that dividends are taxed at a rate of 40 percent but that capital gains are taxed at only 20 percent. The stocks of firms A and B are equally risky, and investors demand an expected *after-tax* rate of return of 10 percent on each. Investors expect A to be worth $112.50 per share next year. The share price of B is expected to be only $102.50, but a $10 dividend is also forecast, so the total pretax payoff is the same—$112.50.

Both stocks offer the same pretax dollar payoff. Yet B's stock sells for less than A's. The reason is obvious: Investors are willing to pay more for stock A because its return comes in the form of

TABLE 18.3 Effects of a shift in dividend policy when dividends are taxed more heavily than capital gains. The high-payout stock (firm B) must sell at a lower price in order to provide the same after-tax return.

	Firm A	Firm B
Next year's price	$112.50	$102.50
Dividend	$ 0	$ 10
Total *pretax* payoff	$112.50	$112.50
Today's stock price	$ 100	$ 97.78
Capital gain	$ 12.50	$ 4.72
Before-tax rate of return (%)	$\frac{12.5}{100} = .125 = 12.5\%$	$\frac{14.72}{97.78} = .1505 = 15.05\%$
Tax on dividend at 40%	$0	$.40 \times \$10 = \$4$
Tax on capital gain at 20%	$.20 \times \$12.50 = \$2.50$	$.20 \times \$4.72 = \$.94$
Total after-tax income (dividends plus capital gains less taxes)	$(0 + 12.50) - 2.50 = \$10.00$	$(10 + 4.72) - (4.00 + .94) = \$9.78$
After-tax rate of return (%)	$\frac{10}{100} = .10 = 10\%$	$\frac{9.78}{97.78} = .10 = 10\%$

low-taxed capital gains. After tax, both stocks offer the same 10 percent expected return despite the fact that B's *pretax* return is higher. Suppose the management of firm B eliminates the $10 dividend and uses the cash to repurchase stock instead. We saw earlier that a stock repurchase is equivalent to a cash dividend but it is treated differently by the tax authorities. Stockholders who sell shares back to their firm pay tax only on any capital gains realized in the sale. By substituting a repurchase for a dividend, B's new policy would reduce the taxes paid by stockholders, and its stock price should rise.

Check Point 18.6 Look again at Table 18.3. What would happen to the price and pretax rate of return on stock B if the tax on capital gains were eliminated?

WHY PAY ANY DIVIDENDS AT ALL?

If dividends are taxed more heavily than capital gains, why should any firm ever pay a cash dividend? If cash is to be distributed to stockholders, isn't share repurchase the best channel for doing so? Few would go that far. The Canada Revenue Agency (CRA) would like to prevent firms from disguising dividends as repurchases. A firm that eliminates dividends and starts repurchasing shares on a regular basis may find that the CRA would recognize the repurchase program for what it really is and would tax the payments accordingly. That is why financial managers seldom announce that they are repurchasing stock to save stockholders taxes; they give some other reason.[14]

DIVIDENDS VERSUS CAPITAL GAINS

We must keep in mind that tax laws tend to change over time and the relationship between dividends and pretax rates of return should change as well. Capital gains were taxed for the first time in Canada in 1972. Before that year, many investors were taxed at higher rates on dividend income than on capital gains income. Consequently, we would expect high-dividend–paying stocks to earn a higher pretax rate of return to compensate for the extra taxes. Since the 1980s, new reforms have increased the tax on capital gains. For example, a $100,000 lifetime capital gain exemption, introduced in the mid-1980s, was ended in 1994. However, in 2000, the federal budget lowered the taxable portion of capital gains from 75 percent to 50 percent. Overall, the net effect of these changes has generally been to reduce the difference in the taxes on dividends and capital gains.[15]

In Chapter 3, we discussed the treatment of income from dividends and capital gains under Canadian tax laws. Canadian public corporations do not pay any tax on dividend income received from another Canadian corporation, whereas individual investors receive some tax relief through a *dividend tax credit (DTC)*. The dividend tax credit reduces the burden of double taxation on shareholder income, which occurs because the cash flows that produce such income are taxed at both corporate and personal levels. On the other hand, corporations and individual investors pay tax on capital gains that are realized when the asset is sold. Currently, only 50 percent of such realized capital gains are taxable. Tax law is on the side of capital gains in another important respect. Taxes on dividends have to be paid immediately, but taxes on capital gains can be deferred until shares are sold and capital gains are realized. Stockholders can choose when to sell their shares and thus when to pay the capital gains tax.[16] Other countries have also sought to

[14] They might say, "Our stock is a good investment," or "The repurchase program will enhance shareholder value." What do you think of these rationales?

[15] Although a study by I.G. Morgan, "Dividends and Stock Price Behaviour in Canada," *Journal of Business Administration* 12 (Fall 1980): 91–106, found no difference in the before-tax rates of return between high- and low-dividend-paying stocks between 1972 and 1977, another study has examined the issue: B. Amoako-adu, M. Rashid, and M. Stebbens, "Capital Gains Tax and Equity Values: Empirical Test of Stock Price Reaction to the Introduction and Reduction of Capital Gains Tax Exemption," *Journal of Banking and Finance* 16 (1992): 275–287.

[16] Suppose the discount rate is 8 percent, and an investor in a combined 40 percent federal and provincial tax bracket has a $100 capital gain. If the stock is sold today, the tax on capital gain will be $20 (that is, $.5 \times .4 \times 100$), but by virtue of delaying the sale for a year, the present value of the tax falls to $20/1.08 = $18.52. The effective tax rate falls to 18.52 percent. The longer the sale is deferred, the lower the effective tax rate.

ameliorate the effects of double taxation of dividend income. Recently, the United States has also moved to reduce the burden of double taxation on dividend income under legislation introduced in 2003. Now, dividends received from domestic U.S. companies and some qualified foreign corporations are taxed at a maximum rate of 15 percent and not at ordinary income tax rates. The top rate of tax on capital gains in the U.S. is also 15 percent.

Overall, for some investors, dividends are taxed more heavily than capital gains, whereas for others, capital gains suffer more tax than dividends. For instance, refer back to the solution to Check Point 3.9 in Chapter 3. Notice that a British Columbia–based investor in the lowest tax bracket (combined tax rate of 20.56 percent) has a dividend tax rate of 4.79 percent (assuming the dividend is non-eligible), but a higher capital gains tax rate of 10.28 percent. On the other hand, the investor in the highest tax bracket with a combined tax rate of 43.7 percent has a dividend tax rate of 33.71 percent, but a lower capital gains tax rate of 21.85 percent.[17] The conclusion would be different, however, if the dividend income was eligible, as then the tax rates on dividend income would be lower than capital gains tax rates for both categories of investors.

DIVIDEND CLIENTELE EFFECTS

From our discussion above, some groups of investors, such as rich individuals, may prefer to receive capital gains and little or no dividends, while other groups, such as corporate investors, may prefer high-dividend payouts. Different investor groups, or clienteles, therefore prefer different payouts; this is the **dividend clientele effect**. The dividend-clientele effect argument is that changing the dividend policy of the firm would attract a new investor clientele but may not change the value of the firm.

dividend clientele effect Different investor groups prefer different dividend yields. Changing the firm's dividend policy may attract a new investor clientele but may not change firm value.

Suppose a firm with a low dividend payout switches to a high-dividend-payout policy. It will now attract clienteles seeking high-dividend-payout stocks. However, its share price may not go up as long as enough firms satisfy the demand for high-dividend-paying stocks. Essentially, this is a supply and demand argument. If the demand from investor clienteles is more for high-dividend-paying stocks relative to the supply of such stocks, the prices of high-dividend-paying stocks should rise. However, low-dividend-paying firms will now find it advantageous to switch to high-dividend-payout policies until prices stabilize and the "market for dividends" is in equilibrium. In such an environment, a dividend policy change by an individual firm will have no effect on its share value.

[17] See Chapter 3, Table 3.7, for a table of tax rates on ordinary income.

18.7 SUMMARY

1. **How are dividends paid and how do companies decide on dividend payments? LO1**

   Dividends come in many forms. The most common is the regular cash dividend, but sometimes companies pay an extra cash dividend, and sometimes they pay a stock dividend. A firm is not free to pay dividends at will. For example, it may have accepted restrictions on dividends as a condition for borrowing money.

Dividends do not go up and down with every change in the firm's earnings. Instead, managers aim for smooth dividends and increase dividends gradually as earnings grow.

2. **How are repurchases used to distribute cash to shareholders? LO2**

Companies also distribute cash to shareholders by repurchasing their shares. Share repurchases have grown rapidly in recent years, but they do not substitute for dividends. Firms that repurchase usually also pay dividends.

Repurchases are used to distribute excess cash. Firms also use repurchases to replace equity with debt financing. In this case, the proceeds of new debt issues are paid out to equity investors via repurchases.

3. **Why are dividend increases and repurchases usually good news for investors? Why are dividend cuts bad news? LO3**

Managers do not increase dividends unless they are confident that the firm will generate enough earnings to cover the payout. Announcement of a dividend increase conveys the managers' confidence to investors. This **information content of dividends** is the main reason that stock price usually increases when a dividend increase is announced. A dividend cut, on the other hand, conveys a lack of confidence.

Repurchases are also good news for investors. Announcement of a repurchase program can reveal the managers' view that the stock is a "good buy" at its current price. Repurchases can also reassure investors who worry that managers will spend excess cash on unprofitable investments.

4. **Why would payout policy not affect firm value in an ideal world? LO4**

If we hold the company's investment policy and capital structure constant, then dividend policy is a trade-off between cash dividends and the issue or repurchase of common stock. In an ideally simple and perfect world, the choice would have no effect on market value. This is the MM dividend-irrelevance proposition. MM's proposition is controversial in some quarters. A common—though by no means universal—view is that high dividends enhance share price. This could be true if there were a restricted supply of high pay-out stocks.

5. **How might differences in the tax treatment of dividends and capital gains affect payout policy? LO5**

Instead of paying dividends, the company can repurchase its own stock. The Canada Revenue Agency (CRA) taxes shareholders on the capital gains that they realize as a result of the repurchase.

Are capital gains taxed at lower rates than dividend income? For some investor groups, dividend income can offer some tax advantages over realized capital gains income. However, investors who do not realize capital gains can defer, and thereby lower, the present value of any capital gains tax liability. This suggests the existence of different investor clienteles preferring different dividend payouts. The dividend-clientele-effect argument is that changing the dividend policy of the firm would attract a new investor clientele but may not change the value of the firm.

If dividends are seriously tax-disadvantaged for some investors, we would expect such investors to demand a higher before-tax return on high-payout stocks. Instead of paying high dividends, companies should then use the cash to repurchase shares or to reduce the amount of share issues. In this way, the company would in effect convert dividend income into capital gains. This is one reason a low-dividend policy might be preferred.

Related Web Links

cfonews.com Current dividend news

dripcentral.com Information about dividend reinvestment plans

companyboardroom.com Data on recent dividend declarations

ndir.com/SI/DRPs.shtml Information on Canadian dividend reinvestment plans and share purchase plans

Key Terms

cash dividend	585	ex-dividend date	586	share purchase plan	588
dividend clientele effect	600	information content of dividends	593	share repurchase	588
dividend payout ratio	591	MM dividend-irrelevance proposition	594	stock dividend	587
dividend reinvestment plan	588	reverse split	588	stock split	587

Questions and Problems

connect Practise and learn online with *Connect*. Questions with online Excel templates or datasets are marked with .

*Answers in Appendix B

BASIC

1. **Dividend Sequence.** Cash Cow International paid a regular quarterly dividend of $.075 a share. (LO1)
   a. Connect each of the following dates to the correct term:

May 7	Record date
June 6	Payment date
June 7	Ex-dividend date
June 9	Last with-dividend date
July 2	Declaration date

   *b. On one of these dates the stock price is likely to fall by about the value of the dividend. Why?
   *c. The stock price in early January was $27. What was the prospective dividend yield?
   *d. The earnings per share were forecast at around $1.90. What was the percentage payout rate?
   *e. Suppose that the company paid a 10 percent stock dividend. What would be the expected fall in the stock price?
2. **Institutional Background.** True or false? If false, correct the statement. (LO1)
   a. A company may not generally pay a dividend out of legal capital.
   b. A company may not generally pay a dividend if it is insolvent.
   c. The *effective* tax rate on capital gains can be less than the stated tax rate on such gains.
   d. Corporations are not taxed on dividends received from other corporations.

*3. **Splits and Dividends.** Shares in Raven Products are selling for $40 per share. There are one million shares outstanding. What will be the share price in each of the following situations? Ignore taxes. (LO1)
   a. The stock splits five-for-four.
   b. The company pays a 25 percent stock dividend.
   c. The company repurchases 100,000 shares.

4. **Dividend-Irrelevance.** You own 1,000 shares of Patriot Corporation, which is about to raise its dividend from $.75 to $1 per share. The share price is currently $50. You would prefer that the dividend remain at its current level. What would you do to offset the effects of the increase in the dividend? (LO4)
5. **DRIPs.** A firm considers initiating an aggressive dividend reinvestment plan (DRIP) in which it allows its investors to use dividends to buy shares at a discount of 40 percent from current market value. The firm's financial manager argues that the policy will benefit shareholders by giving them the opportunity to buy additional shares at a deep discount and will benefit the firm by providing a source of cash. Is the manager correct? (LO4)

INTERMEDIATE

6. **Dividends and Repurchases.** While dividend yields in the United States in the late 1990s were at historically low levels, share repurchases were at historical highs. Was this a coincidence? (LO2)
7. **Dividend-Irrelevance.** Respond to the following comment: "It's all very well saying that I can sell shares to cover cash needs, but that may mean selling at the bottom of the market. If the company pays a regular dividend, investors avoid the risk." (LO1)
8. **Cash Dividends.** The stock of Payout Corp. will go ex-dividend tomorrow. The dividend will be $1 per share, and there are 20,000 shares of stock outstanding. The market-value balance sheet for Payout is shown below. (LO1)
   a. What price is Payout stock selling for today?
   b. What price will it sell for tomorrow? Ignore taxes.

Assets		**Liabilities and Equity**	
Cash	$100,000	Equity	$1,000,000
Fixed assets	900,000		

*9. **Repurchases.** Now suppose that Payout from problem 8 announces its intention to repurchase $20,000 worth of stock instead of paying out the dividend. (LO2)
   a. What effect will the repurchase have on an investor who currently holds 100 shares and sells two of those shares back to the company in the repurchase?
   b. Compare the effects of the repurchase to the effects of the cash dividend that you worked out in problem 8.

10. **Stock Dividend.** Now suppose that Payout again changes its mind and decides to issue a 2 percent stock dividend instead of either issuing the cash dividend or repurchasing 2 percent of the outstanding stock. How would this

action affect a shareholder who owns 100 shares of stock? Compare with your answers to problems 8 and 9. (LO1)

*11. **Dividend-Irrelevance.** Suppose Mr. Dente from Example 18.2 changes his mind and cuts out Consolidated's year 1 dividend entirely, instead spending $10 million to buy back stock. Are shareholders any better or worse off than if Consolidated had paid out $10 million as cash dividends? *Hints:* How many shares will be repurchased? The purchase price at year 1 will be $110. (LO4)

*12. **Dividends and Taxes.** Suppose that the tax rate on dividends is 28 percent, and the tax rate on capital gains is zero. Eagle Net Resources is about to pay a $2 per share dividend. (LO1)
   a. By how much will Eagle Net's share price fall when the stock goes ex-dividend?
   b. Will anything happen to the share price on the payment date when the dividend cheques are sent out?

*13. **Stock Dividends and Splits.** Suppose that you own 1,000 shares of Nocash Corp., and the company is about to pay a 25 percent stock dividend. The stock currently sells at $50 per share. (LO1)
   a. What will be the number of shares that you hold and the total value of your equity position after the dividend is paid?
   b. What will happen to the number of shares that you hold and the value of your equity position if the firm splits five-for-four instead of paying the stock dividend?

*14. **Dividends and Taxes.** Good Values, Inc., is all equity-financed. The total market value of the firm currently is $100,000 and there are 2,000 shares outstanding.
   a. The firm has declared a $5 per share dividend. The stock will go ex-dividend tomorrow. At what price will the stock sell today? Ignore taxes. (LO1)
   b. Now assume that the federal marginal tax rate is 26 percent and the provincial marginal tax rate is 13.39 percent, the federal dividend tax credit is 13.33 percent of the grossed-up dividend, and the provincial dividend tax credit is 5.1 percent of grossed-up dividend. The applicable gross-up for dividend tax credits is 25 percent. What is the dividend tax rate? (LO5)
   c. Using your result for the dividend tax rate from part (b) and assuming a capital gains tax rate of zero, at what price will the stock sell today? (LO5)

15. **Repurchases and Taxes.** Now suppose that instead of paying a dividend, Good Values (from problem 14) plans to repurchase $10,000 worth of stock.
   a. What will be the stock price before and after the repurchase? (LO2)
   b. Suppose an investor who holds 200 shares sells 20 of her shares back to the firm. If there are no taxes on dividends or capital gains, show that she should be indifferent toward the repurchase and the dividend. (LO2)
   c. For this part, use the dividend tax rate from your answer to part (b) in problem 14 and assume that capital gains are not taxed. Is the value of the firm higher or lower if it pursues the share repurchase instead of the dividend? (LO5)

*16. **Dividends and Taxes.** Investors require an after-tax rate of return of 10 percent on their stock investments. Assume that the tax rate on dividends is 28 percent while capital gains escape taxation. A firm will pay a $2 per share dividend 1 year from now, after which it is expected to sell at a price of $20. (LO5)
   a. Find the current price of the stock.
   b. Find the expected before-tax rate of return for a one-year holding period.
   c. Now suppose that the dividend will be $3 per share. If the expected after-tax rate of return is still 10 percent, and investors still expect the stock to sell at $20 in 1 year, at what price must the stock now sell?
   d. What is the before-tax rate of return? Why is it now higher than in part (b)?

17. **Internet.**
   a. Log in to a search engine such as Yahoo or Google and search the news section to find information on recent or planned stock repurchases. What reasons have the companies given for the repurchases? Look up the companies on **finance.yahoo.com**. Do the repurchase programs appear to be a substitute for dividends? (LO2)
   b. Log in to **www.ndir.com/SI/DRPs.shtml** and look under Canadian DRPs and SPPs to find out which companies offer dividend reinvestment plans and share purchase plans. What are the advantages and drawbacks to investing in such plans? (LO1)
   c. Log in to **www.companyboardroom.com** and click on "Dividends" to find a recent list of dividend declarations. Can you explain what each of the dates means? What is the typical interval between each event? (LO1)

18. **Dividends and Taxes.** Suppose all investments offered the same expected return before tax. Consider two equally risky shares, Hi and Lo. Hi shares pay a generous dividend and offer low expected capital gains. Lo shares pay low dividends and offer high expected capital gains. Which of the following investors would prefer the Lo shares? Which would prefer the Hi shares? Which wouldn't care? Explain. Assume that any stock purchased will be sold after one year. (LO5)

a. A pension fund
b. An individual
c. A corporation

19. **Signalling.** It is well documented that stock prices tend to rise when firms announce an increase in their dividend payouts. How then can it be said that dividend policy is irrelevant? (LO3)

20. **Dividend Policy.** Here are several assertions about typical corporate dividend policies. Which of them are true? Write out a corrected version of any false statements. (LO1)
    a. Most companies set a target dividend payout ratio.
    b. Companies set each year's dividend equal to the target payout ratio times that year's earnings.
    c. Managers and investors seem more concerned with dividend changes than dividend levels.
    d. Managers often increase dividends temporarily when earnings are unexpectedly high for a year or two.

21. **Dividend Policy.** For each of the following four groups of companies, state whether you would expect them to distribute a relatively high or low proportion of current earnings and whether you would expect them to have a relatively high or low price-earnings ratio. (LO1)
    a. High-risk companies
    b. Companies that have recently experienced a temporary decline in profits
    c. Companies that expect to experience a decline in profits
    d. "Growth" companies with valuable future investment opportunities

22. **Dividend Policy.** "Risky companies tend to have lower target payout ratios and more gradual adjustment rates." Explain what is meant by this statement. Why do you think it is so? (LO1)

23. **Globe and Mail Investor.** Go to *The Globe and Mail*'s Investors page (**www.theglobeandmail.com/globe-investor**). Review the dividend policy of Enbridge (ENB), BCE (BCE), and the Royal Bank of Canada (RY). Review the dividend yield, dividend payout ratio, and retention rate for each firm. What factors might explain the differences in dividend policies among the companies? (LO1)

CHALLENGE

24. **Dividends and Taxes.** The expected pretax return on three stocks is divided between dividends and capital gains in the following way: (LO5)

Stock	Expected Dividend	Expected Capital Gain
A	$ 0	$10
B	5	5
C	10	0

    a. If each stock is priced at $100, what are the expected net returns on each stock to (1) a pension fund that does not pay taxes; (2) an Ontario corporation engaged in manufacturing activity, paying tax at a combined federal and provincial rate of 28 percent; and (3) an individual based in Ontario, paying a federal marginal tax rate of 29 percent and a provincial marginal tax rate of 11.16 percent? The gross-up for dividend tax credits is 25 percent. The federal dividend tax credit is 13.33 percent of the grossed-up dividend, and the provincial dividend tax credit is 4.5 percent of grossed-up dividend.
    b. Suppose that stocks A, B, and C were priced to yield an 8 percent after-tax return to individual investors paying federal tax of 16 percent and provincial tax of 6.2 percent. The gross-up for dividend tax credits is 25 percent. The federal dividend tax credit is 13.33 percent of the grossed-up dividend and the provincial dividend tax credit is 4.5 percent of grossed-up dividend. What would A, B, and C each sell for?

25. **Dividends Versus Repurchases.** Big Industries has the following market-value balance sheet. The stock currently sells for $20 a share, and there are 1,000 shares outstanding. The firm will either pay a $1 per share dividend or repurchase $1,000 worth of stock. Ignore taxes. (LO4)

Assets		Liabilities and Equity	
Cash	$ 2,000	Debt	$10,000
Fixed assets	28,000	Equity	20,000

    *a. What will be the price per share under each alternative (dividend versus repurchase)?
    *b. If total earnings of the firm are $2,000 a year, find earnings per share under each alternative.
    *c. Find the price-earnings ratio under each alternative.
    d. Adherents of the "dividends are good" school sometimes cite the fact that stocks with high dividend payout ratios tend to sell at above-average price-earnings multiples. Is this evidence convincing? Discuss this argument with regard to your answers to parts (a) through (c).

26. **Dividends and Taxes.** Shares in Growth Products Inc. are priced at $100. Investors expect the total *pretax* rate of return to be 10 percent. The tax rate on both capital gains and dividends is 15 percent. (LO5)
    a. If the entire return on the shares is in the form of dividends, what is the investor's annualized *after-tax* rate of return for a holding period of 1 year? 5 years? 10 years? 20 years?
    b. What is the investor's annualized *after-tax* rate of return for each holding period if all of the pretax return is in the form of capital gains?
    c. Explain why capital gains may be preferred to dividends even if the tax rate on the two are equal.

Solutions to Check Points

18.1 The ex-dividend date is June 1. Therefore Mick buys the stock ex-dividend and will not receive the dividend. The cheques will be mailed on June 30.

18.2

Assets		Liabilities and Equity	
After cash dividend:			
Cash	$ 0	Debt	$ 0
Other assets	850,000	Equity	850,000
Value of firm	$850,000	Value of firm	$850,000
Shares outstanding = 100,000			
Price per share = $850,000/100,000 = $8.50			
After stock repurchase:			
Cash	$ 0	Debt	$ 0
Other assets	850,000	Equity	850,000
Value of firm	$850,000	Value of firm	$850,000
Shares outstanding = 85,000			
Price per share = $850,000/85,000 = $10			

If a dividend is paid, the stock price falls by the amount of the dividend. If the company instead uses the cash for a share repurchase, the stock price remains unchanged, but with fewer shares left outstanding, the market value of the firm falls by the same amount as if the dividend had been paid. If a shareholder wants to receive the same amount of cash as if the firm had paid a dividend, he or she must sell shares, and the market value of the remaining stock will be the same as if the firm had paid a dividend.

18.3 The stock price dropped despite the increase in earnings because investors interpreted the dividend cut as a signal that future earnings would be lower than investors had previously expected. The dividend cut conveyed bad news about the future prospects of the firm.

18.4 The total value of the firm remains at $100 million. Since the firm issues $10 million in new preferred stock and the total value of the firm is fixed, the total value of common equity must fall by $10 million, which translates into the same $1 per share price drop as when equity was issued. If the firm starts out all equity-financed, the market-value balance sheet of the firm will be as follows (in millions):

Assets		Liabilities and Equity	
Assets	$100	Preferred stock	$ 10
		Common equity	90
Value of firm	$100	Value of firm	$100
Shares outstanding = 1 million			
Price per share = $90 million/1 million = $90			

18.5 An investor who prefers a zero-dividend policy can reinvest any dividends received. This will cause the value of the shares held to be unaffected by payouts. The price drop on the ex-dividend date is offset by the reinvestment of the dividends. However, if the investor had to pay brokerage fees on the newly purchased shares, she would be harmed by a high-payout policy since part of the proceeds of the dividends would go toward paying the broker. On the other hand, if the firm offers a dividend reinvestment plan (DRIP) with a 5 percent discount, she is better off with a high-dividend policy. The DRIP is like a "negative trading cost." She can increase the value of her stock by 5 percent of the dividend just by participating in the DRIP.

18.6 The price of the stock will equal the after-tax cash flows discounted by the required (after-tax) rate of return:

$$P = \frac{102.5 + 10 \times (1 - .4)}{1.10} = 98.64$$

Notice that the after-tax proceeds from the stock would increase by the amount that previously went to pay capital gains taxes, .20 × $4.72 = $.944. The present value of this tax saving is $.944/1.10 = $.86. Therefore, the price increases to $97.78 + $.86 = $98.64. The pretax rate of return falls to (102.50 − 98.64 + 10)/98.64 = .1405, or 14.05 percent, but the after-tax rate of return remains at 10 percent.

MINI CASE

George Liu, the CEO of Penn Schumann, was a creature of habit. Every month he and Jennifer Rodriguez, the company's chief financial officer, met for lunch and an informal chat at Pierre's. Nothing was ever discussed until George had finished his favourite *escalope de foie gras chaude*. At their last meeting in March he had then toyed thoughtfully with his glass of Chateau Haut-Brion Blanc before suddenly asking, "What do you think we should be doing about our payout policy?"

Penn Schumann was a large and successful pharmaceutical company. It had an enviable list of highly profitable drugs, many of which had 5 or more further years of patent protection. Earnings in the latest 4 years had increased rapidly, but it was difficult to see that such rates of growth could continue. The company had traditionally paid out about 40 percent of earnings as dividends, though the figure in 2005 was only 35 percent. Penn was spending over $4 billion a year on R&D, but the strong operating cash flow and conservative dividend policy had resulted in a buildup of cash. Penn's recent income statements, balance sheets, and cash-flow statements are summarized in Tables 18.4 to 18.6.

The problem, as Mr. Liu explained, was that Penn's dividend policy was more conservative than that of its main competitors. "Share prices depend on dividends," he said. "If we raise our dividend, we'll raise our share price, and that's the name of the game." Ms. Rodriguez suggested that the real issue was how much cash the company wanted to hold. The current cash holding was more than adequate for the company's immediate needs. On the other hand, the research staff had been analyzing a number of new compounds with promising applications in the treatment of liver diseases. If this research were to lead to a marketable product, Penn would need to make a large investment. In addition, the company might require cash for possible acquisitions in the biotech field. "What worries me," Ms. Rodriguez said, "is that investors don't give us credit for this and think that we are going to fritter away the cash on negative-NPV investments or easy living. I don't think we should commit to paying out high dividends, but perhaps we could use some of our cash to repurchase stock."

"I don't know where anyone gets the idea that we fritter away cash on easy living," replied Mr. Liu, as he took another sip of wine, "but I like the idea of buying back our stock. We can tell shareholders that we are so confident about the future that we believe buying our own stock is the best investment we can make." He scribbled briefly on his napkin. "Suppose we bought back 50 million shares at $105. That would reduce the shares outstanding to 488 million. Net income last year was nearly $4.8 billion, so earnings per share would increase to $9.84. If the price-earnings multiple stays at 11.8, the stock price should rise to $116. That's an increase of over 10 percent." A smile came over Mr. Liu's face. "Wonderful, he exclaimed, "here comes my *homard à la nage*. Let's come back to this idea over dessert."

Evaluate the arguments of Jennifer Rodriguez and George Liu. Do you think the company is holding too much cash? If you do, how do you think it could be best paid out?

TABLE 18.4
Penn Schumann, Inc., balance sheet (figures in millions of dollars).

	2005	2004
Cash and short-term investments	7,061	5,551
Receivables	2,590	2,214
Inventory	1,942	2,435
Total current assets	11,593	10,200
Property, plant, and equipment	21,088	19,025
Less accumulated depreciation	5,780	4,852
Net fixed assets	15,308	14,173
Total assets	26,901	24,373
Payables	6,827	6,215
Short-term debt	1,557	2,620
Total current liabilities	8,384	8,835
Long-term debt	3,349	3,484
Shareholders' equity	15,168	12,054
Total liabilities and equity	26,901	24,373
Note:		
Shares outstanding, millions	538	516
Market price per share ($)	105	88

TABLE 18.5
Penn Schumann, Inc., income statement (figures in millions of dollars).

	2005	2004
Revenue	16,378	13,378
Costs	8,402	7,800
Depreciation	928	850
EBIT	7,048	4,728
Interest	323	353
Tax	1,933	1,160
Net income	4,792	3,215
Dividends	1,678	1,350
Earnings per share ($)	8.91	6.23
Dividends per share ($)	3.12	2.62

TABLE 18.6
Penn Schumann, Inc., statement of cash flows (figures in millions of dollars).

	2005
Net income	4,792
Depreciation	928
Decrease (increase) in receivables	(376)
Decrease (increase) in inventories	493
Increase (decrease) in payables	612
Total cash from operations	6,446
Capital expenditures	(2,063)
Increase (decrease) in short-term debt	(1,063)
Increase (decrease) in long-term debt	(135)
Dividends paid	(1,678)
Cash provided by financing activities	(2,876)
Net increase in cash	1,510

PART 6

Financial Planning

19 Long-Term Financial Planning
- 19.1 What Is Financial Planning?
- 19.2 Financial Planning Models
- 19.3 Tips for Planners
- 19.4 External Financing and Growth
- 19.5 Summary

20 Short-Term Financial Planning

CHAPTER 19

Long-Term Financial Planning

LEARNING OBJECTIVES

After studying this chapter, you should be able to:

LO1 Describe the contents and uses of a financial plan.

LO2 Construct a simple financial planning model.

LO3 Explain the assumptions of percentage-of-sales model. Explain why the investment in some assets and some costs may not be reasonably predicted using the percentage-of-sales model.

LO4 Estimate the effect of growth on the need for external financing.

Financial planning? Financial planners don't guess the future—they prepare for it.

It's been said that a camel looks like a horse designed by committee. If a firm made all its financial decisions piecemeal, it would end up with a financial camel. That is why smart financial managers consider the overall effect of future investment and financing decisions.

Think back to Chapter 1, where we discussed the job of the financial manager. The manager must consider what investments the firm should undertake and how the firm should raise the cash to pay for those investments. By now you know a fair amount about how to make investment decisions that increase shareholder value and about the different securities that the firm can issue. But because new investments need to be paid for, those decisions cannot be made independently. They must add up to a sensible whole. That's why financial planning is needed. The financial plan allows managers to think about the implications of alternative financial strategies and to tease out any inconsistencies in the firm's goals.

Financial planning also helps managers avoid some surprises and think about how they should react to those surprises that *cannot* be avoided. In Chapter 10 we stressed that good financial managers insist on understanding what makes projects work and what could go wrong with them. The same approach should be taken when investment and financing decisions are considered as a whole.

Finally, financial planning helps establish goals to motivate managers and provide standards for measuring performance.

We start the chapter by summarizing what financial planning involves and we describe the contents of a typical financial plan. We then discuss the use of financial models in the planning process. Finally, we examine the relationship between a firm's growth and its need for new financing.

LO1 19.1 WHAT IS FINANCIAL PLANNING?

Firms must plan for both the short term and the long term. Short-term planning rarely looks further ahead than the next 12 months. It is largely the process of ensuring that the firm has enough cash to pay its bills and that short-term borrowing and lending are arranged to the best advantage. We discuss short-term planning in Chapter 20.

planning horizon Time horizon for a financial plan.

Here we are focusing on long-term planning, where a typical **planning horizon** is five years, although some firms look ahead ten years or more. For example, it can take at least ten years for an electric utility to design, obtain approval for, build, and test a major power-generating plant. So in this chapter, the term "financial planning" refers to building long-term financial plans.

Long-term financial plans focus on the firm's long-term goals, the investments that will be needed to meet those goals, and the financing that must be raised to fund the investments. But you can't think about these things without also tackling other important issues. For example, you need to consider possible dividend policies, because the more cash that is paid out to shareholders, the more the external financing that will be needed. You also need to think about what is an appropriate debt ratio for the firm. A conservative capital structure may mean greater reliance on new share issues. The financial plan is used to enforce consistency in the way that these questions are answered and to highlight the choices that the firm needs to make. Finally, by establishing a set of consistent goals, the plan enables subsequent evaluation of the firm's performance in meeting those goals.

FINANCIAL PLANNING FOCUSES ON THE BIG PICTURE

Many of the firm's capital expenditures are proposed by operation managers. But the final budget must also reflect strategic plans made by senior management. Positive-NPV opportunities occur in those businesses of a firm where the firm has a real competitive advantage. Strategic plans identify such businesses and look to expand them. These plans also seek to identify businesses to sell or liquidate as well as businesses that should be allowed to run down. These decisions are not the sole responsibility of the financial manager. The company's chief executive together with specialists in functional areas, such as marketing, production, and human resources, will be closely involved in the planning process. The final plan will also be subject to approval by the board of directors.

Strategic planning involves capital budgeting on a grand scale. In this process, financial planners look at the investment by each line of business and avoid getting bogged down in details. Of course, some individual projects are large enough to have significant individual impact. For example, the telecommunications and entertainment giant Shaw Communications announced plans to enter the cell phone service in 2012, increasing competition in Canada's wireless industry. The Calgary-based cable company said it plans to spend hundreds of millions of dollars over the next few years building a wireless network, initially in Western Canada. You can bet that this project was explicitly analyzed as part of Shaw's long-range financial plan. Normally, however, financial planners do not work on a project-by-project basis. Smaller projects are aggregated into a unit that is treated as a single project.

At the beginning of the planning process the corporate staff might ask each division to submit three alternative business plans covering the next five years:

1. A *best case* or *aggressive growth* plan calling for heavy capital investment and rapid growth of existing markets.
2. A *normal growth* plan in which the division grows with its markets but not significantly at the expense of its competitors.
3. A plan of *retrenchment* if the firm's markets contract. This is planning for lean economic times.

Each type of plan will contain a summary of capital expenditures, working-capital requirements, and strategies to raise funds for these investments.

WHY BUILD FINANCIAL PLANS?

Firms spend considerable energy, time, and resources building elaborate financial plans. What do they get for this investment? They learn about the financing requirements to support their investment plans and also have a tool for exploring implications of various scenarios.

Contingency Planning Planning is not just forecasting. Forecasting concentrates on the most likely outcomes, but planners need to worry about unlikely events as well as likely ones. If you think ahead about what could go wrong, then you are less likely to ignore the danger signals and you can respond faster to trouble.

Companies have developed a number of ways of asking "what if" questions about both individual projects and the overall firm. For example, as we saw in Chapter 10, managers often work through the consequences of investment decisions under different scenarios. One scenario might envisage high interest rates contributing to a slowdown in world economic growth and lower commodity prices. A second scenario might involve a buoyant domestic economy, high inflation, and a weak currency.

The idea is to formulate responses to inevitable surprises. What will you do, for example, if sales in the first year turn out to be 10 percent below forecast? A good financial plan should help you adapt as events unfold.

Considering Options Planners need to determine whether there are opportunities for the company to exploit its existing strengths by moving into a wholly new area. Often they might recommend entering a market for "strategic" reasons—that is, not because the immediate investment has a positive net present value but because it establishes the firm in a new market and creates options for possibly valuable follow-on investments.

For example, Shaw's costly cell phone initiative might not be profitable strictly in terms of ordinary cell phone use. But the wireless technology gives Shaw *options* to deliver broadcast content, now that they own Canwest's broadcasting assets, across multiple platforms, including smart phones and cable systems. The justification for the huge investment includes these potential growth options.

Forcing Consistency Financial plans draw out the connections between the firm's plans for growth and the financing requirements. For example, a forecast of 25 percent sales growth might require the firm to issue securities to raise cash to pay for necessary capital expenditures while a 5 percent growth rate might enable the firm to finance capital expenditures by using only reinvested profits.

Financial plans should help to ensure that the firm's goals are mutually consistent. For example, the chief executive might say that she is shooting for a profit margin of 10 percent and sales growth of 20 percent, but financial planners need to think whether the higher sales growth may require price cuts that will reduce profit margin.

Financial plans help managers ensure that their financing strategies are consistent with their capital budgets. They highlight the financing decisions necessary to support the firm's production and investment goals.

Moreover, a goal that is stated in terms of accounting ratios is not operational unless it is translated back into what that means for business decisions. For example, a higher profit margin can result from higher prices, lower costs, or a move into new, high-margin products. Why then do managers define objectives in this way? In part, such goals may be a code to communicate real concerns. For example, a target profit margin may be a way of saying that in pursuing sales growth, the firm has allowed costs to get out of control.

The danger is that everyone may forget the code and the accounting targets may be seen as goals in themselves. No one should be surprised when lower-level managers focus on the goals for which they are rewarded. For example, when Volkswagen set a goal of 6.5 percent profit margin, some VW groups responded by developing and promoting expensive, high-margin cars. Less attention was paid to marketing cheaper models, which had lower profit margins but higher sales volume. In 2002 Volkswagen announced that it would deemphasize its profit margin goal and would instead focus on return on investment. This, it hoped, would encourage managers to get the most profit out of every dollar of invested capital.

LO2 19.2 FINANCIAL PLANNING MODELS

Financial planners often use a financial planning model to help them explore the consequences of alternative financial strategies. These models range from simple models, such as the one presented in this chapter, to more complex models that incorporate more details about the firm's operations and financing alternatives.

FIGURE 19.1
The components of a financial plan.

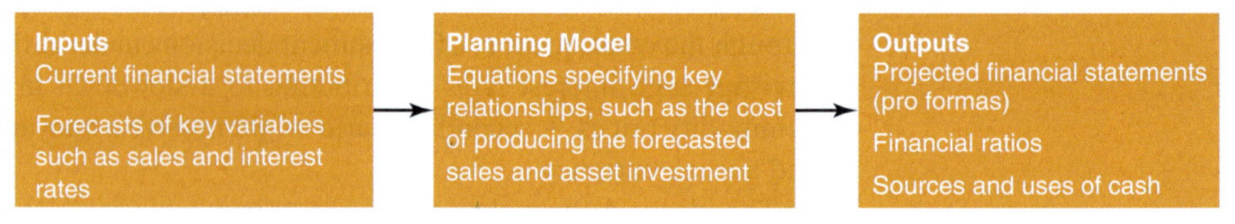

Typically financial planning models are constructed using spreadsheet programs such as Microsoft Excel. Using a spreadsheet program, rather than doing calculations on paper, makes it easier and cheaper to create pro forma (forecasted) financial statements and to explore the impact of changes in assumptions.

COMPONENTS OF A FINANCIAL PLANNING MODEL

A completed financial plan for a large company is a substantial document. A smaller corporation's plan has the same elements but less detail. For the smallest, youngest businesses, financial plans may be entirely in the financial manager's head. However, the basic elements of the plans will be similar for firms of any size.

Financial plans include three components: inputs, the planning model, and outputs. The relationship among these components is represented in Figure 19.1. Let's look at these components in turn.

Inputs The inputs to the financial plan consist of the firm's current financial statements and its forecasts about the future. Usually, the principal forecast is the likely growth in sales, since many of the other variables such as labour requirements and inventory levels are tied to sales. These forecasts are only in part the responsibility of the financial manager. Obviously, the marketing department will play a key role in forecasting sales. Their analysis of sales potential is based on their market research, including their assessment of competitors' plans. In addition, because sales will depend on the state of the overall economy, large firms will seek forecasting help from firms that specialize in preparing macroeconomic and industry forecasts.

The Planning Model The financial planning model calculates the implications of the manager's sales forecasts for profits, new investment, and financing. The model consists of equations relating output variables to forecasts. For example, the equations can show how a change in sales is likely to affect costs, working capital, long-term operating assets, and financing requirements. The financial model could specify that the total cost of goods produced will increase by 80 cents for every $1 increase in total sales, that accounts receivable will be a fixed proportion of sales, and that the firm will need to increase fixed assets by 8 percent for every 10 percent increase in sales.

pro formas Projected or forecasted financial statements.

Outputs The output of the financial model consists of financial statements such as income statements, balance sheets, and cash flow statements. These statements are called **pro formas**, which are forecasted based on the inputs and the assumptions built into the plan. As we discussed in Chapter 3, public Canadian companies must use International Financial Reporting Standards (IFRS) to create their public financial statements. The IFRS name for the income statement is the *statement of comprehensive income* and for the balance sheet is the *statement of financial position*. The pro forma statements typically have the same name as the current financial statements but do not have to meet any accounting standards. Usually the output of financial models also includes many of the financial ratios we discussed in Chapter 4. These ratios are used to help in the assessment of the firm's financial health at the end of the planning period.

PERCENTAGE-OF-SALES MODELS

We can illustrate the basic components of a planning model with a very simple example. In the next section we will start to add some complexity.

Suppose that Executive Cheese Company has prepared the simple balance sheet and income statement for the year just ended, 2011, that are shown in Table 19.1. The firm's financial planners forecast that total sales over the next year, 2012, will increase by 10 percent from this year's level. They expect that costs will be a fixed proportion of sales, so costs will also increase by 10 percent. Almost all the forecasts for Executive Cheese are proportional to the forecast of sales. Such models are therefore called **percentage-of-sales models**. The result is the pro forma, or forecast, income statement in Table 19.2, which shows that next year's income will be $\$200 \times 1.10 = \$220$.

percentage-of-sales models Planning model in which sales forecasts are the driving variables and most other variables are proportional to sales.

Executive Cheese has no spare capacity, and in order to sustain this higher level of output, it must increase plant and equipment by 10 percent, $0.1 \times \$2{,}000$ or \$200. Therefore, the left-hand side of the balance sheet, which lists total assets, must increase to \$2,200. What about the right-hand side? The firm must decide how it intends to finance its new assets. Suppose it decides to maintain its current debt-equity ratio. To do this, both debt and equity must be increased by the same percentage. We have already figured out that assets must grow by 10 percent, and since the balance sheet must balance, both debt and equity must also grow by 10 percent. This implies the firm must issue \$80 in additional debt, 10 percent of the original debt of \$800. Also, equity must increase by \$120, 10 percent of the original \$1,200 in equity. However, no new equity needs to be issued. The 10 percent increase in equity can be accomplished by retaining \$120 of net income. The pro forma balance sheet for this financing plan is in Table 19.2.[1]

TABLE 19.1 Financial statements of Executive Cheese Company for the past year, 2011.

Income Statement For the Year Ending December 31, 2011			
Sales			$1,200
Costs			1,000
Net income			$ 200
Balance Sheet As of December 31, 2011			
Assets	$2,000	Debt	$ 800
		Equity	1,200
Total	$2,000	Total	$2,000

TABLE 19.2 Pro forma financial statements of Executive Cheese Company for the next year, 2012, with fixed debt-equity ratio.

Pro Forma Income Statement For the Year Ending December 31, 2012			
Sales			$1,320
Costs			1,100
Net income			$ 220
Pro Forma Balance Sheet As of December 31, 2012			
Assets	$2,200	Debt	$ 880
		Equity	1,320
Total	$2,200	Total	$2,200

[1] The new financing required can be figured out another way. If the debt-equity ratio is fixed, so too is the debt-asset ratio. The current debt-asset ratio is 800/2,000, or 40 percent. This tells us that the \$200 increase in assets must be financed with 40 percent new debt, $.4 \times \$200 = \$80$, and 60 percent new equity, $.6 \times \$200 = \$120$, the same values we found above.

This raises a question, however. If income is forecast at $220, why does equity increase by only $120? The answer is that the firm must be planning to pay a dividend of $220 − $120 = $100. Notice that this dividend payment is not chosen independently but is a *consequence* of the other decisions. Given the company's need for funds and its decision to maintain the debt-equity ratio, dividend policy is completely determined. Any other dividend payment would be inconsistent with the two conditions that (1) the right-hand side of the balance sheet increase by $200 and (2) both debt and equity increase by 10 percent. For this reason we call dividends the **balancing item**, or plug. The balancing item is the variable that adjusts to make the sources of funds equal to the uses.

balancing item Variable that adjusts to maintain the consistency of a financial plan. Also called the *plug*.

Of course, most firms would be reluctant to vary dividends simply because they have a temporary need for cash; instead, they like to maintain a steady progression of dividends. In this case Executive Cheese could commit to some other dividend payment and allow the debt-equity ratio to vary. The amount of debt would therefore become the balancing item.

EXAMPLE 19.1 BALANCING ITEM

Suppose the firm commits to a dividend level of $180, and raises any extra money it needs by an issue of debt. In this case the amount of debt becomes the balancing item. With the dividend set at $180, addition to retained earnings would be only $40, so the firm would have to issue $160 in new debt to help pay for the additional $200 of assets. Table 19.3, panel A, is the new balance sheet.

Now suppose instead that the firm commits to the $180 dividend but decides that it will issue at most $100 in new debt. In that case, new equity issue becomes the balancing item. With $40 of earnings retained, and $100 of new debt, an additional $60 of equity needs to be raised to support the total addition of $200 to the firm's assets. Table 19.3, panel B, is the resulting balance sheet.

TABLE 19.3 Executive Cheese Company pro forma balance sheets with different balancing items. Panel A: Dividends are fixed and debt is the balancing item. Panel B: Dividends and debt are fixed and equity issues is the balancing item.

Pro Forma Balance Sheets for 2012, Based on Different Balancing Items							
Panel A				Panel B			
Assets	$2,200	Debt	$ 960	Assets	$2,200	Debt	$ 900
		Equity	1,240			Equity	1,300
Total	$2,200	Total	$2,200	Total	$2,200	Total	$2,200

Financial models ensure consistency between growth assumptions and financing plans, but they do not identify the best financing plan.

Is one of these plans better than the others? It's hard to give a simple answer. The choice of dividend payment depends partly on how investors will interpret the decision. If last year's dividend was only $50, investors might regard a dividend payment of $100 as a sign of a confident management; if last year's dividend was $150, investors might not be so content with a payment of $100. The alternative of paying $180 in dividends and making up the shortfall by issuing more debt leaves the company with a debt-equity ratio of 77 percent. That is unlikely to make your bankers edgy but you may worry about how long you can continue to finance expansion predominantly by borrowing.

Our example shows how experiments with a financial model, including changes in the model's balancing item, can raise important financial questions. But the model does not answer these questions.

Check Point 19.1

Suppose that the firm decides to maintain its debt-equity ratio at 800/1,200 = 2/3. It is committed to increasing assets by 10 percent to support the forecast increase in sales, and it strongly believes that a dividend payment of $180 is in the best interests of the firm. What must be the balancing items? What is the implication for the firm's financing activities in the next year?

AN IMPROVED MODEL

Now that you have grasped the idea behind financial planning models, we can move on to a more sophisticated example.

Table 19.4 shows simplified financial statements for Yummy Food Company in 2012. Its 2012 earnings before interest and taxes, EBIT, were 10 percent of sales revenue. Net income was $96,000 after payment of taxes and 10 percent interest paid on $400,000 of long-term debt. The company paid out two-thirds of its net income as dividends.

net operating working capital (NOWC) Operating current assets minus operating current liabilities, excluding interest-bearing debt.

The first entry on the balance sheet is **net operating working capital, NOWC**, operating current assets minus operating current liabilities. Operating current assets consist of current assets needed for the operation of the business, including trade receivables, prepaid expenses, inventory and cash needed to operate the business. Non-operating current assets include excess cash, marketable securities, and other investments. Operating current liabilities include trade payables, accruals, and any other liabilities spontaneously generated by the operation of the firm. For example, when Yummy Food orders more supplies, its trade payables are automatically increased, on the basis of the credit policy of its suppliers, generating spontaneous financing. Discretionary sources of financing, such as bank loans and other interest-bearing debt, are the result of successful negotiations by the financial managers of Yummy Food with banks and other lenders and are not automatically generated by the firm's operations. So interest-bearing debt are non-operating liabilities. Yummy Food does not have any non-operating assets or non-operating liabilities. Currently, Yummy Food has only long-term debt.

Next to each item on the financial statements in Table 19.4 we have entered a comment about the relationship between that variable and sales. In most cases, the comment gives the value of each item as a percentage of sales. This may be useful for forecasting purposes. For example, it would be reasonable to assume that cost of goods sold will remain at 90 percent of sales even if

TABLE 19.4 Financial statements for Yummy Food Company, 2012.

Income Statement For the Year Ending December 31, 2012 ($000s)		
Revenue	$2,000	**Comment**
Cost of goods sold	(1,800)	90% of sales, 1,800/2,000
EBIT	200	Difference = 10% of sales, 200/2,000
Interest expense	(40)	10% of debt at start of year, .1 × 400,000
Earnings before taxes	160	EBIT − interest expense
Corporate tax	(64)	40% of (EBIT − interest expense), .4 × 160
Net income	$ 96	EBIT − interest expense − taxes
Dividends	$ (64)	Payout ratio = 2/3, 64/96
Addition to retained earnings	$ 32	Net income − dividends
Balance Sheet As of December 31, 2012 Assets		
Net operating working capital	$ 200	10% of sales, 200/2,000
Property, plant, and equipment	800	40% of sales, 800/2,000
Total assets	$1,000	50% of sales, 1,000/2,000
Liabilities and Shareholders' Equity		
Long-term debt	$ 400	
Shareholders' equity	600	
Total liabilities and shareholders' equity	$1,000	Equals total assets

sales grow by 10 percent next year. Similarly, it is reasonable to assume that net operating working capital will remain at 10 percent of sales.

On the other hand, the fact that long-term debt currently is 20 percent of sales does not mean that we should assume that this ratio will continue to hold next period. Many alternative financing plans with varying combinations of debt issues, equity issues, and dividend payouts may be considered without affecting the firm's operations.

Now suppose that you are asked to prepare pro forma financial statements for Yummy Food for 2013. You are told to assume that (1) sales and operating costs are expected to be up 10 percent over 2012, (2) interest expense will remain at current level, (3) the firm will stick to its traditional dividend policy of paying out two-thirds of earnings, and (4) property, plant, and equipment (PPE) and net operating working capital must increase 10 percent to support the higher sales volume.

In Table 19.5 we present the resulting first-stage pro forma calculations for Yummy Food. These calculations show what would happen if the size of the firm increases along with sales, but at this preliminary stage, the plan does not specify a particular mix of new security issues.

Without any new financing, the balance sheet at the start of the year will not balance: assets increase to $1,100,000 while debt plus shareholders' equity will amount to only $1,036,000. Somehow the firm will need to raise an extra $64,000 to help pay for the increase in assets necessary to support the higher projected level of sales in 2013. In this first pass, external financing is the balancing item. Given the firm's growth forecasts and its dividend policy, the financial plan calculates how much money the firm needs to raise but does not yet specify how those funds will be raised.

In the second-stage pro forma, the firm must decide on the financing mix that best meets its needs for additional funds. It must choose some combination of new debt and/or new equity that supports the contemplated acquisition of additional assets. For example, it could issue $64,000

TABLE 19.5 First-stage pro forma statements for Yummy Food Company, 2013 (figures in thousands).

Pro Forma Income Statement for 2013		
		Comment
Revenue	$2,200	10% higher
Cost of goods sold	(1,980)	10% higher; 90 percent of sales
EBIT	220	10% higher
Interest	(40)	Unchanged
Earnings before taxes	180	EBIT − interest
Corporate tax	(72)	40% of (EBIT − interest)
Net income	$ 108	EBIT − interest − taxes
Dividends	$ (72)	2/3 of net income
Addition to retained earnings	$ 36	Net income − dividends
Pro Forma Balance Sheet as of December 31, 2013		
Assets		
Net operating working capital	$ 220	10% higher; 10 percent of sales
Property, plant, and equipment	880	10% higher; 40 percent of sales
Total assets	$1,100	10% higher
Liabilities and Shareholders' Equity		
Long-term debt	$ 400	Temporarily held fixed
Shareholders' equity	636	Increased by addition to retained earnings, 600 + 36
Total liabilities and shareholders' equity	$1,036	Sum of debt plus equity
Required external financing	$ 64	Balancing item or plug (= $1,100 − $1,036)

of equity or debt, or it could choose to maintain its long-term debt-equity ratio at two-thirds by issuing both debt and equity.

Table 19.6 shows the second-stage pro forma balance sheet if the required funds are raised by issuing $64,000 of debt. Therefore, in this table debt is treated as the balancing item. Notice that while the plan requires the firm to specify a financing plan *consistent* with its growth projections, it does not provide guidance as to the *best* financing mix.

Table 19.7 sets out the firm's sources and uses of funds for the year, 2013. It shows that net operating working capital must be increased by $20,000 and property, plant, and equipment by $80,000. The firm reinvested $36,000 of this year's profits, so $64,000 must be raised from the capital markets. Under the financing plan presented in Table 19.6, the firm borrows the entire $64,000.

Another way to describe the flow of funds is to calculate the cash flow from assets and the financing flows, as shown in Chapter 3. In Table 19.8 is the cash flow from assets. There were no noncash deductions in the calculation of net income, so no adjustments are needed to convert net income to cash. Yummy Food generated $8,000 cash flow from its operating activities, after its investment in net operating working capital and PPE. Table 19.9 shows the cash flow to

TABLE 19.6
Second-stage pro forma balance sheet for Yummy Food Company, at December 31, 2013, with debt as the balancing item (figures in thousands).

Pro Forma Balance Sheet as of December 31, 2013		
		Comment
Assets		
Net operating working capital	$ 220	10% of sales
Property, plant, and equipment	880	40% of sales
Total assets	$1,100	10% higher
Liabilities and Shareholders' Equity		
Long-term debt	$ 464	16% higher (new borrowing = $64; this is the balancing item)
Shareholders' equity	$ 636	Increased by 2013 addition to retained earnings
Total liabilities and shareholders' equity	$1,100	Again equals total assets equity

TABLE 19.7
Pro forma statement of sources and uses of funds for Yummy Food, for 2013 (figures in thousands).

Pro Forma Sources and Uses of Funds			
Sources		**Uses**	
Addition to retained earnings	$ 36	Investment in net operating working capital	$ 20
New borrowing	64	Investment in property, plant, and equipment	80
Total sources	$100	Total uses	$100

TABLE 19.8
Pro forma cash flow from assets for Yummy Food, 2013 (figures in thousands).

Pro Forma Cash Flow from Assets	
Net income	$108
Investment in net operating working capital	(20)
Investment in property, plant, and equipment	(80)
Total cash flow from assets	$ 8

TABLE 19.9
Pro forma cash flow to bondholders and shareholders for Yummy Food, 2013 (figures in thousands).

Pro Forma Cash Flow to Bondholders and Shareholders	
New borrowing	($64)
Dividends	72
Total cash flow to bondholders and shareholders	$ 8

FIGURE 19.2 Yummy Food spreadsheet.

	A	B	C	D	E	F	G	H
1	**Model Inputs**				**Base Year**			**Formula**
2				**Income Statement**	**2012**	**2013**	**2014**	**for Column G**
3	Sales growth rate	0.1		Revenue	2,000	2,200.0	2,420.0	=F3*(1+$B$3)
4	Tax rate	0.4		Cost of goods sold	1,800	1,980.0	2,178.0	=G3*$B$8
5	Interest rate	0.1		EBIT	200	220.0	242.0	=G3−G4
6	NWC/sales	0.1		Interest expense	40	40.0	46.4	=$B$5*F20
7	Fixed assets/sales	0.4		Earnings before taxes	160	180.0	195.6	=G5−G6
8	COGS/sales	0.9		Taxes	64	72.0	78.2	=$B$4*G7
9	Payout ratio	2/3		Net income	96	108.0	117.4	=G7−G8
10				*Dividends*	64	72.0	78.2	=G9*$B$9
11				Addition to retained earnings	32	36.0	39.1	=G9−G10
12								
13				**Balance Sheet (year-end)**				
14				Assets:				
15				Net operating working capital	200	220.0	242.0	=$B$6*G3
16				Property, plant & equipment	800	880.0	968.0	=$B$7*G3
17				Total assets	1,000	1,100.0	1,210.0	=G15+G16
18								
19				Liabilities and equity:				
20				Long-term debt (note a)	400	464.0	534.9	=F20+G24
21				Shareholders' equity (note b)	600	636.0	675.1	=F21+G11
22				Total liab. & share. equity	1,000	1,100.0	1,210.0	=G20+G21
23								
24				Required external financing		64.0	70.9	=G17−F17−G11
25								
26								
27	**Notes**							
28	(a) Long-term debt, the balancing item, increases by required external financing.							
29	(b) Shareholders' equity equals its value in the previous year plus addition to earnings retained for the year.							
30								

bondholders and shareholders. Since it only generated \$8,000 from its operations, Yummy Food had to borrow \$64,000 in order to pay \$72,000 dividend to shareholders (\$64,000 + \$8,000 = \$72,000). Thus, the net financing flow to bondholders and shareholders was \$72,000 − \$64,000 = \$8,000.

We have spared you the trouble of actually calculating the figures necessary for all these tables. The calculations do not take more than a few minutes for this simple example, *provided* you set up the calculations correctly and make no arithmetic mistakes. If that time requirement seems trivial, remember that in reality you probably would be asked for four similar sets of statements covering each year from 2013 to 2017. Also you would likely be asked for alternative projections under different assumptions (for example, 5 percent instead of 10 percent growth rate of revenue) or different financial strategies (for example, freeze dividends at their 2012 level of \$64,000). This would be far more time-consuming. Moreover, actual plans will have many more line items than this simple one. Building a model and letting the computer toil in your place has obvious attractions.

Figure 19.2 is the spreadsheet we used for the Yummy Food model. Column E contains the values that appear in Table 19.4. Columns F and G are pro forma statements using the growth rate given in cell B3. Column H presents the formulas used to obtain each value in column G. The same formulas but with difference cell numbers are used to calculate the values in column F.

We assume the firm will maintain its dividend payout ratios at 2/3 and that debt will be the balancing item, increasing in each year by required external financing (row 24). Required external financing in 2013 equals total assets required to support that year's sales (cell F17) minus the previous year's assets (cell E17) minus the addition to earnings retained during year (cell F11). Since the previous year's assets equals the total previous year's financing, this method assumes that all existing financing will continue in the next year. In other words, no existing debt must be repaid in 2013. Long-term debt (cell F20) equals its previous value (cell E20) plus the required external financing (cell F24). Shareholders' equity (cell F21) equals its previous value (cell E21) plus addition to retained earnings from the year (cell F11).

Built into the spreadsheet is the assumption that the interest expense in each year is based on the debt level at the start of the year. For example, the interest expense in 2014 is the interest rate, 10 percent, times the debt outstanding at the end of 2013. Calculating interest expense on the basis of the debt at the start of the year implies that the new debt is raised at the end of the year, because new debt does not affect that year's interest expense.

Now that the spreadsheet is set up, it is easy to explore the consequences of various assumptions. For example, you can change the assumed sales growth rate (cell B3) or experiment with different policies, such as changing the dividend payout ratio or forcing debt or equity finance (or both) to absorb the required external financing.

EXAMPLE 19.2 WHAT HAPPENS IF THE GROWTH RATE CHANGES?

Let's use the spreadsheet to explore the effect of sales growth on the need for external financing. We can alter the assumed growth rate in cell B3 and see the effect on required external finance in 2014, cell F24. For example, we saw in Figure 19.2 that when the sales growth rate was 10 percent, required external finance was $64,000. In our model, assets are proportional to sales, so as we assume a higher growth rate of sales, assets also increase at a higher rate. The additional funds necessary to pay for those additional assets imply greater external finance.

Table 19.10 shows how the required external finance changes if the forecasted growth rate changes. Notice that at a 3.33 percent growth rate, required external finance is indeed zero. At higher growth rates, the firm requires external finance; at lower rates, retained earnings exceed the addition to assets and there is a surplus of funds from internal sources, that shows up as negative required external financing. Later in the chapter, we will explore the limits to internal growth more systematically.

TABLE 19.10 Required external financing for Yummy Food. Higher growth rates require greater amounts of external capital.

Growth Rate (%)	Required External Finance ($000s)
0	−32
2	−12.8
3.33	0
5	16
10	64
15	112
20	160

Check Point 19.2

a. Suppose that Yummy Food is committed to a 10 percent growth rate and to paying out two-thirds of its profits as dividends. However, it now wishes to maintain its debt-equity ratio as 2/3. What are the implications for external financing in 2013?
b. If the company is prepared to reduce dividends paid in 2013 to $60,000, how much external financing would be needed?

LO3 19.3 TIPS FOR PLANNERS

PITFALLS IN MODEL DESIGN

The Yummy Food model is still too simple for practical application. You have probably already noticed several ways to improve it. For example, we ignored the capital cost allowance, CCA, associated with the fixed asset. CCA is important because it provides a tax shield. If Yummy Food deducts CCA before calculating its tax bill, it could plow back more money into new investments and would need to borrow less. We've also simplified the firm's borrowing plans, ignoring the possibility of issuing short-term debt and assuming that the firm will be able to issue small amounts of additional long-term debt at the same interest rate of its existing long-term debt. This ignores the interest rate change due to changes in market conditions and also ignores the impact of the firm's increased leverage, increasing the riskiness of debt and resulting in investors requiring a higher interest rate.

You would certainly want to make the obvious improvements. But beware: there is always the temptation to make a model bigger and more detailed. You may end up with an exhaustive model that is too cumbersome for routine use.

Excessive detail gets in the way of the intended use of corporate planning models, which is to project the financial consequences of a variety of strategies and assumptions. The fascination of detail, if you give in to it, distracts attention from crucial decisions like stock issues and dividend policy and allocation of capital by business area.

THE ASSUMPTION IN PERCENTAGE-OF-SALES MODELS

A key factor in any planning exercise is the sales forecast. Ensure the plan reflects reality. For example, if a plan is based on aggressive growth and increase in market share, ask where the sales growth will come from. Put yourself in your competitors' shoes and think how they are likely to react. Although the firm cannot perfectly predict future sales, managers must strive for the most reasonable forecasts.

The percentage-of-sales forecasting method assumes that costs and assets increase proportionately with sales. In Yummy Food's forecast, the 2013 percentage-of-sales forecasting factors are taken from the 2012 sales, costs, and assets. These forecasting assumptions are listed as the "Model Inputs" in column A of Figure 19.2. Are these sensible forecasting factors? When building planning models, financial managers must not naively accept the previous year's percent-of-sales factors as necessarily valid for the future. The specific expansion plans may change the cost-to-sales ratios and the need for assets. For example, to increase Yummy Food's sales, what if the price of products needs to be reduced? Then COGS/Sales will be higher and EBIT/Sales will be lower.

When forecasting Yummy Food's capital requirements, we assumed that both PPE and net operating working capital increase proportionately with sales and assumed that the 2011 percentage-of-sales numbers were sensible forecast factors. For example, line (a) in Figure 19.3 shows that net operating working capital is a constant 10 percent of sales.

Percentage-of-sales models are useful first approximations for financial planning. However, in reality, assets may not be proportional to sales. For example, we will see in Chapter 21 that important components of net operating working capital such as inventories and cash balances will generally rise less than proportionately with sales. Suppose that Yummy Food looks back at past variations in sales and estimates that on average a \$1 rise in sales requires only a \$.075 increase in net operating working capital. Line (b) in Figure 19.3 shows the level of net operating working capital that would now be needed for different levels of sales. To allow for this in the Yummy Food model, we would need to set net operating working capital equal to (\$50,000 $+ .075 \times$ sales).

A further complication is that typically non-current assets such as property, plant, and equipment are not added in small increments as sales increase. Instead, the picture is more likely to resemble Figure 19.4. If Yummy Food's factories are operating at less than full capacity (point A, for example), then the firm can expand sales without any additional investment in plant.

FIGURE 19.3
Net operating working capital (NOWC) as a function of sales: line (a) shows net operating working capital equal to .10 × sales. Line (b) depicts net operating working capital as $50,000 + (.075 × sales), so that NOWC increases less than proportionately with sales.

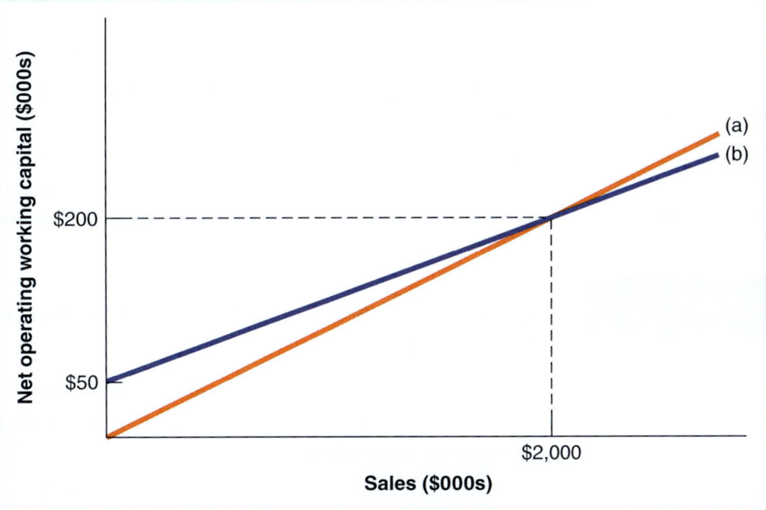

FIGURE 19.4
If factories are operating below full capacity, sales can increase without investment in property, plant, and equipment or other long-term assets (point A). Beyond some sales level (point B), new capacity must be added.

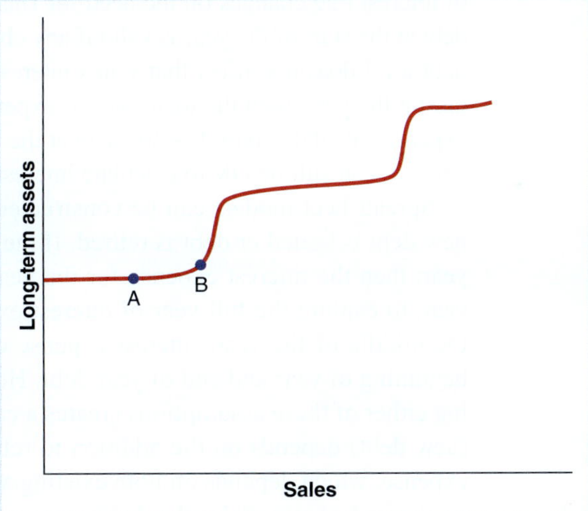

Ultimately, however, if sales continue to increase, say beyond point B, Yummy Food will need to add new capacity. This is shown by the occasional large changes to long-term (non-current) assets in Figure 19.4. These "lumpy" changes to long-term assets need to be recognized when devising the financial plan. If there is considerable excess capacity, even rapid sales growth may not require big additions to long-term assets. On the other hand, if the firm is already operating at capacity, even small sales growth may call for large investment in plant and equipment.

EXAMPLE 19.3 **REQUIRED EXTERNAL FUNDS AND EXCESS CAPACITY**

Suppose that Carter Tools has $50 million invested in property, plant and equipment and generates sales of $60 million. The company is currently working at 80 percent of capacity. Suppose that a 50 percent increase in sales is forecast. How much investment in these assets would be required?

(Continued)

(Concluded)

Sales can increase the need for new investments in long-term assets until the company is at 100 percent of capacity. Therefore, sales can increase to \$60 million × 100/80 = \$75 million before the firm reaches full capacity given its current level of long-term assets. At full capacity, therefore, the ratio of long-term assets to sales would be \$50 million/\$75 million = $^2/_3$.

The 50 percent increase in forecast sales would imply a sales level of \$60 million × 1.5 = \$90 million. To support this level of sales, the company needs at least \$90 million × $^2/_3$ = \$60 million of fixed assets. This calls for a \$10 million investment in additional long-term assets.

Check Point 19.3

Suppose that at its current level of assets and sales, Carter Tools in Example 19.3 is working at 75 percent of capacity.

a. How much can sales expand without any further investment in long-term assets?
b. How much investment in long-term assets would be required to support a 50 percent expansion in sales?

FORECASTING INTEREST EXPENSE

In Figure 19.2 Yummy Food's 2014 forecasted interest expense is the interest rate, 10 percent, times the debt outstanding at the end of 2013 (start of 2014), \$46,400. Use Excel to explore the impact of interest rate changes on the need for financing. Calculating interest expense on the basis of the debt at the start of the year is valid if any change in debt occurs at the end of the year, because new debt level does not affect that year's interest expense. If the firm repays and/or borrows new debt during the year, then the total interest expense for the year may be very different than the interest expense calculated based on the debt at the beginning of the year. However, if the change in debt is small, it can still be OK to calculate interest expense based on the beginning of year debt.

Spreadsheet models can be constructed to accommodate different assumptions about when new debt is issued or debt is retired. If the change in debt is assumed to occur at the start of the year, then the interest expense for the year is calculated using the debt level at the end of the year, to capture the full year of interest expense on the total debt. If the debt change occurs in the middle of the year, interest expense can be calculated on the basis of the average of the beginning of year and end of year debt. However, if debt is also the balancing item, implementing either of these assumptions creates a calculation problem, as the required external financing (new debt) depends on the addition to retained earnings, which depends on the year's interest expense, which depends on both existing and new debt. Assuming that interest expense depends on the end-of-year debt, the 2014 interest expense (cell G6) is based on the debt at the end of 2014 (cell G20). The revised Excel equation is =\$B\$5*G20. So 2014 addition to retained earnings (cell G11) is also connected to the 2014 debt level because of the subtraction of the interest expense.

Adding this new interest expense equation creates what Excel calls a *circular reference*, because interest expense and the required external financing equations are linked to each other by the amount of debt. Remember the required external financing equals the 2014 change in assets (G17–F17) minus the 2014 Addition to retained earnings (G11). To deal with a circular reference Excel uses *iterative calculations*, meaning that it does repeated calculations using different numbers to solve the equations. You must activate circular references to accommodate the new interest expense equation. In 2007 Excel, click on Office>Excel Options>Formulas, and the Enable iterative calculation check box. The 2014 interest expense based on the end-of-year debt increases the required external financing and 2014 debt by \$1,400. The new required external financing is \$72,300 and the 2014 debt to \$536,300. So the new 2014 interest expense is also higher, .1*\$536,300 = \$53,630. To calculate interest expense on the basis of average debt, the 2014 interest expense equation would be =\$B\$5*average(F20:G20) and creates a circular reference for the same reasons. Using average debt in interest expense calculation is a typical assumption used in financial planning, because it is less extreme than using either the beginning- or end-of-year debt.

THE ROLE OF FINANCIAL PLANNING MODELS

Models such as the one that we constructed for Yummy Food help the financial manager avoid surprises. If the planned rate of growth will require the company to raise external finance, the manager can start planning how best to do so.

We commented earlier that financial planners are concerned about unlikely events as well as likely ones. For example, Yummy Food's manager may wish to consider how the company's capital requirement would change if profit margins come under pressure and the company generates less cash from its operations. Planning models make it easy to explore the consequences of such events.

However, there are limits to what you can learn from planning models. Although they help to trace through the consequences of alternative plans, they do not tell the manager which plan is best. For example, we saw that Yummy Food is proposing to grow its sales and earnings per share. Is that good news for shareholders? Well, not necessarily; it depends on the opportunity cost of the additional capital that the company needs to achieve that growth. In 2013 the company proposes to invest $100,000 in PPE and net operating working capital. Comparing net income in Tables 19.4 and 19.5 showed that this extra investment is expected to generate $12,000 of additional net income, 2013 net income − 2012 net income = $108,000 − $96,000 = $12,000. This equivalent to a return of 12 percent on the new investment.[2] If the cost of that capital is less than 12 percent, the new investment will have a positive NPV and will add to shareholder wealth. But suppose that the cost of capital is higher at, say, 15 percent. In this case Yummy Food's investment makes shareholders *worse off*, even though the company is recording steady growth in earnings per share and dividends. Yummy Food's planning model tells us how much money the firm must raise to fund the planned growth, but it cannot tell us whether that growth contributes to shareholder value. Nor can it tell us whether the company should raise the cash by issuing new debt or equity.

Check Point 19.4

Which of the following questions will a financial plan help to answer?

a. Is the firm's assumption for asset growth consistent with its plans for debt and equity issues and dividend policy?
b. Will accounts receivable increase in direct proportion to sales?
c. Will the contemplated debt-equity mix maximize the value of the firm?

LO4 19.4 EXTERNAL FINANCING AND GROWTH

Financial *plans* force managers to be consistent in their goals for growth, investments, and financing. The nearby Finance in Action box describes how one company was brought to its knees in part by fundamental inconsistencies between its growth strategy and its financing plans.

Financial *models*, such as the one that we have developed for Yummy Food, can help managers trace through the financial consequences of their growth plans and avoid such disasters. But there is a danger that the complexities of a full-blown financial model can obscure the basic issues. Therefore, managers also use some simple rules of thumb to draw out the relationship between a firm's growth objectives and its requirement for external financing.

Recall Table 19.4, which showed that in 2012 Yummy Food ended the year with $1,000,000 of property, plant, and equipment and net operating working capital and it had $2,000,000 of sales. In other words, each dollar of sales required $.50 of net assets. These are *net* assets because operating current liabilities have been subtracted from operating current assets. Operating current liabilities are subtracted from operating current assets if they vary with sales. The company forecasts that sales in 2013 will increase by $200,000. Therefore, if the ratio of sales to net assets remains constant, assets will need to rise by $.50 × $200,000 = $100,000.[3] Part of this increase

[2] We assume this additional $12,000 income is a perpetuity and the rate of return is the IRR of the investment. Recall that the IRR is the rate of return that makes the NPV of the $100,000 investment equal zero: NPV = 0 = − $100,000 + $12,000/IRR. So IRR = $12,000/$100,000 = .12 or 12%.

[3] However, remember our earlier warning that the ratio of sales to net assets may change as the firm grows.

Finance in Action

The Collapse of Vivendi: A Failure in Planning

In 1994 39-year-old Jean-Marie Messier became CEO of the French company Générale des Eaux. He immediately set out to transform it from a sleepy water and sewage business into a multinational media and telecommunications group. The company, now renamed Vivendi, entered into a series of major acquisitions, including a $42 billion purchase of Seagram, owner of Universal Studios. To finance its expansion, Vivendi increased its borrowing to $35 billion, and it increased its leverage further by repurchasing 104 million shares for $6.3 billion. Confident that its share price would rise, the company raised the stakes even more by selling a large number of put options on its own stock.

Vivendi's strategy made it very vulnerable to any decline in operating cash flow. As profits began to evaporate, the company faced a severe cash shortage. Its banks were reluctant to extend further credit, and its bonds were downgraded to junk status. By July 2002 the share price had fallen to less than 10 percent of its level 2 years earlier. With the company facing imminent bankruptcy, M. Messier was ousted and the new management set about slashing costs and selling assets to reduce the debt burden.*

Vivendi's problems were exacerbated by considerable waste and ostentatious extravagance, but its brush with bankruptcy was a result of a lack of financial planning. The company's goals for growth were unsustainable, and it had few options for surviving a decline in operating cash flow.

However, Vivendi did survive its financial crisis. Over the years it sold various assets and bought other assets, changing its operating strategy. It now creates, publishes, assembles, and distributes digital content for consumers and businesses, primarily in France, Europe, the United States, Morocco, and Brazil. It is the owner of the world's largest music company, Universal Music Group, and largest video game company, Activision Blizzard. In June 2011 it raised 1.75 billion euros (US$2.5 billion) from its first bond sale in more than a year. You can learn more about the company at Yahoo finance and its Web site, **www.vivendi.com**.

*The rise and fall of Vivendi is chronicled in J. Johnson and M. Orange, *The Man Who Tried to Buy the World: Jean-Marie Messier and Vivendi Universal* (New York: Portfolio, 2003).

can be financed by additional retained earnings, which in 2013 are $36,000. So the amount of external finance needed is

$$\begin{aligned}\text{Required external financing} &= (\text{net assets/sales}) \times \text{increase in sales} \\ &\quad - \text{addition to retained earnings} \\ &= (.50 \times 200{,}000) - 36{,}000 = \$64{,}000\end{aligned}$$

Sometimes it is useful to write this calculation in terms of growth rates. Yummy Food's forecasted increase in sales is equivalent to a rise of 10 percent. So, if net assets are a constant proportion of sales, the higher sales volume will also require a 10 percent addition to net assets. Thus

$$\begin{aligned}\text{New investment} &= \text{growth rate} \times \text{initial net assets} \\ \$100{,}000 &= .10 \times \$1{,}000{,}000\end{aligned}$$

Part of the funds to pay for the new assets will be provided by the forecasted addition to retained earnings. The remainder must come from external financing. Therefore,

$$\begin{aligned}\textbf{Required external financing} &= \textbf{new investment} - \textbf{addition to retained earnings} \\ &= (\textbf{growth rate} \times \textbf{assets}) - \textbf{addition to retained earnings}\end{aligned} \qquad \textbf{(19.1)}$$

The assets used in equation 19.1 are those that vary with sales and are net of operating liabilities that also vary with sales. If liabilities do not vary with sales they are not subtracted. To save space, we use the term "assets," but they might be net assets. This simple equation highlights that the amount of external financing depends on the firm's projected growth. The faster the firm grows, the more it needs to invest and therefore the more it needs to raise new capital.

In the case of Yummy Food,

$$\begin{aligned}\text{Required external financing} &= (.10 \times \$1{,}000{,}000) - \$36{,}000 \\ &= \$100{,}000 - \$36{,}000 = \$64{,}000\end{aligned}$$

FIGURE 19.5
External financing and growth.

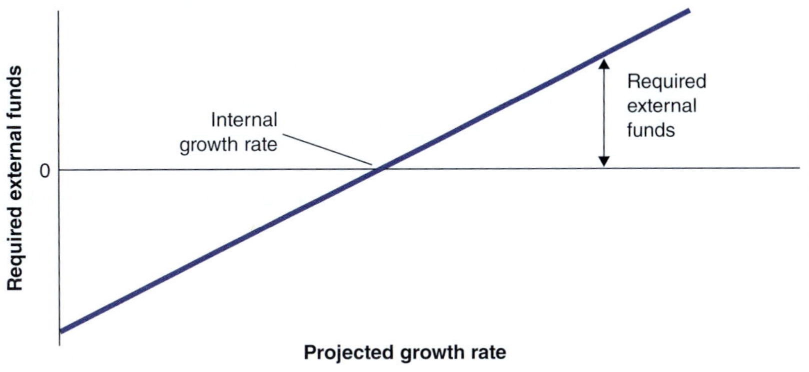

If Yummy Food's assets remain a constant percentage of sales, then the company needs to raise \$64,000 to produce a 10 percent addition to sales.

The sloping line in Figure 19.5 illustrates how required external financing increases with the growth rate. At low growth rates, the firm generates more funds than necessary for expansion. In this sense, its requirement for further external funds is negative. It may choose to use its surplus to pay off some of its debt or buy back its stock. In fact, the vertical intercept in Figure 19.5, at zero growth, is the negative of the addition to retained earnings. When growth is zero, no funds are needed for expansion, so all the additions to retained earnings are surplus.

As the firm's projected growth rate increases, more funds are needed to pay for the necessary investments. Therefore, the plot in Figure 19.5 is upward-sloping. For high rates of growth the firm must issue new securities to pay for new investments.

internal growth rate Maximum rate of growth without external financing.

Where the sloping line crosses the horizontal axis, external financing is zero: the firm is growing as fast as possible without resorting to new security issues. This is called the **internal growth rate**. The growth rate is "internal" because it can be maintained without resort to additional external sources of capital.

If we set required external financing to zero in equation 19.1, we can solve for the internal growth rate as

$$\textbf{Internal growth rate} = \frac{\textbf{addition to retained earnings}}{\textbf{assets}} \qquad \textbf{(19.2)}$$

Thus the firm's rate of growth without additional external sources of capital will equal the ratio of the addition to retained earnings to assets. This means that a firm with a high volume of retained earnings relative to its assets can generate a higher growth rate without needing to raise more capital.

We can gain more insight into what determines the internal growth rate by multiplying the top and bottom of the expression for internal growth by net income and equity as follows:

$$\textbf{Internal growth rate} = \frac{\textbf{addition to retained earnings}}{\textbf{net income}} \times \frac{\textbf{net income}}{\textbf{equity}} \times \frac{\textbf{initial equity}}{\textbf{assets}}$$

$$= \textbf{plowback ratio} \times \textbf{return on equity} \times \frac{\textbf{equity}}{\textbf{assets}} \qquad \textbf{(19.3)}$$

A firm can achieve a higher growth rate without raising external capital if (1) it plows back a high proportion of its earnings, (2) it has a high return on equity (ROE), and (3) it has a low debt-to-asset ratio.

EXAMPLE 19.4 **INTERNAL GROWTH RATE FOR YUMMY FOOD**

Yummy Food has chosen a plowback ratio of one-third. As Table 19.4 shows, at the beginning of 2013 (also the end of 2012), the outstanding assets were \$1,000 and outstanding equity was \$600. Yummy Food's return on equity[4] is ROE = 16.67 percent and its ratio of equity to assets is 600/1,000 = .60. If it is unwilling to raise new capital, its maximum growth rate is

$$\text{Internal growth rate} = \text{plowback ratio} \times \text{ROE} \times \frac{\text{equity}}{\text{assets}}$$

$$= \frac{1}{3} \times .1667 \times .60 = .0333, \text{ or } 3.33\%$$

Look back at Table 19.10, and you will see that at this growth rate, external financing is in fact zero. This growth rate is much less than the 10 percent growth it projects, which explains its need for external financing.

---

sustainable growth rate Steady rate at which a firm can grow without changing leverage; plowback ratio × return on equity.

Instead of focusing on the maximum growth rate that can be supported without *any* external financing, firms also may be interested in the growth rate that can be sustained without additional *equity* issues. Of course, if the firm is able to issue enough debt, virtually any growth rate can be financed. However, it makes more sense to assume that the firm has settled on an optimal capital structure that it will maintain even as equity is augmented by the addition to retained earnings. The firm issues only enough debt to keep its debt-equity ratio constant. The **sustainable growth rate** is the highest growth rate the firm can maintain without increasing its financial leverage. It turns out that the sustainable growth rate depends only on the plowback ratio and return on equity:[5]

$$\textbf{Sustainable growth rate} = \textbf{plowback ratio} \times \textbf{return on equity} \qquad \textbf{(19.4)}$$

You might remember this formula from Chapter 7, where we first used it when we looked at the valuation of the firm and the dividend discount model. Example 19.5 shows how to calculate the sustainable growth rate and use it to calculate the required external financing. The ROE used in both the internal and sustainable growth rate formulas is net income divided by equity at the start of the year.

---

[4] Actually, calculating ROE to find the internal growth rate can be a bit tricky. Yummy Food is forecasting a growth rate of 10 percent and an ROE of 108/600 = 18 percent, but if it grows more slowly, sales, net income and ROE will be lower. In other words, ROE may depend on the growth rate. We saw in Table 19.10 that a growth rate of 3.33 percent implies external financing of zero; we will choose the ROE corresponding to the internal growth rate of 3.33 percent. If you input .0333 as the growth rate in the Yummy Food spreadsheet (Figure 19.2), you will find that net income in 2013 is \$100,000 while equity outstanding at the beginning of 2013 (end of 2012) is \$600,000, which implies an ROE of 100/600 = .1667. Notice that although it is common to calculate ROE by dividing income by either end-of-year or year-average shareholders' equity, neither of those conventions will work in this application. To find the internal growth rate, we need to view ROE as analogous to the rate of return on a stock, that is, as money earned *during* the year per dollar of shareholders' equity at the *start* of the year.

[5] Here is proof:

$$\text{Required equity issues} = \text{growth rate} \times \text{assets} - \text{addition to retained earnings} - \text{new debt issues}$$

We find the sustainable growth rate by setting required new equity issues to zero and solving for growth:

$$\text{Sustainable growth rate} = \frac{\text{addition to retained earnings} + \text{new debt issues}}{\text{assets}}$$

$$= \frac{\text{addition to retained earnings} + \text{new debt issues}}{\text{debt} + \text{equity}}$$

However, because both debt and equity are growing at the same rate, new debt issues must equal the addition to retained earnings multiplied by the ratio of debt to equity, D/E. Therefore, we can write the sustainable growth rate as

$$\text{Sustainable growth rate} = \frac{\text{addition to retained earnings} \times (1 + D/E)}{\text{debt} + \text{equity}}$$

$$= \frac{\text{addition to retained earnings} \times (1 \times D/E)}{\text{equity} \times (1 + D/E)} = \frac{\text{addition to retained earnings}}{\text{equity}}$$

$$= \frac{\text{addition to retained earnings}}{\text{net income}} \times \frac{\text{net income}}{\text{equity}} = \text{plowback} \times \text{ROE}$$

EXAMPLE 19.5 SUSTAINABLE GROWTH OF EXECUTIVE SUITES

Executive Suites, Inc., currently has an equity-to-asset ratio of .8 and has $3,000 assets. So, its current equity is $.8 \times \$3{,}000 = \$2{,}400$ and current debt is $(1 - .8) \times \$3{,}000 = \$600$. Its ROE is 18 percent, current year's net income divided by equity at the beginning of the year. The firm currently reinvests one-third of its earnings back into the firm. Moreover, it plans to keep leverage unchanged, it will issue an additional 20 cents of debt for every 80 cents of reinvested earnings, maintaining .25 debt-to-equity ratio. Given this policy, its maximum growth rate is

$$\text{Sustainable growth rate} = \text{plowback ratio} \times \text{ROE} = \frac{1}{3} \times .18 = .06, \text{ or } 6\%$$

If it grows at 6 percent, use equation 19.1 to calculate the required external financing. The investment in new assets is the growth rate times assets $= .06 \times \$3{,}000 = \$180$. Then calculate the forecasted addition to retained earnings by forecasting net income and multiplying by the plowback ratio. The forecasted net income is the forecasted ROE times the current equity. Forecasted addition to retained earnings:

$$\begin{aligned}\text{Forecasted addition to retained earnings} &= \text{plowback ratio} \times \text{ROE} \times \text{equity}\\ &= 1/3 \times .18 \times 2{,}400 = \$144\\ \text{Required external financing} &= \text{new assets} - \text{addition to retained earnings}\\ &= \$180 - \$144 = \$36\end{aligned}$$

So the new debt level will be $\$600 + \$36 = \$636$ and the new equity level will be $\$2{,}400 + \$144 = \$2{,}544$ and the debt-to-equity ratio is $\$636/\$2{,}544 = .25$, unchanged.

If the firm is willing to plow back a higher proportion of its earnings, it can issue more debt without increasing its leverage. Both the greater reinvested profits and the additional debt issues would allow it to grow more rapidly. You can confirm in the following Check Point problem that, if the firm increases its plowback ratio, its sustainable growth rate will be higher.

Check Point 19.5

Suppose Executive Suites reduces the dividend payout ratio to 25 percent. Calculate its growth rate and required external financing for each of these assumptions: (a) that no new debt or equity will be issued and (b) that the firm maintains its current debt-to-equity ratio.

19.5 SUMMARY

1. **What are the contents and uses of a financial plan?** LO1

Most firms take financial planning seriously and devote considerable resources to it. The tangible product of the planning process is a financial plan describing the firm's financial strategy and projecting its future consequences by means of **pro forma** balance sheets, income statements, and statements of sources and uses of funds. The plan establishes financial goals and is a benchmark for evaluating subsequent performance. Usually it also describes why that strategy was chosen and how the plan's financial goals are to be achieved.

Planning, if it is done right, forces the financial manager to think about events that could upset the firm's progress and to devise strategies to be held in reserve for counterattack when unfortunate surprises occur. Planning is more than forecasting, because forecasting deals with the most likely outcome. Planners also have to think about events that may occur even though they are unlikely.

In long-range, or strategic, planning, the **planning horizon** is usually five years or more. This kind of planning deals with aggregate decisions; for example, the planner would worry about whether one of the firm's divisions should commit to heavy capital investment and rapid growth, but not whether the division should choose machine tool A versus tool B. In fact, planners must be constantly on guard against the fascination of detail, because giving in to it means slighting crucial issues like investment strategy, debt policy, and the choice of a target dividend payout ratio.

The plan is the end result. The process that produces the plan is valuable in its own right. Planning forces the financial manager to consider the combined effects of all the firm's investment and financing decisions. This is important, because these decisions interact and should not be made independently.

2. **How are financial planning models constructed?** LO2

There is no theory or model that leads straight to *the* optimal financial strategy. Consequently, financial planning proceeds by trial and error. Many different strategies may be projected under a range of assumptions about the future before one strategy is finally chosen. Constructing a corporate planning model using spreadsheet software, rather than doing calculations by hand, makes it easier to forecast the financial consequences of specified strategies and assumptions about the future.

The fundamentals of financial planning involve creating the pro forma financial statement using forecasted sales, costs, assets, and investment necessary to implement the firm's strategy. A key aspect of constructing the pro forma financial statements is the assumed **balancing item**, the variable that adjusts to make the sources of funds equal the uses of fund.

3. **The percentage-of-sales model and why it is not necessarily a reasonable model for forecasting all assets and costs.** LO3

One very simple starting point is the **percentage-of-sales** model in which key variables are assumed to be directly proportional to sales. However, it is not necessary that all costs and assets increase proportionately with sales. For example, if the firm can increase sales without increasing its investment in property, plant, and equipment, that asset won't vary directly with sales. Also, forecasting interest expense as a percentage of sales is not necessarily reasonable, because the interest expense depends both on the quantity of debt and on future interest rates.

Planning models are efficient and widely used. But remember that there is not much finance in them. Their primary purpose is to produce accounting statements. The models do not search for the best financial strategy but only trace out the consequences of a strategy specified by the model user.

4. **What is the effect of growth on the need for external financing?** LO4

Higher growth rates will lead to greater need for investments in long-term operating assets, such as property, plant, and equipment, and **net operating working capital**. The **internal growth rate** is the maximum rate that the firm can grow if it relies entirely on reinvested profits to finance its growth, that is, the maximum rate of growth without requiring external financing. The **sustainable growth rate** is the rate at which the firm can grow without changing its leverage ratio.

Related Web Links

canadabusiness.ca Government of Canada gateway to information on starting a business in Canada

jaxworks.com/bpindex.htm Helpful materials on development of a financial plan

toolkit.cch.com Tool kit for small businesses

finance.yahoo.com Analyst estimates of future growth rates

Key Terms

balancing item	614	percentage-of-sales models	613
internal growth rate	625	planning horizon	609
net operating working capital (NOWC)	615	pro formas	612
		sustainable growth rate	626

Questions and Problems

connect™ Practise and learn online with *Connect*. Questions with online Excel templates or datasets are marked with .

*Answers in Appendix B

BASIC

1. **Financial Planning.** True or false? Explain. (LO1)
   a. Financial planning should attempt to minimize risk.
   b. The primary aim of financial planning is to obtain better forecasts of future cash flows and earnings.
   c. Financial planning is necessary because financing and investment decisions interact and should not be made independently.
   d. Firms' planning horizons rarely exceed three years.
   e. Individual capital investment projects are not considered in a financial plan unless they are very large.
   f. Financial planning requires accurate and consistent forecasting.
   g. Financial planning models should include as much detail as possible.
2. **Financial Models.** What are the dangers and disadvantages of using a financial model? Discuss. (LO1)
3. **Using Financial Plans.** Corporate financial plans are often used as a basis for judging subsequent performance. What can be learned from such comparisons? What problems might arise and how might you cope with such problems? (LO1)

*4. **Growth Rates.** Find the sustainable and internal growth rates for a firm with the following ratios: asset turnover (sales/initial assets) = 1.40; profit margin (net income/sales) = 5 percent; payout ratio = 25 percent; initial equity/initial assets = .60. (LO4)

5. **Percentage-of-Sales Models.** Percentage-of-sales models often assume that costs, long-term assets, and net operating working capital all increase at the same rate as sales. When do you think that these assumptions do not make sense? Would you feel happier using a percentage-of-sales model for short-term or long-term planning? (LO2)
6. **Relationships Among Variables.** Comebaq Computers is aiming to increase its market share by slashing the price of its new range of personal computers. Are costs and assets likely to increase or decrease as a proportion of sales? Explain. (LO2)

*7. **Balancing Items.** What are the possible choices of balancing items when using a financial planning model? Discuss whether some are generally preferable to others. (LO2)

8. **Financial Targets.** Managers sometimes state a target growth rate for sales or earnings per share. Do you think that either one makes sense as a corporate goal? If not, why do you think that managers focus on them? (LO1)

INTERMEDIATE

*9. **Percentage-of-Sales Models.** Here are the abbreviated financial statements for Planners Peanuts:

Income Statement, 2012	
Sales	$2,000
Costs	1,500
Net income	$ 500

Balance Sheet, Year-End					
	2011	2012		2011	2012
Assets	$2,500	$3,000	Debt	$ 833	$1,000
			Equity	1,667	2,000
Total	$2,500	$3,000	Total	$2,500	$3,000

If sales increase by 20 percent in 2013, and the company uses a strict percentage-of-sales planning model (meaning that all items on the income and balance sheet also increase by 20 percent), what must be the balancing item? What will be its value? (LO2)

10. **Required External Financing.** If the dividend payout ratio in problem 9 is fixed at 50 percent, calculate the required total external financing for growth rates in 2013 of 15 percent, 20 percent, and 25 percent. (LO4)

*11. **Feasible Growth Rates.**
   a. What is the maximum possible growth rate in 2013 for Planners Peanuts (see problem 9) if the payout ratio remains at 50 percent and
      i. No external debt or equity is to be issued? (LO4)
      ii. The firm maintains its 2012 debt-to-equity ratio but issues no equity? (LO4)
   b. Calculate the required external financing and the new capital structure for the two growth rates. (LO4)

12. **Using Percentage of Sales.** Eagle Sports Supply has the following financial statements. Assume that Eagle's assets and costs are proportional to its sales. (LO2)

Income Statement, 2012	
Sales	$950
Costs	250
EBIT	700
Taxes	200
Net income	$500

Balance Sheet, Year-End

	2011	2012		2011	2012
Assets	$2,700	$3,000	Debt	$ 900	$1,000
	———	———	Equity	1,800	2,000
Total	$2,700	$3,000	Total	$2,700	$3,000

a. Find Eagle's required external funds if it maintains a dividend payout ratio of 70 percent and plans a growth rate of 15 percent in 2013.

b. If Eagle chooses not to issue new shares of stock in 2013, what variable must be the balancing item? What will its value be?

c. Now suppose that the firm plans instead to increase long-term debt only to $1,100 and does not wish to issue any new shares of stock. Why must the dividend payment now be the balancing item? What will its value be? What is the dividend payout ratio?

13. **Feasible Growth Rates.** (LO4) If Eagle Sports (see problem 12) 2013 dividend payout ratio is 70 percent and the equity-to-asset ratio is 2/3 what is the 2013 internal growth rate and sustainable growth rate? Calculate the required external financing and the new capital structure for the two growth rates.

14. **Required External Financing.** How would Yummy Food's 2013 required external financing change if the 2013 dividend payout ratio were cut to one-third? Use this revision to the financing model to generate a new financial plan for 2013 assuming that debt is the balancing item. Show how the financial statement given in Table 19.6 would change. What would be required external financing? (LO2)

*15. **Building Financial Models.** Yummy Food's financial manager believes that sales in 2013 could rise by as much as 20 percent or by as little as 2 percent. The planned dividend payout ratio is 2/3, interest expense is based on the debt at the start of the year and the percentage of sales factors are unchanged. (LO2)

a. Recalculate the first-stage pro forma financial statements (Table 19.5) for each of these growth rates. How do the forecasted sales growth rates affect the firm's need for external funds?

b. Assume any required external funds will be raised by issuing long-term debt and that any surplus funds will be used to retire debt. Prepare the completed (second-stage) pro forma balance sheet (Table 19.6).

16. **Building Financial Models.** The following tables contain financial statements for Dynastatics Corporation. Although the company has not been growing, it now plans to expand and will increase net long-term assets (gross long-term assets minus accumulated depreciation) by $200,000 in 2013 and forecasts that the ratio of revenue to total assets will remain at 1.5. Net operating working capital will equal 50 percent of net long-term assets. Annual depreciation is 10 percent of net long-term assets at the end of the year. Fixed costs are expected to remain at $56,000 and variable costs at 80 percent of revenue. The company's policy is to pay out two-thirds of net income as dividends and to maintain a book debt ratio of 25 percent of total capital. (LO3)

Income Statement 2012 ($000s)		
Revenue		$1,800
Fixed costs		56
Variable costs (80% of revenue)		1,440
Depreciation		80
Interest (8% of beginning-of-year debt)		24
Taxable income		200
Taxes (at 40%)		80
Net income		$ 120
Dividends	$80	
Addition to retained earnings	$40	

Balance Sheet, Year-End ($000s)	2012
Assets	
Net operating working capital	$ 400
Net long-term assets	800
Total assets	$1,200
Liabilities and Shareholders' Equity	
Debt	$ 300
Equity	900
Total liabilities and shareholders' equity	$1,200

a. Produce a set of financial statements for 2013 based on all of the assumptions and policies. What is the required external financing and what is the source of external financing?

b. Now assume that the balancing item is debt, and that no equity is to be issued. Prepare a completed pro forma balance sheet for 2013. What is the projected debt ratio for 2013?

*17. **Sustainable Growth.** Plank's Plants had net income of $2,000 on sales of $50,000 last year. The firm paid a dividend of $500. Total assets at the end of last year were $100,000, of which $40,000 was financed by debt. (LO4)
   a. What is the firm's sustainable growth rate?
   b. If the firm grows at its sustainable growth rate, how much debt will have to be raised in the coming year? Confirm that the firm maintains its current debt/asset ratio.
   c. What would be the maximum possible growth rate if the firm did not sell any new debt or equity in the coming year?

18. **Sustainable Growth.** A firm wants to maintain its capital structure and is currently 100 percent equity financed. It perceives its optimal dividend policy to be a 40 percent payout ratio. Current asset turnover (sales/initial assets) = .8 and the profit margin (net income/sales) is 10 percent. The firm has a target growth rate of 5 percent for the next year but will not issue any equity. (LO4)
   a. Is the firm's target growth rate consistent with its other goals?
   b. If not, by how much does it need to increase asset turnover to achieve its goals?
   c. How much would it need to increase the profit margin instead?

19. **Internal Growth.** Go Go Industries is growing at 30 percent per year. It is all-equity financed and has total assets of $1 million. Its return on equity is 25 percent. Its plowback ratio is 40 percent. (LO4)
   a. What is the internal growth rate?
   b. What is the firm's need for external financing this year?
   c. By how much would the firm increase its internal growth rate if it reduced its payout ratio to zero?
   d. If the payout ratio is zero what is the change in the need for external financing given its planned 30 percent growth? What do you conclude about the relationship between dividend policy and requirements for external financing?

20. **Sustainable Growth.** A firm's profit margin is 10 percent and its asset turnover ratio is .6. It has no debt, has net income of $10 per share, and pays dividends of $4 per share. What is the sustainable growth rate? (LO4)

*21. **Internal Growth.** An all-equity-financed firm plans to grow at an annual rate of at least 10 percent. Its return on equity is 18 percent. What is the maximum possible dividend payout rate the firm can maintain without resorting to additional equity issues? (LO4)

22. **Internal Growth.** Suppose the firm in the previous question has a debt-equity ratio of one-third. What is the maximum dividend payout ratio it can maintain without resorting to any external financing? (LO4)

*23. **Internal Growth.** A firm has an asset turnover ratio of 2.0. Its plowback ratio is 50 percent, and it is all equity-financed. What must its profit margin be if it wishes to finance 10 percent growth using only internally generated funds? (LO4)

24. **Internal Growth.** If the profit margin of the firm in the previous problem is 6 percent, what is the maximum payout ratio that will allow it to grow at 8 percent without resorting to external financing? (LO4)

*25. **Internal Growth.** If the profit margin of the firm in problem 23 is 6 percent, what is the maximum possible growth rate that can be sustained without external financing? (LO4)

26. **Using Percentage of Sales.** The 2012 financial statements for Growth Industries are presented here. Sales and costs in 2013 are projected to be 20 percent higher than in 2012. Both current assets and accounts payable are projected to rise in proportion to sales. The firm is currently operating at full capacity, so it plans to increase long-term assets in proportion to sales. What external financing will be required by the firm? Interest expense in 2013 will equal 10 percent of long-term debt outstanding at the start of the year. The firm will maintain a dividend payout ratio of .4. (LO2)

Income Statement, 2012

Sales	$200,000
Costs	150,000
EBIT	50,000
Interest expense	10,000
Taxable income	40,000
Taxes (at 35%)	14,000
Net income	$ 26,000
Dividends	10,400
Addition to retained earnings	15,600

Balance Sheet, 2012

Assets		**Liabilities**	
Current assets:		Current liabilities:	
Cash	$ 3,000	Accounts payable	$ 10,000
Accounts receivable	8,000	Total current liabilities	10,000
Inventories	29,000	Long-term debt	100,000
Total current assets	$ 40,000	**Shareholders' Equity**	
Net plant and equipment	160,000	Common stock	15,000
		Retained earnings	75,000
Total assets	$200,000	Total liabilities and shareholders' equity	$200,000

CHALLENGE

27. **Capacity Use and External Financing.** Now suppose that the long-term assets of Growth Industries (from the previous problem) are operating at only 75 percent of capacity. What is required external financing over the next year? (LO4)

28. **Capacity Use and External Financing.** If Growth Industries from problem 26 is operating at only 75 percent of capacity, how much can sales grow before the firm will need to raise any external funds? Assume that once long-term assets are operating at capacity, they will need to grow thereafter in direct proportion to sales. (LO3)

29. **Internal Growth.** We will see in Chapter 21 that for many firms, cash and inventory needs may grow less than proportionally with sales. When we recognize this fact, will the firm's internal growth rate be higher or lower than the level predicted by the formula: (LO4)

$$\text{Internal growth rate} = \frac{\text{addition to retained earnings}}{\text{assets}}$$

30. **Spreadsheet Problem.** Use a spreadsheet like that in Figure 19.2 to answer the following questions about Yummy Food: (LO2)
    a. What would be required external financing each year if the growth rate is 15 percent and the dividend payout ratio is 60 percent in 2013 and 2014?
    b. Given the assumptions in part (a), what would be the amount of debt and equity issued if the firm wants to maintain its debt-equity ratio at a level of two-thirds?
    c. What formulas would you put in cells H20 and H21 (as well as the corresponding cells in columns F and G) of the spreadsheet in Figure 19.2 to maintain the debt-equity ratio at two-thirds, while forcing the balance sheet to balance (that is, forcing debt + equity = total assets)?

31. **Integrative: Financial Planning and Financial Ratios.** Use the spreadsheet from problem 30 to examine the impact of various scenarios. Add formulas to calculate ratios to examine the effect on leverage (debt ratio and times interest earned), profitability (profit margin, operating profit margin, EBIT/revenue, EBIT/assets), and accounting rates of return (ROA, ROC, ROE). You will need to calculate NOPAT, net operating profit after taxes (NOPAT = net income + (1 − tax rate) × interest expense). See Chapter 4 for ratio definitions. Unless otherwise stated, use the forecasting assumptions from the original Yummy Food problem, as seen in Figure 19.2. Forecast annual pro forma statements for 2013 to 2016. In each scenario, what do the financial ratios tell you about the financial plan? Explain the difference between accounting rates of return based on NOPAT and on net income. (LO2)
    a. Annual sales growth is 10 percent and all required external financing will be debt. Will the company breach the bank's requirement that the company's debt ratio not exceed 60 percent?
    b. Same scenario as (a), except that the interest rate on debt is 15 percent.
    c. Same scenario as (a), except that Yummy Food keeps its debt ratio at 40 percent.
    d. Same scenario as (a), except that cost of goods sold is 95 percent of sales each year.
    e. Same scenario as (a), except each year's interest expense equals the average of the beginning-of-year and end-of-year debt. For help with this question read "Forecasting Interest Expense" in Section 19.3.

32. **Comprehensive.** Use the 2012 financial statements for Dynastatics, problem 16, and build a financial plan using a spreadsheet like that in Figure 19.2. Add \$3,000,000 gross long-term assets and accumulated depreciation of (\$2,200,000) to the 2012 balance sheet. Thus 2012 net long-term assets are \$3,000,000 − \$2,200,000 = \$800,000. Dynastatics is planning annual capital expenditure of \$200,000 a year for the next five years, which will be added to gross long-term assets. Annual depreciation will be 10 percent net long-term assets of the previous year and added to the accumulated depreciation on the balance sheet. Maintain all other assumptions in problem 16. Add to the spreadsheet the financial ratios listed in problem 31. (LO2)
    a. Assuming that Dynastatics pays out two-thirds of net income as dividends and maintains a book debt ratio of 25 percent of total capital, produce financial statements for 2013 to 2017.
    b. Maintaining the two-thirds dividend payout, but assuming that the balancing item is debt, prepare the five years of pro formas and compare the financial ratios to those in (a).

33. **Integrative.** Use Dynastatics' pro forma income statements and balance sheet from problem 32(a) to assess the cash flows for each forecast year. (LO2)
    a. What is the capital expenditure each year? *Hint:* Look at Check Point 3.1 in Chapter 3 where this equation was used: Capital expenditure = Change in net PP&E + depreciation and impairment expense.
    b. Start the statement of cash flow with net income. Look at Chapter 3 for the structure of the statement of cash flow.
    c. Calculate the cash flow from assets and the financing flow (cash flow to bondholders and shareholders), treating interest as an operating expense. See Chapter 3 for help with this.
    d. Calculate the cash flow from assets and the financing flow (cash flow to bondholders and shareholders) treating after-tax interest expense as a cash flow to bondholders.

34. **Comprehensive.** Go back to problem 12 and build a financial planning model based on percentage of sales

for Eagle Sports Supply using a spreadsheet similar to Figure 19.2. (LO2, LO4)

a. Assume 2013 sales grow at the sustainable growth rate calculated in problem 13 and produce the pro forma income statement and balance sheet. Is the forecasted capital structure consistent with 2012 capital structure?

b. Assuming 2013 sales grow at the internal growth rate calculated in problem 13, produce the pro forma income statement and balance sheet. Is the required external financing zero, the same as what you found in problem 13? Is the forecasted net income the same as the forecasted net income in problem 13? What is going on?

c. Calculate an alternative growth rate using the following formula.

$$\text{Growth rate} = \frac{\text{plowback ratio} \times \text{return on equity}}{\dfrac{\text{2012 assets}}{\text{2011 equity}} - \begin{matrix}\text{plowback ratio} \\ \times \text{ return on equity}\end{matrix}}$$

The ROE is the same as the one used in the other growth rate formulas. It is based on beginning equity, 2012 net income/2011 equity. Use this new growth rate to produce the 2013 pro forma statements. What is the required external financing? How does it compare to the result in 34(b)?

35. **Internet.** Go to **finance.yahoo.com** or **ca.moneycentral.msn.com** to get financial statements for companies to calculate and compare their internal growth rates and sustainable growth rates. At Yahoo dividend payout ratio is listed in key statistics and at MSN it is in highlights. How does each company's growth rate compare to their recent sales and asset growth rates? Look at the statement of cash flows for information on new financing. (LO4)

36. **Internet.** The Web site at **www.canadabusiness.ca/eng/125** is designed to help people plan the successful start of their own business. Check into each of the nine topics. The one most related to this chapter is "Developing your business plan." Click on that, and then look at "Writing your business plan" and identify the links to the content of this chapter. Click on "Business Plans—templates and samples" and download some financial spreadsheets to play with. (LO1, LO2)

Solutions to Check Points

19.1 Total assets will rise to \$2,200. The debt-equity ratio is to be maintained at 2/3. Therefore, debt rises by \$80 to \$880 and equity rises by \$120 to \$1,320. Net income will be \$220. (See Table 19.2.) If the dividend is fixed at \$180, addition to retained earnings will be \$40. Therefore, the firm needs to issue \$120 + \$40 = \$80 of new equity and \$80 of new debt.

19.2 a. The *total amount* of external financing is unchanged, since the dividend payout is unchanged. The \$100,000 increase in total assets will now be financed by a mixture of debt and equity. If the debt-equity ratio is to remain at two-thirds, the firm will need to increase equity by \$60,000 and debt by \$40,000. Since addition to retained earnings already increases shareholders' equity by \$36,000, the firm needs to issue an additional \$24,000 of new equity and \$40,000 of debt.

b. If dividends are reduced from \$72,000 to \$60,000 then the required external funds fall by \$12,000, from \$64,000 to \$52,000.

19.3 a. The company currently runs at 75 percent of capacity given the current level of long-term assets. Sales can increase until the company is at 100 percent of capacity; therefore, sales can increase to \$60 million × (100/75) = \$80 million.

b. If sales were to increase by 50 percent to \$90 million, new long-term assets would need to be added. The ratio of long-term assets to sales when the company is operating at 100 percent of capacity (from part (a)) is \$50 million/\$80 million = 5/8. Therefore, to support sales of \$90 million, the company needs at least \$90 million × 5/8 = \$56.25 million of long-term assets. This calls for a \$6.25 million investment in additional long-term assets.

19.4 a. This question is answered by the planning model. Given assumptions for asset growth, the model will show the need for external financing, and this value can be compared to the firm's plans for such financing.

b. Such a relationship may be assumed and built into the model. However, the model does not help to determine whether it is a reasonable assumption.

c. Financial models do not shed light on the best capital structure. They can tell us only whether contemplated financing decisions are consistent with asset growth.

19.5 a. The equity-to-asset ratio is .8. If the payout ratio were reduced to 25 percent, the maximum growth rate assuming no external financing would be .75 × 18 percent × .8 = 10.8 percent. Required external financing = new assets − addition to retained earnings = .108 × \$3,000 − .75 × .18 × \$2,400 = 0, achieving internally financed growth.

b. If the firm also can issue enough debt to maintain its equity-to-asset ratio unchanged, the sustainable growth rate will be .75 × 18 percent = 13.5 percent. Required external financing = .135 × \$3,000 − .75 × .18 × \$2,400 = \$405 − \$324 = \$81. The new-debt-to-new-equity ratio is \$81/\$324 = .25, maintaining the current debt-to-equity ratio.

MINI CASE

Garnett Jackson, the founder and CEO of Tech Tune-Ups, stared out the window as he finished his customary peanut butter and jelly sandwich, contemplating the dilemma currently facing his firm. Tech Tune-Ups is a startup firm, offering a wide range of computer services to its clients, including online technical assistance, remote maintenance and backup of client computers through the Internet, and virus prevention and recovery. The firm has been highly successful in the two years since it was founded in 2010; its reputation for fair pricing and good service is spreading, and Mr. Jackson believes the firm is in a good position to expand its customer base rapidly. But he is not sure that the firm has the financing in place to support that rapid growth.

Tech Tune-Ups' main capital investments are its own powerful computers, and its major operating expense is salary for its consultants. To a reasonably good approximation, both of these factors grow in proportion to the number of clients the firm serves.

Currently, the firm is a privately held corporation. Mr. Jackson and his partners, two classmates from his undergraduate days, contributed $250,000 in equity capital in 2010, largely raised from their parents and other family members. The firm has a line of credit with a bank that allows it to borrow up to $400,000 at an interest rate of 8 percent. As of the start of 2011 the firm had used $125,000 of its credit line and shareholders' equity was $250,000. If and when the firm reaches its borrowing limit, it will need to raise equity capital and will probably seek funding from a venture capital firm. The firm is growing rapidly, requiring continual investment in additional computers, and Mr. Jackson is concerned that it is approaching its borrowing limit faster than anticipated.

Mr. Jackson thumbed through 2011 financial data and estimated that each of the firm's 15 computers cost $10,000, and could support revenues of $80,000 per year but that the salary and benefits paid to each consultant using one of the computers was $70,000. The end of 2011 book value of long-term assets is $150,000. Sales revenue in 2011 was $1,200,000 million. Jackson assumes that sales will grow at a 20 percent annual rate in the next four years. The firm pays taxes at a rate of 35 percent. Its customers pay their bills with an average delay of 3 months. Net operating working capital is usually around 25 percent of that year's sales.

Mr. Jackson and his co-owners receive minimal formal salary from the firm, instead taking 70 percent of profits as a "dividend," which accounts for a substantial portion of their personal incomes. The remainder of the profits are reinvested in the firm. If reinvested profits are not sufficient to support new purchases of computers, the firm borrows the required additional funds using its line of credit with the bank.

Mr. Jackson doesn't think Tech Tune-Ups can raise venture funding until after 2013. He decides to develop a financial plan to determine whether the firm can sustain its growth plans using its line of credit and reinvested earnings until then. If not, he and his partners will have to consider scaling back their hoped-for rate of growth, negotiate with their bankers to increase the line of credit, or consider taking a smaller share of profits out of the firm until further financing can be arranged.

Mr. Jackson wiped the last piece of jelly from the keyboard and settled down to work.

Can you help Mr. Jackson develop a financial plan for the next four years? You will have to put together the 2011 financial statements, based on the information provided by Mr. Jackson. Calculate interest expense based on debt at the start of the year. Use the percentage of sales method to forecast the financial statements after 2011. Do you think his growth plan is feasible?

PART 6

Financial Planning

19 Long-Term Financial Planning

20 Short-Term Financial Planning

20.1 Links Between Long-Term and Short-Term Financing

20.2 Working Capital

20.3 Tracing Changes in Cash and Working Capital

20.4 Cash Budgeting

20.5 A Short-Term Financing Plan

20.6 Sources of Short-Term Financing

20.7 The Cost of Bank Loans

20.8 Summary

CHAPTER 20

Short-Term Financial Planning

LEARNING OBJECTIVES

After studying this chapter, you should be able to:

LO1 Show how long-term financing policy affects short-term financing requirements.

LO2 Explain why the firm needs to invest in net working capital.

LO3 Trace a firm's sources and uses of cash and evaluate its need for short-term borrowing.

LO4 Develop a short-term financing plan that meets the firm's need for cash.

LO5 Determine the costs of various sources of short-term financing.

Short-term financial planning ensures that you have enough cash on hand to pay the bills.

Much of this book is devoted to long-term investment decisions, such as capital budgeting, and long-term financing decisions, such as the choice of capital structure. These are called *long-term* decisions for two reasons. First, they usually involve long-lived assets or liabilities. Second, they are not easily reversed and thus may commit the firm to a particular course of action for several years.

Short-term financial decisions generally involve short-lived assets and liabilities, and usually they are easily reversed. Compare, for example, a 60-day bank loan for $50 million with a $50 million issue of 20-year bonds. The bank loan is clearly a short-term decision. The firm can repay it two months later and be right back where it started. A firm might conceivably issue a 20-year bond in January and retire it in March, but it would be extremely inconvenient and expensive to do so. In practice, such a bond issue is a long-term decision, not only because of the bond's 20-year maturity, but because the decision to issue it cannot be reversed on short notice.

A financial manager responsible for short-term financial decisions does not have to look far into the future. The decision to take the 60-day bank loan could properly be based on cash flow forecasts for the next few months only. The bond-issue decision will normally reflect forecast cash requirements 5, 10, or more years into the future.

Short-term financial decisions do not involve many of the difficult conceptual issues encountered elsewhere in this book. In a sense, short-term decisions are easier than long-term decisions—but they are not less important. A firm can identify extremely valuable capital investment opportunities, find the precise optimal debt ratio, follow the perfect dividend policy, and yet run into trouble because no one bothers to raise the cash to pay this year's bills. Hence the need for short-term financial planning.

We start by showing how long-term financing decisions, introduced in the previous chapter, affect the firm's short-term financial planning problem. Next we review the components of working capital and describe the cash conversion cycle that dictates the types and amount of working capital a firm might maintain. We demonstrate how financial managers forecast month-by-month cash requirements or surpluses and how they develop short-term financing strategies. We conclude with an examination of various sources of short-term finance.

LO1 20.1 LINKS BETWEEN LONG-TERM AND SHORT-TERM FINANCING

When you plan your personal finances, you have to choose the factors central to your decision making and decide which ones are merely distractions. Often, this will depend on your time horizon. For example, at very long horizons such as for retirement planning, you don't think too carefully about when you will need to purchase your next car. At shorter horizons, covering perhaps the next three to five years, specific big-ticket items such as that potential car purchase need to be accounted for explicitly. At the shortest horizons, your planning might involve details down to the cash balance you maintain in your chequing account and in your pocket.

It is the same with firms. When formulating long-term financial plans such as those considered in the previous chapter, firms may plan year by year. They often will be content with rules of thumb that relate average levels of long-term and short-term assets to annual sales, and not worry so much about seasonal variations in these relationships. When making a long-term plan, for example, the likelihood that trade receivables will rise as sales peak in the Christmas season would be a needless detail that would distract from more important strategic decisions. But such considerations become crucial when firms focus on their near-term needs for cash and working capital. Short-term financing issues are conceptually easier than those involved in capital budgeting, but woe to the firm that takes them for granted.

Moreover, short-term financing needs are tied to the firm's long-term decisions. For example, businesses require capital—that is, money invested in plant, machinery, inventories, accounts receivable, and all the other assets it takes to run a company efficiently. Typically, these assets are not purchased all at once but are obtained gradually over time as the firm grows. The total cost of these assets is called the firm's *total capital requirement*.

When we discussed long-term planning in Chapter 19, we showed how the firm needs to develop a sensible strategy that allows it to finance its long-term goals and cope with possible setbacks. But the firm's total capital requirement does not grow smoothly and the company must be able to meet temporary demands for cash.

Figure 20.1 illustrates the growth in the firm's total capital requirements. The upward-sloping line shows that as the business grows, it is likely to need additional long-term assets and current assets. You can think of this trend line as showing the base level of capital that is required. In addition to this base capital requirement, there may be seasonal fluctuations in the business that require an additional investment in current assets. Thus the wavy line in the illustration shows that the total capital requirement peaks late in each year. In practice, there would also be week-to-week and month-to-month fluctuations in the capital requirement, but these are not shown in Figure 20.1.

The total capital requirement can be met through long-term and/or short-term financing. When long-term financing does not cover the total capital requirement, the firm must raise short-term financing to make up the difference. When long-term financing *more* than covers the total capital requirement, the firm has surplus cash available for short-term investment. Thus the difference between the long-term financing raised and the total capital requirement determines whether the firm is a short-term borrower or lender.

The three panels in Figure 20.2 illustrate this. Each depicts a different long-term financing strategy. The "relaxed strategy" in panel (a) implies a permanent short-term cash surplus. This surplus will be invested in marketable securities. The "restrictive" policy illustrated in panel (c) implies a permanent need for short-term borrowing. Finally, panel (b) illustrates an intermediate strategy: the firm has spare cash, which it can lend out during the part of the year when total capital requirements are relatively low, but it is a borrower during the rest of the year when capital requirements are relatively high.

FIGURE 20.1
The firm's total capital requirement grows over time. It also exhibits seasonal variation around the trend.

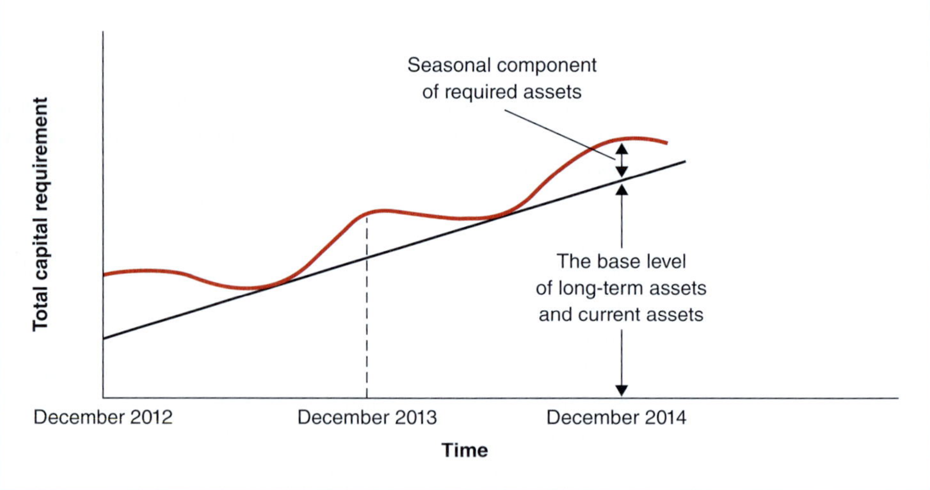

FIGURE 20.2
Alternative approaches to long- versus short-term financing:

(a) Relaxed strategy, in which the firm is always a short-term lender

(b) Middle-of-the-road policy, in which the firm is sometimes a short-term borrower and sometimes a short-term lender

(c) Restrictive policy, in which the firm is always a short-term borrower

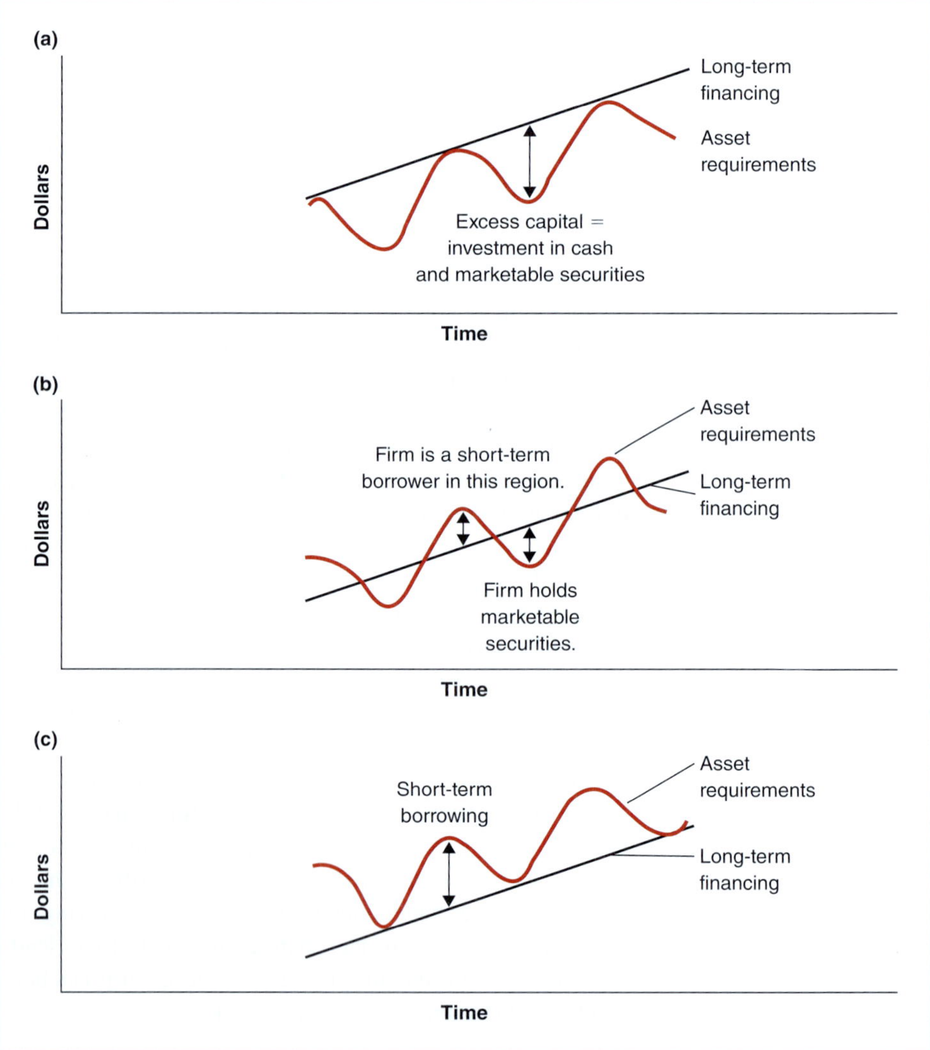

What is the *best* level of long-term financing relative to the total capital requirement? It is hard to say. We can make several practical observations, however.

1. *Matching maturities.* When financial managers are asked the most important reason for choosing short-term rather than long-term debt, they generally say that they try to "match" the maturities of the firm's assets and liabilities.[1] That is, they finance long-lived assets like plant and machinery with long-term borrowing and equity. Short-term assets like inventory and accounts receivable are financed with short-term bank loans or by issuing short-term debt such as commercial paper.
2. *Permanent working capital requirements.* Most firms have a permanent investment in net working capital (current assets less current liabilities). By this we mean that they plan to have a positive amount of net working capital at all times. This is financed from long-term sources. This is an extension of the maturity-matching principle. Since the working capital is permanent, it is funded with long-term sources of financing.
3. *The advantages of liquidity.* Current assets can be converted into cash more easily than can long-term assets. So firms with large holdings of current assets enjoy greater liquidity. Of course, some current assets are more liquid than others. Inventories are converted into cash only when the goods are produced, sold, and paid for. Receivables are more liquid; they become cash as customers pay their outstanding bills. Short-term securities can generally be sold if the firm needs cash on short notice and are therefore more liquid still.

Some firms choose to hold more liquidity than others. For example, many high-tech companies, such as Research In Motion and Apple, hold huge amounts of cash and short-term securities. On the other hand, firms in old-line manufacturing industries—such as chemicals, paper, or steel—manage with a far smaller reservoir of liquidity. Why is this? One reason is that companies with rapidly growing profits may generate cash faster than they can redeploy it in new positive-NPV investments. This produces a surplus of cash that can be invested in short-term securities and kept for future investment.

There are some advantages to holding a large reservoir of cash, particularly for smaller firms that face relatively high costs to raise funds on short notice and also in some industries. For example, biotechnology firms require large amounts of cash if their drugs succeed in gaining regulatory approval. Therefore, these firms generally have substantial cash holdings to fund their possible investment needs.[2]

Financial managers of firms with a surplus of long-term financing and with cash in the bank don't have to worry about finding the money to pay next month's bills. They would feel more comfortable under the relaxed strategy illustrated in Figure 20.2(a) than the restrictive strategy in panel (c). But there are also costs to having surplus cash. Holdings of marketable securities are at best a zero-NPV investment for a taxpaying firm.[3] Also, managers of firms with large cash surpluses may be tempted to run a less tight ship. The Finance in Action box here describes how the fashion company L.A. Gear was able to use its cash to survive six years of large losses and to employ a variety of radical, though ultimately unsuccessful, strategies to stave off bankruptcy. For shareholders, it may be best for firms with excess cash to go on a diet and use the money to retire some of their long-term securities. Indeed, we saw in Chapter 18 that companies reduce cash positions by paying a special dividend and repurchasing its stock.

---

[1] A survey by Graham and Harvey found that 63 percent of managers believed that maturity matching was the most important factor in their choice of debt maturity. See J.R. Graham and C.R. Harvey, "The Theory and Practice of Corporate Finance: Evidence from the Field," *Journal of Financial Economics* 61 (2001): 187–243.

[2] Look back at Table 4.7 in Chapter 4. You can see that the quick ratio, a liquidity measure, of the firms in the biotechnology industry is much higher most other industry averages.

[3] Why do we say *at best* zero NPV? Not because we worry that the Treasury bills may be overpriced. Instead, we worry that when the firm holds Treasury bills, the interest income is subject to double taxation, first at the corporate level, and then again at the personal level when the income is passed through to investors as dividends. The extra layer of taxation can make corporate holdings of Treasury bills a negative-NPV investment, even if the bills would provide a fair rate of interest to an individual investor.

Finance in Action

The Rise and Fall of L.A. Gear

Fashion company L.A. Gear was one of the stars of the 1980s. Teenieboppers loved its pink sequined sneakers and silver and gold lamé workout shoes. Investors preferred the 1,300 percent growth in the company's stock price in the space of four years. But as the company failed to react to changes in fashion during the 1990s, sales and profits fell away rapidly. In January 1998 it filed for Chapter 11 bankruptcy.

The decline illustrates how a company's liquid assets can provide the financial slack that allows it to evade market discipline and survive repeated losses. The following table summarizes the changes in L.A. Gear's profitability and its assets:

Sales, Income, and Assets of L.A. Gear 1989–1996 (US$ millions)

	1989	1990	1991	1992	1993	1994	1995	1996
Sales	617	820	619	430	398	416	297	196
Net income	55	31	−66	−72	−33	−22	−51	−62
Cash and securities	0	3	1	84	28	50	36	34
Receivables	101	156	112	56	73	77	47	24
Inventory	140	161	141	62	110	58	52	33
Current assets	257	338	297	230	220	194	138	93
Total assets	267	364	326	250	255	225	160	101

The first two rows show that after 1990 L.A. Gear's sales declined sharply and the firm produced losses for the rest of its life. The remaining rows show the company's assets. Since L.A. Gear farmed out shoe and clothing production, it had few fixed assets and owned largely cash, receivables, and inventory. As sales declined, two things happened. First, the company was able to reduce its inventory of finished goods. Second, customers paid off their outstanding bills. Thus, despite making steady losses, the company's holdings of cash and short-term securities initially increased.

The following table shows L.A. Gear's capital structure. Notice that after 1991 the company had almost no short-term bank debt, so that it was largely free from the discipline exerted whenever a company has to approach its bank for a loan renewal. As losses accumulated, common equity dwindled and the debt ratio climbed to 92 percent. Yet, even in 1996, the company's cash holdings were over eight times that year's interest payments.

	1989	1990	1991	1992	1993	1994	1995	1996
Bank debt	37	94	20	0	4	1	1	0
Long-term debt	0	0	0	0	50	50	50	50
Preferred stock	0	0	100	100	100	100	108	116
Common equity	168	206	132	88	47	18	−41	−111

Because the company could liquidate its inventories and receivables and had no maturing debt, it was able to survive six years of large losses and to try a variety of radical new strategies, including a new emphasis on performance athletic shoes and then on children's shoes. All these strategies were ultimately unsuccessful. A company with large fixed assets that are not so easily liquidated would have found it less easy to survive so long.

Source: The decline of L.A. Gear is chronicled in H. DeAngelo, L. DeAngelo, and K.H. Wruck, "Asset Liquidity, Debt Covenants, and Managerial Discretion in Financial Distress: The Collapse of L.A. Gear," *Journal of Financial Economics* 64 (2002): 3–34.

LO2 20.2 WORKING CAPITAL

Current, or short-term, assets and liabilities are collectively known as *working capital*. Much of short-term financial planning focuses on variation in working capital. *Current* assets and liabilities such as cash, trade receivables, inventories, and trade payables vary considerably as firms move through a cycle in which raw materials are purchased, goods are produced and sold, and customers pay their bills. In order to plan for the variation, it is best to begin by considering the various components of working capital and the factors that determine the level of each component.

TABLE 20.1
Current assets and current liabilities for CCL Industries Inc. at end of the first quarter of 2011, March 31, 2011 (millions of Canadian dollars).

Current Assets		Current Liabilities	
Cash and cash equivalents	$ 92.134	Bank advances	$ 0.669
Trade and other receivables	198.369	Trade and other payables	208.736
Prepaid expenses	6.764	Income and other taxes payable	11.994
Inventories	82.311	Current portion of long-term debt	16.440
Total current assets	$379.578	**Total current liabilities**	$237.839

Note: Net working capital (current assets − current liabilities) equals $379.578 − $237.839 = $141.739 million.

Source: Adapted from CCL Industries Inc. Consolidated Condensed Interim Financial Statements, March 31, 2011, **www.cclind.com/investors/financials.html**.

THE COMPONENTS OF WORKING CAPITAL

Table 20.1 shows the current assets and current liabilities for CCL Industries Inc. (CCL) as of March 31, 2011, taken from its first statement of financial position (balance sheet) prepared in accordance with International Financial Reporting Standards (IFRS). As a Canadian public company listed on the Toronto Stock Exchange, it had to switch to IFRS. CCL is a world-leading specialty packaging company that provides superior, innovate packaging and labelling for healthcare, food, and beverage products. Its headquarters are in Toronto, but it has global operations. As of March 31, 2011 total current assets were $379.578 million and total current liabilities were $237.839 million.

Current Assets One important current asset are *trade receivables*.[4] Trade receivables arise because companies do not usually require customers to pay for their purchases immediately. These unpaid bills are a valuable asset that companies expect to be able to turn into cash in the near future, as their customers pay their bills. The bulk of trade receivables consist of unpaid bills from sales to other companies and are known as *trade credit*. The remainder arises from the sale of goods to the final consumers. The unpaid bills of final consumers are known as *consumer credit*. Since CCL sells products to other firms, all of its trade receivables are trade credit. In a typical IFRS statement of financial position trade receivables are included in an entry called *trade and other receivables*. *Other receivables* are amounts that are owed but are not unpaid bills of customers. CCL's trade receivables were $186.235 million, reported in financial statement note 10. *Prepaid expenses* are purchases made by CCL for goods and services from suppliers that haven't been delivered yet.

Another important current asset is *inventory*. Inventories may consist of raw materials, work in process, or finished goods awaiting sale and shipment. CCL inventories investment was about 44 percent of its trade receivables and consisted of $36.070 million of raw material, $9.048 million of work in progress and $37.193 million of finished goods (in note 11).

The remaining current assets are *cash and cash equivalents*. *Cash* consists of currency on hand (such as Canadian dollar bills and foreign currency) and bank *demand deposits* (money in chequing or current accounts that the firm can withdraw immediately). *Cash equivalents* include bank *term deposits* (money in savings accounts that can be paid out only with a delay of a maximum of three months) and interest-bearing money market securities that are easily sold, making them equivalent to cash. Money market instruments include *commercial paper* (short-term unsecured debt sold by other firms) and *Treasury bills*, which are short-term debt sold by the Canadian and other governments, and provincial and local government securities. Some firms' current assets also include *other investments*, which are marketable securities intended to held for less than a year. These include other firm's debt and equity securities but are not as liquid as those classified as cash equivalents.[5]

---

[4] On a U.S. GAAP statement, the same entry would be called *accounts receivable* and would include trade receivables and other receivables.

[5] You might also see *other current assets*, which are current assets typically not directly linked to the firm's operating activities.

In managing their cash, companies face much the same problem you do. There are always advantages to holding large amounts of ready cash—they reduce the risk of running out of cash and having to borrow more on short notice. On the other hand, there is a cost to holding idle cash balances rather than putting the money to work earning interest. In Chapter 21 we will tell you how the financial manager decides on an optimal cash balance.

Current Liabilities We have seen that a significant current asset consists of unpaid bills of its customers. One firm's credit must be another's debit. Therefore, it is not surprising that one of a company's current liabilities consists of *trade payables* (also known as *accounts payable*)—that is, outstanding payments due to suppliers that provide materials used in the production and sale of goods and/or services. Added to trade payables are *other payables* include non-trade payables (bills not due to operations) plus accrued expenses (expenses recorded on the income statement that have not been paid yet). CCL had $135.680 million of unpaid bills to its suppliers and also $73.056 million of non-trade payables and accrued expenses (note 13). *Income and other taxes payable* are also bills due within one year but were recorded as expenses on the income statement but no cash was paid.

Bank advances are short-term bank loans, due to be repaid within a year, and *current portion of long-term debt* are the part of the long-term debt that must be repaid within a year. Both of these items are interest-bearing debt that CCL raised by negotiating with lenders, such as banks and investors. We will have more to say about this later in the chapter.

NET WORKING CAPITAL, OPERATING CYCLE, AND THE CASH CONVERSION CYCLE

net working capital Current assets minus current liabilities. Often called *working capital.*

The difference between current assets and current liabilities is known as **net working capital**, but some financial managers refer to the difference simply (but imprecisely) as *working capital*. Usually current assets exceed current liabilities—that is, firms have positive net working capital. CCL Industries' net working capital was $142,739,000. Some current assets and current liabilities are directly linked to the firm's operating activities and some are not. *Operating current assets* consist of current assets needed for the operation of the business, including trade receivables, prepaid expenses, inventory and cash needed to operate the business. *Non-operating current assets* include excess cash, marketable securities and other investments. *Operating current liabilities* include trade payables, accruals and any other liabilities that are spontaneously generated by the operation of the firm. *Non-operating liabilities* include interest-bearing loans because these liabilities occur because the firm negotiates with lenders. So now we are really focusing on *net operating working capital*, the difference between operating current assets and operating current liabilities.

To see why firms need net operating working capital, imagine a small company, Simple Souvenirs, that makes small novelty items for sale at gift shops. It buys raw materials such as leather, beads, and rhinestones for cash, processes them into finished goods such as wallets or costume jewellery, and then sells these goods on credit and eventually receives cash when its customers pay their bills. Figure 20.3 shows the firm's cycle of operations.

If you prepare Simple Souvenirs's balance sheet (statement of financial position) at the beginning of the operating cycle, you see cash (a current asset). If you delay a little, you find the cash replaced first by inventories of raw materials and then by inventories of finished goods (also current assets). When the goods are sold, the inventories give way to trade receivables (another current asset), and finally, when the customers pay their bills, the firm takes out its profit and replenishes the cash balance. Simple Souvenirs has cash tied up in inventory and trade receivables because it takes time to convert raw materials into finished goods and to collect cash from their sale.

Figure 20.4 depicts four key dates in the production cycle that influence the firm's investment in operating working capital. The firm starts the cycle by purchasing raw materials, but it does not pay for them immediately. This delay is called the *trade payables period*. The firm processes the raw material into finished goods and then sells these goods on credit. The delay between the

FIGURE 20.3
Simple cycle of operations.

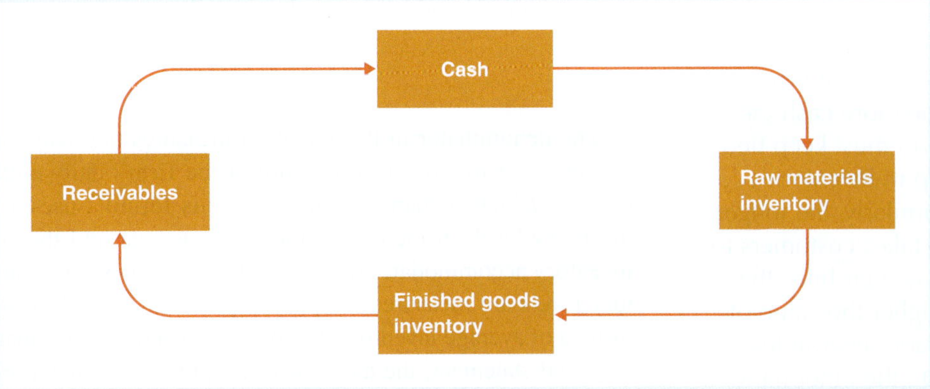

FIGURE 20.4
Cash conversion cycle.

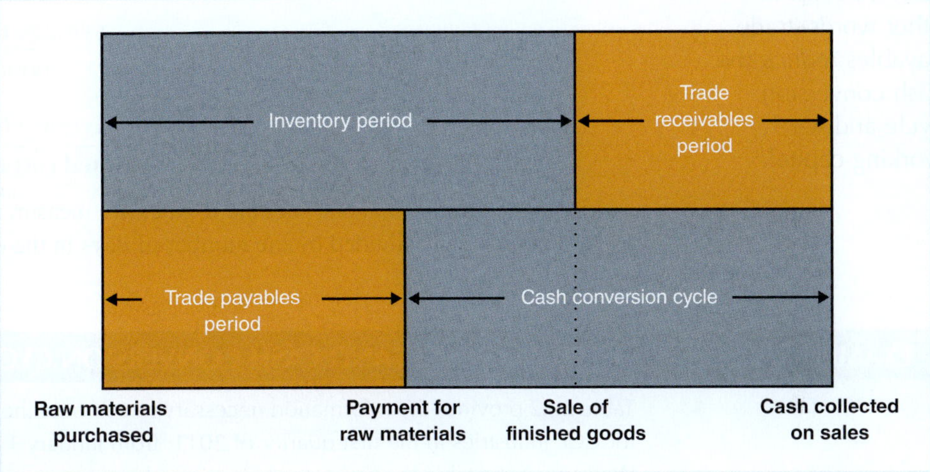

initial investment in inventories and the sale date is the *inventory period*. Some time after the firm has sold the goods, its customers pay their bills. The delay between the date of sale and the date at which the firm is paid is the *trade receivables period*.

The top part of Figure 20.4 shows that the *total* delay between initial purchase of raw materials and ultimate payments from customers is the sum of the inventory and trade receivables periods: first the raw materials must be purchased, processed, and sold, and then the bills must be collected. The sum of the inventory period and trade receivables period is the **operating cycle**.

operating cycle Period of time from the purchase of raw materials to the collection of cash from the sale of finished goods.

$$\text{Operating cycle} = \text{inventory period} + \text{trade receivables period} \quad (20.1)$$

However, the *net* time that the company is out of cash is reduced by the time it takes to pay its own bills. The length of time between the firm's payment for its raw materials and the collection of payment from the customer is known as the firm's **cash conversion cycle**, or the **cash gap**. To summarize,

cash conversion cycle or **cash gap** Period of time between firm's payment for materials and collection on its sales.

$$\begin{aligned}\text{Cash conversion cycle} &= (\text{inventory period} + \text{trade receivables period}) \\ &\quad - \text{accounts payable period} \quad (20.2) \\ &= \text{operating cycle} - \text{trade payables period}\end{aligned}$$

The longer the production process, the more cash the firm must keep tied up in inventories. Similarly, the longer it takes customers to pay their bills, the higher the value of trade receivables. On the other hand, if a firm can delay paying for its own materials, it may reduce the amount of cash it needs. In other words, trade payables *reduce* the cash conversion cycle and net working capital.

In Chapter 4 we showed you how the firm's annual financial statement can be used to estimate the inventory period, also called days' sales in inventory:

$$\textbf{Inventory period} = \frac{\textbf{average inventory}}{\textbf{annual cost of sales/365}} \quad \textbf{(20.3)}$$

The denominator in this equation measures the daily average cost of the products produced by the company, so it is a measure of the firm's daily output. Some firms use the term *cost of goods sold* rather than cost of sales. This formula uses average inventory, calculated with the inventory levels at the end of the previous year and the current year. Using the year's average inventory accommodates the fact that cost of sales is measured over the entire year but the inventory levels are measured at specific points of time. End of year inventory level could be used instead of average inventory. If data is from a quarterly financial statement, rather than an annual financial statement, the daily cost of inputs is calculated by dividing the quarterly cost of sales by the number of days in the quarter and there is no need to average the inventories. The ratio of inventory to daily cost of inputs used to produce output measures the average number of days from the purchase of the inventories to the final sale.

We can estimate the trade receivables period and the trade payables period in a similar way using data from annual financial statement:[6]

$$\textbf{Trade receivables period} = \frac{\textbf{average trade receivables}}{\textbf{annual sales/365}} \quad \textbf{(20.4)}$$

$$\textbf{Trade payables period} = \frac{\textbf{average trade payables}}{\textbf{annual cost of goods sold/365}} \quad \textbf{(20.5)}$$

If using quarterly financial statement, sales are measured for the quarter so the sales per day equal quarterly sales divided by the number of days in the quarter.

EXAMPLE 20.1 OPERATING CYCLE AND CASH CONVERSION CYCLE FOR CCL INDUSTRIES INC.

Table 20.2 provides the information necessary to compute the operating and cash conversion cycles for CCL Industries in the first quarter of 2011, from January 1 to March 31, 2011, which is 90 days. We can use the table to answer four questions: How long on average did it take CCL to produce and sell their product? How long did it take to collect bills? How long did it take to pay bills? What was the operating cycle and the cash conversion cycle?

The operating cycle—the number of days it takes to produce and sell the products—is the delay in collecting cash and equals the sum of inventory and receivables periods. The delay in paying bills

TABLE 20.2
These data can be used to calculate the operating and cash conversion cycles for CCL ($ millions).

Income Statement Data		Balance Sheet Data	
	1st Quarter Ending March 31, 2011		March 31, 2011
Revenue	$315.625	Inventory	$ 82.311
Production costs	238.037	Trade receivables	186.235
		Trade payables	135.680

Source: Adapted from CCL Industries Inc. Consolidated Condensed Interim Financial Statements, March 31, 2011.

[6] Because inventories are valued at cost, we divide inventory levels by cost of sales or COGS rather than revenue to obtain the inventory period. This way, both numerator and denominator are measured by cost. The same reasoning applies to the payables period. On the other hand, because trade receivables are valued at product price, we divide average receivables by daily sales revenue to find the receivables period. If a company does not report cost of sales, then you divide by either revenues or operating expenses.

is given by the payables period. The net delay in collecting payments is the cash conversion cycle. Because we are a using data from a quarterly report the daily cost of sales and daily revenues are calculated by dividing the reported costs and revenue by 90, the number of days in the quarter. We calculate these periods as follows:

$$\textbf{Inventory period} = \frac{\textbf{inventory}}{\textbf{cost of sales per day}} \tag{20.6}$$

$$= \frac{82.311}{238.037/90} = 31.1 \text{ days}$$

$$\textbf{receivables period} = \frac{\textbf{trade receivables}}{\textbf{revenues per day}} \tag{20.7}$$

$$= \frac{186.235}{315.625/90} = 53.1 \text{ days}$$

$$\textbf{payables period} = \frac{\textbf{trade payables}}{\textbf{daily cost of sales}} \tag{20.8}$$

$$= \frac{135.680}{238.037/90} = 51.3 \text{ days}$$

The operating cycle is

$$\begin{aligned} &\text{Inventory period} + \text{trade receivables period} \\ &= 31.1 + 53.1 = 84.2 \text{ days} \end{aligned}$$

On average, it takes about 84 days to convert raw materials into finished goods, sell the goods and collect cash from the customers.

The cash conversion cycle is

$$\begin{aligned} &\text{Inventory period} + \text{trade receivables period} - \text{trade payables period} \\ &= \text{operating cycle} - \text{trade payables period} \\ &= 84.2 - 51.3 = 32.9 \text{ days} \end{aligned}$$

It takes CCL an average of about 33 days from the time they lay out money on inventories to collect payment from their customers. CCL must be able to fund this cash gap.

Check Point 20.1

a. Suppose CCL is able to reduce inventory levels to $60 million and trade receivables to $150 million. By how many days will this change the operating cycle and the cash conversion cycle?

b. Suppose that, with the same level of inventories, trade receivables, and trade payables as shown in Table 20.2, CCL can increase production and sales by 10 percent. What will the effect be on the operating cycle and cash conversion cycle?

THE WORKING CAPITAL TRADE-OFF

Of course, the operating cycle and cash conversion cycle are not cast in stone. To a large extent they are within management's control. Working capital can be *managed*. For example, trade receivables are affected by the terms of credit the firm offers to its customers. You can cut the amount of money tied up in receivables by getting tough with customers who are slow in paying their bills. (You may find, however, that in the future they take their business elsewhere.) Similarly, the firm can reduce its investment in inventories of raw materials. (Here the risk is that it may one day run out of inventories and production will grind to a halt.)

Finance in Action

The Importance of Working Capital Management to Dealing with Financial Crisis

The current financial crisis has elevated decision-making related to working capital and short-term financing to top-of-mind for today's executives. Although working capital is a simple concept, managing it is made difficult by the complexity of the business around it. A focus on short-term earnings without concurrent discipline on cash and working capital has deflected the attention of many companies from the basics, where "cash is king."

As a result of the global nature of large organizations—along with the diversity of systems, processes, organizations and measures of performance—many companies are surprised to find that they are holding excessive levels of working capital. Since free cash flow is a key influencer of shareholder value, and may be critical to a company's survival, organizations are striving to free up the internal cash trapped within their different working capital components.

Rather than relying on external bank financing, we are seeing savvy companies targeting working capital reductions to unlock and accelerate cash invested in the business. Cash-optimization efforts should be "recession-proof." Not only does it pay to optimize cash throughout the enterprise during an economic downturn, but tough times actually demand added emphasis. In many companies, the current liquidity crisis has exposed flaws around properly managing cash and working capital. It has elevated the status of cash optimization from a sporadically considered option to an ongoing business imperative. Those companies that are able to release their trapped cash, that have the means to forecast cash effectively and accurately and that adhere to tight working capital standards will have a competitive advantage in these troubled economic times over those companies that do not address working capital aggressively.

Conversely, complacent companies could find themselves facing disastrous liquidity shocks or, worst case, bankruptcy. Reducing the need to finance working capital is critical. By far, the best source of liquidity and the cheapest financing stem from reducing the need to finance working capital. Small changes in Days Working Capital outstanding can have a dramatic impact on cash flow acceleration. In our experience, simple improvements to receivables, payables and inventory processes typically result in lower operating costs, improved cash flows and better cash-forecast accuracy.

From where we stand, WCM is an effective lever to increase cash flow and preserve, or even to enhance company value. But more importantly, for many companies today, it may be the necessary key to survival. Effectively managing the relationship between a firm's short-term assets and liabilities will accelerate cash flow. Well-capitalized companies are positioned not only to survive the financial crisis today, but also to emerge victorious and thrive when skies turn blue again. Establishing and adhering to tight working capital standards enables a firm to continue its operations with sufficient funds to both satisfy maturing short-term debt and meet upcoming operational expenses.

Source: Excerpted from Timothy T. Hesler and Laura Greenberg, "Liberating Cash: Reducing Working Capital Levels," *AFP Exchange*, April 2009, **www.treasury-management.com/docs/TMANY_Liberating_Cash__4-09.pdf**, accessed October 5, 2011.

carrying costs Costs of maintaining current assets, including opportunity cost of capital.

shortage costs Costs incurred from shortages in current assets.

> An important job of the financial manager is to strike a balance between the costs and benefits of current assets—that is, to find the level of current assets that minimizes the sum of carrying costs and shortage costs.

These considerations show that investment in working capital has both costs and benefits. For example, the cost of the firm's investment in receivables is the interest that could have been earned if customers had paid their bills earlier. The firm also forgoes interest income when it holds idle cash balances rather than putting the money to work in marketable securities. The cost of holding inventory includes not only the opportunity cost of capital but also storage and insurance costs and the risk of spoilage or obsolescence. All of these **carrying costs** encourage firms to hold current assets to a minimum.

While carrying costs discourage large investments in current assets, too low a level of current assets makes it more likely that the firm will face **shortage costs**. For example, if the firm runs out of inventory of raw materials, it may have to shut down production. Similarly, a producer holding a small finished goods inventory is more likely to be caught short, unable to fill orders promptly. There are also disadvantages to holding small "inventories" of cash. If the firm runs out of cash, it may have to sell securities and incur unnecessary trading costs. The firm may also maintain too low a level of trade receivables. If the firm tries to minimize trade receivables by restricting credit sales, it may lose customers and total revenues will be lower.

The financial crisis that began in mid-2007 and led to global economic recession created financial problems for companies, due to sales reductions, limited financing available from banks and higher interest rates. Firms had to deal with the availability of cash, because cash is needed for the survival of a company. Strategies for dealing with a recession include trying to find ways to reduce operating costs, delay capital expenditures but also by improving working capital management. In the nearby Finance in Action box is a discussion of the impact of the recent financial crisis on attention given to working capital management as an effective way of dealing with credit crunch of the financial crisis.

We will look more carefully at the costs and benefits of working capital in the next two chapters.

Check Point 20.2

How will the following affect the size of the firm's optimal investment in current operating assets?

a. The interest rate rises from 6 percent to 8 percent.
b. A just-in-time inventory system is introduced that reduces the risk of inventory shortages.
c. Customers pressure the firm for a more lenient credit sales policy.

LO3 20.3

TRACING CHANGES IN CASH AND WORKING CAPITAL

Table 20.3 compares 2011 and 2012 year-end balance sheets for Dynamic Mattress Company. Table 20.4 shows the firm's income statement for 2012. Note that Dynamic's cash balance increases from $4 million to $5 million in 2012. What caused this increase? Did the extra cash come from Dynamic Mattress Company's additional long-term borrowing? From reinvested earnings? From cash released by reducing inventory? Perhaps it came from extra credit extended by Dynamic's suppliers. (Note the increase in trade payables.)

The correct answer? All of the above. There is rarely any point in linking a particular source of funds with a particular use. Instead, financial analysts list the various sources and uses of cash

TABLE 20.3
Year-end balance sheets for Dynamic Mattress Company ($ millions).

Assets	2011	2012	Liabilities and Shareholders' Equity	2011	2012
Current assets:			Current liabilities:		
Cash	$ 4	$ 5	Bank loans	$ 5	$ 0
Marketable securities	0	5	Trade payables	20	27
Inventory	26	25	Total current liabilities	$25	$ 27
Trade receivables	25	30	Long-term debt	5	12
Total current assets	$55	$ 65	Net worth (equity and retained earnings)	65	76
Non-current assets:			Total liabilities and owners' equity	$95	$115
Gross investment	$56	$ 70			
Less depreciation	(16)	(20)			
Net long-term assets	$40	$ 50			
Total assets	$95	$115			

TABLE 20.4
Income statement for Dynamic Mattress Company, 2012 ($ millions).

Sales	$350
Operating costs	(321)
Depreciation	(4)
EBIT	25
Interest	(1)
Pretax income	24
Tax at 50 percent	(12)
Net income	$ 12

Note: Dividends = $1 million; Addition to retained earnings = $11 million.

TABLE 20.5
Sources and uses of cash for Dynamic Mattress Company, 2012 ($ millions).

Sources	
Issued long-term debt	$ 7
Reduced inventories	1
Increased trade payables	7
Cash from operations:	
Net income	12
Depreciation	4
Total sources	$31
Uses	
Repaid short-term bank loan	$ 5
Invested in long-term assets	14
Purchased marketable securities	5
Increased trade receivables	5
Dividend	1
Total uses	$30
Increase in cash balance	$ 1

in a statement like the one shown in Table 20.5. The statement shows that Dynamic *generated* cash from the following sources:

1. It issued $7 million of long-term debt: Change in long-term debt = $12 million − $5 million.
2. It reduced inventory, releasing $1 million: Change in inventory = $25 million − $26 million.
3. It increased its trade payables, in effect borrowing an additional $7 million from its suppliers: Change in trade payables = $27 million − $20 million.
4. By far the largest source of cash was Dynamic's operations, which generated $16 million. Note that the $12 million net income reported in Table 20.4 understates cash flow because depreciation is deducted in calculating income. Depreciation is not a cash outlay. Thus it must be added back in order to obtain operating cash flow: Cash flow from operations = Net income + depreciation = $12 million + $4 million = $16 million.

Dynamic *used* cash for the following purposes:

1. It paid a $1 million dividend. (*Note:* The $11 million increase in Dynamic's equity is due to addition to retained earnings: $12 million of equity income, less the $1 million dividend.)
2. It repaid a $5 million short-term bank loan: $0 − $5 million.
3. It invested $14 million in long-term assets: Investment in long-term assets = Closing net long-term assets − opening net long-term assets + depreciation = $50 million − $40 million + $4 million.
4. It purchased $5 million of marketable securities: Change in marketable securities = $5 million − $0.
5. It allowed trade receivables to expand by $5 million. In effect, it lent this additional amount to its customers: Change in trade receivables = $30 million − $25 million.

Check Point 20.3

How will the following affect cash and net working capital?

a. The firm takes out a short-term bank loan and uses the funds to pay off some of its trade payables.
b. The firm uses cash on hand to buy raw materials.
c. The firm repurchases outstanding shares of stock.
d. The firm sells long-term bonds and puts the proceeds in its bank account.

In Chapter 3 we introduced the statement of cash flow. The sources and uses of cash information in Table 20.5 is the very same information that would be found in Dynamic's statement of cash flow. The only difference is the way the data is organized. In a statement of cash flow, the information is organized into three sections: cash flow from operations, cash flow from investments, and cash flow from financing activities. When you create a sources and uses of cash statement, you simply organize according to whether the item increased or decreased cash. How you organize the information depends on what you are interested in learning.

Check Point 20.4

Using the information in Table 20.5 and the statement of cash flow for AstraZeneca in Chapter 3 as an example, create the statement of cash flow for Dynamic Mattress. Start with net income, treat interest as an operating expense and the purchase of marketable securities as an investment activity. What is the net cash inflow (outflow)?

LO4 20.4

CASH BUDGETING

The financial manager's task is to forecast *future* sources and uses of cash. These forecasts serve two purposes. First, they alert the financial manager to future cash needs, giving the manager time to develop and implement a plan to manage the forecasted cash shortage or cash surplus. Second, the cash flow forecasts provide a standard, or budget, against which subsequent performance can be judged.

Cash budgets can be based on a highly detailed operating forecast or on a less detailed forecast. But no matter what method is chosen, there are three common steps to preparing a cash budget:

Step 1. Forecast the sources of cash. The largest inflow of cash comes from payments by the firm's customers.
Step 2. Forecast uses of cash.
Step 3. Calculate whether the firm is facing a cash shortage or surplus.

The financial plan sets out a strategy for investing a cash surplus or financing any deficit. We will illustrate these issues by continuing the example of Dynamic Mattress.

FORECAST SOURCES OF CASH

Most of Dynamic's cash inflow comes from the sale of mattresses. We therefore start with a sales forecast by quarter for 2013:[7]

Quarter:	First	Second	Third	Fourth
Sales, millions of dollars	87.5	78.5	116	131

However, unless customers pay cash on delivery, sales become trade receivables before they become cash. Cash flow comes from *collections* on trade receivables.

Most firms keep track of the average time it takes customers to pay their bills. From this they can forecast what proportion of a quarter's sales is likely to be converted into cash in that quarter and what proportion is likely to be carried over to the next quarter as trade receivables. This proportion depends on the lags with which customers pay their bills. For example, if customers wait one month to pay their bills, then on average one-third of each quarter's bills will not be paid until the following quarter. If the payment delay is two months, then two-thirds of quarterly sales will be collected in the following quarter.

[7] For simplicity, we present a quarterly forecast. However, most firms would forecast by month instead of by quarter. Sometimes weekly or even daily forecasts are made.

TABLE 20.6
Dynamic Mattress's cash budget for 2013 (figures in $ millions).

	A	B	C	D	E
1	Quarter:	First	Second	Third	Fourth
2					
3	**Panel A: Accounts Receivable**				
4	Receivables (beginning period)	30.0	32.5	30.7	38.2
5	Sales	87.5	78.5	116.0	131.0
6	Collections:				
7	On sales in current period (80%)	70	62.8	92.8	104.8
8	On sales in previous period (20%)	15[a]	17.5	15.7	23.2
9	Total collections	$ 85	$80.3	$108.5	$ 128
10	Receivables (end of period) = rows 4+5−9	$32.5	$30.7	$ 38.2	$41.2
11					
12	**Panel B: Cash Budget**				
13	**Sources of cash:**				
14	Collections of trade receivable (from row 9)	85.0	80.3	108.5	128.0
15	Other	1.5	0.0	12.5	0.0
16	Total sources	86.5	80.3	121.0	128.0
17	**Uses:**				
18	Materials: Payments of trade payables	65.0	60.0	55.0	50.0
19	Labour and administrative expenses	30.0	30.0	30.0	30.0
20	Capital expenses	32.5	1.3	5.5	8.0
21	Taxes, interest, and dividends	4.0	4.0	4.5	5.0
22	Total uses	131.5	95.3	95.0	93.0
23					
24	**Net cash inflow = sources − uses**	−45.0	−15.0	26.0	35.0
25					
26	**Panel C: Short-Term Financing Requirements**				
27	Cash at start of period	5.0	−40.0	−55.0	−29.0
28	+ Net cash inflow (from row 24)	−45.0	−15.0	26.0	35.0
29	= Cash at end of period[b]	−40.0	−55.0	−29.0	6.0
30	Minimum operating balance	5.0	5.0	5.0	5.0
31	Cumulative financing required[c] (row 30 − 29)	45.0	60.0	34.0	−1.0

[a] Sales in the fourth quarter of the previous year were $75 million.
[b] Of course, firms cannot literally hold a negative amount of cash. This line shows the amount of cash the firm will have to raise to pay its bills.
[c] A negative sign indicates that no short-term financing is required. Instead the firm has a cash surplus.

Suppose that 80 percent of sales are collected in the immediate quarter and the remaining 20 percent in the next. Panel A of Table 20.6 shows forecast collections under this assumption.

In the first quarter, for example, collections from current sales are 80 percent of $87.5 million, or $70 million. But the firm also collects 20 percent of the previous quarter's sales, or .20 × $75 million = $15 million. Therefore, total collections are $70 million + $15 million = $85 million.

Dynamic started the first quarter with $30 million of trade receivables. The quarter's sales of $87.5 million were *added* to trade receivables, but $85 million of collections was *subtracted*. Therefore, as Table 20.6 shows, Dynamic ended the quarter with trade receivables of $30 million + $87.5 million − $85 million = $32.5 million. The general formula is

Ending trade receivables = beginning trade receivables + sales − collections (20.9)

The top section of panel B of Table 20.6 shows forecast sources of cash for Dynamic Mattress. Collection of receivables is the main source but it is not the only one. Perhaps the firm plans to dispose of some land or expects a tax refund or payment of an insurance claim. All such items are included as "other" sources. It is also possible that you may raise additional capital by borrowing or selling stock, but we don't want to prejudge that question. Therefore, for the moment we just assume that Dynamic will not raise further long-term finance.

FORECAST USES OF CASH

There always seem to be many more uses for cash than there are sources. The second section of panel B of Table 20.6 shows how Dynamic expects to use cash. For simplicity, we condensed the uses into four categories:

1. *Materials: Payments of trade payables.* Dynamic has to purchase the raw materials, parts, electricity, and so on needed for its planned production schedule. The production schedule is based on planned sales and desired inventory levels. Once the purchases are known, then Dynamic must plan for the payment for the purchases. Little thought is needed to plan the payment for any purchases that require cash payment: cash is used immediately. However, all purchases made on credit generate trade payables. Just as Dynamic has a collection schedule for its trade receivables, it has a payment schedule for its trade payables. This cash flow forecast assumes all purchases are made on credit and these bills are paid on time, according to the payment terms offered by suppliers. Dynamic could probably delay payment to some extent. Delayed payment is sometimes called *stretching your payables*. Stretching is one source of short-term financing, but for most firms it is an expensive source, because by stretching they lose discounts given to firms that pay promptly. (This is discussed in more detail in Chapter 22.)
2. *Labour, administrative, and other expenses.* This category includes all other regular business expenses.
3. *Capital expenditures.* Note that Dynamic Mattress plans a major outlay of cash in the first quarter to pay for a long-term asset.
4. *Taxes, interest, and dividend payments.* This includes all required taxes, interest on currently outstanding long-term debt, and dividend payments to shareholders.

The forecast net inflow of cash (sources minus uses) is shown in row 24. Note the large negative figure for the first quarter: a $45 million forecast *outflow*. There is a smaller forecast *outflow* in the second quarter and then substantial cash inflows in the second half of the year.

THE CASH BALANCE

So far, Dynamic Mattress does not know how much it will have to borrow or, for that matter, if it will have to borrow at all. These calculations are presented in Table 20.6, panel C, which shows how much financing Dynamic will have to raise if its cash-flow forecasts are right. It starts the year with $5 million in cash. There is a $45 million cash outflow in the first quarter, which in the absence of external financing would create a $40 million cash shortfall at the end of the period (row 29). This deficit is carried to the beginning of the next quarter (cell C27). At the very least, Dynamic must obtain $40 million of additional financing just to cover the forecast cash deficit. This would leave the firm with a forecast cash balance of exactly zero at the start of the second quarter.

Most financial managers regard a planned cash balance of zero as driving too close to the edge of the cliff. They establish a *minimum operating cash balance* to absorb unexpected cash inflows and outflows. We assume in Table 20.6 that Dynamic's minimum operating cash balance is $5 million. That means it will have to raise $45 million instead of $40 million in the first quarter, and $15 million more in the second quarter. Thus its *cumulative* financing requirement is $60 million in the second quarter. Fortunately, this is the peak; the cumulative requirement declines in the third quarter when its $26 million net cash inflow reduces its cumulative financing requirement to $34 million. (Notice that cumulative short-term financing falls by the net cash inflow in that quarter, found in row 24.) In the final quarter Dynamic is out of the woods. Its $35 million net cash inflow is enough to eliminate short-term financing and actually increase cash balances above the $5 million minimum acceptable balance.

Excel Spreadsheet

Dynamic Mattress's Short-Term Plan

	A	B	C	D	E
1	**Quarter:**	**First**	**Second**	**Third**	**Fourth**
2					
3	**Panel A: Trade Receivables**				
4	Receivables (beginning period)	30	=B10	=C10	=D10
5	Sales	87.5	78.5	116.0	131.0
6	Collections				
7	On sales in current period (80%)	=0.8*B5	=0.8*C5	=0.8*D5	=0.8*E5
8	On sales in previous period (20%)	=0.2*75	=0.2*B5	=0.2*C5	=0.2*D5
9	Total collections	=B7+B8	=C7+C8	=D7+D8	=E7+E8
10	Receivables (end period)	=B4+B5−B6	=C4+C5−C6	=D4+D5−D6	=E4+E5−E6
11					
12	**Panel B: Cash Budget**				
13	**Sources of cash**				
14	Collections of trade receivables	=B9	=C9	=D9	=E9
15	Other	1.5	0.0	12.5	0.0
16	Total sources	=B14+B15	=C14+C15	=D14+D15	=E14+E15
17	**Uses**				
18	Materials: Payments of trade payables	65.0	60.0	55.0	50.0
19	Labour and administrative expenses	30.0	30.0	30.0	30.0
20	Capital expenses	32.5	1.3	5.5	8.0
21	Taxes, interest, and dividends	4.0	4.0	4.5	5.0
22	Total uses	=SUM(B18:B21)	=SUM(C18:C21)	=SUM(D18:D21)	=SUM(E18:E21)
23					
24	**Net cash inflow = sources − uses**	=B16−B22	=C16−C22	=D16−D22	=E16−E22
25					
26	**Panel C: Short-Term Financing Requirements**				
27	Cash at start of period	5.0	=B29	=C29	=D29
28	+ Net cash inflow	=B24	=C24	=D24	=E24
29	= Cash at end of period	=B27+B28	=C27+C28	=D27+D28	=E27+E28
30	Minimum operating balance	5.0	=B30	=C30	=D30
31	Cumulative financing required	=B30−B29	=C30−C29	=D30−D29	=E30−E29

Before moving on, we offer two general observations about this example:

1. The large cash outflows in the first two quarters do not necessarily spell trouble for Dynamic Mattress. In part they reflect the capital investment made in the first quarter: Dynamic is spending $32.5 million, but it should be acquiring an asset worth that much or more. The cash outflows also reflect low sales in the first half of the year; sales recover in the second half.[8] If this is a predictable seasonal pattern, the firm should have no trouble borrowing to help it get through the slow months.
2. Table 20.6 is only a best guess about future cash flows. It is a good idea to think about the *uncertainty* in your estimates. For example, you could undertake a sensitivity analysis, in which you inspect how Dynamic's cash requirements would be affected by a shortfall in sales or by a delay in collections.

[8] Maybe people buy more mattresses late in the year when the nights are longer.

Check Point 20.5 Calculate Dynamic Mattress's quarterly cash receipts, net cash inflow, and cumulative short-term financing required if customers pay for only 60 percent of purchases in the current quarter and pay the remaining 40 percent in the following quarter.

Our next step will be to develop a short-term financing plan that covers the forecast requirements in the most economical way possible. Before presenting such a plan, however, we should pause briefly to point out that short-term financial planning, like long-term planning, is best done on a computer. The nearby Excel Spreadsheet box presents the formula view of the spreadsheet underlying Table 20.6. Examine those formulas and note which items are inputs (for example, rows 18–21) and which are calculated from equations. The formulas also indicate the links from one panel to another. For example, in the spreadsheet, collections of receivables are calculated in panel A, row 9, and passed through as inputs in panel B, row 14. Similarly, net cash inflow in panel B, row 24, is passed along to panel C, row 28.

Once the spreadsheet is set up, it becomes easy to explore the consequences of many what-if questions. For example, Check Point 20.5 asks you to recalculate the quarterly cash receipts, net cash inflow, and cumulative short-term financing required if the firm's collections on accounts receivable slow down. You could do this by hand, but it is quicker and easier to do it in a spreadsheet—especially when you might have to work through dozens of scenarios!

LO4 20.5 A SHORT-TERM FINANCING PLAN

Dynamic's cash budget defines its problem. Its financial manager must find short-term financing to cover the firm's forecasted cash requirements. There are dozens of sources of short-term financing, but for simplicity we will consider only two: obtaining bank loans or stretching payables.

We assume that Dynamic can borrow up to $40 million from the bank at an interest cost of 8 percent per year or 2 percent per quarter. It can borrow and repay the loan whenever it wants to, but it may not exceed its credit limit.

Alternatively, Dynamic can also raise capital by putting off paying its bills. The financial manager believes that Dynamic can defer the following amounts in each quarter:

Quarter:	First	Second	Third	Fourth
Amount deferrable, millions of dollars	52	48	44	40

That is, $52 million can be saved in the first quarter by not paying bills in that quarter. (Note that Table 20.6 was prepared assuming these bills *are* paid in the first quarter.) If deferred, these payments *must* be made in the second quarter. Similarly, $48 million of the second quarter's bills can be deferred to the third quarter and so on.

Stretching payables is often costly, however, even if no ill will is incurred.[9] This is because many suppliers offer discounts for prompt payment, so that Dynamic loses the discount if it pays late. In this example we assume the lost discount is 5 percent of the amount deferred. In other words, if a $52 million payment is delayed in the first quarter, the firm must pay 5 percent more, or $54.6 million in the next quarter. This is like borrowing at an annual interest rate of over 20 percent ($1.05^4 - 1 = .216$, or 21.6 percent).

[9] In fact, ill will is likely to be incurred. Firms that stretch payments risk being labelled as credit risks. Since stretching is so expensive, suppliers reason that only customers that cannot obtain credit at reasonable rates elsewhere will resort to it. Suppliers naturally are reluctant to act as the lender of last resort.

DYNAMIC MATTRESS'S FINANCING PLAN

With these two options, the short-term financing strategy is obvious: use the lower-cost bank loan first. Stretch payables only if you can't borrow enough from the bank.

Table 20.7 shows the resulting plan. Panel A (cash requirements) sets out the cash that needs to be raised in each quarter. Panel B (cash raised in quarter) describes the various sources of financing the firm plans to use. Panels C and D describe how the firm will use net cash inflows when they turn positive. Panel E keeps track of the bank loan.

In the first quarter, the plan calls for borrowing the full amount available from the bank ($40 million). In addition, the firm sells the $5 million of marketable securities it held at the end of 2012. Thus, under this plan, it raises the necessary $45 million in the first quarter.

In the second quarter, an additional $15 million must be raised to cover the net cash outflow predicted in Table 20.6. In addition, $.8 million must be raised to pay interest on the bank loan. Therefore, the plan calls for Dynamic to maintain its bank borrowing and to stretch $15.8 million in payables. Notice that in the first two quarters, when net cash flow from operations is negative, the firm maintains its cash balance at the minimum acceptable level. Additions to cash balances are zero. Similarly, repayments of outstanding debt are zero. In fact, outstanding debt rises in each of these quarters.

In the third and fourth quarters, the firm generates a cash flow surplus, so the plan calls for Dynamic to pay off its debt. First it pays off stretched payables, as it is required to do, and then it uses any remaining cash flow surplus to pay down its bank loan. In the third quarter, all of the net cash inflow is used to reduce outstanding short-term borrowing. In the fourth quarter, the firm pays off its remaining short-term borrowing and uses the extra $2.98 million to increase its cash balances.

TABLE 20.7 Dynamic Mattress's financing plan ($ millions).

	A	B	C	D	E
1	**Quarter:**	**First**	**Second**	**Third**	**Fourth**
2	**Panel A: Cash Requirements**				
3	Cash required for operations[a]	$45	$ 15	−$ 26	−$ 35
4	Interest on bank loan[b]	0	0.8	0.8	0.6
5	Interest on stretched payables[c]	0	0	0.8	0
6	Total cash required	$45	$15.8	−$24.4	−$34.4
7					
8	**Panel B: Cash Raised in Quarter**				
9	Bank loan	$40	$ 0	$ 0	$ 0
10	Stretched payables	0	15.8	0	0
11	Securities sold	5	0	0	0
12	Total cash raised	$45	$15.8	$ 0	$ 0
13					
14	**Panel C: Repayments**				
15	Of stretched payables	0	0	$15.8	$ 0
16	Of bank loan	0	0	8.6	$31.4
17					
18	**Panel D: Addition to Cash Balances**	$ 0	$ 0	$ 0	$ 3
19					
20	**Panel E: Bank Loan**				
21	Beginning of quarter	$ 0	$ 40	$ 40	$31.4
22	End of quarter	40	40	31.4	0

[a] A negative cash requirement implies positive cash flow from operations.

[b] The interest rate on the bank loan is 2 percent per quarter applied to the bank loan outstanding at the start of the quarter. Thus the interest due in the second quarter is .02 × $40 million = $.8 million.

[c] The "interest" cost of the stretched payables is 5 percent of the amount of payment deferred. For example, in the third quarter, 5 percent of the $15.8 million stretched in the second quarter is about $.8 million.

Check Point 20.6

Revise Dynamic Mattress's short-term financial plan assuming it can borrow up to $45 million through its line of credit. Assume that the firm will still sell its $5 million of short-term securities in the first quarter.

EVALUATING THE PLAN

Does the plan shown in Table 20.7 solve Dynamic's short-term financing problem? No—the plan is feasible but Dynamic can probably do better. The most glaring weakness of this plan is its reliance on stretching payables, an extremely expensive financing device. Remember that it costs Dynamic 5 percent *per quarter* to delay paying bills—20 percent per year at simple interest. This first plan should merely stimulate the financial manager to search for cheaper sources of short-term borrowing.

The financial manager would ask several other questions as well. For example:

1. Does Dynamic need a larger reserve of cash or marketable securities, say, to guard against its customers stretching *their* payables (thus slowing down collections on trade receivables)?
2. Does the plan yield satisfactory current and quick ratios?[10] Its bankers may be worried if these ratios deteriorate.
3. Are there hidden costs to stretching payables? Will suppliers begin to doubt Dynamic's creditworthiness?
4. Does the plan for 2013 leave Dynamic in good financial shape for 2014? (Here the answer is yes, since Dynamic will have paid off all short-term borrowing by the end of the year.)
5. Should Dynamic try to arrange long-term financing for the major capital expenditure in the first quarter? This seems sensible, following the rule of thumb that long-term assets deserve long-term financing. It would also dramatically reduce the need for short-term borrowing. A counter argument is that Dynamic is financing the capital investment *only temporarily* by short-term borrowing. By year-end, the investment is paid for by cash from operations. Thus Dynamic's initial decision not to seek immediate long-term financing may reflect a preference for ultimately financing the investment with retained earnings, which means it is equity financed.
6. Perhaps the firm's operating and investment plans can be adjusted to make the short-term financing problem easier. Is there any easy way of deferring the first quarter's large cash outflow? For example, suppose that the large capital investment in the first quarter is for new mattress-stuffing machines to be delivered and installed in the first half of the year. The new machines are not scheduled to be ready for full-scale use until August. Perhaps the machine manufacturer could be persuaded to accept 60 percent of the purchase price on delivery and 40 percent when the machines are installed and operating satisfactorily.

Short-term financing plans must be developed by trial and error. You lay out one plan, think about it, then try again with different assumptions about financing and investment alternatives. You continue until you can think of no further improvements.

Once these and other questions are answered and incorporated into the short-term financial plan, managers will have a sense of the need for short-term financing. Developing the best short-term financial plan requires assessing the consequences of different assumptions.

LO5 20.6 SOURCES OF SHORT-TERM FINANCING

Dynamic solved the greater part of its cash shortage by borrowing from a bank. Banks offer various types of loans and one type may make more sense for you than another. Also, banks are not the only source of short-term borrowing. For example, firms may obtain loans from finance companies, which specialize in lending to businesses and individuals. Unlike banks, finance

[10] These ratios are discussed in Chapter 4.

companies obtain funds through selling securities rather than by taking deposits. Firms may also raise money by selling their own short-term debt directly to investors. Let's look at some of these alternative sources of short-term financing.

BANK LOANS

line of credit Agreement by a bank that a company may borrow at any time up to an established limit.

commitment fee Fee charged by the lender on the unused portion of a line of credit.

The simplest and most common source of short-term financing is a loan from a bank. Companies sometimes wait until they need the money before they apply for a bank loan, but in the majority of cases the firm will arrange a **line of credit** that permits it to borrow from the bank up to an agreed-upon limit. Lines of credit are typically reviewed annually, and it is possible that the bank may seek to cancel it if the firm's creditworthiness deteriorates. If the firm wants to be sure that it will be able to borrow, it can enter into a *revolving credit agreement* with the bank. Revolving credit arrangements usually last for a few years and formally commit the bank to lending up to the agreed limit. In return the bank will require the firm to pay a **commitment fee**; for example, it might be .25 percent of the unused amount.

EXAMPLE 20.2 COMMITMENT FEES

Goofy Eatery Inc. has entered into a $1,000,000 revolving credit arrangement with its bank with a commitment fee of .5 percent, which will apply on the average unused portion of the loan. The interest on any funds borrowed will be 6 percent per year. At the end of the year, it is determined that the firm has, on average, used up only $600,000 of its credit limit. The interest on the loan for the year is, therefore, $600,000 × 0.06 = $36,000. In addition, a commitment fee is applicable on the average funds unused, that is $1,000,000 − $600,000 = $400,000. This works out to .5 percent of $400,000, or $2,000. The interest and commitment fee together total $36,000 + $2,000 = $38,000.

For example, in July 2011, Churchill Corporation, a construction and industrial services company in western Canada, announced that it had negotiated improved terms and conditions for its $200 million senior secured revolving credit facility (the "Revolver"). Churchill's new credit agreement included 100 basis point reduction in the applicable interest rate, relaxation or elimination of certain financial covenants, an increase in the term from three to four years (new maturity date of July 12, 2015), and additional flexibility on consents regarding dividends and acquisitions. As a *revolver* the company can borrow and repay whenever it wants until 2015, as long as it does not exceed the agreed limit. However, Churchill's Revolver continues to include a $75 million *accordion feature*. An accordion feature is an option that a company can buy that gives it the right to increase its line of credit or similar type of liability with a lender. Companies typically purchase an accordion feature in anticipation of the need for more working capital for possible expansion opportunities.

term loans Bank loans for one or more years.

The alternative to a line of credit is a loan which provides the all of the money at the start of the loan and has a specified repayment schedule. Some bank loans have durations of only a few months. For example, Dynamic may need a loan to cover a seasonal increase in inventories, and the loan is then repaid as the goods are sold. However, banks also make **term loans**, which could last for one to ten years.

syndicated loan Loan provided by a group of banks that combine to provide the loan amount.

Some lines of credits and term loans involve huge sums of money and are too large for a single lender. In these cases the borrower may pay an arrangement fee to a lead bank, which then parcels out the loan or line of credit among a syndicate of commercial and investment banks, creating a **syndicated loan**. For example, Churchill Corp's $200 million line of credit was provided by a syndicate of lenders, a group of Canadian banks. A report from Bloomberg[11] noted that the overall Canadian syndicated loan market had continued to improve from the low in

[11] Sean B. Pasternak, "TD Securities Tops RBC in Syndicated Loans Race: Canada Credit," *Bloomberg Businessweek*, April 12, 2011, **www.businessweek.com/news/2011-04-12/td-securities-tops-rbc-in-syndicated-loans-race-canada-credit.html**, accessed October 5, 2011.

2008–2009. In the first half of 2011 there were a total of 229 new deals of term loans and revolving-credit facilities for a total of $81.4 billion, up 58 percent by volume compared to the same time period last year. In Bloomberg's syndicated loan rankings, TD and CIBC are followed by Scotia Capital, RBC Capital and BMO Capital Markets. RBC, the unit of Toronto-based Royal Bank of Canada, topped the Bloomberg rankings from 2001 to 2009, before TD Securities led all Canadian banks in 2010.

SECURED LOANS

Banks do not make loans without assessing the firm's credit risk because the riskiness of the borrower affects the bank's risk. Typically the firm's credit risk will affect whether the firm will need to provide security or collateral for the loan, meaning a *secured loan*. For example, TD bank won't provide unsecured loans unless the firm credit risk is investment grade (BBB or higher). If a bank is lending on a short-term basis, the security generally consists of liquid assets such as receivables, inventories, or securities. For example, a small firm may decide to borrow short-term money secured by its accounts receivable. In return for giving the bank the legal right to seize assets in the event the firm is unable to repay its debt, the firm is able to borrow money at a lower rate of interest than if it had arranged an unsecured line of credit. When its customers pay their bills, it can use the cash collected to repay the loan.

Banks will not usually lend the full value of the assets that are used as security. For example, a firm that puts up $100,000 of receivables as security may find that the bank is prepared to lend only $75,000. The safety margin (or haircut, as it is called) is likely to be even larger in the case of loans that are secured by inventory. Typical maximum loan amounts are between 50 and 75 percent of accounts receivable, 50 percent of finished goods inventories, and zero for raw material and work-in-progress inventories.

pledged accounts receivable Accounts receivable that are collateral, the security, for a loan.

Accounts Receivable Financing

When a loan is secured by receivables, the firm *assigns* or *pledges* the receivables to the bank so the receivables are the collateral for the loan. If the firm fails to repay the loan, the bank can collect the **pledged accounts receivable** from the firm's customers and use the cash to pay off the debt. However, the firm is still responsible for the loan even if ultimately the receivables cannot be collected. The risk of default on the receivables is therefore borne by the firm. Depending on the arrangement between the borrowing firm and the bank, the customer whose receivable has been assigned may or may not be notified about such a pledge. Typically, in such an arrangement, in addition to the interest on the loan, the bank may also charge a service fee to cover administrative costs. For instance, the interest rate could be set at a premium of, say, 3 percent above the prime rate, while the service fee could be at 2 percent of the receivables amount pledged. Since accounts receivable tend to be relatively liquid current assets, pledging them provides good collateral value to the lender.

EXAMPLE 20.3 ACCOUNTS RECEIVABLE PLEDGING

Suppose Mid-life Gym Equipment is negotiating a bank loan by assigning its receivables totalling $150,000. The bank has agreed to lend to the extent of 70 percent of the amount pledged at an interest rate of 3 percent points above the prime rate, which is currently at 5 percent. In this instance, the bank has also agreed to waive the service fee as a goodwill gesture to Mid-life Gym. Mid-life Gym's average collection period is 30 days. The amount of the bank loan will be $150,000 × 0.7 = $105,000. Interest costs, at an annual percentage rate of 8 percent are calculated over the average collection period as $105,000 × 0.08 × 30/365 = $690.41.

factoring A firm sells its accounts receivable at a discount for the purpose of obtaining short-term financing.

An alternative procedure is **factoring**, that is, to *sell* the trade receivables at a discount to a financial institution known as a factor and let it collect the money. In other words, some companies solve their financing problem by borrowing on the strength of their current assets; others solve it by selling their current assets. With factoring, once the firm has sold its receivables, the factor bears the responsibility for collecting on the trade receivables. There are two types of factors: non-recourse factors and recourse factors. They differ in who takes responsibility for bad debts. In recourse factoring, the factor does not take on the risk of bad debts. Put another way, the factor will be able to reclaim their money from borrower if the customer does not pay. The factoring agreement will specify how many days after the due date for payment the borrower must refund the advance. In non-recourse factoring, the factor takes on the bad debt risk. It accepts specified risks around the debtor's failure to pay, but it does not insure against debts that are unpaid because of genuine disputes. Because of this, non-recourse factoring will be more expensive than recourse factoring.

EXAMPLE 20.4 FACTORING

Suppose that the firm sells its trade receivables to a non-recourse factor at a 2 percent discount. This means that the factor pays 98 cents for each dollar of trade receivables. If the average collection period is 1 month, then in a month the factor should be able to collect $1 for every 98 cents it paid today. Therefore, the implicit interest rate is $2/98 = 2.04$ percent per month, which corresponds to an effective annual interest rate of $(1.0204)^{12} - 1 = .274$, or 27.4 percent.

While factoring would appear to be an expensive source of financing for the firm, from this example, part of the apparently steep interest rate represents payment for the assumption of default risk as well as for the cost of running the credit operation.

Inventory Financing Banks also lend on the security of inventory, but they are choosy about the inventory they will accept. They want to make sure that they can identify and sell it if you default. Automobiles and other standardized, non-perishable commodities are good security for a loan; work in progress and ripe strawberries are poor collateral.

Banks need to monitor companies to be sure they don't sell their assets and run off with the money. Consider, for example, the story of the great salad oil swindle. Fifty-one banks and companies made loans for nearly US$200 million to the Allied Crude Vegetable Oil Refining Corporation in the belief that these loans were secured on valuable salad oil. Unfortunately, they did not notice that Allied's tanks contained false compartments filled mainly with seawater. When the fraud was discovered, the president of Allied went to jail and the 51 lenders were left out in the cold looking for their $200 million. The nearby Finance in Action box presents a similar story that illustrates the pitfalls of secured lending. Here, too, the loans were not as "secured" as they looked: the supposed collateral did not exist.

To protect themselves against this sort of risk, lenders often insist on *field warehousing*. An independent warehouse company hired by the bank supervises the inventory pledged as collateral. As the firm sells its product and uses the revenue to pay back the loan, the bank directs the warehouse company to release the inventory back to the firm. If the firm defaults on the loan, the bank keeps the inventory and sells it to recover the debt.

All secured loans are types of asset-based lending, in which the lender has a legal claim to the assets in the event of default. The main focus of an asset-based lender is on the quality and the liquidity of the assets providing the security for the loan. Asset-based lenders actively monitor the assets. In contrast, a traditional unsecured bank lender is focused on the quality of the borrower's management and the cash flow of the company. To reduce the risk of not being paid, the unsecured lender typically imposes financial covenants, such as minimum interest coverage ratio, to ensure that the firm has enough cash flow to service the loan.

COMMERCIAL PAPER

When banks lend money, they provide two services. They match up would-be borrowers and lenders, and they check that the borrower is likely to repay the loan. Banks recover the costs of providing these services by charging borrowers on average a higher interest rate than they pay to lenders. These services are less necessary for large, well-known companies that regularly need

Finance in Action

The Hazards of Secured Bank Lending

The National Safety Council of Australia's Victoria Division had been a sleepy outfit until John Friedrich took over. Under its new management, NSC members trained like commandos and were prepared to go anywhere and do anything. They saved people from drowning, they fought fires, found lost bushwalkers, and went down mines. Their lavish equipment included 22 helicopters, eight aircraft, and a mini-submarine. Soon the NSC began selling its services internationally.

Unfortunately the NSC's paramilitary outfit cost millions of dollars to run—far more than it earned in revenue. Friedrich bridged the gap by borrowing AU$236 million of debt. The banks were happy to lend because the NSC's debt appeared well secured. At one point the company showed AU$107 million of receivables (that is, money owed by its customers), which it pledged as security for bank loans. Later checks revealed that many of these customers did not owe the NSC a cent. In other cases, banks took comfort in the fact that their loans were secured by containers of valuable rescue gear. There were more than 100 containers stacked around the NSC's main base. Only a handful contained any equipment, but these were the ones that the bankers saw when they came to check that their loans were safe. Sometimes a suspicious banker would ask to inspect a particular container. Friedrich would then explain that it was away on exercise, fly the banker across the country in a light plane and point to a container well out in the bush. The container would of course be empty, but the banker had no way to know that.

Six years after Friedrich was appointed CEO, his massive fraud was uncovered. But a few days before a warrant could be issued, Friedrich disappeared. Although he was eventually caught and arrested, he shot himself before he could come to trial. Investigations revealed that Friedrich was operating under an assumed name, having fled from his native Germany where he was wanted by the police. Many rumours continued to circulate about Friedrich. He was variously alleged to have been a plant of the CIA and the KGB, and the NSC was said to have been behind an attempted counter-coup in Fiji. For the banks there was only one hard truth. Their loans to the NSC, which had appeared so well secured, would never be repaid.

Source: Adapted from Chap. 7 of T. Sykes, *The Bold Riders* (St. Leonards, NSW, Australia: Allen & Unwin, 1994).

commercial paper Short-term unsecured notes issued by large corporations.

to raise large amounts of cash. These companies have increasingly found it profitable to bypass the bank and to sell short-term debt, known as **commercial paper**, directly to large investors. Corporate commercial paper is backed by the quality of the corporation's assets and its operating cash flows. Banks have been forced to respond by reducing the interest rates on their loans to blue-chip customers.

Commercial paper issued by corporations needing financing for current assets is not the same as *asset-backed commercial paper (ABCP)*. Like corporate commercial paper, ABCP is a short-term security but is issued by financial companies who use the funds to purchase accounts receivable and mortgages of other companies. We will have more to say about ABCP in Chapter 21, when we look at securities used by companies with idle cash.

In Canada, commercial paper can sometimes have a maturity of a year, although corporations mostly issue these instruments for periods of one, two, or three months. Commercial paper is not secured, but companies generally back up their issue of paper by arranging a special line of credit with a bank. This guarantees that they can find the money to repay the paper and the risk of default is therefore small. Commercial paper can have a zero interest rate, so is issued below face value and is called discount paper but some commercial paper is interest-bearing.

Some companies regularly sell commercial paper in huge amounts. For example, the Canadian Wheat Board had $1.322 billion of commercial paper outstanding as of January 31, 2011. The rating of this commercial paper by Dominion Bond Rating Service (DBRS) is R-1, the highest ranking.

Rating organizations often provide information to investors regarding the quality and risk of different commercial paper issues. For instance, Dominion Bond Rating Service provides the following categories of ratings for commercial paper issues:[12]

- *R-1 (high, medium, or low).* Prime credit quality securities
- *R-2 (high, medium, or low).* Adequate credit quality securities

[12] For details, see Dominion Bond Rating Service's Web site at **www.dbrs.com**.

- *R-3 (high, medium, or low).* Speculative securities
- *D.* Securities in, or likely to be in, arrears

An R-1 (high) rating indicates the best possible credit rating whereas an R-3 (low) rating signifies a highly speculative issue. Firms with R-3 rated issues are likely to have unstable earnings and low profitability. If a security is rated D, it means that the issuer has missed a scheduled payment, such as interest, or is going to miss such a payment in the near future. The rate of return, or yield, on commercial paper tends to differ according to the issue's credit rating. Higher-rated issues carry lower yields than lower-rated ones. Commercial paper issues may carry yields of one or two percentage points below the prime rate, which tends to fluctuate with changing economic conditions and general levels of interest rates.

EXAMPLE 20.5 **COST OF COMMERCIAL PAPER**

Suppose Maya Entertainment has issued discount commercial paper for $492,000. Its face value is $500,000 and will mature in 60 days. Interest paid on the paper is, therefore, $500,000 − $492,000 = $8,000. Over a 60-day period, the effective interest rate is $8,000/$492,000 = 1.63 percent. The annualized rate is calculated by solving for *i* in the following equation:

$$\text{Face value of the commercial paper} = \text{price} \times [1 + (i \times t)/365]$$

Inserting numbers, we get $500,000 = $492,000 × [1 + (*i* × 60)/365]. With some algebraic manipulation, we get *i* = (8,000 × 365)/(492,000 × 60), which works out to .0989 or 9.89 percent.

BANKER'S ACCEPTANCE

banker's acceptance A firm's time draft that has been accepted by a bank and may be sold to investors as a short-term unsecured note issued by the firm and guaranteed by the bank.

A firm may also raise short-term financing through a **banker's acceptance**. This instrument is created when a firm submits a time draft (which is much like a postdated cheque) to its bank for acceptance. When the bank stamps "accepted" on the draft, it becomes a *banker's acceptance* and represents an unconditional promise of the bank to pay the amount stated on the draft when it matures. As such, it becomes the bank's IOU and can be sold to portfolio investors in the acceptance market. Such investors may include money market funds, pension funds, and banks.

LO5 20.7 THE COST OF BANK LOANS

Bank loans often extend for several years. Interest payments on these loans are sometimes fixed for the term of the loan but more commonly they are *floating rates*, adjusted up or down as the general level of interest rates changes.

The interest rate on bank loans of less than a year is almost invariably fixed for the term of the loan. However, you need to be careful when comparing rates on these shorter-term bank loans, for the rates may be calculated in different ways.

SIMPLE INTEREST

The interest rate on bank loans frequently is quoted as simple interest. For example, if the bank quotes an annual rate of 12 percent on a simple interest loan of $100,000 for 1 month, then at the end of the month you would need to repay $100,000 plus 1 month's interest. This interest is calculated as

$$\text{Amount of loan} \times \frac{\text{annual interest rate}}{\text{number of periods in the year}} = \$100{,}000 \times \frac{.12}{12} = \$1{,}000$$

Your total payment at the end of the month would be

$$\text{Repayment of face value } plus \text{ interest} = \$100{,}000 + \$1{,}000 = \$101{,}000$$

In Chapter 5 you learned to distinguish between simple interest and compound interest. We have just seen that your 12 percent simple interest bank loan costs 1 percent per month. One percent per month compounded for 1 year cumulates to $1.01^{12} = 1.1268$. Thus the compound, or *effective*, annual interest rate on the bank loan is 12.68 percent, not the quoted rate of 12 percent.

The general formula for the equivalent compound interest rate on a simple interest loan is

$$\text{Effective annual rate} = 1 + \left(\frac{\text{quoted annual interest rate}}{m}\right)^m - 1$$

where the annual interest rate is stated as a fraction (.12 in our example) and m is the number of periods in the year (12 in our example).

DISCOUNT INTEREST

The interest rate on a bank loan is often calculated on a discount basis. Similarly, when companies issue commercial paper, they also usually quote the interest rate as a discount. With a discount interest loan, the bank deducts the interest up front. For example, suppose that you borrow \$100,000 on a discount basis for 1 year at 12 percent. In this case the bank hands you \$100,000 less 12 percent, or \$88,000. Then at the end of the year you repay the bank the \$100,000 face value of the loan. This is equivalent to paying interest of \$12,000 on a loan of \$88,000. The effective interest rate on such a loan is therefore \$12,000/\$88,000 = .1364, or 13.64 percent.

Now suppose that you borrow \$100,000 on a discount basis for 1 month at 12 percent. In this case the bank deducts 1 percent up-front interest and hands you

$$\text{Face value of loan} \times \left(1 - \frac{\text{quoted annual interest rate}}{\text{number of periods in the year}}\right)$$

$$= \$100{,}000 \times \left(1 - \frac{.12}{12}\right) = \$99{,}000$$

At the end of the month you repay the bank the \$100,000 face value of the loan, so you are effectively paying interest of \$1,000 on a loan of \$99,000. The *monthly* interest rate on such a loan is \$1,000/\$99,000 = 1.01 percent and the compound, or effective, annual interest rate on this loan is $1.0101^{12} - 1 = .1282$, or 12.82 percent. The effective interest rate is higher than on the simple interest rate loan because the interest is paid at the beginning of the month rather than the end.

The general formula for the equivalent compound interest rate on a discount interest loan is

$$\text{Effective annual rate on a discount loan} = \left(\frac{1}{1 - \dfrac{\text{quoted annual interest rate}}{m}}\right)^m - 1$$

where the quoted annual interest rate is stated as a fraction (.12 in our example) and m is the number of periods in the year (12 in our example).

INTEREST WITH COMPENSATING BALANCES

In the United States, some bank loans require the firm to maintain an amount of money on balance at the bank. This is called a *compensating balance*. You won't see compensating balances for loans in Canada because the *Bank Act* does not permit banks operating in Canada to require them.

Suppose a firm operating in the United States obtains a \$100,000 loan from a U.S. bank and must maintain a balance of 20 percent of the amount of the loan in its account. In other words, it gets to use only \$80,000, because \$20,000 (20 percent of \$100,000) must be left on deposit in the bank. If the compensating balance does not pay interest (or pays a below-market rate of interest), the actual interest rate on the loan is higher than the stated rate. The reason is that the borrower must pay interest on the full amount borrowed but has access to only part of the funds.

For example, we calculated above that a firm borrowing \$100,000 for 1 month at 12 percent simple interest must pay interest at the end of the month of \$1,000. If the firm gets the use of only \$80,000, the effective monthly interest rate is \$1,000/\$80,000 = .0125, or 1.25 percent. This is equivalent to a compound annual interest rate of $1.0125^{12} - 1 = .1608$, or 16.08 percent.

In general, the compound annual interest rate on a loan with compensating balances is

$$\text{Effective annual rate on a loan with compensating balances} = \left(1 + \frac{\text{actual interest paid}}{\text{borrowed funds available}}\right)^m - 1$$

where m is the number of periods in the year (again, 12 in our example).

Check Point 20.7

Suppose that Dynamic Mattress needs to raise \$20 million for 6 months. Bank A quotes a simple interest rate of 7 percent but requires the firm to maintain an interest-free compensating balance of 20 percent. Bank B quotes a simple interest rate of 8 percent but does not require any compensating balances. Bank C quotes a discount interest rate of 7.5 percent and also does not require compensating balances. What is the effective (or compound) annual interest rate on each of these loans?

20.8 SUMMARY

1. **How does long-term financing policy affect short-term financing requirements? LO1**

   The nature of the firm's short-term financial planning problem is determined by the amount of long-term capital it raises. A firm that issues large amounts of long-term debt or common stock, or that retains a large part of its earnings, may find that it has permanent excess cash. Other firms raise relatively little long-term capital and end up as permanent short-term debtors. Most firms attempt to find a happy balance by financing all long-term assets and part of current assets with equity and long-term debt. Such firms may invest cash surpluses during part of the year and borrow during the rest of the year.

2. **Why do firms need to invest in net working capital? LO2**

   Short-term financial planning is concerned with the management of the firm's short-term, or current, assets and liabilities. The most important current assets are cash, marketable securities, inventory, and trade receivables. The most important current liabilities are bank loans and trade payables. The difference between current assets and current liabilities is called **net working capital**. Net working capital arises from lags between the time the firm obtains the raw materials for its product and the time it finally collects its bills from customers. The operating cycle is the length of time from the purchase of raw materials to the collection of cash from customers. The cash **conversion cycle** is the length of time between the firm's payment for materials and the date that it gets paid by its customers. **The cash conversion cycle** is partly within management's control. For example, it can choose to have a higher or lower level of inventories. Management needs to trade off the benefits and costs of investing in current assets. Higher investments in current assets entail higher **carrying costs** but lower expected **shortage costs**.

3. **How do the firm's sources and uses of cash relate to its need for short-term borrowing? LO3**

   The starting point for short-term financial planning is an understanding of sources and uses of cash. Firms forecast their net cash requirement by forecasting collections on trade receivables, adding other cash inflows, and subtracting all forecast cash outlays. If the forecast cash balance is insufficient to cover day-to-day operations and to provide a buffer against contingencies, you will need to find additional finance. For example, you may borrow from a bank on a **line of credit**, you may borrow by offering receivables or inventory as security, or you may issue your own short-term notes known as **commercial paper**. You may also seek a short-term financing through a **banker's acceptance**.

4. **How do firms develop a short-term financing plan that meets their need for cash?** LO4

The search for the best short-term financial plan inevitably proceeds by trial and error. The financial manager must explore the consequences of different assumptions about cash requirements, interest rates, limits on financing from particular sources, and so on. Firms use computerized financial models to help in this process. Remember the key differences between the various sources of short-term financing—for example, the differences between bank lines of credit and commercial paper. Remember too that firms often raise money on the strength of their current assets, especially accounts receivable and inventories.

5. **What are some of the major sources of short-term financing, and how are interest rates on these loans quoted?** LO5

A major source of short-term financing is bank loans. Often, firms pay a regular fee for a **line of credit** that allows them to borrow from the bank up to an agreed amount. The interest rate on short-term bank loans is usually quoted as a simple interest rate (or APR). Sometimes the interest rate is quoted as a discount, so that the interest is deducted up front. Two other important sources of short-term finance are **commercial paper** and **factoring**.

Related Web Links

businessfinancemag.com Resources and software reviews for financial planning

toolkit.cch.com Financial planning resources of all kinds

imoneynet.com Short-term investment and money fund rates

dbrs.com Dominion Bond Rating Service

pages.stern.nyu.edu/~adamodar Aswath Damodaran's home page; includes data on working-capital requirements by U.S. industry sector

gelending.com Information on types of short-term finance

treasuryandrisk.com Web site of *Treasury & Risk Management* magazine

americanbanker.com Host of information for bankers and finance professionals

intltreasurer.com Articles on short-term financial management

Key Terms

banker's acceptance	660	factoring	657	shortage costs	646
carrying costs	646	line of credit	656	syndicated loan	656
cash conversion cycle *or* cash gap	643	net working capital	642	term loans	656
commercial paper	659	operating cycle	643		
commitment fee	656	pledged accounts receivable	657		

Questions and Problems

connect™ Practise and learn online with *Connect*. Questions with online Excel templates or datasets are marked with .

*Answers in Appendix B

BASIC

1. **Working Capital Management.** Indicate how each of the following six different transactions that Dynamic Mattress might make would affect (i) cash and (ii) net working capital: (LO2)
   *a. Paying out a $2 million cash dividend.
   *b. A customer paying a $2,500 bill resulting from a previous sale.
   c. Paying $5,000 previously owed to one of its suppliers.
   *d. Borrowing $1 million long-term debt and investing the proceeds in inventory.
   e. Borrowing $1 million short-term debt and investing the proceeds in inventory.
   *f. Selling $5 million of marketable securities for cash.

*2. **Short-Term Financial Plans.** Fill in the blanks in the following statements: (LO3)
   a. A firm has a cash surplus when its ______ exceeds its ______. The surplus is normally invested in ______.
   b. In developing the short-term financial plan, the financial manager starts with a(n) ______ budget for the next year. This budget shows the ______ generated or absorbed by the firm's operations and also the minimum ______ needed to support these operations. The financial manager may also wish to invest in ______ as a reserve for unexpected cash requirements.

3. **Sources and Uses of Cash.** State how each of the following events would affect the firm's balance sheet. State whether each change is a source or use of cash. (LO3)
   a. An automobile manufacturer increases production in response to a forecast increase in demand. Unfortunately, the demand does not increase.
   b. Competition forces the firm to give customers more time to pay for their purchases.
   c. The firm sells a parcel of land for $100,000. The land was purchased 5 years earlier for $200,000.
   d. The firm repurchases its own common stock.
   e. The firm pays its quarterly dividend.
   f. The firm issues $1 million of long-term debt and uses the proceeds to repay a short-term bank loan.

4. **Operating and Cash Conversion Cycle.** What effect will the following events have on the operating and cash conversion cycles? (LO2)
   a. Higher financing rates induce the firm to reduce its level of inventory.
   b. The firm obtains a new line of credit that enables it to avoid stretching payables to its suppliers.
   c. The firm factors its trade receivables.
   d. A recession occurs and the firm's customers increasingly stretch their payables.
   e. The new production process shortens the time needed to manufacture products.

*5. **Managing Working Capital.** A new computer system allows your firm to more accurately monitor finished goods inventory and anticipate future inventory shortfalls. As a result, the firm feels more able to pare down its inventory levels. What effect will the new system have on working capital and on the cash conversion cycle? (LO2)

6. **Operating and Cash Conversion Cycles.** Calculate the trade receivables period, trade payable periods, inventory period, operating cycle, and cash conversion cycle for the following firm: (LO2)

Income statement data:

Sales	5,000
Cost of goods sold	4,200

Balance sheet data:

	Beginning of Year	End of Year
Inventory	500	600
Trade receivables	100	120
Trade payables	250	290

7. **Operating and Cash Conversion Cycle.** What effect will the following have on the operating and cash conversion cycles? (LO2)
   *a. Customers are given a larger discount for cash transactions.
   *b. The inventory turnover ratio falls from 8 to 6.
   *c. New technology streamlines the production process.
   *d. The firm adopts a policy of reducing outstanding trade payables.
   e. The firm starts producing more goods in response to customers' advance orders instead of producing for inventory.
   f. A temporary glut in the commodity market induces the firm to stock up on raw materials while prices are low.

INTERMEDIATE

8. **Compensating Balances.** Suppose that Dynamic Sofa (a subsidiary of Dynamic Mattress) has a line of credit with a stated interest rate of 10 percent and a compensating balance of 25 percent. The compensating balance earns no interest. (LO5)
   a. If the firm needs $10,000, how much will it need to borrow?
   b. Suppose that Dynamic's bank offers to forget about the compensating balance requirement if the firm pays interest at a rate of 12 percent. Should the firm accept this offer? Why or why not?
   c. Redo part (b) if the compensating balance pays interest of 4 percent. *Warning:* You cannot use the formula in the chapter for the effective interest rate when the compensating balance pays interest. Think about how to measure the effective interest rate on this loan.

*9. **Compensating Balances.** The stated bank loan rate is 8 percent, payable annually, but the loan requires a compensating balance of 10 percent on which no interest is earned. What is the effective interest rate on the loan? What happens to the effective rate if the compensating balance is doubled to 20 percent? (LO5)

10. **Factoring.** A firm sells its trade receivables to a factor at a 1.5 percent discount. The average collection period is one month. What is the implicit effective annual interest rate on the factoring arrangement? Suppose the average collection period is 1.5 months. How does this affect the implicit effective annual interest rate? (LO5)

*11. **Discount Loan.** A discount bank loan has a quoted annual rate of 6 percent. (LO5)
   a. What is the effective rate of interest if the loan is for one year and is paid off in one payment at the end of the year?
   b. What is the effective rate of interest if the loan is for one month?

12. **Compensating Balances.** A bank loan has a quoted annual rate of 6 percent. However, the borrower must maintain a balance of 25 percent of the amount of the loan, and the balance does not earn any interest. (LO5)
   a. What is the effective rate of interest if the loan is for one year and is paid off in one payment at the end of the year?
   b. What is the effective rate of interest if the loan is for one month?

13. **Forecasting Collections.** Here is a forecast of sales by National Bromide for the first 4 months of 2013 (figures in thousands of dollars):

Month:	1	2	3	4
Cash sales	15	24	18	14
Sales on credit	100	120	90	70

On average, 50 percent of credit sales are paid for in the current month, 30 percent in the next month, and the remainder in the month after that. What are expected cash collections in months 3 and 4? (LO4)

14. **Forecasting Payments.** If a firm pays its bills with a 30-day delay, what fraction of its purchases will be paid for in the current quarter? In the following quarter? What if its payment delay is 60 days? (LO4)

*15. **Short-Term Planning.** Paymore Products places orders for goods equal to 75 percent of its sales forecast in the next quarter. What will be orders in each quarter of the year if the sales forecasts for the next five quarters are as follows? (LO4)

	Quarter in Coming Year				Following Year
	First	Second	Third	Fourth	First Quarter
Sales forecast	$372	$360	$336	$384	$384

16. **Forecasting Payments.** Calculate Paymore's cash payments to its suppliers under the assumption that the firm pays for its goods with a one-month delay. Therefore, on average, two-thirds of purchases are paid for in the quarter that they are purchased and one-third are paid in the following quarter. (LO4)

17. **Forecasting Collections.** Now suppose that Paymore's customers pay their bills with a two-month delay. What is the forecast for Paymore's cash receipts in each quarter of the coming year? Assume that sales in the last quarter of the previous year were $336. (LO4)

18. **Forecasting Net Cash Flow.** Assuming that Paymore's labour and administrative expenses are $65 per quarter and that interest on long-term debt is $40 per quarter, work out the net cash inflow for Paymore for the coming year using a table like Table 20.6, panel B. (LO4)

*19. **Short-Term Financing Requirements.** Suppose that Paymore's cash balance at the start of the first quarter is $40 and its minimum acceptable cash balance is $30. Work out the short-term financing requirements for the firm in the coming year using a table like Table 20.6, panel C. The firm pays no dividends. (LO4)

20. **Short-Term Financing Plan.** Now assume that Paymore can borrow up to $100 from a line of credit at an interest rate of 2 percent per quarter. Prepare a short-term financing plan. Use Table 20.7 to guide your answer. (LO4)

21. **Short-Term Plan.** Recalculate Dynamic Mattress's financing plan (Table 20.7) assuming that the firm wishes to maintain a minimum cash balance of $10 million instead of $5 million. Assume the firm can convince the bank to extend its line of credit to $45 million. (LO4)

22. **Internet.** Industries differ substantially in the amount of working capital that they need to hold. Which industries would you expect to involve large investments in working capital? Which would involve small investments in working capital? Check your answers by looking at the table of working-capital requirements by industry sector on Professor Aswath Damodaran's home page (**pages.stern.nyu.edu/~adamodar**), clicking on "updated" under "Recent Additions" and "6. Data." (LO2)

23. **Internet.** The Treasury Management Association of Canada is Canada's only association of treasury and finance professionals. They list treasury management career opportunities on their Web site at **www.tmac-toronto.ca/careers**. Pick one job posting and read the job description. Describe each of the activities required for the position and where possible relate each activity to the material presented in this textbook. (LO2)

24. **Internet.** We mentioned that the interest rate on longer-term bank loans is not usually fixed for the term of the loan, but is adjusted up or down as the general level of interest rates changes. Often the interest rate is linked to the bank's prime rate or to the London Interbank Offered Rate (LIBOR), which is the interest rate at which major international banks lend to one another. Suppose you are offered the choice between a 3-year loan at the bank's prime rate or at 1 percent above LIBOR. Which would you prefer based on information about current rates? Go to **www.bloomberg.com/markets** to find current rates. (LO5)

*25. **Sources and Uses of Cash and Free Cash Flow.** The accompanying tables show Dynamic Mattress's year-end 2010 balance sheet and its income statement for 2011. Use these tables (and Table 20.3) to work out a statement of sources and uses of cash and the statement of cash flow for 2011. Use Table 20.5 and the solution to Check Point 20.4 as guides. (LO4)

Year-End Balance Sheet for 2010
($ millions)

Assets		**Liabilities**	
Current assets:		Current liabilities:	
Cash	4	Bank loans	4
Marketable securities	2	Trade payables	15
Inventory	20	Total current liabilities	19
Trade receivables	22	Long-term debt	5
Total current assets	48	Net worth (equity and retained earnings)	60
Non-current assets:			
Gross investment	50		
Less depreciation	14	Total liabilities and net worth	84
Net long-term assets	36		
Total assets	84		

Income Statement for 2011
($ millions)

Sales	300
Operating costs	−285
EBITDA	15
Depreciation	− 2
EBIT	13
Interest	− 1
Pretax income	12
Tax at 50 percent	− 6
Net income	6

Note: Dividend = $1 million and addition to retained earnings = $5 million.

CHALLENGE

26. **Internet.** Go to **www.finance.yahoo.com** and look up the financial statements for Walmart Stores and Sears Holding Corp., two retailers at opposite ends of the performance scale. Calculate the net working capital, the operating cycle, and the cash conversion cycle, discussed in Section 20.2, for each firm. By how much would the investment in working capital fall if each firm could reduce its cash conversion cycle by one day? Using the number of employees listed on the

"Competitors" page, compare and contrast revenues per employee. Choose some financial ratios to compare the financial performance and use stock prices to calculate each stock's rate of return. Do you think that the market has reacted to the performance differences between the companies? (LO3)

*27. **Cash Budget.** The following data are from the budget of Ritewell Publishers. Half the company's sales are transacted on a cash basis. The other half are paid for with a one-month delay. The company pays all of its credit purchases with a one-month delay. Credit purchases in January were $30 and total sales in January were $180. (LO4)

	February	March	April
Total sales	200	220	180
Cash purchases	70	80	60
Credit purchases	40	30	40
Labour and administrative expenses	30	30	30
Taxes, interest, and dividends	10	10	10
Capital expenditures	100	0	0

Complete the following cash budget:

	February	March	April
Sources of cash:			
Collections on current sales			
Collections on trade receivables			
Total sources of cash			
Uses of cash:			
Payments of trade payables			
Cash purchases			
Labour and administrative expenses			
Capital expenditures			
Taxes, interest, and dividends			
Total uses of cash			
Net cash inflow:			
Cash at start of period	100		
+ Net cash inflow			
= Cash at end of period			
+ Minimum operating cash balance	100	100	100
= Cumulative short-term financing required			

28. **Financial Plan.** What does the cash budget in problem 27 reveal about Ritewell's short-term financing requirements? Propose a short-term financing plan. (LO3)

Solutions to Check Points

20.1 a. The new values for the accounts receivable period and inventory period are as follows.

$$\text{Days in inventory} = \frac{60}{238.037/90} = 22.7 \text{ days}$$

This is a reduction of 8.4 days from the original value of 31.1 days.

$$\text{Days in receivables} = \frac{150}{315.625/90} = 42.8 \text{ days}$$

This is a reduction of 10.3 days from the original value of 53.1 days.

Both the operating cycle and the cash conversion cycle fall by a total of 8.4 + 10.3 = 18.7 days.

b. Costs and revenues increase 10 percent. The inventory period, accounts receivable period, and accounts payable period will all fall by a factor of 1.10. (The numerators are unchanged, but the denominators are higher by 10 percent.) Therefore, the operating cycle will fall from 84.2 days to 84.2/1.1 to 76.5 days and cash conversion cycle will fall from 32.9 days to 32.9/1.10 = 29.9 days.

20.2 a. An increase in the interest rate will increase the cost of carrying current assets. The effect is to reduce the optimal level of such assets.

b. The just-in-time system lowers the expected level of shortage costs and reduces the amount of goods the firm ought to be willing to keep in inventory.

c. If the firm decides that more lenient credit terms are necessary to avoid lost sales, it must then expect customers to pay their bills more slowly. Trade receivables will increase.

20.3 a. This transaction merely substitutes one current liability (short-term debt) for another (trade payables). Neither cash nor net working capital is affected.

b. This transaction will increase inventory at the expense of cash. Cash falls but net working capital is unaffected.

c. The firm will use cash to buy back the stock. Both cash and net working capital will fall.

d. The proceeds from the bond sale will increase both cash and net working capital.

20.4

Statement of Cash Flow	
Cash Flow from Operating Activities	
Net income	$ 12
Depreciation	4
Decrease (increase) in trade receivables	(5)
Decrease (increase) in inventory	1
Increase (decrease) in trade payables	7
Cash inflow (outflow) from operating activities	$ 19
Cash Flow from Investing Activities	
Purchase of marketable securities	$ (5)
Investment in fixed assets	$ (14)
Cash inflow(outflow) from investing activities	$ (19)
Cash Flow from Financing Activities	
Increase in long-term debt	$ 7
Repayment of short-term loan	(5)
Cash dividend	(1)
Cash inflow (outflow) from financing activities	$ 1
Increase in cash balance	$ 1

Net cash inflow = cash inflow (outflow) from operating activities + cash inflow (outflow) from investment activities + cash inflow (outflow) from financing activities = 19 − 19 + 1 = 1

20.5

Quarter:	First	Second	Third	Fourth
Trade Receivables				
Receivables (beginning period)	30	35	31.4	46.4
Sales	87.5	78.5	116	131
Collections[a]	82.5	82.1	101	125
Receivables (end period)	35	31.4	46.4	52.4
Cash Budget				
Sources of cash:				
Collections of trade receivables	82.5	82.1	101	125
Other	1.5	0	12.5	0
Total sources	84	82.1	113.5	125
Uses:				
Payments of trade payables	65	60	55	50
Labour and administrative expenses	30	30	30	30
Capital expenses	32.5	1.3	5.5	8
Taxes, interest, and dividends	4	4	4.5	5
Total uses	131.5	95.3	95	93
Net cash inflow	−47.5	−13.2	18.5	32
Short-Term Financing Requirements				
Cash at start of period	5	−42.5	−55.7	−37.2
+ Net cash inflow	−47.5	−13.2	18.5	32
= Cash at end of period	−42.5	−55.7	−37.2	−5.2
Minimum operating balance	5	5	5	5
Cumulative short-term financing required	47.5	60.7	42.2	10.2

[a] Sales in fourth quarter of the previous year totalled $75 million.

20.6 The major change in the plan is the substitution of the extra $5 million of borrowing via the line of credit (bank loan) in the second quarter and the corresponding reduction in the stretched payables. This substitution is advantageous because the bank loan is a cheaper source of funds. Notice that the cash balance at the end of the year is higher under this plan than in the original plan.

Quarter:	First	Second	Third	Fourth
Cash Requirements				
1. Cash required for operations	45	15	−26.0	−35
2. Interest on line of credit	0	0.8	0.9	0.6
3. Interest on stretched payables	0	0	0.5	0
4. Total cash required	45	15.8	−24.6	−34.4
Cash Raised				
5. Bank loan	40	5	0	0
6. Stretched payables	0	10.8	0	0
7. Securities sold	5	0	0	0
8. Total cash raised	45	15.8	0	0
Repayments				
9. Of stretched payables	0	0	10.8	0
10. Of bank loan	0	0	13.8	31.2
Increase in Cash Balances				
11. Addition to cash balances	0	0	0	3.2
Bank Loan				
12. Beginning of quarter	0	40	45	31.2
13. End of quarter	40	45	31.2	0

20.7 Bank A: The interest paid on the \$20 million loan over the 6-month period will be \$20 million × .07/2 = \$.7 million. With a 20 percent compensating balance, \$16 million is available to the firm. The effective annual interest rate is

$$\text{Effective annual rate on a loan with compensating balances} = \left(1 + \frac{\text{actual interest paid}}{\text{borrowed funds available}}\right)^m - 1$$

$$= \left(1 + \frac{\$.7 \text{ million}}{\$16 \text{ million}}\right)^2 - 1$$

$$= .0894, \text{ or } 8.94\%$$

Bank B: The compound annual interest rate on the simple loan is

$$\text{Effective annual rate} = \left(1 + \frac{\text{quoted interest rate}}{m}\right)^m - 1$$

$$= \left(1 + \frac{.08}{2}\right)^2 - 1 = 1.04^2 - 1$$

$$= .0816, \text{ or } 8.16\%$$

Bank C: The compound annual interest rate is

$$\text{Effective annual rate on a discount loan} = \left(\frac{1}{1 - \frac{\text{annual interest rate}}{m}}\right)^m - 1$$

$$= \left(\frac{1}{1 - \frac{.075}{2}}\right)^2 - 1 = \left(\frac{1}{.9625}\right)^2 - 1$$

$$= .0794, \text{ or } 7.94\%$$

MINI CASE

Capstan Autos operated a dealership in the Maritime provinces for a major Japanese car manufacturer. Capstan's owner, Sidney Capstan, attributed much of the business's success to its no-frills policy of competitive pricing and immediate cash payment. The business was basically a simple one—the firm imported cars at the beginning of each quarter and paid the manufacturer at the end of the quarter. The revenues from the sale of these cars covered the payment to the manufacturer and the expenses of running the business, as well as providing Sidney with a good return on his equity investment.

By the fourth quarter of 2012, sales were running at 250 cars a quarter. Since the average sale price of each car was about $20,000, this translated into quarterly revenues of 250 × $20,000 = $5 million. The average cost to Capstan of each imported car was $18,000. After paying wages, rent, and other recurring costs of $200,000 per quarter and deducting depreciation of $80,000, the company was left with earnings before interest and taxes (EBIT) of $220,000 a quarter and net profits of $140,000.

The year 2013 was not a happy one for car importers in Canada. Recession led to a general decline in auto sales, while the fall in the value of the dollar shaved profit margins for many dealers in imported cars. Capstan, more than most firms, foresaw the difficulties ahead and reacted at once by offering six months' free credit while holding the sale price of its cars constant. Wages and other costs were pared by 25 percent to $150,000 a quarter and the company effectively eliminated all capital expenditures. The policy appeared successful. Unit sales fell by 20 percent to 200 units a quarter, but the company continued to operate at a satisfactory profit (see table).

The slump in sales lasted for six months, but as consumer confidence began to return, auto sales began to recover. The company's new policy of six months' free credit was proving sufficiently popular that Sidney Capstan decided to maintain the policy. In the third quarter of 2013, sales had recovered to 225 units; by the fourth quarter they were 250 units; and by the first quarter of the next year they had reached 275 units. It looked as if the company could expect to sell 300 cars by the second quarter of 2009. Earnings before interest and tax were already in excess of their previous high and Sidney was able to congratulate himself on weathering what looked to be a tricky period. Over the 18-month period the firm had earned net profits of over half a million dollars, and the equity had grown from just under $1 million to about $2 million. Sidney was first and foremost a superb salesman and always left the financial aspects of the business to his financial manager. However, one feature of the financial statements disturbed him: the mounting level of debt, which had reached $9.7 million by the end of the first quarter of 2014. This unease turned to alarm when the financial manager phoned to say that the bank was reluctant to extend further credit and was even questioning its current level of exposure to the company.

Sidney found it impossible to understand how such a successful year could have landed the company in financial difficulties. The company had always had good relationships with its bank, and the interest rate on its bank loans was a reasonable 8 percent per year (or about 2 percent per quarter). Surely, he reasoned, when the bank saw the projected sales growth for the rest of 2014, it would realize that there were plenty of profits to enable the company to start repaying its loans.

Questions

1. Is Capstan Autos in trouble?
2. Is the bank correct to withhold further credit?
3. Why is Capstan's indebtedness increasing if its profits are higher than ever?

Summary Income Statement
(all figures except unit sales in $000s)

Year:	2012	2013				2014
Quarter:	**4**	**1**	**2**	**3**	**4**	**1**
1. Number of cars sold	250	200	200	225	250	275
2. Unit price	20	20	20	20	20	20
3. Unit cost	18	18	18	18	18	18
4. Revenues (1 × 2)	5,000	4,000	4,000	4,500	5,000	5,500
5. Cost of goods sold (1 × 3)	4,500	3,600	3,600	4,050	4,500	4,950
6. Wages and other costs	200	150	150	150	150	150
7. Depreciation	80	80	80	80	80	80
8. EBIT (4 − 5 − 6 − 7)	220	170	170	220	270	320
9. Net interest	4	0	76	153	161	178
10. Pretax profit (8 − 9)	216	170	94	67	109	142
11. Tax (.35 × 10)	76	60	33	23	38	50
12. Net profit (10 − 11)	140	110	61	44	71	92

Summary Balance Sheets
($000s)

	End of 3rd Quarter 2012	End of 1st Quarter 2013
Cash	10	10
Receivables	0	10,500
Inventory	4,500	5,400
Total current assets	4,510	15,910
Fixed assets, net	1,760	1,280
Total assets	6,270	17,190
Bank loan	230	9,731
Payables	4,500	5,400
Total current liabilities	4,730	15,131
Shareholders' equity	1,540	2,059
Total liabilities	6,270	17,190

21 Cash and Inventory Management
21.1 Cash Collection, Disbursement, and Float
21.2 The Payment System and the Float
21.3 Managing Float
21.4 Managing Inventories and Cash Balances
21.5 Investing Idle Cash: The Money Market
21.6 Summary
22 Credit Management and Collection

CHAPTER 21

Cash and Inventory Management

LEARNING OBJECTIVES

After studying this chapter, you should be able to:

LO1 Measure float, explain why it arises and calculate the value of changes in float.

LO2 Explain how the float can be controlled.

LO3 Analyze the costs and benefits of holding inventories and calculate the optimal order size.

LO4 Cite the costs and benefits of holding cash.

LO5 Explain why and how an understanding inventory management can be useful for cash management.

LO6 Identify where firms can invest excess funds.

Not the right way to manage cash. Why hoard cash when you could invest it? Still, you need some cash on hand to pay bills. What's the right cash inventory?

The Kobal Collection/Walt Disney Productions.

In December 2010 citizens and corporations in Canada held nearly $1,528 billion in cash and bank deposits. Cash pays no interest and most bank deposits pay no or low interest. Why, then, do sensible people and companies hold so much cash? Why, for example, don't you take all your cash and invest it in interest-bearing securities? The answer is that cash gives more *liquidity* than securities. By this we mean it can be used it to buy things. It is hard enough getting cab drivers to give you change for a $100 bill, but try asking them to split a Treasury bill. There might be myriad reasons for firms wanting to hold cash balances, but we can categorize the main ones as follows:

- *Meet transactions needs.* Firms have to carry certain minimum cash balances to meet day-to-day cash expenditures, which include routine items such as paying monthly bills or spending on regular supplies. Cash is also needed for major recurring expenses such as wage and salary disbursements as well as tax and dividend payments.
- *Hedge against uncertain future.* Firms often hold some additional cash over and above their transaction requirement as a provision for the future. These funds are typically held as marketable securities. Alternatively, firms may choose to hedge against uncertainty by obtaining a line of credit. With a line of credit from a bank, the firm can borrow up to a specified maximum amount over a stipulated period of time. However, lines of credit can require a commitment fee, whether they are used or not.
- *Speculation.* Firms may hold liquid assets in anticipation of taking advantage of unforeseen investment opportunities.
- *Compensating balance requirement.* We saw in Chapter 20 that although this requirement is rare in Canada, a firm in the United States might be required to maintain a specified amount on deposit in its chequing account in lieu of loans and services provided by its bank. Usually, the amount of the compensating balance is determined by the size of the loan and the amount and range of services provided.

Of course, rational investors will not hold an asset like cash unless it provides the same benefit on the margin as other assets such as Treasury bills. The benefit from holding Treasury bills is the interest received; the benefit of holding cash is convenience of liquidity. When you have only a small proportion of your assets in cash, a little extra liquidity can be extremely useful; when you have a substantial holding, any additional liquidity is not worth much. Therefore, financial managers want to hold cash balances up to the point where the value of any additional liquidity is equal to the value of the interest forgone.

Cash is simply a raw material that companies need to carry out operations. As we will explain later, the financial manager's decision to stock up on cash is in many ways similar to the production manager's decision to stock up on inventories of raw materials. We will therefore look at the problem of managing inventories and then show how this helps us to understand how much cash should be held.

But first you need to learn about the mechanics of cash collection and disbursement. This may seem a rather humdrum topic, but you will find that it involves some interesting and important decisions.

LO1 21.1 CASH COLLECTION, DISBURSEMENT, AND FLOAT

Companies don't keep their cash in a little tin box; they keep it in a bank deposit. To understand how they can make best use of that deposit, you need to understand what happens when companies withdraw money from their bank accounts or pay money into them.

FLOAT

Suppose that the United Carbon Company has $1 million in a chequing account with its bank. It now pays one of its suppliers by writing and mailing a cheque for $200,000. The company's records are immediately adjusted to show a cash balance of $800,000. Thus the company is said to have a *ledger balance* of $800,000.

But the company's bank won't learn anything about this cheque until it has been received by the supplier, deposited at the supplier's bank, processed through the cheque-clearing system, and presented to United Carbon's bank for payment. During this time United Carbon's bank continues to show in its ledger that United Carbon has a chequing account balance of $1 million.

While the cheque is clearing, the company obtains the benefit of an extra $200,000 in the bank. This sum is often called **disbursement float**, or **payment float**.

payment or **disbursement float** Cheques written by a company that have not yet cleared the banking system.

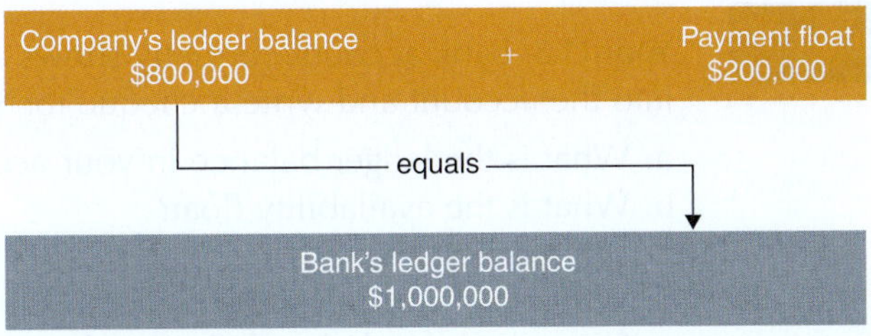

Float sounds like a marvellous invention; every time you write and mail a cheque, it takes time for your bank to learn about it. Unfortunately it can also work in reverse. Suppose that in addition to paying its supplier, United Carbon *receives* a cheque for $120,000 from a customer. It first processes the cheque through its collections department and then deposits it in the bank. At this point both the company and the bank increase the ledger balance by $120,000:

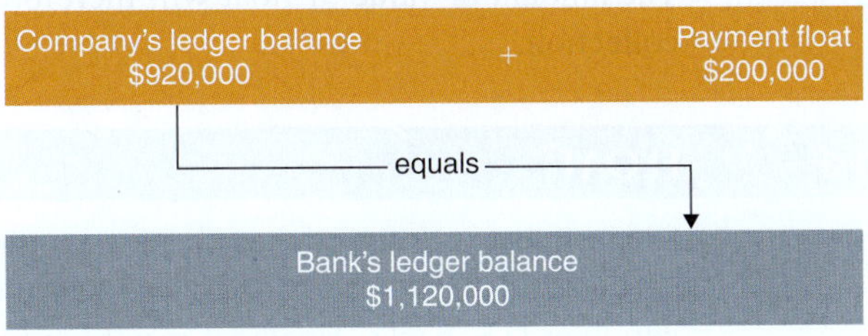

But is this money immediately available to United Carbon? Or does United Carbon's bank put a *hold* on the cheque until it has sent the cheque to customer's bank and received payment? In many countries, if the bank has to wait, it makes the depositor wait too. In the United States, with more than 1,800 different banks, it typically takes one or two business days to clear cheques. In Canada, with six major banks and a central cheque-clearing system, cheques are cleared within a day and funds are often immediately available on deposit. If the bank puts a hold on the cheque, the bank will show that United Carbon still has an available balance of only $1 million. The extra $120,000 has been deposited but is not yet available. This uncleared money is known as the **availability float**. In Canada, the availability float can be zero!

availability float Cheques already deposited that have not yet been cleared.

net float Difference between payment float and availability float.

Notice that the company gains as a result of the payment float and loses as a result of availability float. The **net float** available to the firm is the difference between payment and availability float:

$$\text{Net float} = \text{payment float} - \text{availability float}$$

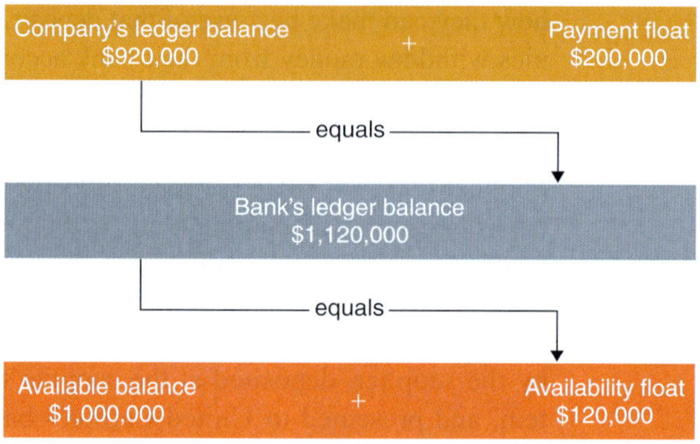

In our example, the net float is $80,000. The company's available balance is $80,000 greater than the balance shown in its ledger.

Check Point 21.1

Your U.S. bank account currently shows a balance of $940. You deposit a $100 cheque into the account and write a cheque for $40.

a. What is the ledger balance in your account?
b. What is the availability float?
c. What is payment float?
d. What is the bank's ledger balance?
e. Show that your ledger balance plus payment float equals the bank's ledger balance, which in turn equals the available balance plus availability float.

VALUING FLOAT

Float results from the delay between writing a cheque and the reduction in the bank balance. The amount or value of float will therefore depend on the size of the cheque and the delay in collection.

EXAMPLE 21.1 FLOAT

Suppose that your firm writes cheques worth $6,000 per day. It may take three days to mail these cheques to your U.S.-based suppliers, who then take a day to process the cheques and deposit them into their U.S. banks. Finally, it may be a further three days before the suppliers' banks send the cheques to your bank, which then debits your account. The total delay is 7 days and the payment float is $7 \times \$6,000 = \$42,000$. On average, the available balance at your bank will be $42,000 more than what is shown in your firm's ledger.

As a financial manager your concern is with the available bank balance, not with the company's ledger balance. If you know that it is going to be a week before some of your cheques are presented for payment, you may be able to get by on a smaller cash balance. The smaller you can keep your cash balance, the more funds you can hold in interest-earning accounts or securities. This game is often called *playing the float*.

You can increase your available cash balance by increasing your net float. This means ensuring that cheques received from customers are cleared rapidly and those paid to suppliers are cleared slowly. Perhaps this may sound like small potatoes, but think what it could mean to a company like Ford Motor Company. In 2010 Ford's average daily auto sales was about \$327 million. If it could speed up collections by one day, and the interest rate is .015 percent per day (about 5.6 percent per year), it would increase earnings by .00015 × \$327 million = \$49,050 per day.

What would be the present value to Ford if it could *permanently* reduce its collection period by one day? The extra interest income would then be a perpetuity, and the present value of the income would be \$49,050/.00015 = \$327 million, exactly equal to the reduction in float.

Why should this be? Think about the company's cash flow stream. It receives \$327 million per day. At any time, suppose that four days' worth of payments are deposited and "in the pipeline." When the company speeds up the collection period by a day, the pipeline will shrink to three days' worth of payments. At that point, Ford receives an extra \$327 million cash flow: it receives the "usual" payment of \$327 million, and it also receives the \$327 million for which it ordinarily would have had to wait an extra day. From that day forward, it continues to receive \$327 million per day, exactly as before. So the net effect of reducing the payment pipeline from four days to three is that GM gets an extra up-front payment equal to one day of float, or \$327 million. Therefore, the present value of a permanent reduction in float is simply the amount by which float is reduced.

However, be careful not to become overenthusiastic about managing the float. Writing cheques on your account for the sole purpose of creating float and earning interest is called *cheque kiting* and is illegal. In 1985 the American brokerage firm E.F. Hutton pleaded guilty to 2,000 separate counts of mail and wire fraud. Hutton admitted that it had created nearly \$1 billion of float by shuffling funds between its branches and through various accounts at different banks.

Check Point 21.2

In April 2011 General Motor's stock price was US\$31 per share, and there were 1.56 billion shares of General Motors outstanding. The annual auto sales was US\$135 billion, so daily sales average is US\$370 million. Now suppose that technological improvements in the cheque-clearing process reduce availability float from four days to two days. Assume that the daily interest rate is 0.015 percent. What would happen to the stock price? How much should General Motors be willing to pay for a new computer system that would reduce availability float by two days?

LO1 21.2 THE PAYMENT SYSTEM AND THE FLOAT

Managing the float of a company requires an understanding of how payments are made. There are a variety of ways that you can pay for purchases or send payments to another location. Some of the more important payment methods are set out in Table 21.1.

Look now at Figure 21.1. You can see that there are large differences in how people around the world pay for their purchases. For example, cheques are almost unknown in Germany, the Netherlands, Sweden, and Switzerland. Most payments in these countries are made by direct debits and credit transfers with credit and debit cards; however, in Germany, these cards are used less frequently than in the other countries. By contrast, Americans love to write cheques, although the use of cheques in the U.S. has been declining over time. In 2009 U.S. individuals and firms made about 25 billion payments by cheque, about 24 percent of cashless transactions. Back in 2005, about 33 billion cheques were used, about 37 percent of transactions. In Canada,

TABLE 21.1 Small purchases are often paid for in cash, but here are some other ways you can pay your bills.

Cheque	When you write a cheque, you are instructing your bank to pay a specified sum on demand to the particular firm or person named on the cheque.
Credit card	A credit card, such as Visa or MasterCard, gives you a line of credit that allows you to make purchases up to a stated limit. At the end of each month, either you pay the credit card company for these purchases or you will be charged interest on any outstanding balance.
Charge card	(or travel and entertainment card) A charge card might look like a credit card and you might be able to spend money with it like a credit card, but with a charge card the day of reckoning comes at the end of each month, when you have to pay for all purchases. In other words, you have to pay off your entire balance every month.
Debit card	A debit card allows you to have your purchases from a store charged directly to your bank account. The deduction is usually made electronically and is immediate. Often, debit cards may also be used to make withdrawals from a cash machine (ATM).
Credit transfer	With a credit transfer you ask your bank to set up a standing order to make a regular set payment to a supplier. For example, standing orders are often used to make regular fixed mortgage payments.
Direct debit	A direct debit is an instruction to your bank to allow a company to collect varying amounts from your account, as long as you have been given advance notice of the collection amounts and dates. For example, an electric utility company might ask you to set up a direct debit that allows it to receive automatic payment of your electricity bills from your bank account.
E-money payment transactions	These are transactions in which a holder of e-money transfers e-money value from his/her balance to the balance of the merchant. This can be done either with an e-money card or through other e-money storages.

FIGURE 21.1 How purchases are paid for. Percentages of total volume of cashless transactions, 2009.

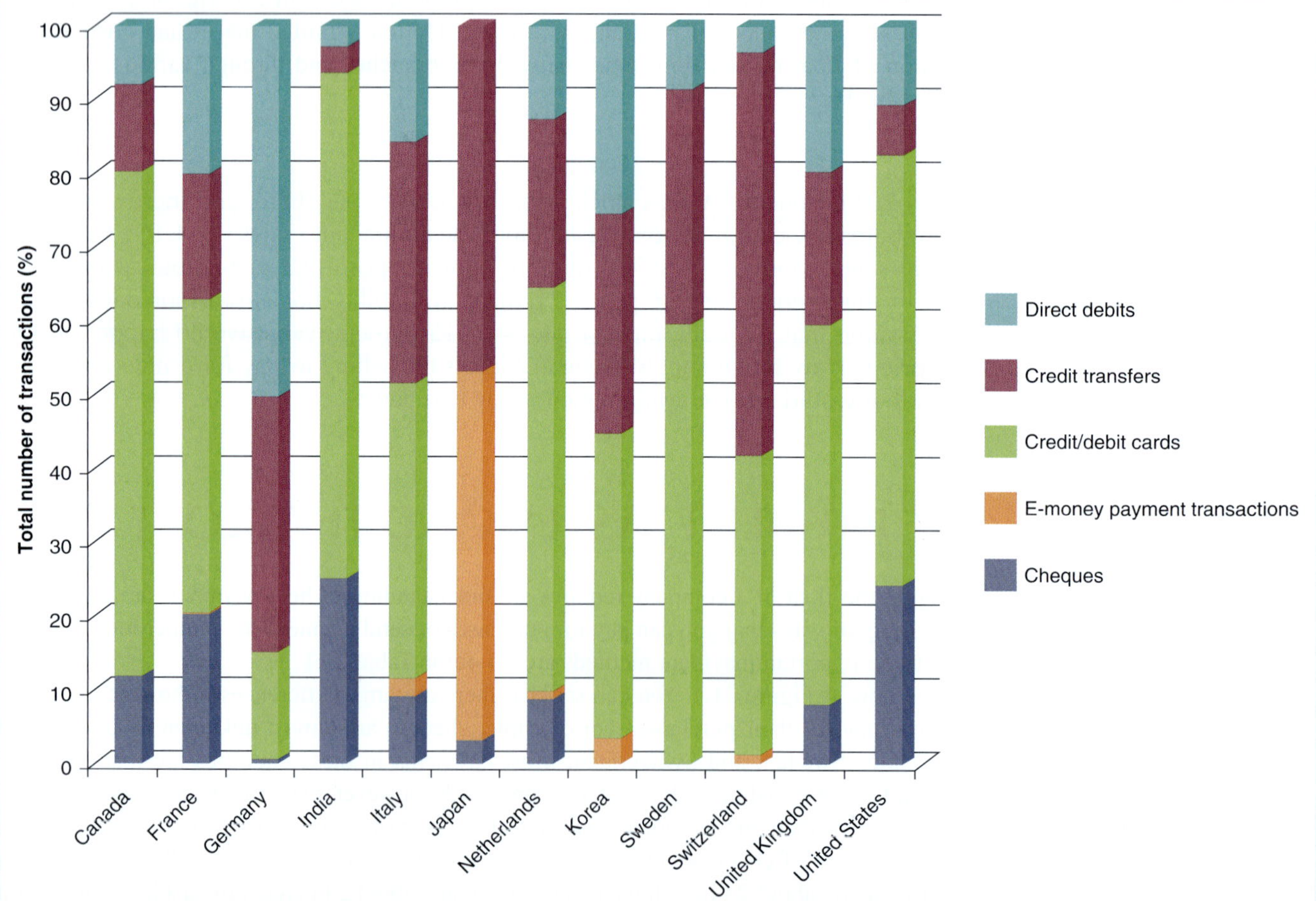

Source: Calculated with data provided by Bank for International Settlements, "Statistics on Payment and Settlement Systems in the CPSS (Committee on Payment and Settlement Systems) countries—Figures for 2009," *CPSS Publications* 95, **www.bis.org/publ/cpss95.htm**, accessed October 10, 2011.

the use of cheques has dropped significantly. In 1990, 87 percent of payments were made by cheque and only 13 percent were electronic, but by 2007 the volume of cheques was only 20 percent and electronic payments had risen to 80 percent. In 2009, 1.1 million cheques were written, about 12 percent of cashless transactions.

One key determinant of float is the time taken for payments to clear through the payment system. Canada's clearing and settlement system is among the most efficient in the world, enabling consumers and businesses to make and receive payments throughout the country quickly and reliably. The vast majority of payments involve moving funds between accounts at different financial institutions. The Canadian Payments Association (CPA) operates national clearing and settlement systems that facilitate this flow of funds between institutions and mitigate risk to payment system participants. On average, some 24 million payment items, representing $170 billion in transactions, were cleared and settled through the CPA's systems every business day during 2010. These include cheques, wire transfers, direct deposits, preauthorized debits, bill payments, point-of-sale debits, and online payments.

The CPA owns and operates two major payment systems: the *Automated Clearing Settlement System (ACSS)* and the *Large Value Transfer System (LVTS)*. The ACSS is the system by which cheques and certain types of automated payments (such as direct deposits) are cleared and settled. The core of the ACSS is an information system used to track the volume and value of payment items exchanged between CPA members and to determine the balances due to and from participants. LVTS, introduced in 1999, is an electronic wire transfer system, which can be used by Canadian companies for their domestic and international payments. The members of the CPA are financing institutions including banks, trust companies, credit unions, and caisses populaires that take deposits and offer chequing privileges.

There are three steps in the process of clearing and settling payments:[1]

Step 1. Payment—by cheque, debit card, direct deposit, or other means

Step 2. Clearing—the daily process by which CPA members exchange deposited payment items and then determine the net amounts owed to each other

Step 3. Settlement—the procedure by which CPA members use funds on deposit at the Bank of Canada to meet their net payment obligations to other member institutions

Suppose, for example, that you renew your auto insurance by writing a cheque for $1,000, which you mail to your insurance company. A day or so later the insurance company receives your cheque and deposits it in its bank account. Your cheque and all of the others deposited at that bank branch that day are sent to a data centre operated by that bank's direct clearer, one of the CPA member financial institutions. The cheques are sorted according to the bank they are drawn on, bundled for delivery to the data centre responsible for that bank's payments. The corresponding total number and value of the cheques to be delivered to every other direct clearer is enter into the ACSS. After your cheque gets sorted, it will be forwarded to the data centre of your bank. Most cheques, regardless of how far they have to travel, are received at the branch level no later than two days after they are deposited. Until the cheque reaches the branch, it is not known whether there are sufficient funds in the account to honour it.

Canadians usually receive credit immediately for the cheques they deposit, even if they do so at another branch on the other side of the country. The computerized network enables same-day settlement for cheques. In contrast, in the United States, a cheque might be placed on hold until it is verified that the person who wrote it has the funds in his or her account. In the United Kingdom, it can take three or four days for a cheque to clear.

Innovations continue to reduce the time it takes to clear cheques. In 2004, the U.S. payment system changed to allow the exchange of digital images of paper cheques. The use of such images is currently being implemented in Canada. As the new technology becomes more widespread, there will be ever-fewer cargo planes and trucks crisscrossing the country to take bundles of cheques from one bank to another, and it will become possible to clear cheques in hours.

---

[1] Much of our discussion here and elsewhere in this section is based on information provided on the Canadian Payment Association's Web site at **www.cdnpay.ca**.

LO2 21.3 MANAGING FLOAT

Delays that help the payer hurt the recipient. Recipients try to speed up collections. Payers try to slow down disbursements. Both attempt to minimize net float.

Several kinds of delay create float, so people in the cash management business refer to several kinds of float. Figure 21.2 shows the three sources of float:

- The time it takes to mail a cheque
- The time it takes the company to process the cheque after it has been received
- The time it takes the bank to clear the cheque and adjust the firm's account[2]

The total collection time is the sum of these three sources of delay. Delays that help the payer hurt the recipient. Recipients try to speed up collections. Payers try to slow down disbursements. Both attempt to minimize net float.

SPEEDING UP CHEQUE COLLECTIONS

lockbox system System whereby customers send payments to a post office box and a bank collects and processes cheques.

Firms that receive a large volume of cheques have devised a number of ways to make sure that the cash becomes available as soon as possible. One way to speed up collections is by using a **lockbox system**. In a lockbox system, you pay your bank to take on the administrative chores of processing and depositing cheques, speeding up your access to your customers' payments. It works as follows: The company rents a locked post office box in each principal region. All customers within a region are instructed to send their payments to the post office box. The bank empties the box at regular intervals (as often as several times per day) and deposits the cheques in your company's account.

Lockbox services are provided in many countries, including Canada. For example, CIBC offers lockbox services in Halifax, Montréal, Toronto, Winnipeg, Calgary, and Vancouver. They also provide an electronic file listing details for all invoices paid, helping their clients manage their accounts receivable.[3] Despite the increased use of electronic payments, many businesses

FIGURE 21.2
Delays create float. Each arrow represents a source of delay. Recipients try to reduce delay to get available cash sooner. Payers prefer delay so they can use their cash longer.

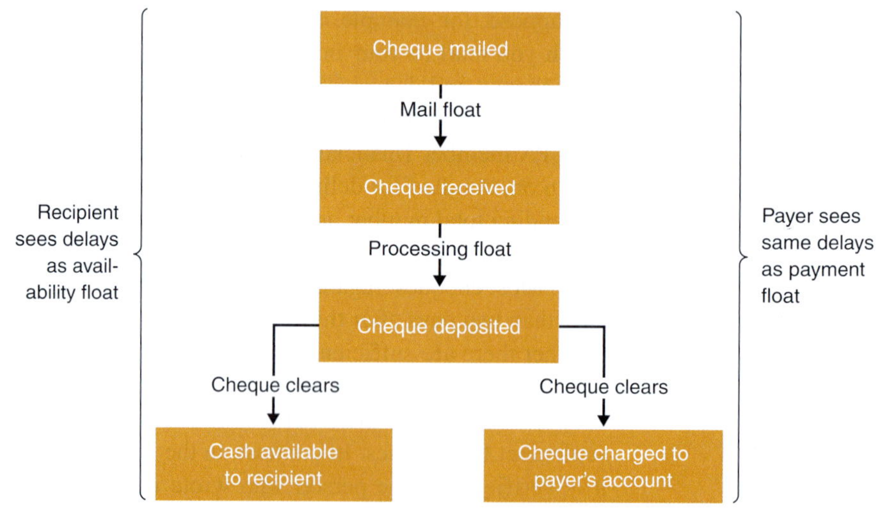

[2] In the earlier discussion of Canada's payments system, we saw that Canadians often receive immediate credit for the cheques they deposit, and so this type of float is not significant here. However, this might be important if you are doing business in other countries such as the United States or the United Kingdom, where the delay is longer.

[3] For more information on CIBC's lockbox service, visit **www.cibc.com/ca/lrg-corporate/cash-management/lockbox.html**.

and individuals still pay by cheque, making lockboxes useful. Look at the mailing address on your credit card bill. You will likely see a post office box address, suggesting that your cheque is going to a lockbox.

How many collection points do you need if you use a lockbox system? The answer depends on where your customers are and on the speed of Canada Post.

EXAMPLE 21.2 LOCKBOX SYSTEMS

Suppose you are thinking of opening a lockbox. The bank shows you a map of mail delivery times. From that information and knowledge of your customers' locations, you come up with the following data:

Average number of daily payments to lockbox	= 150
Average size of payment	= 1,200
Rate of interest *per day*	= .02 percent
Saving in mailing time	= 1.2 days
Saving in processing time	= .8 of a day

On this basis, the lockbox would reduce collection float by

$$150 \text{ items per day} \times \$1,200 \text{ per item} \times (1.2 + .8) \text{ days saved} = \$360,000$$

Invested at .02 percent per day, that gives a daily return of

$$.0002 \times \$360,000 = \$72$$

The bank's charge for operating the lockbox system depends on the number of cheques processed. Suppose that the bank charges \$.26 per cheque. That works out to 150 × \$.26 = \$39 per day. You are ahead by \$72 − \$39 = \$33 per day, plus whatever your firm saves from not having to process the cheques itself.

Check Point 21.3

How will the following conditions affect the price that a firm should be willing to pay for a lockbox service?

a. The average size of its payments increases.
b. The number of payments per day increases (with no change in average size of payments).
c. The interest rate increases.
d. The average mail time saved by the lockbox system increases.
e. The processing time saved by the lockbox system increases.

CONTROLLING CHEQUE DISBURSEMENTS

Speeding up collections is not the only way to increase the net float. You can also do this by slowing down disbursements. One tempting strategy is to increase mail time. For example, United Carbon could pay its Halifax suppliers with cheques mailed from Prince George, B.C., and its Vancouver suppliers with cheques mailed from Charlottetown, P.E.I.

But on second thought you realize that these kinds of post office tricks are unlikely to help you. Suppose you have promised to pay a Halifax supplier on March 29. Does it matter whether you mail the cheque from Prince George on the 26th or from Halifax on the 28th? Such mailing games would buy you time only if your creditor cares more about the date you mailed the cheque than the day it arrives. This is unlikely: with the notable exception of tax returns sent to Canada Revenue Agency, mailing dates are irrelevant. Of course, you could use a remote

Finance in Action

How Laidlaw Restructured Its Cash Management

The Canadian company Laidlaw Inc. has more than 4,000 facilities throughout the United States, operating school bus services, ambulance services, and Greyhound coaches. During the 1990s the company expanded rapidly through acquisition, and its number of banking relationships multiplied until it had 1,000 separate bank accounts with more than 200 different banks. The head office had no way of knowing how much cash was stashed in these accounts until the end of each quarter, when it was able to construct a consolidated balance sheet.

To economize on the use of cash, Laidlaw's financial manager sought to cut the company's average float from five days to two. At the same time management decided to consolidate cash management at five key banks. This enabled cash to be zero-balanced to a single account for each division and swept daily to Laidlaw's disbursement bank. Because the head office could obtain daily reports of the company's cash position, cash forecasting was improved and the company could reduce its cash needs still further.

Source: Cash management at Laidlaw is described in G. Mann and S. Hutchinson, "Driving Down Working Capital: Laidlaw's Story," *Canadian Treasurer Magazine*, August/September 1999. Reprinted by permission of Canadian Treasurer Magazine, **www.canadiantreasurer.com**

---

mailing address as an *excuse* to pay late, but that's a trick easily seen through. If you have to pay late, you might as well mail late.

Remote Disbursement You might try to pay the Toronto supplier with a cheque drawn on your account at the Prince George branch of your bank. This technique, known as *remote disbursement*, works in the United States, where banks do not have widespread branches and the process for clearing cheques tends to be slow. Some American firms even maintain disbursement accounts in different parts of the country. The computer looks up each supplier's zip code and automatically produces a cheque on the most distant bank.[4] In Canada where most cheques are settled on the same day, there is little scope for creating float through the clearing system, making remote disbursement a waste of effort.

Zero-Balance Accounts A company cannot predict exactly when cheques will be presented for payment. Either it must keep a large cash balance to cover contingencies or it must be prepared to borrow. With a **zero-balance account**, enough funds are moved from a concentration account into the disbursement account to cover the required payments. The nearby Finance in Action box describes how one company has been able to economize on the use of cash by means of a zero-balance account.

zero-balance account Bank account to which just enough funds are transferred daily to pay each day's bills.

ELECTRONIC FUNDS TRANSFER

electronic funds transfer (EFT) Payments made electronically instead of using paper-based cheques.

Throughout the world the use of cheques is in decline, being replaced with the electronic payment methods listed in Table 21.1, known as **electronic funds transfer (EFT)**. EFT makes float management much less important. You probably have encountered companies' efforts to reduce their float and transaction costs by changing the payment format. For example, some stores encourage you to pay bills with your bank debit card instead of a credit card, and do not accept cheques. The debit card payment is automatically taken from your bank account on the day of the transaction, which eliminates the considerable float you otherwise would enjoy until you were billed by your credit card company and paid your bill. The stores save on any transaction costs that would have been payable to the credit card companies. Also, by receiving payment through debit cards, the stores have almost immediate use of cash and are able to eliminate accounts receivable.

---

[4] This way, the company hopes to gain a few days of additional float. However, the suppliers won't object to these machinations, because the U.S. Federal Reserve guarantees a maximum clearing time of two days on all cheques cleared through the Federal Reserve system. Therefore, the supplier never gives up more than two days of float; instead, the victim of remote disbursement is the Federal Reserve, which loses float if it takes more than two days to collect funds. The Fed has been trying to prevent remote disbursement.

Similarly, many companies arrange *preauthorized payments* or *preauthorized debits (PADs)* with their customers. For example, if you have a mortgage payment on a house, the lender can arrange to have your bank account debited by the amount of the payment each month. The funds are automatically transferred to the lender. You save the work of paying the bill by cheque, and the lender saves the float time during which your cheque would have been processed through the banking system.

Traditionally, insurance companies and mortgage providers, such as banks, have offered PADs as a convenient way for their customers to meet monthly premium and loan payments. In recent years, other businesses such as utility companies and satellite and cable TV suppliers have realized the convenience and efficiency of this type of payment and are also offering PAD services. Many firms routinely deposit employees' pay cheques directly into their bank accounts, which saves the employees a few days of float.

In addition, mobile phone technology and the Internet are encouraging the development of new payment systems. Electronic bill presentment and payment (or EBPP) allows companies to bill customers and receive payments through the Internet. For example, Canada Post operates a EBPP service for companies and their customers at **epost.ca**. You can sign up to electronically receive your bills and make your payments to your suppliers.

A recent survey of Canadian businesses asked 190 Canadian businesses about their use of electronic payment systems for buying and selling transactions.[5] Of the firms, 73 percent used wire transfers, 49 percent used electronic bill payments, including online banking, 48 percent used credit cards, 47 percent used preauthorized payments, and 31 percent used automatic fund transfers in transactions every year. However, 57 percent received cheques for the payments of receivables and 85 percent used cheques to pay their accounts payable. When asked about the benefits of electronic payments 60 percent identified the convenience for the business, 43 percent mentioned improved cash flow, and 39 percent found reduced transactional costs. Only 27 percent of respondents surveyed report that more than half their transactions are electronic. Yet 86 percent of respondents say they would prefer using electronic transactions in the payment process. Of course, the 2011 Canada Post strike has certainly encouraged the switchover!

electronic data interchange (EDI) Direct, electronic information exchange between enterprises, eliminating the mailing and handling of paper invoices.

There is also a growing practice of the exchange of financial information, or **electronic data interchange (EDI)**, between enterprises. EDI allows companies to electronically send purchase orders, shipping notices, and invoices to customers, which is then followed by electronic payments. EDI and EFT allow companies to eliminate the use of paper invoices and cheques, thereby avoiding the mail.

Electronic payment options, such as automated payments under the ACSS and electronic wire transfers through the LVTS, have enabled businesses to become more efficient in their cash management procedures. The net effect of the electronic transfer of funds is a reduction in the importance of managing the float, because the float is much smaller.

All these electronic payment systems have several advantages:

- Record keeping and routine transactions are easy to automate when money moves electronically.
- The marginal cost of transactions on ACSS and LVTS is very low. For example, it can cost less than $10 to transfer huge sums of money through electronic wire transfers.
- Float is drastically reduced, generating substantial savings. For example, cash managers at Occidental Petroleum found that one plant was sending out about cheques totalling US$8 million per month several days early, to avoid late fees due to mail delays. The solution was obvious: the plant's managers switched to paying large bills electronically, ensuring payments arrived exactly on time.[6]

---

[5] The survey results are from "Electronic Payments in Canada: What's the Hold Up?" published by the Canadian Financial Executives Research Foundation and available at **www.feicanada.org/page/cferf/cferf2**.

[6] R.J. Pisapia, "The Cash Manager's Expanding Role: Working Capital," *Journal of Cash Management* 10 (November/December 1990): 11–14.

LO3, 4, 5 21.4 MANAGING INVENTORIES AND CASH BALANCES

Cash management involves a trade-off. If the cash were invested in securities, it would earn interest. But you can't use securities to pay the firm's bills. If you had to sell those securities every time you needed to pay a bill, you would incur heavy transactions costs. The art of cash management is to balance these costs and benefits.

So far we have focused on managing the *flow* of cash efficiently. We have seen how efficient float management can improve a firm's income and its net worth. Now we turn to the management of the *stock* of cash that a firm chooses to keep on hand and ask: How much cash does it make sense for a firm to hold?

Recall that cash management involves a trade-off. If the cash were invested in securities, it would earn interest. But you can't use securities to pay the firm's bills. If you had to sell those securities every time you needed to pay a bill, you would incur heavy transactions costs. The art of cash management is to balance these costs and benefits.

If that seems easier said than done, you may be comforted to know that production managers have to make a similar trade-off. Ask yourself why they carry inventories of raw materials, work in process, and finished goods. They are not obliged to carry these inventories. For example, they could simply buy materials day by day, as needed. But then they would pay higher prices for ordering in small numbers, and risk production delays if the materials arrived late. They avoid that risk by ordering more than the firm's immediate needs. Similarly, firms might do away with inventories of finished goods by producing only what they expect to sell tomorrow. But this also could be a dangerous strategy. A producer with only a small inventory of finished goods is more likely to be caught short and unable to fill orders if demand rises unexpectedly. Moreover, a large inventory of finished goods may allow longer, more economical production runs.

But there are costs to holding inventories that must be set against these benefits. These are called *carrying costs*. For example, money tied up in inventories does not earn interest, storage and insurance must be paid for, and often there is spoilage and deterioration. Production managers must try to strike a sensible balance between the benefits of holding inventory and the costs of holding inventory.

In this sense, cash is just another raw material needed for production. There are costs to keeping an excessive inventory of cash (lost interest) and costs to keeping an inventory too small (the cost of repeated sales of securities).

INVENTORY MANAGEMENT MODELS

As the firm increases its order size, the number of orders falls and therefore the order costs decline. However, an increase in order size also increases the average amount in inventory, so that the carrying cost of inventory rises. The trick is to strike a balance.

Let us look at what economists have had to say about managing inventories and then see whether some of these ideas can help us manage cash balances.

Here is a simple inventory problem. A builder's merchant faces steady demand for engineering bricks. Every so often, when the merchant runs out of inventory, it orders more bricks from the manufacturer.

There are two costs associated with the inventory of bricks. First, there is the *order cost*; every order placed with a supplier involves a fixed handling expense and delivery charge.[7] The second type of cost is the *carrying cost*, which comprises the cost of space, insurance, and losses due to spoilage or theft. The opportunity cost of the capital tied up in the inventory is also part of the carrying cost.

The essence of the inventory problem is that, as the firm increases its order size, the number of orders falls and therefore the order costs decline. However, an increase in order size also increases the average amount in inventory, so that the carrying cost of inventory rises. The trick is to strike a balance between these two costs.

Let's insert some numbers to illustrate. Suppose that the merchant plans to buy 1 million bricks over the coming year. Each order it places costs \$90, and the annual carrying cost of the inventory is \$.05 per brick. To minimize order costs, the merchant would need to place a single order for the entire million bricks on January 1 and would then work off the inventory over the remainder of the year. The *average* inventory over the year would be 500,000 bricks, and

[7] Some components of order costs, such as delivery charges, may at times include a variable component as well. For simplicity, we assume order costs, in general, to be fixed.

therefore carrying costs would be 500,000 × \$.05 = \$25,000. The first row of Table 21.2 shows that if the firm places just this one order, total costs are \$25,090:

$$\text{Total costs} = \text{order costs} + \text{carrying costs}$$
$$\$25{,}090 = \$90 + \$25{,}000$$

To minimize *carrying costs*, the merchant would need to minimize inventory by placing a large number of very small orders. For example, the bottom row of Table 21.2 shows the costs of placing 100 orders a year for 10,000 bricks each. The average inventory is now only 5,000 bricks, and therefore the carrying costs are only 5,000 × \$.05 = \$250. But the order costs have risen to 100 × \$90 = \$9,000.

Each row in Table 21.2 illustrates how changes in the order size affect the inventory costs. You can see that as the order size decreases and the number of orders rises, total inventory costs decline at first because carrying costs fall faster than order costs rise. Eventually, however, the curve turns up as order costs rise faster than carrying costs fall. Figure 21.3 illustrates this

TABLE 21.2 How inventory costs vary with the number of orders.

Order Size = Bricks per Order	Orders per Year = Annual Puchases / Bricks per Order	Average Inventory = Order Size / 2	Order Costs = \$90 per Order	Carrying Costs = \$.05 per Brick	Total Cost = Order Costs plus Carrying Costs
1,000,000	1	500,000	\$ 90	\$25,000	\$25,090
500,000	2	250,000	180	12,500	12,680
200,000	5	100,000	450	5,000	5,450
100,000	10	50,000	900	2,500	3,400
60,000	16.7	30,000	1,500	1,500	3,000
50,000	20	25,000	1,800	1,250	3,050
20,000	50	10,000	4,500	500	5,000
10,000	100	5,000	9,000	250	9,250

FIGURE 21.3
Determination of optimal order size.

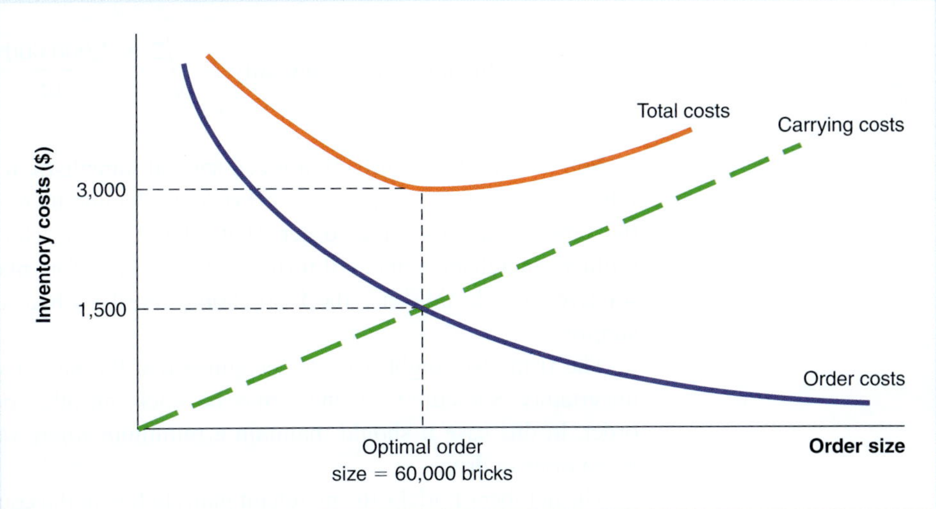

FIGURE 21.4
The builder's merchant minimizes inventory costs by placing about 17 orders per year for 60,000 bricks each. That is, it places orders at about three-week intervals.

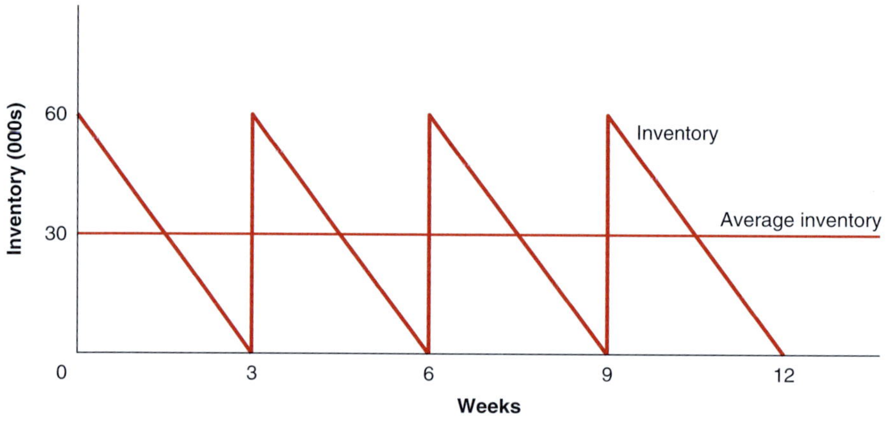

graphically. The downward-sloping curve charts annual order costs, and the upward-sloping straight line charts carrying costs. The U-shaped curve is the sum of these two costs. Total costs are minimized in this example when the order size is 60,000 bricks. About 17 times per year the merchant should place an order for 60,000 bricks, and it should work off this inventory over a period of about three weeks. Its inventory will therefore follow the sawtooth pattern in Figure 21.4.

Note that it is worth increasing order size as long as the decrease in total order costs outweighs the increase in carrying costs. The optimal order size is the point at which these two effects offset each other. This order size is called the **economic order quantity**. There is a formula for calculating the economic order quantity:

economic order quantity
Order size that minimizes total inventory costs.

$$\text{Economic order quantity} = \sqrt{\frac{2 \times \text{annual sales} \times \text{cost per order}}{\text{carrying cost}}} \qquad (21.1)$$

In the present example,

$$\text{Economic order quantity} - \sqrt{\frac{2 \times 1{,}000{,}000 \times 90}{.05}} = 60{,}000 \text{ bricks}$$

You have probably already noticed several unrealistic features in our simple example. First, rather than allowing inventories of bricks to decline to zero, the firm would want to allow for the time it takes to fill an order. If it takes five days for the bricks to be delivered and the builder's merchant waits until it runs out of stock before placing an order, it will be out of stock for five days. In this case the firm should reorder when its stock of bricks falls to a five-day supply.

The firm also might want to recognize that the rate at which it sells its goods is subject to uncertainty. Sometimes business may be slack; on other occasions, the firm may land a large order. In this case it should maintain a minimum *safety stock* below which it would not want inventories to drop.

The number of bricks the merchant plans to buy in the course of the year, in this case 1 million, is also a forecast that is subject to uncertainty. The optimal order size is proportional to the square root of the forecast of annual sales.

The economic order quantity is a simplified, and even simplistic, version of the inventory management process in real firms, but it does capture the four essential features of inventory management:

1. Carrying costs include both the cost of storing goods and the cost of capital tied up in inventory.
2. Optimal inventory levels are lower when carrying costs are high, and they are higher when the cost of restocking inventories is high. This makes sense. If order costs are high, you will want to make larger and therefore less frequent orders, even at the expense of somewhat higher average carrying costs.
3. Average inventory levels are higher when there is more uncertainty about sales and the flow of goods out of inventory.
4. Optimal levels of inventories do not rise in direct proportion to sales. As sales increase, the inventory level rises, but less than proportionately.

Check Point 21.4

The builder's merchant has experienced an increase in demand for engineering bricks. It now expects to sell 1.25 million bricks a year. Unfortunately, interest rates have risen and the annual carrying cost of the inventory has increased to $.09 per brick. Order costs have remained steady at $90 per order.

a. Rework Table 21.2 for each of the eight order sizes shown in the table.
b. Has the optimal inventory level risen or fallen? Explain why.

JUST-IN-TIME INVENTORY MANAGEMENT

just-in-time inventory management A system of inventory management in which materials are delivered to the firm just when needed.

In recent years a number of firms have used a technique known as **just-in-time inventory management** to make dramatic reductions in inventory levels. This technique, first implemented by Toyota Motor Corp. in Japan, is particularly useful to manufacturers that produce a variety of different products. Firms that use the just-in-time system receive a nearly continuous flow of deliveries with no more than two or three hours' worth of parts inventory on hand at any time. For these firms the extra cost of restocking is completely outweighed by the savings in carrying cost. Just-in-time inventory management entails detailed and careful planning of material requirements and much greater coordination with suppliers to avoid the costs of stockouts, however. Suppliers should be able to maintain frequent deliveries of smaller orders with meticulous timing.

Just-in-time inventory management also can reduce costs by allowing suppliers to produce and transport goods on a steadier schedule. However, these systems rely heavily on the predictability of the production process. A firm with shaky labour relations, for example, adopts a just-in-time system at its peril; having essentially no inventory on hand, it would be particularly vulnerable to a strike.

Just before we return to the problem of managing the firm's inventory of cash, see the nearby Finance in Action box, which describes how automobile manufacturers have been able to use just-in-time and other systems to reduce not only their inventories of parts and finished product but also some of the risks of reduced inventory.

MANAGING INVENTORIES OF CASH

William Baumol was the first to notice that this simple inventory model can tell us something about the management of cash balances.[8] Suppose that you keep a reservoir of cash that is steadily drawn down to pay bills. When it runs out, you replenish the cash balance by selling short-term securities. In these circumstances your inventory of cash also follows a sawtooth pattern like that for inventories we saw in Figure 21.4.

---

[8] See W.J. Baumol, "The Transactions Demand for Cash: An Inventory Theoretic Approach," *Quarterly Journal of Economics* 66 (November 1952): 545–556.

Finance in Action

The Benefits and Costs of Just-in-Time Inventory Management

Inventories tie up capital, they take up floor space, and they deteriorate. So it is not surprising that managers are constantly looking for ways to reduce these costs. One way companies have reduced inventories is by moving to a just-in-time (JIT) approach. JIT was pioneered by Toyota in Japan, but it has since been adopted throughout the world.

With JIT a company calls up supplies only when needed. For example, deliveries to Toyota plants are made throughout the day at intervals as short as one hour for air conditioners and heaters, and as long as a day for wipers, seatbelts, and trim parts. Toyota's largest supplier, Denso Corp., makes hundreds of shipments every day to the automaker's assembly plants throughout Japan. Denso's Nishio plant alone dispatches 16 truckloads of air conditioners and heaters to Takaoka, nearly one every hour, covering a distance of 24 kilometres.

To keep production running requires careful planning and coordination between manufacturer and its suppliers. Just-in-time systems have helped reduce inventories of parts and materials. At the same time many firms are cutting inventories of finished goods by building their products to order. For example, in the automobile industry the traditional policy has been to produce batches of different colours or with different options, according to forecasts of likely demand. The cost of producing cars this way to meet a demand that sometimes never materializes has been estimated at $80 billion a year. So automobile manufacturers are increasingly trying to reduce unwanted inventory by building cars in response to customer orders. They observe how a similar policy of build-to-order enabled Dell Computer to become the largest producer of personal computers. Dell customers use the Internet to specify what features they want on their PC. The machine is then assembled to order and dispatched, usually arriving within three days.

Reducing inventory and using just-in-time technique is not without risk. A strike at a supplier's plant or transportation difficulties in delivering components can wreak havoc. Also, natural disasters have caused chaos for manufacturers who don't hold large inventories of supplies. For example, Toyota once had to shut down its Georgetown, Kentucky, plant for nearly a day because an ice storm in the Midwest had made roads impassable. Toyota's response was to hire a forecasting company to monitor weather conditions between the Georgetown plant and its 330 suppliers.

Iceland's volcanic ash in 2010 disrupted air transport across Europe and gave the world's manufacturing supply chain one of its biggest tests since the advent of the low-inventory, just-in-time era. Then Japan's 2011 earthquake, tsunami, nuclear alert, and power shortages put the supply chain under far greater stress. General Motors temporarily shut a truck plant in Louisiana because it could not get enough Japanese-made parts. Production slowdowns at auto plants in North America, such as Honda, Toyota, and Nissan, occurred because of the slowdown in auto supplies from Japan.

In June 2011 Toyota announced that its North American vehicle production levels were expected to return to 100 percent in September, 2011. Production recovered earlier than originally anticipated following the March 11 earthquake and tsunami in Japan. Said Toyota Motor Manufacturing Canada president Brian Krinock: "We applaud the many, many team members and suppliers who have worked tirelessly to help get us back to 100 per cent production volume. Considering the devastation in Japan, we are very appreciative of the incredible effort required to make this happen. Over the next months, we will focus on recovering as much production as possible at TMMC."

Over the past decade or so, the just-in-time concept of having supplies delivered at the last minute, so as to keep inventories down, has spread down the global manufacturing chain. Now, some economists are predicting that this chain may be fortified with "just-in-case" systems to limit the damage from disruptions. For instance, suppliers who have near-monopolies on crucial parts and materials may be pressed to spread their production facilities geographically. As a precaution, their customers may also switch part of their orders to smaller rivals.

Sources: Toyota, "Updated Statement Regarding Earthquake and Tsunami in Japan," press release, **media.toyota.ca/pr/tci/en/toyota-statement-regarding-earthquake-197650.aspx**; T. Murphy, "JIT: When ASAP Isn't Good Enough," *Ward's Auto World*, May 1999, pp. 67–73; R. Schreffler, "Alive and Well," *Ward's Auto World*, May 1999, pp. 73–77; "A Long March: Mass Customisation," *The Economist*, July 14, 2001, pp. 63–65; "Manufacturers Feel the Jolt of Japanese Quake—Disaster May Spark New Industry That Holds Inventory for Firms," *Winnipeg Free Press*, April 2, 2011; "Lacking Parts, G.M. Will Close Plant," *New York Times*, March 18, 2011.

In other words, your cash management problem is just like the problem of finding the optimal order size faced by the builder's merchant. You simply need to redefine the variables. Instead of bricks per order, the order size is defined as the value of short-term securities sold whenever the cash balance is replenished. Total cash outflow takes the place of the total number of bricks sold. Cost per order becomes the cost per sale of securities, and the carrying cost is just the interest rate. Our formula for the number of securities to be sold or, equivalently, the initial cash balance is therefore

$$\textbf{Initial cash balance} = \sqrt{\frac{\textbf{2} \times \textbf{annual cash outflows} \times \textbf{cost per sale of securities}}{\textbf{interest rate}}} \qquad \textbf{(21.2)}$$

Baumol's model of optimal cash balances illustrates the basic trade-offs that managers must make:

- When the cost of selling securities is high, you should hold larger average cash balances.
- When interest rates are high, you should hold smaller cash balances.
- When annual cash outflows increase, the optimal level of cash increases less than proportionally.

EXAMPLE 21.3 **THE OPTIMAL CASH BALANCE**

Suppose that you can invest spare cash in Canadian Treasury bills at an interest rate of 8 percent, but every sale of bills costs you $20. Your firm pays out cash at a rate of $105,000 per month, or $1,260,000 per year. Our formula for the initial cash balance tells us that the optimal number of Treasury bills that you should sell at one time is

$$\sqrt{\frac{2 \times 1{,}260{,}000 \times 20}{.08}} = \$25{,}100$$

Thus your firm would sell approximately $25,000 of Treasury bills four times a month—about once a week. Its average cash balance will be $25,000/2, or $12,500.

In Baumol's model a higher interest rate implies smaller sales of bills. In other words, when interest rates are high, you should hold more of your funds in interest-bearing securities and make small sales of these securities when you need the cash. On the other hand, if you use up cash at a high rate or there are high costs to selling securities, you want to hold large average cash balances. Think about that for a moment. *You can hold too little cash.* Many financial managers proudly point out the extra interest they have earned; these benefits are highly visible. The costs are less visible, but they can be very high. When you allow for the time that a manager spends in monitoring the cash balance, it may make some sense to forgo some of that extra interest.

Check Point 21.5

Suppose now that the interest rate is only 4 percent. How will this affect the optimal initial cash balance derived in Example 21.3? What will be the average cash balance? What will be annual trading costs? Explain why the optimal cash position now involves fewer trades.

UNCERTAIN CASH FLOWS

Baumol's model stresses the essential similarity between the inventory problem and the cash management problem. It also demonstrates the relationship between the optimal cash balance on the one hand, and the level of interest rates and the cost of transactions on the other. However, it is clearly too simple for practical use. For example, firms do not pay out cash at a steady rate day after day and week after week. Sometimes the firm may collect a large unpaid bill and therefore receive a net *inflow* of cash. On other occasions it may pay its suppliers and so incur a net *outflow* of cash.

Economists and management scientists have developed a variety of more elaborate and realistic models that allow for the possibility of both cash inflows and outflows. For example, Figure 21.5 illustrates how the firm should manage its cash balance if it cannot predict day-to-day cash inflows and outflows. You can see that the cash balance meanders unpredictably until it reaches an upper limit, which we denote as U. At this point the firm buys enough securities to return the cash balance to a more normal level, C^*. The firm will move $U - C^*$ dollars from its cash holdings into securities. Once again the cash balance is allowed to meander until this time

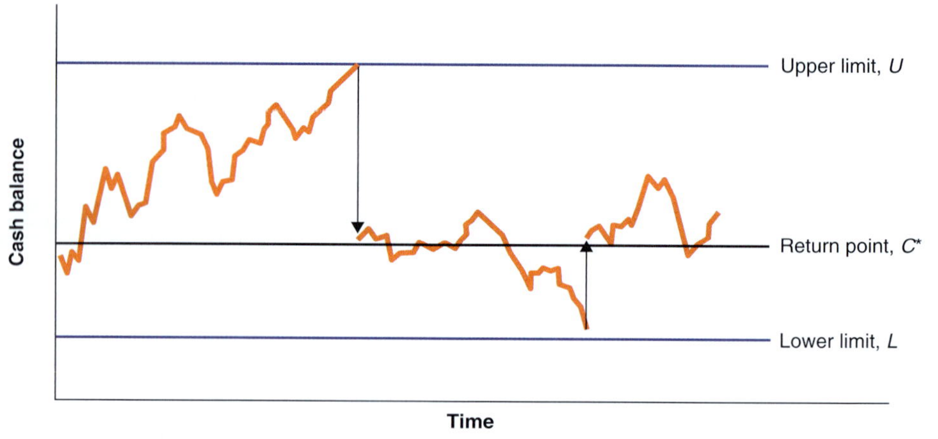

FIGURE 21.5
If cash flows are unpredictable, the cash balance should be allowed to meander until it hits an upper or lower limit. At this point the firm buys or sells securities to restore the balance to the return point, which is the lower limit plus one-third of the spread between the upper and lower limits.

it hits a lower limit, L. This may be zero, a minimum safety margin above zero, or a balance necessary to keep the bank happy. When the cash balance hits the lower limit, the firm *sells* enough securities to restore the balance to a normal level. In this instance, the amount of securities sold is given by $C^* - L$ dollars. Thus the rule is to allow the cash holding to wander freely until it hits an upper or lower limit. When this happens, the firm should buy or sell securities to regain the desired balance.

How far should the firm allow its cash balance to wander? The answer depends on three factors. If the day-to-day variability in cash flows is large or if the cost of buying and selling securities is high, then the firm should set the upper and lower limits far apart. The firm allows wider limits when cash flow volatility is high to keep down the frequency of costly security sales and purchases. Similarly, the firm tolerates wider limits if the cost of security transactions is high. Conversely, if the rate of interest is high and the incentives to manage cash are correspondingly more important, the firm will set the limits close together.[9]

Have you noticed one odd feature about Figure 21.5? The cash balance does not return to a point halfway between the lower and upper limits. It always comes back to a point one-third of the distance from the lower to the upper limit. Always starting at this return point means the firm hits the lower limit more often than the upper limit. This does not minimize the number of transactions—that would require always starting exactly at the middle of the spread. However, always starting at the middle would mean a higher average cash balance and higher interest costs. The lower return point minimizes the sum of transaction costs and interest costs.

If F represents the fixed cost per transaction of buying and selling marketable securities, and I is the interest rate per period on marketable securities,[10] then, according to the Miller-Orr model (see footnote 9), the upper limit to the amount of cash, U, the target cash balance, C^*, and the average cash balance, $AvgC^*$, can be represented by the following equations:

$$U = [(3 \times C^*) - (2 \times L)]$$
$$C^* = L + (3/4 \times F \times \sigma^2/I)^{1/3}$$
$$AvgC^* = [4 \times (C^* - L)]/3$$

where σ^2 is the variance of the firm's monthly net cash flows.

[9] See M.H. Miller and D. Orr, "A Model of the Demand for Money by Firms," *Quarterly Journal of Economics* 80 (August 1966): 413–435.

[10] I can also be regarded as the opportunity cost of holding cash.

To illustrate, suppose $F = \$8$ and $I = 0.75$ percent per month. Also, assume that the lower limit to the firm's target cash balance, L, is \$150 and the standard deviation of its monthly net cash flows, σ, is \$125. The variance, $\sigma^2 = (\$125)^2 = \$15{,}625$. Inserting the numbers into our equations for U, C^*, and $AvgC^*$, we get

$$C^* = \$150 + (3/4 \times \$8 \times \$15{,}625/.0075)^{1/3}, \text{ or}$$
$$C^* = \$150 + (\$12{,}500{,}000)^{1/3} = \$150 + \$232 = \$381$$
$$U = 3 \times \$382 - 2 \times \$150 = \$1{,}146 - \$300 = \$846$$
$$AvgC^* = [4(\$382 - \$150)]/3 = \$309$$

Recognizing uncertainty in cash flows is realistic, but few managers would concede that cash inflows and outflows are entirely unpredictable. The manager of Toys 'R' Us knows that there will be substantial cash inflows around Christmas. Financial managers know when dividends will be paid and when taxes will be due. In Chapter 20 we described how firms forecast cash inflows and outflows and how they arrange short-term investment and financing decisions to supply cash when needed and put cash to work earning interest when it is not needed.

This kind of short-term financial plan is usually designed to produce a cash balance that is stable at some lower limit. But there are always fluctuations that financial managers cannot plan for, certainly not on a day-to-day basis. You can think of the decision rule depicted in Figure 21.5 as a way to cope with the cash inflows and outflows, which cannot be predicted or that are not *worth* predicting. Trying to predict *all* cash flows would chew up enormous amounts of management time.

You should therefore think of these cash management rules as helping us understand the problem of cash management. But they are not generally used for day-to-day management and would probably not yield substantial savings compared with policies based on a manager's judgment, providing of course that the manager understands the trade-offs we have discussed.

Check Point 21.6

How would you expect the firm's cash balance to respond to the following changes?

a. Interest rates increase.
b. The volatility of daily cash flow decreases.
c. The transaction cost of buying or selling marketable securities goes up.

CASH MANAGEMENT IN LARGE DOMESTIC AND INTERNATIONAL CORPORATIONS

For large domestic corporations, the transaction costs of buying and selling securities become trivial compared with the opportunity cost of holding idle cash balances. Suppose that the interest rate is 4 percent per year, or roughly $4/365 = .011$ percent per day. Then the daily interest earned on \$1 million is $.00011 \times \$1{,}000{,}000 = \$110$. Even at a cost of \$50 per transaction, which is generous, it pays to buy Treasury bills today and sell them tomorrow rather than leave \$1 million idle overnight.

A corporation with \$1 billion of annual sales has an average daily cash flow of \$1,000,000,000/365, about \$2.7 million. Firms of this size end up buying or selling securities once a day, every day, unless by chance they have only a small positive cash balance at the end of the day.

Why do such firms hold any significant amounts of cash? For two reasons. First, cash may be left in non-interest-bearing accounts to compensate banks for the services they provide. Second, large corporations in a country without national banks, may have, literally, hundreds of accounts with dozens of different banks. It is often less expensive to leave idle cash in some of these accounts than to monitor each account daily and make daily transfers between them. However, since Canadian banks have branches across Canada, a domestic firm can use the same bank across Canada, so it is less expensive to manage the cash.

One major reason for the proliferation of bank accounts is decentralized management. You cannot give a subsidiary operating freedom to manage its own affairs without giving it the right to spend and receive cash.

Good cash management nevertheless implies some degree of centralization. You cannot maintain your desired inventory of cash if all the subsidiaries in the group are responsible for their own private pools of cash. And you certainly want to avoid situations in which one subsidiary is investing its spare cash at 8 percent while another is borrowing at 10 percent. It is not surprising, therefore, that even in highly decentralized companies, generally, there is central control over cash balances and bank relations.

Cash management in domestic firms is child's play compared with managing cash in large multinational corporations operating in dozens of different countries, each with its own currency, banking system, and legal structure. Each foreign subsidiary must have its own bank accounts in its country of operation.

For example, suppose that you are treasurer of a large multinational company with operations throughout Europe. You could allow the separate businesses to manage their own cash, but that would be costly and would almost certainly result in each one accumulating little hoards of cash. The solution is to set up a regional system. In this case the company establishes a local concentration account with a bank in each country. Any surplus cash is swept daily into central multicurrency accounts in London or another European banking centre. This cash is then invested in marketable securities or used to finance any subsidiaries that have a cash shortage.

Payments can also be made out of the regional centre. For example, to pay wages in each European country, the company just needs to send its principal bank a computer file with details of the payments to be made. The bank then finds the least costly way to transfer the cash from the company's central accounts and arranges for the funds to be credited on the correct day to the employees in each country.

Most large multinationals have several banks in each country, but the more banks they use, the less control they have over their cash balances. So development of regional cash management systems favours banks that can offer a worldwide branch network. These banks can also afford the high costs of setting up computer systems for handling cash payments and receipts in different countries. Some Canadian banks, including CIBC, TD, RBC, and Scotiabank, have subsidiary and affiliate banks in different countries. A bank's foreign operations provide banking services in these other countries and also provide cash transfer between its various banks. So cash management by a Canadian multinational business, with global operations, can be easier and cheaper if the bank accounts of its global operations are with the foreign operations of the parent company's Canadian bank. An example of global banking services is ScotiaGlobal electronic banking, an Internet-based banking platform providing a single point of access to Scotiabank accounts in Canada, the United States and Mexico. Using ScotiaGlobal, a company can monitor and control its cash position and manage cross-border operations with convenience from one centralized location. With the growing number of multinational corporations and electronic connections, it is becoming easier for firms to manage their cash.

LO6 21.5 INVESTING IDLE CASH: THE MONEY MARKET

money market Market for short-term financial assets.

When firms have excess funds, they can invest the surplus in interest-bearing securities. Treasury bills are only one of many securities that might be appropriate for such short-term investments. More generally, firms may invest in a variety of securities in the **money market**, the market for short-term financial assets. Larger firms usually invest directly in these securities. However, smaller firms often park their spare cash in a money market mutual fund or money market exchange-traded fund (ETF), which holds a portfolio of money market investments.

Only fixed-income securities with maturities less than one year are considered to be part of the money market. In fact, however, most instruments in the money market have considerably shorter maturity. Limiting maturity has two advantages for the cash manager. First, short-term securities entail little interest rate risk. Recall from Chapter 6 that price risk due to interest rate fluctuations increases with maturity. Very-short-term securities, therefore, have almost no interest rate risk. Second, it is far easier to gauge financial stability over very short horizons. It isn't necessary to worry as much about deterioration in financial strength over a 90-day horizon compared to the 30-year life of a bond. These considerations imply that high-quality money market securities are a safe "parking spot" for idle balances until they are converted back to cash.

Most money market securities are also highly marketable, or *liquid*, meaning that it is easy and cheap to sell the asset for cash. This property, too, is an attractive feature of securities used as temporary investments until cash is needed. Some important money market instruments are described below.[11] Also, Table 21.3 provides information on recent rates for some Canadian money market securities.

TABLE 21.3
Money market rates, April 11, 2012.

1-month Treasury bills	.94%
2-month Treasury bills	.96%
3-month Treasury bills	.97%
6-month Treasury bills	1.12%
1-year Treasury bills	1.45%
1-month banker's acceptance	1.13%
3-month banker's acceptance	1.21%
1-month prime corporate paper*	1.07%
2-month prime corporate paper	1.11%
3-month prime corporate paper	1.18%

**Prime corporate paper* is the Bank of Canada's term for commercial paper.

Source: Bank of Canada, April 11, 2011, **www.bankofcanada.ca**.

Treasury Bills Treasury bills are sold in weekly auctions by the Canadian government with original maturities of either one, three, six or twelve months. These are the safest and most liquid of assets and are traded actively over-the-counter by banks and security dealers.

Commercial Paper We introduced commercial paper in Chapter 20 when we were looking at ways for companies to raise cash to finance short-term assets. Large corporations sell commercial paper, which is typically unsecured, as an alternative to a short-term loan from a bank. While maturities can go up to 365 days, commercial paper usually is issued with maturities ranging from one to three months. Commercial paper is typically sold by financial institutions, such as Canadian banks, who are hired as sale agents by the issuer. Because there is no active trading in commercial paper, it has low marketability. Therefore, it would not be an appropriate investment for a firm that could not hold it until maturity. Dominion Bond Rating Service rates commercial paper in terms of the default risk of the issuer. A corporation with idle cash might consider purchasing the corporate commercial paper of such issuers as Loblaws, EnCana, or BCE, knowing that they will earn a higher rate of return than a Treasury bill but also take on a higher risk of default than the Government of Canada.

asset-backed commercial paper (ABCP) Short-term security with cash flows coming from a pool of assets such as mortgage or credit card receivables.

A second type of commercial paper market is **asset-backed commercial paper (ABCP)**. ABCP is also issued to raise short-term financing. The difference is that ABCP is issued by a limited purpose trust (or a "conduit") or a finance company to fund purchases of assets that back up the ABCP and generate cash flow. When the asset-backed commercial paper was first established, those underlying assets were principally mortgages and various types of consumer loans and receivables. As people paid interest and repaid their loans, cash flowed into the ABCP trusts and then on to commercial paper owners. However, the asset pool was expanded to include more complex derivative securities whose value was tied to pools of mortgages and other securities.

[11] We have not included a discussion of the *banker's acceptance* here. This instrument is discussed in detail in Chapters 20 and 22.

Finance in Action

Asset-Backed Commercial Paper Crisis and Resolution

Prior to the 2007 financial crisis, asset-based commercial paper (ABCP) was a popular investment, because it provided higher returns than banks due to bank interest rates being cut. The various ABCPs were highly rated and sold by some of the world's biggest banks. In 2006 ABCP accounted for 30 percent of Canada's $360 billion short-term debt market. Some of it was issued by Canadian banks, but some was issued by non-bank finance companies, such as Coventree.

The ABCP sector was struck down in August 2007 by the crisis in U.S. subprime mortgages. It was revealed that an unknown amount of ABCP was tied to dodgy U.S. housing loans. Buyers disappeared and the market froze.

Canada's non-bank funds were unable to turn to banks for emergency funds to refinance maturing commercial paper, because the banks that committed to back these trusts only had to do so in the case of a "market disruption."

To stop the trusts that issued the paper from going into default and being liquidated, a group of major financial players, led by the Caisse de dépôt et placement du Québec, called for a standstill in the market to avoid a meltdown and seek a solution. Known as the "Montreal Accord," the $35 billion market for non-bank asset-backed commercial paper was frozen. Investors holding the frozen ABCP were stuck with commercial paper that they had expected would be turned into cash in 30 to 60 days.

A committee lead by Toronto lawyer Purdy Crawford crafted a plan to exchange the short-term notes for ones that matured in as long as nine years. On April 25, 2008, almost 96 percent of 1,932 noteholders voted in favour of the restructuring plan. In June 4, 2008, an Ontario judge approved the plan to restructure $32 billion of asset-backed commercial paper, moving individual and corporate investors closer to recovering troubled investments that had been frozen since August. The plan included shielding the issuers from lawsuit. Subsequently, several appeals were made but made. In January 2009, the restructuring plan was approved by Ontario Superior Court, clearing the way for investors to exchange $32 billion of frozen asset-backed commercial paper for a new long-term bond. Investors who had bought less than $1 million in ABC paper got a cash refund from the brokerage firms that initially sold them the financial vehicle and the others exchanged their ABCP for long-term notes.

Finally, in April 2011, the Canadian Securities Administrators, a group for Canada's provincial securities commissions, unveiled proposed reforms to govern the sale of securitized products, responding to calls for tighter regulation following the meltdown of Canada's $32 billion market for non-bank ABCP in the summer of 2007. The CSA proposed that the sale of securitized financial products, including ABCP, be restricted to sophisticated investors. Also, the CSA proposed a framework for regulation of securitized products in Canada that would improve investor protection through enhanced transparency and disclosure requirements for securitized products, and modify the current exemptions investors use to access these products in the exempt market. Under the proposed framework, reporting issuers would be required to provide investors with information on the features and risks of securitized products. This information was to be provided to investors at the time of product distribution, and on an ongoing basis.

The new disclosure requirements were designed to be consistent with international developments. In addition, non-reporting issuers that distributed securitized products in the exempt market would also be subject to certain initial and ongoing disclosure requirements.

Sources: Tara Perkins, "The ABCs of Asset-Backed Commercial Paper," *The Globe and Mail*, April 25, 2008; John Greenwood, "Judge Approves ABCP Debt Restructure: $32-Billion," *Financial Post*, June 6, 2008; John Greenwood, "Ruling Clears Way for ABCP Restructuring: Investors Relieved," *Financial Post*, January 13, 2009; and CSA, "Canadian Securities Regulators Propose Enhanced Oversight of Securitized Products," press release, April 1, 2011, **www.securities-administrators.ca/aboutcsa.aspx?id=960**, accessed October 10, 2011.

In August 2007, the U.S. mortgage crisis, or "subprime crisis," caused concern that the underlying mortgages were not going to generate cash flow, and the market for the ABCP dried up. As ABCP matured, the conduits tried to sell new paper but investors did not want to buy the new issues. The nearby Finance in Action box talks about the asset-backed commercial paper crisis of 2007/08.

In 2010, three years after being demonized for its association with the credit crisis, asset-backed commercial paper reemerged as a credible investment alternative. As of May 31, 2011, the outstanding amount in the Canadian ABCP market stood at $24.1 billion. One issuer of ABCP in May was Prime Trust, a seller of various asset-based securities based on assets they acquire from various companies. The assets typically consisting of trade receivables, auto loans and leases, and residential mortgages. The deal in May was based on increased account receivables from communications companies. The ABCP market is dominated by residential mortgage securitizations representing 35.7 percent of the market, followed by secured lines of credit (22 percent) and auto-related finance (17 percent). The Dominion Bond Rating Service, **www.dbrs.com**, produces a monthly report on the state of the ABCP market and puts it on the Structured Finance page. DBRS plays a very important role in evaluating and ranking various asset-based funds, including ABCP.

Guaranteed Investment Certificates GICs are term deposits at Canadian banks that provide rates of return over fixed periods, between six months and 10 years, and have minimum and maximum deposits that range between $500 and $999,999. Most GICs have a fixed interest rate, but some banks also offer variable-rate ones, whose interest rate is linked to the bank prime rate or to other market rates. For example, the interest rate for the TD Bank's GIC Plus equals the S&P/TSX index return but has a 10 percent maximum rate.

Unlike demand deposits (chequing accounts), not all GICs can be withdrawn from the bank before the maturity date. Some banks permit early withdrawal but charge a penalty, and others allow the withdrawal only once a year and at lower interest than GICs with no withdrawal option.

The U.S. equivalent to the GIC is a certificate of deposit (CD), which generally has more restrictions than most GICs.

Repurchase Agreements Repurchase agreements, also known as *repos* or *buybacks*, are in effect collateralized loans. A government bond dealer sells Treasury bills to an investor, with an agreement to repurchase them at a later date at a higher price. The increase in price serves as implicit interest, so the investor is, in effect, lending money to the dealer, first giving money to the dealer and later getting it back with interest. The bills serve as collateral for the loan: if the dealer fails and cannot buy back the bill, the investor can keep it. Repurchase agreements are usually very short-term, with maturities of only a few days and sometimes overnight. These are usually transacted in minimum denominations of $100,000.

21.6 SUMMARY

1. **What is float and why can it be valuable? LO1**

   The cash shown in the company ledger is not the same as the available balance in its bank account. When you write a cheque, it takes time before your bank balance is adjusted downward. This is **payment float**. During this time the available balance will be larger than the ledger balance. When you deposit a cheque, there is a delay before it gets credited to your bank account. In this case the available balance will be smaller than the ledger balance. This is **availability float**. The difference between payment float and availability float is the **net float**. If you can predict how long it will take cheques to clear, you may be able to "play the float" and get by on a smaller cash balance. The interest you can thereby earn on the net float is a source of value.

2. **What are some tactics to increase net float? LO2**

   You can manage the float by speeding collections and slowing payments. One way to speed collections is by using a **lockbox system**, in which customers send their cheques to a local post office box. A bank empties the box at regular intervals and clears the cheques. Lockbox banking reduces mailing time and the time required to clear cheques. Another way to reduce the float is with a **zero-balance account**, a bank account to which just enough funds are transferred each day to pay that day's bills. Also encourage customers to use electronic transfer payments, rather than cheques.

3. **What are the costs and benefits of holding inventories? LO3**

   The benefit of higher inventory levels is the reduction in order costs associated with restocking and the reduced chances of running out of material. The costs are the carrying costs, which include the cost of space, insurance, spoilage, and the opportunity cost of the capital tied up in inventory. The **economic order quantity** is the order size that minimizes the sum of order costs plus carrying costs.

4. **What are the costs and benefits of holding cash? LO4**

Cash provides liquidity, but it doesn't pay interest. Securities pay interest, but you can't use them to buy things. As financial manager, you want to hold cash up to the point at which the incremental or marginal benefit of liquidity is equal to the cost of holding cash, that is, the interest you could earn on securities.

5. **Why is an understanding of inventory management useful for cash management? LO5**

Cash is simply a raw material—like inventories of other goods—that you need to do business. Capital that is tied up in large inventories of any raw material rather than earning interest is expensive. So why do you hold inventories at all? Why not order materials when you need them? The answer is that placing many small orders is also expensive. The principles of optimal inventory management and optimal cash management are similar.

Try to strike a balance between holding an inventory of cash that's too large (and losing interest on the money) and making too many small adjustments to your inventory (and incurring additional transaction or administrative costs). If interest rates are high, you want to hold relatively small inventories of cash. If your cash needs are variable and your transaction or administrative costs are high, you will want to hold relatively large inventories.

6. **Where do firms invest excess funds until they are needed to pay bills? LO6**

Firms can invest idle cash in the **money market**, the market for short-term financial assets. These assets tend to be short term, low risk, and highly liquid, making them ideal instruments in which to invest funds for short periods of time before cash is needed.

Related Web Links

fpsc.com Web site of Financial Publishing Services, with useful and current information for Treasury management professionals

ioma.com An online management library with some articles on cash management

nacha.org U.S. automated collection systems for cash management

cdnpay.ca Canadian Payments Association

federalreserve.gov and ny.frb.org Information on U.S. money market and interest rates

bankofcanada.ca Information on Canadian money market and interest rates

phoenixhecht.com A comprehensive Web site on cash management with useful links

treasuryandrisk.com Web site of Treasury & Risk: The Future of Finance Today

americanbanker.com Provides a host of information for bankers and finance professionals

intltreasurer.com Articles on short-term financial management

Key Terms

asset-backed commercial paper (ABCP)	693	electronic data interchange (EDI)	683	money market	692
availability float	675	electronic funds transfer (ETF)	682	net float	676
economic order quantity	686	just-in-time inventory management	687	payment *or* disbursement float	675
		lockbox system	680	zero-balance account	682

Questions and Problems

connect™ Practise and learn online with *Connect*. Questions with online Excel templates or datasets are marked with [icon].

*Answers in Appendix B

BASIC

*1. **Float.** On January 25, Coot Company has $250,000 deposited with a local bank. On January 27, the company writes and mails cheques of $20,000 and $60,000 to suppliers. At the end of the month, Coot's financial manager deposits a $45,000 cheque received from a customer in the morning mail and picks up the end-of-month account summary from the bank. The manager notes that only the $20,000 payment of the 27th has cleared the bank. What are the company's ledger balance and payment float? What is the company's net float? (LO1)

2. **Float.** A company has the following cash balances:

Company's ledger balance = $600,000

Bank's ledger balance = $625,000

Available balance = $550,000

a. Calculate the payment float and availability float. (LO1)

b. Why does the company gain from the payment float? (LO1)

c. Suppose the company operates in the United States and adopts a policy of writing cheques on a remote U.S. bank. How is this likely to affect the three measures of cash balance? (LO2)

3. **Float.** General Products writes cheques that average $20,000 daily. These cheques take an average of six days to clear. It receives payments that average $22,000 daily. It takes three days before these cheques are available to the firm. (LO1)

   a. Calculate payment float, availability float, and net float.

   b. What would be General Products' annual savings if it could reduce availability float to two days? The interest rate is 6 percent per year. What would be the present value of these savings?

4. **Lockboxes.** Anne Teak, the financial manager of a furniture manufacturer, is considering operating a lockbox system. She forecasts that 300 payments per day will be made to lockboxes with an average payment size of $1,500. The bank's charge for operating the lockboxes is $.40 per cheque. The interest rate is .015 percent per day. (LO2)

   a. If the lockbox saves two days in collection float, is it worthwhile to adopt the system?

   b. What minimum reduction in the time to collect and process each cheque is needed to justify use of the lockbox system?

5. **Cash Management.** Complete the following passage by choosing the appropriate term from the following list: lockbox banking, payment float, availability float, net float. (LO2)

   The firm's available balance is equal to its ledger balance plus the _______ and minus the _______. The difference between the available balance and the ledger balance is often called the _______. Firms can increase their cash resources by speeding up collections. One way to do this to arrange for a bank to collect the cheques directly from a post office box. This is known as _______.

INTERMEDIATE

*6. **Lockboxes.** Sherman's Sherbet currently takes about six days to collect and deposit cheques from customers. A lockbox system could reduce this time to four days. Collections average $10,000 daily. The interest rate is .02 percent per day. (LO2)

   a. By how much will the lockbox system reduce collection float?

   b. What is the daily interest savings of the system?

   c. Suppose the lockbox service is offered for a fixed monthly fee instead of payment per cheque. What is the maximum monthly fee that Sherman's should be willing to pay for this service? (Assume a 30-day month.)

7. **Lockboxes.** The financial manager of JAC Cosmetics is considering opening a lockbox in Calgary. Cheques cleared through the lockbox will amount to $300,000 per month. The lockbox will make cash available to the company three days earlier. (LO2)

   a. Suppose that the bank offers to run the lockbox for a $20,000 compensating balance. Is the lockbox worthwhile?

   b. Suppose that the bank offers to run the lockbox for a fee of $.10 per cheque cleared instead of a compensating balance. What must the average cheque size be for the fee alternative to be less costly? Assume an interest rate of 6 percent per year.

   c. Why did you need to know the interest rate to answer (b) but not to answer (a)?

*8. **Collection Policy.** Major Manufacturing has a big market for its products in the United States. It currently has one bank account located in New York to handle all of its collections. The firm keeps a compensating balance of US$300,000 to pay for these services (see Section 20.7). It is considering opening a bank account with West Coast National Bank to speed up collections from its many California-based customers. Major estimates that the West Coast account would reduce collection time by one day on the $1 million a day of business that it does with its California-based customers. If it opens the account, it can reduce the compensating balance with its New York bank to $200,000, since it will do less business in that city. However, West Coast also will require a compensating balance of $200,000. Should Major open the new account? (LO2)

9. **Economic Order Quantity.** Assume that Everyman's Bookstore uses up cash at a steady rate of $200,000 per year. The interest rate is 2 percent and each sale of securities costs $20. (LO4)

   a. How many times a year should the store sell securities?

   b. What is its average cash balance?

*10. **Economic Order Quantity.** Genuine Gems orders a full month's worth of precious stones at the beginning of every month. Over the course of the month, it sells off its stock, at which point it restocks inventory for the following month. It sells 200 gems per month, and the monthly carrying cost is $1 per gem. The fixed order cost is $20 per order. Should the firm adjust its inventory policy? If so, should it order smaller stocks more frequently or larger stocks less frequently? (LO3)

11. **Economic Order Quantity.** Patty's Pancakes orders pancake mix once a week. The mix is used up by the end of the week, at which point more is reordered. Each time Patty orders pancake mix, she spends about a half hour of her time, which she estimates is worth $20. Patty sells 200 pounds of reconstituted pancake each week. The carrying cost of each pound of the mix is $.05 per week. Should Patty restock more or less frequently? What is the cost-minimizing order size? How many times per month should Patty restock? (LO3)

12. **Economic Order Quantity.** A large consulting firm orders photocopying paper by the carton. The firm pays a $30 delivery charge on each order. The total cost of storing the paper, including forgone interest, storage space, and deterioration comes to about $1.50 per carton per month. The firm uses about 1,000 cartons of paper per month. (LO3)
    a. Fill in the following table:

	Order Size			
	100	200	250	500
Orders per month	______	______	______	______
Total order cost	______	______	______	______
Average inventory	______	______	______	______
Total carrying costs	______	______	______	______
Total inventory costs	______	______	______	______

    b. Calculate the economic order quantity. Is your answer consistent with your findings in part (a)?

*13. **Economic Order Quantity.** Micro-Encapsulator Corp. (MEC) expects to sell 7,200 miniature home encapsulators this year. The cost of placing an order from its supplier is $250. Each unit costs $50 and carrying costs are 20 percent of the purchase price. (LO3)
    a. What is the economic order quantity?
    b. What are total costs—order costs plus carrying costs—of inventory over the course of the year?

14. **Inventory Management.** Suppose now that the supplier in the previous problem offers a 1 percent discount on orders of 1,800 units or more. Should MEC accept the supplier's offer? (LO3)

*15. **Inventory Management.** A just-in-time inventory system reduces the cost of ordering additional inventory by a factor of 100. What is the change in the optimal order size predicted by the economic order quantity model? (LO3)

*16. **Cash Management.** A firm maintains a separate account for cash disbursements. Total disbursements are $100,000 per month, spread evenly over the month. Administrative and transaction costs of transferring cash to the disbursement account are $10 per transfer. Marketable securities yield 1 percent per month. Determine the size and number of transfers that will minimize the cost of maintaining the special account. (LO4)

17. **Float Management in the United States and Canada.** The Automated Clearinghouse (ACH) system in the United States uses electronic communication to provide next-day delivery of payments. The processing cost of making a payment through the ACH system is roughly half the cost of making the same payment by cheque. (LO2)
    a. Why then do American firms often rationally choose to make payments by cheque?
    b. Two major payment systems in Canada are the Automated Clearing Settlement System (ACSS) and the Large Value Transfer System (LVTS). Would your answer in the context of Canada's payment system be different from part (a) above?

18. **Internet.** Banks allow you to pay your bills over the Internet. You log on to your account to tell the bank which payments it should send out on your behalf. Most banks allow you to connect to epost, Canada Post's free online service that allows you to receive, view, pay, print, and store your bills or other documents online. Go to **www.epost.ca** and learn about how epost works. Click on Find Your Mailers, select your province, and look at all of the companies willing to send bills electronically. If you have bills to pay, create yourself an account, and start using epost. You will be helping the environment by reducing paper bills. Learn more at **www.canadapost.ca/cpo/mc/personal/epost/tour/help_environment.jsf** and fill in the order numbers. (LO2)

19. **Internet.** Current money market rates are available at the Bank of Canada, **www.bankofcanada.ca/rates/interest-rates/money-market-yields**. Compare the interest rates on Treasury bills to corporate (commercial) paper of the same maturity. What do you observe? Why do you think the rates are different? (LO6)

20. **Cash Management.** If cash flows change unpredictably, the firm should allow the cash balance to move within limits. (LO4)
    *a. What three factors determine how far apart these limits are?
    *b. How far should the firm adjust its cash balance when it reaches the upper or lower limit?
    c. Why does it not restore the cash balance to the halfway point?

*21. **Optimal Cash Balances.** Suppose that your weekly cash expenses are $80. Every time you withdraw money from the automated teller at your bank, you are charged

$.15. Your bank account pays interest of 3 percent annually. (LO4)

a. How often should you withdraw funds from the bank?
b. What is the optimal-sized withdrawal?
c. What is your average amount of cash on hand?

*22. **Cash Management.** Suppose that the rate of interest increases from 4 to 8 percent per year. Would firms' cash balances go up or down relative to sales? Explain. (LO4)

23. **Cash and Inventory Management.** According to the economic-order-quantity-inventory model and the Baumol model of cash management, what will happen to cash balances and inventory levels if the firm's production and sales both double? What is the implication of your answer for percentage-of-sales financial planning models (see Section 19.2)? (LO5)

24. **Internet.** Go to the Web page of a major bank such as TD Commercial Banking (**www.tdcommercialbanking.com/index.jsp**) or Scotiabank (**www.scotiabank.com/cda/index/0,,LIDen_SID87,00.html**). How do these banks help corporations to manage their cash? (LO2)

25. **Internet.** Your company has some spare cash to invest for three months. You are wondering whether to invest it in Canadian or U.S. Treasury bills, commercial paper, GICS, or CDs. Go to the Bank of Canada site (**www.bankofcanada.ca/rates/daily-digest**) and the U.S. Federal Reserve System site (**www.federalreserve.gov/releases/h15/update/default.htm**) and find the latest rates on these investments. Why might you not choose to take the investment offering the highest rate? (LO6)

26. **Identify the Model.** The Asian Tigers Conglomerate is seeking appropriate ways to manage its cash balances. The firm has established a lower limit with regard to its cash balance holdings of $40,000. It faces quite a bit of volatility in its daily cash flows, with a variance of $300,000. The annual interest rate on marketable securities is 6 percent. The fixed cost per transaction of buying and selling securities is $50. (LO5)

a. Calculate the target cash balance and the upper limit to holding cash for the firm.
b. Which cash balance model did you use for your computation?

CHALLENGE

27. **Float Management.** Some years ago, Merrill Lynch, the American investment bank, increased its float by mailing cheques drawn on West Coast banks to customers in the east and cheques drawn on East Coast banks to customers in the west. A subsequent class action suit against Merrill Lynch revealed that in 28 months from September 1976, Merrill Lynch disbursed US$1.25 billion in 365,000 cheques to New York State customers alone. The plaintiff's lawyer calculated that by using a remote bank Merrill Lynch had increased its average float by 1.5 days.[12] (LO2)

1. How much did Merrill Lynch disburse per day to New York State customers?
2. What was the total gain to Merrill Lynch over the 28 months, assuming an interest rate of 8 percent?
3. What was the present value of the increase in float, if the benefits were expected to be permanent?
4. Suppose that the use of remote banks had involved Merrill Lynch in extra expenses. What was the maximum extra cost per cheque that Merrill Lynch would have been prepared to pay?

Solutions to Check Points

21.1 a. The ledger balance is $940 + $100 − $40 = $1,000.

b. Availability float is $100, since you do not yet have access to the funds you have deposited.

c. Payment float is $40, since the cheque that you wrote has not yet cleared.

d. The bank's ledger balance is $940 + $100 = $1,040. The bank is aware of the cheque you deposited but is not aware of the cheque you wrote.

e. Ledger balance plus payment float = $1,000 + $40 = $1,040, which equals the bank's ledger balance. Available balance + availability float = $940 + $100 = $1,040, also equal to the bank's ledger balance.

21.2 The current market value of GM is 1.56 billion shares × $31/share = $48.36 billion. The 2-day reduction in float is worth $740 million (= 2 × .00015 × 370/.00015) This increases the value of GM to $49.1 billion (= $48.36 billion + $.74 billion). The new stock price will be 49.1/1.56 = $31.47 per share. GM should be willing to pay up to $740 million for the system, since the present value of the savings is $740 million.

21.3 The benefit of the lockbox system, and the price the firm should be willing to pay for the system, is higher when

[12] See I. Ross, "The Race Is to the Slow Player," *Fortune*, April 1983, pp. 75–80.

a. Payment size is higher (since interest is earned on more funds).
b. Payments per day are higher (since interest is earned on more funds).
c. The interest rate is higher (since the cost of float is higher).
d. Mail time saved is higher (since more float is saved).
e. Processing time saved is higher (since more float is saved).

21.4 a.

Order Size	Orders per Year	Average Inventory	Order Costs	Carrying Costs	Total Costs
Bricks per Order	1,250,000 / Bricks per Order	Order Size / 2	\$90 per Order	\$.09 per Brick	Order Costs Plus Carrying Costs
1,000,000	1.25	500,000	\$ 113	\$45,000	\$45,113
500,000	2.50	250,000	225	22,500	22,725
200,000	6.25	100,000	563	9,000	9,563
100,000	12.50	50,000	1,125	4,500	5,625
60,000	20.83	30,000	1,875	2,700	4,575
50,000	25.00	25,000	2,250	2,250	4,500
20,000	62.50	10,000	5,625	900	6,525
10,000	125.00	5,000	11,250	450	11,700

b. The optimal order size decreases to 50,000 bricks:

$$\text{Economic order quantity} = \sqrt{\frac{2 \times \text{annual sales} \times \text{costs per order}}{\text{carrying cost}}}$$

$$= \sqrt{\frac{2 \times 1{,}250{,}000 \times 90}{.09}} = 50{,}000$$

Therefore, the average inventory level will fall to 25,000 bricks. The effect of the higher carrying costs more than offsets the effect of the higher sales.

21.5 At an interest rate of 4 percent, the optimal initial cash balance is

$$\sqrt{\frac{2 \times 1{,}260{,}000 \times 20}{.04}} = \$35{,}496$$

The average cash balance will be one-half this amount, or \$17,748. The firm will need to sell securities 1,260,000/35,496 = 35.5 times per year. Therefore, annual trading costs will be 35.5 × \$20 = \$710 per year. Because the interest rate is lower, the firm is willing to hold larger cash balances.

21.6 a. Higher interest rates will lead to lower cash balances.
b. Higher (lower) volatility will lead to higher (lower) cash balances.
c. Higher transaction costs will lead to higher cash balances.

PART 7

Short-Term Financial Decisions

21 Cash and Inventory Management

22 Credit Management and Collection

22.1 Terms of Sale

22.2 Credit Agreements

22.3 Credit Analysis

22.4 The Credit Decision

22.5 Collection Policy

22.6 Summary

CHAPTER 22

Credit Management and Collection

LEARNING OBJECTIVES

After studying this chapter, you should be able to:

LO1 Identify the steps in credit management.

LO2 Measure the implicit interest rate on credit.

LO3 Decide whether it makes sense to ask the customer for a formal IOU.

LO4 Explain how firms can assess the probability that a customer will pay its bills.

LO5 Explain how to assess whether it makes sense to grant credit to customers.

LO6 Explain collection policy and how it is implemented.

Collection policy is an important part of credit management. After deciding to allow customers to buy on credit, management must be prepared to deal with customers who are slow to pay their bills.

When companies sell their products, they sometimes demand cash on delivery, but in most cases they allow a delay in payment. The customers' promises to pay for their purchases constitute a valuable asset; therefore, the accountant enters these promises in the balance sheet as trade receivables. For example, CCL's trade receivables, the $186,235,000 reported in Table 20.2, constitute almost 50 percent of its current assets, the $379,578,000 reported in Table 20.1. These receivables are trade credit, since CCL sells to other firms, not to consumers. Trade credit is larger by far than consumer credit and will therefore be the main focus of this chapter.

Customers may be attracted by the opportunity to buy goods on credit, but there is a cost to the seller who provides the credit. In Chapter 20 we saw that in the 90 days of the first quarter of 2011, CCL had $315,625,000 sales, or about $3,506,944 per a day. Thus CCL's customers were taking an average of $186,235,000/$3,506,944 = 53 days to pay their bills. Suppose that CCL could collect this cash one day earlier without affecting sales. In that case receivables would decline by about $3.5 million, and CCL would have an extra $3.5 million in the bank, which it could either hand back to shareholders or invest to earn interest.

Credit management involves the following steps, which we will discuss in turn:

1. You must establish the *terms of sale* on which you propose to sell your goods. How long are you going to give customers to pay their bills? Are you prepared to offer a cash discount for prompt payment?
2. You must decide what evidence you need to have that shows the customer owes you money. Do you just ask the buyer to sign a receipt, or do you insist on a more formal IOU?
3. You must consider which customers are likely to pay their bills. This is called *credit analysis*. Do you judge this from the customer's past payment record or past financial statements? Do you also rely on bank references?
4. You must decide on *credit policy*. How much credit are you prepared to extend to each customer? Do you play it safe by turning down any doubtful prospects? Or do you accept the risk of a few bad debts as part of the cost of building up a large, regular clientele?
5. Finally, after you have granted credit, you have the problem of collecting the money when it becomes due. This is called *collection policy*. How do you keep track of payments and pursue slow payers? If all goes well, this is the end of the matter. But sometimes you will find that the customers go bankrupt and cannot pay. In this case you need to understand how bankruptcy works. Bankruptcy procedures are discussed in Chapter 16, Section 16.5.

LO1, 2 22.1

TERMS OF SALE

terms of sale Credit, discount, and payment terms offered on a sale.

Whenever you sell goods, you need to set the **terms of sale**. For example, if you are supplying goods to a wide variety of irregular customers, you may require cash on delivery (COD), demanding payment when the goods are delivered. And if you are producing goods to the customer's specification or incurring heavy delivery costs, then it may be sensible to ask for cash before delivery (CBD).

Some contracts provide for *progress payments* as work is carried out. For example, a large consulting contract might call for 30 percent payment after completion of field research, 30 percent more on submission of a draft report, and the remaining 40 percent when the project is finally completed.

In many other cases, payment is not made until after delivery, so the buyer receives *credit*. Each industry seems to have its own typical credit arrangements. These arrangements have a rough logic. For example, the seller will naturally demand earlier payment if its customers are financially less secure, if their accounts are small, or if the goods are perishable or quickly resold.

Whenever you buy goods on credit, the supplier is providing short-term financing and the terms of sale set the final payment date. To encourage you to pay *before* the final date, it is common to offer a cash discount for prompt settlement. For example, a manufacturer may require payment within 30 days but offer a 5 percent discount to customers who pay within 10 days. These terms would be referred to as 5/10, net 30:

5 /	10,	net 30
↑	↑	↑
Percent discount for early payment	Number of days discount is available	Number of days before payment is due

Similarly, if a firm sells goods on terms of 2/30, net 60, customers receive a 2 percent discount for payment within 30 days or else must pay in full within 60 days. If the terms are simply net 30, then customers must pay within 30 days of the invoice date, and no discounts are offered for early payment.

Check Point 22.1

Suppose that a firm sells goods on terms of 2/10, net 20. On May 1 you buy goods from the company with an invoice value of $20,000. How much would you need to pay if you took the cash discount? What is the latest date on which the cash discount is available? By what date should you pay for your purchase if you decide not to take the cash discount?

For many items that are bought regularly, it is inconvenient to require separate payment for each delivery. A common solution is to pretend that all sales during the month in fact occur at the end of the month (EOM). Thus goods may be sold on terms of 8/10, EOM, net 60. This allows the customer a cash discount of 8 percent if the bill is paid within 10 days of the end of the month; otherwise, the full payment is due within 60 days of the invoice date.

When purchases are subject to seasonal fluctuations, manufacturers often encourage customers to take early delivery, allowing them to delay payment until the usual order season. This practice is known as *season dating*. For example, summer products might have terms of 2/10, net 30, but the invoice might be dated May 1, even if the sale takes place in February. The discount is then available until May 11, and the bill is not due until May 31.

What is the cost of using trade credit as a source of financing? Of course, an interest-free loan is always worth having. However, if you pass up a cash discount, the loan may prove to be very expensive. For example, a customer who buys on terms of 3/10, net 30, may decide to forgo the

A firm that buys on credit is in effect borrowing from its supplier. Trade credit is a form of short-term financing. Getting the goods or services without paying the cash is effectively an implicit loan from the supplier. The saved cash will be paid later, ending the loan.

cash discount and pay on the 30th day. The customer obtains an extra 20 days' credit by deferring payment from 10 to 30 days after the sale but pays about 3 percent more for the goods. This is equivalent to borrowing money at a rate of 74.3 percent a year.

To see why, consider an order of \$100. If the firm pays within 10 days, it gets a 3 percent discount, saving $.03 \times \$100 = \$3$, and pays only \$97. So during the first 10 days, the firm owes \$97 and effectively has an interest-free loan of \$97—it borrows \$97 and pays back only \$97. If it waits the full 30 days, it has to pay \$100. This extra 20 days of credit means that the loan of \$97 has to be repaid as \$100, so the implied interest rate is $\$100/\$97 - 1 = 3.09$ percent.

The implied rate can be calculated several other ways. The extra 20 days of credit increases the payment by the fraction $3/97 = .0309$, or 3.09 percent. Notice that this is also equal to the ratio of the cash discount rate/(1 − cash discount rate) $= .03/(1 - .03) = .0309$. Therefore, the implicit interest charged to extend the trade credit is 3.09 percent *per 20 days*. There are $365/20 = 18.25$ twenty-day periods in a year, so the effective annual rate of interest on the loan is $(1.0309)^{18.25} - 1 = .743$, or 74.3 percent.

Thus the implicit annual interest rate for customers who do not take the cash discount use the ratio of the cash discount to the discounted price can be calculated three ways but give the same answers. The third version is the more common use formula:

$$\textbf{Effective annual rate} = \left(\frac{\text{undiscounted price}}{\text{discounted price}}\right)^{365/\text{extra days' credit}} - 1$$

$$= \left(1 + \frac{\text{discount}}{\text{discounted price}}\right)^{365/\text{extra days' credit}} - 1 \qquad (22.1)$$

$$= \left(1 + \frac{\text{cash discount rate}}{1 - \text{cash discounted rate}}\right)^{365/\text{extra days' credit}} - 1$$

In all three versions, the term inside the bracket is one plus the percentage increase in price paid by a customer who forgoes the discount. This is the per-period implicit rate of interest. The period of the loan is the number of extra days of credit that you can obtain by forgoing the discount. In our example, this is 20 days. To annualize this rate, we compound the per-period rate by the number of periods in a year. Of course, any firm that delays payment beyond day 30 gains a cheaper loan but damages its reputation for creditworthiness.

EXAMPLE 22.1 TRADE CREDIT RATES

A customer purchases \$500 and the credit terms are 5/10, net 60. If the customer pays the bill within 10 days, they get the cash discount so the amount owed is $\$500 - .05 \times \$500 = \$500 - \$25 = \$475$. So the implied interest rate if the bill is paid within 10 days is zero.

If the customer chooses not to take the discount they receive an extra $60 - 10 = 50$ days credit. The interest rate for the 50 days of credit $.05/(1 - .05) = 5/95 = .05263$. Given the \$500 purchase, the interest rate can also be calculated as $1 - \$500/\$475 = .05263$. So the implied effective annual interest can be calculated as:

$$\text{Effective annual rate} = \left(1 + \frac{\text{cash discount rate}}{1 - \text{cash discount rate}}\right)^{365/\text{extra days' credit}} - 1$$

$$= \left(1 + \frac{.05}{1 - .05}\right)^{365/50} - 1 = .454, \text{ or } 45.4\%$$

In this case the customer who does not take the discount is effectively borrowing money at an annual interest rate of 45.4 percent.

You might wonder why the effective interest rate on trade credit is typically so high. Part of the rate should be viewed as compensation for the costs the firm anticipates in collecting from slow payers. After all, at such steep effective rates, most purchasers will choose to pay early and receive the discount. Therefore, you might interpret the choice to not to take the cash discount as a sign of financial difficulties. It makes sense to charge these firms a high rate of interest.

Check Point 22.2

The trade receivables of a firm are the trade payables of its customers. In Chapter 20 we talked about stretching payables as a source of financing. When payables are stretched, payment is delayed past its due date. What would be the effective annual interest rate in Example 22.1 if the customer did not pay until 80 days? Why has the rate changed? Why are customers tempted to stretch their payables?

LO3

22.2 CREDIT AGREEMENTS

open account Agreement whereby sales are made with no formal debt contract.

The terms of sale define the amount of credit but not the nature of the contract. Repetitive sales are almost always made on **open account** and involve only an implicit contract. There is simply a record in the seller's books and a receipt signed by the buyer.

Sometimes you might want a more formal agreement stating that the customer owes you money. When the order is very large and there is no complicated cash discount, the customer may be asked to sign a *promissory note*. This is just a straightforward IOU, worded along the following lines:

> Vancouver
> April 1, 2013
>
> Sixty days after date, ABC, Inc., promises to pay to the order of the XYZ Company ten thousand dollars ($10,000) for value received.
>
> Signature

Such an arrangement is not common but it does eliminate the possibility of any subsequent disputes about the amount and existence of the debt; the customer knows that he may be sued immediately for failure to pay on the due date.

If you want a clear commitment from the buyer, it is more useful to have it *before* you deliver the goods. In this case the common procedure is to arrange a *commercial draft*. This is simply jargon for an order to pay.[1] It works as follows. The seller prepares a draft ordering payment by the customer and sends this draft to the customer's bank. If immediate payment is required, the draft is termed a *sight draft*; otherwise it is known as a *time draft*. Depending on whether it is a sight or a time draft, the customer either tells the bank to pay up or acknowledges the debt by adding the word *accepted* and a signature. Once accepted, a time draft is like a postdated cheque and is called a *trade acceptance*. This trade acceptance is then forwarded to the seller, who holds it until the payment becomes due.

If the customer's credit is for any reason suspect, the seller may ask the customer to arrange for her bank to accept the time draft. In this case, the bank guarantees the customer's debt and the draft is called a *banker's acceptance*. Banker's acceptances are often used in overseas trade. They are actively bought and sold in the money market—the market for short-term high-quality debt.

If you sell goods to a customer who proves unable to pay, you cannot get your goods back. You simply become a general creditor similar to other unfortunate companies. You can avoid this situation by making a *conditional sale*, so that ownership of the goods remains with the seller until full payment is made. The conditional sale is common in Europe. In Canada it is used only for goods that are bought on instalment. In this case, if the customer fails to make the agreed number of payments, then the equipment can be immediately repossessed by the seller.

---

[1] For example, a cheque is an example of a draft. Whenever you write a cheque, you are ordering the bank to make a payment.

LO4 22.3 CREDIT ANALYSIS

credit analysis Procedure to determine the likelihood a customer will pay its bills.

There are a number of ways to find out whether customers are likely to pay their debts, that is, to carry out **credit analysis**. The most obvious indication is whether they have paid promptly in the past. Prompt payment is usually a good omen, but beware of the customer who establishes a high credit limit based on small payments, and then disappears, leaving you with a large unpaid bill.

If you are dealing with a new customer, you will probably check with a credit agency. Dun & Bradstreet, which is by far the largest of these agencies, provides credit ratings on 120 million businesses from around the world, including 1.5 million Canadian businesses. In addition to its rating service, Dun & Bradstreet provides, on request, a full credit report on a potential customer. Similarly, TransUnion Canada offers consumer credit-related products and services throughout Canada to its subscribers.

Credit agencies usually report the experience that other firms have had with your customer, but you can also get this information by contacting those firms directly or through a credit bureau.

Your bank can also make a credit check. It will contact the customer's bank and ask for information on the customer's average bank balance, access to bank credit, and general reputation.

In addition to checking with your customer's bank, it might make sense to check what everybody else in the financial community thinks about your customer's credit standing. Does that sound expensive? Not if your customer is a public company. You just look at Dominion Bond Rating Service's or Standard & Poor's rating for the customer's bonds.[2] You can also compare prices of these bonds to the prices of other firms' bonds. (Of course, the comparisons should be between bonds of similar maturity, coupon, and so on.) Finally, you can look at how the customer's stock price has been behaving recently. A sharp fall in price doesn't mean that the company is in trouble, but it does suggest that prospects are less bright than they were formerly.

FINANCIAL RATIO ANALYSIS

We have suggested a number of ways to check whether your customer is a good risk. You can ask your collection manager, a specialized credit agency, credit bureau, banker, or the financial community at large. But if you don't like relying on the judgment of others, you can do your own homework. Ideally this would involve a detailed analysis of the company's business prospects and financing, but this is usually too expensive. Therefore, credit analysts concentrate on the company's financial statements, using rough rules of thumb to judge whether the firm is a good credit risk. The rules of thumb are based on *financial ratios*. Chapter 4 described how these ratios are calculated and interpreted.

NUMERICAL CREDIT SCORING

Analyzing credit risk is like detective work. You have a lot of clues—some important, some fitting into a neat pattern, others contradictory. You must weigh these clues to come up with an overall judgment.

When the firm has a small, regular clientele, the credit manager can easily handle the process informally and make a judgment about what are often termed the *five Cs of credit*:

1. The customer's *character*
2. The customer's *capacity to pay*
3. The customer's *capital*

---

[2] Many large Canadian companies borrow regularly in the United States and other countries, and their bonds are rated by other prominent rating firms such as Moody's. We described bond ratings in Chapter 6, Section 6.6.

4. The *collateral* provided by the customer[3]
5. The *condition* of the customer's business

When the company is dealing directly with consumers or with a large number of small trade accounts, some streamlining is essential. In these cases a scoring system might be used to prescreen credit applications.

For example, if you apply for a credit card or a bank loan, you will be asked about your job, home, and financial position. The information you provide is used to calculate an overall credit score. Applicants who do not make the grade on the score are likely to be refused credit or subjected to more detailed analysis.

Banks and the credit departments of industrial firms also use mechanical credit scoring systems to cut the costs of assessing commercial credit applications. One bank claimed that by introducing a credit scoring system, it cut the cost of reviewing loan applications by two-thirds. It cited the case of an application for a $5,000 line of credit from a small business. A clerk entered information from the loan application into a computer and checked the firm's deposit balances with the bank, as well as the owner's personal and business credit files. Immediately the loan officer could see the applicant's score: 240 on a scale of 100 to 300, well above the bank's cutoff figure. All that remained for the bank was to check that there was nothing obviously suspicious about the application. "We don't want to lend to set up an alligator farm in the desert," said one bank official.[4]

Firms use several statistical techniques to separate the creditworthy customers from the impecunious ones. One common method employs *multiple discriminant analysis* to produce a measure of solvency called a *Z score*. For example, a study of Canadian firms by Edward Altman and Mario Lavallee suggested the following relationship between a firm's financial ratios and its creditworthiness (Z_C):[5]

$$Z_C = .972\frac{\text{net profit after tax}}{\text{total debt}} + .234\frac{\text{sales}}{\text{total assets}} - .531\frac{\text{total debt}}{\text{total assets}}$$
$$+ 1.002\frac{\text{current assets}}{\text{current liabilities}} + .612 \times (\text{rate of growth of equity} - \text{rate of growth of assets})$$

Net profit after tax (NOPAT) is net income plus after-tax interest expense. This equation did a good job of distinguishing between the bankrupt and non-bankrupt firms. Of the former, 85.2 percent had Z scores *less* than 1.626 the year before they went bankrupt. In contrast, 81.5 percent of the non-bankrupt firms had Z scores *above* this level.[6] However, now that Canadian public companies have to use IFRS when preparing their financial statements, it is quite likely that the Z score formula will need to be revised to reflect the impact of IFRS on firms' financial statements.

---

[3] For example, the customer can offer bonds as collateral. These bonds can then be seized by the seller if the customer fails to pay.

[4] Quoted in S. Hansell, "Need a Loan? Ask the Computer; 'Credit Scoring' Changes Small-Business Lending," *The New York Times*, April 18, 1995, D1.

[5] E.I. Altman and M. Lavallee, "Business Failure Classification in Canada," *Journal of Business Administration* 12 (Fall 1980): 147–164.

[6] E.I. Altman, "Financial Ratios, Discriminant Analysis and the Prediction of Corporate Bankruptcy," *Journal of Finance* 23 (September 1968): 589–609, provides this equation for U.S. firms:

$$Z = 3.3\frac{\text{EBIT}}{\text{total assets}} + 1.0\frac{\text{sales}}{\text{total assets}} + .6\frac{\text{market value of equity}}{\text{total book debt}}$$
$$+ 1.4\frac{\text{retained earnings}}{\text{total assets}} + 1.2\frac{\text{working capital}}{\text{total assets}}$$

The cut-off Z score is 2.7. Of the firms going bankrupt, 94 percent has a Z score less than 2.7. Of the non-bankrupt firms, 97 percent had scores above 2.7.

EXAMPLE 22.2 **CREDIT SCORING**

Consider a firm with the following financial ratios:

$$\frac{\text{Net profit after tax}}{\text{Total debt}} = .34 \quad \frac{\text{Sales}}{\text{Total assets}} = 4.5 \quad \frac{\text{Total debt}}{\text{Total assets}} = .58$$

$$\frac{\text{Current assets}}{\text{Current liabilities}} = 1.2 \text{ rate of growth of equity} - \text{rate of growth of assets} = .3$$

The firm's Z score is thus

$$(.972 \times .34) + (.234 \times 4.5) - (.531 \times .58) + (1.002 \times 1.2) + (.612 \times .3) = 2.4615$$

This score is above the cut-off level for predicting bankruptcy and, thus, would be considered favourable in terms of evaluating the firm's creditworthiness.

The nearby Finance in Action box describes how statistical scoring systems similar to the Z score can provide timely first-cut estimates of creditworthiness. These assessments can streamline the credit decision and free up labour for other, less mechanical tasks. These scoring systems can be used in conjunction with large databases, such as Dun & Bradstreet's, to provide quick credit scores for thousands of firms.

WHEN TO STOP LOOKING FOR CLUES

Credit analysis is worthwhile only if the expected savings exceed the cost.

We told you earlier where to start looking for clues about a customer's creditworthiness, but we never said anything about when to stop. A detailed credit analysis costs money, so you need to keep in mind one basic principle: that credit analysis is worthwhile only if the expected savings exceed the cost.

This simple rule has two immediate implications:

1. *Don't undertake a full credit analysis unless the order is big enough to justify it.* If the maximum profit on an order is $100, it is foolish to spend $200 to check whether the customer is a good prospect. Rely on a less detailed credit check for the smaller orders and save your energy and your money for the big orders.
2. *Undertake a full credit analysis for the doubtful orders.* If a preliminary check suggests that a customer is almost certainly a good prospect, then searching further is unlikely to justify the costs. That is why many firms use a numerical credit scoring system to identify borderline applicants, who are then the subject of a full-blown detailed credit check. Other applicants are either accepted or rejected without further question.

LO5 22.4 THE CREDIT DECISION

credit policy Standards set to determine the amount and nature of credit to extend to customers.

The decision to offer credit depends on the probability of payment. You should grant credit if the expected profit is greater than the profit from refusing.

You have taken the first three steps toward an effective credit operation. In other words, you have fixed your terms of sale; you have decided whether to sell on open account or to ask your customers to sign an IOU; and you have established a procedure for estimating the probability of customers paying up. Your next step is to decide on **credit policy**.

If there is no possibility of repeat orders, the credit decision is relatively simple. Figure 22.1 summarizes your choice. On the one hand, you can refuse credit and pass up the sale. In this case you make neither profit nor loss. The alternative is to offer credit. If you offer credit and the customer pays, you benefit by the profit margin on the sale. If the customer defaults, you lose the cost of the goods delivered.

Suppose that the probability that the customer will pay up is p. If the customer does pay, you receive additional revenues (REV), and you deliver goods that you incurred costs to produce; your net gain is the present value of REV − COST. Unfortunately, you can't be certain that the customer will pay; there is a probability $(1 - p)$ of default. Default means you receive nothing

Finance in Action

Credit Scoring: What Your Lender Won't Tell You

To hear bankers tell it, credit scoring is the best thing to happen to small-business borrowers since the invention of compound interest. Forget haggling over things like how well your business is doing or what your competitors are up to. Just hand in some predetermined data about yourself and your company, let the computer crunch the numbers, and voila: Out comes a "credit score" that predicts the chances that you'll actually pay off the loan. Score high enough, and you get approved, sometimes within minutes.

Scoring is already ubiquitous in consumer lending, and 22 of the 25 biggest players in the small-business loan market use the system, according to Fair, Isaac & Co., a pioneer in the development of credit-scoring software. Almost any loan of $50,000 or less issued by a national financial services company will have gone through a credit-scoring system.

Credit-scoring models assign points for up to 20 factors. The more points you get, the better credit risk you represent. The best-known credit-scoring models are provided by Fair, Isaac. The score on its Small Business Scoring Service ranges from 50 to 350, with most small businesses falling into the 150 to 250 area. While lenders set their own cutoff points, if you score above 220, that's generally good, while scores below 170 are considered high risk.

The overriding factor in a small-business credit score is your personal credit history. Specifically, the system looks at whether you pay your personal bills on time. The later you pay, the fewer points you get, and the more bills you pay late, the more your score gets knocked down.

The next key input is how much credit you've already got access to and balances on your accounts. If lines of credit are maxed out, lenders worry that there is little room to maneuver if the business runs into trouble. Other major red flags include bankruptcies, debts turned over to a collection agency, liens, and even overdue child-support payments. You can even get penalized for shopping too hard for credit.

Finally, specific business characteristics are weighed. They include the size of the company; its age; the industry in which it does business; and whether it's a corporation, partnership, or sole proprietorship. A sole proprietorship gets fewer points than a partnership, and a partnership gets fewer points than a corporation. After all, if you're a sole proprietor and you get hit by a bus, all bets are off on your business. By the same token, a manufacturer gets higher points than bars or restaurants because it's less likely to go under quickly.

Source: V.M. Kahn, "Credit Scoring: What Your Lender Won't Tell You," *BusinessWeek*, May 22, 2000, F30.

but still incur the additional costs of the delivered goods. The *expected profit*[7] from the two sources of action is therefore as follows:

Action	*Expected Profit*	
Refuse credit:	0	**(22.2)**
Grant credit:	$p \times \text{PV(REV} - \text{COST)} - (1 - p) \times \text{PV(COST)}$	

You should grant credit if the expected profit from doing so is positive.

FIGURE 22.1
If you refuse credit, you make neither profit nor loss. If you offer credit, there is a probability (p) that the customer will pay and you will make REV − COST; there is a probability ($1 - p$) that the customer will default and you will lose COST.

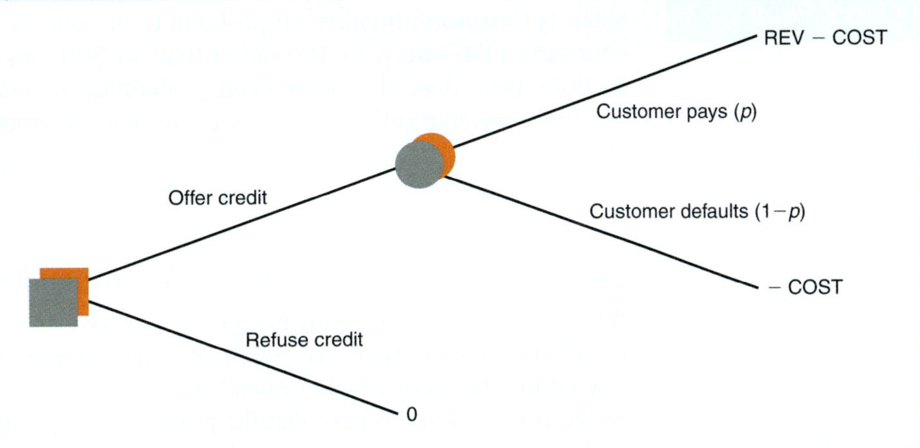

[7] Notice that we use the present values of costs and revenues. This is because there are sometimes significant lags between costs incurred and revenues generated. Also, while we follow convention in referring to the "expected profit" of the decision, it should be clear that our equation for expected profit is, in fact, the net present value of the decision to grant credit. As we emphasized in Chapter 1, the manager's task is to add value, not to maximize accounting profits.

EXAMPLE 22.3 THE CREDIT DECISION

Consider the case of the Cast Iron Company. On each non-delinquent sale, Cast Iron receives revenues with a present value of $1,200 and incurs costs with a present value of $1,000. Therefore, the company's expected profit if it offers credit is

$$p \times \text{PV(REV} - \text{COST)} - (1 - p) \times \text{PV(COST)} = p \times 200 - (1 - p) \times 1{,}000$$

If the probability of collection is 5/6, Cast Iron can expect to break even:

$$\text{Expected profit} = 5/6 \times 200 - (1 - 5/6) \times 1{,}000 = 0$$

Thus Cast Iron's policy should be to grant credit whenever the chances of collection are better than 5 out of 6.

In this last example, the net present value of granting credit is positive if the probability of collection exceeds 5/6. In general, this break-even probability can be found by setting the net present value of granting credit equal to zero, and solving for p:

$$p \times \text{PV(REV} - \text{COST)} - (1 - p) \times \text{PV(COST)} = 0$$

It turns out that the formula for break-even probability is simply the ratio of the present value of costs to revenues. Break-even probability of collection, then, is

$$p = \frac{\text{PV(COST)}}{\text{PV(REV)}}$$

and the break-even probability of *default* is

$$(1 - p) = 1 - \text{PV(COST)/PV(REV)} = \text{PV(PROFIT)/PV(REV)}$$

In other words, the break-even probability of default is simply the profit margin on each sale. If the default probability is larger than the profit margin, you should not extend credit.

Think what this implies. Companies that operate on low profit margins should be cautious about granting credit to high-risk customers. Firms with high margins can afford to deal with more doubtful ones.

Check Point 22.3

What is Cast-Iron's break-even probability of collection if the present value of the revenues from the sale is $1,100 rather than $1,200 and the present value of cost are still $1,000? Why does the break-even probability increase? Use your answer to decide whether firms that sell high- or low-profit-margin goods should be more willing to issue credit.

CREDIT DECISIONS WITH REPEAT ORDERS

What effect does the possibility of repeat orders have on your credit decision? One of the reasons for offering credit today is that you might acquire a good, regular customer.

Cast Iron has been asked to extend credit to a new customer. You can find little information on the firm, and you believe that the probability of payment is no better than .8. If you grant credit, the expected profit on this order is

$$\begin{aligned}\text{Expected profit on initial order} &= p \times \text{PV(REV} - \text{COST)} - (1 - p) \times \text{PV(COST)} \\ &= (.8 \times 200) - (.2 \times 1{,}000) = -\$40\end{aligned}$$

You decide to refuse credit.

If one sale may lead to profitable repeat sales, the firm should be inclined to grant credit on the initial purchase.

This is the correct decision *if* there is no chance of a repeat order. But now consider the future. If the customer does pay up, there will be a reorder next year. Having paid once, the customer will seem less of a risk. For this reason, any repeat orders are very profitable.

Think back to Chapter 10, and you will recognize that the credit decision bears many similarities to our earlier discussion of real options. By granting credit now, the firm retains the option to grant credit on an entire sequence of potentially profitable repeat sales. This option can be very valuable and can tilt the decision toward granting credit. Even a dubious prospect may warrant some initial credit if there is a chance that it will develop into a profitable steady customer.

EXAMPLE 22.4 CREDIT DECISIONS WITH REPEAT ORDERS

To illustrate, let's look at an extreme case. Suppose that if a customer pays up on the first sale, you can be *sure* you will have a regular and completely reliable customer. In this case, the value of such a customer is not the profit of one order but an entire stream of profits from repeat purchases. For example, suppose that the customer will make one purchase each year from Cast Iron. If the discount rate is 10 percent and the profit on each order is \$200 per year, then the present value of an indefinite stream of business from a good customer is not \$200 but \$200/.10 = \$2,000. There is a probability (p) that Cast Iron will secure a good customer with a value of \$2,000. There is a probability of $(1 - p)$ that the customer will default, resulting in a loss of \$1,000. So, once we recognize the benefits of securing a good and permanent customer, the expected profit from granting credit is

$$\text{Expected profit} = (p \times 2{,}000) - (1 - p) \times 1{,}000$$

This is positive for any probability of collection above .33. Thus the break-even probability falls from 5/6 to 1/3.

Check Point 22.4

How will the break-even probability vary with the discount rate? Try a rate of 20 percent in Example 22.4. What is the thinking behind your answer?

EXAMPLE 22.5 THE CREDIT DECISION: A COMPREHENSIVE LOOK

Careerbuild Publishers sells motivational guides on how to be successful at different careers. The books are priced at \$125. The present value of the cost of producing one such career enhancement book is \$100. Careerbuild sells the books on terms of net 30 and estimates that about 10 percent of all orders will not be collectible. If the interest rate is 1 percent per month, should the firm extend credit for a one-time order?

To work through this problem, we need to first determine present values of production costs and revenues. We know the present value of production costs to be \$100. The present value of revenues is \$125/1.01 = \$123.76. The expected profit from a sale will be

$$\begin{aligned} &.9(\$123.76 - \$100) - .1(\$100) \\ &= \$21.38 - \$10 = \$11.38 \end{aligned}$$

What would be the steps to figure out the breakeven probability of collection? We know that breakeven probability, which we denote as p, implies zero expected profits. We solve for p as follows:

$$\begin{aligned} p(\$123.76 - \$100) - (1 - p)(\$100) &= 0 \\ \text{or } 23.76p - \$100 + 100p &= 0 \\ \text{or } p = 100/123.76 &= .808 \end{aligned}$$

(Continued)

(Concluded)

Let us now see what happens with repeat orders. In such instances, a paying customer will potentially generate a perpetuity of profits of \$123.76 − \$100 = \$23.76 per month. At an interest rate of 1 percent per month, the present value of the perpetuity is \$23.76/.01 = \$2,376. If we continue to assume a 10 percent default rate, the present value of a sale will work out to

$$.9(\$2{,}376) - .1(\$100) = \$2{,}138.4 - \$10 = \$2{,}128.4$$

Notice that for repeat orders it is much easier to justify extending credit to paying customers. To calculate the breakeven probability of collection, p, in the case of repeat orders, we solve for

$$p(\$2{,}376) - (1 - p)(\$100) = 0$$
$$\text{or } 2{,}376p - \$100 + 100p = 0$$
$$\text{or } p = 100/2{,}476 = .04$$

So, for repeat orders, the probability of payments needs to be greater than only 4 percent to justify extending credit.

EVALUATING A CREDIT POLICY SWITCH

Let us look at an example to help us evaluate the efficacy of switching from a cash-only policy to a new credit policy.

EXAMPLE 22.6 THE CREDIT DECISION: EVALUATING A CREDIT POLICY SWITCH

Start-me-up Inc. specializes in manufacturing a type of component used in automotive transmissions. To help boost its unit sales, the firm is contemplating switching from a cash-only policy to a new credit policy of net 30 days on sales. The cost of capital rate for Start-me-up is 1 percent per month. The firm's price per unit of automotive transmission parts is \$120, and variable cost per unit is \$95. These numbers are likely to remain unchanged even after a switch to a new credit policy. The new credit policy is, however, likely to increase unit sales from 900 to 1,000 per month. Notice that by introducing the new credit policy, Start-me-up has, in effect, increased its sales by 100 additional units per month in perpetuity. The incremental cash inflow each month from the extra sales is 100(\$120 − \$95) = \$2,500. Since this amount is expected to be generated in perpetuity, the present value of this perpetuity is \$2,500/.01 = \$250,000.

What about the cost of switching to the new credit policy? One component of this cost is the variable cost associated with producing the extra units; that is, 100 × \$95 = \$9,500. Another component of the cost is the monthly sales revenue under the old policy, which, with the new policy, will no longer be available to Start-me-up in the same month but only in the following month; this works out to \$120 × 900 = \$108,000. The total cost of the switch is, therefore, \$9,500 + \$108,000 = \$117,500.

The net present value of the credit policy switch is \$250,000 − \$117,500 = \$132,500. Clearly, in this instance, the switch in credit policy is worthwhile.

SOME GENERAL PRINCIPLES

Real-life situations are generally far more complex than our simple examples. Customers are not all good or all bad. Many pay late consistently; you get your money, but it costs more to collect, and you lose a few months' interest. And estimating the probability that a customer will pay up is far from an exact science.

Like almost all financial decisions, credit allocation involves a strong dose of judgment. Our examples are intended as reminders of the issues involved rather than as "cookbook" formulas. Here are the basic things to remember:

1. *Maximize profit.* As credit manager, your job is not to minimize the number of bad accounts; it is to maximize profits. You are faced with a trade-off. The best that can happen is that the

customer pays promptly; the worst is default. In the one case the firm receives the full additional revenues from the sale less the additional costs; in the other it receives nothing and loses the costs. You must weigh the chances of these alternative outcomes. If the margin of profit is high, you are justified in a liberal credit policy; if it is low, you cannot afford many bad debts.

2. *Concentrate on the dangerous accounts.* You should not expend the same effort on analyzing all credit decisions. If an application is small or clear-cut, your decision should be largely routine; if it is large or dubious, you might do better to move forward to a detailed credit appraisal. Most credit managers don't make credit decisions on an order-by-order basis. Instead they set a credit limit for each customer. The sales representative is required to refer the order for approval only if the customer exceeds this limit.
3. *Look beyond the immediate order.* Sometimes it may be worth accepting a relatively poor risk as long as there is a likelihood that the customer will grow into a regular and reliable buyer. (This is why credit card companies are eager to sign up university and college students even though few students can point to an established credit history.) New businesses must be prepared to incur more bad debts than established businesses because they have not yet formed relationships with low-risk customers. This is part of the cost of building up a good customer list.

LO6 22.5 COLLECTION POLICY

It would be nice if all customers paid their bills by the due date. But they don't, and since you may also "stretch" your payables, you can't really blame them.

Slow payers impose two costs on the firm. First, they require the firm to spend more resources in collecting payments. They also force the firm to invest more in working capital. Recall from Chapter 4 that trade receivables are proportional to the average collection period (also known as days' sales in receivables):

$$\text{Trade receivables} = \text{daily sales} \times \text{average collection period}$$

When your customers stretch payables, you end up with a longer collection period and a greater investment in trade receivables. Thus you must establish a **collection policy**.

collection policy Procedures to collect and monitor receivables.

The credit manager keeps a record of payment experiences with each customer. In addition, the manager monitors overdue payments by drawing up a schedule of the aging of receivables. The **aging schedule** classifies trade receivables by the length of time they are outstanding. This may look similar to Table 22.1. The table shows that customer A, for example, is fully current: no bills are outstanding for more than a month. Customer Z, however, might present problems, as there are $15,000 in bills that have been outstanding for more than three months.

aging schedule Classification of trades receivables by time outstanding.

When a customer is in arrears, the usual procedure is to send a *statement of account* and to follow this at intervals with increasingly insistent letters, telephone calls, or fax messages. If none of these has any effect, most companies turn the debt over to a collection agency or an attorney.

TABLE 22.1 An aging schedule of receivables.

Customer	Less Than 1 Month	1–2 Months	2–3 Months	More Than 3 Months	Total Owed
A	$ 10,000	$ 0	$ 0	$ 0	$ 10,000
B	8,000	3,000	0	0	11,000
•	•	•	•	•	•
•	•	•	•	•	•
•	•	•	•	•	•
Z	5,000	4,000	6,000	15,000	30,000
Total	$200,000	$40,000	$15,000	$43,000	$298,000

Check Point 22.5 Suppose a customer who buys goods on terms 1/10, net 45, always forgoes the cash discount and pays on the 45th day after sale. If the firm typically buys $10,000 of goods per month, spread evenly over the month, what will the aging schedule look like?

Good collection policy balances conflicting goals. The company wants cordial relations with its customers. It also wants them to pay their bills on time.

There is always a potential conflict of interest between the collection department and the sales department. Sales representatives commonly complain that they no sooner win new customers than the collection department frightens them off with threatening letters. The collection manager, on the other hand, bemoans the fact that the sales force is concerned only with winning orders and does not care whether the goods are subsequently paid for. This conflict is another example of the agency problem introduced in Chapter 1.

There are instances of cooperation between sales managers and the financial managers who worry about collections. For example, the specialty chemicals division of a major pharmaceutical company actually made a business loan to an important customer that had been suddenly cut off by its bank. The pharmaceutical company bet it knew its customer better than the bank did—and it was right. The customer arranged alternative bank financing, paid back the pharmaceutical company, and became a more loyal customer. This is a nice example of financial management supporting sales.

22.6 SUMMARY

1. **What are the usual steps in credit management?** LO1

The first step in credit management is to set normal **terms of sale**. This means that you must decide the length of the payment period and the size of any cash discounts. In most industries these conditions are standardized.

Your second step is to decide the form of the contract with your customer. Most domestic sales are made on **open account**. In this case the only evidence that the customer owes you money is the entry in your ledger and a receipt signed by the customer. Sometimes, you may require a more formal commitment before you deliver the goods. For example, the supplier may arrange for the customer to provide a trade acceptance.

The third task is to assess each customer's creditworthiness. When you have made an assessment of the customer's credit standing, the fourth step is to establish sensible credit policy. Finally, once the credit policy is set, you need to establish a collection policy to identify and pursue slow payers.

2. **How do we measure the implicit interest rate on credit?** LO2

The effective interest rate for customers who buy goods on credit rather than taking the discount for quicker payment is

$$\left(1 + \frac{\text{discount}}{\text{discounted price}}\right)^{365/\text{extra days' credit}} - 1$$

3. **When does it make sense to ask the customer for a formal IOU?** LO3

When a customer places a large order, and you want to eliminate the possibility of any subsequent disputes about the existence, amount, and scheduled payment date of the debt, a formal IOU such as a signed commercial draft may be appropriate.

4. **How do firms assess the probability that a customer will pay?** LO4

   Credit analysis is the process of deciding which customers are likely to pay their bills. There are various sources of information: your own experience with the customer, the experience of other creditors, the assessment of a credit agency, a check with the customer's bank, the market value of the customer's securities, and an analysis of the customer's financial statements. Firms that handle a large volume of credit information often use a formal system for combining the various sources into an overall credit score.

5. **How do firms decide whether it makes sense to grant credit to a customer?** LO5

   Credit policy refers to the decision to extend credit to a customer. The job of the credit manager is not to minimize the number of bad debts; it is to maximize profits. This means that you need to weigh the odds that the customer will pay, providing you with a profit, against the odds that the customer will default, resulting in a loss. Remember not to be too short-sighted when reckoning the expected profit. It is often worth accepting the marginal applicant if there is a chance the applicant might become a regular and reliable customer.

6. **What is a firm's collection policy, and how is it implemented?** LO6

   If credit is granted, the next problem is to set a **collection policy**. This requires tact and judgment. You want to be firm with the truly delinquent customer, but you don't want to offend the good one by writing demanding letters just because a cheque has been delayed in the mail. You will find it easier to spot troublesome accounts if you keep a careful **aging schedule** of outstanding accounts.

Related Web Links

nacm.org Site of the National Association of Credit Management

creditedu.org Site of the Credit Institute of Canada

dnb.com Dun & Bradstreet's site; the premier guide to corporate credit decisions

creditworthy.com Useful tips and online resources for credit management

tuc.ca TransUnion Canada

strategis.gc.ca Site maintained by Industry Canada, providing a variety of trade, business, and consumer information

jaxworks.com/zscore2.htm To calculate *Z* scores

Key Terms

aging schedule	713	credit analysis	706	open account	705
collection policy	713	credit policy	708	terms of sale	703

Questions and Problems

connect Practise and learn online with *Connect*. Questions with online Excel templates or datasets are marked with ✎.

*Answers in Appendix B

BASIC

*1. **Trade Credit Rates.** Company X sells on a 1/20, net 60, basis. Customer Y buys goods with an invoice of $1,000. (LO2)
   a. How much can Y deduct from the bill if it pays on day 20?
   b. How many extra days of credit can Y receive if it passes up the cash discount?
   c. What is the effective annual rate of interest if Y pays on the due date rather than day 20?

2. **Terms of Sale.** Complete the following passage by selecting the appropriate terms from the following list (some terms may be used more than once): acceptance, open, commercial, trade, Canada, his or her own, note, draft, account, promissory, bank, banker's, the customer's. (LO1)

Most goods are sold on _____ _____. In this case the only evidence of the debt is a record in the seller's books and a signed receipt. When the order is very large, the customer may be asked to sign a(n) _____ _____, which is just a simple IOU. An alternative is for the seller to arrange a(n) _____ _____ ordering payment by the customer. In order to obtain the goods, the customer must acknowledge this order and sign the document. This signed acknowledgment is known as a(n) _____ _____. Sometimes the seller may also ask _____ _____ bank to sign the document. In this case it is known as a(n) _____ _____.

3. **Terms of Sale.** Indicate which firm, of each pair, you would expect to grant shorter or longer credit periods: (LO4)
   a. One firm sells hardware; the other bread.
   b. One firm's customers have an inventory turnover ratio of 10; the other's a turnover of 15.
   c. One firm sells mainly to electric utilities; the other mainly to fashion boutiques.

4. **Payment Lag.** The lag between purchase date and the date at which payment is due is known as the *terms lag*. The lag between the due date and the date on which the buyer actually pays is termed the *due lag*, and the lag between the purchase and actual payment dates is the *pay lag*. Thus

   $$\text{Pay lag} = \text{terms lag} + \text{due lag}$$

   State how you would expect the following events to affect each type of lag: (LO5)
   *a. The company imposes a service charge on late payers.
   b. A recession causes customers to be short of cash.
   *c. The company changes its terms from net 10 to net 20.

5. **Trade Credit Rates.** A firm currently offers terms of sale of 3/20, net 40. What effect will the following actions have on the implicit interest rate charged to customers that pass up the cash discount? State whether the implicit interest rate will increase or decrease. (LO2)
   a. The terms are changed to 4/20, net 40.
   b. The terms are changed to 3/30, net 40.
   c. The terms are changed to 3/20, net 30.

INTERMEDIATE

*6. **Trade Credit and Receivables.** A firm offers terms of 2/15, net 30. Currently, two-thirds of all customers take advantage of the trade discount; the remainder pay bills at the due date. (LO5)
   a. What will be the firm's typical value for its trade receivables period? (See Section 20.2 for a review of the trade receivables period.)
   b. What is the average investment in trade receivables if annual sales are $20 million?
   c. What would likely happen to the firm's trade receivables period if it changed its terms to 3/15, net 30?

7. **Terms of Sale.** Microbiotics currently sells all of its frozen dinners cash on delivery but believes it can increase sales by offering supermarkets one month of free credit. The price per carton is $50 and the cost per carton is $40. (LO5)
   a. If unit sales will increase from 1,000 cartons to 1,060 per month, should the firm offer the credit? The interest rate is 1 percent per month, and all customers will pay their bills.
   b. What if the interest rate is 1.5 percent per month?
   c. What if the interest rate is 1.5 percent per month, but the firm offers the credit only as a special deal to new customers, while old customers continue to pay cash on delivery?

*8. **Credit Decision/Repeat Sales.** Locust Software sells computer training packages to its business customers at a price of $101. The cost of production (in present value terms) is $95. Locust sells its packages on terms of net 30 and estimates that about 7 percent of all orders will be uncollectible. An order comes in for 20 units. The interest rate is 1 percent per month. (LO5)
   a. Should the firm extend credit if this is a one-time order? The sale will not be made unless credit is extended.
   b. What is the break-even probability of collection?
   c. Now suppose that if a customer pays this month's bill, it will place an identical order in each month indefinitely and can be safely assumed to pose no risk of default. Should credit be extended?
   d. What is the break-even probability of collection in the repeat-sales case?

9. **Credit Decision.** Look back at Example 22.3. Cast Iron's costs have increased from $1,000 to $1,050. Assuming there is no possibility of repeat orders, and that the probability of successful collection from the customer is $p = .9$, answer the following: (LO5)
   a. Should Cast Iron grant or refuse credit?
   b. What is the break-even probability of collection?

10. **Credit Analysis.** Financial ratios were described in Chapter 4. If you were the credit manager, to which financial ratios would you pay most attention? (LO4)

11. **Credit Decision.** The Branding Iron Company sells its irons for $50 apiece wholesale. Production cost is $40 per iron. There is a 25 percent chance that a prospective customer will go bankrupt within the next half year. The customer orders 1,000 irons and asks for 6 months' credit. Should you accept the order? Assume a 10 percent per year discount rate, no chance of a repeat order, and that the customer will pay either in full or not at all. (LO5)

12. **Credit Policy.** As treasurer of the Universal Bed Corporation, Aristotle Procrustes is worried about his bad debt ratio, which is currently running at 6 percent. He believes that imposing a more stringent credit policy might reduce sales by 5 percent and reduce the bad debt ratio to 4 percent. If the cost of goods sold is 80 percent of the selling price, should Mr. Procrustes adopt the more stringent policy? (LO5)

13. **Credit Decision/Repeat Sales.** Surf City sells its network browsing software for $15 per copy to computer software distributors and allows its customers 1 month to pay their bills. The cost of the software is $10 per copy. The industry is very new and unsettled, however, and the probability that a new customer granted credit will go bankrupt within the next month is 25 percent. The firm is considering switching to a cash-on-delivery credit policy to reduce its exposure to defaults on trade credit. The discount rate is 1 percent per month. (LO5)
    a. Should the firm switch to a cash-on-delivery policy? If it does so, its sales will fall by 40 percent.
    b. How would your answer change if a customer that is granted credit pays its bills, and is expected to generate repeat orders with negligible likelihood of default for each of the next six months? Similarly, customers that pay cash also will generate on average six months of repeat sales.

*14. **Credit Policy.** A firm currently makes only cash sales. It estimates that allowing trade credit on terms of net 30 would increase monthly sales from 200 to 220 units per month. The price per unit is $101 and the cost (in present value terms) is $80. The interest rate is 1 percent per month.
    a. Should the firm change its credit policy? (LO5)
    b. Would your answer to part (a) change if 5 percent of all customers fail to pay their bills under the new credit policy? (LO5)
    c. What if 5 percent of only the new customers fail to pay their bills? The current customers take advantage of the 30 days of free credit but remain safe credit risks. (LO5)
    d. If a firm allows trade credit, does it need a collection policy? (LO6)

CHALLENGE

*15. **Credit Analysis.** Use the data in Example 22.3. Now suppose, however, that 10 percent of Cast Iron's customers are slow payers, and that slow payers have a probability of 30 percent of defaulting on their bills. If it costs $5 to determine whether a customer has been a prompt or slow payer in the past, should Cast Iron undertake such a check? *Hint:* What is the expected savings from the credit check? It will depend on both the probability of uncovering a slow payer and the savings from denying these payers credit. (LO5)

16. **Credit Analysis.** Look back at the previous problem, but now suppose that if a customer defaults on a payment, you can eventually collect about half the amount owed to you. Will you be more or less tempted to pay for a credit check once you account for the possibility of partial recovery of debts? (LO5)

*17. **Credit Policy.** Jim Khana, the credit manager of Velcro Saddles, is reappraising the company's credit policy. Velcro sells on terms of net 30. Cost of goods sold is 85 percent of sales. Velcro classifies customers on a scale of 1 to 4. During the past five years, the collection experience was as follows: (LO5)

Classification	Defaults as Percentage of Sales	Average Collection Period in Days for Non-defaulting Accounts
1	0	45
2	2	42
3	10	50
4	20	80

The average interest rate was 15 percent. What conclusions (if any) can you draw about Velcro's credit policy? Should the firm deny credit to any of its customers? What other factors should be taken into account before changing this policy?

18. **Credit Analysis.** Galenic, Inc., is a wholesaler for a range of pharmaceutical products. Before deducting any losses from bad debts, Galenic operates on a profit margin of 5 percent. For a long time the firm has employed a numerical credit scoring system based on a small number of key ratios. This has resulted in a bad debt ratio of 1 percent.

    Galenic has recently commissioned a detailed statistical study of the payment record of its customers over the past eight years and, after considerable experimentation, has identified five variables that could form the basis of a new credit-scoring system. On the evidence of the past eight years, Galenic calculates that for every 10,000 accounts it would have experienced the following default rates: (LO5)

Credit Score Under Proposed System	Number of Accounts Defaulting	Paying	Total
Better than 80	60	9,100	9,160
Worse than 80	40	800	840
Total	100	9,900	10,000

By refusing credit to firms with a poor credit score (less than 80), Galenic calculates that it would reduce its bad debt ratio to 60/9,160 net, or just under .7 percent. While this may not seem like a big deal, Galenic's credit manager reasons that this is equivalent to a decrease of one-third in the bad debt ratio and would result in a significant improvement in the profit margin.

a. What is Galenic's current profit margin allowing for bad debts?
b. Assuming that the firm's estimates of default rates are right, how would the new credit-scoring system affect profits?
c. Why might you suspect that Galenic's estimates of default rates will not be realized in practice?
d. Suppose that one of the variables in the proposed new scoring system is whether the customer has an existing account with Galenic (new customers are more likely to default). How would this affect your assessment of the proposal? *Hint:* Think about repeat sales.

19. **Internet.** Log in to the Bankruptcy Calculator at **www.jaxworks.com/calc2a.htm** and calculate the *Z* scores for two U.S. companies (say Exxon and American Airlines). You will need to find some financial data for each firm, which you can get from its annual report, available on each company's Web site. Another convenient source for U.S. companies is **finance.yahoo.com**. At this site, go to the company's profile and then click on the highlights page. Which of your two companies appears more likely to encounter financial distress? (LO4)

20. **Internet.** When credit managers need a credit check on a small business, they often look up the Dun & Bradstreet report on the company. Go to **www.dnb.com**, put your mouse on the "Small Business" button, then click "Credit Report on Another Business." In the box with the heading "Comprehensive Insight Plus Report" click on "View a sample report." Review the company snapshot and supporting pages of information. On the basis of this report, would you be prepared to extend credit to this company? Why or why not? (LO4)

21. **Internet.** Go to **finance.yahoo.com**. Compare and contrast the trade (account) receivables turnover and days' sales outstanding of Winn-Dixie Stores Inc., Dean Foods Co., and Lifeway Foods Inc. Read the business profiles for information that might explain the level of each company's investment in trade receivables. (LO4)

Solutions to Check Points

22.1 To get the cash discount, you have to pay the bill within 10 days, that is, by May 11. With the 2 percent discount, the amount that needs to be paid by May 11 is $\$20,000 \times .98 = \$19,600$. If you forgo the cash discount, you do not have to pay your bill until May 21, but on that date, the amount due is $20,000.

22.2 The cash discount in this case is 5 percent and the customer who stretches their payables and does not pay until day 80 receives an $80 - 10 = 70$ days of extra credit. So the effective annual interest is

Effective annual rate

$$= \left(1 + \frac{\text{cash discount rate}}{1 - \text{cash discount rate}}\right)^{365/\text{extra days' credit}} - 1$$

$$= \left(1 + \frac{.05}{.95}\right)^{365/70} - 1 = .307, \text{ or } 30.7\%$$

In this case the customer who delays paying is effectively borrowing money at an annual interest rate of 30.7 percent. This is lower than the rate in Example 22.1, because the customer is getting more days of credit with the same cost of giving up the cash discount. Companies short of funds are tempted to stretch their payables, because they can borrow longer at an effectively lower interest rate.

22.3 The present value of costs is still $1,000. Present value of revenues is now $1,100. The break-even probability is

$$p = \frac{\text{PV(COST)}}{\text{PV(REV)}} = \frac{1{,}000}{1{,}100} = .909$$

The break-even probability is higher because the profit margin is now lower. The firm cannot afford as high a bad-debt ratio as before since it is not making as much on its successful sales. We conclude that high-margin goods will be offered with more liberal credit terms.

22.4 The higher the discount rate the less important future sales are. Because the value of repeat sales is lower, the break-even probability on the initial sale is higher. For instance, we saw that the break-even probability was one-third when the discount rate was 10 percent. When the discount rate is 20 percent, the value of a perpetual flow of repeat sales falls to $\$200/.20 = \$1{,}000$, and the break-even probability increases to one-half:

$$1/2 \times \$1{,}000 - 1/2 \times \$1{,}000 = 0$$

22.5 The customer pays bills 45 days after the invoice date. Because goods are purchased daily, at any given time there will be bills outstanding with "ages" ranging from 1 to 45 days. At any given time, the customer will have 30 days' worth of purchases, or \$10,000, outstanding for a period of up to 1 month, and 15 days' worth of purchases, or \$5,000, outstanding for between 1 month and 45 days. The aging schedule will appear as follows:

Age of Account	Amount
< month	\$10,000
1–2 months	\$ 5,000

MINI CASE

George Stamper, a credit analyst with Micro-Encapsulators Corp. (MEC), needed to respond to an urgent e-mail request from the western Canada sales office. The local sales manager reported that she had an opportunity to clinch an order from Surrey Spice (SS) for 50 encapsulators at $10,000 each. She added that she was particularly keen to secure this order since SS was likely to have a continuing need for 50 encapsulators a year and could therefore prove to be a very valuable customer. However, orders of this size for a new customer generally required head office agreement. It was therefore George's responsibility to make a rapid assessment of SS's creditworthiness and to approve or disapprove the sale.

George knew that SS was a medium-sized company with a patchy earnings record. After growing rapidly in the 1990s, SS had encountered strong competition in its principal markets and earnings had fallen sharply. George Stamper was not exactly sure to what extent this was a bad omen. New management had been brought in to cut costs and there were some indications that the worst was over for the company. Investors appeared to agree with this assessment, because the stock price had risen to $5.80 from its low of $4.25 the previous year. George had in front of him SS's latest financial statements, which are summarized in Table 22.2. He rapidly calculated a few key financial ratios and the company's *Z* score.

George also made a number of other checks on SS. The company had a small issue of bonds outstanding, which were rated BB by Dominion Bond Rating Service. Inquiries through MEC's bank indicated that SS had unused lines of credit totalling $5 million but had entered into discussions with its bank for a renewal of a $15 million bank loan that was due to be repaid at the end of the year. Telephone calls to SS's other suppliers suggested that the company had recently been 30 days late in paying its bills.

George also needed to take into account the profit that the company could make on SS's order. Encapsulators were sold on standard terms of 2/30, net 60. So if SS paid promptly, MEC would receive additional revenues of $50 \times \$9{,}800 = \$490{,}000$. However, given SS's cash position, it was more than likely that it would forgo the cash discount and would not pay until sometime after the 60 days. Since interest rates were about 8 percent, any such delays in payment would reduce the present value to MEC of the revenues. George also recognized that there were production and transportation costs in filling SS's order. These worked out at $475,000, or $9,500, a unit. Corporate profits were taxed at 35 percent.

Questions

1. What can you say about Surrey Spice's creditworthiness?
2. What is the break-even probability of default? How is it affected by the delay before SS pays its bills?
3. How should George Stamper's decision be affected by the possibility of repeat orders?

TABLE 22.2
Surrey Spice: Summary financial statements ($ millions).

	2012	2011
Assets		
Current assets:		
Cash and marketable securities	5.0	12.2
Trade receivables	16.2	15.7
Inventories	27.5	32.5
Total current assets	48.7	60.4
Fixed assets:		
Property, plant, and equipment	228.5	228.1
Less accumulated depreciation	129.5	127.6
Net fixed assets	99.0	100.5
Total assets	147.7	160.9
Liabilities and Shareholders' Equity		
Current liabilities:		
Debt due for repayment	22.8	28.0
Trade payables	19.0	16.2
Total current liabilities	41.8	44.2
Long-term debt	40.8	42.3
Shareholders' equity:		
Common stock[a]	10.0	10.0
Retained earnings	55.1	64.4
Total shareholders' equity	65.1	74.4
Total liabilities and shareholders' equity	147.7	160.9
Income Statement		
Revenue	149.8	134.4
Cost of goods sold	131.0	124.2
Other expenses	1.7	8.7
Depreciation	8.1	8.6
Earnings before interest and taxes	9.0	−7.1
Interest expense	5.1	5.6
Income taxes	1.4	−4.4
Net income	2.5	−8.3
Allocation of net income:		
Addition to retained earnings	1.5	−9.3
Dividends	1.0	1.0

[a] 10 million shares.

PART 8

Special Topics

23 Mergers, Acquisitions, and Corporate Control
- 23.1 Sensible Motives for Mergers
- 23.2 Dubious Reasons for Mergers
- 23.3 Mechanics of a Merger
- 23.4 Evaluating Mergers
- 23.5 The Market for Corporate Control
- 23.6 Method 1: Proxy Contests
- 23.7 Method 2: Takeover Bids
- 23.8 Method 3: Leveraged Buyouts
- 23.9 Method 4: Divestitures, Spin-Offs, and Equity Carve-Outs
- 23.10 The Benefits and Costs of Mergers
- 23.11 Summary

24 International Financial Management

25 Options

26 Risk Management

CHAPTER 23

Mergers, Acquisitions, and Corporate Control

LEARNING OBJECTIVES

After studying this chapter, you should be able to:

LO1 Explain why it might make sense for companies to merge.

LO2 Describe the mechanics of mergers.

LO3 Estimate the gains and costs of mergers to the acquiring firm.

LO4 Describe ways that companies change their ownership or management.

LO5 Describe merger takeover defences.

LO6 Explain some of the motivations for leveraged and management buyouts of the firm.

LO7 Summarize the evidence on whether mergers increase efficiency and on how the gains from mergers are distributed between shareholders of the acquired and acquiring firms.

Peter Thomson (left), David Thomson, and Geoff Beattie (right) applaud after ringing the opening bell to celebrate the launch of Thomson Reuters on the Toronto Stock Exchange in Toronto on Thursday, April 17, 2008.

Mergers involve business combinations. The pace and scale of merger activity tend to vary over time. Figure 23.1 shows the number of merger deals involving Canadian companies each year from 1995 to 2010. The peak of merger activities occurred in 2006 and 2007, with nearly 1,400 deals each year. The financial market crisis caused merger activity to drop in 2008 and 2009, but in 2010 merger activity started to increase again. With increased availability of debt financing, stronger economies, and increased global activity, more businesses are engaging in business combinations.

During periods of intense merger activity, financial managers spend considerable time either searching for firms to acquire or worrying whether some other firm is about to take over their company.

When one company buys another, it is making an investment, and the basic principle of capital investment decisions applies: Go ahead with the purchase if it makes a net contribution to shareholders' wealth. But mergers and acquisitions are often awkward transactions to evaluate, and you have to be careful to define benefits and costs properly.

Many mergers between companies are amicable, but sometimes one firm wants to stop the merger. We will review these so-called *hostile* takeover bids and the principal methods of attack and defence.

When a firm is taken over, its senior management is often replaced. That is why we describe takeovers as part of a broader market for corporate control. Activity in this market goes far beyond ordinary acquisitions. Ownership or management also changes if there is a proxy contest, a leveraged buyout, or a divestiture. We therefore look at these ways to change control of the firm.

We close the chapter with a discussion of who gains and loses from mergers, and we discuss whether mergers are beneficial on balance.

FIGURE 23.1
The number of mergers involving Canadian firms, 1995–2010.

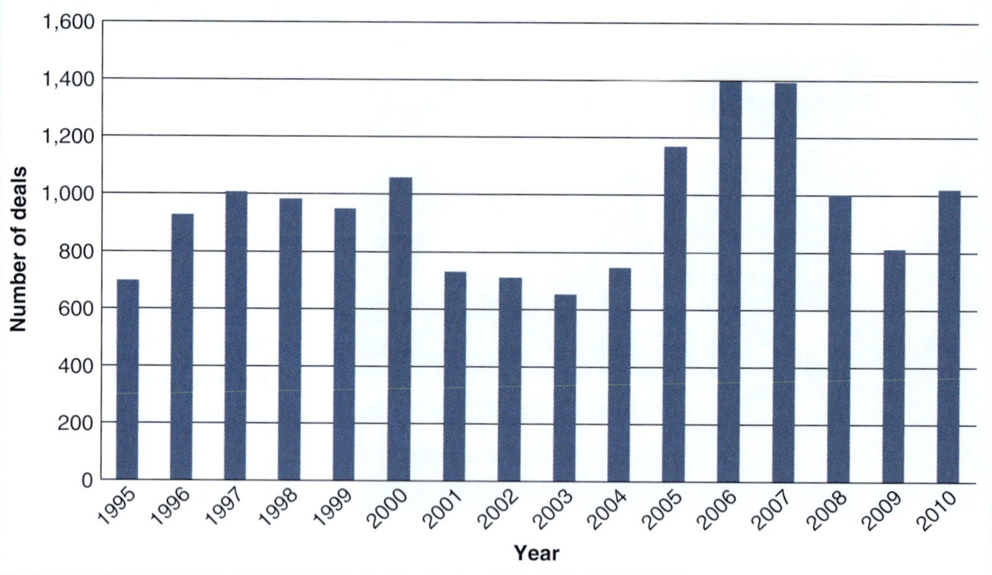

Source: FP Advisor—Financial Post Crosbie Mergers & Acquisitions in Canada. Material reprinted with the express permission of National Post, a division of Postmedia Network Inc.

LO1 23.1 SENSIBLE MOTIVES FOR MERGERS

In a typical business purchase, a business, *the buyer*, purchases equity (shares) of another business, *the seller or target*, and the buyer becomes a majority shareholder of the seller. In some deals, the buyer pays cash for the shares of the seller but in other deals the buyer gives shares of its company in exchange for the shares of the seller. The term *acquisition* is a common name given to this corporate action in which a company buys most, if not all, of the target company's shares in order to assume control of the target firm. In the Canadian *Federal Government Competition Act*, the term *merger* includes any manner in which control over, or a significant interest in, the whole or a part of a business of another person is acquired or established.[1] So we use the term **merger** to refer to acquisition of control of another business. *Mergers and acquisitions, M&A*, is another term used to refer to any kind of business purchase.

merger The acquisition of control of a business by another business.

What happens after the acquisition depends on the nature of the buyer and the seller and also on the terms of the deal. In some cases, the buyer and seller firms continue to exist and operate as separate businesses but are commonly controlled. In some cases the assets and liabilities of the businesses are combined to create a new company, or one company continues to exist but includes the assets and liabilities of the other company so that it no longer exists. There are various aspects to the combination of the businesses, depending on the relevant laws. In Section 23.3 we will review the mechanics of acquisitions and deal with some of the legal aspects of business combinations. Now let's look at reasons for mergers. Table 23.1 lists eight of the largest mergers in 2008 to 2010 involving Canadian companies as either the buyer or seller.

Mergers are categorized as *horizontal*, *vertical*, or *conglomerate*. A *horizontal merger* is one that takes place between two firms in the same line of business; the merged firms are former competitors. Five deals listed in Table 23.1 are horizontal mergers. Thomson Corp and Reuters Groups were both competitors in the financial information market. The two acquired

[1] This interpretation of the definition of merger was posted on the Web site of the Canadian Competition Bureau, **www.competitionbureau.gc.ca/eic/site/cb-bc.nsf/eng/01245.html#part1acquisition**. The Bureau is the organization responsible for ensuring that the Canadian marketplace is competitive, on the basis of the *Federal Competition Act*.

TABLE 23.1 Some large recent mergers involving Canadian companies.

Year	Buying Company	Selling Company	Selling Company Industry	Value ($ millions)
2010	Onex Corporation (Canada); CPP Investment Board (Canada)	Tomkins Limited (UK)	Engineering and manufacturing	5,502
2010	Kinross Gold Corporation (US)	Red Back Mining Inc. (Canada)	Gold mining	6,942
2009	Leonard Green & Partners LP (US); TPG Capital (US); CPP Investment Board (Canada)	IMS Health Inc. (US)	Pharmaceutical	5,718
2009	CPP Investment Board (Canada)	CPPIB Communications Infrastructure Group (Australia)	Communication services	6,620
2009	Mirror Lake Oil and Gas Co. Ltd. (Canada)	Addax Petroleum Corp. (Switzerland)	Oil and gas exploration	10,165
2008	Suncor Energy Inc. (Canada)	Petro-Canada (Canada)	Oil and gas exploration, refining and retail	24,083
2008	Teck Resources Limited (Canada)	Fording Canadian Coal Trust (Canada)	Coal mining	11,618
2008	The Thomson Corp (Canada)	Reuters Group PLC (UK)	Market data provider	18,979

Source: *S&P Capital IQ*, **www.capitaliq.com**, accessed March 10, 2011.

mining companies, Red Back Mining and Fording Canadian Coal, and the two acquired oil and gas exploration companies, Addax Petroleum and Petro-Canada, were each bought by a company in the same industry. In a typical horizontal merger, the assets and liabilities of the acquired company are combined with the assets and liabilities of the buyer to create one company. However, the acquired company can continue to exist but becomes a subsidiary of the buyer. For example, Petro-Canada is a wholly owned subsidiary of Suncor Energy and still exists as a corporation.

A *vertical merger* involves companies at different stages of production. The buyer expands back toward the source of raw materials or forward in the direction of the ultimate consumer. Thus, a soft-drink manufacturer might buy a sugar producer (expanding backward) or a fast-food chain as an outlet for its product (expanding forward). Suncor Energy's acquisition of Petro-Canada had vertical and horizontal merger aspects, because Petro-Canada is in both oil and gas exploration and gasoline retail. Another example of a vertical merger was eBay's acquisition of PayPal. Customers use PayPal's electronic payment system as a secure way to pay for goods they have purchased in eBay's online auction.

A *conglomerate merger* involves companies in unrelated lines of business. For example, before it went belly-up in 1999, the Korean conglomerate, Daewoo, had nearly 400 different subsidiaries and 150,000 employees. It built ships in Korea; manufactured microwaves in France, TVs in Mexico, cars in Poland, and fertilizers in Vietnam; and managed hotels in China and a bank in Hungary. No Canadian or U.S. company is as diversified as Daewoo, but in the 1960s and 1970s it was common in both Canada and the United States for unrelated businesses to merge. However, the number of conglomerate mergers declined in the 1980s. In fact, much of the merger action in the 1980s came from breaking up the conglomerates that had been formed 10 to 20 years earlier.

Three of the deals in Table 23.1 were acquisitions made by companies not in the same industry. However, the acquirers are private equity investors, including the Canada Pension Plan (CPP) Investment Board, Onex Corporation, Leonard Green, and TPG. The private equity investors own the equity of the companies they acquire, but typically they do not integrate the operations of the companies they acquire. We will talk more about private equity investments in the section on leveraged buyouts.

Check Point 23.1

Are the following hypothetical mergers horizontal, vertical, or conglomerate?

a. IBM acquires Apple Computer.
b. Research In Motion acquires Empire Company (owner of Sobeys retail grocery stores).
c. Loblaws acquires Lassonde Industries (a fruit and vegetable juice manufacturer).
d. EnCana (natural gas producer) acquires Canada Bread (manufacturer of flour based food).

synergy The principle by which the value generated by the combination of companies is greater than the sum of their individual values.

Many mergers are motivated by possible gains in efficiency from combining operations through the phenomenon known as **synergy**. By this we mean that the two firms are worth more together than apart. A merger adds value, creates synergy, because of better management or other changes make the two firms worth more together than apart. Synergy generated by the merger of company A and company B equals the value of the combined business AB, V_{AB}, minus the sum of the pre-merger value of company A, V_A, and company B, V_B: Synergy $= V_{AB} - (V_A + V_B)$.

A merger adds value, creates synergy, because of better management or other changes make the two firms worth more together than apart. Synergy generated by the merger of company A and company B equals the value of the combined business AB.

It would be convenient if we could say that certain types of mergers are usually successful and other types fail. Unfortunately, there are no such simple generalizations. Many mergers that appear to make sense nevertheless fail because managers cannot handle the complex task of integrating two firms with different production processes, accounting methods, and corporate cultures. Moreover, the value of most businesses depends on *human assets*—managers, skilled workers, scientists, and engineers. If these people are not happy in their new roles in the acquiring firm, many of them will leave. Beware of paying too much for assets that go down in the elevator and out to the parking lot at the close of each business day.

Consider the $38 billion merger between Daimler Benz and Chrysler. Although it was hailed as a model for consolidation in the auto industry, the early years were bedevilled by conflicts between two very different cultures:

> German management-board members had executive assistants who prepared detailed position papers on any number of issues. The Americans didn't have assigned aides and formulated their decisions by talking directly to engineers or other specialists. A German decision worked its way through the bureaucracy for final approval at the top. Then it was set in stone. The Americans allowed mid-level employees to proceed on their own initiative, sometimes without waiting for executive-level approval. . . . Cultural integration also was proving to be a slippery commodity. The yawning gap in pay scales fuelled an undercurrent of tension. The Americans earned two, three, and, in some cases, four times as much as their German counterparts. But the expenses of US workers were tightly controlled compared with the German system. Daimler-side employees thought nothing of flying to Paris or New York for a half-day meeting, then capping the visit with a fancy dinner and a night in an expensive hotel. The Americans blanched at the extravagance.[2]

Nine years after acquiring Chrysler, Daimler threw in the towel and announced that it was offloading an 80 percent stake in Chrysler to a leveraged-buyout firm, Cerberus Capital Management. Daimler actually paid Cerberus $677 million to take Chrysler off its hands. Cerberus in return assumed about $18 billion in pension and employee healthcare liabilities and agreed to invest $6 billion in Chrysler and its finance subsidiary.

These observations illustrate the difficulties in realizing the benefits of merger. There are also occasions when the merger does achieve the intended synergies, but the buyer nevertheless loses because it pays too much. For example, the buyer may overestimate the value of stale inventory or underestimate the costs of renovating old plant and equipment, or it may overlook the warranties on a defective product.

With these caveats in mind, we will now consider some possible sources of synergy.

[2] Bill Vlasic and Bradley A. Stertz, "Taken for a Ride," *Businessweek*, June 5, 2000.

INCREASED REVENUES

Mergers are frequently justified on the belief that revenues of the combined companies will exceed the sum of the revenues of the two companies run separately. However, revenue synergies are difficult to estimate accurately because they are out of the direct control of management. For revenues to increase, customers must buy more than they used to or be willing to pay a higher price and, also, competitors must not lower their prices in response to the acquisition.

Potentially, the most effective way to increase revenues is a horizontal merger. By combining with a competitor in the same business, market share and market power of the companies may be increased, allowing the merged company to raise its prices with the expectation of raising revenues. Although this may sound like a great idea to an enterprising capitalist, from society's perspective, mergers that lessen competition to the detriment of customers are not acceptable. Many countries have regulations dealing with mergers to have the power to stop or demand modifications to mergers that are assessed to reduce competition. Some information about merger regulations is in Section 23.3.

ECONOMIES OF SCALE

Just as most of us believe that we would be happier if only we were a little richer, so managers always seem to believe their firm would be more competitive if only it were just a little bigger. They hope for *economies of scale*, that is, the opportunity to spread fixed costs across a larger volume of output. The banking industry provides many examples. As a result of bank regulation, the United States had too many small, local banks. When these regulations were relaxed, some banks grew by systematically buying up smaller banks and streamlining their operations. Most of the cost savings came from consolidating "back-office" operations, such as computer systems for processing cheques and credit-card transactions and payments. Other buyers of U.S. banks were Canadian banks, including Royal Bank, TD Bank, and Bank of Montreal. Similarly, TD Bank management argued it should be permitted to merge with its competitor Canada Trust to increase the scale and scope of its operations, and thereby, better compete with its larger domestic and foreign competitors. In addition to increasing the scale of back-office operations, the merger permitted the companies to reduce the number of branches. The effect is to create increased economies of scale, with higher volume at the remaining branches and lower costs per transaction.

These economies of scale are the natural goal of horizontal mergers, to create synergy. But economies of scale have been claimed in conglomerate mergers, too. The architects of these mergers have pointed to the savings that come from sharing central services such as accounting, financial control, and top-level management.

ECONOMIES OF VERTICAL INTEGRATION

Large industrial companies commonly like to gain as much control and coordination as possible over the production process by expanding back toward the output of the raw material and forward to the ultimate consumer. One way to achieve this is to merge with a supplier or a customer. Consider DuPont's purchase of an oil company, Conoco. This was vertical integration because petroleum is the ultimate raw material for much of DuPont's chemical production.

Do not assume that more vertical integration is necessarily better than less. Carried to extremes, it is absurdly inefficient. For example, before the Polish economy was restructured, LOT, the Polish state airline, found itself raising pigs to make sure that its employees had fresh meat on their tables. (Of course, in a centrally managed economy it may prove necessary to grow your own meat, since you can't be sure you'll be able to buy it.)

Some people mistakenly think that vertical integration is a good idea because if you own your supplier, you will pay less for materials. However, if you pay less, the supplier's profits will fall. No synergy is created if the merger simply moves profits but does not increase total profit. The gains from vertical integration are achieved through improved coordination and control of production.

Vertical integration is now less popular. The advent of just-in-time inventory systems and computerized ordering systems makes it much easier for a company to manage its supply chain without having to own its suppliers. Many companies are finding it more efficient to *outsource* many activities. For example, automobile manufacturers used to manufacture most of the parts used to make cars. Now companies such as General Motors and Ford are primarily car assemblers, building vehicles with components purchased from parts manufacturers such as Magna International. Even DuPont seems to have become less convinced of the benefits of vertical integration: in 1999, it sold off Conoco.

COMBINING COMPLEMENTARY RESOURCES

Many small firms are acquired by large firms that can provide the missing ingredients necessary for the firm's success. The small firm may have a unique product but lack the engineering and sales organization necessary to produce and market it on a large scale. The firm could develop engineering and sales talent from scratch, but it may be quicker and cheaper to merge with a firm that already has ample talent. The two firms have *complementary resources*—each has what the other needs—so it may make sense for them to merge. Also the merger may open up opportunities that neither firm would pursue otherwise. Google's purchase of DocVerse, a small team of talented software developers, in 2010 is an example. With DocVerse software, people can begin to experience some of the benefits of Web-based collaboration using the traditional Microsoft Word, Excel, and PowerPoint desktop applications. Google plans to integrate DocVerse technology into some Google apps. Combining complementary resources may increase total revenues, decrease total costs, or both.

MERGING TO REDUCE TAXES

The tax implications of a merger or acquisition are often very complicated. However, it may be possible to reduce the total taxes of the combined companies if one of the companies has tax shields it is unable to use. For example, if a company with operating losses merges with another company in the same business that has taxable income, the losses may be a valuable tax deduction. However, merging for the sole purpose of using operating losses is not permitted and CRA may disallow the tax deductions.

Unused interest tax shields are another merger motive. As we saw in Chapter 16, the interest on debt generates an interest tax shield. A company with unused debt capacity, perhaps due to poor management, may be an attractive target. The acquirer will increase the target's debt/equity ratio, taking advantage of the interest deduction to reduce taxes and increase target firm value. This is one explanation offered for leveraged buyouts.

MERGERS AS A USE FOR SURPLUS FUNDS

Suppose that your firm is in a mature industry. It is generating a substantial amount of cash but has few profitable investment opportunities. Ideally such a firm should distribute the surplus cash to shareholders by increasing its dividend payment or by repurchasing its shares. Unfortunately, energetic managers are often reluctant to shrink their firm in this way. Furthermore, some shareholders may pay taxes on the dividends and repurchased shares.

If the firm is not willing to purchase its own shares, it can instead purchase someone else's. Thus firms with a surplus of cash and a shortage of good investment opportunities often turn to mergers *financed by cash* as a way of deploying their capital. This also avoids the tax consequences of dividends and share repurchases.

Firms that have excess cash and do not pay it out or re-deploy it by acquisition often find themselves targets for takeover by other firms that propose to re-deploy the cash for them. During the oil price slump of the early 1980s, many cash-rich oil companies found themselves threatened by takeover. This was not because their cash was a unique asset. The acquirers wanted to capture the companies' cash flow to make sure it was not frittered away on negative-NPV oil exploration projects. We return to this *free-cash-flow* motive for takeovers later in this chapter.

LO1 23.2 DUBIOUS REASONS FOR MERGERS

The benefits that we have described so far all make economic sense. Other arguments sometimes given for mergers are more dubious. Here are two.

DIVERSIFICATION

We have suggested that the managers of a cash-rich company may prefer to see that cash used for acquisitions. That is why we often see cash-rich firms in stagnant industries merging their way into fresh woods and new pastures. What about diversification as an end in itself? It is obvious that diversification reduces risk. Isn't that a gain from merging?

The trouble with this argument is that diversification is easier and cheaper for the shareholder than for the corporation. Why should firm A buy firm B to diversify when the shareholders of firm A can buy shares in firm B to diversify their own portfolios? It is far easier and cheaper for individual investors to diversify than it is for firms to combine operations.

THE BOOTSTRAP GAME

During the 1960s some conglomerate companies made acquisitions that offered no evident economic gains. Nevertheless, the conglomerates' aggressive strategy produced several years of rising earnings per share. To see how this can happen, let us look at the acquisition of Muck and Slurry by the well-known conglomerate World Enterprises.

EXAMPLE 23.1 THE BOOTSTRAP GAME

The position before the merger is set out in the first two columns of Table 23.2. Notice that because Muck and Slurry has relatively poor growth prospects, its stock sells at a lower price-earnings ratio than World Enterprises (line 3). The merger, we assume, produces no economic benefits, so the firms should be worth exactly the same together as apart. The value of World Enterprises after the merger is therefore equal to the sum of the separate values of the two firms (line 6).

Since World Enterprises stock is selling for double the price of Muck and Slurry stock (line 2), World Enterprises can acquire the 100,000 Muck and Slurry shares for 50,000 of its own shares. Thus World will have 150,000 shares outstanding after the merger.

World's total earnings double as a result of the acquisition (line 5), but the number of shares increases by only 50 percent. Its earnings *per share* rise from $2 to $2.67. We call this a *bootstrap effect*, because there is no real gain created by the merger and no increase in the two firms' combined value. Since World's stock price is unchanged by the acquisition of Muck and Slurry, the price-earnings ratio falls (line 3).

Before the merger, $1 invested in World Enterprises bought 5 cents of current earnings and rapid growth prospects. On the other hand, $1 invested in Muck and Slurry bought 10 cents of current earnings but slower growth prospects. If the *total* market value is not altered by the merger, then $1 invested in the merged firm gives World shareholders 6.7 cents of immediate earnings but slower growth than before the merger. Muck and Slurry shareholders get lower immediate earnings but faster growth. Neither side gains or loses *provided* that everybody understands the deal.

Financial manipulators sometimes try to ensure that the market does not understand the deal. Suppose that investors are fooled by the exuberance of the president of World Enterprises and mistake the 33 percent post-merger increase in earnings per share for *sustainable* growth. If they do, the price of World Enterprises stock rises and the shareholders of both companies receive something for nothing.

You should now see how to play the bootstrap game. Suppose that you manage a company enjoying a high price-earnings ratio. The reason it is high is that investors anticipate rapid growth in future earnings. You achieve this growth not by capital investment, product improvement,

TABLE 23.2
Impact of merger on market value and earnings per share of World Enterprises.

	World Enterprises (before merger)	Muck and Slurry	World Enterprises (after acquiring Muck and Slurry)
1. Earnings per share	$ 2	$ 2	$ 2.67
2. Price per share	$ 40	$ 20	$ 40
3. Price-earnings ratio	20	10	15
4. Number of shares	100,000	100,000	150,000
5. Total earnings	$ 200,000	$ 200,000	$ 400,000
6. Total market value	$4,000,000	$2,000,000	$6,000,000
7. Current earnings per dollar invested in stock (line 1 divided by line 2)	$ .05	$ .10	$ .067

Note: When World Enterprises purchases Muck and Slurry, there are no gains. Therefore, total earnings and total market value should be unaffected by the merger. But earnings per share increase. World Enterprises issues only 50,000 of its shares (priced at $40) to acquire the 100,000 Muck and Slurry shares (priced at $20).

Buying a firm with a lower P/E ratio can increase earnings per share. But the increase should not result in a higher share price. The short-term increase in earnings should be offset by lower future earnings growth.

or increased operating efficiency, but by purchasing slow-growing firms with low price-earnings ratios. The long-run result will be slower growth and a depressed price-earnings ratio, but in the short run earnings per share can increase dramatically. If this fools investors, you may be able to achieve the higher earnings per share without suffering a decline in your price-earnings ratio. But in order to keep fooling investors, you must continue to expand by merger at the same compound rate. Obviously you cannot do this forever; one day expansion must slow down or stop. Then earnings growth will cease, and your house of cards will fall.

Check Point 23.2

Suppose that Muck and Slurry has even worse growth prospects than in our example and its share price is only $10. Recalculate the effects of the merger in this case. You should find that earnings per share increase by a greater amount, since World Enterprises can now buy the same current earnings for fewer shares.

LO2 23.3 THE MECHANICS OF A MERGER

Buying a company is much more complicated than buying a piece of machinery. We will describe the different forms an acquisition can take and the way an acquisition can be blocked by an anti-competition (or antitrust) ruling, foreign ownership rules or political pressure.

THE FORM OF ACQUISITION

There are three ways for one firm to acquire another firm: (1) amalgamate with it, (2) purchase a majority of its shares, or (3) purchase its assets.

amalgamation The combination of the assets and liabilities of two firms into one. Called a *merger* in the United States.

In Canada when the assets and liabilities of two companies are combined into one company this is an **amalgamation**. The laws governing amalgamations are found in the federal and provincial business corporations acts. The legal vehicles are "plan of arrangement" and "statutory amalgamation." These laws provide the procedure for combining the assets and liabilities of two companies. For an amalgamation to succeed in Canada, a large majority of shareholders has to approve it by voting in favour at a special shareholders' meeting, at least 66 2/3 percent of votes. In the United States the legal term for the combination of the assets and liabilities of two companies is *merger*. The percentage of shareholder approval for a U.S. merger can be as low as 50 percent, but it might be higher, depending on the relevant state laws and the company's corporate charter. Note, we will continue to use "merger" to refer to acquisition of control of another business, despite the fact that the term has a different meaning in the United States.

In an acquisition by amalgamation deal, the boards of directors of both companies meet to agree on the terms of the deal and then must get shareholders to approve the deal. Here's an example of an acquisition by amalgamation.

EXAMPLE 23.2 PROPOSED AMALGAMATION OF NORTHGATE MINERALS AND PRIMERO MINING

In July 2011, Northgate Minerals Corp. and Primero Mining Corp. announced an amalgamation agreement to combine their business and create new, leading mid-tier gold producer. Northgate will acquire all of the common shares of Primero for 1.50 Northgate common shares per Primero Share (the "exchange ratio"). Northgate's offer represents a value of $4.215 for each Primero common share based on the July 12, 2011, closing price of Northgate common shares ($2.81) on the Toronto Stock Exchange. It is a premium of approximately 13.9 percent to Primero's closing price on July 12, 2011, and a premium of approximately 20.5 percent and 11.7 percent calculated on the 10-day and 20-day volume weighted average price (VWAP) of each respective company on the Toronto Stock Exchange.

The transaction will be carried out by way of a court-approved Plan of Arrangement and will require approval by at least 66⅔ percent of the votes cast by the shareholders of Primero at a special meeting of Primero shareholders. The transaction is also subject to obtaining approval by a majority of votes cast by the shareholders of Northgate at a special meeting of Northgate shareholders expected to take place the same date as the Primero meeting. In addition to the shareholder and court approvals, the transaction is subject to applicable regulatory approvals and the satisfaction of certain other closing conditions customary in transactions of this nature. It is anticipated that the shareholder meetings will be held in September 2011.

In some amalgamations an acquiring company takes all the assets and the liabilities of the target company, which ceases to exist. The former shareholders of the target firm receive cash and/or securities in the acquiring firm. However, sometimes an entirely new company is created through the amalgamation and both original companies disappear. Such is the case when the companies involved are considered equals, with management from both firms having a major say in the running of the new company. For example, the combination of Molson and Adolph Coors in 2004 was a merger of equals creating Molson Coors Brewing Company. The merger of Thomson and Reuters was similar.

EXAMPLE 23.3 THE MERGER OF THOMSON CORP AND REUTERS PLC

In May 2007, the boards of directors of Thomson Corp, one of the world's largest information companies, and Reuters Group, a leading news service and financial information provider, announced their agreement to combine the two businesses. The acquisition involved payment of both cash and shares to Reuters's shareholders. The total payment was approximately US$17.6 billion. The deal required the approval of both Thomson and Reuters's shareholders. Each company had a special shareholders' meeting to vote on the deal. Finally, in April 2008, the merger was completed and created Thomson Reuters Corp., the world's largest provider of information to businesses and professionals.

---

takeover bid or **tender offer** Takeover attempt in which outsiders make an offer to buy the stock of the target firm's shareholders.

A second acquisition method is for the acquiring firm to buy the target firm's stock for cash, or in exchange for its share. The offer to purchase stock is called a **takeover bid** in Canada and a **tender offer** in the United States. By offering to buy shares directly from shareholders, the acquiring firm can bypass the target firm's management and board of directors. Whenever a takeover bid is made, the board of directors of the target firm has to tell their shareholders whether they approve or reject the bid. A takeover bid is *friendly* if management and board of directors of the target company are in favour of the offer. If target management and the board disapprove of the takeover bid, then it is called a *hostile* takeover bid. If the takeover bid is successful, the buyer obtains enough shares to control the target and can, if it chooses, toss out incumbent management. The acquired firm may continue to exist as a separate entity, but it is now owned by the acquirer. The approval and cooperation of the target firm's managers are generally sought, but even if they resist, the acquirer can attempt to purchase a majority of the outstanding shares.

Frequently, a takeover bid is the first step toward the final goal of amalgamation of the companies. Consequently, many takeover bids are conditional on acquiring a minimum of two-thirds of the outstanding shares. Why two-thirds, you ask? With two-thirds of the shares, the acquiring firm ensures it will win the subsequent vote to approve the amalgamation of the target company with the acquirer.

The third approach for one firm to acquire another is to buy the target firm's assets. In this case ownership of the assets is transferred, and payment is made to the selling firm rather than directly to its shareholders. Usually the target firm sells only some of its assets, but occasionally it sells all of them. In this case, the selling firm continues to exist as an independent entity, but it becomes an empty shell—a corporation engaged in no business activity. In any asset sale, the board of directors of the selling firm must agree to the terms of the sale.

MERGERS, ANTITRUST LAW, AND POPULAR OPPOSITION

Any business merger may be blocked by a government if it is assessed as likely to substantially increase the market power of the merged firms and so to result in prevention or lessening of competition. In Canada, the *Competition Act*, administered by the Competition Bureau and the Competition Tribunal, prohibits mergers that severely limit competition. As we noted in Section 23.1, in the *Competition Act* a merger means control of a business is acquired by someone else. However, merger proposals are rarely turned down for anti-competitive reasons in Canada. Instead, the Competition Bureau requests that the companies sell some of their assets to a third company, thereby limiting the reduction in competition. When Canada Trust and TD Bank proposed to merge, the Bureau required that they sell branches to competitors in certain geographic areas to reduce the anti-competitive impact.

Like Canada, many countries will often object to a merger because of the impact on competition, but then relent if the companies agree to divest certain assets and operations. So mergers between companies with global operations might require approval in various countries. For example, GE's US$46 billion takeover bid for Honeywell was blocked by the European Commission, which argued that the combined company would have too much power in the aircraft industry.

EXAMPLE 23.4 REGULATORY RESPONSES TO MERGER OF NOVARTIS AND ALCON

In August 2010 the Canadian Competition Bureau assessed that the proposed acquisition of Alcon Inc. by Novartis, AG was going to substantially reduce competition in Canada for the supply of certain ophthalmic (eyecare) products. Novartis is a Swiss-based company in the research, development, manufacture, and marketing of healthcare products worldwide; Alcon, Inc., is a U.S.-based company in the development, manufacture, and marketing of pharmaceuticals, surgical equipment and devices, and consumer eyecare products to treat primarily diseases and disorders of the eye in the U.S. and internationally. To resolve Canadian competition issues, Novartis and Alcon were required to divest assets and associated licences related to the sale in Canada of ophthalmic products. In March 2011, the Bureau announced its approval of the divestiture of certain assets and associated licences related to the sale in Canada of ophthalmic products belonging to Novartis, as part of a remedy required to address competition concerns resulting from Novartis's acquisition of control of Alcon.

In the United States, Novartis and Alcon were required to divest products given to cataract surgery patients to prevent infection, because the two companies are the only ones producing this class of drugs. Also, China's Ministry of Commerce ordered two major divestitures, which it deemed necessary to preserve competition in China's eyecare sector. The Ministry said Novartis-Alcon enjoyed a 55 percent stake in the affected markets worldwide and a 60 percent share in China.

Mergers may also be stymied by political pressures and popular resentment even when no formal antitrust issues arise. Economic nationalism rears its head in many countries, including Canada. For example, in 2008, the Canadian federal government blocked the $1.3 billion sale of the space technology division of Vancouver-based MacDonald, Dettwiler and Associates (MDA) to a major U.S. defence contractor, Alliant Techsystems Inc. Critics of the sale, including former Canadian Space Agency head Marc Garneau, asked the government to stop the deal, saying it handed over taxpayer-funded technology and gave away technology designed to protect Canada's sovereignty. The government did so, using the Investment Canada legislation, having assessed the deal as of no net benefit to Canada.

In 2005 the news that Pepsi-Cola might bid for Danone aroused considerable hostility in France. The French prime minister added his support to opponents of the merger and announced that his government was drawing up a list of strategic industries that should be protected from foreign ownership. It was unclear whether yogurt production would be one of these strategic industries. However, Pepsi ended up not making a takeover bid for Danone.

In 2005 the China National Offshore Oil Corporation felt obliged to withdraw its bid for Unocal, after what it described as "unprecedented political opposition" in U.S. Congress. The following year Congress voiced its opposition to the takeover of Britain's P&O by the Dubai company, DP World. The acquisition went ahead only after P&O's ports in the United States were removed from the deal.

LO3 23.4 EVALUATING MERGERS

If you are given the responsibility for evaluating a proposed merger, you must think hard about the following two questions:

1. Is there an overall economic gain to the merger? In other words, is the merger value enhancing? Are the two firms worth more together than apart?
2. Do the terms of the merger make my company and its shareholders better off? There is no point in merging if the cost is too high and all the economic gain goes to the other company.

Answering these deceptively simple questions is rarely easy. Some economic gains can be nearly impossible to quantify, and complex merger financing can obscure the true terms of the deal. But the basic principles for evaluating mergers are not too difficult.

MERGERS FINANCED BY CASH

We will concentrate on a simple numerical example. Your company, Cislunar Foods, is considering acquisition of a smaller food company, Targetco. Cislunar is proposing to make a takeover bid of $19 per share for all of Targetco's outstanding stock. Some financial information on the two companies is given in the left and centre columns of Table 23.3.

Question 1 Why would Cislunar and Targetco be worth more together than apart? Suppose that operating costs can be reduced by combining the companies' marketing, distribution, and administration. Revenues can also be increased in Targetco's region. The right column of Table 23.3 contains projected revenues, costs, and earnings for the two firms operating together: annual operating costs post-merger will be $2 million less than the sum of the separate companies' costs, and revenues will be $2 million more. Therefore, projected earnings increase by $4 million.[3] We will assume that the increased earnings are the only synergy to be generated by the merger.

[3] To keep things simple, the example ignores taxes and assumes that both companies are all equity-financed. We also ignore the interest income that could have been earned by investing the cash used to finance the merger.

TABLE 23.3
Cislunar Foods is considering an acquisition of Targetco. The merger would increase the companies' combined earnings by $4 million.

	Cislunar Foods	Targetco	Combined Companies	
Revenues	$150	$20	$172	(+2)
Operating costs	118	16	132	(−2)
Earnings	$ 32	$ 4	$ 40	(+4)
Cash	$ 55	$ 2.5		
Other assets' book value	185	17		
Total assets	$240	$19.5		
Price per share	$ 48	$16		
Number of shares	10	2.5		
Market value	$480	$40		

Note: Figures in millions except price per share.

The economic gain to the merger is the present value of the extra earnings. If the earnings increase is permanent (a level perpetuity), and the cost of capital is 20 percent,

$$\text{Economic gain} = \text{PV(increased earnings)}\frac{4}{.20} = \$20 \text{ million}$$

This additional value is the basic motivation for the merger. The next step is to determine how the economic gain to the merger is divided between the shareholders of Cislunar and Targetco. This division is determined by the *terms of the merger*.

Question 2 What are the terms of the merger? What is the cost to Cislunar and its shareholders of acquiring Targetco's shares?

Targetco's management and shareholders will not consent to the merger unless they receive at least the stand-alone value of their shares. They can be paid in cash or by new shares issued by Cislunar. In this case we are considering a cash offer of $19 per Targetco share, $3 per share over the prior share price. Targetco has 2.5 million shares outstanding, so Cislunar will have to pay out $47.5 million, a premium of $7.5 million over Targetco's prior market value. On these terms, Targetco shareholders will capture $7.5 million out of the $20 million gain from the merger. That ought to leave $12.5 million for Cislunar.

This is confirmed in the Cash Purchase column of Table 23.4. Start at the *bottom* of the column, where the total market value of the merged firms is $492.5 million. This is derived as follows:

Cislunar market value prior to merger	$480 million
Targetco stand-alone market value	40
Present value of gain to merger	20
Less cash paid out to Targetco shareholders	−47.5
Post-merger market value of Cislunar	$492.5 million

TABLE 23.4
Financial forecasts after the Cislunar–Targetco merger: The left column assumes a cash purchase at $19 per Targetco share. The right column assumes Targetco shareholders receive one new Cislunar share for every three Targetco shares.

Merged Firm	Cash Purchase	Exchange of Shares
Earnings	$ 40	$ 40
Cash	$ 10	$ 57.5
Other assets' book value	202	202
Total assets	$212	$259.5
Price per share	$ 49.25	$ 49.85
Number of shares	10	10.833
Market value	$492.5	$540

Note: Figures in millions except price per share.

The post-merger share price for Cislunar will be \$49.25, an increase of \$1.25 per share. There are 10 million shares now outstanding, so the total increase in the value of Cislunar shares is \$12.5 million.

Now let's summarize. The merger makes sense for Cislunar for two reasons. First, the merger adds \$20 million of overall value. Second, the terms of the merger give only \$7.5 million of the \$20 million overall gain to Targetco's shareholders, leaving \$12.5 million for Cislunar. You might say that the *cost* of acquiring Targetco is \$7.5 million, the difference between the cash payment and the value of Targetco as a separate company.

$$\text{Cost} = \text{cash paid out} - \text{Targetco stand-alone value} = \$47.5 - 40 = \$7.5 \text{ million}$$

Of course, the Targetco shareholders are ahead by \$7.5 million. *Their gain is your cost.* As we've already seen, Cislunar shareholders come out \$12.5 million ahead. This is the merger's NPV for Cislunar:

$$\text{NPV} = \text{economic gain} - \text{cost} = \$20 - 7.5 = \$12.5 \text{ million}$$

Writing down the economic gain and cost of a merger in this way separates the motive for the merger (the economic gain, or value added) from the terms of the merger (the *division* of the gain between the two merging companies).

Check Point 23.3

Killer Shark Inc. makes a surprise cash offer of \$22 a share for Goldfish Industries. Before the offer, Goldfish was selling for \$18 a share. Goldfish has 1 million shares outstanding. What must Killer Shark believe about the present value of the improvement it can bring to Goldfish's operations?

MERGERS FINANCED BY STOCK

What if Cislunar wants to conserve its cash for other investments, and therefore decides to pay for the Targetco acquisition with new Cislunar shares? The deal calls for Targetco shareholders to receive one Cislunar share in exchange for every three Targetco shares.

It's the same merger, but the financing is different. The right column of Table 23.4 works out the consequences. Again, start at the *bottom* of the column. Note that the market value of Cislunar's shares after the merger is \$540 million, \$47.5 million higher than in the cash deal, because that cash is kept rather than paid out to Targetco shareholders. On the other hand, there are more shares outstanding, since 833,333 new shares have to be issued in exchange for the 2.5 million Targetco shares (a 1 to 3 ratio). Therefore, the price per share is 540/10.833 = \$49.85, which is 60 cents higher than in the cash offer.

> There is a key distinction between cash and stock for financing mergers. If cash is offered, the cost of the merger is not affected by the size of the merger gains. If stock is offered, the cost depends on the gains because the gains show up in the post-merger share price, and these shares are used to pay for the acquired firm.

Why do Cislunar shareholders do better from the share exchange? The economic gain from the merger is the same, but the Targetco shareholders capture less of it. They get 833,333 shares at \$49.85, or \$41.5 million, a premium of only \$1.5 million over Targetco's prior market value.

$$\begin{aligned}\text{Cost} &= \text{value of shares issued} - \text{Targetco stand-alone value}\\ &= \$41.5 - 40 = \$1.5\end{aligned}$$

The merger's NPV to Cislunar's original shareholders is

$$\text{NPV} = \text{economic gain} - \text{cost} = \$20 - 1.5 = \$18.5 \text{ million}$$

Note that Cislunar stock rises by \$1.85 from its pre-merger share price of \$48. The total increase in value for Cislunar's original shareholders, who retain 10 million shares, is \$18.5 million.

Evaluating the terms of a merger can be tricky when there is an exchange of shares. The target company's shareholders will retain a stake in the merged firms, so you have to figure out what the firm's shares will be worth after the merger is announced and its benefits appreciated by investors. Notice that we started with the total market value of Cislunar and Targetco post-merger, took account of the merger terms (833,333 new shares issued), and worked back to the post-merger share price. Only then could we work out the division of the merger gains between the two companies.

Stock financing also mitigates the effects of over- or undervaluation of either firm. Suppose, for example, that A overestimates B's value as a separate entity, perhaps because it has overlooked some hidden liability. Thus A makes too generous an offer. Other things being equal, A's shareholders are better off if it is a stock rather than a cash offer. With a stock offer, the inevitable bad news about B's value will fall partly on B's former shareholders.

Check Point 23.4

Suppose Targetco shareholders demand one Cislunar share for every 2.5 Targetco shares. Otherwise they will not accept the merger. Under these revised terms, is the merger still a good deal for Cislunar?

SOME TAX ISSUES

An acquisition may be either taxable or tax-free. If the form of payment is cash, the acquisition is regarded as taxable. Why? The selling shareholders have *sold* their shares, and they must pay tax on any capital gains. On the other hand, if the payment is largely in the form of shares, the acquisition is tax-free. In this case, the selling shareholders have *exchanged* their old shares for new ones; no capital gains or losses are realized. The rules determining the tax-free status of amalgamations, stocks, and assets are complex but the basic message is the same: the selling shareholders must continue to be shareholders or capital gains will be assessed from the share sale.

The tax status of the acquisition also affects the taxation of the company afterward. In a taxable acquisition, the assets of the target are revalued for tax purposes, allowing the acquirer to take more CCA deductions and reduce taxable income. This is called *stepping up the asset pool*. In a tax-free acquisition, the assets are not revalued and no incremental tax savings are generated.

As you can see, the selling shareholders would prefer a tax-free acquisition, while the buyer pays less tax in the future if the acquisition is taxable. If possible, the merger deal will be struck to reduce the total tax consequences of the transaction.

Always ask why the two firms should be worth more together than apart. Remember, you add value only if you can generate *additional economic benefits*—some competitive edge that other firms can't match and that the target firm's managers can't achieve on their own.

A WARNING

The cost of a merger is the premium the acquirer pays for the target firm over its value as a separate company. If the target is a public company, you can measure its separate value by multiplying its stock price by the number of outstanding shares. Watch out, though: if investors expect the target to be acquired, its stock price may overstate the company's separate value. The target company's stock price might already have risen in anticipation of a premium to be paid by an acquiring firm.

ANOTHER WARNING

Some companies begin their merger analyses with a forecast of the target firm's future cash flows. Any revenue increases or cost reductions attributable to the merger are included in the forecasts, which are then discounted back to the present and compared with the purchase price:

$$\text{Estimated net gain} = \text{DCF valuation of target including merger benefits} - \text{cash required for acquisition}$$

This is a dangerous procedure. Even the brightest and best-trained analyst can make large errors in valuing a business. The estimated net gain might come up positive, not because the merger makes sense, but simply because the analyst's cash flow forecasts are too optimistic. On the other hand, a good merger might not be pursued if the analyst fails to recognize the target's potential as a stand-alone business.

A better procedure *starts* with the target's current and stand-alone market value and concentrates instead on the *changes* in cash flow that would result from the merger.

It makes sense to keep an eye on the value that investors put on the gains from merging. If A's stock price falls when the deal is announced, investors are sending a message that the merger benefits are doubtful *or* that A is paying too much for these benefits.

LO4 23.5 THE MARKET FOR CORPORATE CONTROL

The shareholders are the owners of the firm. But most shareholders do not feel like the boss, and with good reason. Try buying a share of Royal Bank stock and marching into the boardroom for a chat with your employee, the chief executive officer.

The *ownership* and *management* of large public corporations are often separated. Shareholders do not directly appoint or supervise the firm's managers. They elect the board of directors, who act as their agents in choosing and monitoring the managers of the firm. Shareholders have a direct say in very few matters. Control of the firm is in the hands of the managers, subject to the general oversight of the board of directors.

This system of governance creates potential *agency costs*. Agency costs occur when managers or directors take actions adverse to shareholders' interests.

The temptation to take such actions may be ever-present, but there are many forces and constraints working to keep managers' and shareholders' interests in line. As we pointed out in Chapter 1, managers' paycheques in large corporations are almost always tied to the profitability of the firm and the performance of its shares. Boards of directors take their responsibilities seriously—they may face lawsuits if they don't—and therefore are reluctant to rubber-stamp obviously bad financial decisions.

But what ensures that the board has engaged the most talented managers? What happens if managers are inadequate? What if the board of directors is derelict in monitoring the performance of managers? Or what if the firm's managers are fine, but resources of the firm could be used more efficiently by merging with another firm? Can we count on managers to pursue arrangements that would put them out of jobs?

These are all questions about *the market for corporate control*, the mechanisms by which firms are matched up with management teams and owners who can make the most of the firm's resources. You should not take a firm's current ownership and management for granted. If it is possible for the value of the firm to be enhanced by changing management or by reorganizing under new owners, there will be incentives for someone to make a change.

There are four ways to change the management of a firm: (1) a successful proxy contest in which a group of shareholders votes in a new group of directors, who then pick a new management team; (2) the purchase of one firm by another in a merger or acquisition; (3) a leveraged buyout of the firm by a private group of investors; and (4) a divestiture, in which a firm either sells part of its operations to another company or spins it off as an independent firm.

OWNERSHIP STRUCTURE AND THE EFFECTIVENESS OF THE MARKET FOR CORPORATE CONTROL

The ownership structure—how shares are distributed among shareholders—affects the extent of the separation of ownership and control and also the effectiveness of the market for corporate control. At one extreme are privately owned companies with no publicly traded common shares and only one or a few shareholders. In Canada, most of the largest private companies are owned by other corporations. Rio Tinto Alcan, ranked the 5th-largest private Canadian company with 2010 revenues of US$15.2 billion, is 100 percent by Rio Tinto Group Corporation, its Australian parent. A few of the large private corporations are owned by individuals or families. For example, McCain Foods, the 24th-largest private company in Canada, with 2010 revenues of $6.5 billion, is 100 percent owned by the McCain family.[4]

In a personally owned private company, such as McCain Foods, shareholders are actively involved in the management of the company, often holding senior management positions, as well as sitting on the board of directors. Thus problems of the separation of ownership from control are much less important than in a publicly owned company. Of course, if the sole shareholder of the company is another company, the shareholders of the parent company are still separated from the control of the various companies they own. A private company, however, will never be sold unless the shareholders want it to happen. Proxy contests and hostile takeover bids cannot occur.

Some publicly traded companies have a controlling shareholder or shareholder group who owns a significant percentage of the votes. These closely held but publicly traded companies use a variety of methods to maintain control while still allowing outsiders to invest in the company's equity. Having multiple classes of equity is a commonly used structure. For example, Canadian Tire has two classes of equity: one with one vote per share and the other with no votes. The Billes family controls about 60 percent of the voting shares. Many Canadian public companies have a controlling shareholder; however, most U.S. public companies do not.

A closely held public company has less separation between management and the controlling shareholders. However, minority, non-controlling shareholders have less influence and are unlikely to be able to change management through the market for corporate control mechanisms. If the large shareholder owns more than 50 percent of the votes, any proxy fight or hostile bid is doomed to fail. If the controlling shareholder does not want to sell his shares, control cannot be changed.[5]

Finally, some public companies are widely held, where no one shareholder or shareholder group owns a significant number of votes. In these companies, the separation of ownership from control is the most evident. Likewise, the corporate control mechanisms have the greatest chance to succeed. We will review each of the methods for changing corporate control in the next four Sections. But remember, if the firm has a shareholder who owns more than 50 percent of the equity, these methods for changing corporate control won't work unless the controlling shareholder agrees to support the change in control.

LO4 23.6 METHOD 1: PROXY CONTESTS

Shareholders elect the board of directors to keep watch on management and replace unsatisfactory managers. If the board is lax, shareholders are free to elect a different board. In theory this ensures that the corporation is run in the best interests of shareholders.

In practice things are not so clear-cut. Ownership in large public corporations is sometimes widely dispersed and even the largest single shareholder may hold only a small fraction of the shares. Most shareholders have little notion who is on the board or what the members stand for. Management, on the other hand, deals directly with the board and has a personal relationship with its members. In many corporations, management sits on the committee that nominates candidates for the board. It is not surprising that some boards seem less than aggressive in forcing managers to run a lean, efficient operation and to act primarily in the interests of shareholders.

---

[4] The corporations' rankings are from the *Report on Business* magazine, July/August 2011, available online at **www.theglobeandmail.com/report-on-business/rob-magazine/top-1000**. Many of the largest private companies are subsidiaries of others.

[5] To protect non-controlling public shareholders, Canadian securities commissions have implemented special rules governing non–arm's length transactions by controlling shareholders. For example, if the majority shareholder wants to take the company private by purchasing all the shares held by other shareholders, the company must get an independent valuation of the company and a majority of the minority shareholders must approve the transaction.

proxy contest An event in which outsiders compete with management for shareholders' votes in order to take control of the company. Also called *proxy fight* and *proxy battle*.

When a group of investors believes that the board and its management team should be replaced, they can launch a **proxy contest**. A *proxy* is the right to vote another shareholder's shares. In a proxy contest, the dissident shareholders attempt to obtain enough proxies to elect their own slate to the board of directors. Once the new board is in control, management can be replaced and company policy changed. A proxy contest is therefore a direct battle for control of the corporation.

Proxy contests can cost millions of dollars. Dissidents who engage in such fights must use their own money, while management can use the corporation's funds and lines of communication with shareholders to defend itself. The pressure for change often comes from institutional shareholders such as hedge funds and pension funds. Some of these funds have been able to gain concessions from firms without initiating proxy contests. For example, firms have agreed to split the jobs of chief executive officer and chairperson of the board of directors. This ensures that an outsider is responsible for keeping watch over the company. Nevertheless, a proxy contest can be an effective means of forcing change.

EXAMPLE 23.5 MAPLE LEAF FOODS PROXY CONTEST

In December 2010 West Face Capital Inc., a hedge fund that owned about 11 percent of Maple Leaf Foods shares, announced it was launching a proxy battle to reduce the McCain family's influence at Maple Leaf Foods by initiating a process to nominate a new slate of independent directors. West Face Capital expressed concerns that the lack of independence of the board meant that the board did not adequate evaluate management proposals. At the heart of the dispute was a conflict over CEO Michael McCain's ambitious plan to spend $1 billion to expand and modernize the company's facilities.

In February 2011 Maple Leaf Foods ended the fight by agreeing to implement a number of governance reforms, addressing criticism that its board was too closely tied to the McCain family. Maple Leaf Foods gave the chief executive of West Face Capital Inc. a seat on the board of directors, and placed him on number of committees, including the one that helped determine executive compensation. So West Face Capital won the battle.

LO4, 5 23.7 METHOD 2: TAKEOVER BIDS

Poorly performing managers face a greater risk of takeover attempt than from a proxy contest. If the management of one firm believes that another company's management is not acting in the best interest of investors, it can go over the heads of that firm's management and make a takeover bid directly to its shareholders. The management of the target firm may advise its shareholders to accept the offer to sell their shares, or it may fight the bid in hope that the acquirer will either raise its offer or walk away from the deal. If the takeover bid is successful, the new owner can install its own management team. Thus corporate takeovers are the arenas where contests for corporate control are often fought.

EXAMPLE 23.6 THE BATTLE FOR POTASH INC.

In August 2010, British-Australian mining giant BHP Billiton approached the board of directors of Potash Corporation, Canadian base world leading miner of potash, with an offer of US$130 cash per share. BHP's initial offer was rejected by the Potash board of directors, calling it "grossly inadequate" and saying it "substantially undervalues" the company. Then BHP launched a US$40 billion hostile takeover bid for Potash Corp, making a tender offer of US$130 cash per share. Subsequently, Potash Corp management and Saskatchewan Premier worked to stop the takeover by lobbying the Canadian federal government to not approve the bid. After a long battle, the government rejected the bid in November 2010 because they decided it did not have a net benefit for Canada. BHP then withdrew its offer.

TAKEOVER BID TACTICS

The rules of merger warfare are largely set by the *Ontario Securities Act* and are administered by the Ontario Securities Commission (OSC). Ontario dominates in this area because the Toronto Stock Exchange is located in Ontario. However, the various provincial securities acts tend to be similar, and the provincial securities commissions try to work together. The courts act as referee to see that contests are conducted fairly. We will look at one contest that illustrates the tactics and weapons employed.

EXAMPLE 23.7 A HOSTILE TAKEOVER BID: TRILOGY/INDIGO GOES AFTER CHAPTERS

In late November 2000, Trilogy Retail Enterprises, a private company owned by Gerald Schwartz, CEO of Onex Corp., and his wife, Heather Reisman, CEO of Indigo Books, offered $63.5 million ($13 cash per share) for 50.1 percent of Chapters, Canada's largest Canadian book retailer at the time. Schwartz and Reisman, majority shareholders of Indigo, the second-largest Canadian book retailer, suggested they combine Chapters and Indigo and reduce the number of stores. The two companies had been engaged in a tough battle for supremacy in the bookselling business; both had expanded aggressively and both were losing money.

The market reacted favourably, increasing Chapters's price to $11.10 from the previous day's price of $9.10. However, the offer was far below Chapters's $35 peak share price in mid-1999.

Quickly, Chapters's board of directors advised shareholders to reject the bid. Chapters CEO Larry Stevenson called the offer "completely inadequate."

"Shareholders are much better served by us continuing to run this company the way it should be and doing the things we can to maximize shareholder value," he said in an interview. "Shareholders should hold on to their shares."[6]

In a move viewed by many as defensive, Chapters also announced a $25.5 million plan to buy back the 31 percent of Chapters Online shares it did not own, for $3.40 per share. Funds for the buyback would be raised through additional borrowing by Chapters, which would make the company less attractive to a buyer. Those Chapters Online shares had been sold in an initial public offering in September 1999 at $13.50 per share.

Trilogy continued to purchase Chapters shares on the open market, increasing its stake from 9 percent to 14 percent. In early January, Trilogy raised its bid to $15 per share, for a 50.1 percent stake in Chapters.

Chapters's management felt the bid was too low and disliked the fact that it was a partial bid—offering to purchase only 50.1 percent of the shares. They were concerned that accepting Trilogy's partial bid left shareholders in the dark about the potential value of the shares not taken up in the tender offer.

Chapters's management worked hard to thwart the takeover. On several occasions they asked the OSC to order Reisman to allow Chapters to look at Indigo's financial statements. They wanted to estimate the postmerger price of the remaining Chapters shares. The OSC determined that it was not necessary for Indigo to reveal its financial situation to Chapters.

shareholders' rights plan or **poison pill** Measures taken by the target firm to avoid acquisition; for example, the right of existing shareholders to buy additional shares at an attractive price if a bidder acquires a significant holding.

Trilogy, on the other hand, appealed to the OSC to kill Chapters's **shareholders' rights plan**. The rights plan, or **poison pill**, put in place in April 2000, stipulated that anyone who acquired 20 percent or more of the company without meeting the requirements of the Chapters board would find their shareholding diluted through a rights issue. All shareholders other than the raider would be given rights to purchase additional Chapters shares at a low price.

The daily reporting of the very hostile, very public battle for Chapters filled the business press for several months as both sides argued why they were right and the other side was wrong.

white knight Friendly potential acquirer sought by a target company threatened by an unwelcome bidder.

On January 18, 2001, Future Shop unexpectedly entered as a **white knight**. Supported by Chapters's board and management, Future Shop bid $200 million for all of Chapters's common shares. The bid was $16 cash or two Future Shop shares for each Chapters share. Had Trilogy been

[6] G. Livingston, "Indigo CEO Reisman and Husband Gerry Schwartz Bid for Bookseller Chapters," *Canadian Press Newswire*, November 28, 2000.

trumped? Would they come back with a higher bid? The business press speculated that Schwartz and Reisman had been beaten.

However, on January 20, 2001, Trilogy raised its bid to $121.5 million, $17 a share for all Chapters shares except the 30 percent locked up in the Future Shop deal. It was revealed that Schwartz and Reisman would be providing half of the money to pay for the purchase, the other half coming from bank financing. A condition of the revised bid was the removal of Chapters's poison pill. At an unusual Sunday hearing on January 21, 2001, the OSC ruled that Chapters's shareholders' rights plan had served its purpose and it was in the public interest to end it. Schwartz and Reisman had won this round.

At the same time, Schwartz and Reisman met with the federal Competition Bureau to negotiate a plan to deal with the Bureau's concern about the lessening of competition if the two top book retailers were allowed to merge.

With two bids on the table for Chapters, its board of directors formed a special committee of independent (non-management) directors to examine the bids and inform shareholders which bid was better.

In the end, Chapters's board recommended the Trilogy bid to its shareholders, and Schwartz and Reisman's bid for Chapters was successful. The Competition Bureau gave its approval, conditional on the sale of 13 superstores and 10 mall stores of Chapters and Indigo.

The Chapters–Indigo battle illustrates many of the features of Canadian merger warfare. Firms frequently attempt to deter potential bidders by adopting poison pills, which make the company unappealing. In a typical poison pill, or shareholders' rights plan, existing shareholders are given the right to buy additional shares at a low price as soon as the bidder acquires more than 20 percent of the shares. The bidder is not entitled to the discount and finds itself unable to acquire the needed shares.

In Canada, shareholders' rights plans have never been activated, and are typically killed by the OSC at the request of the bidder. Their main value is to extend the bid, giving other bidders time to make an offer.

In addition, bidders and targets ask the securities commissions and the courts to make rulings to prevent or require their opponent to take some action, hoping to help their cause.

The search for a white knight is also typical of many hostile bids. White knights play an important role in raising the bid. Sometimes they successfully acquire the target, sometimes they lose the battle.

shark repellent Amendments to a company charter made to forestall takeover attempts.

Another merger tactic, rare in Canada but used frequently in the United States, is known as **shark repellent**. Managers who are worried about the possibility of a hostile bid will ask shareholders to agree to changes in the corporate charter that make it more difficult for a successful bidder to get control of the board of directors. For example, the charter may be amended to stagger the election of board members, making only one-third of the board up for reelection each year. This means that the bidder cannot obtain majority control of the board immediately after acquiring a majority of the shares. Another example is to require a supermajority of 80 percent of the shares to approve the merger rather than the normal 50 percent. In Canada, most mergers require a two-thirds majority by law.

LO4, 6 23.8 METHOD 3: LEVERAGED BUYOUTS

leveraged buyout (LBO) Acquisition of the firm by a private group using substantial borrowed funds.

Leveraged buyouts (LBOs) differ from ordinary acquisitions in two ways. First, a large fraction of the purchase price is debt-financed. Some, perhaps all, of this debt is *junk*, that is, below investment grade. Second, if the target company was publicly traded, after the LBO the shares no longer trade on the open market. The remaining equity in the LBO is privately held by a small group of (usually institutional) investors and known as *private equity investors*. Thus, the leveraged buyout of a

management buyout (MBO) Acquisition of the firm by its own management in a leveraged buyout.

public company is a *going private transaction*. When the buyout group is led by the company's management, the acquisition is called a **management buyout (MBO)**. Many LBOs are in fact MBOs.

In the 1970s and 1980s many management buyouts were arranged for unwanted divisions of large, diversified companies. Smaller divisions outside the companies' main lines of business often lacked top management's interest and commitment, and divisional management chafed under corporate bureaucracy. Many such divisions flowered when spun off as MBOs. Their managers, pushed by the need to generate cash for debt service and encouraged by a substantial personal stake in the business, found ways to cut costs and compete more effectively.

During the 1980s private-equity activity expanded to include buyouts of entire businesses, including large, mature public corporations. The largest, most dramatic, and best-documented LBO of them all was the $25 billion takeover of RJR Nabisco[7] in 1988 by Kohlberg Kravis Roberts. The players, tactics, and controversies of LBOs are writ large in this case.

EXAMPLE 23.8 RJR NABISCO

On October 28, 1988, the board of directors of RJR Nabisco revealed that Ross Johnson, the company's chief executive officer, had formed a group of investors prepared to buy all the firm's stock for $75 per share in cash and take the company private. Johnson's group was backed up and advised by Shearson Lehman Hutton, the investment bank subsidiary of American Express.

RJR's share price immediately moved to about $75, handing shareholders a 36 percent gain over the previous day's price of $56. At the same time RJR's bonds fell, since it was clear that RJR would be adding a lot more debt.

Johnson's offer lifted RJR onto the auction block. Once the company was in play, its board of directors was obliged to consider other offers. Four days later, a group of investors led by LBO specialists Kohlberg Kravis Roberts (KKR) bid $90 per share, $79 in cash plus preferred stock valued at $11.

The bidding finally closed on November 30, some 32 days after the initial offer was revealed. In the end it was Johnson's group against KKR. KKR offered $109 per share, after adding $1 per share (roughly $230 million) at the last hour. The KKR bid was $81 in cash, convertible subordinated debentures valued at about $10, and preferred shares valued at about $18. Johnson's group bid $112 in cash and securities.

But the RJR board chose KKR. True, Johnson's group had offered $3 per share more, but its security valuations were viewed as "softer" and perhaps overstated. Also, KKR's planned asset sales were less drastic; perhaps their plans for managing the business inspired more confidence. Finally, the Johnson group's proposal contained a management compensation package that seemed extremely generous and had generated an avalanche of bad press.

But where did the merger benefits come from? What could justify offering $109 per share, about $25 billion in all, for a company that only 33 days previously had been selling for $56 per share?

KKR and other bidders were betting on two things. First, they expected to generate billions of additional dollars from interest tax shields, reduced capital expenditures, and sales of assets not strictly necessary to RJR's core businesses. Asset sales alone were projected to generate $5 billion. Second, they expected to make those core businesses significantly more profitable, mainly by cutting back on expenses and bureaucracy. Apparently there was plenty to cut, including the RJR "Air Force," which at one point operated 10 corporate jets.

In the year after KKR took over, new management was installed. This group sold assets and cut back operating expenses and capital spending. There were also layoffs. As expected, high interest charges meant a net loss of $976 million for 1989, but pretax operating income actually increased, despite extensive asset sales, including the sale of RJR's European food operations.

While management was cutting costs and selling assets, prices in the junk bond market were rapidly declining, implying much higher future interest charges for RJR and stricter terms on any

[7] The story of the RJR Nabisco buyout is reconstructed by B. Burrough and J. Helyar in *Barbarians at the Gate: The Fall of RJR Nabisco* (New York: Harper & Row, 1990) and is the subject of a movie with the same title.

refinancing. In mid-1990 KKR made an additional equity investment, and later that year the company announced an offer of cash and new shares in exchange for $753 million of junk bonds. By 1993 the burden of debt had been reduced from $26 billion to $14 billion. For RJR, the world's largest LBO, it seemed that high debt was a temporary, not permanent, virtue.

BARBARIANS AT THE GATE?

The buyout of RJR crystallized views on LBOs, the junk bond market, and the takeover business. For many it exemplified all that was wrong with finance in the 1980s, especially the willingness of "raiders" to carve up established companies, leaving them with enormous debt burdens, basically in order to get rich quick.

There was plenty of confusion, stupidity, and greed in the LBO business. On the other hand, LBOs generated enormous increases in market value, and most of the gains went to selling shareholders, not raiders. For example, the biggest winners in the RJR Nabisco LBO were the company's shareholders.

We should therefore consider briefly where these gains may have come from before we try to pass judgment on LBOs. There are several possibilities.

The Junk Bond Markets LBOs and debt-financed takeovers may have been driven by artificially cheap funding from the junk bond markets. With hindsight it seems that investors in junk bonds underestimated the risks of default. Default rates climbed painfully between 1989 and 1991. At the same time, the junk bond market became much less liquid after the demise of Drexel Burnham Lambert, the chief market maker. Yields rose dramatically, and new issues dried up. For a while junk-financed LBOs disappeared from the scene.

Leverage and Taxes As we explained in Chapter 16, borrowing money saves taxes. But taxes were not the main driving force behind LBOs. The value of interest tax shields was just not big enough to explain the observed gains in market value.

Of course, if interest tax shields were the main motive for LBOs' high debt, then LBO managers would not be so concerned to pay off debt. We saw that this was one of the first tasks facing RJR Nabisco's new management.

Other Stakeholders It is possible that the gain to the selling shareholders is just someone else's loss and that no value is generated overall. Therefore, we should look at the total gain to all investors in an LBO, not just the selling shareholders.

Bondholders are the obvious losers. The debt they thought was well secured may turn into junk when the borrower goes through an LBO. We noted how market prices of RJR Nabisco debt fell sharply when Ross Johnson's first LBO offer was announced. But again, the value losses suffered by bondholders in LBOs are not nearly large enough to explain shareholder gains.

Leverage and Incentives Managers and employees of LBOs work harder and often smarter. They have to generate cash to service the extra debt. Moreover, managers' personal fortunes are riding on the buyout's success. They become owners rather than organization men or women.

It is hard to measure the payoff from better incentives, but there is some evidence of improved operating efficiency in LBOs. Kaplan, who studied 48 management buyouts between 1980 and 1986, found average increases in operating income of 24 percent over the following three years. Ratios of operating income and net cash flow to assets and sales increased dramatically. He observed cutbacks in capital expenditures but not in employment. Kaplan suggests that these operating changes "are due to improved incentives rather than layoffs or managerial exploitation of shareholders through inside information."[8]

[8] S. Kaplan, "The Effects of Management Buyouts on Operating Performance and Value," *Journal of Financial Economics* 24 (October 1989): 217–254.

Free Cash Flow The free-cash-flow theory of takeovers states that mature firms with a surplus of cash will tend to waste it. This contrasts with standard finance theory, which says that firms with more cash than positive-NPV investment opportunities should give the cash back to investors through higher dividends or share repurchases. But we see firms like RJR Nabisco spending on corporate luxuries and questionable capital investments. One benefit of LBOs is to put such companies on a diet and force them to pay out cash to service debt.

The free-cash-flow theory predicts that mature, "cash cow" companies will be the most likely targets of LBOs. We can find many examples that fit the theory, including RJR Nabisco. The theory says that the gains in market value generated by LBOs are just the present values of the future cash flows that would otherwise have been frittered away.[9]

We do not endorse the free-cash-flow theory as the sole explanation for LBOs. We have mentioned several other plausible rationales, and we suspect that most LBOs are driven by a mixture of motives. Nor do we say that all LBOs are beneficial. On the contrary, there are many mistakes, and even soundly motivated LBOs can be dangerous, as the bankruptcies of Campeau, Revco, National Gypsum, and many other highly leveraged companies prove. However, we do take issue with those who portray LBOs simply as Bay Street or Wall Street barbarians breaking up the traditional strengths of corporate North America. In many cases LBOs have generated true gains.

RECENT LBO ACTIVITY

The buyout of RJR Nabisco illustrates how during the merger boom of the 1980s even very large companies were not immune from attack by a rival management team. But by the end of the 1980s the merger environment had changed. Many of the obvious targets had disappeared and the battle for RJR Nabisco highlighted the increasing cost of victory. Institutions were reluctant to increase their holdings of junk bonds. Moreover, the market for these bonds had depended to a remarkable extent on one individual, Michael Milken, of the investment bank Drexel Burnham Lambert. By the late 1980s Milken and his employer were in trouble. Milken was indicted by a grand jury on 98 counts and was subsequently sentenced to jail. Drexel filed for bankruptcy, but by that time the junk bond market was moribund and the finance for highly leveraged buyouts had largely dried up.[10] Finally, in reaction to the perceived excesses of the merger boom, the state legislatures and the courts began to lean against hostile takeovers.

Toward the end of the 1990s, leveraged buyouts began making a comeback, encouraged by low interest rates and easy access to debt financing. The trend continued into the 2000s, with LBOs escalating in number around the world, involving larger companies and with increasingly higher leverage. Financed by the substantial increase in private equity funds, plus the availability of cheap debt financing, private equity buyouts around the world hit a peak in 2006 and the first half of 2007. In 2007, about 26 percent of all North American acquisitions were leveraged buyouts. In June 2007, BCE was the target of leveraged buyout for $34.8 million. Had the deal succeed, it would have been the world's largest LBO. However, the financial market crisis caused the deal to fail. The deal's auditors assessed that BCE would be insolvent with all of the debt.

The largest private equity investors in Canada include Teachers' Private Capital, the private equity arm of the Ontario Teachers' Pension Plan, and Onex, a Canadian publicly owned private equity investor, and its buyout funds, Onex Partners I and II and ONCAP. Canadian mid-sized private equity players include Birch Hill Equity Partners, EdgeStone Capital Partners, and

---

[9] The free-cash-flow theory's chief proponent is Michael Jensen. See M.C. Jensen, "The Eclipse of the Public Corporation," *Harvard Business Review* 67 (September/October 1989): 61–74, and "The Agency Costs of Free Cash Flow, Corporate Finance and Takeovers," *American Economic Review* 76 (May 1986): 323–329.

[10] For a history of the role of Milken in the development of the junk bond market, see C. Bruck, *The Predator's Ball: The Junk Bond Raiders and the Man Who Staked Them* (New York: Simon and Schuster, 1988).

Finance in Action

Predictions of Growth in Leveraged Buyouts

Expect more debt-backed takeover bids like Valeant Pharmaceuticals's offer for Cephalon Inc. now that credit markets are largely recovered from the financial crisis, top bankers said on Tuesday.

Large leveraged deals, which were wildly popular just before the crisis, will gather steam both globally and in Canada given interest rates still at or near historic lows and increased investors confidence, bankers told the Toronto leg of the Reuters Global Mergers and Acquisitions Summit.

"Credit is a lot more available. You're seeing leverage multiples go up. You have private equity buyers who are sitting on a lot of investment capital," said "You're definitely going to see more transactions of that nature." Private equity-style takeovers—known as leveraged buyouts or LBOs—plunged after the credit crisis as access to debt financing froze.

CIBC's Michael Boyd, the bank's head of M&A, said he was surprised how quickly and dramatically the credit markets have bounced back and at the magnitude of leverage available to fund deals. "If you'd asked me a year ago if you'd see a $5 billion LBO in the next two years, I probably would have said 'no' because people's memories of the financial crisis were pretty fresh," he told Reuters. "Now we're seeing deals of that size. People are talking about LBOs larger than that—$10 billion, $15 billion."

Recent deals by private equity firms include Blackstone Group LP's plans to buy Australia's Centro Property Group for about $9.4 billion and KKR & Co LP's plans to buy the hard capsules unit of Pfizer Inc for nearly $2.38 billion. One of last year's largest leveraged buyouts was the acquisition of British car parts maker Tomkins Plc by Onex, Canada's largest private equity firm, and the Canada Pension Plan Investment Board for about $5 billion.

While private equity firms are the ones who typically finance their acquisitions with large amounts of debt, the Valeant move indicates companies are also taking advantage of the strength in the credit markets.

However, the amount of leverage as a percentage of deals is likely to be tempered this time and not go to extreme levels seen before the financial crisis hit, said Andre Hidi, head of global M&A at BMO Capital Markets, a unit of BMO Financial Group.

"We'll continue to see large leveraged transactions, whether by sponsors or in even some cases by corporates who want to offer cash," he said. The availability of debt has helped drive up deal sizes. Hidi estimated the average deal size, excluding those below $100 million, in Canada has surged to $1 billion, compared with $500 million a year ago.

Source: S. John Tilak and Pav Jordan, "Reuters Summit: Bankers See Rebound in Leveraged Deals," ed. Jeffrey Hodgson and Tim Dobbyn, Yahoo News, April 6, 2011, **in.reuters.com/article/2011/04/05/idINIndia-56144220110405**.

TorQuest Partners. The largest private equity funds in the US include Kohlberg Kravis Roberts (KKR), and the Blackstone Group.[11]

In a typical LBO, the private equity investor, also known as the *equity sponsor*, identifies a company to be bought out and works with lenders to determine how much debt financing the lenders are willing to provide to finance the buyout. The equity sponsor provides the equity financing for the LBO. In a typical deal, senior secured financing is provided by banks and junior unsecured financing is provided by investment funds specializing in providing debt financing to leveraged buyouts.

The extent of the leverage varies with market conditions and the ability of the target company to produce cash flow to meet interest and principal payments. For the peak years of the LBO boom, debt provided between 50 and 75 percent of the funds needed for the buyout. When the U.S. subprime crisis hit in mid-2007, interest rates rose and the amount of debt available to fund LBOs decreased dramatically. The number of leveraged buyouts plummeted. Some of the companies that had been bought out with LBOs went bankrupt because of the economic slowdown, causing revenues to fall, and high interest rates.

In 2011 economies were recovering from the financial crisis, debt markets had are largely recovered from the financial crisis and banks were more willing to provide debt financing for acquisitions. Leveraged buyouts are starting to occur again. See the nearby Finance in Action box for a prediction of their growth.

[11] See the McKinsey & Company site, at **www.mckinsey.com/client_service/private_equity/** for information on the Canadian private equity industry.

LO3 23.9 METHOD 4: DIVESTITURES, SPIN-OFFS, AND EQUITY CARVE-OUTS

In the market for corporate control, fusion—mergers and acquisitions—gets the most publicity. But fission—the divestiture of assets or entire businesses—can be just as important. Often one firm may sell part of its business to another firm. For example, in March 2011, Yellow Media announced the sale of one of its wholly owned subsidiary, Trader Corp., to British-based Apax Partners for $745 million cash to reduce debt and focus on its transition to a digital company. Yellow Media is in the paper and online phone directory business (Yellow Pages) and Trader Corp has about 160 publications and 22 Web sites on auto, property, general merchandise, and jobs. The CEO of Yellow Media said that the divestiture would be attractive to shareholders and would provide the company with money to invest in their core digital business. Another way to do a divestiture of a subsidiary is to make an initial public offering (IPO), of the shares of the subsidiary. An IPO sells the business to investors.

Instead of selling a business to another firm or to investors, companies may *spin off* the business: separate it from the parent firm and distribute stock in the newly independent company to the shareholders of the parent. For example, BCE decided to spin off almost all of its holdings of Nortel Networks to BCE shareholders. Although at one time BCE owned all of Nortel, by January 2000 it was a minority shareholder, owning 39 percent of Nortel's stock. These shares accounted for about 78 percent of BCE's value. BCE management and some analysts felt that the non-Nortel assets of BCE were not being fully valued, overshadowed by the Nortel holdings. BCE shareholders received .78 Nortel share for each BCE share. On the announcement of the widely anticipated spin-off, BCE's share price rose about 5 percent. Given the colossal crash of Nortel's stock value in 2001, BCE's management looks pretty smart (or lucky) to have disconnected from Nortel.

A special case of a spin-off is a split-up, in which the entire company is separated into new companies and then all shares of the original company are exchanged for shares of the new companies. Example 23.9 explains the split-up of Canadian Pacific. Because Canadian Pacific was a huge company, the executive called it a "starburst split."

EXAMPLE 23.9 CANADIAN PACIFIC "STARBURST" SPLIT

Another major Canadian spin-off was announced in February 2001, when Canadian Pacific (CP) revealed its plans to split into five companies, each of which was to be publicly traded.

In July 2001, the details were finalized. Each common share of CP was to be exchanged for .5 CP Railway common shares, .25 CP Ships common shares, .25 Fairmont Hotel and Resorts common shares, .684 PanCanadian Energy common shares, and .166 Fording common shares.

CP stated that the reorganization was designed to maximize value for its shareholders by unlocking the current value of the businesses and strengthening their ability to pursue further success as independent companies. The stated hope of management was that the sum of the value of shares of the new companies would exceed the current market value of the pre-split Canadian Pacific common shares.

Investors clearly welcomed the split: the stock price jumped nearly 11 percent on the day the plan was announced.

Probably the most frequent motive for divestitures and spin-offs is improved efficiency. Companies sometimes refer to a business as being a "poor fit." By spinning off a poor fit, the management of the parent company can concentrate on its main activity. If every business has to stand on its own two feet, there is no risk that funds will be siphoned off from one to support unprofitable investments in the other. Moreover, if the two parts are independent, it is easy to see the value of each and to reward managers accordingly.

In an equity *carve-out*, rather than shares in the new company being given to existing stockholders, some are sold in a public offering. Thus, cash is raised. Unlike an IPO, in which most of the shares are sold to investors, in a carve-out typically only 20 percent of the equity is sold. As a result the firm still owns 80 percent of its subsidiary but now there is a stock price for the subsidiary, which can be a useful tool for motivating the managers of the subsidiary. Sometimes companies do the equity carve-out to establish a market in the subsidiary and subsequently spin off the remainder of the shares to the company's shareholders.

Tim Hortons, founded as private company in 1964, was bought by Wendy's International in 1995. Wendy's planned to grow the company in the United States. However, poor performance by Wendy's hamburger chain and the strong performance of the Hortons chain put pressure on Wendy's to sell Hortons to provide money for Wendy's shareholders. Therefore, in March 2006, Wendy's International did an equity carve-out, keeping about 85 percent of the Hortons shares. Then, in September 2006, Wendy's International did a spin-off its Tim Hortons shares through a special dividend to Wendy's International shareholders, creating Tim Hortons as a stand-alone public company.

LO7 23.10 THE BENEFITS AND COSTS OF MERGERS

Merger activity comes in waves and is concentrated in a relatively small number of industries. This urge to merge frequently seems to be prompted by deregulation and by changes in technology or the pattern of demand. Take the merger wave of the 1990s, for example. Deregulation of telecoms and financial services in the United States and Canada earlier in the decade led to a spate of mergers in both industries. In the entertainment industry the prospective advantages from controlling both content and distribution led to mergers between such giants as AOL and Time Warner. Canadian companies followed, including the merger of CTV and *The Globe and Mail* to create Bell Globemedia. Now, many mergers involve companies from different countries and are called cross-border deals.

There are undoubtedly good acquisitions and bad acquisitions, but economists find it hard to agree on whether acquisitions are beneficial on balance. In general, shareholders of the target firm make a healthy gain. For example, a Canadian study found that following the announcement of a bid for all of the company's shares, the stock price of the target company jumped by 22 percent on average but when the bid was for less than all of the shares, the target's stock price rose 13 percent on average.[12] On the other hand, studies have shown that investors expected the acquiring companies to just about break even. In a Canadian study the price of bidder firms' shares rose about 1 percent but in a U.S. study, bidder shares fell by .7 percent.[13] Generally, studies have found that the value of the total package—buyer plus seller—has increased. Of course, these are averages; selling shareholders, for example, have sometimes obtained much higher returns. When IBM took over Lotus Corporation, it paid a premium of 100 percent, or about \$1.7 billion, for Lotus stock.

Since buyers roughly break even and sellers make substantial gains, it seems that there are positive overall benefits from mergers. But not everybody is convinced. Some believe that investors analyzing mergers pay too much attention to short-term earnings gains, and don't notice that these gains are at the expense of long-term prospects.

Since we can't observe how companies would have fared in the absence of a merger, it is difficult to measure the effects on profitability. However, several studies of merger activity suggest that mergers do seem to improve real productivity. For example, Healy, Palepu, and Ruback

[12] See B. Amoako-Adu and B. Smith, "Comparative Study of Complete Tender Offers and Partial Acquisitions," *Journal of Banking and Finance* 17 (1993): 1097–1110.

[13] The Canadian study is B.E. Eckbo, "Mergers and the Market for Corporate Control: The Canadian Evidence," *Canadian Journal of Economics* 19 (1986): 236–260. The U.S. study is G. Andrade, M. Mitchell, and E. Stafford, "New Evidence and Perspectives on Mergers," *Journal of Economic Perspectives* 15 (Spring 2001): 103–120.

examined 50 large mergers between 1979 and 1983 and found an average increase in the companies' pretax returns of 2.4 percentage points.[14] They argue that this gain came from generating a higher level of sales from the same assets. There was no evidence that the companies were mortgaging their long-term futures by cutting back on long-term investments; expenditures on capital equipment and research and development tracked the industry average.

If you are concerned with public policy toward mergers, you do not want to look only at their impact on the shareholders of the companies concerned. For instance, we have already seen that in the case of RJR Nabisco, some part of the shareholders' gain was at the expense of the bondholders and the U.S. government (through the enlarged interest tax shield). The acquirer's shareholders may also gain at the expense of the target firm's employees, who in some cases are laid off or are forced to take pay cuts after takeovers.

Perhaps the most important effect of acquisition is felt by the managers of companies that are not taken over. For example, one effect of LBOs was that the managers of even the largest corporations could not feel safe from challenge. Perhaps the threat of takeover spurs every employee to try harder. Unfortunately, we don't know whether on balance the threat of merger makes for more active days or sleepless nights.

The threat of takeover may be a spur to inefficient management, but it is also costly. It can soak up large amounts of management time and effort. When a company is planning a takeover, it can be difficult to give as much attention as one should to the firm's existing business. In addition, the companies need to pay for the services provided by the investment bankers, lawyers, and accountants. In 2000, merging companies paid in total more than $2 billion for professional assistance.

Even if the gains to the community exceed these costs, one wonders whether the same benefits could not be achieved more cheaply another way. For example, are leveraged buyouts necessary to make managers work harder? Perhaps the problem lies in the way that many corporations reward and penalize their managers. Perhaps many of the gains from takeover could be captured by linking management compensation more closely to performance.

[14] See P. Healy, K. Palepu, and R. Ruback, "Does Corporate Performance Improve After Mergers?" *Journal of Financial Economics* 31 (April 1992): 135–175. The study examined the pretax returns of the merged companies relative to industry averages.

23.11 SUMMARY

1. Why might it make sense for companies to merge? LO1

A merger may be undertaken in order to replace an inefficient management. But sometimes two businesses may be more valuable together than apart, the merger creates **synergy**. Gains, the sources of synergy, may stem from increased revenues, economies of scale, economies of vertical integration, the combination of complementary resources, reduced taxes, or redeployment of surplus funds. We don't know how frequently these benefits occur, but they do make economic sense. Sometimes mergers are undertaken to diversify risks or artificially increase growth of earnings per share. These motives are dubious.

2. How do mergers occur? LO2

A merger, the acquisition of control of another firm, can occur through negotiations with the board of directors of the target firm to arrange an **amalgamation**, the combination of the assets and liabilities of the two firms. Then the shareholders of both firms need to vote to approve the amalgamation. Or a **takeover bid** (a tender offer in the U.S.) can be made to buy the stock of the target firm's shareholders, without negotiating with the target firm's board of directors. Also, the acquisition can be the purchase of individual assets of the target, arranged through negotiations with the target board of directors.

3. **How should the gains and costs of mergers to the acquiring firm be measured? LO3**

   A merger generates an economic gain if the two firms are worth more together than apart. The *gain* is the difference between the value of the merged firm and the value of the two firms run independently. The *cost* is the premium that the buyer pays for the selling firm over its value as a separate entity. When payment is in the form of shares, the value of this payment naturally depends on what those shares are worth after the merger is complete. You should go ahead with the merger if the gain exceeds the cost.

4. **In what ways do companies change the composition of their ownership or management? LO4**

   If the board of directors fails to replace an inefficient management, there are four ways to effect a change: (1) shareholders may engage in a **proxy contest** to replace the board; (2) the firm may be acquired by another; (3) the firm may be purchased by a private group of investors in a leveraged buyout; or (4) it may sell off part of its operations to another company.

5. **What are some takeover defences? LO5**

   Mergers are often amicably negotiated between the management and directors of the two companies, but if the seller is reluctant, the would-be buyer can decide to make a tender offer for the stock. We sketched some of the offensive and defensive tactics used in takeover battles. These defences include **shark repellents** (changes in the company charter meant to make a takeover more difficult to achieve), **shareholders' rights plans** or **poison pills** (measures that make takeover of the firm more costly), and the search for **white knights** (the attempt to find a friendly acquirer before the unfriendly one takes over the firm).

6. **What are some of the motivations for leveraged and management buyouts of the firm? LO6**

   In a **leveraged buyout** (LBO) or **management buyout** (MBO), all public shares are repurchased and the company "goes private." LBOs tend to involve mature businesses with ample cash flow and modest growth opportunities. LBOs and other debt-financed takeovers are driven by a mixture of motives, including (1) the value of interest tax shields, (2) transfers of value from bondholders, who may see the value of their bonds fall as the firm piles up more debt, and (3) the opportunity to create better incentives for managers and employees, who have a personal stake in the company. In addition, many LBOs have been designed to force firms with surplus cash to distribute it to shareholders rather than plowing it back. Investors feared such companies would otherwise channel free cash flow into negative-NPV investments.

7. **Do mergers increase efficiency and how are the gains from mergers distributed between shareholders of the acquired and acquiring firms? LO7**

   We observed that when the target firm is acquired, its shareholders typically win: target firms' shareholders earn abnormally large returns. The bidding firm's shareholders roughly break even. This suggests that the typical merger appears to generate positive net benefits, but competition among bidders and active defence by management of the target firm pushes most of the gains toward selling shareholders.

Related Web Links

crosbieco.com/ma/index.html Canadian merger data

mergernetwork.com Information about companies for sale

corpgov.net The Corporate Governance Network

biz.yahoo.com/topic/m-a Yahoo's merger site

blackstone.com Blackstone Group, private equity and other investment fund manager

kkr.com Kohlberg Kravis Roberts, large private equity and other investment funds

onex.ca Onex, Canada's largest publicly owned private equity investor

otpp.com/web/website.nsf/web/privatecapital Teachers' Private Capital, the private equity fund of the Ontario Teachers' Pension Plan

Key Terms

amalgamation	730
leveraged buyout (LBO)	741
management buyout (MBO)	742
merger	724
proxy contest	739
shareholders' rights plan *or* poison pill	740
shark repellent	741
synergy	726
takeover bid *or* tender offer	731
white knight	740

Questions and Problems

connect Practise and learn online with *Connect*. Questions with online Excel templates or datasets are marked with [Excel icon].

*Answers in Appendix B

BASIC

1. **Merger Motives.** Which of the following motives for mergers make economic sense? (LO1)
   a. Merging to achieve economies of scale
   b. Merging to reduce risk by diversification
   c. Merging to redeploy cash generated by a firm with ample profits but limited growth opportunities
   d. Merging to increase earnings per share
2. **Merger Motives.** Explain why it might make sense for Northeast Heating and Northeast Air Conditioning to merge into one company. (LO1)
3. **Empirical Facts.** True or false? (LO7)
   a. Sellers almost always gain in mergers.
   b. Buyers almost always gain in mergers.
   c. Firms that do unusually well tend to be acquisition targets.
   d. Merger activity in Canada varies dramatically from year to year.
   e. On the average, mergers produce substantial economic gains.
   f. Tender offers (or takeover bids) require the approval of the selling firm's management.
   g. The cost of a merger is always independent of the economic gain produced by the merger.
4. **Merger Tactics.** Connect each term to its correct definition or description: (LO7)

A. LBO	1. Attempt to gain control of a firm by winning the votes of its shareholders.
B. Poison pill	2. Changes in corporate charter designed to deter an unwelcome takeover.
C. Takeover bid	3. Friendly potential acquirer sought by a threatened target firm.
D. Shark repellent	4. Shareholders are issued rights to buy shares if a bidder acquires a large stake in the firm.
E. Proxy contest	5. Offer to buy shares directly from shareholders.
F. White knight	6. Company or business bought out by private investors, largely debt financed

5. **LBO Facts.** True or false? (LO7)
   a. One of the first tasks of an LBO's financial manager is to pay down debt.
   b. The cost of a merger is affected by the size of the merger gains only when the merger is financed with cash.
   c. Targets for LBOs in the 1980s tended to be profitable companies in mature industries with limited investment opportunities.

INTERMEDIATE

*6. **Merger Gains.** Acquiring Corp. is considering a takeover of Takeover Target Inc. Acquiring has 10 million shares outstanding, which sell for $40 each. Takeover Target has 5 million shares outstanding, which sell for $20 each. If the merger gains are estimated at $20 million, what is the highest price per share that Acquiring should be willing to pay to Takeover Target shareholders? What is Acquiring's NPV if it pays the maximum price? (LO3)

7. **Mergers and P/E Ratios.** If Acquiring Corp. from the previous problem has a price-earnings ratio of 12, and Takeover Target has a P/E ratio of 8, what should be the P/E ratio of the merged firm? Assume in this case that the merger is financed by an issue of new Acquiring Corp. shares. Takeover Target will get one Acquiring share for every two Takeover Target shares held. (LO1)

*8. **Merger Gains and Costs.** Velcro Saddles is contemplating the acquisition of Pogo Ski Sticks, Inc. The values of the two companies as separate entities are $20 million and $10 million, respectively. Velcro Saddles estimates that by combining the two companies, it will reduce after-tax marketing and administrative costs by $500,000 per year in perpetuity. Velcro Saddles is willing to pay $14 million cash for Pogo. The opportunity cost of capital is 8 percent and the tax rate is 30 percent. (LO3)
   a. What would be the gain from the merger?
   b. What is the cost of the cash offer?
   c. What is the NPV of the acquisition under the cash offer?

9. **Stock Versus Cash Offers.** Suppose that instead of making a cash offer as in the previous problem, Velcro Saddles considers offering Pogo shareholders a 50 percent holding in Velcro Saddles. (LO3)
   a. What is the value of the stock in the merged company held by the original Pogo shareholders?

b. What is the cost of the stock alternative?
c. What is its NPV under the stock offer?

10. **Merger Gains.** Immense Appetite, Inc., believes that it can acquire Sleepy Industries and improve efficiency to the extent that the market value of Sleepy will increase by $5 million. Sleepy currently sells for $20 a share, and there are 1 million shares outstanding. (LO3)
    a. Sleepy's management is willing to accept a cash offer of $25 a share. Can the merger be accomplished on a friendly basis?
    b. What will happen if Sleepy's management holds out for an offer of $28 a share?

11. **Mergers and P/E Ratios.** Castles in the Sand currently sells at a price-earnings multiple of 10. The firm has 2 million shares outstanding and sells at a price per share of $40. Firm Foundation has a P/E multiple of 8, has 1 million shares outstanding, and sells at a price per share of $20. (LO1)
    a. If Castles acquires the other firm by exchanging one of its shares for every two of Firm Foundation's, what will be the earnings per share of the merged firm?
    b. What should be the P/E of the new firm if the merger has no economic gains? What will happen to Castles's price per share? Show that shareholders of neither Castles nor Firm Foundation realize any change in wealth.
    c. What will happen to Castles's price per share if the market does not realize that the P/E ratio of the merged firm ought to differ from Castles's pre-merger ratio?
    d. How are the gains from the merger split between shareholders of the two firms if the market is fooled as in part (c)?

*12. **Stock Versus Cash Offers.** Sweet Cola Corp. (SCC) is bidding to take over Salty Dog Pretzels (SDP). SCC has 3,000 shares outstanding, selling at $50 per share. SDP has 2,000 shares outstanding, selling at $17.50 a share. SCC estimates the economic gain from the merger to be $10,000. (LO3)
    a. If SDP can be acquired for $20 a share, what is the NPV of the merger to SCC?
    b. What will SCC sell for when the market learns that it plans to acquire SDP for $20 a share? What will SDP sell for? What are the percentage gains to the shareholders of each firm? What fraction of the economic gain do SCC's shareholders receive? What fraction goes to SDP's shareholders?
    c. Now suppose that the merger takes place through an exchange of stock. Based on the pre-merger prices of the firms, SCC issues .40 of its shares for every SDP share. What will be the price of the merged firm?
    d. What is the NPV of the merger to SCC when it uses an exchange of stock? What fraction of the economic gain do SCC's shareholders receive? Why does your answer differ from parts (a) and (b)? Calculate the share exchange equivalent to the cash offer in part (a).

CHALLENGE

13. **Internet.** *Mergers and Acquisitions in Canada* reports on current merger activity in Canada. It is available in libraries and parts of it can be found at **www.crosbieco.com/ma/index.html**. Select "Press Release" for recent summaries of merger activity in Canada. Read the most current and the oldest press releases and compare them. Is the same industry experiencing the greatest M&A activity? How have the cross-border transactions changed? (LO7)

14. **Bootstrap Game.** The Muck and Slurry merger has fallen through (see Section 23.2). But World Enterprises is determined to report earnings per share of $2.67. It therefore acquires the Wheelrim and Axle Company.

    Once again there are no gains from merging. In exchange for Wheelrim and Axle shares, World Enterprises issues just enough of its own shares to ensure its $2.67 earnings per share objective. Here are the facts you are given: (LO1)

	World Enterprises	Wheelrim and Axle	Merged Firm
Earnings per share	$ 2	$ 2.50	$2.67
Price per share	$ 40	$ 25	_____
Price-earnings ratio	20	10	_____
Number of shares	100,000	200,000	_____
Total earnings	$ 200,000	$ 500,000	_____
Total market value	$4,000,000	$5,000,000	_____

    a. Complete the above table for the merged firm.
    b. How many shares of World Enterprises are exchanged for each share of Wheelrim and Axle?
    c. What is the cost of the merger to World Enterprises?
    d. What is the change in the total market value of those World Enterprises shares that were outstanding before the merger?

15. **Integrative.** As treasurer of Leisure Products, Inc., you are investigating the possible acquisition of Plastitoys. You have the following basic data:

	Leisure Products	Plastitoys
Forecast earnings per share	$ 5	$1.50
Forecast dividend per share	$ 3	$ .80
Number of shares	1,000,000	600,000
Stock price	$90	$ 20

You estimate that investors currently expect a steady growth of about 6 percent in Plastitoys's earnings and dividends. You believe that Leisure Products could increase Plastitoys's growth rate to 8 percent per year, after 1 year, without any additional capital investment required. (LO3)

a. What is the economic gain from the acquisition?
b. What is the cost of the acquisition if Leisure Products pays $25 in cash for each share of Plastitoys? What is the NPV to Leisure of acquiring Plastitoys?
c. What is the cost of the acquisition if Leisure Products offers 1 share of Leisure Products for every 3.96 shares of Plastitoys? What is the NPV to Leisure of acquiring Plastitoy?
d. Suppose immediately after the completion of the merger, everyone realizes that the expected growth rate will not be improved. Reassess the cost and NPV of the cash and share offers. Explain what you find.

16. **Internet.** The Ontario Teachers Pension Plan Board (Teachers), **www.otpp.com**, and the Ontario Municipal Employees Retirement System (OMERS), **www.omers.com**, manage very large investment portfolios. (LO7)
    a. What are the current sizes of their portfolios?
    b. As active shareholders, they closely monitor the activities of the companies they own. Review their corporate governance policies. What issues concern them?
    c. Click on the "Proxy Votes" at the Teachers Web site and then look under "Upcoming Meetings" and pick a company. You will see a list of issues to be voted at an upcoming shareholders meeting and how Teachers intends to vote. Click on the little "i" and read the reasons for Teachers' position. Do you agree?
    d. At the OMERS Web site, click on "Investments," "What we do," "Read our investments," and then "Learn more about our proxy voting." What proposals has OMERS voted against?
17. **Internet.** You might be interested in becoming a Chartered Business Valuator, CBV, an expert in business valuation. You can read about this program of study at the Web site of the Canadian Institute of Chartered Business Valuators, **www.cicbv.ca**. The site also provides a list of valuation terms, **cicbv.ca/glossary**. (LO1)

Solutions to Check Points

23.1 a. *Horizontal merger.* IBM is in the same industry as Apple Computer.
b. *Conglomerate merger.* RIM and Empire Company are in different industries.
c. *Vertical merger.* Loblaws is expanding backward to acquire one of its suppliers, Lassonde Industries.
d. *Conglomerate merger.* EnCana and Canada Bread are in different industries.

23.2 Given current earnings of $2 a share, and a share price of $10, Muck and Slurry would have a market value of $1,000,000 and a price-earnings ratio of only 5. It can be acquired for only half as many shares of World Enterprises, 25,000 shares. Therefore, the merged firm will have 125,000 shares outstanding and earnings of $400,000, resulting in earnings per share of $3.20, higher than the $2.67 value in the third column of Table 23.2.

23.3 The cost of the merger is $4 million: the $4 per share premium offered to Goldfish shareholders × 1 million shares. If the merger has positive NPV to Killer Shark, the gain must be greater than $4 million.

23.4 Yes. Look again at Table 23.4. Total market value is still $540, but Cislunar will have to issue 1 million shares to complete the merger. Total shares in the merged firm will be 11 million. The post-merger share price is $49.09, so Cislunar and its shareholders still come out ahead.

MINI CASE

McPhee Food Halls operated a chain of supermarkets in western Scotland. The company had had a lacklustre record, and, since the death of its founder in late 2005, it had been regarded as a prime target for takeover. In anticipation of a bid, McPhee's share price moved up from £4.90 in March 2006 to a 12-month high of £5.80 on June 10, despite the fact that the London stock market index as a whole was largely unchanged.

Almost nobody anticipated a bid coming from Fenton, a diversified retail business with a chain of clothing and department stores. Though Fenton operated food halls in several of its department stores, it had relatively little experience in food retailing. Fenton's management, however, had been contemplating a merger with McPhee for some time. They not only felt that they could make use of McPhee's food retailing skills within their department stores, but they believed that better management and inventory control in McPhee's business could result in cost savings worth £10 million.

Fenton's offer of 8 Fenton shares for every 10 McPhee shares was announced after the market close on June 10. Since McPhee had 5 million shares outstanding, the acquisition would add $5 \times (8/10) = 4$ million shares to the 10 million already outstanding. While Fenton's management believed that it would be difficult for McPhee to mount a successful takeover defence, the company and its investment bankers privately agreed that the company could afford to raise the offer if it proved necessary.

Investors were not persuaded of the benefits of combining a supermarket with a department store company, and on June 11, Fenton's shares opened lower and drifted down £.10 to close the day at £7.90. McPhee's shares, however, jumped to £6.32 a share.

Fenton's financial manager was due to attend a meeting with the company's investment bankers that evening, but before doing so he decided to run the numbers once again. First he reestimated the gain and the cost of the merger. Then he analyzed that day's fall in Fenton's stock price to see whether investors believed there were any gains to be had from merging. Finally, he decided to revisit the issue of whether Fenton could afford to raise its bid at a later stage. If the effect was simply a further fall in the price of Fenton stock, the move could be self-defeating.

PART 8

Special Topics

23 Mergers, Acquisitions, and Corporate Control
24 International Financial Management
24.1 Foreign Exchange Markets
24.2 Some Basic Relationships
24.3 Hedging Exchange Rate Risk
24.4 International Capital Budgeting
24.5 Summary
25 Options
26 Risk Management

CHAPTER 24

International Financial Management

LEARNING OBJECTIVES

After studying this chapter, you should be able to:

LO1 Explain the difference between spot and forward exchange rates.

LO2 Explain the basic relationships between spot exchange rates, forward exchange rates, interest rates, and inflation rates.

LO3 Formulate simple strategies to protect the firm against exchange rate risk.

LO4 Perform an NPV analysis for projects with cash flows in foreign currencies.

Bombardier's train manufacturing business, Bombardier Transportation, has its worldwide headquarters in Berlin, Germany. Bombardier does business in many countries around the world.

Courtesy of Bombardier Inc.

Thus far we have talked principally about doing business at home. But many companies have substantial overseas interests. Of course, the objectives of international financial management are still the same. You want to buy assets that are worth *more* than they cost, and you want to pay for them by issuing liabilities that are worth *less* than the money raised. But when you try to apply these criteria to an international business, you come up against some new wrinkles.

You must, for example, know how to deal with more than one currency. Therefore we open this chapter with a look at foreign exchange markets.

The financial manager must also remember that interest rates differ from country to country. For example, at the end of February 2011 the short-term rate of interest was about .1 percent in Japan, 1.0 percent in Canada, .125 percent in the United States, and 1.0 percent in the euro countries. We will discuss the reasons for these differences in interest rates, along with some of the implications for financing overseas operations.

Exchange rate fluctuations can knock companies off course and transform black ink into red. We will therefore discuss how firms can protect themselves against exchange risks.

We will also discuss how international companies decide on capital investments. How do they choose the discount rate? You'll find that the basic principles of capital budgeting are the same as for domestic projects, but there are a few pitfalls to watch for.

LO1 24.1 FOREIGN EXCHANGE MARKETS

A Canadian company that imports goods from Switzerland may need to exchange its dollars for Swiss francs in order to pay for its purchases. A Canadian company exporting to Switzerland may *receive* Swiss francs, which it sells in exchange for dollars. Both firms must make use of the foreign exchange market, where currencies are traded.

The foreign exchange market has no central marketplace. All business is conducted by computer and telephone. The principal dealers are the large commercial banks, and any corporation that wants to buy or sell currency usually does so through a commercial bank.

Turnover in the foreign exchange markets is huge. In London alone about US$1,480 billion of currency changes hands every day. That is equivalent to an annual turnover of US$370 trillion ($370,000,000,000,000). New York and Tokyo together account for a further $880 billion of turnover per day. Compare this to the trading volume of the New York Stock Exchange, in which no more than US$70 billion of stock might change hands on a typical day.

TABLE 24.1 Currency exchange rates on March 22, 2011.

Closing Midpoint Rates at 4:00 p.m. London Time, March 22, 2011							
		1 US$ in C$ =	1 C$ in US$ =	Country/Region	Currency	C$ per Unit*	US$ per Unit
U.S./Canada Spot		0.9770	1.023541	**India**	**Rupee**	0.021728	0.022240
1 month forward		0.9777	1.022809	**Indonesia**	**Rupiah**	0.000112	0.000115
3 months forward		0.9790	1.021450	**Iran**	**Rial**	0.000094	0.000096
12 months forward		0.9868	1.013377	**Israel**	**Shekel**	0.276810	0.283326
Country/Region	Currency	C$ per Unit*	US$ per Unit	**Korea South**	**Won**	0.000872	0.000892
Britain	**Pound**	1.601010	1.6387	**Kuwait**	**Dinar**	3.528350	3.611412
1 month forward		1.601570	1.6381	**Malaysia**	**Ringgit**	0.322495	0.330087
3 months forward		1.602329	1.6367	**Mexico**	**Peso**	0.081498	0.083417
12 months forward		1.605622	1.6271	**New Zealand**	**Dollar**	0.724186	0.741235
Europe	**Euro**	1.388512	1.4212	**Norway**	**Nor. Krone**	0.175410	0.179540
1 month forward		1.388725	1.4204	**Peru**	**New Sol**	0.350997	0.359260
3 months forward		1.389103	1.4189	**Philippines**	**Peso**	0.022548	0.023079
12 months forward		1.389020	1.4076	**Poland**	**Zloty**	0.344135	0.352237
Japan	**Yen**	0.012061	0.012345	**Russia**	**Rouble**	0.034629	0.035445
1 month forward		0.012072	0.012347	**Saudi Arabia**	**Riyal**	0.260512	0.266645
3 months forward		0.012094	0.012353	**Singapore**	**Dollar**	0.773433	0.791640
12 months forward		0.012244	0.012408	**South Africa**	**Rand**	0.141820	0.145159
Argentina	**Peso**	0.241754	0.247445	**Sweden**	**Krona**	0.155001	0.158650
Australia	**Dollar**	0.988466	1.011736	**Switzerland**	**Fr**	1.080513	1.105950
Brazil	**Real**	0.587245	0.601070	**Taiwan**	**Dollar**	0.033075	0.033854
Czech Rep.	**Koruna**	0.056849	0.058188	**Thailand**	**Baht**	0.032314	0.033074
Denmark	**Danish Krone**	0.186191	0.190574	**Turkey**	**New Lira**	0.624122	0.638814
Hong Kong	**Dollar**	0.125371	0.128322	**UAE**	**Dirham**	0.266002	0.272264
Hungary	**Forint**	0.005139	0.005260	**Special Drawing Right**	**SDR**	1.555732	1.592357

*Canadian dollar rates have been calculated by multiplying the U.S. dollar rates by U.S./Canada spot and forward rates.

Source: Financial Times Markets, "Currencies," **markets.ft.com/research/Markets/Currencies**, accessed October 15, 2011. U.S. dollar rates excerpted from Financial Times Markets, "Dollar Spot Forward Against the Dollar," **markets.ft.com/RESEARCH/markets/DataArchiveFetchReport?Category=CU&Type=DSP&Date=03/22/2011**, accessed October 15, 2011.

SPOT EXCHANGE RATES

exchange rate Amount of one currency needed to purchase one unit of another.

Suppose you ask someone the price of bread. He may tell you that you can buy two loaves for a dollar, or he may say that one loaf costs 50 cents. Similarly, if you ask a foreign exchange dealer to quote you a price for Ruritanian francs, she may tell you that you can buy two francs for a dollar or that one franc costs $.50. The first quote (the number of francs that you can buy for a dollar) is known as an *indirect quote* of the **exchange rate**. The second quote (the number of dollars that it costs to buy one franc) is known as a *direct quote*. Of course, both quotes provide the same information. If you can buy two francs for a dollar, then you can easily calculate that the cost of one franc is 1/2 = $.50.

Now look at Table 24.1, which has been adapted from the daily archives of spot and forward rates in *Financial Times*. The table provides exchange rate information for 34 currencies on March 22, 2011. The price of the U.S. dollar is expressed as indirect and direct quotes, while all other currency prices are expressed as direct quotes. Thus you could buy .0815 Canadian dollars with one Mexican peso, or converting to an indirect quote, 12.27 pesos for one Canadian dollar.[1]

EXAMPLE 24.1 A YEN FOR TRADE

How many yen will it cost a Japanese importer to purchase $1,000 worth of potatoes from a Prince Edward Island farmer? How many dollars will it take for that farmer to buy a Japanese DVD player priced in Japan at 30,000 yen (¥)?

The exchange rate is $.012061 per yen. The $1,000 worth of potatoes will require the Japanese importer to come up with 1,000 ÷ .012061 = ¥82,911.865. The DVD player will require the Canadian importer to come up with 30,000 × .012061 = $361.83.

Check Point 24.1

Use the exchange rates in Table 24.1. How many euros can you buy for one Canadian dollar (an indirect quote)? How many dollars can you buy for one yen (a direct quote)?

spot rate of exchange Exchange rate for an immediate transaction.

Table 24.1 provides information on spot rates and also forward rates that are described later. The **spot rate of exchange** is the price of currency for immediate delivery. For example, the spot rate of exchange for Canadian dollars in terms of Mexican pesos is $.081498/peso. In other words, it costs .081498 dollars to buy one Mexican peso. We might also express the spot rate of exchange for Mexican pesos as 1/.081498 = 12.2702 pesos/$. That is, it will cost 12.2702 pesos to buy one dollar. Notice that the table provides spot and forward rates for a few selected currencies: the U.S. dollar, British pound, euro, and Japanese yen. Only spot rates are available for currencies of 32 other countries.

Many countries allow their currencies to float, so that the exchange rate fluctuates from day to day, and from minute to minute. When the currency increases in value, meaning that you need less of the foreign currency to buy one dollar, the currency is said to *appreciate*. When you need more of the currency to buy one dollar, the currency is said to *depreciate*.

Check Point 24.2

Table 24.1 shows the exchange rate for the Swiss franc on March 22, 2011. The next day the spot rate of exchange for the Swiss franc was $1.083278/SFr, or SFr.923124/$. Thus you could buy less Swiss francs for your dollar than one day earlier. Had the Swiss franc appreciated or depreciated?

Some countries try to avoid fluctuations in the value of their currency and seek instead to maintain a fixed exchange rate. But fixed rates seldom last forever. If everybody tries to sell the currency, eventually the country will be forced to allow the currency to depreciate. When this happens, exchange rates can change dramatically. For example, when Indonesia gave up trying to fix its exchange rate in fall 1997, the value of the Indonesian rupiah fell by 80 percent in a few months.

[1] In the United States, prices of most currencies are customarily expressed as indirect quotes in terms of the U.S. dollar. However, the price of the euro and the British pound are generally expressed as direct quotes.

FORWARD EXCHANGE RATES

These fluctuations in exchange rates can get companies into hot water. For example, suppose you have agreed to buy a shipment of Japanese DVD players for ¥100 million and to make the payment when you take delivery of the DVD players at the end of 12 months. You could wait until the 12 months have passed and then buy 100 million yen at the spot exchange rate. If the spot rate is unchanged at \$.012061/¥, then the DVD players will cost you 100 million × .012061 = \$1.2061 million. But you are taking a risk by waiting, for the yen may become more expensive. For example, if the yen appreciates from the existing rate of 1/.012061 = ¥82.912/\$ to ¥70/\$, then you will have to pay out 100 million/70 = \$1.429 million. For much of 2010 and 2011, the Canadian dollar appreciated against the U.S. dollar. The nearby Finance in Action box discusses whether this rise is sustainable.

You can avoid exchange rate risk and fix the dollar cost of DVD players by "buying the yen forward," that is, by arranging *now* to buy yen in the future. A foreign exchange *forward contract* is an agreement to exchange at a future date a given amount of currency at an exchange rate agreed to *today*. The **forward exchange rate** is the price of currency for delivery at some time in the future. Table 24.1 shows forward exchange rates for four currencies, namely the U.S. dollar, British pound, euro, and Japanese yen.[2] For example, the 12-month forward rate for the yen is quoted at .012244 dollars per yen, or 81.673 yen per dollar. If you buy 100 million yen forward, you don't pay anything today; you simply fix today the price that you will pay for your yen in the future. At the end of the year you receive your 100 million yen and hand over 100 million/81.673 = \$1.2244 million in payment.

forward exchange rate Exchange rate for a forward transaction.

Notice that if you buy Japanese yen forward, you get fewer yen for your dollar than if you buy spot. In this case, the yen is said to trade at a forward *premium* relative to the dollar. Expressed as a percentage, the 12-month forward premium is

$$\frac{82.912 - 81.673}{81.673} \times 100 = 1.517\%$$

You might also say the dollar was selling at a *forward discount* of about 1.517 percent.[3]

A forward purchase or sale is a made-to-order transaction between you and the bank. It can be for any currency, any amount, and any delivery day. You could buy, say, 99,999 Sudanese dinar or Slovakian koruna for a year and a day forward as long as you can find a bank ready to deal. From Table 24.1, we see that forward rates are quoted for most currencies for periods ranging from a month to a year. However, banks are prepared to buy or sell the U.S. dollar, Canada's major trading currency, for up to 10 years forward.

There is also an organized market for currency for future delivery known as the currency *futures* market. Futures contracts are highly standardized versions of forward contracts—they exist only for the main currencies, they are for specified amounts, and choice of delivery dates is limited. The advantage of this standardization is that there is a very low-cost market in

---

[2] Although forward rates are not quoted for the remaining currencies in Canadian dollars, such rates are available for several currencies in terms of the U.S. dollar, which is recognized as the major international trading currency. For instance, daily spot and forward rate quotes in U.S. dollars are available for Swedish krona, Mexican pesos, and Australian, Hong Kong, and Singapore dollars.

[3] Here is a minor point that sometimes causes confusion. To calculate the forward premium, we divide by the *forward* rate as long as the exchange quotes are *indirect*. If you use *direct* quotes, the correct formula is

$$\text{Forward premium} = \frac{\text{forward rate} - \text{spot rate}}{\text{spot rate}}$$

In our example, the corresponding direct quote for spot yen is .012061, while the direct forward quote is .012244. Substituting these rates in our revised formula gives

$$\text{Forward premium} = \frac{.012244 - .012061}{.012061} = .01517\text{, or } 1.517\%$$

The two methods give the same answer.

Finance in Action

Loonie Looks Ripe for a Pullback, Economists Say

The Canadian dollar and other commodity currencies, which have outperformed since the financial crisis, are now overvalued and look ripe for a pullback, says a new report from Barclays Capital Markets. The only question is when.

"The traffic light has changed from green to amber for the commodity currencies," said Paul Robinson, a currency analyst at the London-based bank. "It is too early to expect rapid depreciation, but we do not expect further appreciation over the next three months."

According to Mr. Robinson's estimates of purchasing power parity, a measure of relative inflation differentials, the Canadian dollar is 17% overvalued relative to the U.S. dollar, while the New Zealand dollar is 26% overvalued and the Australian dollar is 33% too expensive.

He thinks all three currencies are likely to start depreciating in the second half of this year and the risks are generally to the downside.

Those risks include a quicker slowdown than expected for Chinese growth, negative oil supply shocks, which are bad for the Australian and New Zealand dollars but not the loonie, and an increase in risk aversion, due to the incredible rally in equities.

In addition, Mr. Robinson thinks commodity currencies are susceptible to the possibility that G4 nations, in particular the United States, could move quicker than expected on tightening monetary policy.

Since the recovery from the financial crisis began in March 9, 2009, the Canadian dollar has risen 31% against the U.S. dollar, the Australian dollar has appreciated 59% and New Zealand's dollar is up almost 50%.

Mr. Robinson said increases in all three currencies are due to strong commodity prices, good economic fundamentals and tighter monetary policy by Australia and New Zealand in particular.

In addition, he said G10 commodity currencies may have benefited from emerging market nations actively limiting the appreciation of their real exchange rates in the face of tighter monetary policy and global capital seeking relatively strong returns.

George Vasic, a UBS strategist, said the Canadian dollar has benefited mostly from the rise in commodity prices and very little if at all from its sound fundamentals and monetary policy that remains relatively loose despite three rate hikes in 2010.

He said in a note to clients that there is a 0.95 correlation between commodities and the loonie since 1995. "An important implication of the tight linkage between commodities and the CAD is that the usual currency fundamentals, such as economic conditions and monetary/fiscal policy, don't actually mean that much for the currency," he said.

"And neither does purchasing power parity. This is underscored by the fact that PPP was at a similar level between 1998 and 2003, when the Canadian dollar traded around US65¢. and when commodity prices were depressed."

Source: Excerpted from David Pett, "Loonie Looks Ripe for a Pullback, Economists Say," *Financial Post*, March 29, 2011, accessed April 2, 2011, at **www.financialpost.com/news/Loonie+looks+ripe+pullback+economists/4518919/story.html**. Material reprinted with the express permission of National Post, a division of Postmedia Network Inc.

currency futures. Huge numbers of contracts are bought and sold daily on the futures exchanges. In North America, the most important market for foreign currency futures is the International Monetary Market (IMM), a division of the Chicago Mercantile Exchange.

When you buy a forward or futures contract, you are committed to taking delivery of the currency. As an alternative, you can take out an *option* to buy or sell currency in the future at a price that is fixed today. Made-to-measure currency options can be bought from the major banks, and standardized options are traded on the options exchanges. We discuss futures, forwards, and options in more detail in Chapters 25 and 26.

Check Point 24.3

A skiing vacation in Switzerland costs SFr1,500.

a. How many dollars does that represent? Use the exchange rates in Table 24.1.
b. Suppose the dollar depreciates by 10 percent relative to the Swiss franc, so that each dollar buys 10 percent fewer Swiss francs than before. What will be the new value of the (1) direct exchange rate and (2) indirect exchange rate?
c. If the Swiss vacation continues to cost the same amount of Swiss francs, what will happen to the cost in dollars?
d. If the tour company that is offering the vacation keeps the price fixed in dollars, what will happen to the amount of Swiss francs that it will receive?

LO2 24.2 SOME BASIC RELATIONSHIPS

The financial manager of an international business must cope with fluctuations in exchange rates and must be aware of the distinction between spot and forward exchange rates. She must also recognize that two countries may have different interest rates. To develop a consistent international financial policy, the financial manager needs to understand how exchange rates are determined and why one country may have a lower interest rate than another. Here are four questions managers need to consider:

1. Why do interest rates in different countries differ?
2. What explains the difference between the forward exchange rate and the spot rate?
3. What is the relationship between the spot exchange rate today and the expected exchange rate at some future date?
4. How do different rates of inflation in two countries affect each country's interest rate as well as the exchange rate between the currencies of those countries?

These are complex issues, but as a first cut we suggest that you think of spot and forward exchange rates, interest rates, and inflation rates as being linked as shown in Figure 24.1. Let's explain.

EXCHANGE RATES AND INFLATION

Consider first the relationship between changes in the spot exchange rate and inflation rates (the two boxes on the right of Figure 24.1). The idea here is simple: if country X suffers a higher rate of inflation than country Y, then the value of X's currency will decline relative to Y's. The decline in value shows up in the spot exchange rate for X's currency.

But let's slow down and consider why changes in inflation and spot interest rates are linked. Think first about the prices of the same good or service in two different countries and currencies.

Suppose you notice that gold can be bought in Toronto for \$1,400 an ounce and sold in Mexico City for 20,000 pesos an ounce. If there are no restrictions on the import of gold, you could be on to a good thing. You buy gold for \$1,400 and put it on the first plane to Mexico City, where you sell it for 20,000 pesos. Then (using the exchange rates from Table 24.1) you can exchange your 20,000 pesos for $20{,}000 \times .081498 = \$1{,}630$. You have made a gross profit of

FIGURE 24.1
Some simple theories linking spot and forward exchange rates, interest rates, and inflation rates.

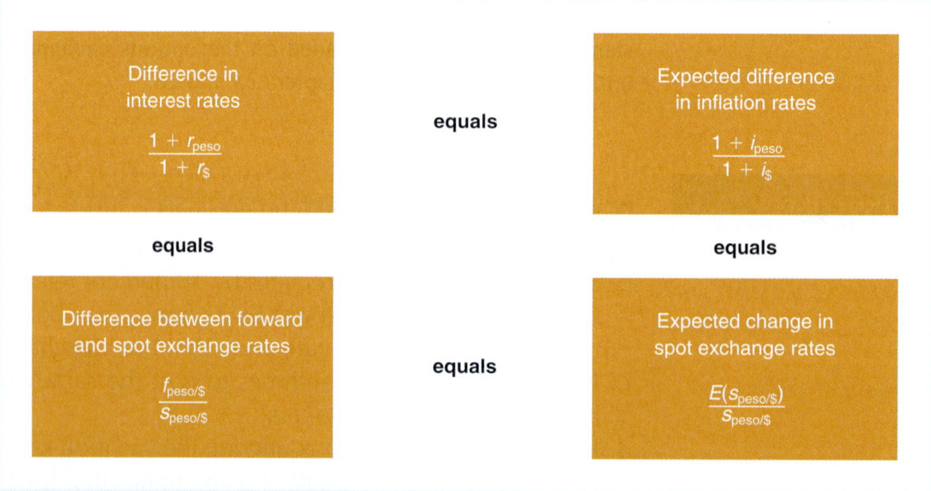

$230 an ounce. Of course, you have to pay transportation and insurance costs out of this, but there should still be something left over for you.

You returned from your trip with a sure-fire profit. But sure-fire profits don't exist—not for long. As others notice the disparity between the price of gold in Mexico and the price in Toronto, the price will be forced down in Mexico and up in Toronto until the profit opportunity disappears. This ensures that the dollar price of gold is about the same in the two countries.[4]

Gold is a standard and easily transportable commodity, but to some degree you might expect that the same forces would be acting to equalize the domestic and foreign prices of other goods. Those goods that can be bought more cheaply abroad will be imported, and that will force down the price of the domestic product. Similarly, those goods that can be bought more cheaply in Canada will be exported, and that will force down the price of the foreign product.

law of one price Theory that prices of goods in all countries should be equal when translated to a common currency.

This conclusion is often called the **law of one price**. Just as the price of goods in Provigo must be roughly the same as the price of goods in Sobeys, so the price of goods in Mexico, when converted into dollars, must be roughly the same as the price in Canada:

$$\text{Dollar price of goods in Canada} = \text{peso price of goods in Mexico} \times \text{number of dollars per peso}$$

$$\$1{,}400 = \text{peso price of goods in Mexico} \times .081498$$

$$\text{Price of gold in Mexico} = \frac{1{,}400}{.081498} = 17{,}178 \text{ pesos}$$

No one who has compared prices in foreign stores with prices at home really believes that the law of one price holds exactly. Look at Table 24.2, which shows the local price of a McDonald's Big Mac converted to U.S. dollars for different countries. You can see that the price varies considerably across countries. For example, Big Macs were 83 percent more expensive in Switzerland than in the United States, but they were a little more than half the price in China.[5]

This suggests a possible way to make a quick buck. Why don't you buy a hamburger to go in China for $2.18 and take it for resale to Switzerland where the price in dollars is $6.78? The answer, of course, is that the gain would not cover the costs. The law of one price works very well for commodities like gold, where transportation costs are relatively small; it works far less well for Big Macs, and very badly indeed for haircuts and appendectomies, which cannot be transported at all.

purchasing power parity (PPP) Theory that the cost of living in different countries is equal and exchange rates adjust to offset inflation differentials across countries.

A weaker version of the law of one price is known as **purchasing power parity (PPP)**. PPP states that although some goods may cost different amounts in different countries, the general cost of living should be the same in any two countries.

TABLE 24.2
Price of McDonald's Big Mac hamburgers in different currencies.

Country	Local Price Converted to U.S. Dollars	Country	Local Price Converted to U.S. Dollars
Brazil	5.26	Singapore	3.46
Canada	4.18	South Africa	2.79
China	2.18	South Korea	3.03
Euro area	4.79	Switzerland	6.78
Japan	3.91	Thailand	2.44
Malaysia	2.25	United Kingdom	3.63
Mexico	2.58	United States	3.71
Russia	2.39		

Source: "Big Mac Index," *The Economist*, October 14, 2010, **www.economist.com/node/17257797?story_id=17257797**, accessed October 15, 2011.

[4] Activity of this kind is known as *arbitrage*. The arbitrageur makes a riskless profit by noticing discrepancies in prices.

[5] Of course, it could also be that Big Macs come with a bigger smile in Switzerland. If the quality of the hamburgers or the service differs, we are not comparing like with like.

FIGURE 24.2
A decline in the exchange rate and a decline in a country's purchasing power usually go hand in hand. In this diagram, each point represents the experience of a different country between 1995 and 2000.

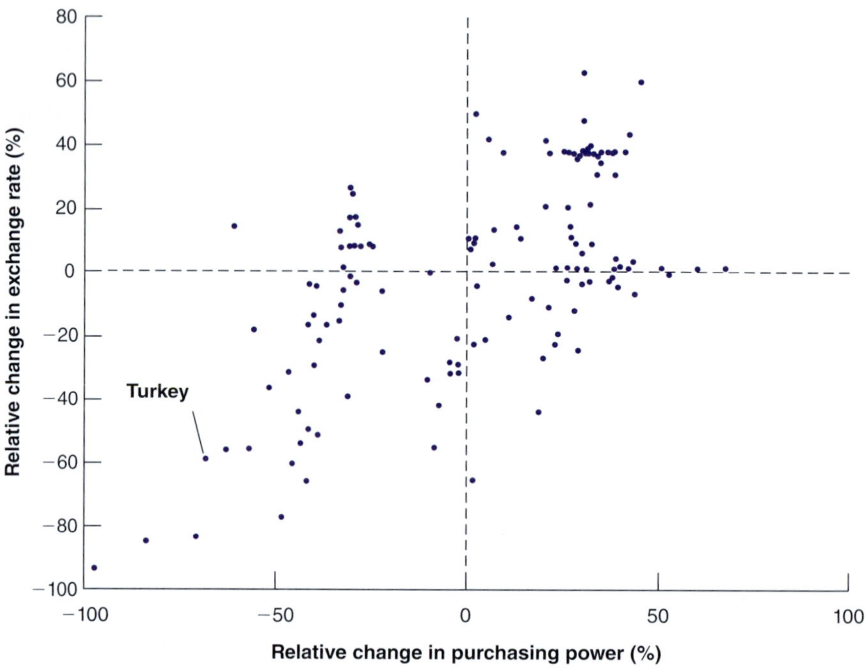

Purchasing power parity implies that the relative costs of living in two countries will not be affected by differences in their inflation rates. Instead, the different inflation rates in local currencies will be offset by changes in the exchange rate between the two currencies.

For example, between 1999 and 2004, prices in Turkey rose 4.7 times. As prices in Turkey increased, Turkish exporters would have found it impossible to sell their goods if the exchange rate had not also changed. But, of course, the exchange rate did adjust. In fact, by the end of the period the Turkish lira bought about 60 percent less foreign currency than it did before.

In Figure 24.2 we have plotted the relative change in purchasing power against the change in the exchange rate for a sample of countries. Turkey is toward the bottom left-hand corner. You can see that although the relationship is far from exact, large differences in inflation rates are generally accompanied by an offsetting change in the exchange rate. In fact, if you have to make a long-term forecast of the exchange rate, it is very difficult to do much better than to assume that it will offset the effect of any differences in the inflation rates.

If purchasing power parity holds, then your forecast of the difference in inflation rates is also your best forecast of the change in the spot rate of exchange. Thus the expected difference between inflation rates in Mexico and the United States was given by the right-hand boxes in Figure 24.1:

Expected difference in inflation rates		Expected change in spot exchange rate
$\dfrac{1+i_{peso}}{1+i_{\$}}$	equals	$\dfrac{E(s_{peso/\$})}{s_{peso/\$}}$

For example, from Table 24.1, the present spot exchange rate between the U.S. dollar and Mexican peso is US\$.083417/peso, or peso 11.988/US\$. If inflation is 2 percent in the United

States and 6 percent in Mexico, then purchasing power parity implies that the expected spot rate for the peso at the end of the year is peso 12.458/US$:

$$\text{Current spot rate} \times \text{expected difference in inflation rates} = \text{expected spot rate}$$

$$11.988 \times \frac{1.06}{1.02} = 12.458$$

Check Point 24.4

Suppose that gold currently costs \$1320 an ounce in the United States and £880 an ounce in Great Britain.

a. What must be the pound/dollar exchange rate?
b. Suppose that gold prices rise by 2 percent in the United States and by 5 percent in Great Britain. What will be the price of gold in the two currencies at the end of the year? What must be the exchange rate at the end of the year?
c. Show that at the end of the year each dollar buys about 3 percent more pounds, as predicted by PPP.

INFLATION AND INTEREST RATES

Interest rates in Turkey in 2008 were about 15 percent. So why didn't you (and a few million other investors) put your cash in an Istanbul bank deposit where the return seemed to be so attractive?

The answer lies in the distinction that we made in Chapter 4 between nominal and real rates of interest. Bank deposits usually promise you a fixed nominal rate of interest but they don't promise what that money will buy. If you invested 100 lira for a year at an interest rate of 15 percent, you would have 15 percent more lira at the end of the year than you did at the start. But you wouldn't be 15 percent better off. A good part of the gain would be needed to compensate for inflation.

The nominal rate of interest in 2008 was much lower in Canada, but then so was the inflation rate. The real rates of interest were much closer than the nominal rates.

There is a general law at work here. Just as water always flows downhill, so capital always flows where returns are greatest. But it is the real returns that concern investors, not the *nominal* returns. Two countries might have a different nominal interest rate but the same expected real interest rate.

international Fisher effect
Theory that real interest rates in all countries should be equal, with differences in nominal rates reflecting differences in expected inflation.

Recall Irving Fisher's theory from Chapter 6 that changes in the expected inflation rate are reflected in the nominal interest rate. We have just described here the **international Fisher effect**—international variations in the expected inflation rate are reflected in the nominal interest rates:

$$\text{Difference in interest rates } \frac{1+r_{\text{lira}}}{1+r_{\$}} \text{ — equals — } \text{Expected difference in inflation rates } \frac{1+i_{\text{lira}}}{1+i_{\$}}$$

In other words, capital market equilibrium requires that real interest rates be the same in any two countries.

How similar are real interest rates around the world? It is hard to say, because we cannot directly observe expected inflation. In Figure 24.3 we have plotted the average interest rate in each of 55 countries against the inflation that in fact occurred. You can see that the countries with the highest interest rates generally had the highest inflation rates. Turkey had high interest rates which in recent years have come down.

EXAMPLE 24.2 INTERNATIONAL FISHER EFFECT

If the nominal interest rate in Turkey is 15 percent and the expected inflation is 8 percent, then

$$r_{\text{lira}}(\text{real}) = \frac{1 + r_{\text{lira}}}{E(1 + i_{\text{lira}})} = \frac{1.15}{1.08} - 1 = .065, \text{ or } 6.5\%$$

In Canada, where the nominal interest rate is about 4.0 percent and the expected inflation rate is about 2.2 percent,

$$r_{\$}(\text{real}) = \frac{1 + r_{\$}}{E(1 + i_{\$})} = \frac{1.04}{1.022} - 1 = .018, \text{ or } 1.8\%$$

The real interest rate is higher in Turkey than in Canada, but the difference in the real rates is much smaller than the difference in nominal rates.

Check Point 24.5

Canadian investors can invest $1,000 at an interest rate of 4 percent. Alternatively, they can convert those funds to 8,064,516 rupiah at the current exchange rate and invest at 8 percent in Indonesia. If the expected inflation rate in Canada is 2.2 percent, what must be investors' forecast of the inflation rate in Indonesia?

INTEREST RATES AND EXCHANGE RATES

You are an investor with $1 million to invest for 1 year. Suppose the interest rate in Canada is 1.6 percent and in Japan it is .1 percent. Is it better to make a yen loan or a dollar loan?

The answer might seem obvious: Isn't it better to earn an interest rate of 4 percent in Canada than .37 percent in Japan? But appearances are deceptive. If you lend in Japan, you first need to convert your $1 million into yen. When the loan is repaid at the end of the year, you need to convert your yen back into dollars. Of course, you don't know what the exchange rate will be at the end of the year but you can fix the future value of your yen by selling them forward. If the forward rate of exchange is sufficiently high, you might do just as well investing your money in Japan.

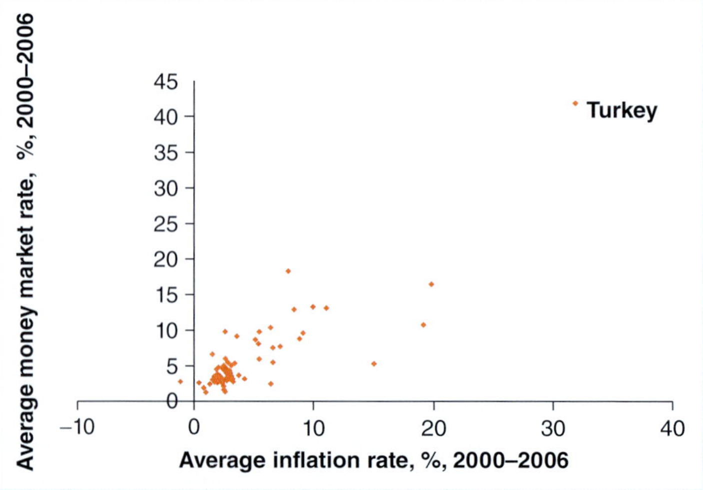

FIGURE 24.3
Countries with the highest interest rates generally have the highest subsequent inflation rates. In this diagram, each point represents a different country.

Let's use the data from Table 24.1 to check which loan is the better deal:

- *Dollar loan.* The rate of interest on a dollar loan is 1.6 percent. Therefore, at the end of the year you get 1,000,000 × 1.016 = \$1,016,000.
- *Yen loan.* The current rate of exchange (from Table 24.1) is \$.012061/¥. Therefore, for \$1 million, you can buy 1,000,000 ÷ .012061 = 82,911,865 yen. The rate of interest on a one-year yen loan is .1 percent. So at the end of the year, you get ¥82,911,865 × 1.001 = ¥82,994,777. Of course, you don't know what the exchange rate will be at the end of the year. But that doesn't matter. You can nail down the price at which you sell your yen. The 12-month forward rate is \$.012244¥. Therefore, by selling the ¥82,994,777 forward, you make sure that you will get 82,994,777 × .012244 = \$1,016,188.

A difference in interest rates must be offset by a difference between spot and forward exchange rates. If the risk-free interest rate in country X is higher than in country Y, then country X's currency will buy less of Y's in a forward transaction than in a spot transaction.

Thus the two investments offer almost exactly the same rate of return. They have to—they are both risk-free. If the domestic interest rate were different from the "covered" foreign rate, you would have a money machine: you could borrow in the market with the lower rate and lend in the market with the higher rate.

When you make a yen loan, you lose because you get a lower interest rate. But you gain because you sell the yen forward at a higher price than you have to pay for them today. The interest rate differential is

$$\frac{1 + r_{¥}}{1 + r_{\$}} = \frac{1.001}{1.016} = .9852$$

and the differential between the forward and spot exchange rates is virtually identical:[6]

$$\frac{f_{¥/\$}}{s_{¥/\$}} = \frac{81.673}{82.912} = .9851$$

interest rate parity Theory that forward premium equals interest rate differential.

Interest rate parity theory says that the interest rate differential must equal the differential between the forward and spot exchange rates. Thus

Difference in interest rates — equals — Difference between forward and spot rates

$$\frac{1+r_{¥}}{1+r_{\$}} \quad \text{equals} \quad \frac{f_{¥/\$}}{s_{¥/\$}}$$

EXAMPLE 24.3 WHAT HAPPENS IF INTEREST RATE PARITY THEORY DOES NOT HOLD?

Suppose that the forward rate on the yen is not ¥81.673/\$ (or \$.012244/¥) but ¥82.50/\$ (or \$.012121/¥). Here is what you do.

Borrow 1 million yen at an interest rate of .1 percent and change these yen into dollars at the spot exchange rate of ¥82.912/\$ (or \$.012061/¥). This gives you \$12,061, which you invest for a year at 1.6 percent. At the end of the year you will have 12,061 × 1.016 = \$12,254. Of course, this is not money to spend, because you have to repay your yen loan. The amount you need to repay is

(Continued)

[6] In our discussion so far, we have used direct quotes from Table 24.1. The indirect quote for the forward rate, $f_{yen}/\$$, is 1/.012244 = ¥81.673/\$. The indirect spot quote, $s_{yen}/\$$, is 1/.012061 = ¥82.912.

(Concluded)

1,000,000 × 1.001 = ¥1,001,000. If you buy these yen forward, you can fix in advance the number of dollars that you will need to lay out. With a forward rate of ¥82.50/$, you need to set aside 1,001,000/82.50 = $12,133. Thus, after paying off your yen loan, you walk away with a risk-free profit of $12,254 − $12,133 = $121.

While this amount is small, notice that you would have made a profit of $1,210 had you invested 10 million yen. It is a pity that in practice interest rate parity almost always holds, and the opportunities for such easy profits are rare.

Check Point 24.6

Look at the exchange rates in Table 24.1. Does the British pound sell at a forward premium or discount on the dollar? Does this suggest that the interest rate in Britain is higher or lower than in Canada? Use the interest rate parity relationship to estimate the 1-year interest rate in Britain. Assume the Canadian interest rate is 1.6 percent.

THE FORWARD RATE AND THE EXPECTED SPOT RATE

If you buy yen forward, you get fewer yen for your dollar than if you buy them spot. So the yen is selling at a forward premium. Now let us think how this premium is related to expected changes in spot rates of exchange.

The 12-month forward rate for the yen is $.012244/¥. Would you sell yen at this rate if you expected the yen to rise in value? Probably not. You would be tempted to wait until the end of the year and get a better price for your yen in the spot market. If other traders felt the same way, nobody would sell yen forward and everybody would want to buy. The result would be that the number of yen that you could get for your dollar in the forward market would fall. Similarly, if traders expected the yen to fall sharply in value, they might be reluctant to *buy* forward and, in order to attract buyers, the number of yen that you could buy for a dollar in the forward market would need to rise.[7]

expectations theory of exchange rates Theory that the expected spot exchange rate equals the forward rate.

This is the reasoning behind the **expectations theory of exchange rates**, which predicts that the forward rate equals the expected future spot exchange rate: $f_{¥/\$} = E(s_{¥/\$})$. Equivalently, we can say that the *percentage* difference between the forward rate and today's spot rate is equal to the expected *percentage* change in the spot rate:

> The expectations theory of forward rates does not imply that managers are perfect forecasters. Sometimes the *actual* future spot rate will turn out to be above the previous forward rate. Sometimes it will fall below. But if the theory is correct, we should find that on *average* the forward rate is equal to the future spot rate.

Difference between forward and spot rates		Expected change in spot exchange rate
$\frac{f_{¥/\$}}{s_{¥/\$}}$	equals	$\frac{E(s_{¥/\$})}{s_{¥/\$}}$

This is the final leg of our quadrilateral in Figure 24.1.

How well does the expectations theory explain the level of forward rates? Scholars who have studied exchange rates have found that forward rates typically exaggerate the likely change in the spot rate. When the forward rate appears to predict a sharp rise in the spot rate, the forward

[7] This reasoning ignores risk. If a forward purchase reduces your risk sufficiently, you *might* be prepared to buy forward even if you expected to pay more as a result. Similarly, if a forward sale reduces risk, you *might* be prepared to sell forward even if you expected to receive less as a result.

rate tends to overestimate the rise in the spot rate. Conversely, when the forward rate appears to predict a fall in the currency, it tends to overestimate this fall.[8]

This finding is *not* consistent with the expectations theory. Instead it seems that companies are sometimes prepared to give up return in order to buy forward currency and other times they are prepared to give up return in order to sell forward currency. Almost half the time the forward rate *overstates* the likely future spot rate and half the time it *understates* the likely spot rate. This is important news for the financial manager; it means that a company that always covers its foreign exchange commitments by buying or selling currency in the forward market does not have to pay a premium to avoid exchange rate risk: *on average*, the forward price at which it agrees to exchange currency will equal the eventual spot exchange rate; no better but no worse.

We should, however, warn you that the forward rate does not tell you very much about the future spot rate. For example, when the forward rate appears to suggest that the spot rate is likely to appreciate, you will find that the spot rate is about equally likely to head off in the opposite direction.

SOME IMPLICATIONS

Our four simple relationships ignore many of the complexities of interest rates and exchange rates. But they capture the more important features and emphasize that international capital markets and currency markets function well and offer no free lunches. When managers forget this, it can be costly. For example, in the late 1980s, several Australian banks observed that interest rates in Switzerland were about 8 percentage points lower than those in Australia and advised their clients to borrow Swiss francs. Was this advice correct? According to the international Fisher effect, the lower Swiss interest rate indicated that investors were expecting a lower inflation rate in Switzerland than in Australia and this in turn would result in an appreciation of the Swiss franc relative to the Australian dollar. Thus it was likely that the advantage of the low Swiss interest rate would be offset by the fact that it would cost the borrowers more Australian dollars to repay the loan. As it turned out, the Swiss franc appreciated very rapidly, and the Australian banks found that they had a number of very irate clients and agreed to compensate them for the losses they had incurred. The moral: Don't assume automatically that it is cheaper to borrow in a currency with a low nominal rate of interest.

Check Point 24.7

Starlight Corporation borrows 100 million Japanese yen at an apparently attractive interest rate of 1 percent, when the exchange rate between the yen and the U.S. dollar is ¥81.00/US$. Suppose that one year later, when Starlight has to repay its loan, the exchange rate is ¥80.60/US$. Calculate in U.S. dollars the amount Starlight borrows and the amounts it pays in interest and principal (assume annual interest payments). What effective U.S. dollar interest rate has Starlight paid on the loan?

Here is another case where our simple relationships can stop you from falling into a trap. Managers sometimes talk as if you make money simply by buying currencies that go up in value and selling those that go down. But if investors anticipate the change in the exchange rate, then it will be reflected in the interest rate differential; therefore, what you gain on the currency you will lose in terms of interest income. You make money from currency speculation only if you can predict whether the exchange rate will change by more or less than the interest rate differential. In other words, you must be able to predict whether the exchange rate will change by more or less than the forward premium.

[8] Many researchers have even found that, when the forward rate predicts a rise, the spot rate is more likely to fall, and vice versa. For a readable discussion of this puzzling finding, see K.A. Froot and R.H. Thaler, "Anomalies: Foreign Exchange," *Journal of Political Economy* 4 (1990): 179–192.

EXAMPLE 24.4 **MEASURING CURRENCY GAINS**

The financial manager of Universal Waffle is proud of his acumen. Instead of keeping his cash in U.S. dollars, he for many years invested it in deposits denominated in deutschemarks, which used to be the German currency before the country adopted the euro. He calculates that between the end of 1980 and the end of 1998, the deutschemark increased in value by nearly 47 percent, or about 2.1 percent a year. But did the manager really gain from investing in foreign currency? Let's check.

The compound rate of interest on U.S. dollar deposits during the period was 9.0 percent, while the compound rate of interest on deutschemark deposits was only 6.9 percent. So the 2.1 percent a year appreciation in the value of the deutschemark was almost exactly offset by the lower rate of interest on deutschemark deposits.

The interest rate differential (which by interest rate parity is equal to the forward premium) is a measure of the market's expectation of the change in the value of the currency. The difference between the German and U.S. interest rates during this period suggests that the market was expecting the deutschemark to appreciate by just over 2 percent a year,[9] and that is almost exactly what happened.

LO3 24.3 HEDGING EXCHANGE RATE RISK

TRANSACTION RISK

Firms with international operations are subject to exchange rate risk. As exchange rates fluctuate, the dollar value of their revenues or expenses also fluctuates. It helps to distinguish two types of exchange rate risk: *transaction risk* and *economic risk*. Transaction risk arises when the firm agrees to pay or receive a known amount of foreign currency. For example, our DVD player importer was committed to pay ¥100 million at the end of 12 months. If the value of the yen appreciates rapidly over this period, those DVD players will cost more dollars than the firm expected.

Transaction risk is easily identified and hedged. For every yen our importer is committed to pay, for example, she can buy one yen forward. If she buys ¥100 million forward, the importer fixes the entire dollar cost of the DVD players and avoids the risk of an appreciation of the yen.

Of course, it is possible that the yen will *depreciate* over the year, in which case the importer would regret that she did not wait to buy the yen more cheaply in the spot market. Unfortunately, you cannot have your cake and eat it too. By fixing the dollar cost of the DVD players, the importer forfeits the chance of pleasant as well as unpleasant surprises.

Is there any other way the importer might hedge against exchange rate loss? Of course. She might borrow dollars, convert them into yen today, put the proceeds into a Japanese bank deposit, and withdraw the ¥100 million at the end of the year to pay her bill. Interest rate parity tells us that the cost of buying yen forward is exactly the same as the cost of borrowing dollars, buying yen in the spot market, and leaving them on deposit.

What is the cost of protection against currency risk? You sometimes hear managers say that it is equal to the difference between the forward rate and *today's* spot rate. This is wrong. If our importer did not hedge, she would pay the spot price for yen when the payment is due at the end of the year. Therefore, the cost of hedging is the difference between the forward rate and the expected spot rate when payment is due.

---

[9] If the interest rate is 9 percent on U.S. dollar deposits and 6.9 percent on deutschemark deposits, our simple relationship implies that the expected change in the value of the deutschemark was $(1 + r_{US\$})/(1 + r_{DM}) - 1 = 1.090/1.069 - 1 = .020$, or 2 percent per year.

Check Point 24.8

Interest rate parity theory implies that the cost of buying yen forward is exactly the same as the cost of borrowing dollars, buying yen in the spot market, and leaving them on deposit. Use the exchange rates for U.S. dollars and Japanese yen in Table 24.1 to show that this is the case. Assume a U.S. dollar interest rate of 0.6 percent and a yen rate of 0.1 percent.

Hedge or speculate? We generally vote for hedging. First, it makes life simpler for the firm and allows it to concentrate on its own business. Second, it does not cost much. (In fact, the cost is zero if the forward rate equals the expected spot rate, as our simple theories imply.) Third, the foreign exchange market seems reasonably efficient, at least for the major currencies. Speculation should be a zero-sum game unless financial managers have superior information to that of the pros who make the market.

ECONOMIC RISK

Even if a firm neither owes nor is owed foreign currency, it still may be affected by currency fluctuations. Consider, for example, the competitive position of foreign auto producers such as Volkswagen or Toyota when the value of the U.S. dollar fell dramatically in 2006 and 2007. These firms faced a difficult choice between maintaining the dollar price of their product, thus accepting a reduced price in their home currencies, or raising the dollar price and becoming less competitive against U.S. producers such as Ford and General Motors. *Economic exposure* to the exchange rate arises because exchange rate fluctuations affect the competitive position of the firm.

One solution is for the company to undertake operational hedging by balancing production closely with sales. For example, 38 percent of Ford's sales are outside North America, but so is 44 percent of its production. Because its costs and revenues in each currency are reasonably closely balanced, exchange rate changes do not affect its profits nearly as much as would be the case if its production were concentrated in one country.

Other manufacturers, particularly the Japanese firms, have less operational hedging. For example, Toyota produces 63 percent of its output in Japan, but only 37 percent is sold there. Exchange rate fluctuations are potentially a more serious risk for Toyota. On the other hand, the Japanese companies operate in a wider range of markets than do U.S. firms. They have therefore diversified away a good part of their currency risk.

Operational hedging rarely eliminates all exchange risk. Think again of Toyota. It is a net exporter of autos to North America and is therefore exposed to a decline in the value of the dollar. So, in addition to its operational hedging, Toyota also controls exchange rate risk by using *financial hedges*. For example, it borrows some of its funds in dollars. So, if the dollar falls, the pressure on Toyota's profits is offset in part by a reduction in the number of yen needed to service this debt.

Check Point 24.9

Suppose that the current spot rate for the euro is \$1.388512/€ and that the 3-month forward rate is \$1.389103/€. What is the cost to a Canadian company of hedging its future need for euros by buying them in the forward market? Assume the expectations theory of exchange rates.

LO4 24.4 INTERNATIONAL CAPITAL BUDGETING

NET PRESENT VALUE ANALYSIS

KW Corporation is a Canadian firm manufacturing flat-packed kit wardrobes. Its export business has risen to the point that it is considering establishing a small manufacturing operation overseas in Narnia. KW's decision to invest overseas should be based on the same criteria as a decision to invest in Canada—that is, the company needs to forecast the incremental cash flows from the project, discount the cash flows at the opportunity cost of capital, and accept those projects with a positive NPV.

Suppose KW's Narnian facility is expected to generate the following cash flows in the currency known as "Narnian leos" (L):

Year:	0	1	2	3	4	5
Cash flow (millions of L)	−7.6	2.0	2.5	3.0	3.5	4.0

You cannot compare the project's return measured in one currency with the return that you require from investing in another currency. If the opportunity cost of capital is measured as a dollar-denominated return, consistency demands that the forecast cash flows should also be stated in dollars.

The interest rate in Canada is 5 percent. KW's financial manager estimates that the company requires an additional expected return of 10 percent to compensate for the risk of the project, so the opportunity cost of capital for the project is 5 + 10 = 15 percent.

Notice that KW's opportunity cost of capital is stated in terms of the return on a dollar-denominated investment, but the cash flows are given in leos. A project that offers a 15 percent expected return in leos could fall far short of offering the required return in dollars if the value of the leo is expected to decline. Conversely, a project that offers an expected return of less than 15 percent in leos may be worthwhile if the leo is likely to appreciate.

To translate the leo cash flows into dollars, KW needs a forecast of the leo/dollar exchange rate. Where does this come from? We suggest using the simple parity relationships in Figure 24.1. These tell us that the expected annual change in the spot exchange rate (the bottom right box in Figure 24.1) is equal to the difference between the interest rates in the two countries (the upper left box). For example, suppose that the financial manager looks in the newspaper and finds that the current exchange rate is 2 leos to the dollar ($s_{L/\$} = 2.0$), while the interest rate is 5 percent in Canada ($r_\$ = .05$) and 10 percent in Narnia ($r_L = .10$). Thus the manager sees right away that the leo is likely to depreciate by about 5 percent a year.[10] For example, at the end of one year

$$\text{Expected spot rate in year 1} = \text{spot rate in year 0} \times \text{expected change in spot rate}$$

$$= 2.0 \times \frac{1.10}{1.05} = \text{L}2.095/\$$$

The forecast exchange rates for each year of the project are calculated in a similar way, as follows:

Year	Forecast Exchange Rate		
0	Spot exchange rate	=	L2.0/$
1	$2.0 \times (1.10/1.05)$	=	L2.095/$
2	$2.0 \times (1.10/1.05)^2$	=	L2.195/$
3	$2.0 \times (1.10/1.05)^3$	=	L2.300/$
4	$2.0 \times (1.10/1.05)^4$	=	L2.409/$
5	$2.0 \times (1.10/1.05)^5$	=	L2.524/$

[10] The financial manager could use the forward exchange rate ($f_{L/\$}$) equally well to estimate the expected spot rate. In practice, it is usually easier to find interest rates in the financial press than yearly forward rates.

The financial manager can use these projected exchange rates to convert the leo cash flows into dollars:[11]

Year:	0	1	2	3	4	5
Cash flow ($ millions)	$\frac{-7.6}{2.00} = -\$3.8$	$\frac{2.0}{2.095} = \$.95$	$\frac{2.5}{2.195} = \$1.14$	$\frac{3.0}{2.300} = \$1.30$	$\frac{3.5}{2.409} = \$1.45$	$\frac{4.0}{2.524} = \$1.58$

Now the manager discounts these *dollar* cash flows at the 15 percent *dollar* cost of capital:

$$\text{NPV} = -3.8 + \frac{.95}{1.15} + \frac{1.14}{1.15^2} + \frac{1.30}{1.15^3} + \frac{1.45}{1.15^4} + \frac{1.58}{1.15^5}$$
$$= \$.36 \text{ million, or } \$360{,}000$$

Notice that the manager discounted cash flows at 15 percent, not the Canadian risk-free interest rate of 5 percent. The cash flows are risky, so a risk-adjusted interest rate is appropriate. The positive NPV tells the manager that the project is worth undertaking; it increases shareholder wealth by $360,000.

Check Point 24.10

Suppose that the nominal interest rate in Narnia is 3 percent rather than 10 percent. The spot exchange rate is still L2.0/$ and the forecast leo cash flows on KW's project are also the same as before.

a. What do you deduce about the likely difference in the inflation rates in Narnia and Canada?
b. Would you now forecast that the leo will appreciate or depreciate against the dollar?
c. Do you think that the NPV of KW's project will now be higher or lower than the figure we calculated above? Check your answer by calculating NPV under this new assumption.

THE COST OF CAPITAL FOR FOREIGN INVESTMENT

We did not say how KW arrived at a 15 percent dollar discount rate for its Narnian project. That depends on the risk of overseas investment and the reward that investors require for taking this risk. These are issues on which few economists can agree, but we will tell you where we stand.[12]

Remember that the risk of an investment cannot be considered in isolation; it depends on the securities that the investor holds in his or her portfolio. For example, suppose KW's shareholders invest mainly in companies that do business in Canada. They would find that the value of KW's Narnian venture was relatively unaffected by fluctuations in the value of Canadian shares. So an investment in the Narnian furniture business would appear to be a

[11] Suppose KW's managers do not go along with what market prices are telling them. For example, perhaps they believe that the leo is likely to appreciate relative to the dollar. Should they plug their own currency forecasts into their present value calculations? We think not. It would be unwise to undertake what might be an unprofitable investment just because management is optimistic about the currency. Given its exchange rate forecast, KW would do better to pass up the investment in wardrobe manufacturing and buy leos instead.

[12] Why don't economists agree? One fundamental reason is that economists have never been able to agree on what makes one country different from another. Is it just that they have different currencies? Or is it that their citizens have different tastes? Or is it that they are subject to different regulations and taxes? The answer affects the relationship between security prices in different countries.

TABLE 24.3
The top 10 least risky and top 10 most risky countries for investment, July 2010.

10 Least Risky Countries	10 Riskiest Countries
Norway	Venezuela
Switzerland	Guinea
Brunei	Liberia
Luxembourg	Niger
Taiwan	Sudan
Canada	Myanmar
Finland	Haiti
Kuwait	Congo, Democratic Republic of
Singapore	Zimbabwe
Sweden	Somalia

Source: PRS Group, "International Country Risk Guide," **www.prsgroup.com/ICRG_TableDef.aspx**, accessed October 15, 2011.

relatively low-risk project to KW's shareholders. That would not be true of a Narnian company, whose shareholders are already exposed to the fortunes of the Narnian market. To them an investment in the Narnian furniture business might seem a relatively high-risk project. They would therefore demand a higher return (*measured in dollars*) than KW's shareholders.

POLITICAL RISK

So far we have focused on the management of exchange rate risk, but managers also worry about the threat that a government will change the rules of the game—that is, break a promise or understanding—after the investment is made. Of course, such risks are not confined to overseas investments. At worst, the government might expropriate the company's assets without compensation. Or it might simply insist that the company keep any profits it makes in the country. Businesses in every country are exposed to the risk of unanticipated actions by governments or the courts. But in some parts of the world, foreign companies are particularly vulnerable to what is called "political risk."

political risk A change in firm value arising from political events.

Political risk refers to any change in the value of a firm arising from political events, which are often unanticipated. A number of consultancy services offer analyses of political and economic risks and draw up country rankings.[13] For example, the PRS Group places countries on a scale of 1 to 100 based on factors such as regime stability, financial transfer, and turmoil. Table 24.3 presents the 10 least risky and 10 riskiest countries based on these factors. Norway tops the list, while Somalia is ranked as riskiest. Notice that risk perceptions change with global events. Some experts feel that the recent pro-democracy movement in several countries in the Middle East, such as Egypt, Libya, and Syria, may also have an impact on Kuwait, increasing the level of political risk in that country.

Some managers dismiss political risk as an "act of God," like a hurricane or earthquake.

Sometimes, such risk can spread from one country to other countries, as has recently happened in the case of the eurozone nations. Two nearby Finance in Action boxes describe the crisis in the eurozone. The first box describes the wider implications of the fiscal meltdown in Greece; the second describes how the crisis has deepened as Portugal, Ireland, and Spain also grapple with dire fiscal and economic circumstances.

[13] For a discussion of these services, see C. Erb, C.R. Harvey, and T. Viskanta, "Political Risk, Financial Risk, and Economic Risk," *Financial Analysts Journal* 52 (1996): 28–46. Campbell Harvey's Web page (**www.duke.edu/~charvey**) is also a useful source of information on political risk.

Finance in Action

Greece Could Be Your Problem Too

Greece said yesterday its fiscal meltdown is part of a wider eurozone problem. Investors could find it becomes their problem, too.

The issue is not that Greece's economy is so big that it will topple the global recovery. To the contrary, the country's output is less than 1% of the world's gross domestic product.

But its growing debt load is having a negative impact on the value of the euro, which has very real implications for investors.

"The strong U.S. dollar relative to the euro is not good news," said Chen Zhao, managing editor of BCA Research in Montreal. "If the euro tumbles, the correction in the U.S. equity market could turn ugly."

Struggling with a massive debt of €294-billion ($434.12-billion) that is greater than its GDP, Greece's sovereign debt ratings were cut severely at the end of the last year. That prompted a rise in bond yields that so far has culminated in a record spread of 405 basis points between the Greek and German 10-year bonds.

While the Greek government has scrambled to introduce austerity measures, the euro has weakened relative to other world currencies and other eurozone bond markets—in Spain and Portugal—have come under the microscope.

In particular, the U.S. dollar has strengthened 8% against the euro since early December, threatening to undo some of the benefits from the weak greenback on earnings growth south of the border. The 3.7% drop in U.S. stocks in January can at least be partially attributed to the sovereign debt worries across the Atlantic.

With no easy way out of the Greek debt crisis and further euro weakness possible, Mr. Zhao said U.S. equities could come under further downward pressure.

When the U.S. dollar rises on a better economy, it is often welcomed by equities, he wrote. However, when it climbs on weakness elsewhere in the world, it often results in falling stock prices.

Commission president Jose Barroso said yesterday the magnitude of Greece's debt must be decisively corrected, adding the planned correction of the deficit by 2012, which includes a wage freeze of all state workers and higher fuel taxes, is "feasible but subject to risks."

Meanwhile, Greece Finance Minister George Papaconstantinou warned at an economic conference yesterday that his country's credit crunch is part of a broader eurozone issue, with Spain and Portugal just two countries also in dire fiscal straits.

"An [EU] endorsement would be a step in the right direction, but there is still a lot of wood to chop," said Stewart Hall, economist, HSBC Securities Canada. "There's some pretty aggressive work to be done and a political constituency that seems to have little patience."

One of the issues being highlighted by the Greek crisis, said Mr. Hall, is the fact that the European Union lacks the infrastructure to help member nations in distress, not least of which is a lack of a bailout program.

Mr. Chen ruled out recent speculation that either Germany or China may bail out Greece—at least not without major concessions. The only viable solution to preventing solvency default in the member countries is through direct purchases of the government debt of troubled economies by the European Central Bank, but with existing laws preventing outright purchases, the ECB will need to bypass regulations to monetize the troubled debt.

"This would imply that the ECB's balance sheet will inevitably grow at a time when the Federal Reserve is ready to unwind its quantitative easing program," he said.

"This is unambiguously bearish for the euro, not to mention that the euro area yield curve has already flattened dramatically relative to the U.S., suggesting that the euro's earlier strength is beginning to bite."

Source: Excerpted from David Pett, "Greece Could Be Your Problem Too," *Financial Post*, February 3, 2010, FP1. Material reprinted with the express permission of National Post, a division of Postmedia Network Inc.

The next Finance in Action box provides an update on the crisis in Greece, which has worsened considerably amid speculation that the country may have to pull out of the eurozone altogether in order to survive.

But the most successful multinational companies structure their business to reduce political risk. Foreign governments are not likely to expropriate a local business if it cannot operate without the support of its parent. For example, the foreign subsidiaries of American computer manufacturers or pharmaceutical companies would have relatively little value if they were cut off from the know-how of their parents. Such operations are much less likely to be expropriated than, say, a mining operation that can be operated as a stand-alone venture.

We are not recommending that you turn your silver mine into a pharmaceutical company, but you may be able to plan your overseas manufacturing operations to improve your bargaining position with foreign governments. For example, Ford has integrated its overseas operations so that the manufacture of components, subassemblies, and complete automobiles is spread across plants in a number of countries. None of these plants would have much value on its own, and Ford can switch production between plants if the political climate in one country deteriorates.

Finance in Action

Eurozone Debt Crisis Deepens on Summit Eve

Germany refused to be rushed into boosting the eurozone's rescue fund after Moody Investors Service Inc. cut Spain's credit rating on Thursday and markets piled pressure on Portugal on the eve of a summit of the currency bloc.

The euro fell to a one-week low of US$1.3804, the risk premium on Spanish bonds widened and the cost of insuring Spanish, Greek and Portuguese debt against default rose as a fresh wave of eurozone jitters hit financial markets.

Leaders of the 17-nation currency area are expected to back a watered-down version of a German-French plan to boost economic competitiveness at Friday's Brussels summit but are unlikely to overcome sharp differences over the size and scope of the rescue fund.

A German official lowered any expectation of a breakthrough, saying no decisions would be taken on strengthening the European Financial Stability Facility on Friday.

"The German government does not believe it is the right time to discuss this," he told a pre-summit briefing.

The question of raising the fund's lending capacity would be decided in a package at the end of March, he said, and Berlin opposed giving the EFSF or its successor any direct or indirect role in buying troubled states' bonds on the secondary market.

EU diplomats said France and several other countries want at least an outline agreement on Friday on the remit of a planned permanent financial rescue mechanism for the eurozone.

"The quicker we get a deal the quicker we calm the markets," one senior diplomat said.

Traders said the euro could fall further due to market concerns that Friday's 17-nation meeting and a summit of the full 27-nation European Union on March 24-25 may fail to agree on decisive action to tackle the debt crisis.

"If officials make no progress and Germans remain unwavering in their demands, the likelihood of a capitulation [in the euro] will be significantly higher," said Jessica Hoversen, currency strategist at MF Global in Chicago.

Moody's cut Spain's sovereign debt rating one notch to Aa2 and warned of further downgrades, estimating that restructuring savings banks will cost more than double the government's ¤20-billion (US$27.6-billion) forecast.

"[Moody's] believes there is a meaningful risk that the eventual cost of the recapitalization effort could considerably exceed the government's current projections," the credit ratings agency said.

It said the overall cost was likely to be nearer ¤40-billion to ¤50-billion and in a more stressed scenario, recapitalization needs could even rise to as high as ¤120-billion.

Bond market pressure on Portugal to become the third eurozone state to seek an European Union/International Monetary Fund rescue after Greece and Ireland has risen this week with 10-year bond yields at euro lifetime highs above 7.5%, a level Lisbon says is unsustainable.

A French presidential source said eurozone leaders would discuss Portugal's measures to cope with its financial problems at Friday's summit but they were not working on a rescue plan.

EU sources said Portuguese Prime Minister José Sôcrates is under intense pressure from his peers and the European Central Bank to announce additional austerity measures and accelerate economic reforms. The sources said he would make a statement to the leaders at the start of a summit on his commitment to deeper reforms, including to the labour market.

Source: Excerpted from E. O'Leary and J. Toyer, "Eurozone Debt Crisis Deepens on Summit Eve," *National Post*, March 11, 2011, **www.nationalpost.com/todays-paper/Eurozone+debt+crisis+deepens+summit/4420832/story.html**, accessed April 6, 2011.

Multinational corporations have also devised financing arrangements to help keep foreign governments honest. For example, suppose your firm is contemplating an investment of $500 million to reopen the San Tomé silver mine in Costaguana with modern machinery, smelting equipment, and shipping facilities. The Costaguanan government agrees to invest in roads and other infrastructure and to take 20 percent of the silver produced by the mine in lieu of taxes. The agreement is to run for 25 years.

The project's NPV on these assumptions is quite attractive. But what happens if a new government comes into power five years from now and imposes a 50 percent tax on "any precious metals exported from the Republic of Costaguana"? Or changes the government's share of output from 20 to 50 percent? Or simply takes over the mine "with fair compensation to be determined in due course by the Minister of Natural Resources of the Republic of Costaguana"?

No contract can absolutely restrain sovereign power. But you can arrange project financing to make these acts as painful as possible for the foreign government. For example, you might set up the mine as a subsidiary corporation, which then borrows a large fraction of the required

Finance in Action

Will Greece Give Have to Give Up the Euro?

Dismissed as foolish fantasy a year ago, the prospect of Greece leaving the euro zone has become a topic worthy of serious discussion among experts handling the crisis in recent weeks.

In public, the official line remains that no member will exit the single currency bloc, but policymakers are at least willing to exchange views on an intellectual level.

In bailing out Greece, Ireland and Portugal, the bloc has already broken its rule that member states cannot assume the liabilities of others—the supposed "no bailout" clause.

The euro project is at best faltering, but it is unclear whether the sovereign debt crisis will bring it to an end or whether it will emerge from a difficult teenage phase.

The 1992 Maastricht Treaty, which laid out the goal of establishing economic and monetary union, resolved to converge as well as strengthen the EU's economies. A levelling-out of wealth and prices across the region was a long-term aim.

Critics, and the evidence, suggest that has been a failure.

In 2010, prices for consumer goods and services were more than 20 percent above the EU average in Finland and some 30 percent below in fellow euro zone member Slovakia.

Income inequality has also increased, although not shot up, in the past decade, with the richest 20 percent in the euro zone now earning five times more than the poorest 20 percent.

While few actually expect a country to abandon the single currency, the chances of it happening have substantially increased since the crisis began in late 2009, with a growing consensus that Greece will prove unable to pay its bills.

It could default and stay within the euro zone, but it is unlikely to achieve the necessary improvement of its competitive position without devaluing, by exiting the single currency.

Emergency aid may take the form of loans not hand-outs, but many economists believe a Greek default is inevitable and that its bailout, set to be doubled, is only buying time.

Financial markets certainly seem to think so.

The prices of credit default swaps imply a 80 percent chance of Greece defaulting and a probability just short of 50 percent for Ireland and Portugal.

Jean Pisani-Ferry, director of the Brussels-based Bruegel thinktank, says that to return to markets, Greece would need to reduce its debt-to-GDP ratio considerably below a current level of some 150 percent. That would require creating a sustained primary surplus of more than 8 percent, he said.

However, no advanced economy other than oil-rich Norway has consistently been able to achieve a surplus above 6 percent.

"The situation is so exceptionally severe that it's hard to see how it can work," Pisani-Ferry said.

There is a risk that, as Greece struggles to push through austerity and is chastised on a regular basis by the EU, IMF and European Central Bank—the troika of experts who oversee Athens' progress—further market turmoil will be triggered.

Bank of America Merrill Lynch economists believe troika reviews at the end of November 2011 and of February 2012 will be particularly important in assessing Greece's progress.

Policymakers have consistently said a default would be catastrophic, but if it is indeed inevitable, all that can be controlled is when it should happen and how to contain it.

Senior EU officials repeatedly said there was no "Plan B" for Greece in the run-up to last month's Greek parliamentary votes in favour of austerity measures.

But the EU's top economic official, Olli Rehn, said there was "no Plan B to avoid default," implying that a contingency plan might have existed, albeit one which involved a Greek default taking place—which would break another taboo.

If you believe a Greek default is inevitable, the question is how it should proceed.

Greece could skip interest payments or reduce the principal owed and still stay within the euro zone. Creditors, banks and taxpayers within and outside Greece would take a huge hit, but Greece would still be forced to carry out savage austerity just to cut its primary deficit to zero.

A devaluation via a Greek exit from the euro would be even more tumultuous, with a likely run on Greek banks as savers withdraw their euro-denominated assets.

Greece, with a modest export to GDP ratio of some 20-25 percent, would still struggle.

"Devaluation works best if you have a strong export sector. For Greece it is small and on average imports deducted from growth more than exports added," said Carsten Brzeski, an economist with ING in Brussels.

However, for an increasingly vocal number of commentators, devaluation is the only viable option.

"To have an economic future Greece has to be competitive," said Martin Jacomb, the chairman of Shire Plc and a former Bank of England director. "This involves, especially for sectors such as the tourist industry, lower real wages and that is almost impossible to achieve harmoniously without devaluation."

He points to Argentina, Latin America's third-largest economy which defaulted on $100 billion of debt in 2002 and dropped the peso's link to the U.S. dollar, and also to the post-split successor states of Czechoslovakia and Yugoslavia, which proved able to adopt different currencies.

Argentina rapidly returned to economic growth of around 9 percent, but the reputation it earned and its failure since to return to global capital markets in the face of U.S. litigation mean euro zone policymakers do not see it as a model to follow.

"This was less messy because they still had the peso, albeit devalued, but we have seen countries split and each part develop their own currencies successfully," Jacomb said.

Source: Excerpted from P. Blenkinsop, "Greece's Euro Exit No Longer Taboo Subject," *National Post*, July 8, 2011, **www.nationalpost.com**, accessed July 11, 2011. Material reprinted with the express permission of National Post, a division of Postmedia Network Inc.

investment from a consortium of major international banks. If your firm guarantees the loan, make sure the guarantee stands only if the Costaguanan government honours its contract. The government will be reluctant to break the contract if that causes a default on the loans and undercuts the country's credit standing with the international banking system.

AVOIDING FUDGE FACTORS

We certainly don't pretend that we can put a precise figure on the cost of capital for foreign investment. But you can see that we disagree with the frequent practice of *automatically* increasing the domestic cost of capital when foreign investment is considered. We suspect that managers mark up the required return for foreign investment because it is more costly to manage an operation in a foreign country and to cover the risk of expropriation, foreign exchange restrictions, or unfavourable tax changes. A fudge factor is added to the discount factor to cover costs associated with political risk.

We think managers should leave the discount rate alone and reduce expected cash flows instead. For example, suppose that KW is expected to earn L2.5 million in the first year *if no penalties are placed on the operations of foreign firms*. Suppose also that there is a 20 percent chance that KW's cash flow may be expropriated without compensation. The expected cash flow is not L2.5 million but $.8 \times 2.5$ million $=$ L2 million.

The end result may be the same if you pretend that the expected cash flow is L2.5 million but add a fudge factor to the discount rate. Nevertheless, adjusting cash flows brings management's assumptions about "political risk" out in the open for scrutiny and sensitivity analysis.

24.5 SUMMARY

1. What is the difference between spot and forward exchange rates? LO1

The exchange rate is the amount of one currency needed to purchase one unit of another currency. The **spot rate of exchange** is the exchange rate for an immediate transaction. The **forward rate** is the exchange rate for a forward transaction, that is, a transaction at a specified future date.

2. What are the basic relationships between spot exchange rates, forward exchange rates, interest rates, and inflation rates? LO2

To produce order out of chaos, the international financial manager needs some model of the relationships between exchange rates, interest rates, and inflation rates. Four very simple theories prove useful:

- In its strictest form, **purchasing power parity** states that \$1 must have the same purchasing power in every country. You only need to take a vacation abroad to know that this doesn't square well with the facts. Nevertheless, on average, changes in exchange rates match differences in inflation rates, and if you need a long-term forecast of the exchange rate, it is difficult to do much better than to assume that the exchange rate will offset the effect of any differences in the inflation rates.
- In an open world-capital market, real rates of interest would have to be the same. Thus differences in nominal interest rates result from differences in expected inflation rates. The **international Fisher effect** suggests that firms should not simply borrow where interest rates are lowest. Those countries are also likely to have the lowest inflation rates and the strongest currencies.

- **Interest rate parity theory** states that the interest differential between two countries must be equal to the difference between the forward and spot exchange rates. In the international markets, arbitrage ensures that parity almost always holds.
- The **expectations theory of exchange rates** tells us that the forward rate equals the expected spot rate (though it is very far from being a perfect forecaster of the spot rate).

3. **What are some simple strategies to protect the firm against exchange rate risk?** LO3

Our simple theories about forward rates have two practical implications for the problem of hedging overseas operations. First, the expectations theory suggests that hedging exchange risk is on average cost free. Second, there are two ways to hedge against exchange risk—one is to buy or sell currency forward, the other is to lend or borrow abroad. Interest rate parity tells us that the cost of the two methods should be the same.

4. **How do we perform an NPV analysis for projects with cash flows in foreign currencies?** LO4

Overseas investment decisions are no different in principle from domestic decisions. You need to forecast the project's cash flows and then discount them at the opportunity cost of capital. But it is important to remember that if the opportunity cost of capital is stated in dollars, the cash flows must also be converted to dollars. This requires a forecast of foreign exchange rates. We suggest that you rely on the simple parity relationships and use the interest rate differential to produce these forecasts. In international capital budgeting, the return that shareholders require from foreign investments must be estimated. Adding a premium for the "extra risks," such as political risk, of overseas investment is not a good solution.

Related Web Links

stls.frb.org Web site of the Federal Reserve Bank of St. Louis; a good source of exchange rate data

globalfinancialdata.com Good data source for major currencies

newyorkfed.org Federal Reserve Bank of New York; forward exchange rates for the yen and euro, and other data

corporateinformation.com For data on overseas companies and useful links to finance-related sites for each country

prsgroup.com For estimates of the political risk of different countries

cmegroup.com/education The Chicago Mercantile Exchange's information centre on a variety of products including foreign currency futures and options

bloomberg.com/markets Data on current exchange rates and securities

global-investor.com Financial information and resources including information on international markets

emgmkts.com/index.htm Analysis of economic, political, and financial events in emerging markets

forbes.com/markets News and information about financial markets

florin.com/v4/valore4.html Issues in currency risk management

globeandmail.ca *The Globe and Mail* Web site

ft.com *Financial Times* Web site

fx.sauder.ubc.ca/data.html Foreign exchange data, teaching- and research-related information from the Pacific Exchange Rate Service, Sauder School of Business, University of British Columbia

Key Terms

exchange rate	756	interest rate parity	765	political risk	772
expectations theory of exchange rates	766	international Fisher effect	763	purchasing power parity (PPP)	761
forward exchange rate	758	law of one price	761	spot rate of exchange	757

Questions and Problems

connect Practise and learn online with *Connect*. Questions with online Excel templates or datasets are marked with ✓.

*Answers in Appendix B

BASIC

*1. **Exchange Rates.** Use Table 24.1 to answer these questions: (LO1)
   a. How many euros can you buy for $100? How many dollars can you buy for 100 euros?
   b. How many Swiss francs can you buy for $100? How many dollars can you buy for 100 Swiss francs?
   c. If the euro depreciates with respect to the dollar, will the direct exchange rate quoted in Table 24.1 increase or decrease? What about the indirect exchange rate?
   d. Is a United States or an Australian dollar worth more?

2. **Exchange Rate Relationships.** Look at Table 24.1. (LO2)
   a. How many Japanese yen do you get for your dollar?
   b. What is the 12-month forward rate for the yen?
   c. Is the yen at a forward discount or premium on the dollar?
   d. Calculate the annual percentage discount or premium on the yen.
   e. If the interest rate on dollars is 1.6 percent, what do you think is the interest rate on yen?
   f. According to the expectations theory, what is the expected spot rate for the yen in one year's time?
   g. According to purchasing power parity, what is the expected difference in the rate of price inflation in Canada and Japan?

3. **Exchange Rate Relationships.** Define each of the following theories in a sentence or simple equation: (LO2)
   a. Interest rate parity theory
   b. Expectations theory of forward rates
   c. Law of one price
   *d. International Fisher effect (relationship between interest rates in different countries)

4. **International Capital Budgeting.** Which of the following items do you need if you do all your capital budgeting calculations in your own currency? (LO4)
   a. Forecasts of future exchange rates
   b. Forecasts of the foreign inflation rate
   c. Forecasts of the domestic inflation rate
   d. Foreign interest rates
   e. Domestic interest rates

5. **Foreign Currency Management.** Rosetta Stone, the treasurer of International Reprints, Inc., has noticed that the interest rate in Switzerland is below the rates in most other countries. She is therefore suggesting that the company should make an issue of Swiss franc bonds. What considerations should she first take into account? (LO3)

*6. **Hedging Exchange Rate Risk.** An importer in Canada is due to take delivery of silk scarves from Europe in six months. The price is fixed in euros. Which of the following transactions could eliminate the importer's exchange risk? (LO3)
   a. Buy euros forward.
   b. Sell euros forward.
   c. Borrow euros, buy dollars at the spot exchange rate.
   d. Sell euros at the spot exchange rate, lend dollars.

INTERMEDIATE

7. **Currency Risk.** Sanyo produces audio and video consumer goods and exports a large fraction of its output to the United States under its own name and the Fisher brand name. It prices its products in yen, meaning that it seeks to maintain a fixed price in terms of yen. Suppose the yen moves from ¥118.39/US$ to ¥110/US$. What currency risk does Sanyo face? How can it reduce its exposure? (LO3)

*8. **Managing Exchange Rate Risk.** A firm in the United States is due to receive payment of 1 million Australian dollars in 8 years' time. It would like to protect itself against a decline in the value of the Australian dollar, but finds it difficult to arrange a forward sale for such a long period. Is there any other way it can protect itself? (LO3)

9. **Interest Rate Parity.** The following table shows interest rates and exchange rates for the U.S. dollar and Mexican peso. The spot exchange rate is 9.5 pesos per U.S. dollar. Complete the missing entries:

	1 Month	1 Year
U.S. dollar interest rate (annually compounded)	5.5%	7%
Peso interest rate (annually compounded)	20%	—
Forward pesos per U.S. dollar	—	11.2

Hint: When calculating the 1-month forward rate, remember to translate the annual interest rate into a monthly interest rate. (LO2)

*10. **Exchange Rate Risk.** An American investor buys 100 shares of London Enterprises at a price of £50 when the exchange rate is US$1.60/£. A year later the shares are selling at £52. No dividends have been paid. (LO3)

a. What is the rate of return to an American investor if the exchange rate is still US$1.60/£?
b. What if the exchange rate is US$1.70/£?
c. What if the exchange rate is US$1.50/£?

*11. **Interest Rate Parity.** Look at Table 24.1. If the 3-month interest rate on dollars is 6 percent (annualized), what do you think is the 3-month sterling (U.K.) interest rate? Explain what would happen if the rate were substantially above your figure. *Hint:* In your calculations remember to convert the annually compounded interest rate into a rate for three months. (LO2)

12. **Expectations Theory.** Table 24.1 shows the 12-month forward rate on the U.S. dollar. (LO2)

a. Is the U.S. dollar at a forward discount or a premium on the Canadian dollar?
b. What is the annualized percentage discount or premium?
c. If you have no other information about the two currencies, what is your best guess about the spot rate in one year?
d. Suppose that you expect to receive 100,000 U.S. dollars in 1 year. How many Canadian dollars is this likely to be worth?

13. **Interest Rate Parity.** Suppose the interest rate on 1-year loans in the United States is 5 percent while in the United Kingdom the interest rate is 6 percent. The spot exchange rate is US$1.55/£ and the forward rate is US$1.54/£. In what country would you choose to borrow? To lend? Can you profit from this situation? (LO2)

*14. **Purchasing Power Parity.** Suppose that the inflation rate in the United States is 4 percent and in Canada it is 5 percent. What would you expect is happening to the exchange rate between the United States and Canadian dollars? (LO2)

15. **Cross Rates.** Look at Table 24.1. How many Swiss francs can you buy for $1? How many yen can you buy? What rate do you think a Japanese bank would quote for buying or selling Swiss francs? Explain what would happen if it quoted a rate that was substantially less than your figure. (LO1)

*16. **International Capital Budgeting.** Suppose that you apply your own views about exchange rates when valuing an overseas investment proposal. Specifically, suppose that you believe that the leo will depreciate by 2 percent per year. Recalculate the NPV of KW's project. (LO4)

17. **Currency Risk.** You have bid for a possible export order that would provide a cash inflow of €1 million in one year. The spot exchange rate is €.687/$ and the 12-month forward rate is €.691/$. There are two sources of uncertainty: (1) the euro could appreciate or depreciate, and (2) you may or may not receive the export order. Illustrate in each case the profits or losses that you would make if you sell €1 million forward by filling in the following table. Assume that the exchange rate in 1 year will be either €.65/$ or €.74/$. (LO3)

	Profit/Loss	
Spot Rate	**Receive Order**	**Lose Order**
€.65/$	_____	_____
€.74/$	_____	_____

18. **Managing Currency Risk.** General Gadget Corp. (GGC) is a Canada-based multinational firm that makes electrical coconut scrapers. These gadgets are made only in Canada using local inputs. The scrapers are sold mainly to Asian and West Indian countries where coconuts are grown. (LO3)

a. If GGC sells scrapers in Trinidad, what is the currency risk faced by the firm?
b. In what currency should GGC borrow funds to pay for its investment in order to mitigate its foreign exchange exposure?
c. Suppose that GGC begins manufacturing its products in Trinidad using local (Trinidadian) inputs and labour. How does this affect its exchange rate risk?

19. **Currency Risk.** If investors recognize the impacts of inflation and exchange rate changes on a firm's cash flows, changes in exchange rates should be reflected in stock prices. How would the stock price of each of the following Swiss companies be affected by an unanticipated appreciation in the Swiss franc of 10 percent, only 2 percent of which could be justified by comparing Swiss inflation to that in the rest of the world? (LO3)

a. *Swiss Air.* More than two-thirds of its employees are Swiss. Most revenues come from international fares set in U.S. dollars.
b. *Nestlé.* Fewer than 5 percent of its employees are Swiss. Most revenues are derived from sales of consumer goods in a wide range of countries with competition from local producers.
c. *Union Bank of Switzerland.* Most employees are Swiss. All non–Swiss franc monetary positions are fully hedged.

20. **Internet.** The *Financial Times* maintains a "special reports" Web site on the euro: **specials.ft.com/euro/index.html**. Go to the site and trace the chronology of events that led to the European Monetary Union and the creation of this single currency. (LO1)

21. **Internet.** The euro has replaced 16 national currencies. Browse through the European Commission's Web site at **ec.europa.eu** to find and list these 16 countries. What is the permanent conversion rate of the euro against these eurozone currencies? (LO1)

22. **Internet.** Go to **stats.oecd.org**, the Statistics section of the Web site of the Organisation for Economic Co-Operation and Development (OECD). Can you retrieve information on the most recent purchasing-power parity rates for all of the OECD countries? (LO2)

23. **Internet.** There are plenty of good sites that show current and past spot rates of exchange. One excellent site is the Pacific Exchange Rate Service of Sauder School of Business, University of British Columbia, which can be accessed at **fx.sauder.ubc.ca**. Forward rates are less easy to come by, but the Pacific Exchange Rate Service site shows daily forward rates for the Canadian and U.S. dollars. Can you deduce from these whether the interest rate is higher in Canada than in the United States? (*Warning:* Look out for the difference between direct and indirect quotes). (LO2)

24. **Internet.** The Organisation for Economic Cooperation and Development (OECD) provides data on nominal and effective (that is, real) exchange rates. Log in to **www.oecd.org** and then click on "Statistics," and choose "Finance" topic. You need the tables on interest rates and exchange rates. Look at the effective exchange rate for the dollar against other currencies. Has the U.S. dollar been appreciating or declining in real terms? Is this helping or hurting U.S. exporters? Which country has experienced the sharpest fall in the real value of its currency? (LO2)

25. **Internet.** Go to Yahoo Finance Website at **ca.finance.yahoo.com**. In February 2010, a Japanese investor bought 2,000 shares of Magna International, Inc. (MG.TO), for $60 through his Toronto-based broker. What is the return over the latest calendar year on his investment in Canadian dollars and in Japanese yen? What has been the percentage change in the yen/dollar exchange rate over the 1-year period since he made his investment? (To obtain dollar/yen exchange rates, go to **www.bank-banque-canada.ca/en/exchange.htm**.) (LO1)

CHALLENGE

26. **International Capital Budgeting.** A Canadian firm is evaluating an investment in Indonesia. The project costs 500 billion Indonesian rupiah and it is expected to produce an income of 250 billion Indonesian rupiah a year in real terms for each of the next 3 years. The expected inflation rate in Indonesia is 12 percent per year and the firm estimates that an appropriate discount rate for the project would be about 8 percent above the risk-free rate of interest. Calculate the net present value of the project in dollars. Exchange rates are given in Table 24.1. The interest rate is about 15 percent in Indonesia and 5 percent in Canada. (LO4)

27. **Hedging Exchange Rate Risk.** You have decided to purchase a deluxe condominium apartment in a newly built residential complex in South Florida. Your agreement with the real estate developer specifies that construction of the apartment will be completed and its keys will be handed to you three months from today. The purchase price is US$200,000 to be paid at the time of possession. The current spot exchange rate is $.9770/US$ and the current 3-month forward rate is $.9790/US$.

    You intend to pay for the apartment using your dollar savings from a bank account in Canada. These dollars are earning interest at 5 percent per annum in Canada. Interest rates in the United States are 3 percent per annum.

    What options are available to you to pay for the condominium apartment if you want to avoid all foreign exchange risk associated with the transaction? Show which of the choices will work out best for you. (LO3)

28. **Integrative.** Fleximetals Inc. of Canada is considering a capital investment in Zamboana. The currency of Zamboana is the Zamboa peso (symbol: Zp). Details regarding the project are provided below (all currency amounts are reported in the nearest thousands).
    - *Initial project cost (in 2008).* $3,500 (Zp7000) for plant and equipment and $250 (Zp500) for working capital.
    - *Sales.* First year = Zp13,000. It is expected to grow at 10 percent per annum over the next 3 years.
    - *Costs.* Variable costs will be 30 percent of sales, and fixed cash costs are Zp1,000 per year.
    - *Working capital.* Gross working capital (that is, cash, receivables and inventory) = 20 percent of sales. Half financed by local accruals and accounts payable, but other half financed externally.
    - *Depreciation.* Straight-line over three years. No salvage value.
    - *Taxes.* Income taxes are 30 percent in both Zamboana and Canada.
    - *Liquidation values (after 3 years).* Zp5,000 (free of all Zamboana and Canadian taxes).
    - *Weighted average cost of capital (WACC).* The WACC used in Zamboana and Canada for projects of this type is 18 percent.
    - *Exchange rate in 2008.* Zp/$ is 2.0 and is expected to increase by 10 percent in each subsequent year.

    Assume that 50 percent of the project's net income after taxes are remitted to the Canadian parent company as dividend. (LO4)

a. Compute the net present value of the project from the point of view of the affiliate in Zamboana as well as the parent in Canada.

b. Is the project acceptable under both circumstances? If not, briefly comment on factors to be considered in the decision process.

Solutions to Check Points

24.1 *Direct quote.* \$1.388512/€
Indirect quote. 1/1.388512 = €.720120/\$
Direct quote. \$.012061/¥
Indirect quote. 1/.012061 = ¥82.912/\$

24.2 The dollar buys less Swiss francs, so the franc has appreciated with respect to the dollar.

24.3 a. SFr1,500 × 1.080513 = \$1,620.77 using the direct (that is, \$/SFr) quote.
b. (1) Direct exchange rate: SFr1 = 1.080513/.9 = \$1.20057
(2) Indirect exchange rate: \$1 = .9 × .925486 = .832937 francs
c. 1,500 × 1.20057 = \$1,800.86
d. 1,620.77/1.20057 = 1,350 francs

24.4 a. £880 = \$1320. Therefore £1 = 1320/880 = \$1.50. The £/\$ exchange rate = 1/1.50 = .67.
b. In the United States, price = \$1320 × 1.02 = \$1346.40. In Great Britain, price = £880 × 1.05 = £924. The new exchange rate = \$1346.40/£924 = \$1.457/£.
c. Initially \$1 buys 1/1.50 = £.667. At the end of the year, \$1 buys 1/1.457 = £.686, which is about 3 percent higher than the original value of £.667.

24.5 The real interest rate in Canada is 1.04/1.022 − 1 = .018, or 1.8 percent. If the real rate is the same in Indonesia, then expected inflation must be

$$(1 + \text{nominal rate})/(1 + \text{real rate}) - 1 = 1.08/1.018 - 1 = .061, \text{ or } 6.1\%$$

24.6 The pound is at a forward premium (that is, you get fewer pounds for \$1, or conversely, more dollars for £1 in the forward market). This implies that the interest rates in Great Britain are lower than those in Canada.

The interest rate in Canada is 1.6 percent. Interest rate parity states

$$(1 + r_£)/(1 + r_\$) = f_{£/\$}/S_{£/\$}$$

Therefore,

$$r_£ = 1.016 \times (.6228/.6246) - 1 = .013, \text{ or } 1.3\%$$

24.7 Stellar borrows ¥100 million now. It pays ¥1 million in interest after 1 year, when it also repays the loan. Cash flows in U.S. dollars are

$$\text{Now: } \frac{100 \text{ million}}{81.00} = \text{US\$}1,234,568$$

$$\text{In one year: Interest} = \frac{1 \text{ million}}{80.60} = \text{US\$}12,407$$

$$\text{Principal} = \frac{100 \text{ million}}{80.60} = \text{US\$}1,240,695$$

$$\text{Total} = \text{US\$}1,253,102$$

To find the U.S. dollar interest rate, solve

$$1,234,568 \times (1 + r_{US\$}) = \$1,253,102$$

$$r_{US\$} = \frac{1,253,102}{1,234,568} - 1 = .015, \text{ or } 1.5\%$$

24.8 If you buy yen in the forward market, you will exchange ¥80.60 per U.S. dollar in 1 year. Suppose instead that you borrow US\$1, convert the dollar to ¥81.00 in the spot market, and invest the funds in Japan. You will have to repay the U.S. dollar loan with .6 percent interest and will earn .1 percent interest on your yen investment. Therefore, in 1 year, you will receive ¥81.00 × 1.001 = ¥81.081, but will have to pay US\$1.006. This is effectively an exchange rate of ¥81 for US\$1, corresponding to a forward exchange rate of ¥81.081/US\$1.006 = ¥80.597, which except for minor rounding error matches the rate in the forward market.

24.9 According to the expectations theory of exchange rates, the forward rate equals the expected future spot exchange rate. Therefore, the expected cost of the hedge—the difference between the forward rate and expected spot rate is zero!

24.10 a. The lower interest rate in Narnia than in Canada suggests that forecast inflation is lower in Narnia. If real interest rates are the same in the two countries, then the difference in inflation rates is about 5 − 3 = 2 percent.
b. The lower interest rate (and lower expected inflation rate) in Narnia suggests that investors are expecting the leo to appreciate against the dollar.
c. Since KW can now expect to change its leo cash flows into more dollars than before, the project's NPV is increased. Forecast exchange rates will be as follows:

Year	Forecast Exchange Rate		
0	Spot exchange rate	=	L2.0/\$
1	$2.0 \times (1.03/1.05)$	=	L1.962/\$
2	$2.0 \times (1.03/1.05)^2$	=	L1.925/\$
3	$2.0 \times (1.03/1.05)^3$	=	L1.888/\$
4	$2.0 \times (1.03/1.05)^4$	=	L1.852/\$
5	$2.0 \times (1.03/1.05)^5$	=	L1.817/\$

The expected dollar cash flows from the project are:

Year:	0	1	2	3	4	5
Cash flow ($ millions)	$\frac{-7.6}{2.00} = -\$3.8$	$\frac{2.0}{1.962} = \$1.02$	$\frac{2.5}{1.925} = \$1.30$	$\frac{3.0}{1.888} = \$1.59$	$\frac{3.5}{1.852} = \$1.89$	$\frac{4.0}{1.817} = \$2.20$

Discounting these dollar cash flows at the 15 percent dollar cost of capital gives

$$\text{NPV} = -3.8 + \frac{1.02}{1.15} + \frac{1.30}{1.15^2} + \frac{1.59}{1.15^3} + \frac{1.89}{1.15^4} + \frac{2.20}{1.15^5}$$

$$= \$1.29 \text{ million, or } \$1{,}290{,}000$$

The project is worth more because the reduced interest rate in Narnia suggests that investors expect the leo to appreciate in value. Thus the dollar cash flows from the project are higher than in Section 24.4.

MINI CASE

"Jumping jackasses! Not another one!" groaned Mike Luger. It was the third memo he had received that morning from the CEO of DVD player Importers:

From: CEO's Office
To: Company Treasurer

Mike,

I have been looking at some of our foreign exchange deals and they don't seem to make sense.

First, we have been buying yen forward to cover the cost of our imports. You have explained that this insures us against the risk that the dollar may depreciate over the next year, but it is incredibly expensive insurance. Each dollar buys only 81.68 yen when we buy forward, compared with the current spot rate of 82.91 yen to the dollar. We could save a fortune by buying yen as and when we need them rather than buying them forward.

Another possibility has occurred to me. If we are worried that the dollar may depreciate (or do I mean "appreciate"?), why don't we buy yen at the low spot rate of ¥82.91 to the dollar and then put them on deposit until we have to pay for the DVD players? That way we can make sure we get a good rate for our yen.

I am also worried that we are missing out on some cheap financing. We are paying about 8 percent to borrow dollars for one year, but Ben Hur was telling me at lunch that we could get a 1-year yen loan for about 1.75 percent. I find that a bit surprising, but if that's the case, why don't we repay our dollar loans and borrow yen instead?

Perhaps we could discuss these ideas at next Wednesday's meeting. I would be interested in your views on the matter.

Jill Edison

PART 8 Special Topics

23 Mergers, Acquisitions, and Corporate Control

24 International Financial Management

25 Options

25.1 Calls and Puts

25.2 What Determines Option Values?

25.3 Spotting the Option

25.4 Summary

Appendix 25A The Black-Scholes Option Valuation Model (see the Online Learning Centre)

26 Risk Management

CHAPTER 25

Options

LEARNING OBJECTIVES

After studying this chapter, you should be able to:

LO1 Calculate the payoff to buyers and sellers of call and put options.

LO2 Describe how option values are determined.

LO3 Point out examples of options in capital investment proposals.

LO4 Identify options that are provided in financial securities.

Just another day at the Montréal Exchange, home of the Canadian Derivatives Exchange. But why does the financial manager of an industrial company need to understand options?

When the Chicago Board Options Exchange (CBOE) was established in 1973, few observers guessed what a success it would be. By creating standardized, listed stock options, the CBOE revolutionized options trading. Today the CBOE is one of the world's largest options exchange, each year trading options to buy or sell more than 50 billion shares of stock in 2,200 companies. Other exchanges around the world have copied the CBOE model, and in addition to options on individual stocks, options can be traded on stock indexes, bonds, commodities, and foreign exchanges. For example, options on Canadian stocks and bonds are traded on the Montréal Exchange, home of the Canadian Derivatives Exchange, **www.m-x.ca**.

You will see that options can be valuable tools for managing the risk characteristics of an investment portfolio. But why should the financial manager of an industrial company read further? There are several reasons. First, most capital budgeting projects have options embedded in them that allow the company to expand at a future date or to bail out. These options allow the company to profit if things go well but give downside protection when they don't.

Second, many of the securities that firms issue include an option. For example, companies often issue convertible bonds. The holder has the option to exchange the bond for common stock. Some corporate bonds also contain a call provision, meaning that the issuer has the option to buy back the bond from the investor.

Finally, managers routinely use currency, commodity, and interest rate options to protect the firm against a variety of risks. (We will have more to say about this in Chapter 26.)

In one chapter we can provide you with only a brief introduction to options. Our first goal in this chapter is to explain how options work and how option value is determined. Then we will tell you how to recognize some of the options that crop up in capital investment proposals and in company financing.

LO1 25.1 CALLS AND PUTS

call option Right to buy an asset at a specified exercise price on or before the expiration (or expiry) date.

A **call option** gives its holder the right to buy stock for a fixed *exercise price* (also called the *strike price*) on or before a specified expiration (or expiry) date.[1] For example, if you buy a call option on The Toronto-Dominion Bank (TD) stock with an expiry (or expiration) date[2] in

[1] In some cases, the option can be exercised only on one particular day, which is conventionally known as a *European call*; in other cases, it can be exercised on or before that day, which is called an *American call*.

[2] For the Montréal Exchange, the expiry date is the Saturday following the last trading day of the expiration month. The last trading day is the third Friday of the expiration month, providing it is a business day; if not, the first preceding business day. These details vary among the options exchanges.

October and an exercise price of $84, you have the right to buy shares of TD at a price of $84 per share at any time until October.

You need not exercise a call option; it will be profitable to do so only if the share price exceeds the exercise price. If it does not, the option will be left unexercised and will be valueless. But suppose that when the call option expires TD shares are selling above the $84 exercise price, say at $90. In this case you choose to exercise your option to pay $84 for shares worth $90. Your payoff will equal the difference between the $90 for which you can sell the shares and the $84 that you pay when you exercise the option. More generally, when the stock price is greater than exercise price, the payoff from your call option is equal to the difference between the stock price and the exercise price.

In summary, the value of the call option at expiration is as follows:

Stock Price at Expiration	Value of Call at Expiration
Greater than exercise price	Stock price − exercise price
Less than exercise price	Zero

Of course, that payoff is not all profit: You have to pay for the option. The price of the call is called the option *premium*. Option buyers pay the premium for the right to exercise later. Your *profit* equals the ultimate payoff to the call option (which may be zero) minus the initial premium.

EXAMPLE 25.1 CALL OPTIONS ON TORONTO-DOMINION BANK

On March 25, 2011, a call option on TD common shares with a October 2011 expiration and an exercise price of $84 per share sold for $4.60. If you had purchased the call on this date, you would have had the right to purchase shares of TD for $84 any time until the option expired in October. On March 25, the closing TD stock price was $84.45. Immediate exercise of the call would have resulted in a payoff of $84.45 − $84 = $0.45. Obviously, anyone who paid $4.60 for the call on March 25 had no intention of exercising it immediately. If the stock price did not rise by October, the call would not be worth exercising and you would lose your investment of $4.60. On the other hand, even a relatively modest rise in the stock price could give you a rich profit on your option. For example, if TD sold for $90 in October, the proceeds from exercising the call would have been

$$\text{Proceeds} = \text{stock price} - \text{exercise price} = \$90 - \$84 = \$6$$

and the net profit on the call would have been

$$\text{Profits} = \text{proceeds} - \text{original investment} = \$6 - \$4.60 = \$1.40$$

In seven months, you would have earned a return of $1.40/$4.60 = .304 or 30.4 percent.

put option Right to sell an asset at a specified exercise price on or before the expiration (or expiry) date.

Whereas a call option gives you the right to buy a share of stock, a **put option** gives you the right to *sell* it for the exercise price. If you own a put on a share of stock and the stock price turns out to be greater than the exercise price, you will not want to exercise your option to sell the shares for the exercise price. The put will be left unexercised and will expire valueless. But if the stock price turns out to be less than the exercise price, it will pay to buy the share in the market at the low price and then exercise your option to sell it for the exercise price. The put would then be worth the difference between the exercise price and the stock price.

EXAMPLE 25.2 PUT OPTIONS ON TORONTO-DOMINION BANK

On March 25, 2011, it cost $4.45 to buy a put option on TD shares with a October 2011 expiration and an exercise price of $84. Suppose TD is selling for $78 just before the put option expires. Then if you hold a put, you can buy a share of stock in the market for $78 and exercise your right to sell it for $84. The put will be worth $84 − $78 = $6. Because you paid $4.45 for the put originally, your net profit is $6 − $4.45 = $1.55. As a put buyer, your worry is that the stock price will rise above the $84 exercise price. If that happens, you will let the put option expire worthless and your loss is the $4.45 you originally paid for it.

In general, the value of the put option at expiration is as follows:

Stock Price at Expiration	Value of Put Option at Expiration
Greater than exercise price	Zero
Less than exercise price	Exercise price − stock price

Table 25.1 shows how the values of TD calls and puts are affected by the level of the TD stock price on the expiration date. You can see that once the stock price is above the exercise price, the call value rises dollar for dollar with the stock price, and once the stock price is below the exercise price, the put value rises a dollar for each dollar *decrease* in the stock price. Figure 25.1 plots the values of each option on the expiration date, for various possible stock prices.

Table 25.2 shows the prices of nine call and nine put options on shares of TD on March 25, 2011.

Notice that for any particular expiration date, calls are worth more when the exercise price is lower, while puts are worth more when the exercise price is higher. This makes sense. You would rather have the right to buy at a low price and the right to sell at high price. Notice also that for any particular exercise price, the longer-dated options are the most valuable. This also makes sense. An option that expires in January 2012 gives you everything that a shorter-dated option offers and more. Naturally, you would be prepared to pay for the chance of keeping your options open for as long as possible.

TABLE 25.1
How the value of a TD option on its expiration date varies with the price of stock on that date (exercise price = $84).

Stock Price	$76	$80	$84	$88	$92
Call value	$0	$0	$0	$4	$8
Put value	$8	$4	$0	$0	$0

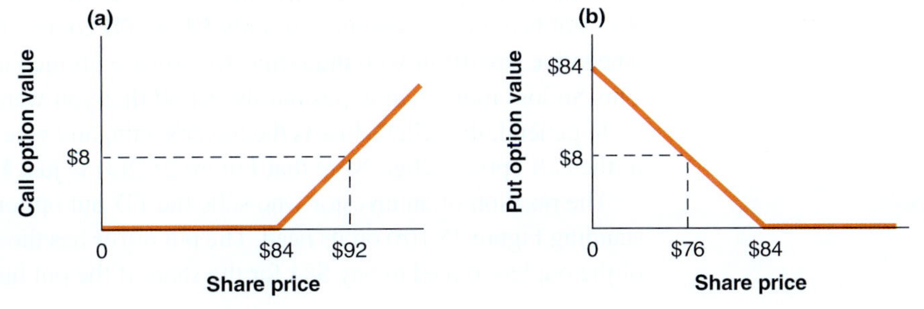

FIGURE 25.1
Values of call options and put options on TD stock on option expiration date (exercise price = $84).

TABLE 25.2
Examples of option prices on TD shares on March 25, 2011, when TD stock was selling for $84.45.

Expiration Date	Exercise Price	Call Price	Put Price
July 2011	$80	$5.70	$1.58
	84	$3.00	$2.86
	88	$1.27	$5.15
October 2011	$80	$7.10	$2.85
	84	$4.60	$4.45
	88	$2.25	$6.50
January 2012	$80	$7.95	$3.95
	84	$5.50	$5.75
	88	$3.55	$7.75

Source: Montréal Exchange, **www.m-x.ca**.

Check Point 25.1

a. What will be the proceeds and profits (that is, net of the option premium) to an investor who purchases the July-expiration TD call options with exercise price $84 if the stock price at maturity is $80? What if the stock price at maturity is $92? Use the data in Table 25.2.
b. Now answer part (a) for an investor who purchases a July-expiration TD put option with exercise price $84.

SELLING CALLS AND PUTS

The traded options that you see quoted in the financial Web sites are not sold by the companies themselves but by other investors. If one investor buys an option on TD stock, some other investor must be on the other side of the transaction. We will look now at the position of the investor who sells an option.[3]

We have already seen that the October-expiration TD calls with exercise price $84 are trading at $4.60. Thus if you *sell* the October call option on TD stock, the buyer pays you $4.60. However, in return you promise to *sell* TD shares at a price of $84 if the call buyer decides to exercise his option. The option seller's obligation to *sell* TD is just the other side of the coin to the option holder's right to *buy* the stock. The buyer *pays* the option premium for the right to exercise; the seller *receives* the premium but may be required at a later date to deliver the stock for an exercise price that is less than the market price of the stock. If the share price is below the exercise price of $84 when the option expires in October, holders of the call will not exercise their option, and you, the seller, will have no further liability. However, if the price of TD is greater than $84, it will pay the buyer to exercise, and you must give up your shares for $84 each. You lose the difference between the share price and the $84 that you receive from the buyer.

Suppose that TD's stock price turns out to be $90. In this case the buyer will exercise the call option and will pay $84 for stock that can be resold for $90. The buyer therefore has a payoff of $6—not bad on an investment of only $4.60. Of course, that positive payoff for the *buyer* means a negative payoff for you, the *seller*, for you are obliged to sell TD stock worth $90 for only $84. This $6 loss more than wipes out the $4.60 that you were originally paid for selling the option.

In general, the seller's loss is the buyer's gain, and vice versa. Figure 25.2(a) shows the payoffs to the call option seller. Note that Figure 25.2(a) is just Figure 25.1(a) drawn upside down.

The position of an investor who sells the TD put option can be shown in just the same way by standing Figure 25.1(b) on its head. The put *buyer* has the right to sell a share for $84; so the *seller* of the put has agreed to pay $84 for the share if the put buyer should demand it. Clearly the seller

[3] The option seller is known as the *writer*.

FIGURE 25.2
Payoffs to sellers of call and put options on TD stock (exercise price = $84).

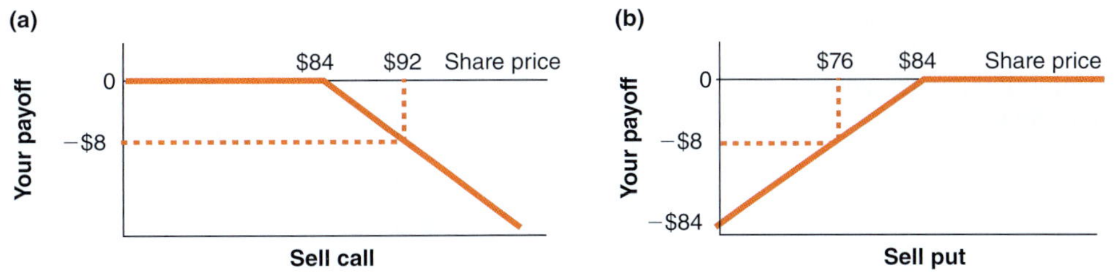

TABLE 25.3
Rights and obligations of various options positions.

	Buyer	Seller
Call option	Right to buy asset	Obligation to sell asset
Put option	Right to sell asset	Obligation to buy asset

will be safe as long as the share price remains above $84, but will payout money if the share price falls below this figure. The worst thing that can happen to the put seller is for the stock to be worthless. The seller would then be obliged to pay $84 for a worthless stock. The payoff to the seller would be −$84. Note that the advantage (choice and flexibility) always lies with the option buyer, the obligation with the seller. Therefore, the buyer must pay the seller to acquire the option.

Table 25.3 summarizes the rights and obligation of buyers and sellers of calls and puts.

Check Point 25.2

a. What will be the proceeds and profits to an investor who sells the July-expiration TD call options with exercise price $84 if the stock price at maturity is $80? What if the stock price at maturity is $92? Use the data in Table 25.2.

b. Now answer part (a) for an investor who sells a July-expiration TD put option with exercise price $84.

PAYOFF DIAGRAMS ARE NOT PROFIT DIAGRAMS

Figures 25.1 and 25.2 show *only* the possible payoffs when the option expires; they do not account for the initial cost of buying the option or the initial proceeds from selling it.

This is a common point of confusion. For example, the payoff diagram in Figure 25.1(a) makes purchase of a call look like a sure thing—the payoff is at worst zero, with plenty of upside if TD's stock price goes above $84 by October 2011. But compare this with the *profit diagram* in Figure 25.3, which subtracts the $4.60 cost of the call in March 2011 from the payoff at expiration. The call buyer loses money at all share prices less than $84 + $4.60 = $88.60.

FIGURE 25.3
Payoff and profit for a purchaser of a call option on Toronto-Dominion Bank with exercise price of $84.

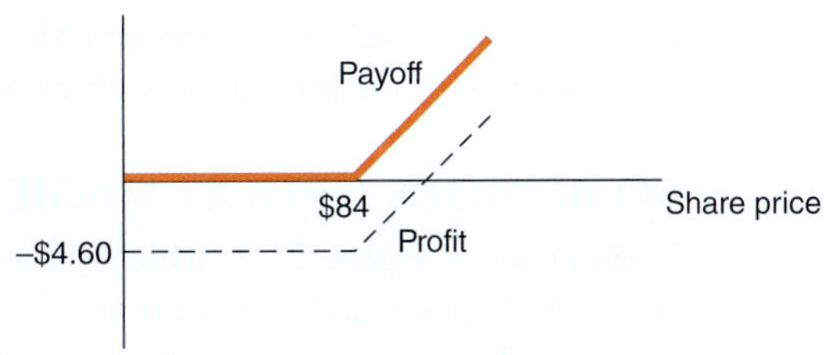

FIGURE 25.4
Payoff and profit for a seller of a put option on Toronto-Dominion Bank with exercise price of $84.

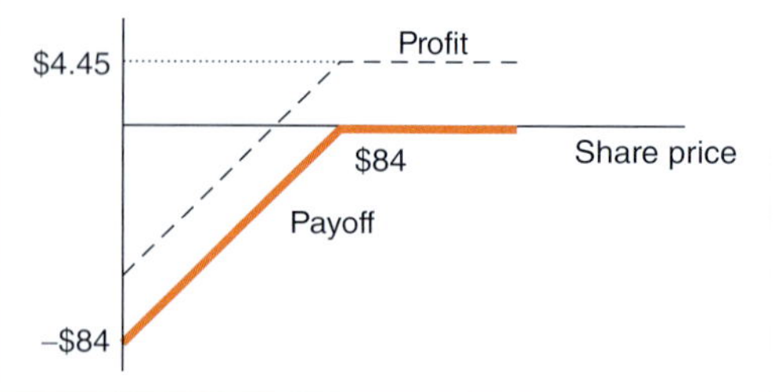

Take another example: The payoff diagram in Figure 25.2(b) makes selling a put look like a sure loser—the *best* payoff is zero. But the profit diagram in Figure 25.4, which recognizes the $4.45 received by the seller, shows that the seller gains at all prices above $84 − $4.45 = $79.55.

Profit diagrams like those in Figures 25.3 and 25.4 might be helpful to the options beginner, but options experts rarely draw them. Now that you've graduated from the first options class, we won't draw them either. We will stick to payoff diagrams, because you have to focus on payoffs at expiration to understand options and to value them properly.

FINANCIAL ALCHEMY WITH OPTIONS

Options can be used to modify the risk characteristics of a portfolio. Suppose, for example, that you are generally optimistic about TD's prospects, but you understand that a large investment in the stock is a risk and would cause you to have sleepless nights. Here is a strategy that might appeal to you: Buy the stock, but also buy a put option on the stock with exercise price $84. If the stock price rises from its current level of $84, your put turns out to be worthless, but you win on the stock investment. If the stock price falls, your losses are limited, since the put gives you the right to sell the stock for the $84 exercise price. Thus the value of your stock-plus-put position cannot be less than $84.

Here is another way to view your overall position. You hold the stock and the put option. The value of each component of the portfolio will be as follows:

	Stock Price < $84	**Stock Price ≥ $84**
Value of stock	Stock price	Stock price
Value of put option	$84 − stock price	$0
Total value	$84	Stock price

No matter how far the stock price falls, the total value of your portfolio cannot fall below the $84 exercise price.

The value of your position when the options expire is graphed in Figure 25.5. You have downside protection at $84 but still share in potential gains on the stock. This strategy is called a *protective put*, because the put option gives protection against losses. Of course, such protection is not free. Look again at Table 25.2 and you will find the cost of such protection. "Stock price insurance" at a level of $84 between March 25, 2011 and October 2011 cost $4.45 per share; this was the price of the put option with exercise price $84 and October expiration.

SOME MORE OPTION MAGIC

Look again at Figure 25.5, which shows the possible payoffs at maturity from holding both a share of TD stock and a put option to sell it for $84. Does this picture look somewhat familiar? It should. Turn back to Figure 25.1(a), which shows the payoffs from holding a call option on TD stock with an exercise price of $84. The only difference between the two sets of payoffs is that

FIGURE 25.5
Payoff to protective put strategy. If the ultimate stock price exceeds $84, the put is valueless but you own the stock. If it is less than $84, you can sell the stock for the exercise price.

the combination of the stock and put option always provides exactly $84 more than the call option. In other words, regardless of the final stock price, holding the stock plus a put option gives the same payoff as the alternative strategy of buying a call option plus investing the present value of $84 in a bank deposit.

Think what happens if you follow this second strategy. If the stock price is below $84 when the option expires, your call option will be valueless but you will still have $84 in the bank. On the other hand, if the stock price rises above $84, you will take your money out of the bank, use it to exercise the call, and own the stock. The following table confirms that this second investment package gives you exactly the same payoffs as you get from holding the stock and a put option:

	Payoffs at Expiration	
	Stock Price < $84	**Stock Price ≥ $84**
Call option	Zero	Stock price − $84
Bank deposit paying $84	$84	$84
Total value	$84	Stock price

If you plan to hold each of these packages until the options expire, the packages must sell for the same price today. This gives us a fundamental relationship between the value of a call and the value of a put:[4]

$$\text{Value of stock} + \text{value of put} = \text{value of call} + \text{present value of exercise price}$$

This basic relationship between share price, call and put values, and the present value of the exercise price is called *put-call parity*.

Check Point 25.3

A one-year call option on Big Canoe Inc. stock with an exercise price of $60 costs $8.05. The stock price is $55 and the interest rate on a bank deposit is 4 percent. What is the value of a one-year put option on Big Canoe with an exercise price of $60?

[4] This relationship assumes that the two options have the same exercise price and maturity. Note that the present value of the exercise price is simply the amount that you would need to set aside in a bank deposit in order to receive the exercise price at maturity.

LO2 25.2 WHAT DETERMINES OPTION VALUES?

Table 25.2 shows prices of different TD options. But we have said nothing about how the market values of options are determined. It is time we deal with option valuation.

UPPER AND LOWER LIMITS ON OPTION VALUES

We know what an option is worth when it expires. Consider, for example, the option to buy TD stock at \$84. If the stock price is below \$84 at the expiration date, the call will be worthless; if the stock price is above \$84, the call will be worth the value of the stock minus the \$84 exercise price. The relationship is depicted by the heavy blue line in Figure 25.6.

Even before expiration, the price of the option can never remain *below* the heavy blue line in Figure 25.6. For example, if our option were priced at \$3 and the stock at \$92, it would pay any investor to buy the option, exercise it for an additional \$84, and then sell the stock for \$92. That would give a "money machine" with a profit of \$92 − (\$3 + \$84) = \$5. Money machines can't last; the demand for options from investors using this strategy would quickly force the option price up at least to the heavy blue line in the figure. The heavy blue line is therefore a *lower* limit on the market price of the option. Thus

$$\text{Lower limit on value of call option} = \text{the greater of } \textit{zero} \text{ or } \textit{(stock price} - \textit{exercise price)}$$

The diagonal gold line in Figure 25.6, which is the plot of the stock price, is the *upper* limit to the option price. Why? Because the stock itself gives a higher final payoff whatever happens. If when the option expires the stock price ends up above the exercise price, the option is worth the stock price *less* the exercise price. If the stock price ends up below the exercise price, the

FIGURE 25.6
Value of a call before its expiration date (dashed line). The value depends on the stock price. The call is always worth more than its value if exercised now (heavy blue line). It is never worth more than the stock price itself.

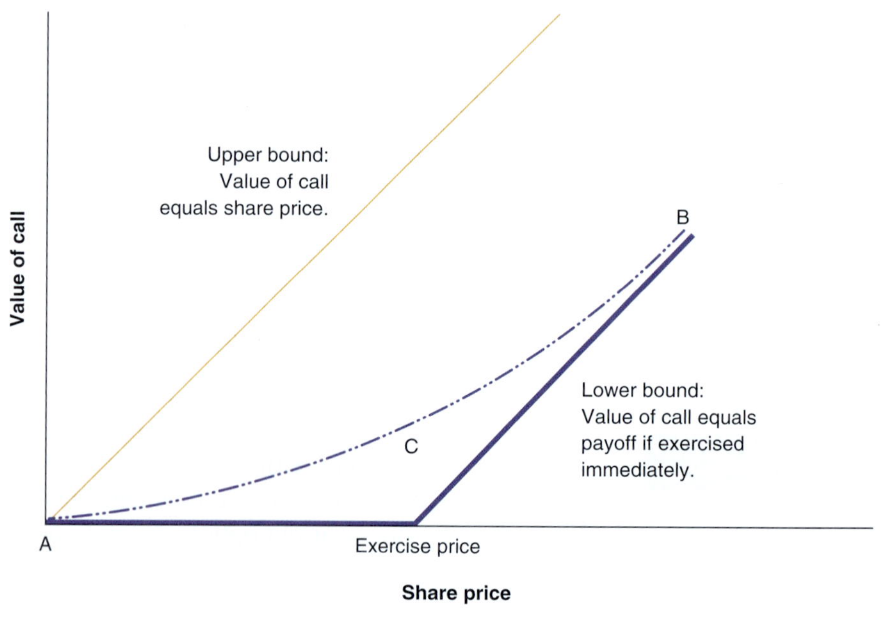

option is worthless, but the stock's owner still has a valuable security. Thus the extra payoff to holding the stock rather than the option is as follows:

Stock Price at Expiration	Stock Payoff	Option Payoff	Extra Payoff from Holding Stock Rather Than Option
Greater than \$84	Stock price	Stock price − \$84	\$84
Less than or equal to \$84	Stock price	\$0	Stock price

THE DETERMINANTS OF OPTION VALUE

The call option price must lie between the upper and lower limits in Figure 25.6. In fact, the price will lie on a curved, upward-sloping line like the dashed curve shown in the figure. This line begins its travels where the upper and lower bounds meet (at zero). Then it rises, gradually becoming parallel to the lower bound. This line tells us an important fact about option values: Given the exercise price, *the value of a call option increases as the stock price increases*.

That should come as no surprise. Owners of call options clearly hope for the stock price to rise, and are happy when it does. But let us look more carefully at the shape and location of the dashed line. Three points, A, B, and C, are marked on the dashed line. As we explain each point, you will see why the option price has to behave as the dashed line predicts.

Point A. When the stock is worthless, the option is worthless. A stock price of zero means that there is no possibility the stock will ever have any future value.[5] If so, the option is sure to expire unexercised and worthless, and it is worthless today.

Point B. When the stock price becomes very high, the option price approaches the stock price less the present value of the exercise price. Notice that the dashed line representing the option price in Figure 25.6 eventually becomes parallel to the ascending heavy blue line representing the lower bound on the option price. The reason is as follows. The higher the stock price, the greater the odds that the option will eventually be exercised. If the stock price is high enough, exercise becomes a virtual certainty; the probability that the stock price will fall below the exercise price before the option expires becomes trivial.

If you own an option that you *know* will be exchanged for a share of stock, you effectively own the stock now. The only difference is that you don't have to pay for the stock (by handing over the exercise price) until later, when formal exercise occurs. In these circumstances, buying the call is equivalent to buying the stock now with deferred payment and delivery. The value of the call is therefore equal to the stock price less the present value of the exercise price.[6]

This brings us to another important point about options. Investors who acquire stock by way of a call option are buying on "instalment credit." They pay the purchase price of the option today, but they do not pay the exercise price until they actually exercise the option. The delay in payment is particularly valuable if interest rates are high and the option has a long maturity. Thus *the value of a call option increases with both the rate of interest and the time to expiration*.

Check Point 25.4 How would the value of a put option be affected by an increase in the stock price? How would the value of a put option be affected by an increase in the exercise price? Explain.

[5] If a stock *can* be worth something in the future then investors will pay *something* for it today, although possibly a very small amount.

[6] We assume here that the stock pays no dividends until after the option matures. If dividends were paid, you *would* care about when you get to own the stock because the option holder misses out on any dividends.

Point C. The option price always exceeds its minimum value (except at maturity or when stock price is zero). We have seen that the dashed and heavy lines in Figure 25.6 coincide when stock price is zero (point A), but elsewhere the lines diverge; that is, the option price must exceed the minimum value given by the heavy blue line. You can see why by examining point C.

At point C, the stock price exactly equals the exercise price. The option therefore would be worthless if it expired today. However, suppose that the option will not expire until 3 months hence. Of course, we do not know what the stock price will be at the expiration date. There is roughly a 50 percent chance that it will be higher than the exercise price, and a 50 percent chance that it will be lower. The possible payoffs to the option are therefore:

Outcome	**Payoff**
Stock price rises (50 percent probability)	Stock price − exercise price (option is exercised)
Stock price falls (50 percent probability)	Zero (option expires worthless)

If there is some chance of a positive payoff, and if the worst payoff is zero, then the option must be valuable. That means the option price at point C exceeds its lower bound, which at point C is zero. In general, the option price will exceed the lower bound as long as there is time left before expiration.

One of the most important determinants of the *height* of the dashed curve (that is, of the difference between actual and lower-bound value) is the likelihood of substantial movements in the stock price. An option on a stock whose price is unlikely to change by more than 1 or 2 percent is not worth much; an option on a stock whose price may halve or double is very valuable.

For example, suppose that a call option has an exercise price of $84, and the stock price will be either $80 or $88 when the option expires. The possible payoffs to the option are as follows:

Stock price at expiration	$80	$88
Call value at expiration	$ 0	$ 4

Now suppose that the value of the stock when the option expires can be $70 or $98. The *average* of the possible stock prices is the same as before, $84, but the volatility is greater. In this case the payoffs to the call are

Stock price at expiration	$70	$98
Call value at expiration	$ 0	$14

A comparison of the two cases highlights the valuable asymmetry that options offer. If the stock price turns out to be below the exercise price when the option expires, the option is valueless regardless of whether the shortfall is a cent or a dollar. However, the option holder reaps all the benefits of stock price advances. Thus in our example the option is worth only $4 if the stock price reaches $88, but it is worth $14 if the stock price rises to $98. Therefore, volatility helps the option holder.

The probability of large stock price changes during the remaining life of an option depend on two things: (1) the variability of the stock price *per unit of time*, and (2) the length of time until the option expires. Other things being equal, you would like to hold an option on a volatile stock. Given volatility, you would like to hold an option with a long life ahead of it, since that longer life means that there is more opportunity for the stock price to change.

The value of an option increases with both the variability of the share price and the time to expiration.

It's hard to keep all these properties straight at first reading. Therefore, we have summed them up in Table 25.4.

TABLE 25.4
What the prices of a call option and a put option depend on.

If the following variables *increase:*	. . . the value of a call option will:	. . . the value of a put option will:
Stock price	increase	decrease
Exercise price	decrease	increase
Interest rate	increase	decrease
Time to expiration	increase	increase
Volatility of stock price	increase	increase

Check Point 25.5

Rework our numerical example for a put option with an exercise price of $84. Show that put options also are more valuable when the stock price is more volatile.

OPTION-VALUATION MODELS

If you want to value an option, you need to go beyond the qualitative statements of Table 25.4; you need an exact option-valuation model—a formula that you can plug numbers into and come up with a figure for option value.

Valuing complex options is a high-tech business and well beyond the scope of this book. Our aim here is not to instantly make you into option whizzes but to illustrate the basics of option valuation by walking you through an example. The trick to option valuation is to find a combination of borrowing and an investment in the stock that exactly replicates the option. The nearby Finance in Action box illustrates a simple version of one of these option-valuation models.

This model achieves simplicity by assuming that the share price can take on only two values at the expiration date of the option. This assumption is clearly unrealistic, but it turns out that this approach can be generalized to allow for a large number of possible future share prices rather than just the two values in our example.

In 1973, Fischer Black, Myron Scholes, and Robert Merton came up with a formula that showed that even when share prices are changing continuously, you can still replicate an option by a series of levered investments in the stock. The Black-Scholes formula is regularly used by option traders, investment bankers, and financial managers to value a wide variety of options. Scholes and Merton shared the 1997 Nobel Prize in economics for their work on the development of this formula.[7] The nearby Excel Spreadsheet box shows you how to set up a Black-Scholes calculator in Excel. In Appendix 25A (available on the Online Learning Centre) we present the basics of their remarkable option pricing formula.

Today, there are many more sophisticated variants of the Black-Scholes formula that can better capture some aspect of real-life markets. As computer power continues to increase, these models can be made more complex and increasingly accurate.

Check Point 25.6

Use the Finance in Action box "A Simple Option-Valuation Model" as a model to help you answer this question. Suppose that the price of Dollarama stock is $30 and could either double to $60 or halve to $15 over the next 3 months. Show that the following two strategies have exactly the same payoffs regardless of whether the stock price rises or falls: strategy A—buy three call options with an exercise price of $30 and a 3-month expiration date; strategy B—buy two shares and borrow the present value of $30. What is your cash outflow today if you follow strategy B? What does this tell you about the value of three call options? Assume that the interest rate is .5 percent per 3 months.

[7] Fischer Black passed away in 1995. Nobel prizes are not awarded posthumously. Both Black and Merton were born in America but Scholes was born in Timmins, Ontario, and started his university education at McMaster University, Hamilton, Ontario!

Finance in Action

A Simple Option-Valuation Model

It is March 2011 and you are contemplating the purchase of a call option on TD stock. The call has an October 2011 expiration date and an exercise price of \$84. TD's stock price is currently \$84, so the option will be valueless unless the stock price appreciates over the next 7 months. The outlook for TD stock is uncertain, and all you know is that at the end of the 7 months it will be either \$92 or \$78. Finally, the rate of interest on a bank loan at this time is 2 percent a year, or about 1.16 percent for 7 months.[1]

The following table depicts the outlook for three alternative investments:

TD Stock		Call Option		Bank Loan	
March	Oct.	March	Oct.	March	Oct.
\$84	\$92	?	\$8	\$100	\$101.16
	\$78		\$0		\$101.16

The first investment is TD stock. Its current price is \$84 but the price could rise to \$92 or fall to \$78. The second investment is the call option. When the call expires in October, the option will be valueless if the stock price falls to \$78, and it will be worth \$92 − \$84 = \$8 if the stock price rises to \$92. We don't know (yet) how much the call is worth today, so for the time being we put a question mark against the March value. Our third investment is a bank loan at an interest rate of 1.16 percent per 7 months. The payoff on a \$100 bank loan is 1.0116 × \$100 = \$101.16 no matter what happens to the price of TD stock.

Consider now two investment strategies. The first (strategy A) is to buy seven call options. The second (strategy B) is to buy four TD shares, at a total cost of \$336 (= 4 × \$84), and to borrow the present value of \$312 from the bank. Table 25.5 shows the possible payoffs from the two strategies. Notice that when you borrow from the bank, you receive a *positive* cash flow now but have a *negative flow* when the loan is repaid in October.

You can see that *regardless of whether the stock price falls to \$78 or rises to \$92*, the payoffs from the two strategies are identical. To put it another way, you can exactly *replicate* an investment in call options by a combination of a bank loan and an investment in the stock.[2] If two investments give the same payoffs in all circumstances, then their value must be the same today. In other words, the cost of buying 7 call options must be exactly the same as borrowing PV(\$312) from the bank and buying 4 TD shares:

$$\text{Price of 7 calls} = \$336 - \$308.42 = \$27.58$$

$$\text{Price of 1 call} = \frac{\$27.58}{7} = \$3.94$$

Presto! You have just valued a call option.

TABLE 25.5
It is possible to replicate the payoffs from TD call options by borrowing to invest in TD stock.

	Cash Flow in March 2011	Payoff in Oct. 2011 If Stock Price Equals: \$78	\$92
Strategy A:			
Buy 7 calls	?	\$0	+\$56 (= 7 × \$8)
Strategy B:			
Buy 4 shares	−\$336	+\$312	+\$368
Borrow PV (\$312)	+\$308.42	−\$312	−\$312
	−\$27.58	\$0	+\$56

Note: The present value of \$312 paid 7 months from now at an interest rate of 1.16 percent is PV(\$312) = 312/1.0116 = 308.42.

[1] The 7-month interest rate, y, is calculated with the formula from Chapter 5: $y = (1 + \text{annual rate})^{7/12} - 1 = (1.02)^{7/12} - 1 = .0116$, or 1.16%.

[2] The only tricky part in valuing the TD option is to work out the number of shares that are needed to replicate one option. Fortunately, there is a simple formula that says that the number of shares needed is equal to one call option:

$$\frac{\text{Spread of possible option prices}}{\text{Spread of possible stock prices}} = \frac{\$8 - \$0}{\$92 - \$78} = \frac{\$8}{\$14} = \frac{4}{7}$$

To replicate one call option, you need to buy 4/7 of a share. To replicate 7 calls, you need to buy 7 × (4/7) shares = 4 shares of stock. This ratio is called the *hedge ratio* or the *option delta*.

Excel Spreadsheet

Using the Black-Scholes Formula

	A	B	C	D	E	F	G	H	I	J
1	**Inputs**			**Outputs**			**Formulas for Output in Column E**			
2	Standard deviation (annual)	0.1664		PV(Ex. Price)	83.035		B6/(1+B4)^B3			
3	Maturity (in years)	0.583		d1	0.154		(LN(B5/E2)+(0.5*B2^2)*B3)/(B2*SQRT(B3))			
4	Risk-free rate (effective annual rate)	0.02		d2	0.027		E3−B2*SQRT(B3)			
5	Stock price	84		N(d1)	0.561		NORMSDIST(E3)			
6	Exercise price	84		N(d2)	0.511		NORMSDIST(E4)			
7				B/S call value	4.731		B5*E5−E2*E6			
8				B/S put value	3.767		E7+E2 − B5			

You might like to try your hand at using the Black-Scholes option-pricing formula to value a call option. A number of Web sites include a Black Scholes calculator (for example **www.numa.com**), but it takes only a few moments to construct your own Excel program to calculate Black-Scholes values. The spreadsheet shows how you do it. First, type in the formulas shown on the right side of the spreadsheet in cells E2 to E8. Now enter the data for the TD October 2011 call, with $84 exercise in cells B2 to B6. We want the price as of October 2011, giving the option 7 months or .583 (7/12) of a year to expiration. Notice that the values for the standard deviation and interest rate are entered as decimals, not as percentages.[8] On past evidence, the standard deviation of TD's annual returns has been about 16.64 percent, so we enter the standard deviation in cell B2 as .1664, not 16.44. Historical volatility for TD and other Canadian options is available on the option quotes pages at the Montréal Exchange, **www.m-x.ca**. The last two lines of the output column show that the Black-Scholes formula gives a value of $4.73 for the TD call option, slightly higher than its market price in March 2011 and the corresponding put option, $3.767, slightly lower than the put market price.

LO3, 4 25.3 SPOTTING THE OPTION

In our discussion so far we may have given you the impression that financial managers are concerned only with traded options to buy or sell shares. But once you have learned to recognize the different kinds of options, you will find that they are everywhere. Unfortunately, they rarely come with a large label attached. Often the trickiest part of the problem is to identify the option.

We will start by looking briefly at options on real assets and then turn to options on financial assets. You should find that you have already encountered many of these options in earlier chapters.

OPTIONS ON REAL ASSETS

In Chapter 10 we pointed out that the capital investment projects that you accept today may affect the opportunities you have tomorrow. Today's capital budgeting decisions need to recognize these future opportunities.

real options Options to invest in, modify, or dispose of a capital investment project.

Other things being equal, a capital investment project that generates new opportunities is more valuable than one that doesn't. A flexible project—one that doesn't commit management to a fixed operating strategy—is more valuable than an inflexible one. When a project is flexible or generates new opportunities for the firm, it is said to contain **real options**.

[8] Chapter 11 described how to calculate standard deviations. Notice also that in cell E2, we compute the present value of the exercise price by treating the interest rate as an effective annual yield. You should be aware, however, that many Black-Scholes calculators require that the interest rate be expressed as a continuously compounded rate. See Chapter 5 if you need a review of continuous compounding.

Finance in Action

Allegheny Acquires a Real Option

Allegheny Energy Corporation acquired open gas-fired power plants in Mississippi and Tennessee. These plants were expected to sit idle most of the year and, when operating, to produce electricity at a cost at least 50 percent higher than the most efficient state-of-the-art facilities. Allegheny's decision to buy these power plants resulted from a sophisticated application of real options analysis.

The firm observed that electricity prices in an increasingly free energy market can be wildly volatile. For example, during some power shortages in the Midwest during hot summer months the cost of 1 megawatt-hour of electricity increased briefly from a typical level of $40 to several thousand dollars. The option to obtain additional energy in these situations obviously would be quite valuable.

Allegheny concluded that it would pay to acquire some cheap power plants, even if they were relatively high-cost electricity producers. Most of the time, the plants will sit idle, with market prices for electricity below the marginal cost of production. But every so often, when electricity prices spike, the plants can be fired up to produce electricity—at a great profit. Even if they operate only a few weeks a year, they can be positive-NPV investments.

These plants are in effect call options on electrical power. The options are currently out of the money, but the possibility that prices will increase makes these calls worth more than their price. The decision to buy them therefore makes the firm more valuable.

If you look out for real options, you'll find them almost everywhere. Whenever management can decide in the future how best to operate a project—for example, to expand, contract, delay, or abandon it—the project contains a real option. The nearby Finance in Action box provides an illustration of a firm that took real options into account in an important capital budgeting decision. In Chapter 10 we looked at several ways that companies may build future flexibility into a project. Here is a brief reminder of two types of real options that we introduced in that chapter.

Option to Expand Many capital investment proposals include an option to expand in the future. For example, some of the world's largest oil reserves are found in the oil sands of northern Alberta. Unfortunately, the cost of extracting oil from the sand is substantially higher than the cost of extracting oil from conventional sources. Even when the market price of oil was substantially below the cost of extracting oil from the sands, oil companies paid considerable sums of money to purchase barren tracts of oil sand lands. The reason? Ownership of the oil sands gave the companies an option. The oil companies knew that if the price of oil rose above the extraction cost, the land purchased could prove to be very valuable. Thus ownership gave them a real option—a call option to extract the oil. Now, more than half of Alberta's oil comes from the oil sands. Oil companies have exercised their real option and are extracting oil from the oil sands.

Option to Abandon Suppose that you need a new plant ready to produce turboencabulators in three years. You have a choice of designs. If design A is chosen, construction must begin immediately. Design B is more expensive but you can wait a year before breaking ground.

If you know with certainty that the plant will be needed, you should opt for design A. But suppose that there is some possibility that demand for turboencabulators will fall off and that in a year's time, you will decide the plant is not required. Then design B may be preferable because it gives you the option to bail out at low cost any time during the next 12 months.

You can think of the option to abandon as a put option. The exercise price of the put is the amount that you could recover if you abandon the project. The abandonment option makes design B more attractive by limiting the downside exposure; the worst outcome is that you receive the project's salvage value. The more uncertain the need for the new plant, the more valuable the downside protection offered by the abandonment option.

Check Point 25.7

A real estate developer buys 28 hectares of land in a rural area, planning to build a subdivision on the land if and when the population from the city begins to expand into the area. If population growth is less than anticipated, the developer believes that the land can be sold to a country club that would build a golf course on the property.

a. In what way does the possibility of sale to the country club provide a put option to the developer?
b. What is the exercise price of the option? The asset value?
c. How does the golf course option increase the NPV of the land project to the developer?

OPTIONS ON FINANCIAL ASSETS

The TD options that we examined earlier in this chapter were sold by some investors to other investors. They had no effect on the company's cash flows because they are not issued by TD. However, firms may issue options to employees or to investors, and these do have a potential impact on the companies' cash flows. Here are a few examples of the options that are associated with new financing.

warrant Right to buy shares from a company at a stipulated price before a set date.

Warrants

A **warrant** is like a long-term call option on the company's stock. Unlike the TD options that we considered earlier, a warrant is issued by the company. The company sells the warrant; the investor buys it. If the warrant is exercised, the company issues new shares. So, the exercise of warrants generates cash for the issue but also increases the number of shares outstanding so immediately reduces the earnings per share. The valuation of warrants is not exactly the same as the valuation of call options because the dilution effect of issued stock has to be incorporated. But all of the same factors affect option prices affect warrant prices, such as the stock price, the volatility of the stock price and interest rates.

In December 2010 Western Copper Corporation sold a package of one common share and one-half of a warrant for $2.45. At the time, Western Copper's share price was $2.50. Each whole warrant entitled the holder to buy one common share of Western Copper at a price of $3.45 any time within the next 24 months. So the stock price would need to rise by $.95, or 38 percent, before the options were "in the money." The warrants are traded on the Toronto Stock Exchange, WRN.WT-T, and initially were trading for about $.50 in December 2010. Obviously, warrant investors were anticipating that the Western Copper stock price would rise over time. As it turned out, the warrant holders were in luck because the Western Copper stock, listed on the TSX, has increased from its December price. For example, on July 22, 2011, the stock price was $3.46 and the warrant price $1.05.

Warrants are often given to underwriters as part of their compensation for managing an issue of securities. At other times they may be issued when a firm becomes bankrupt; the bankruptcy court offers the firm's bondholders warrants in the reorganized company as part of the settlement. When a company issues a bond, it will sometimes add some warrants as a "sweetener." Since these warrants are valuable to investors, they are prepared to pay a higher price for a package of bonds and warrants than for the bond on its own. Managers sometimes look with delight at this higher price, forgetting that in return the company has incurred a liability to sell its shares to the warrant holders at what with hindsight may turn out to be a low price.

Executive and Employee Stock Options

Stock options are given to a company's directors, management and other employees as part of their compensation. Like a warrant, when stock options are exercised, the company issues new shares to give to the option holder. The stock option exercise price is set at or above the stock's market price at the time of the option grant.

The TSX does not permit listed companies to set the exercise price below the current stock price. The idea is that options encourage managers to work hard to increase the value of their companies' stock.

In 2010 the cash salary of the CEO of Nvidia Inc., a visual computing technology producer, was only US$1, even though the company's revenues were US$844 million. Does that mean the CEO was condemned to a life of poverty? No, in 2010 he was the 10th-highest-paid CEO in corporate America, with $34.4 million in total compensation. The extra $34,399,999 came from stock options. He exercised some of the options to generate cash.

The example highlights the fact that stock options can be important part of managers' compensation. Employee stock options are valuable and therefore are an expense just like wages and salaries. U.S., Canadian, and International accounting rules require that companies estimate the fair-market value of stock options, using an option pricing model such as the Black-Scholes model. The value of the stock options must be deducted when calculating the firm's profits. Expensing stock options can have a significant impact on company earnings.

However, some companies have illegally boosted the value of the stock options that they have given to managers by backdating the grant of their executive stock options. In 2007 and 2008 over 100 U.S. firms and Research In Motion were investigated by the U.S. Securities and Exchange Commission (SEC) for allegations of stock option *backdating*. Option backdating occurs when a company grants options to employees, but claims it issued them at an earlier date than it actually did. Backdating enables firms to base the exercise price of the options on a lower market price for the issuer's shares. As a result, the options have a built-in profit, making them even more valuable. Investigations by SEC have resulted in fines, resignations, and even a handful of jail sentences for executives of U.S. companies involved in backdating. Research In Motion admitted to backdating their stock options and were charged by both the SEC and the Ontario Securities Commission.

Under the terms of a settlement agreement with the OSC, RIM co-chief executive officers James Balsillie and Mike Lazaridis, as well as chief operating officer Dennis Kavelman, paid a total of US$77 million, of which US$68 million was paid to RIM to reimburse the company for losses from the backdating and for the costs of a long internal investigation and US$9 million of penalties and costs to the OSC. The company and the four accused agreed to settle the SEC case by paying penalties totalling US$1.425 million.

The recent financial crisis caused substantial declines in equity share prices and has significantly impacted the value of stock options held by many employees of public companies. Large numbers of stock options are currently out-of-the-money (or "underwater"), causing the incentive and retention features of many public company stock option programs to be diminished or, in some cases, obliterated. To address this issue some companies put an option exchange program, in which underwater options are exchanged for new options or restricted stock, to a shareholder vote.

EXAMPLE 25.3 SMART BALANCE COMPLETES EMPLOYEE STOCK OPTION EXCHANGE PROGRAM

On March 29, 2011, Smart Balance, a U.S.-based food products company, completed the Stock Option Exchange Program for employees. The Program had been overwhelmingly approved at its February 15, 2011, special meeting of stockholders. The company indicated that a total of 2.5 million stock options were forfeited by eligible employees in exchange for 1.5 million replacement stock options. The average exercise price of the replaced stock options was about US$8.40. The replacement stock options carry an exercise price of US$4.60, based on the closing price of Smart Balance common stock on March 23, 2011, and a new four-year vesting schedule. The company has retired all stock options forfeited under the Stock Option Exchange Program.

convertible bond Bond that the holder may exchange for a specified number of shares.

Convertible Bonds The **convertible bond** is a close relative of the bond-warrant package. It allows the bondholder to exchange the bond for a given number of shares of common stock. Therefore, it is a package of a straight bond (that is, a bond that is not convertible) with a call option. The exercise price of the call option is the value of the straight bond. If the value of the stock exceeds the value of the straight bond, it will be profitable to convert.

The owner of a convertible bond owns a bond and a call option on the firm's stock. So does the owner of a package of a bond and a warrant. However, there are differences, the most important being that a convertible bond's owner must give up the bond to exercise the option. The owner of a package of bonds and warrants exercises the warrants for cash and keeps the bond.

EXAMPLE 25.4 CONVERTIBLE BONDS

In December 2010 Southern Pacific Resources, a Canadian junior oil and gas exploration company, issued 6-year convertible bonds with a coupon rate of 6 percent for $1,000 per bond. Each bond could be converted at any time before maturity into 465.1163 shares of Southern Pacific common shares. In other words, the owner had a 6-year option to return the bond to Southern Pacific and receive 465.1163 shares in exchange. The *conversion ratio* of the bond—the number of shares received for each bond—was 465.1163.

In order to receive 465.1163 shares of Southern Pacific stock, you had to surrender bonds with a face value of $1,000. Therefore, to receive *one* share, you had to surrender a face amount of 1,000/465.1163 = $2.15. This figure is called the *conversion price*. Anybody who bought the bond at $1,000 in order to convert into 465.1163 shares paid the equivalent of $2.15 per share.

On March 1, 2011, Southern Pacific Resources' stock price closed at $1.90. So, if investors were obliged to convert their bond that day, their investment would be worth only 465.1163 × $1.90 = $883.72. This figure is called the bond's *conversion value*. Of course, investors do not need to convert immediately. They hope that Southern Pacific's stock price will zoom up and make conversion profitable. If instead it zooms down, investors will choose not to convert. The value of the bond if it could not be converted is known as its *bond value*.

Since the owner of the convertible always has the option *not* to convert, bond value establishes a lower bound, or *floor*, to the price of a convertible. Of course, this floor is not completely flat. If the firm falls on hard times, the bond may not be worth much. In the extreme case where the firm becomes worthless, the bond is also worthless. In addition, a convertible can never sell for less than its conversion value. If it did, smart investors would buy the convertible, exchange it for stock, and sell the stock. Their profit would be the difference between the conversion value and the price of the convertible.

This means that there are two parts to the lower bound of the price of any convertible: either its bond value or its conversion value. When the firm does well, conversion value exceeds bond value; the investor would choose to convert if forced to make an immediate choice. Bond value exceeds conversion value when the firm does poorly. In these circumstances the investor would hold on to the bonds if forced to choose.

Convertible holders do not have to make a now-or-never choice for or against conversion. They can wait and then, with the benefit of hindsight, take whatever course turns out to give them the highest payoff. Thus a convertible is always worth *more* than both its bond value and its conversion value (except when time runs out at the bond's maturity).

We stated earlier that it is useful to think of a convertible bond as a package of a straight bond and an option to buy the common stock in exchange for the straight bond. The value of this call option is equal to the difference between the convertible's selling price and its bond value.

Check Point 25.8

a. What is the conversion value of the Southern Pacific Resources convertible bond if the stock price is $4? What would happen to its conversion price?
b. Suppose that a straight (non-convertible) six-year bond issued by Southern Pacific Resources at the same time had been priced to yield 9 percent. What would be the bond value of the Southern Pacific 6 percent convertibles at the time of issue? (Assume annual coupon payments.)
c. What is value of call option of the Southern Pacific Convertible bond?

callable bond Bond that may be repurchased by the issuer before maturity at a specified call price.

Callable Bonds Unlike warrants and convertibles, which give the investor an option, a **callable bond** gives an option to the issuer. A company that issues a callable bond has an option to buy the bond back at the stated exercise or "call" price. Therefore, you can think of a callable bond as a *package* of a straight bond (a bond that is not callable) and a call option held by the issuer.

The option to call the bond is obviously attractive to the issuer. If interest rates decline and bond prices rise, the company has the opportunity to repurchase the bond at a fixed call price. Therefore, the option to call the bond puts a ceiling on the bond price.

Of course, when the company issues a callable bond, investors are aware of this ceiling on the bond price and will pay less for a callable bond than for a straight bond. The difference between the value of a straight bond and a callable bond with the same coupon rate and maturity is the value of the call option that investors have given to the company:

$$\text{Value of callable bond} = \text{value of straight bond} - \text{value of the issuer's call option}$$

Check Point 25.9

Extendable or *puttable* bonds allow the investor to redeem the bond at par value or let the bond remain outstanding until maturity. Suppose a 20-year extendable bond is issued with the investor allowed after 5 years to redeem the bond at par value (face value).

a. Why are these called puttable bonds? On what asset is the option written? (What asset do the option holders have the right to sell?) Who holds an implicit put option?
b. What is the exercise price of the option?
c. In what circumstances will the option be exercised?
d. Does the put option make the bond more or less valuable?

25.4 SUMMARY

1. **What is the payoff to buyers and sellers of call and put options?** LO1

There are two basic types of options. A **call option** is the right to buy an asset at a specific exercise price on or before the exercise date. A **put** is the right to sell an asset at a specific exercise price on or before the exercise date.

The payoff to a call is the value of the asset minus the exercise price, if the difference is positive, and zero otherwise. The payoff to a put is the exercise price minus the value of the asset if the difference is positive, and zero otherwise. The payoff to the seller of an option is the negative of the payoff to the option buyer.

2. **What are the determinants of option values?** LO2

The value of a call option depends on the following considerations:

- To exercise the call option you must pay the exercise price. Other things being equal, the less you are obliged to pay, the better. Therefore, the value of the option is higher when the exercise price is low relative to the stock price.
- Investors who buy the stock by way of a call option are buying on instalment credit. They pay the purchase price of the option today, but they do not pay the exercise price until they exercise the option. The higher the rate of interest and the longer the time to expiration, the more this "free credit" is worth.
- No matter how far the stock price falls, the owner of the call cannot lose more than the price of the call. On the other hand, the more the stock price rises above the exercise price, the greater the profit on the call. Therefore, the option holder does not lose from increased variability if things go wrong, but gains if they go right. The value of the option increases with the variability of stock returns. Of course, the longer the time to the final exercise date, the more opportunity there is for the stock price to vary.

3. **What options may be present in capital investment proposals?** LO3

The importance of building flexibility into investment projects (discussed in Chapter 10) can be reformulated in the language of options. For example, many capital investments provide the flexibility to expand capacity in the future if demand turns out to be unusually buoyant. They are in effect providing the firm with a call option on the extra capacity. Firms also think about alternative uses for their assets if things go wrong. The option to abandon a project is a put option; the put's exercise price is the value of the project's assets if shifted to an alternative use. The ability to expand or to abandon are both examples of **real options**.

4. **What options may be provided in financial securities?** LO4

Many of the securities that firms issue contain an option. For example, a **warrant** is nothing but a long-term call option issued by the firm. Executive and employee stock options are similar to warrant but given to employees as part of their salary. **Convertible bonds** give the investor the option to buy the firm's stock in exchange for the value of the underlying bond. Unlike warrants and convertibles, which give an option to the investor, **callable bonds** give the option to the issuing firm. If interest rates decline and the value of the underlying bond rises, the firm can buy the bonds back at a specified exercise price.

Related Web Links

cboe.com Chicago Board Options Exchange

m-x.ca Montréal Exchange, Canada's public derivatives exchange

numa.com Information about financial derivatives of all kinds, including options, warrants, and convertible bond calculators

real-options.com The real-options approach to valuing projects

Key Terms

call option	785	convertible bond	801	real options	797
callable bond	802	put option	786	warrant	799

Questions and Problems

connect™ Practise and learn online with *Connect*. Questions with online Excel templates or datasets are marked with .

*Answers in Appendix B

BASIC

1. **Option Payoffs.** Turn back to Table 25.2, which lists prices of various TD options. Use the data in the table to calculate the payoff and the profits for investments in each of the following January 2012 maturity options, assuming that the stock price on the expiration date is \$84. (LO1)

   a. Put option with exercise price \$80
   *b. Call option with exercise price \$80
   c. Put option with exercise price \$84

d. Call option with exercise price $84
*e. Put option with exercise price $88
f. Call option with exercise price $88

2. **Option Payoffs.** Redo the preceding problem assuming the stock price on the expiration date is (a) $90 (b) $78. (LO1)

*3. **Determinants of Option Value.** Look at the data in Table 25.2. (LO2)
   a. What is the price of a call option with an exercise price of $88 and expiration in July? What if expiration is in January?
   b. Why do you think the January calls cost more than the July calls?
   c. Is the same true of put options? Why? Find a pair of puts in Table 25.2 to illustrate.

4. **Option Contracts.** Fill in the blanks by choosing the appropriate terms from the following list: *call, exercise, put.* (LO1)

   A(n) _____ option gives its owner the opportunity to buy a stock at a specific price that is generally called the _____ price. A(n) _____ option gives its owner the opportunity to sell stock at a specified _____ price.

*5. **Option Payoffs.** Note Figure 25.7(a) and 25.7(b). Match each figure with one of the following positions and draw the figures for the positions not shown. (LO1)
   a. Call buyer
   b. Call seller
   c. Put buyer
   d. Put seller

6. **Puts Versus Calls.** "The buyer of a call and the seller of a put both hope that the stock price will rise. Therefore the two positions are identical." Is the speaker correct? Illustrate with a simple example and show graphically. (LO1)

*7. **Hedging with Options.** Suppose that you hold a share of stock and a put option on that share with an exercise price of $100. Show algebraically and graphically the value of your portfolio when the option expires if
   a. The stock price is below $100. (LO1)
   b. The stock price is above $100. (LO1)

INTERMEDIATE

8. **Option Portfolios.** Mixing options and securities can often create interesting payoffs. For each of the following combinations show what the payoff would be when the option expires if (1) the stock price is below the exercise price, and (2) the stock price is above the exercise price. Illustrate the payoffs with graphs. Assume that each option has the same exercise price and expiration date. (LO1)
   a. Buy a call and invest the present value of the exercise price in a bank deposit.
   b. Buy a share and a put option on the share.
   c. Buy a share, buy a put option on the share, and sell a call option on the share.
   d. Buy a call option and a put option on the share.

9. **Option Portfolios.** Look at Figure 25.8, which shows the possible future payoffs in October 2011 from a

FIGURE 25.7
See problem 5.

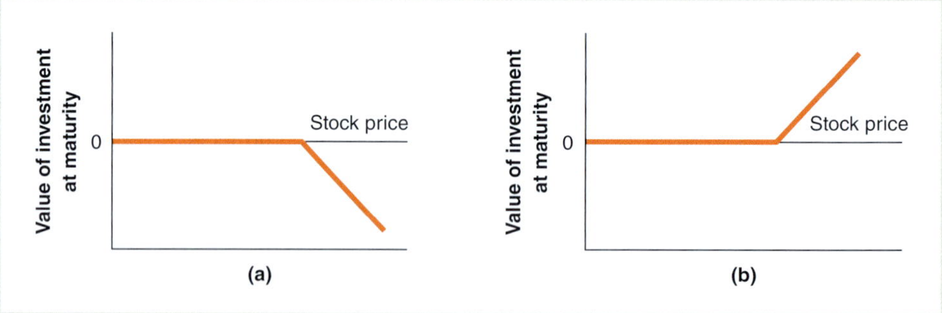

FIGURE 25.8
This strategy provides a payoff of $0 if the TD stock price remains at $84 and a payoff of $84 if TD's stock price either falls to zero or rises to $168. See problem 9.

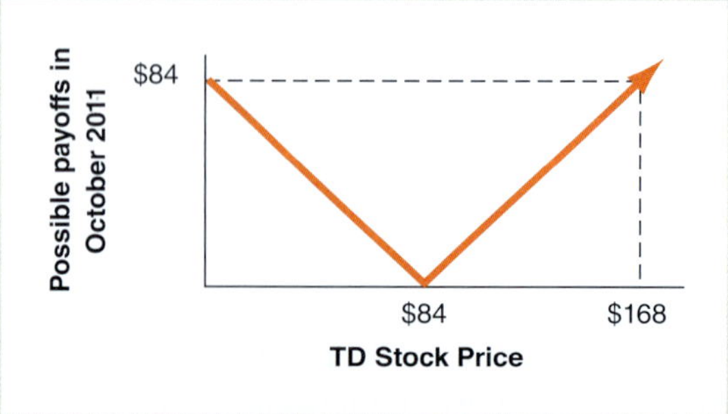

particular package of investments involving TD stock and options. (LO1)

a. What package of investments would provide you with this set of payoffs?
b. How much would the package have cost you in March 2011? (See Table 25.2.)
c. In what circumstances might it make sense to invest in this package? Incidentally, this package of investments is known as a "straddle" by option buffs.

10. **Option Values.** What is the lower bound to the price of a call option? What is the upper bound? (LO2)

11. **Option Values.** What is a call option worth if
  a. The stock price is zero? (LO2)
  b. The stock price is extremely high relative to the exercise price? (LO2)

12. **Option Valuation.** Table 25.2 shows call options on TD stock with the same exercise date in July and with exercise prices \$80, \$84, and \$88. Notice that the March price of the middle call option (with exercise price \$84) is less than halfway between the prices of the other two calls (with exercise prices \$80 and \$88150). Suppose that this were not the case. For example, suppose that the price of the middle call were the average of the prices of the other two calls. Show that if you sell two of the middle calls and use the proceeds to buy one each of the other calls, your proceeds in July may be positive but cannot be negative despite the fact that your net outlay today is zero. What can you deduce from this example about option pricing? (LO2)

13. **Put Prices.** How does the price of a *put* option respond to the following changes, other things being equal? Does the put price go up or down? Explain why. (LO2)
  a. Stock price increases.
  b. Exercise price is increased.
  c. Risk-free interest rate increases.
  d. Expiration date of the option is extended.
  e. Volatility of the stock price falls.
  f. Time passes, so the option's expiration date comes closer.

14. **Internet.** Visit the Montréal Exchange, **www.m-x.ca**, and click on "Trading," then "Quotes," "Options List," and "Equity Options." Pick a stock and look up current prices of call and put options on it by clicking on its option symbol. Find examples to illustrate the effect on the prices of call and put options from an increase in the exercise price holding constant the other factors. Repeat for an increase in the time to expiration. (LO2)

15. **Internet.** What other options are traded on the Montréal Exchange (**www.m-x.ca**)? Try to explain what these options are. (LO3)

*16. **Integrative.** As manager of United Bedstead you own substantial executive stock options. These options entitle you to buy the firm's shares during the next 5 years at a price of \$100 a share. The plant manager has just outlined two alternative proposals to re-equip the plant. Both proposals have the same net present value but one is substantially riskier than the other. At first you are undecided about which to choose, but then you remember your stock options. How might these influence your choice? (LO2)

17. **Real and Financial Options.** Are these put or call options? Fill in the blanks. (LO3, LO4)
  a. An oil company acquires mining rights to a silver deposit. It is not obliged to mine the silver, however. The company has effectively acquired a _____ option, where the exercise price is the cost of opening the mine and extracting the silver.
  b. Some preferred shareholders have the right to redeem their shares at par value after a specified date. (If they hand over their shares, the firm sends them a cheque equal to the shares' par value.) These shareholders have a _____ option.
  c. A firm buys a standard machine with a ready secondhand market. The secondhand market gives the firm a _____ option.

*18. **Real Options.** What is the option in each of the following cases. Is it a call or a put? (LO3)
  a. Western Telecom commits to production of digital switching equipment specifically designed for the European market. As a stand-alone venture, the project has a negative NPV, but it is justified by the need for a strong market position in the rapidly growing, and potentially very profitable, market.
  b. Western Telecom vetoes a fully integrated automated production line for the new digital switches. It will rely on standard, less expensive equipment even though the automated production line would be more efficient overall using the specialized equipment, according to a discounted cash flow calculation.

19. **Real Options.** Describe each of the following situations in the language of options. (LO3)
  a. Mining rights to an undeveloped gold mine in Nunavut. Development and production of the gold now is a negative-NPV endeavour. The break-even price is \$500 per ounce, versus a spot gold price of \$420 per ounce. However, the decision to develop can be put off for up to five years.
  b. A restaurant producing net cash flows, after all out-of-pocket expenses of \$700,000 per year. There is no upward or downward trend in the cash flows, but they fluctuate. The restaurant owns the real estate it occupies and it could be sold for \$5 million.

*20. **Real Options.** Price support systems for various agricultural products have allowed farmers to sell their crops to the government for a specified "support price." What kind of option has the government given to the farmers? What is the exercise price? (LO3)

21. **Hidden Options.** Some investment management contracts give the portfolio manager a bonus proportional to the amount by which a portfolio return exceeds a specified threshold. (LO4)
    a. In what way is this an implicit call option on the portfolio?
    b. Can you think of a way in which such contracts can lead to incentive problems? For example, what happens to the value of the prospective bonus if the manager invests in high-volatility stocks?

*22. **Hidden Options.** The Rank and File Company is considering a stock issue to raise $50 million. An underwriter offers to guarantee the success of the issue by buying any unwanted stock at the $25 issue price. The underwriter's fee is $2 million. (LO4)
    a. What kind of option does Rank and File acquire if it accepts the underwriter's offer?
    b. What determines the value of the option?

23. **Hidden Options.** (LO4)
    a. Some banks have offered their customers an unusual type of time deposit. The deposit does not pay any interest if the market falls, but instead the depositor receives a proportion of any rise in the Standard & Poor's Index. What implicit option do the investors hold? How should the bank invest the money in order to protect itself against the risk of offering this deposit?
    b. You can also make a deposit with a bank that does not pay interest if the market index rises but which makes an increasingly large payment as the market index falls. How should the bank protect itself against the risk of offering this deposit?

24. **Loan Guarantees.** The CDIC (Canadian Deposit Insurance Corporation) insures bank deposits. If a bank's assets are insufficient to pay off all depositors, the CDIC will contribute enough money to ensure that all depositors can be paid off in full. (We ignore the $100,000 maximum coverage on each account.) In what way is this guarantee of deposits the provision of a put option by the CDIC? *Hint:* Write out the funds the CDIC will have to contribute when bank assets are less than deposits owed to depositors. What is the exercise price of the put option? (LO4)

25. **Real Options.** After dramatic increases in oil prices in the 1970s, the United States government funded several projects to create synthetic oil or natural gas from abundant U.S. supplies of coal and oil shale. Although the cost of producing such synthetic fuels at the time was greater than the price of oil, it was argued that the projects still could be justified for their insurance value, since the cost of synthetic fuel would be essentially fixed while the price of oil was risky. Evaluate the synthetic fuel program as an option on fuel sources. Is it a call or a put option? What is the exercise price? How would uncertainty in the future price of oil affect the amount the United States should have been willing to spend on such projects? (LO3)

*26. **Arbitrage Opportunities.** (LO3)
    a. Circular File stock is selling for $25 a share. You see that call options on the stock with exercise price of $20 are selling at $3. What should you do? What will happen to the option price as investors identify this opportunity?
    b. Now you observe that put options on Circular File with exercise price $30 are selling for $4. What should you do?

27. **Convertible Bonds.** A 10-year maturity convertible bond with a 6 percent coupon on a company with a bond rating of AAA is selling for $1,050. Each bond can be exchanged for 20 shares, and the stock price currently is $50 per share. Other AAA-rated bonds with the same maturity would sell at a yield to maturity of 8 percent. What is the value of the implicit call option on the bond? Why is the bond selling for more than the value of the shares it can be converted into? (LO4)

28. **Internet.** The application of option pricing models to real options is a rapidly expanding field of finance. Although the details are beyond this textbook in scope, check out the visual discussion of real options at **www.puc-rio.br/marco.ind/faqs.html**. (LO3)

CHALLENGE

29. **Option Portfolios.** Repeat the three parts of question 9 except that now the problem is to devise a package of investments with the payoffs shown in Figure 25.9. This package of investments is known as a "butterfly." (LO1)

30. **Option Pricing.** Look again at the TD call option that we valued in the previous Finance in Action box titled "A Simple Option-Valuation Model." Suppose that by the end of October the price of TD stock could rise to $94 or fall to $76. The annual interest rate is still 2 percent. (LO2)
    a. What would be the value of the TD call at the end of October if the stock price is $94? If it is $76?
    b. Show that a strategy of buying 9 calls provides exactly the same payoffs as borrowing the present value of $380 from the bank and buying 5 shares.

FIGURE 25.9
This strategy provides a total payoff of $4 if the stock price is $84 and a payoff of zero if the stock price is either (a) $80 or less or (b) $88 or more.

c. What is the net cash flow in March from the policy of borrowing PV($380) and buying 5 shares?
d. What does this tell you about the value of the call option?
e. Why is the value of the call option different from the value that we calculated in the Finance in Action box? What does this tell you about the relationship between the value of a call and the volatility of the share price?

31. **Option Pricing.** Look once more at the TD call option discussed in problem 30. Suppose that the interest rate on bank loans is zero. Recalculate the value of the TD call option. What does this tell you about the relationship between interest rates and the value of a call? (LO2)

32. **Internet.** Following the instructions in question 14, go to Montréal Exchange and get two current call option prices, current stock price and stock 30-day historical volatility for EnCana Ltd. (ECA) and Barrick Gold Corp (ABX). Go to **www.bankofcanada.ca/rates/interest-rates/t-bill-yields** and get the one-year Treasury bill rate for the risk-free rate. Either using the Excel spreadsheet in the previous box titled "Using the Black-Scholes Formula" or the option pricing calculator at **www.numa.com**, calculate the prices for your chosen call options. How different are the prices you obtain from the ones from the Montréal Exchange? What happens to the calculated price if you change the standard deviation? Why? (LO2)

Solutions to Check Points

25.1 a. The call with exercise price $84 costs $3. If the stock price at maturity is $80, the call expires valueless and the investor loses the entire $3. If the stock price is $92, the proceeds from exercising the call is $92 − $84 = $8, and the investor's net profit is $8 − $3 = $5.

b. The put with exercise price $84 costs $2.86. If the stock price at maturity is $80, the proceeds from exercising the put is $84 − $80 = $4 and the investor's net profit is $4 − $2.86 = $1.14. If the stock price is $92, the value of the put is zero, and the investor's loss is the price paid for the put, $2.86.

25.2 a. The call seller receives $3 for writing the call. If the stock price at maturity is $80, the call expires valueless, and the investor keeps the entire $3 as a profit. If the stock price is $92, the value of the call is $92 − $84 = $8. In other words, the call option seller must deliver a stock worth $92 for an exercise price of only $84. The investor's net profit is $3 − $8 = −$5. The call seller will clear a positive net profit as long as the stock price remains below $84 + $3 = $87 (the exercise price plus call option selling price).

b. The put seller receives $2.86 for writing the put. If the stock price at maturity is $80 the put value at expiration is $84 − $80 = $4. In other words, the put option seller must pay an exercise price of $84 to buy a stock worth only $80. The put seller's net profit is $2.86 − $4 = −$1.14. If the stock price is $92, the final value of the put is zero, and the put seller's profit is the price originally received for selling the put, $2.86. The put seller will clear a positive net profit as long as the value of the put at expiration is less than the initial premium received for writing the option; this requires that the stock price remain above $84 − $2.86 = $81.14 (the exercise price minus the put option selling price).

25.3 Put-call parity states: value of stock + value of put = value of call + present value of exercise price. Therefore, in the case of Big Canoe,

$$\$55 + \text{value of put} = \$8.05 + \frac{\$60}{1.04}$$

and

$$\text{Value of put} = \$8.05 + \$57.69 - \$55 = \$10.74$$

25.4 Given the exercise price, the value of a put option is lower when the stock price is higher. The put gives you the right to sell the stock at the exercise price. The higher the stock price, the less attractive the put. The value of a put option is higher when the exercise price is higher. You would be willing to pay more for the right to sell a stock at a high price than the right to sell it at a low price.

25.5 First consider the payoff to the put holder in the lower stock price volatility scenario:

Stock price	$80	$88
Put value	$ 4	$ 0

In the higher-volatility scenario, the value of the stock can be $70 or $98. Now the payoff to the put is:

Stock price	$70	$98
Put value	$14	$ 0

The expected value of the payoff of the put is higher in the higher stock volatility scenario. Higher stock volatility increases the value of a put option.

25.6 The payoffs are as follows:

		Payoff in 3 Months If Stock Price Equals:	
	Cash Flow Today	**$15**	**$60**
Strategy A:			
Buy three calls	?	$0	+$90 (= 3 × (60 − 30)
Strategy B:			
Buy two shares	−$60	+$30	+$120
Borrow PV ($47)	+$29.85	−$30	−$30
	−$30.15	$0	+$90

Note: PV($30) at an interest rate of .5 percent for 3 months is 30/1.005 = $29.85.

The initial net cash outflow from strategy B is $30.15. Since the three calls offer the same payoffs in the future, they also cost $30.15. One call is worth 30.15/3 = $10.05.

25.7 a. The developer has the option to sell the potential housing development to the country club. This abandonment option is like a put that guarantees a minimum payoff from the investment.

b. The exercise price of the option is the price at which it can be sold to the country club. The asset value is the present value of the project if maintained as a housing development. If this value is less than the value as a golf course, the project will be sold.

c. The abandonment option increases NPV by placing a lower bound on the possible payoffs from the project.

25.8 a. Conversion value = 465.1163 × $4 = $1860.4652

Conversion price = $1,000/465.1163 = $2.15 (unchanged)

b. Calculate the bond value of the convertible bond by discounting the annual interest payments (.06 × $1000 = $60) and the principal ($1,000) using the straight bond's yield (9 percent):

Bond value = $60 × 6-year annuity factor at 9% + $1,000 × 6-year PV factor at 9%
= $269.16 + 596.27 = $865.43

c. Convertible bond price at issue was $1,000. The bond price would have been $865.43 if it had been issued without the conversion option. The value of conversion option (call option) is

$1,000 − $865.43 = $134.57

25.9 a. After 5 years, the bond will be a 15-year maturity bond. The bondholder can choose to sell the bond back to the firm at par value. The bondholder therefore has a put option to sell a 15-year bond for par value even if interest rates have risen and the bond would otherwise sell below par.

b. The exercise price is the par value of the bond.

c. The bondholder will extend the loan if interest rates decrease or the company's credit deteriorates

d. More valuable. The bondholder has the right, but not the obligation, to sell the bond at par value in 5 years.

PART 8

Special Topics

23 Mergers, Acquisitions, and Corporate Control

24 International Financial Management

25 Options

26 Risk Management

26.1 Why Hedge?

26.2 Reducing Risk with Options

26.3 Futures Contracts

26.4 Forward Contracts

26.5 Swaps

26.6 Innovation in the Derivatives Market

26.7 Is "Derivative" a Four-Letter Word?

26.8 Summary

CHAPTER 26

Risk Management

LEARNING OBJECTIVES

After studying this chapter, you should be able to:

LO1 Explain why companies hedge to reduce risk.

LO2 Use options, futures, and forward contracts to devise simple hedging strategies.

LO3 Explain how companies can use swaps to change the risk of securities that they have issued.

LO4 Analyze innovations in the derivatives market in the context of recent events involving speculative activities.

Risk management does not mean avoiding risk. It means deciding which risks to take.

We often assume that risk is beyond our control. A business is exposed to unpredictable changes in raw material costs, tax rates, technology, and a long list of other variables. There's nothing the manager can do about it.

This is not wholly true. To some extent a manager can *select* the risks of an asset or business. For example, in the last chapter we saw that companies can consciously affect the risk of an investment by building in flexibility. A company that reduces the cost of bailing out of a project by using standardized equipment is taking less risk than a similar firm that uses specialized equipment with no alternative uses. In this case the option to resell the equipment serves as an insurance policy.

Sometimes, rather than building flexibility into the project, companies accept the risk but then use financial instruments to offset it. This practice of taking offsetting risks is known as *hedging*. In this chapter we will explain how hedging works and we will describe some of the specialized financial instruments that have been devised to help manage risk. These instruments include options, futures, forwards, and swaps. Each of these instruments provides a payoff that depends on the price of some underlying commodity or financial asset. Because their payoffs derive from the prices of other assets, they are often known collectively as *derivative instruments* (*derivatives* for short).[1]

LO1 26.1 WHY HEDGE?

In this chapter we will explain *how* companies use derivatives to hedge the risks of their business. But first we should give some of the reasons *why* they do it.

Surely, the answer to this question is obvious. Isn't less risk always better than more? Well, not necessarily. Even if hedging is costless, transactions undertaken *solely* to reduce risk are unlikely to add value. There are two basic reasons for this:

- *Reason 1: Hedging is a zero-sum game.* A company that hedges a risk does not eliminate it. It simply passes the risk on to someone else. For example, suppose that a heating-oil distributor agrees with a refiner to buy all of next winter's heating-oil deliveries at a fixed price. This contract is a zero-sum game, because the refiner loses what the distributor gains and vice versa. If next winter's price of heating oil turns out to be unusually high, the distributor wins from having locked in a below-market price but the refiner is forced to sell below market.

[1] Derivatives often conjure up an image of wicked speculators. Derivative instruments attract their share of speculators, some of whom may be wicked, but they are also used by sober and prudent businesspeople who simply want to reduce risk.

Conversely, if the price of heating oil is unusually *low*, the refiner wins because the distributor is forced to buy at the high fixed price. Of course, neither party knows next winter's price at the time that the deal is struck, but they consider the range of possible prices and negotiate terms that are fair (zero-NPV) on both sides of the bargain.

- *Reason 2: Investors' do-it-yourself alternative.* Companies cannot increase the value of their shares by undertaking transactions that investors can easily do on their own. We came across this idea when we discussed whether leverage increases company value, and we met it again when we came to dividend policy. It also applies to hedging. For example, when the shareholders in our heating-oil distributor invested in the company, they were presumably aware of the risks of the business. If they did not want to be exposed to the ups and downs of energy prices, they could have protected themselves in several ways. Perhaps they own shares in both the distributor and the refiner and do not care whether one wins at the other's expense.

Of course, shareholders can adjust their exposure only when companies keep investors fully informed of the transactions that they have made. For example, when a group of European central banks announced in 1999 that they would limit their sales of gold, the gold price immediately shot up. Investors in gold-mining shares rubbed their hands at the prospect of rising profits. But when they discovered that some mining companies had protected themselves against price fluctuations and would *not* benefit from the price rise, the hand-rubbing turned to hand-wringing.

Some stockholders of these gold-mining companies wanted to make a bet on rising gold prices; others didn't. But all of them gave the same message to management. The first group said, "Don't hedge! I'm happy to bear the risk of fluctuating gold prices, because I think gold prices will increase." The second group said, "Don't hedge! I'd rather do it myself."

We have seen that although hedging reduces risk, this doesn't in itself increase firm value. So when does it make sense to hedge? Sometimes hedging is worthwhile because it makes financial planning easier and reduces the odds of an embarrassing cash shortfall. A shortfall might mean only an unexpected trip to the bank, but on other occasions the firm might have to forgo worthwhile investments, and in extreme cases the shortfall could trigger bankruptcy. Why not reduce the odds of these awkward outcomes with a hedge?

We saw in our discussion of debt policy in Chapter 16 that financial distress can result in indirect as well as direct costs to a firm. Costs of financial distress arise from disruption to normal business operations as well as from the effect financial distress has on the firm's investment decisions. The better the risk management policies, the less the risk and the lower the expected costs of financial distress. As a side benefit, better risk management increases the firm's debt capacity.

In some cases hedging also makes it easier to decide whether an operating manager deserves a stern lecture or a pat on the back. Suppose that your export division shows a 50 percent decline in profits when the dollar unexpectedly strengthens against other currencies. How much of that decrease is due to the exchange rate shift and how much to poor management? If the company had protected itself against the effect of exchange rate changes, it's probably bad management. If it wasn't protected, you have to make a judgment with hindsight, probably by asking, "What would profits have been if the firm had hedged against exchange rate movements?"

Finally, hedging extraneous events can help focus the operating manager's attention. We know we shouldn't worry about events outside our control, but most of us do anyway. It's naive to expect the manager of the export division not to worry about exchange rate movements if his bottom line and bonus depend on them. The time spent worrying could be better spent if the company hedged itself against such movements.

A sensible risk strategy must answer the following questions:

- *What major risks does the company face and what are the possible consequences?* Some risks are scarcely worth a thought, but there are others that might bankrupt the company.
- *Is the company being paid for taking these risks?* Managers are not paid to avoid all risks, but if they can reduce their exposure to risks for which there are no compensating rewards, they can afford to place larger bets when the odds are stacked in their favour.

- *Can the company take any measures to reduce the probability of a bad outcome or to limit its impact?* For example, most businesses install alarm and sprinkler systems to prevent damage from fire and invest in backup facilities in case damage does occur.
- *Can the company purchase fairly priced insurance to offset any losses?* Insurance companies have some advantages in bearing risk. In particular, they may be able to spread the risk across a portfolio of different insurers.
- *Can the company use derivatives, such as options or futures, to hedge the risk?* In the remainder of this chapter we explain when and how derivatives may be used.

THE EVIDENCE ON RISK MANAGEMENT

There are three principal ways to manage risk. First, the firm can reduce risk by building flexibility into its operations. For example, a petrochemical plant designed to use either oil or natural gas as a feedstock reduces the threat of an unfavourable shift in the price of raw materials. Or think of a company that reduces the risk of disaster by test-marketing a new product before launching it nationally. Both firms are using *real options* to limit their risk. A second way to reduce risk is to buy an insurance policy against such hazards as fire, accidents, and theft. Finally, the firm may enter into specialized financial contracts that fix its costs or prices. These contracts are known collectively as **derivatives**, and they include options, futures, and swaps.

derivatives Securities whose payoffs are determined by the values of other financial variables such as prices, exchange rates, or interest rates.

A survey of the world's 500 largest companies found that almost all the companies use derivatives in some way to manage their risk.[2] Eighty-five percent employ them to control interest rate risk; 78 percent use them to manage currency risk; and 24 percent to manage the risk of fluctuations in commodity prices.

Risk policies differ. For example, some natural resource companies work hard to hedge their exposure to price fluctuations; others shrug their corporate shoulders and let prices wander as they may. Explaining why some hedge and others don't is not easy. One study of oil and gas companies found that the firms hedged most if they had high debt ratios, no debt ratings, and low dividend payouts.[3] It seems that for these firms, hedging programs were designed to reduce the likelihood of financial distress and to improve the firms' access to debt finance.

LO2 26.2 REDUCING RISK WITH OPTIONS

In the last chapter we introduced you to put and call options. Managers regularly buy options on currencies, interest rates, and commodities to limit their downside risk. Many of these options are traded on options exchanges, but often they are simply private deals between the corporation and a bank.

Petrochemical Parfum, Inc., is concerned about potential increases in the price of heavy crude oil, which is one of its major inputs. To protect itself against such increases, Petrochemical buys six-month options to purchase 1,000 barrels of crude oil at an exercise price of $90. These options might cost $.50 per barrel.

If the price of crude is above the $90 exercise price when the options expire, Petrochemical will exercise the options and will receive the difference between the oil price and the exercise price. If the oil price falls below the exercise price, the options will expire worthless. The net cost of oil will therefore be:

	Oil Price, Dollars per Barrel		
	$88	**$90**	**$92**
Cost of 1,000 barrels	$88,000	$90,000	$92,000
− Payoff on call option	0	0	2,000
Net cost	$88,000	$90,000	$90,000

[2] International Swap Dealers Association, "2003 Derivatives Usage Survey," **www.isda.org**.

[3] G.D. Haushalter, "Financing Policy, Basis Risk and Corporate Hedging," *Journal of Finance* 55 (February 2000): 107–152.

You can see that by buying options Petrochemical protects itself against increases in the oil price while continuing to benefit from oil price decreases. If prices fall, it can discard its call option and buy its oil at the market price. If oil prices rise, however, it can exercise its call option to purchase oil for $90 a barrel. Therefore, options create an attractive asymmetry. Of course, this asymmetry comes at a price—the $500 cost of the options.

Consider now the problem of Onnex, Inc., which supplies Petrochemical with crude oil. Its problem is the mirror image of Petrochemical's; it loses when oil prices fall and gains when oil prices rise.

Onnex wants to lock in a minimum price of oil but still benefit from rising oil prices. It can do so by purchasing *put* options that give it the right to *sell* oil at an exercise price of $90 per barrel. If oil prices fall, it will exercise the put. If they rise, it will discard the put and sell oil at the market price:

	Oil Price, Dollars per Barrel		
	$88	**$90**	**$92**
Revenue from 1,000 barrels	$88,000	$90,000	$92,000
+ Payoff on put option	2,000	0	0
Net revenues	$90,000	$90,000	$92,000

Once again you don't get something for nothing. The price Onnex pays for insurance against a fall in the price of oil is the cost of the put option. Similarly, the price Petrochemical paid for insurance against a rise in the price of oil was the cost of the call option. Options provide protection against adverse price changes for a fee—the option premium.

If oil prices rise, Onnex reaps the benefit. But if oil prices fall below $90 a barrel the payoff of the put option exactly offsets the revenue shortfall. As a result, Onnex realizes net revenues of at least $90 a barrel, which is the exercise price of the put option.

Notice that both Petrochemical and Onnex use options to insure against an adverse move in oil prices. But the options do not remove all uncertainty. For example, Onnex may be able to sell oil for much more than the exercise price of the option.

Figure 26.1 illustrates the nature of Onnex's hedge. Panel (a) shows the total revenue derived from selling the 1,000 barrels of oil. The firm is currently exposed to oil price risk: as prices fall, so will the firm's revenue. But, as panel (b) illustrates, the payoff on a put option to sell 1,000 barrels rises as oil prices fall below $90 a barrel and, therefore, can offset the firm's exposure. Panel (c) shows the firm's net revenues after it buys the put option. For prices below $90 per barrel, revenues are $90,000. But revenues rise $1,000 for every dollar that oil prices rise above $90. The profile in panel (c) should be familiar to you: think back to the protective put strategy we first saw in Figure 25.5 in Chapter 25. In both cases, the put provides a floor on the value of the overall position.

Check Point 26.1

Draw three graphs like those in Figure 26.1 to illustrate how Petrochemical hedges its costs by purchasing call options on oil.

LO2 26.3 FUTURES CONTRACTS

Suppose you are a canola farmer.[4] You are optimistic about next year's canola crop, but still you can't sleep. You are worried that when the time comes to sell the canola, prices may have fallen through the floor. The cure for insomnia is to sell canola *futures*. In this case, you agree to deliver so many tonnes of canola in (say) November at a price that is set today. Do not confuse this **futures contract** with an option, in which the holder has a choice whether or not to make delivery; your futures contract is a firm promise to deliver canola at a fixed selling price.

futures contract Exchange-traded promise to buy or sell an asset in the future at a pre-specified price.

[4] Canola is a grain used to make canola oil, which is very low in saturated fat and is believed to be healthier than many other oils. Canada produces about 15 percent of the world's output of canola.

FIGURE 26.1
Onnex can buy put options to place a floor on its overall revenues.

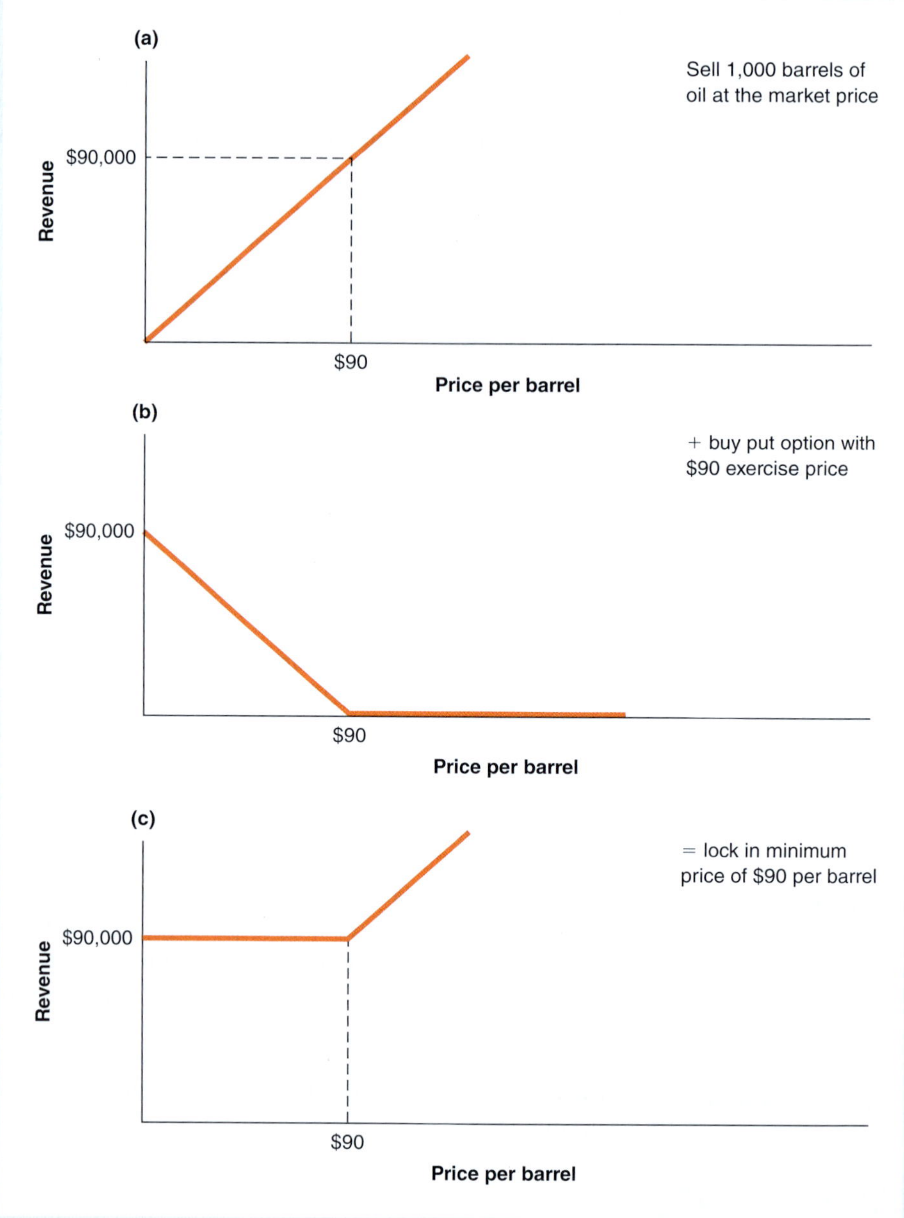

A canola oil processor is in the opposite position. She needs to *buy* canola after the harvest. If she would like to fix the price of this canola ahead of time, she can do so by *buying* canola futures. In other words, she agrees to take delivery of canola in the future at a price that is fixed today. The oil processor also does not have an option; if she still holds the futures contract when it matures, she is obliged to take delivery.

Let's suppose you, the farmer, and the oil processor strike a deal. You enter a futures contract. What happens? First, no money changes hands when the contract is initiated.[5] The oil processor

[5] Actually, each party will be required to set up a margin account to guarantee performance on the contract. Despite this, the futures contract may still be considered as essentially requiring no money down. First, the amount of margin is small. Second, it may be posted in interest-bearing securities, so that the parties to the trade need not suffer opportunity cost from placing assets in the margin account.

No money changes hands when a futures contract is entered into. The contract is a binding obligation to buy or sell at a fixed price at contract maturity.

agrees to buy canola at the futures price on a stated *future* date (the contract maturity date). You agree to sell at the same price and date. Second, the futures contract is a binding obligation, not an option. Options give the right to buy or sell if buying or selling turns out to be profitable. The futures contract *requires* you, the farmer, to sell and the oil processor to buy regardless of who profits and who loses.

The profit on the futures contract is the difference between the initial futures price and the ultimate price of the asset when the contract matures. For example, if the futures price is originally \$580 per tonne and the market price of canola turns out to be \$620, the farmer delivers and the oil processor receives the canola for a price \$40 below market value. The farmer loses \$40 per tonne and the canola oil processor gains \$40 per tonne as a result of the futures transaction. In general, the seller of the contract benefits if the price initially locked in turns out to exceed the price that could have been obtained at contract maturity. Conversely, the buyer of the contract benefits if the ultimate market price of the asset turns out to exceed the initial futures price. Therefore, the profits on the futures contract to each party are

Profit to seller = initial futures price − ultimate market price **(26.1)**

Profit to buyer = ultimate market price − initial futures price **(26.2)**

Now it is easy to see how the farmer and the oil processor can both use the contract to hedge. Consider the farmer's overall cash flows:

	Cash Flow
Sale of canola	Ultimate price of canola
Futures profits	Futures price − ultimate price of canola
Total	Futures price

The profits on the futures contract offset the risk surrounding the sales price of canola and lock in total revenue equal to the futures price. Similarly, the oil processor's all-in cost for the canola is also fixed at the futures price. Any increase in the cost of canola will be offset by a commensurate increase in the profit realized on the futures contract.

Both the farmer and the oil processor have less risk than before. The farmer has hedged (that is, offset) risk by selling canola futures; the oil processor has hedged risk by buying canola futures.[6]

EXAMPLE 26.1 HEDGING WITH FUTURES

Suppose that the farmer originally sold 50 tonnes of November canola futures at a price of \$580 per tonne. In November, when the futures contract matures, the price of canola is only \$530 per tonne. The farmer buys back the canola futures at \$530 just before maturity, giving him a profit of \$50 a tonne on the sale and subsequent repurchase. At the same time he sells his canola at the spot price of \$530 a tonne. His total receipts are therefore \$580 a tonne:

Profit on sale and repurchase of futures	\$ 50
Sale of canola at the November spot price	\$530
Total receipts	\$580

You can see that the futures contract has allowed the farmer to lock in total proceeds of \$580 a tonne.

[6] Neither has eliminated all risk. For example, the farmer still has quantity risk. He does not know for sure how many tonnes of canola he will produce.

Figure 26.2 illustrates how the futures contract enabled the farmer in Example 26.1 to hedge his position. Panel (a) is the value of 50 tonnes of canola as a function of the spot price of canola. The value rises by \$50 for every dollar increase in canola prices. Panel (b) is the profit on a futures contract to deliver 50 tonnes of canola at a futures price of \$580 per tonne. The profit will be zero if the ultimate price of canola equals the original futures price, \$580. The profit on the contract to deliver at \$580 rises by \$50 for every dollar the price of canola *falls* below \$580. The exposures to the price of canola depicted in panels (a) and (b) obviously cancel out. Panel (c) shows that the total value of the 50 tonnes plus the futures position is unaffected by the ultimate price of canola, and equals $\$580 \times 50 = \$29{,}000$. In other words, the farmer has locked in proceeds per tonne equal to the original futures price.

FIGURE 26.2
The farmer can use canola futures to hedge the value of the crop. See Example 26.1.

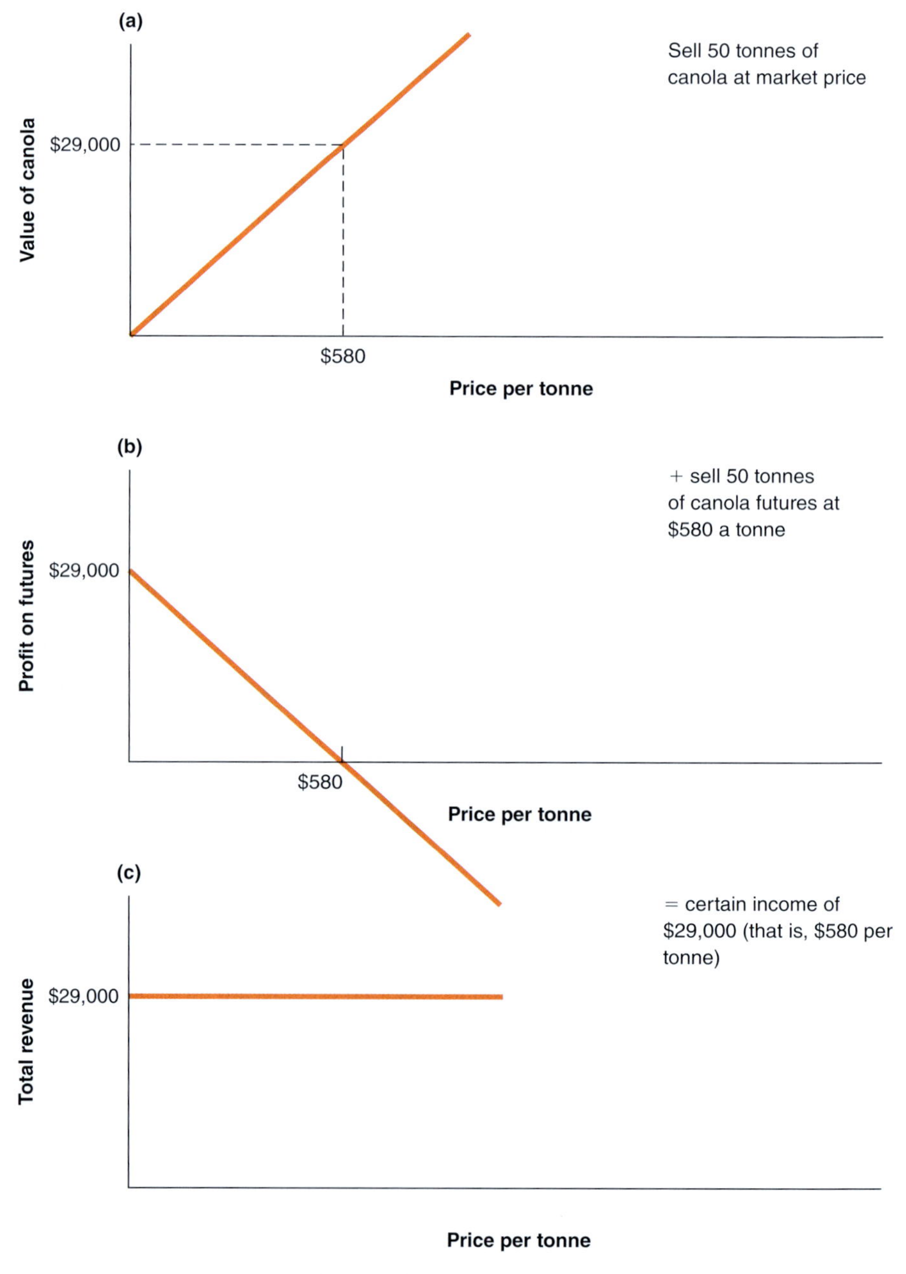

THE MECHANICS OF FUTURES TRADING

In practice, the farmer and canola oil processor would not sign the futures contract face to face. Instead, each would likely go to ICE Futures Canada,[5] the dominant exchange for canola futures and options contracts trading.

Table 26.1 shows the settlement price of canola futures at ICE Futures Canada on April 5, 2011, when the price for immediate delivery was about $576.17 a tonne. Notice that there is a choice of possible delivery dates. If, for example, you were to sell canola for delivery in July, you would get a higher price than by selling May futures.

The oil processor would not be prepared to buy futures contracts if the farmer were free to deliver half-rotten canola to a leaky barn at the end of a cart track. Futures trading is possible only because the contracts are highly standardized. For example, in the case of canola futures, each contract calls for the delivery of 20 tonnes of canola of a specified quality at a warehouse in Saskatchewan.

When you buy or sell a futures contract, the price is fixed today, but payment is not made until later. However, you will be asked to put up some cash or securities as a margin to demonstrate that you are able to honour your side of the bargain.

In addition, futures contracts are *marked to market*. This means that each day any profits or losses on the contract are calculated; you pay the exchange any losses and receive any profits.

For example, our farmer agreed to deliver 50 tonnes of canola in November at $582 a tonne. Suppose that the next day the price of canola futures increases to $587 a tonne. The farmer now has a loss on his sale of $50 \times \$5 = \$250$ and must pay this sum to the exchange. You can think of the farmer as buying back his futures position each day and then opening up a new position. Thus after the first day the farmer has realized a loss on his trade of $5 a tonne and now has an obligation to deliver canola for $587 per tonne.

Of course, our oil processor is in the opposite position. The rise in the futures price leaves her with a *profit* of $5 a tonne. The exchange will therefore pay her this profit. In effect the oil processor sells her futures position at a profit and opens a new contract to take delivery at $587 per tonne.

The price of canola for immediate delivery is known as the *spot price*. When the farmer sells canola futures, the price that he agrees to take for his canola may be very different from the spot price. But the future eventually becomes the present. As the date for delivery approaches, the futures contract becomes more and more like a spot contract and the price of the futures contract approaches the spot price.

The farmer might decide to wait until the futures contract matures and then deliver canola to the buyer. But in practice such delivery is rare, for it is more convenient for the farmer to buy back the canola futures just before maturity.[7]

TABLE 26.1
The settlement prices of canola futures at ICE Futures Canada, on April 5, 2011.

Delivery Date	Price per Tonne
May 2011	$593.20
July 2011	601.80
November 2011	582.50
January 2012	588.40
March 2012	589.50

Source: Courtesy of Intercontinental Exchange, Inc. "End of Day Report," **www.theice.com/marketdata/reports/ReportCenter.shtml**, accessed October 17, 2011.

[7] In the case of some of the financial futures described later, you *cannot* deliver the asset. At maturity the buyer simply receives (or pays) the difference between the spot price and the price at which he or she has agreed to purchase the asset.

Check Point 26.2

Suppose that two days after taking out the futures contracts the price of March canola increases to $590 a tonne. What additional payments will be made by or to the farmer and the oil processor? What will be their remaining obligations at the end of this second day?

COMMODITY AND FINANCIAL FUTURES

Financial futures are similar to commodity futures, but instead of placing an order to buy or sell a commodity at a future date, you place an order to buy or sell a financial asset at a future date. You can use financial futures to protect yourself against fluctuations in short- and long-term interest rates, exchange rates, and the level of share prices.

We have shown how the farmer and the oil processor can both use canola futures to hedge their risk. It is also possible to trade futures in a wide variety of other commodities, such as sugar, soybean oil, pork bellies, orange juice, crude oil, and copper.

Commodity prices can bounce up and down like a bungee jumper. For example, in December 2000 the price of a ton (about .91 tonnes) of cocoa hit a low of $674. Two years later the price had more than tripled to $2,400. For a large buyer of cocoa, such as Hershey, these price fluctuations could knock the company badly off course. Hershey therefore reduces its exposure to movements in cocoa and sugar prices by hedging with commodity futures.

For many firms, the wide fluctuations in interest rates and exchange rates have become at least as important a source of risk as changes in commodity prices. You can use *financial futures* to hedge against these risks.

Financial futures have been a remarkable success. They were invented in 1972; within a few years, trading in financial futures significantly exceeded trading in commodity futures. Table 26.2 lists some of the more popular financial futures contracts and the exchanges on which they are traded. The largest exchanges are the CME Group, recently formed as the result of a merger of the Chicago Board of Trade (CBOT) and Chicago Mercantile Exchange (CME) and Eurex, the European derivatives exchange. In 2010, 3.05 billion futures and options contracts were traded through the CME Group and 1.9 billion contracts were traded on the Eurex. In Canada, all financial futures and options are traded at the Bourse de Montréal.

Check Point 26.3

You plan to issue long-term bonds in nine months but are worried that interest rates may have increased in the meantime. How could you use financial futures to protect yourself against a general rise in interest rates?

TABLE 26.2
Some financial futures contracts and where they are traded.

Future	Principal Exchange
Government of Canada bonds	ME
Standard & Poor's Canada 60 Index	ME
U.S. Treasury notes	CBOT
U.S. Treasury bonds	CBOT
Eurodollar deposits	CME
Standard & Poor's Index	CME
Euro	CME
Yen	CME
German government bonds (bunds)	Eurex

Key to abbreviations:
CBOT Chicago Board of Trade, at the Chicago Mercantile Exchange, **www.cmegroup.com**
CME Chicago Mercantile Exchange, **www.cmegroup.com**
ME Bourse de Montréal, **www.m-x.ca**
Eurex European Derivatives Exchange, **www.eurexchange.com**

LO2 26.4 FORWARD CONTRACTS

Every day, billions of dollars of futures contracts are bought and sold. We have seen that this liquidity is possible only because futures contracts are standardized. Futures contracts mature on a limited number of dates each year (take another look at the canola contracts in Table 26.1), and the contract size is standardized. For example, a contract may call for delivery of 5,000 bushels of wheat, 100 ounces of gold, or 62,500 British pounds. If the terms of a futures contract do not suit your needs, you may be able to buy or sell a **forward contract**.

forward contract Agreement to buy or sell an asset in the future at an agreed price.

Forward contracts are custom-tailored futures contracts.[8] You can write a forward contract with any maturity date for delivery of any quantity of goods. For example, suppose that you know that you will need to pay out yen in three months' time. You can fix the price today that you will pay for the yen by arranging with your bank to buy yen forward. At the end of the three months, you pay the agreed-upon sum and take delivery of the yen.

EXAMPLE 26.2 A PIZZA FORWARD CONTRACT

Have you ever ordered a pizza by phone? If so, you have entered into a forward contract! Your order specifies the pizza type (cheese, pepperoni, and green olives), size (large), the delivery time and location (to be delivered in 30 minutes to your front door) and the price ($15). You don't pay until the product is delivered but you agree on the price at the time the contract is established. You might even be able to trade your forward contract—that is, if your roommate suddenly arrives home very hungry and is willing to buy your pizza contract from you.

EXAMPLE 26.3 FOREIGN CURRENCY FORWARD CONTRACTS

Computer Parts Inc. has ordered memory chips from its supplier in Japan. The bill for ¥53 million must be paid on July 27. The company can arrange with its bank today to buy this number of yen forward for delivery on July 27 at a forward price of ¥110 per dollar. Therefore, on July 27, Computer Parts pays the bank 53 million/110 = $481,818 and receives ¥53 million, which it can use to pay its Japanese supplier. By committing forward to exchange $481,818 for ¥53 million, its dollar costs are locked in. Notice that if the firm had not used the forward contract to hedge and the dollar had depreciated over this period, the firm would have had to pay a greater amount of dollars. For example, if the exchange rate had fallen to ¥100/dollar, the firm would have had to exchange $530,000 for the ¥53 million necessary to pay its bill. The firm could have used a futures contract to hedge its foreign exchange exposure, but standardization of futures would not allow for delivery of precisely ¥53 million on precisely July 27.

The most active trading in forwards is in foreign currencies, but in recent years companies have increasingly entered into forward rate agreements that allow them to fix the interest rate at which they borrow or lend in advance.

LO3 26.5 SWAPS

Suppose Computer Parts from Example 26.3 decides to produce memory chips instead of purchasing them from outside suppliers. It has issued $100 million in floating-rate bonds to help finance the construction of a new plant. (Recall from Chapter 14 that floating-rate bonds make interest payments that go up and down with the general level of interest rates. The coupon payments on the bonds are tied to a specific short-term interest rate.) But the financial manager is

[8] One difference between forward and futures contracts is that forward contracts are not marked to market. Thus with a forward contract you settle up any profits or losses when the contract matures.

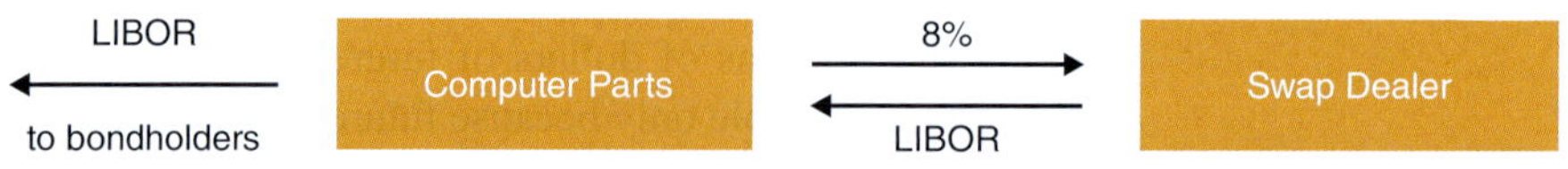

FIGURE 26.3
Interest rate swap: Computer Parts currently pays the LIBOR rate on its outstanding bonds (the arrow on the left). If the firm enters a swap to pay a fixed rate of 8 percent and receive a floating rate of LIBOR, its exposure to LIBOR will cancel out, and its net cash outflow will be a fixed rate of 8 percent.

concerned that interest rates are becoming more volatile, and she would like to lock in the firm's interest expenses. One approach would be to buy back the floating-rate bonds and replace them with a new issue of fixed-rate debt. But it is costly to issue new debt to the public; in addition, buying back the outstanding bonds in the market will result in considerable trading costs.

swap Arrangement by two counterparties to exchange one stream of cash flows for another.

A better approach to hedge out its interest rate exposure is for the firm to enter an interest rate **swap**. The firm will pay or "swap" a fixed payment for another payment that is tied to the level of interest rates. Thus, if rates do rise, increasing the firm's interest expense on its floating-rate debt, its cash flow from the swap agreement will rise as well, offsetting its exposure.

Suppose the firm pays the LIBOR rate on its floating-rate bonds. (Recall that LIBOR, the London Interbank Offer Rate, is the interest rate at which banks borrow from each other in the Eurodollar market. It is the most frequently used short-term interest rate in the swap market.) The firm's interest expense each year therefore equals the LIBOR rate times $100 million. It would like to transform this obligation into one that will not fluctuate with interest rates.

Suppose that current rates in the swaps market are LIBOR for 8 percent fixed. This means that Computer Parts can enter into a swap agreement to pay 8 percent on "notional principal" of $100 million to a swap dealer and receive payment of the LIBOR rate on the same amount of notional principal. The firm pays the dealer .08 × $100 million and receives LIBOR × $100 million. The dealer and the firm are called *counterparties* in the swap. The firm's net cash payment to the dealer is therefore (LIBOR − .08) × $100 million. (If LIBOR exceeds 8 percent, the firm receives money from the dealer; if it is less than 8 percent, the firm pays money to the dealer.) Figure 26.3 illustrates the cash flows paid by Computer Parts and the swap dealer.

Table 26.3 shows Computer Parts' net payments for three possible interest rates. The total payment on the bond-with-swap agreement equals $8,000,000 regardless of the interest rate. The swap has transformed the floating-rate bond into synthetic fixed-rate debt with an effective coupon rate of 8 percent. The firm has thus hedged away its interest rate exposure without actually having to replace its floating-rate bonds with fixed-rate bonds. Swaps offer a much cheaper way to "rearrange the balance sheet."[9]

TABLE 26.3
An interest rate swap can transform floating-rate bonds into synthetic fixed-rate bonds.

	LIBOR Rate		
	7.5%	8.0%	8.5%
Interest paid on floating-rate bonds (= LIBOR × $100 million)	$7,500,000	$8,000,000	$8,500,000
+ Cash payment on swap (= [.08 − LIBOR] × notional principal of $100 million)	500,000	0	−500,000
Total payment	$8,000,000	$8,000,000	$8,000,000

[9] You might wonder what's in this arrangement for the swap dealer. The dealer will profit by charging a bid-ask spread. Since the dealer pays LIBOR in return for 8 percent in this swap, it might search for another trader who wishes to receive a fixed rate and pay LIBOR. The dealer will pay a 7.9 percent rate to that trader in return for the LIBOR rate. So the dealer pays a fixed rate and receives floating with one trader but pays floating and receives fixed with the other. Its net cash flow is thus riskless and equal to .1 percent of notional principal.

There are many other applications of interest rate swaps. A portfolio manager who holds a portfolio of long-term bonds but is worried interest rates might increase, causing a capital loss on the portfolio, can enter a swap to pay a fixed rate and receive a floating rate, converting the holdings into a synthetic floating-rate portfolio (see Check Point 26.4). Or a pension fund manager might identify some money market securities that are paying excellent yields compared to other comparable-risk short-term securities. However, the manager might believe that such short-term assets are inappropriate for the portfolio. The fund can hold these high-yielding securities and enter a swap in which it receives a fixed rate and pays a floating rate. It thus captures the benefit of the advantageous *relative yields* on these securities, but still establishes a portfolio with the fixed-interest-rate risk characteristic of long-term bonds.

Check Point 26.4

Consider the portfolio manager who is holding a $100 million portfolio of long-term bonds and wishes to reduce price risk by transforming the holdings into a synthetic floating-rate portfolio. Assume that the portfolio currently pays an 8 percent fixed rate and that swap dealers currently offer terms of 8 percent fixed for LIBOR. What swap would the manager establish? Show the total income on the fund in a table like Table 26.3, and illustrate the cash flows in a diagram like Figure 26.3.

There are many variations on the interest rate swap. For example, currency swaps allow firms to exchange a series of payments in dollars (which may be tied to a fixed or floating rate) for a series of payments in another currency (which also may be tied to a fixed or floating rate). These swaps can therefore be used to manage exposure to exchange rate fluctuations.

EXAMPLE 26.4 CURRENCY SWAPS

Suppose that the Moose Company wishes to borrow Swiss francs (SFr) to help finance its European operations. Since Moose is better known in Canada, the financial manager believes that the company can obtain more attractive terms on a dollar loan than on a Swiss franc loan. Therefore, the company borrows $10 million for 5 years at 5 percent in Canada. At the same time Moose arranges with a bank to trade its future dollar liability for Swiss francs. Under this arrangement the bank agrees to pay Moose sufficient dollars to service its dollar loan, and in exchange, Moose agrees to make a series of annual payments in Swiss francs to the bank.

Moose's cash flows are set out in Table 26.4. Line 1 shows that when Moose takes out its dollar loan, it contracts to pay annual interest of $.5 million and repay the $10 million that it has borrowed. Lines 2(a) and 2(b) show the cash flows from the swap, assuming that the spot exchange rate for Swiss francs is $1 = SFr2. Moose hands over to the bank the $10 million that it borrowed and receives in exchange 2 × $10 million = SFr20 million. In each of the next 4 years the bank pays Moose $.5 million, which Moose uses to pay the annual interest on its loan. In year 5 the bank pays Moose $10.5 million, which covers both the final year's interest and the repayment of the loan. In return for these future dollar receipts, Moose agrees to pay the bank SFr1.2 million in each of the next 4 years and SFr21.2 million in year 5.

The combined effect of Moose's two steps (line 3) is to convert its 5 percent dollar loan into a 6 percent Swiss franc loan. The device that makes this possible is the currency swap.

TABLE 26.4 Cash flows from Moose's dollar loan and currency swap ($ millions).

	Year 0		Years 1–4		Year 5	
	$	SFr	$	SFr	$	SFr
1. Issue dollar loan	+10		−.5		−10.5	
2. Arrange currency swap						
a. Moose $ cash flows	−10		+.5		+10.5	
b. Moose SFr cash flows	___	+20	___	−1.2	___	−21.2
3. Net cash flow	0	+20	0	−1.2	0	−21.2

Check Point 26.5 Suppose that the spot exchange rate had been $1 = SFr3 and that Swiss interest rates were 8 percent. Recalculate the Swiss franc cash flows that the bank would agree to (line 2(b) of Table 26.4) and Moose's net cash flows (line 3).

LO2, 3 26.6 INNOVATION IN THE DERIVATIVES MARKET

Almost every day some new derivative contract seems to be invented. At first there may be just a few private deals between a bank and its customers, but, if the contract proves popular, one of the futures exchanges may try to muscle in on the business.

Derivatives dealers try to identify the major risks that face businesses and then design a contract that will allow them to lay off these risks. For example, a major hazard for many financial institutions is the possibility that a large customer will get into difficulties and default on its debts. Credit derivatives offer a way for the lender to insure against such a default. The provider of the insurance promises to pay out if the borrower defaults on its debts and in return charges a premium for taking on the risk. The market for credit derivatives has grown very rapidly in recent years.

Farmers, electric utilities, and soft-drink sellers all worry about the weather. So wouldn't it be nice if they could stop worrying and hedge themselves against bad weather? Well, now they can do so, either by entering into a private deal with a derivative firm or by dealing in weather futures and options on the Chicago Mercantile Exchange. Similarly, real estate futures were launched in 2006 and enable participants such as real estate businesses and builders to protect themselves against changes in house prices in 10 U.S. cities.

It seems to be very difficult to predict which new contracts will succeed and which will bomb. By the time you read this, weather contracts may have been forgotten and everyone will be talking about the new growth market in _____ derivatives. Perhaps you can fill in the missing word.

LO2, 3, 4 26.7 IS "DERIVATIVE" A FOUR-LETTER WORD?

Our earlier examples of the farmer and the oil processor showed how derivatives—futures, options, or swaps, for example—can be used to reduce business risk. However, if you were to copy the farmer and sell canola futures without an offsetting holding of canola, you would not be *reducing* risk; you would be *speculating*.

A successful futures market needs speculators who are prepared to take on risk and provide the farmer and the canola oil processor with the protection they need. For example, if an excess of farmers wished to sell canola futures, the price of futures would be forced down until enough speculators were tempted to buy in the hope of a profit. If there is a surplus of oil processors wishing to buy canola futures, the reverse will happen. The price will be forced up until speculators are drawn in to sell.

Speculation may be necessary to a thriving derivatives market, but it can get companies into serious trouble. For example, for 10 years a Japanese trading company, Sumitomo Corporation, used the futures market to place huge bets on the price of copper. Its chief trader, known in the business simply as "Mr. Copper," was lauded for his contributions to the firm's profits. However, in June 1996 the copper market was battered by the revelation that the man with the Midas touch had managed to hide losses amounting to about $1 billion.

Sumitomo has plenty of company. In 1995, Baring Brothers, a blue-chip British merchant bank, became insolvent. The reason: Nick Leeson, a trader in its Singapore office, had lost

Finance in Action

Did Goldman Bury AIG?

We have not spent a lot of time reporting on the various "What caused the financial crisis?" panels and discussions, largely because no regulatory outgrowth has occurred that will affect investors and most of the studies were basically an exercise in political bickering. This morning, however, we have an exception as the NY Times *dug through a the huge stack of documents attached to the Financial Crisis Inquiry Commission (the one Michael Lewis savaged yesterday) and wondered aloud whether Goldman Sachs went out of its way to destroy AIG in search of profits. . . .*

On the exceptionally important but little understood role played by the increasingly lower prices Goldman Sachs placed on the complex mortgage securities on its balance sheet—which helped determine the fate of many of its shakier Wall Street brethren—the commission report, on page 237, is crystalline:

> As the crisis unfolded Goldman marked mortgage-related securities at prices that were significantly lower than those of other companies. Goldman knew that those lower marks might hurt those other companies—including some clients—because they could require marking down those assets and similar assets. In addition, Goldman's marks would get picked up by competitors in dealer surveys. As a result, Goldman's marks could contribute to other companies recording "mark-to-market" losses: that is, the reported value of their assets could fall and their earnings would decline.

In late July 2007, Goldman started a nearly 17-month dispute with A.I.G. Financial Products, a subsidiary of American International Group, the giant insurer, about the value of $23-billion of complex mortgage securities that Goldman had insured through the subsidiary by paying some $10-million in premiums. Goldman's agreement with the A.I.G. Financial Products allowed Goldman to demand collateral payments from the firm under two conditions. First, if A.I.G., the parent company, lost its AAA credit rating, which it did in March 2005. And, second, if Goldman believed the value of the underlying securities being insured had fallen, which by mid-2007 Goldman thought—correctly—had occurred. But the consequences of Goldman's collateral disputes with the financial products subsidiary were profound for A.I.G., and contributed mightily to the government takeover of the insurer after pumping some $180-billion into it.

Source: Excerpted from Scott Barlow, "Market Questions LSE/TMX Deal Completion: Did Goldman Bury AIG?" *National Post*, February 17, 2011, **www.nationalpost.com**.

$1.4 billion speculating in futures contracts on the Japanese stock market index. The same year Daiwa Bank reported that a bond trader in its New York office had managed to hide losses over 11 years of $1.1 billion. In 2008 the French bank Societé générale joined the billion-dollar club when it reported that one of its derivatives traders had lost a record $7.2 billion on unauthorized trades.

As we have discussed in Chapter 1, the origins of the recent financial crisis in the United States lie in the U.S. securitization market, in which mortgages were bundled into mortgage-backed securities (MBS) and sold to private pools of capital. The financial institutions that sold these securities insured all the counterparty risk by buying instruments known as *credit default swaps* (CDS). Some of the world's largest insurance companies, such as U.S.-based AIG sold these credit default swaps in large volumes. When the real estate market in the United States began to weaken significantly, there was a flood of insurance claims from holders of CDS instruments. The insurance companies did not, however, have enough capital to meet all the claims and were unable to pay their obligations. Several of the insurance companies, including AIG, became insolvent. The U.S. federal government was forced to bailout AIG and other financial institutions to the tune of trillions of dollars in order to prevent a catastrophic financial and economic collapse and the virtual shutdown of the banking system.

> If you are no better informed than the highly paid professionals in banks and other institutions, you should use derivatives for hedging, not for speculation.

Two nearby Finance in Action boxes discuss the controversy surrounding the role of a venerable Wall Street financial institution, Goldman Sachs, in the financial crisis.

Do such horror stories mean that firms should ban the use of derivatives? Of course not. But they do illustrate that derivatives need to be used with care. Our view is this that speculation is foolish unless you have reason to think the odds are in your favour. If you are no better informed than the highly paid professionals in banks and other institutions, you should use derivatives for hedging, not for speculation.

Finance in Action

Goldman Says Did Not "Bet Against" Clients

Goldman Sachs Group Inc. said it did not intentionally "bet against" securities in the mortgage market during the financial crisis, dismissing suggestions that it unfairly made money by placing bets against its clients.

"As a market maker, we execute a variety of transactions with clients and other market participants ... which may result in long or short risk exposures to thousands of different instruments at any given time," Goldman said in an annual letter to its shareholders.

Goldman said it did not generate enormous net revenue or profit by betting against residential mortgage-related products.

However, following its decision to reduce its exposure to risky mortgage securities, the bank said it lost less money than it otherwise would have when the residential housing market began to deteriorate rapidly.

In January, Goldman Chief Executive Lloyd Blankfein faced harsh questioning from the chairman of the Financial Crisis Inquiry Commission, who accused Goldman of knowingly creating shoddy subprime-backed securities for customers, and then betting they would default.

In the letter to shareholders, Goldman also defended its relationship with the bailed out U.S. insurer AIG . . . and said the bank bought protection on super-senior collateralized debt obligation (CDO) risk only as part of a trading relationship.

"This protection was designed to hedge equivalent transactions executed with clients taking the other side of the same trades. In so doing, we served as an intermediary in assisting our clients to express a defined view on the market," Goldman said.

Many banks, including Goldman, were among the recipients of tens of billions of federal bailout dollars that were funneled through the insurer at the height of the crisis, saving them from potential losses and causing a public uproar.

The bank said its total exposure on the securities on which it bought protection was roughly $10 billion and it held about $7.5 billion in collateral from AIG. The remainder was covered through other hedges entered with various counterparties.

"If AIG had failed, we would have had the collateral from AIG and the proceeds from the Credit Default Swap (CDS) protection we purchased.

Therefore, we would not have incurred any material economic loss," Goldman said.

Source: Excerpted from "Goldman Says Did Not 'Bet Against' Clients," *National Post*, April 7, 2010, **www.nationalpost.com**.

26.8 SUMMARY

1. **Why do companies hedge to reduce risk?** LO1

   Fluctuations in commodity prices, interest rates, or exchange rates can make planning difficult and can throw companies badly off course. Financial managers therefore look for opportunities to manage these risks, and a number of specialized instruments have been invented to help them. These are collectively known as derivative instruments.

2. **How can options, futures, and forward contracts be used to devise simple hedging strategies?** LO2

   In the last chapter we introduced you to put and call options. **Options** are often used by firms to limit their downside risk. For example, if you own an asset and have the option to sell it at the current price, then you have effectively insured yourself against loss.

   Futures contracts are agreements made today to buy or sell an asset in the future. The price is fixed today, but the final payment does not occur until the delivery date. Futures contracts are highly standardized and are traded on organized exchanges. Commodity futures allow firms to fix the future price that they pay for a wide range of agricultural commodities, metals, and oil. Financial futures help firms to protect themselves against unforeseen movements in interest rates, exchange rates, and stock prices.

   Forward contracts are equivalent to tailor-made futures contracts. For example, firms often enter into forward agreements with a bank to buy or sell foreign exchange or to fix the interest rate on a loan to be made in the future.

3. **How can companies use swaps to change the risk of securities they have issued?** LO3

   Swaps allow firms to exchange one series of future payments for another. For example, the firm might agree to make a series of regular payments in one currency in return for receiving a series of payments in another currency.

4. **Are derivatives used for speculative purposes?** LO4

   Derivatives should be used with care. Recent events have shown that derivatives, when used for speculative purposes, can have unforeseen adverse consequences

Related Web Links

msci.com/insights/risk_management Online papers and webinars about risk management

cisco-futures.com Data on a variety of contracts, including simulations and other information

home.earthlink.net/~green/whatisan.htm Information about swaps

pitnews.com Daily market information on commodity futures and options markets

futuresmag.com, risk.net Journals specializing in derivatives

global-derivatives.com Information on degree program offerings and research on derivatives

Key Terms

derivatives	812	futures contract	813
forward contract	819	swap	820

Questions and Problems

*Answers in Appendix B

BASIC

1. **Risk Management.** Large businesses spend millions of dollars annually on insurance. Why? Should they insure against all risks or does insurance make more sense for some risks than others'? (LO1)
2. **Hedging.** (LO2)
   a. An investor currently holding $1 million in long-term government bonds becomes concerned about increasing volatility in interest rates. She decides to hedge her risk using government bond futures contracts. Should she buy or sell such contracts?
   b. The treasurer of a corporation that will be issuing bonds in 3 months is also concerned about interest rate volatility and wants to lock in the price at which he could sell 8 percent coupon bonds. How would he use government bond futures contracts to hedge his firm's position?
3. **Commodity Futures.** What commodity futures are traded on futures exchanges? Who do you think could usefully reduce risk by buying each of these contracts? Who do you think might wish to sell each contract? (LO1)
4. **Hedging.** "The farmer does not avoid risk by selling canola futures. If canola prices stay above $580 per tonne, then he will actually have lost by selling canola futures at $580." Is this a fair comment? (LO1)
5. **Marking to Market.** Suppose that in the 5 days following a farmer's sale of September wheat futures at a futures price of $3.83 the futures prices are

Day	1	2	3	4	5
Price	$3.83	$3.98	$3.70	$3.50	$3.60

   At the end of day 5 the farmer decides to quit wheat farming and buys back his futures contract. What payments are made between the farmer and the exchange on each day? What is the total payment over the five days? Would the total payment be any different if the contract was not marked to market? The contract size is 5,000 bushels. (LO2)

*6. **Futures Versus Spot Positions.** What do you think are the advantages of holding futures rather than the underlying commodity? What do you think are the disadvantages? (LO2)

INTERMEDIATE

*7. **Hedging with Futures Versus Puts.** A gold mining firm is concerned about short-term volatility in its revenues. Gold currently sells for $1,450 an ounce, but the price is extremely volatile and could fall as low as $1,330 or rise as high as $1,650 in the next month. The company will bring 1,000 ounces to the market next month. (LO2)

a. What will total revenues be if the firm remains unhedged for gold prices of $1,330, $1,450, and $1,650 an ounce?

b. The futures price of gold for 1-month-ahead delivery is $1,460. What will be the firm's total revenues at each gold price if the firm enters a 1-month futures contract to deliver 1,000 ounces of gold?

c. What will total revenues be if the firm buys a 1-month put option to sell gold for $1,450 an ounce? The puts cost $5 per ounce.

8. **Hedging with Calls.** A large dental lab plans to purchase 1,000 ounces of gold in 1 month. Assume again that gold prices can be $1,330, $1,450, or $1,650 an ounce. (LO2)

a. What will total expenses be if the firm purchases call options on 1,000 ounces of gold with an exercise price of $1,450 an ounce? The options cost $3 per ounce.

b. What will total expenses be if the firm purchases call options on 1,000 ounces of gold with an exercise price of $1,445 an ounce? These options cost $7 per ounce.

9. **Forward Contract.** Assume that the 1-year interest rate is 6 percent and the 2-year interest rate is 7 percent per year. You approach a bank and ask at what rate the bank will promise to make a 1-year loan in 12 months' time. The bank offers to make a forward commitment to lend to you at 12 percent. Would you accept the offer? Can you think of a simple, cheaper alternative? (LO2)

10. **Hedging Project Risk.** Your firm has just tendered for a contract in Japan. You won't know for 3 months whether you get the contract but if you do, you will receive a payment of ¥10 million 1 year from now. You are worried that if the yen declines in value, the dollar value of this payment will be less than you expect and the project could even show a loss. Discuss the possible ways that you could protect the firm against a decline in the value of the yen. Illustrate the possible outcomes if you do get the contract and if you don't. (LO2)

*11. **Hedging with Futures.** Show how Petrochemical Parfum (see Section 26.2) can also use futures contracts to protect itself against a rise in the price of crude oil. Show how the payoffs would vary if the oil price is $88, $90, or $92 a barrel. What are the advantages and disadvantages for Petrochemical of using futures rather than options to reduce risk? Repeat the exercise for Onnex. Assume the futures price for oil is $90 per barrel. (LO2)

12. **Futures Contracts.** Look in *The Globe and Mail* or *National Post* at the prices of gold futures quoted on the COMEX futures exchange. What is the date of the most distant contract? Suppose that you buy 100 ounces of gold futures for this date. When do you receive the gold? When do you pay for it? Is the futures price higher or lower than the current spot price? Can you suggest why? (LO2)

13. **Hedging Currency Risk.** When the deutschemark strengthened in 1991 and 1992, German luxury car manufacturers found it increasingly difficult to compete in the United States market. How could they have hedged themselves against this risk? Would a company that was hedged have been in a better position to compete? Explain why or why not. (LO1)

14. **Swaps.** What is a currency swap? An interest rate swap? Give one example of how each might be used. (LO3)

CHALLENGE

15. **Swaps.** Firms A and B face the following borrowing rates for a 5-year fixed-rate debt issue in Canadian dollars or euros:

	Canadian Dollars	Euros
Firm A	10%	7%
Firm B	8%	6%

Suppose that A wishes to borrow Canadian dollars and B wishes to borrow euros. Show how a swap could be used to reduce the borrowing costs of each company. Assume a spot exchange rate of 1 euro to the dollar. (LO3)

16. **Risk Management.** Discuss each of the following statements: (LO1)

a. "The better the risk management policies of a company, the greater a company's debt capacity."

b. "Managers are not paid to avoid all risk."

17. **Internet.** The International Finance Risk Institute provides three case studies on the sources, types, and control of financial risk at **riskinstitute.ch/introduction.htm**. Read the Sumitomo story for insights into the financial trading scandal. (LO1)

18. **Internet.** Risk management extends beyond using financial instruments to hedge. This Web site offers ideas on how to manage a business crisis: **www.smallbusinessnotes.com/business-finances/risk-management-strategies.html**. (LO1)

19. **Internet.** In Canada, futures are traded on the Bourse de Montréal, **www.m-x.ca**. What futures contracts are offered for trading? Why would an investor be interested in purchasing a bond futures? (LO2)

20. **Internet.** Algorithmics is a world leader in risk management systems and a Canadian company. Go to **www.algorithmics.com/EN/careers**. Click on "Worldwide Opportunities" and read a couple of job descriptions. Summarize what skills are needed to be a financial risk management professional, such as a financial engineer. (LO1)

21. **Internet.** Go to the Industry Center of Yahoo Finance Web site at **biz.yahoo.com/ic/ind_index.html**. The "Processed & Packaged Goods" industry is made up of companies that buy commodities and package and/or transform them into food for retail customers. Review the list of companies (under "Industry Browser") in the industry and review the company profile of any firm of interest to you. Link to that company's home page, investor relations, and SEC filings. Review the latest 10K filing or annual report for management's discussion of risk management activities.
    a. What areas of risk does the firm manage with derivative contracts? (LO1)
    b. Given the company's products and the commodities they are derived from, what futures and options contracts would make most sense for hedging price risk? Review the list of futures and options contracts traded on exchanges. (See the menu "Currencies, Agricultural," etc., at **www.site-by-site.com/usa/optfut.htm**.) (LO2)

Solutions to Check Points

26.1 See Figure 26.4.

26.2 The farmer has a further loss of $3 a tonne ($590 − $587) and will be required to pay 50 × $3, or $150 to the exchange. The oil processor has a further profit of $3 a tonne ($590 − $587) and will receive $150 from the exchange for the 50 tonne contract. The farmer is now committed to delivering canola in March for $590 a tonne and the oil processor is committed to paying $590 a tonne.

26.3 You sell long-term bond futures with a delivery date of nine months. Suppose, for example, that you agree to deliver long-term bonds in 9 months at a price of 100. If interest rates fall, the price of the bond futures will rise to (say) 105. (Remember that when interest rates fall, bond prices rise.) In this case the profit that you make on your bond futures offsets the lower price that the firm is likely to receive on the sale of its own bonds. Conversely, if interest rates rise, the company will make a loss on its futures position but will receive a higher price for its own bonds.

26.4 The manager should enter a swap to pay an 8 percent fixed rate and receive LIBOR on notional principal of $100 million. The cash flows will then rise in tandem with the LIBOR rate:

	LIBOR Rate		
	7.5%	**8.0%**	**7.5%**
Interest paid on floating-rate bonds (= LIBOR × $100 million)	$7,500,000	$8,000,000	$8,500,000
+ Cash payment on swap (= [LIBOR − .08] × notional principal of $100 million)	−500,000	0	+500,000
Total payment	$7,500,000	$8,000,000	$8,500,000

The diagram describing the cash flows of each party to the swap is as follows:

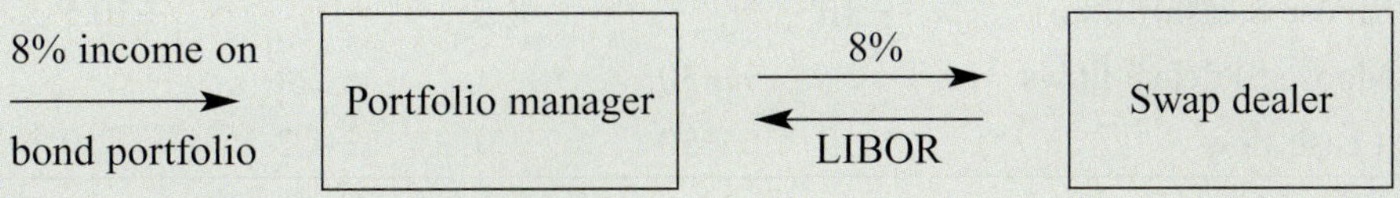

The manager nets a cash flow proportional to the LIBOR rate.

FIGURE 26.4
Diagrams for Check Point 26.1.

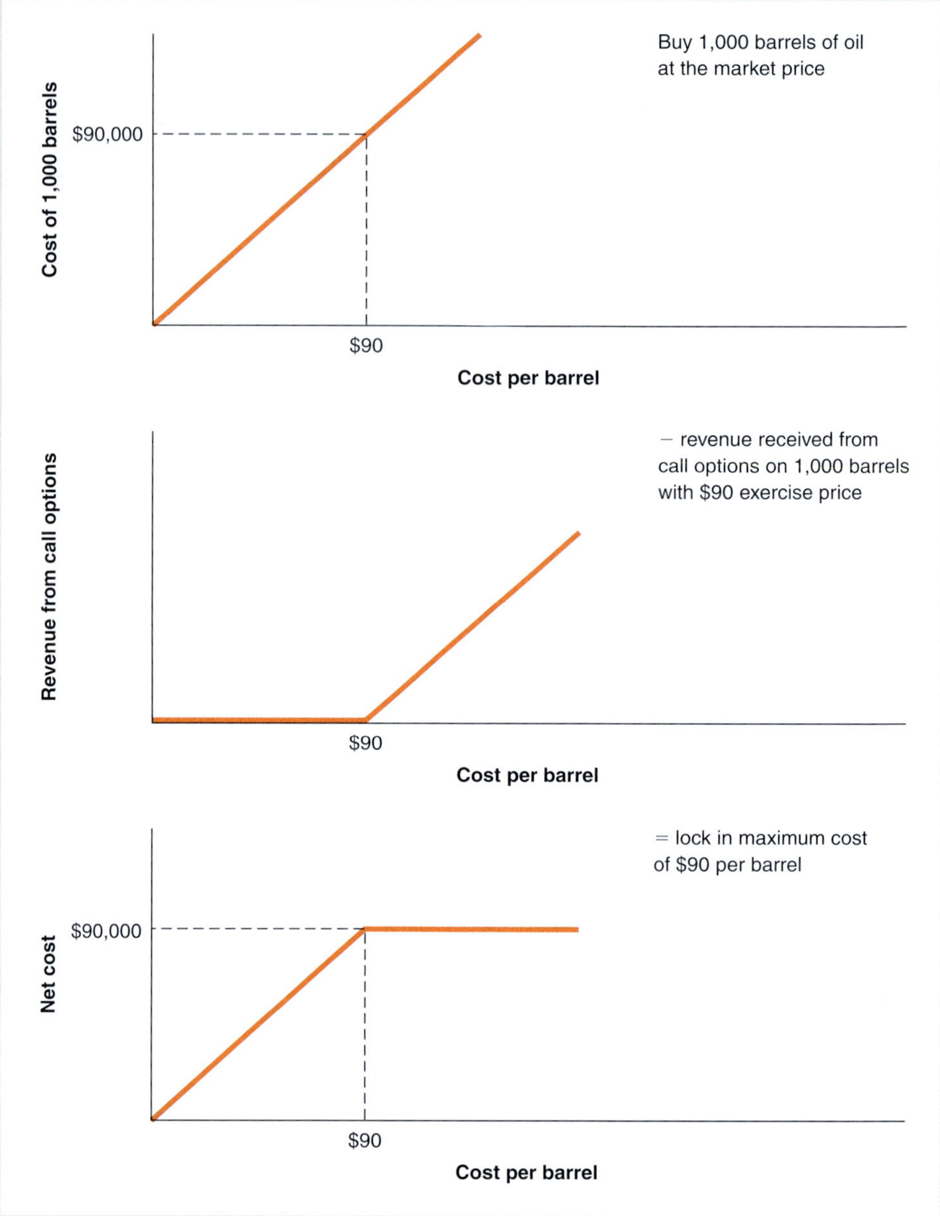

26.5 The following table shows revised cash flows from Moose's dollar loan and currency swap ($ millions):

	Year 0		Years 1–4		Year 5	
	$	SFr	$	SFr	$	SFr
1. Issue dollar loan	+10		−.5		−10.5	
2. Arrange currency swap						
a. Moose $ cash flows	−10		+.5		+10.5	
b. Moose SFr cash flows		+30		−2.4		−32.4
3. Net cash flow	0	+30	0	−1.2	0	−32.4

Notice that in exchange for $10 million today the bank is now prepared to pay SFr30 million. Since the Swiss interest rate is now 8 percent, the bank will expect to earn .08 × 30 = SFr2.4 million interest on its Swiss franc outlay.

APPENDIX A: PRESENT VALUE TABLES

TABLE A.1
Future value of $1 after t periods $= (1 + r)^t$

Number of Periods	Interest Rate per Period														
	1%	2%	3%	4%	5%	6%	7%	8%	9%	10%	11%	12%	13%	14%	15%
1	1.0100	1.0200	1.0300	1.0400	1.0500	1.0600	1.0700	1.0800	1.0900	1.1000	1.1100	1.1200	1.1300	1.1400	1.1500
2	1.0201	1.0404	1.0609	1.0816	1.1025	1.1236	1.1449	1.1664	1.1881	1.2100	1.2321	1.2544	1.2769	1.2996	1.3225
3	1.0303	1.0612	1.0927	1.1249	1.1576	1.1910	1.2250	1.2597	1.2950	1.3310	1.3676	1.4049	1.4429	1.4815	1.5209
4	1.0406	1.0824	1.1255	1.1699	1.2155	1.2625	1.3108	1.3605	1.4116	1.4641	1.5181	1.5735	1.6305	1.6890	1.7490
5	1.0510	1.1041	1.1593	1.2167	1.2763	1.3382	1.4026	1.4693	1.5386	1.6105	1.6851	1.7623	1.8424	1.9254	2.0114
6	1.0615	1.1262	1.1941	1.2653	1.3401	1.4185	1.5007	1.5869	1.6771	1.7716	1.8704	1.9738	2.0820	2.1950	2.3131
7	1.0721	1.1487	1.2299	1.3159	1.4071	1.5036	1.6058	1.7138	1.8280	1.9487	2.0762	2.2107	2.3526	2.5023	2.6600
8	1.0829	1.1717	1.2668	1.3686	1.4775	1.5938	1.7182	1.8509	1.9926	2.1436	2.3045	2.4760	2.6584	2.8526	3.0590
9	1.0937	1.1951	1.3048	1.4233	1.5513	1.6895	1.8385	1.9990	2.1719	2.3579	2.5580	2.7731	3.0040	3.2519	3.5179
10	1.1046	1.2190	1.3439	1.4802	1.6289	1.7908	1.9672	2.1589	2.3674	2.5937	2.8394	3.1058	3.3946	3.7072	4.0456
11	1.1157	1.2434	1.3842	1.5395	1.7103	1.8983	2.1049	2.3316	2.5804	2.8531	3.1518	3.4785	3.8359	4.2262	4.6524
12	1.1268	1.2682	1.4258	1.6010	1.7959	2.0122	2.2522	2.5182	2.8127	3.1384	3.4985	3.8960	4.3345	4.8179	5.3503
13	1.1381	1.2936	1.4685	1.6651	1.8856	2.1329	2.4098	2.7196	3.0658	3.4523	3.8833	4.3635	4.8980	5.4924	6.1528
14	1.1495	1.3195	1.5126	1.7317	1.9799	2.2609	2.5785	2.9372	3.3417	3.7975	4.3104	4.8871	5.5348	6.2613	7.0757
15	1.1610	1.3459	1.5580	1.8009	2.0789	2.3966	2.7590	3.1722	3.6425	4.1772	4.7846	5.4736	6.2543	7.1379	8.1371
16	1.1726	1.3728	1.6047	1.8730	2.1829	2.5404	2.9522	3.4259	3.9703	4.5950	5.3109	6.1304	7.0673	8.1372	9.3576
17	1.1843	1.4002	1.6528	1.9479	2.2920	2.6928	3.1588	3.7000	4.3276	5.0545	5.8951	6.8660	7.9861	9.2765	10.7613
18	1.1961	1.4282	1.7024	2.0258	2.4066	2.8543	3.3799	3.9960	4.7171	5.5599	6.5436	7.6900	9.0243	10.5752	12.3755
19	1.2081	1.4568	1.7535	2.1068	2.5270	3.0256	3.6165	4.3157	5.1417	6.1159	7.2633	8.6128	10.1974	12.0557	14.2318
20	1.2202	1.4859	1.8061	2.1911	2.6533	3.2071	3.8697	4.6610	5.6044	6.7275	8.0623	9.6463	11.5231	13.7435	16.3665
25	1.2824	1.6406	2.0938	2.6658	3.3864	4.2919	5.4274	6.8485	8.6231	10.8347	13.5855	17.0001	21.2305	26.4619	32.9190
30	1.3478	1.8114	2.4273	3.2434	4.3219	5.7435	7.6123	10.0627	13.2677	17.4494	22.8923	29.9599	39.1159	50.9502	66.2118
40	1.4889	2.2080	3.2620	4.8010	7.0400	10.2857	14.9745	21.7245	31.4094	45.2593	65.0009	93.0510	132.7816	188.8835	267.8635
50	1.6446	2.6916	4.3839	7.1067	11.4674	18.4202	29.4570	46.9016	74.3575	117.3909	184.5648	289.0022	450.7359	700.2330	1083.657

TABLE A.1

Future value of $1 after t periods = $(1 + r)^t$ (Concluded)

Number of Periods	Interest Rate per Period														
	16%	17%	18%	19%	20%	21%	22%	23%	24%	25%	26%	27%	28%	29%	30%
1	1.1600	1.1700	1.1800	1.1900	1.2000	1.2100	1.2200	1.2300	1.2400	1.2500	1.2600	1.2700	1.2800	1.2900	1.3000
2	1.3456	1.3689	1.3924	1.4161	1.4400	1.4641	1.4884	1.5129	1.5376	1.5625	1.5876	1.6129	1.6384	1.6641	1.6900
3	1.5609	1.6016	1.6430	1.6852	1.7280	1.7716	1.8158	1.8609	1.9066	1.9531	2.0004	2.0484	2.0972	2.1467	2.1970
4	1.8106	1.8739	1.9388	2.0053	2.0736	2.1436	2.2153	2.2889	2.3642	2.4414	2.5205	2.6014	2.6844	2.7692	2.8561
5	2.1003	2.1924	2.2878	2.3864	2.4883	2.5937	2.7027	2.8153	2.9316	3.0518	3.1758	3.3038	3.4360	3.5723	3.7129
6	2.4364	2.5652	2.6996	2.8398	2.9860	3.1384	3.2973	3.4628	3.6352	3.8147	4.0015	4.1959	4.3980	4.6083	4.8268
7	2.8262	3.0012	3.1855	3.3793	3.5832	3.7975	4.0227	4.2593	4.5077	4.7684	5.0419	5.3288	5.6295	5.9447	6.2749
8	3.2784	3.5115	3.7589	4.0214	4.2998	4.5950	4.9077	5.2389	5.5895	5.9605	6.3528	6.7675	7.2058	7.6686	8.1573
9	3.8030	4.1084	4.4355	4.7854	5.1598	5.5599	5.9874	6.4439	6.9310	7.4506	8.0045	8.5948	9.2234	9.8925	10.6045
10	4.4114	4.8068	5.2338	5.6947	6.1917	6.7275	7.3046	7.9259	8.5944	9.3132	10.0857	10.9153	11.8059	12.7614	13.7858
11	5.1173	5.6240	6.1759	6.7767	7.4301	8.1403	8.9117	9.7489	10.6571	11.6415	12.7080	13.8625	15.1116	16.4622	17.9216
12	5.9360	6.5801	7.2876	8.0642	8.9161	9.8497	10.8722	11.9912	13.2148	14.5519	16.0120	17.6053	19.3428	21.2362	23.2981
13	6.8858	7.6987	8.5994	9.5964	10.6993	11.9182	13.2641	14.7491	16.3863	18.1899	20.1752	22.3588	24.7588	27.3947	30.2875
14	7.9875	9.0075	10.1472	11.4198	12.8392	14.4210	16.1822	18.1414	20.3191	22.7374	25.4207	28.3957	31.6913	35.3391	39.3738
15	9.2655	10.5387	11.9737	13.5895	15.4070	17.4494	19.7423	22.3140	25.1956	28.4217	32.0301	36.0625	40.5648	45.5875	51.1859
16	10.7480	12.3303	14.1290	16.1715	18.4884	21.1138	24.0856	27.4462	31.2426	35.5271	40.3579	45.7994	51.9230	58.8079	66.5417
17	12.4677	14.4265	16.6722	19.2441	22.1861	25.5477	29.3844	33.7588	38.7408	44.4089	50.8510	58.1652	66.4614	75.8621	86.5042
18	14.4625	16.8790	19.6733	22.9005	26.6233	30.9127	35.8490	41.5233	48.0386	55.5112	64.0722	73.8698	85.0706	97.8622	112.4554
19	16.7765	19.7484	23.2144	27.2516	31.9480	37.4043	43.7358	51.0737	59.5679	69.3889	80.7310	93.8147	108.8904	126.2422	146.1920
20	19.4608	23.1056	27.3930	32.4294	38.3376	45.2593	53.3576	62.8206	73.8641	86.7362	101.7211	119.1446	139.3797	162.8524	190.0496
25	40.8742	50.6578	62.6686	77.3881	95.3962	117.3909	144.2101	176.8593	216.5420	264.6978	323.0454	393.6344	478.9049	581.7585	705.6410
30	85.8499	111.0647	143.3706	184.6753	237.3763	304.4816	389.7579	497.9129	634.8199	807.7936	1,025.927	1,300.504	1,645.505	2,078.219	2,619.996
40	378.7212	533.8687	750.3783	1,051.668	1,469.772	2,048.400	2,847.038	3,946.430	5,455.913	7,523.164	10,347.18	14,195.44	19,426.69	26,520.91	36,118.86
50	1,670.704	2,566.215	3,927.357	5,988.914	9,100.438	13,780.61	20,796.56	31,279.20	46,890.43	70,064.92	104,358.4	154,948.0	229,349.9	338,443.0	497,929.2

(E.g., if the interest rate is 10 percent per year, the investment of $1 today will be worth $1.611 at year 5.)

TABLE A.2

Discount factors: Present value of $1 to be received after t periods = $1/(1+r)^t$

Number	Interest Rate per Period														
of Periods	1%	2%	3%	4%	5%	6%	7%	8%	9%	10%	11%	12%	13%	14%	15%
1	0.9901	0.9804	0.9709	0.9615	0.9524	0.9434	0.9346	0.9259	0.9174	0.9091	0.9009	0.8929	0.8850	0.8772	0.8696
2	0.9803	0.9612	0.9426	0.9246	0.9070	0.8900	0.8734	0.8573	0.8417	0.8264	0.8116	0.7972	0.7831	0.7695	0.7561
3	0.9706	0.9423	0.9151	0.8890	0.8638	0.8396	0.8163	0.7938	0.7722	0.7513	0.7312	0.7118	0.6931	0.6750	0.6575
4	0.9610	0.9238	0.8885	0.8548	0.8227	0.7921	0.7629	0.7350	0.7084	0.6830	0.6587	0.6355	0.6133	0.5921	0.5718
5	0.9515	0.9057	0.8626	0.8219	0.7835	0.7473	0.7130	0.6806	0.6499	0.6209	0.5935	0.5674	0.5428	0.5194	0.4972
6	0.9420	0.8880	0.8375	0.7903	0.7462	0.7050	0.6663	0.6302	0.5963	0.5645	0.5346	0.5066	0.4803	0.4556	0.4323
7	0.9327	0.8706	0.8131	0.7599	0.7107	0.6651	0.6227	0.5835	0.5470	0.5132	0.4817	0.4523	0.4251	0.3996	0.3759
8	0.9235	0.8535	0.7894	0.7307	0.6768	0.6274	0.5820	0.5403	0.5019	0.4665	0.4339	0.4039	0.3762	0.3506	0.3269
9	0.9143	0.8368	0.7664	0.7026	0.6446	0.5919	0.5439	0.5002	0.4604	0.4241	0.3909	0.3606	0.3329	0.3075	0.2843
10	0.9053	0.8203	0.7441	0.6756	0.6139	0.5584	0.5083	0.4632	0.4224	0.3855	0.3522	0.3220	0.2946	0.2697	0.2472
11	0.8963	0.8043	0.7224	0.6496	0.5847	0.5268	0.4751	0.4289	0.3875	0.3505	0.3173	0.2875	0.2607	0.2366	0.2149
12	0.8874	0.7885	0.7014	0.6246	0.5568	0.4970	0.4440	0.3971	0.3555	0.3186	0.2858	0.2567	0.2307	0.2076	0.1869
13	0.8787	0.7730	0.6810	0.6006	0.5303	0.4688	0.4150	0.3677	0.3262	0.2897	0.2575	0.2292	0.2042	0.1821	0.1625
14	0.8700	0.7579	0.6611	0.5775	0.5051	0.4423	0.3878	0.3405	0.2992	0.2633	0.2320	0.2046	0.1807	0.1597	0.1413
15	0.8613	0.7430	0.6419	0.5553	0.4810	0.4173	0.3624	0.3152	0.2745	0.2394	0.2090	0.1827	0.1599	0.1401	0.1229
16	0.8528	0.7284	0.6232	0.5339	0.4581	0.3936	0.3387	0.2919	0.2519	0.2176	0.1883	0.1631	0.1415	0.1229	0.1069
17	0.8444	0.7142	0.6050	0.5134	0.4363	0.3714	0.3166	0.2703	0.2311	0.1978	0.1696	0.1456	0.1252	0.1078	0.0929
18	0.8360	0.7002	0.5874	0.4936	0.4155	0.3503	0.2959	0.2502	0.2120	0.1799	0.1528	0.1300	0.1108	0.0946	0.0808
19	0.8277	0.6864	0.5703	0.4746	0.3957	0.3305	0.2765	0.2317	0.1945	0.1635	0.1377	0.1161	0.0981	0.0829	0.0703
20	0.8195	0.6730	0.5537	0.4564	0.3769	0.3118	0.2584	0.2145	0.1784	0.1486	0.1240	0.1037	0.0868	0.0728	0.0611
25	0.7798	0.6095	0.4776	0.3751	0.2953	0.2330	0.1842	0.1460	0.1160	0.0923	0.0736	0.0588	0.0471	0.0378	0.0304
30	0.7419	0.5521	0.4120	0.3083	0.2314	0.1741	0.1314	0.0994	0.0754	0.0573	0.0437	0.0334	0.0256	0.0196	0.0151
40	0.6717	0.4529	0.3066	0.2083	0.1420	0.0972	0.0668	0.0460	0.0318	0.0221	0.0154	0.0107	0.0075	0.0053	0.0037
50	0.6080	0.3715	0.2281	0.1407	0.0872	0.0543	0.0339	0.0213	0.0134	0.0085	0.0054	0.0035	0.0022	0.0014	0.0009

TABLE A.2

Discount factors: Present value of $1 to be received after t periods = $1/(1+r)^t$ (Concluded)

Number of Periods	Interest Rate per Period														
	16%	17%	18%	19%	20%	21%	22%	23%	24%	25%	26%	27%	28%	29%	30%
1	0.8621	0.8547	0.8475	0.8403	0.8333	0.8264	0.8197	0.8130	0.8065	0.8000	0.7937	0.7874	0.7813	0.7752	0.7692
2	0.7432	0.7305	0.7182	0.7062	0.6944	0.6830	0.6719	0.6610	0.6504	0.6400	0.6299	0.6200	0.6104	0.6009	0.5917
3	0.6407	0.6244	0.6086	0.5934	0.5787	0.5645	0.5507	0.5374	0.5245	0.5120	0.4999	0.4882	0.4768	0.4658	0.4552
4	0.5523	0.5337	0.5158	0.4987	0.4823	0.4665	0.4514	0.4369	0.4230	0.4096	0.3968	0.3844	0.3725	0.3611	0.3501
5	0.4761	0.4561	0.4371	0.4190	0.4019	0.3855	0.3700	0.3552	0.3411	0.3277	0.3149	0.3027	0.2910	0.2799	0.2693
6	0.4104	0.3898	0.3704	0.3521	0.3349	0.3186	0.3033	0.2888	0.2751	0.2621	0.2499	0.2383	0.2274	0.2170	0.2072
7	0.3538	0.3332	0.3139	0.2959	0.2791	0.2633	0.2486	0.2348	0.2218	0.2097	0.1983	0.1877	0.1776	0.1682	0.1594
8	0.3050	0.2848	0.2660	0.2487	0.2326	0.2176	0.2038	0.1909	0.1789	0.1678	0.1574	0.1478	0.1388	0.1304	0.1226
9	0.2630	0.2434	0.2255	0.2090	0.1938	0.1799	0.1670	0.1552	0.1443	0.1342	0.1249	0.1164	0.1084	0.1011	0.0943
10	0.2267	0.2080	0.1911	0.1756	0.1615	0.1486	0.1369	0.1262	0.1164	0.1074	0.0992	0.0916	0.0847	0.0784	0.0725
11	0.1954	0.1778	0.1619	0.1476	0.1346	0.1228	0.1122	0.1026	0.0938	0.0859	0.0787	0.0721	0.0662	0.0607	0.0558
12	0.1685	0.1520	0.1372	0.1240	0.1122	0.1015	0.0920	0.0834	0.0757	0.0687	0.0625	0.0568	0.0517	0.0471	0.0429
13	0.1452	0.1299	0.1163	0.1042	0.0935	0.0839	0.0754	0.0678	0.0610	0.0550	0.0496	0.0447	0.0404	0.0365	0.0330
14	0.1252	0.1110	0.0985	0.0876	0.0779	0.0693	0.0618	0.0551	0.0492	0.0440	0.0393	0.0352	0.0316	0.0283	0.0254
15	0.1079	0.0949	0.0835	0.0736	0.0649	0.0573	0.0507	0.0448	0.0397	0.0352	0.0312	0.0277	0.0247	0.0219	0.0195
16	0.0930	0.0811	0.0708	0.0618	0.0541	0.0474	0.0415	0.0364	0.0320	0.0281	0.0248	0.0218	0.0193	0.0170	0.0150
17	0.0802	0.0693	0.0600	0.0520	0.0451	0.0391	0.0340	0.0296	0.0258	0.0225	0.0197	0.0172	0.0150	0.0132	0.0116
18	0.0691	0.0592	0.0508	0.0437	0.0376	0.0323	0.0279	0.0241	0.0208	0.0180	0.0156	0.0135	0.0118	0.0102	0.0089
19	0.0596	0.0506	0.0431	0.0367	0.0313	0.0267	0.0229	0.0196	0.0168	0.0144	0.0124	0.0107	0.0092	0.0079	0.0068
20	0.0514	0.0433	0.0365	0.0308	0.0261	0.0221	0.0187	0.0159	0.0135	0.0115	0.0098	0.0084	0.0072	0.0061	0.0053
25	0.0245	0.0197	0.0160	0.0129	0.0105	0.0085	0.0069	0.0057	0.0046	0.0038	0.0031	0.0025	0.0021	0.0017	0.0014
30	0.0116	0.0090	0.0070	0.0054	0.0042	0.0033	0.0026	0.0020	0.0016	0.0012	0.0010	0.0008	0.0006	0.0005	0.0004
40	0.0026	0.0019	0.0013	0.0010	0.0007	0.0005	0.0004	0.0003	0.0002	0.0001	0.0001	0.0001	0.0001	0.0000	0.0000
50	0.0006	0.0004	0.0003	0.0002	0.0001	0.0001	0.0000	0.0000	0.0000	0.0000	0.0000	0.0000	0.0000	0.0000	0.0000

(E.g., if the interest rate is 10 percent per year, the present value of $1 received at year 5 is $.621.)

TABLE A.3

Annuity table: Present value of $1 per year for each of t periods $= 1/r - 1/[r(1+r)^t]$

Number of Periods	Interest Rate per Period														
	1%	2%	3%	4%	5%	6%	7%	8%	9%	10%	11%	12%	13%	14%	15%
1	0.9901	0.9804	0.9709	0.9615	0.9524	0.9434	0.9346	0.9259	0.9174	0.9091	0.9009	0.8929	0.8850	0.8772	0.8696
2	1.9704	1.9416	1.9135	1.8861	1.8594	1.8334	1.8080	1.7833	1.7591	1.7355	1.7125	1.6901	1.6681	1.6467	1.6257
3	2.9410	2.8839	2.8286	2.7751	2.7232	2.6730	2.6243	2.5771	2.5313	2.4869	2.4437	2.4018	2.3612	2.3216	2.2832
4	3.9020	3.8077	3.7171	3.6299	3.5460	3.4651	3.3872	3.3121	3.2397	3.1699	3.1024	3.0373	2.9745	2.9137	2.8550
5	4.8534	4.7135	4.5797	4.4518	4.3295	4.2124	4.1002	3.9927	3.8897	3.7908	3.6959	3.6048	3.5172	3.4331	3.3522
6	5.7955	5.6014	5.4172	5.2421	5.0757	4.9173	4.7665	4.6229	4.4859	4.3553	4.2305	4.1114	3.9975	3.8887	3.7845
7	6.7282	6.4720	6.2303	6.0021	5.7864	5.5824	5.3893	5.2064	5.0330	4.8684	4.7122	4.5638	4.4226	4.2883	4.1604
8	7.6517	7.3255	7.0197	6.7327	6.4632	6.2098	5.9713	5.7466	5.5348	5.3349	5.1461	4.9676	4.7988	4.6389	4.4873
9	8.5660	8.1622	7.7861	7.4353	7.1078	6.8017	6.5152	6.2469	5.9952	5.7590	5.5370	5.3282	5.1317	4.9464	4.7716
10	9.4713	8.9826	8.5302	8.1109	7.7217	7.3601	7.0236	6.7101	6.4177	6.1446	5.8892	5.6502	5.4262	5.2161	5.0188
11	10.3676	9.7868	9.2526	8.7605	8.3064	7.8869	7.4987	7.1390	6.8052	6.4951	6.2065	5.9377	5.6869	5.4527	5.2337
12	11.2551	10.5753	9.9540	9.3851	8.8633	8.3838	7.9427	7.5361	7.1607	6.8137	6.4924	6.1944	5.9176	5.6603	5.4206
13	12.1337	11.3484	10.6350	9.9856	9.3936	8.8527	8.3577	7.9038	7.4869	7.1034	6.7499	6.4235	6.1218	5.8424	5.5831
14	13.0037	12.1062	11.2961	10.5631	9.8986	9.2950	8.7455	8.2442	7.7862	7.3667	6.9819	6.6282	6.3025	6.0021	5.7245
15	13.8651	12.8493	11.9379	11.1184	10.3797	9.7122	9.1079	8.5595	8.0607	7.6061	7.1909	6.8109	6.4624	6.1422	5.8474
16	14.7179	13.5777	12.5611	11.6523	10.8378	10.1059	9.4466	8.8514	8.3126	7.8237	7.3792	6.9740	6.6039	6.2651	5.9542
17	15.5623	14.2919	13.1661	12.1657	11.2741	10.4773	9.7632	9.1216	8.5436	8.0216	7.5488	7.1196	6.7291	6.3729	6.0472
18	16.3983	14.9920	13.7535	12.6593	11.6896	10.8276	10.0591	9.3719	8.7556	8.2014	7.7016	7.2497	6.8399	6.4674	6.1280
19	17.2260	15.6785	14.3238	13.1339	12.0853	11.1581	10.3356	9.6036	8.9501	8.3649	7.8393	7.3658	6.9380	6.5504	6.1982
20	18.0456	16.3514	14.8775	13.5903	12.4622	11.4699	10.5940	9.8181	9.1285	8.5136	7.9633	7.4694	7.0248	6.6231	6.2593
25	22.0232	19.5235	17.4131	15.6221	14.0939	12.7834	11.6536	10.6748	9.8226	9.0770	8.4217	7.8431	7.3300	6.8729	6.4641
30	25.8077	22.3965	19.6004	17.2920	15.3725	13.7648	12.4090	11.2578	10.2737	9.4269	8.6938	8.0552	7.4957	7.0027	6.5660
40	32.8347	27.3555	23.1148	19.7928	17.1591	15.0463	13.3317	11.9246	10.7574	9.7791	8.9511	8.2438	7.6344	7.1050	6.6418
50	39.1961	31.4236	25.7298	21.4822	18.2559	15.7619	13.8007	12.2335	10.9617	9.9148	9.0417	8.3045	7.6752	7.1327	6.6605

TABLE A.3

Annuity table: Present value of $1 per year for each of t periods $= 1/r - 1/[r(1+r)^t]$ (Concluded)

Number of Periods	Interest Rate per Period														
	16%	17%	18%	19%	20%	21%	22%	23%	24%	25%	26%	27%	28%	29%	30%
1	0.8621	0.8547	0.8475	0.8403	0.8333	0.8264	0.8197	0.8130	0.8065	0.8000	0.7937	0.7874	0.7813	0.7752	0.7692
2	1.6052	1.5852	1.5656	1.5465	1.5278	1.5095	1.4915	1.4740	1.4568	1.4400	1.4235	1.4074	1.3916	1.3761	1.3609
3	2.2459	2.2096	2.1743	2.1399	2.1065	2.0739	2.0422	2.0114	1.9813	1.9520	1.9234	1.8956	1.8684	1.8420	1.8161
4	2.7982	2.7432	2.6901	2.6386	2.5887	2.5404	2.4936	2.4483	2.4043	2.3616	2.3202	2.2800	2.2410	2.2031	2.1662
5	3.2743	3.1993	3.1272	3.0576	2.9906	2.9260	2.8636	2.8035	2.7454	2.6893	2.6351	2.5827	2.5320	2.4830	2.4356
6	3.6847	3.5892	3.4976	3.4098	3.3255	3.2446	3.1669	3.0923	3.0205	2.9514	2.8850	2.8210	2.7594	2.7000	2.6427
7	4.0386	3.9224	3.8115	3.7057	3.6046	3.5079	3.4155	3.3270	3.2423	3.1611	3.0833	3.0087	2.9370	2.8682	2.8021
8	4.3436	4.2072	4.0776	3.9544	3.8372	3.7256	3.6193	3.5179	3.4212	3.3289	3.2407	3.1564	3.0758	2.9986	2.9247
9	4.6065	4.4506	4.3030	4.1633	4.0310	3.9054	3.7863	3.6731	3.5655	3.4631	3.3657	3.2728	3.1842	3.0997	3.0190
10	4.8332	4.6586	4.4941	4.3389	4.1925	4.0541	3.9232	3.7993	3.6819	3.5705	3.4648	3.3644	3.2689	3.1781	3.0915
11	5.0286	4.8364	4.6560	4.4865	4.3271	4.1769	4.0354	3.9018	3.7757	3.6564	3.5435	3.4365	3.3351	3.2388	3.1473
12	5.1971	4.9884	4.7932	4.6105	4.4392	4.2784	4.1274	3.9852	3.8514	3.7251	3.6059	3.4933	3.3868	3.2859	3.1903
13	5.3423	5.1183	4.9095	4.7147	4.5327	4.3624	4.2028	4.0530	3.9124	3.7801	3.6555	3.5381	3.4272	3.3224	3.2233
14	5.4675	5.2293	5.0081	4.8023	4.6106	4.4317	4.2646	4.1082	3.9616	3.8241	3.6949	3.5733	3.4587	3.3507	3.2487
15	5.5755	5.3242	5.0916	4.8759	4.6755	4.4890	4.3152	4.1530	4.0013	3.8593	3.7261	3.6010	3.4834	3.3726	3.2682
16	5.6685	5.4053	5.1624	4.9377	4.7296	4.5364	4.3567	4.1894	4.0333	3.8874	3.7509	3.6228	3.5026	3.3896	3.2832
17	5.7487	5.4746	5.2223	4.9897	4.7746	4.5755	4.3908	4.2190	4.0591	3.9099	3.7705	3.6400	3.5177	3.4028	3.2948
18	5.8178	5.5339	5.2732	5.0333	4.8122	4.6079	4.4187	4.2431	4.0799	3.9279	3.7861	3.6536	3.5294	3.4130	3.3037
19	5.8775	5.5845	5.3162	5.0700	4.8435	4.6346	4.4415	4.2627	4.0967	3.9424	3.7985	3.6642	3.5386	3.4210	3.3105
20	5.9288	5.6278	5.3527	5.1009	4.8696	4.6567	4.4603	4.2786	4.1103	3.9539	3.8083	3.6726	3.5458	3.4271	3.3158
25	6.0971	5.7662	5.4669	5.1951	4.9476	4.7213	4.5139	4.3232	4.1474	3.9849	3.8342	3.6943	3.5640	3.4423	3.3286
30	6.1772	5.8294	5.5168	5.2347	4.9789	4.7463	4.5338	4.3391	4.1601	3.9950	3.8424	3.7009	3.5693	3.4466	3.3321
40	6.2335	5.8713	5.5482	5.2582	4.9966	4.7596	4.5439	4.3467	4.1659	3.9995	3.8458	3.7034	3.5712	3.4481	3.3332
50	6.2463	5.8801	5.5541	5.2623	4.9995	4.7616	4.5452	4.3477	4.1666	3.9999	3.8461	3.7037	3.5714	3.4483	3.3333

(E.g., if the interest rate is 10 percent per year, the present value of $1 received in each of the next 5 years is $3.791.)

TABLE A.4

Annuity table: Future value of $1 per year for each of t periods = $[(1 + r)^t - 1]/r$

Number of Periods	Interest Rate per Period														
	1%	2%	3%	4%	5%	6%	7%	8%	9%	10%	11%	12%	13%	14%	15%
1	1.0000	1.0000	1.0000	1.0000	1.0000	1.0000	1.0000	1.0000	1.0000	1.0000	1.0000	1.0000	1.0000	1.0000	1.0000
2	2.0100	2.0200	2.0300	2.0400	2.0500	2.0600	2.0700	2.0800	2.0900	2.1000	2.1100	2.1200	2.1300	2.1400	2.1500
3	3.0301	3.0604	3.0909	3.1216	3.1525	3.1836	3.2149	3.2464	3.2781	3.3100	3.3421	3.3744	3.4069	3.4396	3.4725
4	4.0604	4.1216	4.1836	4.2465	4.3101	4.3746	4.4399	4.5061	4.5731	4.6410	4.7097	4.7793	4.8498	4.9211	4.9934
5	5.1010	5.2040	5.3091	5.4163	5.5256	5.6371	5.7507	5.8666	5.9847	6.1051	6.2278	6.3528	6.4803	6.6101	6.7424
6	6.1520	6.3081	6.4684	6.6330	6.8019	6.9753	7.1533	7.3359	7.5233	7.7156	7.9129	8.1152	8.3227	8.5355	8.7537
7	7.2135	7.4343	7.6625	7.8983	8.1420	8.3938	8.6540	8.9228	9.2004	9.4872	9.7833	10.0890	10.4047	10.7305	11.0668
8	8.2857	8.5830	8.8923	9.2142	9.5491	9.8975	10.2598	10.6366	11.0285	11.4359	11.8594	12.2997	12.7573	13.2328	13.7268
9	9.3685	9.7546	10.1591	10.5828	11.0266	11.4913	11.9780	12.4876	13.0210	13.5795	14.1640	14.7757	15.4157	16.0853	16.7858
10	10.4622	10.9497	11.4639	12.0061	12.5779	13.1808	13.8164	14.4866	15.1929	15.9374	16.7220	17.5487	18.4197	19.3373	20.3037
11	11.5668	12.1687	12.8078	13.4864	14.2068	14.9716	15.7836	16.6455	17.5603	18.5312	19.5614	20.6546	21.8143	23.0445	24.3493
12	12.6825	13.4121	14.1920	15.0258	15.9171	16.8699	17.8885	18.9771	20.1407	21.3843	22.7132	24.1331	25.6502	27.2707	29.0017
13	13.8093	14.6803	15.6178	16.6268	17.7130	18.8821	20.1406	21.4953	22.9534	24.5227	26.2116	28.0291	29.9847	32.0887	34.3519
14	14.9474	15.9739	17.0863	18.2919	19.5986	21.0151	22.5505	24.2149	26.0192	27.9750	30.0949	32.3926	34.8827	37.5811	40.5047
15	16.0969	17.2934	18.5989	20.0236	21.5786	23.2760	25.1290	27.1521	29.3609	31.7725	34.4054	37.2797	40.4175	43.8424	47.5804
16	17.2579	18.6393	20.1569	21.8245	23.6575	25.6725	27.8881	30.3243	33.0034	35.9497	39.1899	42.7533	46.6717	50.9804	55.7175
17	18.4304	20.0121	21.7616	23.6975	25.8404	28.2129	30.8402	33.7502	36.9737	40.5447	44.5008	48.8837	53.7391	59.1176	65.0751
18	19.6147	21.4123	23.4144	25.6454	28.1324	30.9057	33.9990	37.4502	41.3013	45.5992	50.3959	55.7497	61.7251	68.3941	75.8364
19	20.8109	22.8406	25.1169	27.6712	30.5390	33.7600	37.3790	41.4463	46.0185	51.1591	56.9395	63.4397	70.7494	78.9692	88.2118
20	22.0190	24.2974	26.8704	29.7781	33.0660	36.7856	40.9955	45.7620	51.1601	57.2750	64.2028	72.0524	80.9468	91.0249	102.4436
25	28.2432	32.0303	36.4593	41.6459	47.7271	54.8645	63.2490	73.1059	84.7009	98.3471	114.4133	133.3339	155.6196	181.8708	212.7930
30	34.7849	40.5681	47.5754	56.0849	66.4388	79.0582	94.4608	113.2832	136.3075	164.4940	199.0209	241.3327	293.1992	356.7868	434.7451
40	48.8864	60.4020	75.4013	95.0255	120.7998	154.7620	199.6351	259.0565	337.8824	442.5926	581.8261	767.0914	1,013.704	1,342.025	1,779.0903
50	64.4632	84.5794	112.7969	152.6671	209.3480	290.3359	406.5289	573.7702	815.0836	1,163.909	1,668.771	2,400.018	3,459.507	4,994.521	7,217.7163

TABLE A.4

Annuity table: Future value of $1 per year for each of t periods = $[(1+r)^t - 1]/r$ (Concluded)

Number of Periods	Interest Rate per Period														
	16%	17%	18%	19%	20%	21%	22%	23%	24%	25%	26%	27%	28%	29%	30%
1	1.0000	1.0000	1.0000	1.0000	1.0000	1.0000	1.0000	1.0000	1.0000	1.0000	1.0000	1.0000	1.0000	1.0000	1.0000
2	2.1600	2.1700	2.1800	2.1900	2.2000	2.2100	2.2200	2.2300	2.2400	2.2500	2.2600	2.2700	2.2800	2.2900	2.3000
3	3.5056	3.5389	3.5724	3.6061	3.6400	3.6741	3.7084	3.7429	3.7776	3.8125	3.8476	3.8829	3.9184	3.9541	3.9900
4	5.0665	5.1405	5.2154	5.2913	5.3680	5.4457	5.5242	5.6038	5.6842	5.7656	5.8480	5.9313	6.0156	6.1008	6.1870
5	6.8771	7.0144	7.1542	7.2966	7.4416	7.5892	7.7396	7.8926	8.0484	8.2070	8.3684	8.5327	8.6999	8.8700	9.0431
6	8.9775	9.2068	9.4420	9.6830	9.9299	10.1830	10.4423	10.7079	10.9801	11.2588	11.5442	11.8366	12.1359	12.4423	12.7560
7	11.4139	11.7720	12.1415	12.5227	12.9159	13.3214	13.7396	14.1708	14.6153	15.0735	15.5458	16.0324	16.5339	17.0506	17.5828
8	14.2401	14.7733	15.3270	15.9020	16.4991	17.1189	17.7623	18.4300	19.1229	19.8419	20.5876	21.3612	22.1634	22.9953	23.8577
9	17.5185	18.2847	19.0859	19.9234	20.7989	21.7139	22.6700	23.6690	24.7125	25.8023	26.9404	28.1287	29.3692	30.6639	32.0150
10	21.3215	22.3931	23.5213	24.7089	25.9587	27.2738	28.6574	30.1128	31.6434	33.2529	34.9449	36.7235	38.5926	40.5564	42.6195
11	25.7329	27.1999	28.7551	30.4035	32.1504	34.0013	35.9620	38.0388	40.2379	42.5661	45.0306	47.6388	50.3985	53.3178	56.4053
12	30.8502	32.8239	34.9311	37.1802	39.5805	42.1416	44.8737	47.7877	50.8950	54.2077	57.7386	61.5013	65.5100	69.7800	74.3270
13	36.7862	39.4040	42.2187	45.2445	48.4966	51.9913	55.7459	59.7788	64.1097	68.7596	73.7506	79.1066	84.8529	91.0161	97.6250
14	43.6720	47.1027	50.8180	54.8409	59.1959	63.9095	69.0100	74.5280	80.4961	86.9495	93.9258	101.4654	109.6117	118.4108	127.9125
15	51.6595	56.1101	60.9653	66.2607	72.0351	78.3305	85.1922	92.6694	100.8151	109.6868	119.3465	129.8611	141.3029	153.7500	167.2863
16	60.9250	66.6488	72.9390	79.8502	87.4421	95.7799	104.9345	114.9834	126.0108	138.1085	151.3766	165.9236	181.8677	199.3374	218.4722
17	71.6730	78.9792	87.0680	96.0218	105.9306	116.8937	129.0201	142.4295	157.2534	173.6357	191.7345	211.7230	233.7907	258.1453	285.0139
18	84.1407	93.4056	103.7403	115.2659	128.1167	142.4413	158.4045	176.1883	195.9942	218.0446	242.5855	269.8882	300.2521	334.0074	371.5180
19	98.6032	110.2846	123.4135	138.1664	154.7400	173.3540	194.2535	217.7116	244.0328	273.5558	306.6577	343.7580	385.3227	431.8696	483.9734
20	115.3797	130.0329	146.6280	165.4180	186.6880	210.7584	237.9893	268.7853	303.6006	342.9447	387.3887	437.5726	494.2131	558.1118	630.1655
25	249.2140	292.1049	342.6035	402.0425	471.9811	554.2422	650.9551	764.6054	898.0916	1,054.791	1,238.636	1,454.201	1,706.803	2,002.616	2,348.803
30	530.312	647.439	790.948	966.712	1,181.882	1,445.151	1,767.081	2,160.491	2,640.916	3,227.174	3,942.026	4,812.977	5,873.231	7,162.824	8,729.985
40	2,360.76	3,134.52	4,163.21	5,529.83	7,343.86	9,749.52	12,936.54	17,154.05	22,728.80	30,088.66	39,792.98	52,572.00	69,377.46	91,447.96	120,392.9
50	10,435.65	15,089.50	21,813.09	31,515.34	45,497.19	65,617.20	94,525.28	135,992.2	195,372.6	280,255.7	401,374.5	573,877.9	819,103.1	1,167,041	1,659,761

(E.g., if the interest rate is 10 percent per year, the future value of $1 received in each of the next 5 years is $6.105.)

APPENDIX B: ANSWERS TO SELECTED END-OF-CHAPTER PROBLEMS

CHAPTER 1

1. real, executive airplanes, brand names, financial, stock, investment, capital budgeting, financing
8. A. financial
   D. real
   F. financial
   G. real
14. The contingency arrangement aligns the interests of the lawyer and the client. More appropriate when client doesn't know the lawyer's skill.
16. Such a plan would burden them with a considerable personal risk tied to the fortunes of the firm.
17. Managers who are more securely entrenched in their positions are more able to pursue their own interests.

CHAPTER 2

3. Options markets, foreign exchange markets, futures markets, commodity markets, money market.
4. Buy shares in an exchange-traded fund or a mutual fund.
8. Look up the price of gold in commodity markets, and compare it to $2,500/6 = $416.67/ounce.
19. a. Find the rate of return available on other riskless investments, for example, 1-year-maturity Treasury bills.
    b. The opportunity cost is 20%, the same expected rate of return available on other investments of comparable risk. The sequester is expected to pay $115,000 on a $100,000 investment, a gain of $15,000. If the $100,000 was invested in the London Carbon Exchange, the expected payback is .2 × $100,000, or $20,000. The purchase of additional sequesters is not a worthwhile capital expenditure.

CHAPTER 3

1.

Assets		Liabilities and Shareholders' Equity	
Cash and cash equivalents	$ 10,000	Trade payable	$ 17,000
Trade receivables	22,000	Long-term debt	170,000
Inventory	200,000		
Store & property	100,000	Shareholders' equity	145,000
Total assets	$332,000	Liabilities and shareholders' equity	$332,000

5. b.

	AB	NF
Total tax	$16,291.92	$16,260.53
Average tax rate	27.15%	27.1%
Marginal tax rate	32%	34.5%

7.

Income:	**After-Tax**	**Tax Rate**
Interest	$847.50	43.5%
Dividends	$2,317.92	22.74%
Capital gain	$1,565	21.75%

9. Dividends paid in 2013 = $600,000
11. a. Book value = $1,000,000, Market value = $50,900,000
    b. Price per share = $25.45, Book value per share = $.50
12. a. EBIT = $2,500
    b. Net earnings = $1,300
    c. Cash flow from operating activities = $2,100
    d. Cash flow from assets = $1,200
20. a. 2011 equity = $470
       2012 equity = $680
    b. Net income = $310
    c. Depreciation = $80
    d. ΔNWC = $80
    e. Debt repaid = $110
    f. Cash flow from operations = $310
       Cash flow from assets = $10
    g. Cash flow to bondholders = $110 − $200 = −90
       Cash flow to shareholders = $100
24. Net working capital decreased by $420.
    Noncash net working capital decreased by $40.
26. Earnings per share in 2011 = $2.20
    Earnings per share in 2012 = $2.16
32. Price per share = $7,030,000/500,000 = $14.06

CHAPTER 4

1. a. Long-term debt ratio = .42
   b. Total debt ratio = .65
   c. Times interest earned = 3.75
   d. Cash coverage ratio = 7.42
   e. Current ratio = .74
   f. Quick ratio = .52
   g. Operating profit margin = NOPAT/sales = .135
   h. Inventory turnover = cost of sales/average inventories = 19.11
   i. Days sales in inventory = average inventories/daily cost of sales = 19.1
   j. Average collection period = average receivables/daily sales = 67.39 days
   k. ROE = net income/equity at start of year = .144
   l. ROA = NOPAT/assets at start of year = .065
   m. Payout ratio = .65
3. NOPAT = 1,311 + (1 − .303) × 685 = 1,788.4
   Average total capitalization = (15,954 + 16,742)/2 = 16,348
   EVA = 1,788.4 − 8.3% × 16,348 = 431.516
14. The current ratio is unaffected. The quick ratio falls.
16. Days in inventory = 2 days
18. a. Times interest earned = 1.25
    b. Cash coverage ratio = 1.5
    c. Fixed-payment cash-charge coverage ratio = 1.09
20. Asset turnover = .73, ROA = 3.65%

22. $\frac{\text{Book debt}}{\text{Market equity}} = \frac{.5}{2} = .25$

26. a. The shipping company
 b. Food Producer
 c. The paper mill
 d. The power company

CHAPTER 5

1. a. 46.32
2. a. 215.89
4. PV = $548.47
5. 5%, 8%, 0%
7. PV = $812.44
8. a. $t = 23.36$
9. a. 671.01
10. a. 1,448.66
11. 12.68%, 8.24%, 10.25%
12. 9.57%, 6%, 8%
13. $n = 9.01$ years
15. APR = 52%; EAR = 67.77%
22. a. EAR = 6.78%, APR = 6.57%, compounded monthly,
 b. PMT = 573.14
23. a. $r = 11.11\%$, b. $r = 1/(1 - d) - 1 = d/(1 - d)$
28. a. 277.41, b. 247.69
29. PV = $61,796.71
30. Monthly mortgage payment = $1,119.71.
 Balance remaining after 5 years is $157,215.
35. Real rate of interest is zero. Annual consumption = $15,000.
41. $n = 44.74$ months
42. The present value of your payments is $671. The present value of your receipts is $579. This is a bad deal.
55. a. The present value of the payoff is $1,228. This is a good deal.
 b. PV is $771. This is a bad deal.
58. $4,126.57
59. a. $408,334.38, b. $3,457.40
63. a. 4%, b. 8.16%, c. 10.24%
65. a. $79.38, b. $91.51, c. 4.854%,
 d. $\$91.51/(1.04854)^3 = \$79.38$
69. a. $261,139, b. $16,172
70. 18 years
71. Inflation = 1,099% per year
78. $1.188, $0.8418

CHAPTER 6

1. a. Coupon rate remains unchanged.
 b. Price will fall.
 c. Yield to maturity increases.
 d. Current yield increases.
3. Bond price = $1,142.86
4. Coupon rate = 8%, Current yield = 8.42%,
 Yield to maturity = 9.1185%
9. 15%
10. 12%
11. Rate of return on both bonds = 10%
13. a. Price will be $1,000.
 b. Rate of return = 1.82%
 c. Real return = −4.68%
14. b. Price = $939.20
15 c. 7.1796%
19. 20 years
21. a. Price = $634.34, b. 12.9882%
22. a. YTM today = 8.3%, YTM next year = 6.4978%
 b. Rate of return = 20.41%
26. a. 7.5% per year
 b. 7.63% per year
 c. 8.64% per year
27. 8.64% per year
33. Initial price = $974.33, New price = $954.9
37. a. 3.92%

CHAPTER 7

3. a. $66.67
 b. $66.67
 c. Dividend yield = 12%; capital gains yield = 0%; expected return = 12%
6. a. 14%
 b. $P_0 = \$24$
8. weak, semi-strong, strong, fundamental, technical
11. a. $DIV_1 = \$1.04$, $DIV_2 = \$1.0816$, $DIV_3 = \$1.1249$
 b. $P_0 = \$13$, c. $P_3 = (\$1.04)^4/(.12 - .04) = \$14.6232$
 d. Your payments are:

	Year 1	Year 2	Year 3
DIV	1.04	1.0816	1.1249
Sales price			14.6232
Total cash flow	1.04	1.0816	15.7481
PV of cash flow	0.9286	0.8622	11.2092
Sum of PV of cash flow = $13			

13. a. $P_0 = \$31.50$, b. $P_0 = \$45$, c. $P_0 = \$14.25$
15. a. 9.26%, b. 3.74%, c. 12.5%
18. a. In each case, $P_0 = \$33.33$
 b. (1) Reinvest at 0%: $P_0 = \$33.33$, PVGO = 0
 (2) Reinvest at 40%: $P_0 = \$42.86$, PVGO = $9.53
 (3) Reinvest at 60%: $P_0 = \$66.67$, PVGO = $33.34
 c. In part (a), the return on reinvested earnings was equal to the discount rate. In part (b), the return on reinvested earnings was greater than the discount rate.
21. ROE = 16.6%

22. a. $P_0 = \$18.10$, b. $DIV_1/P_0 = 5.52\%$

24. a. 6%, b. 23.33, c. 6.66, d. 11.665, e. $P_0 = \$16.67$, P/E = 8.335,
 f. High P/E ratios reflect expectations of high PVGO.

26. a. P/E = 33.33/4 = 8.33
 b. P/E increases to 10

28. a. $P_0 = \$125$
 b. Assets in place = \$80, PVGO = \$45

31. a. Market-to-book ratio = \$400/\$100 = 4
 b. Market-to-book ratio = ½

39. Before-tax return is 7.8%, after-tax return is 5.96%.

42. If the price of the shares already reflects this fact, the shares may not be a bargain.

CHAPTER 8

1. Both projects are worth pursuing.

3. $NPV_A = \$11.93$ and $NPV_B = \$12.29$. Choose B.

5. No.

7. Project A has a payback period of 2.5 years. Project B has a payback period of 2 years.

12. .2378

15. $IRR_A = 25.7\%$
 $IRR_B = 20.7\%$
 Project B is best.

16. NPV = −\$197.7. Reject.

17. a. $r = 0$ implies NPV = \$15,750.
 $r = 50\%$ implies NPV = \$4,250.
 $r = 100\%$ implies NPV = 0.
 b. IRR = 100%

19. $NPV_{9\%} = \$2{,}139.28$ and $NPV_{14\%} = -\$1{,}444.54$. The IRR is 11.81%.

22. NPV must be negative.

24. a.

Project	**Payback**	**Discounted Payback**
A	3	4+
B	2	2.12
C	3	3.30

 b. Project B
 c. Project B
 d.

Project	**NPV**
A	−1,011
B	3,378
C	2,405

 e. False

26. a. NPV = \$1,978

30. a. If $r = 2\%$, choose A.
 b. If $r = 12\%$, choose B.
 c. Larger cash flows for project A come later and are more sensitive to discount rate increases.

32. \$22,774

34. b. At 5%, NPV = −\$.443
 c. At 20%, NPV = \$.840
 At 40%, NPV = −\$.634

38. a. The equivalent cost of owning and operating the new machine is \$4,590. The old machine costs \$5,000 a year to operate. You should replace.
 b. If $r = 10\%$, do not replace.

CHAPTER 9

3. \$2.2 million

5. Increase in net cash flow = \$106 million

8. Cash flow = \$3,300

10. Total operating cash flow in thousands (years 1–6) = \$339.45
 Net cash flow at time 0 = −\$1,000

11. a.

Year	**CCA Rate**
1	6,000
2	10,200
3	7,140

 b. and c. See Solutions Manual.

16. After-tax cash flow = \$17.3 million

18. a. Total incremental operating CF = \$6,772 in years 1−6
 Net cash flow at time 0 = −\$4,000
 b. NPV = \$403.14
 c. NPV = −4,000 + 1,300 × annuity factor (15%, 6 years) = \$919.83; IRR = 23.21%

23. NPV = −10,894. Don't buy.

25. Equivalent annual (net-of-tax) capital costs:
 Quick and Dirty: \$2.12 million
 Do-It-Right: \$1.84 million
 Choose Do-It-Right.

27. NPV = −\$372,988

32. NPV = −\$0.1817 million

34. c. NPV = \$24.92 million
 IRR = 31.33%
 d. NPV (with CCA) = \$9.21 million

CHAPTER 10

1. Variable costs = \$.50 per burger
 Fixed costs = \$1.25 million

5. a. NPV = \$5.1 million
 b. NPV = \$2.5 million
 c. NPV = \$6.2 million
 d. Price = \$1.61 per jar

9. a. 4,286 diamonds annually
 b. 5,978 diamonds per year

11. Accounting break-even is unaffected. NPV break-even increases.

12. CF break-even is less than zero-profit break-even sales level.

15. a. Accounting break-even increases.
 b. NPV break-even falls.
 c. The switch to MACRS makes the project more attractive.

17. NPV will be negative.

20. DOL = 1

23. a. Average CF = 0
    b. Average CF = $15,000

28. a. Expected NPV = −$681,728. The firm will reject the project.
    b. Expected NPV = $69,855. The project is now worth pursuing.

CHAPTER 11

1. Return = 15%, Dividend yield = 5%, Capital gains yield = 10%

3. a. Rate of return = 0, Real rate = −2.91%

5.

Asset Class	Real Rate
Treasury bills	1.36%
Government bonds	3.2
Common stock	8.04

9. b. Average TSX risk premium = 6.93%; Average long bond risk premium = 3.81%
   c. TSX risk premium standard deviation = 26.08%; long bond risk premium standard deviation = 7.87%. The riskier TSX has a more variable historic risk premium.

14. Expected return = 23.33%, standard deviation = 77.63%

17. b. r_{stock} = 13%, standard deviation = 9.8%
    r_{bonds} = 8.4%, standard deviation = 3.2%

21. a. General Steel, b. Exotic World Tour Agency

25. a., b.

	Average Return	Standard Deviation
TSX	9.30	25.4%
Long bond	6.17	8.07
Treasury bill	2.37	1.83
Portfolio	5.95	9.63

b. The average standard deviation of the three securities is 11.8%, higher than the portfolio standard deviation of 9.63%, showing the benefit of diversification.

CHAPTER 12

1. a. False, only market risk matters
   b. False, earn risk-free rate
   c. False, beta = 2/3
   d. True
   e. True

7. Required return = 12.75%, overpriced.

9. a. Ford
   b. Ford
   c. $\beta = 1.58$
   d. $\beta = 2.46$, std. dev. = 49.2%
   e. Ford: $r = 23.68\%$, Newmont mining: $r = 10.72\%$, McDonald's: $r = 15.6\%$

11. a. $\beta_A = 1.2$, $\beta_D = .75$
    D's return is less sensitive to the return of the overall market.
    b. $r_m = 12\%$, $r_A = 14\%$, $r_D = 9\%$
    c. $r_A = 13.6\%$, $r_D = 10\%$
    d. Stock A

13. NPV = −$25.29

15. P_1 = $52.625

19. $416,667

24. $\beta_{stock} = 1.51$, $\beta_{bond} = .36$

CHAPTER 13

1. 5.92%

3. 10.03%

4. 13.75%

6. No, the risk of the project determines the appropriate discount rate. Use Geothermal's WACC.

8. The cost of equity capital is 9.6%. WACC = 7.695%

11. WACC = 12.67%

15. a. 10.55%

17. WACC = 11.68%

CHAPTER 14

1. a. 80,000 shares
   b.

After New Issue:	
Common shares	$110,000
Retained earnings	$ 30,000
Common equity	$140,000
Note:	
Authorized shares	$100,000
Issued shares	$ 30,000

3. a. Funded
   b. Eurobond
   d. Sinking fund
   f. Prime rate
   g. Floating rate
   h. Private placement, public issue

6. a. 90 votes
   b. 900 votes

7. a. 200,001 shares
   b. 80,000 shares

11. Similarity: The firm promises to make specified payments. Advantage of income bonds: interest payments are tax-deductible expenses.

CHAPTER 15

1. a. Subsequent issue
   b. Bond issue
   c. Bond issue

3. a. A large issue
   b. A bond issue
   c. Private placements
4. Less underwriter risk; less signalling effect from debt; easier to value
7. a. 10%
   b. Average return = 3.94%
   c. I have suffered the winner's curse.
10. No.
12. 12% of the value of funds raised.
15. a. $12.5 million
    b. $5.80 per share
17. a. $10
    b. $18.333
    c. $8.333
    d. 200 rights

CHAPTER 16

4. $296 million
11. P/E = 10/1.25 = 8 (no leverage)
    P/E = 10/1.33 = 7.5 (leveraged)
13. b. False
    c. True
17. $r_{equity} = 18\%$
23. a. 11.27%
    b. Without the tax shield, the value of equity would fall by $296 million. Market-value balance sheet:

Assets	Liabilities and Equity	
2,404	Debt	0
	Equity	2,404

24. a. PV tax shield = $14
    b. Assuming cost of debt = 8% and cost of equity = 15%, WACC = 12.55%.
    c. $150.47
25. Distorted investment decisions, impeded relations with other firms and creditors
36. a. Stockholders gain; bondholders lose.
    b. Bondholders gain; stockholders lose.
    c. Bondholders lose; stockholders gain.
    d. Original stockholders lose; bondholders gain.

CHAPTER 17

2. a, b, d, f
5. a. $58,803.9
   b. $3,196.09
   c. NPV = −$1,803.91; do not lease.
7. a. Lease cash flows:

	0	1	2	3	4	5
Saved cost	75,000					
CCA tax shield	−3,281	−5,742	−4,307	−3,230	−2,422	−7,267
Lease payment	−15,000	−15,000	−15,000	−15,000	−15,000	−15,000
Lease tax shield	5,250	5,250	5,250	5,250	5,250	0
Lease cash flows	61,969	−15,492	−14,057	−12,980	−12,172	−7,267

   b. Equivalent loan = $53,292; NPV = $8,677
   c. NPV = $1,017
13. a. $188
    b. $1,471
    c. $60
14. a. Minimum lease payment acceptable to lessor = $18,441.5
    b. Maximum lease payment acceptable to lessee = $18,673
17. a. NPV to Nodhead = −$24,599
    b. NPV to Compulease = $17,143
    c. Overall gain = −$24,599 + $17,143 = −$7,456

CHAPTER 18

1. b. The ex-dividend date, June 7
   c. Dividend yield = 1.1%
   d. Payout ratio = 15.8%
   e. New stock price = $24.55
3. a. Price = $32
   b. Price = $32
   c. Price = $40, unchanged
9. a. No effect on total wealth
   b. Identical to position after the stock repurchase
11. No impact on wealth
12. a. The after-tax dividend, $1.44
    b. No
13. a. 1,250 shares. Value of equity remains at $50,000.
    b. Same effect as the stock dividend.
14. a. $50
    b. 26.16%
    c. $48.692
16. a. Price = $19.49
    b. Before-tax return = 12.9%
    c. Price = $20.15
    d. Before-tax return = 14.1%
26. a. $20 per share
    b. If the firm pays a dividend, EPS = $2. If the firm does the repurchase, EPS = $2.105.
    c. If the dividend is paid, the P/E ratio = 9.5. If the stock is repurchased, the P/E ratio = 9.5.

CHAPTER 19

4. Sustainable growth rate = 8.75%
   Internal growth rate = 5.25%
7. Possible balancing items: dividends, borrowing or equity issues. With the tendency to keep dividends steady and raise equity in large amounts, borrowing is the most frequently used balancing item.
9. The balancing item is dividends. Dividends must be $200.
11. a. Internal growth rate = 10%
    b. Sustainable growth rate = 15%
15. a. With 20% growth: Addition to retained earnings = $40,000; increase in net assets = $200,000; required external financing = $160,000.

    With 5% growth: Add. to r.e. = $34,000; increase in net assets = $50,000; required external financing = $16,000. To finance faster growth, more external financing is needed.

    b. **Second-Stage Pro Forma**

Balance Sheet: As of 2013 Year-End	20% Growth
Assets	
Net working capital	240
Fixed assets	960
Net assets	1,200
Liabilities and Shareholders' Equity	
Long-term debt	560
Shareholders' equity	640
Total liabilities and shareholders' equity	1,200

17. a. Sustainable growth rate = 2.564%
    b. Issue $1,025.4 in new debt and new debt-asset ratio = .4.
    c. Internal growth rate = 1.538%
21. Payout ratio can be at most 44.4%.
23. Profit margin = 10%
25. Internal growth rate = 12%

CHAPTER 20

1.

	Cash	Net Working Capital
a.	$2 million decline	$2 million decline
b.	$2,500 increase	Unchanged
d.	Unchanged	$1 million increase
f.	$5 million increase	Unchanged

2. a. Long-term financing, total capital requirement, marketable securities
   b. Cash, cash, cash balance, marketable securities
5. Shorter inventory period and shorter cash conversion cycle; reduce net working capital.
7. a. Shorter operating cycle; shorter cash conversion cycle.
   b. Longer operating cycle; longer cash conversion cycle.
   c. Shorter operating cycle; shorter cash conversion cycle.
   d. No change in operating cycle, longer cash conversion cycle.
9. Effective rate = 8.89%. If the compensating balance is 20%, the effective rate is 10%.
11. a. $[1/(1-.06)]-1=.0638=6.38\%$
    b. $[1/(1-.06/12)]^{12}-1=.0620=6.20\%$
15. The order is .75 times the following quarter's sales forecast:

	Quarter			
	First	Second	Third	Fourth
Order for the quarter	$270	$252	$288	$288

19.

	Quarter			
	First	Second	Third	Fourth
Cash at start of period	$40	$10	$15	−$14
+ Net cash inflow (from problem 18)	−30	+5	−29	−41
= Cash at end of period	10	15	−14	−55
Minimum operating cash balance	30	30	30	30
Cumulative short-term financing required (minimum cash balance minus cash at end of period)	$20	$15	$44	$85

25.

Sources of Cash	
Sale of marketable securities	2
Increase in bank loans	1
Increase in trade payable	5
Cash from operations:	
Net income	6
Depreciation	2
Total	16

Uses of Cash	
Increase in inventories	6
Increase in trade receivable	3
Investment in long-term assets	6
Dividend paid	1
Total	16
Change in cash balance	0

Statement of Cash Flow for 2011	
Operating Activities	
Net income	$6
Depreciation	2
Increase in inventory	−6
Increase in trade receivable	−3
Increase in accounts payable	5
Cash provided by operating activities	$4
Investment Activities	
Sale of marketable securities	$2
Investment in long-term assets	−6
Cash provided by investment activities	−$4
Financing Activities	
Increase in bank loan	$1
Dividends paid	−1
Cash provided by financing activities	$0
Increase in cash balance	$0

27.

	February	March	April
Sources of cash:			
Collections on current sales	$100	$110	$ 90
Collections on trade receivable	90	100	110
Total sources of cash	$190	$210	$200
Uses of cash:			
Payments of trade payable	$ 30	$ 40	$ 30
Cash purchases	70	80	60
Labour and administrative expenses	30	30	30
Capital expenditures	100	0	0
Taxes, interest, and dividends	10	10	10
Total uses of cash	$240	$160	$130
Net cash inflow (sources – uses)	−$50	+$50	+$70
Cash at start of period	$100	$ 50	$100
+ Net cash inflow	−50	+50	+70
= Cash at end of period	$ 50	$100	$170
Minimum operating cash balance	$100	$100	$100
Cumulative short-term financing required (minimum cash balance minus cash at end of period)	$ 50	$ 0	−$ 70

CHAPTER 21

1. Ledger balance = $215,000
   Net float = $15,000
6. a. $20,000
   b. $4
   c. $120
8. Yes
10. The economic order quantity = 90 gems. The firm should place smaller but more frequent orders.
13. a. Economic order quantity = 600
    b. Total costs = $6,000
15. Economic order quantity falls by a factor of 10.
16. Cash balance = $14,142
    Transfers per month = 7.07
20. a. The interest rate, the cost of each transaction, and the variability of each cash flow.
    b. It should restore it to one-third of the distance from the lower to the upper limit.
21. a. Once every 2½ weeks
    b. $204
    c. $102
22. Cash balances fall relative to sales.

CHAPTER 22

1. a. $10
   b. 40 days
   c. 9.6%
4. a. Due lag and pay lag fall, no change in terms lag.
   c. Terms lag and pay lag increase, no change in due lag.
6. a. 20 days
   b. $1.096 million
   c. Average days in receivables will fall.
8. a. The expected profit from a sale is −$2. Do not extend credit.
   b. $p = .95$
   c. The present value of a sale, net of default, is positive, $458.35.
   d. $p = 16\%$
14. a. Yes, NPV of profits increases from $4,200 to $4,400.
    b. Credit should not be advanced. NPV of expected profits falls to $3,300.
    c. Net benefit from advancing credit = $100
15. From Ex. 22.3: PV(REV) = $1,200 and PV(COST) = $1,000. Slow payers have a 70% probability of paying their bills. The expected profit of a sale to a slow payer is therefore .70($1,200 − $1,000) − .30($1,000) = −$160. Expected savings from doing a credit check is the probability of uncovering a slow payer times the expected loss saved by denying credit: expected savings = .1 × $160 = $16. The credit check costs $5, so it is cost-effective.
17. Sell only to groups 1, 2, and 3.

CHAPTER 23

6. $24 per share, NPV = 0.
8. a. $6.25 million
   b. $4 million
   c. NPV = $2.25 million
12. a. NPV = $5,000
    b. SCC will sell for $51.67; SDP will sell for $20. Wealth increase: SCC = 3.34%, SDP = 14.29%; fraction of economic gain: SCC = 50%, SDP = 50%.
    c. Price = $51.32
    d. NPV = $3,947.37; SCC's fraction of economic gain = 39.5%. Share offer equivalent to (a): SCC issues .3871 shares for every SDP share.

CHAPTER 24

1. a. 65.13 euros; $153.55
   b. 106.80 Swiss francs; $93.63
   c. Direct exchange rate will decrease and indirect exchange rate will increase.
   d. U.S. dollar is worth more.
3. d. $\frac{1 + r_x}{1 + r_\$} = \frac{E(1 + i_x)}{E(1 + i_\$)}$
6. a
8. Borrow the present value of 1 million Australian dollars, sell them for U.S. dollars in the spot market, and invest the proceeds in an 8-year U.S. dollar loan. In 8 years, it can repay the Australian loan with the anticipated Australian dollar payment.

10. a. 4.0%
    b. 10.5%
    c. −2.5%
11. 7.44%
14. Canadian dollar should be depreciating relative to the US dollar.
16. Net present value = $.72 million

CHAPTER 25

1.

	Payoff	Profit
b. Call option, $X = 80$	4	$4 - 7.95 = -3.95$
e. Put option, $X = 88$	4	$4 - 7.75 = -3.75$

3. a. The July call costs $1.27. The January call costs $3.35.
   b. Longer time to expiry increases the probability that the stock price will go up, making the call more valuable.
   c. This is true of puts as well.
5. Figure 25.7(a) represents a call seller; Figure 25.7(b) represents a call buyer. For the put buyer, see Figure 25.1*b* and for the put seller, see Figure 25.2*b*.
7.

	a. $S < 100$	b. $S > 100$
Value of put	$100 - S$	0
Value of stock	S	S
Total	100	S

16. You will be more tempted to choose the high-risk proposal.
18. a. Call option to pursue a project.
    b. Put option to sell the equipment.
20. Put option with exercise price equal to support price.
22. a. Option to put (sell) the stock to the underwriter.
    b. Volatility of the stock value; the length of the period for which the underwriter guarantees the issue; the interest rate; the price at which the underwriter is obligated to buy the stock; and the market value of the stock.
26. a. Buy a call option for $3. Exercise the call to purchase stock. Pay the $20 exercise price. Sell the share for $25. Riskless profit equals $2.
    b. Buy a share and put option. Exercise the put. Riskless profit equals $1.

CHAPTER 26

6. Advantages: liquidity, no storage costs, no spoilage.
   Disadvantages: no income or benefits that could accrue from holding asset in portfolio.
7.

	Gold Price		
	$1,330	**$1,450**	**$1,650**
a. Revenues	$1,330,000	$1,450,000	$1,650,000
Futures contract	130,000	10,000	−190,000
b. Total	$1,460,000	$1,460,000	$1,460,000
c. Revenues	$1,330,000	$1,450,000	$1,650,000
+ Put option payoff	120,000	0	0
− Put option cost	5,000	5,000	5,000
Net revenue	$1,445,000	$1,445,000	$1,645,000

11. Petrochemical will take a long position to hedge its cost of buying oil. Onnex will take a short position to hedge its revenue from selling oil.

	Oil Price ($ per barrel)		
	$88	**$90**	**$92**
Cost for Petrochemical			
Cash flow on purchase of oil	−88,000	−90,000	−92,000
+ Cash flow on long futures position	−2,000	0	+2,000
Total cash flow	−90,000	−90,000	−90,000
Revenue for Onnex			
Revenue from 1,000 barrels	$88,000	$90,000	$92,000
+Payoff on short futures position	2,000	0	(2,000)
Net revenue	$90,000	$90,000	$90,000

The benefit of futures is the ability to lock in a riskless position without paying any money. The benefit of the option hedge is that you benefit if prices move in one direction without losing if they move in the other direction. However, this asymmetry comes at a price: the cost of the option.

Glossary

ABCP See ***asset-backed commercial paper***.

accrued interest: Coupon interest earned from the last coupon payment to the purchase date of the bond. 186

additional paid-in capital: Difference between issue price and par value of stock, also called *capital surplus*. 454

aging schedule: Classification of trades receivables by time outstanding. 713

amalgamation: The combination of the assets and liabilities of two firms into one. Called a *merger* in the United States. 730

angel: A wealthy individual investor in early-stage ventures. 490

annual percentage rate (APR): Interest rate that is annualized using simple interest. 166

annuity: Equally spaced and level stream of cash flows. 147

annuity due: Level stream of cash flows starting immediately. 154

annuity factor: Present value of a $1 annuity. 150

APR See ***annual percentage rate***.

asset class: Eligible depreciable assets are grouped into specified asset classes by CRA. Each asset class has a prescribed CCA rate. 312

asset-backed commercial paper (ABCP): Short-term security with cash flows coming from a pool of assets such as mortgage or credit card receivables. 693

authorized share capital: Maximum number of shares that the company is permitted to issue as specified in the firm's articles of incorporation. 454

availability float: Cheques already deposited that have not yet been cleared. 675

balancing item: Variable that adjusts to maintain the consistency of a financial plan. Also called the *plug*. 614

banker's acceptance: A firm's time draft that has been accepted by a bank and may be sold to investors as a short-term unsecured note issued by the firm and guaranteed by the bank. 660

bankruptcy: The reorganization or liquidation of a firm that cannot pay its debts. 548

beta: Sensitivity of a stock's return to the return on the market portfolio. 394

bond: Security that obligates the issuer to make specified payments to the bondholder. 184

book value of equity: Net worth of the firm according to the balance sheet. 225

bought deal: An arrangement in which the underwriter buys securities from the issuing company and sells them to investors. 503

break-even analysis: Analysis of the level of sales at which the company breaks even. 341

call option: Right to buy an asset at a specified exercise price on or before the expiration (or expiry) date. 785

callable bond: Bond that may be repurchased by the firm before maturity at a specified call price. 464, 802

capital asset pricing model (CAPM): Theory of the relationship between risk and return that states that the expected risk premium on any security equals its beta times the market risk premium. 403

capital budget: List of planned investment projects. 335

capital cost allowance (CCA): The amount of write-off on depreciable assets allowed by Canada Revenue Agency (CRA) against taxable income. 311

capital lease See ***financial lease***.

capital rationing: Limit set on the amount of funds available for investment. 286

capital structure: A firm's mix of debt and equity financing. 422, 525

CAPM See ***capital asset pricing model***.

carrying costs: Costs of maintaining current assets, including opportunity cost of capital. 646

carrying value See ***book value***.

cash conversion cycle or **cash gap:** Period of time between firm's payment for materials and collection on its sales. 643

cash dividend: Payment of cash by the firm to its shareholders. 585

CCA See ***capital cost allowance***.

CCA tax shield: Tax savings arising from the capital cost allowance charge. 311

CFO See ***chief financial officer***.

clean bond price: Bond price excluding accrued interest. 186

collection policy: Procedures to collect and monitor receivables. 713

commercial paper: Short-term unsecured notes issued by large corporations. 659

commitment fee: Fee charged by the lender on the unused portion of a line of credit. 656

common stock or **common equity** or **common shares:** Ownership shares in a corporation. 220

company cost of capital: Expected rate of return demanded by investors in a company, determined by the average risk of the company's assets and operations. 409

compound interest: Interest earned on interest. 133

constant-growth dividend discount model: Version of the dividend discount model in which dividends grow at a constant rate. 236

convertible bond: Bond that the holder may exchange for a specified amount of another security. 473, 801

correlation coefficient: Measure of how closely two variables move together. 378

costs of financial distress: Costs arising from bankruptcy or distorted business decisions before bankruptcy. 537

coupon rate: Annual interest payment as a percentage of face value. 184

coupon: The interest payment paid to the bondholder. 184

credit analysis: Procedure to determine the likelihood a customer will pay its bills. 706

credit policy: Standards set to determine the amount and nature of credit to extend to customers. 708

credit risk See ***default risk***.

cumulative voting: Voting system in which all the votes one shareholder is allowed to cast can be cast for one candidate for the board of directors. 456

current yield: Annual coupon payment divided by current bond price. 191

debt-irrelevance proposition See ***MM's proposition I***.

decision tree: Diagram of sequential decisions and possible outcomes. 348

declining balance depreciation: This is computed by applying the depreciation rate to the asset balance for each year. 313

default (or **credit**) **risk:** The risk that a bond issuer will default on its bonds. 204

default premium or **credit spread:** The additional yield on a bond that investors require for bearing credit risk. 204

degree of operating leverage (DOL): Percentage change in profits given a 1 percent change in sales. 346

depreciation tax shield: Reduction in taxes attributable to the depreciation allowance. 309

derivatives: Securities whose payoffs are determined by the values of other financial variables such as prices, exchange rates, or interest rates. 812

dirty bond price: Bond price including accrued interest. 186

discount (or **present value interest**) **factor:** Present value of a $1 future payment. 180

discount bond: Bond that sells for less than its face value. 191

discount rate: Interest rate used to compute present values of future cash flows. 137

discounted payback period: The time until discounted cash flows recover the initial investment in the project. 271

diversifiable risk See ***unique risk***.
diversification: Strategy designed to reduce risk by spreading the portfolio across many investments. 375
dividend clientele effect: Different investor groups prefer different dividend yields. Changing the firm's dividend policy may attract a new investor clientele but may not change firm value. 600
dividend discount model: Discounted cash flow model that states that today's stock price equals the present value of all expected future dividends. 231
dividend payout ratio: Percentage of earnings paid out as dividends. 591
dividend reinvestment plan: Enables shareholders to reinvest dividends into additional new shares. 588
dividend yield: A stock's cash dividend divided by its current price. 223
DOL See ***degree of operating leverage***.
Dow Jones Industrial Average: U.S. index of the investment performance of a portfolio of 30 "blue-chip" stocks. 364
Du Pont formula: ROA equals the product of the asset turnover and operating profit margin. 110

economic order quantity: Order size that minimizes total inventory costs. 686
economic value added (EVA): Operating profit minus a charges for the cost of capital employed. Also called *residual income*. 103
EDI See ***electronic data interchange***.
effective annual interest rate (EAR): Interest rate that is annualized using compound interest. 165
efficient market: Market in which prices reflect all available information. 248
EFT See ***electronic funds transfer***.
electronic data interchange (EDI): Direct, electronic information exchange between enterprises, eliminating the mailing and handling of paper invoices. 683
electronic funds transfer (EFT): Payments made electronically instead of using paper-based cheques. 682
equivalent annual cost: The cost per period with the same present value as the cost of buying and operating a machine. 284
equivalent loan: Present value of the lease cash outflows, discounted at the after-tax cost of borrowing. 572
eurobond: Bond that is denominated in the currency of one country but issued to investors in other countries. 466
eurodollars: Dollars held on deposit in a bank outside the United States. 466
EVA See ***economic value added***.
exchange rate: Amount of one currency needed to purchase one unit of another. 756
ex-dividend date: Date that determines whether a stockholder is entitled to a dividend payment; anyone holding stock before this date is entitled to a dividend. 586
expectations theory of exchange rates: Theory that the expected spot exchange rate equals the forward rate. 766
ex-rights date: This date is usually four business days before the holder-of-record date. 502

face value: Payment at the maturity of the bond. Also called *par value* or *maturity value*. 184
factoring: A firm sells its accounts receivable at a discount for the purpose of obtaining short-term financing. 657
financial lease: Long-term, non-cancellable lease. Also known as *capital* or *full-payout* lease. 562
financial leverage: Debt financing to amplify the effects of changes in operating income on the returns to stockholders. 530
financial risk: Risk to shareholders resulting from the use of debt. 530
financial slack: Ready access to cash or debt financing. 545
Fisher effect: The nominal interest rate is determined by the real interest rate and the expected rate of inflation. 200
fixed costs: Costs that do not depend on the level of output. 338
floating-rate preferred: Preferred stock paying dividends that vary with short-term interest rates. 463
flotation costs: The costs incurred when a firm issues new securities to the public. 495
foreign bond: Bond issued in the currency of its country but the borrower is from another country. 466
forward contract: Agreement to buy or sell an asset in the future at an agreed price. 819
forward exchange rate: Exchange rate for a forward transaction. 758
free cash flow: Cash flow that is not required for investment in fixed assets or working capital and is therefore available to investors. 441
fundamental analysts: Investors who attempt to find mispriced securities by analyzing fundamental information, such as accounting data and business prospects. 247
funded debt: Debt with more than one year remaining to maturity. 464
future value (FV): Amount to which an investment will grow after earning interest. 133
future value interest factor: Future value of a current cash flow of $1. 135
futures contract: Exchange-traded promise to buy or sell an asset in the future at a pre-specified price. 813
FV See ***future value***.

general cash offer: Sale of securities open to all investors by an already-public company. 503
growing annuity: A finite stream of cash flows growing at a constant rate. 158
growing perpetuity: An infinite stream of cash flows growing at a constant rate. 158

half-year rule: Only one-half of the purchase cost of the asset is added to the asset class and used to compute CCA in the year of purchase. 313
high-yield bond See ***junk bond***.
holder-of-record date: The date on which shareholders appearing on company records are entitled to receive the stock rights. 502

IFRS See ***International Financial Reporting Standards***.
inflation: Rate at which prices as a whole are increasing. 160
information content of dividends: Dividend increases send good news about future cash flow and earnings. Dividend cuts send bad news. 593
initial public offering (IPO): First offering of stock to the general public. 221, 492
inside information: Relevant information about a company known by its board of directors, management and/or employees, and other insiders but not by the public. 247
insider trading: Illegal trading of securities, including stocks, bonds, and options, by insiders or those tipped by insiders, on the basis of inside information. 248
insider: Member of the board of directors, management, employees, and others with a close relationship to a company, including lawyers, financial advisors, and accountants. 247
interest rate parity: Theory that forward premium equals interest rate differential. 765
interest rate risk: The risk in bond prices due to fluctuations in interest rates. 202
interest tax shield: Tax savings resulting from deductibility of interest payments. 534
internal growth rate: Maximum rate of growth without external financing. 625
internal rate of return (IRR): The discount rate at which a project NPV = 0. 275
internally generated funds: Cash reinvested in the firm: depreciation plus earnings not paid out as dividends. 473
international Fisher effect: Theory that real interest rates in all countries should be equal, with differences in nominal rates reflecting differences in expected inflation. 763

intrinsic value: Present value of expected future cash flows from a stock or other security. 230
investment-grade bond: Bond rated Baa or above by Moody's, or BBB or above by Standard and Poor's or DBRS. 204
IPO See ***initial public offering***.
IRR See ***internal rate of return***.
issued shares: Shares that have been issued by the company. 454

junk (or **speculative-grade**) **bond:** Bond with a rating below Baa or BBB. Also called *high-yield*. 204
just-in-time inventory management: A system of inventory management in which materials are delivered to the firm just when needed. 687

law of one price: Theory that prices of goods in all countries should be equal when translated to a common currency. 761
LBO See ***leveraged buyout***.
lease: Rental agreement for the use of an asset extending for more than one year and involving a series of fixed payments. 561, 468
lessee: User of the asset in a lease. Responsible for making regular payments to lessor. 561
lessor: Owner of the asset in a lease. Receives regular payments from lessee. 561
leveraged buyout (LBO): Acquisition of the firm by a private group using substantial borrowed funds. 741
levered equity beta: Beta of equity of a firm that has debt, reflecting both the risk arising from the firm's operating activities and the risk created by the leverage (debtholders are entitled to be paid principal and interest before shareholders are paid dividends). 438
line of credit: Agreement by a bank that a company may borrow at any time up to an established limit. 656
liquidation value: Net proceeds that would be realized by selling the firm's assets and paying off its creditors. 226
liquidation: Sale of a bankrupt firm's assets. 549
loan covenant: Agreement between firm and lender requiring the firm to fulfill certain conditions to safeguard the loan. 542
lockbox system: System whereby customers send payments to a post office box and a bank collects and processes cheques. 680

majority voting: Voting system in which each director is voted on separately. 456
management buyout (MBO): Acquisition of the firm by its own management in a leveraged buyout. 742
market capitalization: Total market value of equity, equal to share price times number of shares outstanding. 100
market index: Measure of the investment performance of the overall market. 363
market portfolio: Portfolio of all assets in the economy. In practice, a broad stock market index, such as the S&P/TSX or S&P 500 Composite Index, is used to represent the market. 393
market risk premium (MRP): Risk premium of market portfolio. Expected extra return on the market portfolio relative to the return on risk-free Treasury bills. 401
market risk: Economy-wide (macroeconomic) sources of risk that affect the overall stock market. Also called *systematic risk*. 382
market value added: Market capitalization minus book value of equity. 100
market-to-book ratio: Ratio of market value to book value of equity. 101
market-value balance sheet: Financial statement that uses the market value of all assets and liabilities. 227
maturity premium: Extra average return from investing in long-term bonds versus short-term Treasury securities. 365
maturity value See ***face value***.
MBO See ***management buyout***.
merger: The acquisition of control of a business by another business. See also ***amalgamation***. 724
MM's dividend-irrelevance proposition: Under ideal conditions, the value of the firm is unaffected by dividend policy. 594
MM's proposition I (or **debt-irrelevance proposition**)**:** The principle that the value of a firm is unaffected by its capital structure. 528
MM's proposition II: The principle that the required rate of return on equity increases as the firm's debt-equity ratio increases. 531
money market: Market for short-term financial assets. 692
mutually exclusive projects: Two or more projects that cannot be pursued simultaneously. 269

net float: Difference between payment float and availability float. 676
net operating profit after tax (NOPAT): The after-tax profits from operations, as if the firm had no debt. Equals net income (or net earnings or profit) plus after-tax net finance (or interest) expense. 104
net operating working capital (NOWC): Operating current assets minus operating current liabilities, excluding interest-bearing debt. 615
net present value (NPV): Present value of cash flows minus initial investment. 264
net working capital: Current assets minus current liabilities. Often called *working capital*. 304, 642
net worth: Book value of common shareholders' equity plus preferred stock. 451
nominal interest rate: Rate at which money invested grows. 162
NOPAT See ***net operating profit after tax***.
NOWC See ***net operating working capital***.
NPV break-even point: The level of sales at which NPV is zero. 343
NPV See ***net present value***.

off-balance-sheet financing: Financing that is not shown as a liability on a company's balance sheet. 564
open account: Agreement whereby sales are made with no formal debt contract. 705
operating cycle: Period of time from the purchase of raw materials to the collection of cash from the sale of finished goods. 643
operating lease: Short-term, cancellable lease. 561
operating leverage: Degree to which costs are fixed. 346
operating profit margin: Net-operating profit after taxes (NOPAT) as a percentage of sales. 110
operating risk or **business risk:** Risk in a firm's operating income. 529
opportunity cost of capital: Expected rate of return given up by investing in a project. 264
opportunity cost: Benefit or cash flow forgone as a result of an action. 304
outstanding shares: Shares that have been issued by the company and are held by investors. 454
oversubscription privilege: A privilege given to shareholders in a rights issue, enabling them to purchase any unsold shares at the subscription price. 502

par value: Value of security shown on certificate. See also ***face value***. 454
partnership: Business owned by two or more people who are personally responsible for all its liabilities. 11
payback period: Time until cash flows recover the initial investment of the project. 270
payment or **disbursement float:** Cheques written by a company that have not yet cleared the banking system. 675
payout ratio: Fraction of earnings paid out as dividends. 241
pecking-order theory: Firms prefer to issue debt rather than equity if internal finance is insufficient. 545
pension fund: Investment plan set up by an employer to provide for employees' retirement. 42
percentage-of-sales models: Planning model in which sales forecasts are the driving variables and most other variables are proportional to sales. 613

perpetuity: Stream of level cash payments that never ends. 147
planning horizon: Time horizon for a financial plan. 609
pledged accounts receivable: Accounts receivable that are collateral, the security, for a loan. 657
plowback ratio: Fraction of earnings retained by the firm. Also called *retention ratio*. 241
plug See ***balancing item***.
political risk: A change in firm value arising from political events. 772
POP See ***prompt offering prospectus***.
PPP See ***purchasing power parity***.
preferred stock: Stock that takes priority over common stock in regard to dividends. 225, 451
premium bond: Bond that sells for more than its face value. 191
present value (PV): Value today of a future cash flow. 136
present value of growth opportunities (PVGO): Net present value of a firm's future investments. 242
price-earnings multiple or **P/E ratio:** Ratio of stock price to earnings per share. 223
primary market: Market for the sale of new securities issued by corporations. 221
prime rate: Benchmark interest rate charged by banks. 464
private company: Corporation whose shares are privately owned. 8
private equity fund: Investment fund focused on investing in equity of privately owned businesses. 42
private placement: Sale of securities to a limited number of investors without a public offering. 466, 505
pro formas: Projected or forecasted financial statements. 612
profitability index: Ratio of net present value to initial investment. 287
project cost of capital: Minimum acceptable expected rate of return on a project given its risk. 409
prompt offering prospectus (POP) system: Allows qualified firms quicker access to capital markets by enabling them to use a short-form filing process rather than a full prospectus. 503
prospectus: Formal summary that provides information on an issue of securities. 493
protective covenant: Restriction on a firm to protect bondholders. 467
proxy contest: An event in which outsiders compete with management for shareholders' votes in order to take control of the company. Also called *proxy fight* and *proxy battle*. 457, 739
proxy fight (battle) See ***proxy contest***.
public company: Corporation whose shares are listed for trading on a stock exchange. 8
purchasing power parity (PPP): Theory that the cost of living in different countries is equal and exchange rates adjust to offset inflation differentials across countries. 761
pure-play approach: Estimating project cost of capital using the cost of capital of another company involved exclusively in the same type of project. 410
put option: Right to sell an asset at a specified exercise price on or before the expiration (or expiry) date. 786
PV See ***present value***.
PVGO See ***present value of growth opportunities***.

random walk: The movement of security prices that change randomly, with no predictable trends or patterns. 244
rate of return: Total income per period per dollar invested. 193
real assets: Assets used to produce goods and services. 8
real interest rate: Rate at which the purchasing power of an investment increases. 162
real options: Options to invest in, modify, or dispose of a capital investment project. 349, 797
real return bond (RRB): Bond with variable nominal coupon payments, determined by a fixed real coupon payment and the inflation rate. 199
real value of $1: Purchasing power-adjusted value of a dollar. 161
recaptured depreciation: The negative balance that is caused in an asset class by the sale of an asset. Recaptured depreciation is added to taxable income. 314
refunding: Replacing an old bond issue with a new one by the firm. Often done when interest rates decline, and the firm can save on the interest cost of the new issue. 465
reorganization: Restructuring of financial claims on a failing firm to allow it to keep operating. 549
residual income See ***economic value added (EVA)***.
restructuring: Process of changing the firm's capital structure without changing its assets. 526
retained earnings: Earnings not paid out as dividends. 454
retention ratio See ***plowback ratio***.
return on assets (ROA): Net operating profit after taxes (NOPAT) as a percentage of total assets. 106
return on capital (ROC): Net operating profit after taxes (NOPAT) as a percentage of invested capital (debt plus equity). 105
return on equity (ROE): Net income as a percentage of shareholders' equity. 107
reverse split: Issue of new shares in exchange for old shares, which results in the reduction of outstanding shares. 588
rights issue: Issue of securities offered only to current shareholders. 501
risk premium: Expected return in excess of risk-free return as compensation for risk. 366
ROA See ***return on assets***.
ROC See ***return on capital***.
ROE See ***return on equity***.
RRB See ***real return bond***.

S&P 500 See ***Standard & Poor's Composite Index***.
S&P/TSX Composite Index: Index of the investment performance of a portfolio of the major stocks listed on the Toronto Stock Exchange. Also called the *TSX index*. Formerly called the *TSE 300*. 363
S&P/TSX Composite Total Return Index (TSXT): Measure of the Composite Index based on the prices plus dividends paid by the stocks in the S&P/TSX Composite Index. 363
scenario analysis: Project analysis given a particular combination of assumptions. 340
SCI See ***statement of comprehensive income***.
seasoned equity offering (SEO): Sale of additional stock by a public company 221
seasoned offering: Sale of securities by a firm that is already publicly traded. 501
secondary market: Market in which already-issued securities are traded among investors. 221
secured debt: Debt that has first claim on specified collateral in the event of default. 466
securities See ***financial assets***.
security market line: Relationship between expected return and beta. 404
semi-strong-form efficiency: Market prices rapidly reflect all publicly available information. 248
sensitivity analysis: Analysis of the effects of changes in sales, costs, and so on, on project profitability. 337
SEO See ***seasoned equity offering***.
SFP See ***statement of financial position***.
share purchase plan: Allows shareholders to make cash contributions toward the acquisition of new shares. 588
share repurchase: Firm buys back stock from its shareholders. 588
shareholders' rights plan or **poison pill:** Measures taken by the target firm to avoid acquisition; for example, the right of existing shareholders to buy additional shares at an attractive price if a bidder acquires a significant holding. 740

shark repellent: Amendments to a company charter made to forestall takeover attempts. 741

shelf registration: A procedure followed in the United States that allows firms to file one registration statement for several issues of the same security. 503

shortage costs: Costs incurred from shortages in current assets. 646

simple interest: Interest earned only on the original investment; no interest is earned on interest. 135

simulation analysis: Estimation of the probabilities of different possible outcomes—for example, from an investment project. 341

sinking fund: Fund established to retire debt before maturity. 464

sole proprietor: Sole owner of a business that has no partners and no shareholders. Personally liable for all the firm's obligations. 10

specific risk See ***unique risk***.

speculative-grade bond See ***junk bond***.

spot rate of exchange: Exchange rate for an immediate transaction. 757

spread: Difference between public offer price and price paid by underwriter. 493

stakeholder: Anyone with a financial interest in the firm. 17

Standard & Poor's Composite Index: U.S. index of the investment performance of a portfolio of 500 large stocks. Also called the *S&P 500*. 364

standard deviation: Square root of variance. Another measure of volatility. 369

standby underwriting agreement: An underwriting agreement in which underwriter stands ready to purchase any unsold shares. 502

statement of cash flows: Financial statement that shows the firm's cash receipts and cash payments over a period of time. 75

statement of changes in equity: Financial statement that explains the change from the previous period of each component of equity on the statement of financial position (balance sheet). 70

statement of comprehensive income (SCI): Financial statement that shows profits and other comprehensive income of a firm over a period of time. Without an income statement, SCI starts with the profit section, which has the same content as the income statement. 69

statement of financial position (SFP) or **balance sheet:** Financial statement that shows the book value of the firm's assets, liabilities, and equity as of a specific date. 61

stock dividend: Distribution of additional shares to a firm's shareholders. 587

stock split: Issue of additional shares to firm's shareholders. 587

straight-line depreciation: Constant depreciation for each year of the asset's accounting life. 313

strong-form efficiency: Market prices rapidly reflect all information that could in principle be used to determine true value. 248

subordinated debt: Debt that may be repaid in bankruptcy only after senior debt is paid. 465

subsidiary: A business controlled by another business. 60

sustainable growth rate: Steady rate at which a firm can grow without changing leverage; plowback ratio × return on equity. 117, 241, 626

swap: Arrangement by two counterparties to exchange one stream of cash flows for another. 820

syndicated loan: Loan provided by a group of banks that combine to provide the loan amount. 656

synergy: The principle by which the value generated by the combination of companies is greater than the sum of their individual values. 726

systematic risk See ***market risk***.

takeover bid: Takeover attempt in which outsiders make an offer to buy the stock of the target firm's shareholders. 731

technical analysts: Investors who attempt to identify undervalued stocks by searching for patterns in past stock prices. 244

tender offer See ***takeover bid***.

term loans: Bank loans for one or more years. 656

terminal loss: The positive balance following the disposal of all assets in the class. The UCC of the asset class is set to zero after a terminal loss is recognized. 314

terms of sale: Credit, discount, and payment terms offered on a sale. 703

trade-off theory: The idea that debt levels are chosen to balance interest tax shields against the costs of financial distress. 538

treasurer: Manager responsible for financing, cash management, and relationships with financial markets and institutions. 12

TSE 300 See ***S&P/TSX Composite Index***.

TSX index See ***S&P/TSX Composite Index***.

TSXT See ***S&P/TSX Composite Total Return Index***.

UCC See ***undepreciated capital cost***.

undepreciated capital cost (UCC): The balance remaining in an asset class that has not yet been depreciated in that year. 311

underpricing: Issuing securities at an offering price set below the true value of the security. 494

underwriter: Investment dealer that buys an issue of securities from a company and resells it to the public. 493

unique risk: Risk factors affecting only the particular firm. Also called *specific risk* or *diversifiable risk*. 382

unlevered beta: Beta of equity of a debt-free firm, reflecting the risk arising from the firm's operating activities. 438

variable costs: Costs that change as the level of output changes. 338

variance: Average value of squared deviations from mean. A measure of volatility. 369

venture capital: Money invested to finance a new firm. 490

WACC See ***weighted-average cost of capital***.

warrant: Right to buy shares from a company at a stipulated price before a set date. 472, 799

weak-form efficiency: Market prices rapidly reflect all information contained in the history of past prices. 248

weighted-average cost of capital (WACC): Expected rate of return on a portfolio of all the firm's securities, adjusted for tax savings due to interest payments. 427

white knight: Friendly potential acquirer sought by a target company threatened by an unwelcome bidder. 740

workout: Agreement between a company and its creditors establishing the steps the company must take to avoid bankruptcy. 549

yield curve or **term structure of interest rates:** Graph of the relationship between time to maturity and yield to maturity, for bonds that differ only in their maturity dates. 198

yield to maturity: Interest rate for which the present value of the bond's payments equals the price. 191

zero-balance account: Bank account to which just enough funds are transferred daily to pay each day's bills. 682

Index

A

- ABACUS, 15
- ACA Management LLC, 15
- accordion feature, 656
- accounting fraud, 82
- accounting rates of return, 102–108
- accounting standards, 60, 81, 82, 226, 566. *See also* International Financial Reporting Standards (IFRS)
- Accounting Standards Board (AcSB), 81, 565
- accounting standards for private enterprises (ASPE), 60
- accounts payable, 64
- accounts receivable financing, 657–658
- accounts receivables, 62
- accrual accounting, 72–74
- accrued interest, 186
- accumulated depreciation, 63
- acid-test ratio. *See* quick ratio
- accounting, practice and malpractice, 81–83
- acquisition/buyout stage, 514
- Activision Blizzard, 624
- additional paid-in capital, 454
- adjusted cost of disposal, 314
- Adolph Coors, 731
- agency problem, 17–21
  - compensation plans, 18–19, 21
  - conflicts of interest, 16–18
  - and corporate governance, 38
  - financial crisis of 2007–2009, 53
  - firm value, 17–18
- aging schedule, 713
- Agricultural Bank of China, 492
- AIG, 52, 823
- AIM Canadian Premier Fund, 40–41
- Airbus, 20
- Airbus A380, 263
- Air Canada, 540
- Alcan, 468
- Alcon, Inc., 732
- Allen, Paul, 489
- Alliance Atlantis Communications, 524
- Allied Crude Vegetable Oil Refining, 658
- Allied Irish Bank, 53
- alternative trading systems (ATS), 38, 222
- Altman, Edward, 707
- amalgamation, 730–731
- Amazon.com, 250
- AMC Entertainment, 227
- American Depositary Receipt (ADR), 222
- American Express, 742
- amortization charges, and cash, 72
- angel investor, 490, 517
- annual percentage rate (APR), 166–167
  - comparing rates of return, 362
- annuity, 147, 149–157
  - formula, 150
  - future value, 155–157
  - future value *vs.* annuities due, 157
  - valuing annuities, 149–153
  - vs annuity due, 154
- annuity due, 154, 155n, 157
- annuity factor, 150
- AOL, 747
- Apax Partners, 746
- Apple Computer, 11, 489, 639
- Aramark, 492
- Arthur Anderson, 82
- asked price, 184
- asset-backed bonds, 468–471
- asset-backed commercial paper (ABCP), 17, 470–471, 472, 693–694
- asset class, 312–313
- assets
  - financial, 8
  - intangible, 5, 8, 63–64
  - real, 8
- asset turnover ratio, 108
- asset turnover vs profit margin, 110–111
- AstraZeneca PLC (AZN), 60–69, 99–101, 107, 222
- ATCO, 544
- ATI Technologies Inc, 248
- authorized share capital, 454
- Automated Clearing Settlement System (ACSS), 679
- availability float, 675
- average collection period, 109

B

- bad debt, allowance for, 81
- balance sheet, 61. *See also* statement of financial position (SFP)
  - first-stage financing, 490
  - market-value, 227–228
  - second-stage financing, 490–491
- balancing item, 614
- Balsillie, Jim, 3, 800
- banker's acceptance, 660, 705
- banking group. *See* syndicate
- bank loans, 656–657, 660–662
- Bank of America, 52
- Bank of Canada, 198
- Bank of Nova Scotia, 472
- bankruptcy, 548
- *Bankruptcy and Insolvency Act of 1992,* 539, 549
- bankruptcy costs, 538–540
- bankruptcy procedures, 548–552
- banks, 43
  - financial careers, 22
  - investment, 221, 499
- Barclays Capital Markets, 759
- Baring Brothers, 822–823
- Barrick Gold, 229, 458
- Baumol, William, 687
- BCE, 547, 744, 746
- Bear Stearns, 52*n*
- Bechtel, 492
- behavioural finance, 250–251
- Bell Globemedia, 747
- best-efforts basis, 493
- beta
  - defined, 394
  - of portfolio, 399–400
  - risk, 403–404
  - of stocks, 394–398
- BHP Billiton, 739
- bid price, 184
- Bill C-198, 20, 38, 459
- Birch Hill Equity Partners, 744
- Black, Conrad, 19
- Black, Fischer, 795
- Black-Scholes formula, 795
- Blackstone Group LP, 745
- Blankfein, Lloyd, 15
- BMO Nesbitt Burns, 11
- board of directors, 9, 19–20, 456, 459, 460, 738–739
- Boeing, 19
- Bombardier, 457
- bond rates of return, 192–198
  - defined, 193
  - formula, 193
  - multiperiod rates of return, 197–198
  - taxes and, 196–197
  - yield to maturity and, 194–196
- bonds, 182–218. *See also* yield curve
  - accrued interest, 186
  - asked price, 184
  - asset-backed, 468–471
  - bid price, 184
  - Canadian corporate, 45–46
  - clean price, 186
  - convertible, 472–473, 801
  - coupon, 184, 463
  - coupon rate, 184, 190
  - current yield, 190–191
  - default premium, 204
  - default risk, 203–204, 466
  - dirty price, 186
  - discount, 191
  - eurobonds, 466
  - eurodollars, 466
  - expected return on, 432
  - face value, 184
  - foreign, 466
  - forward interest rate, 216
  - function of, 184
  - government, 38, 184, 200, 203, 365–367
  - indexed, 468
  - inflation-indexed, 199–200
  - interest rate risk, 202
  - investment-grade, 204
  - junk, 204, 743, 744
  - liquidity premium, 203
  - market data, 184–186
  - market interest rate, 187, 190
  - maturity premium, 365
  - premium, 191
  - prices, 186–190, 195–196
  - ratings, 204
  - real return bond, 199–200
  - refunding decision, 465

reverse floaters, 471
Rio Tinto Group bond issue, 469
security markets, 38–39, 185
semi-annual coupon payments, 188, 192
spot rates, 216
spread, 184–185
subordinated debt, 465
yield to maturity, 190–192
zero-coupon, 139n, 464
book value, 61, 65, 66–68
of equity, 225, 228, 455
fair value, 67
historical value, 67
and stock price, 226
vs. market value, 66–68, 455
bought deals, 503
Bowie, David, 468
Boyd, Michael, 745
break-even probability of collection, 710
Brin, Sergey, 489
Bristol-Myers Squibb, 464
British Gas, 492
British Petroleum (BP) shares, 497
Bromley, David, 567
Brookfield Properties, 470
Buffett, Warren, 21
Business Development Corporation (BDC), 512–513
business organizations, 8–12
corporation, 8–10
hybrid forms, 11–12
partnership, 11
sole proprietorship, 10–11
business trusts, 547

C
Caisse de dépôt et placement du Québec, 24, 457, 694
caisses populaires. *See* credit unions
calculator method
annity due, 155n
annuity problems, 159
bond valuation, 193
net present value, 276
time value of money, 142–143
Caldwell Securities, 22
callable bonds, 464–465, 802
call option, 785–786
call price
bonds, 464
stocks, 462
calls and puts, 785–791
Cameco, 229
Canaccord Financial Ltd., 472
Canada Business Corporation Act, 9, 454, 587
Canada Pension Plan Investment Board, 506, 745
Canada Post, 683
Canadian accounting standards, 60, 81, 83. *See also* Accounting Standards Board (AcSB); International Financial Reporting Standards (IFRS)
Canadian Airlines, 20
Canadian Coalition for Good Governance, 460
Canadian Competition Bureau, 732
Canadian dollar, 759
Canadian Energy Services & Technology Corp (CEU), 230
Canadian Imperial Bank of Commerce, 472, 498
Canadian National Railway, 492
Canadian National Stock Exchange (CNSX), 37
Canadian Natural Resources Ltd., 587
Canadian Oil Sands Trust, 263
Canadian Pacific, 694
Canadian Pacific Railway, 229, 464
Canadian Payments Association (CPA), 679
Canadian Securities Administrators (CSA), 59, 694
Canadian Tire, 457
Canadian Wheat Board, 659
capital
company cost of, 409, 424–425
cost of, 51, 421–423
opportunity cost of, 51, 264, 408–409
project cost of, 409, 440
Capital, Octagon, 586
capital asset pricing model (CAPM), 403–408
"beta" risk, 403–404
described, 403–405
expected returns, 408
formula, 403
performance of model, 405–408
security market line, 404–405
capital budgeting decision. *See* investment decisions
capital cost allowance (CCA)
asset class system, 312–313
declining balance depreciation, 313
depreciation, 311–313
half-year rule, 313, 313n
nominal amount of, 324
and NPV of project, 320–321
recaptured depreciation, 314–315
sale of assets, 314
terminal loss, 314
termination of asset pool, 314
undepreciated capital cost, 331
capital cost allowance (CCA) tax shield
defined, 311
leasing, 564
present values of, 315–317
capital expenditure, 63
capital gain
after-tax, 196
percentage, 362
vs. dividends, 599–600
capital lease. *See* financial lease
capital markets, 39
and corporate financing, 476
cost of capital, based on historical evidence, 367–368
historical returns of market indexes, 363–368
international, 466
Capital One Bank, 43
capital rationing, 286–288
defined, 286
hard rationing, 286–287
profitability index, 287–288, 287n
soft rationing, 286
capital structure, 422, 525
and corporate taxes, 533–537
corporate taxes and, 536–537
decisions, 6
and increased efficiency, 546
measurement, 430–432
MM proposition, 525–526, 528–530
restructuring, 526
capital surplus. *See* additional paid-in capital
carrying costs, 646, 685
carrying value. *See* book value
carve-out, 747
cash
changes in, 647–649
depreciation and, 72
idle, 692–695
working capital trade-off, 645–646
cash and cash equivalents, 62
cash budgeting, 649–653
cash balance, 651–653
forecast sources of cash, 649–651
forecast uses of cash, 651
cash collection, 675–677
cash conversion cycle, 642–645
cash coverage ratio, 113
cash flow
accrual accounting, 72–74
total, 73–74
cash flow from assets, 78, 79–81
cash gap, 643
cash management, 675–684
Baumol's model of optimal cash balances, 687–689
cheque collections, 680–681
cheque disbursement, 681–682
electronic funds transfer, 682–683
float, 675–679
in large domestic and international corporations, 691–692
uncertain cash flows, 689–691
cash ratio, 116
Cedara Software Corp., 498
Centro Property Group, 745
Cephalon Inc., 745
Cerberus Capital Management, 726
certificate of deposit (CD), 695
chaebol, 461
Chagnon family, 457
Chang, Joanne, 248
"channel stuffing," 81
Chapters, 20, 740
charge card, 678
cheque collection, 680–681
cheque disbursements, 681–682
cheque kiting, 677
cheques, 675–679
Chicago Board Options Exchange (CBOE), 785
Chicago Mercantile Exchange, 40, 759
chief financial officer (CFO), 12, 13
Chrysler, 726
Churchill Corporation, 656
CIBC. *See* Canadian Imperial Bank of Commerce
CIBC World Markets, 11, 470, 498
Citibank Canada, 43
Citigroup, 19, 45, 471
Citron, Robert, 471
CJ CGV, 227
clean bond price, 186

coattail provision, 458
collateralized debt obligation (CDO), 15
collection policy, 713–714
commercial draft, 705
commercial paper, 17, 658–660, 693–694
commitment fee, 656
commodities markets, 39
commodity and financial futures, 818
commodity prices, 48
common equity, 220
common shares, 220. *See also* common stock
common stock, 220, 365
  classes of stock, 457–458
  comparables, valuation by, 228–229
  dividends, 456
  expected return on, 432–434
  issued shares, 454
  outstanding shares, 454
  price and intrinsic values, 229–231
  restricted shares, 457
  share repurchase, 455, 474, 588–590
  valuation, 228–234
Companies' Creditors Arrangement Act, 539, 549–550
Companies House, 59
company cost of capital, 409, 424–425
company value, 49–50
compensating balance, 661
compensation plans, 18–19, 21
composition, 549
compound interest
  future value and, 132–136
  future value formula, 133
comprehensive income, 68–69
conditional sale, 705
Confederation Bridge, 263
conglomerate mergers, 725
consolidated statement of changes in equity, 70–72
consolidated statement of financial position, 61, 65
constant-growth dividend discount model, 235–236, 237
consumer price index (CPI), 161
controller, 12, 13
convertible bond, 472–473, 801
convertible securities, 472–473
convertible stocks, 462
Co-operators Insurance, 45
corporate control
  carve-out, 747
  divestitures, 746
  leveraged buyouts (LBOs), 741–745
  market for, 737–747
  ownership structure and, 737–738
  proxy contests, 738–739
  spin-off, 747
  takeover bids, 739–741
corporate debt, 463–472. *See also* bonds
  capital markets, 466
  currency, 466
  default risk, 466
  interest rate, 463–664
  private *vs.* public placement, 466–467
  protective covenants, 467–468
  repayment provisions, 464–465
  security, 465–466
  seniority, 465
  sinking fund, 464
corporate financing
  Canadian corporations, 474–476
  external sources of capital, 474–476
  internally generated funds, 473–474
  patterns of, 473–476
  total, 45–46
corporate financing choices
  trade-off theory, 539–544
corporate governance, 38, 458–461
corporate venture capital funds, 513
corporation
  board of directors, 9, 19–20, 456, 459, 460, 738–739
  control of, 737–747
  current market value, maximizing, 14
  drawbacks, 10
  as form of business organization, 8–10
  goals of, 13–21
  legal entity, 9
  ownership of, 456
  private *vs.* public company, 8
  profit maximization, 13
  takeovers, 20
correlation, 378–381
correlation coefficient, 378–379
cost method, 62
coupon, 184, 463
coupon income, after-tax, 186
coupon rate, 184, 190
covariance, 378–379, 397
Coventree Inc, 472
cram-down, 550
Crawford, Purdy, 694
credit agreements, 705
credit analysis, 706–708
credit card, 678
credit decision, 708–713
  policy switch, 712–713
  probability of default, 708–710
  repeat orders, 710–712
credit default swaps (CDS), 823
credit policy, 708
credit risk, 204
credit scoring, numerical, 706–708, 709
credit spread, 204
credit transfer, 678
credit unions, 43–44
CTV, 747
cumulative voting, 457
currency futures market, 758
current assts, 62
current liabilities, 64
current ratio, 116
current yield, 190–191

D
Daimler, 726
Daiwa Bank, 823
Daviau, Dan, 498
days' sales in inventory. *See* inventory period
debit card, 678
debt
  cash flows and firm value, in tax-free economy, 525–526
  and cost of equity, 530–533
  risk and return, 529–530
  and taxes, 533–537
debt capacity, 566
debt financing, 6
debt ratio, 111–113
debt securities, 38–39
declining balance depreciation, 313
default premium, 204
default risk, 203–204, 466
deferred tax liabilities, 65, 103
Dell Computer, 688
Denso Corp., 688
depreciation, 62–63
  and capital cost allowance, 311–313
  declining balance, 313
  deduction for, 72
  defined, 62
  expense, 63
  purpose of, 67
  straight-line method, 63, 313
derivatives, 62
  forward contracts, 819–820
  futures contracts, 613–818
  markets, 39
  swaps, 819–821
Desjardins-Laurentian Financial Corporation, 24
Desmarais, Paul, Jr., 460
Desmarais, Paul, Sr., 460
Deutsche Bank AG, 43
Deutsche Telekom, 20
Diageo, 4, 5
Dimson, Elroy, 424
direct debit, 678
dirty bond price, 186
disaster-out clause. *See* market-out clause
disbursement float, 675
discounted cash-flow analysis, 272, 276, 289. *See also* capital cost allowance (CCA)
  calculating cash flows, 307–311
  example, 317–324
  identifying cash flows, 301–307
discounted cash flow (DCF) rate of return, 275. *See also* internal rate of return (IRR)
discounted payback, 271–272
discounted payback period, 273
discount factor, 138–139
discount interest, 661
discount rate, 137, 424
diversification
  correlation and, 379–381
  merger and, 729
  portfolio, 375
  risk and, 374–383
divestiture, 746–747
dividend clientele effect, 600
dividend discount model, 231–234
  constant-growth dividend discount model, 235–236
  with no growth, 234–235
dividend payout ratio, 591
dividend reinvestment plan (DRIP), 588

dividends, 456
cash, 585–586
ex-dividend date, 586
extra, 585–586
and firm value, 597–600
information content of, 592–594
legal limitations, 587
MM's dividend-irrelevance proposition, 594–597
noncash, 587–588
policies, 591–592, 593
regular, 585
reinvestment plans, 588
share purchase plans, 588
stock, 587
vs capital gains, 599–600
dividend tax credit, 599
dividend yield, 361
DocVerse, 728
Dodd-Frank Wall Street Reform and Consumer Protection Act, 493
Dominion Bond Rating Service (DBRS), 204, 694, 706
dot-com boom, 250, 251, 499
Drexel Burnham Lambert, 744
Dubai Islamic Bank, 45
Dun & Bradstreet, 706
Dunlap, "Chainsaw" Al, 81
DuPont Canada, 524
Dupont system, 109–111
Dylex, 551

E
easy-money policies, 52
Eaton's, 551
Ebbers, Bernie, 459
EBITDA (earnings before interest, depreciation, and amortization), 113–114
economic order quantity, 686–687
economic value added (EVA), 102–105, 107–108
EdgeStone Capital Partners, 744
E.F. Hutton, 677
effective annual interest rates, 165–168
efficiency, 108–109
efficiency measures
asset turnover, 108
average collection period, 109
inventory turnover, 108–109
receivables turnover, 109
efficient market, 248
Eggertson, Gunnar, 498
electronic auction houses, 222
electronic bill presentment and payment (EBPP), 683
electronic communication networks (ECNs), 38, 222
electronic data interchange (EDI), 683
electronic fund transfer (EFT), 682–683
e-money payment transactions, 678
EnCana Corporation, 4, 6, 38, 223
Enron, 14, 82, 122, 539
Epstein, Barry, 82
equity financing, 6, 454–461
Canadian corporate shares, holdings of, 45, 46
initial public offering (IPO), 221
issued shares, 65, 454
net worth, 461
outstanding shares, 65, 454
seasoned equity offering (SEO), 221
equity market. *See* stock market
equivalent loan, 572–573
eruozone debt crisis, 773, 774, 775
Esteireiro, John, 498
ethics
accounting misdeeds, 14
conflicts of interest, 16–18
and management objectives, 14–16
of maximizing value, 14–16
reputation, 15, 17
unspoken understandings, 18
eurobonds, 466
eurodollars, 466
European Central Bank, 53
European Commission, 53
European Depositary Receipts, 222
Eurotunnel, 267–269
Evershed, Phil, 498
exchange rates, and inflation, 760–767
exchange-traded funds (ETFs), 40, 41, 400
ex-dividend date, 586
expansion stage, 514
expectations theory of exchange rates, 766–767
expectation theory, 201, 216–217
expected risk premium, 402–403
ex-rights date, 502
extension, 549
extra earning power, 226
ExxonMobilis, 263

F
face value, 184, 454
factoring, 657–658
fair value, 62, 67
Fannie Mae, 52, 82
fiduciary enterprises, 60n
finance
banks, 22
careers in, 22–24
corporations, 22
financial analyst, 23–24
insurance industry, 23
investment dealers, 22
salaries in, 24
Financial Accounting Standards Board (FASB), 82, 566
financial assets, 8
financial crisis of 2007–2009, 52–53, 823
financial distress
and assets, 542–543
costs of, 537–543
direct *vs.* indirect costs of bankruptcy, 540
shareholders' *vs.* debtholders' interests, 541–542
without bankruptcy, 540–542
financial institutions, 43–44
financial intermediaries, 39–42
defined, 39
exchange-traded funds (ETFs), 40, 41
functions of, 46–50
hedge funds, 41–42
mutual funds, 40–41, 400
pension funds, 42–43, 44
private equity funds, 42
financial lease, 562, 568–571
cash flows of, 568–570
discount rate, 571–572
evaluation with formulas, 575–576
lease *vs.* borrow decision, 568
legal ownership of asset, 570–571
net financial lease and salvage value, 575
NPV, 571–572, 574–576
and secured loan, 570–571
financial leverage, 111–115, 530
cash coverage ratio, 113
debt ratio, 111–113
EBITDA (earnings before interest, depreciation, and amortization), 113–114
measures, 111–115
and return on equity, 114–115
times interest earned ratio, 113
financial manager, 12–13
financial market, defined, 37
financial markets, 37–39, 453
capital markets, 39
commodities markets, 39
debt securities, 38–39, 185
derivative markets, 39
fixed-income market, 39
foreign-exchange markets, 39
functions of, 46–50
in historical perspective, 26
information, providing, 48–50
liquidity, 48
money markets, 39
payment mechanism, 48
risk transfer and diversification, 47
stock market, 37–38
transporting cash across time, 47
financial planning
balancing item, 614
consistent goals, 611
contingency planning, 610–611
external financing and growth, 623–627
inputs, 612
liquidity, 639
long-term and short-term planning, 637–640
long-term planning, 609–610
maturity-matching principle, 639
model design, 620
net working capital, 639
outputs, 612
pro forma financial statements, 615–619
purposes, 610–611
short-term, 653–655
strategic planning, 610
total capital requirement, 637–639
financial planning models, 611–619
components, 612
forecasting interest expense, 622
percentage-of-sales models, 613–614, 620–622
role of, 623
spreadsheet, 615–619
financial ratios
credit analysis, 706
efficiency measures, 108–109

financial ratios—*Cont.*
growth measures, 116–117
interpretation of, 117–120
leverage measures, 111–115
liquidity measures, 115–116
performance measures, 100–102
profitability measures, 105–108
financial reporting, legal requirement, 59–60
financial risk, 530
financial slack, 545–546, 640
financing decisions, 3, 4, 6–8
capital structure decisions, 6
creating value, 453
debt financing, 6
defined, 6
equity financing, 6
relationship with investment decisions, 7
sources of financing, 34
financing flow, 78, 79–80, 81
firm commitment, 493
firm-specific risk. *See* unique risk
firm value, 14, 16–21
agency problem, 17–18
ethics of maximizing value, 14–16
Fisher, Irving, 200
Fisher effect, 200
fixed-income market, 39
float
availability float, 675
management, 680–683
net, 676
payment float, 675
payment system and, 677–679
valuing, 676–677
floating interest rate, 464
floating-rate preferred, 463
Florida Power & Light Company, 593
flotation costs, 495
follow-on offers. *See* seasoned equity offers
Forbes Magazine, 244
Ford Motor Company, 677, 773
foreign bonds, 466
foreign exchange markets, 755–759
foreign-exchange markets, 39
"FOREX," 39
Fortis, 53
forward contracts, 819
forward exchange rates, 758–759
forward interest rate, 216
407 International Inc., 200
FPL Group, 593
fraud. *See* accounting fraud
Freddie Mac, 52
free cash flow, 78, 80, 81, 441, 646. *See also* cash flow from assets
free cash flow "problem," 546–547
free-cash-flow theory of takeovers, 744
Fregin, Doug, 2
Friedrich, John, 659
full-payout lease. *See* financial lease
fundamental analysts, 247
funded debt, 464
fund manager, 41
future investments, value of, 227
futures contracts, 813–818
commodity and financial futures, 818
trading, 817–818
Future Shop, 740
future value
calculator for, 134, 142, 143, 159
and compound interest, 132–136
formula, 133
future cash payments, valuing, 164–165
(interest) factor, 135
interest rate, 143
multiple cash flows, 142–143, 145
tables, 134–135
"FX," 39

G
GAAP (generally accepted accounting principles). *See* U.S. GAAP accounting standards
Gates, Bill, 489
Générale des Eaux, 624
General Motors, 688
Genuity Capital Markets, 498
George Weston Ltd. (GW), 454–455, 461–462, 474, 586
Gibson, Robert, 586
Gildan Activewear, 229
GlaxoSmithKline PLC, 222
Global Crossing, 82
Global Depositary Receipts, 222
Globe and Mail, 747
GMAC Residential Lending, 470
going-concern value, 226–227
Goldman Sachs, 11, 15, 823, 824
goodwill, 64
Google, 242, 489, 728
"go public," 37, 492
Gordon, Myron, 236
Gordon growth model. *See* constant-growth dividend discount model
Government bonds, 38, 184, 200, 203, 365–367
government debt, 203
government venture capital funds, 513
Gradley, Richard, 23
Graham, J. R., 81
Grameen Bank, 35
Great-West Life Assurance and Investors Group, 24
Great West Lifeco Inc., 460
Greece, debt crisis, 53, 775
green-shoe option. *See* overallotment option
Greenspan, Alan, 251n
Groupe Eurotunnel, 269
Groupe Videotron Ltée, 457
growing perpetuity, 158–160
growth measures, 116–117
growth stocks, 240–242
guaranteed investment certificates (GICs), 695

H
half-year rule, 313, 313n
hard rationing, 286–287
Harvey, C. R., 81
hedge fund, 41–42
hedging, 810–812
hedging exchange rate risk, 768–769
Heinz, 467–468
Hewlett-Packard, 40
Hickey, Robert, 467
Hidi, Andre, 745
high-yield bond, 204
Hinkley Point C., 424
Hirst, Ted, 498
historical cost, 226
historical value, 67
historic cost, 226
holder-of-record date, 502
Hollinger International, 19, 20, 456
Home Depot, 21
horizon value, 442
Host Marriott Corp., 467
HSBC, 45
HSBC Bank Canada, 43, 472
Hudson's Bay Company, 9
Hunkin, John, 498
hybrid forms, of business organizations, 11–12
Hypo Group, 53

I
IBM, 747
IGM Financial Inc., 460
IMAX, 227, 229
impairment losses, and cash, 72
income statement, 68–74. *See also* statement of comprehensive income (SCI)
income stocks, 240–242
income tax payable, 64
income trust, 11, 547
indexed bonds, 468
index funds, 41, 244, 400
Indigo Books, 740
inflation
defined, 160
exchange rates and, 760–767
and interest rates, 162–163
prices, 160–161
and time value of money, 160–165
inflation-indexed bonds, 199–200
ING, 53
initial public offering (IPO), 221, 492–497, 500
divestiture, 746
flotation costs, 495–496
issue price, 493–494
lockup period clause, 493
preliminary prospectus, 493
primary offering, 492
"roadshow," 494
secondary offering, 492
stock market listing, 500–501
underpricing, 494–495
underwriters, 493, 497–500, 503
Innovation Strategy Canada, 3
inside information, 247
insider, 247
insider trading, 247–248
insurance companies, 44, 513
intangible assets, 5, 8, 63–64, 226–227
Intel, 491
interest-bearing loans and borrowings, 65

interest payments
    classification of, 80
    and reduction of corporate taxes, 84
interest rate risk, 202
interest rate risk premium. *See* liquidity premium
interest rates, 49
    annual percentage rate (APR), 166–167
    approximation rule, 163, 163n
    and bond prices, 186–190
    calculator for, 143
    compounding frequency, 167–168
    effective annual rates, 165–168
    floating rate, 464
    London Interbank Offered Rate (LIBOR), 464
    market rate, 187, 190
    mortgage rates, 167–168
    nominal rate, 162–163, 200, 362
    per-period interest rate, 166–167
    prime rate, 464
    real rate, 162–163, 362
    spreadsheets calculation, 144
interest tax shield, 534–536. *See also* capital cost allowance (CCA) tax shield
internal growth rate, 625
internally generated funds, 473
internal rate of return (IRR), 197, 272–281, 289
    calculator method, 276
    calculating, 274–277
    modified, 279–280
    multiple rates of return, 278–279
    mutually exclusive projects, 280–281
    and opportunity cost, 277, 278
    pitfalls of IRR rule, 277–281
    rate of return rule, 273–274
international budgeting decisions, 770–776
international capital budgeting
    avoiding fudge factors, 776
    cost of capital, 771–772
    net present value, 770–771
    political risk, 772–775
International Financial Reporting Standards (IFRS), 60
    cost method, 62
    criticisms of, 83
    fair value, 62
    principles-based approach, 82
    and retail industry, 567
    revaluation method, 62
    transportation sector and, 568
international Fisher effect, 763–764
International Monetary Fund (IMF), 53
International Monetary Market (IMM), 759
intrinsic values, 229–231
inventories, 62
inventory management, 687, 688
inventory management models, 684–687
inventory period, 643, 644
inventory turnover, 108–109
investment banks, 221, 499. *See also* underwriters
investment dealers, 11n, 22–23, 37
Investment Dealers Association, 23
investment decisions, 3, 4, 5–6
    business taxes and, 311–324
    comparison of decision rules, 288
    costs and risks, 5–6
    defined, 5
    intangible assets, 5
    international, 770–776
    relationship with financing decisions, 7
    and uncertain future cash inflows, 6
investment-grade bond, 204
investment horizon, 232–234
Investment Industry Regulatory Organization of Canada, 472
Iowa Electronic Market, 40
IPO (initial public offering), 37
Iridium, 5
"irrational exuberance," 251n
iShares DEX Universe Bond Index Fund ETF (XBB), 41
Islamic Development Bank, 45
Islamic financial sector, 44, 45
issued shares, 454
Ivaco, Inc., 549

J
Jarislowsky, Stephen, 460
Jean Coutu Group, 11
Jensen, Michael, 546
Jetsgo, 540
Jobs, Steve, 489
Johnson, Ross, 742
Johnson & Johnson, 491, 544
junk bonds, 204, 743, 744
just-in-time inventory management, 687, 688

K
Kaplan, S., 743
Kassie, David, 498
Kavelman, Dennis, 800
keiretsu, 460–461
Kohlberg Kravis Roberts (KKR), 742, 743, 745
Kuletsky, Emma, 23

L
L.A. Gear, 639, 640
labour-sponsored funds, 513
Laidlaw Inc., 682
Large Value Transfer System (LVTS), 679
Laricina Energy Inc., 506
Laurentian Bank, 472
Lavallee, Mario, 707
law of one price, 761
Lazaridis, Mike, 2, 489, 800
leases, 468, 561
    described, 561–562
    direct, 562
    evaluating, 574–576
    financial, 562, 568–571
    lessor's criterion, 576–577
    net, 562
    operating, 561, 567–568
    rental, 562
    sale and lease back arrangement, 562
    and secured loan, 570–571
    valuing, 567–576
leasing
    accounting rules, 565, 566
    and book income, 566–567
    cancellation option, 563
    dubious reasons for, 564
    and financial leverage of firm, 566
    long-term obligations, 566
    low administrative and transaction costs, 564
    and maintenance, 563
    off-balance-sheet financing, 564–566
    short-term, 563–564
    and tax shield, 564
    vs. equivalent loan, 571–574
leasing industry, 562–563
Leeson, Nick, 822–823
legal and regulatory requirements, 10, 20
Lehman Brothers, 52
lessee, 561
lessor, 561
level cash flows, 147–160
    annuity, 147, 148–157
    growing perpetuity, 158–160
    perpetuities, 147–149
leverage. *See* financial leverage
leveraged buyouts (LBOs), 741–745
levered equity beta, 439
Levi Strauss, 492
liabilities, 64
limited liability, 8
limited liability companies (LLCs), 11
limited liability partnerships (LLPs), 11
limited voting shares, 457
line of credit, 656
liquid assets, 61
liquidation, 549, 551
liquidation value, 226, 228
liquidity, 48
    cash ratio, 116
    current ratio, 116
    measures, 115–116
    net working capital to total assets ratio, 115–116
    quick ratio, 116
liquidity-preference theory, 217
liquidity premium, 203
Livent, 456
loan covenant, 542
Loblaw Companies, 462, 543
lockbox system, 680–681
lockup period clause, 493
London England Stock Exchange, 60, 66, 222
London Interbank Offered Rate (LIBOR), 464
long-lived projects
    net present value (NPV), 264–267
    rate of return, 274–281
Lord & Taylor, 9n
loss, 69
Lotus Corporation, 747

M
Madoff, Bernard, 16
Magna International, 457
majority voting, 457
management
    agency problem, 17–18, 20–21
    compensation plans, 18–19, 21
    legal duty of, 20
    specialist monitoring, 20

management buyout (MBO), 742
Manville Corporation, 551
Maple Leaf Foods Inc. (MLFI), 585–586, 739
market anomalies, 249–250
market capitalization, 99–100
market interest rate, 187, 190
market-out clause, 503
market portfolio, 367–368
market risk, 382, 384–385
market risk premium (MRP), 368, 401–403
market-to-book value, 101–102
market value
measuring, 99–102
performance measures, 102
vs. book value, 66–68
market value added, 100–101
market-value balance sheet, 227–228
market-value statement of financial position, 67
market weights, 426
Marriott Corp., 467
Marriott International, Inc., 467
maturity-matching principle, 639
maturity premium, 365
maturity risk premium. *See* liquidity premium
maturity value. *See* face value
McCain, Michael, 739
McCain Foods, 4, 8, 492, 738
McKelvey, Andrew, 21
mergers. *See also* corporate control
amalgamation, 730–731
antitrust law and, 732–733
benefits and costs, 747–748
cash, financed by, 733–735
and complementary resources, 728
conglomerate, 725
dubious reasons for, 729
and economies of scale, 727
and economies of vertical integration, 727–728
evaluating, 733–737
and increased revenues, 727
mechanics of, 730–733
and popular opposition, 733
stocks, financed by, 735–736
and surplus funds, 728
and tax reduction, 728
vertical, 725
Merge Technologies Inc., 498
Merrill Lynch, 11, 19, 52
Merton, Robert, 795
Messier, Jean-Marie, 624
microcredit movement, 35
Microsoft, 11, 228, 489, 585
Milken, Michael, 744
Miller, Merton, 525
Missouri Pacific Railroad, 551
Mitsubishi keiretsu, 460–461
MM debt-irrelevance proposition, 528–530
MM proposition, 525–526
MM's dividend-irrelevance proposition, 594–597
MM's proposition I. *See* MM debt-irrelevance proposition
MM's proposition II, 531–532
Modigliani, Franco, 525
Molson, 731
Molson Coors Brewing Company, 731
money market funds, 17
money markets, 39, 692–695
Monster Worldwide, 21
"Montreal Accord," 694
Moody's, 204
Morgan Stanley, 11
Morrison, David, 498
mortgage-backed securities, 52
mortgage rates, 167–168
Mouvement des caisses Desjardins, 44
multiclass mortgage pass-through certificates, 470
multiple cash flows, 142–147
future value, 142–143, 145
present value, 145–147
multiple discriminant analysis, 707
multiple rates of return, 278–279
mutual funds, 40–41, 400
mutual fund trust. *See* income trust
mutually exclusive projects, 269, 280–286
with different outlays, 281
investment timing decision, 282–283
and IRR, 280–281
long- *vs.* short-lived equipment, 283–284
replacement decision, 285–286

N
Nasdaq, 37–38, 221
National Amusements, 227
National Bank of Canada, 16, 17, 24, 472
National Safety Council of Australia, 659
negative profit. *See* loss
net acquisitions rule, 314
net common equity, 454
net current assets. *See* working capital
net earnings, 69, 72, 103
net float, 676
net income. *See* net earlnings
net operating profit after taxes (NOPAT), 104
net operating working capital (NOWC), 615
net present value (NPV), 263–269, 273, 288–289
calculator method, 276
choosing between projects, 269
defined, 264
long-lived projects, 264–267
positive, 269
profile, 274
and total present value of cash flows, 320
net working capital, 639, 642
net working capital to total assets ratio, 115–116
net worth, 461
New York Stock Exchange (NYSE), 37, 221, 222
Nippon Telegraph and Telephone, 492
Nokia, 4, 5–6
nominal interest rate, 162–163, 200, 362
non-constant growth, 238
non-controlling interest, 65
non-current assets, 62–63
cost method, 62
depreciation, 63
revaluation method, 62
non-current liabilities, 64, 65
non-operating assets, 64
non-voting shares, 457
Nortel Networks, 14, 19, 82, 250, 459, 746
Northgate Minerals Corp, 731
Novartis, AG, 732
NPV profile, 274
NRDC Equity Partners, 9n
numerical credit scoring, 706–708, 709

O
Occidental Petroleum, 683
Odeon & UCI Cinemas, 227
off-balance-sheet financing, 564–566
Office of the Superintendent of Bankruptcy (OSB), 548
one price, law of, 761
Onex, 740, 744, 745
Ontario Securities Act, 493
Ontario Securities Commission, 20, 248
Ontario Teachers' Pension Plan, 42, 44, 491, 513, 744
open account, 705
operating cycle, 642–645
operating lease, 561–562, 567–568
operating profit margin, 110
operating risk, 529
operational hedging, 769
opportunity cost, 51–52, 187, 264, 408–409
optimal cash balances, 687–689
option backdating, 800
options
to abandon, 798
callable bonds, 802
convertible bonds, 801
to expand, 798
on financial assets, 799–802
on real assets, 797–799
and risk management, 812–813
option-valuation models, 795–797
option values, 792–797
other receivables, 62
outstanding shares, 454
overallotment option, 503
oversubscription privilege, 501

P
Pacific Northern Gas, 227, 229
Page, Larry, 489
paid-in surplus. *See* additional paid-in capital
Palamat, 82, 459
Parmalat, 14
partnership, 11
par value. *See* face value
Paulson, John, 15
Paulson & Co, 15
payback, 270–271
payback period, 270
payback rule, 270
payment float, 675
payment system, 677–679
payout ratio, 117, 241
pecking-order theory, 544–545
Penn Central Corporation, 550
pension funds, 42, 44, 491, 513
P/E ratio, 223, 229, 242
percentage capital gain, 362
percentage-of-sales models, 613–614, 620–622
percentage points, 368n
percentage return, 361
performance measures, 102
market-to-book value, 101–102
market value added, 100–101

per-period interest rate, 166–167
perpetuities, 147–149
Pfizer, 20, 745
Placer Dome Inc., 460
planning horizon, 609
pledged accounts receivable, 657
plowback ratio, 117, 241
plug, 614
poison pill, 740
political risk, 772–775
Ponzi scheme, 16
population variance, 372
portfolio diversification
 correlation and, 378–381
 international, 383
 and risk, 374–375
portfolio standard deviation, 380
positive net present value, 269
Potash Corporation, 739
Power Corporation, 457, 460
preauthorized debits (PADs), 683
prediction markets, 40
preferred stock, 227, 235, 428, 461–463
present value of its growth opportunities (PVGO), 242
present values, 136–142
 alternative patterns of payment, 139–140
 of bond, 187
 calculator for, 143, 159
 discount rate, 137
 formula, 137–138
 interest rate, finding, 140–141, 143
 investment period, finding, 141–142, 143
 multiple cash flows, 145–147
 present value interest factor, 138–139
 Rule of 72, 141
price-earnings multiple, 223. *See also* P/E ratio
price-to-book-value ratios, 229
PricewaterhouseCoopers, 567
primary market, 37, 221
primary offering, 492
prime rate, 464
Primero Mining Corp., 731
Prime Trust, 694
principal. *See* face value
private company, 8, 240, 738
private equity fund, 42
private equity investing, 491
private equity investors, 741
private independent firms, as source of venture capital, 512–513
private placement, 466–467, 505–506
probability of default, 708–710
professional corporation (PC), 11
profit, in accounting, 69
profitability index, 287–288, 287n
profitability measures, 105–108
 economic value added (EVA), 102–105, 107–108
 operating profit margin, 110
 return on capital (ROC), 105–106
 return on equity (ROE), 107
profit margin, 109–110
profit maximization, 13
profits vs.cash flow, 72–74
pro formas, 612
project cost of capital, 409, 440
project risk, 408–412
 company risk *vs.*, 409–410
 determinants of, 410–411
promissory note, 705
prompt offering prospectus (POP) system, 503
property, plant, and equipment (PP&E), 62–63
 book values *vs.* market values, 67
 non-current assets, 62–63
prospectus, 493, 504–505, 519–522
protective covenants, 467–468
proxy contest, 457, 738–739
public company, 8, 58–59
Public Company Accounting Oversight Board, 82, 122, 459
purchasing power parity (PPP), 761–763
pure-play approach, 410–411
Pure Trading, 38
put-call parity, 791
put option, 786

Q
quasi equity. *See* deferred tax liabilities
Quebecor, 457
quick ratio, 116
Qwest Communications, 82

R
Rajgopal, S., 81
random walk, 244–245
rate of return
 after-tax, 196–197
 bond, 192–198
 and cost of capital, 51–52
 estimation, 237
RBC Capital Markets, 22, 499
RBC Dominion Securities, 22
real assets, 8
real interest rate, 162–163, 362
real options, 797
real return bond (RRB), 199–200
real value of $1, 161
recaptured depreciation, 314–315
receivables turnover, 109
redeemable shares, 462
refunding, bond, 465
Regal Cinemas, Inc., 227
Reisman, Heather, 740, 741
remote disbursement, 682
reorganization, 549–551
repurchase agreement, 695
research and development (R&D), 5, 227
Research In Motion (RIM), 2–3, 5, 21, 34–35, 37, 225–227, 229, 489, 543, 544, 639, 800
residual income. *See* economic value added (EVA)
restricted shares, 457
restructuring, 526
retained earnings, 65, 454
return on assets (ROA), 106
return on capital (ROC), 105–106
return on equity (ROE), 107
Reuters Group, 731
revenue recognition, 81
reverse floaters, 471
reverse split, 588
rights issues, 501–503
Rio Tinto Group, 468, 469, 738
risk management
 forward contracts, 819–820
 future contracts, 813–818
 hedging, 810–812
 and options, 812–813
 swaps, 619–822
risk measurement, 369–374, 385
 beta of stocks, 394–398
 market risk, 393–400
 portfolio betas, 399–400
 standard deviation, 369–371, 374–375, 379–380
 total risk *vs.* market risk, 398–399
 variance, 369–374
risk premium, 366
risks
 asset *vs.* portfolio risk, 375–378
 business risk, 529
 correlation, 378–381
 covariance, 378–379, 397
 default, 203–204
 fudge factors, 411–412
 market portfolio, 367–368
 market *vs.* unique risk, 382–385
 and present value, 265
 and profit maximization, 50
 and return, 400–408
RJR Nabisco, 456, 468, 742–743, 744, 748
Robinson, Paul, 759
Rodriguez, Albert, 23
Rogers Communications, 457, 524
Rosen, Al, 83
Rotman, Earl, 498
Royal Bank Financial Group, 23
Royal Bank of Canada, 4, 23, 229, 587
Royal Bank of Scotland, 53, 502
royalty trusts, 547
Rule of 72, 141

S
Sable Island Offshore Energy Project, 263
sale, terms of, 703–705
Salole, Ron, 83
Salomon, Smith Barney, 11
salvage value, 321
sample variance, 372
Saputo Inc., 11, 229, 238–240
Sarbanes-Oxley (SOX) *Act,* 10, 19, 20, 38, 82, 122, 459
savings, flow of, 35–37
Schedule I banks, 43
Schedule II banks, 43
Schedule III banks, 43
Scholes, Myron, 795
Schwartz, Gerald, 740, 741
Scotia Capital, 11, 472
Seagram, 624
Sealed Air Corporation, 524, 546
season dating, 703
seasoned equity offering (SEO), 221
seasoned equity offers, 37
seasoned offering, 501
secondary market, 37
secondary offering, 492
secured debt, 466

Securities and Exchange Commission (SEC), 15, 59
securities dealers, 221
securities (financial assets), 8
security market line, 404–405
seed stage, 514
semi-annual coupon payments, 188, 192
semi-strong-form efficiency, 248
724 Solutions, 221, 494
share capital, 65
shareholders, 8
  and corporate governance, 458–459
  financial objective, 13
  oversubscription privilege, 501
  ownership of corporation, 456
  of record date, 585
  rights issue, 501–503
  voting procedures, 456–457
shareholders' equity, 66, 67
  book values *vs.* market values, 67
  interest tax shields and, 535
shareholders' rights plan, 740
share purchase plans (SPP), 588
share repurchase, 455, 474, 588–590
  decisions, 592
  information content of, 592–594
  methods of, 589
  and share valuation, 590
  vs. cash dividends, 589–590
Sharia-compliant products, 44, 45
shark repellent, 741
Sharpe, William F., 393
Shaw Communications, 5, 6, 610
Shaw-Rimmington, Carolyn, 472
Shearson Lehman Hutton, 742
shelf registration, 503–505
shortage costs, 646
short selling, 42
"short term," 39
short-term financial planning, 653–655
short-term financing, 655–660
  accounts receivable financing, 657–658
  banker's acceptance, 660
  bank loans, 656–657
  commercial paper, 658–660
  secured loans, 657–658
sight draft, 705
simple interest, 133, 660–661
sinking fund, 464
Smith, Adam, 15
Societé générale, 823
soft rationing, 286
sole proprietorship, 10–11
sovereign debt, 203
"special purpose entities" (SPEs), 14, 122
speculative-grade, 204
speculative-grade bond, 204
Spider-Man 3, 263
"spinning," 495, 499
spinoff, 746
Spitzer, Eliot, 499
split-up, 746
spot exchange rates, 756–757
spot rates, 216
spread, 184–185, 493
spreadsheet method
  annuities, 160
  beta of stocks, 398
  Black-Scholes formula, 797
  bond valuation, 194–195
  discounted cash flow analysis, 322–323
  discounted payback period, 273
  interest-rate functions, 144
  internal rate of return, 277
  multiple cash flows, 148
  present value of series of cash flows, 270
  short-term plan, 652
  variance and standard deviation, 373
stakeholders, 18
standard deviation, 369–371, 374–375, 379–380
Standard & Poor's (S&P), 204, 706
standby underwriting agreement, 501
startup stage, 514
statement of cash flows, 75–78
statement of comprehensive income (SCI), 68–74
  finance income, 70
  operating costs, 69
  organization of, 69–70
  profit section, 69
  total comprehensive income, 70
statement of financial position (SFP), 49–69
  accounts receivables, 62
  assets, value of, 226
  book values *vs.* market values, 67–69
  cash and cash equivalents, 62
  consolidated statement, 61, 65
  current assts, 62
  current liabilities, 64
  function of, 60–61
  intangible assets, 63–64
  inventories, 62
  liabilities, 64
  liquid assets, 61
  market-value, 67
  non-current assets, 62–63
  non-current liabilities, 64, 65
  other receivables, 62
  retained earnings, 65
  sequence of assets, 61–62
  share capital, 65
  shareholders' equity, 66
  tangible assets, 62
  working capital, 65
Stelco, 8, 549–550
Stern Stewart & Co., 103
stock dividends, 587
stockholders. *See* shareholders
stock issue. *See also* initial public offering (IPO)
  general cash offers, 503–504
  market reaction, 504–505
  rights issue, 501–503
  seasoned offering, 501
stock market, 37–38, 220–225
  initial public offerings, 500–501
  listings, 222–225
  major Canadian exchanges, 221
  primary market, 37, 221
  secondary market, 37, 221
  volatility, 373–374
stock options, 21, 799–800
stock price, 225–227
stocks. *See also* common stock
  call price, 462
  common shares, 220
  floating-rate preferred, 463
  growth, 240–242
  high-payout, 597–598
  income, 240–242
  payout ratio, 241
  P/E ratio, 223
  plowback ratio, 241
  preferred shares, 227, 235, 428, 461–463
stock split, 587
stock valuation, 220–251
  behavioural finance, 250–251
  constant-growth dividend discount model, 235–236, 237
  dividend discount model, 231–234
  dividend discount model with no growth, 234–235
  efficient market theory, 248
  estimation, 238–240
  fundamental analysis, 247–248
  market anomalies, 249–250
  non-constant growth, 238
  ratio of value comparison method (EV/EBITDA), 240
  technical analysis, 244–245
stock value, 49–50
Stone, David, 248
straight-line method, depreciation, 63, 313
strike price, 785
strong-form efficiency, 248
structured investments vehicles (SIVs), 115
subordinated debt, 465
subordinate voting shares, 457
subprime mortgages, 15, 52, 52n, 53, 470–471, 472, 694
subsidiary, 60
"Sukuk market," 45
Sumitomo Corporation, 822
Sunbeam Corporation, 81
Sun Microsystems, 19–20, 491
sustainable growth, 116–117, 626–627
sustainable growth rate, 626
sustainable rate of growth, 117
swaps, 819–821
syndicate, 497
syndicated loan, 656
synergy, 726
systematic risk. *See* market risk
System for Electronic Documents and Retrieval (SEDAR), 493

T
takeover bid, 731
takeovers, 20
  debt-financed, 743
  free-cash-flow theory, 744
  hostile bid, 732
  incentives, 743
  leveraged buyouts (LBOs), 741–745
  tactics, 740–741
  threat of, 748
Tal, Benjamin, 470, 471

tangible assets, 62
taxes, 83–89. *See also* capital cost allowance (CCA)
  acquisition and, 736
  bankruptcy, 549
  and bond rate of return, 196–197
  capital gains tax, 89, 230, 231
  and capital structure, 533–537
  corporate tax, 83–85
  dividends, tax on, 87–89, 230, 231, 598–600
  and leasing, 571
  leverage and, 743
  personal tax, 85–87
  preferred shares, 462–463
  and rate of return, 230, 231
  and weighted-average cost of capital, 427–428
Taylor, Jay, 460
Teachers' Private Capital, 513, 744
technical analysis, 244–245
technical analysts, 244
tender offer, 731
Tennant Company, 459
terminal loss, 314
terminal value, 238
term loans, 656
term structure of interest rates. *See* yield curve
Thomson Corp, 731
Thomson Reuters Corp., 731
time draft, 705
times interest earned ratio, 113
time value of money
  future value, 132–136
  level cash flows, 147–160
  multiple cash flows, 142–147
  present values, 136–142
Time Warner, 747
Tim Hortons, 747
TMX Venture Exchange, 500, 501
Tokyu Cinemas, 227
Tomkins Plc, 745
Toronto Stock Exchange (TMX), 37, 59, 66, 221, 500, 501
TorQuest Partners, 745
total capitalization, 103
total equity. *See* shareholders' equity
Total risk, 398–399
Tourre, Fabrice, 15
Toyota, 263, 688
trade credit, 703–705
trade-off theory, 539
trade payables, 64, 651
trade payables period, 642
Trader Corp., 746
trade receivables period, 643
TransCanada, 4, 229
transparency, 122–123
TransUnion Canada, 706
treasurer, 12, 13
treasury bills, 17, 365–367, 400–402, 435, 693
Treasury Inflation-Protected Securities (TIPs), 200
Trilogy Retail Enterprises, 740
true value, concept, 453
trust companies, 43
TSX Venture Exchange (TSX-V), 37, 59
turnaround stage, 514
TWA, 551

U
UBS, 20, 53
UM Financial Inc., 45
undepreciated capital cost (UCC), 311, 313
underpricing, 494–495
underwriters, 493, 497–500, 503
unique risk, 382, 383
Universal Music Group, 624
Universal Studios, 624
unlevered equity beta, 438
unspoken understandings, 18
U.S. *Bankruptcy Reform Act,* 539
U.S. Federal Reserve, 52, 52*n,* 53
U.S. GAAP accounting standards, 60, 226
U.S. government, 52–53, 200

V
Vachon, Louis, 17
Valeant Pharmaceuticals, 745
VA Linux, 498
valuation. *See also* stock valuation
  common stocks, 228–234
  of entire business, 440–442
value maximization, 50–52
Van Kampen Merritt, 467
variance
  diversification and, 375, 379–381
  individual stocks and portfolios, 374–375
  measurement, 369–372
  in stock returns, 372–374
venture capital, 490–491, 512–517
venture capital companies, 491
venture capital exits, 516–517
venture capital funds, 512–514
Verizon, 263
vertical merger, 725
Vivendi, 624
Vivendi Universal, 82
Volcker, Paul, 21
Volkswagen, 20
"vulture funds," 42

W
Wahl, Ivan, 470
Walmart, 4
Wanda Cinema Line Co. Ltd., 227
warrant, 472, 473, 799
weak-form efficiency, 248
Webb, Susan, 23
weighted-average cost of capital (WACC), 103n, 421–430
  bonds, expected return on, 432
  calculating, 434–435
  and capital structure, 430–432
  CAPM, estimates based on, 432–433
  changes in capital structure without corporate tax and, 437–438
  common mistakes to avoid, 436
  common stock, expected return on, 432–434
  company cost of capital, 424–426
  corporate taxes and changes in capital structure, effect of, 438–439
  cost of capital as weighted average, 424–426
  and debt policy, 536
  dividend discount model, estimates based on, 433
  expected return demanded by investors, 426
  formula for calculating, 424–430
  general formula, 427
  imprecise nature of estimates, 433–434
  interpreting, 435–439
  levered equity beta, 439
  market weights, 426
  multiple sources of financing, 428
  preferred stock, expected return on, 434
  project cost of capital, 440
  project net present value, 428–430
  and required rates of return, 432–434
  tax benefit of debt and, 535–536
  taxes and, 427–428
  unlevered equity beta, 438
  use of, 435–436
  valuing entire business, 440–443
Wells Fargo, 470
Wendy's International, 747
West Face Capital Inc., 739
West Lb, 53
white knight, 740, 741
Wickes Corp., 549
Winding-Up and Restructuring Act, 539
Wolfond, Greg, 494
working capital, 65, 640–649
  changes in, 647–649
  components of, 641–642
  current assets, 641–642
  current liabilities, 642
  management, 646
  trade-off, 645–647
workout, 549
WorldCom, 14, 82, 204, 459, 539
Wozniak, Steve, 489

X
Xceed Mortgage Corp., 470

Y
Yahoo, 250
Yahoo Finance, 66
Yellow Media, 746
yield curve, 198–203, 216–217
  determinants of, 201–203
  expectations theory, 201, 216–217
  interest rate risk, 202–203
  liquidity-preference theory, 217
  liquidity premium, 203
  nominal and real rates of interest, 199–201
yield to maturity, 190–192
Yunus, Muhammad, 35

Z
zero-balance account, 682
zero-coupon bonds, 139n, 464
Zucker, Jerry, 9